- rather strange
  chronology /
  Order

- document disc
  has some
  interesting stuff,
  but none of it
  is annotated
  - go through - print out contents)

T...GE

CIVILIZATIONS

THE HERITAGE OF WORLD CIVILIZATIONS

COMBINED VOLUME
BRIEF EDITION

Albert M. Craig
Harvard University

William A. Graham
Harvard University

Donald Kagan
Yale University

Steven Ozment
Harvard University

Frank M. Turner
Yale University

Prentice Hall, Upper Saddle River, NJ 07458

Library of Congress Cataloging–in–Publication Data

The heritage of world civilizations/ Albert M. Craig...[et al.].—Brief ed., combined ed.
    p.   cm.
    Includes bibliographical references and index.
    ISBN 0-13-034065-0
    1. Civilization--History. I. Craig. Albert M.
    CB69.H45 2002
    909--dc21   00-067812

Editorial Director: *Charlyce Jones Owen*
Senior Acquisitions Editor: *Charles Cavaliere*
Editor-in-Chief, Development: *Susanna Lesan*
Assistant Editor: *Emsal Hasan*
Development Editor of Brief Edition: *Gerald Lombardi*
AVP, Director of Production and Manufacturing:
    Barbara Kittle
Project Manager: *Harriet Tellem*
Manufacturing Manager: *Nick Sklitsis*
Prepress and Manufacturing Buyer: *Lynn Pearlman*

Creative Design Director: *Leslie Osher*
Art Director, Interior, and Cover Designer:
    Kathryn Foot
Cover Art: Taj Mahal, India. *Luis Villota/Corbis Stock*
Cartographers: *GEOSYSTEMS, Mirella Signoretto*
Line Art Coordinator: *Guy Ruggiero*
Copy Editor: *Karen Verde*
Photo Permission Manager: *Kay Dellosa*
Photo Permission Specialist: *Tara Gardner*

This book was set in 10/12.5 Caslon 540 by Color Associates and was printed and bound by Web Crafters.
The cover was printed by Lehigh Press, Inc.

 © 2002 by Pearson Education, Inc.
Upper Saddle River, NJ 07458

Printed in the United States of America
10 9 8 7 6 5 4 3 2 1

ISBN 0-13-034065-0

Pearson Education LTD., London
Pearson Education Australia PTY, Limited, Sydney
Pearson Education Singapore, Pte. LTD.
Pearson Education North Asia LTD., Hong Kong
Pearson Education Canada, LTD., Toronto
Pearson Educación de Mexico, S.A. de C.V.
Pearson Education--Japan, Tokyo
Pearson Education Malaysia, Pte. LTD.
Pearson Education, Upper Saddle River, New Jersey

BRIEF CONTENTS

CONTENTS

12 The Early Middle Ages in the West to 1000: The Birth of Europe — 146

13 The High Middle Ages (1000–1300) — 160

14 The Islamic Heartlands and India (ca. 1000–1500) — 181

26 Europe and North America 1815–1850: Political Reform, Economic Advance, and Social Unrest **355**

PART VI — INTO THE MODERN WORLD 367

27 Political Consolidation in Europe and North America **370**

28 The Building of Northern Transatlantic Supremacy: Society and Politics to World War I **382**

DOCUMENTS

MAPS

PREFACE

The twenty-first century is upon us, and its arrival demands, as never before, an understanding of human history in a global context. The pressures of the present—of a new century and a new millennium—draw us to seek a more certain understanding of the past.

The idea of globalization was once just that, an idea. It is now a pressing reality in the life of nations, affecting the standard of living, the environment, and war and peace. Globalization is also a daily reality in the lives of ordinary people. Not only are global markets linked as never before, but the internet quickly delivers all manner of information to the readers of this book. People with different cultural heritages, religious beliefs, and economic and political expectations are being drawn into ever closer contact with one another. If that experience is to be one of peace and mutual respect, then understanding the historical experiences that have informed and shaped the world's cultures is essential. Globalization demands of world citizens greater historical knowledge than ever before. *The Heritage of World Civilizations* provides a path to such knowledge.

The Roots of Globalization

Globalization itself has resulted from two major historical developments: the closing of the European era of world history and the rise of technology. From approximately 1500 to the middle of the twentieth century, Europeans gradually came to dominate the world through colonization (most particularly in North and South America), political organization, economic productivity, and military power.

That era ended during the third quarter of the twentieth century after Europe had brought unprecedented destruction on itself during World War II and as the nations of Asia, the Near East, and Africa achieved new positions on the world scene. Their new political independence, their control over strategic natural resources, and the expansion of their economies (particularly those of the nations of the Pacific rim of Asia), and in some cases their access to nuclear weapons have changed the shape of world affairs.

The second historical development that continues to fuel the pace of globalization is technology, associated most importantly with transportation, military weapons, and electronic communication. The advances in transportation over the past two centuries including ships, railways, and airplanes made more parts of the world and its resources accessible to more people in ever shorter spans of time. Military weapons of increasingly destructive power over the past century and a half enabled Europeans to dominate other regions of the globe. Now, the spread of these weapons means that any nation with sophisticated military technology can threaten any other nation, no matter how far away. Most recently, the electronic revolution associated with computer technology in all its forms has sparked an unprecedented speed and complexity in global communications. It is astonishing to recall that personal computers have been generally available for less than twenty years and that rapid communication associated with them has existed for less than a decade.

Why not, then, focus only on new factors in the modern world, such as the impact of technology and the end of the European era? To do that would ignore the very deep roots that these developments have in the past. Modern technology and society were shaped by the values, ingenuity, and expectations of people centuries old. For that reason, *The Heritage of World Civilizations* continues to pay particular attention to the emergence of the major religious traditions. These link today's civilizations to their most ancient roots and continue to exert a powerful influence worldwide. We believe this emphasis on the great religious traditions recognizes not only a factor that has shaped the past but also one of the most dynamic, influential forces of today.

We also bring a comparative perspective to our survey, tracing the threads of interaction that have linked civilizations throughout history. In the end, students should emerge more culturally sensitive citizens of the global, twenty-first century.

The Brief Edition

We prepared the brief version of our text, *The Heritage of World Civilizations*, Fifth Edition, in response to the demand for abridged textbooks in the field, by instructors who wanted to use readings, computer simulations, or a variety of other sources of information as well as a textbook in their courses.

The brief edition is about half as long as the complete version. We eliminated 25 percent of the text, and made up the rest of the cuts by removing some photographs, maps, and source documents. We also eliminated the part essays, comparative perspectives, and religions of the world essays from the complete version of the text, but these, as well as the source documents cut from this version, may be found on the companion website for this text, at www.prenhall.com/craig. Throughout the abridgement process we made sure that the text retained the coherency of the full-length version. Every effort was made to keep the narrative lively and engaging.

Strengths of the Text

Balanced and Flexible Presentation In this edition, as in past editions, we have sought to present world history fairly, accurately, and in a way that does justice to its great variety. History has many facets, no one of which can account for the others. Any attempt to tell the story of civilization from a single perspective, no matter how timely, is bound to neglect or suppress some important part of that story.

Historians have recently brought a vast array of new tools and concepts to bear on the study of history. Our coverage introduces students to various aspects of social and intellectual history as well as to the more traditional political, diplomatic, and military coverage. We firmly believe that only through an appreciation of all pathways to understanding of the past can the real heritage of world civilizations be claimed.

The Heritage of World Civilizations is designed to accommodate a variety of approaches to a course in world civilization, allowing teachers to stress what is most important to them. Some teachers will ask students to read all the chapters. Others will select among them to reinforce assigned readings and lectures.

Clarity and Accessibility Good narrative history requires clear, vigorous prose. Our goal has been to make our presentation fully accessible to students without compromising on vocabulary or conceptual level. We hope this effort will benefit both teachers and students.

Recent Scholarship As in previous editions, changes in this edition reflect our determination to incorporate the most recent developments in historical scholarship and the expanding concerns of professional historians.

Pedagogical Features This edition retains the pedagogical features of the last edition, helping to make the text accessible to students, reinforcing key concepts, and providing a global, comparative perspective.

◆ *Chapter Topics* introduce each chapter.
◆ *Questions accompanying the source documents* direct students toward important, thought-provoking issues and help them relate the documents to the material in the text. They can be used to stimulate class discussion or as topics for essays and study groups.
◆ *Chapter review questions* help students focus on and interpret the broad themes of a chapter. These questions, too, can be used for class discussion and essay topics.
◆ *Chronologies* within each chapter help students organize a time sequence for key events.
◆ *Primary Source Documents*, including selections from sacred books, poems, philosophy, political manifestos, letters, and travel accounts, introduce students to the raw material of history, providing an intimate contact with the people of the past and their concerns.
◆ *In World Perspective* sections conclude most chapters. These brief essays place important developments in the chapter into a world context.

New in the Fifth Edition

Content and Organization The many changes in content and organization in the 5th edition of *The Heritage of World Civilizations* reflect our ongoing effort to present a truly global survey of world civilization that at the same time gives a rich picture of the history of individual regions.

In an effort to draw students into both a comparative and, in this case, transatlantic perspective, we have omitted the separate chapter on North America in the nineteenth century, transferring most of that material to chapters which deal with related topics in European history. Thus, for example, the Civil War in the United States appears in the chapter on nineteenth-century nation-state consolidation (Chapter 27). Similarly, the late nineteenth-century social development of the United States now appears with the contemporaneous developments in Europe (Chapter 28). We hope that such integration will enable students to understand the broad strands of the development of the United States in a broader context.

Revisions of specific chapters include the following:

◆ Chapter 17, "The Age of Reformation and Religious Wars" includes new sections on the social significance of the Reformation in Western Europe, the changing role of women, and family life in early modern Europe.
◆ Chapter 20, "East Asia in the Late Traditional Era" includes a considerable revision of the section on

Vietnam. As a group, the chapters on East Asia include more documents relating to the position of women.

- Chapter 25, "Revolutions in the Transatlantic World" includes a new section on the crusade to abolish the slave trade in the transatlantic economy. The discussion integrates the themes of the eighteenth-century Enlightenment and Revolutions, developed in Chapter 24.
- Chapter 26, "Europe and North America 1815–1850: Political Reform, Economic Advance, and Social Unrest" now includes the topic, Testing the New American Republic, a discussion of sectional conflict and the rise of abolitionism in the North.
- Chapter 27, "Political Consolidation in Europe and North America" now includes a section on The United States: Civil War, Reconstruction, and Progressive Politics and another on The Canadian Experience.
- Chapter 28, "The Building of Northern Transatlantic Supremacy: Society and Politics to World War I" now includes discussions of The New Industrial Economy and The Progressives in a new section on North America.
- Our discussion of the "New Imperialism" in Europe has been moved to Chapter 33, "Imperialism and World War I."
- Chapter 37, "East Asia in the Late Twentieth Century" has been expanded to include more social history.

A Note on Dates and Transliterations We have used B.C.E. (before the common era) and C.E. (common era) instead of B.C. (before Christ) and A.D. (*anno domini*, the year of our Lord) to designate dates.

Until recently, most scholarship on China used the Wade-Giles system of romanization for Chinese names and terms. In order that students may move easily from the present text to the existing body of advanced scholarship on Chinese history, we have used the Wade-Giles system throughout. China today, however, uses another system known as *pinyin*. Virtually all Western newspapers have adopted it. Therefore, for Chinese history since 1949 we have included the *pinyin* spellings in parentheses after the Wade-Giles.

Also, we have followed the currently accepted English transliterations of Arabic words. For example, today *Koran* is being replaced by the more accurate *Qur'an;* similarly *Muhammad* is preferable to *Mohammed* and *Muslim* to *Moslem.* We have not tried to distinguish the letters *'ayn* and *hamza;* both are rendered by a simple apostrophe ('), as in *shi'ite.*

With regard to Sanskritic transliteration, we have not distinguished linguals and dentals, and both palatal and lingual *s* are rendered *sh*, as in *Shiva* and *Upanishad.*

Ancillary Instructional Materials

The Heritage of World Civilizations, Brief Edition, comes with an extensive package of ancillary materials.

- *Instructor's Manual* with tests provides summary and multiple choice questions for each part essay, as well as chapter summaries, outlines of key points and concepts, identification questions, and multiple choice and essay questions to be used for tests, and a suggested list of relevant films and videos for each chapter.
- A *Study Guide* (Volumes I and II) includes chapter summaries, key concepts, identification questions, short-answer exercises, and essay questions.
- A *Test Item File* provides more than 1,000 test questions.
- *Prentice Hall Custom Test,* Prentice Hall's new testing software program, permits instructors to edit any or all items in the Test Item File and add their own questions. Other special features of this program, which is available for DOS, Windows, and Macintosh, include random generation of an item set, creation of alternative versions of the same test, scrambling question sequence, and test preview before printing.
- *Color Transparencies* of maps, charts, and graphs from the text provide strong visual support for lectures.
- A *Map Workbook* helps students develop geographical knowledge. This workbook is free to students using new copies of this text.
- *Understanding and Answering Essay Questions*, prepared by Mary L. Kelley, San Antonio College. This brief guide suggests helpful study techniques as well as specific analytical tools for understanding different types of essay questions and provides precise guidelines for preparing well-crafted essay answers. The guide is available free to students when packaged with *The Heritage of World Civilizations.*
- *Reading Critically About History,* prepared by Rose Wassman and Lee Rinsky, both of DeAnza College. This brief guide provides students with helpful strategies for reading a history textbook. It is available free when packaged with *The Heritage of World Civilizations.*
- *Themes of the Times* is a newspaper supplement prepared jointly by Prentice Hall and the premier news publication, *The New York Times.* Issued twice a year, it contains recent articles pertinent to American history. These articles connect the classroom to the world. For information about a reduced-rate subscription to *The New York Times,* call toll free: (800) 631-1222.

The ancillary package also includes an extensive list of multimedia supplements.

History on the Internet. This guide focuses on developing the critical thinking skills necessary to evaluate and use online sources. The guide also provides a brief introduction to navigating the Internet, along with complete references related specifically to the History discipline and how to use the *Companion Website*™ available for *The Heritage of World Civilizations*. This supplementary book is free to students when shrink-wrapped with the text.

◆ *The Heritage of World Civilizations*, Companion Website (http://www.prenhall.com/craig) works in tandem with the text to help students use the World Wide Web to enrich their understanding of world history. Featuring chapter objectives, study questions, new updates, labeling exercises, and much more, it links the text with related material available on the Internet.

◆ *Documents CD-Rom* Functional in both Windows and Macintosh environments, this resource contains all the primary source readings from the print Documents Set in easy-to-read Adobe Acrobat™. Additionally, all the document questions are linked directly to the *Compan-ion Website*, enhancing an already useful study tool. This CD-ROM comes packaged free with all new copies of *The Heritage of World Civilizations, Brief Edition*.

◆ *Powerpoint*™ *Images CD-Rom* Available for Windows and Macintosh environments, this resource includes the maps from the text for use in Powerpoint™. Organized by chapters in the text, this collection of images is useful for classroom presentations and lectures.

Finally, we would like to thank the dedicated people who helped produce this brief edition: our acquisitions editor, Charles Cavaliere; our development editor, Gerald Lombardi; Kathy Foot, who created the handsome new design for this edition; Harriet Tellem, our project manager; and Lynn Pearlman, our manufacturing buyer.

A.M.C.
W.A.G.
D.K.
S.O.
F.M.T.

ABOUT THE AUTHORS

Albert M. Craig is the Harvard-Yenching Professor of History at Harvard University, where he has taught since 1959. A graduate of Northwestern University, he took his Ph.D. at Harvard University. He has studied at Strasbourg University and at Kyoto, Keio, and Tokyo universities in Japan. He is the author of *Choshu in the Meiji Restoration* (1961), and, with others, of *East Asia, Tradition and Transformation* (1978). He is the editor of *Japan, A Comparative View* (1973) and co-editor of *Personality in Japanese History* (1970). At present he is engaged in research on the thought of Fukuzawa Yukichi. For eleven years (1976–1987) he was the director of the Harvard-Yenching Institute. He has also been a visiting professor at Kyoto and Tokyo Universities. He has received Guggenheim, Fulbright, and Japan Foundation Fellowships. In 1988 he was awarded the Order of the Rising Sun by the Japanese government.

William A. Graham is a Professor of the History of Religion and Islamic Studies, Chairman of the Near Eastern Languages and Civilizations, and Master of Currier House at Harvard University. From 1990–1996 he directed Harvard's Center for Middle Eastern Studies. He has taught for twenty-six years at Harvard, where he received the A.M. and Ph.D. degrees after graduating with an A.B. in comparative literature from the University of North Carolina at Chapel Hill. He also studied in Göttingen, Tübingen, and Lebanon. He is the author of *Divine Word and Prophetic Word in Early Islam* (1977); awarded the American Council of Learned Societies History of Religions book prize in 1978, and of *Beyond the Written Word: Oral Aspects of Scripture in the History of Religion* (1987). He has published a variety of articles in both Islamic studies and the general history of religion and is one of the editors of the forthcoming *Encyclopedia of the Qur'an*. He serves currently on the editorial board of several journals and has held John Simon Guggenheim and Alexander von Humboldt research fellowships.

Donald Kagan is Hillhouse Professor of History and Classics at Yale University, where he has taught since 1969. He received the A.B. degree in history from Brooklyn College, the M.A. in classics from Brown University, and the Ph.D. in history from Ohio State University. During 1958–1959 he studied at the American School of Classical Studies as a Fulbright Scholar. He has received four awards for undergraduate teaching at Cornell and Yale. He is the author of a history of Greek political thought, *The Great Dialogue* (1965); a four-volume history of the Peloponnesian War, *The Origins of the Peloponnesian War* (1969), *The Archidamian War* (1974), *The Peace of Nicias and the Sicilian Expedition* (1981), and *The Fall of the Athenian Empire* (1987); a biography of Pericles, *Pericles of Athens and the Birth of Democracy* (1991); and *On the Origins of War* (1995). With Brian Tierney and L. Pearce Williams, he is the editor of *Great Issues in Western Civilization*, a collection of readings.

Steven Ozment is McLean Professor of Ancient and Modern History at Harvard University. He has taught Western Civilization at Yale, Stanford, and Harvard. He is the author of nine books. *The Age of Reform, 1250–1550* (1980) won the Schaff Prize and was nominated for the 1981 National Book Award. Four of his books: *Magdalena and Balthasar: An Intimate Portrait of Life in Sixteenth Century Europe* (1986), *Three Behaim Boys: Growing Up in Early Modern Germany* (1990), *Protestants: The Birth of a Revolution* (1992), and *The Bürgermeister's Daughter: Scandal in a Sixteenth Century German Town* (1996) were selections of the History Book Club. His most recent book is *Flesh and Spirit: Private Life in Early Modern Germany* (1999).

Frank M. Turner is John Hay Whitney Professor of History at Yale University, where he served as University Provost from 1988 to 1992. He received his B.A. degree at the College of William and Mary and his Ph.D. from Yale. He has received the Yale College Award for Distinguished Undergraduate Teaching. He has directed a National Endowment for the Humanities Summer Institute. His scholarly research has received the support of fellowships from the National Endowment for the Humanities and the Guggenheim Foundation. He is the author of *Between Science and Religion: The Reaction to Scientific Naturalism in Late Victorian England* (1974), *The Greek Heritage in Victorian Britain* (1981), which received the British Council Prize of the Conference on British Studies and the Yale Press Governors Award, and *Contesting Cultural Authority: Essays in Victorian Intellectual Life* (1993). He has also contributed numerous articles to journals and has served on the editorial advisory boards of *The Journal of Modern History, Isis*, and *Victorian Studies*. He edited *John Henry Newman, The Idea of a University* (1996). Since 1996 he has served as a Trustee of Connecticut College.

THE HERITAGE
OF WORLD
CIVILIZATIONS

THE COMING OF CIVILIZATION

Homo sapiens—modern humans—first appeared about 100,000 years ago. Since then the pace of human control over the environment has constantly accelerated. It took us tens of thousands of years to domesticate animals and to master the rudiments of agriculture. It took us another 7,000–9,000 years to develop cities, systems of writing, then bronze and iron. Several hundred years later, the great religious and philosophical revolutions of the ancient world occurred, followed by the empires of China, India, Iran, and Rome.

The timetable for the development of river-valley civilizations varied. The Near Eastern cultures began earlier, followed by India and China. But the parallelism in stages of development is remarkable. First came agriculture and pottery; then cities, writing, and bronze; and, finally, iron and empire. In the Americas the civilizations of Mesoamerica and the Andes followed a similar sequence from agriculture to urbanism to empire. Does the logic of nature dictate that once agriculture develops, cities will arise in alluvial river valleys favorable to intensive cultivation?

That is to say, did agriculture set in motion a chain of similar events in widely separated regions? Or is diffusion a more likely cause? Both hypotheses—diffusion and independent origins—are plausible. However, a definitive answer cannot be given.

In or near the same Eurasian and African river valleys that saw the birth of civilization occurred the religious and philosophical revolutions that permanently marked the world thereafter: monotheistic Judaism, from which would later develop Christianity and Islam; Hinduism and Buddhism in southern Asia; and the philosophies of China and Greece. The simultaneity of their appearance was striking. The Hebrew prophets, Buddha, Confucius, and Socrates were grouped within a few hundred years of each other in the first millennium B.C.E.

The coming of the bronze and iron ages led to a series of crises of the early civilizations across the world. The founders of the great religions and philosophies responded to these crises with new visions of humanity's place in the universe, and with new and more universal ethics. Buddhism, Christianity, and Islam differed from the Shinto of Japan, the religions of the Egyptians or Mayas in contending that their answers were true for all peoples and times. This universalism made them missionary religions.

Similarly, the philosophies of China and Greece were more universal than previous systems of thought. Confucianism eventually spread to Korea, Japan, and Vietnam, where it became the basis for laws because its ethics transcended Chinese institutions.

Greek ideas played an equivalent role in the west. They joined Judaic concepts to form Christianity. Universal Greek conceptions also lay at the base of the Roman law code (*ius gentium*) used to govern peoples with widely varying customs. This last example says something about the transition from the older civilizations to the empires of the ancient world. For their leaders to govern and their bureaucracies to function, they had to have philosophies and laws.

1 BIRTH OF CIVILIZATION

The earliest humans lived by hunting, fishing, and collecting wild plants. Only some 10,000 years ago did they learn to cultivate plants, herd animals, and make airtight pottery for storage. These discoveries transformed them from gatherers to producers and allowed them to grow in number and to lead a settled life. Beginning about 5,000 years ago a far more complex way of life began to appear in some parts of the world. In these places, humans learned how to increase harvests through irrigation and other methods, making possible much larger populations. They came together in cities and other centers, where industry and commerce flourished. They developed writing. Specialized occupations emerged, complex religions took form, and social divisions increased. These changes marked the birth of civilization.

Early Human Beings and Their Culture

Humans, unlike other animals, are cultural beings. *Culture* may be defined as the ways of living built up by a group and passed on from one generation to another. Language, apparently a uniquely human trait, lies behind our ability to transmit culture from one generation to another.

The Paleolithic Age

Anthropologists designate early human cultures by their tools. The earliest cultural period—the Paleolithic (from Greek, "old stone")—dates from the first use of stone tools some 1 or 2 million years ago to about 10,000 B.C.E. During this long span, people were hunters, fishers, and gatherers—but not producers—of food. They learned to make and use increasingly sophisticated tools, to make and control fire, and to acquire language.

Paleolithic technology could support only a sparsely settled society. If hunters were too numerous, game would not suffice. Paleolithic society was probably characterized by a division of labor by sex. Men most likely hunted, fished, and fought. Women, less mobile because of childbearing, most likely gathered nuts, berries, and wild grains, wove baskets, and made clothing. Women gathering food probably discovered how to plant and care for seeds, knowledge that eventually led to agriculture and the Neolithic revolution.

The Neolithic Age

However it happened, some 10,000 years ago parts of what we now call the Near East began to shift from a hunter-gatherer way of life to a settled agricultural one characteristic of the Neolithic ("new stone") Age. Neolithic people domesticated animals as well as plants. They invented pottery. They learned to weave cloth from flax and wool. And to give their crops the constant care they required from planting to harvest, Neolithic people built permanent buildings, usually in clusters near the best fields.

Over time, in the regions where agriculture and animal husbandry appeared, the number of human beings grew. The Neolithic revolution was a major step in human control of nature, and it was a vital precondition for the emergence of civilization. The earliest Neolithic societies appeared in the Near East about 8000 B.C.E., in China about 4000 B.C.E., and in India about 5500 B.C.E. In Mesoamerica (modern Mexico and Central America) and in the Andean region of South America, settled agricultural societies were becoming prevalent by about 2500 B.C.E.

The Emergence of Civilization

Beginning between 4000 and 3000 B.C.E., civilization first appeared in the valley of the Tigris and Euphrates Rivers in the region called Mesopotamia, later in the valley of the Nile River in Egypt, and somewhat later still in the Indus Valley in India and the Yellow River basin in China (see Map 1–1). It was marked by the appearance of urban centers, monumental architecture, hierarchical societies, and the invention of writing. The period is known as the Bronze Age because it coincided with the discovery of the technique for smelting tin and copper to make bronze, a stronger and more useful metal.

Early Civilizations in the Near East

About 4000 B.C.E., people began to move in large numbers into the river-watered lowlands of Mesopotamia and Egypt. By about 3000 B.C.E., when the invention of writing gave birth to history, urban life and the organization of society into centralized states was established in the valleys of the Tigris and Euphrates Rivers in Mesopotamia and the Nile River in Egypt.

The concentration of people in cities created something new. Unlike Neolithic villages, cities served as administrative, religious, manufacturing, entertainment, and commercial centers. Great temples were built. Commerce supported a merchant class. The earliest written records

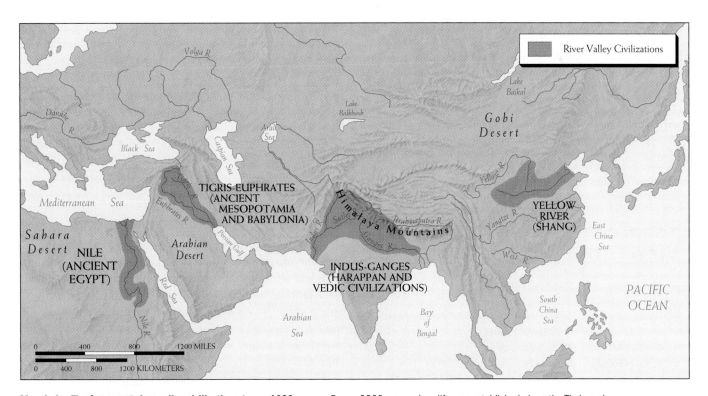

Map 1–1 The four great river valley civilizations to ca. 1000 B.C.E. By ca. 2000 B.C.E. urban life was established along the Tigris and Euphrates Rivers in Mesopotamia, the Nile River in Egypt, the Indus and Ganges Rivers in India, and the Yellow River in China.

reflect this increasing complexity. City governments recorded their acts and laws. Because early writing was so difficult, scribes emerged.

The typical king in a river valley civilization was regarded as divine. Beneath the monarch were military aristocrats and priests; below them were mostly peasants; and at the bottom were slaves. Most of the land was owned or controlled by the king, the nobility, and the priests.

Mesopotamian Civilization

The oldest Mesopotamian cities seem to have been founded by the Sumerians, around 3000 B.C.E. From about 2800 to 2370 B.C.E., several Sumerian city-states arose in southern Mesopotamia. In time, stronger towns conquered weaker ones and expanded to form larger units, usually kingdoms.

The region immediately upstream from the principal Sumerian city-states was occupied mostly by people who spoke a Semitic language (in the same family as Arabic and Hebrew). These people established their own kingdom, with its capital at Akkad, near the site of a later city known to us as Babylon. Under Sargon, the Akkadians conquered the Sumerian cities and created an empire. Sargon ruled from about 2370 B.C.E. and established a family, or dynasty, of Semitic kings that ruled Sumer and Akkad for two centuries.

External attack and internal weakness destroyed Akkad. Then, about 1900 B.C.E., a people called the Amorites gained control of the region, establishing their capital at Babylon.

The Amorite, or Old Babylonian, dynasty dominated Mesopotamia for about 300 years. Its high point was the reign of Hammurabi (r. ca. 1792–1750 B.C.E.), best known for the law code that bears his name. The Code of Hammurabi reveals a society strictly divided by class; there were nobles, commoners, and slaves, and the law did not treat them equally. Punishments were harsh. The code makes it clear that law and justice came from the gods through the king.

About 1600 B.C.E., the Babylonian kingdom fell apart under the impact of invasions from the north and east.

Government The first historical city-states had kings or priest-kings who led the army, administered the economy, and served as judges and as intermediaries between their people and the gods. Later, on some occasions and for relatively short periods, they were worshiped as divine.

This union of church and state (to use modern terminology) in the person of the king reflected the centralization of power typical of Mesopotamian life. The economy was managed from the center by the priests and the king. Each year the land was surveyed, fields were assigned to specific farmers, and the amount of seed to be used was designated. The government estimated the size of the crop and planned its distribution even before it was planted.

This process required a large and competent staff, the ability to observe and record natural phenomena, a good knowledge of mathematics, and, for all of this, a system of writing. The Sumerians invented the writing system known as *cuneiform* (from the Latin *cuneus*, "wedge") because of the wedge-shaped stylus with which they wrote on clay tablets.

Religion The Sumerians and their successors worshiped gods with human forms, each of whom was usually identified with some natural phenomenon. Expert knowledge was required to influence the gods, and so the priesthood flourished. The Babylonians, in an effort to discover the will and intentions of the gods, sought evidence of divine action in the movements of the heavenly bodies and gave birth to astrology. This religious activity required armies of scribes to keep records and learned priests to interpret them.

Religion, in the form of myth, played a large part in the literature and art of Mesopotamia. The Babylonians told tales of the creation of the world, of a great flood that almost destroyed human life, of an island paradise from which the god Enki was expelled for eating forbidden plants, and many more.

Society The many sections of the Code of Hammurabi devoted to debts, rates of interest, security, and default indicate the importance of Babylonian commercial life. Sections also deal with builders, surgeons, and other professionals, with land tenure, and with the family. Marriages were arranged by the parents. A husband whose wife was childless or ill could take a second wife. Extramarital relations between the husband and concubines, slaves, and prostitutes were accepted.

The wife seems to have been treated as an individual with rights protected by the law. Divorce was relatively easy, and women divorced by their husbands without good cause received

Key Events and People in Mesopotamian History

ca. 3500 B.C.E.	Sumerians arrive
ca. 2800–2370 B.C.E.	Sumerian city-states
ca. 2370 B.C.E.	Sargon establishes Semitic dynasty at Akkad
ca. 2125–2027 B.C.E.	Third Dynasty of Ur
ca. 1900 B.C.E.	Amorites at Babylon
ca. 1792–1750 B.C.E.	Reign of Hammurabi
ca. 1600 B.C.E.	Invasion by Hittites and Kassites

Hammurabi's Code on Women, Marriage, and Divorce in Babylonia

Hammurabi, of the Old Babylonian, or Amorite, dynasty, was king of Babylonia from 1792 to 1750 B.C.E. His empire extended from the Mediterranean Sea to the Persian Gulf, with its capital at Babylon in what is now Iraq. His greatest legacy is his code of written law, derived and refined from a long tradition of law codes in ancient Mesopotamia. It is a uniquely valuable source for understanding the character of society at that time. The following laws from Hammurabi's law code focus on the place of women and marriage in that society.

What rights and protections did women have in Hammurabi's Babylonia? Under what conditions could a man divorce his wife? What might deter him from such a divorce? Was betrothal protected by law? How do the institutions of marriage and divorce in Babylonia compare with those in modern America? What do you think are some consequences of the differences?

If a seignior wishes to divorce his wife who did not bear him children, he shall give her money to the full amount of her marriage-price and he shall also make good to her the dowry which she brought from her father's house and then he may divorce her.

If there was no marriage-price, he shall give her one mina of silver as the divorce-settlement.

If he is a peasant, he shall give her one-third mina of silver.

If a seignior's wife, who was living in the house of the seignior, has made up her mind to leave in order that she may engage in business, thus neglecting her house (and) humiliating her husband, they shall prove it against her; and if her husband has then decided on her divorce, he may divorce her, with nothing to be given her as her divorce-settlement upon her departure. If her husband has not decided on her divorce, her husband may marry another woman, with the former woman living in the house of her husband like a maidservant.

If a woman so hated her husband that she has declared, "You may not have me," her record shall be investigated at her city council, and if she was careful and was not at fault, even though her husband has been going out and disparaging her greatly, that woman, without incurring any blame at all, may take her dowry and go off to her father's house.

If she was not careful, but was a gadabout, thus neglecting her house (and) humiliating her husband, they shall throw that woman into the water.

When a seignior married a woman and a fever has then seized her, if he has made up his mind to marry another, he may marry (her), without divorcing his wife whom the fever seized; she shall live in the house which he built and he shall continue to support her as long as she lives.

If that woman has refused to live in her husband's house, he shall make good her dowry to her which she brought from her father's house and then she may leave.

If a seignior, upon presenting a field, orchard, house, or goods to his wife, left a sealed document with her, her children may not enter a claim against her after (the death of) her husband, since the mother may give her inheritance to that son of hers whom she likes, (but) she may not give (it) to an outsider.

If a seignior, who had the betrothal-gift brought to the house of his (prospective) father-in-law (and) paid the marriage-price, has then fallen in love with another woman and has said to his (prospective) father-in-law, "I will not marry your daughter," the father of the daughter shall keep whatever was brought to him.

If a seignior, who had the betrothal-gift brought to the house of the (prospective) father-in-law (and) paid the marriage-price, has the daughter has then said, "I will not give my daughter to you," he shall pay back double the full amount that was brought to him.

If a seignior, who had the betrothal-gift brought to the house of his (prospective) father-in-law (and) paid the marriage-price, and then a friend of his has so maligned him that his (prospective) father-in-law has said to the (prospective) husband, "You may not marry my daughter," he shall pay back double the full amount that was brought to him, but his friend may not marry his (intended) wife.

From "The Code of Hammurabi," translated by Theophile J. Meek in James B. Pritchard, ed., *Ancient Near Eastern Texts*, 3d Ed., © 1969, renewed 1978 by Princeton University Press, pp. 172–173. Reprinted by permission of Princeton University Press.

---

their dowry back. A woman seeking divorce could also recover her dowry if her husband could not convict her of wrongdoing. On the other hand, a woman's place was thought to be in the home.

For most of Mesopotamian history slavery arose from debt. Parents could sell their children into slavery or pledge themselves and their family as surety for a loan. Some slaves worked for the king and the state, others for the temple and the priests, and still others for private citizens.

Slaves could engage in business and hold property. They could marry free men or women, and the resulting children would be free. Slaves who acquired wealth could buy their freedom. Nevertheless, slaves were property, were subject to their master's will, and had little legal protection.

Egyptian Civilization

The center of Egyptian civilization was the Nile River. From its source in central Africa, the Nile runs north some 4,000 miles to the Mediterranean, with long navigable stretches broken by several cataracts. Ancient Egypt included the 750 miles of the valley from the First Cataract to the sea. Upper (southern) Egypt consisted of the narrow valley of the Nile. Lower (northern) Egypt consisted of the broad delta, which branches out about 150 miles along the Mediterranean coast.

The Nile alone made life possible in Egypt's almost rainless desert. Each year the river flooded and covered the land, and when it receded it left a fertile mud that could produce two crops a year. The construction and maintenance of irrigation ditches to preserve the river's water, along with careful planning and organization of planting and harvesting, produced agricultural prosperity unmatched in the ancient world.

The Nile also served as a highway connecting the long, narrow country and encouraging its unification. By 3100 B.C.E., Upper and Lower Egypt had been united into a single kingdom. Nature helped protect and isolate the ancient Egyptians from outsiders. The cataracts, the sea, and the desert made it difficult for foreigners to reach Egypt for either friendly or hostile purposes. Egypt knew far more peace and security than Mesopotamia. This security, along with the sunny, predictable climate, gave Egyptian civilization a more optimistic

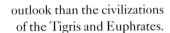

Seated Egyptian scribe, height 21 in. (53 cm) painted limestone, Fifth Dynasty, ca. 2510–2460 B.C.E. One of the hallmarks of the early river valley civilizations was the development of writing. Ancient Egyptian scribes had to undergo rigorous training, but were rewarded with a position of respect and privilege. [Musee du Louvre, Paris. © Giraudon/Art Resource, N.Y.]

outlook than the civilizations of the Tigris and Euphrates. Events in the more than 3,000-year span of ancient Egyptian history are traditionally dated by reference to the reigns of thirty-one royal dynasties, which modern historians have clustered into eight periods.

The Old Kingdom (2700–2200 B.C.E.) By the time of the Third Dynasty, Egypt's kings had achieved supremacy. Ruling from their capital at Memphis, in Upper Egypt, just above the opening of the delta, they had the resources of a huge, prosperous nation at their disposal. Royal power was absolute. The king (the title *pharaoh*, meaning "great house" or "palace," was not used until later in Egyptian history) governed through his family, appointing and removing officials at his pleasure. Peasants were carefully regulated and were taxed heavily.

An Egyptian king was considered a god, on whom the lives, safety, and prosperity of his people depended. The land was his own personal possession, and the people his servants. Because he was the direct source of law and justice, Egypt needed no law codes. Government was merely an aspect of religion, and religion dominated Egyptian life. The gods of Egypt took many forms: animals, humans, and natural forces.

The Egyptians buried their dead according to elaborate conventions, supplying the grave with things the departed would need for a pleasant life after death. Bodies were preserved as mummies. Tombs were beautifully decorated with paintings; offerings of food were regularly brought to the dead.

Periods in Ancient Egyptian History (dynasties in Roman numerals)

ca. 3100–2700 B.C.E.	Early Dynastic Period (I–II)
ca. 2700–2200 B.C.E.	Old Kingdom (III–VI)
ca. 2200–2052 B.C.E.	First Intermediate Period (VII–X)
ca. 2052–1786 B.C.E.	Middle Kingdom (XI–XII)
ca. 1786–1575 B.C.E.	Second Intermediate Period (XIII–XVII)
ca. 1700 B.C.E.	Hyksos invasion
ca. 1575–1087 B.C.E.	New Kingdom (or Empire) (XVIII–XX)
ca. 1087–30 B.C.E.	Post-Empire (XXI–XXXI)

Nothing better illustrates the extent of royal power than the three great pyramids built as tombs by the kings of the Fourth Dynasty. They are remarkable for the great technical skill they demonstrate, but even more for the concentration of resources they represent.

Though the idea of writing may have come from Mesopotamia, Egyptian script developed independently. It was a difficult and complicated script that the Greeks later called *hieroglyph* ("sacred carvings"). Egyptian literature consisted of hymns, myths, magical formulas, tales of travel, and "wisdom literature" (bits of advice to help one get on well in the world).

The Middle Kingdom (2052–1786 B.C.E.) About 2200 B.C.E. the Old Kingdom collapsed. After a period of confusion (the First Intermediate Period, ca. 2200–2052 B.C.E.), the governors of Thebes in Upper Egypt established the Middle Kingdom in 2052 B.C.E.

The rulers of the Twelfth Dynasty brought order, peace, and prosperity after the troubles of the First Intermediate Period. They encouraged trade and extended Egyptian power and influence toward Palestine and Ethiopia.

The New Kingdom (Empire) (1575–1087 B.C.E.) and After The resurgent power of the local nobility and the erosion of central authority mark the end of the Middle Kingdom and the beginning of the Second Intermediate Period (1786–1575 B.C.E.). About 1700 B.C.E., a people called the Hyksos—Semitic peoples from the eastern Mediterranean—conquered the Nile Delta. About 1575 B.C.E., a dynasty from Thebes drove out the Hyksos and reunited Egypt, marking the beginning of the New Kingdom, or Empire Period.

The kings of the New Kingdom built a powerful army and pushed out Egypt's frontiers to the south and east and forged an empire that extended across Palestine and Syria to the upper Euphrates. Egyptian expansion was finally checked by the powerful Hittite Empire of Asia Minor. Egypt survived, but its period of glory had passed. Throughout the Post–Empire period (1087–30 B.C.E.) it repeatedly fell victim to foreign invasion and rule.

Ancient Near Eastern Empires

In the time of the Eighteenth Dynasty in Egypt, new groups of peoples established themselves in the Near East: the Kassites in Babylonia, the Hittites in Asia Minor. The Hittites forged an empire that lasted 200 years.

The Hittites

By about 1500 B.C.E., the Hittites had established a strong, centralized kingdom near Ankara, the capital of modern Turkey. Between 1400 and 1200 B.C.E., they contested Egypt's control of Palestine and Syria, but by 1200 B.C.E., their kingdom was gone, swept away by new Indo-European migrants. The Hittites appear to have been responsible for a great technological advance, the smelting of iron. They also played an important role in transmitting the ancient cultures of Mesopotamia and Egypt to the Greeks, who lived on their frontiers.

The Assyrians

The fall of the Hittites was followed by the rise of the Assyrians. Their homeland was in the valleys and hills of northern Mesopotamia and the area east of the Tigris River. They had a series of capitals, of which Nineveh is perhaps the best known. They spoke a Semitic language and were culturally a part of Mesopotamia.

After 1000 B.C.E., the Assyrians began a period of steady expansion, and by 665 B.C.E., they controlled all of Mesopotamia, much of Asia Minor, Syria, Palestine, and Egypt. They succeeded thanks to a large, well-disciplined army and a society that valued military virtues. Fierce and cruel, they boasted of their own brutality, at least in part to terrorize real and potential enemies.

Unlike earlier empires, the Assyrian Empire systematically exploited the area it held. The Assyrians used various methods of control, ranging from collecting tribute to stationing garrisons in conquered territory to scattering populations away from their homelands.

In the seventh century B.C.E., a new dynasty in Babylon threw off Assyrian rule, joined with the rising kingdom of Media to the east (in modern Iran), and defeated the Assyrians, destroying Nineveh in 612 B.C.E. The successor kingdoms, the Chaldean (or Neo-Babylonian) and the Median, did not last long. By 539 B.C.E., they were swallowed by yet another great eastern empire, that of the Persians (see Chapter 4).

Key Events in the History of Ancient Near Eastern Empires	
ca. 1400–1200 B.C.E.	Hittite Empire
ca. 1100 B.C.E.	Rise of Assyrian power
ca. 732–722 B.C.E.	Assyrian conquest of Palestine-Syria
ca. 671 B.C.E.	Assyrian conquest of Egypt
ca. 612 B.C.E.	Destruction of Assyrian capital at Nineveh
ca. 612–539 B.C.E.	Neo-Babylonian (Chaldean) Empire

Early Indian Civilization

The Indian subcontinent's earliest literate, urban civilization arose in the valley of the Indus River sometime after 2600, and by about 2300 B.C.E. was trading with Mesopotamia. Known as the Indus-Valley Culture (or Harappan), it lasted only a few centuries. The region's second identifiable civilization is known as the Vedic Aryan civilization after the originally nomadic Indo-European (or "Aryan") immigrant people who founded it and their holy texts, or Vedas. It dates to about 1500 B.C.E. and endured for nearly a millennium without cities or writing, but with religious and social traditions that commingled with older traditions to form the Indian civilization as it has developed in the past two and a half millennia.

The Indus Civilization

No one knew of the existence of the Indus culture until archaeologists discovered it at the site of Harappa in the 1920s. Since then, some seventy cities, the largest being Harappa and Mohenjo-Daro, have been identified. This urban civilization had bronze tools, writing, covered drainage systems, and a diversified social and economic organization. Though it remains the least understood of the early river valley civilizations, archaeological evidence and inferences from later Indian life allow us to reconstruct something of its culture.

Indus stone stamp seal. Note the familiar humped bull of India.

[© Scala/Art Resource, N.Y.]

General Character   The Indus culture was remarkably homogeneous. City layouts, building construction, highly developed weights and measures, seal inscriptions, fine-patterned pottery and figurines, and even the burnt brick used for buildings and floodwalls are unusually uniform in all Indus towns, suggesting an integrated economic system and good internal communications.

Indus culture was also remarkably constant over time. Because the main cities and towns lay in river lowlands subject to periodic flooding, they were rebuilt often, each new level of construction closely following its precursor's pattern. Similarly, the Indus script shows no evidence of change over time. This stability, regularity, and traditionalism have led scholars to speculate that this far-flung society had a centralized government, perhaps a conservative (priestly) theocracy rather than a more unstable royal dynasty.

Cities   Harappa and Mohenjo-Daro both apparently had populations of more than 35,000 and were meticulously laid out. To the west of each stood a large, walled citadel on a raised rectangular platform. The town proper was laid out on a north-south, east-west grid of main avenues. The citadel apparently contained the main public buildings.

The town "blocks" formed by the main avenues were crisscrossed by small, less rigidly planned lanes, off of which opened private houses. The typical house was built around a central courtyard and presented only blank walls to the lanes or streets outside.

Perhaps the most striking feature of these cities was a complex system of covered drains and sewers. Private houses were serviced by wells, bathrooms, and latrines. The drainage system that served these facilities was an engineering feat unrivaled in the ancient world until the time of the Romans, nearly 2,000 years later.

Economic Life   The economy of the Indus state or states was based on a thriving agriculture. The people wove cloth from cotton, made metal tools, and used the potter's wheel. Evidence points to trade between the Indus culture and Mesopotamia. Metals and semiprecious stones were apparently imported from present-day Iran, Afghanistan, and Central Asia, from farther south on the Indian peninsula, and perhaps from Arabia. Artistic styles suggest that trade contacts resulted in cultural borrowings.

Material Culture   Among the most striking accomplishments of the Indus culture are fine sculptures and artifacts, including copper and bronze tools and vessels, painted pottery, stonework, figurines and toys, jewelry, and dyed fabric. However, except for some decorative brickwork, no monumental friezes, mosaics, or sculpture have been found.

Religion   The elaborate bath facilities suggest that ritual bathing and water purification rites were important. The many images of male animals such as the humped bull might be symbols of power and fertility or might indicate animal worship. A recurring image of a male figure with leafy headdress and horns, often seated in a posture associated later in India with yogic meditation, has been likened to the Vedic Aryan "Lord of All Creatures." Terra-cotta figurines of females, often pregnant or carrying a child, are suggestive of similar female images in several prehistoric cultures. They may also represent an element of pre-Aryan religion that reemerged later to figure in "Hindu" culture.

The Passing of Indus Civilization   Some time from about 1800 to 1700 B.C.E., Indus civilization declined and disappeared. It is not clear whether its demise was related to the warlike Aryan invaders or to abnormal flooding or a long period of dessication. Whatever the reason, the Indus culture remains still too much in the shadows of prehistory for its proper influence to be gauged.

The Vedic Aryan Civilization

The Aryan culture effectively "refounded" Indian civilization around 1500 B.C.E. Yet virtually our only source of knowledge about ancient Aryan life is the "winged words" of the Vedas, the Aryan sacred texts—hence we know the culture as "Vedic." The Vedas are ritual, priestly, and speculative, not historical works. They tell us little about events but do offer insight into the religion, society, values, and thought of early Aryan India.

Veda means "knowledge." We speak of "the Vedas" to refer to the four major compilations of Vedic ritual texts. The most significant of the four for the history of the early Aryans is the collection of 1,028 religious hymns known as the *Rig Veda*, which represent the oldest materials of the Vedas, dating from ca. 1000 B.C.E., to perhaps 1700–1200 B.C.E., when the Aryans spread across the northern plains to the upper reaches of the Ganges.

"Aryan" is a different kind of term. It was apparently the original name of peoples who migrated out of the steppeland between Eastern Europe and Central Asia into Europe, Greece, Anatolia, the Iranian plateau, and India during the second and first millennia B.C.E. Those who came to India are thus more precisely designated *Indo-Aryans*, or *Vedic Aryans*.

In the nineteenth century, "Aryan" was the term applied to the widespread language group known more commonly today as *Indo-European*. To this widely distributed family belong Greek, Latin, the Romance and Germanic languages, the Slavic tongues, and the Indo-Iranian languages, including Persian and Sanskrit and their derivatives. The Nazis perversely misused "Aryan" to refer to a white "master race." Today *Aryan* usually only refers to the Indo-European speakers who invaded India and the Iranian plateau in the second millennium B.C.E., and in linguistics as a name for the Indo-Iranian languages.

"Aryanizing" of North India   The Vedic Aryans were seminomadic warriors who reached India through the mountain passes of the Hindu Kush. Theirs was probably a gradual migration of small tribal groups. They were horsemen and cattle herders rather than farmers and city builders. They left their mark not in material culture but in the changes that their conquests brought to the regions they overran: a new language, a new social organization, new techniques of warfare, and new religious forms and ideas.

They penetrated first into the Punjab and the Indus Valley around 1800–1500 B.C.E. Their horses, chariots, and copper-bronze weapons likely gave them military superiority. Echos of early conflicts can be heard in some Rigvedic hymns.

How far they penetrated during the *Rigvedic age* (ca. 1700–1000 B.C.E.) is not clear, but their main locus remained the Punjab and the plains west of the Yamuna River. Then, between about 1000 and 500 B.C.E., the *Later Vedic age*, they spread across the plain between the Yamuna and the Ganges, northeast to the Himalayan foothills and southeast along the Ganges, in what was to be the cradle of subsequent Indian civilization.

The Later Vedic period is also called the *Brahmanic age* because it was dominated by the priestly religion of the Brahman class, as evidenced in commentaries called the *Brahmanas* (ca. 1000–800 or 600 B.C.E.). It also provided the setting for India's two classical epics, the *Mahabharata* and the *Ramayana*, both of which reflect the complex cultural and social mixing of Aryan and other earlier subcontinent peoples.

By about 200 C.E., this mixing was to produce a distinctive new "Indian" civilization over most of the subcontinent. Its basis was clearly Aryan, but its language, society, and religion incorporated many non-Aryan elements.

Vedic Aryan Society   Aryan society was apparently patrilineal—with succession and inheritance in the male line—and its gods were likewise predominantly male. Marriage appears to have been monogamous, and widows could remarry. Related families formed larger kin groups. The largest social grouping was the tribe, ruled by a chieftain or *raja* ("king" in Sanskrit). By the Brahmanic age, the power of the priestly class increased, along with that of the king, who, with the sanction of the priestly establishment, became a hereditary ruler claiming divine qualities.

Aryan society seems originally to have had only two basic divisions: noble and common. The *Dasas*—the darker, conquered peoples—came to form a third group of the socially excluded. Over time, a more rigid scheme of four social classes (excluding the non-Aryan *Dasas*) evolved. By the late Rigvedic period, these four divisions, or *varnas*—the priestly *(Brahman)*, the warrior/noble *(Kshatriya)*, the peasant/tradesman *(Vaishya)*, and the servant *(Shudra)*—had become so basic as to be sanctioned explicitly in religious theory. Only the members of the three upper classes participated fully in social, political, and religious life. This scheme underlies the rigid caste system that later became fundamental to Indian society.

Material Culture   The early, seminomadic Aryans had little impressive material culture. They lived simply in wood and thatch or, later, mud-walled dwellings. They measured wealth in cattle, and were accomplished at carpentry and bronze working. They cultivated some crops, especially grains.

The Brahmanic age is also poor in material remains. Urban culture remained undeveloped, although mud-brick towns appeared. Established kingdoms with fixed capitals now existed. Trade was growing. Later texts mention artisans, including goldsmiths, basketmakers, weavers, potters, and entertainers.

To judge from references to its common use by around 500 B.C.E., writing had been reintroduced to India some time earlier, perhaps about 700 B.C.E. The prestige of oral transmission for the Vedas remained so high among the Brahman class, however, that writing continued to be scorned for truly sacred texts.

Religion   The earliest Indo-Aryans seem to have worshiped numerous gods. The Rigvedic hymns are addressed to anthropomorphic deities linked to natural phenomena such as the sky, the clouds, and the sun. Chief among them was Indra, god of war and the storm.

Ritual sacrifice was the central focus of Vedic religion, its goal apparently to invoke the presence of the gods to whom an offering was made rather than to expiate sins or express thanksgiving. The drinking of soma juice, an intoxicant, was a prominent aspect of the sacrificial ritual. A recurring theme of the Vedic hymns that accompanied the rituals is the desire for the good things of this life: prosperity, health, and victory. Fire sacrifices, both public and domestic, were particularly important.

By Brahmanic times, a considerable body of mystical speculation had developed around the sacrificial ritual. The god, the offering, the sacrifice, and the sacrificer, for example, were all identified with one another. The word *Brahman*, originally used to designate the ritual utterance or word of power, came to refer also to the generalized divine power present in the sacrifice. In the Upanishads, some of the latest Vedic texts and the ones most concerned with speculation about the universe, *Brahman* was extended to refer to the Absolute, the transcendent principle of reality. As the guardian of ritual and the master of the sacred word, the priest was known throughout the Vedic Aryan period by a related word, *Brahmana*, for which the English is *Brahman*. Echoes of these associations were to lend force in later Hindu tradition to the special status of the Brahman caste groups as the highest social class (see Chapter 4).

Early Chinese Civilization
Neolithic Origins in the Yellow River Valley

Agriculture began in China about 4000 B.C.E. in the basin of the southern bend of the Yellow River. The chief crop of China's agricultural revolution was millet. The early Chinese cleared land and burned its cover to plant millet and cabbage and, later, rice and soybeans. When the soil became exhausted, fields and sometimes early villages were abandoned. Tools were of stone: axes, hoes, spades, and sickle-shaped knives. The early Chinese domesticated pigs, sheep, cattle, dogs, and chickens. Grain was stored in pottery.

The earliest cultivators lived in wattle-and-daub pit dwellings with wooden support posts and sunken, plastered floors. Their villages were located in isolated clearings along slopes of river valleys. They buried their dead in cemeteries with jars of food. Tribal leaders wore rings and beads of jade.

Early Bronze Age: The Shang

The traditional history of China tells of three ancient dynasties: Hsia (2205–1766 B.C.E.), Shang (1766–1050 B.C.E.), and

---

Ancient India

ca. 2250–1750 (2500–1500?) B.C.E.	Indus (Harappan) civilization (written script still undeciphered)
ca. 1800–1500 B.C.E.	Aryan peoples invade northwestern India
ca. 1500–1000 B.C.E.	Rigvedic period: composition of Rigvedic hymns; Punjab as center of Indo-Aryan civilization
ca. 1000–500 B.C.E.	Later Vedic period: Doab as center of Indo-Aryan civilization
ca. 1000–800/600 B.C.E.	Composition of *Brahmanas* and other Vedic texts
ca. 800–500 B.C.E.	Composition of major Upanishads
ca. 700–500 B.C.E.	Probable reintroduction of writing
ca. 400 B.C.E.–200 C.E.	Composition of great epics, the *Mahabharata* and *Ramayana*

Chou (1050–256 B.C.E.). Until early in the twentieth century, modern historians saw the first two as legendary. Then, in the 1920s, archaeological excavations near present-day An Yang uncovered the ruins of a walled city that had been a late Shang capital. Other Shang cities have been discovered more recently. The ruins contained the archives of the department of divination of the Shang court, with thousands of "oracle bones" incised with archaic Chinese writing. The names of kings on the bones fit almost perfectly those of the traditional historical record. The recognition that the Shang actually existed has led historians to suggest that the Hsia may also have been an actual dynasty.

The characteristic political institution of Bronze Age China was the city-state. The walled city contained public buildings, altars, and the residences of the aristocracy; it was surrounded by a sea of Neolithic tribal villages. By late Shang times, several such cities were spotted across the north China plain.

The military aristocracy went to war in chariots, supported by levies of foot soldiers. The Shang fought against barbarian tribes and, occasionally, against other city-states in rebellion against Shang rule. Captured prisoners were enslaved.

The three most notable features of Shang China were writing, bronzes, and the appearance of social classes. Scribes at the Shang court kept records on strips of bamboo, but few of these have survived. What have survived in great numbers are inscriptions on bronze artifacts and the oracle bones. Some bones contain the question put to the oracle, the answer, and the outcome of the matter. Representative questions were: Which ancestor is causing the king's earache? Will the king's child be a son? Was a sacrifice acceptable to ancestral deities?

What we know of Shang religion is based on the bones. The Shang believed in a supreme "Deity Above," who had authority over the human world. There were also lesser natural deities—the sun, moon, earth, rain, wind, and the six clouds—who served at the court of the Deity Above. Even the Shang king sacrificed not to the Deity Above but to his ancestors, who interceded with the Deity Above on the king's behalf. Kings, while alive at least, were not considered divine but were regarded as the high priests of the state.

In Shang times, as later, religion in China was closely associated with cosmology. The Shang people observed the movements of the planets and stars and reported eclipses. Celestial happenings were seen as omens from the gods. The chief cosmologists also recorded events at the court. The Shang calendar had a month of 30 days and a year of 360 days. Adjustments were made periodically by adding an extra month. The calendar was used by the king to tell his people when to sow and when to reap.

Bronze appeared in China about 2000 B.C.E. It was used for weapons, armor, and chariot fittings, and for ceremonial vessels.

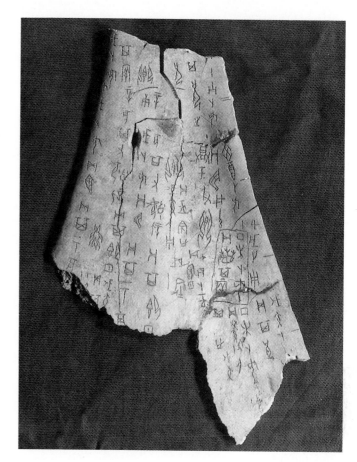

Inscribed oracle bone from the Shang Dynasty city of An Yang. [From the Collection of the C.V. Starr East Asian Library, Columbia University]

A hierarchy of class defined life in the Chinese city-state. The king and the officials of his court lived within the walled city. Their lifestyle was, for ancient times, opulent. In contrast, a far larger population of agricultural workers lived outside the city in cramped pit dwellings. Their life was meager and hard.

Nowhere was the gulf between the royal lineage and the baseborn more apparent than in the Shang institution of human sacrifice. When a king died, hundreds of slaves or prisoners of war, sometimes together with those who had served the king during his lifetime, might be buried with him. Sacrifices also were made when a palace or an altar was built.

Later Bronze Age: The Western Chou

To the west of the area of Shang rule lived the Chou people. They were less civilized and more warlike than the Shang. By 1050 B.C.E., the last Shang kings had been debilitated by campaigns against nomads in the north and rebellious tribes in the east. Taking advantage of this opportunity, the Chou swept in, conquering the Shang.

The Chou continued the Shang pattern of life and rule. The agrarian-based city-state remained the basic unit of society, and there were about 200 of them in the eighth century B.C.E. The Chou also assimilated Shang culture, continuing without interruption the development of China's ideographic writing.

The Chou kept their capital in the west but set up a secondary capital at Loyang, along the southern bend of the Yellow River. They appointed their kinsmen or other aristocratic allies to rule in other city-states. Blood or lineage ties were essential to the Chou pattern of rule. The Chou king was the head of the senior branch of the family. He performed the sacrifices to the Deity Above for the entire family. The rankings of the lords of other princely states reflected their degree of closeness to the senior line of Chou kings.

The Chou, having conquered the Shang, needed a rationale for why they, and not the Shang, were now the rightful rulers. Their argument was that Heaven had withdrawn its mandate to rule from the Shang, awarding it instead to the Chou. This concept of the Mandate of Heaven was subsequently invoked by every dynasty in China down to the twentieth century.

Iron Age: The Eastern Chou

In 771 B.C.E., the Wei valley capital of the Western Chou was overrun by barbarians. The heir to the throne escaped to the secondary capital at Loyang, beginning the Eastern Chou period.

The first phase of the Eastern Chou lasted until 481 B.C.E. After their flight to Loyang, the Chou kings were never able to reestablish their old authority. By the early seventh century B.C.E., kinship and religious ties to the Chou house had worn thin, and it no longer had the military strength to reimpose its rule. During the seventh and sixth centuries B.C.E., the political configuration was an equilibrium of many small principalities on the north-central plain surrounded by larger, wholly autonomous territorial states along the borders of the plain. The larger states expanded, conquering states on their periphery.

The second phase of the Eastern Chou is known as the Warring States period after a chronicle of the same name treating the years from 401 to 256 B.C.E. By the fifth century B.C.E., all defensive alliances had collapsed. Strong states swallowed their weaker neighbors. The border states grew

Early China

4000 B.C.E.	Neolithic agricultural villages
1766 B.C.E.	Bronze Age city-states
771 B.C.E.	Iron Age territorial states
500 B.C.E.	Age of philosophers
221 B.C.E.	China is unified

in size and power. Interstate stability disappeared. By the fourth century B.C.E., only eight or nine great territorial states remained as contenders. The only question was which one would defeat the others and go on to unify China.

Three basic changes in Chinese society contributed to the rise of large territorial states. One was the expansion of population and agricultural lands. The walled cities of the Shang and Western Chou had been like oases in the wilds, bounded by plains, marshes, and forests. But in the Eastern Chou, as population grew, wilds began to disappear. Friction arose over boundaries as states began to abut. These changes accelerated in the late sixth century B.C.E. after the start of the Iron Age. With iron tools, farmers cleared new lands and plowed deeper, raising yields and increasing agricultural surpluses. Irrigation and drainage canals became important for the first time. By the third century B.C.E., China had about 20 million people, making it the most populous country in the world, a distinction it has never lost.

A second development was the rise of commerce. Roads built for war were used by merchants. The products of one region were traded for those of another. Copper coins joined bolts of silk and precious metals as media of exchange. Chou tombs show that the material and artistic culture of China leaped ahead during this period, despite its endemic wars.

A third change that doomed the city-state was the rise of a new kind of army. The war chariots of the old aristocracy, practical only on level terrain, gave way to cavalry armed with crossbows. Most of the fighting was done by conscript foot soldiers. Armies of the territorial states numbered in the hundreds of thousands. The old nobility gave way to professional commanders. Military tactics became bloody and ruthless. Prisoners were often massacred.

Change also affected government. Lords of the new territorial states began to style themselves as kings, taking the title that previously only Chou royalty had enjoyed. The hereditary nobility began to decline, supplanted by ministers appointed for their knowledge of statecraft. To survive, new states had to transform their agricultural and commercial wealth into military strength. To administer the affairs of state, a literate bureaucracy developed. Its members were referred to as *shih*, a term that came to mean "scholar-bureaucrat." The *shih* included petty nobility, warriors, landlords, merchants, and commoners. From this class, as we will see in Chapter 2, came the philosophers who transformed the culture of China.

The Rise of Civilization in the Americas

During the last ice age, the Bering region between Siberia and Alaska was dry land. Perhaps as early as 30,000 years ago, humans crossed this land bridge. These Asian immigrants moved south and east until they eventually reached the tip of South America and the eastern regions of North America.

The earliest immigrants to the Americas, like all other Paleolithic peoples, lived by hunting, fishing, and gathering. However, compared to Africa and Eurasia, many parts of North and South America were poor in animal resources. Neither horses nor cattle populated the American continents. Where fishing or small game was not sufficiently plentiful, people had to rely on protein from vegetable sources. One result was that American production of plants providing protein far outpaced that of European agriculture. One of the most important early developments was the cultivation of maize. Wherever maize could be extensively grown, a major ingredient in the food supply was secured. The cultivation of maize appears to have been in place in Mexico by approximately 4000 B.C.E. Other important foods were potatoes, manioc, squash, beans, peppers, and tomatoes.

Early Civilizations of Mesoamerica

1500–400 B.C.E.	The Olmec
200 C.E.–750 C.E.	The Classic period in Central Mexico. Dominance of Teotihuacán in the Valley of Mexico and Monte Alban in the Valley of Oaxaca
150 C.E.–900 C.E.	The Classic period of Maya civilization in the Yucatán and Guatemala

Eventually, Mesoamerica and the Andean region of South America saw the emergence of strong, long-lasting states. In other regions with maize agriculture and settled village life—notably the North American Southwest—food supplies might have been too insecure to support the development of states.

Mesoamerica, which extends from the central part of modern Mexico into Central America, ranges from tropical rainforest to semiarid mountains (see Map 1–2). Archaeologists

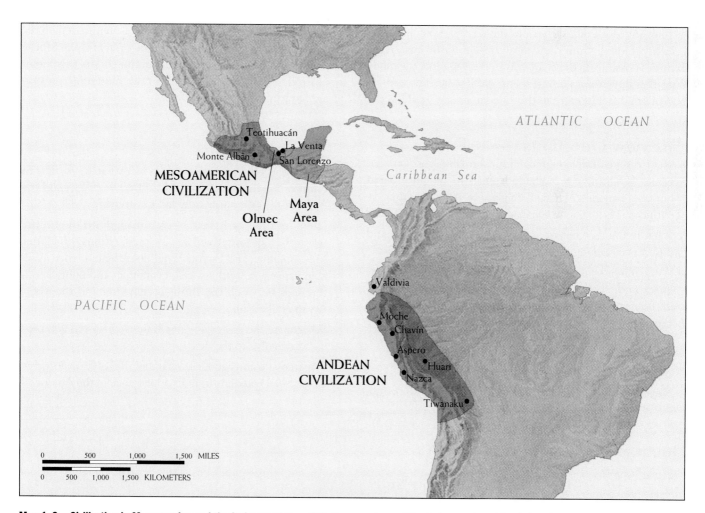

Map 1–2   Civilization in Mesoamerica and the Andean region.   Both Mesoamerica and the Andean region of South America saw the development of a series of civilizations beginning between 1500 and 1000 B.C.E.

Early Civilization of the Andes

ca. 2750 B.C.E.	Monumental architecture at Aspero
800–200 B.C.E.	Chavín (Early) Horizon
200 B.C.E.–600 C.E.	Early Intermediate period (Moche on the northern coast of Peru, Nazca on the southern coast)

divide its preconquest history into three broad periods: Preclassic or Formative (2000 B.C.E.–150 C.E.), Classic (150–900 C.E.), and Post-Classic (900–1521). The earliest Mesoamerican civilization, that of the Olmecs, arose during the Preclassic on the Gulf Coast beginning approximately 1500 B.C.E. The Olmec centers at San Lorenzo (ca. 1200–ca. 900 B.C.E.) and La Venta (ca. 900–ca. 400 B.C.E.) exhibit many of the characteristics of later Mesoamerican cities, including the symmetrical arrangement of large platforms, plazas, and other monumental structures along a central axis. Writing developed in Mesoamerica during the late Formative period.

The Andes rise abruptly from the coastal plain and then descend gradually into the Amazon basin to the east. Agriculture is possible on the coast only in the valleys of the many rivers that flow from the Andes into the Pacific. The earliest monumental architecture in the Andean region, built on the coast at the site of Aspero by people who depended on a combination of agriculture and the Pacific's rich marine resources, dates to about 2750 B.C.E., contemporary with the Great Pyramids of Egypt's Old Kingdom.

From 800 B.C.E. to 200 B.C.E., a civilization associated with the site of Chavín de Huantar in the highlands of Peru exerted great influence in the Andes. Artifacts in the distinctive Chavín style can be found over a large area dating to this period, which archaeologists call the Early Horizon. This was a time of technical innovation in many areas, including pottery, textiles, and metallurgy. Whether the spread of the Chavín style represents actual political integration or the influence of a strong religious center is not known. The period following the decline of Chavín, which archaeologists call the Early Intermediate period, saw the development of distinctive cultures in several regions. Notable among these are the Moche culture on the northern coast of Peru and the Nazca culture on the southern coast. A second period of transregional integration—called the Middle Horizon—occurred around 600 C.E., this time probably associated with empires centered on the highland sites of Huari and Tiahuanaco. The succeeding Late Intermediate period was dominated on the northern coast of Peru by the Chimu successors of the Moche state. This period ended with the founding of the vast, tightly controlled empire of the Incas in the fourteenth and fifteenth centuries C.E.

Review Questions

1. How was life during the Paleolithic Age different from that in the Neolithic Age? What advances in agriculture and human development had taken place by the end of the Neolithic era? Is it valid to speak of a "Neolithic Revolution"?

2. What defines civilization? What are the similarities and differences among the world's earliest civilizations?

3. What general conclusions can you draw about the differences in the political and intellectual outlooks of the civilizations of Egypt and Mesopotamia? Compare especially Egyptian and Mesopotamian religious views. In what ways did the regional geography influence the religious outlooks of these two civilizations?

4. Why were the Assyrians so successful in establishing their Near Eastern Empire? How did their empire differ from that of the Hittites or Egyptians? In what ways did this empire benefit the civilized Middle East? Why did the Assyrian Empire ultimately fail to survive?

5. How does the early history of Indian civilization differ from that of the river valley civilizations of China, Mesopotamia, and Egypt? What does the evidence available suggest were the social, economic, and political differences between the Indus civilization and the Vedic Aryan civilization?

6. What were the stages of early Chinese history? What led each to evolve to the next?

7. What conclusions about the factors that give rise to civilization can you draw from its appearance in the Americas?

Documents CD-ROM

1. Hittite Laws
2. "Hymn to the Nile" and "Hymn to the Sun"
3. *The Epic of Gilgamesh*
4. An Alumnus Reminisces about Scribal School in Ancient Sumeria
5. *The Book of Shang*
6. *The Book of Songs*

2 THE FOUR GREAT REVOLUTIONS IN THOUGHT AND RELIGION

CHAPTER TOPICS

- ◆ Comparing the Four Great Revolutions
- ◆ Philosophy in China
- ◆ Religion in India

- ◆ The Religion of the Israelites
- ◆ Greek Philosophy

Between 800 B.C.E. and 300 B.C.E., four philosophical or religious revolutions shaped the subsequent history of the world. The names of many involved in these revolutions—Socrates, Aristotle, the Buddha, Isaiah, and Confucious—are world famous. All the revolutions occurred in or near the four heartland areas in which the river valley civilizations (described in Chapter 1) had appeared one and a half or more millennia earlier. The transition from the early river valley civilizations to the intellectual and spiritual breakthroughs of the middle of the first millennium B.C.E. is schematized in the chart on the following page.

Comparing the Four Great Revolutions

Before considering each of the original breakthroughs that occurred between 800 and 300 B.C.E., we might ask whether they have anything in common. Five points are worth noting.

1. All the philosophical or religious revolutions occurred in or near the original river valley civilizations. These areas had the material preconditions for breakthroughs in religion and thought.

2. Each of the revolutions in thought and ethos was born of a crisis in the ancient world. Old societies began to change and then to disintegrate. Old aristocratic and priestly codes of behavior broke down, producing a demand for more universalized rules of behavior, for ethics. This predicament led to new visions of social and political order.

3. The number of philosophical and religious revolutions can be counted on the fingers of one hand. Subsequent breakthroughs and advances tended to occur within the original traditions, which continued to evolve.

4. After the first- and second-stage transformations, much of the cultural history of the world involves the spread of cultures derived from these original heartlands to ever wider spheres. Typically, the process spread out over centuries.

5. Once a cultural pattern was set, it usually endured. Each major culture was resistant to the others and only rarely displaced. These major cultures endured because they were not only responses to particular crises, but also attempts to answer universal questions concerning the human condition: What are human beings? What is our relation to the universe? How should we relate to others?

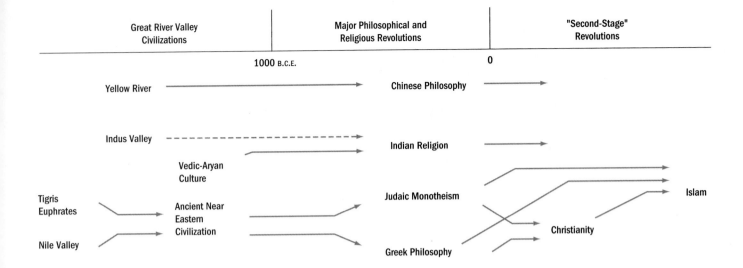

Great River Valley Civilizations	Major Philosophical and Religious Revolutions	"Second-Stage" Revolutions

1000 B.C.E.   0

Yellow River → Chinese Philosophy →

Indus Valley - - - - → Indian Religion →

Vedic-Aryan Culture

Tigris Euphrates → Ancient Near Eastern Civilization

Nile Valley →

Judaic Monotheism

Greek Philosophy

Christianity

Islam

Philosophy in China

Of the four great revolutions in thought of the first millennium B.C.E., the Chinese was more akin, perhaps, to the Greek than to the Indian religious transformations or to Judaic monotheism. Just as Greece had a gamut of philosophies, so in China there were the "one hundred schools." Whereas Greek thought was speculative and more concerned with the world of nature, Chinese thought was sociopolitical and more practical. Chinese thought also had far greater staying power than Greek thought, which only a few centuries after the glory of Athens was submerged by Christianity. It became the handmaiden of theology and did not reemerge as an independent force until the Renaissance. In contrast, Chinese philosophy, although challenged by Buddhism, remained dominant until the early twentieth century. How were these early philosophies able to maintain such a grip on China when the cultures of every other part of the world fell under the sway of religions?

Part of the answer is that most Chinese philosophy had a religious dimension. But it was a different kind of religion, with assumptions unlike those derived from Judaic roots. In the Christian or Islamic worldview, there is a God who, however concerned with humankind, is not of this world. This worldview leads to dualism, the distinction between an otherworld, which is supernatural, and this world, which is natural.

In the Chinese worldview, the two spheres are not separate: The cosmos is single, continuous, and nondualistic. It includes Heaven, Earth, and man. Heaven is above. Earth is below. Man, ideally guided by a wise and virtuous ruler, stands in between and regulates or harmonizes the cosmological forces of Heaven and Earth by the power of his virtue and by performing the sacrifices.

Confucianism

Confucius was born in 551 B.C.E. in a minor state in northeastern China. Since he received an education in writing, music, and rituals, he probably belonged to the lower nobility or the knightly class. His father died when Confucius was young, so he may have known privation. He made his living by teaching. He traveled with his disciples from state to state, seeking a ruler who would put his ideas into practice. His ideas, however, were rejected as impractical, although he may once have held a minor position. He died in 479 B.C.E., honored as a teacher and scholar but having failed to find a ruler to advise. The name *Confucius* is the Latinized form of *K'ung Fu-tzu,* or *Master K'ung,* as he is known in China.

We know of Confucius only through the *Analects,* his sayings collected by his disciples. The picture that emerges is of a man of moderation, propriety, optimism, good sense, and wisdom. In an age of cruelty and superstition, he was humane, rational, and upright, demanding much of others and more of himself. Asked about death, he replied, "You do not understand even life. How can you understand death?"[1]

Confucius described himself as a transmitter and a conservator of tradition, not an innovator. He idealized the early Shang and Chou kings as paragons of virtue and particularly saw early Chou society as a golden age. He sought the secrets of this golden age in its writings. Some of these writings, along with later texts, became the Confucian classics, which through most of Chinese history had an authority not unlike Scripture in the West.

Basing his teachings on these writings, Confucius proposed to resolve the turmoil of his own age by a return to the good old ways of the early Chou. When asked about government, he said, "Let the ruler be a ruler, the subject a subject, the father

---

[1]This quotation and all quotations from Confucius in this passage are from Confucius, *The Analects,* trans. by D. C. Lau (Penguin Books, 1979).

a father, the son a son." (The five Confucian relationships were ruler-subject, father-son, husband-wife, older brother-younger brother, and friend-friend.) His vision was of an unbroken social harmony extending from the individual family member to the monarch.

But China was undergoing a dynamic transition. It was thus not enough to stress basic human relationships. The genius of Confucius was to transform the old aristocratic code into a new ethic that any educated Chinese could practice. His reinterpretation of the early Chou tradition can be seen in the concept of the *chun-tzu*. This term literally meant "the son of the ruler" (or the aristocrat). Confucius redefined it to mean one of noble behavior, a person with the inner virtues of humanity, integrity, righteousness, altruism, and loyalty, and an outward demeanor and propriety to match.

This redefinition was not unlike the change in the meaning of *gentleman* in England, from "one who is gentle-born" to "one who is gentle-behaved." But whereas *gentleman* remained a fairly superficial category in the West, in China *chun-tzu* went deeper. Confucius saw ethics as grounded in nature. The true gentleman was in touch with his own basic nature, which in turn was a part of the cosmic order.

Good government for Confucius depended on the appointment to office of good men, who would serve as models for the multitude: "The virtue of the gentleman is like wind; the virtue of the small man is like grass. Let the wind blow over the grass and it is sure to bend." Beyond the gentleman was the sage-king, who possessed an almost mystical virtue and power.

Confucianism was not adopted as the official philosophy of China until the second century B.C.E., during the Han dynasty (202 B.C.E.–9 C.E.; see Chapter 7). But two other important Confucian philosophers had appeared in the meantime. Mencius (370–290 B.C.E.) is famous for his argument that humans tend toward the good just as water runs downward. The role of education, therefore, is to uncover and cultivate that innate goodness. Moreover, just as humans tend toward the good, so does Heaven possess a moral will. The will of Heaven is that a government should see to the education and well-being of its people. The rebellion of people against a government is the primary evidence that Heaven has withdrawn its mandate. At times in Chinese history, only lip service was paid to a concern for the people. But the idea that government ought to care for the people became a permanent part of the Confucian tradition.

The other influential Confucian philosopher was Hsun-tzu (300–237 B.C.E.), who felt Heaven was amoral, indifferent to whether China was ruled by a tyrant or a sage. He believed human nature was bad or at least that desires and emotions, if unchecked and unrefined, led to social conflict. So he emphasized etiquette and education as restraints on an unruly human nature, and good institutions, including punishments and rewards, as a means for shaping behavior. These ideas influenced the thinkers of the Legalist school.

Confucius, depicted wearing the robes of a scholar of a later age. [Collection of the National Palace Museum, Taiwan, Republic of China]

Taoism

Taoism (pronounced "Dah-oh-ism") offered a refuge from the burden of social responsibilities. The classics of the school are the *Lao-tzu*, dating from the fourth century B.C.E., and the *Chuang-tzu*, dating from about a century later.

The central concept is the *Tao*, or way. It is mysterious and cannot be named. It is the creator, the sustainer, and the process or flux of the universe. The Tao functions on a cosmic scale. As the *Lao-tzu* put it, "Heaven and Earth are ruthless, and treat the myriad creatures as straw dogs; the sage (in accord with the Tao) is ruthless, and treats the people as straw dogs."[2] But the sage is also described as one who "excels in saving people." By realizing the Tao, he transcends the forms of morality and becomes moral by his very nature.

What does it mean to be a sage? How does a human join the rhythms of nature? The answer given by the *Lao-tzu* is by regaining or returning to an original simplicity. To attain this

[2]All quotations from the *Lao-tzu* are from Lao-Tzu, *Tao Te Ching*, trans. by D. C. Lau (Penguin Books, 1963).

state, one must "learn to be without learning." Knowledge is bad because it creates distinctions, and because it leads to the succession of ideas and images that interfere with participation in the Tao. One must also learn to be without desires beyond the immediate and simple needs of nature.

Along with the basic Taoist prescription of becoming one with the Tao are two other assumptions or principles. One is that any action pushed to an extreme will initiate a countervailing reaction in the direction of the opposite extreme. The other is that too much government, even good government, can become oppressive by its very weight. As the *Lao-tzu* put it, "Govern a large state as you would cook small fish," that is, without too much stirring.

Legalism

A third great current in classical Chinese thought was Legalism. The Legalists were also concerned to end the wars that plagued China. True peace, they felt, required a strong state. The Legalists did not seek a model in the distant past nor model their state on a heavenly order of values. Human nature is selfish, argued the leading Legalists. If laws are severe and impartial, if what strengthens the state is rewarded and what weakens the state is punished, then a strong state and a good society will follow.

Legalism was the philosophy of the state of Ch'in, which destroyed the Chou in 256 B.C.E. and unified China in 221 B.C.E. Because Ch'in laws were cruel and severe, and because Legalism put human laws above an ethic modeled on Heaven, later generations of Chinese have execrated its doctrines. Yet its legacy of administrative and criminal laws became a vital part of subsequent dynastic China. Even Confucian statesmen could not do without them.

Religion in India

By 400 B.C.E., new social and religious forms took shape in the Indian subcontinent. A tradition was created whose fundamental institutions and ideas came to prevail virtually throughout the subcontinent. Despite staggering internal diversity and divisions, and long periods of foreign rule, this Indian culture has survived for over 2,000 years.

"Hindu" and "Indian"

The word *Hindu* lumps together an immense diversity of social, racial, linguistic, and religious groups. It is not a term for any single or uniform religious community.

"Indian," on the other hand, commonly refers today to all native inhabitants of the subcontinent, including Muslims, Sikhs, and Christians. However, for the period before the arrival of Muslim culture (ca. 1000 C.E.), we shall use *Indian* to refer to the distinctively Indian tradition of thought and culture that achieved its classical formulation in the Hindu society and religion of the first millennium C.E. The Jains of India and the Buddhists of wider Asia were also its legitimate heirs.

Historical Background

We saw in Chapter 1 how, in the later Vedic or Brahmanic period, a priest-centered cult dominated the upper classes of Aryanized northern Indian society. By the sixth century B.C.E., this cult had apparently grown so extreme that most people had little or no access to it. Elaborate animal sacrifices on behalf of Aryan rulers were an economic burden on the peasants and largely irrelevant to the religious concerns of peasant and town dweller alike.

The latest Vedic texts themselves reflected a reaction against excessive emphasis on the power of sacrifice and ritual formulas, accumulation of worldly wealth and power, and hope for an afterlife in paradise. The treatises of the *Brahmanas* (ca. 1000–800 B.C.E.) dealt with the ritual application of the old Vedic texts, the explanation of Vedic rites and mythology, and the theory of the sacrifice. Early on they focused on controlling the sacred power (*Brahman*) of the sacrificial ritual, but they gradually stressed acquiring this power through knowledge instead of ritual acts.

This tendency became central in the Upanishads (ca. 800–500 B.C.E.), which were extended meditations on the meaning of ritual and the nature of *Brahman*. The Upanishadic sages and the early Jains and Buddhists shared certain revolutionary ideas and concerns. Their thinking and piety influenced not only all later Indian intellectual thought but, through the spread of the Buddhist tradition, much of the intellectual and religious life of East and Southeast Asia as well. Thus, the middle centuries of the first millennium B.C.E. in India began a religious and philosophical revolution that ranks alongside those of Chinese philosophy and religion, Judaic monotheism, and Greek philosophy as a turning point in the history of civilization.

The Upanishadic Worldview

In the Upanishads we see two new emphases: on knowledge over ritual and on immortality in terms not of an afterlife but of escape from existence itself. These were already evident in two sentences from the prayer of an early Upanishadic thinker who said, "From the unreal lead me to the Real. . . . From death lead me to immortality." The first sentence points to the Upanishadic focus on speculation about the nature of things, the quest for ultimate truth. Here ritual takes a back seat to meditation; knowledge, not the sacred word or act, has become the ultimate source of power. The second sentence reflects a new concern with life after death. Immortality is now interpreted in terms of escape from existence in any earthly, heavenly, or other form. These two Upanishadic emphases gave birth to ideas that were to change the shape of Indian thought forever. They also provide the key to its basic worldview.

The Nature of Reality   The quest for knowledge by the Upanishadic sages focused on the nature of the individual self (*atman*) and its relation to ultimate reality (*Brahman*). The gods are now merely part of the total scheme of things, subject to the laws of existence, and not to be put on the same plane with the transcendent Absolute. Prayer and sacrifice to particular gods for their help continue; but the higher goal is realization of *Brahman* through mental action alone, not ritual.

The culmination of Upanishadic speculation is the recognition that the way to the Absolute is through the self. Through contemplation, *Atman-Brahman* is recognized not as a deity, but as the very principle of reality itself: the unborn, unmade, unchanging infinite. Of this reality, all that can be said is that it is "neither this nor that," because the ultimate cannot be conceptualized or described in finite terms. Beneath the impermanence of ordinary reality is the changeless *Brahman*, to which every being's immortal self belongs. The difficulty is recognizing this self, and with it the Absolute, while one is enmeshed in mortal existence.

A second, related focus of Upanishadic inquiry was the nature of "normal" existence. The realm of life is seen to be ultimately impermanent, ever in change. What seem to be "solid" things—the physical world, our bodies and personalities, worldly success—are revealed in the Upanishads as finally insubstantial, impermanent, ephemeral. Even happiness is transient. Existence is neither satisfying nor lasting in any fundamental sense. Only *Brahman* is enduring, eternal, unchanging—the unmoved ground of existence. This perception already shows a marked tendency toward the eventual emphasis of the Buddhists on impermanence and suffering as the fundamental facts of existence as we know it.

Life After Death   The Upanishadic sages conceived of existence as a ceaseless cycle, a never-ending alternation between life and death. This idea became the basic assumption of all Indian thought and religious life. The idea of the endless cycle of existence, or *samsara*, is for Indians the key to

understanding reality. It refers to the terrifying prospect of endless "redeath" as the normal lot of all beings in this world. This is the fundamental problem for all later Indian thought.

Karma   The key to resolving the dilemma of *samsara* lies in the concept of *karma*. At base, it is the concept that every action has its inevitable effects, sooner or later. Good deeds bring good results, perhaps even rebirth in a heaven or as a god, and evil ones bring evil consequences, whether in this life or by rebirth in the next. Because of the fundamental impermanence of everything in existence, both good and evil are temporary. The flux of existence knows only movement, change, endless cause and effect far transcending a mere human life span.

Solutions   The Indian tradition developed two kinds of solutions to the problem of *samsara*. The first involves a strategy of maximizing good actions and minimizing bad actions to achieve the best possible rebirth in one's next round of existence. The second, and more radical, solution seeks "liberation" (*moksha*) from existence: escaping all karmic effects by escaping action itself.

The first strategy has been characterized as the "ordinary norm," as opposed to the "extraordinary norm," the path of only the select elite. Essentially, the ordinary norm aims at living according to a code of social and moral responsibility. The most significant such codes in Indian history are those of the masses of Hindus, Buddhists, and Jains over the centuries. On the other hand, the seekers of the extraordinary norm usually follow an ascetic discipline aimed at withdrawal from the karmic cycle altogether and the consequent release (*moksha*) from cause and effect, good and evil, birth and rebirth. These two characteristic Indian responses to the problem posed by *samsara* underlie the fundamental forms of Indian thought and piety that took shape in the mid- to late-first millennium B.C.E.

Social Responsibility: *Dharma* as Ideal   The "ordinary norm" of life in the various traditions of Indian religiousness can be summarized as life lived according to *dharma*. Although *dharma* has many meanings, its most common is "the right (order of things)," "moral law," "right conduct," or even "duty." It includes the cosmic order (compare the Chinese Tao) as well as the right conduct of political, commercial, social, and religious affairs and individual moral responsibility. For most people, life according to *dharma* is the life of moral action that will lead to a better birth in the next round of existence.

Life according to *dharma* has several implications. First, it accepts action in the world of *samsara* as necessary and legitimate. Second, it demands acceptance of the responsibilities appropriate to one's sex, class and caste group, stage in life, and other circumstances. Third, it allows for legitimate self-interest: One's duty is to do things that acquire merit for one's eternal *atman* and to avoid those that bring evil consequences. Fourth, rebirth in heaven, in paradise, is the highest goal attainable through the life of *dharma*. However (fifth), all achievement in the world of *dharma* (which is also the world of *samsara*), even the attainment of Heaven, is ultimately impermanent and is subject to change.

Ascetic Discipline: *Moksha* as Ideal   For those who have the mental and physical capacity to abandon the world of ordinary life to gain freedom from *samsara*, the implications for living are in direct contrast to those of the ordinary norm. First, any action, good or bad, is at least counterproductive, for action produces only more action, more *karma*, more rebirth. Second, nonaction is achieved only by withdrawal from "normal" existence. The person seeking release from *samsara* has to move beyond the usual responsibilities of family and society. Most often, this involves becoming a "renouncer" (*sannyasi*)—whether a Hindu hermit, yogi, or wanderer, or a Jain or Buddhist monk. Third, this renunciation of the world and its goals demands selflessness, absence of ego. One must give up the desires and attachments that the self normally needs to function in the world. Fourth, the highest goal is not rebirth in Heaven at all, but liberation (*moksha*) from all rebirth and redeath. Finally, this *moksha* is lasting, permanent. Its realization means no more becoming, no more suffering in the realm of *samsara*. Permanence, eternity, transcendence, and freedom from suffering are its attributes.

Mahavira and the Jain Tradition

The Jains are an Indian community that traces its tradition to Vardhamana, known as Mahavira ("the great hero"), who is traditionally believed to have lived from about 540 to 468 B.C.E. Mahavira is hailed by the Jains as the final Jina ("victor" over *samsara*). The Jains (or *Jainas*, "adherents of the *Jina*") see in Mahavira not a god, but a human teacher who found and taught the way to extricate the self, or soul, from the bonds of the material world and its karmic accretions.

In the Jain view, there are only innumerable, ceaseless cycles of generation and degeneration. The universe is alive with an infinite number of souls, all immortal, omniscient,

and pure, but trapped in *samsara*. Any thought, word, or deed attracts karmic matter that encumbers the soul. The greatest amounts come from evil acts, especially those done out of cruelty to any other being.

Mahavira's path to release focused on the elimination of evil thoughts and acts, especially those harmful to others. His radical ascetic practice aimed at destroying karmic defilements and, ultimately, all actions leading to further karmic bondage.

Today, as in earlier centuries, there is a thriving lay community of perhaps 3 million Jains, most in western India. They are vegetarians and regard *ahimsa* ("noninjury") to any being as paramount. Compassion is the great virtue for them, as for Buddhists.

The Buddha's "Middle Path"

The Buddhist tradition remains one of the great universalist forms of faith in the world today, but few people in India proper are Buddhists. Yet there it was born, there it developed its basic contours, and there it left its mark on Hindu and Jain religion and culture. Like the two other great universalist traditions, Christianity and Islam, it traces its origins to a single figure who has loomed larger than life in the community of the faithful for centuries.

This figure is Siddhartha Gautama, known as the Buddha, or "enlightened/awakened one." A contemporary of Mahavira, Gautama was also born (ca. 566 B.C.E.) in apparently comfortable circumstances.

At the age of twenty-nine, Gautama first perceived the reality of aging, sickness, and death as the human lot. He abandoned his home and family to seek an answer to the dilemma of the endless cycle of mortal existence. After this "Great Renunciation," he studied first with renowned teachers, then took up extreme ascetic disciplines of penance and self-mortification. Still unsatisfied, Gautama turned finally to intense yogic meditation under a pipal tree in the place near Varanasi (Banaras) known as Gaya. In one historic night, he moved through different levels of trance, during which he realized all of his past lives, the reality of the cycle of existence of all beings, and how to stop the karmic outflows that fuel suffering. Thus he became the Buddha; that is, he achieved full enlightenment—the omniscient consciousness of reality as it truly is.

Gautama devoted the last of his earthly lives before his final release to teaching others his "middle path" between asceticism and indulgence. This path has been the core of Buddhist faith and practice ever since. It begins with realizing the "four noble truths": (1) all life is *dukkha*, or suffering; (2) the source of suffering is desiring; (3) the cessation of desiring is the way to end suffering; and (4) the path to this end is eightfold: right understanding, thought, speech, action,

India	
ca. 800–500 B.C.E.	The Upanishads
540–ca. 468 B.C.E.	Mahavira, the Jina/Vardamana
ca. 566–ca. 486 B.C.E.	Siddhartha Gautama, the Buddha

The "Turning of the Wheel of the *Dharma*": Basic Teachings of the Buddha

The following are selections from the sermon said to have been the first preached by the Buddha. It was directed at five former companions with whom he had practiced extreme austerities. When he abandoned asceticism to meditate under the Bodh tree, they had left him. This sermon is said to have made them the first to follow him. Because it set in motion the Buddha's teaching, or dharma, *on earth, it is usually described as "setting in motion the wheel of* dharma.*" The text is from the* Dhammacakkappavattanasutta.

What are the extremes that the "Middle Path" tries to avoid? What emotion drives the chain of suffering? How does the "knowledge" that brings salvation compare to the knowledge sought in the Hindu tradition?

Thus have I heard. The Blessed One was once living in the Deer Park at Isipatana (the Resort of Seers) near Baranasi (Benares). There he addressed the group of five bhikkhus.

"Bhikkhus, these two extremes ought not to be practiced by one who has gone forth from the household life. What are the two? There is devotion to the indulgence of sense-pleasures, which is low, common, the way of ordinary people, unworthy and unprofitable; and there is devotion to self-mortification, which is painful, unworthy and unprofitable.

"Avoiding both these extremes, the Tathagata has realized the Middle Path: it gives vision, it gives knowledge, and it leads to calm, to insight, to enlightenment, to Nibbana. And what is that Middle Path? It is simply the Noble Eightfold Path, namely, right view, right thought, right speech, right action, right livelihood, right effort, right mindfulness, right concentration. This is the Middle Path realized by the Tathagata, which gives vision, which gives knowledge, and which leads to calm, to insight, to enlightenment, to Nibbana. . . .

"The Noble Truth of suffering *(Dukkha)* is this: Birth is suffering; aging is suffering; sickness is suffering; death is suffering; sorrow and lamentation, pain, grief and despair are suffering; association with the unpleasant is suffering; dissociation from the pleasant is suffering; not to get what one wants is suffering—in brief, the five aggregates of attachment are suffering.

"The Noble Truth of the origin of suffering is this: It is this thirst (craving) which produces re-existence and re-becoming, bound up with passionate greed. It finds fresh delight now here and now there, namely, thirst for non-existence (self-annihilation).

"The Noble Truth of the Cessation of suffering is this: It is the complete cessation of that very thirst, giving it up, renouncing it, emancipating oneself from it, detaching oneself from it.

"The Noble Truth of the Path leading to the Cessation of suffering is this: It is simply the Noble Eightfold Path. . . .

" 'This is the Noble Truth of Suffering *(Dukkha)*': such was the vision, the knowledge, the wisdom, the science, the light, that arose in me with regard to things not heard before. 'This suffering, as a noble truth, should be fully understood.'

" 'This is the Noble Truth of the Cessation of suffering': such was the vision 'This Cessation of suffering, as a noble truth, should be realized.'

" 'This is the Noble Truth of the Path leading to the Cessation of suffering': such was the vision, 'This Path leading to the Cessation of suffering, as a noble truth, has been followed (cultivated).'

"As long as my vision of true knowledge was not fully clear regarding the Four Noble Truths, I did not claim to have realized the perfect Enlightenment that is supreme in the world with its gods, in this world with its recluses and brahmanas, with its princes and men. But when my vision of true knowledge was fully clear regarding the Four Noble Truths, then I claimed to have realized the perfect Enlightenment that is supreme in the world with its gods, in this world with its recluses and brahmanas, with its princes and men. And a vision of true knowledge arose in me thus: My heart's deliverance is unassailable. This is the last birth. Now there is no more rebecoming (rebirth)."

This the Blessed One said. The group of five bhikkhus was glad, and they rejoiced at his words.

—*Samyutta-nikaya*, LVI, II

From *What the Buddha Taught* by Walpola Rahula. Copyright © 1974 by W. Rahula, pp. 92–94. Used by permission of Grove Atlantic Inc.

livelihood, effort, mindfulness, and concentration. The key idea of the Buddha's teaching, or *dharma,* is that everything in the world of existence is causally linked. The essential fact of existence is *dukkha:* All existing is suffering, for no pleasure—however great—is permanent (here we see the Buddhist variation on the central Indian theme of *samsara*). *Dukkha* comes from desire, from craving, from attachment to self.

Thus, Buddhist discipline focuses on the moral "eightfold path," and the cardinal virtue of compassion for all beings, as the way to eliminate the selfish desiring that is the root of *samsara* and its unavoidable suffering. The Buddha himself had attained this goal; when he died (ca. 486 B.C.E.) after a life of teaching others how to master desiring, he passed from the round of existence forever. In Buddhist terminology, he attained nirvana, the extinguishing of karmic bondage. This attainment became the starting point for the growth and eventual spread of the Buddhist *Dharma*, which was to assume new and diverse forms in its long history.

The Buddhist movement, like the Jain, included not only those who were willing to renounce marriage and normal occupations to become part of the Buddha's communities of monks or nuns, but also laypersons who would strive to live by the high moral standards of the tradition and support those willing and able to become mendicants in attaining full release. Buddhist tradition encompassed seekers of both the extraordinary and the ordinary norms in their present lives. This dual community has remained characteristic of all forms of Buddhism wherever it is practiced.

The Religion of the Israelites

The ancient Near East was a polytheistic world. Everywhere people worshiped local or regional gods and goddesses who were represented largely as capricious, amoral beings, no more affected by the actions of humans than were the natural forces that some of them represented. Out of this polytheistic world came the great tradition of ethical monotheistic faith represented historically in the Jewish, Christian, and Islamic communities. This tradition traces its origin to the small nation of the Israelites, or Hebrews.

Monotheism, faith in a single, all-powerful God as the sole creator, sustainer, and ruler of the universe, may be older than the Hebrews, but its first clear historical manifestation was with them. It was among the Hebrew tribes that emphasis on the moral demands and responsibilities that the one God placed on individual and community was first definitively linked to human history itself, and that history to a divine plan.

The Israelites	
ca. 1000–961 B.C.E.	Reign of King David
ca. 961–922 B.C.E.	Reign of King Solomon
722 B.C.E.	Assyrian conquest of Israel (northern kingdom)
586 B.C.E.	Destruction of Jerusalem; fall of Judah (southern kingdom); Babylonian captivity
539 B.C.E.	Restoration of temple; return of exiles

From Hebrew Nomads to the Israelite Nation

The history of the Hebrews, later known as Israelites, must be pieced together from various sources. They are mentioned only rarely in the records of their ancient Near Eastern neighbors, so we must rely on their own accounts as compiled in the Hebrew Bible (the "Old Testament" of Christian terminology). Scholars once tended to discard the Bible as a source for historians, but the trend today is to use it cautiously and critically.

We need not reject the core reality of the tradition that the Hebrew Abraham came from Ur in southern Mesopotamia and wandered west with his Hebrew clan to the land later known as Palestine. Precise dating of the arrival of the Hebrews in Palestine is impossible, but it was likely between 1900 and 1600 B.C.E.

It is, however, with Moses, at about the beginning of the thirteenth century B.C.E., that the Hebrews tread clearly upon the stage of history. Some of Abraham's people had settled in the Palestinian region, but others apparently wandered farther, into Egypt. By about 1400 B.C.E., as the biblical narrative tells it, they had become a settled but subjected, even enslaved, people there. Under Moses, part of the Egyptian Israelites fled Egypt to find a new homeland in Canaan, the province of Palestine that is described in the Bible as their promised homeland. The Bible presents this experience as the key event in Israel's history: the forging of the covenant, or mutual pact, between God, or *Yahweh*, and His people. We interpret this Exodus as the time when the Israelites emerged as a nation, a people with a sense of community and common faith.

By about 1200 B.C.E., they had displaced the Canaanite inhabitants of ancient Palestine. After perhaps two centuries, the now-settled nation reached its peak as a kingdom under David (r. ca. 1000–961 B.C.E.) and Solomon (r. ca. 961–922 B.C.E.). But the kingdom split into two parts in the ninth century B.C.E.: Israel in the north and Judah, with its capital at Jerusalem, in the south (see Map 2–1).

The rise of great empires around them brought disaster to the Israelites. The northern kingdom fell to the Assyrians in 722 B.C.E. Only Judah remained, and henceforward we may call the Israelites Jews. In 586 B.C.E., Judah was defeated by the Neo-Babylonian king Nebuchadnezzar II (d. 562 B.C.E.). He destroyed the Jewish cult center, the great temple built by Solomon, and carried off the cream of the Jewish nation as exiles in Babylon. There, in the "Babylonian captivity" of the Exile, without a temple, the Jews clung to their traditions and faith. After the Persians defeated the Babylonians in 539 B.C.E., the Jews were allowed to return, and by about 516 B.C.E., a second temple was erected in Jerusalem.

The new Judaic state continued for centuries to be dominated by foreign peoples but was able to maintain its religious and national identity. However, it was again destroyed and its people dispersed after the Romans' destruction of Jerusalem, in 70 C.E. and again in 132 C.E. By this era, however, the Jews had developed a religious worldview that would long outlive any Judaic national state.

The Monotheistic Revolution

This small nation developed a tradition of faith that amounted to a revolution in ways of thinking about the human condition, the meaning of life and history, and the nature of the Divine. The revolutionary character of this interpretation lay in its uniquely moralistic understanding of human life and history and the uncompromising monotheism on which it was based.

At the root of this monotheistic tradition stands Abraham. Jews, Christians, and Muslims look to him as the symbolic founder of their faith. Abraham probably conceived of his Lord as his chosen deity among the many divinities who might be worshiped. Yet the biblical account recognizes him as the "Father of the Faithful," the first Hebrew patriarch to make a covenant with the God who would become unique and supreme. Abraham promised to serve only Him, and his God promised to guide his descendants as His special people.

As with Abraham's faith, it is difficult to say how much the Mosaic covenant at Sinai actually marked an exclusively monotheistic faith. Certainly, the covenant united the Israelites as a people with a special relationship to God. At Sinai, they received both God's holy Law (the Torah) and his promise of protection as long as they kept the law. This was the pivotal moment in the monotheistic revolution that came to fruition several hundred years later. From Sinai, the Israelites saw themselves as God's chosen people.

The monotheistic revolution might thus be said to have begun with Abraham or Moses. Historically, we can trace it primarily from the division of the Israelite kingdom in 922 B.C.E. After this, the *prophets*—inspired messengers of God—were sent to call their people back from false gods to faith in the one true God and to obedience to God's commandments. Their concern with purifying Jewish faith, and with morality, focused on two ideas that proved central to Judaic monotheism.

The first was the significance of history in the divine plan. The prophets saw in Israel's troubles God's punishment for failing in their covenant duties. But they saw Israel as the "suffering servant," the people who would purify other nations and bring them ultimately to God. Here the nationalistic focus of Israelite religion gave way to a universalist monotheism: Yahweh was now God of all.

The second idea centered on the nature of Yahweh. God was a righteous God who expected righteousness from human beings. He was a moral God who demanded goodness, not blood offerings or empty prayers.

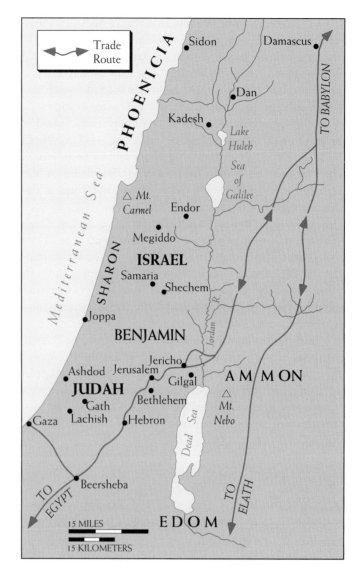

Map 2–1 Ancient Palestine. The Hebrews established a unified kingdom under Kings David and Solomon in the tenth century B.C.E. After Solomon, the kingdom was divided into Israel in the north and Judah, with its capital, Jerusalem, in the south. North of Israel were the great commercial cities of Phoenicia.

The crux of the breakthrough to ethical monotheism lay in linking the Lord of the Universe to history and morality. The Almighty Creator was seen as concerned with the actions and fates of His human creatures as exemplified in Israel. History thus took on transcendent meaning. God had created humankind for a good purpose; they were called to be just and good like their Creator, for they were involved in the fulfillment of His divine purpose. This fulfillment would come in the restoration of Israel as a people purified of their sins.

However, even after the Exile, the realization of the prophesied days of peace and blessedness under God's rule still had not come. This brought forth the concept that history's culmination would come in a future Messianic age. Faith and morality were tied to human destiny, even without the still later Jewish idea that a day of judgment would cap the golden age of the Messiah. These ideas played a key role in similar Christian and Muslim ideas of a Messianic deliverer, resurrection of the body, and a life after death.

The other key element in the monotheistic revolution of the Jews was the Law embodied in the five books of Torah (Genesis, Exodus, Leviticus, Numbers, and Deuteronomy). The Law enabled the Jews in exile to survive the loss of the Temple and its priestly cult, thereby fixing the Torah as the ultimate earthly focus of faith in God.

In the second century B.C.E., the enduring role of Torah was ensured by its physical compilation, together with the books of the prophets and other writings, into the Holy Scriptures, or Bible (from Greek *bibloi*, "books"). A holy, authoritative, divinely revealed scripture put the seal on the monotheistic revolution that had made the sovereignty and righteousness of God the foci of faith.

In the evolution of Judaic monotheistic faith, we see the beginning of one of the major traditions of world religion. For the first time we find a nation defined by shared religious faith and practice. This was new in human history. It was later to have still greater effects when not only Judaic but also Christian and Muslim tradition would change the face of much of the world.

Greek Philosophy

Many, if not most, Greeks in the ancient world must have lived with notions similar to those held by other peoples. But some Greeks developed ideas that were different and thereby set a part of humankind on a new path. As early as the sixth century B.C.E., Greeks raised questions about nature that produced an intellectual revolution. They made guesses that included no reference to supernatural powers. As one historian, discussing the views of Thales (624–545 B.C.E.), the first Greek philosopher, put it:

> In one of the Babylonian legends it says: "All the lands were sea. Marduk bound a rush mat upon the face of the waters, he made dirt and piled it beside the rush mat." What Thales did was to leave Marduk out. He, too, said that everything was once water. But he thought that earth and everything else had been formed out of water by a natural process, like the silting up of the Delta of the Nile. It is an admirable beginning, the whole point of which is that it gathers together into a coherent picture a number of observed facts without letting Marduk in.[3]

[3]Benjamin Farrington, *Greek Science* (London: Penguin Books, 1953), p. 37.

By putting the question of the world's origin in a naturalistic form, Thales may have initiated the unreservedly rational investigation of the universe, and in so doing, initiated both Western philosophy and Western science.

The same relentlessly rational approach was applied even to the gods themselves. In the same century as Thales, Xenophanes of Colophon expressed the opinion that humans think of the gods as resembling themselves. Thus Africans believed in flat-nosed, black-faced gods, and the Thracians in gods with blue eyes and red hair.[4] In the fifth century B.C.E., Protagoras of Abdera (ca. 490–ca. 420 B.C.E.) went so far in the direction of agnosticism as to say, "About the gods I can have no knowledge either that they are or that they are not or what is their nature."[5]

This rationalistic, skeptical way of thinking carried over into practical matters. Hippocrates of Cos (ca. 400 B.C.E.) attempted to understand and cure disease without recourse to supernatural forces.

By the fifth century B.C.E., the historian Thucydides (ca. 460–ca. 400 B.C.E.) could analyze and explain events completely in terms of human nature and chance, leaving no place for the gods.

The relative unimportance of divine or supernatural forces also characterized Greek views of law and justice. Greeks understood that laws were made by humans and should be obeyed because they represented the consent of the citizens.

These ideas, so different from any that came before the Greeks, open the discussion of most of the issues that appear in the long history of civilization and that remain major concerns in the modern world: What is the nature of the universe and how can it be controlled? Are there divine powers, and if so, what is humanity's relationship to them? Are law and justice human, divine, or both? What is the place in human society of freedom, obedience, and reverence? These and many other problems were confronted and intensified by the Greeks.

Reason and the Scientific Spirit

The rational spirit characteristic of Greek culture blossomed in the sixth century B.C.E. into the intellectual examination of the physical world and the place of humankind in it that we call *philosophy*. The first steps along this path were taken in Ionia on the coast of Asia Minor, which was in touch with the learning of the East.

We have already met Thales of Miletus. He believed that the Earth floated on water and that water was the primary substance. Thales observed, as any person can, that water has many forms: liquid, solid, and gaseous. He saw that it could "create" land by alluvial deposit and that it was necessary for all life. These observations he organized by reason into a sin-

[4]Frankfort et al., *Before Philosophy* (1949), pp. 14–16.
[5]Hermann Diels, *Fragmente der Vorsokratiker*, 5th ed., by Walther Kranz (Berlin: Weidmann, 1934–1938), Frg. 4.

gle explanation that accounted for many phenomena without any need for the supernatural. Greek philosophers assumed that the world was knowable, rational, and simple.

Another Milesian, Anaximander (ca. 611–546 B.C.E.), imagined that the basic element was something undefined, "unlimited." The world emerged from this basic element as the result of an interaction of opposite forces—wet and dry, hot and cold. Anaximander pictured the universe in eternal motion, with all sensible things emerging from the "unlimited," then decaying and returning to it. He also argued that human beings originated in water and had evolved to the present state through several stages, including that of a fish.

Heraclitus of Ephesus, who lived near the end of the sixth century B.C.E., carried the dialogue further. His famous saying, "All is motion," raised important problems. If all is constantly in motion, nothing ever really exists. Yet Heraclitus believed that the world order was governed by a guiding principle, the *logos*, and that though phenomena changed, the *logos* did not. *Logos* has several meanings, among them "word," "language," "speech," and "reason." So Heraclitus implied that the physical world could be explained by reason. What we would call natural science thus soon led toward philosophical speculations about language, the manner of human thought, and knowledge itself.

In opposition to Heraclitus, Parmenides of Elea and his pupil Zeno argued that change was only an illusion of the senses. Reality was fixed and unchanging because it seemed evident that nothing could be created out of nothingness. Empedocles of Acragas (flourished ca. 450 B.C.E.) spoke of four basic elements: fire, water, earth, and air. Like Parmenides, he thought that reality was permanent but not immobile, for the four elements were moved by two primary forces, Love and Strife, or, as we might say, attraction and repulsion.

This theory was clearly a step on the road to the atomic theory of Leucippus of Miletus (flourished fifth century B.C.E.) and Democritus of Abdera (ca. 460–370 B.C.E.). They believed that the world consisted of tiny, solid particles (atoms) that could not be divided or modified and that moved about in the void. The size of the atoms and the arrangement in which they were joined produced the secondary qualities that the senses could perceive, such as color and shape. These qualities—unlike the atoms themselves, which were natural—were merely conventional. Anaxagoras of Clazomenae (ca. 500–428 B.C.E.) had previously spoken of tiny fundamental particles called *seeds* that were put together on a rational basis by a force called *nous*, or "mind." Thus, he suggested a distinction between matter and mind. The atomists, however, regarded "mind" as material and believed that everything was guided by purely physical laws. In these arguments we have the beginning of the continuing debate between materialism and idealism.

Most Greeks were suspicious of such speculations. A more influential debate was begun by professional teachers in the mid-fifth century B.C.E. Called *Sophists*, they traveled about and received pay for teaching practical techniques of persuasion, such as rhetoric. They did not speculate about the physical universe but applied reasoned analysis to human beliefs and institutions. This human focus was characteristic of fifth-century-B.C.E. thought, as was the central problem that the Sophists considered: They discovered the tension and even the contradiction between nature and custom, or law. The more traditional among them argued that law was in accord with nature, and this view fortified the traditional beliefs about the *polis*, the Greek city-state (see Chapter 3).

Others argued, however, that laws were not in accord with nature, merely the result of an agreement among people, which prevented them from harming each other. The most extreme Sophists argued that law was contrary to nature, a trick whereby the weak controlled the strong.

Political and Moral Philosophy

Like thinkers in other parts of the world around the middle of the first millennium B.C.E., some Greeks were vitally concerned with the formulation of moral principles for the governance of the state and the regulation of individual life, as well as with more abstract problems of the nature of existence and transcendence. Nowhere is the Greek concern with ethical, political, and religious issues clearer than in the philosophical tradition that began with Socrates in the latter half of the fifth century B.C.E. That tradition continued with Socrates' pupil Plato and with Plato's pupil Aristotle. Aristotle also had great interest in and made great contributions to the scientific understanding of the physical world, but perhaps his more important impact was on later Western and Islamic metaphysics.

The starting point for all three was the social and political reality of the Greek city-state, or *polis*. The greatest crisis for the *polis* was the Great Peloponnesian War (435–404 B.C.E.), which is discussed in Chapter 3. Probably the most complicated response to this crisis may be found in the life and teachings of Socrates (469–399 B.C.E.). Our knowledge of him comes chiefly from his disciples Plato and Xenophon (ca. 435–354 B.C.E.) and from later tradition.

Socrates was committed to the search for truth and for the knowledge about human affairs that he believed reason could reveal. His method was to go among men to question and cross-examine them. The result was always the same: Those he questioned might have technical information and skills but seldom had any knowledge of the fundamental principles of human behavior. It is understandable that Athenians so exposed should become angry with their examiner, and it is not surprising that they thought Socrates was undermining the beliefs and values of the *polis*. Socrates' unconcealed contempt for democracy, which seemingly relied on ignorant amateurs to make important political decisions without any certain knowledge, created further hostility. Moreover, his insistence on the primacy of his own individualism and his determination to pursue philosophy even against the wishes of his fellow citizens reinforced this hostility and the prejudice that went with it.

But Socrates, unlike the Sophists, did not accept pay for his teaching: It was not wealth or pleasure or power that he urged people to seek, but "the greatest improvement of the soul." He also thought that the *polis* had a legitimate claim on the citizen, and he proved it in 399 B.C.E., when he was condemned to death by an Athenian jury. He was given a chance to escape, but refused to do so because of his veneration of the laws.

Socrates' career set the stage for later responses to the travail of the *polis;* he recognized its difficulties and criticized its shortcomings. Although he turned away from an active political life, he did not abandon the idea of the *polis.* He fought as a soldier in its defense, obeyed its laws, and sought to use reason to put its values on a sound foundation.

Plato

Plato (429–347 B.C.E.) was the most important of Socrates' associates. He was the first systematic philosopher and therefore the first to place political ideas in their full philosophical context. He was also a writer of genius, leaving us twenty-six philosophical discussions. In 386 B.C.E., Plato founded the Academy, a center of philosophical investigation and a school for training statesmen and citizens that endured until it was closed in the sixth century C.E.

Like Socrates, Plato firmly believed in the *polis* and its values. Its virtues were order, harmony, and justice, and one of its main objects was to produce good people. He accepted Socrates' doctrine of the identity of virtue and knowledge and made it plain what that knowledge was: *episteme,* science, a body of true and unchanging wisdom open to only a few philosophers whose training, character, and intellect allowed them to see reality. Only such people were qualified to rule; they themselves would prefer the life of pure contemplation but would accept their responsibility and take their turn as philosopher-kings. The training of such men required a specialization of function and a subordination of the individual to the community. This specialization would lead to Plato's definition of justice: that each man should do only that one thing to which his nature was best suited.

Plato understood that the *polis* of his day suffered from terrible internal stress, class struggle, and factional divisions. His solution was moral and political reform. The way to

harmony was to destroy the causes of strife: private property, the family—anything, in short, that stood between the individual citizen and devotion to the *polis.*

Plato began by asking the traditional questions: What is a good man, and how is he made? The goodness of a human being was a theme that belonged to moral philosophy, and when it became a function of the state, the question became part of political philosophy. Because goodness depended on knowledge of the good, it required a theory of knowledge and an investigation of what the knowledge was that was required for goodness. The answer must be metaphysical and so required a full examination of metaphysics. Even when the philosopher knew the good, however, the question remained of how the state could bring its citizens to the necessary comprehension of that knowledge. The answer required a theory of education. Even purely logical and metaphysical questions, therefore, were subordinate to the overriding political questions. Plato's need to find a satisfactory foundation for the beleaguered *polis* thus contributed to the birth of systematic philosophy.

Aristotle

Aristotle (384–322 B.C.E.) was a pupil of Plato whose different experience and cast of mind led him in new directions. In 336, he founded his own school at Athens, the Lyceum. The Lyceum was different from the Academy. Its members were concerned with gathering, ordering, and analyzing all human knowledge. Aristotle and his students also prepared collections of information to serve as the basis for scientific works. The range of treated subjects includes logic, physics, astronomy, biology, ethics, rhetoric, literary criticism, and politics.

In each field, the method was the same. Aristotle began with observation of the empirical evidence, which in some cases was physical and in others was common opinion. To this body of information he applied reason and discovered inconsistencies or difficulties. To deal with these he introduced metaphysical principles to explain the problems or to reconcile the inconsistencies. His view on all subjects, like Plato's, was teleological; that is, he recognized purposes apart from and greater than the will of the individual human being. Plato's purposes, however, were contained in the Ideas, or Forms—transcendental concepts outside the experience of most people. For Aristotle, the purposes of most things were easily inferred by observing their behavior in the world.

Aristotle's most striking characteristics are his moderation and common sense. His epistemology finds room for both reason and experience; his metaphysics gives meaning and reality to both mind and body; his ethics aims at the good life, which is the contemplative life, but recognizes the necessity for moderate wealth, comfort, and pleasure.

All these qualities are evident in Aristotle's political thought. Like Plato, he opposed the Sophists' assertion that the *polis* was contrary to nature and the result of mere convention. His response was to apply the teleology that he saw in all nature to

Major Greek Philosophers

469–399 B.C.E.	Socrates
429–347 B.C.E.	Plato
384–322 B.C.E.	Aristotle

Plato on the Role of Women in His Utopian Republic

The Greek invention of reasoned intellectual analysis of all things led the philosopher Plato to consider the problem of justice, which is the subject of his most famous dialogue, the Republic. *This leads him to sketch out a utopian state in which justice may be found and where the most radical arrangements may be necessary. These include the equality of the sexes and the destruction of the family in favor of the practice of men having wives and children in common. In the following excerpts he argues for the fundamental equality of men and women and that women are no less appropriate as Guardians, leaders of the state, than men.*

What are Plato's reasons for treating men and women the same? What objections could be raised to that practice? Would that policy, even if appropriate in Plato's utopia, also be suitable to conditions in the real world of classical Athens? In the world of today?

"If, then, we use the women for the same things as the men, they must also be taught the same things."

"Yes."

"Now music and gymnastics were given to the men."

"Yes."

"Then these two arts, and what has to do with war, must be assigned to the women also, and they must be used in the same ways."

"On the basis of what you say," he said, "it's likely."

"Perhaps," I said, "compared to what is habitual, many of the things now being said would look ridiculous if they were to be done as is said."

"Indeed they would," he said.

"Well," I said, "since we've started to speak, we mustn't be afraid of all the jokes—of whatever kind—the wits might make if such a change took place in gymnastic, in music and, not the least, in the bearing of arms and the riding of horses."

"Then," I said, "if either the class of men or that of women shows its superiority in some art or other practice, then we'll say that that art must be assigned to it. But if they look as though they differ in this alone, that the female bears and the male mounts, we'll assert that it has not thereby yet been proved that a woman differs from a man with respect to what we're talking about; rather, we'll still suppose that our guardians and their women must practice the same things."

"And rightly," he said.

"Therefore, my friend, there is no practice of a city's governors which belongs to woman because she's woman, or to man because he's man; but the natures are scattered alike among both animals; and woman participates according to nature in all practices, and man in all, but in all of them woman is weaker than man."

"Certainly."

"So, shall we assign all of them to men and none to women?"

"How could we?"

"For I suppose there is, as we shall assert, one woman apt at medicine and another not, one woman apt at music and another unmusical by nature."

"Of course."

"And isn't there then also one apt at gymnastic and at war, and another unwarlike and no lover of gymnastic?"

"I suppose so."

"And what about this? Is there a lover of wisdom and a hater of wisdom? And one who is spirited and another without spirit?"

"Yes, there are these too."

"There is, therefore, one woman fit for guarding and another not. or wasn't it a nature of this sort we also selected for the men fit for guarding?"

"Certainly, that was it."

From *The Republic of Plato*, 2nd ed., translated by Allan Bloom. Copyright © 1968 by Allan Bloom. Preface to paperback edition, © 1991 by Allan Bloom, pp. 130–134. Reprinted by permission of Basic Books, a member of Perseus Books, L.L.C.

politics. In his view, matter existed to achieve an end, and it developed until it achieved its form, which was its end. There was constant development from matter to form, from potential to actual. Therefore, human primitive instincts could be seen as the matter out of which the human's potential as a political being could be realized. The *polis* made individuals self-sufficient and allowed the full realization of their potentiality. It was therefore natural. It was also the highest point in the evolution of the social institutions that serve the human need to continue the species: marriage, household, village, and finally, *polis*. For Aris-

totle, the purpose of the *polis* was neither economic nor military, but moral: "The end of the state is the good life," the life lived "for the sake of noble actions," a life of virtue and morality.[6]

Characteristically, Aristotle was less interested in the best state—the utopia that required philosophers to rule it—than in the best state practically possible, one that would combine justice with stability. The constitution for that state he called *politeia*, not the best constitution, but the next best, the one

[6]Aristotle, *Politics*, 1280b, 1281a.

This is believed to be an ancient copy of an actual portrait of the philosopher Aristotle (384–322 B.C.E.). [Kunsthistorisches Museum, Vienna]

the most numerous. The middle class possessed many virtues: Because of its moderate wealth, it was free of the arrogance of the rich and the malice of the poor. For this reason, it was the most stable class. The stability of the constitution also came from being a mixed constitution, blending in some way the laws of democracy and those of oligarchy. Aristotle's scheme was unique because of its realism and the breadth of its vision.

The concern with an understanding of nature in a purely rational, scientific way remained strong through the fifth century B.C.E., culminating in the work of the formulators of the atomic theory, Democritus and Leucippus, and in that of the medical school founded by Hippocrates of Cos. In the mid-fifth century B.C.E., however, men like the Sophists and Socrates turned their attention to humankind and to ethical, political, and religious questions. This latter tradition of inquiry led, by way of Plato, Aristotle (in his metaphysical thought), and the Stoics, to Christianity; it had, as well, a substantial impact on Judaic and Islamic thought. The former tradition of thought, following a line from the natural philosophers, the Sophists, Aristotle (in his scientific thought), and the Epicureans, had to wait until the Renaissance in western Europe to exert an influence. Since the eighteenth century, this line of Greek thought has been the more influential force in Western civilization. It may not be too much to say that since the Enlightenment of that century, the Western world has been engaged in a debate between the two strands of the Greek intellectual tradition. As Western influence has spread over the world in recent times, that debate has become of universal importance, for other societies have not separated the religious and philosophical from the scientific and physical realms as radically as has the modern West.

most suited to and most possible for most states. Its quality was moderation, and it naturally gave power to neither the rich nor the poor but to the middle class, which also had to be

Review Questions

1. What do you think are the reasons for the emergence of so many revolutionary philosophical and religious ideas at about the same time in many different regions? Do these ideas share any fundamental concerns?

2. Is your outlook on life closer to Confucianism, Taoism, or Legalism? What makes you favor one over the others?

3. What fundamental assumptions about the world, the individual, and reality do the Jain, Hindu, and Buddhist traditions share? How do these assumptions compare with those that underlie Chinese philosophy, Jewish religious thought, and Greek philosophy?

4. To what extent did their faith bind the Jews politically? Why was the concept of monotheism so radical for Near Eastern civilization?

5. In what ways did the ideas of the Greeks differ from those of other ancient peoples? How do Aristotle's political and ethical ideas compare with those of Confucius? What were Socrates' contributions to the development of philosophy?

Documents CD-ROM

1. Confucius, *Analects*

2. "Upanishads": A Mirror into the Underpinnings of the Ancient Hindu Faith

3. The Path of Mindfulness

4. Isaiah: From "The Book of Isaiah"

5. Plato, *The Apology*

6. Aristotle, *Nichomachean Ethics*

EMPIRES AND CULTURES OF THE ANCIENT WORLD

The last 500 years before the beginning of the common era and the two centuries that followed saw the appearance of great empires in Iran, India, and China, and of the Roman Empire in the Mediterranean. Each empire replaced a confusion of local sovereign units. Each had large, efficient armies and well-organized bureaucracies.

The military, political, and economic unification of vast territories produced relative peace and prosperity, and encouraged the use of a common tongue and the formation of a common culture. The Greeks, the Romans, the Hindus, and the Chinese produced great literature, and the prosperity of all the empires gave great impetus to painting, sculpture, and architecture.

The rise of these empires fostered religious movements like Buddhism and Christianity that stressed morality and the search for personal immortality.

But none of the great empires could avoid a cycle of growth and decline. There was never enough wealth to sustain the cost of an empire for long. Taxes rose beyond the citizens' capacity to pay. Bureaucracies become ineffective. Talented leadership was not always available. Civilization drew the envy of barbarians, while internal problems reduced the capacity of the empires to resist. Invaders eventually triumphed. Imperial authority collapsed. But the conquering tribes were themselves often conquered by the religions or philosophies of their victims. In India, China, and Rome, moreover, the cultural achievements of the great empires eventually became the bases for new advances in civilization.

3000 B.C.E.

ca. **2500–1100** Minoan civilization on Crete
ca. **1600–1100** Mycenaean civilization on Greek mainland

ca. **3500–3000** Emergence of Sumerian city-states
ca. **3000** Emergence of civilization along the Nile River
ca. **2300** Emergence of Harappan civilization in Indus Valley
2276–2221 Sargon of Akkad creates the first Mesopotamian Empire
ca. **2000** Epic of Gilgamesh
1750 Hammurabi's Code

1500 B.C.E.

Sixth century B.C.E. attic jar. (The British Museum)

ca. **1100–800** Greek "Dark Ages"
800 Etruscan civilization begins in Italy
ca. **750–550** Rise of the *polis*
594 Solon's legislation at Athens
509 Foundation of the Roman Republic
508 Democracy established in Athens

ca. **1500** Aryan peoples migrate into northwestern India
960–933 Rule of Hebrew King Solomon
ca. **628–551** Traditional dates of Zarathushtra
ca. **537–486** Siddhartha Gautama
559–529 Cyrus the Great creates the Persian Empire

500 B.C.E.

480–479 Persian invasion of Greece
478 Foundation of Delian League/Athenian Empire
431–404 Peloponnesian Wars
338 Battle of Chaeronia; Macedonian conquest of Greece
336–323 Career of Alexander the Great

ca. **540–468** Vardhamana Mahavira, founder of Jain tradition
334 Alexander begins conquest of the Near East; invades India in 327
321–181 Mauryan Empire in India

300 B.C.E.

264 Rome rules all of Italy
146 Rome destroys Carthage; rules all of western Mediterranean
44–31 Civil wars destroy Republic
31 Rome rules Mediterranean
31 B.C.E.–**14** C.E. Principate of Augustus

ca. **300** Foundation of Seleucid dynasty in Anatolia, Syria, and Mesopotamia; Ptolemaic dynasty in Egypt
269–232 Mauryan Emperor, Ashoka, patronizes Buddhism
247 B.C.E.–**224** C.E. Parthian dynasty controls Persia
180 B.C.E.–**320** C.E. India politically divided

1 C.E.

96–180 The Good Emperors rule Rome
180–284 Breakdown of the *Pax Romana*
306–337 Constantine reigns
313 Edict of Milan
325 Council of Nicaea
391 Theodosius makes Christianity the official imperial religion
ca. **400–500** The Germanic invasions
426 *The City of God*, by Augustine
476 The last Western emperor is deposed

30 Crucifixion of Jesus
70 Romans destroy the Temple at Jerusalem
216–277 Mani
ca. **224** Fall of Parthians, rise of Sasanids, in Persia
ca. **320–500** Gupta dynasty in India
ca. **400** Chandra Gupta (r. 375–415) conquers western India; increases trade with Near East and China
ca. **450** The Huns invade India

ca. 4000 Neolithic cultures in China **ca. 8000–300** Jōmon culture in Japan **ca. 1766–1050** Shang dynasty in China with city-states and writing	**ca. 3000** Practice of agriculture spreads from Nile River Valley to the Sudan **ca. 2000** Ivory and gold trade between Kush (Nubia) and Egypt **ca. 1500** Practice of agriculture spreads from the Sudan to Abyssinia and the savannah region	**ca. 4000** Maize already domesticated in Mexico

1027–771 Western Chou dynasty, China **771–256** Eastern Chou dynasty in China **ca. 771** Iron Age territorial states in China **551–479** Confucius in China	**750** Kushite king Kashta conquers Upper Egypt; founds 25th Egyptian dynasty **ca. 720** Kushite king Piankhy completes conquest of Egypt and reigns as king of Kush and Egypt **ca. 600** Meroitic period of Kushan civilization begins	**ca. 1500–800** Olmec civilization in Mesoamerica **ca. 800–200** Chavín (Early) Horizon in Andean South America

Olmec monument, La Venta. (Robert and Linda Mitchell Photography)

ca. 500–200 Rise of Mohist, Taoist, and Legalist schools of thought in China **401–256** Period of the Warring States in China **ca. 300** Old Stone Age Jōmon culture in Japan replaced by Yayoi culture		**ca. 500–200** Founding of Monte Alban

256–206 Ch'in dynasty in China **221** Ch'in emperor unites all of China **206 B.C.E.–8 C.E.** Former Han dynasty in China **179–104** Han philosopher, Tung Chung-shu **145–90** Han historian, Ssu-ma Chien **141–187** Emperor Wu Ti of China reigns	**25** Romans sack Kushite capital of Napata **100 B.C.E.–1 C.E.** Probable first Indonesian migrations to East African coast	

Han dynasty sculpture. (Eric Lessing/Art Resource, N.Y.)

25–220 The Later Han dynasty, China **ca. 220–590** Spread of Buddhism in China **220–589** Six Dynasties period in China **ca. 300–500** Barbarian invasions of China **ca. 300–680** Archaic Yamato state in Japan	**ca. 200** Camel first used for trans-Saharan transport **ca. 200–900** Expansion of Bantu people **ca. 250** Aksum (Ethiopia) controls the Red Sea trade **ca. 300–400** Rise of kingdom of Ghana **ca. 350** Kush ceases to exist	**ca. 200–600** Early Intermediate period in Andean South America; Moche and Nazca cultures **ca. 150–900** Classic period. Dominance of Teotihuacán in central Mexico, Tikal in southern Yucatán.

3 GREEK AND HELLENISTIC CIVILIZATION

About 2000 B.C.E., Greek-speaking peoples settled the lands surrounding the Aegean Sea, where they came in touch with the more advanced and earlier civilizations of the Near East. Adapting from these predecessors, the Greeks forged their own way of life, forming a set of ideas, values, and institutions that would spread far beyond their homeland. The foundation of this way of life was the independent city-state, or *polis* (plural *poleis*).

Bronze Age on Crete and on the Mainland to ca. 1150 B.C.E.

The culture of the large island of Crete was a cultural bridge between the older civilizations and the new one of the Greeks.

The Minoans

In the third and second millennia B.C.E., a Bronze Age civilization arose on Crete that powerfully influenced the islands of the Aegean and the mainland of Greece. This civilization has been given the name *Minoan*, after Minos, the legendary king of Crete. Scholars have divided Minoan history into three major periods—Early, Middle, and Late Minoan.

The civilization of the Middle and Late Minoan periods in eastern and central Crete centered around several great palaces. The distinctive and striking art and architecture of these palaces reflect the influence of Syria, Asia Minor, and Egypt, but have a uniquely Cretan style and quality. Minoan cities lacked strong defensive walls, suggesting that they were not built with defense in mind.

Excavations at Minoan sites have revealed clay writing tablets like those found in Mesopotamia. Tablets found at the royal palace at Cnossus, accidentally preserved when a great fire that destroyed the palace hardened them, have three distinct kinds of writing on them. One has proved to be an early form of Greek. The contents of the tablets reveal an organization centered on the palace and ruled by a king who was supported by an extensive bureaucracy. This sort of organization is typical of early civilizations in the

Near East but is nothing like that of the Greeks after the Bronze Age. Yet some of the inventories were written in a form of Greek. Why should Minoans, who were not Greek, write in a language not their own? This question raises the larger one of what the relationship was between Crete and the Greek mainland during the Bronze Age, leading us to an examination of mainland, or Helladic, culture.

The Mycenaeans

In the third millennium B.C.E., most of the Greek mainland, including many of the sites of later Greek cities, was settled by people who used metal, built some impressive houses, and traded with Crete and the islands of the Aegean. The names they gave to places make it clear that they were not Greeks and that they spoke a language that was not Indo-European (the language family to which Greek belongs).

Not long after 2000 B.C.E., many of the Early Helladic sites were destroyed, abandoned, or yielded to an invading people. These signs of invasion probably signal the arrival of the Greeks.

The shaft graves cut into the rock at the royal palace-fortress of Mycenae show that by the Late Helladic, the conquerors had prospered. At Mycenae the richest finds come from the period after 1600 B.C.E. The city's wealth and power reached their peak during this time, and the culture of the whole mainland during this period goes by the name *Mycenaean*. Greek invaders also established themselves in Crete, and at the height of Mycenaean power (1400–1200 B.C.E.), Crete was part of the Mycenaean world.

Excavations at Mycenaean sites reveal a culture influenced by, but different from, Minoan culture. Mycenaean cities were built on hills commanding the neighboring territory. The Mycenaean people were warriors led by strong kings who, with their retainers, lived in palaces protected by defensive walls while most of the population lived outside the walls. Like the palaces of Crete, Mycenaean palaces were adorned with murals, but instead of the peaceful scenery and games depicted on the Cretan murals, the Mycenaean murals depicted scenes of war and boar hunting.

About 1500 B.C.E., *tholos* tombs—large, beehivelike chambers cut into hillsides—replaced the shaft graves. The *tholos* tombs, built of enormous, well-cut, fitted stones, were approached through an unroofed passage cut horizontally into the side of the hill. Only a strong king could undertake such a project. His wealth probably came from plundering raids, piracy, and trade. Some of this trade went to Italy and Sicily, but most was with the Aegean islands, Asia Minor, Syria, Egypt, and Crete. The Mycenaeans exchanged pottery, olive oil, and animal hides for jewels and other luxuries.

Further evidence that the Mycenaean world was made up of a number of independent, powerful, and well-organized monarchies comes from the many clay tablets with Mycenaean writing found throughout the mainland. These reveal a society similar to that of Cnossus on Crete. A king, whose title was *wanax*, held a royal domain, appointed officials, commanded servants, and kept a close record of what he owned and what was owed to him.

The Fall of Mycenaean Power At the height of their power (1400–1200 B.C.E.), the Mycenaeans enlarged their cities, expanded their trade, and even established commercial colonies in the east. Sometime about 1250 B.C.E. they probably sacked Troy, on the coast of northwestern Asia Minor, giving rise to the epic poems of Homer, *The Iliad* and *The Odyssey*. Around the year 1200 B.C.E., however, the Mycenaean world showed signs of great trouble; by 1100 B.C.E. it was gone.

The reasons for the collapse of Mycenaean civilization are unclear. Greek legends attribute it to a new wave of Greek invaders, the Dorians, from the north. The legends identify the Dorians as a rude people who spoke a different Greek dialect from that of the Mycenaean peoples.

Greek "Middle Age" to ca. 750 B.C.E.

The immediate effects of the Mycenaean collapse were disastrous. Palaces were destroyed, the kings and bureaucrats were swept away, and the wealth and organization evaporated. Greece entered a dark "Middle Age" about which little is known.

Another result of the turmoil surrounding the Mycenaean collapse was the spread of the Greek people eastward from the mainland to the Aegean islands and the coast of Asia Minor, which came to be called Ionia. These migrations made the Aegean a Greek lake. Trade, however, was virtually ended. The Greeks were forced to turn inward, and each community was left largely to its own devices. The Near East was also in disarray, and no great power arose to impose its ways on the helpless people who lived around the Aegean. The Greeks were allowed to create their unique style of life.

Age of Homer

For a picture of society in these "dark ages," the best source is Homer. His epic poems, *The Iliad* and *The Odyssey*, emerged from a tradition of oral poetry whose roots extend into the Mycenaean Age. Through the centuries bards had sung tales of the heroes who had fought at Troy. In this way, some very old material was preserved into the eighth century B.C.E., when the poems attributed to Homer were finally written down. Although the poems tell of the deeds of Mycenaean heroes, the world they describe seems to be that of the tenth and ninth centuries B.C.E. rather than Mycenaean.

Government

In the Homeric poems the power of the kings is much less than that of the Mycenaean rulers. Homeric kings were limited in their ability to make important decisions by the need to consult a council of nobles.

The right to speak in council was limited to noblemen, but the common people could not be ignored. If a king planned a major change of policy, he would call the common soldiers to an assembly; they could express their feelings by acclamation, though they could not take part in the debate. Homer shows that even in these early times the Greeks practiced some forms of constitutional government.

Society

Homeric society was aristocratic. Birth determined noble status, and wealth usually accompanied it. Below the nobles were two other classes: *thetes* and slaves.

Thetes, who were landless laborers, endured the worst conditions in Homeric society. Slaves, at least, were attached to family households and so were protected and fed. In a world where membership in a settled group provided the only security, free laborers were desperately vulnerable. Slaves were few in number and were mostly women who served as maids and concubines. Agriculture depended chiefly on free labor throughout Greek history.

Homeric Values

The Homeric poems reflect an aristocratic code of values that influenced all future Greek thought. Homer was the schoolbook of the Greeks. They memorized his texts and emulated the behavior and cherished the values they found in them. Those values were physical prowess; courage; and fierce protection of one's family, friends, property, and above all, personal honor and reputation. Speed of foot, strength, and excellence at fighting make a man great, and these attributes serve to promote personal honor. The great hero of *The Iliad*, Achilles, refuses to fight in battle, allowing his fellow Greeks to be almost defeated, because Agamemnon has wounded his honor. He returns to the army not out of a sense of duty but to avenge the death of his dear friend Patroclus.

The highest virtue in Homeric society was *arete*—manliness, the excellence proper to a hero. This quality was best revealed in a contest, or *agon*. Homeric battles are primarily individual contests between champions, and one of the prime forms of entertainment is the athletic contest.

The central ethical idea in Homer can be found in the instructions that the fathers of heroes give to their sons: "Always be the best and distinguished above others," and "Do not bring shame on the family of your fathers." Here we have the chief values of the aristocrats of Homer's world: to vie for individual supremacy in *arete* and to defend and increase the honor of the family. These would remain prominent aristocratic values long after Homeric society was only a memory.

The "Trojan Horse," depicted on a seventh-century-B.C.E. Greek vase. According to legend, the Greeks finally defeated Troy by pretending to abandon their siege of the city, leaving a giant wooden horse behind. Soldiers hidden in the horse opened the gates of the city to their compatriots after the Trojans had brought it within their walls. Note the wheels on the horse and the Greek soldiers who are hiding inside it holding weapons and armor. [Deutsches Archäologisches Institut, Athens]

The Polis

The characteristic Greek institution was the *polis*. The common translation of that word as "city-state" says both too much and too little. All Greek *poleis* began as agricultural villages or towns, and many stayed that way, so the word "city" is inappropriate. All of them were states, in the sense of being independent political units, but they were much more than that. The *polis* was thought of as a community of relatives; all its citizens, who were theoretically descended from a common ancestor, belonged to subgroups such as fighting brotherhoods (*phratries*), clans, and tribes. They worshiped the gods in common ceremonies.

Aristotle (see Chapter 2) argued that the *polis* was a natural growth and that the human being is by nature "an animal who lives in a *polis*." Humans alone have the power of speech and from it derive the ability to distinguish good from bad and right from wrong, "and the sharing of these things is what makes a household and a *polis*." Without law and justice, humans are the worst and most dangerous of the animals. With them, they can be the best, and justice exists only in the *polis*.

Development of the Polis

Originally the word *polis* referred only to a citadel, an elevated, defensible rock to which the farmers of the neighboring area could retreat in case of attack. The Acropolis in Athens and the hill called Acrocorinth in Corinth are examples. For some time such high places and the adjacent farms made up the *polis*. The towns grew gradually and without planning. For centuries they had no walls. The availability of farmland and of a natural fortress determined their location. They were placed either well inland or far enough away from the sea to avoid piratical raids. Only later and gradually did the *agora*— a marketplace and civic center—appear within the *polis*. The agora was to become the heart of the Greeks' remarkable social life, distinguished by conversation and argument carried on in the open air.

Some *poleis* probably came into existence early in the eighth century B.C.E., and all the colonies established by the Greeks after 750 B.C.E. took the form of the *polis*. Once the new institution had been fully established, true monarchy disappeared. The original form of the *polis* was an aristocratic republic dominated by the nobility through its council of nobles and its monopoly of the magistracies.

The Hoplite Phalanx

A new military strategy was crucial to the development of the *polis*. In earlier times the brunt of fighting had been carried on by small troops of cavalry and individual "champions." Toward the end of the eighth century B.C.E., however, the hoplite phalanx came into being and remained the basis of Greek warfare thereafter.

The hoplite was a heavily armed infantryman who fought with a spear and a large shield. These soldiers were arrayed in close order, usually at least eight ranks deep, to form a phalanx. All depended on the discipline, strength, and courage of the individual soldier. At its best, the phalanx could withstand cavalry charges and defeat infantries not as well protected or disciplined. Until defeated by the Roman legion, it was the dominant military force in the eastern Mediterranean.

The usual hoplite battle in Greece was between the armies of two *poleis* quarreling over a piece of land. One army invaded the territory of the other when its crops were almost ready for harvest. The defending army had to protect the fields. If the defenders were beaten, the fields were captured or destroyed. This style of fighting produced a single decisive battle and perfectly suited the farmer-soldier-citizen who was the backbone of the *polis*. By keeping wars short and limiting their destructiveness and expense, it helped the *polis* prosper.

The phalanx and the *polis* arose together and created a bond between aristocrats and family farmers who fought in it side by side. This bond helps to explain why class conflicts were muted for some time in Greece. It also guaranteed, however, that the aristocrats, who dominated the *poleis* at first, would not always be unchallenged.

Expansion of the Greek World

From the mid-eighth century B.C.E. until well into the sixth, a burst of colonizing activity placed *poleis* from Spain to the Black Sea. A century earlier a few Greeks had established trading posts in Syria. There, in about 750 B.C.E., they borrowed a writing system from one of the Semitic scripts and added vowels to create the first true alphabet. The new Greek alphabet was easier to learn than any earlier writing system and made possible a widely literate society.

Greek Colonies

Syria and its neighboring territory were too strong to penetrate, so the Greeks settled more sparsely populated areas. Before long, there were so many Greek colonies in Italy and Sicily that the Romans called the whole region *Magna Graecia* ("Great Greece"). The Greeks also put colonies in Spain, southern France, on the Black Sea, and on the north African coast. Most colonies, although independent, were friendly with their mother cities.

Colonization relieved the pressure and land hunger of a growing population. By confronting them with the differences between themselves and new peoples, it gave the Greeks a sense of cultural identity and fostered a Panhellenic ("all-Greek") spirit that led to the establishment of common religious festivals. The most important of these were at Olympia, Delphi, Corinth, and Nemea.

Colonization also encouraged trade and industry. The influx of new wealth and the increased demand for goods stimulated a more intensive use of the land, an emphasis on crops for export, chiefly the olive and the wine grape, and the manufacture of pottery, tools, weapons, and fine metalwork as well as perfumed oil, the soap of the ancient Mediterranean. New opportunities allowed some men outside the nobility to become wealthy and important. These newly enriched became a troublesome element in the aristocratic *poleis*, for they were barred from political power, religious privileges, and social acceptance by the ruling aristocrats. These conditions soon created a crisis in many states. Between 700 and 500 B.C.E., the result was often the establishment of a tyranny.

The Tyrants (ca. 700–500 B.C.E.)

A tyrant was a monarch who had gained power in an unorthodox but not necessarily wicked way and who exercised a strong one-man rule that might well be beneficent and popular.

The founding tyrant was usually a member of the ruling aristocracy who either had a personal grievance or led an unsuccessful faction. He generally had the support of the politically powerless newly wealthy and of poor farmers. He often expelled his aristocratic opponents and divided their land among his supporters. He destroyed the privileges of the old aristocracy and fostered trade and colonization.

The tyrants presided over a period of population growth. They responded with a program of public works, new local festivals, and patronage of the arts. This activity contributed to the tyrant's popularity, to the prosperity of his city, and to his self-esteem.

Chronology of the Rise of Greece	
ca. 2900–1150 B.C.E.	Minoan period
ca. 1900 B.C.E.	Probable date of the arrival of the Greeks on the mainland
ca. 1600–1150 B.C.E.	Mycenaean period
ca. 1250 B.C.E.	Sack of Troy (?)
ca. 1200–1150 B.C.E.	Destruction of Mycenaean centers in Greece
ca. 1100–750 B.C.E.	Dark Ages
ca. 750–500 B.C.E.	Major period of Greek colonization
ca. 725 B.C.E.	Probable date of Homer
ca. 700 B.C.E.	Probable date of Hesiod
ca. 700–500 B.C.E.	Major period of Greek tyranny

By the end of the sixth century B.C.E., tyranny had disappeared from the Greek states. The last tyrants left bitter memories everywhere. There was something about the concept of tyranny that was inimical to the idea of the *polis*. The notion of the *polis* as a community to which every member must be responsible, the connection of justice with that community, and the natural aristocratic hatred of monarchy all made tyranny seem alien and offensive.

However, the tyrants made important contributions. They helped secure the future prosperity of Greece and cultivated technology, the arts, and literature. Most important, they broke the grip of the aristocracy.

Life in Archaic Greece

Society

As the "dark ages" came to an end, the features that would distinguish Greek society took shape. The role of the artisan and the merchant grew more important, but most people were farmers.

Farmers The poet Hesiod (ca. 700 B.C.E.) presented himself as a small farmer, and his *Works and Days* gives some idea of the life of such a farmer. The crops included grain, chiefly barley but also wheat; grapes for wine; olives, mainly for oil used for cooking, lighting, and washing; green vegetables; and fruit. Sheep and goats provided milk and cheese, but small farmers tasted meat chiefly from sacrificial animals at festivals. Life was continual toil under the burning sun and in the freezing cold, and pleasures were few.

Aristocrats Most aristocrats employed hired laborers, sharecroppers, and even slaves, to work their lands, so they could enjoy leisure for other activities. The center of aristocratic social life was the drinking party, or *symposion*, a carefully organized occasion in which only men took part. There were games or entertainment, or the participants provided their own amusements with songs, poetry, or even philosophical disputes. Characteristically, these took the form of contests, with a prize for the winner, for aristocratic values continued to emphasize competition and the need to excel.

This aspect of aristocratic life appears in the athletic contests that became widespread early in the sixth century B.C.E. The games included running events, boxing, wrestling, and the chariot race. Only the rich could afford race horses, so the chariot race was a special preserve of aristocracy. Wrestling, however, was also especially favored by the nobility, and the *palaestra* where they practiced became an important social center for the aristocracy. The contrast between the hard, drab life of the peasants and the leisured and lively one of the aristocrats could hardly be greater.

Religion

Like most ancient peoples, the Greeks were polytheists, and religion played an important part in their lives.

The Greek pantheon consisted of the twelve gods who lived on Mount Olympus. These were

- Zeus, the father of the gods
- Hera, his wife
- Zeus's siblings:
  Poseidon, his brother, god of the seas and earthquakes
  Hestia, his sister, goddess of the hearth
  Demeter, his sister, goddess of agriculture and marriage
- Zeus's children:
  Aphrodite, goddess of love and beauty
  Apollo, god of the sun, music, poetry, and prophecy
  Ares, god of war
  Artemis, goddess of the moon and the hunt
  Athena, goddess of wisdom and the arts
  Hephaestus, god of fire and metallurgy
  Hermes, messenger of the gods, connected with commerce and cunning

The gods were seen as behaving like mortal humans, except in their strength and immortality. On the other hand, Zeus, at least, was seen as a source of justice, and even the Olympians were understood to be subordinate to the Fates. Each *polis* had one of the Olympians as its guardian deity and worshiped that god in its own special way, but all the gods were Panhellenic. In the eighth and seventh centuries B.C.E., common shrines were established at Olympia for the worship of Zeus, at Delphi for Apollo, and at Corinth for Poseidon. Each held athletic contests in honor of its deity, to which all Greeks were invited and for which a sacred truce was declared.

The worship of these deities did not involve great emotion. Worshipers offered a god prayer, libations, and gifts in hopes of protection and favors. Greek religion offered little moral teaching. Most Greeks seem to have thought that civic virtue consisted of worshiping the state deities in the traditional way, performing required public services, and fighting in defense of the state. To them, private morality meant to do good to one's friends and harm to one's enemies.

In the sixth century B.C.E., the influence of the cult of Apollo at Delphi and of his oracle there became great. The priests of Apollo preached moderation; their advice was exemplified in two famous sayings: "Know thyself" and "Nothing in excess." Humans need self-control. Its opposite is arrogance (*hubris*), which leads to moral blindness and divine vengeance.

To assuage human fears, hopes, and passions, the Greeks turned to other deities and rites. Of them, the most popular was Dionysus, a god of nature and fertility, of the grapevine and drunkenness and sexual abandon.

Poetry

The great changes sweeping through the Greek world were also reflected in poetry. The lyric style predominated. Sappho of Lesbos, Anacreon of Teos, and Simonides of Cous composed personal poetry, often speaking of the pleasure and agony of love. Alcaeus of Mytilene, an aristocrat driven from his city by a tyrant, wrote bitter invective.

But the most interesting poet from a political point of view was Theognis of Megara, the spokesman for the old, defeated aristocracy of birth. He divided everyone into two classes—the noble and the base; the former were good, the latter bad. Only nobles could aspire to virtue and possessed the critical moral and intellectual qualities: respect (or honor) and judgment. These qualities could not be taught; they were innate. Intermarriage between the noble and the base was condemned. These ideas remained alive in aristocratic hearts throughout the next century and greatly influenced later thinkers, Plato among them.

Major City-States

Generalization about the *polis* is difficult, for although the states had much in common, some of them developed in unique ways. Sparta and Athens became the two most powerful Greek states.

Sparta

About 725 B.C.E., population pressure and land hunger led the Spartans to conquer their western neighbor, Messenia. The Spartans now had as much land as they would ever need, and because they reduced the Messenians to serfs, or Helots, they no longer had to work this land themselves. When the Helots rebelled in about 650 B.C.E., the Spartans faced a turning point. To keep down the Helots, who outnumbered them perhaps ten to one, they turned their city forever after into a military academy and camp.

Society   The new system exerted control over each Spartan from birth, when officials of the state decided which infants, male and female, were physically fit to survive. At age seven, the Spartan boy was taken from his mother and turned over to young instructors who trained him in athletics and the military arts. The Spartan youth was enrolled in the army at twenty and lived in barracks until he was thirty. He could marry, but could visit his wife only by stealth. At thirty he became a full citizen, an "equal," and was allowed to live in his own house with his wife, although he took his meals at a public mess in the company of fifteen comrades. His food, a simple diet without much meat or wine, was provided by his own plot of land, which was worked by Helots. Only when he

The Greek and Persian Ways of War— Autocracy versus Freedom under the Law

The Greek historian Herodotus, who wrote his account of the wars between the Greeks and Persians more than half a century after they ended, was very interested in the differences between the ways of the Greeks and other peoples of the world. In the following passage he describes a conversation between Demaratus, an exiled king of Sparta, and Xerxes, the Great King of Persia. Demaratus had come to Xerxes' court after his exile. Xerxes received him kindly and made him a royal adviser.

On what does Xerxes rely for Persian military success? What is the source of Demaratus's confidence in the Spartans? Does the claim he makes hold for other Greeks as well as the Spartans? How is it possible to reconcile freedom with obedience to the laws?

'How is it possible that a thousand men, or ten thousand, or fifty thousand, should stand up to an army as big as mine, especially if they were not under a single master, but all perfectly free to do as they pleased? Suppose them to have five thousand men: in that case we should be more than a thousand to one! If, like ours, their troops were subject to the control of a single man, then possibly for fear of him, in spite of the disparity in numbers, they might show some sort of factitious courage, or let themselves be whipped into battle; but, as every man is free to follow his fancy, it is not conceivable that they should do either. Indeed, my own opinion is that even on equal terms the Greeks could hardly face the Persians alone. We, too, have this thing that you were speaking of—I do not say it is common, but it does exist; for instance, amongst the Persians in my bodyguard there are men who would willingly fight with three Greeks together. But you know nothing of such things, or you could not talk such nonsense.'

'My lord,' Demaratus answered, 'I knew before I began that if I spoke the truth you would not like it. But, as you demanded the plain truth and nothing less, I told you how things are with the Spartans. Yet you are well aware that I now feel but little affection for my countrymen, who robbed me of my hereditary power and privileges and made me a fugitive without a home—whereas your father welcomed me at his court and gave me the means of livelihood and somewhere to live. Surely it is unreasonable to reject kindness; any sensible man will cherish it. Personally I do not claim to be able to fight ten men—or two; indeed I should prefer not even to fight with one. But should it be necessary—should there be some great cause to urge me on—then nothing would give me more pleasure than to stand up to one of those men of yours who claim to be a match for three Greeks. So it is with the Spartans; fighting singly, they are as good as any, but fighting together they are the best soldiers in the world. They are free— yes—but not entirely free; for they have a master, and that master is Law, which they fear much more than your subjects fear you. Whatever this master commands they do; and his command never varies: it is never to retreat in battle, however great the odds, but always to stand firm, and to conquer or die. If, my lord, you think that what I have said is nonsense—very well; I am willing henceforward to hold my tongue. This time I spoke because you forced me to speak. In any case, I pray that all may turn out as you desire.'

Xerxes burst out laughing at Demaratus's answer, and goodhumouredly let him go.

From *The Histories* by Herodotus, trans. by Aubrey de Selincourt, revised by A. R. Burn (Penguin Classics 1954, Revised edition, 1972). Copyright © The Estate of Aubrey de Silincourt, 1954. Copyright © A. R. Burn, 1972.

reached sixty could the Spartan retire from military service to his home and family.

Spartan girls were permitted greater freedom than among other Greeks and were also indoctrinated with the idea of service to Sparta. The entire system was designed to change the natural feelings of devotion to family into a more powerful commitment to the *polis*. Privacy, luxury, and even comfort were sacrificed to produce the best soldiers in the world. Nothing that might turn the mind away from duty was permitted.

Government Sparta was governed by two kings, a council of elders, and an assembly. The power of the kings was limited by law. The council of elders—twenty-eight men over sixty who were elected for life—was consulted before any proposal was put before the assembly. The assembly, which consisted of all males over thirty, served only to ratify the decisions of magistrates, elders, and kings.

Sparta also had a board of ephors, five men elected annually by the assembly. The ephors controlled foreign policy, oversaw the generalship of the kings, presided at the assembly, and guarded against rebellion by the Helots.

Suppression of the Helots required all the effort and energy the Spartans had. They could not expand their borders, but they forced their neighbors to follow Sparta's lead in foreign affairs and supply Sparta with a fixed number of troops on demand. This formed an alliance known as the Peloponnesian League that made Sparta the most powerful *polis* in Greece.

Athens

In the seventh century B.C.E., Athens and the region of Attica constituted a typical aristocratic *polis*. The state was governed by the Areopagus, a council of nobles. Annually the council elected nine magistrates, called *archons*, who joined the Areopagus after their year in office. A broad-based citizens' assembly, which had little power, represented the four tribes into which Attica's inhabitants were traditionally divided.

Pressure for Change In the seventh century B.C.E., quarrels within the nobility and the beginnings of an agrarian crisis disturbed the peaceful life of Athens. A shift to more intensive agricultural techniques forced the less successful farmers to borrow from wealthy neighbors. Many defaulted and were enslaved. Some were even sold abroad. The poor began to demand the abolition of debt and a redistribution of the land.

Reforms of Solon In the year 594 B.C.E., as tradition has it, the Athenians elected Solon (ca. 639–559 B.C.E.) to revise Athens' governing institutions. Solon immediately canceled current debts, forbade debt slavery, and brought back Athenians enslaved abroad. He encouraged commerce and forbade the export of wheat, but encouraged the export of olive oil and wine, thus diverting Athenian land to the cultivation of olive trees and vines as cash crops.

Solon changed the way Athens was governed. He expanded citizenship to include immigrant artisans and merchants, and divided the citizenry into four classes on the basis of wealth. Only men of the wealthiest two classes could be archons and sit on the Areopagus. Men of the third class could serve as hoplites and on a council of four hundred chosen by the assembly of all male citizens.

Pisistratus the Tyrant Despite Solon's reforms, Pisistratus (605?–527 B.C.E.), a nobleman and military hero, seized power in 546 B.C.E. and made himself the city's first tyrant. Pisistratus sought to increase the power of the central government at the expense of the nobles. He made no formal change in the institutions of government, but saw to it that his supporters filled key offices. The unintended effect was to give the Athenians more experience in the procedures of self-government and a growing taste for it.

Pisistratus's son, Hippias (r. 527–510 B.C.E.), whose rule became increasingly harsh, was driven into exile in 510 B.C.E. The tyranny was over.

<table>
<tr><td colspan="2">**Key Events in the Early History of Sparta and Athens**</td></tr>
<tr><td>ca. 725–710 B.C.E.</td><td>First Messenian War</td></tr>
<tr><td>ca. 650–625 B.C.E.</td><td>Second Messenian War; Solon institutes reforms at Athens</td></tr>
<tr><td>ca. 560–550 B.C.E.</td><td>Sparta defeats Tegea: beginning of Peloponnesian League</td></tr>
<tr><td>546–527 B.C.E.</td><td>Pisistratus reigns as tyrant at Athens (main period)</td></tr>
<tr><td>510 B.C.E.</td><td>Hippias, son of Pisistratus, deposed as tyrant of Athens</td></tr>
<tr><td>ca. 508–501 B.C.E.</td><td>Clisthenes institutes reforms at Athens</td></tr>
</table>

Clisthenes, the Founder of Democracy Some factions in the Athenian aristocracy then tried to restore the aristocracy to the position of dominance it held before Solon. One aristocratic rival, Clisthenes, turned to the people for support and won it with a program of great popular appeal. A central aim of Clisthenes' reforms was to diminish the influence of traditional regions in Athenian life, for they were an important source of power for the nobility. Clisthenes replaced Attica's traditional four tribes with ten new tribes organized to guarantee that no region would dominate any of them. The new organization increased devotion to the *polis*, weakening regional loyalties.

Clisthenes vested final authority in all things in the assembly of all adult male Athenian citizens. Debate in the assembly was free and open; any Athenian could now submit legislation, offer amendments, or argue the merits of any question.

The Persian Wars

The Greeks' period of isolation and freedom ended in the sixth century B.C.E. when the Greek cities on the coast of Asia Minor came under the control of the powerful Persian Empire (see Chapter 4).

Ionian Rebellion

Initially the cities of Ionia (those on the central part of the west coast of Asia Minor and nearby islands) prospered under Persian rule and remained obedient. The private troubles of the ambitious tyrant of Miletus, Aristagoras, however, ended this calm. Aristagoras had urged a Persian expedition against the island of Naxos; when it failed, he feared the consequences and organized a rebellion in Ionia in 499 B.C.E., and turned to the mainland Greeks for help. Athens agreed to send a fleet and in 498 B.C.E., the Athenians and their allies burned Sardis, the seat of the Persian governor. The revolt spread, but the Athenians withdrew and the Persians gradually reimposed their will. In 494 B.C.E. they wiped out Miletus, and the Ionian rebellion was over.

The War in Greece

In 490 B.C.E. the Persian king, Darius (r. 521–486 B.C.E.), sent an expedition to punish Athens. Miltiades (d. 489 B.C.E.), an Athenian who had fled from Persian service, led the city's army to a confrontation with the invaders at Marathon and won a decisive victory.

The Great Invasion For the Persians, however, Marathon was only a temporary defeat. In 481 B.C.E., Darius's successor, Xerxes (r. 486–465 B.C.E.), gathered an army of at least 150,000 men and a navy of more than 600 ships for the conquest of Greece. In Athens, Themistocles (ca. 525–462 B.C.E.), who favored making Athens into a naval power, had become the leading politician. By 480 B.C.E. Athens had more than 200 ships, the backbone of a navy that was to defeat the Persians.

In the spring of 480 B.C.E. Xerxes launched his invasion. The Persian strategy was to march into Greece, destroy Athens, defeat the Greek army, and add the Greeks to the number of Persian subjects. The huge Persian army needed to keep in touch with the fleet for supplies. If the Greeks could defeat the Persian navy, the army could not remain in Greece. Themistocles' strategy was to delay the Persian army and then to bring on the kind of naval battle he might hope to win.

The fate of Greece was decided in a sea battle in the narrow straits to the east of the island of Salamis. There the Greeks destroyed more than half the Persian fleet, forcing the rest to retreat to Asia with a good part of the Persian army.

The danger, however, was not over yet. The Persian general Mardonius spent the winter in central Greece. The Spartan regent, Pausanias (d. ca. 470 B.C.E.), then led the largest Greek army yet assembled to confront Mardonius. At Plataea, in the summer of 479 B.C.E., Mardonius died in battle, and his army fled home. Meanwhile, the Ionian Greeks urged King

Leotychidas, the Spartan commander of the fleet, to fight the Persian fleet. At Mycale, near Samos, he destroyed the Persian camp and its fleet offshore. The Persians fled the Aegean and Ionia.

Classical Greece

The repulse of the Persians marks the beginning of the Classical Period in Greece, 150 years of intense cultural achievement that has rarely if ever been matched anywhere since (see Map 3–1). The Classical Period was also a time of destructive conflicts among the *poleis* that left them weakened and vulnerable.

The Delian League

Greek unity gave way within two years of the Persian retreat. Two spheres of influence emerged—one dominated by Sparta, the other by Athens. The reasons for the split lay in the Ionian Greeks' need for protection against the Persians and the desire for revenge. Athens, the leading naval power in Greece, led the effort to drive the Persians from the Aegean.

In the winter of 478–477 B.C.E., the islanders, the Greeks from the coast of Asia Minor, and some from other Greek cities on the Aegean met with the Athenians on the sacred island of Delos to swear a permanent alliance. Athens was clearly designated leader. Known as the Delian League, the alliance drove the Persians from Europe and cleared the Aegean of pirates. For their common safety, the members forced some states into the league and prevented others from leaving.

Leading Athens and the Delian League in this succession of victories was the statesman and soldier Cimon (d. 449 B.C.E.). Cimon pursued a policy of aggressive attacks on Persia and friendly relations with Sparta. In domestic affairs, he accepted the democratic constitution of Clisthenes.

The First Peloponnesian War

The Fall of Cimon In 465 B.C.E., the island of Thasos rebelled against the league. Cimon's suppression of this rebellion was a significant step in the evolution of the league into an Athenian empire. Despite his success, Cimon faced a challenge at home from a faction whose chief supporter was Pericles (ca. 495–429 B.C.E.), a member of a distinguished Athenian family. This faction wanted to increase the power of ordinary people in Athens and break with Sparta.

In 461 B.C.E. Cimon was exiled, and Athens made an alliance with Argos, Sparta's traditional enemy. Almost overnight, Cimon's domestic and foreign policies had been overturned.

Greek Wars Against Persia	
ca. 560–546 B.C.E.	Greek cities of Asia Minor conquered by Croesus of Lydia
546 B.C.E.	Cyrus of Persia conquers Lydia and gains control of Greek cities
499–494 B.C.E.	Greek cities rebel (Ionian rebellion)
490 B.C.E.	Battle of Marathon
480–479 B.C.E.	Xerxes' invasion of Greece
480 B.C.E.	Battles of Thermopylae, Artemisium, and Salamis
479 B.C.E.	Battles of Plataea and Mycale

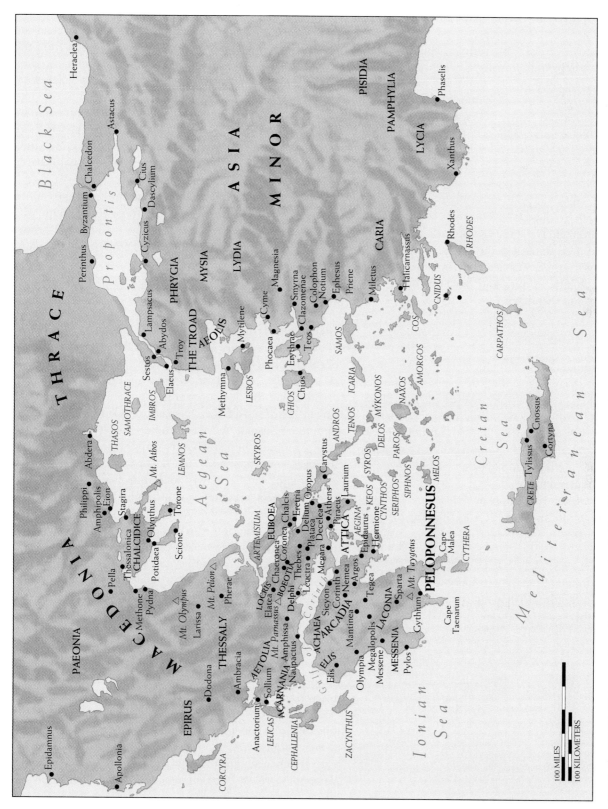

Map 3–1 Classical Greece.   Greece in the classical period (ca. 480–338 B.C.E.) centered on the Aegean Sea. Although there were important Greek settlements in Italy, Sicily, and all around the Black Sea, the area shown in this general reference map embraced the vast majority of Greek states.

Outbreak of War The policies of the new regime at Athens helped bring on a conflict with Sparta known as The First Peloponnesian War. The Athenians made great gains during the war's early years. They appeared supreme and invulnerable, controlling neighboring states and dominating the sea.

In 454 B.C.E., however, the tide turned. The Athenian fleet, dispatched to help an Egyptian rebellion against Persia, suffered a defeat. Rebellions broke out within the Delian League. Pericles, the commander of the Athenian army, agreed to a peace of thirty years. Greece was now divided into two blocs: Sparta and its alliance on the mainland and Athens and what had become the Athenian Empire in the Aegean.

The Athenian Empire

The Athenians moved the Delian League's treasury to Athens and began to keep one-sixtieth of the league's annual revenues for themselves. Athens was clearly the master and its allies mere subjects. The empire had become the key to Athens' prosperity and security.

Athenian Democracy

Even as the Athenians were tightening their control over their empire, they were expanding democracy at home. Under the leadership of Pericles they evolved the freest government the world had yet seen. No adult male was barred from office on the basis of property. Pericles introduced pay for jury service, opening that important duty to the poor. Circuit judges made swift impartial justice available even to the poor in the countryside.

However, citizenship was sharply restricted to those who had two citizen parents. In Greek terms this was natural.

Key Events in Athenian History Between the Persian War and the Great Peloponnesian War

478–477 B.C.E.	Delian League founded
ca. 474–462 B.C.E.	Cimon leading politician
467 B.C.E.	Victory over Persians at Eurymedon River
465–463 B.C.E.	Rebellion of Thasos
462 B.C.E.	Pericles rises to leadership
461 B.C.E.	Cimon ostracized
ca. 460 B.C.E.	First Peloponnesian War begins
454 B.C.E.	Athens defeated in Egypt; crisis in the Delian League
445 B.C.E.	Thirty Years' Peace ends First Peloponnesian War

Democracy was the privilege of citizenship, making citizenship a valuable commodity.

Among citizens, however, the extent of the democracy was remarkable. Every decision of the state had to be approved by the popular assembly—a collection of the people, not their representatives. Every judicial decision was subject to appeal to a popular court chosen from the Athenian male population. Most officials were selected by lot, without regard to class. The main elected officials were generally nobles and almost always rich men, but the people were free to choose others. All public officials could be removed from office and were held to a compulsory accounting at the end of their terms. There was no standing army; no police force, open or secret; and no way to coerce the people.

Pericles was elected to the generalship (a military office with important political influence) fifteen years in a row and thirty times in all. He favored a conservative policy after the First Peloponnesian War: to retain the empire in the Aegean and live at peace with the Spartans.

Women of Athens

Greek society was dominated by men. This was equally true of democratic Athens. Women were excluded from most aspects of public life. They could not vote, take part in political assemblies, or hold office.

In private life, women were always under the control of a male guardian—a father, husband, or relative. Women married young, usually between the ages of twelve and eighteen, whereas their husbands were typically over thirty. Marriages were arranged; the woman normally had no choice of husband, and her dowry was controlled by a male relative. To obtain a divorce, a woman needed the approval of a male relative.

The main function of an Athenian woman of a citizen family was to produce male heirs for the household (*oikos*) of her husband. Because the pure and legitimate lineage of the offspring was important, women were carefully segregated from men outside the family and were confined to the women's quarters in the house. Men might seek sexual gratification outside the house with prostitutes. Respectable women stayed home to raise the children and oversee the household. The only public function of women—an important one—was in the various rituals and festivals of the state religion.

However, evidence from mythology, pictorial art, and the tragedies and comedies often shows women as central characters and powerful figures in both the public and the private spheres, suggesting that the role played by Athenian women may have been more complex than their legal status suggests.

The Acropolis was both the religious and civic center of Athens. In its final form it is the work of Pericles and his successors in the late fifth century B.C.E. This photograph shows the Parthenon and, to its left, the Erechtheum. [Meredith Pillon, Greek National Tourism Organization]

The Great Peloponnesian War

The Thirty Years' Peace of 445 B.C.E. endured little more than ten years. About 435 B.C.E., Athens and Sparta plunged back into conflict. This new war shook the foundations of Greek civilization.

The Spartan strategy was traditional: to invade the enemy's country and threaten the crops, forcing the enemy to defend them in a hoplite battle. The Athenian strategy was to allow the devastation of their own land and raid the Peloponnesian coast to hurt Sparta's allies. The Athenian plan required restraint, but Pericles died in 429 B.C.E. Ten years of war ended in stalemate.

In 415 B.C.E., Alcibiades (ca. 450–404 B.C.E.), a young and ambitious leader, persuaded the Athenians to attack Sicily to bring it under their control, but the entire expedition was destroyed. This disaster shook Athenian prestige, reduced its power, provoked rebellions, and brought Persia into the war on Sparta's side.

The Athenians continued fighting despite the disaster and won several important victories at sea. As their allies rebelled, however, the Athenians saw their financial resources disappear. When their fleet was destroyed at Aegospotami in 405 B.C.E., they could not build another. The Spartans, under Lysander (d. 395 B.C.E.) cut off the food supply to Athens. In 404 B.C.E. Athens surrendered unconditionally. The Great Peloponnesian War was over.

Struggle for Greek Leadership

The Hegemony of Sparta

The collapse of the Athenian empire opened the way for Spartan leadership, or hegemony. Lysander installed a board of ten local oligarchs loyal to him and supported by a Spartan garrison in most of the cities along the European coast and the islands of the Aegean. These tributaries brought Sparta almost as much revenue as the Athenians had collected.

Some of Sparta's allies, especially Thebes and Corinth, were alienated by Sparta's increasingly arrogant policies. In 404 B.C.E., Lysander installed an oligarchic government in Athens whose outrageous behavior earned it the title "Thirty Tyrants." Democratic exiles took refuge in Thebes and Corinth and created an army to challenge the oligarchy. Sparta's conservative king, Pausanias, arranged a peaceful settlement and ultimately the restoration of democracy. Thereafter, Athenian foreign policy remained under Spartan control, but otherwise Athens was free.

Sparta's actions, however, grew increasingly arrogant and lawless. In 382 B.C.E., Sparta seized Thebes during peacetime without warning or pretext. In 379 B.C.E., a Spartan army made a similar attempt on Athens. That action per-

The Great Peloponnesian War	
435 B.C.E.	Civil war at Epidamnus
432 B.C.E.	Sparta declares war on Athens
431 B.C.E.	Peloponnesian invasion of Athens
421 B.C.E.	Peace of Nicias
415–413 B.C.E.	Athenian invasion of Sicily
405 B.C.E.	Battle of Aegospotami
404 B.C.E.	Athens surrenders

Athenian Democracy: An Unfriendly View

The following selection comes from an anonymous pamphlet thought to have been written in late fifth century B.C.E. The obviously antidemocratic views of its author were common among members of the upper classes in Athens late in the fifth century and thereafter.

What are the author's objections to democracy? Does he describe the workings of the Athenian democracy accurately? How would a defender of the Athenian constitution and way of life meet his complaints? Is there any merit in his criticisms? For other perspectives on law, leadership, and government, see "Hammurabi's Code on Women, Marriage, and Divorce in Babylon" (Chapter 1) and "The Edicts of Ashoka" (Chapter 4).

Now, in discussing the Athenian constitution, I cannot commend their present method of running the state, because in choosing it they preferred that the masses should do better than the respectable citizens; this, then, is my reason for not commending it. Since, however, they have made this choice, I will demonstrate how well they preserve their constitution and handle the other affairs for which the rest of the Greeks criticise them.

Again, some people are surprised at the fact that in all fields they give more power to the masses, the poor and the common people than they do to the respectable elements of society, but it will become clear that they preserve the democracy by doing precisely this. When the poor, the ordinary people and the lower classes flourish and increase in numbers, then the power of the democracy will be increased; if, however, the rich and the respectable flourish, the democrats increase the strength of their opponents. Throughout the world the aristocracy are opposed to democracy, for they are naturally least liable to loss of self-control and injustice and most meticulous in their regard for what is respectable, whereas the masses display extreme ignorance, indiscipline and wickedness, for poverty gives them a tendency towards the ignoble, and in some cases lack of money leads to their being uneducated and ignorant.

It may be objected that they ought not to grant each and every man the right of speaking in the Ekklesia and serving on the Boule, but only the ablest and best of them; however, in this also they are acting in their own best interests by allowing the mob also a voice. If none but the respectable spoke in the Ekklesia and the Boule, the result would benefit that class and harm the masses; as it is, anyone who wishes rises and speaks, and as a member of the mob he discovers what is to his own advantage and that of those like him.

But someone may say: 'How could such a man find out what was advantageous to himself and the common people?' The Athenians realise that this man, despite his ignorance and badness, brings them more advantage because he is well disposed to them than the ill-disposed respectable man would, despite his virtue and wisdom. Such practices do not produce the best city, but they are the best way of preserving democracy. For the common people do not wish to be deprived of their rights in an admirably governed city, but to be free and to rule the city; they are not disturbed by inferior laws, for the common people get their strength and freedom from what you define as inferior laws.

From *Aristotle and Xenophon on Democracy and Oligarchy*, trans. with introductions and commentary by J. M. Moore, pp. 37–38. Copyright © 1975 J. M. Moore. Published by University of California Press. Reprinted by permission.

Spartan and Theban Hegemonies

404–403 B.C.E.	Thirty Tyrants rule at Athens
401 B.C.E.	Expedition of Cyrus, rebellious prince of Persia; Battle of Cunaxa
400–387 B.C.E.	Spartan War against Persia
398–360 B.C.E.	Reign of Agesilaus at Sparta
395–387 B.C.E.	Corinthian War
382 B.C.E.	Sparta seizes Thebes
378 B.C.E.	Second Athenian Confederation founded
371 B.C.E.	Thebans defeat Sparta at Leuctra; end of Spartan hegemony
362 B.C.E.	Battle of Mantinea; end of Theban hegemony

suaded the Athenians to join with Thebes, which had rebelled from Sparta. In 371 B.C.E. the Thebans defeated the Spartans at Leuctra. They then encouraged the Arcadian cities of the central Peloponnesus to form a federal league and freed the Helots, helping them found a city of their own. Sparta's population had already been shrinking. Now, hemmed in by hostile neighbors, deprived of much of its farmland and of the slaves who had worked it, Sparta ceased to be a first-rank power. Its aggressive policies had led to ruin. After two centuries of almost continual warfare, the Greeks returned to the chaotic disorganization that characterized the time before the founding of the Peloponnesian League.

Culture of Classical Greece

The term *classical* often suggests calm and serenity, but the word that best describes Greek life, thought, art, and literature during the classical period is *tension*. Among the achievements of this era, discussed in Chapter 2, were the philosophical works of Socrates (469–399 B.C.E.), Plato (427?–347 B.C.E.), and Aristotle (384–322 B.C.E.). The same concern with the nature and place in the universe of human beings animated all the arts of the time.

Fifth Century B.C.E.

Two sources of tension contributed to the artistic outpouring of fifth-century-B.C.E. Greece. One arose from the conflict between the Greeks' pride in their accomplishments and their concern that overreaching would bring retribution. The second was the conflict between the hopes and achievements of individuals and the claims and limits put on them by their fellow citizens in the *polis*. These tensions were felt throughout Greece. They had the most spectacular consequences, however, in Athens in its Golden Age, between the Persian and Peloponnesian Wars.

Attic Tragedy Nothing reflects these concerns better than Attic (Athenian) tragedy, which emerged in the fifth century B.C.E. The tragedies were selected in a contest and presented as part of public religious observations in honor of the god Dionysus.

Poets who wished to compete submitted their works to the archon. The three best competitors were each awarded three actors and a chorus. The actors were paid by the state, and the chorus was provided by a wealthy citizen. Most of the tragedies were performed in the theater of Dionysus, where as many as 30,000 Athenians could attend.

Attic tragedy raised vital issues. Until late in the century the tragedies, drawing mostly on mythological subjects, dealt solemnly with religion, politics, ethics, or morality. The plays of the dramatists Aeschylus (525–456 B.C.E.) and Sophocles (ca. 496–406 B.C.E.) follow this pattern. The plays of Euripides (ca. 480–406 B.C.E.) are more concerned with individual psychology.

Old Comedy Comedy was introduced into the Dionysian festival early in the fifth century B.C.E. The great master of the genre called Old Comedy, Aristophanes (ca. 450–385 B.C.E.), wrote political comedies filled with scathing invective and satire.

Architecture and Sculpture Beginning in 448 B.C.E., Pericles undertook a great building program on the Acropolis with funds from the empire. The new buildings visually projected Athenian greatness, emphasizing the city's intellectual and artistic achievements and providing tangible proof that Athens was the intellectual center of Greece.

History The first prose history ever written was an account of the Persian War by Herodotus (484?–425? B.C.E.), "the father of history." His account attempts to explain human actions and draw instruction from them.

Herodotus accepted legends and oracles, although not uncritically, and often explained human events in terms of divine intervention. Yet his *History* also celebrates the influence of human intelligence on events. Herodotus also recognized the importance of institutions, pointing to the way the Greek *polis* inspired a voluntary obedience to the law in its citizen soldiers, in contrast to the fear of punishment that motivated the Persians.

Thucydides, the historian of the Peloponnesian War, was born about 460 B.C.E. and died about 400. He took great pains to achieve factual accuracy and tried to use his evidence to discover meaningful patterns of human behavior. He believed human nature was essentially unchanging, so that a wise person equipped with an understanding of history might accurately foresee events and help to guide them.

The striding god from Artemisium is a bronze statue dating from about 460 B.C.E. It was found in the sea near Artemisium, the northern tip of the large Greek island of Euboea, and is now on display in the Athens archaeological museum. Exactly whom this god represents is not known. Some have thought him to be Poseidon holding a trident; others believe that he is Zeus hurling a thunderbolt. In either case he is a splendid representative of the early classical period of Greek sculpture. [Helenic Republic Ministry of Culture, National Archaeological Museum, Athens]

Emergence of the Hellenistic World

The term *Hellenistic* was coined in the nineteenth century to describe a period of three centuries during which Greek culture spread from its homeland to Egypt and Asia. The result was a new civilization that combined Greek and Asian elements. The Hellenistic world was larger than the world of classical Greece, and its major political units were much larger than the *poleis*. Hellenistic civilization had its roots in the rise to power of a dynasty in Macedonia whose armies conquered Greece and the Persian Empire.

Macedonian Conquest

The kingdom of Macedon, north of Thessaly, had long served as a buffer between the Greek states and barbarian tribes farther to the north. The Macedonians were of the same stock as the Greeks and spoke a Greek dialect. Macedon's kings sought to bring Greek culture to their court. By Greek standards, however, Macedon was semibarbaric. It had no *poleis*. The king gained legitimacy only with the acclamation of the army assembly. A council of nobles checked the royal power. Plagued by constant war, Macedon played no great part in Greek affairs up to the fourth century B.C.E. Once unified under a strong king, however, that changed.

Philip of Macedon   That king was Philip II (r. 359–336 B.C.E.). Like many of his predecessors, he admired Greek culture. His natural talents for war and diplomacy and his boundless ambition made him the ablest king in Macedonian history. Gaining control of a lucrative gold and silver mining region, he began to reorganize his army into the finest fighting force in the world.

Invasion of Greece   So armed, Philip turned south toward central Greece, threatening the vital interest of Athens. In 340 B.C.E., he besieged Perinthus and Byzantium, the lifeline of Athenian commerce, and declared war. The Athenian fleet saved both cities, so Philip marched into Greece and in 338 B.C.E., defeated Athens and Thebes at Chaeronea in Boeotia. Chaeronea ended Greek freedom and autonomy. Although it maintained its form and internal life for some time, the *polis* had lost control of its own affairs and the special conditions that had made it unique.

In 337 B.C.E., Philip announced his intention to invade Persia. In the spring of 336 B.C.E., however, as he prepared to begin the campaign, Philip was assassinated.

Alexander the Great and His Successors

Philip's son, Alexander III (356–323 B.C.E.), later called Alexander the Great, succeeded his father at the age of twenty, and inherited his plans for the conquest of Persia.

The Conquest of Persia   In 334 B.C.E., Alexander crossed into Asia. His army consisted of about 30,000 infantry and 5,000 cavalry; he had no navy and little money. Consequently, he sought quick and decisive battles.

Alexander met the Persian forces of Asia Minor at the Granicus River (see Map 3–2), where he won a smashing victory. Alexander then captured the coastal cities, denying them to the Persian fleet.

In 333 B.C.E., Alexander marched inland to Syria, meeting the main Persian army under King Darius III (r. 336–330 B.C.E.) at Issus, and sent Darius fleeing to the east. In Egypt he was greeted as liberator, pharaoh, and son of the god Re.

In the spring of 331 B.C.E., Alexander marched into Mesopotamia. At Gaugamela, near the ancient Assyrian city of Nineveh, he met Darius again. Alexander's tactical genius and personal leadership carried the day. The Persians were broken. Alexander entered Babylon and burned Persepolis, the Persian capital.

Setting off after Darius, Alexander found him murdered by his relative Bessus. Alexander soon captured Bessus, but his desire to see the most distant places took him to the frontier of India. As a part of his grand scheme of amalgamation and conquest, he married the Bactrian princess Roxane and enrolled 30,000 young Bactrians to be trained for his army.

In 327 B.C.E., Alexander conquered the lands around the Indus River (modern Pakistan) and pushed on to the river called Ocean that the Greeks believed encircled the world. Finally, his weary men refused to go on. By the spring of 324 B.C.E., the army was back at the Persian Gulf.

Alexander's Successors   Alexander was filled with plans for the future, but in June of 323 B.C.E. he was overcome by a fever and died in Babylon at the age of thirty-three. His sudden death left his enormous empire with no clear, strong heir. After prolonged warfare, three of his generals founded dynasties of significance in the spread of Hellenistic culture:

- Ptolemy I, 367?–283 B.C.E.; founder of the thirty-first dynasty in Egypt, the Ptolemies, of whom Cleopatra, who died in 30 B.C.E., was the last
- Seleucus I, 358?–280 B.C.E.; founder of the Seleucid dynasty in Mesopotamia
- Antigonus I, 382–301 B.C.E.; founder of the Antigonid dynasty in Asia Minor and Macedon

For the first seventy-five years or so after the death of Alexander, the world ruled by his successors enjoyed prosperity. The vast sums of money he and they had put into circulation increased economic activity. The opening of vast new territories to Greek trade, the increased demand for Greek products, and the new availability of things Greeks wanted all helped stimulate commerce. The new prosperity, however, was not evenly distributed. The urban Greeks, the

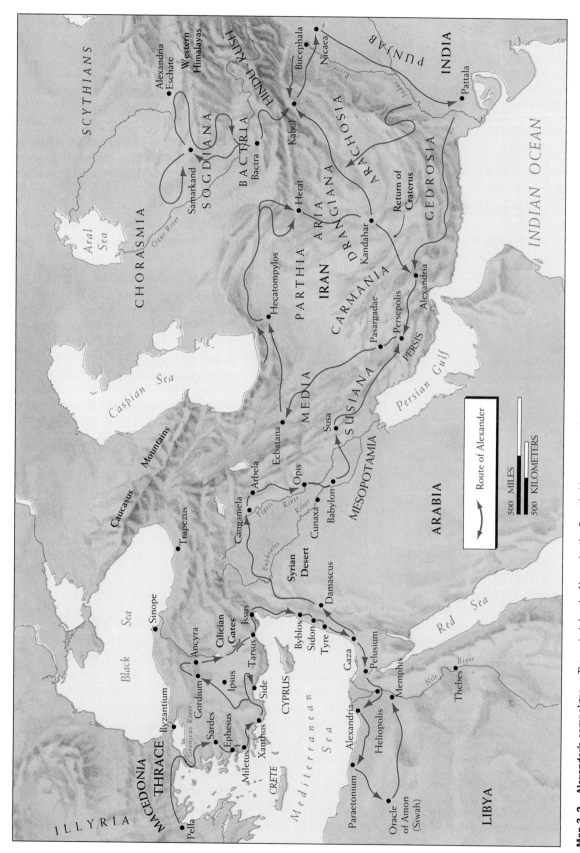

Map 3-2 Alexander's campaigns. The route taken by Alexander the Great in his conquest of the Persian Empire, 334–323 B.C.E. Starting from the Macedonian capital at Pella, he reached the Indus valley before being turned back by his own restive troops. He died of fever in Mesopotamia.

Rise of Macedon

359–336 B.C.E.	Reign of Philip II
338 B.C.E.	Battle of Chaeronea; Philip conquers Greece; founding of League of Corinth
336–323 B.C.E.	Reign of Alexander III, the Great
334 B.C.E.	Alexander invades Asia
333 B.C.E.	Battle of Issus
331 B.C.E.	Battle of Gaugamela
330 B.C.E.	Fall of Persepolis
327 B.C.E.	Alexander reaches Indus Valley
323 B.C.E.	Death of Alexander

Macedonians, and the Hellenized natives who made up the upper and middle classes lived lives of comfort and even luxury, but native peasants did not.

After a while, however, war and inflation led to economic crisis. The kings bore down heavily, but the middle classes were skilled in avoiding their responsibilities, and peasants and city laborers responded by slowing work and even by striking. In Greece, economic pressures brought clashes between rich and poor and even civil war.

These internal divisions made the Hellenistic kingdoms vulnerable to outside attack, and by the middle of the second century B.C.E. Rome had absorbed all but Egypt. The two centuries of Hellenistic rule, however, saw the entire eastern Mediterranean coast, Greece, Egypt, Mesopotamia, and the old Persian Empire formed into a single political, economic, and cultural unit.

Hellenistic Culture

Alexander's conquests and the successor kingdoms, by ending the central role of the *polis*, marked a turning point in Greek literature, philosophy, religion, and art.

The postclassical cities lost the kind of political freedom that was basic to the old outlook. They were cities but not *poleis*. As time passed, they became municipalities within military empires. The Greeks after Alexander turned inward, away from politics, to address their hopes and fears. The confident, sometimes arrogant, humanism of the fifth century B.C.E. gave way to a kind of resignation to fate, a recognition of helplessness before forces too great for humans to manage.

Philosophy

These developments are noticeable in the emergence of two new and influential groups of philosophers, the Epicureans and the Stoics.

Epicureans   Epicurus of Athens (342–271 B.C.E.), formulated a philosophy in which the goal was happiness, which Epicurus believed could be achieved through a life based on reason.

The Epicureans took sense perception to be the basis of all human knowledge. According to Epicurus, atoms were continually falling through the void and giving off images in direct contact with the senses. These falling atoms produced the combinations seen in the world. When a person died, the atoms that composed the body dispersed so that the person had no further existence or perception and therefore nothing to fear after death. The gods took no interest in human affairs. This belief amounted to atheism, and the Epicureans were often thought to be atheists.

The purpose of Epicurean physics was to liberate people from the fear of death and the supernatural. Epicurean ethics identified happiness with pleasure. But *pleasure* for Epicurus was chiefly negative: the absence of pain and trouble. The goal was *ataraxia*, the condition of being undisturbed, without trouble, pain, or responsibility. To achieve it, one should ideally have sufficient means to withdraw from worldly affairs; Epicurus even advised against marriage and children. He preached a life of restrained selfishness, which might appeal to intellectuals of means but was not widely attractive.

Stoics   The Stoic school, established by Zeno of Citium (335–263 B.C.E.), took its name from the *Stoa Poikile*, or Painted Portico, in the Athenian Agora, where Zeno and his disciples met.

The Stoics also sought the happiness of the individual; but Stoic philosophy was almost indistinguishable from religion. The Stoics believed that god and nature are the same and that humans must live in harmony within themselves and with nature. The guiding principle in nature is divine reason (*logos*), or fire. Every human has a spark of this divinity, and after death it returns to the eternal divine spirit. From time to time the world is destroyed by fire, from the ashes of which a new world arises.

Human happiness, according to the Stoics, lies in the virtuous life, lived in accordance with natural law. Only the wise—who know what is good, what is evil, and what is "indifferent"—can live such a life. Good and evil are dispositions of the mind or soul. Thus prudence, justice, courage, and temperance are good; folly, injustice, and cowardice are evil. Life, health, pleasure, beauty, strength, and wealth are morally "indifferent." The source of misery is passion, an irrational mental contraction that arises from morally indifferent things. The wise seek *apatheia*, or freedom from passion.

The Stoics viewed the world as a single large *polis* and all people as children of god. Many Stoics were politically active, but they believed the usual subjects of political argument to be indifferent. With their striving for inner harmony and a life lived in accordance with the divine will, their fatalistic attitude, and their goal a form of apathy, the Stoics fit the post-Alexandrian world well. The spread of Stoicism eased the creation of a new political system that relied on the docile submission of the governed.

Literature

The literary center of the Hellenistic world in the third and second centuries B.C.E. was Alexandria, Egypt. There, the Ptolemies had founded the museum—a great research institute where royal funds supported scientists and scholars—and a library that housed much of the great body of past Greek literature, most of which has since been lost. Alexandrian scholars had what they judged to be the best works copied, editing and criticizing them from the point of view of language, form, and content, and writing biographies of the authors. To this work we owe the preservation of most of what remains of ancient literature.

Architecture and Sculpture

The Hellenistic monarchies greatly increased the opportunities open to architects and sculptors, and leading artists who accepted commissions wherever they were attractive. In general, Hellenistic sculpture continued the trend that emerged in the fourth century B.C.E. toward the sentimental, emotional, and realistic.

Mathematics and Science

Among the most spectacular intellectual accomplishments of the Hellenistic age were those in mathematics and science. Indeed, Alexandrian scholars were responsible for most of the scientific knowledge available to the West until the Scientific Revolution of the sixteenth and seventeenth centuries C.E.

Euclid's Elements (written early in the third century B.C.E.) is still the foundation for courses in plane and solid geometry. Archimedes of Syracuse (ca. 287–212 B.C.E.), who also made advances in geometry, established the theory of the lever in mechanics and invented hydrostatics.

As early as the fourth century, Heraclides of Pontus (ca. 390–310 B.C.E.) had argued that Mercury and Venus circulate around the sun and not the Earth. He appears to have made other suggestions leading in the direction of a heliocentric theory of the universe. It was Aristarchus of Samos (ca. 310–230 B.C.E.), however, who asserted that the sun, along with the other fixed stars, did not move and that the Earth revolved around the sun and rotated on its axis while doing so. The heliocentric theory, however, did not take hold. Hipparchus of Nicea (b. ca. 190 B.C.E.) constructed a complicated geocentric model of the universe that did a good job of accounting for the movements of the sun, the moon, and the planets. Ptolemy of Alexandria (second century C.E.) adopted Hipparchus's system with a few improvements, and it remained dominant until the work of Copernicus, in the sixteenth century C.E.

Hellenistic scientists mapped the Earth as well as the sky. Eratosthenes of Cyrene (ca. 275–195 B.C.E.) accurately calculated the circumference of the Earth and wrote a treatise on geography based on mathematical and physical reasoning and the reports of travelers.

IN WORLD PERSPECTIVE

The Achievement of Greek and Hellenistic Civilization

Hellenic civilization lies at the root of western civilization. The Classical Age was a period of unparalleled achievement. Athens developed democratic government to an extent not seen again until modern times. Athenian citizenship—although limited to adult males of native parentage—granted full and active participation in every decision of the state without regard to wealth or class.

It was in Athens that the greatest artistic, literary, and philosophical achievements of the Classical Period took place. Classical writers and thinkers created many still-vital literary genres and forms. Among their accomplishments are analytical, secular history; tragedy and comedy; the philosophical dialogue; systematic logic; and philosophical treatises on almost every conceivable subject. Greek artists developed a naturalistic style that has had an enduring impact on western art.

These accomplishments, diverging sharply from those of other civilizations, sprang largely from the unique political experience of the Greeks, which was based on the independent *polis* rather than on powerful monarchies and great, extended land empires. With the Macedonian conquest of Greece and the onset of the Hellenistic Period, however, the age of the *polis* came to an end.

The conquests of Alexander and the Hellenistic states that followed, spread Greek culture over a wide area and made a significant and lasting impression on the conquered societies and their neighbors. As it spread, Greek culture of the Hellenistic period became simpler and more unified as it became more accessible to outsiders. Alexandrian scholars established canons of literary excellence and the scholarly tools with which to make the great treasures of Greek literature and art understandable to later generations. Shared over a wide area, Hellenistic culture helped widely differing peoples accommodate one another. It powerfully impressed the conquering Romans who, although they captured the Hellenistic world, became, as the Roman poet Horace said, captives of its culture.

Review Questions

1. Describe the Minoan civilization of Crete. How did the later Bronze Age Mycenaean civilization differ from the Minoan civilization in political organization, art motifs, and military posture? How valuable are the Homeric epics as sources of early Greek history?

2. Define the concept of *polis*. What role did geography play in its development, and why did the Greeks consider it a unique and valuable institution?

3. Compare the fundamental political, social, and economic institutions of Athens and Sparta about 500 B.C.E. Why did Sparta develop its unique form of government? What were the main stages in the transformation of Athens from an aristocratic state to a democracy between 600 and 500 B.C.E.?

4. Why did the Greeks and Persians go to war in 490 and 480 B.C.E.? What benefit could the Persians have derived from conquering Greece? Why were the Greeks able to defeat the Persians, and how did they benefit from the victory?

5. How was the Delian League transformed into the Athenian Empire during the fifth century B.C.E.? Did the empire offer any advantages to its subjects? Why was there such resistance to Athenian efforts to unify the Greek world in the fifth and fourth centuries B.C.E.?

6. Why did Athens and Sparta come to blows in the Great Peloponnesian War? What was each side's strategy for victory? Why did Sparta win the war?

7. Give examples from art, literature, and philosophy of the tension that characterized Greek life and thought in the Classical Period. How does Hellenistic art differ from that of the Classical Period?

8. Between 431 and 362 B.C.E., Athens, Sparta, and Thebes each tried to impose hegemony over the city-states of Greece, but none succeeded except for short periods of time. Why did each state fail? How was Philip II of Macedon able to conquer Greece? Where does more of the credit for Philip's success lie: in Macedon's strength, or in the weakness of the Greek city-states? What does your analysis tell you about the components of successful rule?

9. What were the major consequences of Alexander's death? Assess the achievement of Alexander. Was he a conscious promoter of Greek civilization, or just an egomaniac drunk with a lust for conquest?

Documents CD-ROM

1. *Pericles' Funeral Oration* by Thucydides

2. *Antigone* by Sophocles

3. Homer: From *The Iliad*

4. Tyrtaeus, *The Spartan Creed*

5. Thucydides: From *The History of the Peloponnesian War*

4 IRAN, INDIA, AND INNER ASIA TO 200 C.E.

From the Mediterranean to China, the period from about 600 B.C.E. to 200 C.E. saw the rise of centralized empires on an unprecedented scale. Well before the Ch'in unification (221–207 B.C.E.) or the Han dynasty (202 B.C.E.–9 C.E.) in China, and long before *imperium* replaced republic in Rome, imperial states flourished in Iran. The Achaemenids (ca. 539–330 B.C.E.), an Aryan dynasty from the mountains of southwestern Iran, created an empire based in Babylonia and Iran that was the greatest yet seen anywhere. Two centuries later the Mauryans, a northeast Indian dynasty centered in the Ganges basin, founded the first great Indian empire (ca. 321–ca. 185 B.C.E.). Both of these empires, like their later Chinese and Roman counterparts, built sophisticated bureaucracies, professional armies, and strong communication systems. They also contributed to new cultural, political, and religious developments in their domains.

Another characteristic of this period was increased and sustained contact among the major centers of culture from the Mediterranean to China. Alexander the Great's conquest (334–323 B.C.E.) of the Persian Empire and the regions eastward to North India increased the growing contact among diverse cultures, races, and religious traditions.

A third characteristic of this period was the rise, spread, and consolidation of major religious traditions that would affect later history from Africa to China.

IRAN

"Iran" designates the vast expanse of southwest Asia bounded by the Caspian Sea and Jaxartes (Syr Darya) River to the north and northeast, the Indus Valley to the southeast, the Arabian Sea and Gulf to the south, the Tigris-Euphrates to the west, and the Caucasus to the northwest. The heart of this region is the vast Iranian plateau, bounded on all sides by mountains.

The great Asian trade routes put Iran at the heart of east-west interchange. Their location, as well as the locations of the cities and towns that flourished because of them, was determined largely by mountain passes, river fords, and plateau crossings.

Ancient Background

The Iranians

The forefathers of the Iranian dynasts were Aryans. The oldest texts in ancient Persian dialects show that Aryan peoples settled on the Iranian plateau sometime around 1100 B.C.E. Like their Vedic or Indo-Aryan relations in North India, these peoples were evidently pastoralists—horse-breeders—from the Eurasian or Central Asian steppes. The most prominent of these ancient Iranians were the Medes and the Persians. By the eighth century B.C.E., they had spread around the deserts of the plateau to settle and control its western and southwestern reaches, to which they gave their names, Media and Persis (later Fars).

The Medes developed a tribal confederacy in western Iran. By 612 B.C.E., they and the Neo-Babylonians had defeated the mighty Assyrians. The rise of Persian power under the Achaemenid clan from the seventh century B.C.E. led to the end of Median supremacy on the Iranian plateau by the time of the Achaemenid ruler Cyrus the Great around 550 B.C.E. Many of the institutions that developed in the ensuing empire (such as the satrapy system of provincial administration) were apparently based on Median practices, which in turn had often been drawn from Babylonian and Assyrian models. The Achaemenids' unparalleled imperial success used existing institutions to build their own state and administer far-flung dominions.

Ancient Iranian Religion

We know more about religious traditions of ancient Iran than about other aspects of its culture because our only pre-Achaemenid texts are religious. They suggest that old Iranian culture and religion were similar to those of the Vedic Aryans. The emphasis was on moral order, or the "Right." The supreme heavenly deity was Ahura Mazda, the "Wise Lord."

Zoroaster and the Zoroastrian Tradition

The first person who stands out in Iranian history was not Cyrus, the famous founder of the Achaemenid Empire, but the great prophet-reformer of Iranian religion, Zarathushtra, commonly known in the West as Zoroaster. It is clear from his hymns that, like the Hebrew prophets, the Buddha, and Confucius, Zoroaster presented a message of moral reform in an age of materialism, political opportunism, and ethical indifference.

Zoroaster was evidently trained as a priest in the old Iranian tradition, but his hymns reflect the new religious vision he championed. Zoroaster's personal experience of Ahura Mazda as the supreme deity led him to reinterpret the old sacrificial fire as Ahura's symbol. He called on people to abandon worship of and sacrifice to all lesser deities, whom he identified as demons, not gods. He tried to reform his people's morality by exhorting them to turn from the "Lie" to the "Truth." He warned of a "final reckoning," when the good would be rewarded with "future glory" but the wicked with "long-lasting darkness, ill food, and wailing."

By the mid-fourth century B.C.E., the Zoroastrian reform had spread into western as well as eastern Iran. The quasi-monotheistic worship of Ahura Mazda, the Wise Lord, was rapidly accommodated to the veneration of older Iranian gods. The old Iranian priestly clan of the *Magi* may have integrated Zoroastrian ideas and texts into their older, polytheistic tradition, becoming thereby architects of a reformed tradition. Certainly the name "magi" was later used for the priests of the tradition that we call "Zoroastrian."

Zoroastrianism probably influenced not only Jewish, Christian, and Muslim ideas of angels, devils, the messiah, the last judgment, and afterlife, but some important Buddhist concepts as well. Zoroastrianism was wiped out as a major force in Iran by the spread of Islamic rule in the seventh and eighth centuries C.E. and later. However, its tradition continues in the faith and practice of the Parsis, most of whom live in western India.

The First Iranian Empire (550–330 B.C.E.)

The Achaemenids

Achaemenid regional power in southwestern Iran (Persis) went back at least to Cyrus I (d. 600 B.C.E.), but the rise of Iran as a major civilization and empire is usually dated from the reign of his famous grandson, Cyrus the Great (559–530 B.C.E.). The empire the latter founded was anticipated in many ways by the large but loosely controlled empire of his predecessors, the Medes. Cyrus defeated the last Median king about 550 B.C.E. He then subdued northern Assyria, Cilicia, and the kingdom of Lydia, near the Aegean coast of Asia Minor. The Lydian capital, Sardis, became a provincial capital of the growing Persian state. Next, Cyrus defeated the last Babylonian king.

This event, in 539 B.C.E., symbolically marks the beginning of the Achaemenid Empire, for it joined the Mesopotamian and Iranian spheres for the first time under one rule (see Map 4–1). One of its results was the end of the Babylonian Exile of the Jews (see Chapter 2). Cyrus subsequently extended Achaemenid rule in the east before he was killed fighting steppe tribes there. His readiness to rule through local elites and institutions rather than to impose new political superstructures was perhaps his most notable legacy to his heirs.

He and his successors, in what was really a tribal confederation, adopted Median administrative practice, and many Medes were highly placed in the new state. Thus it is not surprising that the Achaemenid rulers are referred to in the Bible and other sources as the "Medes and Persians." What the Medes had set in motion, Cyrus and his heirs consolidated and expanded, so that the new Iranian Empire became the most extensive the world had ever seen.

Cyrus's successor, Cambyses (r. 529–522 B.C.E.), added Egypt to the Achaemenid dominions. His brief reign was followed by a succession struggle. The winner, Darius I (521–486 B.C.E.), enjoyed a prosperous reign in which the Achaemenid Empire reached its greatest extent—from Egypt northeast to southern Russia and Sogdiana (Transoxiana) and east to the Indus Valley.

The next five rulers (486–359 B.C.E.) fared less well, and after 478 B.C.E., the Persians found themselves militarily inferior to the Greeks. Although they kept the divided Greeks at bay by clever diplomacy, Greek cultural influence steadily grew in Asia Minor. Egyptian rebellions, succession struggles, renewed conflict with Scythian steppe tribes, and poor leadership now plagued Achaemenid rule. Much might have

been recouped by the able, energetic Artaxerxes III (r. 359–338 B.C.E.) had he not been poisoned in a palace coup just as Philip of Macedon was unifying the Greeks. When Philip's son Alexander succeeded him, the days of Achaemenid rule were numbered.

Iran to the Third Century C.E.

ca. 2000-1000 B.C.E.	Indo-Iranian (Aryan) tribes move south into the Punjab of India and the Iranian Plateau
ca. 628-551 B.C.E. (or before 1000 B.C.E.?)	Traditional life of Zoroaster, probably in eastern/northeastern Iran (perhaps originally in Herat?)
559-530 B.C.E.	Reign of Cyrus the Great Persian Achaemenid ruler
539-330 B.C.E.	Achaemenid Empire
331-330 B.C.E.	Alexander (d. 323 B.C.E.) conquers Achaemenid Empire
312-ca. 125 B.C.E.	Seleucid rule in part of Achaemenid realm
ca. 248 B.C.E.-224 C.E.	Parthian Empire of the Arsacids in Iran, Babylonia

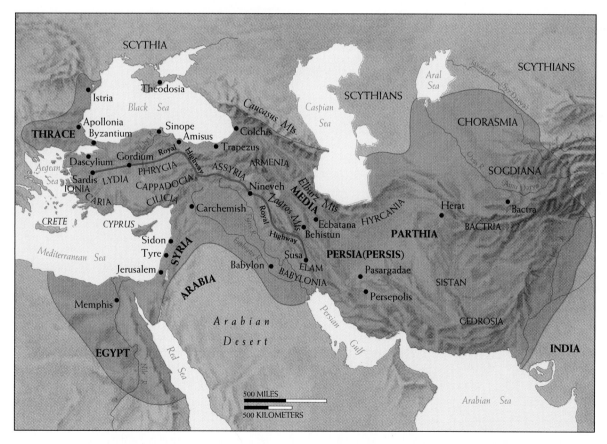

Map 4–1 The Achaemenid Persian Empire. The empire created by Cyrus had reached its fullest extent under Darius when Persia attacked Greece in 490 B.C.E. It extended from India to the Aegean, and even into Europe, including the lands formerly ruled by Egyptians, Hittites, Babylonians, and Assyrians.

The Achaemenid State

Perhaps the greatest achievement of the Achaemenids was the relative stability of their rule. To justify their sovereignty—and the title of *Shahanshah*, "king of kings"—they claimed that Ahura Mazda had entrusted them with universal sovereignty. The ruler acted as priest and sacrificer in the court rituals; his role as cosmic ruler was symbolized by a special royal fire that burned throughout his reign. The Achaemenids were, however, tolerant of other cultural and religious traditions in ways earlier empires had not been.

The Achaemenids built a powerful army, but much of their success lay in their administrative abilities and willingness to learn and to borrow from predecessors like the Medes or Babylonians. Most of their leaders worked to establish what

has been termed a *pax Achaemenica*.[1] They were able to maintain continuity as their state evolved from a tribal confederation into a sophisticated monarchy supported by a noble class, professional armies (led by Persian elite troops), provinces ruled by governors called *satraps*, and fixed-yield levies of revenue.

The excellence of Achaemenid administration can also be seen in their communication and propaganda systems. Couriers linked imperial outposts with the heartlands over a well-kept highway system. Herodotus called the greatest of these highways, from Sardis to Susa, "the King's Road." A network of observers and royal inspectors kept the court abreast of activities outside the capital. An efficient chancery

[1]Richard N. Frye, *The Heritage of Persia* (New York: New American Library, 1966), p. 110.

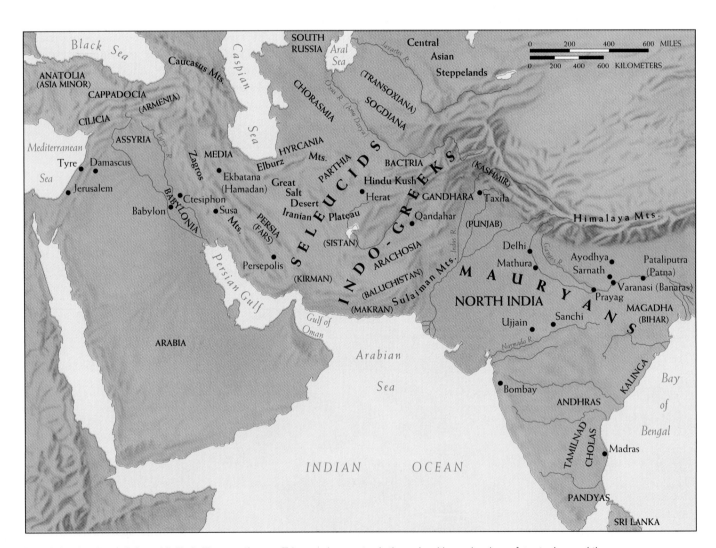

Map 4–2   Southwest Asia and India in Mauryan times.   This map shows not only the major cities and regions of greater Iran and the Indian subcontinent, but also the neighboring eastern Mediterranean world. Although the Mediterranean was closely tied to Iran from Achaemenid times onward, its contacts with India in the wake of the conquests of Alexander the Great were many and varied.

served administrative needs. The bureaucratic adoption of Aramaic helped link east and west. Achaemenid inscriptions reflect a strong emphasis on universal justice through the rule of law.

The Achaemenids moved the court as needed from one to another of their palaces and never had a single fixed capital. The satrapy divisions usually reflected the borders of former states incorporated into the empire. Although some satraps revolted, the centralized power of the "king of kings" held together the diverse provinces.

The Achaemenid Economy

Economic life from Greece to India received a substantial boost from Achaemenid success. Coinage gradually displaced in-kind payment altogether and stimulated banking operations. The Achaemenids levied taxes on estates, livestock, mines, trade, and production. Wages were regulated and money-goods equivalences published (thus a sheep might be set at three shekels).

Agriculture remained the basic industry and normal occupation of free men. Serfs and slaves formed most of the labor force. Where water was scarce, the government dug both subterranean and surface canals for irrigation.

The empire's overall stability for over two centuries testifies to the quality of the *pax Achaemenica*. Within this stable environment, the cosmopolitan basis for the coming Hellenization of western Asia in the wake of Alexander's conquests was laid.

INDIA

Large-scale imperial expansion came much later to the South Asian, or Indian, subcontinent than to Iran. A cultural and religious heritage going back to the Aryan invaders of North India left its mark on the subsequent history of the vast and diverse subcontinent. However, only on four occasions has a substantial part of the whole come under a single rule: in the Mauryan, Gupta, Mughal, and British imperial epochs.

The First Indian Empire (321–185 B.C.E.)

The Mauryans

The first true Indian empire was established by Chandragupta Maurya (r. ca. 321–297 B.C.E.), an adventurer who made Pataliputra (modern Patna) his capital (see Map 4–2). He next marched westward into the vacuum created by Alexander's departure (326 B.C.E.) and brought the Indus re-

India from the Sixth Century B.C.E. to the End of Mauryan Rule	
ca. 600–400 B.C.E.	Late Upanishadic age: local/regional kingdoms and tribal republics along the Ganges and in Himalayan foothills, the Punjab, and northwestern India
ca. 540–ca. 468 B.C.E.	Vardhamana Mahavira, Jain founder
ca. 537–ca. 486 B.C.E.	Siddhartha Gautama, the Buddha
ca. 550–324 B.C.E.	Regional empire of Maghadan kings
330–325 B.C.E.	Alexander campaigns in Indus Valley, Soghdiana, Bactria, and Punjab
324–ca. 185 B.C.E.	Mauryan empire controls most of northern India and the Deccan
ca. 272–232 B.C.E.	Reign of the Mauryan emperor Ashoka

gion and much of west-central India under his control. A treaty with the invading Seleucus (ca. 358–280 B.C.E.), Alexander's successor in Bactria, added Gandhara and Arachosia to his empire.

Chandragupta's son and successor, Bindusara (r. ca. 297–272 B.C.E.), took up his father's imperial aspirations. He moved swiftly to conquer the Deccan, the great plateau that covers central India and divides the far south (Tamilnad) from North India.

Ashoka The third and greatest Mauryan, Ashoka (r. ca. 272–232 B.C.E.), left numerous rock inscriptions. From them, we can piece together much of his reign and glimpse something of his character. He conquered Kalinga, the last independent kingdom in North India and the Deccan. He thus extended Mauryan control over the whole subcontinent except the far south.

Apparently revolted by the bloody Kalinga war, Ashoka underwent a religious conversion. Thereafter he pursued the Buddhist "middle path" in both personal and state relations. Accordingly, he forsook hunting and meat eating, championing nonviolence. He eschewed aggression in favor of the ideal of "conquest by righteousness" (*dharma*). He sought by moral example to win over others to humanitarian values. Within his realm he looked on all his subjects as his "children." His edicts show that he pursued the laity's norm of the Buddhist *dharma*, striving to attain Heaven by the merit of good actions. He stressed tolerance for all traditions, but sent envoys abroad to spread Buddhist teaching. He appointed "*dharma* officials" to investigate public welfare problems and foster just government at the local level.

Ashoka did ease burdens imposed on the populace by earlier governments, and instituted beneficial public works. However, by the end of his reign, the empire's size hampered administration, and under his successors, Mauryan rule fell apart.

Ashoka provided the model of the ideal king for later Hindu and Buddhist thought. His name lives on as a symbol of enlightened rule with few equals in the history of East or West.

The Mauryan State Mauryan bureaucracy was marked by centralization, standardization, and efficiency in communications, civil and military organization, tax collection, and information gathering (by a secret service). The fundamental unit of government was the village, with its headman and council. Groups of villages formed districts within the larger provincial unit. The provinces were controlled through governors sent from the capital or local rulers, as under the Achaemenids (who were probably a model for Mauryan imperialism).

The administration of the empire depended on the king himself, who had an advisory council to assist him. Revenues came primarily from taxing the produce of the land, which was regarded as the king's property. Urban trade and production were also taxed heavily. The Mauryan economic system involved slavery, although most of it was domestic labor.

The Mauryan Legacy An imperial ideal, a strengthened Buddhist movement, and strong central administration were not the Mauryans' only gifts to Indian culture. They left behind new cosmopolitan traditions of external relations and internal communication that encouraged cultural development and discouraged provincialism. Their many contacts with the West reflect their international perspective, as do the Ashokan edicts, which were executed in various languages and scripts. Writing and reading must have been common by this time, or the edicts would have had no purpose. The Mauryans' excellent road system would later be the routes for Buddhism's spread to Central Asia and China,

The Lion Capital of Sarnath. This famous Ashokan column capital was taken by India as its state seal after independence in 1947. It reflects both Persian and Greek influences. Originally the capital stood atop a mighty pillar some fifty feet high; the lions supported a huge stone chakra, the Buddhist "Wheel of the Dharma," the symbol of universal law. [Giraudon/Art Resource, N.Y.]

as well as corridors for successive invaders of the subcontinent.

This era also saw the flourishing of cities across the empire. They were centers for arts, crafts, industry, literature, and education. The stone buildings and sculpture of the Ashokan period reflect sophisticated aesthetics and technique, as well as strong Persian and Greek influence.

Consolidation of Indian Civilization (ca. 200 B.C.E.– 300 C.E.)

In the post-Mauryan period, North India was dominated by the influx of various foreign peoples. In the rest of the subcontinent, indigenous Indian dynasties held sway. A general pattern of regional and local political autonomy would be broken only by the empire built by the Guptas (320 C.E.–ca. 550; see Chapter 10). However, religiously and culturally, the centuries between the Mauryans and Guptas still saw the consolidation of transregional patterns and styles that helped to shape Indian and, through the diffusion of Buddhism, Asian civilization ever after.

The Edicts of Ashoka

In the first of the two following excerpts from Ashokan edicts, we see the monarch's explanation of his change of heart and conversion to nonviolence after the Kalinga war and a statement of his determination to follow dharma. "The Beloved of the Gods" was the common royal epithet used by Ashoka for himself. The second excerpt is from the end of Ashoka's reign and speaks of his efforts to better his and other people's lives by rule according to the dictates of dharma.

What does Ashoka suggest is the role of the monarch? What is his concept of "conquest"? What does he think of those of other faiths and what does he want for them? What reforms does Ashoka propose, and why? Can you reconcile his expressed abhorrence of killing with his words to the forest tribes? How do these edicts compare to other approaches to law, leadership, and government? See, for example, "Athenian Democracy: An Unfriendly View" (Chapter 3).

From the Thirteenth Rock Edict

When the king, Beloved of the Gods and of Gracious Mien, had been consecrated eight years Kalinga was conquered, 150,000 people were deported, 100,000 were killed, and many times that number died. But after the conquest of Kalinga, the Beloved of the Gods began to follow Righteousness [*dharma*], to love Righteousness, and to give instruction in Righteousness. Now the Beloved of the Gods regrets the conquest of Kalinga, for when an independent country is conquered people are killed, they die, or are deported, and that the Beloved of the Gods finds very painful and grievous. . . . The Beloved of the Gods will forgive as far as he can, and he even conciliates the forest tribes of his dominions; but he warns them that there is power even in the remorse of the Beloved of the Gods, and he tells them to reform, lest they be killed.

For all beings the Beloved of the Gods desires security, self-control, calm of mind, and gentleness. The Beloved of the Gods considers that the greatest victory is the victory of Righteousness; and this he has won here [in India] and even five hundred leagues beyond his frontiers in the realm of the Greek king Antiochus, and beyond Antiochus among the four kings Ptolemy, Antigonus, Magas, and Alexander. Even where the envoys of the Beloved of the Gods have not been sent men hear of the way in which he follows and teaches Righteousness, and they too follow it and will follow it. Thus he achieves a universal conquest, and conquest always gives a feeling of pleasure; yet it is but a slight pleasure, for the Beloved of the Gods only looks on that which concerns the next life as of great importance. . . .

From the Seventh Pillar Edict

In the past kings sought to make the people progress in Righteousness, but they did not progress. . . . And I asked myself how I might uplift them through progress in Righteousness. . . . Thus I decided to have them instructed in Righteousness, and to issue ordinances of Righteousness, so that by hearing them the people might conform, advance in the progress of Righteousness, and themselves make great progress. . . . For that purpose many officials are employed among the people to instruct them in Righteousness and to explain it to them. . . .

Moreover I have had banyan trees planted on the roads to give shade to man and beast; I have planted mango groves, and I have had ponds dug and shelters erected along the roads at every eight kos. Everywhere I have had wells dug for the benefit of man and beast. But this benefit is but small, for in many ways the kings of olden time have worked for the welfare of the world; but what I have done has been done that men may conform to Righteousness. . . .

I have enforced the law against killing certain animals and many others, but the greatest progress of Righteousness among men comes from exhortation in favor of non-injury to life and abstention from killing living beings.

I have done this that it may endure as long as the moon and sun, and that my sons and my great-grandsons may support it; for by supporting it they will gain both this world and the next.

From *Sources of Indian Tradition* by William Theodore de Bary. Copyright © 1988 by Columbia University Press. Reprinted with permission of the publisher.

The Economic Base

Although agriculture remained the basis of the economy, commerce flourished amid the post-Mauryan political fragmentation. The fine Mauryan road system facilitated trade throughout India. Chinese and Roman demand for Indian luxury goods made India a center of world trade. Wealth flowed in. Within India, guild organizations provided technical education in crafts. Kings as well as the merchant classes invested in guilds. Coin minting increased after Mauryan times, and banking flourished.[2]

---

[2]Romila Thapar, *A History of India*, Vol. 1 (Harmondsworth, U. K.: Penguin Books, 1966), pp. 105–118.

High Culture

In the arts, the great achievements of this era were primarily Buddhist in inspiration. Northwestern India saw the rise of the Gandharan school of Buddhist art. In Gandharan sculpture, Hellenistic naturalism joined with the more recent Indian tradition of Buddha images to produce relief and free-standing sculptural figures with flowing draped garments through which the muscular lines of the human body are readily discernible. In central India as early as the first century B.C.E., artists were producing stone-relief sculpture with the naturalistic, yet flowing, plastic human and animal forms that would become earmarks of the "classical" style of Indian art.

Language and literature during this period rested on the sophisticated Sanskrit grammar of Panini (ca. 300 B.C.E.?). Two masterpieces of Sanskrit culture, the epics of the *Mahabharata* and the *Ramayana*, probably took general shape by 200 C.E. The first is a composite work concerned largely with the nature of *dharma* (see Chapter 2). Included in its earlier, narrative portions is the Bhagavad Gita, or "Song of the Blessed Lord," the most influential of all Indian religious texts.

Religion and Society

The post-Mauryan period saw Buddhist monasticism and lay devotionalism thrive across the subcontinent. However, the Brahmans continued to dominate Vedic learning and ritual. Toward the end of this age, Buddhism in its Mahayana form began to spread from India to Central Asia and eventually to China and Japan.

Hindu Tradition What we now call Hinduism emerged in this era. The major developments shaping a Hindu tradition were (1) the consolidation of the caste system, Brahman ascendancy, and the "high" culture of Sanskrit learning; (2) the increasing dominance of theistic devotionalism (especially the cults of Vishnu and Shiva); and (3) the intellectual reconciliation of these developments with the older ascetic and speculative traditions deriving from the Upanishadic age.

Buddhist Tradition Indian Buddhist monastic communities prospered under mercantile and royal patronage. Buddhist lay devotion figured prominently in Indian religious life, especially in the Ganges basin. The Buddha and Buddhist saints were naturally identified with popular Indian deities, and popular Buddhist practice was indistinguishable from countless other devotional cults that began to dominate the Indian scene. One reason that Buddhist tradition remained only one among many Indian religious paths was its absorption into the religious variety that then and now typifies the Hindu religious scene.

GREEK AND ASIAN DYNASTIES

Seleucids

Alexander's successors in Achaemenid lands, the Greek general Seleucus and his heirs, ruled most of the former Achaemenid realm from about 312 to 246 B.C.E. and lesser portions until about 125 B.C.E. Alexander's policies of Greco-Persian fusion helped make the Seleucid rule of many eastern areas viable. The new "cities" that Alexander left behind provided bases for Seleucid control. As a foreign minority, the Seleucids had to maintain control with mercenary troops. It was, however, the leaders of their own troops and satrapies whose imperial aspirations gradually whittled away at Seleucid rule. Neither Seleucus (r. 311–281 B.C.E.; see Chapter 3) nor the greatest of his successors, Antiochus the Great (r. 223–187 B.C.E.), ever secured lasting dominion on the scale of the Achaemenids.

In the end, Alexander's policy of linking Hellenes with Iranians in political power, marriage, and culture bore fruit more lasting than empire. During the second century B.C.E., Hellenistic culture and law became new ideals among the Seleucid elites. The Seleucids welcomed into the ruling classes those non-Hellenes willing to become hellenized.

Zoroastrian religious tradition declined with the loss of its imperial-cult status. The many syncretic cults of the Mediterranean Hellenistic world made inroads even in the East in Seleucid and Parthian times. Mystery and savior cults were becoming more popular. The new Hellenistic urban centers

---

**Indo-Greek, Iranian, Indian,
and Steppe Dynasties After Alexander**

312–ca. 125 B.C.E.	Seleucid rule in part of the old Achaemenid realm
ca. 248 B.C.E.–224 C.E.	Parthian Empire of the Arsacids in Iran, Babylonia
246–ca. 50 B.C.E.	Indo-Greek ("Graeco-Bactrian," "Euthydemid") rulers of region from modern Afghanistan to Oxus
ca. 171–138 B.C.E.	Reign of Arsacid king Mithradates I
ca. 140 B.C.E.–ca. 100 C.E.	Movements west and south of Yüeh Chih (including Kushans) and Sythians (Sakas) into Sogdiana, then Bactria, then northwestern India
ca. C.E. 50–ca. 250	Height of Kushan power in Oxus to Ganges region
ca. 105 C.E.	Accession of King Kanishka to Kushan throne in Taxila (ruled about 28 years)

---

may have provided an environment in which the individual was less rooted in established traditions of culture and religious life. This would have enhanced the attractiveness of the focus on individual salvation common to many lesser Hellenistic cults and to emerging traditions like the Christian, Mahayana Buddhist, Manichaean, and Hindu devotionalist that came to dominate Eurasia.

Indo-Greeks

The farthest reach of Hellenization in the East came not under the Seleucids but with the Indo-Greeks of Bactria. About 246 B.C.E., Bactria's Greek satrap broke away from the Seleucids. His successor, Euthydemus (r. ca. 235–ca. 200 B.C.E.), extended his sway north and southwest. His son Demetrius exploited the growing Mauryan weakness to conquer Arachosia. Demetrius and his successor, Menander, made Taxila their capital. Most of the Indo-Greeks were Indian in language, culture, and religion, as their coins and inscriptions show.

Before their demise at the hands of invading steppe peoples (ca. 130–100 B.C.E.), these Indo-Greeks left their mark on civilization in all the areas around their Bactrian center. Bactria was a major source of the later Greco-Buddhist art of Gandhara, one of history's remarkable examples of cross-cultural influence. The Indo-Greeks also probably helped spread Buddhism from India to Central Asia.

Steppe Peoples

The history of North India and the Iranian plateau was dominated from about 250 B.C.E. to 300 C.E. by incursions of Iranian tribal peoples originally from the Central Asian steppes. Although commonly ignored, the nomadic steppe peoples have been a major force in Eurasian history.

Parthians

The Parni, said to be related to the Scythians, were probably the major group of Iranian steppe peoples who first settled the area south of the Aral Sea and Oxus. In late Achaemenid times, they moved south into Parthia. Thenceforward we can call them Parthians. The independent control of Parthia by the dynastic family of the Arsacids dates from about 247 B.C.E. For decades only a regional power, they emerged under Mithradates I (ca. 171–138 B.C.E.) as a new Eurasian imperial force, the true Achaemenid successors.

The Parthian Empire stretched across the Iranian plateau from Mesopotamia to Arachosia, and its center was Ctesiphon, on the Tigris. From their victory over the Romans at Carrhae in 53 B.C.E. (see Chapter 5) until their fall in 233 C.E., the Parthians were the major Eurasian power alongside Rome. Eventually the constant Roman wars of the last century and the pressure of the Kushan Empire in the east weakened them sufficiently for a new Persian dynasty to replace them.

Culturally, the Parthians were oriented toward the Hellenistic world of their Seleucid predecessors until the mid-first century C.E., when they experienced a kind of Iranian revival. Similarly, the Magi preserved the worship of Ahura Mazda despite the success of other eastern and western cults and the common assimilation of Greek gods to Iranian ones. Still, the Parthians seem to have tolerated religious plurality.

Sakas and Kushans

The successors of the Indo-Greeks were steppe peoples who played a major political and cultural role in Asia for several centuries. They reflect the cosmopolitan nature of Central Asia, eastern Iran, and northwestern India at this time.

Beginning about 130 B.C.E., Scythian (Saka) tribes from beyond the Jaxartes (Syr Darya) overran northeastern Iran, taking Sogdiana's Hellenic cities and then Bactria. One group of Sakas soon extended their domain into North India. Another went southwest into Herat and Sistan. In northwestern India the Sakas were in turn defeated by invading Iranians known as the Pahlavas.[3]

The Sakas had been displaced earlier in Sogdiana by another steppe people, known from Chinese sources as the Yüeh Chih. These peoples, led by the Kushan tribe, drove the Sakas out of Bactria in the mid-first century B.C.E. About a hundred years later, they swept over the mountains into northwestern India. Here they ended Pahlava rule and founded a long-lived Indian Kushan dynasty.

The Kushan kingdom of India was—along with Rome, China, and the weakened Parthian Empire of Iran—one of four major centers of civilization in Eurasia around 100 C.E. Its greatest ruler, Kanishka, reigned either around 100 or possibly 150 C.E. He was the greatest patron of Buddhism since Ashoka. In their heyday (the first to third centuries C.E.), Kushan power in Central Asia facilitated the missionary activity that carried Buddhism across the steppes into China. A lasting Kushan contribution was the school of Greco-Buddhist art fostered in Gandhara by Kanishka and his successors and supported by a later Kushan dynasty for another 500 years.

---

[3]Tradition gives one of their rulers, Gondophares, the role of host to Saint Thomas, who is said to have brought Christianity to India. But because Gondophares probably ruled in the early to mid-first century C.E., it may be a confused report. Even if traditions of Thomas's mission to India are correct, some connect him instead with southern India.

IN WORLD PERSPECTIVE

Iran, India, and Inner Asia to the Third Century C.E.

By the second century C.E., we see in the Indo-Iranian world the development of imperial governments with power and influence far surpassing those of any before them. Such empires are indices of the security and wealth requisite for progress in these areas. In this respect, developments in these regions paralleled those in the wider world, where Greek, Hellenistic, and Roman Empires, like the Han Empire of China, provided contexts in which civilization could flourish, grow, and spread.

In Asia this was also an era in which widely influential, lasting religious traditions came of age, and there was an increase in cross-cultural contact. The Central Asian reaches of Iran and India especially provided the great meeting ground of Iranian, Indian, Greek, and steppe-people languages, customs, ideas, arts, and religious practices. These contacts and influences were manifested in new peoples, governmental structures, technological innovations, specialized skills and arts, and ethico-religious ideas.

Review Questions

1. What were key factors in the success and long survival of the Achaemenid Empire? What aspects of government control expanded the Achaemenid power base?

2. How was the Mauryan Empire created? What role did Greeks play in its creation? What role did Ashoka play in the development of Mauryan power and prestige?

3. Referring to this chapter and Chapter 2, compare the major religious developments in Iran and India down to 200 C.E. How did the role of religion in the Achaemenid Empire compare to its role in the Mauryan Empire?

4. Compare the Achaemenid and Mauryan Empires. What was their respective historical importance? How did each affect the world beyond its borders?

5. Compare the major features of the Hindu and Buddhist traditions. Why do you think Buddhism spread to southeast and east Asia whereas Hinduism did not?

6. In what ways did the Kushans, Sakas, and other inner Asian groups play important roles in world history?

Documents CD-ROM

1. *The Laws of Manu*
2. *Bhagavad-Gita*

3. Cyrus of Persia: A Study in Imperial Success
4. Kuan-yin: Compassion of the Bodhisattva

5 REPUBLICAN AND IMPERIAL ROME

The ancient Romans were responsible for one of the most remarkable achievements in history. From their city in central Italy, they conquered most of the Near East and much of Europe. Their unifying government brought peace and prosperity to this vast region, which has never been unified again.

Rome's legacy was not just of military prowess and superb political organization. The Romans transformed the intellectual and cultural achievements of the Greeks, creating the Graeco-Roman tradition in literature, philosophy, and art. This tradition remains the heart of Western civilization.

The Etruscans

Etruscan civilization, which was to have a powerful influence on the Romans, arose about 800 B.C.E. The Etruscans constituted a military ruling class, dominating the native people they had dispossessed.

Royal Rome

In the sixth century B.C.E., Rome in Latium came under Etruscan control. It was a natural center for communication and trade. Led by Etruscan kings, the Roman army conquered most of Latium.

Government

Roman kings had the awesome power of *imperium*, the right to issue commands and enforce them by fines, arrests, and physical punishment, including execution. Although it tended to remain in families, kingship was elective. The Roman Senate approved the candidate, and the Roman people, voting in assembly, formally granted the *imperium*. This procedure—the granting of great power to executive officers contingent on the approval of the Senate and ultimately the people—would remain a basic characteristic of Roman government.

The Senate, the second branch of the early Roman government, ostensibly had neither executive nor legislative power. In reality its authority was great, for the senators, like the king, served for life. The Senate therefore had continuity and experience, and it was composed of the most powerful men in the state.

The third branch of government, the curiate assembly, was made up of all citizens as divided into thirty groups. Voting was by group; a majority within each group determined its vote, and the decisions were made by majority vote of the groups. Group voting would be typical of all future forms of Roman assembly.

Family

The center of Roman life was the family. At its head stood the father, whose power and authority resembled those of the king within the state. Over his children he held broad powers analogous to *imperium;* he could sell his children into slavery, and might even kill them. Over his wife he had less power; he could not sell or kill her. In practice his power to dispose of his children was limited by other family members, by public opinion, and, most of all, by tradition. A wife could be divorced only for serious offenses. The Roman woman had a respected position and the main responsibility for managing the household.

Clientage

Clientage was one of Rome's most important institutions. The client was said to be in the *fides*, or trust, of his patron, giving the relationship a moral dimension. The patron provided his client with physical and legal protection and economic support. In return the client would fight for his patron, work his land, and support him politically. These mutual obligations were enforced by public opinion and tradition. Because the client-patron relationship was hereditary and was sanctioned by religion and custom, it played an important part in the life of the Roman Republic.

Patricians and Plebeians

In the royal period, Roman society was divided into two classes based on birth. The wealthy patrician upper class held a monopoly of power and influence. Its members alone could conduct state religious ceremonies, sit in the Senate, or hold office. They formed a closed caste by forbidding marriage outside their own group.

The plebeian lower class must have consisted originally of poor, dependent small farmers, laborers, and artisans, the clients of the nobility. As Rome grew, nonpatrician families acquired wealth. From early times, therefore, there were rich plebeians and patrician families that fell into poverty from incompetence or bad luck. The line between the classes and the monopoly of privileges nevertheless remained firm.

The Republic

According to Roman tradition, the outrageous behavior of the last kings provoked the noble families to revolt in 509 B.C.E., leading to the creation of the republic.

Constitution

The Roman constitution was an unwritten accumulation of laws and customs.

Consuls   The Romans were never willing to deprive their chief magistrates of the great powers their kings had exercised. They elected two patricians to the office of consul and endowed them with *imperium*. Assisting the consuls were financial officials called *quaestors*. Like the kings, the consuls led the army, had religious duties, and served as judges.

The power of the consulship was granted for a year only. Each consul could overrule the other. Even the *imperium* was limited. Although the consuls had full powers of life and death while leading an army, within the city of Rome, citizens could appeal to the popular assembly all cases involving capital punishment. Besides, after their year in office, the consuls would spend the rest of their lives as members of the Senate, so only a reckless consul would ignore its advice. In serious crises, the consuls could, with the advice of the Senate, appoint a *dictator*, who would have *imperium* not subject to appeal both inside and outside the city for six months.

In 325 B.C.E., the Romans created the office of proconsul, which permitted a consul in the field to retain command during a long campaign. Another new office, that of *praetor*, was primarily judicial. After the middle of the fifth century B.C.E., the job of identifying citizens and classifying them according to age and property was delegated to a *censor*. The Senate elected two censors every five years. They conducted a census and drew up the citizen rolls, and by the fourth century B.C.E. could exclude senators from the Senate on moral as well as financial grounds. The office came to be considered the ultimate prize of a political career.

Senate and Assembly   The end of the monarchy increased the power of the Senate. It became the only ongoing deliberative body in the Roman state and soon controlled finances and foreign policy.

The *centuriate assemble*, the early republic's most important popular assembly, was, in a sense, the Roman army acting in a political capacity. Its basic unit was the century, theoretically 100 fighting men who fought with the same kind of equipment. Because each man equipped himself, this organization divided the assembly into classes according to wealth.

Struggle of the Orders   Patricians monopolized power in the early republic. In response, the plebeians launched the "struggle of the orders," a fight for political, legal, and social equality that lasted 200 years.

Plebeians made up much of the Roman army, giving them great political leverage. They formed the plebeian tribal assembly, and elected *tribunes*. A tribune could veto any action of a magistrate or any bill in a Roman assembly or the Senate.

It was not until 367 B.C.E. that one of the consuls was allowed to be of plebeian rank. In 287 B.C.E., the plebeians secured the passage of a law making the decisions of the plebeian assembly binding on all Romans without the approval of the Senate.

The victory of the plebeians allowed wealthy plebeian families to share the privileges of the patrician aristocracy. The *nobiles*—a small group of wealthy families, both patrician and plebeian—dominated the Senate and controlled the highest offices of the state.

Conquest of Italy

Initial Expansion and Gallic Invasion   By the beginning of the fourth century B.C.E., the Romans were the chief power in central Italy. In 340 B.C.E., the city's Latin neighbors, the Latin League, sought to curtail Rome's expansion. In 338 B.C.E., the Romans defeated the league and dissolved it.

Roman Policy Toward the Conquered   The Romans did not destroy any of the Latin cities. To some near Rome they granted full citizenship. To others farther away they granted municipal status, which included the right to local self-government and the right to trade and intermarry with Romans. Still other states became allies of Rome. The Romans established permanent colonies of veteran soldiers in conquered lands. The colonists remained Roman citizens and deterred rebellion. A network of durable roads—some still in use—connected the colonies to Rome.

Rome divided its enemies and extended its influence through military force and diplomatic skill. Rebels were pun-

Lictors, pictured here, attended the chief Roman magistrates when they appeared in public. The axe carried by one of the lictors and the bound bundle of staffs carried by the others symbolize both the power of Roman magistrates to inflict corporal punishment on Roman citizens and the limits on that power. The bound staffs symbolize the right of citizens within the city of Rome not to be punished without a trial. The axe symbolizes the power of the magistrates, as commanders of the army, to put anyone to death without a trial outside the city walls. [Alinari/Art Resource, N.Y.]

ished harshly. But Rome was generous to those who submitted. Loyal allies could gain full Roman citizenship. This policy gave allies a stake in Rome's future and, as a result, most remained loyal.

Rome and Carthage

In the ninth century B.C.E., the Phoenician city of Tyre had planted a colony on the North African coast, calling it Carthage. In the sixth century B.C.E., Carthage became independent and expanded west and east. Carthage claimed an absolute monopoly on trade in the western Mediterranean.

First Punic War (264–241 B.C.E.)   Sicily was strategically important to both Carthage and Rome. It was there, in 264 B.C.E., that the two expanding powers first came to blows. Because the Romans called the Carthaginians *Poeni* or *Puni* (meaning "Phoenician"), the conflicts between them are called the Punic Wars.

Neither side made any progress until the Romans built a fleet to blockade the Carthaginian ports in Sicily. Carthage capitulated in 241 B.C.E., giving up Sicily and agreeing to

A Women's Uprising in Republican Rome

In 195 B.C.E., Roman women staged a rare public political protest when they demanded the repeal of a law passed two decades earlier during the Second Punic War that they judged to limit their rights unfairly. Livy (59 B.C.E.–17 C.E.) describes the affair and the response of the traditionalist Marcus Porcius Cato (234–149 B.C.E.).

Of what did the women complain? How did they try to achieve their goals? Which of Cato's objections to their behavior do you think were most important? Since women did not vote or sit in assemblies, how can the outcome of the affair be explained?

Amid the anxieties of great wars, either scarce finished or soon to come, an incident occurred, trivial to relate, but which, by reason of the passions it aroused, developed into a violent contention. Marcus Fundanius and Lucius Valerius, tribunes of the people, proposed to the assembly the abrogation of the Oppian law. The tribune Gaius Oppius had carried this law in the heat of the Punic War, in the consulship of Quintus Fabius and Tiberius Sempronius, that no woman should possess more than half an ounce of gold or wear a parti-coloured garment or ride in a carriage in the City or in a town within a mile thereof, except on the occasion of a religious festival. The tribunes Marcus and Publius Iunius Brutus were supporting the Oppian law, and averred that they would not permit its repeal; many distinguished men came forward to speak for and against it; the Capitoline was filled with crowds of supporters and opponents of the bill. The matrons could not be kept at home by advice or modesty or their husbands' orders, but blocked all the streets and approaches to the Forum, begging the men as they came down to the Forum that, in the prosperous condition of the state, when the private fortunes of all men were daily increasing, they should allow the woman too to have their former distinctions restored. The crowd of women grew larger day by day; for they were now coming in from the towns and rural districts. Soon they dared even to approach and appeal to the consuls, the praetors, and the other officials, but one consul, at least, they found adamant, Marcus Porcius Cato, who spoke thus in favour of the law whose repeal was being urged.

"If each of us, citizens, had determined to assert his rights and dignity as a husband with respect to his own spouse, we should have less trouble with the sex as a

---

pay a war indemnity. Neither side was to attack the allies of the other.

Second Punic War (218–202 B.C.E.)

After 241 B.C.E., Carthage recovered strength by building a rich empire in Spain. In 221 B.C.E., Hannibal (247–182 B.C.E.) took command of Carthaginian forces in Spain. A few years earlier, Rome had received an offer from the Spanish town of Saguntum to become the friends of Rome. The Romans accepted, thereby taking on the responsibilities of friendship with a foreign state. At first the Saguntines, confident of Rome's protection, began

The Punic Wars	
264–241 B.C.E.	First Punic War
238 B.C.E.	Rome seizes Sardinia and Corsica
221 B.C.E.	Hannibal takes command of Punic army in Spain
218–202 B.C.E.	Second Punic War
216 B.C.E.	Battle of Cannae
202 B.C.E.	Battle of Zama
149–146 B.C.E.	Third Punic War
146 B.C.E.	Destruction of Carthage

to interfere with Spanish tribes allied with Hannibal. The Romans warned Hannibal to let Saguntum alone, but he ignored Rome's warning and captured it.

Rome declared war in 218 B.C.E. Hannibal launched a swift and daring invasion of Italy. His army defeated the Romans in three battles, but his chances of prevailing would depend on Rome's ability to retain its allies.

In 216 B.C.E., at Cannae, Hannibal destroyed a Roman army of 80,000 men. It was the worst defeat in Roman history, and many of its allies went over to Hannibal. In 215 B.C.E., Philip V (r. 221–179 B.C.E.), king of Macedon, made an alliance with Hannibal and launched a war to recover his influence on the Adriatic. For more than a decade Hannibal was free to roam Italy and do as he pleased.

But crucial allies remained loyal to Rome, preventing Hannibal's victory. He had neither the numbers nor the supplies to besiege Rome. The Romans appointed Publius Cornelius Scipio (237–183 B.C.E.), later called Scipio Africanus, to the command in Spain. He was almost as talented as Hannibal. Within a few years Scipio had conquered all Spain and deprived Hannibal of help from that region.

In 204 B.C.E., Scipio landed in Africa. In 202 B.C.E., Scipio and Hannibal faced each other at Zama. Rome won and the new peace terms reduced Carthage to a dependent ally of whole; as it is, our liberty, destroyed at home by female violence, even here in the Forum is crushed and trodden underfoot, and because we have not kept them individually under control, we dread them collectively. . . . But from no class is there not the greatest danger if you permit them meetings and gatherings and secret consultations. . . .

"I should have said, 'What sort of practice is this, of running out into the streets and blocking the roads and speaking to other women's husbands? Could you not have made the same requests, each of your own husband, at home? Or are you more attractive outside and to other women's husbands than to your own? And yet, not even at home, if modesty would keep matrons within the limits of their proper rights, did it become you to concern yourselves with the question of what laws should be adopted in this place or repealed.' Our ancestors permitted no woman to conduct even personal business without a guardian to intervene in her behalf; they wished them to be under the control of fathers, brothers, husbands; we (Heaven help us!) allow them now even to interfere in public affairs, yes, and to visit the Forum and our informal and formal sessions. What else are they doing now on the streets and at the corners except urging the bill of the tribunes and voting for the repeal of the law? Give loose rein to their uncontrollable nature and to this untamed creature and expect that they will themselves set bounds to their licence; unless you act, this is the least of the things enjoined upon women by custom or law and to which they submit with a feeling of injustice. It is complete liberty or, rather, if we wish to speak the truth, complete licence that they desire.

"If they win in this, what will they not attempt? Review all the laws with which your forefathers restrained their licence and made them subject to their husbands; even with all these bonds you can scarcely control them. What of this? If you suffer them to seize these bonds one by one and wrench themselves free and finally to be placed on a parity with their husbands, do you think that you will be able to endure them? The moment they begin to be your equals, they will be your superiors. . . . "

The next day an even greater crowd of women appeared in public, and all of them in a body beset the doors of those tribunes, who were vetoing their colleagues' proposal, and they did not desist until the threat of veto was withdrawn by the tribunes. After that there was no question that all the tribes would vote to repeal the law. The law was repealed twenty years after it was passed.

From *Livy*, trans. by Evan T. Stage (Cambridge, Mass.: Harvard University Press, 1935), XXXIV, pp. i–iii, viii, 413–419, 439.

Rome. Rome ruled the seas and the entire Mediterranean coast from Italy westward.

The New Imperial System The old practice of extending citizenship and with it loyalty to Rome stopped at the borders of Italy. The Romans made Sicily, Sardinia, and Corsica provinces. It became common to extend the term of the governors of these provinces beyond a year. The governors exercised full *imperium*, free of the limits put on the power of officials in Rome. The new populations were subjects who paid tribute. Rome collected the new taxes by "farming them out" at auction to the highest bidder. The tax collectors became powerful and wealthy by squeezing the provincials hard. These innovations in time so strained the constitution and traditions of Rome that the existence of the republic was threatened.

The Republic's Conquest of the Hellenistic World

The East By the mid-third century B.C.E., the eastern Mediterranean had reached a stable balance of power. That equilibrium was threatened by two aggressive monarchs, Philip V of Macedon and the Seleucid Antiochus III (223–187 B.C.E.). In 200 B.C.E., the Romans ordered Philip not to attack any Greek city and to pay reparations to the kingdom of Pergamum in Asia Minor. Philip refused. Two years later, the Romans demanded that Philip withdraw from Greece entirely. In 197 B.C.E., with Greek support, they defeated Philip in Thessaly. The Greek cities taken from Philip were made autonomous and the freedom of the Greeks was proclaimed.

Soon after, Antiochus landed an army on the Greek mainland. The Romans drove him from Greece, and in 189 B.C.E. they crushed his army at Magnesia in Asia Minor. The Romans left Greek cities in Asia free. They continued to regard Greece, and now Asia Minor, as a kind of protectorate in which they could intervene as they chose.

In 179 B.C.E., Perseus (r. 179–168 B.C.E.) succeeded Philip V as king of Macedon. He tried to gain popularity in Greece by favoring the democratic and revolutionary forces in the cities. The Romans defeated him in 168 B.C.E. and divided Macedon into four separate republics.

The new policy reflected the stern and businesslike approach favored by the conservative censor Cato (234–149 B.C.E.). Leaders of anti-Roman factions in the Greek cities were punished severely. In 146 B.C.E., for instance, the city of Corinth was destroyed.

The public treasury benefited to such a degree from these wars that the direct property tax on Roman citizens was abolished. Foreign campaigns could bring profit to the state, rewards to the army, and wealth, fame, and power to the general.

The West   Roman treatment of Carthage was no better. Although Carthage posed no threat, some Romans refused to abandon their hatred and fear of the traditional enemy. In 146 B.C.E., Scipio Aemilianus took the city, and the Romans incorporated Carthage as the province of Africa.

Civilization in the Early Roman Republic: Greek Influence

Among the most important changes wrought by Roman expansion overseas were those in the Roman style of life and thought. Such Roman aristocrats as the Scipios surrounded themselves with Greek intellectuals. Even conservatives, such as Cato, learned Greek and absorbed Greek culture.

Religion

Almost from the beginning, the Romans identified their own gods with Greek equivalents and incorporated Greek mythology into their own. However, the third century B.C.E. brought important new influences from the east: the worship of Cybele, the Great Mother goddess from Asia Minor, and of Dionysus, or Bacchus. Interest in Babylonian astrology also grew.

Education

Education was entirely the responsibility of the Roman family. It is not clear whether girls received any education in early Rome, although they did later on. Boys' education aimed at making them moral, pious, patriotic, law-abiding, and respectful of tradition.

Contact with the Greeks of southern Italy produced momentous changes. Greek teachers introduced the study of language, literature, and philosophy, as well as the idea of a liberal education, or what the Romans called *humanitas*.

Schools were established in which the teacher taught his students the Greek language and its literature, particularly the works of Homer. Thereafter, educated Romans were expected to be bilingual. Roman boys of the upper classes then studied rhetoric which was of great use in legal disputes and political life.

By the last century of the Roman Republic, the new Hellenized education had become dominant. Latin literature formed part of the course of study. Many schools were established, and the number of educated people grew.

Girls of the upper classes were educated similarly to boys. They were probably taught by tutors at home, although they were usually married by the age when men were pursuing higher education. Still, some women became prose writers or poets.

A rich and ambitious Roman could support a Greek philosopher in his own home, so that his son could acquire through conversation the learning and polished thought necessary for the fully cultured gentleman. Some, like the great orator Cicero (106–43 B.C.E.), traveled to Greece to study with great teachers of rhetoric and philosophy. This style of education made the Romans part of the culture of the Hellenistic world, a world they needed to understand.

Roman Imperialism

Rome's expansion in Italy and overseas was accomplished without a grand general plan. But whether intended or not, it brought the Romans an empire, and with it, power, wealth, and responsibilities.

Aftermath of Conquest

War and expansion changed the economic, social, and political life of Italy. The Second Punic War did terrible damage to Italian farmland. Many veterans found it impossible or unprofitable to go back to their farms. Most became tenant farmers or hired hands. Often the land they abandoned was acquired by the wealthy who converted these farms, later called *latifundia*, into large plantations.

Land was cheap, and slaves conquered in war provided cheap labor. By fair means and foul, large landholders obtained sizable quantities of public land and forced small farmers off it. These changes separated the people of Rome and Italy more sharply into rich and poor, landed and landless, privileged and deprived. The result was conflict that threatened the republic.

The Gracchi

By the middle of the second century B.C.E., the problems caused by Rome's rapid expansion troubled perceptive Roman nobles. Tiberius Gracchus (168–133 B.C.E.) tried to solve these problems. He became tribune in 133 B.C.E. on a program of land reform. The program aroused great hostility. When Tiberius put it before the tribal assembly, another tribune interposed his veto.

Tiberius then proposed a second bill, harsher than the first and more appealing to the people, for he had despaired of conciliating the Senate. There could be no compromise: Either Tiberius or the Roman constitution must go under.

Tiberius understood the danger he would face if he stepped down from the tribunate, so he announced his candidacy for a second successive term, a blow at tradition. At the elections, a mob of senators and their clients killed Tiberius and some 300 of his followers and threw their bodies into the Tiber River.

The tribunate of Tiberius Gracchus and the senatorial resort to bloodshed created a new situation. From then on, Romans could pursue a political career that was not based solely on influence within the aristocracy; pressure from the people might be an effective substitute. In the last century of the republic, such politicians were called *populares*, whereas those who supported the traditional role of the Senate were called *optimates* ("the best men").

The tribunate of Gaius Gracchus (ca. 159–121 B.C.E.), brother of Tiberius, was much more dangerous to the Senate than that of Tiberius because all the tribunes were Gaius's supporters. There could be no veto, and tribunes could now be reelected. Gaius proposed to establish new colonies for landless veterans and passed a law stabilizing the price of grain in Rome.

Gaius also appealed to the equestrian order in his struggle against the Senate. The equestrians were rich men who supplied goods and services to the Roman state and collected its taxes in the provinces. They had a special interest in Roman expansion and in the exploitation of the provinces. When Pergamum became the Roman province of Asia in 129 B.C.E., Gaius gave them the right to collect taxes there.

Gaius easily won reelection as tribune for 122 B.C.E. He aimed at giving citizenship to the Italians, but the common people did not want to share the advantages of Roman citizenship. The Senate seized on this proposal to drive a wedge between Gaius and his supporters.

The Romans did not reelect Gaius in 121 B.C.E., and a hostile consul provoked an incident that led to violence. Gaius was killed, and 3,000 of his followers were put to death without trial.

Marius and Sulla

Before long the senatorial oligarchy faced more serious dangers arising from war with Jugurtha (d. 104 B.C.E.), king of Numidia. The war dragged on until the people elected Gaius Marius (157–86 B.C.E.) to the consulship for 107 B.C.E. Marius quickly defeated Jugurtha, but guerrilla warfare continued. Finally, Marius's subordinate, Lucius Cornelius Sulla (138–78 B.C.E.), brought the war to an end. Marius celebrated the victory, but Sulla resented being cheated of the credit.

Marius made important changes in the army. He began using volunteers, mostly dispossessed farmers and rural proletarians. They enlisted for a long term of service and looked on the army as a career. They became semiprofessional clients

Roman Overseas Engagements	
215–205 B.C.E.	First Macedonian War
200–197 B.C.E.	Second Macedonian War
196 B.C.E.	Proclamation of Greek Freedom
189 B.C.E.	Battle of Magnesia; Antiochus defeated in Asia Minor
172–168 B.C.E.	Third Macedonian War
168 B.C.E.	Battle of Pydna
154–133 B.C.E.	Roman wars in Spain
134 B.C.E.	Numantia taken

of their general and came to expect land as a bonus when they retired. Volunteers were most likely to join a man influential enough to obtain what they wanted. They looked to him rather than to the state for their rewards. He, on the other hand, had to obtain grants from the Senate to maintain his power and reputation.

Marius's innovation created both the opportunity and the necessity for military leaders to gain enough power to challenge civilian authority. The promise of rewards won these leaders the personal loyalty of their troops that allowed them to frighten the Senate into granting their demands.

War Against the Italian Allies (90–88 B.C.E.)

For a decade, Rome ignored Italian discontent. In frustration, the Italians revolted. By 88 B.C.E., the war was over. The Italians became Roman citizens, but retained local self-government and a dedication to their own municipalities that made Italy flourish. The passage of time forged Romans and Italians into a single nation.

Sulla's Dictatorship

Sulla was elected consul for 88 B.C.E. A champion of senatorial control, he won a civil war against Marius and his friends. He had himself appointed dictator to restore senatorial government and then retired to a life of luxury in 79 B.C.E. He could not, however, undo the effect of his example: a general using the loyalty of his own troops to take power and massacre his opponents.

Fall of the Republic
Pompey, Crassus, and Caesar

Marcus Licinius Crassus (115–53 B.C.E.) and Cnaeus Pompey (106–48 B.C.E.) were ambitious men who demanded special honors and election to the consulship for the year

70 B.C.E. They both won election and repealed most of Sulla's constitution.

In 67 B.C.E., a special law gave Pompey *imperium* for three years over the entire Mediterranean and fifty miles in from the coast to rid the area of pirates. When he returned to Rome in 62 B.C.E., he had more power, prestige, and popular support than any Roman in history.

Crassus had the most reason to fear Pompey's return. Although rich and influential, he did not have the confidence of the Senate, a firm political base of his own, or the kind of military glory to rival Pompey. During the 60s B.C.E., therefore, he allied himself with Gaius Julius Caesar (100–44 B.C.E.).

First Triumvirate

To general surprise, Pompey disbanded his army and returned to private life. He wanted the Senate to give land to his veterans. But the jealous and fearful Senate refused. Pompey was thus driven to an alliance with Crassus and Caesar. So was born the First Triumvirate.

Dictatorship of Julius Caesar

Caesar was elected consul for 59 B.C.E. The Triumvirate's program was enacted, and Caesar got the governorship of Illyricum and Gaul for five years. By the time he was ready to return, after conquering Gaul, the Triumvirate had dissolved. At Carrhae in 53 B.C.E., Crassus died trying to conquer the Parthians. Pompey joined the Senate in opposing Caesar.

Early in January of 49 B.C.E., the Senate ordered Pompey to defend the state and Caesar to lay down his command. Caesar ordered his legions to cross the Rubicon River, the boundary of his province. This action was the first act of a civil war that ended in 45 B.C.E. with Caesar's victory.

Caesar made few changes in the government of Rome, but his monopoly of military power made the whole structure a sham. He treated the Senate as his creature. His enemies conspired against him. On March 15, 44 B.C.E., Caesar was stabbed to death in the Senate. The assassins expected the republic to be restored. Instead, thirteen more years of civil war ensued, at the end of which the republic received its final burial.

Second Triumvirate and the Emergence of Octavian

Caesar's heir was his grandnephew, Octavian (63 B.C.E.–14 C.E.). He joined Marcus Antonius (Mark Antony) (ca. 83–30 B.C.E.) and Lepidus (d. 13 B.C.E.), two of Caesar's officers, in the Second Triumvirate to fight the assassins. The new triumvirs defeated the enemy in 42 B.C.E., but soon quarreled. Octavian gained control of the western part of the empire. Antonius, together with Cleopatra (r. 51–30 B.C.E.), queen of Egypt, ruled the east. In 31 B.C.E., Octavian crushed the fleet and army of Antony and Cleopatra at Actium.

The civil wars were over, and Octavian was master of the Mediterranean world. He had to restore peace, prosperity, and confidence, without offending unduly the traditional republican prejudices of Rome and Italy.

The Augustan Principate

Octavian's constitutional solution proved to be successful. Behind the republican trappings and the apparent sharing of authority with the Senate, his government was a monarchy. All real power lay with the ruler, whether he was called by the unofficial title of "first citizen" (*princeps*) like Octavian, or "emperor" (*imperator*) like those who followed.

In 27 B.C.E., he put forward a new plan: He would rule the provinces of Spain, Gaul, and Syria with proconsular power for military command and retain the consulship in Rome. The Senate would govern the other provinces as before. His provinces contained twenty of the twenty-six legions. The Senate voted him many honors, including the semireligious title "Augustus," which connoted veneration, majesty, and holiness. Historians thus speak of Rome's first emperor as Augustus and of his regime as the Principate. This helps conceal the unrepublican nature of the regime and the naked power on which it rested.

Administration

Augustus made important changes in the government of Rome, Italy, and the provinces to reduce inefficiency and corruption, eliminate the threat to peace and order by ambitious

---

Fall of the Roman Republic

133 B.C.E.	Tribunate of Tiberius Gracchus
123–122 B.C.E.	Tribunate of Gaius Gracchus
111–105 B.C.E.	Jugurthine War
104–100 B.C.E.	Consecutive consulships of Marius
90–88 B.C.E.	War against the Italian allies
70 B.C.E.	Consulship of Crassus and Pompey
60 B.C.E.	Formation of First Triumvirate
58–50 B.C.E.	Caesar in Gaul
53 B.C.E.	Crassus killed in Battle of Carrhae
49 B.C.E.	Caesar crosses Rubicon; civil war begins
46–44 B.C.E.	Caesar's dictatorship
45 B.C.E.	End of civil war
43 B.C.E.	Formation of Second Triumvirate
42 B.C.E.	Battle of Philippi
31 B.C.E.	Octavian defeats Antony at Actium

---

individuals, and reduce the distinction between Romans and Italians, senators and equestrians. Augustus controlled the elections and saw to it that promising young men, whatever their origin, served the state. Thus, equestrians and Italians who had no connection with the Roman aristocracy entered the Senate, which Augustus treated with respect and honor.

The Augustan period was one of prosperity, based on the wealth brought in by the conquest of Egypt, on the increase in commerce and industry made possible by general peace and a vast program of public works, and on a revival of small farming by Augustus's veterans.

The Army and Defense

Under Augustus, members of the armed forces became true professionals. Enlistment was for twenty years, but the pay was good, and there were bonuses and a pension on retirement. Together with the auxiliaries from the provinces, these forces formed a frontier army of about 300,000 men. This was barely enough to hold the line. The army in the provinces brought Roman culture to the natives. The soldiers spread their language and customs, often marrying local women and settling down there. They attracted merchants, who became the nuclei of new towns that became centers of Roman civilization. As time passed, the provincials on the frontiers became Roman citizens and helped strengthen Rome's defenses against the barbarians.

Religion and Morality

A century of political strife and civil war had undermined Roman society. Augustus undertook to restore the traditional values of the family and religion. He curbed adultery and divorce and encouraged marriage and the procreation of legitimate children.

Augustus also restored the dignity of formal Roman religion, building temples, reviving cults, and invigorating the priestly colleges. He was deified after his death; as with Julius Caesar, a state cult was dedicated to his worship.

Civilization of the Ciceronian and Augustan Ages

The high point of Roman culture came in the last century of the republic and during the Principate of Augustus.

The Late Republic

Cicero (106–43 B.C.E.) Cicero is most famous for his orations delivered in the law courts and the Senate. Together with many of his letters, the speeches give us a fuller insight

This statue of Emperor Augustus (r. 27 B.C.E.–14 C.E.), now in the Vatican, stood in the villa of Augustus's wife Livia. The figures on the elaborate breastplate are all of symbolic significance. At the top, for example, Dawn in her chariot brings in a new day under the protective mantle of the sky god; in the center, Tiberius, Augustus's successor, accepts the return of captured Roman army standards from a barbarian prince; and at the bottom, Mother Earth offers a horn of plenty. [Charitable Foundation, Leonard von Matt]

into his mind than the works of any other figure in antiquity. He also wrote treatises on rhetoric, ethics, and politics, and believed in a world governed by divine and natural law. He looked to law, custom, and tradition to produce both stability and liberty.

Law The period from the Gracchi to the fall of the Republic was important in the development of Roman law. The edicts of the magistrates who dealt with foreigners developed the idea of the *jus gentium*, or "law of peoples," as opposed to that arising strictly from the experience of the Romans. In the first century B.C.E., the influence of Greek thought made the idea of *jus gentium* identical to that of the *jus naturale*, or "natural law," taught by the Stoics.

Poetry   This was also the period of two of Rome's greatest poets, Lucretius and Catullus. The Hellenistic literary theorists saw poets as entertainers and teachers, and Lucretius (ca. 99–ca. 55 B.C.E.) pursued this path in his epic poem *De Rerum Natura (On the Nature of Things)*. In it, he set forth the scientific and philosophical ideas of Epicurus and Democritus with the zeal of a missionary trying to save society from fear and superstition.

Catullus's (ca. 84–ca. 54 B.C.E.) poems were personal. He wrote of the joys and pains of love, and amused himself in witty poetic exchanges. He is an example of the proud, independent, pleasure-seeking nobleman at the end of the republic.

Age of Augustus

The Augustan Age, the Golden Age of Roman literature, reflected the new conditions of society. The old aristocratic order was gone. So was the world of poets receiving patronage from individual aristocrats. All patronage now flowed from the *princeps*.

Virgil   Virgil (70–19 B.C.E.) was the most important of the Augustan poets. His greatest work is the *Aeneid*, a long national epic that placed the history of Rome in the great tradition of the Greeks and the Trojan War. Its hero, the Trojan Aeneas, personifies the ideal Roman qualities of duty, responsibility, serious purpose, and patriotism. As the Romans' equivalent to Homer, Virgil glorified the peace and prosperity that Augustus had given to imperial Rome.

Horace   Horace's (65–8 B.C.E.) great skills as a lyric poet are best revealed in his *Odes*. Many of them glorify the new Augustan order, the imperial family, and the empire.

Ovid   Ovid (43 B.C.E.–18 C.E.) wrote entertaining love elegies that reveal the sophistication and the loose sexual code of the Roman aristocracy. His most popular work is *Metamorphoses*, a kind of mythological epic that turns Greek myths into charming stories in a graceful and lively style.

History   The most important and influential prose writer of the time was Livy (59 B.C.E.–17 C.E.). His *History of Rome* treated the period from the legendary origins of Rome until 9 B.C.E. Only one-fourth of his work survives. His great achievement was to tell the story of Rome in a continuous and impressive narrative. Its purpose was moral and patriotic. He glorified Rome's greatness and connected it with Rome's past, just as Augustus tried to do.

Architecture and Sculpture   Augustus embarked on a building program that beautified Rome, glorified his reign, and contributed to the general prosperity and his own popularity. The greatest monument of the age is the Altar of Peace (*Ara Pacis*), dedicated in 9 B.C.E. Its walls show a procession in which Augustus and his family appear to move forward, followed by the magistrates, the Senate, and the people of Rome. There is no better symbol of the new order.

Peace and Prosperity: Imperial Rome (14–180 C.E.)

Augustus tried to cloak the monarchical nature of his government, but his successors soon abandoned all pretense. The rulers came to be called *imperator*—from which comes our word *emperor*—as well as *Caesar*. The latter title signified connection with the imperial house, and the former indicated the military power on which their authority was based. Augustus designated his heirs by giving them a share in the imperial power and responsibility (see Map 5–1).

Tiberius (emperor 14–37 C.E.), Gaius (Caligula, 37–41 C.E.), Claudius (41–54 C.E.), and Nero (54–68 C.E.) were all descended from Augustus's family. The year 69 C.E., however, saw four different emperors as different Roman armies took turns placing their commanders on the throne.

Vespasian (69–79 C.E.) emerged victorious from the chaos, and his sons, Titus (79–81 C.E.) and Domitian (81–96 C.E.), carried forward his line, the Flavian Dynasty. Vespasian was the first emperor who did not come from the old Roman nobility.

Nerva (96–98 C.E.) was the first of the five "good emperors," who included Trajan (98–117 C.E.), Hadrian (117–138

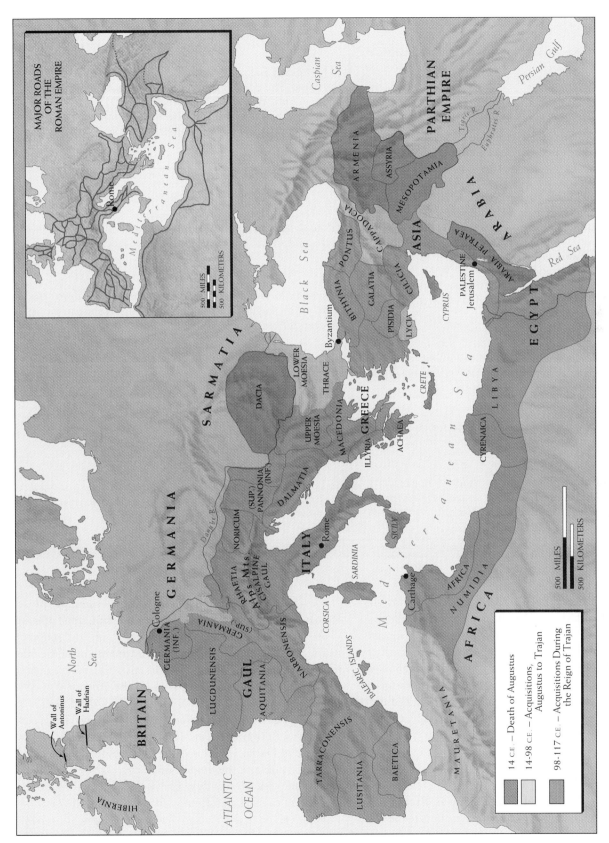

Map 5-1 Provinces of the Roman Empire to 117 C.E. The growth of the empire to its greatest extent is shown in three states—at the death of Augustus in 14 C.E., at the death of Nerva in 98 C.E., and at the death of Trajan in 117 C.E. The division into provinces is also indicated. The inset outlines the main roads that tied the far-flung empire together.

Daily Life in a Roman Provincial Town: Graffiti from Pompeii

On the walls of the houses of Pompeii, buried and preserved by the eruption of Mount Vesuvius in 79 C.E., are many scribblings that give us an idea of what the life of ordinary people was like.

How do these graffiti differ from those one sees in a modern American city? What do they reveal about the similarities and differences between the ordinary people of ancient Rome and the people of today? How would you account for the differences?

I

Twenty pairs of gladiators of Decimus Lucretius Satrius Valens, lifetime flamen of Nero son of Caesar Augustus, and ten pairs of gladiators of Decimus Lucretius Valens, his son, will fight at Pompeii on April 8, 9, 10, 11, 12. There will be a full card of wild beast combats, and awnings [for the spectators]. Aemilius Celer [painted this sign], all alone in the moonlight.

II

Market days: Saturday in Pompeii, Sunday in Nuceria, Monday in Atella, Tuesday in Nola, Wednesday in Cumae, Thursday in Puteoli, Friday in Rome.

III

Pleasure says: "You can get a drink here for an as [a few cents], a better drink for two, Falernian for four."

IV

A copper pot is missing from this shop. 65 sesterces reward if anybody brings it back, 20 sesterces if he reveals the thief so we can get our property back.

V

The weaver Successus loves the innkeeper's slave girl, Iris by name. She doesn't care for him, but he begs her to take pity on him. Written by his rival. So long.

[Answer by the rival:] Just because you're bursting with envy, don't pick on a handsomer man, a lady-killer and a gallant.

[Answer by the first writer:] There's nothing more to say or write. You love Iris, who doesn't care for you.

VI

Take your lewd looks and flirting eyes off another man's wife, and show some decency on your face!

VII

Anybody in love, come here. I want to break Venus' ribs with a club and cripple the goddess' loins. If she can pierce my tender breast, why can't I break her head with a club?

VIII

I write at Love's dictation and Cupid's instruction;
But damn it! I don't want to be a god without you.

IX

[A prostitute's sign:] I am yours for 2 asses cash.

From *Roman Civilization*, edited by Naphtali Lewis and Meyer Reinhold. Copyright © 1955 by Columbia University Press. Reprinted with permission of the publisher.

C.E.), Antoninus Pius (138–161 C.E.), and Marcus Aurelius (161–180 C.E.). Until Marcus Aurelius, none of these emperors had sons, so they each adopted an able senator as successor. The result was almost a century of competent rule, which ended when Marcus Aurelius allowed his incompetent son, Commodus (180–192 C.E.), to succeed him, with unfortunate results. From Nerva to Marcus Aurelius, however, the emperors enlisted the cooperation of the upper class by courteous and modest deportment.

Administration of the Empire

The empire was a collection of cities and towns. Roman policy during the Principate was to raise urban centers to the status of Roman municipalities. The Romans enlisted the upper classes of the provinces in their own government, spread Roman culture, and won the loyalty of the influential people.

As the bureaucracy became more efficient, the scope of its functions grew. The importance and autonomy of the municipalities shrank as the central administration took a greater part in local affairs. The price paid for the efficiency of centralized control was the loss of the vitality of the cities.

Trajan was the first emperor to take the offensive in a sustained way. Between 101 and 106 C.E., he established the new province of Dacia. He probably was pursuing a new general strategy: to defend the empire more aggressively by driving wedges into enemy territory. The same strategy dictated the invasion of the Parthian Empire in the east (113–117 C.E.).

Under Hadrian the Roman defense became rigid, and initiative passed to the barbarians. Marcus Aurelius spent most of his reign resisting dangerous attacks on the frontier. These attacks put enormous pressure on the empire's resources.

Culture of the Early Empire

Literature   In Latin literature, the years between the death of Augustus and Marcus Aurelius are known as the Silver Age. The writers of the Silver Age were gloomy, negative, and pessimistic. Criticism and satire lurk everywhere in their work. Historical writing was about remote periods, so there was less danger of irritating imperial sensibilities. Scholarship was encouraged, but we hear little of poetry. Romances written in Greek became popular as an escape from contemporary realities.

Architecture   The prosperity and relative stability of the first two centuries of imperial Rome allowed the full development of Roman architecture. The main contribution of the Romans lay in the size of the structures they could build and in the advances in engineering that made them possible. To the basic post-and-lintel construction used by the Greeks, the Romans added the semicircular arch, borrowed from the Etruscans. They also made good use of concrete, a building material first used by the Hellenistic Greeks. The arch combined with the post and lintel produced the great Colosseum built by the Flavian emperors. When used internally in the form of vaults and domes, the arch permitted great buildings like the baths.

The Pantheon combines all these elements. The new engineering also made possible the construction of bridges and aqueducts.

Society   The first two centuries of the Roman Empire deserve their reputation as a Golden Age, but by the second century C.E., troubles had arisen—troubles that foreshadowed the difficult times ahead. In the first century C.E., the upper classes vied for election to municipal office. By the second century, much of their zeal had disappeared, and the emperors had to force the ruling classes to accept public office. The reluctance to serve was caused largely by the imperial practice of holding magistrates and councilmen personally and collectively responsible for revenues that were due.

All of these difficulties reflected more basic problems. The prosperity brought by the end of civil war and the influx of wealth from the east could not sustain itself. The population also seems to have declined. The cost of government kept rising as the emperors were required to maintain an expensive standing army, to keep the people in Rome happy with "bread and circuses," to pay for an increasingly large bureaucracy, and to defend the frontiers against dangerous and determined enemies.

The ever-increasing need for money compelled the emperors to oppress their subjects and debase the coinage. These elements were to bring on the crises that destroyed the empire.

Rise of Christianity

The story of how Christianity ultimately conquered the Roman Empire is one of the most remarkable in history. Christianity faced the hostility of the established religious institutions of its native Judaea and had to compete not only against the official cults of Rome and the sophisticated philosophies of the educated classes, but also against "mystery" religions like the cults of Mithra, Isis, and Osiris. The Christians also suffered formal persecution, yet Christianity finally became the official religion of the empire.

Jesus of Nazareth

An attempt to understand this amazing outcome must begin with Jesus of Nazareth. The Gospel authors believed that Jesus was the son of God who came to redeem humanity and bring immortality to those who followed his way; to the Gospel writers, Jesus' resurrection was striking proof of his teachings.

Jesus was born in Judaea in the time of Augustus and was a most effective teacher in the tradition of the Jewish prophets. This tradition promised the coming of a Messiah (in Greek, *christos*—so *Jesus Christ* means "Jesus the Messiah"), the redeemer who would make Israel triumph over its enemies and establish the kingdom of God on Earth. In fact, Jesus seems to have insisted that the Messiah would not establish an earthly kingdom but, at the Day of Judgment, God would reward the righteous and condemn the wicked. Until that day, which his followers believed would come soon, Jesus taught the faithful to abandon sin and worldly concerns; to follow the moral code described in the Sermon on the Mount, which preached love, charity, and humility; and to believe in him and his divine mission.

Jesus won a following, especially among the poor. This provoked the hostility of the religious establishment in Jerusalem. They convinced the Roman governor that Jesus and his followers might be dangerous revolutionaries. He was put to death in Jerusalem by the cruel and degrading method of crucifixion, probably in 30 C.E. His followers believed that he was resurrected on the third day after his death, and that belief became a critical element in their religion.

Although the new belief spread to the Jewish communities of Syria and Asia Minor, without Saint Paul it might have been only a Jewish heresy.

Paul of Tarsus

Paul (?5–67 C.E.) was born Saul, a citizen of Tarsus in Asia Minor. Even though he was trained in Hellenistic culture and was a Roman citizen, he was a Pharisee, the strictest adherents of the Jewish law. He persecuted the early Christians until his own conversion outside Damascus about 35 C.E. The great problem facing the early Christians was their relationship to Judaism. If the new faith was a version of Judaism, then it must adhere to the Jewish law and seek converts only among Jews. James, called the brother of Jesus, held that view, whereas Hellenist Jews tended to see Christianity as a new and universal religion.

Paul, converted and with his new name, supported the position of the Hellenists and soon won many converts among the gentiles. Paul believed it important that the followers of Jesus be evangelists ("messengers"), to spread the gospel ("good news") of God's gracious gift. He taught that Jesus would soon return for the Day of Judgment, and that all should believe in him and accept his way. Faith in Jesus as the Christ was necessary but not sufficient for salvation, nor could good deeds achieve it. Salvation was a gift of God's grace.

Organization

The new religion had its greatest success in the cities and among the poor and uneducated. The rites of the early communities appear to have been simple and few. Baptism by water removed original sin and permitted participation in the community and its activities. The central ritual was a common meal called the *agape* ("love feast"), followed by the ceremony of the *eucharist* ("thanksgiving"), a celebration of the Lord's Supper in which unleavened bread was eaten and unfermented wine drunk. There were also prayers, hymns, and readings from the Gospels.

At first the churches had little formal organization. By the second century C.E., the Christians of each city tended to accept the authority and leadership of bishops (*episkopoi* or "overseers"). The authority of the bishops was soon enhanced by the doctrine of Apostolic Succession, which asserted that the powers Jesus had given his original disciples were passed on from bishop to bishop by the rite of ordination.

The bishops kept internal discipline and dealt with the civil authorities. In time they began coming together in councils to settle difficult questions, establish orthodox opinion, and expel those who would not accept it. Christianity could probably not have survived without such strong internal organization and government.

Persecution of Christians

The new faith soon incurred the distrust of the pagan world and of the imperial government. The Christians' refusal to worship the emperor was considered treason. By the end of the first century, membership in the Christian community was a crime.

Emergence of Catholicism

Most Christians held to traditional, simple, conservative beliefs. This body of majority opinion and the church that enshrined it came to be called *Catholic*, which means "universal." Its doctrines were deemed orthodox; those holding contrary opinions were heretics.

By the end of the second century, an orthodox canon had been shaped that included the Old Testament, the Gospels, and the Epistles of Paul. The orthodox declared the church itself to be the depository of Christian teaching and the bishops to be its receivers. They also drew up creeds, brief statements of faith to which true Christians should adhere. By the end of the second century, an orthodox Christian—that is, a member of the Catholic Church—had to accept its creed, its canon of holy writings, and the authority of the bishops.

Rome as a Center of the Early Church

During this same period the church in the city of Rome came to have special prominence. Rome benefited from the tradition that both Jesus' apostles Peter and Paul were martyred there. Peter was thought to be the first bishop of Rome, and the Gospel of Matthew (16:18) reported Jesus' statement to Peter: "Thou art Peter [in Greek, *Petros*] and upon this rock [in Greek, *petra*] I will build my church." As a result, later bishops of Rome were to claim supremacy in the Catholic Church.

The Crisis of the Third Century

The pressure on Rome's frontiers reached massive proportions in the third century C.E. In the east, a new Iranian dynasty, the Sassanids, reinvigorated Persia (see Chapter 10) and raided Roman territory.

Barbarian Invasions

On the western and northern frontiers the threat came from German tribes. There was a danger that Rome would be unable to meet this challenge.

Septimius Severus (emperor 193–211 C.E.) and his successors transformed the character of the Roman army. Septimius was prepared to make Rome into a military monarchy. Septimius drew recruits for the army increasingly from peasants of the less civilized provinces, and the result was a barbarization of Rome's military forces.

Economic Difficulties

Inflation had forced Commodus (r. 180–192 C.E.) to raise the soldiers' pay, but the Severan emperors had to double it to keep up with prices, which increased the imperial budget by as much as 25 percent. The emperors invented new taxes, debased the coinage, and even sold the palace furniture to raise money. Even then it was hard to recruit troops.

As external threats distracted the emperors, they were less able to preserve domestic peace. Piracy, brigandage, and the neglect of roads and harbors hampered trade. So, too, did inflation. The government now had to demand food, supplies, money, and labor. The upper classes in the cities were made to serve as administrators without pay and to meet deficits in revenue out of their own pockets. There were provincial rebellions, and peasants and even town administrators fled to escape their burdens. These difficulties weakened Rome's economic strength.

Civil Disorder

The new conditions caused important changes in the social order. The whole state began to take on a military appearance. People's clothing became a kind of uniform that revealed their status. Titles were assigned to ranks in society as to ranks in the army. The most important distinction was the one formally established by Septimius Severus between the *honestiores* (senators, equestrians, the municipal aristocracy, and the soldiers) and the lower classes, or *humiliores*. Septimius gave the *honestiores* a privileged position before the law. They were given lighter punishments, could not be tortured, and alone had the right of appeal to the emperor.

It became more difficult to move from the lower order to the higher. Freedom and private initiative yielded to the needs of the state and its ever expanding control of its citizens. Hereafter, the army was composed largely of Germanic mercenaries whose officers gave personal loyalty to the emperor rather than to the empire. These officers became a foreign, hereditary caste of aristocrats that increasingly supplied high administrators and even emperors. In effect, the Roman people hired an army of mercenaries to protect them.

Reigns of Selected Late Empire Rulers (all dates are C.E.)

180–192	Commodus
193–211	Septimius Severus
284–305	Diocletian
306–337	Constantine
324–337	Constantine sole emperor
337–361	Constantius II
361–363	Julian the Apostate
364–375	Valentinian
364–378	Valens
379–395	Theodosius

The Late Empire

The Fourth Century and Imperial Reorganization

The period from Diocletian (r. 284–305 C.E.) to Constantine (r. 306–337 C.E.) was one of reconstruction and reorganization.

Diocletian Diocletian rose to the throne through the army. He knew that the job of defending and governing the entire empire was too great for one man. He therefore decreed the introduction of the tetrarchy, the rule of the empire by four men with power divided on a territorial basis.

Constantine In 305, Diocletian retired and compelled his co-emperor to do the same. But his plan for a smooth succession failed. In 310, there were five competing emperors. Out of this chaos, Constantine in 324 made himself sole emperor.

The emperor had now become almost unapproachable. Those admitted to his presence had to prostrate themselves before him and kiss the hem of his robe. The emperor was addressed as *dominus* ("lord"), and his right to rule was derived from God. This remoteness and ceremony enhanced the dignity of the emperor and safeguarded him against assassination.

Constantine erected the new city of Constantinople on the site of ancient Byzantium on the Bosphorus and made it the new capital of the empire. Its strategic location was excellent for protecting the eastern and Danubian frontiers, and, surrounded on three sides by water, it was easily defended.

Administration and Finance The autocratic rule of the emperors was carried out by a civilian bureaucracy, which was separated from the military service to reduce rebellion. The entire system was supervised by a network of spies and secret police. Despite these efforts, the system was corrupt and inefficient.

The cost of maintaining a 400,000-man army, the vast civilian bureaucracy, and the expensive imperial court, strained the weak economy. Peasants unable to pay their taxes and officials unable to collect them tried to escape. The terror of the third century had turned many peasants into tenant farmers on the country estates of powerful landowners. They were tied to the land, as were their descendants, as the caste system hardened.

Division of the Empire The peace and unity established by Constantine did not last. The Germans in the west attacked along the Rhine, but even greater trouble was brewing along the Danube where the Visigoths had been driven from their home in the Ukraine by the Huns. The Emperor Valentinian (r. 364–375) saw that he could not defend the empire alone and appointed his brother Valens (r. 364–378) as co-ruler in the east. The empire was again divided in two. The two halves of the empire became increasingly separate. Latin was the language of the west and Greek of the east.

In 376, when the Goths began to plunder the Balkan provinces, Valens attacked them and died, along with most of his army, at Adrianople in Thrace in 378. Theodosius (r. 379–395), an able and experienced general, tried to unify the empire again, but his death in 395 left it divided and weak.

Thereafter, the two parts of the empire went their separate ways. The west became increasingly rural as barbarian invasions grew. The villa, a fortified country estate, became the basic unit of life. There, *coloni* (tenant farmers) gave their services to the local magnate in return for economic assistance and protection. Many cities shrank to tiny walled fortresses ruled by military commanders and bishops. The upper classes moved to the country and asserted ever greater independence of imperial authority. The failure of the central authority to maintain the roads and the danger from robber bands curtailed trade and communications, forcing a more primitive style of life. By the fifth century, the west was made up of isolated units of rural aristocrats and their dependent laborers. The only unifying institution was the Christian church. The pattern for the early Middle Ages in the west was formed.

The east was different. Constantinople became the center of a flourishing culture that we call *Byzantine* and that lasted until the fifteenth century. Due to its defensible location, the skill of its emperors, and the firmness and strength of its base in Asia Minor, it was able to deflect and repulse barbarian attacks. A strong navy allowed commerce to flourish. Cities continued to prosper, and the emperors controlled the nobility. Byzantine civilization was a unique combination of classical culture, the Christian religion, Roman law, and eastern artistic influences. While the west was being overrun by barbarians, the Roman Empire, in altered form, persisted in the east. Constantinople flourished as the seat of empire, the "New Rome," and the Byzantines called themselves "Romans." When we contemplate the decline and fall of the Roman Empire in the fourth and fifth centuries, we are speaking only of the west. A form of classical culture persisted in the Byzantine east for another thousand years.

Triumph of Christianity

In 303, Diocletian launched the most serious persecution inflicted on the Christians in the Roman Empire. Because the martyrs often aroused pity and because ancient states were unable to carry out a program of terror with the thoroughness of modern totalitarian governments, the Christians and their church survived to enjoy what they must have considered a miraculous change of fortune.

The victory of Constantine and his emergence as sole ruler of the empire transformed Christianity to the religion favored by the emperor. In 394, Theodosius forbade the celebration of pagan cults. At his death, Christianity was the official religion of the Roman Empire.

The favored position of the church diluted the moral excellence and spiritual fervor of its adherents. The relationship between church and state presented the possibility that religion would become subordinate to the state, as it traditionally had been. In the east, that largely happened. In the west, the weakness of the emperors permitted church leaders to exercise independence. In 390, Ambrose (ca. 339–397), bishop of Milan, excommunicated Emperor Theodosius, and the emperor did humble penance. This act provided an important precedent for future assertions of the church's autonomy and authority.

Arianism and the Council of Nicea   Internal divisions within the church proved to be even more troubling as new heresies emerged. The most important was Arianism, founded by a priest named Arius of Alexandria (ca. 280–336) in the fourth century. Arius's view that Jesus was not co-equal and co-eternal with God the Father did away with the mysterious concept of the Trinity, the difficult doctrine that holds that God is three persons (the Father, the Son, and the Holy Spirit) but also one in substance and essence.

Athanasius (ca. 293–373) saw the Arian view as an impediment to salvation. Only if Jesus were both fully human and fully God could the transformation of humanity to divinity have taken place in Him and be transmitted by Him to his disciples.

To deal with the growing controversy, Constantine called a council of Christian bishops at Nicea in 325, where the view expounded by Athanasius won out, became orthodox, and was embodied in the Nicene Creed. The Christian emperors hoped to unify their increasingly decentralized realms by imposing a single religion, but it also introduced new divisions where none had previously existed.

Arts and Letters in the Late Empire

The art and literature of the late empire reflect both the confluence of pagan and Christian ideas and traditions and the conflict between them. Much of the literature is polemical, and much of the art is propaganda.

Preservation of Classical Culture

One of the main needs and accomplishments of this period was to preserve classical culture. The great classical authors were reproduced in many copies. Scholars also digested long works like Livy's *History of Rome* into shorter versions and wrote learned commentaries and compiled grammars.

Christian Writers

Christianity could also boast important scholars. Jerome (348–420), thoroughly trained in classical Latin literature and rhetoric, produced a revised version of the Bible in Latin, commonly called the Vulgate, which became the Bible used by the Catholic Church.

Probably the most important eastern scholar was Eusebius of Caesarea (ca. 260–ca. 340). His most important contribution was his *Ecclesiastical History*, an attempt to set forth the Christian view of history. He saw history as the working out of God's will. All of history, therefore, had a purpose and a direction, and Constantine's victory and the subsequent unity of empire and church was its culmination.

The closeness and complexity of the relationship between classical pagan culture and the Christianity of the late empire are nowhere better displayed than in the career and writings of Augustine (354–430), bishop of Hippo in North Africa. His skill in pagan rhetoric and philosophy made him peerless among his contemporaries as a defender of Christianity and a theologian. His greatest works are his *Confessions*, an autobiography describing the road to his conversion, and *The City of God*. The latter was a response to Rome's sack by the Goths in 410. Augustine sought to separate the fate of Christianity from that of the Roman Empire. He contrasted the secular world—the city of Man—with the spiritual—the City of God. The former was selfish, the latter unselfish; the former evil, the latter good. All states, even a Christian Rome, were part of the City of Man and therefore corrupt and mortal. Only the City of God was immortal, and it was untouched by earthly calamities.

The Problem of the Decline and Fall of the Empire in the West

The massive barbarian invasions of the fifth century ended effective imperial government in the west. For centuries people have speculated about why the ancient world collapsed. Soil exhaustion, plague, climatic change, and even poisoning from lead water pipes have been suggested as reasons for Rome's decline. Perhaps a more simple and obvious explanation can be found. We may do well to think of the decline of Rome as the historian Edward Gibbon did:

> The decline of Rome was the natural and inevitable effect of immoderate greatness. Prosperity ripened the principle of decay; the cause of the destruction

multiplied with the extent of conquest; and, as soon as time or accident had removed the artificial supports, the stupendous fabric yielded to the pressure of its own weight. The story of the ruin is simple and obvious; and instead of inquiring why the Roman Empire was destroyed, we should rather be surprised that it had subsisted so long.[1]

This explanation allows us to see the Roman Empire as one among several great empires around the world that had similar experiences.

IN WORLD PERSPECTIVE

Republican and Imperial Rome

The history of the Roman republic reflects almost as sharp a departure from the common experience of ancient civilizations as that of the Greek city-states. The force of Roman arms, the high quality of Roman roads and bridges, and the pragmatic character of Roman law helped create something unique: an empire ruled by a republic. Rome achieved its greatness with an army of citizens and allies, without a monarchy or a regular bureaucracy.

The temptations and responsibilities of governing a vast and rich empire, however, finally proved too much for the republican constitution. Out of the civil wars and chaos that brought down the republic, Augustus brought unity, peace, order, and prosperity. For almost 200 years, the empire was generally prosperous, peaceful, and well run, but problems developed. In the late empire, the government's control over the lives of its people became ever greater and the society more rigid. Many measures were tried in an effort to save the empire, but ultimately they all failed.

The conquest of a vast empire had moved the Romans away from their unusual historical traditions toward the more familiar path of empire trodden by rulers in Egypt, Mesopotamia, China, India, and Iran. It is especially instructive to look at Rome from the perspective of the historians who discern a "dynastic cycle" in China (see Chapter 7). The development of the Roman Empire, although by no means the same as the Chinese, fits the same pattern fairly well. Like the Former Han Dynasty in China, the Roman Empire in the west fell, leaving disunity, insecurity, disorder, and poverty. Like similar empires in the ancient world, it had been unable to sustain its "immoderate greatness."

---

[1]Edward Gibbon, *Decline and Fall of the Roman Empire*, ed. by J. B. Bury, 2nd ed., Vol. 4 (London: J. Murray, 1909), pp. 173–174.

Review Questions

1. How did the institutions of family and clientage and the establishment of patrician and plebeian classes contribute to the stability of the early Roman republic? How important was education to the success of the republic?

2. Discuss Rome's expansion to 265 B.C.E. How was Rome able to conquer and control Italy? In their relations with Greece and Asia Minor in the second century B.C.E., were the Romans looking for security? Wealth? Power? Fame?

3. Explain the clash between the Romans and the Carthaginians in the First and Second Punic Wars. Could the wars have been avoided? How did Rome benefit from its victory over Carthage? What problems were created by this victory?

4. What were the problems that plagued the Roman republic in the last century B.C.E.? What caused these problems and how did the Romans try to solve them? To what extent was the republic destroyed by ambitious generals who loved power more than Rome itself?

5. Discuss the Augustan constitution and government. What solutions did Augustus provide for the problems that had plagued the Roman republic? Why was the Roman population willing to accept Augustus as head of the state?

6. Despite unpromising beginnings, Christianity was enormously popular by the fourth century C.E. Why were Christians persecuted by Roman authorities? What were the more important reasons for Christianity's success?

7. What are the difficulties involved in explaining the fall of the Roman Empire? What explanation would you give?

Documents CD-ROM

1. The Speech of Camillus: "All Things Went Well When We Obeyed the Gods, but Badly When We Disobeyed Them"

2. Polybius: "Why Romans and Not Greeks Govern the World"

3. Marcus Tullius Cicero: *The Laws*

4. Overture: *The Gospel of Jesus*

5. *The Gospel According to John*

6. *The Letter of Paul to the Romans*

6 AFRICA: EARLY HISTORY TO 1000 C.E.

Africa forms the southern frontier of the Mediterranean world and connects to Asia through the Arabian peninsula and the Indian Ocean. The evidence suggests that the first humans emerged from eastern Africa, and the continent's subsequent history is one of ongoing interaction, both internally and with the rest of the world.

African history has flourished in recent decades, but there is much we do not know. A major reason for this is the paucity of sources, especially for the small, local societies without writing, centralized governmental bureaucracies, or large urban centers that characterize much of sub-Saharan African history.

Physical Description of the Continent

Africa makes up over one-fifth of the Earth's landmass. It is geologically massive, with unusually high relief over virtually its entire expanse. The result is a dearth of natural harbors and islands and generally steep escarpments surmounting narrow coasts. This has made access to, as well as egress from, its interior difficult. All of Africa's major rivers (the Niger, Kongo

[Zaïre], Nile, Zambezi, and Orange) lie largely in plateau basins and are navigable in their inland reaches. They are not, however, navigable across the cataracts they traverse before they reach the coastlands. (Only the Nile has a relatively long navigable reach below its cataracts in upper Egypt.) The vast size and sharp physical variations, from high mountains to swamplands, tropical forest, and deserts, have also made rapid long-distance communication and movement difficult.

The special character of various regions is due in considerable part to Africa's position astride the equator. As a whole, its climate is unusually hot. North and south of the equator, dense rain forests dominate a west-east band of tropical woodland territory. North and south of this band, the lush rain forests give way to the *savannah*—open woodlands and grassy plains. This in turn passes into steppe and semidesert known as the Sahel, and finally into true desert as Africa contains two of the world's greatest and driest deserts. The Sahara is the world's largest desert and historically has hindered contact between the Mediterranean world and sub-Saharan Africa. The Kalahari in southwestern Africa partially cuts off the southern plateau and coastal regions from central Africa.

Other natural factors are of importance to Africa's history. Its soils are devoid of much humus, or vegetable mold, and generally are easily leached of mineral and nutrient content. Thus they are not highly productive for extended periods. Water shortage is also a perennial problem for agriculture in most of Africa and a potent factor in its history. Crop pests and insects have also been enemies of both farming and pastoralism in Africa; the tsetse fly has blocked the spread of domesticated cattle and horses to the forest regions of the continent. Still, abundant animal life has made hunting and fishing important, from early times to the present in most regions.

Africa's great mineral wealth has shaped human activity. Salt, for example, was an important focus of the trans-Saharan trade between the western Sudan and North Africa from as early as the first millennium C.E. Iron, copper, and gold were also significant trading commodities.

Finally, Africa is often discussed in terms of several major regions: *North Africa*—all the Mediterranean coastal regions from modern Morocco through modern Libya and the northern Sahara, including the Sahel that marks the transition from mountains to true desert; *Nilotic Africa* (i.e., the lands of the Nile), roughly the area of modern Egypt and Sudan; *the Sudan*, the broad belt of Sahel and savannah below the Sahara, stretching from the Atlantic east across the entire continent; *West Africa*, including the woodland coastal regions and the desert, Sahel, and savannah of the western Sudan as far east as the Lake Chad basin; *East Africa*, from the Ethiopian highlands south over modern Kenya and Tanzania; *central Africa*, the region north of the Kalahari, from the Chad basin across the Zaïre basin and southeast to Lake Tanganyika and south to the Zambezi River; and *southern Africa*, from the Kalahari desert and Zambezi south to the Cape of Good Hope.

African Peoples

Africa and Early Human Culture

Archaeological research indicates that our hominid ancestors evolved in the Great Rift region of highland East Africa at least 1.5 to 1.8 million years ago. It was probably also here that, sometime before 100,000 B.C.E., modern humans—the species *homo sapiens* (*sapiens*)—appeared and moved out to populate the rest of Africa and the world.

The once popular view of sub-Saharan Africa as a vast region isolated from civilization until its "discovery" by Europeans distorts reality. Although its interior and southern reaches were isolated from direct contact with Eurasia until relatively recent centuries, African goods circulated for centuries through Indian Ocean and Mediterranean trade. Archaeological research is documenting the existence and substantial internal movements of peoples—and hence languages, cultures, and technologies—both north-south and east-west within the continent in ancient times.

The Sahara and the Sudan to the Beginning of the Christian Era

Early Saharan Cultures

One of the most striking and imposing physical features of the African continent is the Sahara. Since the second millennium B.C.E., this vast arid wilderness has separated the North African and Egyptian worlds from the wide expanse of the Sudan and, farther south, West and central Africa. Still, this desert barrier never fully blocked north-south contact and exchange. The Nile Valley and the Great Rift plateau provided one corridor for movement of ideas and peoples south to north and vice versa. Similarly, the Red Sea, the Atlantic and Indian Ocean coasts, and a few routes through the Sahara itself allowed people, goods, and ideas to breach the great Saharan barrier as far back as our evidence takes us.

What is hard for us to imagine, however, is that until about 2500 B.C.E. the Sahara was arable land with lakes and rivers, trees, grasses, and a reasonable climate. Then climatic changes caused the Sahara to undergo a relatively rapid dessication. By 1000 B.C.E., the dessication process had made the Sahara an immense east-west expanse of largely uninhabitable desert separating the greater part of the African continent from the Mediterranean coastal rim and the Near Eastern centers of early civilization.

Neolithic Sudanic Cultures

Most interesting to speculate about are the repercussions of the Saharan dessication for later settled communities, especially those in the Sahel and savannah of the Sudan. From the first millennium B.C.E., preliterate but complex agricultural communities of Neolithic and early Iron Age culture dotted the central and western reaches of the great belt of the sub-Saharan Sudan. We may surmise that these peoples had once been spread farther north, in the then-arable Saharan lands they would have shared with ancestors of the Berber-speaking peoples of contemporary west-Saharan and North Africa.

One theory proposes that the progressive dessication of the second millennium B.C.E. forced these peoples farther south. Pottery found in the first-millennium settlements in places such as Jenne (in Mali) are clearly "offshoots of a Saharan pottery tradition."[1] These migrants carried with them both languages and techniques of settled agriculture, especially those based on cereal grains, and of animal husbandry. Assisted ultimately by knowledge of iron working (probably passed on from North Africa or the Nilotic kingdom of Kush),

---

[1]S. J. and R. J. McIntosh, *Prehistoric Investigations at Jenne, Mali* (Oxford, U.K.: B.A.R., 1980), p. 436.

they were able to effect an agricultural revolution. This meant considerable population growth in the more fertile Sudanic regions, especially near the great river basins of the Niger and Senegal, and the Lake Chad basin. (A similar spread of agricultural techniques and cattle and sheep raising seems to have occurred down the Rift valley of the East African highlands.) This agricultural revolution, completed during the first millennium B.C.E., paved the way for the growth of new cultural centers in the sub-Saharan regions.

Whatever their earlier history, we know that in the first millennium B.C.E. the Sudanic peoples developed and refined techniques of settled agriculture. They must have carried these together with their languages eastward through the savannahs and southward, largely along the rivers, into the tropical rain forests of central and West Africa. The result changed the face of sub-Saharan Africa, where before small groups of hunter-gatherers had predominated. With the advent of iron smelting, these settled peoples were able to develop larger and more complex societies than their predecessors.

The Early Iron Age and the Nok Culture

The common features of the oldest iron-smelting furnaces found in widely scattered sites across Africa suggest that smelting in Africa was invented within the continent, probably in Egypt and Nubia, or possibly in the central Saharan highlands of the Tibesti, Ahaggar, and Aïr. Thence it likely spread southward into western, central, and eastern parts of the continent.

Some of the most significant Iron Age sites have been found in what is today northeastern Nigeria. Here, near the village of Jos, archaeological digs have yielded evidence of an Iron Age people labeled the Nok culture, dating between 900 B.C.E. and 200 C.E. The Nok people cleared substantial woodlands from the plateau, and combined agriculture as their mainstay with cattleherding.

The Nok culture is significant for two reasons. The first is that the Nok people, who mastered the relatively difficult art of smelting by at least 500 B.C.E., had the earliest Iron Age culture of West Africa. That they likely acquired this art by way of the Aïr Mountains to the north is further evi-

A terra-cotta head (20 cm high) from the Iron Age Nok culture, which occupied what is today northeastern Nigeria from about 900 B.C.E. to about 200 C.E. [Werner Forman Archive/Art Resource, N.Y./Jos Museum, Nigeria]

dence of early contact among African cultures. The second important aspect of Nok culture is its extraordinary sculptural art, most vividly evident in magnificent burial or ritual masks. The apparent continuities of Nok sculptural traditions with those of other, later West African cultures to the south suggest that this culture had an important impact on later West and central African life. These continuities indicate that ancient communities of considerable sophistication laid a basis on which later, better-known Sudanic civilizations must have built.

Nilotic Africa and the Ethiopian Highlands

The Kingdom of Kush

If we move east across the Sudan to the upper Nile basin, just above the first cataract, we come to the lower Nubian land of Kush. It was here that an Egyptianized segment of Nilo-Saharan-speaking Nubians built the earliest known literate and politically unified civilization in Africa after Pharaonic Egypt. The Old Kingdom pharaohs had subjugated and colonized Nubia. In the early second millennium B.C.E., however, an independent kingdom arose in Kush just above the third cataract of the Nile. As early as 2000 B.C.E., its capital, Kerma, had been a major trading outpost for Middle Kingdom Egypt.

The early Kushite kingdom reached its zenith between the Middle and New kingdoms of Egypt, or about 1700–1500 B.C.E. Kush appears to have been a wealthy and prosperous

The Lion Temple and Kiosk at Naga in the Butana Desert, about 60 miles northeast of Khartoum. Naga, founded in the early first century C.E., was a Meroitic caravanserai on the Red Sea trade routes. Initially, Kushite religion appears to have followed Egyptian tradition. By the third century B.C.E., however, gods who were unknown to Egypt rose in importance. Judging by the presence of many temples like this, the lion-headed god Apedemak was one of the most important of these gods. [Tim Kendall]

kingdom by any standard. After the Hyksos invasions, with Egypt's recovery (from about 1500 B.C.E.) under the New Kingdom rulers, Kush came once more under Egyptian colonial rule and hence stronger Egyptian cultural influence. Then, sometime after 1000 B.C.E., as the New Kingdom floundered, a new Kushite state reasserted itself and by about 900 B.C.E. conquered lower as well as upper Nubia.

The Napatan Empire

This new Kushite empire, centered first at Napata and then at Meroe, survived from the tenth century B.C.E. until the fourth century C.E., when the Ethiopian Aksumites replaced Kush as the dominant power in northeastern Africa.

The new Nubian state and culture was the true successor to Pharaonic Egypt. The royal line that ruled at Napata saw themselves as Egyptian. They practiced the Pharaonic custom of marrying their own sisters. They buried their royalty embalmed in pyramids in traditional Egyptian style. They used Egyptian protocol and titles. In the eighth century B.C.E., they conquered Egypt and ruled it for about a century as the twenty-fifth Pharaonic dynasty. This Kushite dynasty was driven out of Egypt proper only by Assyria around the middle of the seventh century B.C.E.

The Meroitic Empire

Forced back above the lower cataracts of the Nile by the Assyrians and kept there by the Persians, the Napatan kingdom became increasingly isolated and developed in its own distinctive ways. Napata itself was sacked by an Egyptian army in 591 B.C.E. Meroe then became the kingdom's densely populated political and cultural capital. In the sixth century B.C.E., it was the center of a flourishing iron industry, from which iron smelting may first have spread west and south to the sub-Saharan world. Certainly the Kushites traded widely to the west across the Sudan as well as with the Hellenistic world and beyond. The Meroitic state was built on a wide network of internal African as well as external, intercontinental commercial relations. The empire lasted until it was defeated and divided in the fourth century C.E. by Nuba peoples from west of the upper Nile and replaced as the dominant regional power by the rival trading state of Aksum on the Abyssinian plateau.

Culture and Economy The heyday of Meroitic culture was from the mid-third century B.C.E. to the first century C.E. The kingdom was "middleman" for varied African goods in demand in the Mediterranean and Near East: animal skins, ebony and ivory, gold, oils and perfumes, and slaves. The Kushites traded with the Hellenistic-Roman world, southern Arabia, and India. They shipped quality iron to Aksum and the Red Sea, and the Kushite lands between the Nile and the Red Sea were a major source of gold for Egypt and the Mediterranean world. Cattle breeding and other animal husbandry were their economic mainstays along with agriculture. Cotton cultivation in Kush preceded that of Egypt and may have been an early export.

Many monuments were built, including royal pyramids and the storied palace and walls of the capital. Meroitic culture is especially renowned for its two kinds of pottery: The first, turned on wheels, was the product of an all-male industry attuned apparently to market demands; the second, made exclusively by hand by women, was largely for domestic use. This latter pottery seems to have come from an older tradition of African pottery craft found well outside the region of Kush—an indication of ancient traditions shared in varied regions of Africa and of the antiquity of African internal trade.

Rule and Administration

The political system of the Meroitic Empire, like the Pharaonic, was evidently stable over many centuries. The king seems to have ruled strictly by customary law. According to Greek accounts, his actions were limited by firm taboos. There was also a royal election system. The priests presented several candidates for king, and from this group the god would choose the new sacred king. The priests apparently considered the king a living god, an idea found in both ancient Egypt and many other African societies.

Royal succession was not from father to son, but within the royal family, often through the maternal rather than the paternal line, which would be in line with the evidence of matrilineal succession as a widespread norm in ancient Africa. The role of the queen mother in the election appears to have been crucial—another parallel to African practices elsewhere. Indeed, the queen mother seems to have adopted formally her son's wife upon his succession. By the second century B.C.E., a woman had become monarch, initiating a long line of queens.

We know very little of Meroitic administration. The empire seems to have been under the autocratic rule of the sovereign, perhaps on the Egyptian model. He or she presided over a central administration run by numerous high officials. The provinces were delegated to princes.

Society and Religion

Because of the limited sources, we have to speculate about the social structure outside the ruling class of monarch and relatives, priests, courtiers, and nobility. We do find mention of slaves, most commonly female domestics, but also male laborers drawn largely from prisoners of war. Cattle breeders, farmers, traders, artisans, and minor government functionaries probably formed an intermediate class or classes between slaves and rulers.

Kushite religious practices followed Egyptian traditions for centuries. To judge from the great temples dedicated to him, Amon was the highest god for the earlier kings. By the third century B.C.E., however, gods unknown to Egypt rose in importance alongside Amon and other Egyptian gods. Most notable was Apedemak, a warrior god with a lion's head. The many lion temples associated with him reflect his importance. Such gods likely represented local deities who gradually rose to take their places alongside the highest Egyptian gods.

Early African Civilizations

ca. 7500–2500 B.C.E.	"Wet Holocene" period
ca. 2500 B.C.E.	Rapid dessication of Saharan region begins
ca. 2000–1000 B.C.E.	Increasing Egyptian influence in Nubia
ca. 1000–900 B.C.E.	Kushite kingdom with capital at Napata becomes independent of Egypt
751–663 B.C.E.	Kushite kings Piankhi and Taharqa rule all Egypt
ca. 600–500 B.C.E.	Meroe becomes new Kushite capital
ca. 500 B.C.E.–330 C.E.	Meroitic kingdom of Kush (height of Meroitic Kushite power ca. 250 B.C.E.–50 C.E.)
ca. 500 B.C.E.–500 C.E.?	Nok culture flourishes on Jos plateau in western Sudan (modern central Nigeria)
First century C.E.	Rise of Aksum as trading power on Ethiopian (Abyssinian) plateau
ca. 330 C.E.	Aksumite conquest of Kush

The Aksumite Empire

A highland people who had developed their own commercially powerful trading state to the south of Kush delivered the *coup de grâce* to the weakened Kushite Empire, apparently about 330 C.E. This was the newly Christianized state of Aksum, which centered in the northern Ethiopian, or Abyssinian, highlands where the Blue Nile rises. With the ascendancy of Aksum, our sources lapse into relative silence concerning the Nubian regions of the Nile. Not until the rise of new Christian Nubian states in the mid-sixth century can we again find clear evidence of the inheritors of the land of Kush.

The peoples of Aksum were the product of a linguistic, cultural, and genetic mixing of African Kushitic speakers with Semitic speakers from Yemenite southern Arabia. This mixing occurred after southern Arabians settled on the Ethiopian plateau around 500 B.C.E., giving Aksum, and later Ethiopia, Semitic speech and script closely related to South Arabian. Greek and Roman sources attest to the existence of an Aksumite kingdom from at least the first century C.E. By this time, the kingdom, through its chief port of Adulis, had already become the major ivory and elephant market of northeastern Africa.

In the first two centuries C.E., their Red Sea location gave the Aksumites a strategic seat astride the increasingly important Indian Ocean trade routes that linked India and the East Indies, Iran, Arabia, and the East African coast with the Roman Mediterranean. Aksum also controlled trade between the African interior and the extra-African world, from Rome to Southeast Asia—notably exports of ivory, but also of elephants, obsidian, slaves, gold dust, and other inland products.

By the third century C.E., Aksum was one of the most impressive states of its age in the African or western Asian world, as the remains of its major cities—Aksum, Adulis, and Matara—attest. From the late second century onward, the Aksumites often held tributary territories across the Red Sea in southern Arabia. They also gained control of northern Ethiopia and conquered Meroitic Kush. Thus, by the third and fourth centuries they controlled some of the most fertile cultivated regions of the ancient world: their own plateau, the rich Yemenite highlands of southern Arabia, and much of the eastern Sudan across the upper Nile as far as the Sahara.

The resulting empire was ruled by a king of kings in Aksum through tribute-paying vassal kings in the other subject states. Aksum's minting of coinage in gold, silver, and copper (it was the first tropical African state to do so) was a symbol of both its political and economic power. The Aksumites enjoyed a long-lived economic prosperity. Goods of the Roman-Byzantine world and India and Sri Lanka, as well as of neighboring Meroe, flowed into Aksum, and vast herds and good agricultural produce gave a firm base to its prosperity.

In religion, the pre-Christian paganism of Aksum resembled the pre-Islamic paganism of southern Arabia, with various gods and goddesses closely tied to natural phenomena such as the sun, moon, and stars. There is also evidence of Jewish, Meroitic, and even Buddhist minorities living in the major cities of Aksum—an index of its cosmopolitanism.

In an inscription of the powerful fourth-century ruler King Ezana, we read of his conversion to Christianity, which led to the Christianizing of the kingdom as a whole. The conversion of Ezana and his realm was the work of Frumentius, a Syrian bishop of Aksum who served as secretary and treasurer to the king. Subsequently, under Alexandrian influence, the Ethiopian church became Monophysite in doctrine (that is, it adhered to the dogma of the single, unitary nature of Christ). Yet this did not end Aksumite trade with Byzantium, however much Constantinople persecuted Monophysites at home. In the fifth century C.E., the native Semitic language, Ge'ez, began to replace Greek in the liturgy, which proved a major step in the unique development of the Ethiopic or Abyssinian Christian Church over the succeeding centuries.

Isolation of Christian Ethiopia

Aksumite trade continued to thrive through the sixth century, despite the decay of Rome. Strong enough at times to extend to the Yemen, Aksumite power was eclipsed in the end by the rise of Arab Islamic power. Aksum ceased to be a center of foreign trade and became increasingly isolated. Its center of gravity shifted south from the coast to the more rugged parts of the plateau. Here a Monophysite Christian, Ge'ez-speaking culture emerged in the region of modern Ethiopia and lasted in relative isolation until modern times, surrounded largely by Muslim peoples and states.

Ethiopia's northern neighbors, the Christian states of Maqurra and Alwa, also survived for centuries in the former Meroitic lands of the Nilotic Sudan. However, incursions from Muslim Egypt in the fourteenth and fifteenth centuries and Arab migration from about 1300 led ultimately to the Islamization of the whole Nubian region. Ethiopia was left as the sole predominantly Christian state in Africa.

The Western and Central Sudan

Agriculture, Trade, and the Rise of Urban Centers

By the first or second century C.E., settled agriculture, augmented by iron tools, had become the way of life of most inhabitants of the western Sudan; it had even made considerable progress in the forest regions farther south. The savannah areas seem to have experienced a substantial population explosion, especially around major water sources: along the Senegal River, around the great northern bend in the Niger River, and in the Lake Chad basin. Villages, and some chiefdoms consisting of several villages, remained normally the largest political units. As time went on, their growth provided the basis (and need) for the development of larger towns and political units.

Trade was another element that promoted or at least accompanied the eventual rise of larger political entities in the western and central Sudan. Regional and interregional trade networks in the western and central Sudan date to ancient times. Extensive east-west trade connected the western Sahel to Egypt and the Nilotic Sudan. From the western Sahel, this trade connected to Saharan routes and sites to the north (see Map 6–1).

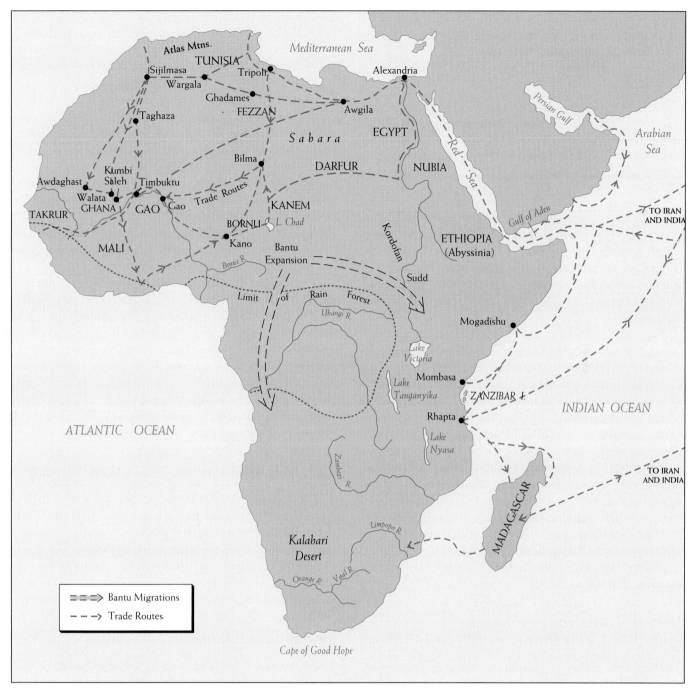

Map 6–1   Africa: Early trade routes and early states of the western and central Sudan.   This map shows some of the major routes of north-south trans-Saharan caravan trade and their links with Egypt and with Sudanic and forest West Africa.

By the latter half of the first millennium B.C.E., substantial urban settlements—such as Gao, Kumbi (or Kumbi Saleh), and Jenne—emerged in the western Sahel. Excavations at Jenne, in the upper Niger (the so-called Inland Delta) indicate that it dates from 250 B.C.E. and that its

population reached more than 10,000 by the late first millennium C.E.[2]

[2]S. K. and R. J. McIntosh, pp. 41–59, 434–461; and R. Oliver, *The African Experience* (1991), p. 90. The ensuing discussion of West African urban settlement is also taken primarily from Oliver, pp. 90–101.

These early urbanized areas were characterized by an economy based on a mix of farming, fishing, and hunting, and all developed in oasis or river regions rich enough to support dense populations and trade. The existence of relatively autonomous settlements made possible rather loose confederations or even widely dispersed imperial networks as time went on.

The introduction of the domesticated camel from the east around the beginning of the Christian era greatly increased the viability of trans-Saharan trade. By the early Christian centuries, the West African settled communities had developed trading centers of considerable importance on their northern peripheries, in the Sahel near the edge of the true desert. Salt and gold were the prime commodities exchanged.

Towns such as Awdaghast, Walata, Timbuktu, Gao, Tadmekka, and Agades were the most famous southern terminals for this trade over the centuries. These centers allowed the largely Berber middlemen who plied the desert routes to cross the ever-dangerous Sahara via oasis stations en route to the North African coasts or even Egypt. Since a typical crossing could take two to three months, this was not an easy means of transporting goods.

Formation of Sudanic Kingdoms in the First Millennium

The first millennium C.E. saw the growth of settled agricultural populations and the expansion of trans-Saharan and other internal trade. These developments coincided with the rise of sizable states in the western and central Sudan. The most important states were located in Takrur on the Senegal River, from perhaps the fifth century, if not earlier; Ghana, between the northern bends of the Senegal and the Niger, from the fifth or sixth century; Gao, on the Niger southeast of the great bend, from before the eighth century; and Kanem, northeast of Lake Chad, from the eighth or ninth century. Each represents the first of a series of large political entities in its region. All continued to figure prominently in subsequent West African history (see Chapter 18).

The states developed by the Fulbe people of Takrur and the Soninke people of Ghana depended on their ability to draw gold for the Saharan trade with Morocco from the savannah region west of the upper Senegal. Of all the sub-Saharan kingdoms of the late first millennium, Ghana was the most famous outside of the region, largely owing to its substantial control of the gold trade. Its people built a large regional empire centered at its capital of Kumbi (or Kumbi Saleh). Inheriting his throne by matrilineal descent, the ruler was treated as a semidivine personage whose interaction with his subjects was mediated by a hierarchy of government ministers. In contrast to the Soninke of Ghana, the Songhai rulers of Gao had no gold trade until the fourteenth century. Unlike its western neighbors, Gao was oriented in its forest trade toward the lower, not the upper, Niger basin and in its Saharan trade toward eastern Algeria, not Morocco.

These states were based on agriculture and settled populations. By contrast, the power of Kanem, on the northwestern side of Lake Chad, originated in the borderlands of the central Sudan and southern Sahara with a nomadic federation of black tribal peoples that persisted long enough for the separate tribes to merge and form a single people, the Kanuri. Their kingdom controlled the southern terminus of perhaps the best trans-Saharan route—that running north via good watering stations to the oasis region of Fezzan in modern central Libya and then to the Mediterranean.

Central, Southern, and East Africa

The African subcontinent is that part of central, southern, and East Africa that lies south of a line from roughly the Niger delta and Cameroon across to southern Somalia on the east coast. Paucity of sources makes it difficult to reconstruct in any detail the history of this region before 1000 C.E. Some relatively certain facts and reasonable hypotheses have, however, emerged from linguistic, archaeological, and other research.

Bantu Migrations and Diffusion

In the southern subcontinent, most people speak one of more than four hundred languages that belong to a single language group known as *Bantu*. All of these languages are as closely related as are the Germanic or Romance tongues of Europe. Although the place of origin and routes of diffusion of Bantu tongues have long been debated, there is increasing consensus that the location of the proto-Bantu language must have been in the region south of the Benue River, in eastern Nigeria and modern Cameroon. Thence, during the later centuries B.C.E. and the first millennium C.E., migrations of Bantu-speaking peoples must have carried their languages in two basic directions: (1) south into the lower Zaïre (Kongo) basin and ultimately to the southern edge of the equatorial

A Tenth-Century Arab Description of the East African Coast

This selection is from the famous Baghdadi scholar, al-Mas'udi, who died in Cairo about 956 C.E. It treats the country of the Zanj, by which he means the coastal region of East Africa from the Horn down to Mozambique, a region that he himself visited on a voyage from Oman.

In what ways does this Muslim observer seem to be critical, and in what ways laudatory, of the East Africans?

The sea of the Zanj reaches down to the country of Sofala and of the Wak-Wak which produces gold in abundance and other marvels; its climate is warm and its soil fertile. It is there that the Zanj built their capital; then they elected a king whom they called *Waklimi*. . . .

The *Waklimi* has under him all the other Zanj kings, and commands three hundred thousand men. The Zanj use the ox as a beast of burden, for their country has no horses or mules or camels and they do not even know these animals. Snow and hail are unknown to them as to all the Abyssinians. Some of their tribes have sharpened teeth and are cannibals. The territory of the Zanj begins at the canal which flows from the Upper Nile and goes down as far as the country of Sofala and the Wak-Wak. Their settlements extend over an area of about seven hundred parasangs in length and in breadth; this country is divided by valleys, mountains and stony deserts; it abounds in wild elephants but there is not so much as a single tame elephant. . . .

Although constantly employed in hunting elephants and gathering ivory, the Zanj make no use of ivory for their own domestic purposes. They wear iron instead of gold and silver. . . .

. . . *Waklimi* . . . means supreme lord; they give this title to their sovereign because he has been chosen to govern them with equity. But once he becomes tyrannical and departs from the rules of justice, they cause him to die and exclude his posterity from succession to the throne, for they claim that in thus conducting himself he ceases to be the son of the Master, that to say of the king of heaven and earth. They call God by the name of Maklandjalu, which means supreme Master. . . .

The Zanj speak elegantly, and they have orators in their own language. . . . These peoples have no code of religion; their kings follow custom, and conform in their government to a few political rules. . . . Each worships what he pleases, a plant, an animal, a mineral.

They possess a great number of islands where the coconut grows, a fruit that is eaten by all the peoples of the Zanj. One of these islands, placed one or two days' journey from the coast, has a Muslim population who provide the royal family. . . .

Translated from the French version of de Meynard and de Courteille (1864) by Basil Davidson, *The African Past* (New York: Grosset and Dunlap, 1967), pp. 108–109.

---

forest in present-day northern Katanga; and (2) east around the equatorial forests into the lakes of highland East Africa.

How the Bantu peoples managed to impose their languages on the earlier cultures of these regions remains unexplained. In any case, Bantu cultures became fully interwoven with those of the peoples among whom they settled. For example, Bantu-Arab mixing on the eastern coasts produced the Swahili culture, which we shall treat in Chapter 18. We find Bantu-speaking peoples as slash-and-burn farmers in the Zaïre River savannah, as cattle herders in the East African high plains, as perennial floodplain cultivators on the Zambezi River, and as terracing and irrigating farmers among the highland Kikuyu and Chagga peoples.

East Africa

The history of East Africa along the coast before Islam differed from that of the inland highlands. Long-distance travel was easy and common along the seashore but less so inland.

The coast had had maritime contact with India, Arabia, and the Mediterranean via the Indian Ocean and Red Sea trade routes from at least as early as the second century B.C.E. By contrast, we know little about the long-distance contacts of inland regions with the coastal areas until after 1000 C.E. Nonetheless, both regional inland and coastal trade must also be ancient. Both coastal and overseas trade remained important and interdependent over the centuries, because the Indian Ocean trade depended on the monsoon winds and could use only the northernmost coastal trading harbors of East Africa for round-trip voyages in the same year. The monsoon winds blow from the northeast from December to March and thus can carry sailing ships south from Iran, Arabia, and India only during those months; they blow from the southwest from April to August, so ships can sail from Africa northeast during those months. Local coastal shipping thus had to haul cargoes from south of Zanzibar and then transfer them to other ships for the annual round-trip voyages to Arabia and beyond.

ca. 1300–1000 B.C.E.	Kushitic-speaking peoples migrate from Ethiopian plateau south along Rift valley
ca. 400 B.C.E.–1000 C.E.	Probable era of major Bantu migrations into central, East, and southeastern Africa
200–100 B.C.E.	East African coast or earlier becomes involved in Indian Ocean trade
ca. 100 B.C.E.	Probable time of first Indonesian immigration to East African coast
ca. 100–1500 C.E.	Nilotic-speaking peoples spread over upper Nile valley; Nilotic peoples spread over Rift valley region

Long-distance trade came into its own in Islamic times—about the ninth century—as an Arab monopoly. However, long before the coming of Islam, trade was apparently largely in the hands of Arabs, many of whom had settled in the East African coastal towns and in Iran and India to handle this international commerce. We have documentation of Greco-Roman contact with these East African centers of Red Sea and Indian Ocean trade from as early as the first century C.E.

The overseas trade was, however, evidently even more international than the earliest sources indicate. Today, Malagasy, the imported Malayo-Polynesian language of Madagascar, points to the antiquity of substantial contact with the East Indies via the coastal trading routes of Asia's ancient southern rim. Evidence of an Indonesian migration even before the beginning of our era is seen in the spread of bananas, coconut palms, and other food crops indigenous to Southeast Asia across the entire African continent as staple foods. Further, as a result of the early regular commercial ties to distant lands of Asia, extra-African ethnic and cultural mixing has long been the rule for the East African coast; even today, its linguistic and cultural traditions are rich and varied (see Chapter 18).

Other African imports included such items as Persian Gulf pottery, Chinese porcelain, and cotton cloth. The major African export good around which the east coast trade revolved was ivory. The slave trade was another major business. Slaves were exported to the Arab and Persian world, as well as to India or China.

The history of inland East Africa south of Ethiopia is much more difficult to trace than that of the coast, again because of the absence of written sources and the immense difficulty of access until relatively recent times. We can, however, use linguistic clues and other evidence to note some key developments in the eastern highlands. These regions had seen an early diffusion of peoples from the north, and

changing conditions of subsistence over the centuries continued to propel movements of small groups into new areas. Of the early migrants from the north, first came peoples speaking Kushitic languages of the Afro-Asiatic family, likely cattle herders and grain cultivators. Perhaps as early as 2000 B.C.E., they pushed from their homeland on the Ethiopian plateau south down the Rift valley as far as the southern end of Lake Tanganyika.

Later, Nilotic-Saharan speakers moved from the southwestern side of the Ethiopian plateau west over the upper Nile valley by about 1000 C.E. Then they pushed east and south, following older Kushite paths, to spread over the Rift valley area by the fifteenth century and subsequently much of the East African highlands of modern-day Uganda, Kenya, and Tanzania. Here they all but completely supplanted their Kushite predecessors. Two of these Nilotic peoples were the Lwo and Maasai. The Lwo spread over a 900-mile-long swath of modern Uganda and parts of southern Sudan and western Kenya. They mixed readily with other peoples, absorbing new cultural elements and adapting to new situations wherever they went. The Maasai, on the other hand, were and still are cattle pastoralists fiercely proud of their separate language, way of life, and cultural traditions. These features have distinguished them sharply from the farming or hunting peoples whose settlements abutted their pasturages at the top of the southern Rift valley in modern Kenya and Tanzania. Here, the Maasai have concentrated and remained.

These migrations from the north and those of the Bantu peoples, who also entered the eastern highlands over many centuries from the west, have made the highlands a melting pot of their immense diversity of languages and cultures. Here, as well as anywhere, we can see the radical diversity of peoples and cultures of the entire African continent mirrored in a single region.

IN WORLD PERSPECTIVE

Africa to ca. 1000 C.E.

Pre-Islamic Africa is often viewed as a relatively isolated landmass that contributed little to political, cultural, and religious developments in the ancient world and was little engaged on the world scene. This view cannot withstand close scrutiny. To begin with, the human species probably originated in Africa. Pharaonic Egypt most notably, but also the Kushite kingdoms of Napata and Meroe and the Ethiopian state of Aksum, were all major political-military powers with highly developed cultures in regular interchange with other lands of the ancient world, from Rome to India and beyond.

Thus, from a world perspective, Africa was engaged with lands far and near from at least the first millennium B.C.E.—in trading, in conflict and cooperation, in religious life, and in cultural life. An active internal trade brought goods from the interior of the continent to the centers of external exchange. In Africa, however, as in much of Eurasia, the imminent coming of the last major world religious and cultural tradition—that of Islam—would affect, redefine, or even eliminate the overt presence of many previous centers of civilization.

Review Questions

1. How has the term "civilization" been interpreted to imply that Africa societies early and late lacked true "civilization"? What is your opinion on this?

2. What are the primary sources for study of Africa to 1000 C.E.? What are their advantages and drawbacks as reliable sources for early African history?

3. Do you find it a problem to think of Africa as a "dark" continent until European voyages of discovery and interior expeditions "discovered" it? Why? Discuss.

4. Discuss the diffusion of peoples and languages in African history. What does it tell us about early African history?

5. How was the political system of the Meroitic Empire similar to and different from that of Egyptian rule?

6. How did Aksum become a Christian state? What effect did it have on relations with Byzantium?

7. What were the most important goods for African internal trade? Which products were traded abroad? What can we learn from these trade patterns?

8. In what ways did geography "control" early African history? What about the specific case of Ghana? Of North Africa? Of the East African littoral? Of southern Africa?

Documents CD-ROM

1. Bumba Vomits the World, Bushongo (Bantu), Zaire

2. Cagn Orders the World, Bushman, and Southern Africa

3. The Separation of God from Man (Krachi), Togo

4. Traditional Songs of Africa

7 CHINA'S FIRST EMPIRE (221 B.C.E.–220 C.E.)

CHAPTER TOPICS

◆ Ch'in Unification of China

◆ Former Han Dynasty (206 B.C.E.–8 C.E.)

◆ Later Han (25–220 C.E.) and Its Aftermath

◆ Han Thought and Religion

In World Perspective China's First Empire

One hallmark of Chinese history is its striking continuity of culture, language, and geography. The Shang and Chou dynasties were centered in north China along the Yellow River or its tributary, the Wei. The capitals of China's first empire were in exactly the same areas, and north China would remain China's political center through history to the present. If Western civilization had experienced similar continuity, it would have progressed from Thebes in the valley of the Nile to Athens on the Nile; Rome on the Nile; and then, in time, to Paris, London, and Berlin on the Nile; and each of these centers of civilization would have spoken Egyptian and written in Egyptian hieroglyphics.

The many continuities of its history, however, did not mean that China was unchanging. One key turning point came in the third century B.C.E. when the old, quasi-feudal, multistate Chou system gave way to a centralized bureaucratic government under the Ch'in. The new centralized state built an empire stretching from the steppe in the north to Vietnam in the south.

The two succeeding Han dynasties each lasted about 200 years, from 206 B.C.E. to 220 C.E. So deep was the impression left by these two dynasties on the Chinese that even today they call themselves the "Han people."

Ch'in Unification of China

Of the territorial states of the late Chou era, none was more innovative and ruthless than the Ch'in. Other states regarded the Ch'in as tough, crude, and brutal, but recognized their formidable strengths.

In 246 B.C.E., the man who would unify China succeeded to the Ch'in throne at the age of thirteen. He is famous as a Legalist autocrat but was also well liked by his ministers, whose advice he usually followed. (See Chapter 2 for a description of Legalism.) In 232 B.C.E., at the age of twenty-seven, he began the campaigns that destroyed the six remaining territorial states. On completing his conquests in 221 B.C.E., he adopted the glorious title we translate as "emperor," to raise himself above the kings of the former territorial states. Then, aided by officials of great talent, this First Ch'in Emperor set about applying to all of China the reforms that had been tried and found effective in his own realm. His accomplishments in the eleven years before his death in 210 B.C.E. were stupendous.

Having conquered the civilized world of north China and the Yangtze River basin, the First Emperor sent his armies to conquer new lands. They reached the northern edge of the

Red River basin in what is now Vietnam. They occupied China's southeastern coast and the area about the present-day city of Canton, and in the north border states built long walls to protect settled lands from incursions by horse-riding raiders. The Ch'in emperor had them joined into a single Great Wall that extended 1,400 miles.

The most significant Ch'in reform extended the Ch'in system of bureaucratic government to the entire empire. The Legalist minister, Li Ssu divided China into forty prefectures, which were further subdivided into counties. The county heads were responsible to prefects, who, in turn, were responsible to the central government. Officials were chosen by ability. Bureaucratic administration was impersonal, based on laws to which all were subject. Furthermore, to ensure the smooth functioning of local government offices, former aristocrats of the territorial states were resettled in the Ch'in capital.

Other reforms further unified the First Emperor's vast domain. Roads were built radiating out from the capital. The emperor decreed a system of uniform weights and measures. He unified the Chinese writing system. He established uniform axle lengths for carts. Even ideas did not escape the drive toward uniformity. Following the precepts of Legalism, the emperor and his advisers collected and burned the books of Confucianism and other schools, and were said to have buried alive several hundred scholars opposed to the Legalist philosophy. Only useful books on agriculture, medicine, or Legalist teachings were spared.

But the Ch'in had changed too much too quickly. After the First Emperor died in 210 B.C.E., intrigues broke out at court and rebellions arose. The dynasty collapsed in 206 B.C.E.

Former Han Dynasty (206 B.C.E.–8 C.E.)

The Dynastic Cycle

Confucian historians of China have seen a pattern in every dynasty of long duration. They call it the *dynastic cycle*. The stages of the cycle are interpreted in terms of the "Mandate of Heaven." The cycle begins with internal wars that eventually lead to the unification of China. Unification is proof

Tomb figure of standing attendant from the Former Han dynasty, second century B.C.E. [The Asia Society, N.Y.: Mr. and Mrs. John D. Rockefeller 3rd Collection]

that Heaven has given the unifier the mandate to rule. Strong and vigorous, the first ruler, in the process of consolidating his political power, restores peace and order. Economic growth follows. The peak of the cycle is marked by public works, energetic reforms, and military expansion. China appears invincible. But then the cycle turns downward. The costs of expansion, coupled with an increasing opulence at the court, place a heavy burden on tax revenues just as they are beginning to decline. The vigor of the monarchs wanes. Intrigues develop. Central controls loosen. Finally, public works fall into disrepair, floods and pestilence occur, rebellions break out, and the dynasty collapses. For Confucian historians, the last emperors in a cycle are morally culpable.

Early Years of the Former Han Dynasty

The first sixty years of the Han may be thought of as the early phase of its dynastic cycle. After the collapse of the Ch'in, one rebel general became the first emperor of the Han dynasty and is known by his posthumous title of Kao Tsu (r. 206–195 B.C.E.). Kao Tsu built his capital at Ch'ang-an, not far from the former capitals of the Western Chou and the Ch'in. Kao Tsu and his immediate successors consciously avoided actions that would remind the populace of the hated Ch'in despotism. They made punishments less severe and reduced taxes. Good government prevailed, the economy rebounded, granaries were filled, and vast cash reserves were accumulated. Later historians often singled out the early Han rulers as model sage emperors.

Han Wu Ti

The second phase of the dynastic cycle began with the rule of Wu Ti, who came to the throne at the age of sixteen and remained there for fifty-four years (141–87 B.C.E.). Wu Ti wielded tremendous personal authority.

Building on the prosperity achieved by his predecessors, Wu Ti initiated new economic policies. A canal was built from the Yellow River to the capital in northwest China, linking the two major economic regions of north China. "Ever level granaries" were established throughout the country so that the surplus from bumper crops could be bought and then resold in time of scarcity. To increase revenues, taxes were levied on merchants, the currency was debased, and some offices were sold. Wu Ti also reestablished government monopolies on copper coins, salt, iron, and liquor. Thereafter, state monopolies became a regular part of Chinese government finance.

Wu Ti also expanded Chinese borders—a policy that would characterize every strong dynasty. His armies swept south into what is today northern Vietnam and northeast across Manchuria to northern Korea.

The principal threat to the Han was from the Hsiung Nu Empire to the north. Their mounted archers could raid China and flee before an army could be sent against them. To combat them, Wu Ti employed the entire repertoire of policies that would become standard thereafter. When possible he "used the barbarian to control the barbarian," making allies of border nomads against those more distant. Allies were permitted to trade with Chinese merchants; they were awarded titles and honors; and their kings were sent Chinese princesses as brides. When this method did not work, he used force. Between 129 and 119 B.C.E., Wu Ti sent several armies of over 100,000 troops into the steppe, destroying Hsiung Nu power south of the Gobi Desert in southern Mongolia. To establish a strategic line of defense aimed at the heart of the Hsiung Nu Empire further to the west, Wu Ti then sent 700,000 Chinese colonists to the arid Kansu panhandle and extended the Great Wall to the Jade Gate outpost at the eastern end of the Tarim Basin. From this outpost, Chinese influence was extended over the rim oases of Central Asia, establishing the Silk Road that linked Ch'ang-an with Rome (see Map 7–1).

Government During the Former Han

Despite its repudiation of the Ch'in and all its works, the Han continued the Ch'in form of centralized bureaucratic administration. Officials were organized by grades and were paid salaries in grain, plus cash or silk. The bureaucracy grew until, by the first century B.C.E., there were more than 130,000 officials for a population that had reached 60 million.

Under the Han dynasty, this "Legalist" structure of government became partially Confucianized. Confucian ideas proved useful. The mandate of Heaven provided an ethical justification for dynastic rule. A respect for old records and the written word fit in well with the vast bookkeeping the empire entailed. The Confucian classics gradually became the standard for education. Confucianism was seen as shaping moral men who would be upright officials, even in the absence of external constraints. For Confucius had taught the transformation of self through ethical cultivation and had presented a vision of benevolent government by men who were virtuous as well as talented. Increasingly, laws were interpreted and applied by men with a Confucian education.

The court during the Han dynasty exhibited features that would appear in later dynasties as well. The emperor was the all-powerful "son of Heaven." The will of a strong adult emperor was paramount. When the emperor was weak, however, or ascended to the throne as a child, others competed to rule in his name. Four contenders for this surrogate role appeared and reappeared through Chinese history: court officials, the empress dowager, court eunuchs, and military commanders.

Court officials staffed the apparatus of government and advised the emperor directly. Apart from the emperor himself, they were usually the most powerful men in China. Yet their position was often precarious. Few officials escaped being removed from office or banished once or twice during their careers.

Of the emperor's many wives, the one whose child was named as the heir to the throne became the empress dowager. Her influence sometimes continued even after her child became an adult emperor. But she was most powerful as a regent for a child emperor.

Court eunuchs were brought to the court as boys, castrated, and assigned to work as servants in the emperor's harem. They were thus in contact with the future emperor from the day he was born, they became his childhood confidants, and they often continued to advise him after he had gained the throne. Emperors found eunuchs useful as counterweights to officials. But to the scholars who wrote China's history, the eunuchs were greedy half-men, given to evil intrigues.

Military leaders, whether generals or rebels, were the usual founders of dynasties. In the later phase of most dynasties, regional military commanders often became semi-independent rulers. A few even usurped the throne. Yet

The Dynastic History of China's First Empire

256–206 B.C.E.	Ch'in dynasty
206 B.C.E.–8 C.E.	Former Han dynasty
25–220 C.E.	Later Han dynasty

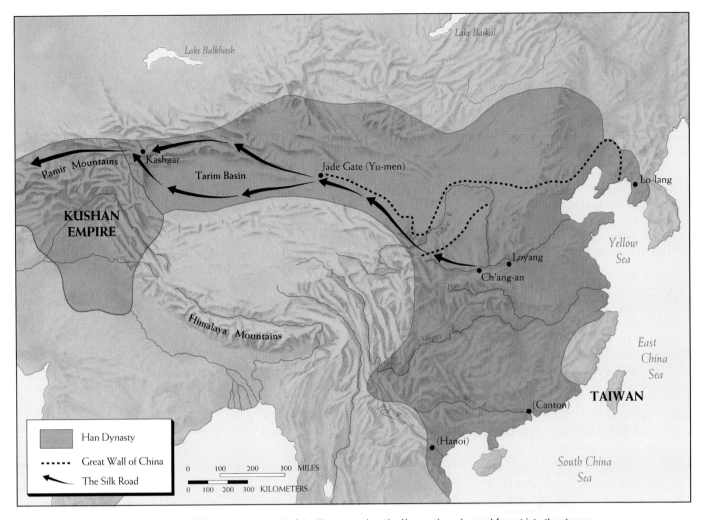

Map 7-1 The Han Empire 206 B.C.E.–220 C.E.   At the peak of the Han expansion, the Han armies advanced far out into the steppe north of the Great Wall and west into Central Asia. The silk road to Rome passed through the Tarim Basin and the Kushan Empire.

they were less powerful at the Chinese court than they were, for example, in imperial Rome, partly because the military constituted a separate category, lower in prestige than the better-educated civil officials. The court also took great pains to prevent its generals from establishing a base of personal power.

Another characteristic of government during the Han and subsequent dynasties was that its functions were limited. It collected taxes, maintained military forces, administered laws, supported the imperial household, and carried out public works. But government in a district that remained orderly and paid its taxes was left largely in the hands of local notables and large landowners.

Decline and Usurpation

During the last decade of Wu Ti's rule in the early first century C.E., military expenses ran ahead of revenues. His successor cut back on military costs, eased economic controls, and reduced taxes. But large landowners began to avoid paying taxes. State revenues declined. The tax burden on smaller landowners and free peasants grew heavier. In 22 B.C.E., rebellions broke out in several parts of the empire. At the court, too, a decline set in. There was a succession of weak emperors. Even officials began to sense that the dynasty no longer had the approval of Heaven.

Many at the court urged Wang Mang, the regent for the infant emperor and the nephew of an empress, to become the emperor and begin a new dynasty. Wang Mang accepted in 8 C.E. He drew up a program of sweeping reforms based on ancient texts. He was a Confucian, yet relied on new institutional arrangements rather than moral reform to improve society. He revived ancient titles, expanded state monopolies, abolished private slavery (about 1 percent of the population), made loans to poor peasants, and then moved to confiscate large private estates.

Pan Chao's Admonitions for Women

Pan Chao (45–116 C.E.) was the sister of the famous historian Pan Ku. Her guide to morality, Admonitions for Woman, *was widely used during the Han Dynasty. Humility is one of the seven womanly virtues about which she wrote; the others are resignation, subservience, self-abasement, obedience, cleanliness, and industry.*

Given the range of female personalities in Chinese society, what are some of the likely responses to this sort of moral education? Are self-control and self-discipline more likely to be associated with weakness or with strength of character?

Humility

In ancient times, on the third day after a girl was born, people placed her at the base of the bed, gave her a pot shard to play with, and made a sacrifice to announce her birth. She was put below the bed to show that she was lowly and weak and should concentrate on humbling herself before others. Playing with a shard showed that she should get accustomed to hard work and concentrate on being diligent. Announcing her birth to the ancestors showed that she should focus on continuing the sacrifices. These three customs convey the unchanging path for women and the ritual traditions.

Humility means yielding and acting respectful, putting others first and oneself last, never mentioning one's own good deeds or denying one's own faults, enduring insults and bearing with mistreatment, all with due trepidation. Industriousness means going to bed late, getting up early, never shirking work morning or night, never refusing to take on domestic work, and completing everything that needs to be done neatly and carefully. Continuing the sacrifices means serving one's husband-master with appropriate demeanor, keeping oneself clean and pure, never joking or laughing, and preparing pure wine and food to offer to the ancestors.

There has never been a woman who had these three traits and yet ruined her reputation or fell into disgrace. If a woman loses these three traits, she will have no name to preserve and will not be able to avoid shame.

Reprinted with the permission of The Free Press, A Division of Simon & Schuster, Inc. From *Chinese Civilizations: A Sourcebook* by Patricia Buckley Ebrey. © 1993 by Patricia Buckley Ebrey.

These reforms, however, alienated many. Merchants disliked the monopolies. Large landowners resisted the expropriation of their lands. The Yellow River overflowed its banks, destroying the northern Chinese irrigation system. Poor harvests produced famines. The Hsiung Nu overran China's northern borders. In 23 C.E., rebels attacked Ch'ang-an, and Wang Mang was killed and eaten by rebel troops. Internal wars continued in China for two more years, until a rebel army leader, originally a large landowner, emerged triumphant in 25 C.E. Because he was from a branch line of the imperial family, his new dynasty was viewed as a restoration of the Han.

Later Han (25–220 C.E.) and Its Aftermath

First Century

The founder of the Later Han moved his capital east to Loyang. Under the first emperor and his two successors, there was a return to strong central government and a laissez-faire economy. Agriculture and population recovered. By the end of the first century C.E., China was as prosperous as it had been during the good years of the Former Han.

South China and Vietnam were retaken. In 89 C.E., Chinese armies crossed the Gobi Desert and defeated the northern Hsiung Nu. This defeat sparked the migrations, some historians say, that brought the Hsiung Nu to the southern Russian steppes and then, in the fifth century C.E., to Europe, where they were known as the Huns of Attila. In 97 C.E., a Chinese general led an army to the Caspian Sea. The Chinese expansion in inner Asia, coupled with more lenient policies toward merchants, facilitated the caravans that carried Chinese silk across the Tarim Basin to Iran, Palestine, and Rome.

Decline During the Second Century

Until 88 C.E., the emperors of the Later Han were vigorous; afterward they were ineffective and short lived. In the countryside, large landowners harbored private armies. Farmers on the estates of the mighty were reduced to serfs. The landowners used their influence to avoid taxes. The remaining freeholders paid ever heavier taxes and labor services. In 184 C.E., rebellions broke out against the government. Han generals suppressed the rebellions but stayed on to rule in the provinces they had pacified. In 220 C.E., they deposed the last Han emperor.

Aftermath of Empire

For more than three and a half centuries after the fall of the Han, China was disunited. Chinese history during the post-Han centuries had two characteristics. The first was the dominant role played by the great aristocratic landowning families. With vast estates, huge numbers of serfs, fortified manor houses, and private armies, they were beyond the control of most governments. The second was that northern and southern China developed in different ways.

In the south, there followed a succession of ever weaker dynasties with capitals at Nanking. Although these six southern states were called dynasties—and the entire period of Chinese history from 220 C.E. to 589 C.E. is called the Six Dynasties era after them—they were in fact short-lived kingdoms. The main developments in the south were (1) continuing economic growth and the emergence of Nanking as a thriving center of commerce; (2) the ongoing absorption of tribal peoples into Chinese society and culture; (3) large-scale immigrations of Chinese fleeing the north; and (4) the spread of Buddhism and its penetration to the heart of Chinese culture.

In the north, state formation depended on the interaction of nomads and Chinese. During the Han dynasty, Chinese invasions of the steppe had led to the incorporation of semi-Sinicized Hsiung Nu as the northernmost tier of the Chinese defense system—just as Germanic tribes had acted as the teeth and claws of the late Roman Empire. But as the Chinese state weakened, the highly mobile nomads began to invade China. The short-lived states that they formed are usually referred to as the "Sixteen Kingdoms." Most spoke Altaic languages: the Hsien Pi (proto-Mongols), the Toba (proto-Turks), and the Juan Juan (who would later appear in eastern Europe as the Avars). But differences of language and stock were less important than these tribes' similarities:

1. All began as steppe nomads.

2. All became at least partially Sinicized.

3. All were involved in wars—among themselves, against southern dynasties, or against conservative steppe tribes that resisted Sinicization.

4. Buddhism was as powerful in the north as in the south. As a universal religion, it acted as a bridge between "barbarians" and Chinese—just as Christianity was a unifying force in post-Roman Europe. The barbarian rulers of the north were especially attracted to its magical side. Usually Buddhism was made the state religion.

Han Thought and Religion

Poems describe the splendor of Ch'ang-an and Loyang; today little remains of the grandeur of the Han. Only from the pottery, bronzes, musical instruments, gold and silver jewelry, lacquerware, and clay figurines that were buried in tombs do we gain an inkling of the rich material culture of the Han period. And only from paintings on the walls of tombs do we know of its art.

But a wealth of written records conveys the sophistication and depth of Han culture. Perhaps the two most important areas were philosophy and history.

Han Confucianism

A major accomplishment of the early Han was the recovery of texts that had been lost during the Ch'in persecution of scholars. In 51 B.C.E. and again in 79 C.E., councils were held to determine the true meaning of the Confucian classics. In 175 C.E., an approved, official version of the texts was inscribed on stone tablets.

In about 100 C.E., the first dictionary was compiled. Containing about 9,000 characters, it helped promote a uniform system of writing. In Han times, as today, Chinese from the north could not converse with Chinese from the southeastern coast. But a common written language bridged differences of pronunciation, contributing to Chinese unity.

It was also in Han times that scholars began writing commentaries on the classics, a major scholarly activity throughout Chinese history. Scholars learned the classics by heart and used classical allusions in their writing.

Han philosophers also extended Chou Confucianism by adding to it the teachings of cosmological naturalism. Chou Confucianists had assumed that the moral force of a virtuous emperor would not only order society but also harmonize nature. Han Confucianists explained why. Tung Chung-shu (ca. 179–104 B.C.E.), for example, held that all nature was a single, interrelated system. Just as summer always follows spring, so does one color, one virtue, one planet, one element, one number, and one officer of the court always take precedence over another. All reflect the systematic workings of yang and yin and the five elements. And just as one dresses appropriately to the season, so was it important for the emperor to choose policies appropriate to the sequences inherent in nature. If he acted in accord with Heaven's natural system, all would go well. But if he acted inappropriately, then Heaven would send a portent as a warning. If the portent was not heeded, misfortunes would follow. It was the Confucian scholars, of course, who claimed to understand nature's messages and advised the emperor.

Han philosophy represented a new effort by the Chinese to encompass and comprehend the interrelationships of the natural world. This effort led to inventions like the seismo-graph and to advances in astronomy, music, and medicine. It was also during the Han that the Chinese invented paper, the wheelbarrow, the stern-post rudder, and the compass.

History

The Chinese were the greatest historians of the premodern world, and what they wrote was usually accurate. Why the Chinese were so history-minded has been variously explained: because the Chinese tradition is this-worldly; because Confucianists were scholarly and their veneration for the classics carried over to the written word; because history was seen as a lesson book for statesmen, and thus a necessity for the literate men who operated the centralized Chinese state.

The practice of using actual documents and firsthand accounts of events began with Ssu-ma Ch'ien (d. 85 B.C.E.), who wrote a history of the known world from the most ancient times down to the age of the emperor Wu Ti. A second great work, *The Book of the Han*, was written by Pan Ku (d. 92 C.E.). It applied the analytical schema of Ssu-ma Ch'ien to a single dynasty, the Former Han, and established the pattern by which each dynasty wrote the history of its predecessor.

Neo-Taoism

As the Han dynasty waned, the effort to realize the Confucian ethic in the sociopolitical order became increasingly difficult. Some scholars abandoned Confucianism altogether in favor of Neo-Taoism, or "mysterious learning," as it was called. Other scholars, defining the natural as the pleasurable, withdrew from society to engage in witty "pure conversations." They discussed poetry and philosophy, played the lute, and drank wine.

Another concern of Neo-Taoism was immortality. Some sought it in dietary restrictions and Yoga-like meditation, some in sexual abstinence or orgies. Others, seeking elixirs to prolong life, dabbled in alchemy. The schools of alchemy are credited with the discovery of medicines, dyes, glazes, and gunpowder.

Meanwhile, among the common people, there arose popular religious cults that, because they included the Taoist classics among their sacred texts, are also called Neo-Taoist. Like most folk religions, they contained an amalgam of beliefs, practices, and superstitions. They had a pantheon of gods and immortals and taught that the good or evil done in this life would be rewarded or punished in the innumerable heavens or hells of an afterlife. These cults had priests, shamans who practiced faith healing, seers, and sorceresses. For a time, they also had hierarchical church organizations, but these were discontinued at the end of the second century C.E. Local Taoist temples and monasteries, however, continued until modern times. With many Buddhist accretions, they furnished the religious beliefs of the bulk of the Chinese population. Even today, these sects continue in Taiwan and Chinese communities in Southeast Asia.

Buddhism

Central Asian missionaries brought Buddhism to China in the first century C.E. It was at first viewed as a new Taoist sect because early translators used Taoist terms to render Buddhist concepts. In the second century B.C.E., confusion about the two religions led to the very Chinese view that Lao-tzu had gone to India, where the Buddha had become his disciple, and that Buddhism was the Indian form of Taoism.

Then, as the Han sociopolitical order collapsed in the third century C.E., Buddhism spread rapidly. We are reminded of the spread of Christianity at the end of the Roman Empire. Although an alien religion in China, Buddhism had some advantages over Taoism:

1. It was a doctrine of personal salvation, offering several routes to that goal.

2. It upheld high standards of personal ethics.

3. It had systematic philosophies, and during its early centuries in China, it continued to receive inspiration from India.

4. It drew on the Indian tradition of meditative practices and psychologies, which were the most sophisticated in the world.

By the fifth century C.E., Buddhism had spread over all of China. Occasionally it was persecuted by Taoist emperors, but most courts supported Buddhism. Temples and monasteries abounded. There were communities of women as well as of men. Chinese artists produced Buddhist painting and sculpture of surpassing beauty, and thousands of monk-scholars labored to translate sutras and philosophical treatises. Chinese monks went on pilgrimages to India.

A comparison of Indian and Chinese Buddhism highlights some distinctive features of its spread. Buddhism in India had begun as a reform movement. Followers were to forego speculative philosophies and elaborate metaphysics, and learn the simple truths of Buddhism: Life is suffering, the cause of suffering is desire, death does not stop the endless cycle of birth and rebirth; only the attainment of *nirvana* releases one from the "wheel of *karma*." Thus, in this most otherworldly of the world's religions, all of the cosmic drama of salvation was compressed into the single figure of the Buddha meditating under the Bodhi tree. Over the centuries, however, Indian Buddhism developed contending philosophies and conflicting sects and, having become virtually indistinguishable from Hinduism, was reabsorbed after 1000 C.E.

In China, there were a number of sects with different doctrinal positions. But the Chinese genius was more syncretic. It took in the sutras and meditative practices of early Buddhism. It took in the Mahayana philosophies that depicted a succession of Buddhas, cosmic and historical, past and future, all embodying a single ultimate reality. It also took in the sutras and practices of Buddhist devotional sects. Finally, in the T'ien-t'ai sect, the Chinese joined together these various elements as different levels of a single truth. Thus, the monastic routine of a T'ien-tai monk would include reading sutras, sitting in meditation, and also practicing devotional exercises.

Socially, too, Buddhism adapted to China. Ancestor worship demanded heirs to perform the sacrifices. Without progeny, ancestors might become "hungry ghosts." Hence, the first son would be expected to marry and have children, whereas the second son, if he were so inclined, might become a monk. The practice also arose of holding Buddhist masses for dead ancestors. Still another difference between China and India was the more extensive regulation of Buddhism by the state in China. Just as Buddhism was not to injure the family, so Buddhism was not to reduce the taxes paid on land. As a result, limits were placed on the number of monasteries, nunneries, and monastic lands, and the state had to give its permission before men or women abandoned the world to enter a religious establishment.

IN WORLD PERSPECTIVE
China's First Empire

Were there world-historical forces that produced at roughly the same time great empires in China, India, and the Mediterranean? Certainly there were similar features in these empires. All three came after revolutions in thought. The Han built on Chou thought (it would be hard to imagine the Han bureaucratic state without Legalism and Confucianism), just as Rome used Greek thought, and the Mauryan Empire used Buddhist thought. In each case, the conception of a universal political authority sustaining the empire derived from earlier philosophies. All three were Iron Age empires, joining their respective technologies with new organizational techniques to create superb military forces.

The differences between the empires are also instructive. Take China and Rome. In China the pervasive culture—the only higher culture in the area—was Chinese, even before the first empire arose. Thus, cultural unity had paved the way for political unity.

In contrast, the polyglot empire of Rome encompassed different peoples, including older civilizations. The genius of Rome, in fact, was to fashion a government and a set of laws that could contain its cultural diversity. Geographically, however, Rome had an easier time of it, for the Mediterranean offered direct access to most parts of the empire and was a thoroughfare for commerce. China, in contrast, was largely landlocked. It was composed of several regional economic units, each of which, located in a segment of a river basin separated from the others by natural barriers, looked inward. It was the genius of Chinese administration to overcome physical and spatial barriers, and integrate the country politically.

A second difference was that government in Han China was more orderly, more complex, and more competent than that of Rome. For example, civil officials controlled the Chinese military almost until the end, whereas in later Roman times, emperor after emperor was set on the throne by the army or the Praetorian Guard. The Roman empire was not a Chinese-type, single-family dynasty.

A third salient difference was in the military dynamics of the two empires. Roman power was built over centuries. Its history is the story of one state growing in power by steady increments, imposing its will on others, and gradually piecing together an empire. China, in contrast, remained a multistate system right up to 232 B.C.E., and then, in a sudden surge, was unified by one state in eleven years. The greater dynamism of China during the first empire can be explained, perhaps, by the greater military challenge it faced across its northern border: an immense Hunnish nomadic empire. Because the threat was more serious than that posed to Rome by any European barbarian enemy, the Chinese response was correspondingly massive.

Review Questions

1. How did Legalism help the Ch'in unify China? What other factors played a part? What were the main features of Ch'in administration? Why did the Ch'in collapse?

2. What was the "dynastic cycle"? In what sense was it a Confucian moral rationalization? Was a cycle of administrative and military decline especially true of Chinese government, or can we see the same pattern elsewhere?

3. Who were the players who sought power at the Han court? Did the means they used reflect the difference in their positions?

4. Did Buddhism "triumph" in China in the same sense in which Christianity triumphed in the Roman world? Compare China to the Roman Empire. What problems did both empires face and how did they try to resolve them?

Documents CD-ROM

1. The Yellow Emperor, *Nei-ching (Canon of Medicine)*

2. Song Yu, *On the Wind*

3. Anonymous Folk Songs from the Music Bureau

4. Sima Qian: The Historian's Historian Writes about The Builder of the Great Wall

5. Cai Yan, from *18 Verses Sung to a Tatar Reed Whistle*

6. Zhang Heng, *The Bones of Chuang Tzu*

CONSOLIDATION AND INTERACTION OF WORLD CIVILIZATIONS

Between 500 and 1500, the major civilizations of the world shaped themselves politically and culturally in new and lasting ways. China survived barbarian conquests and three centuries of political fragmentation to reestablish a united empire in 589. The Chinese emperor became more absolute and Chinese government evolved into an imperial bureaucracy based on a civil-service elite. Chinese culture became conservative and inward looking.

In Japan, tribal aristocracies gave way first to the Chinese model of centralized government and then to a Japanese form of military rule by feudal warriors. The same centuries during which these changes occurred were Japan's age of faith, centering on Pure Land and Zen Buddhism.

In the seventh century, the new faith and culture of Islam preached by Muhammad emerged in Arabia. His Arab successors swept over the area from Spain to the Indus Valley within a century. Muslim traders, missionaries, and Turkish and Mongol peoples expanded the presence of Islam still further.

In Africa, this period witnessed the rise of regional empires. The centuries-old trans-Saharan trade routes promoted increased commercial traffic, and interchanges in people and ideas. After 1000, Islam penetrated across the Sahara, and east Africa became part of an international trade network that reached to Indonesia and China.

In Iran, the Sasanids proved easy prey to the Arab armies of Islam. Persian language and culture persisted, however, and enriched Islamic civilization.

In India, Hindu tradition and the caste system gained the general shape they have today, but by 1500 Islam was an important part of the Indian scene.

Western Europe survived barbarian and Muslim invasions to become an aggressor itself in Byzantium and the Near East. While emperor and pope struggled with each other, "national" monarchies emerged in northern Europe, which developed into diverse and competitive nation-states.

500 C.E.–800

511 Death of Clovis, Frankish ruler of Gaul
529 Benedict of Nursia founds Benedictine Order
590–604 Pontificate of Gregory I, "the Great"
768–814 Charles the Great (Charlemagne)

527–565 Justinian's reign
531–579 Reign of Chosroes Anosharvian in Iran
ca. 570-632 Muhammad
622 The Hijra
616–657 Reign of Harsha; neo-Gupta revival in India
651 Death of last Sasanid ruler
ca. 710 First Muslim invasion of India
661–750 Umayyad dynasty
680 Death of Al-Husayn at Karbala; second civil war begins
750–1258 Abbasid dynasty
786–809 Caliph Harun Al-Rashid reigns

Crown of the
Holy Roman Emperor (Kunsthistorisches Museum Wien)

800–1100

ca. 800–1000 Invasions of England and the Carolingian Empire (Vikings, Magyars, and Muslims)
843 Treaty of Verdun divides Carolingian Empire
910 Cluny Monastery founded
1019–1054 Yaroslav the wise reigns; peak of Kievan Russia
1054 Schism between Latin and Greek churches
1066 Norman conquest of England
1073–1085 Investiture controversy
1096–1270 The Crusades

800–1200 Period of "feudal" overlordship in India
900–1100 Golden Age of Muslim learning
909–1171 Fatimids in North Africa and Egypt
945–1055 Buyid rule in Baghdad
994–1186 Ghaznavid rule in northwestern India, Afghanistan, and Iran
1055–1194 Seljuk rule in Baghdad
1071 Seljuk Turks capture Jerusalem
1081–1118 Byzantine emperor Alexius Comnenus reigns
ca. 1000–1300 Turko-Afghan raids into India

1100–1300

1154–1158 Frederick Barbarosa invades Italy
1182–1226 St. Francis of Assisi
1198–1216 Pontificate of Innocent III
ca. 1100–1300 Growth of trade and towns
1215 Magna Carta granted
ca. 1225–1274 St. Thomas Aquinas
1265–1321 Dante Alighieri

1174–1193 Saladin reigns
1192 Muslim conquerors end Buddhism in India
1206–1526 Delhi Sultanate in India; Indian culture divided into Hindu and Muslim
ca. 1220 Mongol invasions of Iran, Iraq, Syria, India
1258 Hulagu Khan, Mongol leader, conquers Baghdad
1260–1335 Il-Khans rule Iran

1300–1500

1337 Hundred Years' War begins
ca. 1340–1400 Geoffrey Chaucer
1347–1349 The Black Death
1375–1527 The Italian Renaissance
1485 Battle of Bosworth Field; accession of Henry Tudor to the throne of England
1492 Columbus's first voyage to the New World

1250–1517 Mamluk rule in Egypt
1366–1405 Timur (Tamerlane) reigns
1405–1494 Timurids rule in Transoxiana and Iran
1453 Byzantine Empire falls to the Ottoman Turks, with capture of Constantinople

589–618 Sui dynasty reunifies China
607 Japan begins embassies to China
618–907 T'ang dynasty in China
701–762 Li Po, T'ang poet
710–784 Nara court, Japan's first permanent capital
712 *Records of Ancient Matters*, in Japan
713–756 Emperor Hsuan Tsung reigns in China
755 An Lu-shan rebellion in China
794–1185 Heian (Kyoto) court in Japan

ca. 500 States of Takrur and Ghana founded
ca. 500–700 Political and commercial ascendancy of Aksum (Ethiopia)
ca. 600–1500 Extensive slave trade from sub-Saharan Africa to Mediterranean
ca. 700–800 Ghanians begin to supply gold to Mediterranean
ca. 700–900 States of Gao and Kanem
ca. 800 Appearance of the Kanuri people around Lake Chad

ca. 150–900 Classic period. Dominance of Teotihuacán in central Mexico, Tikal in southern Yucatán

Stela at Aksum (Werner Forman Archive/Art Resource, N.Y.)

856–1086 Fujiwara dominate Heian court
960–1279 Sung dynasty in China
ca. 1000 *Pillow Book* by Sei Shōnagon and *Tale of Genji* by Murasaki Shikibu
1037–1101 Su Tung-p'o, Sung poet

ca. 800–900 Decline of Aksum
ca. 900–1100 Kingdom of Ghana; capital city, Kumbi Saleh
ca. 1000–1100 Islam penetrates sub-Saharan Africa
1000–1500 "Great Zimbabwe" center of Bantu Kingdom in southeastern Africa

ca. 600–1000 Middle (Huari/Tiwanaku) Horizon in Andean South America

1130–1200 Chu Hsi, Sung philospher
1167–1227 Genghis Khan, founder of Mongol Empire
1185–1333 Kamakura shogunate in Japan
1274, 1281 Mongol invasions of Japan
1279–1368 Mongol (Yuan) dynasty in China

Genghis Khan (Theartarchive)

ca. 1100–1897 Kingdom of Benin of tropical rain forest region
1194–1221 Kanem Empire achieves greatest expansion
1203 Kingdom of Ghana falls to Sosso people
ca. 1230–1450 Kingdom of Mali
1230–1255 King Sundiata, first ruler of Mali Empire; Walata and Timbuktu become centers of trade and culture

ca. 800–1400 Chimu Empire on north coast of Peru

1336–1467 Ashikaga shogunate in Kyoto
1368–1644 Ming dynasty in China
1405–1433 Voyages of Cheng Ho to India and Africa
1467–1568 Warring States era in Japan
1472–1529 Wang Yang-ming, Ming philospher

1307–1332 Mansa Musa, greatest king of Mali
1490s Europeans establish trading posts on western African coast
mid–1400s Decline of Mali Empire; creation of Songhai Empire
1468 Sonni Ali captures Timbuktu
1476–1507 Reign of King Mai Ali of Bornu in central Sudan
1493–1528 Songhai ruler Askia Muhammed reigns; consolidates Songhai Empire

1325 Founding of Aztec capital of Tenochtitlán
1428–1519 Period of Aztec expansion
1492 European encounter with America
1519 Cortes conquers Aztec Empire
ca. 1350–1533 Inca Empire in Peru
1533 Pizarro executes Inca ruler Atahualpa

8 IMPERIAL CHINA (589–1368)

If Chinese dynasties from the late sixth to the mid-fourteenth centuries were given numbers like those of ancient Egypt, the Sui and T'ang dynasties would be called the Second Empire; the Sung, the Third; and the Yuan, the Fourth. Numbers, however, would not convey the distinct personalities of these dynasties. The T'ang (618–907) is everyone's favorite dynasty: open, cosmopolitan, expansionist, exuberant, and creative. It was the example of T'ang China that decisively influenced the formation of states and high cultures in Japan, Korea, and Vietnam. Poetry during the T'ang attained a peak that has not been equaled since. The Sung (960–1279) rivaled the T'ang in the arts; it was China's great age of painting and the most significant period for philosophy since the Chou, when Chinese philosophy began. The

Sung dynasty also witnessed an important commercial revolution. The Yuan (1279–1368) was a short-lived dynasty of rule by Mongols.

Reestablishment of Empire: Sui (589–618) and T'ang (618–907) Dynasties

In the period corresponding to the European early Middle Ages, the most notable feature of Chinese history was the reunification of China. Reunification, as usual, began in the north. The first steps were taken by the Northern Wei (386–534). It moved its court south to Loyang, made Chinese the language of the court, and adopted Chinese dress and surnames. The Northern Wei was followed by several short-lived kingdoms.

The Sui Dynasty

Sui Wen-ti (d. 605), who came to power in 581 and began the Sui dynasty (589–618), displayed great talent. He unified the north, restored the tax base, reestablished a centralized

Imperial China	
589–618	Sui dynasty
618–907	T'ang dynasty
960–1279	Sung dynasty
1279–1368	Yuan (Mongol) dynasty

bureaucratic government, and went on to unify the country. The Great Wall was rebuilt. The Grand Canal was constructed, linking the Yellow and Yangtze Rivers. This canal enabled the northern conquerors to tap the wealth of central and southern China.

The early years of the Second Sui emperor were also constructive, but then, Chinese attempts to meddle in steppe politics led to wars and produced discontent. Natural disasters occurred. The court became bankrupt and demoralized. Rebellions broke out, and once again, there was a free-for-all among the armies of aristocratic military commanders. The winner, and the founder of the T'ang dynasty, was a relative of the Sui empress and a Sino-barbarian aristocrat of the same social background as those who had ruled before him.

The T'ang Dynasty

The first T'ang emperor renamed the Sui capital Ch'ang-an, and made it his own. Within a decade the T'ang had extended its authority over all of China; tax revenues were adequate to government needs; and Chinese armies had begun to push Chinese borders out farther than ever (see Map 8–1). Confucian scholars were employed at the court, Buddhist temples and monasteries flourished, and peace and order prevailed in the land. The years from 624 to 755 were the good years of the dynasty.

Government   The first T'ang emperor and his successors had to reconcile two conflicting sets of interests. On the one hand, the emperor wanted a bureaucratic government in which authority was centralized in his own person. On the other hand, he had to make concessions to the aristocrats who staffed his government and dominated early T'ang society.

The degree to which political authority was centralized was apparent in the organization of the bureaucracy. At the highest level were three organs: Military Affairs, the Censorate, and the Council of State. Military Affairs supervised the T'ang armies, with the emperor, in effect, the commander-in-chief. The Censorate had watchdog functions: It reported instances of misgovernment directly to the emperor and could also remonstrate with the emperor when it considered his behavior improper. The Council of State met daily with the emperor and was made up of the heads of the Secretariat, which drafted policies; the Chancellery, which reviewed them; and State Affairs, which carried them out. Beneath State Affairs were the Six Ministries, which continued as the core of the

During the T'ang dynasty (618–907), well-to-do families placed glazed pottery figurines in the tombs of their dead. Perhaps they were intended to accompany and amuse the dead in the afterlife. Note the fancy chignon hairstyle of this female flutist, one figure in a musical ensemble. Today these figurines are sought by collectors around the world. [Art Resource, N.Y., Werner Forman Archive. Idemitsu Museum of Arts, Tokyo]

central government down to the twentieth century; beneath them was local administration.

Concessions to the aristocratic families were embodied in the tax system. All land was the property of the emperor and was then redistributed to cultivators, who paid taxes in labor and grain. Because all able-bodied adult males received an equal allotment of land (women got less), the land-tax system was called the "equal field system." But aristocrats enjoyed special exemptions and grants of "rank" and "office" lands that, in effect, confirmed their estate holdings.

Most officials were drawn from the aristocracy. Only a tiny percentage were recruited by examinations. Those who passed the examinations were more likely to have brilliant careers. But as only well-to-do families could afford the years of study needed to pass the rigorous examinations, even the examination bureaucrats were usually the able among the noble.

Ch'ang-an   Ch'ang-an was an administrative city that lived on taxes. It was designed to exhibit the power of the emperor and the majesty of his court. At the far north of the city, the palace faced south. In front of the palace was a complex of government offices from which an imposing 500-feet-wide avenue led to the main southern gate. The city was laid out on a north-south, east-west grid. Each block of the city was administered as a ward with interior streets and gates that were locked at night. Enclosed by great walls, the city covered thirty square miles. Its population was over

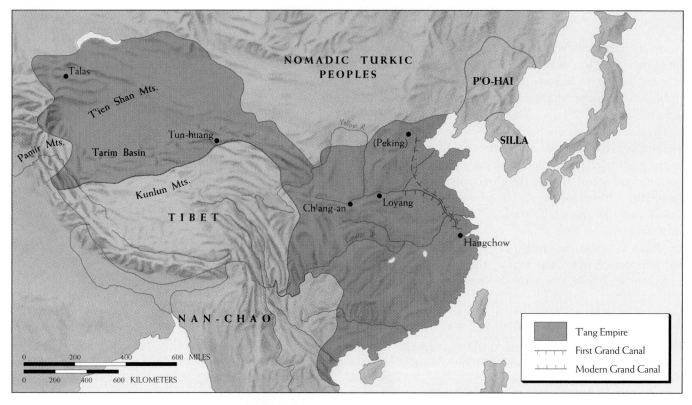

Map 8–1 The T'ang Empire at its peak during the eighth century. The T'ang expansion into Central Asia reopened trade routes to the Middle East and Europe. Students from P'o-Hai, Silla (Korea), and Japan studied in the T'ang capital of Ch'ang-an and then returned, carrying with them T'ang books and technology.

a million: half within the walls, the other half in suburbs—the largest city in the world. (The population of China in the year 750 was about 50 million.) Ch'ang-an was also a trade center from which caravans set out across Central Asia. Merchants from India, Iran, Syria, and Arabia hawked the wares of the Near East and all of Asia in its two government-controlled markets.

The T'ang Empire

A Chinese dynasty is like an accordion, first expanding into the territories of its barbarian neighbors and then contracting back to its core area. The principal threats to the T'ang state were from Tibetans in the west, Turks in the northwest and north, and Khitan Mongols in Manchuria.

To protect their border, the T'ang employed a four-tier policy. When nothing else would work, the T'ang sent armies. But armies were expensive, and using them against nomads was like sweeping back the waves with a broom. A victory might dissolve a tribal confederation, but a decade or two later it would reappear under a new leader. Even during the good years of the T'ang, no final victory was possible.

The second tier of Chinese defenses was to use nomads against other nomads. The critical development for the T'ang was the rise to power of the Uighur Turks. From 744 to 840, the Uighurs controlled Central Asia and were staunch allies of the T'ang. Without their support, the T'ang dynasty would have ended sooner.

A third tier was the defense along China's borders, including the Great Wall. At mid-dynasty, frontier provinces in the north and the northwest were put under military commanders, who came to control the provinces' civil governments. At times their autonomy and potential as rebels were as much a threat to the T'ang court as to the nomadic enemy.

Diplomacy is always cheaper than war. The fourth line of defense was to bring the potential enemy into the empire as a tributary. The T'ang defined the position of "tributary" with great elasticity. It included principalities truly dependent on China; Central Asian states conquered by China; enemy states, when they were not at war with China; the Korean state Silla, which had unified the peninsula with T'ang aid; and wholly independent states, such as Japan. All sent embassies bearing gifts to the T'ang court, which housed and fed them and sent back costly gifts in return.

As the only "developed nation" in eastern Asia, China was a model for countries still forming a state. An embassy gained access to T'ang culture and technology: its philosophy and writing; governmental and land systems; Buddhism; and the arts, architecture, and medicine. Never again would China exert such an influence, for never again would its neighbors be at that formative stage of development.

Rebellion and Decline   From the mid-eighth century, signs of decline began to appear. China's frontiers started to contract. In 751, a T'ang army was defeated by Arabs in western Asia, shutting down China's caravan trade with the West. In 755, a Sogdian general, An Lu-shan, who commanded three Chinese provinces on the northeastern frontier, swept across northern China, capturing Loyang and then Ch'ang-an. The emperor fled to Szechwan.

After a decade of wars and much devastation, a new emperor restored the dynasty with the help of the Uighur Turks, who then looted Ch'ang-an as part of their reward. The century of relative peace and prosperity that followed illustrates the resilience of T'ang institutions. China was smaller, but military governors maintained the diminished frontiers. Provincial governors were more autonomous, but taxes were still sent to the capital. Rebellions were suppressed by imperial armies. Most of the emperors were weak, but reforms were carried out.

Of the reforms of this era, none was more important than that of the land system. The government replaced the equal field system with a tax collected twice a year. The new system, begun in 780, lasted until the sixteenth century. Under it, a fixed quota of taxes was levied on each province. Government revenues from salt and iron surpassed those from land.

During the second half of the ninth century, the government weakened further. By the 880s, warlords had carved all of China into independent kingdoms, and in 907, the T'ang dynasty fell. But the fall of the T'ang did not lead to the centuries of division that had followed the Han. Something had changed within China.

T'ang Culture   The creativity of the T'ang period arose from the juxtaposition and interaction of cosmopolitan, medieval Buddhist, and secular elements. The rise of each of these cultural spheres was rooted in the wealth and the social order of the recreated empire.

T'ang culture was cosmopolitan not just because of its broad contacts with other cultures and peoples, but also because of its openness to them. Commercial contacts were widespread. Foreign goods were vended in Ch'ang-an marketplaces. Communities of central and western Asians were established in the capital, and Arab and Iranian quarters grew up in the seaports of southeastern China. Merchants brought their religions with them. Nestorian Christianity, Zoroastrianism, Manichaeism, Judaism, and Islam entered China at this time.

Central Asian music and musical instruments became so popular as almost to displace the native tradition. T'ang ladies adopted foreign hairstyles. Foreign dramas and acrobatic performances by western Asians could be seen in the streets of the capital. Even among the pottery figurines customarily placed in tombs there were representations of western Asian traders and central Asian grooms, along with those of horses, camels, and court ladies. In T'ang poetry, too, what was foreign was not shunned but judged on its own merits or even presented as exotically attractive.

The T'ang dynasty was the golden age of Buddhism in China. Temples and monasteries were constructed throughout China. Only during the T'ang did China have a "church" establishment that was at all comparable to that of medieval Europe, and even then it was subservient to the T'ang state. Buddhist wealth and learning brought with them secular functions. T'ang temples served as schools, inns, or even bathhouses. They lent money. Priests performed funerals and dispensed medicines.

During the early T'ang, the principal Buddhist sect was the T'ien-t'ai, but after the mid-ninth-century suppression, other sects came to the fore:

1. One devotional sect focused on Maitreya, a Buddha of the future, who will appear and create a paradise on Earth. Maitreya (Mi Lo in Chinese and Miroku in Japanese) was a cosmic messiah, not a human figure. The messianic teachings of the sect often furnished the ideology for popular uprisings and rebellions like the White Lotus, which claimed that it was renewing the world in anticipation of Maitreya's coming.

2. Another devotional or faith sect worshiped the Amitabha (A Mi T'o in Chinese, Amida in Japanese) Buddha, the Lord of the Western Paradise or Pure Land. This sect taught that the Buddha's teachings had become so distorted that only by reliance on Amitabha could humans obtain salvation. All who called on Amitabha with a pure heart and perfect faith would be saved. This sect deeply influenced Chinese popular religion.

3. A third sect, and the most influential among the Chinese elites, is known in China, where it began, as Ch'an and is better known in the West by its Japanese name, Zen. Zen taught that the historical Buddha was only a man and exhorted each person to attain enlightenment by his or her own efforts. Although its monks were often the most learned in China, Zen was anti-intellectual in its emphasis on direct intuition into one's own Buddha-nature. Enlightenment was to be obtained by a regimen of physical labor and meditation. To jolt the monk into enlightenment—after he had been readied by long hours of meditation—some Zen

sects used little problems not answerable by normal ratiocination: "What was your face before you were conceived?" "If all things return to the One, what does the One return to?" "From the top of a hundred-foot pole, how do you step forward?" The discipline of meditation, combined with a Zen view of nature, profoundly influenced the arts in China and subsequently in Korea and Japan.

A third characteristic of T'ang culture was the reappearance of secular scholarship and letters. Most men of letters were also officials, and most high-ranking officials painted or wrote poems. This secular stream of T'ang culture was not ideologically anti-Buddhist. Officials were often privately sympathetic to Buddhism. But as men involved themselves in the affairs of government, their values became increasingly this-worldly.

Court historians of the T'ang revived the Han practice of writing an official history of the previous dynasty. For the first time scholars wrote comprehensive institutional histories and regional and local gazetteers. They compiled dictionaries and wrote commentaries on the Confucian classics. Other scholars wrote ghost stories or tales of adventure. More paintings were Buddhist than secular, but Chinese landscape painting had its origins during the T'ang. Nowhere, however, was the growth of a secular culture more evident than in poetry, the greatest achievement of T'ang letters.

Whether Li Po (701–762) can be called wholly secular is questionable. He might better be called Taoist. But he clearly was not Buddhist. Born in Szechwan, he was exceptional among T'ang poets in never having sat for the civil service examinations, although he briefly held an official post at Ch'ang-an, given in recognition of his poetry. Large and muscular, he was a swordsman and a carouser. Of the 20,000 poems he is said to have composed, 1,800 have survived, and a fair number have titles like "Bring on the Wine" or "Drinking Alone in the Moonlight." According to legend, he drowned while drunkenly attempting to embrace the reflection of the moon in a lake. His poetry is clear, powerful, passionate, and always sensitive to beauty. According to Li Po, life is brief and the universe is large, but this view did not lead him to renounce the world. Rather, he exulted in it, identifying with the primal flux of yin and yang:

I'll wrap this Mighty Mudball of a world all up in a bag
And be wild and free like Chaos itself![1]

---

[1]S. Owen, *The Great Age of Chinese Poetry: The High T'ang.* © 1980, New Haven, CT: Yale University Press, p. 130. Reprinted by permission.

Transition to Late Imperial China: The Sung Dynasty (960–1279)

Most traditional Chinese history was written in terms of the dynastic cycle, and for good reason: The pattern of rise and fall, of expansion and contraction, within each dynasty cannot be denied. Certainly the Sung can be viewed from this perspective. It reunified China in 960, establishing its capital at Kaifeng (see Map 8–2). It ruled for 170 years; this period is called the Northern Sung. Then it weakened. In 1127 it lost the north but for another 150 years continued to rule the south from Hangchow. The Southern Sung fell before the Mongol onslaught in 1279.

But there is more to Chinese history than the inner logic of the dynastic cycle. Longer term changes that cut across dynastic lines were ultimately more important. One such set of changes began during the late T'ang period and continued on into the Sung period, affecting its economy, society, state, and culture. Taken together, these changes help to explain why China after the T'ang did not relapse into centuries of disunity as it had after the Han, and why China would never again experience more than brief intervals of disunity. In this section we will focus on fundamental transformations.

Agricultural Revolution of the Sung: From Serfs to Free Farmers

Landed aristocrats had dominated local society in China during the Sui and the T'ang periods. The tillers of their lands were little better than serfs. Labor service was the heaviest tax, and it created conditions of social subordination.

The aristocracy weakened, however, under the T'ang and after its fall. Estates were divided among male children at each change of generation. Drawn to the capital, the aristocracy became less a landed, and more a metropolitan, elite. After the fall of the T'ang, the aristocratic estates were often seized by warlords. As the aristocracy declined, the claims of those who worked the soil grew stronger, aided by changes in the land and tax systems. With the collapse of the equal field system (described earlier), farmers could buy and sell land and move about as they pleased. Taxes paid in grain gave way during the Sung to taxes in money. The commutation of the labor tax to a money tax gave the farmers more control over their own time. Conscription disappeared as conscript armies gave way to professional armies.

Changes in technology also benefited the cultivator. New strains of an early-ripening rice permitted double cropping. In the Yangtze region, extensive water-control projects were carried out, and more fertilizers were used.

New commercial crops were developed. Tea and cotton became widely cultivated.

The disappearance of the aristocrats also increased the authority of the district magistrate. The Sung magistrate became the sole representative of imperial authority in local society. But as long as taxes were paid and order maintained, affairs were left in the hands of the village elites. So the Sung farmer enjoyed not only a rising income and more freedom, but also substantial self-government.

One other development that began during the Sung—and became vastly more important later—was the appearance of a scholar-gentry class. The typical gentry family contained at least one member who had passed the provincial civil-service examination and lived in the district seats or market towns. Socially and culturally, these gentry were closer to magistrates than to villagers. But they usually owned land in the villages, took a hand in local affairs, and functioned as a buffer between the village and the magistrate's office.

Commercial Revolution of the Sung

Stimulated by changes in the countryside, and contributing to them as well, were demographic shifts, innovative technologies, the growth of cities, the spread of money, and trade.

Emergence of the Yangtze Basin From the late ninth century, the center of gravity of China's population, agricultural production, and culture shifted to the lower and eastern Yangtze region. Between 800 and 1100, the population of the region tripled as China's total population increased to about 100 million. Its rice paddies yielded more per acre than the wheat or millet fields of the north, making rice the tax base of the empire.

New Technology During the Northern Sung, a coal and iron-smelting industry developed in north China that provided China with better tools and weapons and was the most advanced in the world. Printing began in China with the use of carved seals. The earliest woodblock texts appeared in the seventh century, and by the mid-Sung, books printed with movable type were common. Other advances during the Sung were the abacus, the use of gunpowder in grenades and projectiles, and improvements in textiles and porcelains.

Rise of a Money Economy Exchange during the T'ang had been based on silk. During the Northern Sung, large amounts of copper cash were coined, but the demand rose more rapidly than the supply. Beginning in the Southern Sung, silver was minted to complement copper cash. Letters of credit were used by merchants, and various kinds of paper

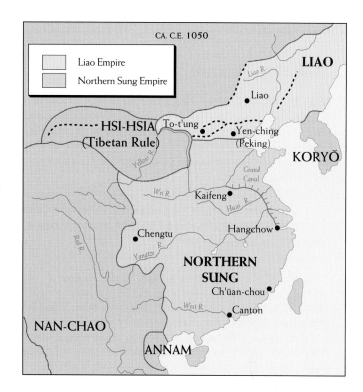

Map 8–2   The Northern Sung and Liao Empires (top) and the Southern Sung and Chin Empires (bottom).   During the Northern Sung, the Mongol Liao dynasty ruled only the extreme northern edge of China. During the Southern Sung, in contrast, the Manchurian Chin dynasty ruled half of China.

"Chaste Woman" Shi

Hung Mai (1123–1202 C.E.) was a collector of stories—fantastic, folkloric, and factual. Unlike the usual Confucian homilies on the proper virtues of women, his stories, and those told by other Sung storytellers reflected the actual diversity of Chinese society. In this story the Chinese belief in ghosts enables the wronged Ning to have a hand in the villain's downfall.

Is the moral of this tale simply that justice ultimately prevails? Can a more complex interpretation be made? What does it say about the dynamics of Sung society?

Ning Six of South Meadow village, in the southern suburbs of Jianchang, was a simple-minded man who concentrated on his farming. His younger brother's wife, Miss Shi, was a little sleeker than her peers. She was also ruthless and licentious, and had an adulterous affair with a youth who lived there. Whenever Ning looked askance at her she would scold him and there was not much he could do.

Once Miss Shi took a chicken, wanting to cook it. When Ning learned of it, he went into her room, demanded that she give it to him, then left with it. Miss Shi quickly cut her arm with a knife, then went to the neighbors screaming, "Because my husband is not home, brother-in-law offered me a chicken and tried to force me to have sex with him. I resisted, threatening to kill myself with the knife I was holding, and so just managed to escape."

Ning at that time had no wife, so the neighbors thought she might be telling the truth. They took them to the village headman, then the county jail. The clerks at the jail reviewed the evidence and demanded 10,000 cash to set things right. Ning was poor and stingy, and moreover, knew himself to be in the right, so stubbornly refused. The clerks sent up the dossier to the prefect Dai Qi. Dai was unable to examine it but noted that it involved an ordinary village wife who was able to protect her virtue and her body and not be violated. The administrative supervisor, Zhao Shiqing, concurred with Qi, and they sent up the case making Ning look guilty. Ning received the death penalty and Miss Shi was granted 100,000 cash, regular visits from the local officials, and a banner honoring her for her chastity. From this, she acquired a reputation as a chaste wife. The local people all realized Ning had been wronged and resented how overboard she had gone.

In the end Miss Shi had an affair with a monk at the nearby Lintian temple. Charges were brought and she received a beating and soon became ill. She saw Ning as a vengeful demon and then died. The date was the sixth month of 1177.

Reprinted with permission of The Free Press, a Division of Simon & Schuster, Inc. from *Chinese Civilization: A Sourcebook* by Patricia Buckley Ebrey. Copyright © 1993 Patricia Buckley Ebrey.

---

money were issued. By 1065, tax receipts paid in money had risen to 38 million strings of cash—in comparison with a mere 2 million in mid-T'ang.

Trade   The growth of trade spurred the demand for money. During the Sung, in the capital and in the economically advanced regions along the Yangtze, cities became the hubs of regional commercial networks, with district seats or market towns serving as the local markets beneath them.

As this transition occurred, cities with more than 100,000 households almost quadrupled in number. Kaifeng is recorded as having 260,000 households—probably more than one million inhabitants—and Hangchow as 391,000 households. Compare these capitals to those of backward Europe: London during the Northern Sung had a population of about 18,000; Rome during the Southern Sung had 35,000; and Paris even a century later had fewer than 60,000.

These Sung capitals spread beyond their outer walls. Their main avenues were lined with shops. Growing wealth also led to a taste for luxury and an increasingly secular lifestyle. Restaurants, theaters, wine shops, and brothels abounded. They catered to traders and rich merchants as well as to officials.

Trade between regions during the Sung was limited mainly to luxury goods. Only where transport was cheap—along rivers, canals, or the coast—was interregional trade in bulk commodities economical.

Foreign trade also reached new heights during the Sung. In the north, Chinese traders bought horses from border states, and sold silks and tea. Along the coast, Chinese merchants took over the port trade. The new hegemony of Chinese merchants was based on improved ships using both sail and oars and equipped with watertight compartments and better rudders. Chinese captains, navigating with the aid of the compass, came to dominate the sea routes from Japan in the north to Sumatra in the south. The content of the overseas trade reflected China's advanced economy: It imported raw materials and exported finished goods.

Government: From Aristocracy to Autocracy

The millennium of late imperial China after the T'ang is often spoken of as China's age of absolute monarchy. Beginning with the Sung, changes occurred that made it easier for emperors to be autocrats.

Sung emperors had direct personal control over more offices than their T'ang predecessors. The emperor could thus prevent bureaucrats from dominating the government. The central government was also better funded, partly because of the growth of population and agricultural wealth, and partly because of government monopolies and taxes levied on trade.

The emperors were also strengthened by the disappearance of the aristocracy. During the T'ang, the emperor had come from the same aristocracy as his ministers. They called him the Son of Heaven, but they knew he was one of them. During the Sung, in contrast, government officials were commoners, mostly products of the examination system. They were separated from the emperor by an enormous social gulf and saw him as a person apart.

Only 10 percent of officials had been recruited by examination during the T'ang; the Sung figure rose to over 50 percent and included the most important officials. The first examination was given at regional centers under close supervision. To ensure impartiality, his answers were recopied and his name replaced by a number before his examination was graded. Only a tiny percentage passed. The second hurdle was the metropolitan examination at the national capital, where the precautions were equally elaborate. Only about 200 a year passed. The average successful applicant was in his mid-thirties. The final hurdle was the palace examination, which rejected a few and assigned a ranking to the others.

To pass the examinations, the candidate had to memorize the Confucian classics, interpret selected passages, write in the literary style, compose poems on themes given by the examiners, and propose solutions to contemporary problems in terms of Confucian philosophy. The quality of the officials produced by the Sung system was impressive. The Chinese examination system continued into the twentieth century. The continuity of Chinese government during this millennium rested on the examination elite, with its common culture and values.

The social base for this examination meritocracy was triangular, consisting of land, education, and office. Landed wealth paid the costs of education. A poor peasant or city dweller could not afford the years of study needed to pass the examinations. Without passing the examinations, official position was out of reach. And without office, family wealth could not be preserved. The Chinese pattern of inheritance led to the division of property at each change of generation. Some families passed the civil-service examinations for sev-

eral generations running. More often, the sons of well-to-do officials did not study as hard as those with bare means. As China had an extended family or clan system, a wealthy official often provided education for the bright children of poor relations.

Merchants had wealth but were despised by scholar-officials as grubby profit seekers and were barred from taking the examinations. Some merchants avoided the system altogether—a thorough education in the Confucian classics did little to fit a merchant's son for a career in commerce. Others bought land for status and security, and their sons became eligible to take the exams. Similarly, a small peasant might become a landlord and educate a son. The system was hierarchical but not closed; nor did it produce a new, self-perpetuating aristocracy.

Sung Culture

Sung culture retained some of the energy of the T'ang while becoming more Chinese. The preconditions for the rich Sung culture were a rising economy, an increase in literacy, and the spread of printing. Sung culture was less aristocratic, less cosmopolitan, and more closely associated with the officials and the scholar-gentry, who were both its practitioners and its patrons. It also was less Buddhist than the T'ang had been. Many Confucians were outspokenly anti-Buddhist and anti-Taoist. In sum, the secular culture of officials became the mainstream during the Sung.

Chinese consider the Sung dynasty the peak of their traditional culture. It was, for example, China's greatest age of pottery and porcelains. It was also an age of great historians. The greatest achievements of the Sung, however, were in philosophy, poetry, and painting.

Philosophy The Sung was second only to the Chou as a creative age in philosophy. A series of original thinkers culminated in the towering figure of Chu Hsi (1130–1200). A brilliant student, he passed the metropolitan examination at the age of eighteen. During his thirties he focused his attention on Confucianism, deepening and making more systematic its social and political ethics by joining to it Buddhist and native metaphysical elements. As a consequence, the new Confucianism became a viable alternative to Buddhism for Chinese intellectuals. Chu Hsi became famous as a teacher, and his writings were widely distributed. His Confucianism remained the standard interpretation used in the civil-service examinations until the twentieth century. If we search for comparable figures in other traditions, we might pick Saint Thomas Aquinas (1224–1274) of medieval Europe or the Islamic theologian al-Ghazali (1058–1111), each of whom produced a new synthesis or worldview that lasted for centuries.

Chu Hsi himself advocated the selection of scholar-officials through schools, rather than by examinations. It is ironic that his teachings became a new orthodoxy that was maintained by the civil-service examinations. Historians argue that Chu Hsi's teachings were a source of stability in late imperial China. Like the examination system, the imperial institution, the scholar-gentry class, and the land system, his interpretation of Confucianism contributed to continuity and impeded change.

Poetry   Sung poets were among China's best. The most famous poet of the Northern Sung was Su Tung-p'o (1037–1101). He was a painter and calligrapher; he practiced Zen and wrote commentaries on the Confucian classics; he superintended engineering projects; and he was a connoisseur of cooking and wine. His life was shaped by politics. He was a conservative, believing in a limited role for government and social control through morality.

Su rose through a succession of posts to become the governor of a province—a position of immense power. While considering death sentences, which could not be carried over into the new year, he wrote

New Year's Eve—you'd think I could go home early
But official business keeps me.
I hold the brush and face them with tears:
Pitiful convicts in chains,
Little men who tried to fill their bellies,
Fell into the law's net, don't understand disgrace.
And I? In love with a meager stipend
I hold on to my job and miss the chance to retire.
Do not ask who is foolish or wise;
All of us alike scheme for a meal.
The ancients would have freed them a while at New
    Year's—
Would I dare do likewise? I am silent with shame.[2]

Painting   In the West, penmanship and painting are separate—one a skill, the other an art. In China, calligraphy and painting are seen as related. A scholar spent his life with brush in hand. The same qualities of line, balance, and strength needed for calligraphy carried over to painting.

Sung painting was varied, but its crowning achievement was landscapes. Sung landscapes are different from those of the West. Each stroke of the brush on silk or paper was final. Mistakes could not be covered up. Each element of a painting was presented in its most pleasing aspect; the painting was not constrained by single-point perspective. Paintings had no single source of illumination with light and shadow but contained an overall diffusion of light. Space was an integral part of the painting. A typical painting might have craggy rocks or pine trees in the foreground, then mist or clouds to create distance, and in the background the outlines of mountains or cliffs fading into space. If human figures appeared at all, they were small, almost unnoticeable. Chinese painting thus reflected the same worldview as Chinese philosophy or poetry. The painter sought to grasp the inner reality of the scene and not be bound up by surface details.

China in the Mongol World Empire: The Yuan Dynasty (1279–1368)

The Mongols created the greatest empire in the history of the world. It extended from the Caspian Sea to the Pacific Ocean; from Russia and Korea to Persia and Burma. Mongol rule in China is one chapter of this larger story.

Rise of the Mongol Empire

The Mongols, a nomadic people, lived to the north of China where they raised horses and herded sheep. Women performed much of the work and were freer than women in China. Families belonged to clans, and clans to tribes. Tribes would gather during the annual migration from the summer plains to winter pasturage. Chiefs were elected—most often from noble lineages—for their courage, military prowess, judgment, and leadership. Politically divided, they traded and warred among themselves and with settled peoples on the borders of their domains.

The founder of the Mongol Empire, Temujin, was born in 1167, the son of a tribal chief. While Temujin was still a child, his father was poisoned. He fled, and after wandering, became chief himself. Through his shrewd policy of alliances and remarkable survival qualities, by the time he was forty, he had united all Mongol tribes and been elected their great khan, or ruler. It is by the title *Genghis Khan* that he is known to history. Genghis possessed an extraordinary charisma, and his sons and grandsons also became wise and talented leaders.

The Mongols, who numbered only about a million and a half, created an army that conquered vastly denser populations. Genghis organized his armies into "myriads" of 10,000 troops, with decimal subdivisions of 1,000, 100, and 10. Elaborate signals were devised so that large units could be manipulated like the fingers of a hand. Mongol tactics were superb: Units would retreat, turn, flank, and destroy their enemies. Genghis's nomadic cavalry had a paralytic effect on the peoples they encountered. Peerless horsemen, the Mongols' most dreaded weapon was the compound bow, short enough to be used from the saddle yet more powerful than the English longbow.

---

[2]Kojiro Yoshikawa, *An Introduction to Sung Poetry*, trans. by Burton Watson (Cambridge: Harvard University Press, Harvard-Yenching Institute Monograph Series, 1967), p. 37.

The troops were astonishingly mobile. Each man carried his own supplies, and they covered vast distances quickly. In 1241, for example, a Mongol army had reached Hungary, Poland, and the shore of the Adriatic. But when word arrived of the death of the great khan, the army galloped back to Mongolia to help choose his successor.

When the army encountered walled cities, it employed siege weapons. The Mongols also used terror as a weapon. Inhabitants of cities that refused to surrender were put to the sword. Large areas in north China and Szechwan were depopulated. Descriptions of the Mongols by the conquered dwell on their toughness and cruelty.

But the Mongols had strengths that went beyond the strictly military. Genghis opened his armies to recruits from the Uighur Turks, the Manchus, and other nomadic peoples. As long as they complied with military discipline, they could participate in his triumphs. In 1206, Genghis promulgated laws designed to prevent the normal wrangling and warring between tribes that would undermine his empire. Genghis also obtained thousands of pledges of personal loyalty from his followers, and he appointed these "vassals" to command his armies and staff his government. This policy countered the divisive effect of tribal loyalties. The Mongol conquests were all the more impressive in that, unlike the earlier Arab expansion, they lacked the unifying force of religious zeal.

Genghis divided his far-flung empire among his four sons. Over several generations, each of the four khanates became independent. The khanate in central Asia remained nomadic. A second khanate ruled Russia. The third was in Persia, and the fourth, led by those who succeeded Genghis as great khans, centered first in Mongolia and then in China.

Mongol Rule in China

The standard theory used in explaining Chinese history is the dynastic cycle. A second theory explains Chinese history in terms of the interaction between the settled people of China and the nomads of the steppe. When strong states emerged in China, their wealth and population enabled them to expand militarily onto the steppe. But when China was weak, as was more often the case, the steppe peoples overran China.

From the start of the Mongol pursuit of world hegemony, the riches of China were a target. But Genghis first disposed of the Tibetan state to the northwest of China and then the Manchu state of Chin that ruled north China. Mongol forces took Peking in 1227, the year Genghis died. They went on to take Loyang and the southern reaches of the Yellow River in 1234, and all of north China by 1241.

Kublai, a grandson of Genghis, was chosen as the great khan in 1260. In 1264, he moved his capital from Mongolia to Peking. Only in 1271 did he adopt a Chinese dynastic name

and go to war with the Southern Sung. The last Sung stronghold fell in 1279.

Kublai Khan's rule in Peking reflected the mixture of cultural elements in Mongol China. From Peking, Kublai ruled as a Chinese emperor. He adopted the Chinese custom of hereditary succession. He rebuilt Peking as a walled city in the Chinese style. But as it was far to the north of any previous capital; to provision it, he had the Grand Canal extended. From Peking, Kublai could look out onto Manchuria and Mongolia and maintain ties with the other khanates. The city proper was for the Mongols. Chinese were segregated in an adjoining walled city. Kublai also maintained a summer palace in Inner Mongolia, where he could hawk and ride and hunt in Mongol style.

Early Mongol rule in northern China was rapacious and exploitative, but it later shifted toward Chinese forms of government and taxation, especially in the south and at the local level. Because it was a foreign military occupation, civil administration was highly centralized, accelerating the trend toward absolutism that had started during the previous dynasty.

About 400,000 Mongols lived in China during the Yuan period. For such a tiny minority to control the Chinese, it had to stay separate. One measure was to make military service a monopoly of Mongols and their nomadic allies. Garrisons were established throughout China. Military officers were regarded as more important than civil officials. A second measure was to use ethnic classifications in appointing civil officials. Mongols held the top civil and military posts. The second category included Persians, Turks, and other non-Chinese, who were given high civil posts. The third category was the northern Chinese, including Manchus and other border peoples, and the fourth was the southern Chinese.

The net result was an uneasy symbiosis. Chinese officials directly governed the Chinese populace, collecting taxes, settling disputes, and maintaining the local order. Without their cooperation, Mongol rule in China would have been impossible. The Mongols, concentrated in large cities and garrisons, usually did not bother to learn Chinese. Communication was through interpreters.

Foreign Contacts and Chinese Culture

Diplomacy and trade within the greater Mongol Empire brought China into contact with other higher civilizations for the first time since the T'ang period. Persia and the Arab world were especially important. The Arab communities in Canton and other ports were larger than they had been during the Sung. Camel caravans carrying silks and ceramics left Peking for Baghdad. Chinese communities became established in Tabriz, the center of trading in western Asia, and in Moscow and Novgorod. Knowledge of printing, gunpowder, and Chinese medicine spread to western Asia.

In Europe, knowledge of China was transmitted by the Venetian trader Marco Polo, who said he had served Kublai as an official between 1275 and 1292. His book, *A Description of the World*, was translated into most European languages. Many readers doubted that a land of such wealth and culture could exist so far from Europe, but the book excited an interest in geography. When Christopher Columbus set sail in 1492, his goal was to reach Polo's Zipangu (Japan).

Other cultural contacts were fostered by the Mongol toleration or encouragement of religion. Nestorian Christianity reentered China during the Mongol era. Papal missions were sent from Rome to the Mongol court. An archbishopric was established in Peking. Kublai sent Marco Polo's father and uncle with a letter to the pope asking for 100 men acquainted with the seven arts.

Tibetan Buddhism with its magical doctrines and elaborate rites was the religion most favored by the Mongols. But Chinese Buddhism also flourished. Priests and monks of all religions were given tax exemptions. The foreign religion that made the greatest gains was Islam, which became permanently established in Central Asia and western China. Even Confucianism was regarded as a religion by the Mongols, but as the scholar-gentry rarely obtained important offices, they saw the Mongol era as a time of hardship.

Despite these wide contacts with other peoples and religions, the high culture of China appears to have been influenced almost not at all—partly because China had little to learn from other areas, and partly because the centers of Chinese culture were in the south, the area least affected by Mongol rule. Also, in reaction to the Mongol conquest, Chinese culture became conservative and turned in on itself.

The major contribution to Chinese arts during the Yuan was by dramatists, who combined poetic arias with vaudeville theater to produce a new operatic drama. Performed by traveling troupes, the operas relied for effect on makeup, costumes, pantomime, and stylized gestures. The women's roles were usually played by men. Except for the arias, the dramas used vernacular Chinese, appealing to a popular audience. Yuan drama continued almost unchanged in later dynasties, and during the nineteenth century it merged with a form of southern Chinese theater to become today's Peking Opera.

Last Years of the Yuan

The Yuan was the shortest of China's major dynasties. The dynasty collapsed in 1368. By then, the khanates had become separated by religion, culture, and distance. Even tribesmen in Mongolia rebelled against the great khans in Peking, who, in their eyes, had become too Chinese. The court at Peking, too, had never really gained legitimacy. Most Chinese saw Mongol rule as a military occupation. When succession disputes, bureaucratic factionalism, and pitched battles between Mongol generals broke out, Chinese showed little inclination to support the dynasty.

Problems also arose in the countryside. Taxes were heavy, and some local officials were corrupt. The government issued excessive paper money and then refused to accept it in payment for taxes. The Yellow River flooded the canals that carried grain to the capital. Further natural disasters during the 1350s led to popular uprisings. Warlords arose. Important economic regions were devastated. At the end, the last Mongol emperor and his court fled into Mongolia.

IN WORLD PERSPECTIVE
Imperial China

Rough parallels between China and Europe persisted until the sixth century C.E. Both saw the rise and fall of great empires. At first glance, the three-and-one-half centuries that followed the Han dynasty appear remarkably similar to the period after the collapse of the Roman Empire: Central authority broke down, private armies arose, and aristocratic estates were established. Barbarian tribes invaded. Otherworldly religions challenged official worldviews. In China, Neo-Taoism and then Buddhism challenged Confucianism, just as Christianity challenged Roman conceptions of the sociopolitical order.

But from the late sixth century C.E., a fundamental divergence occurred. Europe tailed off into centuries of feudal disunity and backwardness. Tiny areas like France (one-seventeenth the size of China), Italy (one thirty-second), or Germany (one twenty-seventh) found it difficult to establish an internal unity, much less recreate a pan-European empire. This pattern of separate little states has persisted in Europe until today. In contrast, China, which is about the size of Europe and geographically no more natural a political unit, attained new wealth, power, culture, and unified rule that has continued until the present. What is the explanation?

One reason the empire was reconstituted in China was that the victory of Buddhism in China was less complete than that of Christianity in Europe. Confucianism survived, and the idea of a united empire was integral to it. It is difficult even to think of Confucianism apart from the idea of a universal ruler, aided by men of virtue and ability, ruling according to Heaven's Mandate. In contrast, the Roman concept of political order was not maintained as an independent doctrine. Moreover, empire was not a vital element in Christian thought—except perhaps in Byzantium, where the empire lasted longer than it did in western Europe. Basically, the kingdom sought by Jesus was not of this world.

A second consideration was China's greater cultural homogeneity. It had a common written language, and minority peoples and even barbarian conquerors were rapidly Sinicized. In contrast, after Rome, the Mediterranean fell apart into its component cultures. Latin became for most Christians a foreign language. Even in Italy it became an artificial language, separate from the living tongue. The European languages and cultures were divisive forces.

A third factor was the combination in the post-Han northern Chinese states of economic strength based on Chinese agriculture with the military striking force of a nomadic cavalry. There was nothing like it in Europe. Such a northern state had reunified China in C.E. 589.

A fourth factor was China's greater population density. The province of Hopei had a registered population of 10,559,728 during the eighth century C.E. Hopei was about one-third the size of France, which in the eleventh century had a population of about 2 million. That is to say, even comparing China with France three centuries later, China's population density was fifteen times as great. The far higher population density resulted in a different kind of history.

Population density explains why the Chinese could absorb barbarian conquerors so much more quickly than Europe. More cultivators provided a larger agricultural surplus than that enjoyed in Europe. Greater numbers of people also meant better communications and a better base for commerce. To be sure, the centuries that followed the Han saw a decline in commerce and cities. But the economic level remained higher than in early medieval Europe.

Several of the factors that explain the Sui-T'ang regeneration of a unified empire apply equally to the Sung and subsequent dynasties. As schools were established and literacy rose, Confucianism and the ideal of a unified China became widely accepted. Chinese culture was more homogeneous and less open to outside influences in the tenth century than it had been four centuries earlier. The population had also grown.

The cyclic regeneration of centralized bureaucratic government can also be analyzed in terms of the interests it served. For the military figure who established the dynasty, the bureaucratic state was a huge tax machine that supported his armies and bestowed on him revenues beyond the imaginings of contemporary European monarchs. Government by civilian officials also acted as a counterweight against other military figures. For the scholar-gentry class, service to the state was the means to maintain family wealth, power, and status. For merchants, a strong state provided order and stability. More often than not, commerce expanded during such periods. For farmers, orderly exploitation was usually preferable to warlords, bandits, or marauding armies.

It seems likely that T'ang and Sung China had longer stretches of good government than any other part of the contemporary world. Not until the nineteenth century would comparable bureaucracies of talent and virtue appear in the West.

Review Questions

1. Why could China recreate its empire—just 400 years after the fall of the Han—but Rome could not? Are there similarities between the Ch'in-Han transition and that of the Sui-T'ang? Between Han and T'ang expansion and contraction?

2. How did the Chinese economy change from the T'ang to the Northern Sung to the Southern Sung? The polity? China's relationships to surrounding states?

3. What do Chinese poetry and art tell us about Chinese society? What position did poets occupy in Chinese society?

4. What drove the Mongols to conquer most of the known world? How could their military accomplish the task? Once they conquered China, how did they rule it? What was the Chinese response to Mongol rule?

Documents CD-ROM

1. Emperor T'ai-tsung: "On the Art of Government"

2. Poems by Wang Wei

3. Du Fu: *Ballad of the War Wagons*

4. Li Qingzhao: Poems

5. The Zen Teachings of Huang Po

6. Ssu-Ma Kwang

9 JAPAN: EARLY HISTORY TO 1467

Japanese history has three main turning points, each marked by a major influx of an outside culture and each followed by a massive restructuring of Japanese institutions. The first was in the third century B.C.E., when an Old Stone Age Japan became an agricultural, metal-working society. The second turning point came during the seventh century, when whole complexes of Chinese culture entered Japan directly, and Japan made the leap to a higher historical civilization, associated with the writing system, technologies, and philosophies of China, and with Chinese forms of Buddhism. Japan would remain a part of this cultural sphere until the third turning point, in the nineteenth century, when it encountered the West.

Japanese Origins

The earliest evidence of human habitation in Japan dates from about 30,000 B.C.E. From about 10,000 B.C.E. there exists pottery, the oldest in the world, and from about 8000 B.C.E. Jōmon or "cord-pattern" pottery. Archaeologists are baffled by its appearance in an Old Stone Age society—when in all other early societies pottery developed as a part of New Stone Age culture.

The Yayoi Revolution

After 8,000 years of Jōmon culture, the second phase of Japanese prehistory began about 300 B.C.E. It is called the Yayoi culture, after a place in Tokyo where its distinctive hard, pale orange pottery was first unearthed. There is no greater break in the entire Japanese record than that between the Jōmon and the Yayoi. For at the beginning of the third century B.C.E., the agricultural revolution, the bronze revolution, and the iron revolution burst into Japan simultaneously.

The new technologies were brought to Japan from Korea and rapidly replaced Jōmon culture as far east in Japan as the present-day city of Nagoya. After that the Yayoi culture diffused overland into eastern Japan more slowly. Conditions were less favorable for agriculture, and a mixed agricultural-hunting economy lasted longer.

By the first century C.E., the Yayoi population had so expanded that wars were fought for the best land. From these wars emerged a more peaceful order of regional states and a ruling class of aristocratic warriors. During the third century C.E., a temporary hegemony was achieved over a number of such regional states.

Tomb Culture and the Yamato State

Emerging directly from the Yayoi culture was a period, 300–600 C.E., characterized by giant tomb mounds, which even today dot the landscape of the Nara-Osaka region. The early tombs—patterned on those in Korea—were circular mounds of earth built atop megalithic burial chambers. Early tombs, like the Yayoi graves that preceded them, contained mirrors, jewels, and other ceremonial objects. From the fifth century C.E., these objects were replaced by armor, swords, spears, and military trappings. The change reflected a new wave of continental influences. The flow of people and culture from the Korean peninsula into Japan that began with Yayoi was continuous into historical times.

The fifth century C.E. was treated in the earliest Japanese accounts of their own history, the *Records of Ancient Matters (Kojiki)* and the *Records of Japan (Nihongi)*, compiled in 712 and 720. The picture that emerges is of regional aristocracies under the loose hegemony of the Yamato "great kings" whose courts were located on the Yamato plain, near present-day Osaka, the richest agricultural region of ancient Japan. The Yamato rulers also held lands and granaries throughout Japan. The tomb of the great king Nintoku is 486 meters long and 36 meters high, with twice the volume of the Great Pyramid of Egypt. By the fifth century C.E., the great kings possessed sufficient authority to commandeer laborers for such a project.

The great kings awarded Korean-type titles to court and regional aristocrats, titles that implied a national hierarchy centering on the Yamato court. Regional rulers had the same kind of political authority over their populations.

The basic social unit of Yamato aristocratic society was the extended family *(uji)*, close in size to a Scottish clan. Attached to these aristocratic families were groups of specialist workers and peasants called *be*. Yamato society had a small class of slaves, and many peasants were neither slaves nor members of aristocratic clans or specialized workers' groups.

The court was the scene of incessant struggles for power between aristocratic families. There were also continuing efforts by the court to control outlying regions. Rebellions were frequent. Finally, there were constant wars with "barbarian tribes" in southern Kyushu and eastern Honshu on the frontiers of "civilized" Japan.

The Yamato Court and Korea

Under the Yamato court, a three-cornered military balance had emerged on the Korean peninsula between the states of Paekche, Silla, and Koguryo (see Map 9–1). Japan was an ally of Paekche.

The Paekche connection enabled the Yamato court to expand its power within Japan. Imports of iron weapons and tools gave it military strength. The migration to Japan of Korean artisans increased its wealth and influence. Many immigrants became established as noble families. Paekche also served as a conduit for elements of Chinese culture. Chinese writing was adopted for the transcription of Japanese names during the fifth or sixth century. Confucianism entered in 513, Buddhism in 538.

In 532, Paekche turned against Japan, but by this time Japan had established direct relations with China.

A clay statue of a warrior in armor from an ancient tomb.

[Tokyo National Museum]

Chronology of Early Japanese History	
8000–300 B.C.E.	Jōmon culture
Early Continental Influences	
300 B.C.E.–300 C.E.	Yayoi culture
300–680 C.E.	Tomb culture and the Yamato state
680–850 C.E.	Chinese T'ang pattern in Nara and Early Heian Japan

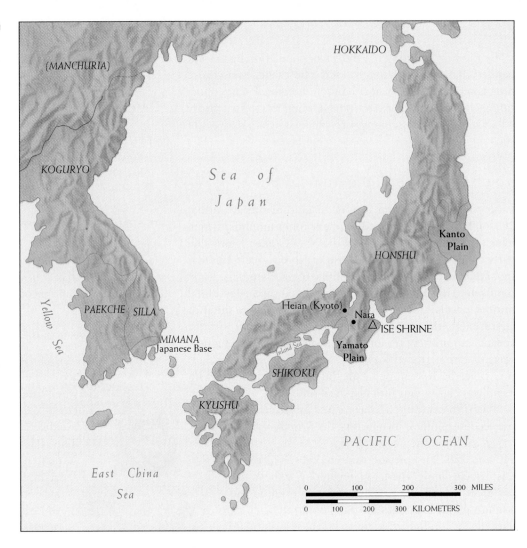

Map 9–1 Yamato Japan and Korea (ca. 500 C.E.). Paekche was Japan's ally on the Korean peninsula. Silla, Japan's enemy, was the state that would eventually unify Korea. (Note: Nara was founded in 710; Heian in 794.)

Religion in Early Japan

The indigenous religion of Yamato Japan was an animistic worship of the forces of nature, later given the name of *Shinto*, or "the way of the gods," to distinguish it from Buddhism. Shinto probably entered Japan as part of Yayoi culture. The underlying forces of nature might be embodied in a waterfall, a twisted tree, a strangely shaped boulder, a mountain, or in a great leader who would be worshiped as a deity after his death. Mount Fuji was holy not as the abode of a god but because the mountain itself was an upwelling of a vital natural force. Even today in Japan, a gnarled tree trunk may be girdled with a straw rope and set aside as an object of veneration. The sensitivity to nature and natural beauty that pervades Japanese art and poetry owes much to Shinto.

A second aspect of early Shinto was its connection with the state and the aristocracy. The more potent forces of nature such as the sea, the sun, the moon, the wind, and thunder and lightning became personified as deities. Each clan, or extended family, had its own myth centering on a nature deity *(kami)* that it claimed as its original ancestor. Aristocratic families possessed genealogies tracing their descent from the deity. The head of a clan was also its chief priest. When Japan was unified by the Yamato court, the myths of several clans apparently were joined into a composite national myth. The deity of the Yamato great kings was the sun goddess, so she became the chief deity.

The *Records of Ancient Matters* and *Records of Japan* tell of the creation of Japan, of the deeds and misdeeds of gods. In mid-volume, the stories of the gods give way to stories of early emperors and Japanese history. The Japanese emperors, today the oldest royal family in the world, were viewed as the lineal descendants of the sun goddess and as "living gods." The Great Shrine of the sun goddess at Ise has always been the most important in Japan.

Nara and Heian Japan

The second major turning point in Japanese history was its adoption of the higher civilization of China. This is a prime example of the worldwide process (described in Chapter 2) by which the heartland civilizations spread into outlying areas. In Japan the process occurred between the seventh and twelfth centuries and can best be understood in terms of three stages. The first was learning about China. The second stage, during the eighth and ninth centuries, saw the implantation of Chinese T'ang-type institutions. The third involved the transformation of these institutions to fit conditions in Japan. By the eleventh century, the creative reworking of Chinese elements had led to a distinctive Japanese culture.

Seventh Century

The official embassies to China that began in 607 C.E. included traders, students, and Buddhist monks. Like Third World students who study abroad today, Japanese who studied in China brought back with them technology, art, Buddhism, and knowledge of T'ang legal and governmental systems. Large-scale institutional changes using the T'ang model began in the 680s with the Emperor Temmu and his successor, the Empress Jitō (r. 686–697).

Temmu came to power by usurping the throne from his nephew. He then used Chinese systems to consolidate his authority. He promulgated a Chinese-type law code that greatly augmented the powers of the ruler. He styled himself as the "heavenly emperor" *(tennō)*, which thereafter replaced the title of "great king." He rewarded his supporters with court ranks and positions in government patterned after the T'ang example. He extended the authority of the court and increased its revenues by a survey of agricultural lands and a census of their population. In short, although the admiration for Chinese things must have been enormous, much of the borrowing was dictated by immediate Japanese concerns.

Nara and Early Heian Court Government

Until the eighth century, the capital was usually moved each time an emperor died. Then, in 710 a new capital, intended to be permanent, was established at Nara. It was laid out on a checkerboard grid like the Chinese capital at Ch'ang-an. But then it was moved again in 794 to Heian (later Kyoto) on the plain north of Nara. This site remained the imperial capital until the move to Tokyo in 1869.

The superimposition of a Chinese-type capital on a still backward Japan produced a stark contrast. In the villages, peasants lived in pit dwellings and either planted in crude paddy fields or used slash-and-burn techniques of dry-land farming. In the capital stood pillared palaces in which dwelt the emperor and nobles, descended from the gods. They drank wine, wore silk, and enjoyed the paintings, perfumes, and pottery of the T'ang. Clustered about the capital were Buddhist temples with soaring pagodas and tile roofs.

The emperors at the Heian court were seen both as Confucian rulers with the majesty accorded by Chinese law and as Shinto rulers descended from the sun goddess. Their lineage was never usurped. Japanese history constitutes a single dynasty, although a few emperors were killed and replaced by other family members.

Beneath the emperor, the same modified Chinese pattern prevailed. Like the T'ang, Japan had a Council of State. It was the office from which leading clans manipulated the authority of an emperor, who usually reigned but did not rule. Beneath this council were eight ministries, including the Imperial Household Ministry. Size affected function: Where T'ang China had a population of 60 million, Japan had only 4 or 5 million. There were no significant external enemies; local rule, in the Yamato tradition, was mostly in the hands of local clans. Consequently, much of the business of court government was with the court itself. Of the 6,000 persons in the central ministries, more than 4,000 were concerned with the care of the imperial house.

Under the central court government were sixty-odd provinces, subdivided into districts and villages. Provincial governors were sent out from the capital. This change reduced the regional aristocrats to district magistrates and increased the power of the central aristocracy.

Japanese court government, in other regards, was unlike that of China. There were no eunuchs. There was little tension between the emperor and the bureaucracy—the main struggles were between clans. The T'ang movement from aristocracy toward meritocracy also was absent in Japan. Only aristocrats were appointed to important official posts. A feeble attempt to establish an examination meritocracy on the Chinese model failed completely.

Land and Taxes

The last Japanese embassy to China was in 839. By that time, the Japanese were sufficiently self-confident to use Chinese ideas in innovative ways. The 350 years that followed until the end of the twelfth century were a time of assimilation and evolutionary change. Nowhere was this more evident than in the system of taxation.

The land system of early Heian Japan was the equal field system of the early T'ang. All land belonged to the emperor; it was redistributed every six years, and taxes were levied on people, not land. The system was complex, requiring land surveys, the redrawing of boundaries, and elaborate land and population registers. Its implementation speaks of the immense ability of the early Japanese, who so quickly absorbed Chinese administrative techniques.

Of course the system was even less equal than in China. Imperial princes and high nobles received thousands or hundreds of units of lands, along with the labor to work them; local officials got less, and the cultivators did the work.

When changes in a society are imposed from above, the results tend to be uniform. But when changes occur willy-nilly within a social system, the results are usually messy. The evolution of the land system and taxation in late Heian Japan was of the second type.

One big change was from the equal field system to one of tax quotas payable in grain. First, land holdings became hereditary. Officials discovered that peasants did not care for land that was redistributed every six years. Second, the main tax of labor service was converted to a grain tax. Officials found it more efficient to pay hired workers in grain than to use the labor of peasants who had no incentive to work. Third, the taxes levied on provinces and districts became fixed quotas. Court officials gave each governor a quota; the governor in turn gave one to each district magistrate and kept any amount collected over the quota. Local notables used their part of the surplus to become a new local ruling class.

Another big change was the conversion of tax-paying lands to tax-free estates. Nobles and powerful temples in Kyoto used their influence at court to obtain exemptions from taxation for their lands. From the ninth century many cultivators began to commend their small holdings to such nobles, judging that they would be better off as serfs on tax-free estates than as free farmers subject to taxation. The estates were managed by stewards, appointed from among local notables. They took a share of the surplus grain for themselves and thus had a vital interest in upholding local order.

Rise of the Samurai

In 792, the court began to rely on local mounted warriors. Some were stationed in the capital and some in the provinces. They were official troops whose taxes were remitted in exchange for military service. The Japanese verb "to serve" is *samurau*, so those who served became known as *samurai*. Then, the officially recruited local warriors were replaced by nonofficial private bands of local warriors. They constituted

Who Was in Charge at the Nara and Heian Courts

710–856	Emperors or combinations of nobles
856–1086	Fujiwara nobles
1086–1160	Retired emperors
1160–1180	Military house of Taira

the military of Japan until the foot-soldier revolution of the fifteenth and sixteenth centuries.

Being a samurai was expensive. Horses, armor, and weapons were costly, and their use required long training. The primary weapon was the bow and arrow, used from the saddle. Most samurai were from well-to-do local families. Their initial function was to preserve local order and, possibly, to help with tax collection. But at times they contributed to disorder. District magistrates led local forces against provincial governors in protests against taxes.

Regional military coalitions or confederations first broke into history in 935–940, when a regional military leader, a descendant of an emperor, became involved in a tax dispute. He captured several provinces and called himself the new emperor. The Kyoto court recruited another military band as its champion, and the rebellion was quelled.

This rebellion was the first of a number of conflicts between regional military bands. By the mid-twelfth century, there were local and regional military bands in every part of Japan.

Late Heian Court Government

By the early Heian period, the actual functions of government were taken over by three new offices outside the Chinese system:

1. *Audit officers.* A newly appointed provincial governor had to report on the accounts of his predecessor. Agreement was rare. So officers were sent to examine the books and then to superintend the collection of taxes and other capital-province relationships. They tried to halt the erosion of tax revenues, but as the quota and estate systems developed, this office had less and less to do.

2. *Bureau of archivists.* The bureau was established in 810 to record imperial decrees. Eventually it took over the executive function at the Heian court, attending to all aspects of the emperor's life.

3. *Police commissioners.* Established in the second decade of the ninth century, the commissioners became responsible for law and order in the capital.

While new institutions were evolving, there also occurred shifts in the control of the court. The key figure remained the emperor, who had the power of appointments. Until the mid-ninth century, some emperors actually ruled or shared power with nobles of leading clans. From 856, the northern branch of the Fujiwara clan became preeminent; from 986 to 1086 its stranglehold on the court was absolute, and the Fujiwara family monopolized key government posts. They controlled the court by marrying their daughters to the emperor, forcing the emperor to retire after a son was born, and then ruling as regents in place of the new infant emperor. At times they even ruled as regents for adult emperors.

Imperial control of government was reasserted by Emperor Shirakawa, who reigned from 1072 to 1086 and, abdicating at the age of thirty-three, ruled for forty-three years as retired emperor. After his death, another retired emperor continued in the same pattern until 1156.

Ex-Emperor Shirakawa garnered huge estates for the imperial family and developed strong ties to regional military leaders. But Shirakawa's powers were exercised in a capital city that was increasingly isolated, and even the city itself was plagued by fires, banditry, and a sense of impending catastrophe.

In 1156, the death of the ruling retired emperor precipitated a struggle for power between another retired emperor and the reigning one. Each called on a Fujiwara and a local military force for backing. The force led by Taira Kiyomori won. Taira Kiyomori's pattern of rule was quite Japanese: Court nobles kept their Chinese court offices; the reigning emperor retired and took control of the offices of the retired emperor and of the estates of the imperial family; the head of the Fujiwara family kept the post of regent, while Taira Kiyomori married his daughter to the new emperor, and when a son was born, Kiyomori forced the emperor to retire and ruled as the maternal grandfather of the infant emperor. That is to say, the Taira ruled as a new stratum atop the old court hierarchy.

Aristocratic Culture and Buddhism in Nara and Heian Japan

If the parts of a culture could be put on a scale and weighed, we would conclude that the culture of Nara and early Heian Japan was overwhelmingly one of Shinto religious practices and village folkways, an extension of the culture of the late Yamato period. The aristocracy was small and encapsulated in court life, just as the Buddhist monks were contained within their monastic life. The early Heian aristocracy comprised one-tenth of 1 percent of Japan's population. Most of the court culture had only recently been imported from China. There had not been time for commoners to ape their betters or for the powerful force of the indigenous culture to reshape that of the elite.

The resulting cultural gap helps explain why the aristocrats believed that commoners were hardly human. The writings of courtiers reflect little sympathy for the people. Heian high culture resembled a hothouse plant. It was protected by the political influence of the court. It was nourished by the flow of tax revenues and income from estates. Under these conditions, aristocrats indulged in a unique way of life and created canons of elegance and taste that are striking even today.

Chinese Tradition in Japan

Education at the Nara and Heian courts was largely a matter of reading Chinese books and acquiring the skills to compose poetry and prose in Chinese. These were daunting tasks, but the challenge was met. From the Nara period until the nineteenth century, most philosophical and legal writings, as well as most of the histories, essays, and religious texts in Japan, were written in Chinese.

Not only were Japanese writings in Chinese a vital part of the Japanese cultural tradition, but the original Chinese works themselves also became a part of the same tradition. Chinese history was read, and its stock figures were among the heroes and villains of the Japanese historical consciousness. Chinese history became the mirror in which Japan saw itself, despite the differences between the two societies. Buddhist stories and the books of Confucianism also became Japanese classics, consulted over the centuries for their wisdom and philosophy. The parallel might be the acceptance of "foreign books" such as the Bible and works of Plato and Aristotle in medieval and Renaissance England.

Birth of Japanese Literature

Stimulated by Chinese models, the Japanese began to compose poetry in their native tongue. The first major anthology was the *Collection of Ten Thousand Leaves (Man'yōshū)*, compiled in about 760. It contained 4,516 poems. The sentiments in the poems reveal a deep sensitivity to nature and strong human relationships between husband and wife, parents and children. They also display a love for the land of Japan and links to a Shinto past.

An early obstacle to the development of a Japanese poetic tradition was the difficulty of transcribing Japanese sounds. In the *Ten Thousand Leaves*, Chinese characters were used as phonetic symbols. But there was no standardization, and the transcription soon became unintelligible. In 951, a committee of poets deciphered the work and put it into *kana*, the new syllabic script or alphabet that had developed during the ninth century.

The invention of *kana* opened the gate to the most brilliant developments of the Heian period. Most of the new works and certainly the greatest were by women. The greatest works of the Heian period were by Sei Shōnagon and Murasaki Shikibu. Both were daughters of provincial officials serving at the Heian court. The *Pillow Book* of Sei Shōnagon contains sharp, satirical, amusing essays and literary jottings that reveal the demanding aristocratic taste of the early-eleventh-century Heian court.

The *Tale of Genji*, written by Murasaki Shikibu in about 1010, was the world's first novel. *Genji* is a work of sensitivity, originality, and acute psychological delineation of character, for which there was no Chinese model. It tells of the life, loves, and sorrows of Prince Genji, the son of an imperial concubine, and, after his death, of his son Kaoru. The novel spans three-quarters of a century and may be seen as having had a "definite and serious purpose." In one passage Genji twits a court lady whom he finds reading an extravagant romance. But then Genji says:

> I think far better of this art than I have led you to suppose. Even its practical value is immense. Without it what should we know of how people lived in the past, from the Age of the Gods down to the present day? For history books such as the *Chronicles of Japan* show us only one small corner of life; whereas these diaries and romances, which I see piled around you contain, I am sure, the most minute information about all sorts of people's private affairs.[1]

Nara and Heian Buddhism

The Six Sects of the Nara period each represented a separate philosophical doctrine within Mahayana Buddhism. Their monks trained in monastic communities set apart from the larger society. They studied, read sutras, copied texts, meditated, and joined in rituals.

As in China, monasteries and temples were involved with the state. Tax revenues were assigned for their support. Monks prayed for the health of the emperor and for rain in time of drought.

Japan in the seventh and eighth centuries was much less culturally developed than China. The Japanese came to Buddhism not from the philosophical perspectives of Confucianism or Taoism but from the magic and mystery of Shinto. The appeal of Buddhism to the early Japanese was, consequently, in its colorful and elaborate rituals; in the gods, demons, and angels of the Mahayana pantheon; and, above all, in the beauty of Buddhist art. The philosophy took longer to establish itself.

Japan's cultural identity was also different. In China, Buddhism was always viewed as Indian and alien. That was one factor leading to the Chinese persecution of Buddhists during the ninth century. In contrast, Japan's cultural identity or cultural self-consciousness took shape only during the Nara and early Heian periods. One element in that identity was the imperial cult derived from Shinto. But as a religion, Shinto was no match for Buddhism. Buddhism was no more foreign than Confucianism and the rest of the T'ang culture that had helped reshape the Japanese identity, so there was no bias against it. Consequently, Buddhism entered deeply into Japanese culture and retained its vitality longer. Not until

[1]R. Tsunoda, W. T. deBary, and D. Keene, eds., *Sources of the Japanese Tradition* (New York: Columbia University Press, 1958), p. 181.

the seventeenth or eighteenth centuries did Japanese elites became so Confucian as to be anti-Buddhist. In 794, the court moved to Heian (Kyoto). The two great new Buddhist sects of the Heian era were Tendai and Shingon.

Saichō (767–822) had founded a temple on Mount Hiei to the northwest of Kyoto in 785. He went to China as a student monk in 804 and returned the following year with the teachings of the Tendai sect. He spread in Japan the doctrine that salvation could be attained by all who led a life of contemplation and moral purity. He instituted strict monastic rules and a twelve-year training curriculum for novice monks at his monastery. The sect grew until thousands of temples had been built on Mount Hiei. Many later Japanese sects emerged from within the Tendai fold.

The Shingon sect was begun by Kūkai (774–835), who became a monk at the age of eighteen. In 804 he went to China with Saichō. He returned two years later bearing the Shingon doctrines and founded a monastery on Mount Kōya. Kūkai was a bridge builder, a poet, an artist, and one of the three great calligraphers of his age. He is sometimes credited with inventing the *kana* syllabary and with introducing tea into Japan. Shingon doctrines center on an eternal and cosmic Buddha, of whom all other Buddhas are manifestations. *Shingon* means "true word" or "mantra," a verbal formula with mystical powers. It is sometimes called *esoteric Buddhism* in that it had secret teachings that were passed from master to disciple. In China, Shingon died out as a sect in the persecutions of the mid-ninth century, but in Japan its doctrines even spread to the Tendai center on Mount Hiei.

During the later Heian period, Buddhism began to be assimilated. At the village level, the folk religion of Shinto took in many Buddhist elements. In the high culture of the capital, Shinto was almost absorbed by Buddhism. Shinto deities came to be seen as the local manifestations of universal Buddhas. The cosmic or "Great Sun Buddha" of the Shingon sect, for example, was easily identified with the sun goddess. Often, great Buddhist temples had smaller Shinto shrines on their grounds. Not until the mid-nineteenth century was Shinto disentangled from Buddhism, and even then for political ends.

Japan's Early Feudal Age

The year 1185, or 1160, if we include Taira rule in Kyoto, marked the shift from centuries of rule by a civil aristocracy to centuries of rule by one that was military. It saw the formation of the *bakufu* (tent government), a completely non-Chinese type of government. It saw the emergence of the *shōgun* as the de facto ruler of Japan, although in theory he was a military official of the emperor. It marked the beginning of new cultural forms and initiated changes in family and social organization.

Rise of Minamoto Yoritomo

Taira Kiyomori's seizure of Kyoto in 1160 fell short of being a national military hegemony, for other bands flourished in Japan. After Kiyomori's victory, the Taira embraced the elegant lifestyle of the Kyoto court. They assumed that their tutelage over the court would be as enduring as had been that of the Fujiwara. In 1180, Minamoto Yoritomo (1147–1199) responded to a call to arms by a disaffected prince, seized control of eastern Japan (the rich Kanto plain), and began the war that ended in 1185 with the downfall of the Taira.

Yoritomo's victory in 1185 was national, for his armies had ranged over most of Japan. After his victory, warriors from every area became his vassals. Wary of Kyoto, Yoritomo set up his headquarters at Kamakura, thirty miles south of present-day Tokyo, at the edge of his base of power in eastern Japan. He called his government the *bakufu* in contrast to the civil government in Kyoto. The offices he established were few and practical: one to deal with his samurai retainers, one to administer and execute his policies, and one to hear legal suits. Each office was staffed by vassals. Yoritomo also appointed military governors in each province and military stewards on the former estates of the Taira and others who had fought against him. These appointments carried the right to income from the land. The rest of the income went to Kyoto as taxes or as revenues to the noble owners of the estates.

The Question of Feudalism

Scholars often contend that Yoritomo's rule marks the start of feudalism in Japan. Feudalism may be defined in terms of three criteria: lord-vassal relationships, fiefs given in return for military service, and a warrior ethic. Do these apply to Kamakura Japan?

Certainly, the mounted warriors who made up the armies of Yoritomo were predominantly his vassals, not his kin. As for fiefs, the answer is ambiguous. Kamakura vassals received rights to income from land in exchange for military service. But fiefs, as such, did not appear until the late fifteenth century.

However, the warrior ethic had been developing among regional military bands for several centuries before 1185. The samurai prized bravery, cunning, physical strength, and endurance. They gave their swords names. Their sports were hunting, hawking, and archery. Warriors thought of themselves as a military aristocracy that practiced "the way of the bow and arrow," "the way of the bow and horse," "the way of the warriors," and so on.

The Kamakura military band thus pretty well fits our definition of feudalism. Nonetheless, warrior bands were only one part of the whole society. Kamakura Japan had two political centers. The *bakufu* had military authority, but the Kyoto court continued the late Heian pattern of civil rule. It

Government by Military Houses	
1160–1180	Taira rule in Kyoto
1185–1333	Kamakura *bakufu*
1185	Founded by Minamoto Yoritomo
1219	Usurped by Hōjō
1221	Armed uprising by Kyoto court
1232	Formation of Jōei Code
1274 and 1281	Invasion by Mongols
1336–1467	Ashikaga *bakufu*
1336	Begun by Ashikaga Takauji
1392	End of Southern Court
1467	Start of warring states period

appointed civil governors, received tax revenues, and controlled the region about Kyoto. Noble families, retired emperors, and the great Buddhist temples also contributed to Kyoto's power. It also remained the fount of rank and honors. After his victory in 1185, Yoritomo asked the emperor for the title of "barbarian-quelling generalissimo" (*Sei i tai shōgun*, shortened to *shōgun*). He was refused, and only in 1192 did Yoritomo get the title. Even then, the award was justified because Yoritomo was a Minamoto offshoot of the imperial line.

The small size of Yoritomo's vassal band is an even more telling argument against viewing Japan as fully feudal at this time. Numbering about 2,000 before 1221 and 3,000 thereafter, most of the band were concentrated in eastern Japan. But even if as many as half were distributed about the rest of the country as military governors and stewards, there would have been only 100 in a region the size of Massachusetts. (Japan in 1180 was about fifteen times larger than that state.) How could so few control such a large area? The answer is that they did not have to.

The local social order of the late Heian era continued into the Kamakura period. The Kyoto court, governors, district magistrates, and local notables functioned more or less as they had earlier. To influence the local scene, the newly appointed Kamakura vassals had to win the cooperation of the existing local power-holders. In short, even if the Kamakura vassals themselves could be called feudal, they were only a thin skin on the surface of a society constructed according to older principles.

Kamakura Rule after Yoritomo

As soon as Yoritomo died in 1199, his widow and her Hōjō kinsmen moved to usurp the power of the Minamoto house. The widow, having taken holy orders after her husband's death, was known as the Nun Shōgun. One of her sons was pushed aside. The other became shōgun but was murdered in 1219. After that, the Hōjō ruled as regents for a puppet shōgun. The Kyoto court led an armed uprising against Kamakura in 1221, but it was suppressed. Any society based on personal bonds faces the problem of how to transfer loyalty from one generation to another. That the Kamakura vassals fought for the Hōjō in 1221 suggests that they were loyal to the *bakufu*, which guaranteed their income from land. Their personal loyalty to the Minamoto had ended with the death of Yoritomo.

In 1266, Kublai Khan (see Chapter 8) sent envoys demanding that Japan submit to his rule. He had subjugated Korea in 1258. The Hōjō at Kamakura refused. The first Mongol invasion fleet arrived with 30,000 troops in 1274, but withdrew after initial victories. A second invasion force arrived in 1281. Carrying 140,000 troops, it was an amphibious operation on a scale unprecedented in world history. With gunpowder bombs and phalanxes of archers protected by a forward wall of soldiers carrying overlapping shields, the Mongol forces were formidable.

The Japanese tactics of fierce individual combat were not appropriate to their foe. But the Mongols were held off until *kamikaze*, or "divine winds," sank a portion of their fleet and forced the rest to retreat.

Women in Warrior Society

The Nun Shōgun was one of a long line of important women in Japan. The central figure of Japanese mythology was the sun goddess, who ruled the Plain of High Heaven. The empresses of the Yamato and Nara courts were followed by the great women writers of the Heian period. Under the Kamakura *bakufu*, the daughters of warrior families often trained in archery and other military arts. Women also occasionally

inherited the position of military steward. But as fighting became more common in the fourteenth century, their position began to decline; as warfare became endemic in the fifteenth, their status plummeted. To protect the integrity of the military fief—the warrior's reward for serving his lord in battle and the lord's guarantee that his warriors would continue their service—multigeniture, in which daughters as well as sons inherited property, gave way to inheritance by the most able son.

The Ashikaga Era

By 1331, various tensions had developed within Kamakura society. The patrimony of a warrior was divided among his children. Over several generations vassals became poorer, often falling into debt. High-ranking vassals of Kamakura were dissatisfied with the Hōjō monopolization of key *bakufu* posts. In the meantime, the ties of vassals to Kamakura were weakening, while the ties to other warriors within their region were growing stronger. New regional bands were ready to emerge. The precipitating event was a revolt in 1331 by an emperor who thought emperors should actually rule. Kamakura sent Ashikaga Takauji (1305–1358), the head of a branch family of the Minamoto line, to put down the revolt. Instead, he joined it. Other regional lords then destroyed the Hōjō *bakufu* in Kamakura.

What emerged from the turmoil of the years from 1331 to 1336 was a regional multistate system centering on Kyoto. Each region was based on a warrior band. In the central Kyoto region, Ashikaga Takauji established his *bakufu*. Its offices were simple and functional: a samurai office for police and military matters, an administrative office for financial matters, a documents office for land records, and a judicial board

Mongol invaders battling with an intrepid samurai horseman. Note the bomb bursting in the air at the upper right of this late thirteenth-century Japanese scroll painting. [© Museum of Imperial Collections—Sannomaru Shozo Kan, Courtesy of the International Society for Educational Information, Inc.]

to settle disputes. The offices were staffed by Takauji's vassals. They were lords (now called daimyo) in their own right who also usually held appointments as military governors in the provinces surrounding Kyoto. The *bakufu* also appointed vassals to watch over its interests in the far north, in eastern Japan, and in Kyushu.

Government in the outlying regions was more diverse. Some lords held several provinces, some only one. Some had integrated most of the warriors in their areas into their bands. Others had several unassimilated military bands in their territories, forcing them to rely more on the authority of Kyoto. Formally, all regional lords or *daimyo* were the vassals of the shōgun. But the relationship was often nominal. Sometimes the regional lords lived on their lands; sometimes they lived in Kyoto.

The relationship between the Kyoto *bakufu* and the regional lords fluctuated from 1336 to 1467. At times, able lords made their regions into virtually independent states. At other times, the Kyoto *bakufu* became stronger. The third shōgun, for example, even relinquished the military post of shōgun—giving it to his son in 1394—to take the highest civil post of grand minister of state. He improved relations with the great Buddhist temples and Shinto shrines and established ties with Ming China. His military campaigns dented the autonomy of regional lords outside of the inner Kyoto circle.

But even the third shōgun had to rely on his vassals. He gave them the authority to levy taxes; to unify in their own hands all judicial, administrative, and military authority in their regions; and to take on unaffiliated warriors as their direct vassals. But this left problems for his successors. As ties of personal loyalty wore thin, new local warrior bands began to form.

Agriculture, Commerce, and Medieval Guilds

Population figures for medieval Japan were about 6 million for the year 1200 and 12 million for 1600. The increase was brought about by land reclamation and improvements in agricultural technology. Iron-edged tools became available to all. New strains of rice were developed. Irrigation and diking improved. Vegetables were planted during the fall and winter in dry fields, which were flooded and planted with rice during the spring and summer.

In the Nara and early Heian periods, the economy was almost exclusively agricultural. The government had established a mint, but little money actually circulated. Taxes were paid in grain and labor. Commercial transactions were largely barter, with silk or grain as the medium of exchange. Artisans produced for the noble households or temples to which they were attached. Peasants were self-sufficient.

From the late Heian period, more of the growing agricultural surplus stayed in local hands. During the Kamakura and Ashikaga periods, there was a transfer of income from the court aristocrats to the warrior class. As this transfer occurred, artisans began to produce for the market. Military equipment was an early staple of commerce, but gradually *sake*, lumber, paper, vegetable oils, salt, and products of the sea also became commercialized. A demand for copper coins appeared, and they were imported in huge quantities from China.

During the Kamakura period, merchants appeared to handle the products of artisans. Trade networks spread over all Japan. Artisan and merchant guilds, not unlike those of medieval Europe, paid a fee in exchange for monopoly rights in a given area. From the Kamakura period onward, markets were held periodically in many parts of Japan. During the fourteenth and fifteenth centuries, such markets were held with increasing frequency until permanent towns were established.

Buddhism and Medieval Culture

The Nara and Heian periods are often referred to as Japan's classical age. The period that followed—say, from 1200 to 1600—is often called medieval. It was medieval in the root sense of the word in that it lay between the other two major spans of premodern Japanese history. It was also medieval in that it shared some characteristics that we label medieval in Europe and China. However, there was an important difference. Medieval Japan grew directly out of its classical era—the two even overlapped during the early Kamakura. Whereas in Europe, torn by barbarian invasions, a millennium separated classical Rome from the high medieval era, and in China, too, there were 400 years of political disunity and barbarian invasions.

The historical continuity in Japan is visible throughout its culture. The earlier poetic tradition continued with vigor. The style of painting that had reached a peak in the *Genji Scrolls* continued into the medieval era with scrolls on historical and religious themes or fairy-tale adventures. Artisanal production continued without a break. In short, Heian culture extended into medieval Japan. Nonetheless, medieval Japanese culture had some new characteristics. First, as the leadership of society shifted from court aristocrats to military aristocrats, new forms of literature appeared. The medieval military tales were as different from the *Tale of Genji* as the elaborate armor of the mounted warrior was from the colorful silken robes of the court nobility. Second, a new wave of culture entered from Sung China. Third, and most important, the medieval centuries were Japan's age of Buddhist faith. A religious revolution occurred and deeply influenced the arts of Japan.

Japanese Pietism: Pure Land and Nichiren Buddhism

Among the doctrines of the Heian Tendai sect was the belief that the true teachings of the historical Buddha had been lost and that salvation could be had only by calling on the name of Amida, the Buddha who ruled over the Western Paradise (or Pure Land). During the tenth and eleventh centuries, itinerant preachers began to spread Pure Land doctrines and practices beyond Kyoto. The doctrine that the world had fallen on evil times and that only faith would suffice was given credence by earthquakes, epidemics, fires, banditry, and wars.

In the early Kamakura era, two figures stand out as religious geniuses who experienced the truth of Pure Land Buddhism within themselves. Hōnen (1133–1212) was perhaps the first to say that the invocation of the name of Amida alone was enough for salvation and that only faith counted. These claims brought Hōnen into conflict with the older Buddhist establishment and marked the emergence of Pure Land as a separate sect. Shinran (1173–1262) taught that even a single invocation in praise of Amida, if done with perfect faith, was sufficient for salvation. But perfect faith was a gift from Amida. Shinran taught that pride was an obstacle to purity of heart. One of his most famous sayings is "If even a good man can be reborn in the Pure Land, how much more so a wicked man." In other words, the evil man is less inclined to assume that he is the source of his own salvation and is, therefore, more inclined to trust in Amida.

Shinran's emphasis on faith alone led him to break many of the monastic rules of earlier Buddhism: He ate meat; he married a nun, and thereafter the Pure Land sect had a married clergy. He also taught that all occupations were equally "heavenly" if performed with a pure heart. He traveled about Japan establishing "True Pure Land" congregations.

The congregation often developed political and military power. As a religion of faith, the sect built a strong church as a protection for the saved while they were still in this world. During the fifteenth century, some Pure Land village congregations created self-defense forces. At times they rebelled against feudal lords. These congregations were smashed during the late sixteenth century, and the sect was depoliticized. Still, as a result of a line of distinguished teachers after Shinran, its doctrinal simplicity, and its reliance on piety, Pure Land Buddhism remains the dominant form of Buddhism in Japan today.

A second devotional sect was founded by Nichiren (1222–1282), who believed that the Lotus Sutra perfectly embodied the teachings of the Buddha. He instructed his adherents to chant, over and over, "Praise to the Lotus Sutra of the Wondrous Law," usually to the accompaniment of rapid drumbeats. The chanting optimally induced a state of religious rapture. Nichiren was remarkable for a Buddhist in being both intolerant and nationalistic. He blamed the ills of his age on rival sects and asserted that only his sect could protect Japan. Even his adopted Buddhist name, the Sun Lotus, combined the term for the rising sun of Japan with that of the flower that had become the symbol of Buddhism.

Zen Buddhism

Meditation had long been a part of Japanese monastic practice. Zen meditation and doctrines were introduced by monks returning from study in Sung China. Zen in Japan was a religion of paradox. Its monks were learned, yet it stressed a return to the uncluttered "original mind," attained in a flash of intuitive understanding. Zen was punctiliously traditional, the most Chinese of Japanese medieval sects. The authority of the Zen master over his pupil-monks was absolute. Yet Zen was also iconoclastic. Its sages were depicted tearing up sutras to make the point that it is religious experience and not words that count. Within a rigidly structured monastic regimen, monks tested their understanding, gained through long hours of meditation, in encounters with their master. Buddhism stressed compassion for all sentient beings, yet in Japan the Zen sect included many samurai whose duty it was to fight and kill. A few military leaders encouraged the practice of Zen among their retainers in the hope of instilling a single-minded attention to duty.

The most remarkable aspect of Zen was its influence on the arts of medieval Japan. The most beautiful gardens, for example, were in Zen temples. Zen monks, such as Josetsu, Shūbun (ca. 1415), and Sesshū (1420–1506) are among the masters of ink painting in East Asia. Because the artist's creativity itself was seen as grounded in his experience of meditation, a painting of a waterfall or a crow on a leafless branch in late fall was viewed as no less religious than a painting of the mythic Zen founder Bodhidharma.

Nō Plays

Another fascinating product of medieval culture was the Nō play, a kind of mystery drama without parallels in East Asia. The play was performed on an almost square, bare wooden stage (often outdoors) by male actors wearing robes of great beauty and carved, painted masks of enigmatic expressions. Many such masks and robes number among Japan's national treasures. The chorus was chanted to the accompaniment of flute and drums. The language was poetic. The action was slow and highly stylized. At a critical juncture in most plays, the protagonist was possessed by the spirit of another and performed a dance. Spirit possession was a commonplace in Japanese folk religion and also occurred in the *Tale of Genji*.

The Arts and Zen Buddhism

Zen Buddhism in Japan developed a theory of art that influenced every department of high medieval culture. Put simply, the theory is that intuitive action is better than conscious, purposive action. The best painter is one so skilled that he no longer needs to think of technique but paints as a natural act. Substitute a sword for a brush, and the same theory applies: A warrior who has to stop to consider his next move is at a disadvantage in battle. To this concern with direct, intuitive action is added the Zen distinction between the deluded mind and the "original mind." The latter is also referred to as the "no mind," or the mind in the enlightened state. The highest intuitive action proceeds from such a state of being. This theory was applied, in time, to the performance of the actor, to the skill of the potter, to archery, to flower arrangement, and to the tea ceremony. Compare the following two passages, one by Seami (1363–1443), the author of many Nō plays, and the other by Takuan Sōhō (1573–1645), a famous Zen master of the early Tokugawa era (see Chapter 20).

Could the same theory be applied to baseball? If it were, would baseball change?

Sometimes spectators of the Nō say, "The moments of 'no-action' are the most enjoyable." This is an art which the actor keeps secret. Dancing and singing, movements and the different types of miming are all acts performed by the body. Moments of "no-action" occur in between. When we examine why such moments without actions are enjoyable, we find that it is due to the underlying spiritual strength of the actor which unremittingly holds the attention. He does not relax the tension when the dancing or singing come to an end or at intervals between the dialogue and the different types of miming, but maintains an unwavering inner strength. This feeling of inner strength will faintly reveal itself and bring enjoyment. However, it is undesirable for the actor to permit this inner strength to become obvious to the audience. If it is obvious, it becomes an act, and is no longer "no-action." The actions before and after an interval of "no-action" must be linked by entering the state of mindlessness in which one conceals even from oneself one's intent. This, then, is the faculty of moving audiences, by linking all the artistic powers with one mind.

Where should a swordsman fix his mind? If he puts his mind on the physical movement of his opponent, it will be seized by the movement; if he places it on the sword of his opponent, it will be arrested by the sword; if he focuses his mind on the thought of striking his opponent, it will be carried away by the very thought; if the mind stays on his own sword, it will be captured by his sword; if he centers it on the thought of not being killed by his opponent, his mind will be overtaken by this very thought; if he keeps his mind firmly on his own or on his opponent's posture, likewise, it will be blocked by them. Thus the mind should not be fixed anywhere.

1. From *Sources of Japanese Tradition*, trans. by William Theodore de Bary. Copyright © 1958 by Columbia University. Reprinted with permission of the publisher. 2. From *The Buddhist Tradition* by William Theodore de Bary. Copyright © 1969 by William Theodore de Bary. Reprinted by permission of Random House Inc.

IN WORLD PERSPECTIVE

Early Japanese History

During the first millennium C.E., the major development in world history was the spread of the civilizations that had risen out of the earlier philosophical and religious revolutions. In the West, the process began with the spread of civilization from Greece to Rome, continued with the rise of Christianity and its diffusion within the late Roman Empire, and entered a third phase when the countries of northern Europe became civilized by borrowing Mediterranean culture. The spread was slow because Rome was no longer a vital center. By contrast, in East Asia the spread of civilization from its Chinese heartland was more rapid because in the early seventh century the centralized T'ang empire had been reestablished—more vital, exuberant, and powerful than ever before. Within the East Asian culture zone, and apart from post-T'ang China itself, there were three major developing areas: Vietnam, Korea, and Japan.

All three used Chinese writing during most of their history, combined indigenous and Chinese elements to create distinctive cultures and national identities, and in premodern times built independent states. The contrast between these countries and other areas around China is interesting. Vietnam, Korea, and Japan were more Chinese in their culture than Tibet, Mongolia, or Manchuria. Yet during the modern era it is the latter areas that have been swallowed up by China, whereas Korea, Vietnam, and Japan have preserved their independence. These three nations had used Chinese culture to forge self-identities that could resist Chinese domination, just as present-day Third World nations borrow Western systems and ideas to build states that are politically anti-Western.

For all their political independence and unique social institutions, Vietnam and Korea would absorb increasingly large amounts of Chinese culture as the centuries passed. But Japan because it was bigger, more populous, and more distant, became the major variant to the Chinese pattern within East Asian civilization. It reflected, often brilliantly, the potentials of East Asian culture in a non-Chinese milieu.

Of particular interest to Western students are the striking parallels that developed between Japan and northwestern Europe. Both had centuries of feudalism: peasant-farmers on the estates or manors of nobles; castles and mounted warriors who wore armor and fought for their lords; cultures in which the glorification of valor and military prowess conflicted with the gentler virtues of their religions; merchant guilds and decentralized political economies. These parallels should not be surprising since both Japan and northwestern Europe began as backward tribal or post-tribal societies onto which heartland cultures were grafted during the first millennium C.E.

Review Questions

1. Discuss the sense in which Yayoi society was defined by its eastern frontier. What changes in this early frontier society led to the building of tombs and the emergence of the Yamato great kings?

2. Discuss Japan's cultural ties with China during the Nara and Heian periods. How did Chinese culture affect Japan in government and religion? How did the Japanese change what they borrowed?

3. How did the Buddhism of the Nara and Heian periods differ from that of the early medieval era?

4. Trace the rise in Japan of a society dominated by military lords and their vassals. Do the late Heian, the Kamakura, and the Ashikaga represent different stages in the development of Japanese feudalism?

5. Contrast the Heian court culture with the "feudal" culture of the Kamakura and Ashikaga eras. Was the one not as aristocratic as the other? How did the role of women change over time?

Documents CD-ROM

1. Futo No Yasumaro: *The Kojiki*

2. Prince Shōtoku's Seventeen Article Constitution

3. "Kagerō Nikki": A Noblewoman's Lot in Ancient Japan

4. *Tale of the Heike*

5. Kamo No Chōmei (Memoir)

6. Japanese Zen Poetry

10 IRAN AND INDIA BEFORE ISLAM

CHAPTER TOPICS

IRAN

◆ The Parthians

◆ The Sasanid Empire (224–651 C.E.)

INDIA

◆ Golden Age of the Guptas (ca. 320–450 C.E.)

◆ The Development of "Classical" Traditions in Indian Civilization (ca. 300–1000 C.E.)

In World Perspective Pre-Islamic Iran and India

In this chapter we look at southwest and south Asia before the spread of Muslim faith and Islamic rule. In Iran, the period was one of relative political stability under one long-lived dynasty of Persian imperial rulers, the Sasanids. Although Zoroastrian traditions regained their vitality in this period, the social and political systems came to be dominated by a small ruling nobility, and foreign policy focused on constant competition with the Byzantine empire. This competition finally exhausted both empires, which were ripe for defeat at the hands of the Arabs, whose armies, flying the banner of Islam, moved out of the Arabian peninsula in the mid-seventh century.

India experienced a similarly spectacular imperial revival under the Gupta kings, who presided over a cultural efflorescence of unprecedented magnificence. Then incursions of new waves of steppe peoples from about 500 C.E. led to political fragmentation. Nevertheless, regional empires lasted until the thirteenth century, when Islamic power under the Delhi sultans began to forge new patterns of power and culture.

The coming of Islamic civilization took place at different times and with differing consequences in each of these two major cultural areas. In Iran, Islamic presence was a prominent factor in government and public life from the early years of the Arab conquests in the mid-seventh century. In northwestern India, Arab armies penetrated the Indus region as early as 711, and Muslim rulers controlled the Panjab from around 1000. The establishment of the so-called Delhi Sultanate in 1205 marked the entrenchment of Muslim ruling dynasties in the Indian heartlands.

IRAN

The Parthians

Parthian Arsacid rule (ca. 247 B.C.E.–223 C.E.) began in the eastern Iranian province of Parthia in Seleucid times, and eventually dominated the Iranian heartlands (see Chapter 4). The Parthian dynasty also continued the Iranian imperial and cultural traditions of the Achaemenids. The relative Parthian tolerance of religious diversity was paralleled by the growth of regionalism in political and cultural affairs. A growing nobility built strong local power bases and became the backbone of the military power of the realm.

Despite their general religious tolerance, the Parthians still upheld such Zoroastrian traditions as maintenance of a royal sacred fire at a shrine in their Parthian homeland and inclusion of priestly advisers on the emperor's council. The last century or so of their rule saw increased emphasis on Iranian traditions, perhaps in reaction to the constant warfare with the Romans on their west flank and the Greco-Bactrian Kushan threat to the east. By this time Christianity and Buddhism were making sufficient converts to directly threaten Zoroastrian tradition for the first time. These threats may have stimulated Parthian attempts to collect the largely oral Zoroastrian textual heritage. In such ways, Parthian rule laid the groundwork for the nationalistic emphases of subsequent centuries.

The Sasanid Empire (224–651 C.E.)

The Sasanids, like the earlier Achaemenids, were a Persian dynasty. They championed Iranian legitimacy and tried to brand the Parthians as outside invaders who followed foreign ways.

The first Sasanid king, Ardashir (224 C.E.–ca. 239), was a Persian warrior noble of priestly background. Ardashir and his son, Shapur I (r. ca. 239–272), built a strong internal administration in Persia (Fars), extended their sway to Ctesiphon, and took Bactria from the Kushans. Under Shapur, the empire extended beyond the Caucasus and into Syria, Armenia, and parts of Anatolia. Shapur inflicted humiliating defeats on three Roman emperors, even capturing one of them, Valerian (r. 253–260). Thus he could claim to be a restorer of Iranian glory and a "king of kings," or *shahanshah*. He also centralized and rationalized taxation, the civil ministries, and the military.

With the shift of the Roman Empire east to Byzantium in the early fourth century C.E., the stage of imperial conflict was set

Sasanid Iran	
223–224 C.E.	Ardashir (r. 224–ca. 239) defeats the last Arsacid ruler, becomes *shahanshah* of Iran
ca. 225–ca. 239	Tosar chief priest (Mobad) of realm
239–272	Reign of Shapur I; expansion of the empire east and west
ca. 239–293	Kirdir chief priest (Mobad) of the realm
216–277	Mani
ca. 307–379	Reign of Shapur II
488–531	Reign of Kavad I; height of Mazdakite movement
528	Mazdak and many of his followers massacred
531–579	Reign of Chosroes Anosharvan at Ctesiphon
651	Death of last Sasanid; Arabs conquer Persian empire

for the next 350 years: Byzantium (Constantinople) and Ctesiphon were home to the two mightiest thrones of Eurasia until the coming of the Arabs. Each won victories and championed a different religious orthodoxy, but neither could conquer the other. In the sixth century, each produced its greatest emperor: the Byzantine Justinian (r. 527–565) and the Sasanid Chosroes Anosharvan ("Chosroes of the Immortal Soul," r. 531–579). Yet less than a century after their deaths, the new Arab power reduced one empire and destroyed the other. Byzantium survived for another 800 years, but the Sasanid imperial order was swept away in 651. Memory of the Sasanids did not, however, die. Chosroes, for example, became a model of greatness for Persians and a symbol of splendor among the Arabs.

Society and Economy

Sasanid society was like that of earlier times. The extended family was the basic social unit. Zoroastrian orthodoxy recognized four classes: priests, warriors, scribes, and peasants. However, a great divide separated the royal house, the priesthood, and the warrior nobility from the common people.

The basis of the economy remained agriculture. The growth of great estates was similar to that in Roman domains and similarly responsible for a growing imbalance between the rich few and the impoverished many. Small farmers were reduced to serfdom. The burden of land taxation, like that of conscript labor work and army duty, hit hardest those least able to afford it.

The Sasanids heavily taxed the caravan trade that traversed their territory, as well as trade by sea. Silk and glass production increased under government monopoly, and the state also controlled mining. The empire's many urban centers and its foreign trade relied on a money system. It was from Jewish bankers in Babylonia and their Persian counterparts that the rest of the world acquired the use of bills of exchange (the term *check* comes from a Pahlavi word).[1]

Sasanid aristocratic culture drew on traditions from Roman, Hellenistic, and Bactrian-Indian to Achaemenid and other native Iranian ones. Its heyday was the reign of Chosroes. Indian influences—religious in the case of Buddhist ideas, but also artistic and scientific—were strong.

Religion

Zoroastrian Revival Religion played a significant role in Sasanid life. The Sasanids institutionalized Zoroastrian ritual and theology as state orthodoxy and claimed to be restoring the true faith after centuries of neglect. The initial

[1]R. Girshman, *Iran* (Harmondsworth, U.K.: Penguin Books, 1954), pp. 341–346. "Pahlavi" is the name of the middle Persian language that gradually replaced Aramaic as the Iranian *lingua franca* in Sasanid times.

architect of this propaganda and the Zoroastrian revival was the first chief priest of the empire, Tosar. Under Ardashir, Tosar instituted a state church and began the fixation of a written canon of the Avesta, the scriptural texts that include the hymns of Zarathushtra (see Chapter 4).

The most influential figure in Sasanid religious history was Tosar's successor, Kartir (or Kirdir), who served as chief priest to Shapur I and three successors (ca. 239–293). He seems to have tried to convert not only pagans, but also Christians, Buddhists, and others. His chief opponents were the Manichaeans, whom he considered Zoroastrian heretics.

Manichaeism   Mani (216–277 C.E.) was born of a noble Parthian family. He preached a message similar to, but at crucial points sharply divergent from, its Zoroastrian, Judaic, and Christian forerunners. It centered on a dualistic and moralistic view of reality in which good and evil, spirit and matter, warred. His preaching was missionary, presenting itself as the culmination and restoration of the original unity of Zoroastrian, Christian, and Buddhist teachings. Mani may have been the first person in history consciously to "found" a new religious tradition or to seek to create a "scripture" for his followers. He called his new system "Justice," although it is known as *Manichaeism*. Mani's movement proved attractive.

Kirdir had Mani executed as a heretic in 277, but Mani's movement spread westward to challenge the young Christian church (Saint Augustine was once a Manichaean) and eastward along the silk route to coexist in Central Asia with Nestorian Christian and Mahayana Buddhist communities as a third major universalistic tradition until after the coming of Islam. Its ideas figured in both Christian and Islamic heresies.

Zoroastrian Orthodoxy   Kartir had firmly grounded Zoroastrian orthodoxy despite the persistence of challenges to it, such as that of Mani. This orthodoxy became the backbone of Sasanid culture. Throughout Sasanid times, the priesthood increased its power as the jurists and legal interpreters as well as the liturgists and scholars of the land. With increasing endowments of new fire temples, the church establishment also eventually controlled much of Iran's wealth.

Later Sasanid Developments

The Sasanid ideal of justice did not include equal distribution of the empire's bounty. The radical inequalities between the aristocracy and the masses erupted at least once in conflict with the Mazdakite movement at the end of the fifth century. Its leader, Mazdak, preached asceticism, pessimism about the evil state of the material world, and vegetarianism,

tolerance, and brotherly love—all ideas apparently drawn from Manichaeism. Mazdak included a demand for a more equal distribution of society's goods. This was attractive especially to the oppressed classes, although even one Sasanid ruler, Kavad I (r. 488–531), was sympathetic for a time to Mazdak's ideas of social justice. However, in 528, Kavad's third son, the later Chosroes Anosharvan, massacred Mazdak and his most important followers.

Golden Age of the Guptas

Indians have always considered the Gupta era a high point of their civilization. Historians have seen in it the source of "classical" norms for Hindu religion and Indian culture—the symbolic equivalent of Periclean Athens, Augustan Rome, or Han China. The Guptas ruled when the various facets of Indian life took on the recognizable patterns of a single civilization that extended its influence over the whole subcontinent. A major factor in this development was the peace and stability that marked the Guptas' reign.

Gupta Rule

The first Gupta king was Chandragupta (r. 320–ca. 330 C.E.). He ruled first in Magadha and then became prominent in the whole Ganges basin after he married Princess Kumaradevi, daughter of a powerful tribal leader north of the Ganges. Their son, Samudragupta (r. ca. 330–375), and their grandson, Chandragupta II (r. ca. 375–415), turned kingdom into empire and presided over the Gupta "golden age."

India from the Gupta Age to ca. 1000 C.E.

320 C.E.–ca. 467	Gupta period
320–330	Reign of Chandragupta, first Gupta king
376–454	Reigns of Chandragupta II and Kumaragupta: Kalidasa flourishes; heyday of Gupta culture
ca. 440	Beginning of Hun invasions from Central Asia
399–414	Chinese Buddhist monk, Fa-Hsien, travels in India
616–657	Reign of Harsha; revival of Gupta splendor and power
820	Death of Vedantin philosopher-theologian, Shankara
550–ca. 1000	Regional Indian kingdoms in north and south; major Puranas composed; age of first great Vaishnava and Shaivite devotional poets in southern India

The Gupta realm extended from the Panjab and Kashmir south to the western Deccan and east to modern Assam (see Map 10–1). The Gupta sphere of influence included some of the Kushan and Saka kingdoms of the northwest as well as much of the eastern coast of India and possibly Ceylon (Sri Lanka). The Guptas were usually ready to accept a defeated ruler as a vassal rather than place his kingdom under direct rule. Seated at the old Mauryan capital, Pataliputra, Gupta splendor and power had no rival. Under Chandragupta II, India was arguably the most civilized and peaceful country in the world.

Two further Gupta kings sustained this prosperity for another half century, despite invasions by the Huns, after about 440. By about 500, the Huns had overrun western India. The Gupta empire collapsed about 550. Harsha, a descendant of the Guptas through his grandmother, did revive a semblance of Gupta splendor between 616 and 657. But when he died without heirs, the empire broke up, and the final echo of Gupta grandeur was gone.

The succeeding centuries before the arrival of Muslim invaders about 1000 C.E. saw no unified rule of any duration. In this period, the main centers of Indian civilization shifted to the Deccan and the south.

Gupta Culture

With the decline of Rome in the West, Indian culture experienced little new outside influence from Gupta until Muslim times. India's chief contacts were now with Southeast Asia and China, and most of the cultural transmission was from India eastward, not vice versa.

The Gupta period and later centuries saw great artistic and literary productivity. The claim of the Gupta era to being India's golden age of culture could be sustained solely on the

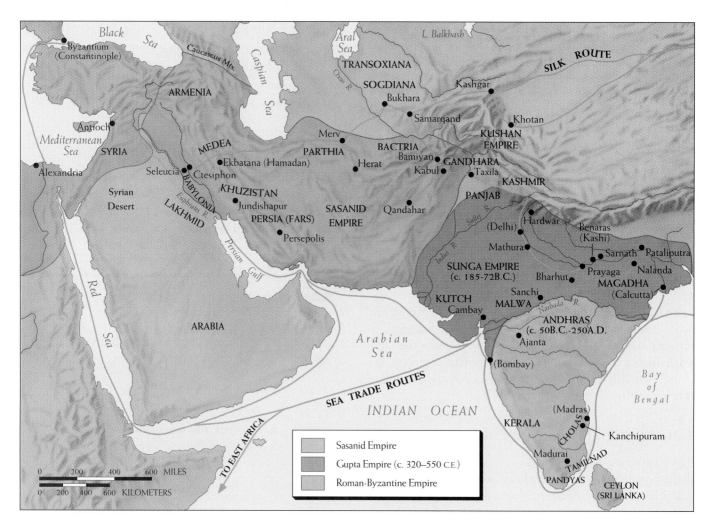

Map 10–1 International trade routes in Gupta and Sasanid times. This map shows the Gupta and Sasanid Empires and the trade routes that linked them to each other and to other areas of the world.

basis of its magnificent architecture and sculpture, the wall paintings of the Ajanta caves, and Kalidasa's matchless drama and verse. The "Shakespeare" of Sanskrit letters, Kalidasa flourished under Chandragupta II and his successor.

The depth of Gupta culture can be seen in the strong emphasis on education. In addition to religious texts, typical subjects included rhetoric, prose and poetic composition, grammar, logic, medicine, and metaphysics. Using an Indian number system that was transmitted by the Arabs to the West as "Arabic numerals," Gupta scholars cultivated mathematics.

In sculpture, the monastic complex at Sarnath was a great center of activity. The superb technique and expressive serenity of Gupta style grew out of native Mathura and Greco-Roman schools. Hindu, Jain, and Buddhist works all shared the same style and conventions. Gupta products were in great demand abroad: silks, muslin, linen, ivory and other carvings, bronze metalwork, gold and silver work, and cut stones, among others.

The Development of "Classical" Traditions in Indian Civilization (ca. 300–1000 C.E.)

The Guptas' support of Brahmanic traditions and Vaishnava[2] devotionalism reflected the waning of Buddhist traditions in Indian religious life. In Gupta times, Indian civilization assumed its classical shape, its enduring "Hindu" social, religious, and cultural life.

Society

In these centuries, the fundamentally hierarchical character of Hindu/Indian society solidified in practice and theory. The oldest manual of legal and ethical theory, the *Dharmashastra* of Manu, dates from about 200 C.E. Based on Vedic tradition, it treats the dharma appropriate to one's class and stage of life, rules for rites and study of the Veda, pollution and purification measures, dietary restrictions, royal duties and prerogatives, and other legal and moral questions.

In it we find the classic statement of the four-class theory of social hierarchy. This ideal rests on the principle that every person is born into a particular station in life (as a result of *karma* from earlier lives), and every station has its particular *dharma*, or appropriate duties and responsibilities. The Brahmans' ancient division of Aryans into the four *varnas*, or classes, of *Brahman* (priest), *Kshatriya* (noble/warrior), *Vaishya*

Fifth century C.E. statue of Lokanatha from Sarnath, which despite damage, shows the fine sculptural work of the important school of Gupta artists at Sarnath and the influence on them of both Greco-Roman antecedents and native Indian traditions and conventions. [Scala/Art Resource, N.Y.]

(tradesperson), and *Shudra* (servant) provides a schematic structure. These divisions reflect an attempt to fix the status and power of the upper three groups, especially the Brahmans, at the expense of the Shudras and the "fifth estate" of non-Aryan "outcasts," who performed the most polluting jobs in society. Although class distinctions had already hardened before 500 B.C.E., the classes were, in practice, somewhat fluid. If the traditional occupation of a varna was closed to a member, he could often take up another, all theory to the contrary. When Brahmans, Vaishyas, or even Shudras gained political power as rulers, their family gradually became recognized as *Kshatriyas*, the appropriate class for princes.

Although the four classes, or *varnas*, are the theoretical basis for caste relations, much smaller and far more numerous subgroups, or *jatis*, are the units to which our English term

---

[2]*Vaishnava* or *Vaishnavite* means "related to Vishnu"; similarly, *Shaiva* or *Shaivite* refers to Shiva worship (compare with *Jaina/Jain* for devotees of the way of the *Jinas* such as Mahavira).

caste best refers. These basic and lasting divisions (most representing occupational groups) were already the primary units of social distinction in Gupta times. *Jati* groupings are hereditarily determined and distinguished essentially on principles of purity and pollution, which are expressed in three kinds of regulation: (1) commensality (one may take food only from or with persons of the same or a higher group); (2) endogamy (one may marry only within the group); and (3) trade or craft limitation (one must practice only the trade of one's group).[3]

The caste system has been the basis of Indian social organization for at least two millennia. It enabled Hindus to accommodate foreign cultural, racial, and religious communities within Indian society by treating them as new caste groups. It enabled everyone to tell by dress and other marks how to relate to a given person or group, thus giving stability and security to the individual and society. It represented also the extension of the doctrine of karma into society—whether as justification, result, or partial cause of the system itself (see Chapter 2).

Religion

Hindu Religious Life

Gupta and later times saw the growth of devotional cults of deities, preeminently Vishnu and Shiva. The temple worship of a particular deity has ever since been a basic form of Hindu piety. After Vishnu (especially in his form as the hero-savior Krishna) and Shiva, the chief focus of devotion came to be the Goddess in one of her many forms, such as Parvati, Shakti, Durga, or Kali. Vishnu and Shiva, like Parvati, have always been easily identified with other deities, who are then worshiped as one form of the Supreme Lord or Goddess. Animal or nature deities were presumably part of popular piety from Indus Valley days forward. Indian reverence for all forms of life and stress on *ahimsa*, or "noninjury" to living beings (see Chapter 2), is most vivid in the sacredness of the cow, which has always been a mainstay of life in India.

In the development of Hindu piety and practice, a major strand was the tradition of ardent theism known as *bhakti*, or "loving devotion." The central bhakti strand in Hindu life derives in good part from Tamil and other vernacular poets who first sang the praises of Shiva or Vishnu as Supreme Lord. Of major importance also to devotional piety was the development in this era of the Puranas—epic, mythological, and devotional texts. They are still the functional sacred scriptures of grassroots Hindu religious life.

Whatever god or goddess a Hindu worships, it is usual to pay homage on occasion to other deities as well. Most Hindus view one deity as Supreme Lord but see others as manifestations of the Ultimate at lower levels. Hindu polytheism is not "idolatry" but a vivid affirmation of the infinite forms that transcendence takes in this world. The sense of the presence of the divine everywhere is evident at the popular level in the immense importance attached to sacred places in India. It is the land of religious pilgrimage *par excellence*. Sacred mountains, rivers, trees, and groves are all *tirthas*, or "river fords" to the divine.

The intellectual articulation of Hindu polytheism and relativism found its finest expression in post-Gupta formulations of Vedanta ("the end of the Veda"). This is one of six major Hindu systems of thought based on Vedic texts, especially the Upanishads. The major Vedantin thinker was Shankara (d. 820). He stressed a strict "nonduality" of the Ultimate, teaching that Brahman was the only Reality behind the "illusion" *(maya)* of the world of sense experience. Yet he accepted the worship of a lesser deity as appropriate for those who could not follow his extraordinary norm—the intellectual realization of the formless Absolute beyond all "name and form."

Buddhist Religious Life

The major developments of these centuries were (1) the solidification of the two main strands of Buddhist tradition, the Mahayana and the Theravada, and (2) the spread of Buddhism abroad from its Indian homeland. The Mahayana ("Great Vehicle [of salvation]") arose in the first century B.C.E. Its proponents differentiated it sharply from the older, more conservative traditions of monk-oriented piety and thought, which they labeled the Hinayana ("Little Vehicle"). Mahayana speculation developed in the style of Upanishadic monism: Buddhas were seen as manifestations of a single principle of "Ultimate" Reality, and Sidhartha Gautama was held to be but one Buddha among many. In the Mahayana, the model of the Buddha's infinite compassion for all beings was paramount. The highest goal was not a *nirvana* of "selfish" extinction but the status of a *bodhisattva*, or "Buddha-to-be," who postpones his own nirvana until he has helped all other beings become enlightened.

The *bodhisattva* is capable of offering this aid because of infinite merit gained through his long career of self-sacrifice. Salvation becomes possible not only through individual effort, but through devotion to the Buddhas and *bodhisattvas*. At the popular level, this idea translated into cults of transcendent Buddhas and *bodhisattvas* conceived of as cosmic beings. Of such cults, one of the most important was that of the Buddha Amitabha, who personifies infinite compassion. Amitabha presides over a Western Paradise, or Pure Land, to which all who have faith in him have access. (See Chapter 9 for Pure Land Buddhism in Japan.)

The older, more conservative "way of the elders" (Theravada) was never the totally selfish elite tradition of the few

---

[3]A. L. Basham, *The Wonder That Was India* (New York: 1963), pp. 148–149.

Devoting Oneself to Krishna

The Bhagavad Gita is the most widely revered and often quoted of all Hindu religious texts. In these verses (Bhagavad Gita 9:22–34), Krishna (Vishnu) tells his friend and disciple, the young warrior Arjuna, of the highest path to salvation, which involves both renouncing one's attachment to the objects ("fruits") of one's actions and devoting oneself in pure faith to the Supreme Lord Krishna.

How is the understanding of older Indian religious practices and ideals (about sacrifice, for example) transformed here? How does the Lord Krishna present himself in relation to other deities? Does the passage present a sharp dichotomy between faith and works? What are the social implications of the message here?

God and the Devotee

Those persons who, meditating on Me without any thought of another god, worship Me—to them, who constantly apply themselves [to that worship], I bring attainment [of what they do not have] and preservation [of what they have attained].

Even the devotees of other divinities, who worship them, being endowed with faith—they, too, O son of Kuntī [actually] worship Me alone, though not according to the prescribed rites.

For I am the enjoyer, as also the lord of all sacrifices. But those people do not comprehend Me in My true nature and hence they fall.

Worshipers of the gods go to the gods; worshipers of the manes go to the manes; those who sacrifice to the spirits go to the spirits; and those who worship Me, come to Me.

A leaf, a flower, a fruit, or water, whoever offers to Me with devotion—that same, proffered in devotion by one whose soul is pure, I accept.

Whatever you do, whatever you eat, whatever you offer in sacrifice, whatever you give away, whatever penance you practice—that, O son of Kuntī, do you dedicate to Me.

Thus will you be freed from the good or evil fruits which constitute the bondage of actions. With your mind firmly set on the way of renunciation [of fruits], you will, becoming free, come to Me.

Even-minded am I to all beings; none is hateful nor dear to Me. Those, however, who worship Me with devotion, they abide in Me, and I also in them.

Even if a person of extremely vile conduct worships Me being devoted to none else, he is to be reckoned as righteous, for he has engaged himself in action in the right spirit.

Quickly does he become of righteous soul and obtain eternal peace. O son of Kuntī, know for certain that My devotee perishes not.

For those, O son of Prithā, who take refuge in Me, even though they be lowly born, women, vaishyas, as also shūdras—even they attain to the highest goal.

How much more, then, pious brāhmans, as also devout royal sages? Having come to this impermanent, blissless world, worship Me.

On Me fix your mind; become My devotee, My worshiper; render homage unto Me. Thus having attached yourself to Me, with Me as your goal, you shall come to Me. . . .

From *Sources of Indian Tradition* by William Theodore de Bary. Copyright ©1988 by Columbia University Press. Reprinted with permission of the publisher.

---

that its Mahayana critics claimed it to be. Its focus was the monastic community, but lay devotees were needed to support this community; moreover, their service and gifts were a major source of merit for them. The emphasis on gaining merit for a better rebirth through high standards of conduct was strong. Popular lay devotion to the Buddha and pilgrimage to his relics at various *stupas* also became prominent in Theravada practice. The Mahayana also held up monastic life as the ideal, but some of its greatest attractions were its devotionalism and virtually polytheistic delight in divine Buddhas and *bodhisattvas* to whom one could pray for mercy, help, and rebirth in paradise. The basis of Theravada piety and practice was the scriptural collection of the traditional teachings ascribed to the Buddha, as reported by his disciples. Theravadins rejected the Mahayana claim that later texts (e.g., the Lotus Sutra) contained the highest teachings of the Buddha.

The Theravada was the form of Buddhism that India gave to Ceylon, Burma, and parts of Southeast Asia. The Mahayana was the dominant form carried into Central Asia and China, where it became the major form of religious practice. Tantric Buddhism, an esoteric Mahayana tradition influenced by Hindu Tantric speculation and ritual, entered Tibet from North India in the seventh century and became the dominant tradition there. From China, Mahayana teachings spread in the fifth to eighth centuries to Korea and Japan.

IN WORLD PERSPECTIVE
Pre-Islamic Iran and India

From a Western perspective, the center of the world in the early Christian centuries is seen as having been the Roman-Byzantine Mediterranean basin. Yet in global perspective the loci of major political power, cultural creativity, and religious vitality throughout most of the early centuries C.E. also included Iran, India, and China.

Even in the Roman "West," Africa and southwestern Asia were prominent both politically and culturally. Roman imperial strength rapidly shifted east to Byzantium; Alexandria was the center of Hellenism for centuries; and the major Christian doctrinal councils were held in Asia and Africa. Our perspective changes when we recognize historical realities still farther east before the seventh-century rise of Islam: the Sasanid culture of Iran, the Zoroastrian revival, the Manichaean movement, the compilation of the Babylonian and Palestinian Talmuds, the completion of the *Mahabharata* and *Ramayana*, Gupta imperial power, art and literature, Indian religious thought, and the spread of the Mahayana across Central Asia to China and Japan.

Asia and Africa were thus the settings for momentous developments. Simplistic notions of a progressive "rise of the West" from classical antiquity to modern times do not hold for the first millennium C.E., especially when we take into account the coming of Islam in its last third. To any impartial observer, in these centuries progressiveness and culture seemed best embodied either in Sasanid and Gupta culture in southwest and south Asia, or in China under the Han, Sui, and T'ang dynasties, and Japan in Nara and Heian times.

A revised perspective would thus identify important centers of cultural, religious, and political traditions around the globe, in the Asian kingdoms and also in the Mediterranean empire of Byzantium and in Aksumite Ethiopia. Hindu tradition and Indian culture were undergoing important developments, while Buddhism was finding new and rich fields for conversion in Central Asia, China, Japan, and Southeast Asia. Zoroastrian Iran appeared well on its way into a second millennium of imperial splendor under the Sasanids.

Yet with the imminent rise of the last major world religious and cultural tradition, Islam, Iran would soon face cataclysmic changes—changes that would later overtake much of India and South Asia. Who could have suspected in the time of Chosroes Anoshirvan how radically Persian culture would be recast in Islamic forms within three or four centuries?

Review Questions ——

1. What are the key elements of Manichaean religion? How might it be said to be an offspring of Christian and Zoroastrian traditions?

2. How did the Sasanid Empire develop after the fall of the Parthians? What were the principal economic bases of the Sasanid state?

3. What were the major religious issues in the Sasanid Empire? What role did Zoroastrian "orthodoxy" play in Sasanid affairs? What changes did Zoroastrianism undergo? Who were the main opponents of Zoroastrian tradition?

4. What might have been the importance of the Silk Route in bringing new religious ideas to Central Asia in these centuries?

5. In what ways can the high Gupta period (ca. 320–450) be considered a "golden age"? What was the extent of the empire in these years? Why did it collapse? Where did the locus of Indian culture move after the fifth century and why?

6. Consider Persia and India in the seventh century, just before the coming of Arab invaders. What factors might have made the subsequent conquests in both areas possible for the new forces from the west?

7. What major affinities do you see between the classical Buddhist and Hindu traditions that crystallized in the first half of the first millennium C.E.? What major differences? Discuss some of the main tenets and ideas of each.

Documents CD-ROM

1. Gnostic Texts
2. Duties of a King, Artha Shastra
3. Kalidasa: From *The Seasons*
4. Hsuan-tsang, The Land and People of India

11 THE FORMATION OF ISLAMIC CIVILIZATION (622–945)

CHAPTER TOPICS

- Origins and Early Development
- Early Islamic Conquests
- The New Islamic Order

- The High Caliphate
- The "Classical" Islamic Culture

In World Perspective The Formation of Islamic Civilization

Islamic civilization has been the last great world civilization to appear to date, if one excepts the post-Enlightenment modern West. The basic ideas and ideals of the Islamic worldview derived from a single, prophetic-revelatory event, Muhammad's proclamation of the Qur'an. This event galvanized the Arabs into a new kind of unity—that of the community of Muslims, or "submitters" to God. This community subsequently spread far beyond Arabia, and Persians, Indians, and others raised it to new heights. Their acceptance of a new vision of society (and also of reality) as more compelling than any older vision—Jewish, Greek, Iranian, Christian, Buddhist—allowed an Islamic civilization to come into being.

Origins and Early Development

The Setting

By 600 C.E., the dominant Eurasian political powers, Christian Byzantium and Sasanid Iran, had confronted one another for centuries. This rivalry did not, however, continue much longer. In the wake of one final, mutually exhausting conflict (608–627), a new Arab power humbled the one and destroyed the other.

Pre-Islamic Arabia was not just a land of desert nomads. In the Fertile Crescent, Byzantium and Iran had kept the nomads of the Syrian and northern Arabian steppe at bay by enlisting small Arab client kingdoms on the edge of the desert as buffer states. One of the biggest of these was Christian in faith. There had long been settled Arab kingdoms in the highlands of southern Arabia, which had direct access to the international trade that moved along its coasts (see Chapter 4). Some of these kingdoms, including a Jewish one, had been independent; others had been under Persian or Abyssinian control. In the western Arabian highland of the Hijaz, the town of Mecca was a center of the caravan trade. It was also a pilgrimage center because of its famous sanctuary, the Ka'ba (or Kaaba), where many pagan Arab tribes had gods enshrined. Mecca was a merchant republic in which older tribal values were breaking down under the strains of urban and commercial life. But neither the Meccans nor other settled Arabs were wholly cut off from the nomads. The Arabic language defined and linked the Arab peoples, however divided they were by religion, blood feuds, rivalry, and conflict.

The popular notion of Islam as a "religion of the desert" is largely untrue. Islam began in a commercial center and first flourished in an agricultural oasis. Its first converts were settled Meccan townsfolk and date farmers of Yathrib

The Ka'ba in Mecca. The Ka'ba is viewed in Muslim tradition as the site of the first "house of God" built by Abraham and his son Ishmael at God's command. It is held to have fallen later into idolatrous use until Muhammad's victory over the Meccans and his cleansing of the holy cubical structure (*Ka'ba* means "cube"). The Ka'ba is the geographical point toward which all Muslims face when performing ritual prayer. It and the plain of Arafat outside Mecca are the two foci of the pilgrimage of Hajj that each Muslim aspires to make at least once in a lifetime. [Mehmet Biber/Photo Researchers, Inc.]

(Medina). Before becoming Muslims, most of these Arabs were pagans, but some were Jews or Christians, or influenced by them. Caravans passed north and south through Mecca, and no merchant involved in this traffic, as Muhammad himself was, could have been ignorant of diverse cultures. Early Muslim leaders used the Arabs as warriors and looked to Arab culture for roots long after the locus of Islamic power had left Arabia. But the empire and civilization they built were centered in the heartlands of Eurasian urban culture and based on settled communal existence rather than desert tribal anarchy.

Muhammad and the Qur'an

Muhammad (ca. 570–632) was raised an orphan in one of the commercial families of the old Meccan tribe of Quraysh. Later, in the midst of a successful business career made possible by his marriage to Khadija (d. ca. 619), a wealthy Meccan widow and entrepreneur, he grew troubled by the idolatry, worldliness, and lack of social conscience around him. These traits would have offended Jewish or Christian morality, about which he knew something. Yet these traditions remained foreign to most Arabs, even though some Arab tribes were Jewish or Christian.

Muhammad's discontent paved the way for a religious experience that changed his life when he was about forty years old. He felt himself called by the one true God to "rise and warn" his fellow Arabs about their disregard for morality and the worship due their creator. On repeated occasions, revelation came to him through God's messenger angel, Gabriel. It took the form of a "reciting" *(qur'an)* of God's word—now rendered in "clear Arabic" for the Arabs, just as it had been given to previous prophets in other languages for their peoples.

The message of the Qur'an was clear: The Prophet is to warn his people against false gods and immorality, especially injustice to the poor, orphans, widows, and women in general. At the end of time, on judgment day, every person will be bodily resurrected to face eternal punishment in hellfire or joy in paradise, according to how he or she has lived. The way to paradise lies in gratitude to God for the bounties of creation, His prophetic and revelatory guidance, and His readiness to forgive. Social justice and worship of the one Lord are required of every person. Each is to recognize his or her creatureliness and God's transcendence. The proper response is "submission" *(islam)* to God's will, becoming *muslim* ("submissive" or "surrendering") in one's worship and morality. All of creation praises and serves God by nature except humans, who can choose to obey or to reject Him.

In this Qur'anic message, the ethical monotheism of Judaic and Christian tradition (probably reinforced by Zoroastrian and Manichaean ideas) reached its logical conclusion—it demanded absolute obedience to the one Lord of the Universe. The Qur'anic revelations state that Muhammad is the last in a line of prophets chosen to bring God's word: Noah, Abraham, Moses, Jesus, and nonbiblical Arabian figures like Salih had been sent on similar missions. Because the communities of

The Qur'an, or "Recitation," of God's Word

The Qur'an has many themes, from moral admonition, social justice, eternal punishment for the ungodly, and exemplary stories of past peoples and their prophets, to God's majesty and uniqueness, His bountiful natural world and compassion for humankind, and the joys of paradise.

Can you identify at least four major Qur'anic themes in the selections below? To what end are the bounties of creation cited? What is the image of God conveyed in these selections? What can you infer about the Qur'anic conception of prophethood? Of the Judgment Day?

The revelation of the Book is from God who is mighty and wise. There are signs for men of faith, in the heavens and in the earth, in your being created and in God's scattered throng of creatures—signs for people with a grasp of truth.

There are signs, too—for those with a mind to understand—in the alternation of night and day, and in the gracious rain God sends from heaven to renew the face of the parched earth, and in the veering of the winds.

These are the signs of God which truly We recite to you. Having God and His signs, in what else after that will you believe as a message?

—Sura 45:1–6

Were you set to count up the mercies of God you would not be able to number them. God is truly forgiving and merciful.

—Sura 16:18

Such is God your Lord. There is no god but He, creator of all things. Then worship Him who is guardian over all there is. No human perception comprehends Him, while He comprehends all perception. He is beyond all conceiving, the One who is infinitely aware.

—Sura 6:102–103

To God belong the east and the west, and wheresoever you turn there is the face of God. Truly God is all-pervading, all-knowing.

—Sura 2:115

You people of the Book, why are you so argumentative about Abraham, seeing that the Torah and the Gospel were only sent down after his time? Will you not use your reason? You are people much given to disputing about things within your comprehension: why insist on disputing about things of which you have no knowledge? Knowledge belongs to God and you lack it!

Abraham was not a Jew, nor was he a Christian. He was a man of pure worship (a hanif) and a Muslim: he was not one of those pagan idolaters. . . .

–Sura 3.65–67

Yet you [people] deny the reality of the judgement. There are guardians keeping watch over you, noble beings keeping record, who know your every deed. The righteous will dwell in bliss. The evil-doers will be in *Jahīm*, in the burning on judgement Day, and there will be no absconding for them.

What can make you realize the Day of judgement as it is? . . . the Day when there is no soul that can avail another soul. For the authority on that Day is God's alone.

–Sura 82.1–5, 9, 19

Excerpt from *Readings in the Qur'an* by Kenneth Cragg. Copyright © 1988 by Kenneth Cragg. Reprinted by permission of HarperCollins, Inc.

---

these earlier prophets had strayed from their scriptures' teachings or altered them, Muhammad was given one final iteration of God's message. Jews and Christians, like pagans, were summoned to respond to the moral imperatives of the Qur'an.

The Prophet's preaching fell largely on deaf ears in the first years after his calling. However, a few did follow the lead of his wife, Khadija, in recognizing him as a divinely chosen reformer. But the merchant aristocracy as a whole resisted. His preaching against their traditional gods and goddesses threatened both their ancestral ways and also the Meccan pilgrimage shrine and the lucrative trade it attracted. The Meccans began to persecute Muhammad's followers. After the deaths of Khadija and Muhammad's uncle and protector, Abu Talib, the situation worsened. Then, as a result of his growing reputation as a moral and holy man, Muhammad was

called to Yathrib (an agricultural oasis about 240 miles north of Mecca) as a neutral arbitrator among its five quarrelsome tribes, three of which were Jewish. Having sent his Meccan followers ahead, Muhammad fled Mecca in July 622 for Yathrib, afterward to be known as Medina (al-Madina, "the City [of the Prophet]"). Some dozen years later, this "emigration," or Hegira, became the starting point for the Islamic calendar, the event marking the creation of a distinctive Islamic community, or *Umma*.[1]

---

[1] The twelve-month Muslim lunar year is shorter than the Christian solar year by about eleven days, giving a difference of about three years per century. Muslim dates are reckoned from the month in 622 in which Muhammad began his Hegira (Arabic: *Hijra*). Thus Muslims celebrated the start of their lunar year 1401 in November 1980 (1979–1980 C.E. = A.H. [Anno Hegirae] 1400), whereas it was only 1,358 solar years from 622 to 1980.

Muhammad quickly cemented ties between the Meccan emigrants and the Medinans, many of whom became converts. Raids on his Meccan enemies' caravans established his leadership. The Arab Jews of Medina largely rejected his religious message. They even made contact with his Meccan enemies, moving Muhammad to turn on them and take their lands. Many of the revelations of the Qur'an from this period pertain to communal order or to the Jews and Christians who rejected Islam.

The basic Muslim norms took shape in Medina: allegiance to the *Umma;* honesty; modesty; abstention from alcohol and pork; fair division of inheritances; improved treatment of women, especially as to property and other rights in marriage; regulation of marriage and divorce; ritual ablution before worship, be it Qur'an reciting or prayer; three (later five) daily rites of worship, facing the Meccan shrine of the Ka'ba; payment to support less fortunate Muslims; daytime fasting for one month each year; and, eventually, pilgrimage to Mecca (*Hajj*) at least once in a lifetime, if one can.

Acceptance of Islamic political authority brought tolerance. A Jewish oasis yielded to Muhammad's authority and was allowed, unlike the resistant Medinan Jews, to keep its lands, practice its faith, and receive protection in return for the payment of a head tax. This practice was followed ever after for Jews, Christians, and other "people of Scripture" who accepted Islamic rule. After long conflict, the Meccans surrendered to Muhammad, and his generosity in accepting them into the *Umma* set the pattern for the later Islamic conquests. Muhammad cemented many of his alliances with marriage. In the last years of the Prophet's life, the once tiny band of Muslims became the heart of a pan-Arabian tribal confederation, bound together by personal allegiance to Muhammad, submission (*islam*) to God, and membership in the *Umma* of "submitters."

Early Islamic Conquests

In 632 Muhammad died, leaving neither a son nor a designated successor. The new *Umma* faced its first major crisis. A political struggle between Meccan and Medinan factions ended in a pledge of allegiance to Abu Bakr, the most senior of the early Meccan converts. Many tribes renounced their allegiance to the Prophet at his death. Nevertheless, Abu Bakr's rule (632–634) as Muhammad's successor, or "caliph" (Arabic: *khalifa*), reestablished at least nominal religious conformity for Arabia. The Arabs were forced to recognize in the *Umma* a new kind of supratribal community that demanded more than allegiance to a particular leader.

Course of Conquest

Under the next two caliphs, Umar (634–644) and Uthman (644–656), Arab armies burst out of the peninsula. By 643 they had conquered the Byzantine and Sasanid territories of the Fertile Crescent, Egypt, and most of Iran. For the first time in centuries, the lands from Egypt to Iran came under one rule. Finally, Arab armies swept west over the Byzantine-controlled Libyan coast and in the east defeated the last Sasanid ruler by 651.

An interlude of civil war followed during the contested caliphate of Ali (656–661). Then the fifth caliph, Mu'awiya (661–680), directed further expansion. An Islamic fleet conquered Cyprus, plundered Sicily and Rhodes, and crippled Byzantine sea power. By 680, control of greater Iran was solidified by permanent Arab garrisoning of Khorasan, much of Anatolia was raided, Constantinople was besieged (but not taken), and Armenia was under Islamic rule.

Succeeding decades saw the eastern Berbers of Libyan North Africa defeated and converted to Islam. With their help, "the West" (*al-Maghrib*, modern Morocco and Algeria), fell quickly. By 716, the disunited Spanish Visigoth kingdoms had fallen, and much of Iberia was under Islamic control. Pushing north into France, the Arabs were finally checked by a defeat at the hands of Charles Martel south of Tours (732). In 710, Arab armies reached the Indus region. Islamic power was supreme from the Atlantic to central Asia (see Map 11–1).

Factors of Success

A combination of factors underlay this rapid expansion. The basic one was the weakened military and economic condition of the Byzantines and Sasanids—the result of their chronic warfare with one another. Also basic was the capacity of the new Islamic vision of society and life to unite the Arabs and attract others. Its corollary was the commitment among the Islamic leadership to extend "the abode of submission" (*Dar al-Islam*) abroad. However, assurance of paradise for those engaged in *jihad*, or "struggle (in the path of God)," is less likely to have motivated the average Arab tribesman than booty. The marginal life in the peninsula was such that the hope of greater prosperity must have been compelling.

Still, religious zeal cannot be discounted as time went on. Another major factor was certainly the leadership of the first caliphs and generals. This combined with Byzantine and Iranian exhaustion to give Arab armies an advantage. Also important was the readiness of many subject populations to welcome Islamic rule as a relief from Byzantine or Persian oppression. Crucial here was the Muslim willingness to allow Christian, Jewish, and even Zoroastrian groups to continue as minorities (with their own legal systems and no military obligations) under protection of Islamic rule. In return, they had to recognize Islamic political authority, pay a non-Muslim head tax (*jizya*), and refrain from proselytizing or interfering with Muslim religious practice. (Ironically, as time went on, the head tax and other strictures on non-Muslims encouraged Christians and Jews to convert.)

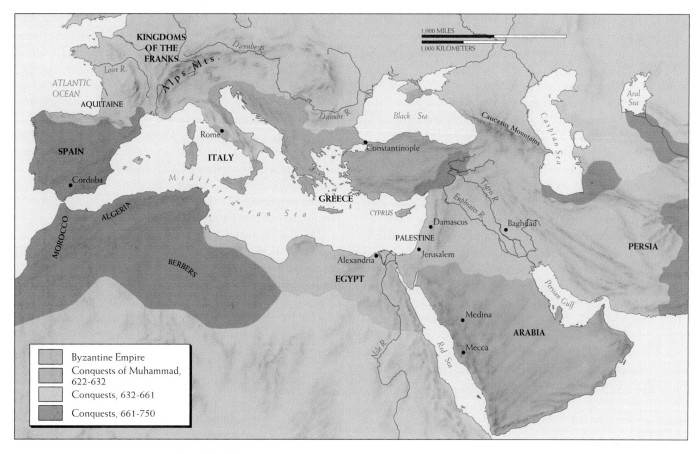

Map 11–1 Muslim conquests and domination of the Mediterranean to about 750 c.e. The rapid spread of Islam (both religion and political-military power) is shown here. Within 125 years of Muhammad's rise, Muslims came to dominate Spain and all areas south and east of the Mediterranean.

Finally, what gave the conquests overall permanence, besides the vitality of the new faith, were the astute policies of the early leaders: relatively little bloodshed, destruction, or disruption in conquest; adoption of existing administrative systems (and personnel) with minimal changes; adjustment of unequal taxation; appointment of capable governors; and strategic siting of new garrison towns like Basra, Kufa, and Fustat (later Cairo).

The New Islamic Order

Although they were quick to adopt and adapt existing traditions, the Muslims brought with them a new worldview that demanded a new political, social, and cultural reality. Beyond military and administrative problems loomed the question of the nature of Islamic society. Under the Prophet, the new community of the *Umma* had replaced, at least in theory, the tribal, blood-based sociopolitical order in Arabia. Yet once the Arabs (most of whom became Muslims) had to rule non-Arabs and non-Muslims, new problems tested the ideal of an Islamic

polity. Chief among these were leadership and membership qualifications, social order, and religious and cultural identity.

The Caliphate

Allegiance to Muhammad had rested on his authority as a divine spokesperson and gifted leader. His first successors were chosen much as were Arab *shaykhs* ("sheiks"), or tribal chieftains: by agreement of the leaders, or elders, of the new religious "tribe" of Muslims, on the basis of superior personal qualities. Added to these qualities was now the precedence in faith conferred by piety and association with the Prophet. Their titles were "successor" (*khalifa*, or caliph), "leader" (*imam*—literally, the one who stands in front to lead the ritual prayer), and "commander (*amir*) of the faithful." These names underscored religious and political authority, both of which most Muslims were willing to recognize in the caliphs Abu Bakr and Umar, and potentially in Uthman and Ali. But by the time of Uthman and Ali, dissension led to civil war. Yet the first four caliphs had all been close to Muhammad, and this closeness gave their reigns a nostalgic aura of pristine purity, especially as the later caliphal institution was based largely on sheer power legitimized by hereditary succession.

The nature of Islamic leadership became an issue with the first civil war (656–661) and the recognition of Mu'awiya, a kinsman of Uthman, as caliph. He founded the first dynastic caliphate, that of his Meccan clan of Umayya (661–750). Umayyad descendants held power until they were ousted in 750 by the Abbasid clan, which based its legitimacy on descent from Abbas, an uncle of the Prophet. The Umayyads had the prestige of the office held by the first four, "rightly guided" caliphs. But they were also judged by many to be worldly kings in comparison to the first four, who were seen as true Muslim successors to Muhammad.

The Abbasids won the caliphate by open rebellion in 750, aided by exploitation of pious dissatisfaction with Umayyad worldliness, non-Arab Muslim resentment of Arab preference (primarily in Iran), and ongoing dissension among Arab tribal factions in the garrison towns. They were scarcely less worldly and continued the hereditary rule begun by the Umayyads. They retained control of most of the Islamic territories until 945. Thereafter, although their line continued until 1258, the caliphate was primarily a titular office representing an Islamic unity that existed politically in name only.

The *Ulama*

The caliph was never "emperor and pope combined." Religious leadership in the *Umma* devolved on another group, those Muslims recognized for piety and learning and sought as authorities. Initially, they were the "Companions" (male and female) of Muhammad. This generation was replaced by those younger followers most concerned with preserving, interpreting, and applying the Qur'an, and with maintaining the norms of the Prophet's original *Umma*. Because the Qur'an contained few actual legal prescriptions, they had to draw on precedents from Meccan and Medinan practice, as well as on oral traditions from and about the Prophet and Companions. They also had to develop and standardize grammatical rules for a common Arabic language based on the Qur'an and pre-Islamic poetry. Furthermore, they had to improve the phonetic, cursive Arabic script, a task done so well that the script was gradually applied as the standard written medium for languages wherever Islamic religion and culture became dominant: among Iranians, Turks, Indians, Indonesians, Malays, East Africans, and others. They also developed an enduring pattern of education based on study under those persons highest in the unbroken temporal chain of trustworthy Muslims linking the current age with that of the earliest *Umma*.

These scholars came to be known as *ulama* ("persons of right knowledge"). Their legal opinions and collective discussions of issues, from theological doctrine to criminal punishments, established a basis for religious and social order. By the ninth century, they had largely defined the understanding of the divine Law, or *Shari'a*, that Muslims ever after have held to be definitive for legal, social, commercial, political, ritual, and moral concerns. This understanding and the methods by which it was derived together form the Muslim science of jurisprudence, the core discipline of Islamic learning.

In Umayyad time, the *ulama* became a new elite. Caliphs and their governors regularly sought their advice, but often only for moral or legal (the two are, in Muslim view, the same) sanction of a contemplated (or accomplished) action. Some *ulama* compromised themselves. Yet incorruptible *ulama* were seldom persecuted for their opinions, mostly because of their status and influence among Muslims.

Thus, without building a formal clergy, Muslims developed a workable moral-legal system based on a formally trained scholarly elite and a tradition of concern with religious ideals in public affairs and social order. The caliphs and their deputies had at least to act with circumspection and support for pious standards in public. Thus, the *ulama* shared the de facto leadership in Muslim societies with the rulers—a pattern that has endured in Islamic states.

The *Umma*

A strength of the Qur'anic message was its universalism, the acceptance into the *Umma* of anyone who would submit to God and follow Muslim precepts. Non-Arab converts had to be accepted, even if it meant loss of tax revenue. The social and political status of new converts was, however, clearly second to that of Arabs. Umar had organized the army register, or *diwan*, according to tribal precedence in conversion to Islam. The *diwan* served as the basis for distribution and taxation of the new wealth, which perpetuated Arab precedence. The new garrisons, which became centers of Islamic culture, kept the Arabs enough apart that they were not simply absorbed into the cultural patterns or traditions of the new lands. The dominance of the Arabic language was ensured by the centrality of the Qur'an in Muslim life and the notion of its perfect Arabic form, together with the increasing administrative use of Arabic to replace Aramaic, Greek, Middle Persian, or Coptic.

Non-Arab converts routinely attached themselves to Arab tribes as "clients," which assured a place in the *diwan*. Still, this attachment also meant second-class citizenship alongside the Arabs. Dissatisfaction among client Muslims was widespread and led to uprisings. Persian-Arab tensions were strong in Umayyad and early Abbasid times. Nevertheless, a Persian cultural renaissance raised the Islamicized modern Persian language to high status in Islamic culture. Consequently, it affected religion, art, and literature in much of the Islamic world.

Caliphal administration joined with the evolution of legal theory and practice and the consolidation of religious norms to give stability to the emerging Islamic society. So powerful was the Muslim vision of society that, upon the demise of a caliph, or even a dynasty such as the Umayyads, the *Umma* and the caliphal office continued. There were, however, conflicting notions of that vision. In the first three Islamic centuries, two major interpretations crystallized that reflected idealistic interpretations of the *Umma*—its leadership and membership. When neither proved viable in the practical world, they failed to win broad-based support. A third, "centrist," vision found favor with the majority because it accommodated inevitable compromises in the higher cause of Islamic unity.

The Kharijites

The most radical idealists traced their political origin to the first civil war (656–661). They were the Kharijites, or "seceders" from Ali's camp because, in their view, he compromised with his enemies. The Kharijites' position was that the Muslim polity must be based on strict Qur'anic principles. They espoused total equality of the faithful and held that the leader of the *Umma* should be the best Muslim, whoever that might be. They took a moralistic view of membership in the *Umma*: Anyone who committed a major sin was no longer a Muslim. Extreme Kharijites were rallying points for opposition to the Umayyads and the Abbasids. Although the movement declined, moderate Kharijite groups survive in Oman and North Africa.

The Shi'a

A second position was defined largely in terms of leadership of the *Umma*. Muhammad had no surviving sons, and his son-in-law and cousin Ali claimed the caliphate in 656, partly on the basis of his blood tie to the Prophet. His claim was contested by Mu'awiya in the first Islamic civil war. Mu'awiya took over after a Kharijite murdered Ali in 661. The "partisans of Ali" (*Shi'at Ali*, or simply the *Shi'a*, or *Shi'ites*) go back to Ali's murder and especially to that of his son Husayn at Karbala, in Iraq, at the hands of Umayyad troops (680).

Whereas all Muslims esteem Ali for his closeness to Muhammad, Shi'ites believe him to be the Prophet's appointed successor. Ali's blood tie with Muhammad was augmented in Shi'ite thinking by belief in the Prophet's designation of him as the true *imam*, or Muslim leader, after him. Numerous rebellions in Umayyad times rallied around persons claiming to be such a true successor, whether as an Alid or merely a member of Muhammad's clan of Hashim. Even the Abbasids based their right to the caliphate on their Hashimite ancestry. The major Shi'ite pretenders who emerged in the ninth and tenth centuries based their claims on both the Prophet's designation and their descent from Ali and Fatima, Muhammad's daughter. They also stressed the idea of a divinely inspired knowledge passed on by Muhammad to his designated heirs. Thus the true Muslim was the faithful follower of the *imams*, who carried Muhammad's blood and spiritual authority.

Origins and Early Development of Islam

ca. 570	Birth of Muhammad
622	The Hijra ("emigration") of Muslims to Yathrib (henceforward *al-Madina*, "The City [of the Prophet]"); beginning of Muslim calendar
632	Death of Muhammad; Abu Bakr becomes first "successor" (*Khalifa*, caliph) to leadership, reigns 632–634
634–644	Caliphate of Umar; rapid conquests in Egypt and Iran
644–656	Caliphate of Uthman (member of Umayyad clan); more conquests; Qur'an text established; growth of sea power
656–661	Contested Caliphate of Ali; first civil war
661–680	Caliphate of Mu'awiya; founding of Umayyad dynasty (661–750); capital moved to Damascus; more expansion
680	Second civil war (680–692) begins with death of al-Husayn at Karbala

Shi'ites saw Ali's assassination by a Kharijite and the massacre of Husayn and his family as proofs of the evil nature of this world's rulers, and as rallying points for true Muslims. True Muslims, like their *imams*, must suffer. But they would be vindicated by a *mahdi*, or "guided one," who would usher in a messianic age and a judgment day that would see the faithful rewarded.

On several occasions, Shi'ite rulers did head Islamic states. But only after 1500, in Iran, did Shi'ism prevail as the majority faith in a major Muslim state. The Shi'ite vision of the true *Umma* has not been able to dominate the larger Islamic world.

The Centrists

It was a third, less sharply defined position on the nature of leadership and membership in the *Umma* that most Muslims accepted. It proved acceptable not only to lukewarm Muslims or pragmatists, but also to persons of piety as intense as that of any Kharijite or Shi'ite. We may term the proponents of this position *centrists*. They called themselves *Sunnis*—followers of the tradition (*sunna*) established by the Prophet and the Qur'an. Neither they, nor the Shi'ites, nor the Kharijites, have ever been a single sect, but have always encompassed a wide range of ideas and groups. They have made up the broad middle spectrum of Muslims who tend to put communal solidarity and maintenance of the Islamic polity above purist adherence to particular theological tenets. They have been inclusivist rather than exclusivist, a trait that has typified the Islamic (unlike the Jewish or Christian) community.

The centrist position was the most workable framework for the new Islamic state. Its basic ideas were: (1) The *Umma* is a theocratic entity, a state under the authority of God's law, the Shari'a. The sources of guidance are, first, the Qur'an; second, Muhammad's precedent; and, third and fourth, the interpretive efforts and consensus of the Muslims (in practice, the *ulama*). (2) The caliph is the absolute temporal ruler, charged with administering and defending the Abode of Islam and protecting Muslim norms and practice; he possesses no greater authority than other Muslims in matters of faith. (3) A person who professes to be Muslim by witnessing that "There is no god but God, and Muhammad is His Messenger" should be considered a Muslim (because "only God knows what is in the heart"), and not even a mortal sin excludes such a person from the *Umma*.

These and other basic premises of Muslim community came to be the theological underpinnings of both the caliphal state and the international Islamic social order.

The High Caliphate

The consolidation of the caliphal institution began with the victory of the Umayyad caliph Abd al-Malik in 692, in the second civil war. The ensuing century and a half mark the era of the "high caliphate" that flourished first under the Umayyads in Damascus and then in the Abbasid capital of Baghdad. The height of caliphal power and splendor came in the first century of Abbasid rule, largely during the caliphates of the fabled Harun al-Rashid (786–809) and his third son, al-Ma'mun (813–833).

The Abbasid State

The Abbasids' victory effectively ended Arab dominance as well as Umayyad ascendancy (except in Spain). The shift of the imperial capital from Damascus to Baghdad on the Tigris (762–766) symbolized the eastward shift in cultural and political orientation under the new regime. More and more Persians entered the bureaucracy. Religiously, the Abbasids' disavowal of Shi'ite hopes for a divinely inspired imamate re-

flected their determination to gain the support of a broad spectrum of Muslims, even if they still stressed their descent from al-Abbas (ca. 565–653), uncle of both Muhammad and Ali.

Whereas the Umayyads had relied on Syrian Arab forces, the Abbasids used Khorasanian Arabs and Iranians. Beginning in the ninth century, however, they enlisted slave soldiers (*mamluks*), mostly Turks from the northern steppes, as their personal troops. The officers of these forces, themselves *mamluks*, soon seized the positions of power in the bureaucracies and the army and dominated the caliphs. This domination led to increasing alienation of the Muslim populace from their own rulers.

Society

The deep division between rulers and populace became typical of Islamic societies. However, even while the independence of ever more provincial rulers reduced Abbasid central power after the mid-ninth century, such rulers generally chose to recognize caliphal authority at least nominally. This underscored their role as guardians of the Islamic order, which found its real cohesiveness in the Muslim ideals propagated by the *ulama*.

However, full conversion of the diverse populace of the Islamic Empire lagged behind centralization of political power and development of Islamic institutions. Iraq and Iran (especially Khorasan, which had substantial early Arab Muslim immigration) saw the fullest Islamization of local elites before the mid-twelfth century. They were followed by Spain, North Africa, and Syria. Conversion and fuller Islamization meant the development of a self-confident Muslim polity and a diminished need for centralized caliphal power.[2]

Decline

The eclipse of the caliphal empire was foreshadowed at the outset of Abbasid rule, when one of the last Umayyads founded a Spanish Islamic state (756–1030) that produced the spectacular Moorish culture of Spain. The Spanish Umayyads even claimed the title of caliph in 929. In all the Abbasid provinces, regional governments were always potential independent states. A separate state in North Africa was set up in 801 by Harun al-Rashid's governor of modern Tunisia. A later North African dynasty, the Fatimids, conquered Egypt and set up Shi'ite rule in 969 that claimed to be the only true caliphate.

In the East, Iran became harder for Baghdad to control. Beginning in 821 in Khorasan, Abbasid governors or rebel groups started independent dynasties repeatedly for two centuries. The caliph usually had to recognize their rule. The

Early Period of the High Caliphate	
680–692	Second civil war
685–705	Caliphate of Abd al-Malik; consolidation, arabization of administration
705–715	Caliphate of al-Walid; Morocco conquered, Spain invaded; Arab armies reach the Indus
ca. 750	Introduction of paper manufacture from China through Samarqand to Islamic world
750	Abbasids seize caliphate from Umayyads, begin new dynasty (750–1258)
756	Some Umayyads escape to Spain, found new dynasty (756–1030)
762–766	New Abbasid capital built at Baghdad

[2]Richard W. Bulliet, *Conversion to Islam in the Medieval Period* (Cambridge: Harvard University Press, 1979), especially pp. 7–15, 128–138.

Samanids of Khorasan and Transoxiana ruled at Bukhara as nominal Abbasid vassals from 875 until 999. They gave northeastern Iran a long period of economic and political security from Turkish steppe invaders. Under their aegis, Persian poetry and Arabic scientific studies began a Persian Islamic cultural renaissance and influential scientific tradition.

Of greatest consequence for the Abbasid caliphate, however, was the rise of a Shi'ite clan, the Buyids, who took over Abbasid rule in 945. The caliph and his descendants were henceforth puppets in the hands of a Buyid "commander" (*amirs* or *emirs; later, sultans*). In 1055, the Buyids were replaced by the more famous Seljuk *sultans.* Abbasid caliphs continued as figureheads of Muslim unity until Mongol invaders killed the last of them in 1258.

The "Classical" Islamic Culture

The splendor of the Abbasid court became the stuff of Islamic legends, such as those in *The Thousand and One Nights.* Their rich cultural legacy similarly outlived the Abbasids themselves. Their achievements were made possible by a strong army and central government and vigorous internal and external trade. The latter may have been stimulated by the T'ang Empire of China, with which the Islamic world had overland and sea contact. Material factors, such as the introduction of paper manufacture (introduced from China about 750) or the flight of Byzantine scholars east to new Abbasid centers of learning, also contributed to making the early Abbasid era special.

Intellectual Traditions

The Abbasid heyday was marked by sophisticated tastes and an insatiable thirst for knowledge—*any* knowledge. Contacts (primarily among intellectuals) between Muslims and Christian, Jewish, Zoroastrian, and other "protected" religious communities contributed to the cosmopolitanism of the age. Some older intellectual traditions experienced a revival in early Abbasid times, as with Hellenistic learning. Philosophy, astronomy, mathematics, medicine, and other natural sciences enjoyed patronage. Islamic culture took over the tradition of rational inquiry from the Hellenistic world and developed and preserved it when Europe was by comparison a cultural wasteland.

Arabic translations of Greek and Sanskrit works stimulated progress in astronomy and medicine. Translation reached its peak in al-Ma'mun's new academy headed by a Nestorian Christian, Hunayn ibn Ishaq (d. 873), noted for his medical and Greek learning. There were Arabic translations of everything from the Greek authors Galen, Ptolemy, Euclid, Aristotle, Plato, and the Neo-Platonists to the Indian fables that had been translated into Middle Persian under the Sasanids.

Such translations stimulated not only Arabic learning, but later also that of the less advanced European world, especially in the twelfth and thirteenth centuries.

Language and Literature

Arabic language and literature developed greatly in the expanded cultural sphere of the new empire. In *belles lettres* there arose a significant genre of Arabic writing known as *adab*, or "manners" literature. It included essays and didactic literature influenced by earlier Persian letters. At the same time, as translations of different literary genres increased the range of the original bedouin idiom, poetry flourished by building on the sophisticated tradition of the Arabic ode, or *qasida.* Grammar was central to the interpretation of the Qur'an that occupied the *ulama* and undergirded an emerging curriculum of Muslim learning. Historical and biographical writings became major genres of Arabic writing. They arose primarily to record, first, the lives and times of the Prophet and earliest Companions, then those of subsequent generations of Muslims. This information was crucial to judging the reliability of the "chains" of transmitters included with each traditional report, or *hadith.* A *hadith* reports words or actions ascribed to Muhammad and the Companions; it became the chief source of Muslim legal and religious norms alongside the Qur'an, as well as the basic unit of most prose genres, from history to Qur'an exegesis. Collections of the *hadith* also formed a separate genre that was mined by preachers and by the developing schools of legal interpretation, whose crowning glory was the work of al-Shafi'i (d. 820) on legal reasoning.

Art and Architecture

In art and architecture the Abbasid era saw the crystallization of a "classical" Islamic style by about 1000 C.E. Except for ceramics and Arabic calligraphy, most of the discrete elements

"Classical" Period of the High Caliphate	
786–809	Caliphate of Harun al-Rashid; apogee of caliphal power
813–833	Caliphate of al-Ma'mun; strong patronage of translations of Greek, Sanskrit, and other works into Arabic; first heavy reliance on slave soldiers (*mamluks*)
875	Rise of Samanid power at Bukhara; patronage of Persian poetry paves way for Persian literary renaissance
945–1055	Buyid amirs rule the eastern empire at Baghdad; the Abbasid caliphs continue largely as figureheads
969	Rise of Shi'ite Fatimid dynasty in North Africa
1055	Buyid amirs replaced by Seljuk sultans as effective rulers at Baghdad and custodians of the caliphate

of Islamic art and architecture had antecedents in Greco-Roman, Byzantine, or Iranian art. What was new was the use of older forms and motifs for new purposes and combinations, and also the spread of such elements to new locales, generally from east (especially the Fertile Crescent) to west (Syria, Egypt, North Africa, and Spain). Also new was the combination and elaboration of discrete forms, as in the case of the colonnade (or hypostyle) mosque or complex arabesque designs.

The Muslims had good reason to be self-confident about their faith and culture and to want to distinguish them from others. Particular formal items, such as calligraphic motifs and inscriptions on buildings, came to characterize Islamic architecture and define its functions. Most striking was the avoidance of pictures or icons in public art. This was, of course, in line with the Muslim aversion to idolatry and to Byzantine Christian art. Although this iconoclasm later diminished, it was a telling expression of the general thrust of Muslim faith and culture.

IN WORLD PERSPECTIVE
The Formation of Islamic Civilization

The rise of Islam as both an international religious tradition and an international civilization is one of the pivotal moments in world history. The new traditions forged first in the Arabian peninsula and then in Syria, Iraq, North Africa, Iran, and beyond were to change much of Asia and Africa and parts of Europe. Religiously, the Islamic movement became, along with the Buddhist and Christian movements, one of the three major universalist, missionary traditions of world religious history. Politically and socially, the Islamic order for society spread far beyond the imagination of Muhammad and his companions.

The Islamic polity was in its first three centuries the most dynamic and expansive imperial state of its day. During the same time, Chinese emperors of the T'ang were rebuilding and improving on the previous Han imperium; Charlemagne and the Carolingians were struggling to hammer out a much smaller, more homogeneous empire and a cultural renaissance in the relatively backward world of western Europe; Byzantium was fighting to survive against Islamic arms and turning inward to conserve its traditions; and post-Gupta India was divided into regional kingdoms and vulnerable to new forces (including those of Islam) moving into northwestern India.

As different as the two were, only China compared favorably with or surpassed the Islamic world during this period in terms of political and military power as well as cultural unity, creativity, and self-consciousness. The T'ang and the Abbasids wielded commensurate power in their heydays, although the Chinese held together as a centralized state much better than the Islamic Empire. Certainly they were the two greatest political and cultural units in the world in their age. They each had one cultural language. They also shared the military primacy of nomadic cavalry as well as the adaptive ability to incorporate new peoples into their larger culture—although Islamic cultures proved more flexible on this count. Indeed, the great elasticity and adaptability of Islam as a religious tradition and a social order belie its present reputation in the West as an inherently inflexible system.

Nevertheless, the bases of Islamic rule were clearly different, spread as the empire was over vastly more culturally heterogeneous and dispersed geographical areas than that of China. Conquest initially fueled the economy of the new Islamic state, but in the long run, trade and urban commercial centers were the backbone of Islamic prosperity, as well as the prime means of dissemination of Muslim faith to new lands. The Islamic Empire was agrarian-based, yet the overall climate, soil, and water conditions for food production were not as good as those in China or western Europe. Most Islamic lands lacked abundant water; therefore, supporting dense populations well was difficult. This hindrance did not stop the development of impressive Islamic states, societies, and cultures, but it did set limits to it.

The Islamic achievement was different from any other in this period primarily in that it resulted from an effort to build something new rather than to recapture old traditions, whether religious, social, or political. In later centuries, the early Arab impress of Islamic culture and religion was tempered and changed by the vast numbers of Persian- and Turkish-speaking Muslims and also the many regional groups, from Swahili-speakers in East Africa to the Malays and Indonesians of Southeast Asia. Nevertheless, Arabic went abroad with the holy Qur'an as the sacred medium of God's final revelation. Since Islam's emergence from the Arabian peninsula, individual Muslims worldwide have always learned something of Arabic and the sacred Book.

This achievement was a new historical phenomenon, at least in its scale. Although Muslim faith can be seen as largely a reformation of Semitic monotheism, it was more fundamentally an effort to do something new—not merely to reform, but to subsume older traditions of Jews or Christians in a more comprehensive vision of God's plan on Earth. Muslims did adopt and adapt the traditions of older Afro-Eurasian cultures. Yet as both a civilization and a religious tradition, Islam developed its own distinctive stamp that persisted wherever Muslims extended the *Umma*.

Review Questions

1. What was Arabian society like before the coming of Islam? What were the prime targets of the Qur'anic message in that society?

2. What are the main features of the Islamic worldview? How do Islamic ideas about history, salvation, law, social justice, and other key issues compare to those of Christianity and Judaism?

3. What were the primary kinds of leadership in the early Islamic polities? To what extent were political and religious leadership separated in different offices and functions?

4. Discuss the conversion of subject populations in the early centuries of the Islamic Empire. What were incentives and obstacles to conversion?

5. What explains the initial rapid conquests of the Arab armies? The decline of the imperial caliphal state? What were some of the lasting accomplishments of the Umayyad and Abbasid Empires?

6. Discuss the "classical" culture of the high caliphate. What role did foreign traditions play in it? What were some of its prominent achievements in various fields?

Documents CD-ROM

1. Al-Tabari: An Early Biography of Islam's Prophet

2. Islam in the Prophet's Absence: Continuation under the Caliphate

3. The Caliphate in Decline: Al-Matawwakil's Murder

4. Al-Tabari: The Perfect State

5. Shi'ism and the Caliph Ali: Controversy over the Prophet's Succession

12 THE EARLY MIDDLE AGES IN THE WEST TO 1000: THE BIRTH OF EUROPE

CHAPTER TOPICS

The early Middle Ages marks the birth of Europe. Within what had been the northern and western provinces of the Roman Empire, Greco-Roman culture combined with Germanic culture and Christianity to create distinctive political and cultural forms. In government, religion, and language, as well as geography, these regions grew separate from the eastern Byzantine world and the Islamic Arab world that extended across North Africa from Spain to the eastern Mediterranean.

Surrounded and assailed from north, east, and south, western Europe became insular and stagnant, its people losing touch with classical, especially Greek, learning and science. But they learned to develop their native resources. The reign of Charlemagne saw a modest renaissance of antiquity. And the social and political forms that emerged during this period—manorialism and feudalism—proved to be fertile seedbeds for the growth of distinctive western institutions.

The Decline of Roman Authority in the West

By the late third century, the Roman Empire faced growing disarray. To strengthen it, the Emperor Diocletian (r. 284–305)

divided it between himself and a co-emperor. The result was a dual empire with its own emperor in the east and the west, and, eventually, independent imperial bureaucracies.

A critical shift of the empire's resources and orientation to the east accompanied these changes. In 330, Emperor Constantine I (r. 306–337) dedicated a new imperial capital, Constantinople, built on the site of ancient Byzantium at the mouth of the Black Sea and a major commercial crossroads. Constantinople gradually became a "new Rome" as the "old" Rome declined in importance. When the barbarian migrations began in the late fourth century, the west was in serious disarray, imperial focus having shifted to Constantinople and the east.

Germanic Migrations

The German tribes did not suddenly arrive in the west. Roman and Germanic cultures had commingled peacefully for centuries. A great influx of Visigoths into the empire in 376 ended this coexistence. The Visigoths had been pushed into the empire by the Huns. In exchange for their services as *foederati*, or special allies, the eastern emperor Valens (r. 364–378) promised the Visigoths the right to settle within the empire. However, the Romans treated their new allies harshly. The Visigoths rebelled and defeated Roman armies under Valens at the Battle of Adrianople in 378.

After Adrianople, the Romans permitted the settlement of barbarians within the heart of the western empire. Although the largest of the tribes numbered at most 100,000 people, the invaders entered a western empire divided by ambitious military commanders and weakened by famine, disease, and overtaxation. By the second half of the fourth century, the Romans could not manage their frontiers in the west. "Barbarizing" the Roman army—that is, recruiting peasants and making the Germanic tribes Roman allies—only weakened it further. The eastern empire retained enough wealth and vitality to field new armies or to buy off invaders. The western empire succumbed.

Fall of the Western Roman Empire

In the early fifth century, Italy and Rome suffered devastating blows. In 410, the Visigoths sacked Rome. In 452, the Huns, led by Attila, invaded Italy. In 455, Rome was overrun by the Vandals.

By the mid-fifth century, power in western Europe had passed to barbarian chieftains. In 476, the barbarian Odovacer (ca. 434–493) deposed the western emperor Romulus Augustulus. The eastern emperor Zeno (r. 474–491) recognized Odovacer as his western viceroy. By the end of the fifth century, the barbarians had overrun the western empire.

The barbarians admired Roman culture and had no desire to destroy it. Except in Britain and northern Gaul, Roman law and government and Latin coexisted with the new Germanic institutions. Only the Vandals and the Anglo-Saxons refused to profess titular obedience to the emperor in Constantinople.

The Visigoths, the Ostrogoths, and the Vandals were followers of the Arian creed, which had been condemned at the Council of Nicea in 325 and was considered heretical in the west. Later, around 500, the Franks, who had settled in Gaul, would convert to the orthodox, or "Catholic," form of Christianity supported by the bishops of Rome. The Franks ultimately helped convert the other barbarians to Roman Christianity.

A gradual interpenetration of two strong cultures marked the period of the Germanic migrations. Despite western military defeat, the Goths and the Franks became far more romanized than the Romans were germanized. Latin, Nicene Christianity, and Roman law and government were to triumph in the west during the Middle Ages.

The Byzantine Empire

As western Europe succumbed to the Germanic invasions, imperial power shifted to the eastern part of the Roman Empire—known as the Byzantine Empire—and its capital, Constantinople. The Byzantine Empire would endure until 1453.

The Reign of Justinian

The first period of Byzantine history (324–632) was by far its greatest. At the height of this period, Emperor Justinian (r. 527–565) ruled with the assistance of his brilliant wife, Empress Theodora, who rose from lowly origins to become a major figure in imperial government.

The imperial goal in the east was to impose legal and doctrinal conformity throughout the empire. To this end, Justinian collated and revised Roman law. Justinian's *Corpus Juris Civilis* (body of civil law) was a fourfold compilation undertaken by a learned committee of lawyers. Beginning with the Renaissance, these works provided the foundation for most subsequent European law down to the nineteenth century.

Religion also served imperial centralization. Since the fifth century, the patriarch of Constantinople had crowned emperors in Constantinople. This practice reflected the close ties between rulers and the church. As clerical ranks grew, the church served the state as a welfare agency for the poor and needy.

During Justinian's reign, the empire's strength was its more than 1,500 cities. Of these, the largest, with perhaps 350,000 inhabitants, was Constantinople, the cultural crossroads of Asian and European civilizations (see Map 12–1). The large provincial cities had populations of 50,000.

Eastern Influences

During the reign of Heraclius (r. 610–641), the empire took an eastern, as opposed to a Roman, direction. Heraclius spoke Greek, not Latin. He spent his reign resisting Persian and Islamic invasions. Islamic armies overran the empire after 632, and attacked Constantinople in 677. Not until Leo III (r. 717–741) were they repulsed and Asia Minor (modern Turkey) was regained by the empire.

Leo, however, perhaps under Islamic influence, forbade the use of images in eastern churches and tried to enforce the ban in the west. His efforts insulted the western church, which had nurtured the adoration of Jesus, Mary, and the saints in images and icons. The banning of images reflected a degree of royal involvement in church affairs, routine in the east, which the western church resisted. The ban was reversed in the late eighth century.

In 1071, the Byzantine Empire suffered a major defeat at Manzikert at the hands of the Muslim Seljuk Turks. The Turks rapidly overran Asia Minor. This defeat marked the beginning of the end of the empire, although the actual end—at the hands of the Ottoman Turks—lay centuries ahead. After two decades of steady Turkish advance, the

(A) The great church of Hagia Sophia (Holy Wisdom). Built in Constantinople (now Instanbul, Turkey) by the emperor Justinian between 532 and 537, this church was one of the most influential achievements of Byzantine art and architecture. This interior view shows part of the great dome of the church (107 feet in diameter) and its rich decoration of marbles and mosaics. [Giraudon/Art Resource, N.Y.]

(A)

(B) The exterior of Hagia Sophia is plain and ordinary compared with the interior—a reflection of the priority the Byzantines attached to the inner life. The four towering minarets were among additions made by the Turkish Muslims after they conquered Constantinople in 1453 and transformed the building into a mosque. Since 1935 it has been a national museum. [Giraudon/Art Resource, N.Y.]

(B)

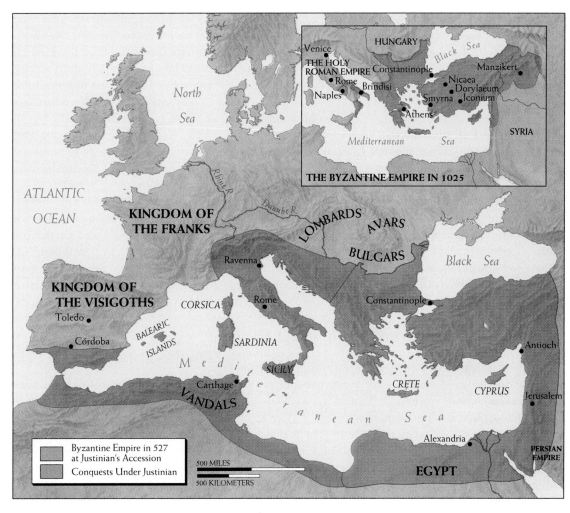

Map 12-1   The Byzantine Empire at the death of Justinian.   The inset shows the empire in 1025, before its losses to the Seljuk Turks.

eastern emperor asked for western aid in 1092. Three years later, the west launched the first Crusade (see Chapter 13). In 1204, the Crusaders would inflict more damage on Constantinople and eastern Christendom than all non-Christian invaders had done.

Throughout the early Middle Ages, the Byzantine Empire protected western Europe from Persian, Arab, and Turkish armies. The Byzantines were also a major conduit of classical learning to the west. While western Europeans were fumbling to create a culture of their own, the Byzantine Empire provided a model of a civilized society.

The Impact of Islam on East and West

A new drama began to unfold in the seventh century with the rise of Islam (see Chapter 11). By the middle of the eighth century, Arabs had conquered the southern and eastern

Mediterranean coastline and occupied parts of Spain. Assaulted from east and west, Christian Europe developed a lasting fear of the Muslims. The Byzantine Emperor Leo III (r. 717–740) stopped Arab armies at Constantinople (717–718); during the next several centuries Byzantine rulers pushed the Arabs back. In the west, the Franks defeated the Arabs near Tours (in central France) in 732, ending the possibility of Arab expansion into Europe by way of Spain. From the end of the seventh century to the middle of the eleventh, the Mediterranean remained something of a Muslim lake. Western trade with East Asia was diminished and carried on in awareness of Muslim dominance.

The Western Debt to Islam

The Arab invasions during the early Middle Ages helped give birth to western Europe as a cultural entity. Arab belligerence forced western Europeans to fall back on their own resources and develop their Germanic and Greco-Roman heritage into a unique culture. By diverting the energies of the Byzantine Empire, the Arabs prevented it from expanding into western Europe, allowing the Franks to gain ascendancy. They also reduced western access to eastern cultural influence.

Despite the hostility of the Christian west to the Islamic world, there was creative interchange between them. The more advanced Arab civilizations taught western farmers how to irrigate fields and western artisans how to tan leather and refine silk. Thanks to Arabic translators, Greek works in astronomy, mathematics, and medicine became available to scholars in the west in Latin translation. And down to the sixteenth century, after the works of the famous ancient physicians Hippocrates and Galen, the basic gynecological and child-care manuals followed by western midwives and physicians were compilations by Arab physicians and scholars.

The Developing Roman Church

Throughout this period, one western institution gained in strength: the Christian church. As the western empire crumbled, local bishops and cathedral chapters (ruling bodies of clergy) filled the resulting vacuum of authority. The local cathedral became the center of urban life and the local bishop the highest authority for those who remained in the cities. In Rome, the pope took control of the city as the western emperors died out. Western Europe discovered that the Christian church was its best repository of Roman administrative skills and classical culture. The church also had a religious message of providential purpose and individual worth that could give solace and meaning to life at its worst. It had a ritual of baptism and a creed that united people beyond the traditional barriers of class, education, and gender. And alone in the west, the church retained an effective hierarchical administration, scattered throughout the old empire, staffed by the best-educated minds in Europe and centered in Rome.

Monastic Culture

The church also enjoyed the services of growing numbers of monks, who were loyal to its mission and objects of popular respect. Monastic culture was a strength of the church during the Middle Ages.

The first monks were hermits who withdrew from society. They were inspired by the Christian ideal of self-denial in imitation of Christ. The popularity of monasticism grew as Christianity became the favored religion of the empire during the fourth century. Embracing the biblical "counsels of perfection" (chastity, poverty, and obedience), the monastic life became the purest form of religious practice.

Hermit monasticism was soon joined by communal monasticism. Basil the Great (329–379) popularized communal monasticism throughout the East, providing a rule that directed monks into such social services as caring for orphans, widows, and the infirm in surrounding communities.

The great organizer of western monasticism was Benedict of Nursia (ca. 480–547). In 529, he established a monastery at Monte Cassino, in Italy, founding the form of monasticism—Benedictine—that came to dominate in the west. Benedict also wrote a *Rule for Monasteries*, which regimented and enriched monastic life. Benedictine monasteries were hierarchically organized under an abbot, whose command was beyond question. Study and religious devotion alternated with manual labor—a program that promoted the religious, intellectual, and physical well-being of the monks. During the early Middle Ages, Benedictine missionaries Christianized both England and Germany. Their disciplined organization and devotion to hard work made the Benedictines an economic and political power as well as a spiritual force.

The Doctrine of Papal Primacy

The eastern emperors looked on the church as a department of the state. The bishops of Rome, however, opposed such royal intervention. Taking advantage of imperial weakness, they developed the doctrine of "papal primacy." This doctrine made the Roman pontiff supreme within the church when it came to church doctrine and clerical allegiance. It also enabled him to make important secular claims, leading to repeated conflicts between church and state, pope and emperor, throughout the Middle Ages.

Pope Damasus I (366–384) took the first step when he declared Rome's "apostolic" primacy. Pointing to Jesus' words to Peter in the Gospel of Matthew (16:18) ("Thou art Peter, and

---

Major Political and Religious Developments of the Early Middle Ages

313	Emperor Constantine issues the Edict of Milan
325	Council of Nicea defines Christian doctrine
410	Rome invaded by Visigoths under Alaric
413–426	St. Augustine writes *The City of God*
451–453	Europe invaded by the Huns under Attila
476	Barbarian Odovacer deposes western emperor and rules as king of the Romans
488	Theodoric establishes kingdom of Ostrogoths in Italy
529	St. Benedict founds monastery at Monte Cassino
533	Justinian codifies Roman law
732	Charles Martel defeats Arabs at Tours
754	Pope Stephen II and Pepin III ally

upon this rock I will build my church"), he claimed all popes to be Peter's successors as the unique "rock" on which the Christian church was built. Pope Leo I (440–461) assumed the title *pontifex maximus*—"supreme priest" and proclaimed himself to be endowed with a "plenitude of power," the supremacy of the bishop of Rome over all other bishops in the church. Pope Gelasius I (492–496) proclaimed the authority of the clergy to be "more weighty" than the power of kings because priests had charge of divine affairs.

Division of Christendom

As these events suggest, the division of Christendom into eastern (Byzantine) and western (Roman Catholic) churches has its roots in the early Middle Ages. The division was due in part to linguistic and cultural differences between the Greek east and the Roman west. As in the west, eastern church organization closely followed that of the secular state. A "patriarch" ruled over "metropolitans" and "archbishops" in the cities and provinces, and they in turn ruled over bishops, who ruled the local clergy. A novel combination of Greek, Roman, and Asian elements, however, shaped Byzantine culture, giving eastern Christianity more of a mystical orientation and a greater preoccupation with the hereafter than western Christianity. This difference in outlook may have predisposed eastern patriarchs to submit more passively than western popes ever could to royal intervention in their affairs.

Three major factors lay behind the religious break between east and west. The first revolved around questions of doctrinal authority. The eastern church put more stress on the authority of the Bible and the ecumenical councils of the church in the definition of Christian doctrine than on the counsel and decrees of the bishop of Rome. The claims of Roman popes were unacceptable to the east. This

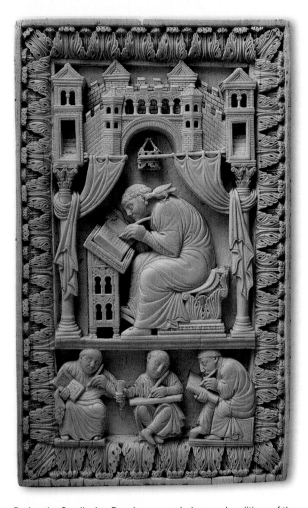

During the Carolingian Renaissance, scholars made editions of the works of Gregory the Great, shown here in a monastic scriptorium (an area devoted to copying and preserving books) receiving the divine word from a dove perched on his shoulder. Below St. Gregory three monks are shown writing. Note the inkwell held by the middle monk. Before the invention of the printing press in about 1450, manuscripts could only be duplicated by laborious hand copying. Much of this painstaking work was done by monks. [Kunsthistorisches Museum, Vienna]

basic issue of authority in matters of faith lay behind the mutual excommunications of Pope Nicholas I and Patriarch Photius in the ninth century and of Pope Leo IX and Patriarch Michael Cerularius in 1054.

A second factor was the western addition of the *filioque* clause to the Nicene Creed. According to this anti-Arian clause, the Holy Spirit proceeds "also from the Son" *(filioque)* as well as from the Father, making clear the western belief that Christ was fully one essence with God the Father and not a lesser being.

The third factor dividing the eastern and western churches was the iconoclastic controversy of the eighth century. As noted earlier, the Byzantine Emperor Leo III (r. 717–741) attempted to force western popes to abolish the use of images in their churches. This stand met fierce resistance and coincided with a threat to Rome from the Lombards of northern Italy. In 754, Pope Stephen II (752–757) enlisted the Franks and their ruler, Pepin III, against the Lombards and as a counterweight to the eastern emperor. This marriage of religion and politics created a new western church and empire; it also determined much of western history into our time.

The Kingdom of the Franks

Merovingians and Carolingians: From Clovis to Charlemagne

Clovis (ca. 466–511), a chieftain who converted to orthodox Christianity around 496, founded the first Frankish dynasty, the Merovingians. Clovis and his successors made the Franks a significant force in western Europe. The Franks' territory extended throughout modern France, Belgium, the Netherlands, and western Germany. In attempting to govern their kingdom, the Merovingians encountered the most persistent problem of medieval political history—the competing claims of the "one" and the "many," with the king (the "one") struggling to impose centralized government and transregional loyalty on local magnates (the "many").

The Merovingian kings addressed this problem by making pacts with the landed nobility and by creating the royal office of count. The counts were men to whom the king gave great lands in the expectation that they would be loyal officers of the kingdom. But like local aristocrats, the Merovingian counts also became territorial rulers, and the Frankish kingdom fragmented into independent regions and tiny principalities. This tendency was aggravated by the Frankish custom of dividing the kingdom among the king's legitimate male heirs.

By the seventh century, the Frankish king had no effective power. Real power was concentrated in the office of the mayor of the palace, who was the spokesman at the king's court for the great landowners. Through this office, the Carolingian dynasty rose to power.

The Carolingians (named for the dynasty's greatest ruler, Carolus, later known as Charlemagne, or Charles the Great) controlled the office of the mayor of the palace from the ascent to that post of Pepin I (d. 639) until 751, when, with the connivance of the pope, they expropriated the Frankish crown. Pepin II (d. 714) ruled in fact if not in title over the Frankish kingdom. His son, Charles Martel ("the Hammer," d. 741), created a great cavalry by bestowing lands known as *benefices* or *fiefs* on nobles, who, in return, served as the king's army. This army checked the Arabs at Tours in 732.

The fiefs bestowed by Charles Martel to create his army came in large part from land usurped from the church. The Carolingians created counts almost entirely out of the landed nobility. The Merovingians, in contrast, had tried to compete with these great aristocrats by raising the landless to power. By playing to strength rather than challenging it, the Carolingians strengthened themselves, at least for the short term. The church had to tolerate the seizure of its lands.

Frankish Church   The church played a large role in the Frankish government. Monasteries were a dominant force. Many had become profitable landed estates, their abbots rich and powerful magnates. The higher clergy were employed as royal agents, and the Carolingians used the church to pacify conquered neighboring tribes, especially the Saxons.

Christian bishops became lords, appointed by and subject to the king. Pope Zacharias (741–752) sanctioned the Carolingian accession to kingship of the Franks. With the pope's blessing, Pepin III was proclaimed king by the nobility in council in 751, and the last of the Merovingians was hustled off to a monastery.

Zacharias's successor, Pope Stephen II (752–757), driven from Rome in 753 by the Lombards, appealed to Pepin to cast out the invaders and guarantee papal claims to central Italy, which was dominated at this time by the eastern emperor. In 754, the Franks and the church formed an alliance against the Lombards and the eastern emperor. Carolingian kings became the protectors of the Catholic Church. Pepin gained the title *patricius Romanorum*, "father-protector of the Romans," a title heretofore borne by the representative of the eastern emperor. In 755, the Franks defeated the Lombards and gave the pope the lands surrounding Rome, creating the Papal States. In this period, a fraudulent document appeared—the *Donation of Constantine* (written between 750 and 800)—that was designed to remind the Franks of the church's importance as the heir of Rome. It was exposed as a forgery in the fifteenth century.

The papacy had looked to the Franks to protect it from the eastern emperors. But the Carolingian dynasty drew almost as slight a boundary between state and church as did eastern emperors. Although preferable to eastern domination, Carolingian patronage of the church proved to be no less constraining.

Reign of Charlemagne (768–814)

Charlemagne, the son of Pepin the Short, continued the role of his father as papal protector in Italy and his policy of territorial conquest in the north. After the Lombards of northern Italy were defeated in 774, Charlemagne took the title "King of the Lombards." He widened the frontiers of his kingdom further by subjugating surrounding pagan tribes, especially the Saxons, whom the Franks Christianized and dispersed. The Danubian plains were brought into the Frankish orbit by the annihilation of the Avars. The Arabs were chased beyond the Pyrenees. By the time of his death on January 28, 814, Charlemagne's kingdom embraced modern France, Belgium, Holland, Switzerland, almost all of Germany, much of Italy, a part of Spain, and Corsica (see Map 12–2).

The New Empire   Charlemagne desired to be a universal emperor. He had his sacred palace city, Aachen, constructed in imitation of the courts of the ancient Roman and of the eastern emperors. He looked after the church with a paternalism almost as great as that of any eastern emperor. He used it to help create a great Frankish Christian empire. Frankish Christians professed the Nicene Creed (with the *filioque* clause) and learned in church to revere Charlemagne.

On Christmas Day, 800, Pope Leo III (795–816) crowned Charlemagne emperor. This event created what would later be called the Holy Roman Empire, a revival, based after 870 in Germany, of the old Roman Empire in the west. The coronation benefited both the church and Charlemagne. Before his coronation, Charlemagne had been a minor western potentate in the eyes of eastern emperors. After the coronation, eastern emperors reluctantly recognized his new imperial dignity.

The New Emperor   Charlemagne was restless, ever ready for a hunt. Informal and gregarious, he was known for his humor and hospitality. Aachen was a festive palace city to which people and gifts came from all over the world.

Charlemagne sired numerous children. This created problems. His oldest son, Pepin, jealous of the attention shown by his father to the sons of his second wife, joined in a conspiracy against his father. He spent the rest of his life in a monastery after the plot was exposed.

Problems of Government   Charlemagne governed his kingdom through counts, strategically located within the ad-ministrative districts into which the kingdom was divided. Carolingian counts tended to be local magnates who already had armed followings and the self-interest to enforce the will of the king. They had three main duties: to maintain a local army loyal to the king, to collect tribute and dues, and to administer justice.

They undertook this last responsibility through a district law court known as the mallus, which heard testimony, passed judgment, and assessed a monetary compensation to be paid to the injured party.

Many counts used their official position and judicial powers to their own advantage, becoming little despots. They came to regard the land grants with which they were paid as

Map 12–2   The empire of Charlemagne to 814.   Building on the successes of his predecessors, Charlemagne greatly increased the Frankish domains. Such traditional enemies as the Saxons and the Lombards fell under his sway.

hereditary positions rather than royal donations. This signaled the fragmentation of Charlemagne's kingdom. Charlemagne tried to supervise his overseers by creating royal envoys known as *missi dominici*, counts and archbishops and bishops who made annual visits to districts other than their own. But their impact was marginal. The king also appointed provincial governors with titles like prefect, duke, or margrave. But they proved no less corruptible than the others.

Charlemagne never created a loyal bureaucracy. Ecclesiastical agents had the same responsibilities and secular lifestyles and aspirations as the royal counts. Except for their attendance to the liturgy and prayers, they were indistinguishable from the lay nobility. Capitularies, or royal decrees, discouraged the more outrageous behavior of the clergy. But Charlemagne also sensed that reform-minded ecclesiastical landowners would be a danger to royal government. Charlemagne treated his bishops as vassals who served at his pleasure.

Alcuin and the Carolingian Renaissance
Charlemagne used his wealth to attract scholars to Aachen, where they developed court culture and education. By rewarding scholarship, Charlemagne attracted such scholars as his biographer Einhard (ca. 770–840) and Alcuin of York (735–804), who became director of the king's palace school in 782. Alcuin brought classical and Christian learning to Aachen and was rewarded with monastic estates.

Although Charlemagne appreciated learning for its own sake, his palace school was intended to upgrade the administrative skills of the officials who staffed the bureaucracy. The school provided training in the basic tools of bureaucracy: reading, writing, speaking, logic, and counting. Charlemagne's scholars also created a new, clear style of handwriting—Carolingian minuscule—and fostered the use of accurate Latin in official documents, developments that helped increase lay literacy. Alcuin created a genuine community of scholars and clerics at court and infused the highest administrative levels with a sense of comradeship and common purpose.

A modest renaissance, or rebirth, of antiquity occurred in the palace school as scholars collected and preserved ancient manuscripts. These scholarly activities served official efforts to bring uniformity to church law and liturgy, educate the clergy, and improve monasteries.

The Manor and Serfdom
The agrarian economy of the Middle Ages was organized and controlled through village farms known as manors. Here peasants labored as farmers in subordination to a lord, that is, a more powerful landowner who gave them land and a dwelling in exchange for their services and a portion of their crops. That part of the land farmed by the peasants for the lord was the demesne, about one-quarter to one-third of the arable land. All crops grown there were harvested for the lord.

Peasants were treated according to their social status and the size of their land holdings. A freeman—that is, a peasant with his own modest property—became a serf by surrendering his property to a lord in exchange for protection and assistance. The freeman received his land back from the lord with a clear definition of his economic and legal rights. Although the land was no longer his property, he had full possession and use of it, and the services and goods he was to supply to the lord were spelled out. Peasants who had little real property to bargain with ended up as unfree serfs and were more vulnerable to the lord's demands. Impoverished peasants were the least protected.

Serfs were subject to dues in kind: firewood for cutting the lord's wood, sheep for grazing their sheep on the lord's land, and the like. Thus the lord, who furnished shacks and small plots of land from his vast domain, had an army of servants who provided him with everything from eggs to boots. Many serfs were discontented, and escaped serfs roamed the land, searching for new masters.

By the time of Charlemagne, the moldboard plow, which was needed in northern Europe where the soil was heavy, and the three-field system were coming into use. These developments improved agricultural productivity. The moldboard cut deep into the soil and turned it to form a ridge, providing a natural drainage system as well as permitting deep planting. Unlike the earlier two-field system, which alternated fallow with planted fields each year, the three-field system increased the amount of cultivated land by leaving only one-third fallow a year.

Religion and the Clergy
As owners of the churches on their lands, the lords had the right to make chosen serfs parish priests. Church law directed the lord to set a serf free before he entered the clergy, but lords preferred a "serf priest," one who not only said mass but continued to serve his lord, waiting on his table and tending his steeds. Frankish lords cultivated a docile parish clergy.

Ordinary people baptized themselves and their children, confessed the Creed at mass, tried to learn the Lord's Prayer, and received last rites from the priest at death. Local priests were no better educated than their congregations, and instruction in Christian doctrine remained at a minimum.

Breakup of the Carolingian Kingdom

In his last years, Charlemagne knew that his empire was ungovernable. The seeds of dissolution lay in the determination of each locality to look to its self-interest. In medieval society, a direct relationship existed between physical proximity to authority and loyalty. Local people obeyed local lords more than a distant king. Charlemagne had enhanced the power of regional magnates to win their support.

The Carolingian Manor

A capitulary (or ordinance) from the reign of Charlemagne (known as "De Villis") itemizes what the king received from his royal manors or village estates. It is a testimony to Carolingian administrative ability and domination over the countryside.

What gave a lord the right to absolutely everything? (Has anything been overlooked?) How did the stewards and workers share in manorial life? Was the arrangement a good deal for them as well as for the lord?

That each steward shall make an annual statement of all our income: an account of our lands cultivated by the oxen which our ploughmen drive and of our lands which the tenants of farms ought to plough; an account of the pigs, of the rents [a payment for the right to keep pigs in the woods], of the obligations and fines; of the game taken in our forests without our permission; of the various compositions; of the mills, of the forest, of the fields, of the bridges, and ships; of the free-men and the hundreds who are under obligations to our treasury; of markets, vineyards, and those who owe wine to us; of the hay, fire-wood, torches, planks, and other kinds of lumber; of the wastelands; of the vegetables, millet, panic; of the wool, flax, and hemp; of the fruits of the trees, of the nut trees, larger and smaller; of the grafted trees of all kinds; of the gardens; of the turnips; of the fish-ponds; of the hides, skins, and horns; of the honey, wax; of the fat, tallow and soap; of the mulberry wine, cooked wine, mead, vinegar, beer, wine new and old; of the new grain and the old; of the hens and eggs; of the geese; the number of fishermen, smiths [workers in metal], sword-makers, and shoemakers; of the bins and boxes; of the turners and saddlers; of the forges and mines, that is iron and other mines; of the lead mines; of the tributaries; of the colts and fillies; they shall make all these known to us, set forth separately and in order, at Christmas, in order that we may know what and how much of each thing we have.

In each of our estates our stewards are to have as many cow-houses, piggeries, sheepfolds, stable for goats, as possible, and they ought never to be without these.

They must provide with the greatest care that whatever is prepared or made with the hands, that is, lard, smoked meat, salt meat, partially salted meat, wine, vinegar, mulberry wine, cooked wine, garns [a kind of fermented liquor], mustard, cheese, butter, malt, beer, mead, honey, wax, flour, all should be prepared and made with the greatest cleanliness.

That each steward on each of our domains shall always have, for the sake of ornament, swans, peacocks, pheasants, ducks, pigeons, partridges, turtle-doves.

For our women's work they are to give at the proper time, as has been ordered, the materials, that is the linen, wool, woad [blue dye], vermillion, madder [red dye], woolcombs, teasels [plant used to create a soft, fuzzy surface on fabrics or leather], soap, grease, vessels and the other objects which are necessary.

Of the food-products other than meat, two-thirds shall be sent each year for our own use, that is of the vegetables, fish, cheese, butter, honey, mustard, vinegar, millet, panic, dried and green herbs, radishes, and in addition of the wax, soap and other small products.

That each steward shall have in his district good workmen, namely, blacksmiths, gold-smiths, silver-smiths, shoemakers, turners [lathe workers], carpenters, swordmakers, fishermen, foilers [sword-makers], soap-makers, men who know how to make beer, cider, berry, and all the other kinds of beverages, bakers to make pastry for our table, net-makers who know how to make nets for hunting, fishing and fowling, and the other who are too numerous to be designated.

Translations and reprints from the *Original Sources of European History*, Vol. 3 (Philadelphia: Department of History, University of Pennsylvania, 1909), pp. 2–4.

Louis the Pious

Charlemagne's successor, Louis the Pious (r. 814–840), had three sons by his first wife; according to Salic or Germanic law, a ruler partitioned his kingdom equally among his surviving sons. Louis tried to break this tradition by making his eldest son, Lothar (d. 855), coregent and sole imperial heir in 817. To Lothar's brothers he gave lesser appanages, or assigned hereditary lands: Pepin (d. 838) became king of Aquitaine; Louis "the German" (d. 876) became king of Bavaria, over the eastern Franks.

In 823 Louis's second wife, Judith of Bavaria, bore him a fourth son, Charles (d. 877). Determined that her son should receive more than just a nominal inheritance, the queen incited Pepin and Louis to war against Lothar, and persuaded Louis to divide the kingdom equally among his four living sons. The pope had an important stake in the preservation of the revived western empire and the imperial title, which Louis's partition of his kingdom threatened to undo. The pope restored Lothar to his inheritance. But Lothar's brothers renewed war against him.

The Treaty of Verdun and Its Aftermath

In 843, with the treaty of Verdun, the Carolingian Empire was partitioned

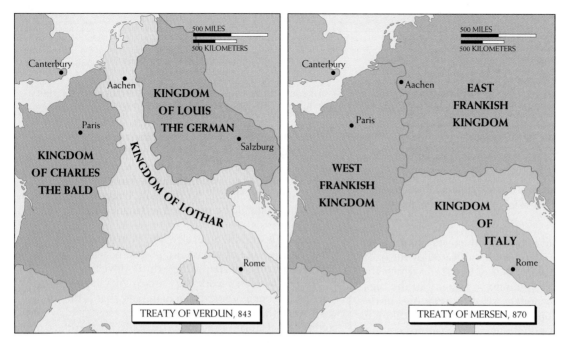

Map 12–3 The Treaty of Verdun (843) and the treaty of Mersen (870).   The Treaty of Verdun divided the kingdom of Louis the Pious among his three feuding children: Charles the Bald, Lothar, and Louis the German. After Lothar's death in 855 the middle kingdom was so weakened by division among his three sons that Charles the Bald and Louis the German divided it between themselves in the Treaty of Mersen.

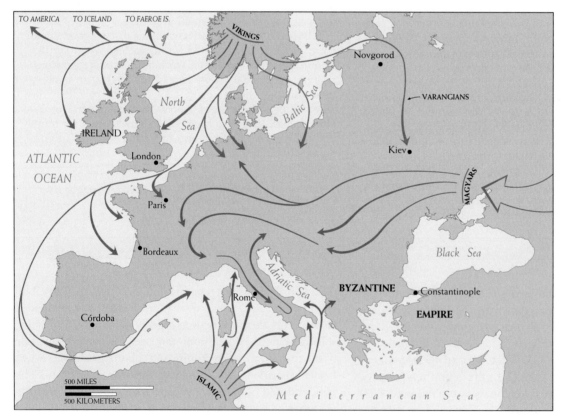

Map 12–4 Viking, Muslim, and Magyar Invasions to the eleventh century.   Western Europe was sorely beset by new waves of outsiders from the ninth to the eleventh century. From north, east, and south a stream of invading Vikings, Magyars, and Muslims brought the west at times to near collapse and of course gravely affected institutions within Europe.

into three equal parts. Lothar received a middle section, which embraced modern Holland, Belgium, Switzerland, Alsace-Lorraine, and Italy. Charles the Bald received roughly modern France, and Louis the German got roughly modern Germany (see Map 12-3). The universal empire of Charlemagne and Louis the Pious now ceased to exist.

The Treaty of Verdun proved to be only the beginning of Carolingian fragmentation. When Lothar died in 855, his kingdom was divided among his three surviving sons. Henceforth, western Europe would be divided into an eastern and a western Frankish kingdom—roughly Germany and France—at war over the fractionalized middle kingdom, a contest that continued into modern times.

The political breakdown of the Carolingian Empire coincided with new external threats. In the late ninth and tenth centuries, waves of Normans (North men), better known as Vikings, swept into Europe from Scandinavia. Magyars, or Hungarians, likewise swept in from the eastern plains, while Muslims made incursions from North Africa (see Map 12-4). The Franks built fortified towns and castles as refuges or bought off the invaders with land and silver. In this turmoil, local populations became more dependent on local strongmen, creating the precondition for feudal society.

Feudal Society

The Middle Ages were characterized by a chronic absence of effective central government and the constant threat of famine, disease, and invasion. The true lords were those who could guarantee protection from rapine and starvation. *Feudal society* refers to the social, political, military, and economic system that emerged from these conditions.

A feudal society is a social order in which a regional prince or a local lord is dominant, and the highest virtues are trust and fidelity. In a feudal society, people require the assurance that others can be depended on in time of need. It is a system of mutual rights and responsibilities.

During the early Middle Ages, the landed nobility ruled over their domains as miniature kingdoms. They maintained their own armies and courts, regulated local tolls, and even minted their own coins. Large groups of warrior vassals were created by bestowals of land, and these developed into a professional military class with its own code of conduct. In feudal society, serfs worked the land, the clergy prayed and gave counsel, and lords and knights maintained law and order.

Origins

The origins of feudal government can be found in the divisions and conflicts of Merovingian society when freemen began placing themselves under the protection of more powerful men. The latter became local magnates, and the former solved the problem of survival. Freemen who so entrusted themselves to others or gave themselves to the king came to be described as *vassi* ("those who serve"), from which evolved the term *vassalage*, meaning the placement of oneself in the personal service of another who promises protection in return.

Landed nobles, like kings, tried to acquire as many vassals as they could, because military strength lay in numbers. To maintain these growing armies, they were granted land, which came to be known as a *benefice*, or a *fief*. Vassals were expected to dwell on it and maintain their accouterments of war in good order. Therefore, vassals originally were gangs-in-waiting.

Vassalage and the Fief

Vassalage involved "fealty" to the lord. To swear fealty was to promise not to act against the lord's well-being and to perform personal services for him on his request. Chief among the expected services was military duty as a mounted knight. Continuous bargaining and bickering occurred over the terms of service.

Limitations were placed on the number of days a lord could require services from a vassal. In France in the eleventh century, about forty days of service per year were considered sufficient. Vassals could also buy their way out of military service by a monetary payment known as *scutage*. The lord, in turn, used this payment to hire mercenaries. The vassal was also expected to give the lord advice and to sit as a member of his court.

The lord's obligations to his vassals were specific. He was obligated to protect the vassal from physical harm and to stand as his advocate. After fealty was sworn and homage

Carolingian Dynasty (751–987)	
751	Pepin III "the Short" becomes king of the Franks
755	Franks drive Lombards out of central Italy; creation of Papal States
768–814	Charlemagne rules as king of the Franks
774	Charlemagne defeats Lombards in northern Italy
750–800	Fraudulent *Donation of Constantine* created in an effort to counter Frankish domination of church
800	Pope Leo III crowns Charlemagne
814–840	Louis the Pious succeeds Charlemagne as "Emperor"
843	Treaty of Verdun partitions the Carolingian Empire
870	Treaty of Mersen further divides Carolingian Empire
875–950	Invasions by Vikings, Muslims, and Magyars
962	Ottonian dynasty succeeds Carolingian in Germany
987	Capetian dynasty succeeds Carolingian in France

paid, the lord bestowed a benefice, or fief. The fief was the physical or material wherewithal to meet the vassal's obligations. It could take the form of liquid wealth. Money fiefs empowered a vassal to receive regular payments from the lord's treasury. Normally, however, the fief consisted of a landed estate or a castle.

In Carolingian times, a benefice, or fief, varied in size from one or more small villas to several *mansi* of twenty-five to forty-eight acres. The king's vassals received benefices of at least thirty and as many as two hundred such mansi. Royal vassalage with a benefice was widely sought by the highest classes of Carolingian society; however, it proved deadly to the king. Although Carolingian kings guarded their rights over property granted in benefice to vassals, vassals were still free to dispose of their benefices as they pleased. Vassals of the king in turn created their own vassals. These vassals created still further vassals of their own—vassals of vassals of vassals—in a reverse pyramiding effect that had fragmented land and authority from the highest to the lowest levels by the late ninth century.

Beginning with the reign of Louis the Pious (r. 814–840), bishops and abbots swore fealty and received their offices from the king as a benefice. The king invested these clerics with a ring and a staff, the symbols of high spiritual office. Lay investiture would eventually provoke a great confrontation between church and state.

Fragmentation and Divided Loyalty

Occupation of the land led to claims of hereditary possession. Hereditary possession became legally recognized in the ninth century and laid the basis for claims to real ownership. Further, to accumulate as much land as possible, one man could become a vassal to several different lords. This led in the ninth century to the concept of a "liege lord"—one master whom the vassal must obey even to the harm of the others, should a direct conflict among them arise.

The problem of loyalty was reflected in the ceremonial development of the act by which a freeman became a vassal. In the mid-eighth century, an "oath of fealty" highlighted the ceremony. A vassal reinforced his promise of fidelity to the lord by swearing a special oath with his hand on a sacred relic or the Bible. In the tenth and eleventh centuries, paying homage also involved placing the vassal's hands between the lord's and sealing the ceremony with a kiss.

Despite their problems, feudal arrangements provided stability in the early Middle Ages and aided the process of political centralization during the High Middle Ages. Feudal government was adaptable. The foundations of the modern nation-state would emerge in France and England from fine-tuning feudal arrangements as kings sought to adapt their goal of centralized government to local power and control.

IN WORLD PERSPECTIVE
The Early Middle Ages

In western Europe, the centuries between 400 and 1000 witnessed the birth of a new European civilization. Beginning with the fifth century, the barbarian invasions separated western Europe culturally from its classical age. No other world culture experienced such a prolonged separation. Western civilization would be recovering its rich classical past in "renaissances" stretching into the sixteenth century. Out of the mixture of barbarian and classical culture, western civilization, as we know it today, was born. Aided by the Christian church, the Carolingians created a new imperial tradition. But western society remained fragmented during the early Middle Ages. Two distinctive institutions arose during this period: manorialism and feudalism. Manorialism helped assure that all were fed and cared for, and feudalism provided for defense.

In China, the T'ang dynasty rulers were also searching for ways to secure their borders against foreign expansion. As in western Europe, religion and philosophy served the state. China was, however, far more cosmopolitan and politically unified than western Europe, and centuries ahead in technology. The authority of Chinese rulers extended far beyond what government Carolingians could imagine.

In Japan, the Yamato court (300–680) also struggled to unify and control the countryside. It too was aided by a religion friendly to royalty—Shinto. As in the West, a Japanese identity evolved through struggle and accommodation with outside cultures, especially with the Chinese. But foreign cultural influence, again as in the West, never eradicated the indigenous culture. By the ninth century, a distinctive Sino-Japanese culture existed. But Japan, again like western Europe, remained fragmented during these centuries, despite a certain allegiance to an imperial court. Throughout Japan, as in western Europe, a system of lordship and vassalage evolved around bands of local mounted warriors, known as samurai. This system maintained local order in Japan until the fifteenth century. Like the Carolingian court, the Japanese court had to tolerate regional rulers.

While western Europe struggled for political and social order in the fourth and fifth centuries, Indian civilization was enjoying a golden age under the Guptas (320–467). Islamic civilization also flourished despite the breakdown of Islamic political unity in the ninth and tenth centuries.

Most of the world's great civilizations were reaching a peak when that of the West was just coming to life. The other world civilizations never experienced cultural disruptions of the magnitude that foreign invaders created in the West during the early Middle Ages.

Review Questions

1. How did the church become a political power in the western Roman Empire?

2. How did the Franks become the dominant force in western Europe? What were the characteristics of Charlemagne's rule? Why did his empire break apart?

3. How and why was the history of the eastern or Byzantine half of the Roman Empire so different from the western half? What were the major political and religious differences?

4. What were the tenets of Islam? How were the Muslims able to build an empire so suddenly? Compare and contrast the teaching of Islam, Roman Catholicism, and Byzantine or Orthodox Christianity. Are they irreconcilable?

5. What were the defining features of feudalism? Is a feudal society a "backward" society?

Documents CD-ROM

1. The Institutes of Justinian from the *Corpus Iuris Civilis*

2. The Book of Emperors and Kings, Charlemagne and Pope Leo III

3. Benedict of Nursia: *The Rule of St. Benedict*

4. Leo I: The Man Who Laid the Foundations for Medieval Papacy

5. Law Code of the Visigoths

13 THE HIGH MIDDLE AGES (1000–1300)

The High Middle Ages were a period of both political expansion and consolidation and intellectual flowering and synthesis. During this time, the borders of western Europe were largely secure from foreign invaders. In the late eleventh and twelfth centuries, western Europe, long the prey of foreign powers, became through the Crusades and foreign trade an aggressor in both the Byzantine and Arab worlds.

During the High Middle Ages, the Latin, or western, church established itself as a spiritual authority independent of secular monarchy, a development that sowed the seeds of the later western separation of church and state.

During the High Middle Ages, powerful monarchies emerged in France, England, and, regionally, Germany. Parliaments and popular assemblies accompanied their rise, seeking to protect local rights and customs and secure the interests of the local nobility, the clergy, and townspeople. The foundations of modern representative institutions can be found in the development of these parliaments and assemblies.

The High Middle Ages saw a revolution in agriculture that increased food supplies and populations. Trade and commerce revived, towns expanded, banking and credit developed, and a "new rich" merchant class, the ancestors of modern capitalists, became ascendant in Europe's cities. Universities came into being, and lasting vernacular and Romance literature was written. New trade with the Arab world, particularly by way of Spain, led to contacts with Muslim intellectuals and the beginning of the recovery of the writings of the ancient Greek philosophers, which would in turn stimulate the great expansion of western education and culture during the late Middle Ages and the Renaissance.

Revival of Empire, Church, and Towns

Otto I and the Revival of the Empire

The Saxon Henry I ("the Fowler"; d. 936), the strongest of the German dukes, became the first non-Frankish king of Germany in 918. Henry rebuilt royal power and secured the imperial borders. Although much smaller than Charlemagne's empire, Henry's German kingdom still placed his son and successor Otto I (r. 936–973) in a strong territorial position.

Otto dealt with each duchy as a subordinate member of a unified kingdom. In 951, Otto invaded Italy and proclaimed himself its king. In 955, he defeated the Hungarians at Lechfeld, a feat comparable to Charles Martel's victory over the Saracens near Tours in 732. Lechfeld secured German borders against new barbarian attack, further unified the German duchies, and earned Otto the title "the Great."

As part of a careful rebuilding program, Otto enlisted the church. Bishops and abbots, men who possessed a sense of universal empire yet did not marry and found competitive dynasties, were made agents of the king. Because these clergy, as royal bureaucrats, received great landholdings and immunity from local counts and dukes, they also found such vassalage to the king attractive.

In 961, Otto, who aspired to the imperial crown, responded to a call for help from Pope John XII (955–964), in return for which John crowned him emperor on February 2, 962. The church was now more than ever under royal control. Its bishops and abbots were Otto's appointees and bureaucrats, and the pope reigned in Rome by the power of the emperor. Recognizing the royal web in which the church had become entangled, Pope John joined the Italian opposition to the new emperor. Otto's revenge was swift. An ecclesiastical synod over which the emperor presided deposed John and proclaimed that no pope could take office without swearing allegiance to the emperor. Under Otto I, popes ruled at the emperor's pleasure.

Otto thus shifted the royal focus from Germany to Italy. His successors became so preoccupied with Italy that their German base began to disintegrate. They might have learned from the Capetian kings, the successor dynasty to the Carolingians in France, who concentrated their resources on securing their immediate royal domain, which was never neglected for foreign adventure. As the revived empire began to crumble in the eleventh century, the church, unhappy with imperial domination, prepared to declare its independence and exact its own vengeance.

The Reviving Catholic Church

During the late ninth and early tenth centuries, the clergy had become tools of kings and magnates, and the papacy a toy of Italian nobles. The Ottonians made bishops their servile princes, and popes served at their pleasure. A new day dawned for the church, however, thanks not only to the failing fortunes of the empire but also to reform within the church itself.

Cluny Reform Movement   In a great monastery at Cluny in east-central France, a reform movement was born. The reformers of Cluny were aided by popular respect for the church that found expression in religious fervor and generous baronial patronage of religious houses. People admired clerics and monks because the church was medieval society's most democratic institution as far as lay participation was concerned. Any man could theoretically become pope, since the pope was supposed to be elected by the people and the clergy of Rome. All people were candidates for the church's grace and salvation. The church promised a better life to come to people who found their existence brutish and without hope.

The tenth and eleventh centuries saw an unprecedented boom in the construction of monasteries. William the Pious, duke of Aquitaine, founded Cluny in 910. It was a Benedictine monastery devoted to the strictest observance of Saint Benedict's *Rule for Monasteries*. The Cluniac reformers were determined to maintain a spiritual church. They rejected the subservience of the clergy to royal authority. They taught that the pope in Rome was sole ruler over the clergy.

No local secular ruler, the Cluniacs asserted, could control their monasteries. They also denounced the concubines of parish clergy.

The Cluny reformers resolved to create an independent and chaste clergy. The distinctive western separation of church and state and the celibacy of the Catholic clergy had their definitive origins in the Cluny reform movement.

From Cluny, reformers were dispatched throughout France and Italy. In time almost 1,500 cloisters were devoted to monastic and church reform. In the later eleventh century, the papacy embraced their reforms.

Popes devoted to reforms like those urged by Cluny came to power during the reign of Emperor Henry III (r. 1039–1056). Pope Leo IX (r. 1049–1054) promoted regional synods to combat simony (that is, the selling of spiritual things, such as church offices) and clerical concubinage. He also placed Cluniacs in key administrative posts in Rome. Pope Stephen IX (r. 1057–1058) reigned without imperial ratification, contrary to the declaration of Otto I. Pope Nicholas II (r. 1059–1061) established a College of Cardinals in 1059, and henceforth this body alone elected the pope.

Investiture Struggle: Gregory VII and Henry IV
Pope Gregory VII (1073–1085) put the church's declaration of independence to the test. In 1075, Pope Gregory condemned under penalty of excommunication the lay investiture of clergy at any level. He had primarily in mind the emperor's custom of installing bishops by presenting them with the ring and staff that symbolized episcopal office. After Gregory's ruling, emperors were no more able to install bishops than they were to install popes. As popes were elected by the College of Cardinals and were not raised up by kings or nobles, so bishops would henceforth be installed by high clerics acting for the pope.

Gregory's prohibition came as a jolt to royal authority. Since the days of Otto I, emperors had passed out bishoprics to favored clergy. Bishops, who received royal estates, were the emperors' appointees and servants of the state. The church and religion were integral parts of government. Henry considered Gregory's action a challenge to his authority. The territorial princes, on the other hand, eager to see the emperor weakened, saw the advantages of Gregory's ruling: if the emperor did not have a bishop's ear, then a territorial prince might. To gain an advantage over both the emperor and the clergy in their territory, the princes supported Gregory's edict.

The lines of battle were drawn. Henry assembled his loyal German bishops at Worms in January 1076 and had them proclaim their independence from Gregory. Gregory excommunicated Henry and absolved Henry's subjects from loyalty to him. The German princes were delighted, and Henry faced a general revolt led by the duchy of Saxony. He had to come to terms with Gregory. In a famous scene, Henry prostrated himself outside Gregory's castle retreat at Canossa in northern Italy on January 25, 1077. There he reportedly stood barefoot in the snow off and on for three days before the pope absolved him. Papal power had reached a pinnacle, the first of several in the High Middle Ages. But Gregory's grandeur was soon to fade. In 1084, Henry forced Gregory into exile and installed his own anti-pope—Clement III—in his place.

The investiture controversy was finally settled in 1122 with the Concordat of Worms. Emperor Henry V (r. 1106–1125) renounced his power to invest bishops with ring and staff. In exchange, Pope Calixtus II (r. 1119–1124) recognized the emperor's right to invest bishops with fiefs before or after their investment with ring and staff by the church. The emperor retained the right to nominate or veto a candidate. The old church-state "back scratching" continued on different terms. The clergy received their offices and religious powers from ecclesiastical authority and no longer from kings and emperors. Rulers continued to bestow lands and worldly goods on high clergy in the hope of influencing them; the Concordat of Worms made the clergy more independent but not less worldly.

The pope had made himself strong by making imperial authority weak. In the end, the local princes profited most from the investiture controversy.

The First Crusades

If an index of popular piety and support for the pope in the High Middle Ages is needed, the Crusades provide it. What

The Crusades

1095	Pope Urban II launches the First Crusade
1099	The crusaders take Jerusalem
1147–1149	The Second Crusade
1187	Jerusalem retaken by the Muslims
1189–1192	Third Crusade
1202–1204	Fourth Crusade

the Cluny reform was to the clergy, the first Crusades to the Holy Land were to the laity: an outlet for the religious zeal of the late eleventh and the twelfth centuries.

Late in the eleventh century, the Byzantine Empire was under severe pressure from the Seljuk Turks, and Emperor Alexius I Comnenus (r. 1081–1118) appealed for western aid. At the Council of Clermont in 1095, Pope Urban II (r. 1088–1099) responded by launching the First Crusade. The pope, the nobility, and western society had much to gain by sending large numbers of nobility temporarily away from Europe. Too many restless noble youths were spending their lives feuding with each other. The pope recognized that peace and tranquility might be gained at home by sending factious aristocrats abroad (100,000 went with the First Crusade). And the nobility recognized there were fortunes to be made in foreign wars. This was especially true of the younger sons of noblemen, who saw the Crusades as an opportunity to become landowners. Pope Urban may also have envisioned the Crusade leading to a reunion with the eastern church.

Religion was not the only motive inspiring the Crusaders; hot blood and greed were equally influential. But the early Crusades were inspired by genuine religious piety and were orchestrated by the papacy. Popes promised participants in the First Crusade a plenary indulgence should they die in battle—that is, a complete remission of any outstanding temporal punishment for their unrepented mortal sins and hence release from suffering for them in purgatory. The Crusaders were also impelled by their enthusiasm for a Holy War against the hated infidel and by the romance of a pilgrimage to the Holy Land. These elements made the First Crusade a rousing success (at least from the Christian point of view). Crusading zeal also sparked anti-Jewish riots and massacres in Europe, an expression of intolerance to Jews that became an enduring feature of militant Christianity.

Three great armies—tens of thousands of Crusaders—gathered in France, Germany, and Italy. Following different routes, they reassembled in Constantinople in 1097 (see Map 13-1). The convergence of these spirited soldiers on the eastern capital deepened eastern antipathy toward the west. Alexis I suspected their motives, and the common people, who were forced to accommodate them, hardly considered them Christian brothers in a common cause—especially since Rome and Constantinople had separated in 1054. Nonetheless, these fanatical Crusaders defeated one Seljuk army after another in a steady advance toward Jerusalem, which fell to them on July 15, 1099. They divided the conquered territory into the "states" of Jerusalem, Edessa, Tripoli, and Antioch, which they held as alleged fiefs from the pope.

The Crusader states, however, were only small islands within a great sea of Muslims, who considered the western invaders savages. After only forty-odd years, the Latin presence in the east began to crumble. A Second Crusade,

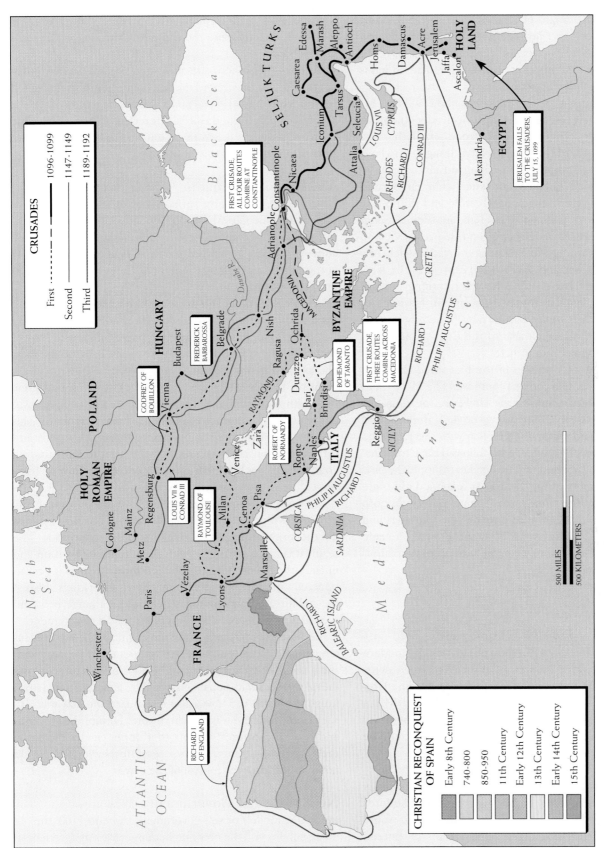

Map 13-1 The early Crusades. Routes and several leaders of the Crusades during the first century of the movement are shown. The names on this map do not exhaust the list of great nobles who went on the First Crusade. The even showier array of monarchs of the Second and Third still left the Crusades, on balance, ineffective in achieving their goals.

preached by Saint Bernard of Clairvaux (1091–1153), was a failure. In October 1187, Jerusalem itself was reconquered by Saladin (r. 1138–1193), king of Egypt and Syria. Save for a brief interlude in the thirteenth century, it remained in Islamic hands until the twentieth century.

A Third Crusade in the twelfth century (1189–1192) attempted yet another rescue, enlisting as its leaders the most powerful western rulers: Emperor Frederick Barbarossa (r. 1152–1190); Richard the Lion-Hearted, king of England (r. 1189–1199); and Philip Augustus, king of France (r. 1179–1223). But Frederick Barbarossa drowned while en route to the Holy Land. Richard the Lion-Hearted and Philip Augustus reached the outskirts of Jerusalem, but their personal rivalry shattered the Crusaders' unity and chances of victory. Philip Augustus returned to France and invaded Richard's continental territories, and Richard fell captive to the Emperor Henry VI (r. 1165–1197) as he was returning to England, forcing the English to pay a ransom for his release. Popular resentment of taxes for this ransom became part of the background of the revolt against the English monarchy that led to the Magna Carta in 1215.

The long-term achievement of the first three Crusades had little to do with their original purpose. The Holy Land remained as firmly Muslim as ever. However, the Crusades did provide a safety valve for violence-prone Europeans and stimulated trade and cultural interaction with the east. The merchants of Venice, Pisa, and Genoa followed the Crusaders' cross to lucrative new markets. The need to resupply the new Christian settlements in the Near East reopened old trade routes and opened new ones. It is a commentary on both the degeneration of the original intent of the Crusades and their true historical importance that the Fourth Crusade (1202–1204) was reduced to a commercial venture manipulated by the Venetians.

Towns and Townspeople

In the eleventh and twelfth centuries, towns held only about 5 percent of western Europe's population. By modern comparison they were small. Of Germany's 3,000 towns, for example, 2,800 had populations under 1,000. The largest European towns were in Italy; Florence and Milan approached 100,000 inhabitants. Yet the whole of medieval society, and especially its most creative segments, could be found in the towns.

The Chartering of Towns   Towns were originally dominated by feudal lords, both lay and clerical. The lords created the towns by granting charters to those who would agree to live and work within them. The charters guaranteed the towns' safety and gave their inhabitants a degree of independence unknown to peasants who worked the land.

The purpose was originally to centralize skilled laborers who could manufacture the finished goods desired by lords and bishops.

As towns beckoned, serfs took their skills to the new urban centers. There they found the freedom and profits that could lift them into higher social ranks. As this migration of serfs to the towns accelerated, lords offered serfs more favorable terms of tenure to keep them on the land. The growth of towns thus improved the lot of serfs.

The Rise of Merchants   The first merchants may also have been enterprising serfs. Some of the long-distance traders were people who had nothing to lose from the enormous risks of foreign trade. They traveled together in armed convoys, buying goods and products as cheaply as possible at the source, and selling them for all they could get in western ports (see Map 13–2).

At first the merchants were disliked because they were outside the traditional social groups of nobility, clergy, and peasantry. Over time, however, the powerful grew to respect them, and the weak tried to imitate them, because the merchants left a trail of wealth.

As the traders established themselves in towns, they grew in wealth and numbers, formed their own protective associations, and soon challenged traditional seigneurial authority. Merchants especially wanted to end the tolls and tariffs regional magnates imposed over the surrounding countryside. Such regulations hampered the flow of commerce in the growing urban export industries.

Townspeople needed simple and uniform laws and a government sympathetic to their new forms of business activity, not the fortress mentality of the lords of the countryside. The result was often a struggle with the old nobility within and outside the towns. This conflict led towns to form independent communes and ally themselves with kings against the nobility, a development that would rearrange power in medieval Europe and dissolve classic feudal government.

Because the merchants were the engine of the urban economy, small shopkeepers and artisans identified far more with them than with aloof lords and bishops, who had been medieval society's traditional masters. The lesser nobility (small knights) outside the towns also recognized the new mercantile economy as the wave of the future. During the eleventh and twelfth centuries, the burgher upper classes increased their economic strength and successfully challenged the old noble urban lords for control of the towns.

New Models of Government   With urban autonomy came new models of self-government. Around 1100, the old urban nobility and the new burgher upper class merged into an urban patriciate. It was a marriage between those wealthy by birth (inherited property) and those who made their fortunes

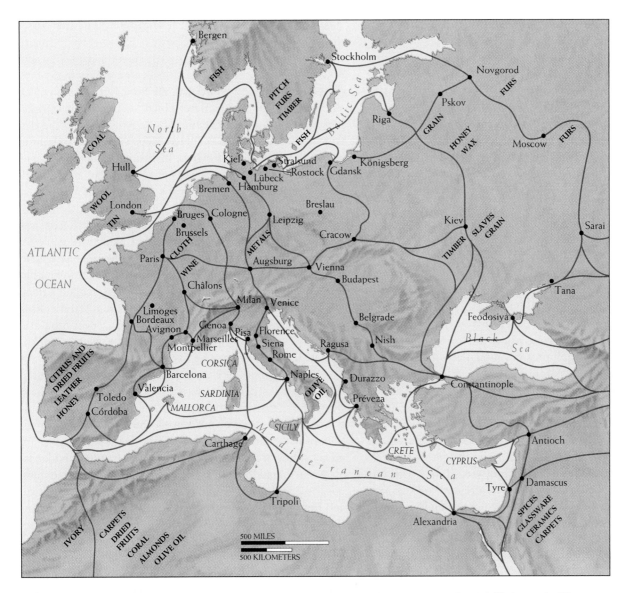

Map 13-2 Medieval trade routes and regional products. Trade in the west varied in intensity and geographical extent in different periods during the Middle Ages. The map shows some of the channels that came to be used in interregional commerce. Labels tell part of what was carried in that commerce.

in long-distance trade. From this new ruling class was born the aristocratic town council, which henceforth governed towns.

Small artisans and craftspeople also developed their own protective associations or guilds and began to gain a voice in government. The towns' opportunities had created the slogan "Town air brings freedom." In the countryside the air still belonged to the lord of the land, but town residents were treated as freemen. Within town walls people thought of themselves as citizens with basic rights, not subjects liable to their masters' whim. Economic hardship continued among the lower urban groups, but social mobility was possible in the towns.

Traditional measures of success had great appeal within towns. Successful merchants wanted to lead the life of a gen-

tleman and a lady on a great manor. When they became rich enough, they took their fortunes to the countryside.

A need to be socially distinguished and distinct pervaded urban society. Towns tried to control this need by defining grades of luxury in dress and residence for the various social groups and vocations. Overly conspicuous consumption was punishable by law. Such sumptuary laws restricted the types and amount of clothing a person could wear and how dwellings might be decorated. People thus were forced to dress and live according to their station in life. Such laws sought to keep everyone in their place.

Over time, artisan guilds gave workers in the trades a direct voice in government. Ironically, this gain limited the social mobility of the poorest artisans. The guilds gained representation on city councils, where, to discourage imports, they enforced quality standards and fair prices on local businesses. These actions created tight restrictions on guild membership, squeezing out poorer artisans and tradespeople. As a result, lesser merchants and artisans found their opportunities limited. The dominant guilds often stifled their own creativity and inflamed the journeypeople whom they excluded from their ranks. Unrepresented artisans and craftspeople constituted a true urban proletariat prevented by law from forming their own guilds or entering existing ones. The efforts by guild-dominated governments to protect local craftspeople and industries tended to narrow trade and depress the economy for everyone.

Towns and Kings

By providing kings with the resources they needed to curb noblemen, towns became a major force in the transition from feudal societies to national governments. Kings and towns often allied against the lords of the land. An exception is England, where the towns joined with the barons against the oppressive monarchy of King John (1199–1216), becoming part of the parliamentary opposition to the crown. But by the fifteenth century, kings and towns had also joined forces in England. Henry VII, the first Tudor monarch (1485–1509), was known as the "burgher king."

Towns attracted monarchs for obvious reasons. They were a source of educated bureaucrats and lawyers who knew Roman law, the tool for running the state. Money was also found in the towns, enabling kings to hire their own armies and free themselves from dependence on the nobility. Towns had the resources to empower kings. By such alliances, towns won royal political recognition and had their constitutions guaranteed. In France, towns became integrated early into royal government. In Germany, they fell under tight control by the princes. In Italy, uniquely, towns expanded to dominate the surrounding countryside, becoming genuine city-states during the Renaissance.

Jews in Christian Society

Towns also attracted Jews, particularly in France and Germany, between the late twelfth and thirteenth centuries. They did so both by choice and for safety in the increasingly hostile Christian world. In cities, Jews plied trades in small businesses, and many became wealthy moneylenders. After the creation of universities, Jews loaned Christian students everything from books to clothes. Jewish intellectual and religious culture had always been sophisticated, both dazzling and threatening to Christians. The separateness of Jews, their economic power, and their cultural strength encouraged suspicion and distrust among Christians, whose religious teaching held Jews responsible for the death of Christ.

Between the late twelfth and early fourteenth centuries, Jews were exiled and persecuted. Two factors were behind this unprecedented anti-Jewish sentiment. The first was a desire by kings to confiscate Jewish wealth and eliminate them as economic competitors with the monarchy. The second factor was the church's political vulnerability to the new dynastic monarchies. Faced with the loss of its political power, the church became more determined to maintain its spiritual hegemony. With the beginning of the Crusades and the creation of new mendicant religious orders, the church reasserted claims to spiritual sovereignty, instigating major campaigns against dissenters, heretics, witches, and Jews at home as well as infidels abroad.

Schools and Universities

In the twelfth century, Byzantine and Spanish Islamic scholars made it possible for the philosophical works of Aristotle, the writings of Euclid and Ptolemy, the texts of Greek physicians and Arab mathematicians, and the corpus of Roman law to circulate among western scholars. Islamic scholars wrote thought-provoking commentaries on Greek texts that were translated into Latin and made available to western scholars. The result was an intellectual ferment that gave rise to western universities.

The first important western university was established in Bologna by Emperor Frederick Barbarossa in 1158. There we find the first formal organizations of students and masters and the first degree programs—the institutional foundations of the modern university. Originally the term university meant simply a corporation of individuals (students and masters) who joined for their mutual protection from overarching episcopal authority (the local bishop oversaw the university) and from the local townspeople. Because townspeople considered students foreigners without civil rights, such protective unions were necessary.

Bolognese students also "unionized" to guarantee fair rents and prices from their often reluctant hosts. And students demanded regular, high-quality teaching from their masters. In Italy, students hired their own teachers, set pay scales, and drew up lecture topics. Price gouging by townspeople was met with the threat to move the university to another town. This could be done because the university did not have a fixed physical plant. Students and masters moved freely from town to town as they chose. Masters also formed their own protective associations and established procedures and standards for certification to teach.

Bologna was famous for the revival of Roman law. From the seventh to the eleventh centuries, only the most rudimentary manuals of Roman law had survived. In the late eleventh century, western scholars had come into contact with the larger and more important parts of Justinian's compilation of civil law. The study and dissemination of this recovered material were undertaken in Bologna under a scholar named Irnerius in the early twelfth century. He and his students thereby expanded legal knowledge. Around 1140 a monk named Gratian, also a resident of Bologna, created the standard legal text in church—or canon—law.

As Bologna was the model for the universities of Spain, Italy, and southern France and for the study of law, so Paris became the model for northern European universities and the study of theology. Oxford, Cambridge, and (much later) Heidelberg were among its imitators. All these universities required a foundation in the liberal arts for advanced study in the higher sciences of medicine, theology, and law. The arts program consisted of the trivium (grammar, rhetoric, and logic) and the quadrivium (arithmetic, geometry, astronomy, and music) or, more simply, the language arts and the mathematical arts.

Cathedral Schools   Before the emergence of universities, the liberal arts had been taught in cathedral and monastery schools. These schools trained the clergy, and their curricula tended to be restricted to this goal. By the late eleventh and twelfth centuries, cathedral schools also began to include training for purely secular vocations. In 1179, a papal decree obliged cathedrals to provide teachers for free to laity.

After 1200, future notaries and merchants who needed Latin and related intellectual disciplines to fill their secular positions studied alongside aspiring priests in cathedral and monastery schools. By the thirteenth century, the demand for secretaries and notaries in government and for literate personnel in merchant firms gave rise to special schools for secular vocations. The church began to lose its monopoly on higher education.

The University of Paris, chartered in 1200 by King Philip Augustus and Pope Innocent III (r. 1198–1216), grew out of the cathedral school of Notre Dame, among others. At Paris the college, or house system, originated. At first a college only provided room and board for poor students. But the educational life of the university quickly expanded into fixed structures and began to thrive on their sure endowments. University-run colleges made the overseeing and protection of students easier and made the university a permanent urban institution.

In Paris, the most famous college was the Sorbonne, founded around 1257 to house theology students. In Oxford and Cambridge, the colleges became the basic unit of student life and were indistinguishable from the university proper. By the end of the Middle Ages, such colleges had tied universities to physical plants and fixed foundations.

As a group, students at Paris had power and prestige. They enjoyed royal protections and privileges denied ordinary citizens. Many Parisian students were well-to-do, spoiled, and petulant. They did not endear themselves to the townspeople, whom they considered their inferiors. Townspeople sometimes let their resentments lead to violence. City law forbade the beating of students. Only those students who had committed serious crimes could be imprisoned. Only in self-defense might a citizen strike a student. All citizens were obligated to testify against anyone seen abusing a student. University laws required all teachers to be examined before being licensed to teach Parisian students. The law thus recognized students as a valuable and vulnerable resource.

The Curriculum   In the High Middle Ages, the learning process was basic. People assumed that truth was already known and only needed to be organized, elucidated, and defended.

This method of study, based on logic and dialectic, was known as scholasticism. It reigned supreme in law, medicine, philosophy, and theology. Students read the traditional authorities in their field, summarized their teaching, disputed them with their peers by elaborating traditional arguments pro and con, and then drew conclusions. Logic and dialectic disciplined knowledge and thought. Dialectic is the art of discovering a truth by finding the contradictions in arguments against it. Medical students did no practical medical work; they studied and debated the authoritative texts in their field just as the law and theology students did in theirs.

Few books existed for students, and because printing with movable type did not yet exist, those available were expensive hand-copied works. So students could not leisurely master a subject in the quiet of their studies; they had to learn it through discussion, lecture, and debate. There was a lot of memorizing, and the ability to think on one's feet was stressed. Rhetoric, or persuasive argument, was the ultimate goal—that is, the ability to defend the knowledge one had clarified by logic and dialectic. Successful students became walking encyclopedias; their education filled their heads with knowledge and enabled them to recite it impressively.

University study normally began between the ages of twelve and fifteen. Students spent four years perfecting their Latin (particularly in the study of the trivium) before attaining the bachelor of arts degree. A master's degree might take three or four more years, during which time students studied classical texts in mathematics, natural science, and philosophy. A degree in theology at Paris could take more than twenty years of study.

The Summa   The twelfth century saw the rise of the summa, the authoritative summary of all that was allegedly known about a subject. The summa's main goal was to conciliate traditional authorities and present a body of clarified truth. Out of this tradition came Saint Thomas Aquinas's (1225–1274) magnificent *Summa Theologiae* (begun in 1265), to many the last word on theology, which the medieval summa was intended to be.

Noblewomen watch a tournament. These mock battles were designed to provide the excitement of war without its mayhem. However, they tended to get out of hand, resulting in bloodshed and even death. [University of Heidelberg]

Society

The Order of Life

In the art and literature of the Middle Ages, three basic social groups were represented: those who fought as mounted knights (the landed nobility), those who prayed (the clergy), and those who labored in fields and shops (the peasantry and village artisans). After the revival of towns in the eleventh century, a fourth social group emerged: the long-distance traders and merchants.

Nobles   As a distinctive social group, not all nobles were originally great men with large hereditary lands. Many rose from the ranks of feudal vassals or warrior knights. The successful vassal attained a special social and legal status based on his landed wealth (accumulated fiefs), his exercise of authority over others, and his distinctive social customs—all of which set him apart in medieval society. By the late Middle

Ages, a higher and lower nobility had evolved, living in both town and country. The higher were the great landowners and territorial magnates, long the dominant powers in their regions, the lower were petty landlords, the descendants of minor knights, newly rich merchants who could buy country estates, or wealthy farmers.

The nobility lived off the labor of others. Basically lords of manors, the nobility of the early and High Middle Ages neither tilled the soil like the peasantry nor engaged in the commerce of merchants—activities they considered beneath their dignity. The nobleman resided in a country mansion or, if he were particularly wealthy, a castle.

Arms were the nobleman's profession. In the eighth century, the adoption of stirrups made cavalry the key ingredient of a successful army. The nobleman's fief provided the means to acquire the expensive military equipment that his rank required. He maintained his enviable position by fighting for his chief.

The nobility celebrated warfare. Warring gave them new riches and an opportunity to gain honor and glory. Knights were paid a share in the plunder of victory. Peace meant economic stagnation and boredom. The peasants and townspeople regarded peace as essential for their occupational success; the nobility despised it as unnatural to their profession.

The nobleman nurtured his sense of distinctiveness by the chivalric ritual of dubbing to knighthood. This ceremonial entrance into the noble class became almost a religious sacrament. It was preceded by a bath of purification, confession, communion, and a prayer vigil. Thereafter, the priest blessed the knight's standard, lance, and sword. As prayers were chanted, the priest girded the knight with his sword and presented him his shield. Dubbing raised the nobleman to a state as sacred in his sphere as clerical ordination made the priest in his. The comparison is legitimate. The clergy and the nobility were medieval society's privileged estates. The appointment of noblemen to high ecclesiastical office and their eager participation in the church's Crusades had strong ideological and social underpinnings.

In the twelfth century, knighthood was legally restricted to men of high birth. This circumscription of noble ranks came in reaction to the growing wealth, political power, and successful social climbing of newly rich townspeople who were competitive with the lower nobility. Kings, however, did not shrink from increasing royal revenues by selling noble titles to wealthy merchants. But the law was building fences between town and countryside in the High Middle Ages.

In peacetime, the nobility had two favorite amusements: hunting and tournaments. Where they could, noblemen forbade commoners from hunting in the "lords'" forests. This practice built resentment. Free game, fishing, and access to wood were basic demands in the revolts of the peasantry throughout the Middle Ages.

Tournaments sowed seeds of social disruption within the ranks of the nobility itself. They were designed to keep men fit for war and provide the excitement of war without maiming and killing prized vassals. But tournaments often got out of hand, ending in bloodshed and animosity. The church came to oppose tournaments as pagan revelry and senseless violence. Kings and princes also turned against them as sources of division within their realms.

From the assemblies in the courts of barons and kings, codes of social conduct, or courtesy, developed in noble circles. With the French leading the way, mannered behavior and etiquette became almost as important as battlefield expertise. Knights became literate gentlemen, and poets sang and moralized at court. The cultivation of a code of behavior and a literature to eulogize it was related to problems within the social life of the nobility. Noblemen were notorious philanderers; their illegitimate children mingled with their legitimate offspring in their houses. Courtesy was an effort to reform this situation.

Although the poetry of courtly love was sprinkled with eroticism, and the beloved were married women pursued by those to whom they were not married, the poet usually recommended love unconsummated by sexual intercourse. It was love without touching and only as such was it considered ennobling. Court poets depicted those who succumbed to illicit carnal love as reaping at least as much suffering as joy from it.

The nobility had strong social divisions within its ranks. Noblemen formed a broad spectrum—from minor vassals to mighty barons, who had many vassals of their own. Dignity and status within the nobility were related to the exercise of authority over others; a chief with many vassals far excelled the small country nobleman who served another and was lord over none but himself.

By the late Middle Ages, several factors forced the landed nobility into a steep economic and political decline from which it never recovered. Climatic changes and agricultural failures created large famines, while the Great Plague (see Chapter 16) brought about unprecedented population losses. The use of infantry and heavy artillery made the noble cavalry nearly obsolete. And the alliance of wealthy towns with the king weakened the nobility within their own domains. One can speak of a waning of the landed nobility after the fourteenth century. Thereafter, land and wealth counted for far more than lineage as qualification for entrance into the highest social class.

Clergy The clergy was an open estate. One was a cleric by religious training and ordination, not because of birth or military prowess.

The regular clergy comprised the orders of monks who lived according to a special rule *(regula)* in cloisters separated from the world. The Gregorian reform led to the creation of new such orders aspiring to a life of poverty and self-sacrifice in imitation of Christ and the first apostles. Founded in 1098, the Cistercians were a reform wing of the Benedictines. They stressed the inner life and spiritual goals of monasticism. They located their houses in remote areas and denied themselves worldly comforts and distractions. The order could count 300 chapter houses within a century of its founding, and others imitated its austere spirituality.

In the thirteenth century, two new orders—the Franciscans and the Dominicans—gained the sanction of the church. The members of these mendicant orders, known as friars, did not confine themselves to the cloister. They went out into the world to preach the church's mission and to combat heresy, begging or working to support themselves (hence the term mendicant). The regular clergy were the spiritual elite among the clergy, and theirs was not a way of life lightly undertaken. Canon law required that one be at least twenty-one years of age before making a final profession of the monastic vows of poverty, chastity, and obedience. The monks' personal sacrifices and high religious ideals earned them great respect.

The regular clergy, however, were never completely cut off from the secular world. They maintained contact with the laity through charitable activities, teaching, and pastoral commissions from the pope, and as preachers and confessors in parish churches during peak religious seasons.

The secular clergy, those who lived and worked directly among the laity in the world *(saeculum)*, formed a vast hierarchy. At the top were the high prelates—the wealthy cardinals, archbishops, and bishops, who were drawn almost exclusively from the nobility—and below them the urban priests, the cathedral canons, and the court clerks. Finally, there was the great mass of poor parish priests, who were neither financially nor intellectually much above the common people they served. Until the Gregorian reform in the eleventh century, parish priests lived with women in a relationship akin to marriage, and their concubines and children were accepted within the communities they served. Because of their relative poverty, priests often moonlighted as teachers, artisans, or farmers. Their parishioners accepted and even admired this practice.

The monasteries and nunneries of the established orders recruited candidates from among the wealthiest social groups. Crowding in the convents and the absence of patronage gave rise in the thirteenth century to lay satellite convents known as *beguine houses.* These housed religiously earnest unmarried women from the upper and middle social strata.

The clergy constituted a far greater proportion of medieval society than modern society. Estimates suggest that 1.5 percent of fourteenth-century Europe was in clerical garb. In late-fourteenth-century England, there was one cleric for every seventy laypeople, and in counties with a cathedral or a university, the proportion rose to one cleric for every fifty laypeople. In large university towns, the clergy could exceed 10 percent of the population.

The clergy as a whole, like the nobility, lived on the labor of others. Their income came from the regular collection of tithes and church taxes. The church was a major landowner and regularly collected rents and fees. Monastic communities and high prelates amassed great fortunes. The immense secular power attached to high clerical posts can be seen in the intensity of the investiture struggle. The loss of the right to present chosen clergy with the ring and staff of episcopal office threatened the emperor's control of his realm. The bishops had become royal agents and were endowed to that purpose with royal lands that the emperor could ill afford to have slip from his control.

During most of the Middle Ages, the clergy were the "first estate," and theology was the queen of the sciences. How did the clergy attain such prominence? A lot of it was self-proclaimed. However, there was also popular respect and reverence for the clergy's role as mediator between God and humanity. The priest brought the Son of God down to Earth when he celebrated the sacrament of the Eucharist; his absolution released penitents from punishment for sin. It was declared improper for mere laypeople to sit in judgment on such a priest.

Theologians elaborated the distinction between the clergy and the laity to the clergy's benefit. The belief in the superior status of the clergy underlay the evolution of clerical privileges and immunities in both person and property. As holy persons, the clergy were not supposed to be taxed by secular rulers without permission from the ecclesiastical authorities. Clerical crimes were under the jurisdiction of special ecclesiastical courts. Churches and monasteries were free from secular taxation and legal jurisdiction. Hunted criminals regularly sought asylum within them. When city officials violated this privilege, ecclesiastical authorities threatened excommunication and interdict. People feared this suspension of the church's sacraments, including Christian burial, almost as much as they feared the criminals to whom the church gave asylum.

By the late Middle Ages, townspeople resented the special immunities of the clergy. Although the separation of church and state and the distinction between clergy and laity have persisted into modern times, after the fifteenth century governments progressively subjected the clergy to the basic responsibilities of citizenship.

Peasants   The largest and lowest social group in medieval society was one on whose labor the welfare of all others depended: the agrarian peasantry. Many peasants lived and worked on the manors of the nobility. Peasants were considered their lord's property. In Frankish times, the manor was a plot of land within a village ranging from twelve to seventy-five acres and assigned by the leaders of a settled tribe or clan to favored members. This member and his family became lords of the land, and those who dwelt there formed a self-sufficient community within a larger village community. In the early Middle Ages, such manors consisted of the dwellings of the lord and his family, the cottages of the peasants, agricultural sheds, and fields.

The landowner or lord of the manor required a certain amount of produce and services from the peasant families that farmed his land. The tenants were free to divide the labor as they wished; and they owned whatever remained after the lord's levies were met. A powerful lord might own many manors. Kings later based their military and tax assessments on the number of manors owned by a vassal. There were manors of a hundred acres or fewer and some of thousands.

There were both servile and free manors. The tenants of the latter had originally been freemen known as *coloni*. They swapped their small possessions for a guarantee of security from a more powerful lord, who thus came to possess their land. Unlike the pure serfdom of the servile manors, whose tenants had no original claim to a part of the land, the tenancy obligations on free manors tended to be limited and the tenants' rights more defined. It was a milder serfdom. Tenants of servile manors were far more vulnerable to the whims of their landlords. These two types of manor tended, however, to merge. In most manors, tenants of greater and lesser degrees of servitude dwelt together. In many regions free, self-governing peasant communities existed without overlords and tenancy obligations.

The lord held both judicial and police powers. He owned and operated the machines that processed crops into food and drink. The lord also had the right to subject his tenants to exactions known as *banalities*. He could force them to breed their cows with his bull, and to pay for the privilege; to grind their bread grains in his mill; to bake their bread in his oven; to make their wine in his wine press; and to buy their beer from his brewery. The lord also collected as an inheritance tax a serf's best animal. Without the lord's permission, a serf could neither travel nor marry outside the manor.

As exploited as the serfs may have been, their status was not chattel slavery. It was to a lord's advantage to keep his serfs healthy and happy; his welfare, like theirs, depended on a successful harvest. Serfs had their own dwellings and strips of land and lived off the produce of their labor. They could also market for their own profit any surpluses that remained after the harvest. They were free to marry within the local village. And serfs could pass their property (their dwellings and field strips) on to their children, along with their worldly goods.

A fifteenth-century rendering of an eleventh- or twelfth-century marketplace. Medieval women were active in all trades, but especially in the food and clothing industries. [Scala/Art Resource, N.Y.]

Two basic changes occurred in the evolution of the manor from the early to the later Middle Ages. The first was the fragmentation of the manor and the predominance of the single-family holding. This development was aided by such technological advances as the collar harness (ca. 800), the horseshoe (ca. 900), and the three-field system of crop rotation, which made it easier for smaller familial units to support themselves. As the lords parceled out their land to new tenants, their own plots became smaller. The increase in tenants and the decrease in the lord's fields reduced the labor services exacted from the tenants. Also, the bringing of new fields into production increased individual holdings and modified labor services. In France, by the reign of Louis IX (1226–1270), only a few days a year were required, whereas under Charlemagne (768–814), peasants had worked the lords' fields several days a week.

As the single-family unit replaced the clan as the basic nuclear group, assessments of goods and services fell on individual fields and households, no longer on manors as a whole. Family farms replaced manorial units. The peasants' carefully nurtured communal life enabled a family to retain its land and dwelling after the death of the head of the household. Land and property thus remained in the possession of a single family from generation to generation.

The second change in the evolution of the manor was the conversion of the serf's dues into money payments, a change made possible by the revival of trade and the rise of the towns. This development, completed by the thirteenth century, permitted serfs to hold their land as rent-paying tenants and to overcome their servile status. But where servile work-ers could have counted on the benevolent assistance of their landlords in hard times, rent-paying workers were left to their own devices. Their independence caused some landlords to treat them with indifference.

Lands and properties that had been occupied by generations of peasants and were recognized as their own were always under the threat of the lord's usurpation. As their demesnes declined, the lords were tempted to encroach on such traditionally common lands. The peasantry resisted such efforts.

By the mid-fourteenth century, a declining nobility in England and France, faced with the ravages of the Great Plague and the Hundred Years' War, tried to increase taxes on the peasantry and restrict their migration to the cities. The response was armed revolt. These revolts were crushed. They stand out at the end of the Middle Ages as violent testimony to the breakup of medieval society. As growing national sentiment would break its political unity and heretical movements end its nominal religious unity, the peasantry's revolts revealed the absence of social unity.

Medieval Women

The image and the reality of medieval women are two different things. The former was influenced by the views of male Christian clergy, whose ideal was a celibate life of chastity, poverty, and obedience. Drawing on classical medical, philosophical, and legal traditions that predated Christianity, as well as on biblical teaching, Christian theologians often depicted women as the physical, mental, and moral inferiors of men.

The clergy considered marriage a debased state by comparison with the religious life, and praised virgins and celibate widows over wives. In marriage the role of a wife was above all to love and obey her husband, and her husband had reciprocal duties of love, protection, and discipline. This image suggests that a medieval woman had only two options in life: either a subjugated housewife or a cloistered nun. In reality, most medieval women were neither.

Image and Status   In chivalric romances and courtly love literature of the twelfth and thirteenth centuries, as also in the contemporaneous cult of the Virgin Mary, women are praised and admired, even treated as superior to men. If the church shared traditional condescending and occasional misogynistic sentiments, it also condemned them and popular bawdy literature as demeaning to women in its eyes.

The learned churchman Peter Lombard (1100–1164) sanctioned an image of women that didactic Christian literature often invoked. Why, Lombard asked, was Eve created from Adam's rib and not taken from his head or his feet? The answer: God wanted woman neither to rule over man nor to be enslaved to him, but rather to be his companion and partner in mutual aid and trust. By insisting on the spiritual equality of men and women and their responsibility to one another within marriage, the church helped to raise the dignity of women.

Under Germanic law, women had basic rights that prevented them from being treated as chattel slaves. There was also far greater equality between the sexes in Germanic than in Roman law. Unlike Roman women, who as teens married much older men, German women married adults of similar age to themselves. Another practice unknown to the Romans was the groom's required conveyance of a dowry to his bride, which remained her own in the event of widowhood. The major Germanic law codes recognized the right of women to inherit, administer, dispose of, and confer family property and wealth on their children. They could also press charges in court against men for bodily injury and rape.

The nunnery was an option open to only a few unmarried women from the higher social classes. Entrance required a dowry (dos) and could be almost as expensive as a wedding. A nun could become abbess or mother superior and exercise authority denied her in much of the secular world. However, nunneries were under male supervision, and even mothers superior had to answer to higher male authority and receive the sacraments from male hands.

Nunneries also provided women an escape from the debilitating effects of multiple pregnancies. In the ninth century, under the influence of Christianity, the Carolingians made monogamous marriage their official policy. The result of the new policy was both a boon and a burden to women.

On one hand, wives gained greater dignity and legal security. On the other hand, a woman's labor as household manager and bearer of children increased.

Most medieval women were workers in fields, trades, and businesses. Evidence suggests that they were respected and loved by their husbands. Between the ages of ten and fifteen, girls were apprenticed in a trade and learned a marketable skill. If they married, they might continue their trade, or become assistants and partners in their husband's shops. Women appeared in virtually every "blue-collar" trade, from butcher to goldsmith; belonged to guilds, just like men; and could become craftmasters. In the later Middle Ages, it became common for townswomen to go to school and gain vernacular literacy.

Women were excluded by reason of gender from the professions of scholarship, law, and medicine. However, the vocational destinies of most men were no less fixed; socially inferior, propertyless men also could not enter these high professions. Women disproportionately filled the ranks of domestic servants and the clothing (sewing, weaving), food, and helping (midwifery, nursing) trades.

Medieval Children

The image and reality of medieval children are also contradictory. Until recently, many historians had believed that medieval parents were emotionally bankrupt and treated their children as little adults.

Some historians maintain that children were rarely portrayed as being different from adults in medieval art and sculpture. There is also evidence of high infant and child mortality, which, it is argued, discouraged parents from making deep emotional commitments to their children. Why should a parent become attached to a child who had a 30–50 percent chance of dying before age five? During the Middle Ages, children also assumed adult responsibilities much earlier in life than children do today. Peasant children labored in the fields as soon as they could manage the work. Urban artisans and burghers sent their children to apprenticeships around the age of ten. That children were expected to grow up fast is also indicated by the canonical ages for marriage: twelve for girls and fourteen for boys. Few actually married at such young ages, and when they did, it was usually a matter of royal dynasties and noble families making long-range political plans. Such unions were more like engagements that were consummated at later ages.

The practice of infanticide has been cited as an even more striking indication of low esteem for children in ancient and early medieval times. According to Tacitus, the Romans exposed unwanted children, especially girls, at birth—that is, abandoned them to die, as a way to control family size and gender. Surviving children, however, appear to have been given attention and affection. The Germanic tribes of medieval Europe, by contrast, had large families, but tended to neglect their children by comparison to the Romans. Infanticide, particularly of girls, continued in the early Middle Ages, as shown by its condemnation in penance books and by church synods.

Among the German tribes, one paid a much lower *wergild*, or compensatory fine, for injury to a child than for injury to an adult, only one-fifth of that for injuring an adult. The *wergild* paid for injury to a female child under fifteen was one half that for injury to a male child. Mothers appear also to have nursed boys longer than they did girls, which favored boys' health and survival. However, a woman's *wergild* increased a full eightfold between infancy and her childbearing years, at which time she had obviously become highly prized.[1]

Despite such varied evidence of parental distance and neglect, the evidence for parental love and responsibility is even stronger. Physicians and theologians portrayed childhood as a distinct and special stage of life. According to the medical authorities, infancy proper extended from birth up to two years and covered the period of speechlessness and suckling. The period thereafter, until age seven, was considered a higher level of infancy, marked by weaning and the beginning of a child's ability to speak. At age seven, when a child could think, act decisively, and speak clearly, childhood proper was seen to begin. After this point, a child could be reasoned with, profit from regular discipline, and begin to train for a vocation. At seven a child was ready for schooling or apprenticeship in a craft or trade. Until physical growth was completed, however—and that could extend to twenty-one years of age—a child or youth was legally under the guardianship of parents or a surrogate authority.

There is evidence that high infant and child mortality actually made parents consider their children all the more precious. The medical authorities of the Middle Ages dealt at length with postnatal care and childhood diseases. When infants and children died, medieval parents grieved as pitiably as modern parents do.

Clear evidence of the special attention children received is also seen in the great variety of children's toys, as well as devices like walkers and potty chairs, that existed in the Middle Ages. The medieval authorities on child rearing condemned child abuse and advocated moderation in the disciplining of children. Parents were urged to love their children as Mary loved Jesus. Early apprenticeships may also be interpreted as

an expression of parental love and concern, for in the Middle Ages, no parental responsibility was thought greater than that of equipping a child for useful and gainful work.

Politics

England and France: Hastings (1066) to Bouvines (1214)

William the Conqueror   The most important change in English political life was occasioned in 1066 by the death of the childless Anglo-Saxon ruler Edward the Confessor (r. 1042–1066), so named because of his reputation of piety. Edward's mother was a Norman princess, which gave Duke William of Normandy (d. 1087) a hereditary claim to the English throne. The Anglo-Saxon assembly, however, chose instead Harold Godwinsson (ca. 1022–1066). That brought the swift conquest of England by the Normans. William's forces defeated Harold at Hastings on October 14, 1066, and William was crowned king of England in Westminster Abbey.

William organized his new English state shrewdly, establishing a strong monarchy whose power was not fragmented by territorial princes. He first embarked on a twenty-year conquest that eventually made every landholder, both large and small, his vassal. He kept the Anglo-Saxon tax system and the practice of court writs (legal warnings) as a flexible form of central control over localities. And he took care not to destroy the Anglo-Saxon quasi-democratic tradition of frequent *parleying*—that is, the holding of conferences between the king and lesser powers who had vested interests in royal decisions. The result was a balancing of monarchical and parliamentary elements that remains true of English government today.

For administration and taxation, William commissioned a county-by-county survey of his new realm, known as the *Domesday Book* (1080–1086). The title of the book reflects the thoroughness of the survey: just as none would escape the doomsday judgment of God, so none was overlooked by William's assessors.

Henry II and Eleanor of Aquitaine   William's son, Henry I (r. 1100–1135), died without a male heir, throwing England into virtual anarchy until Henry II (r. 1154–1189) became king as head of the new Plantagenet dynasty. Henry brought to the throne greatly expanded French holdings, partly by inheritance from his father (Maine, Touraine, and Anjou) and partly by his marriage to Eleanor of Aquitaine (1122–1204), a union that created the so-called Angevin or English-French Empire. Eleanor married Henry while he was still the count of Anjou and not yet king of

---

[1]David Herlihy, "Medieval Children," in *Essays on Medieval Civilization*, ed. by B.K. Lackner and K.R. Phelp (Austin: University of Texas Press, 1978), pp. 109–131.

The English Nobility Imposes Restraints on King John

The gradual building of a sound English constitutional monarchy in the Middle Ages required the king's willingness to share power. He had to be strong but could not act as a despot or rule by fiat. The danger of despotism became acute in England under the rule of King John. In 1215, the English nobility forced him to recognize Magna Carta, which reaffirmed traditional rights and personal liberties that are still enshrined in English law.

Are the rights protected by Magna Carta basic ones or special privileges? Do they suggest there was a sense of "fairness" in the past? Does the granting of such rights in any way weaken the king?

A free man shall not be fined for a small offense, except in proportion to the gravity of the offense; and for a great offense he shall be fined in proportion to the magnitude of the offense, saving his freehold [property]; and a merchant in the same way, saving his merchandise; and the villein [a free serf, bound only to his lord] shall be fined in the same way, saving his wainage [wagon], if he shall be at [the king's] mercy. And none of the above fines shall be imposed except by the oaths of honest men of the neighborhood. . . .

No constable or other bailiff of [the king] shall take anyone's grain or other chattels without immediately paying for them in money, unless he is able to obtain a postponement at the good will of the seller.

No constable shall require any knight to give money in place of his ward of a castle [i.e., standing guard], if he is willing to furnish that ward in his own person, or through another honest man, if he himself is not able to do it for a reasonable cause; and if we shall lead or send him into the army, he shall be free from ward in proportion to the amount of time which he has been in the army through us.

No sheriff or bailiff of [the king], or any one else, shall take horses or wagons of any free man, for carrying purposes, except on the permission of that free man.

Neither we nor our bailiffs will take the wood of another man for castles, or for anything else which we are doing, except by the permission of him to whom the wood belongs. . . .

No free man shall be taken, or imprisoned, or dispossessed, or outlawed, or banished, or in any way injured, nor will we go upon him, nor send upon him, except by the legal judgment of his peers, or by the law of the land.

To no one will we sell, to no one will we deny or delay, right or justice.

James Harvey Robinson, ed., *Readings in European History*, Vol. 1 (Boston: Athenaeum, 1904), pp. 400–402.

England. The marriage occurred only eight weeks after the annulment of Eleanor's marriage to the French king Louis VII (r. 1137–1180) in March 1152. The true reason for the dissolution of the marriage was Louis's suspicion of Eleanor's infidelity.

Eleanor of Aquitaine was a powerful influence on both court politics and culture in twelfth-century France and England. She had accompanied Louis VII on the Second Crusade, becoming an example for women of lesser stature, who were venturing into areas previously considered the province of men. Eleanor spent the years 1154 to 1170 as Henry's queen. She separated from Henry in 1170, partly because of his public philandering and cruel treatment, later (1173) taking revenge by helping provoke a rebellion against him by their three sons.

After separating from Henry, Eleanor lived in Poitiers with her daughter Marie, the countess of Champagne, and the two made the court of Poitiers a famous center for the literature of courtly love. The most enduring example of the latter is the work of Chrétien de Troyes (d. 1183), whose tales of King Arthur and the Knights of the Round Table told the tragic story of Sir Lancelot's secret and illicit love for Arthur's wife, Guinevere.

Eleanor and Henry reunited in 1179, but he kept her under mild house arrest until his death in 1189.

Popular Rebellion and Magna Carta Henry II became autocratic. He forced his will on the clergy in the Constitutions of Clarendon (1164), which limited judicial appeals to Rome, subjected the clergy to the civil courts, and gave the king control over the election of bishops. The result was resistance from both the nobility and the clergy. The archbishop of Canterbury, Thomas à Becket (1118?–1170), once Henry's chancellor, broke with the king. Becket's assassination in 1170 and his canonization by Pope Alexander III (r. 1159–1181) in 1172 helped focus resentment against the king's heavy-handed tactics.

Under Henry's successors, the brothers Richard the Lion-Hearted (r. 1189–1199) and John (r. 1199–1216), burdensome taxation in support of Crusades and war with France turned resistance into rebellion. In 1209 Pope Innocent III (r. 1198–1216), in a dispute with King John over the pope's choice for archbishop of Canterbury, excommunicated the king and placed England under interdict, which forbade church services. To keep his throne, John made humiliating concessions. The last straw for the English came with the defeat of the king's forces by the French at Bouvines in 1214. With the support of the clergy and the townspeople, English barons turned against John in a popular rebellion that ended with the king's grudging recognition of Magna Carta ("Great Charter") in 1215.

This famous cornerstone of modern English law put limits on autocratic behavior of the kind exhibited by Norman kings and their successors, and it secured the rights of the privileged to be represented at the highest levels of government in important matters like taxation. The Great Charter enabled the English to avoid both a dissolution of the monarchy by the nobility and the abridgment of the rights of the nobility by the monarchy.

Philip II Augustus During the century and a half between the Norman Conquest (1066) and the Magna Carta (1215), a strong monarchy was never in question in England. The English struggle in the High Middle Ages was to secure the rights of the many, not the authority of the king. The French faced the reverse problem. Powerful feudal princes dominated France from the beginning of the Capetian dynasty (987) until the reign of Philip II Augustus (1180–1223). During this period the Capetian kings concentrated their limited resources on securing the royal domain surrounding Paris known as the Île-de-France. They did not challenge the more powerful nobility. By the time of Philip II, Paris had become the center of French government and culture, and the Capetian dynasty a secure hereditary monarchy. Thereafter, the kings of France were able to impose their will on the French nobles, who were always in law the king's vassals.

The Norman conquest of England enabled the Capetian kings to establish a truly national monarchy. The duke of Normandy, who after 1066 was master of England, was also a vassal of the French king. Capetian kings watched with alarm as the power of their Norman vassal grew.

Philip Augustus faced both an internal and an international struggle, and he succeeded at both. His armies occupied all the English territories on the French coast, except for Aquitaine. However, the Holy Roman Emperor Otto IV (r. 1198–1215) entered the fray on the side of the English, and the French found themselves assailed from both east and west. Still, when the armies clashed at Bouvines on July 27, 1214, the French defeated the English and the Germans. The victory unified France around the monarchy and laid the foundation for French ascendancy in the later Middle Ages. Philip Augustus also gained control of the lucrative urban industries of Flanders. The defeat so weakened Otto IV that he fell from power in Germany.

France in the Thirteenth Century: Reign of Louis IX

Louis IX (r. 1226–1270), the grandson of Philip Augustus, embodied the medieval view of the perfect ruler. Louis inherited a unified and secure kingdom. Although his moral character far excelled that of his royal and papal contemporaries, he was also at times prey to naiveté. Not beset by the problems of sheer survival, and a reformer at heart, Louis found himself free to concentrate on what medieval people believed to be the business of civilization.

Magnanimity in politics is not always a sign of strength, and Louis could be very magnanimous. Although in a position to drive the English from their French possessions during negotiations for the Treaty of Paris (1259), he refused to take such advantage. Had he confiscated English territories on the French coast, he might have lessened, if not averted altogether, the Hundred Years War (ca. 1337–1453). He instead surrendered territory to the English. Although he chastised popes for their ambitions, Louis remained neutral during the struggle between Emperor Frederick II and the papacy, and his neutrality redounded to the pope's advantage. For their assistance, the Capetian kings of the thirteenth century received many papal favors.

Louis's greatest achievements lay at home. The efficient French bureaucracy became under Louis an instrument of order and fair play in local government. He sent forth royal commissioners (*enqueteurs*) to monitor the royal officials responsible for local administration and ensure justice. These royal ambassadors were received as genuine tribunes of the people. Louis further abolished private wars and serfdom within his own royal domain, gave his subjects the right of appeal from local to higher courts, and made the tax system more equitable. The French people came to associate their king with justice; and national feeling grew strong during his reign.

Louis became an arbiter among the world's powers, having far greater moral authority than the pope. During his reign, French society and culture became an example to all of Europe, a pattern that would continue into the modern period. Northern France became the showcase of monastic reform, chivalry, and Gothic art and architecture. Louis's reign also coincided with the golden age of scholasticism, which saw the convergence of Europe's greatest thinkers on Paris, among them Saint Thomas Aquinas and Saint Bonaventure.

Louis's perfection remained, however, that of a medieval king. Louis was something of a religious fanatic. He sponsored the French Inquisition. He led two disastrous Crusades against the Arabs. During the first (1248–1254), he was captured and had to be ransomed out of Egypt. He died of a fever during the second in 1270. It was especially for this selfless (although useless) service that the church, pressured by the ruthless king Philip the Fair (r. 1285–1314), bestowed sainthood on Louis IX.

The Hohenstaufen Empire (1152–1272)

During the twelfth and thirteenth centuries, stable governments developed in both England and France. The Holy Roman Empire, which embraced Germany, Burgundy, and northern Italy, was a different story (see Map 13–3). There, primarily because of the efforts of the Hohenstaufen dynasty to extend imperial power into southern Italy, Germany fragmented until modern times.

Frederick I Barbarossa

With the accession to the throne of Frederick I Barbarossa (1152–1190), the first of the Hohenstaufens, a new day seemed to dawn for imperial power. The Hohenstaufens not only reestablished imperial authority but also initiated a new phase in the contest between popes and emperors, one that was to prove even more deadly than the investiture struggle had been. Never have rulers and popes despised and persecuted one another more than they did during the Hohenstaufen dynasty.

Frederick I found powerful feudal princes in Germany and Lombardy and a pope in Rome who believed that the emperor should obey his command. There existed, however, widespread disaffection with the incessant warring among the princes and the theocratic pretensions of the papacy. Popular opinion was on the emperor's side, and Fred-

erick attempted to hold the empire together by stressing feudal bonds.

Frederick's reign ended, however, with stalemate in Germany and defeat in Italy. Before his death in 1190, an opportunity had opened to form a new territorial base of power for future emperors by an alliance with Sicily. Sealed in 1186 by the marriage of his son—the future Henry VI (r. 1190–1197)—and Constance, heiress to the kingdom of Sicily, the alliance became a fatal distraction for the Hohenstaufens. Equally ominous, this union of the empire with Sicily left Rome encircled, thereby ensuring the hostility of a papacy already distrustful of the emperor.

When Henry VI died in September 1197, chaos followed. Germany was thrown into anarchy. England gave financial support to anti-Hohenstaufen factions, and helped Otto of Brunswick to become Emperor Otto IV in 1198. With England supporting Otto, the French backed the Hohenstaufens. Meanwhile, Henry VI's four-year-old son, Frederick, who had a direct hereditary claim to the imperial crown, had been made a ward of Pope Innocent III.

Pope Innocent III (1198–1215)

Innocent III was a papal monarch in the Gregorian tradition of papal independence from secular domination. He proclaimed and practiced as none before him the doctrine of the plenitude of papal power. He likened the relationship of the pope to the emperor—or the church to the state—to that of the sun to the moon. As the moon received its light from the sun, so the emperor received his crown from the pope.

Innocent and his successors did not hesitate to act on their ambitions. Innocent had both the will and the means to challenge the Hohenstaufens.

Frederick II

Hohenstaufen support had meanwhile remained alive in Germany despite the dynasty's fall, and Otto IV reigned over a divided kingdom. In October 1209, Pope Innocent crowned him emperor, but then became a mortal enemy when Otto reconquered Sicily and again pursued an imperial policy that left Rome encircled. Within four months of his coronation, Otto received a papal excommunication.

Casting about for a counterweight to Otto, Pope Innocent joined the French, who had remained loyal to the Hohenstaufens. Philip Augustus suggested to the pope that a solution to their problems with Otto IV was close at hand in Innocent's ward, Frederick of Sicily, son of the late Hohenstaufen Emperor Henry VI. In December 1212, young Frederick, with papal, French, and German support, became Emperor Frederick II. Within a year and a half, Philip Augustus defeated Otto IV at Bouvines. After the victory he sent Frederick II Otto's fallen flag, a gesture that suggests the extent to which Frederick was intended to be a French papal puppet.

Church and Empire	
910	Monastary of Cluny founded
918	Henry I becomes King of Germany
951	Otto I invades Italy
955	Otto I defeats the Hungarians at Lechfeld
962	Otto I crowned emperor by Pope John XII
1077	Gregory VII pardons Henry IV at Canossa
1122	Concordat of Worms settles the investiture controversy
1152–1190	Reign of Frederick Barbarossa
1198–1215	Reign of Innocent III
1212	Frederick II crowned emperor
1214	Collapse of the claims of Otto IV
1232	Frederick II devolves authority to the German princes
1257	The German monarchy becomes elective

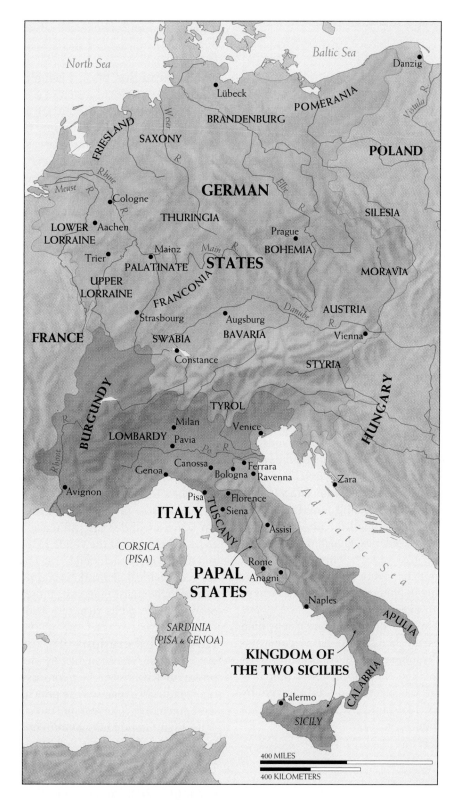

Map 13–3   Germany and Italy in the Middle Ages.   Medieval Germany and Italy were divided lands. The Holy Roman Empire (Germany) embraced hundreds of independent territories that the emperor ruled only in name. The papacy controlled the Rome area and tried to enforce its will in the Romagna. Under the Hohenstaufens (mid-twelfth to mid-thirteenth centuries), internal German divisions and papal conflict reached new heights; German rulers sought to extend their power to southern Italy and Sicily.

Frederick soon disappointed any such hopes. He was Sicilian and dreaded travel beyond the Alps. Frederick desired only one thing from the German princes—the imperial title for himself and his sons—and he gave them what they wanted to secure it. His compliance with their demands laid the foundation for six centuries of German division. The German princes became undisputed lords over their territories, petty kings.

Frederick had an equally disastrous relationship with the papacy, which excommunicated him four times. Pope Innocent IV (1243–1254) organized and led the newly empowered German princes against Frederick, launching the church into European politics on a massive scale. This transformation of the papacy into a formidable political and military power soon made the church highly vulnerable to the criticism of religious reformers and royal apologists alike.

When Frederick died in 1250, the German monarchy died with him. The princes established an informal electoral college in 1257 to pick the emperor, which was formally recognized by the emperor in 1356. The "king of the Romans" became their puppet; he was elected and did not rule by hereditary right. Between 1250 and 1272 the Hohenstaufen dynasty faded into oblivion.

Medieval Russia

In the late tenth century, Prince Vladimir of Kiev (r. 972–1015), then Russia's dominant city, received delegations of Muslims, Roman Catholics, Jews, and Greek Orthodox Christians, each group hoping to win the Russians to its religion. Prince Vladimir chose Greek Orthodoxy, which became the religion of Russia, adding a new cultural bond to the long-standing commercial ties the Russians had with the Byzantine Empire.

Politics and Society   Vladimir's successor, Yaroslav the Wise (r. 1016–1054), developed Kiev into a magnificent political and cultural center. After his death, rivalry among princes slowly split Russians into three cultural groups: the Great Russians, the White Russians, and the Little Russians (Ukrainians). Autonomous principalities also challenged Kiev's dominance, and it became just one of several national centers.

Government in the principalities combined monarchy (the prince), aristocracy (the prince's council of noblemen), and democracy (a popular assembly of all adult males). The broadest social division was between freemen and slaves. Freemen included the clergy, army officers, boyars (wealthy landowners), townsmen, and peasants. Slaves were mostly prisoners of war. Debtors working off their debts made up a large, semi-free, intermediate group.

Mongol Rule (1243–1480)   Ghengis Khan (1155–1227) invaded Russia in 1223, and Kiev fell to Batu Khan in 1240. Russian cities became tribute-paying principalities of the segment of the Mongol (or Tatar) Empire called the *Golden Horde* (a phrase derived from the Tatar words for the color of Batu Khan's tent), which had its capital at Sarai, on the lower Volga. The Golden Horde stationed officials in Russian towns to oversee taxation and the conscription of soldiers into Tatar armies.

Mongol rule further divided Russia from the west. Russian women—under the influence of Islam, which had become the religion of the Golden Horde—began to wear veils and to lead more secluded lives. The Mongols, however, left Russian political institutions and religion largely intact and, thanks to their far-flung trade, brought most Russians greater peace and prosperity than they had enjoyed before.

Russian Liberation   The princes of Moscow grew wealthy under the Mongols. As Mongol rule weakened, the princes took control of the territory surrounding the city. They then gradually expanded the principality of Moscow through land purchases, colonization, and conquest.

In 1380, Grand Duke Dimitri of Moscow (1350–1389) defeated Tatar forces at Kulikov Meadow in a victory that marked the beginning of the decline of Mongolian hegemony. Another century would pass before Ivan III, called Ivan the Great (d. 1505), would bring all of northern Russia under Moscow's control and end Mongol rule in 1480. By the last quarter of the fourteenth century, Moscow had replaced Kiev as the political and religious center of Russia. In Russian eyes it was destined to become the "third Rome" after the fall of Constantinople to the Turks in 1453.

IN WORLD PERSPECTIVE
The High Middle Ages

With its borders finally secured, western Europe concentrated during the High Middle Ages on its political institutions and cultural development. In England and France, modern western nations can be seen in formation. Within the empire, imperial rule both revived (under Otto I) and collapsed (during the Hohenstaufen dynasty). Everywhere, society organized itself from noble to serf. With the flourishing of trade and the expansion of towns, a new wealthy class patronized education. Western Europe's first universities appeared, and scholasticism brought a new order to knowledge. The major disruption of the period, however, was an unprecedented conflict between former allies. The Roman Catholic Church had become a monarchy in its own right, able to compete with secular states and dethrone kings and princes. The foundation was thereby laid both for conflict between popes and rulers, which lasted into early modern times, and for the western separation of church and state.

For western Europe, the High Middle Ages were a period of clearer self-definition during which individual lands gained much of the geographic shape we recognize today. Other world civilizations had by this time become well established and had even begun to depart their "classical" or "golden" periods. For the west, the best still lay ahead.

Under the Sung dynasty (960–1279), before Mongol rule, China continued its technological advance. In addition to the printing press, the Chinese invented the abacus and gunpowder. They also enjoyed a money economy unknown in the west. But culturally, these centuries between 1000 and 1300 were closed and narrow by comparison with those of the T'ang dynasty. Politically, the Sung was far more autocratic. In China (as in western European lands like England and France, although not in Italy and the empire), regional aristocracies ceased to be serious obstacles to a strong centralized government.

Chinese women generally held a lower status and had fewer vocational options than western women, as the practice of foot binding attests. As in the west, a higher degree of freedom and self-government developed in the countryside, especially by the fourteenth century, as peasants gained the right to buy and sell land and to fulfill traditional labor obligations by money payments. Intellectually, China, like the west, had a scholastic movement within its dominant philosophy; Confucianism made religious and philosophical thought more elaborate, systematic, and orthodox. Whereas western scholasticism made Christianity aloof, elitist, and ridiculed by its lay critics, Confucianism remained a philosophy highly adaptable and popular among laypeople.

In the late twelfth century, Japan shifted from civilian to military rule; the Kamakura *bakufu* governed by mounted warriors who were paid with rights to income from land in exchange for their military services. This rise of a military aristocracy marked the beginning of Japan's "medieval," as distinct from its "classical," period. With a civilian court also in existence, Japan actually had a dual government (that is, two emperors and two courts) until the fourteenth century. However, this situation differed greatly from the deep and permanent national divisions developing at this time among the emerging states and autonomous principalities of western Europe.

Japanese women, more like those in western Europe than in China, traditionally played a prominent role in royal government and court culture. The Nun Shogun, for example, succeeded her husband for a brief period of Kamakura rule in the late twelfth century. But the prominence of women in government would also change in Japan by the fourteenth century.

Within the many developing autonomous Islamic lands at this time, the teaching of Muhammad created an international culture. The regular practice of religious fundamentals enabled Muslims to transcend their new and often deep regional divisions. Similarly, Christianity allowed Englishmen, Frenchmen, Germans, and Italians to think of themselves as one people and to unite in Crusades to the Holy Land. As these Crusades began in the late eleventh century, Islam too was on the march, penetrating Anatolia and Afghanistan, and impinging upon India, where it met a new challenge in Hinduism.

Review Questions

1. How did Otto I earn the title "the Great"?

2. How do you account for the success of the Cluny reform movement? Can major features of the modern Catholic Church be found in the Cluny's reforms?

3. Was the investiture controversy a political or a religious conflict? Summarize the respective arguments of Gregory VII and Henry IV. Is the conflict a precedent for the modern doctrine of the separation of church and state?

4. What were the motives behind the Crusades to the Holy Land? Did they have any positive consequences for western Europe?

5. Why did Germany remain divided while France and England began to coalesce into strong states during the High Middle Ages?

6. How did the responsibilities of the nobility differ from those of the clergy and the peasantry during the High Middle Ages? How did each social class contribute to the stability of society?

7. What gave rise to towns, and how did they change traditional medieval society?

8. How did the first universities differ from universities as we know them today?

9. Were the Middle Ages a time of rampant misogyny and child abuse? What were the opportunities of women and the protections for children?

Documents CD-ROM

1. Gregory VII's Letter to the Bishop of Metz, 1081

2. Duke William of Aquitane: "Foundation Charter for the Abbey of Cluny, 909"

3. Saint Thomas Aquinas: *The Summa Against the Gentiles*

4. Saint Thomas Aquinas: "On Kingship or The Governance of Rulers"

5. *The Magna Carta*

6. Robert of Clari, *The Conquest of Constantinople*

14 THE ISLAMIC HEARTLANDS AND INDIA (CA. 1000–1500)

CHAPTER TOPICS

THE ISLAMIC HEARTLANDS

◆ Religion and Society

◆ Regional Developments

◆ The Spread of Islam Beyond the Heartlands

INDIA

◆ The Spread of Islam to India

◆ Muslim-Hindu Encounter

◆ Islamic States and Dynasties

◆ Religious and Cultural Accommodation

◆ Hindu and Other Indian Traditions

In World Perspective The Islamic Heartlands and India, ca. 1000–1500

Centralized caliphal power in the Islamic world had broken down by the mid-tenth century. Regional Islamic states with distinctive political and cultural identities now dominated—a pattern that would endure to modern times (see Map 14–1). Yet the diverse Islamic lands remained part of a larger civilization.

Socially and religiously, the next 500 years saw the growth of a truly international Islamic community, united by shared norms of communal order represented and maintained by the Muslim religious scholars (*ulama*). Sufism, that strand of Islam stressing piety and allegiance to a spiritual master, gained widespread popularity, especially after 1200, through the growth of Sufi affiliations or brotherhoods. Shi'ite ideas also offered an alternative vision of society for many. Movements loyal to Ali and his heirs challenged but failed to reverse centrist, Sunni predominance, even though Shi'ite dynasties ruled much of the Islamic heartlands in the tenth and eleventh centuries.

Culturally, the rise of the New Persian language in the tenth century resulted in a rich new Islamic literature. A cul-

tural renaissance fueled the spread of Persian as the major language of Islam alongside Arabic. The Persian-dominated Iranian and Indian Islamic world became increasingly distinct from the western Islamic lands.

Two Asian steppe peoples, the Mongols and the Turks, came to rule much of the Islamic world in these centuries, while Islam impinged more and more on the Indian subcontinent, Southeast Asia, and sub-Saharan Africa. Although Muslims remained a minority in these regions, Islam became the major new influence in all of them.

THE ISLAMIC HEARTLANDS

Religion and Society

The notable developments in this period for the shape of Islamic society were the consolidation and institutionalization of Sunni and Shi'ite legal and religious norms, and Sufi traditions and personal piety.

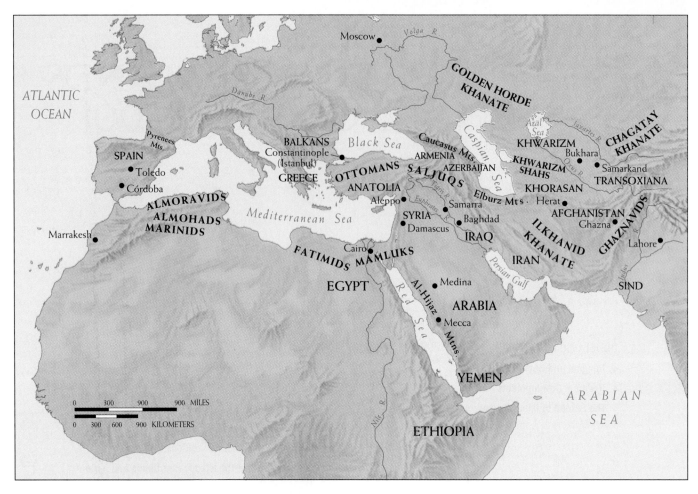

Map 14-1 The Islamic heartlands, 1000–1500. Shown are the major ruling dynasties.

Consolidation of Sunni Orthopraxy

The *ulama* (both Sunni and Shi'ite) gradually became entrenched religious, social, and political elites throughout the Islamic world, especially after the breakdown of centralized power in the tenth century. Their integration into local merchant, landowning, and bureaucratic classes led to stronger identification of these groups with Islam.

From the eleventh century onward, the *ulama's* power and fixity as a class were expressed in the institution of the *madrasa*, or college of higher learning. In contrast to the university, with its corporate organization and institutional degrees, the *madrasa* was a support institution for individual teachers, who personally certified students' mastery of particular subjects. It gave an institutional base (often providing not only teaching space but stipends and student living quarters) to Islam's long-developed system of students seeking out the best teachers and studying texts with them until they received the teachers' formal certification, or "permission" to transmit and teach those same texts themselves.

Popular "unofficial" piety flourished in pilgrimages to saints' tombs, in folk celebrations of Muhammad's birthday, in veneration of him in poetry, and in ecstatic chant and dance among Sufi groups. But the shared traditions that directed family and civil law, the daily worship rituals, fasting in the month of Ramadan, and the yearly Meccan pilgrimage remained the public bond uniting almost all Muslims. The tendency among Muslims, for all their theological disputes, was to define Islam in terms of what Muslims do—namely by ortho*praxy* (practice) rather than by ortho*doxy* (beliefs). The chief arbiters of "normative" Sunni and Shi'i Islam among the *ulama* were the *faqihs*, or legal scholars, not the theologians.

A basic Sunni orthopraxy, discouraging religious or social innovation, was well established by the year 1000 as the dominant tradition. Further, a growing social conservatism among the *ulama* reflected their integration in regional social aristocracies. The *ulama* were often committed to the status quo, as were the rulers.

Sufi Piety and Organization

Sufi piety stresses the spiritual and mystical dimensions of Islam. The term *Sufi* apparently came from the Arabic *suf* ("wool"), based on the old ascetic practice of wearing only a coarse woolen garment. Sufi simplicity and humility developed as a distinctive tendency when, after about 700 C.E., male and female pietists emphasized a godly life over and above mere observance of Muslim duties. Some stressed ascetic avoidance of temptations, others loving devotion to God. Sufi piety bridged the abyss between the human and the divine that is implied in the exalted Muslim concept of the omnipotent God of creation. Sufi piety merged with folk piety in saint veneration, shrine pilgrimage, ecstatic worship, and seasonal festivals. Sufi writers composed some of the world's finest mystical poetry.

Some Sufis were revered as spiritual masters and saints. Their disciples formed brotherhoods that, from about the eleventh century on, became both regional and international organizations. Each had its distinctive mystical teaching, Qur'anic interpretation, and devotional practice. These fraternal orders became the chief instruments of the spread of Muslim faith in almost all Islamic societies. Indeed, Sufi orders became in this age one of the typical social institutions of everyday Muslim life. Whether Sunni or Shi'ite, casually or seriously pious, many Muslims have ever since identified in some degree with one or another Sufi order.

Consolidation of Shi'ite Traditions

Shi'ite traditions crystallized between the tenth and twelfth centuries. Numerous states now came under Shi'ite rulers. Yet a substantial Shi'ite populace developed only in Iran, Iraq, and the lower Indus (Sind).

Two Shi'ite groups emerged as the most influential. The first were the "Seveners," or "Isma'ilis," who recognized Isma'il (d. ca. 760), first son of the sixth Alid *imam*, as the seventh *imam* (rather than his brother). Isma'ili groups were often revolutionary, and one Isma'ili group, the Qarmatians of eastern Arabia, ruled or disrupted Iraq, Syria, and Arabia through much of the tenth century.

By the eleventh century, however, most Shi'ites accepted a line of twelve *imams* (through another son of the sixth *imam*), the last of whom is said to have disappeared in Samarra (Iraq)

The Sultan Hasan Madrasa and Tomb-Mosque. This imposing Mamluk building (1356–1363) was built to house teachers and students studying all four of the major traditions or "schools" of Islamic law. Living and teaching spaces are combined here in a building with a mosque and the Sultan's tomb enclosure. [SuperStock, Inc.]

A Muslim Biographer's Account of Maimonides

The following are excerpts from the entry on Maimonides (Arabic: Musa ibn Maymun) in the biographical dictionary of learned men by Ibn al-Qifti (d. 1248). In one section (omitted here), Ibn al-Qifti describes how this most famous Spanish Jewish savant at first feigned conversion to Islam when a new Berber ruler demanded the expulsion of Christians and Jews from Spain in about 1133. He tells how Maimonides moved his family to the more tolerant Islamic world of Cairo, where he eventually became the court physician. (It was not unusual for Jews or Christians to hold high office under Muslim rulers.) Other omitted material includes treatment of his famous books and his marriage, his death, and his other accomplishments.

Can you identify the probable Islamic dynasty whose rule forced Maimonides to leave Spain for Cairo? Why were the Fatimids in Cairo tolerant of Christians and Jews when their Berber co-religionists were not? From the Muslim biographer's treatment of his subject, what might you infer about Islamic societies and the intellectual atmosphere of the time?

. . . This man was one of the people of Andalus, a Jew by religion. He studied philosophy in Andalus, was expert in mathematics, and devoted attention to some of the logical sciences. He studied medicine there and excelled in it. . . .

. . . After assembling his possessions in the time that was needed for this, he left Andalus and went to Egypt, accompanied by his family. He settled in the town of Fustāt [part of greater Cairo], among its Jews, and practiced his religion openly. He lived in a district called al-Masīsa and made a living by trading in jewels and suchlike. Some people studied philosophy under him. . . .

He married in Cairo the sister of a Jewish scribe called Abu'l-Ma'ālī, the secretary of the mother of Nūr al-Dīn 'Alī, known as al-Afdal, the son of Salāh al-Dīn Yūsuf ibn Ayyūb, and he had a son by her who today is a physician in Cairo after his father. . . .

Mūsā ibn Maymūn died in Cairo in the year 605 [1208–9].[1] He ordered his heirs to carry his body, when the smell had ceased, to Lake Tiberias and bury him there, seeking to be among the graves of the ancient Israelites and their great jurists, which are there. This was done.

He was learned in the law and secrets of the Jews and compiled a commentary on the Talmud, which is a commentary and explanation of the Torah; some of the Jews approve of it. Philosophic doctrines overcame him, and he compiled a treatise denying the canonical resurrection. The leaders of the Jews held this against him, so he

Reading the Torah in a Spanish synagogue. A picture from a Hebrew Haggada, Spain, fourteenth century. Until their expulsion by Christian rulers at the end of the fifteenth century, Jews formed a significant minority in Spain. [By permission of The British Library]

concealed it except from those who shared his opinion in this. . . .

In the latter part of his life he was troubled by a man from Andalus, a jurist called Abu'l-'Arab ibn Ma'īsha, who came to Fustāt and met him. He charged him with having been a Muslim in Andalus, accused him [of apostasy] and wanted to have him punished.[2] 'Abd al-Rahīm ibn 'Alī al-Fādil prevented this, and said to him, "If a man is converted by force, his Islam is not legally valid."

[1] In fact, he died in 1204.
[2] The penalty for apostasy was death.

Excerpt from *Islam from the Prophet Muhammad to the Capture of Constantinople*, Vol. 2 by Bernard Lewis, ed. and trans. Copyright © 1974 by Bernard Lewis. Reprinted by permission of HarperCollins Publishers, Inc.

in 873 into a cosmic concealment from which he will eventually emerge as the Mahdi, or "Guided One," to usher in the messianic age and final judgment. The "Twelvers," the Shi'ite majority, still focus on the martyrdom of the twelve *imams* and look for their intercession on the Day of Judgment. They have flourished best in Iran, the home of most Shi'ite thought, whatever the sect. The Safavids of Iran made Twelver doctrine the "state religion" in the sixteenth century (see Chapter 23).

Regional Developments

The western half of the Islamic world after the tenth century developed two regional foci: (1) Spain, Moroccan North Africa, and to a lesser extent, West Africa; and (2) Egypt, Syria-Palestine, Anatolia, along with Arabia and Libyan North Africa. The history of the eastern half of the Islamic world between 1000 and 1500 was marked by the incursion of the Mongols in the thirteenth century.

The Islamic West: Spain and North Africa

The grandeur of Spanish Islamic ("Moorish") culture is visible still in Córdoba's great mosque and the remnants of the legendary Alhambra castle. Abd al-Rahman I (r. 756–788) was the founder of Umayyad culture at Córdoba, which was the cultural center of the western world for the next two centuries. Renowned for its intellectual life, commercial activity, public baths and gardens, and elegance, Córdoba reached its zenith under Abd al-Rahman III (r. 912–961). He took the title of caliph in 929, and his absolutist but benevolent rule saw a largely unified, peaceful Islamic Spain. The mosque-university of Córdoba that he founded was the earliest of its kind, attracting students from Europe as well as the Islamic world.

A sad irony of this cosmopolitan world was recurring religious exclusivism among both Muslims and Christians, which sparked conflict between them. Abd al-Rahman III checked both the new Fatimid power in North Africa and the Christian kingdoms in northern Spain, making possible a golden era of Moorish power and culture. But after his death, fragmentation into warring Muslim principalities allowed a resurgence of Spain's Christian states between about 1000 and 1085, when the city of Toledo fell permanently into Christian hands.

Brief Islamic revivals in Spain and North Africa came under the African reform movements of the Almoravids and Almohads. The Almoravids originated as a religious-warrior brotherhood among Berber nomads in West Africa. In 1086, they carried their zealotry into Spain and reunited its Islamic

Western Islamic Lands	
756–1021	Spanish Umayyad dynasty
912–961	Rule of Abd al-Rahman III; height of Umayyad power and civilization
969–1171	Fatimid Shi'ite dynasty in Egypt
ca. 1020	Origin of Druze community (Egypt/Syria)
1171	Fatimids fall to Salah al-Din (Saladin), Ayyubid lieutenant of the ruler of Aleppo
1056–1275	Almoravid and Almohad dynasties in North Africa, West Africa, and Spain
1096–1291	Major European Christian crusades into Islamic lands; some European presence in Syria-Palestine
1198	Death of Ibn Rushd (Averroës), philosopher
1204	Death of Musa ibn Maymun (Maimonides), philosopher and Jewish savant
1240	Death of Ibn al-Arabi, theosophical mystic
1250–1517	Mamluk sultanate in Egypt and (from late 1200s) Syria; claim laid to Abbasid Caliphate
1260	Mamluk victory at Ain Jalut halts Mongol advance into Syria
1406	Death of Ibn Khaldun, historian and social philosopher
ca. 1300	Rise of Ottoman state in western Anatolia

kingdoms. Under their rule, arabized Christians (Mozarabs) were persecuted, as were some Moorish Jews. The subsequent wars began the last major phase of the Spanish "Reconquest" (*Reconquista*) in which Christian rulers sought to regain and Christianize the peninsula.

The Almohads ended Almoravid rule in Morocco in 1147 and then conquered much of southern Spain. Before their demise (1225 in Spain; 1275 in Africa), they stimulated a brilliant revival of Moorish culture. During this era, paper manufacture reached Spain and then the rest of western Europe. The long westward odyssey of Indian fable literature ended with Spanish and Latin translations in thirteenth-century Spain. The greatest lights of this Spanish Islamic intellectual world were the philosopher and physician, Ibn Rushd (Averroës, d. 1198); the Muslim mystical thinker, Ibn al-Arabi (d. 1240); and the Arab-Jewish philosopher, Ibn Maymun, or Maimonides (d. 1204).

The Islamic West: Egypt and the Eastern Mediterranean World

The Fatimids The major Islamic presence in the Mediterranean from the tenth to the twelfth century was that of the Shi'ite Fatimids. They took their name from their claim to descent from Muhammad's daughter, Fatima. They began as a Tunisian dynasty, then conquered Morocco, Sicily, and

Egypt (969). In Egypt they built their new capital, Cairo (*al-Qahira,* "the Victorious"), near the original garrison town of the earliest Arab conquest. Their rule as Shi'ite caliphs meant that, for a time, there were three "caliphates"—in Baghdad, Córdoba, and Cairo. The Fatimids were Isma'ilis (see above). They won the allegiance of a Yemeni Shi'ite state and were able, for a time, to take western Arabia and most of Syria.

Fatimid rule spawned two splinter groups. The Druze of modern Lebanon and Syria originated around 1020 with members of the Fatimid court who professed belief in the divinity of one of the Fatimid caliphs. Their tradition is too far from Islam to be considered a Muslim sect. The Isma'ili Assassins, on the other hand, were a radical Muslim movement founded by a Fatimid defector in Iran around 1100. The name "Assassins" comes not from the political assassinations that made them infamous but from the Arabic *Hashishiyyin* ("users of hashish"). It was possibly connected with the story that their assassins were manipulated with drugs to undertake their usually suicidal missions. The Assassins were destroyed by the Mongols in the thirteenth century.

Fatimid rulers treated Egypt's Coptic Christians and Jews generally as well as they did their Sunni majority. Many Copts held high offices. After 1100 the Fatimids weakened, falling in 1171 to Salah al-Din (Saladin, 1137-1193), a general under the Turkish ruler of Syria, Nur al-Din (1118-1174). After Nur al-Din's death, Saladin, a Sunni Kurd, added Syria-Palestine and Mesopotamia to his Egyptian dominions. In so doing, he founded the Ayyubid dynasty that controlled all three areas until Egypt fell to the Mamluks in 1250 and most of Syria and Mesopotamia to the Mongols by 1260.

Like Nur al-Din, and on the model of the Saljuqs (see Chapter 11), Saladin founded *madrasas* to teach and promote Sunni law. His and his Ayyubid successors' reigns in Egypt saw the entrenchment of a self-conscious Sunnism. Shi'ite Islam disappeared from Egypt.

The Mamluks   The heirs of the Fatimids and Saladin in the eastern Mediterranean were the redoubtable sultans of the Mamluk dynasty. The Mamluks were the only Islamic dynasty to withstand the Mongol invasions. Their victory at Ain Jalut in Palestine in 1260 marked the end of the Mongols' westward movement. The first Mamluk sultan, Aybak (r. 1250-1257), and his successors were elite Turkish and Mongol slave officers. Whereas the early Mamluks were often succeeded by sons or brothers, succession after the 1390s was more often a survival of the fittest; no sultan reigned more than a few years. The Mamluk state was based on a military fief system and total control by the slave-officer elite.

The Mamluk sultan Baybars (r. 1260-1277), who took the last Crusader fortresses, is a larger-than-life figure in Arab legend. To legitimize his rule he revived the Abbasid caliphate at least in name after its demise in the fall of Baghdad (1258; discussed later) by installing an uncle of Baghdad's last Abbasid as caliph at Cairo. He extended Mamluk rule south to Nubia and west among the Berbers.

As trade relations with the Mongol domains improved after 1300, the Mamluks enjoyed prosperity. At their zenith, they commanded an empire worthy of the early Abbasids or the later Ottomans. The prosperity and peace of the reign of Ibn Qala'un (1310-1340) marked the heyday of Mamluk rule. The Black Death epidemic of 1347-1348 in the Arab Middle East hurt the Mamluk and other regional states. Still the Mamluks survived even the Ottoman conquest of Egypt in 1517, since Mamluks continued to rule there as Ottoman governors into the nineteenth century.

Architecture, especially that of the reigns of Baybars and al-Nasir (r. 1293-1340), much of which still graces Cairo, remains the most magnificent Mamluk bequest to posterity. In addition, mosaics, calligraphy, and metalwork were of special note. The Mamluks were great patrons of scholars. The most important of these was Ibn Khaldun (d. 1406). He is still recognized as the greatest social historian and philosopher.

The Islamic East: Before the Mongol Conquests

The Iranian dynasties of the Samanids at Bukhara (875-999) and the Buyids at Baghdad (945-1055) were the major usurpers

The Mongol Catastrophe

For the Muslim east, the sudden eruption of the Mongol hordes was an indescribable calamity. Something of the shock and despair of Muslim reaction can be seen in the history of the contemporary historian Ibn al-Athir (d. 1233). He writes here about the year 1220–1221, when the Mongols ("Tartars") burst in on the eastern lands.

Is this a positive, negative, or neutral description of the Mongols? Why might the Mongols be compared to Alexander rather than, say, the Huns (see Chapter 5)?

I say, therefore, that this thing involves the description of the greatest catastrophe and the most dire calamity (of the like of which days and nights are innocent), which befell all men generally, and the Muslims in particular; so that, should one say that the world, since God Almighty created Adam until now, hath not been afflicted with the like thereof, he would but speak the truth. For indeed history doth not contain aught which approaches or comes nigh unto it. . . .

Now this is a thing the like of which ear hath not heard; for Alexander, concerning whom historians agree that he conquered the world, did not do so with such swiftness, but only in the space of about ten years; neither did he slay, but was satisfied that men should be subject to him. But these Tartars conquered most of the habitable globe

and the best, the most flourishing and most populous part thereof, and that whereof the inhabitants were the most advanced in character and conduct, in about [a] year; nor did any country escape their devastations which did not fearfully expect them and dread their arrival.

Moreover they need no commissariat, nor the conveyance of supplies, for they have with them sheep, cows, horses, and the like quadrupeds, the flesh of which they eat, [needing] naught else. As for their beasts which they ride, these dig into the earth with their hoofs and eat the roots of plants, knowing naught of barley. And so, when they alight anywhere, they have need of nothing from without. As for their religion, they worship the sun when it arises, and regard nothing as unlawful, for they eat all beasts, even dogs, pigs, and the like; nor do they recognise the marriage-tie, for several men are in marital relations with one woman, and if a child is born, it knows not who is its father.

Therefore Islâm and the Muslims have been afflicted during this period with calamities wherewith no people hath been visited. These Tartars (may God confound them!) came from the East, and wrought deeds which horrify all who hear of them, and which thou shalt, please God, see set forth in full detail in their proper connection. . . .

From Edward C. Sachau, *Alberuni's Indian*, Vol. I (London: Kegan Paul, Trench, Truebner, 1910), pp. 17, 19, 20.

---

of eastern Abbasid dominions. Their successes epitomized the rise of regional states that had begun to undermine the caliphate by the ninth century. Their demises reflected a second pattern: the ascendancy of Turkish slave-rulers (like the Mamluks in the west) and of Oghuz Turkish peoples, known as Turkomans. With the Saljuk successors of the Buyids, the process begun with the use of Turkish slave troops in ninth-century Baghdad ended in the permanent presence in the Islamic world of Turkish ruling dynasties. As late converts, they became typically the most zealous of Sunni Muslims.

The Ghaznavids The rule of the Samanids in Transoxiana was finally ended by a Turkoman group in 999. But they had already lost all of eastern Iran south of the Oxus in 994 to one of their own slave governors, Subuktigin (r. 976–997). He set up his own state in modern Afghanistan, at Ghazna, whence he and his son and successor, Mahmud of Ghazna (r. 998–1030), launched campaigns against his former masters. The Ghaznavids are notable for their patronage of Persian culture and for their conquests in northwestern India, which began a lasting Muslim presence in India. Mahmud

was their greatest ruler. His empire stretched from western Iran to the Oxus and the Indus.

Mahmud attracted to Ghazna numerous scholars and artists, notably the great scientist and mathematician al-Biruni (d. 1048) and the epic poet Firdawsi (d. ca. 1020). Firdawsi's *Shahnama* ("The Book of Kings") is the masterpiece of Persian literature, an epic of 60,000 verses that helped fix the New Persian language and revive the pre-Islamic Iranian cultural tradition. After Mahmud the empire began to break up, although Ghaznavids ruled at Lahore until 1186.

The Saljuks The Saljuks were the first major Turkish dynasty of Islam. They were a steppe clan who became avid Sunnis. In 1055 they took Baghdad. As the new guardian of the caliphate and master of an Islamic empire, the Saljuk leader Tughril Beg (r. 1037–1063) took the title of *sultan* (authority) to signify his power. He was invested by the caliph as "king of east and west."

As new Turkish tribes joined their ranks, the Saljuks extended Islamic rule into the central Anatolian plateau at Byzantine expense, even capturing the Byzantine emperor

Building the castle of Khawarnaq, ca. 1494. This is one of the magnificent illustrations of the Khamsa, or "Fire Poems" of Nizami, painted by the head of the great art academy of Herat, Bihzad (died ca. 1515). It was Shahrukh's patronage that led to this flourishing school of painting. [By permission of The British Library]

in 1071. They also conquered much of Syria and wrested Mecca and Medina from the Shi'ite Fatimids. Turkish rule in Anatolia dates from 1077, when the Saljuk governor there formed a sultanate. Known as the Saljuks of Rum ("Rome," i.e., Byzantium), these Saljuks were displaced after 1300 by the Ottomans (see Chapter 23).

The most notable figure of Saljuk rule was the vizier Nizam al-Mulk from 1063 to 1092. In his time, new roads and inns (caravanserais) for trade and pilgrimage were built, canals were dug, mosques and other public buildings were founded, and science and culture were patronized. He appointed as professor in his Baghdad *madrasa* Muhammad al-Ghazzali (d. 1111), probably the greatest Muslim religious thinker ever. He also patronized the mathematician and astronomer Umar Khayyam (d. 1123), whose Western fame rests on the poetry of his "Quatrains," or *Ruba'iyat*.

By 1194, Iranian Saljuk rule was erased by another Turkish slave dynasty from Khwarizm in the lower Oxus basin. By 1200, these Khwarizm Shahs had built a large if shaky em-

pire covering Iran and Transoxiana. In the same era, the Abbasid caliph at Baghdad, al-Nasir (r. 1180–1225), established an independent caliphal state in Iraq. But neither his heirs nor the Khwarizm Shahs would long survive.

The Islamic East: The Mongol Age

Mongols and Ilkhanids   The building of a vast Mongol empire (see Chapter 8) proved momentous for Islamic Eurasia and India. The Great Khan, Genghis (ca. 1162–1227) plundered mercilessly (1219–1222) from Transoxiana and Khorasan to the Indus, razing entire cities. After his death, a division of his empire into four khanates under his four sons gave the Islamic world respite. Then in 1255 Hulagu Khan (r. 1256–1265), a grandson of Genghis, again led a massive army across the Oxus. He went from victory to victory, destroying every Iranian state. In 1258, Hulagu's troops smashed Baghdad's defenses and plundered the city, killing at least 80,000 inhabitants, including the caliph and his sons.

Under the influence of his wife and Nestorian Christians and Buddhists in his inner circle, Hulagu spared the Christians of Baghdad. He followed this policy in his other conquests, including the sack of Aleppo. When Damascus surrendered, Western Christians had a vain hope of the impending fall of Mamluk Cairo and a collapse of Islamic power. But Hulagu's drive west was slowed by rivalry with his kinsman Berke. A Muslim convert, Berke ruled the khanate of the Golden Horde, the Mongol state centered in southern Russia. He was in contact with the Mamluks, and some of his Mongol troops even fought with them in their victory over Hulagu in Palestine (1260), which prevented a Mongol advance into Egypt. A treaty in 1261 between the Mamluk sultan and Berke established a formal alliance that confirmed the breakup of Mongol unity and the autonomy of the four khanates: in China (the Yuan dynasty), in Iran (the Ilkhans), in Russia (the Golden Horde), and in Transoxiana (the Chagatays).

Hulagu gave allegiance to the new Great Khan of China. He and his heirs ruled the old Persian Empire from Azerbaijan for some seventy-five years as the Great Khan's viceroys (*Il-Khans;* from which Hulagu's line is named *Ilkhanid*). Here, as elsewhere, the Mongols did not eradicate the society they inherited. Instead, both their native paganism and their Buddhist and Christian leanings yielded to Muslim faith and practice, although religious tolerance remained the norm under their rule. After 1335, Ilkhanid rule fell prey to the familiar pattern of a gradual breaking away of provinces, and for fifty years, Iran was again fragmented.

Timurids and Turkomans   This situation prepared the way for a new Turko-Mongol conquest from Transoxiana, under Timur-i Lang ("Timur the Lame," or "Tamerlane," 1336–1405). Timur's savage campaigns between 1379 and his death in 1405 were aimed at sheer conquest. Timur was a Muslim convert evidently possessed of a strong sense of his role as protector of commerce and punisher of the injustices of regional petty tyrants and extremist groups. Still, his means were brutal. In successive campaigns he swept everything before him in a wave of devastation: eastern Iran (1379–1385); western Iran, Armenia, the Caucasus, and upper Mesopotamia (1385–1387); southwestern Iran, Mesopotamia, and Syria (1391–1393); Central Asia from Transoxiana to the Volga and as far as Moscow (1391–1395); North India (1398); and northern Syria and Anatolia (1400–1402). He left behind him ruins, death, disease, and political chaos across the entire eastern Islamic world. His was, however, the last great steppe invasion, for firearms soon removed the steppe horsemen's advantage forever.

Timur's sons ruled after him with varying results in Transoxiana and Iran (1405–1494). The most successful Timurid was Shahrukh (r. 1405–1447), who ruled a united Iran for a time. His capital, Herat, became an important center of Persian

Islamic culture and Sunni piety. He patronized the famous Herat school of miniature painting as well as Persian literature and philosophy. The Timurids had to share Iran itself with Turkoman dynasties in western Iran, once even losing Herat to one of them. They and the Turkomans were the last Sunnis to rule Iran. Both were eclipsed at the end of the fifteenth century by the militant Shi'ite dynasty of the Safavids, who ushered in a new, Shi'ite era in the Iranian world (see Chapter 23).

The Spread of Islam Beyond the Heartlands

The period from roughly 1000 to 1500 saw the spread of Islam as a lasting religious, cultural, and political force into new areas. India, Malaysia, and Indonesia became major spheres of Islamic political or commercial power even though large numbers, often the majority, of the populace retained their inherited religious traditions.

INDIA

Islamic civilization in India was formed by creative interaction between invading foreigners and indigenous peoples. The early Arab and Turkish invaders were a foreign Muslim minority; their heirs were truly "Indian" as well as Muslim. From then on, Indian civilization would both include and enrich Islamic traditions.

The Spread of Islam to India

Muslim merchants had settled in the port cities of Gujarat and southern India to profit from internal Indian trade as well as from trade with the Indies and China (see Map 14–2). Wherever Muslim traders went, converts to Islam followed. Sufi orders also drew converts.

India	
ca. 900–1300	Chola dynasty in southern India
1137	Death of Ramanuja
1206–1290	Slave-kings of Delhi
1290–1320	Khalji sultans of Delhi
1320–1413	Tughluqid sultans of Delhi
1414–1526	Sayyid sultans of Delhi
1336–1565	Hindu dynasty of Vijayanagar
1347–1527	Muslim Bahmanid dynasty in the Deccan
1398	Timur's sack of Delhi

Muslim-Hindu Encounter

From the outset, Muslim leaders faced the problem of ruling a country dominated by utterly different cultural and religious traditions. The first Arab conquerors in Sind (711) had treated Hindus as "protected peoples" under Muslim sovereignty. These precedents gave later Indian Muslim rulers a legal basis for coexistence with their Hindu subjects. They did not, of course, remove Hindu resistance to Muslim rule.

The chief obstacle to Islamic expansion in India was the military prowess of the Hindu warrior class, known from about the mid-seventh century as *Rajputs*. The Rajputs were a large group of clans bound together by a fierce warrior ethic and strong Hindu cultural and religious traditionalism. They fought the Muslims with tenacity, but their inability to unite brought them under Muslim domination in the sixteenth century (see Chapter 23).

Islamic States and Dynasties

After the Ghaznavids and a brief period of Afghan rule, Turkish-Afghan rulers known as the "Slave Sultans of Delhi" extended Islamic power over North India (1206–1290). Four later Muslim dynasties—the Khaljis, Tughluqs, Sayyids, and Lodis—continued the Delhi sultanate through the fifteenth century, interrupted only by several years of chaos following the Mongol-Turkish invasion and sack of Delhi by Timur in 1398, from which the city took decades to recover. However, throughout its history the Delhi sultanate's authority over its provincial governors was a variable affair, even in the heart of North India. Before the advent of the Mughals in the mid-sixteenth century, many regions split off from the sultanate and became independent. Regional rule predominated across the subcontinent, much as it had before the Ghaznavids.

The most important independent Islamic state was that of the Bahmanids in the Deccan (1347–1527). These rulers were famous for their architecture and the intellectual life of their court, as well as for their role in containing the powerful South Indian Hindu state of Vijayanagar (1336–1565).

Religious and Cultural Accommodation

Despite the enduring division of the subcontinent into multiple and diverse units, the five centuries after Mahmud of Ghazna saw Islam become an enduring, influential, and transregional, if still minority, element of Indian culture—most fully in the north, but also in the Deccan. The Delhi sultans provided a basic political and social framework within which Islam could take root. Although the ruling class remained a Muslim minority of Persianized Turks and Afghans ruling a Hindu majority, conversion went on at various levels of society. *Ghazis* ("warriors") also carried Islam by force of arms to pagan groups in eastern Bengal and Assam. More significantly, Sufi orders converted numerous Hindus among the lower classes across the North. The Muslim aristocracy was usually treated in Indian society as a separate caste group or groups. When lower class or other Hindus converted, they were assimilated into lower "Muslim castes," often identified by occupation.

Sanskrit had long been the Indian scholarly language and lingua franca, but in this period regional languages, such as Tamil in the south, gained status, and Persian became the language of intellectual and cultural life for the ruling elites of North India. However, a new language with both Perso-Arabic and indigenous Indian elements, Urdu-Hindi, would gain wide use and influence in the subcontinent by modern times. It began to take shape not long after the initial Muslim influx in the eleventh century and developed in response to the increasing need of Hindus and Muslims for a shared medium of communication. The name *Urdu* designated the Muslim version that continued to draw on its Perso-Arabic heritage, whereas Hindi ("Indian") was used for the version associated with Hindu culture and oriented toward its Hindu and Sanskritic heritage. Each would later become an official national language: Urdu for modern Pakistan and Hindi for modern India.

Indian Muslims were always susceptible to Hindu influence (in language, marriage customs, and caste consciousness). However, they were never absorbed into Hindu culture. Their identification as Muslims ensured that they remained proud to be distinct.

Nevertheless, reciprocal influence of Muslims and Hindus was inevitable, especially in popular piety. Sufi devotion had an appeal similar to that of Hindu devotional, or *bhakti* movements (see Chapter 10), and each influenced the other. Various theistic mystics preached devotion to a God who saves His worshipers without regard either to Hindu caste obligations or to legalistic observance of Muslim orthopraxy. The poet-saints Ramananda (d. after 1400) and Kabir (d. ca. 1518) were the two most famous such reformers.

Hindu and Other Indian Traditions

The Jain tradition continued to flourish, but in the north by the eleventh century the Muslim conquests effectively ended the Indian Buddhist monastic and lay traditions. Buddhism was already waning long before Islam came to India, and the coming of Islam either dealt the *coup de grâce* to Buddhism in India or coincided with its reduction to small-minority status.

Hindu religion and culture continued to flourish, even under Muslim control. *Bhakti* was especially creative. The great Hindu Vaishnava Brahman, Ramanuja (d. 1137), pro-

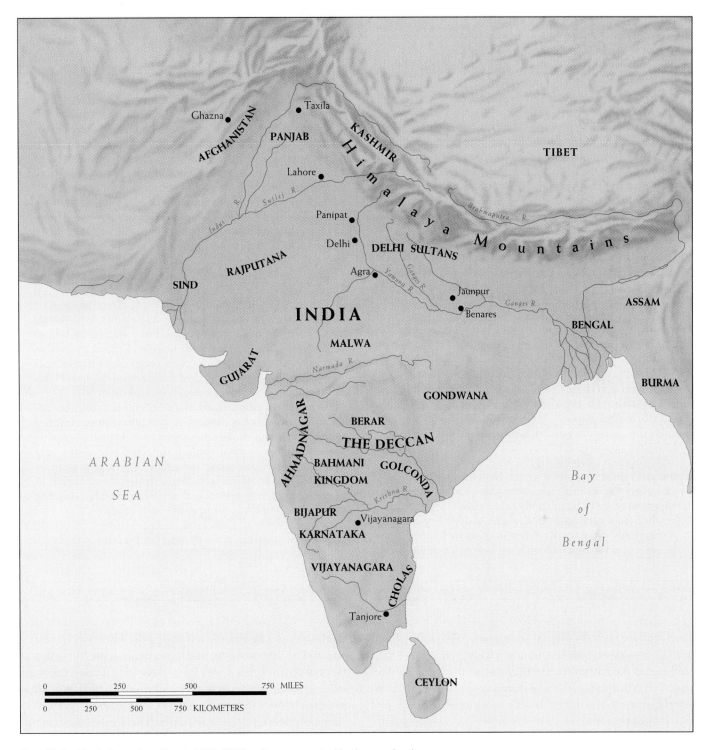

Map 14-2 The Indian subcontinent, 1000–1500. Shown are major kingdoms and regions.

vided a theological basis for *bhakti*, reconciling its ideas with the classical Upanishadic Hindu worldview in the Vedantin tradition. Important examples of *bhakti* movements are the Shaivite and Vaishnavite traditions. *Bhakti* piety underlies the masterpiece of Hindu mystical love poetry, Jayadeva's *Gita Govinda* (twelfth century), which is devoted to Krishna, the most important of Vishnu's incarnations.

The south continued to be the center of Hindu cultural, political, and religious activity. Of several important dynastic states in the south during this age, the foremost was that of

How the Hindus Differ from the Muslims

Al-Biruni (d. ca. 1050), the greatest scholar-scientist of medieval Islam, was born in northeastern Iran. Much of his later life was spent at the court of Mahmud of Ghazna, whom he accompanied on expeditions into northwestern India. Alongside his scientific work, he learned Sanskrit, studied India and the Hindus, and wrote a "History of India." The following selections from the beginning of this work show something of the reach and sophistication of his mind.

How does the emphasis on purity and the impurity of foreigners that Biruni imputes to the Hindus compare with the attitudes of Islam and other religions? Does this passage suggest any possible answers to why the Hindu tradition has remained largely an Indian one, while Islam became an international religion? At what might Biruni's comments about the relative absence of religious controversy among Hindus be aimed?

. . . The barriers which separate Muslims and Hindus rest on different causes.

First, they differ from us in everything which other nations have in common. And here we first mention the language, although the difference of language also exists between other nations. If you want to conquer this difficulty (i.e., to learn Sanskrit), you will not find it easy, because the language is of an enormous range, both in words and inflections, something like the Arabic, calling one and the same thing by various names, both original and derived, and using one and the same word for a variety of subjects, which, in order to be properly understood, must be distinguished from each other by various qualifying epithets. . . .

Secondly, they totally differ from us in religion, as we believe in nothing in which they believe, and vice versá.

On the whole, there is very little disputing about theological topics among themselves; at the utmost, they fight with words, but they will never stake their soul or body or their property on religious controversy. On the contrary, all their fanaticism is directed against those who do not belong to them—against all foreigners. They call them *mleecha*, that is, impure, and forbid having any connection with them, be it by intermarriage or any other kind of relationship, or by sitting, eating, and drinking with them, because thereby, they think, they would be polluted. They consider as impure anything which touches the fire and the water of a foreigner; and no household can exist without these two elements. Besides, they never desire that a thing which once has been polluted should be purified and thus recovered, as, under ordinary circumstances, if anybody or anything has become unclean, he or it would strive to regain the state of purity. They are not allowed to receive anybody who does not belong to them, even if he wished it, or was inclined to their religion. This, too, renders any connection with them quite impossible, and constitutes the widest gulf between us and them.

In the third place, in all manners and usages they differ from us to such a degree as to frighten their children with us, with our dress, and our ways and customs, and as to declare us to be devil's breed, and our doings as the very opposite of all that is good and proper. By the by, we must confess, in order to be just, that a similar depreciation of foreigners not only prevails among us and the Hindus, but is common to all nations towards each other.

From Edward C. Sachau, *Alberuni's India*, Vol. 1 (London: Kegan Paul, Trench, Truebner, 1910), pp. 17, 19, 20.

the Cholas which flourished from about 900–1300. Their mightiest successor, the kingdom of Vijayanagar (1336–1565), subjugated the entire south in the fourteenth century and resisted its Muslim foes longer than any other kingdom. Vijayanagar itself was one of India's most lavishly developed cities and a center of the cult of Shiva.

IN WORLD PERSPECTIVE

The Islamic Heartlands and India, ca. 1000–1500

The spread of Islam to new peoples or their ruling elites has been a theme of this chapter. However, we have also seen that the history of Islam in India is hardly the history of India as a whole. The vast conquests and movements of the Mongols and Central Asian Turks across inner Asia were among the most striking developments in world history in this period; they often had cataclysmic effects, whether on Chinese, south Asian, west Asian, or eastern European societies. These conquests and migrations wiped out existing orders and forced the migration of many who fled their advance. They contributed, even if unintentionally, new and often significant human resources to existing civilizations like those of China and the Islamic heartlands.

In this age, Islam became truly international by being highly adaptable and open to "indigenization" in the seemingly hostile contexts of polytheistic Hindu and African societies. Also in this period, distinct traditions of art, language, and literature became part of a larger Muslim identity.

Islamic civilization had none of the territorial contiguity or linguistic and cultural homogeneity of either Chinese or Japanese civilization. Nevertheless, the Islamic world was an international reality in which a Muslim could travel and meet other Muslims of radically diverse backgrounds with much common ground for understanding.

Indian traditional culture was not bound up with an expanding missionary religious tradition like that of Islam. Yet Hindu kingdoms flourished in Indonesia. Buddhism was expanding across Asia, thereby solidifying its place as an international missionary tradition.

Christianity, by contrast, was not rapidly expanding in Africa, Asia, or Europe; but by 1500 its western European branch was poised on the brink of internal revolution in religion and culture and international proselytism following the fateful "voyages of discovery." In the year 1000, Europe was almost a backwater of culture and power by comparison with major Islamic or Hindu states, let alone that of China. By 1500, however, European civilization was riding the crest of a cultural renaissance, enjoying economic and political growth, and starting the global exploration that would turn into a flood of imperial expansion and affect most of the rest of the globe. Neither Islamic, Indian, African, Chinese, nor Japanese culture and society were so radically changed or changing in their basic ideas and institutions as were those of western Europe over these 500 years.

Review Questions

1. In the period 1000–1500, no Muslim leader built a large-scale Islamic empire of the extent of the early Abbasids. What might be some of the reasons for this?

2. Discuss the role of the *ulama* in Muslim society. How were they educated? What was their relationship to political leadership? What social roles did they play?

3. What was the role and impact of religious sectarianism in this period? Of the institutionalization of Sufi piety and thought?

4. Discuss the cultural developments in Spain before 1500. Why was Córdoba a model of civilized culture?

5. Why was Islam able to survive the invasions by steppe peoples from 945 on? What were the lasting results of these "invasions" for the Islamic world?

6. What were the obstacles to stable rule for India's Muslim invaders and immigrants? How did they deal with them?

Documents CD-ROM

1. William of Rubruck: Impressions of the Medieval Mongols

2. Farid al-Din Attari: *The Conference of Birds*

3. *The Thousand and One Nights*

4. Two Bhakti Poets: Ravidas and Mirabai

15 ANCIENT CIVILIZATIONS OF THE AMERICAS

Humans first settled the American continents between 12,000 and 40,000 years ago. At that time, glaciers locked up much of the world's water, lowering the sea level and opening a bridge of dry land between Siberia and Alaska. When the glaciers receded, the oceans rose, severing Asia from America. The inhabitants of the Americas were now isolated from the inhabitants of Africa and Eurasia, and would remain so until 1492.

Although isolated from one another, the peoples of the Americas, Africa, and Eurasia experienced similar cultural changes at the end of the Paleolithic. People in some regions shifted from hunting and gathering to a settled, agricultural way of life. And in some places civilization emerged.

Mesoamerica, in what is today Mexico and Central America, and the Andean region of South America, have a history of civilization that reaches back thousands of years. At the time of the European conquest of the Americas in the sixteenth century, both regions were dominated by powerful empires—the Aztecs, or Mexica, in Mesoamerica and the Inca in the Andes. Spanish conquerors obliterated both empires. But native American traditions have endured, overlaid, and combined with Hispanic culture, to provide clues to the prehispanic past.

Problems in Reconstructing the History of Native American Civilization

Andean civilizations never developed writing, and in Mesoamerica much of the written record was destroyed by time and conquest. Archaeologists have been able to create a picture of the economic and social organization of ancient American civilizations. But archaeology cannot produce the kind of narrative history that thousands of years of written records have made possible for Eurasian civilization. For one

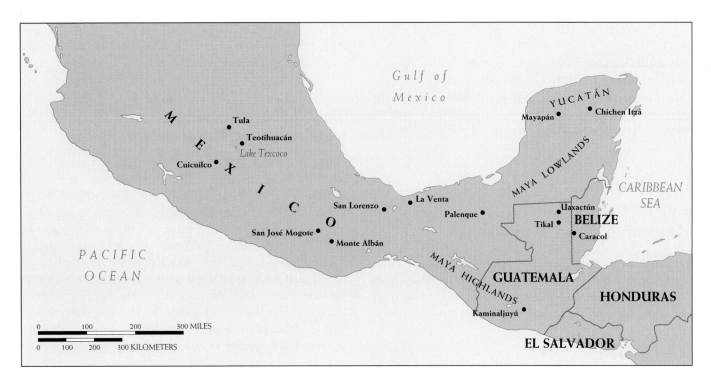

Map 15–1 Pre-Aztec Mesoamerican sites discussed in this chapter.

ancient Mesoamerican people, however—the Maya—scholars have been able to decipher their writing and attach names, dates, and events to silent ruins.

We also have accounts of the history and culture of the Aztecs and Inca that were related to the Spanish in the wake of the conquest. But these accounts are colored by the needs and expectations of the conquerors. This dilemma raises another. Scholars seeking to understand Native American civilization have had to rely on the language and categories of European thought to analyze peoples and cultural experiences that had nothing to do with Europe. Cultural blinders and arrogance have exacerbated this gap.

Mesoamerica

Mesoamerica, which means "middle America," extends from central Mexico into Central America. It also designates a distinctive and enduring cultural tradition that emerged between 1000 and 2000 B.C.E. and manifested itself in a succession of impressive states until the coming of European conquerors in the sixteenth century. The peoples of Mesoamerica were and are ethnically and linguistically diverse. There was no single Mesoamerican civilization or linear development of civilization in the region. Nonetheless, Mesoamerican civilizations shared many traits, including writing, a sophisticated calendrical system, many religious ideas, a ritual ball game, and urban centers with buildings arranged around large plazas.

Throughout its history, the peoples of the region were linked by trade. Metallurgy came late to Mesoamerica and was used primarily for ceremonial objects. Mesoamericans made weapons and tools from obsidian, a volcanic glass capable of holding a razor-sharp edge and thus a valued commodity.

Mesoamerican history before the Spanish conquest is conventionally divided into four major periods: The term "Classic" reflects the view of many early Mesoamericanists that the Classic Period, which corresponds more or less to the time during which the Maya civilizations of the southern Yucatan erected dated stone monuments, was the high point of Mesoamerican civilization. That view is no longer so prevalent, but the terminology has endured. The chronology continues to provide a useful framework for understanding Mesoamerican history.

The transition from hunting and gathering to settled village life occurred gradually in Mesoamerica during the Archaic Period. The cornerstone of the process was the domestication of maize (corn) and other staple crops, including beans, squash, tomatoes, chili peppers, and avocado. Maize and beans together provide a rich source of protein compared to the grains that were the basis of the Neolithic revolution in the Ancient Near East and China, where domesticated animals supplied the protein. Mesoamerica, however, had a few domesticated animals—among them dogs and turkeys—and no large herd animals like the cattle, sheep, and goats of the Old World.

Probably because they had no large draft animals, the people of the Americas, including Mesoamerica, never developed the wheel, although they made wheeled toys. In Mesoamerica humans did the carrying, and warfare was between armies of foot soldiers.

The Formative Period and the Emergence of Mesoamerican Civilization

By about 1500 B.C.E., Mesoamerica's agricultural villages were beginning to coalesce into more complicated societies, with towns and monumental architecture, social classes, trade among regions, and sophisticated artistic traditions.

The Olmec

The most prominent of the early Formative Period cultures is that of the Olmec, centered on the lowlands of Mexico's Gulf Coast. Most of what is known about the Olmecs comes from the archaeological sites of San Lorenzo and La Venta (see Map 15-1). San Lorenzo had developed into a prominent center by about 1200 B.C.E. It included public buildings, a drainage system linked to artificial ponds, and what was probably the earliest court for the Mesoamerican ballgame. It flourished until about 900 B.C.E. but was abandoned by about 400 B.C.E. La Venta flourished from about 900 to 400 B.C.E. Its most conspicuous feature is a 110-foot, scalloped pyramid, known as the Great Pyramid, which stands at one end of a group of platforms and plazas aligned along a north-south axis.

The population of San Lorenzo and La Venta was probably fewer than 1,000 people. The monumental architecture and sculpture at these sites nonetheless suggests that Olmec society was dominated by an elite class of ruler-priests able to command the labor of the rest of the population. The elite probably lived in the centers, supported by farmers who lived in villages.

Major Periods in Ancient Mesoamerican Civilization	
Archaic	8000–2000 B.C.E.
Formative (or Pre-Classic)	2000 B.C.E.–150 C.E.
Classic	150–900 C.E.
Post-Classic	900–1521 C.E.

The raw material for many Olmec artifacts, such as jade and obsidian, comes from other regions of Mesoamerica. Likewise, Olmec goods and iconography are found in other regions, all suggesting that from an early time, the parts of Mesoamerica were linked in a web of trade. These contacts would have contributed to the formation of common Mesoamerican traditions.

The Valley of Oaxaca and the Rise of Monte Alban

Olmec civilization had disappeared by about 200 B.C.E. Other regions, however, were rising to prominence. Some of the most significant developments in the Late Formative Period occurred in the Valley of Oaxaca. Around 500 B.C.E., Monte Alban was built on a hill where three branches of the valley meet. Its population grew to about 5,000, and it emerged as the capital of a state that dominated the Oaxaca region. Carved images of bound prisoners suggest that warfare played a role in establishing its authority. They also suggest an early origin for the ritual human sacrifice that characterized most Mesoamerican cultures. Monte Alban maintained its independence against the growing power of the greatest Classic Period city, Teotihuacán.

The Emergence of Writing and the Mesoamerican Calendar   The earliest evidence of writing and the Mesoamerican calendar have been found in the Valley of Oaxaca. The Mesoamerican calendar is based on two interlocking cycles. One cycle, tied to the solar year, was of 365 days; the other was of 260 days. Combining the two cycles produced a "century" of 52 years, the amount of time required before a combination of days in each cycle would repeat itself.

At the time of the Spanish conquest, all the peoples of Mesoamerica used this 52-year calendrical system. As we will see, only the Maya developed a calendar based on a longer time period, anchored—like the Jewish, Christian, or Muslim calendars—to a fixed starting point in the past.

The Classic Period in Mesoamerica

The Classic Period was a time of cultural florescence. The Maya, who built densely populated cities in the rain forests of the southern Yucatán, developed a sophisticated system of mathematics and Mesoamerica's most advanced hieroglyphic writing. Indeed, Classic Period urban life in Mesoamerica was richer and on a larger scale than in Europe north of the Alps at the same time.

Classic Period cities were religious and administrative centers whose rulers combined secular and religious authority. Warfare was common and rulers used force to expand and maintain their authority. The ritual sacrifice of captive enemies was a feature of Classic Period societies.

The Pyramid of the Sun stands near the southern end of Teotihuacán's great central thoroughfare, the Avenue of the Dead. [Kal Muller/Woodfin Camp & Associates]

Teotihuacán

In the late Formative Period, two centers competed for dominance over the growing population of the Valley of Mexico. One of these, Cuicuilco, was at the southern end of the valley. The other, Teotihuacán, was about thirty miles northeast of Mexico City. When a volcano destroyed Cuicuilco in the first century C.E., Teotihuacán grew into a great city, perhaps Mesoamerica's first true city-state, dominating central Mexico for centuries and influencing the rest of Mesoamerica.

Natural advantages contributed to Teotihuacán's rise. A network of caves recently discovered under its most prominent monument, the Pyramid of the Sun (the name by which the Aztecs knew it), may have been considered an entrance to the underworld. Stone quarried from them was used to construct the city, creating a symbolic link between the city's buildings and its sacred origins. Teotihuacán is also near a source of obsidian, straddling a trade route to the Gulf Coast and southern Mesoamerica. The quarrying of obsidian and the manufacture and trade of obsidian goods were apparently a major source of the city's wealth and influence. Finally, Teotihuacán is surrounded by fertile farmland.

At its height in about 500 C.E., it extended over almost nine square miles and had a population of more than 150,000, making it one of the largest cities in the world at the time. Its size and organization suggest that it was ruled by a powerful, centralized authority. It is laid out on a rigid grid plan dominated by a broad, three-mile-long thoroughfare known as the Avenue of the Dead. Religious and administrative structures and a market occupy the center of the city. At one end of the Avenue of the Dead is the 210-foot-high Pyramid of the Sun. More than 2,000 residential structures surround the city center. The lavish homes of the city's elite lie nearest the center. Most residents lived in walled apartment compounds farther from the center. These compounds were also centers of craft manufacture, with neighborhoods devoted to pottery, obsidian work, and other specialties. Parts of the city were reserved for foreign traders. Murals adorned the interiors of many buildings. The humble dwellings of poor farmers occupied the city's periphery. As the city grew, local farmers had been forced to move to Teotihuacán, another indication of the power of its rulers.

Ruins of Tikal. The structure on the right, towering above the jungle canopy, is known as Temple I or the Temple of the Giant Jaguar. It housed the tomb of Ah Cacao, who ruled Tikal from 682 to about 723. [Robert Frerk/Odyssey Productions]

Teotihuacán's influence extended throughout Mesoamerica. In the central highlands, dispersed settlements were consolidated into larger centers laid out similarly to Teotihuacán, suggesting conquest and direct control—a Teotihuacán empire. The city's influence in more distant regions may have reflected close trading ties rather than conquest. The city's obsidian and pottery were exchanged widely for items like the green feathers of the quetzal bird and jaguar skins, valued for ritual garments.

Many of the buildings in Teotihuacán were decorated with sculptures and murals of the city's gods and ritual practices. Among the deities of Teotihuacán are a storm god and his goddess counterpart, whose representation suggests a link to the Aztec's rain god and his consort. The people of Teotihuacán also worshipped a feathered serpent who is recognizably antecedent to the Aztec god Quetzalcoatl and Maya Kukulcan. Murals also suggest that the Teotihuacán elite, like the Maya and later Mesoamerican peoples, drew their own blood as a form of sacrifice to the gods. They also practiced human sacrifice.

After 500 C.E., Teotihuacán's influence began to wane, and in the eighth century its authority collapsed. A fire destroyed the ritual center and the residences of the elite, hinting at an internal revolt. The city never regained its former status. It retained its hold on the imagination of succeeding generations of Mesoamericans, however, much like the ruins of ancient Greece and Rome on the imaginations of later Europeans. Teotihuacán is an Aztec word meaning "City of the Gods," and it was still a revered pilgrimage site at the time of the Spanish conquest.

The Maya

Maya civilization arose in southern Mesoamerica. During the Classic Period, Maya civilization experienced a remarkable florescence in the lowland jungles of the southern Yucatan.

All the pre-Spanish societies of Mesoamerica were literate, recording historical and religious information on scrolled or screenfold books made with deerhide or bark paper, only a handful of which have survived. The Maya of the Classic Period, who developed Mesoamerica's most advanced writing system, were unique in the extent to which they inscribed writing and calendrical symbols in stone, pottery, and other imperishable materials.

The largest Maya city, Tikal, probably had a population of between 50,000 and 70,000 at its height. Powerful ruling families and their elite retainers dominated Maya cities, supported by a large class of farmer-commoners. Maya inscriptions are almost entirely devoted to recounting important events in the lives of these rulers. Warfare between cities was chronic. As murals and sculptures show, captured prisoners were sacrificed to appease the gods and glorify the victorious ruler.

Religion deeply informed the social and political realm of the Maya. They believed that the world had gone through several cycles of creation, and they recognized no clear distinction between a natural and a supernatural world. As was probably true also of Teotihuacán, rulers and the elite combined religious and political authority, mediating between humans and gods through elaborate rituals. Rulers claimed association with the gods to justify their authority. They wore special regalia that symbolized their power and performed rituals to sustain the gods and the cosmic order. These rituals included bloodletting ceremonies, the sacrifice of captives, and ballgames.

A Maya Myth of Creation

This segment of the Maya creation myth is from the Popol Vuh, *a compendium of Maya mythology and history transcribed into European script by a Quiche Maya noble in the sixteenth century.*

How does this myth describe the world before creation? Who are the beings that exist before creation and decide how it is to be carried out? What did they do to create the Earth?

There was not yet one person, one animal, bird, fish, crab, tree, rock, hollow, canyon, meadow, forest, Only the sky alone is there; the face of the earth is not clear. Only the sea alone is pooled under all the sky; there is nothing whatever gathered together. It is at rest; not a single thing stirs. It is held back; kept at rest under the sky.

Whatever might be is simply not there: only murmurs, ripples, in the dark, in the night. Only the Maker, Modeler alone, Sovereign Plumed Serpent, the Bearers, Begetters are in the water, a glittering light. . . .

So there were three of them, as Heart of Sky, who came to the Sovereign Plumed Serpent, when the dawn of life was conceived:

"How should it be sown, how should it dawn? Who is to be the provider, nurturer?"

"Let it be this way, think about it: this water should be removed, emptied out for the formation of the earth's own plate and platform, then comes the sowing, the dawning of the sky-earth. But there will be no high days and no bright praise for our work, our design, until the rise of the human work, the human design," they said.

And then the earth rose because of them; it was simply their word that brought it forth. For the forming of the earth, they said, "Earth." It arose suddenly, just like a cloud, like a mist, now forming, unfolding. Then the mountains were separated from the water, all at once the great mountains came forth. By their genius alone, by their cutting edge alone they carried out the conception of the mountain-plain, whose face grew instant groves of cypress and pine.

Reprinted with permission of Simon & Schuster, Inc. from *POPOL VUH: The Definitive Edition of the Mayan Book of the Dawn of Life and the Glories of Gods and Kings* by Dennis Tedlock. Copyright © 1985 by Dennis Tedlock.

The significance of sacrifice and the ballgame in Maya ideology is reflected in a Maya creation myth, which tells how the Hero Twins defeated the gods of the underworld in the ballgame and returned to life after being sacrificed. One became the sun and the other Venus, and in their regular rising and setting reenact their descent into the underworld and their subsequent rebirth. All Maya cities had ball courts. The games played there were a symbolic reenactment of the confrontation between the Hero Twins and the lords of the underworld, and the losing team was sometimes sacrificed.[1]

The Classic Period Maya developed a sophisticated mathematics and were among the first peoples in the world to invent the concept of zero. In addition to the 52-year calendar round based on interlocking 260- and 365-day cycles they shared with other Mesoamerican societies, the Maya developed an absolute calendar, known as the Long Count, tied to a fixed point in the past. The calendar had great religious as well as practical significance for the Maya. They viewed the movements of the celestial bodies to which the calendar was tied—including the sun, moon, and Venus—as deities. The complexity and accuracy of their calendar reflect Maya skills in astronomical observation. They adjusted their lunar calendar for the actual length of the lunar cycle (29.53 days) and may have had provisions like our leap years for the actual length of the solar year. They also made accurate observations of Venus and recognized before other peoples that it is both the morning and the evening star. The importance of the calendar, its association with divine forces, and the esoteric knowledge required to master it must have been an important source of prestige and power for its elite guardians.

During the Classic Period, no single center dominated the Maya region. Rather, many independent units, each composed of a capital city and smaller subject towns and villages, rose and fell in prominence. In Tikal, at its height the largest Classic Maya city, the residential center covers more than fourteen square miles and has more than 3,000 structures. The city follows the uneven terrain of the rain forest and is not, like Teotihuacán, laid out on a grid. Monumental causeways link its major structures.

Tikal emerged as an important center in the Late Formative, benefiting from its strategic position. The city is near a source of flint, valued as a raw material for stone tools. It is also near swamps that, with modification, might have been agriculturally productive. And it has access to river systems that lead to the coasts.

A single dynasty of thirty-nine rulers reigned in Tikal from the Early Classic until the eighth century. The early rulers

[1] Robert J. Sharer, *The Ancient Maya*, 5th ed. (Stanford: Stanford University Press, 1994), p. 522.

in this Jaguar Paw line were buried in a structure known as the North Acropolis, and the inscriptions associated with their tombs provide details about them, including in many cases their names and the dates of their rule and military victories.

For about 100 years beginning in the mid-sixth century, Tikal and most other lowland Maya sites experienced little new construction. The city may have suffered a serious defeat at the hands of the city of Caracol. Then in 682 the ruler Ah Cacau (r. 682–723?) initiated a new period of vigor and prosperity for Tikal, expanding its influence through conquest and strategic marriage alliances. He and his two immediate successors began an ambitious building program, creating most of the Tikal's surviving monumental structures, including the dramatic, soaring temples that dominate the site. Chitam (r. 769–?) was the last ruler in the Jaguar Paw dynasty. After he died, Tikal declined and never recovered.

Similar dynastic histories are emerging at other Classic Maya sites. Inscriptions above the tomb of Lord Pacal (r. 615–683), the greatest ruler of the city of Palenque, located in the west of the Maya region, record the city's entire dynastic history back to mythic ancestors. Two of its rulers were women, one of them Pacal's mother, Lady Zac Kuk (r. 612–640), and another predecessor, Lady Kanal Ikal (r. 583–604).

Between 800 and 900 C.E., Classic Period civilization collapsed in the southern lowlands. The ruling dynasties came to an end, and the great cities were virtually abandoned. The cause of the collapse is still not known for sure. However, intensifying warfare, population growth and concentration, and attempts to increase agricultural production that ultimately backfired may have contributed to it. As the urban areas around the ceremonial centers grew, so did the demand for food. Ambitious building projects continued right up to the collapse, and as a growing proportion of the population was employed in these projects, fewer were left to produce food. Overfarming may then have led to soil exhaustion. A major drought may also have occurred. Clearly the Maya exceeded their resources, but why and how remain unknown.

The focus of Maya civilization shifted to the northern Yucatan. There the site of Chichén Itzá, located next to a sacred well, flourished from the ninth to the thirteenth centuries. Stylistic resemblances between Chichén Itzá and Tula, the capital of the Post-Classic Toltec Empire in central Mexico (see the next section), suggest ties between the two cities. After Chichén Itzá's fall, Mayapan became the main Maya center. But by the Spanish conquest, the Maya had divided into small, competing centers.

The Post-Classic Period

After Teotihuacán's collapse in the eighth century, smaller, militaristic states emerged, many centered around fortified hilltop cities. Interregional trade and market systems also became increasingly important, and secular and religious authority began to diverge.

The Toltecs

About 900 C.E., a people known as the Toltecs rose to prominence. Their capital, Tula, is near the northern periphery of Mesoamerica. Like Teotihuacán, it lay close to an important source of obsidian. The Toltecs themselves were apparently descendants of one of many "barbarian" northern peoples (like the later Aztecs) who began migrating into Mesoamerica during the Late Classic.

Aztec mythology glorified the Toltecs as the fount of civilization, attributing to them a vast empire to which the Aztecs were the heirs. Other Mesoamerican peoples also attributed legendary status to the Toltecs. However, Tula, although a substantial city with a population of between 35,000 and 60,000 people, was never as large or as organized as Teotihuacán. Toltec influence reached many regions of Mesoamerica, but archaeologists are uncertain whether that influence translated into political control.

Toltec iconography, which stresses human sacrifice, death, blood, and military symbolism, supports their warlike reputation. But Toltec power was short-lived. By about 1100, Tula was in decline and its influence gone.

The Aztecs

The people commonly known as the Aztecs referred to themselves as the *Mexica*. When the Spanish arrived in 1519, the Aztecs dominated much of Mesoamerica. Their capital city, Tenochtitlán, was the most populous yet seen in Mesoamerica. Built on islands in the southern part of Lake Texcoco in the Valley of Mexico, it was home to some 200,000 to 300,000 people. Its great temples and palaces gleamed in the sun. The city's traders brought goods from distant regions; vast wealth flowed in from subject territories. Yet the Aztecs were relative newcomers, the foundation of their power being less than 200 years old.

According to their legends, the Aztecs were originally a nomadic people from somewhere to the northwest of the Valley of Mexico. At the urging of their patron god Huitzilopochtli, they began to migrate, arriving in the Valley of Mexico early in the thirteenth century. Scorned by the people already there, they settled on the island that became Tenochtitlán in 1325 after seeing an eagle perched there on a prickly pear cactus, an omen Huitzilopochtli had said would identify the end of their wandering.

The Aztecs began as tributaries and mercenaries for Azcazpotzalco, then the most powerful state in the valley, but soon became allies with their own tribute-paying territories. They consolidated their position with marriage alliances to

Nezahualcoyotl of Texcoco Sings of the Giver of Life

Nezahualcoyotl, ruler of Texcoco, lived from 1402 to 1472 and was admired as a philosopher-king. In this poem he sings of the presence of the Giver of Life who invents Himself and of the ability of human beings to invoke this divinity, but at the same time he emphasizes the impossibility of achieving any close relationship with the divinity.

In what ways does this song remind you of the thought and religious traditions of the early civilizations of China, India, Egypt, and Greece? What are the characteristics of "He Who invents Himself"? What kind of relationship can human beings achieve with this being? Why does the singer compare seeking the Giver of Life with seeking someone among flowers?

In no place can be the house of He Who invents
    Himself.
But in all places He is invoked,
in all places He is venerated,
His glory, His fame are sought on the earth.
It is He Who invents everything
He is Who invents Himself: God.
In all places He is invoked,
in all places He is venerated,
His glory, His fame are sought on the earth.
No one here is able,
no one is able to be intimate
with the Giver of Life;

only He is invoked, at His side,
near to Him,
one can live on the earth.
He who finds Him,
knows only one thing; He is invoked,
at His side, near to Him,
one can live on the earth.
In truth no one is intimate with You,
O Giver of Life!
Only as among the flowers,
we might seek someone,
thus we seek You,
we who live on the earth,
while we are at Your side.
Our hearts will be troubled,
only for a short time,
we will be near You and at Your side.
The Giver of Life enrages us,
He intoxicates us here.
No one can be perhaps at His side,
be famous, rule on the earth.
Only You change things
as our hearts know it:
No one can be perhaps at His side,
be famous, rule on the earth.

From *Fifteen Poets of the Aztec World* by Miguel León-Portilla. Copyright © 1992 University of Oklahoma Press, p. 86. Reprinted by permission.

the ruling families of other cities. These alliances gave their own rulers claim to descent from the Toltecs. In 1428, under their fourth ruler, Itzcoatl (r. 1427–1440), the Aztecs formed a triple alliance with Texcoco and Tlacopan and became the dominant power in the Valley of Mexico. Less than 100 years before the arrival of Cortés, the Aztecs, as head of the Triple Alliance, then began the aggressive expansion that brought them their vast tribute-paying empire (see Map 15–2).

Itzcoatl laid the foundation of Aztec imperial ideology. He ordered the burning of all the ancient books in the valley, expunging any history that conflicted with Aztec pretensions, and restructured Aztec religion to support Aztec preeminence. The Aztecs now presented themselves as the divinely ordained successors to the Toltecs.

Aztec conquests ultimately included almost all of central Mexico. To the west, however, they were unable to conquer the rival Tarascan Empire. And within the Aztec realm, several pockets, especially Tlaxcala, remained locked into a pattern of ritual warfare with the Aztecs.

The Aztec Extractive Empire The Aztec Empire was extractive. After a conquest, the Aztecs usually left the local elite in power, but they demanded heavy tribute in goods and labor. Tribute included agricultural products, fine craft goods, gold and jade, textiles, and feathers. For example, as much as 7,000 tons of maize and 2 million cotton cloaks flowed into Tenochtitlán's coffers in a given year. This wealth underwrote the grandeur of Tenochtitlán.

Aztec Religion and Human Sacrifice Aztec imperial exploitation did not end with valued craft goods. Human sacrifice on a prodigious scale was central to Aztec ideology. The Aztecs believed that Huitzilopochtli, as sun god, required human blood to rise again each day, and that it was their responsibility to provide the victims. The prime candidates for sacrifice were war captives, and the Aztecs often engaged in "flowery wars" with traditional enemies just to obtain captives. On major festivals, thousands of victims might perish. Led up the steps of the temple of Huitzilopochtli, a victim was thrown

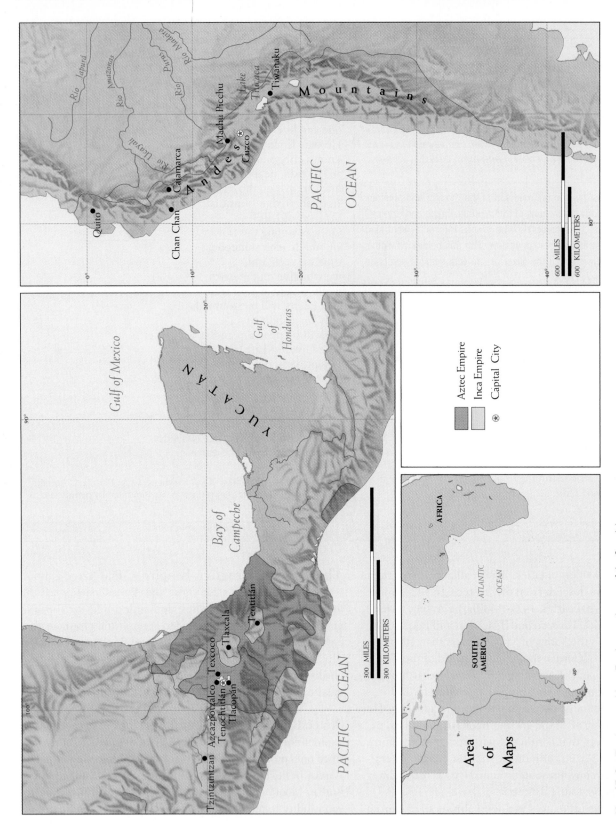

Map 15-2 The Aztec and Inca Empires on the eve of the Spanish conquest.

backward over a stone, his arms and legs pinned, while a priest cut out his heart. He would then be rolled down the steps of the temple, his head placed on a skull rack, and his limbs butchered and distributed to be eaten. Small children were sacrificed to the rain god Tlaloc, who, it was believed, was pleased by their tears.

Victims were also selected as stand-ins for particular gods who were sacrificed after a series of rituals. In the rituals honoring the powerful god Tezcatlipoca, a beautiful male youth was chosen to represent the god for a year, during which he was treated with reverence. He wandered through the city dressed as the god and playing the flute. A month before the end of his reign he was given four wives. Twenty days before his death he was dressed as a warrior and for a few days was virtually ruler of the city. Then he was sacrificed.

No other Mesoamerican people practiced human sacrifice on the scale of the Aztecs. Whatever the other reasons for it might have been, it intimidated subject peoples and reduced their population of fighting-age men and the possibility of rebellion. Together with the heavy burden of tribute, human sacrifice may also have fed resentment and fear, explaining why so many subject peoples were willing to support Cortés when he challenged the Aztecs.

Tenochtitlán   Three great causeways linked Tenochtitlán to the mainland. These met at the ceremonial core of the city, dominated by a temple to Huitzilopochtli and Tlaloc, where most of the Aztec's sacrificial victims met their fate. The palaces of the ruler and high nobles lay just outside the central precinct. The ruler's palace was the empire's administrative center, with government officials, artisans and laborers, gardens, and a zoo. The rest of the city was divided into wards (*calpulli*). Some *calpulli* were specialized, reserved for merchants (*pochteca*) or artisans. The city was laid out on a grid formed of streets and canals. Agricultural plots of great fertility bordered the canals and the lake. Aqueducts carried water into the city. A dike kept the briny water of the northern part of Lake Texcoco from contaminating the waters around Tenochtitlán.

Society   Aztec society was hierarchical, authoritarian, and militaristic. It was divided into two broad classes, noble and commoner, with merchants and certain artisans forming an intermediate category. The nobility enjoyed wealth and luxury. Laws and regulations relating to dress reinforced social divisions. Elaborate and brilliantly colored regalia distinguished nobles from commoners, who were required to wear rough, simple garments.

The Aztecs were morally austere. They valued obedience, respectfulness, discipline, and moderation. Laws were strict and punishment severe. Standards for the nobility were higher than for commoners and punishments for sexual and social offenses were more strictly enforced. Drunkenness was harshly punished among the elite.

The highest rank in the nobility was that of *Tlatoani* (plural *tlatoque*), or ruler of a major political unit. Of these, the highest were the rulers of the three cities of the Triple Alliance; of them, the highest was the *tlatoani* of Tenochtitlán. Below them were the *tetcutin*, lords of subordinate units. And below them were the *pipiltin*, who filled the bureaucracy and the priesthood.

The bulk of the population were commoners. It was they who farmed, harvested fish from the lake, and provided labor for public projects. All commoners belonged to a *calpulli*, each of which had its own temple. Children received training in the song houses attached to these temples. *Calpulli* officials assured that the *calpulli* fulfilled its tribute obligations. Commoners unable to pay debts or tribute might become slaves. They might also become slaves for some criminal offenses. Serfs worked the estates of noblemen.

Traders and merchants—*pochteca*—were important figures in Aztec society. Their activities, backed by Aztec armies, spread Aztec influence. Their far-reaching expeditions brought back luxury goods for the lords of Tenochtitlán. They organized guilds and established laws and customs for doing business. Their wealth put them in an ambiguous position in Aztec society. As a result, they avoided ostentatious display. Artisans of luxury goods also enjoyed a special status.

Markets were central to Aztec economic life. More than 60,000 people went to the great market at Tlatelolco daily. Market administrators, women as well as men, regulated transactions. Cacao beans and cotton cloaks served as mediums of exchange.

Above all, Aztec society was organized for war. The entire society stood on a war footing. All young men received military training. Battles were fought to capture new territory, punish rebellious tributaries, protect trading expeditions, and secure natural resources. The flowery wars were fought just to secure sacrificial victims. Combat was a matter of individual contests, not the confrontation of massed infantry. A warrior's goal was to subdue and capture prisoners for sacrifice. Prowess in battle was key to social advancement and rewards for both commoners and nobles. Failure in battle brought social disgrace.

Women in Aztec society could inherit and own property. They traded in the marketplace and served as market officials. Their craft work provided their families with income. Girls and boys alike were educated in the song houses, and women had access to priestly roles, although they were barred from high religious positions. In general, however, the Aztec emphasis on warfare left women subordinate and excluded from high authority. As a man's primary role was to be a warrior, a woman's was to bear children, and childbirth was compared to battle. Death in childbirth, like death in battle, guaranteed rewards in the afterlife.

Andean South America

The Andean region of South America—primarily modern Peru and Bolivia—had, like Mesoamerica, a long history of civilization when Spanish conquerors arrived in the sixteenth century. Andean civilization is conventionally divided into seven periods: The Early, Middle, and Late Horizons are periods in which a homogeneous art style spread over a wide area. The intermediate periods are characterized by regional stylistic diversity.

The Preceramic and the Initial Period

The earliest monumental architecture in Peru dates to the early third millennium B.C.E., roughly contemporary with the Great Pyramids of Egypt. Located on the coast mostly near the shore, these earliest centers consist of ceremonial mounds and plazas and predate the introduction of pottery to Peru. Coastal people at this time subsisted primarily on the bounties of the sea, supplemented by squash, beans, and chili peppers. They also cultivated cotton. The cotton fishing nets and other textiles of this period represent the beginning of the sophisticated Andean textile tradition.

The earliest public buildings in the highlands date to before 2500 B.C.E. Highland people were more dependent on agriculture than coastal people during the late Preceramic, cultivating maize as well as potatoes and other tubers. Llamas and alpacas were fully domesticated by about 2500 B.C.E.

There is little evidence of social stratification for the late Preceramic. The public structures of both the coast and the highlands appear to have been centers of community ritual for relatively egalitarian societies.

The introduction of pottery to Peru around 2000 B.C.E. marks the beginning of the Initial Period and corresponds to a major shift in settlement and subsistence patterns on the coast. People became dependent on agriculture as well as on maritime resources. They moved their settlements inland, built irriga-tion systems, began cultivating maize, and built large ceremonial centers adorned with sculpture and brightly painted facades. Population grew and society became stratified. Incised carvings of bodies with severed heads suggest growing conflict. Centers apparently remained independent of one another, however.

Chavín de Huantar and the Early Horizon

The large coastal centers of the Initial Period declined early in the first millennium B.C.E. At about the same time, beginning around 800 B.C.E., a site in the highlands, Chavín de Huantar, was growing in influence. Located on a trade route between the coast and the lowland tropical rain forest, Chavín was the center of a powerful religious cult with a population of perhaps 3,000 at its height.

Between about 400 and 200 B.C.E., Chavín influence spread widely throughout Peru. Archaeologists believe Chavín influence reflects the prestige of its cult, not political or military expansion. The florescence of Chavín was also marked by innovations in ceramics, weaving, and metallurgy.

Excavations point to increasing social stratification. Skeletal remains at Chavín, for example, suggest that people who lived closer to the ceremonial center ate better than people living on the margins of the site.

The Early Intermediate Period

Signs of increasing warfare accompany the collapse of the Chavín culture and the ideological unity it had brought to the Andes. The subsequent Early Intermediate Period combine regional diversity with political centralization and the emergence of the first territorial states in the Andes.

Nazca

The Nazca culture, which flourished from about 100 B.C.E. to about 700 C.E., was centered in the Ica and Nazca Valleys. The people of the Nazca Valley built underground aqueducts to divert ground water in the middle of the valley into irrigation canals. Cahuachi, the largest Nazca site, was empty most of the year, filling periodically with pilgrims during religious festivals. It may have been the capital of a Nazca confederation.

The Nazca are renowned for their textiles and fine pottery, decorated with images of Andean plants and animals. They may be most famous, however, for their colossal earthworks, or geoglyphs, the so-called Nazca lines. These were created by brushing away the dark gravel of the desert to reveal a lighter-colored surface. Some are located on hillsides visible to passers-by. Others are only visible from the air.

The Periods of Andean Civilization	
Preceramic	ca. 3000–ca. 2000 B.C.E.
Initial Period	ca. 2000–ca. 800 B.C.E.
Early Horizon	ca. 800–ca. 200 B.C.E.
Early Intermediate Period	ca. 200 B.C.E.–ca. 600 C.E.
Middle Horizon	ca. 600 C.E.–ca. 800/1000 C.E.
Late Intermediate Period	ca. 800/1000–ca. 1475
Late Horizon (Inca Empire)	ca. 1475–1532

Moche

The Moche culture flourished from about 200 to 700 C.E. on the north coast of Peru. The culture takes its name from the Moche Valley. Two huge structures, the Pyramid of the Sun and the Pyramid of the Moon, overlook this site. The cross-shaped Pyramid of the Sun, the largest adobe structure in the Americas, was some 1,200 feet long by 500 feet wide and rose in steps to a height of 60 feet. It was made with more than 143 million adobe bricks.

The Moche were skilled potters. Realistic portrait vessels may depict actual people. Depictions of the sacrifice ceremony show elaborately dressed figures drinking the blood of sacrificed prisoners.

The Moche were also the most sophisticated smiths in the Andes. They developed innovative alloys, cast weapons and agricultural tools, and used the lost-wax process to create small, intricate works.

The Middle Horizon Through the Late Intermediate Period

Tiwanaku and Huari

In the fifth century C.E., when the Germanic invasions were leading to the disintegration of the Roman Empire and as Teotihuacán was reaching its height in Mesoamerica, the first expansionist empires were emerging in the Andean highlands. One of these was centered at Tiwanaku in Bolivia, and the other at Huari in Peru. Both are associated with new agricultural technologies and show evidence of statecraft that foreshadows the administrative practices of the later Inca Empire. The artistic symbolism of both also suggests a shared religious ideology.

Tiwanaku lies more than 12,600 feet above sea level, making it the highest capital in the ancient world. Construction apparently began at the site about 200 C.E. It began its expansionist phase about 500–600 C.E., and collapsed some 500 years later. The city occupied one to two square miles, and may have had a population of 20,000–40,000 people at its height. Laid out on a grid, it is dominated by large public structures and ceremonial gateways. The effort expended in transporting the stone for these monuments was enormous, and indicates the power of the Tiwanaku's rulers.

A system of raised-field agriculture on the shores of Lake Titicaca provided Tiwanaku with its economic base. This system involved farming on artificial platforms capped with rich topsoil and separated by basins of water. Experimental reconstructions have shown it to be extremely productive.

Tiwanaku dominated the Titicaca basin and neighboring regions. It probably exerted its influence through its religious prestige and by establishing colonies and religious-administrative structures in distant territories.

The Huari Empire flourished from about 600 to 800 C.E., dominating the highlands from near Cuzco in the south to Cajamarca in the north. The capital, Huari, covers about 1.5 square miles and had a population of 20,000–30,000 people.

Huari is located in a valley and its rise is associated with techniques for terracing and irrigating the slopes of the valley to increase their productivity. Huari administrative centers were undefended and built in accessible places. Many archaeologists think they may have functioned like later Inca administrative centers, housing a small Huari elite that organized local labor for state projects. Again like the Inca, Huari administrators used *quipu* record-keeping devices made of string.

The Chimu Empire

After the demise of Moche authority, two new states emerged on the north coast. One, named for the site of Sican, was centered in the Lambayeque Valley.

The other new north coast state, known as Chimu, was centered in the Moche Valley. In two waves of expansion, the Chimu built an empire that incorporated the Lambayeque Valley and stretched for 800 miles along the coast. The administrative capital of this empire, Chan Chan, in the Moche Valley, was a vast city. Its walls enclosed eight square miles and its central core covered over two square miles. The focus of the city are some ten immense adobe-walled enclosures that probably housed the empire's ruling elite. Smaller compounds probably housed the lesser nobility. And surrounding these were the homes and workshops of the artisans and workers who served the elite. Two areas were apparently transport centers, where llama caravans brought raw materials to the capital from the empire's territories. The total population of the city was between 30,000 and 40,000.

In about 1470, the Chimu Empire was swept away by the Inca Empire.

The Inca Empire

In 1532, when Francisco Pizarro and his companions happened on it, the Inca Empire was one of the largest states in the world. Its domains encompassed the area between the Pacific Coast and the Amazon basin for some 2,600 miles, from Ecuador to northern Chile (see Map 15–2). Its population numbered in the millions.

The Inca called their domain the Land of the Four Quarters. Their capital, Cuzco, lay at the intersection of these divisions. Home to the ruler (Inca) and the ruling elite, it was a city of great splendor. Its principal temples, dedicated to the sun and moon, gleamed with gold and silver.

The Incas Organize Their Empire

The Incas were remarkable for their ability to organize a vast and diverse empire. One of their chief devices of government was the movement of large groups of people to new, unfamiliar provinces. The Incas were also very sensitive to the power of religion and religious rituals. Once they had moved a population, they required that the chief object of worship belonging to that people be moved to the Inca capital of Cuzco where it was attended by representatives of its original worshippers. This latter group was changed from time to time, allowing portions of the transferred population to become familiar with the language and customs of the court city of Cuzco. These processes of government are described in the following passage by Bernabé Cobo (1582–1657), a Jesuit, whose account is regarded as among the most complete and accurate discussions of Inca culture.

To what extent did the Incas appear to be following a classic mode of rule by dividing and conquering? How did the Incas use one group to balance the threat to their rule from another group? How did they use religion and language to strengthen their authority?

The first thing that these kings did after conquering a province was to remove six or seven thousand families . . . and to transfer these families to the quiet, peaceful provinces, assigning them to different towns. In their stead they introduced the same number of people, taken from the places to which the former families had been sent or from such other places as seemed convenient. . . . In these transfers of population they saw to it that the migrants, both the newly conquered persons and the others, were moved to lands whose climate and conditions were the same as, or similar to, those which they had left behind them. . . .

The Incas introduced these changes of domicile in order to maintain their rule with greater ease, quiet, and security. . . . [T]hey ordered the majority of the *mitimaes* [the groups transferred] whom they sent to the recently conquered towns to make their homes in the provincial capitals, where they served as garrisons. . . . As soldiers they received certain privileges to make them appear of nobler rank, and they were ordered always to obey the slightest commands of their captains and governors. Under this plan, it the natives revolted, the *mitimaes*, being devoted to the governors, soon reduced them to obedience to the Inca; and if the *mitimaes* rioted they were repressed and punished by the natives; thus, through this scheme of domiciling the majority of the people of some province in other parts, the king was made secure against revolts in his dominions. . . . The Incas required everyone to absorb their language, laws, and religion with all the beliefs about these matter that were established at Cuzco. . . . In order to introduce and establish these things more effectively, . . . they would remove the principal idol from a conquered province and set it up in Cuzco with the same attendance and worship that it had formerly had; all this was seen to by persons who had come from that province . . . For this reasons Indians from every province of the kingdom were at all times in residence in the capital and court, occupied in guarding and ministering to their own idols. Thus they learned the usages and customs of the court; and when they were replaced by others . . . they taught their people what they had seen and learned in the court.

From *Historia del Nuevo Mundo* Bernabé Cobe (Seville, 1890–1893), 3: 222–225; Benjamin Keen, trans., as reprinted in Benjamin Keen, ed., *Readings in Latin American Civilization 1492 to the Present* (Boston: Houghton Mifflin Company, 1955), pp. 29–30.

The origins of the Inca are obscure. According to their own traditions, Inca expansion began only in the fifteenth century in the wake of a revolt of the Chanca people that nearly destroyed Cuzco. Inca Yupanqui, son of the city's aging ruler, crushed the revolt. He and his successors expanded their domains to bring civilization to the Andean world. There is an element of imperial propaganda in this legend. Archaeological evidence suggests that the Inca had been expanding for decades and perhaps centuries before the Chanca revolt.

The Inca enlarged their empire through alliance, intimidation, and conquest. They organized their realm into a hierarchical administrative structure and imposed their language, Quechua, as its administrative language. Quechua is still widely spoken in the Peruvian Andes.

The Inca relied on various forms of labor taxation. They divided agricultural lands into categories, allowing local populations to retain some for their own support and reserving others for the state and the gods. In a system known as the *mita*, local people worked for the state on a regular basis, receiving in return gifts and ritual entertainments. Men also served in the army and on public works projects. The Inca also designated entire communities as *Mitimaqs*, moving them about to exploit the resources of their empire. They sometimes settled loyal people in hostile regions and moved hostile people to loyal regions.

The Inca employed several groups of people in what amounted to full-time state service. One of these, the *mamakuna*, consisted of women who lived privileged but celibate and regulated lives in cities and towns throughout the empire.

Mamakuna might also be given in marriage by Inca rulers to cement alliances. These so-called "Virgins of the Sun" played an important economic as well as religious role, weaving cloth and brewing the maize beer known as *chicha* for the Inca elite. Chicha was consumed at state religious festivals. Another group of full-time state workers were men whose duties included tending the royal llama herds.

Cloth and clothing were also a means of communication. Complex textile patterns indicated a person's rank and ethnic affiliation. Inca warehouses were filled with textiles as well as with food and other craft goods.

The Incas made their presence felt in their empire through regional administrative centers and warehouses linked by roads. The centers served to organize, house, and feed people engaged in *mita* labor service and to impress upon them the power and beneficence of the state with feasting and ritual. The wealth of the empire, collected in storehouses, sustained the *mita* laborers, fed and clothed the army, and enriched the Inca elite. Although the Inca lacked writing, they kept detailed administrative records on string accounting devices called *quipu*.

The Inca built more than 14,000 miles of road, from narrow paths to wide thoroughfares. Rope bridges crossed gorges and rivers, and stairways eased the ascent of steep slopes. A system of relay runners sped messages to Cuzco from the reaches of the empire.

Over their long history, the people of the Andes developed an adaptation to their challenging environment that allowed them to prosper and grow, bringing more land under cultivation than today. Building on ancient Andean traditions, the Inca appear to have engineered a productive economy that brought its people a measure of well-being that would not survive the destruction of the empire by Spanish invaders.

IN WORLD PERSPECTIVE

Ancient Civilizations of the Americas

Civilization in the Americas before 1492 developed independently of civilization in the Old World. As the kings of Egypt were erecting their pyramid tombs, the people of the desert coast of Peru were erecting temple platforms. While King Solomon ruled in Jerusalem, the Olmec were creating their monumental stone heads. As Rome reached its apogee and then declined, so did Teotihuacán in the Valley of Mexico. As Islam spread from its heartland, the rulers of Tikal brought their city to its greatest splendor. Maya mathematics and astronomy rivaled that of any in the ancient world. And as the aggressive nation-states of Europe were emerging from their feudal past, the Aztecs and Incas were consolidating their empires.

The encounter between Old World and New, however, would prove devastating for American civilization. The technology that allowed Europeans to embark on the voyages of discovery and fight destructive wars among themselves caught the great native empires unprepared. Uncertain how to respond to these aggressive foreigners, they succumbed.

Review Questions ———

1. Describe the rise of civilization in Mesoamerica and Andean South America. What does it have in common with the rise of civilization in Africa and Eurasia? In what ways was it different?

2. The appearance of monumental architecture in the ancient world was often associated with hierarchical agricultural societies. Was this the case for the Peruvian coast?

3. What were some of the accomplishments of the Classic Period civilizations of Mesoamerica? How do they compare with contemporary civilizations elsewhere in the world?

4. How was the Aztec Empire organized? The Inca Empire? How do they compare to the early empires of the ancient world in the Near East, Europe, and Asia?

5. Both the Aztec and Inca Empires fell in the early sixteenth century when confronted with Spanish forces of a few hundred men. What do you think might have been some of the reasons for their defeat?

Documents CD-ROM

1. The Myth of the Incas: A Case of Double Creation?

2. The Mesoamerican Mind: Tezcatlipoca, Quetzatcoatl, and Music

3. The Mesoamerican Mind: The Aztecs and Holy Warfare

4. *Twenty Sacred Hymns*, Mexico

5. *Florentine Codex*, Mexico

THE WORLD
in TRANSITION

Between 1500 and 1800, the balance of world power shifted toward Europe. That shift was the result of paths Europeans took and other areas of the world did not.

Sixteenth-century Japan was torn by feudal wars, but by 1600, a new political regime was establishing itself on the basis of a "feudal" society like that in medieval Europe. Thereafter, although relatively prosperous, Japan remained separated from the larger world until the mid-nineteenth century.

Spared comparable strife, China entered an epoch of strength and cultural achievement. The bureaucracy governed efficiently. The population expanded. China experienced a commercial revolution. But it did not industrialize.

In the Islamic world, by the mid-1600s, the power of the Ottoman, Safavid, and Mughal Empires was on the wane despite their cultural vitality. The growing military and naval strength of Europe defeated the Ottomans. In Iran, the Safavids neglected political and military structures. In India, Mughal power declined, while Britian was poised to govern the entire subcontinent.

Early in the sixteenth century, western Europe began a century and a half of religious war. Rulers made the most of these religious divisions to consolidate their power and create modern states. Four factors account for the rising power of the West. First, the European monarchies unified their realms. Second, the monarchs encouraged voyages of expansion and discovery through which Europeans penetrated markets across the globe and Europeanized the American continents.

Third, European thinkers carried out the Scientific Revolution, which enabled them to develop their technological skills. Fourth, Europeans industrialized, which enabled them to dominate world markets.

1500–1600

1517–1555 Protestant Reformation
1533–1584 Ivan the Terrible of Russia reigns
1540 Jesuit Order founded by Ignatius Loyola
1543–1727 Scientific Revolution
1556–1598 Philip II of Spain reigns
1558–1603 Elizabeth I of England reigns
1562–1598 French wars of religion
1581 The Netherlands declares its independence from the Spanish Habsburgs
1588 Defeat of the Spanish Armada
1589–1610 Henry IV, Navarre, founds Bourbon dynasty of France

1500–1722 Safavid Shi'ite rule in Iran
1512–1520 Ottoman ruler Selim I
1520–1566 Ottoman ruler Suleiman the Magnificent
1525–1527 Babur founds Mughal dynasty in India
1540 Hungary under Ottoman rule
1571 Battle of Lepanto; Ottomans defeated
1556–1605 Akbar the Great of India reigns
ca. 1571–1640 Safavid philosopher-writer Mullah Sadra
1588–1629 Shah Abbas I of Iran reigns

Queen Elizabeth I (National Portrait Gallery, London)

1600–1700

1618–1648 Thirty Years' War
1640–1688 Frederick William, the Great Elector, reigns in Brandenburg-Prussia
1642–1646 Puritan Revolution in England
1643–1715 Louis XIV of France reigns
1682–1725 Peter the Great of Russia reigns
1688 Glorius Revolution in England
1690 "Second Treatise of Civil Government," by John Locke

1628–1657 Shah Jahan reigns; builds Taj Mahal as mausoleum for his beloved wife
1646 Founding of Maratha Empire
1648 Delhi becomes capital of Mughal Empire
1658–1707 Shah Aurangzeb, the "World Conqueror," reigns in India; end of religious toleration toward Hindus; beginning Mughal decline
1669–1683 Last military expansion by Ottomans: 1669, seize Crete; 1670s, the Ukraine; 1683, Vienna

1700–1800

1701 Act of Settlement provides for Protestant succession to English throne
1702–1713 War of Spanish Succession
1740–1748 War of Austrian Succession
1756–1763 Seven Years' War
ca. 1750 Industrial Revolution begins in England
1772 First partition of Poland
1789 First French Revolution
1793 and 1795 Last two partitions of Poland

ca. 1700 Sikhs and Marathas bring down Mughal imperial power
1708 British East India Company and New East India Company merge
1722 Last Safavid ruler forced to abdicate
1724 Rise in the Deccan of the Islamic state of Hyderabad
1725 Nadir Shah of Afghanistan becomes ruler of Persia
1739 Persian invasion of northern India, by Nadir Shah
1748–1761 Ahmad Shah Durrani of Afghanistan invades India
1757 British victory at Plassey, in Bengal

1500–1800 Commercial revolution in Ming-Ch'ing China; trade with Europe; flourishing of the novel
1543 Portuguese arrive in Japan
1568–1600 Era of unification follows end of Warring States Era in Japan
1587 Spanish arrive in Japan
1588 Hideyoshi's sword hunt in Japan
1592–1598 Ming troops battle Hideyoshi's army in Korea

1506 East coast of Africa under Protuguese domination
1507 Mozambique founded by Portuguese
1517 Spanish crown authorizes slave trade to its South American colonies; rapid increase in importation of slaves to the New World
1554–1659 Sa'did Sultanate in Morocco
1575 Union of Bornu and Kanem by Idris Alawma (r. 1575-1610); Kanem-Bornu state the most fully Islamic in West Africa
1591 Moroccan army defeats Songhai army; Songhai Empire collapses

1519 Conquest of the Aztecs by Cortes; Aztec ruler, Montezuma (r. 1502-1519) killed; Tenochtitlán destroyed
1529 Mexico City becomes capital of the Viceroyalty of New Spain
1533 Pizarro begins his conquest of the Incas
1536 Spanish under Mendoza arrive in Argentina
1544 Lima becomes capital of the Viceroyalty of Peru
1584 Sir Walter Raleigh sends expedition to Roanoke Island (North Carolina)

Algonquin village of Secoton (The Bridgeman Art Library International Ltd.)

1600 Tokugawa Ieyasu wins battle of Sekigahara, completes unification of Japan
1600–1868 Tokugawa shogunate in Edo
1630s Seclusion adopted as national policy in Japan
1644–1694 Bashō, Japanese poet
1644–1911 Ch'ing (Manchu) dynasty in China
1661–1722 K'ang Hsi reign in China
1673–1681 Revolt of southern generals in China
1699 British East India Company arrives in China

1600s English, Dutch, and French enter the slave trade; slaves imported to sugar plantations in the Caribbean
1619 First African slaves in North America land in Virginia
1652 First Cape Colony settlement of Dutch East India Company
1660–1856 Omani domination of East Africa; Omani state centered in Zanzibar; 1698, takes Mozambique from Portuguese

1607 The London Company establishes Jamestown Colony (Virginia)
1608 Champlain founds Quebec
1619 Slave labor introduced at Jamestown (Virginia)

African captives, eighteenth century print (North Wind Picture Archives)

1701 Forty-seven rōnin incident in Japan
1716–1733 Reforms of Tokugawa Yoshimune in Japan
1737–1795 Reign of Ch'ien Lung in China
1742 Christianity banned in China
1784 American traders arrive in China
1787–1793 Matsudaira Sadanobu's reforms in Japan
1798 White Lotus Rebellion in China

1702 Asiento Guinea Trade Company founded for slave trade between Africa and the Americas
1700s Transatlantic slave trade at its height
1741–1856 United Sultanate of Oman and Zanzibar
1754–1817 Usman Dan Fodio, founder of sultanate in northern and central Nigeria; the Fulani become the ruling class in the region
1762 End of Funj Sultanate in eastern Sudanic region

1733 Georgia founded as last English colony in North America
1739–1763 Era of trade wars in Americas between Great Britain and the French and Spanish
1763 Peace of Paris establishes British government in Canada
1776–1781 American Revolution
1783–1830 Simón Bolívar, Latin American soldier, statesman
1789 U.S. Constitution
1791 Negro slave revolt in French Santo Domingo
1791 Canada Constitution Act divides the country into Upper and Lower Canada

16

THE LATE MIDDLE AGES AND THE RENAISSANCE IN THE WEST (1300–1527)

CHAPTER TOPICS

- ◆ Political and Social Breakdown

- ◆ Ecclesiastical Breakdown and Revival: The Late Medieval Church

- ◆ The Renaissance in Italy (1375–1527)

- ◆ Italy's Political Decline: The French Invasions (1494–1527)

- ◆ Revival of Monarchy: Nation Building in the Fifteenth Century

---

The late Middle Ages and the Renaissance were a time of unprecedented calamity and of bold new beginnings in Europe. France and England grappled with each other in a bitter conflict known as the Hundred Years' War (1337–1453). Bubonic plague, known to contemporaries as the Black Death, swept over Europe, killing as much as one-third of the population between 1348 and 1350. A schism emerged within the church that lasted thirty-nine years (1378–1417) and led, by 1409, to the election of three competing popes. In 1453, the Turks captured Constantinople and threatened the west.

But the late Middle Ages also witnessed a rebirth that would continue into the seventeenth century. During this period, scholars criticized medieval assumptions about the nature of God, humankind, and society, and kings worked through parliaments and church councils to limit the pope's temporal power. The principle that sovereigns are accountable to the bodies they head was established. The fifteenth century also saw an unprecedented scholarly renaissance. Italian and northern humanists made cultural changes that would spread throughout Europe. The nation-states of Europe progressively superseded the universal church as the community of highest allegiance, as patriotism and incipient nationalism became major forces.

Political and Social Breakdown

Hundred Years' War and Rise of National Sentiment

Medieval governments were by no means all-powerful and secure. Petty lords kept localities in turmoil; dynastic rivalries could plunge entire lands into war. Late medieval rulers depended on carefully negotiated alliances among a wide range of lesser powers. To maintain the order they required, the Norman kings of England and the Capetian kings of France fine-tuned traditional feudal relationships, stressing the loyalty vassals owed the king. The result was unprecedented centralized royal power and a "national" consciousness that equipped both France and England for international warfare.

The Causes of the War   The conflict that came to be known as the Hundred Years' War began in May 1337 and lasted until October 1453. The English king Edward III (r. 1327–1377), the grandson of Philip the Fair of France (r. 1285–1314), claimed the French throne when the French king Charles IV (r. 1322–1328), the last of Philip the Fair's surviving sons, died without a male heir. The French barons had no intention of placing Edward on the French throne, choosing instead the first cousin of Charles IV, Philip VI of Valois (r. 1328–1350).

But the war was more than a dynastic quarrel. England and France were territorial powers in too close proximity to one another. Edward was a vassal of Philip's, holding several sizable French territories as fiefs. England and France also quarreled over control of Flanders. Compounding these frictions was a long history of animosity between the French and English. The Hundred Years' War was a struggle for national identity as well as for territory.

French Weakness   France had three times the population of England, was wealthier, and fought on its own soil. Yet until after 1415, most of the battles were English victories (see Map 16-1). The primary reason for these French failures was disunity caused by social conflicts. France was still struggling to make the transition from a fragmented feudal society to a centralized modern state.

Desperate to raise money, French kings resorted to financial policies that aggravated internal conflicts. In 1355, the king convened a representative council of townsmen and noblemen that came to be known as the *Estates General*. Although it levied taxes at the king's request, its members also enhanced regional rights and privileges, deepening territorial divisions.

France's defeats also resulted from incompetent leadership and English military superiority. The English infantry was more disciplined than the French, and English archers carried the longbow. With it they could pierce armor at 200 yards.

The war had three major stages, each ending with a seemingly decisive victory. In the first stage, Edward defeated the French fleet in the Bay of Sluys, but his effort to invade France failed. In 1346, Edward defeated the French at Crécy and seized Calais. In 1356, near Poitiers, the English won their greatest victory, and political order in France collapsed. Power now suddenly lay with the Estates General, which received rights similar to those granted the English privileged classes in Magna Carta. Unlike the English Parliament, however, the French Estates General remained too divided for effective government.

To secure their rights, the French privileged classes forced the peasantry to pay more taxes and repair the war-damaged properties of the nobility, inciting a series of bloody rebellions in 1358.

After Edward's death in 1377, the English war effort lessened. During the reign of Richard II (r. 1377–1399), in June 1381, oppressed peasants and artisans revolted. As in France, the revolt was crushed, but left England divided for decades.

In the second stage, Henry V (r. 1413–1422) took advantage of the turmoil created in France by the rise of the duchy of Burgundy. Burgundian power caused such disruption that in 1420 the Treaty of Troyes disinherited the French heir and proclaimed Henry V the successor to the French throne. When Henry and the French king Charles VI both died in 1422, the infant Henry VI (r. 1422–1461) of England was proclaimed king of both France and England.

Joan of Arc and the War's Conclusion   The son of Charles VI became Charles VII (1422–1461) to most of the French people. Displaying unprecedented national feeling, they rallied to his cause, thanks to the inspiring leadership of Joan of Arc (1412–1431). A peasant from Lorraine, Joan presented herself to Charles VII in March 1429, declaring that the King of Heaven had called her to deliver the besieged city of Orléans from the English. Charles's desperation overcame his skepticism, and he gave Joan his leave.

Circumstances worked to her advantage. The English force was already at the point of withdrawing when Joan arrived with fresh French troops. After repulsing the English from Orléans, the French enjoyed a succession of victories they attributed to Joan. She gave the French inspiration and a sense of national identity and self-confidence. Within months of the liberation of Orléans, Charles VII was crowned in Rheims.

Charles forgot his liberator as quickly as he had embraced her. When the Burgundians captured Joan in May 1430, he could have secured her release but did not. The Burgundians and the English wanted her discredited, believing this would demoralize French resistance. She was turned over to the Inquisition in English-held Rouen, where she was executed as a relapsed heretic on May 30, 1431. The war continued, however, until 1453, when all that remained to the English was Calais.

The Hundred Years' War (1337–1443)

1340	English victory at Bay of Sluys
1346	English victory at Crécy and seizure of Calais
1348	Black Death strikes
1356	English victory at Poitiers
1358	*Jacquerie* disrupts France
1360	Peace of Bretigny recognizes English holdings in France
1381	English Peasants Revolt
1422	Treaty of Troyes proclaims Henry VI ruler of both England and France
1429	Joan of Arc leads French to victory at Orléans
1431	Joan of Arc executed as a heretic
1453	War ends; English retain only the coastal town of Calais

Map 16–1 The Hundred Years' War. The Hundred Years' War went on intermittently from the late 1330s to 1453. These maps show the remarkable English territorial gains up to the sudden and decisive turning of the tide of battle in favor of the French by the forces of Joan of Arc in 1429.

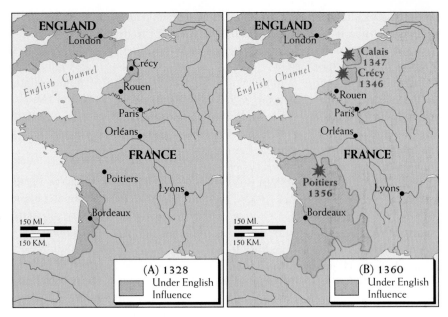

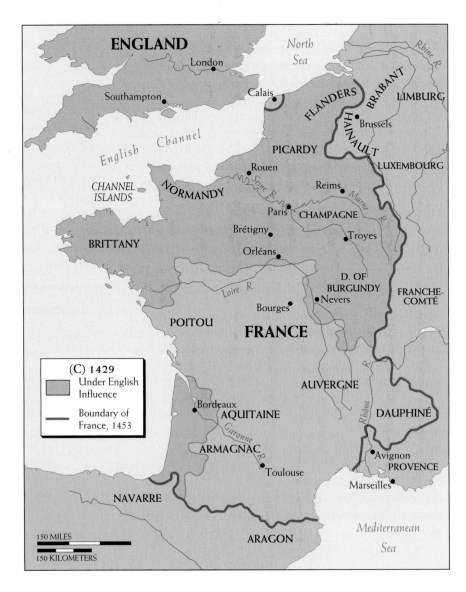

In 1456, Charles VII reopened Joan's trial, and she was found innocent. In 1920, the Church declared her a saint.

The Hundred Years' War devastated France, but it also awakened French nationalism and hastened the country's transition from a feudal monarchy to a centralized state. In both France and England the burden of the war fell most heavily on the peasantry, who were forced to support it with taxes and services.

The Black Death

Preconditions and Causes

In the late Middle Ages, nine-tenths of the population worked the land. The three-field system had increased the food supply. The growth of cities and trade had also stimulated agricultural productivity. But as the food supply grew, so did the population. It is estimated that Europe's population doubled between the years 1000 and 1300, and then began to outstrip food production. There were now more people than food to feed them. The average European faced the probability of famine at least once during his or her expected thirty-five-year life span.

Between 1315 and 1317, crop failures produced the greatest famine of the Middle Ages. Overpopulation, economic depression, famine, and bad health made Europe's population vulnerable to a virulent bubonic plague that struck in 1348.

This Black Death (also called the Great Plague), so called because it discolored the body, followed the trade routes from Asia into Europe. It entered Europe through Venice, Genoa, and Pisa in 1348 and swept through Spain, southern France, and northern Europe. Areas that lay outside the major trade routes appear to have remained unaffected. By the early fifteenth century, it may have killed two-fifths of western Europe's population.

Popular Remedies

The plague, transmitted by fleas, often reached a victim's lungs, from which it could be spread by sneezing and wheezing. Physicians had no understanding of these processes, and thus lacked even the most rudimentary prophylaxis against the disease. To contemporaries, the Black Death was a catastrophe against which there was no defense. It inspired an obsession with death and deep pessimism.

Among the most extreme social reactions were processions of flagellants. These fanatics beat themselves in ritual penance until they bled, believing that such action would bring divine intervention. The flagellants, whose dirty bodies may have helped spread the disease, created a terror that became so threatening that the church outlawed such processions. Jews were cast as scapegoats for the plague. Pogroms occurred, sometimes incited by the flagellants.

Social and Economic Consequences

Whole villages vanished. Among the consequences of this depopulation were a shrunken labor supply and a decline in the value of the estates of the nobility.

As the number of farm laborers decreased, their wages increased, and those of skilled artisans soared. Many serfs replaced their labor services with money payments or abandoned the farm for the cities. Agricultural prices fell, and the price of luxury and manufactured goods rose. Noble landholders were forced to pay more for finished products and farm labor, but received less for their agricultural produce. Their rents declined after the plague.

To recoup their losses, some landowners converted arable land to sheep pasture. Others leased their land. Landowners also sought to reverse their misfortune through repressive legislation that forced peasants to stay on their farms and froze their wages at low levels. In 1351, the English Parliament limited wages to preplague levels and restricted the ability of peasants to leave the land of their traditional masters. Opposition to such legislation helped spark the English Peasants Revolt of 1381.

Although the plague hit urban populations hard, the cities and their skilled industries eventually prospered from its effects. Cities had always regulated competition and immigration from rural areas. After the plague, such laws were extended beyond the cities.

The omnipresence of death whetted the appetite for goods that only skilled urban industries could produce. Jewelry, furs, and silks were in great demand. Initially, this new demand could not be met, as the plague transformed the supply of skilled artisans into a shortage. As a result, the prices of manufactured and luxury items soared, but this encouraged workers to migrate to the city to become artisans. Townspeople profited from the forces that impoverished the landed nobility. As wealth poured into the cities, urban dwellers paid less for agricultural products from the countryside.

New Conflicts and Opportunities

By increasing the importance of skilled artisans, the plague contributed to new conflicts within the cities. The economic and political power of artisans and trade guilds grew along with the demand for their goods and services. As the guilds won political power, they encouraged restrictive legislation to protect local industries. These restrictions brought confrontations between master artisans and the many journeypeople who were eager to become masters. To the long-existing conflict between the guilds and the urban patriciate was now added a conflict within the guilds themselves.

After 1350, and largely as a consequence of the plague, the landed nobility and the church were politically on the defensive. Kings used the new situation to centralize their governments and economies. As already noted, the plague reduced the economic power of the landed nobility, while the battles of the Hundred Years' War demonstrated the military superiority of professional armies over noble cavalry. The plague also killed many of the clergy. The reduction in clerical ranks occurred in the same century in which the residence of the pope in Avignon (1309–1377) and the Schism (1378–1415) undermined the church's popular support.

Ecclesiastical Breakdown and Revival: The Late Medieval Church

The thirteenth-century papacy had become a powerful political institution governed by its own law and courts, serviced by an international bureaucracy, and preoccupied with secular goals.

Boniface VIII and Philip the Fair

By the fourteenth century, popes faced rulers far more powerful than the papacy. Boniface VIII (r. 1294–1303) became pope when England and France were maturing as nation-states and would not be intimidated by the papacy. In England, a long tradition of consultation between the king and powerful members of English society evolved into formal "parliaments" during the reigns of Henry III (1216–1272) and Edward I (1272–1307), and these parliaments helped to create a unified kingdom. During the reign of the French king Philip IV the Fair (1285–1314), France was an efficient, centralized monarchy. Boniface had the further misfortune of bringing to the papal throne memories of the way earlier popes had brought kings and emperors to their knees.

France and England were on the brink of war in 1294. Both countries taxed the clergy heavily. Viewing this as an assault on clerical rights, Boniface issued a bull, *Clericis Laicos*, which forbade lay taxation of the clergy without papal approval.

In England, Edward I retaliated by denying the clergy the right to be heard in the royal court, in effect removing his protection from them. But Philip the Fair forbade the exportation of money from France to Rome, denying the papacy revenues without which it could not operate. Boniface had no choice but to concede Philip the right to tax the French clergy "during an emergency."

In 1300, Boniface's fortunes appeared to revive. Thousands of pilgrims flocked to Rome for the Jubilee celebration. When in 1301 Philip arrested the pope's legate, Boniface informed him that "God has set popes over kings and kingdoms" and demanded his legate's release.

Philip unleashed a ruthless antipapal campaign. Boniface made a last-ditch stand against state control of national churches on November 18, 1302, when he issued the bull

Unam Sanctam, declaring that temporal authority was "subject" to the church.

The French then moved against Boniface with force. Philip's troops surprised the pope in mid-August 1303 at Anagni, beat him, and might even have executed him had not an aroused populace liberated him.

The weakened papacy under Pope Clement V (r. 1305–1314) declared that *Unam Sanctam* did not intend to diminish royal authority. He moved the papal court to Avignon (1309) on the southeastern border of France, where it remained until 1377. Relations between church and state would henceforth tilt toward state control of religion within particular monarchies.

The Great Schism (1378–1417) and the Conciliar Movement to 1449

Pope Gregory XI (r. 1370–1378) reestablished the papacy in Rome in January 1377, ending what had come to be known as the "Babylonian Captivity" of the church in Avignon, a reference to the biblical bondage of the Israelites. The return to Rome proved to be short-lived, however. On Gregory's death, the cardinals, in Rome, elected an Italian as Pope Urban VI (r. 1378–1389). Not wanting to surrender the benefits of a papacy under French influence, the French king, Charles V (r. 1364–1380), supported a schism in the church.

In September 1378, thirteen cardinals, all but one of whom was French, elected a cousin of the French king as Pope Clement VII (r. 1378–1397). Allegiance to the two papal courts divided along political lines: England and its allies (the Holy Roman Empire, Hungary, Bohemia, and Poland) acknowledged Urban VI, whereas France and its orbit (Naples, Scotland, Castile, and Aragon) supported Clement VII. Only the Roman line of popes, however, is recognized by the church.

The Council of Constance (1414–1417)   In 1409, a council in Pisa deposed both the Roman and the Avignon popes and elected its own new pope. But neither Rome nor Avignon accepted its action, so after 1409 there were three contending popes. This intolerable situation ended when the emperor Sigismund (r. 1410–1437) prevailed on the Pisan pope to summon a legal council of the church in Constance in 1414, a council also recognized by the Roman pope. The council fathers asserted their supremacy and proceeded to conduct the business of the church.

They also executed the Bohemian reformer Jan Hus (1369–1415). Hus had advocated communion for laity with both wine and bread (traditionally only the priest had received both, an indication of the clergy's spiritual superiority), denied the dogma of transubstantiation (that wine and bread become the true body and blood of Christ by priestly consecration), and questioned the validity of sacraments performed by priests who led immoral lives. After the three contending popes had either resigned or been deposed, the council elected a new pope, Martin V (r. 1417–1431), in November 1417, reuniting the church.

The Council of Basel (1431–1449)
Conciliar government of the church peaked during the Council of Basel. The council curtailed papal powers of appointment and taxation, but under Pope Eugenius IV (r. 1431–1447), the papacy regained much of its prestige and authority. The notion of conciliar superiority over popes died when the Council of Basel collapsed in 1449. But the conciliar movement had planted deep within the conscience of western peoples the conviction that the leader of an institution must be responsive to its members.

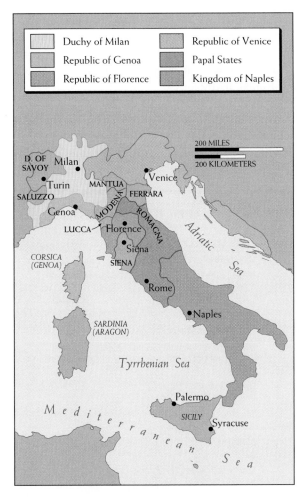

Map 16–2 Renaissance Italy. The city-states of Renaissance Italy were self-contained principalities whose internal strife was monitored by their despots and whose external aggression was long successfully controlled by treaty.

The Renaissance in Italy (1375–1527)

The Renaissance was a transition from the medieval to the modern world. Medieval Europe had been a fragmented feudal society with an agricultural economy, its culture dominated by the church. Renaissance Europe was characterized by growing national consciousness and political centralization, an urban economy based on commerce and capitalism, and ever greater lay and secular control of culture.

The distinctive achievements of the Renaissance are revealed in Italy from 1375 to 1527, the year of the infamous sack of Rome by imperial soldiers. What was achieved in Italy also deeply influenced northern Europe.

The Italian City-State: Social Conflict and Despotism

Renaissance society took shape within the cities of late medieval Italy. Italy was the natural gateway between East and West. Venice, Genoa, and Pisa traded with the Near East throughout the Middle Ages, and maintained vibrant urban societies. During the thirteenth and fourteenth centuries, the Italian cities became powerful city-states. By the fifteenth century, the great Italian cities had become the bankers for Europe.

The growth of Italian cities and urban culture was assisted by the warfare between the emperor and the pope, either of whom might have challenged the cities. They chose instead to weaken one another, strengthening the urban oligarchies. Where northern European cities tended to be dominated by kings and princes, Italian cities absorbed the surrounding countryside and assimilated the local nobility. There were five such major, competitive states in Italy: the duchy of Milan, the republics of Florence and Venice, the Papal States, and the kingdom of Naples (see Map 16–2).

Social strife and competition for political power were so intense within the cities that most had evolved into despotisms by the fifteenth century. Venice was the exception. Elsewhere, the new social classes and divisions within society produced by rapid urban growth fueled chronic, near-anarchic conflict. Florence was the most striking example. There were four distinguishable social groups within the city: the old rich, or *grandi*, the nobles and merchants who had traditionally ruled the city; the emergent new-rich merchant class, capitalists and bankers known as the *popolo grasso*, or "fat people"; the middle-burgher ranks of guild masters, shopkeepers, and professionals; and the omnipresent *popolo minuto*, the "little people" who made up the lower economic classes. In 1457, one-third of the population of Florence, about 30,000 people, were listed as paupers.

These social divisions produced conflict at every level of society. In 1378, a great revolt, known as the Ciompi Revolt, established a chaotic four-year reign of power by the lower Florentine classes. Stability did not return until the ascent to power in 1434 of Cosimo de' Medici (1389–1464). The wealthiest Florentine and an astute statesman, Cosimo controlled the city from behind the scenes, manipulating the constitution. His grandson Lorenzo the Magnificent (1449–1492, r. 1478–1492), ruled Florence in almost totalitarian fashion.

Despotism was less subtle elsewhere. The dominant groups in many cities installed a hired strongman, known as a *podesta*. He held executive, military, and judicial authority, and his mandate was simple: to protect the normal flow of business. These despots operated through mercenary armies.

Political turbulence and warfare gave birth to diplomacy, through which the city-states gained power and advantage without actually going to war. Most city-states established resident embassies during the fifteenth century. Their ambassadors represented them in ceremonies and as negotiators and became their watchful eyes and ears at rival courts. Thought and culture flourished. Renaissance culture was promoted vigorously by despots, republicans, and popes.

Humanism

Some scholars describe humanism as an unchristian philosophy that stressed the dignity of humankind and championed individualism and secular values. Others argue that the humanists were champions of authentic Catholic Christianity, or they see humanism as a form of scholarship designed to promote civic responsibility and political liberty. Others view humanism simply as an educational program that concentrated on rhetoric and sound scholarship for their own sake.

There is truth in each of these definitions. Humanism was the study of the Latin and Greek classics and the ancient Church Fathers, both for their own sake and to promote a rebirth of ancient norms and values. Humanists advocated the *studia humanitatis*, a liberal arts program that embraced grammar, rhetoric, poetry, history, politics, and moral philosophy. The Florentine Leonardo Bruni (1374–1444) first gave this learning the name humanitas ("humanity").

The first humanists were orators and poets. They wrote in both the classical and vernacular languages, inspired by the newly discovered works of the ancients, and they taught rhetoric within the universities. Their talents were sought as secretaries, speech writers, and diplomats in princely and papal courts.

Classical and Christian antiquity had been studied before, during the Carolingian renaissance of the ninth century, for example. However, the Italian Renaissance was more secu-

lar and lay dominated, had broader interests, recovered more manuscripts, and possessed superior technical skills.

Unlike their scholastic rivals, humanists went to the original source and drew their own conclusions. Italian humanists made the full sources of Greek and Latin antiquity available to scholars during the fourteenth and fifteenth centuries. There is a kernel of truth in the humanist boast that the period between themselves and classical civilization was a "dark middle age."

Petrarch, Dante, and Boccaccio   Francesco Petrarch (1304–1374) was the father of humanism. Petrarch celebrated ancient Rome in his writings and collected ancient manuscripts. His critical textual studies, elitism, and contempt for scholastic learning were shared by many later humanists.

Petrarch was far more secular in orientation than Dante Alighieri (1265–1321), whose *Vita Nuova* and *Divine Comedy*, along with Petrarch's sonnets, form the cornerstones of Italian vernacular literature. Giovanni Boccaccio (1313–1375), author of the *Decameron*—100 bawdy tales told by men and women in a country retreat from the plague—also pioneered humanist studies. Boccaccio assembled an encyclopedia of Greek and Roman mythology.

Educational Reforms and Goals   The classical ideal of a useful education that produces well-rounded people inspired reforms in traditional education. Vittorino da Feltre

Major Political Events of the Italian Renaissance (1375–1527)

1378–1382	Ciompi revolt in Florence
1434	Medici rule in Florence established by Cosimo de' Medici
1454–1455	Treaty of Lodi allies Milan, Naples, and Florence (in effect until 1494)
1494	Charles VIII of France invades Italy
1495	League of Venice unites Venice, Milan, the Papal States, the Holy Roman Empire, and Spain against France
1499	Louis XII invades Milan (the second French invasion of Italy)
1500	The Borgias conquer Romagna
1512–1513	The Holy League (Pope Julius II, Ferdinand of Aragon, Emperor Maximilian I, and Venice) defeat the French
1513	Machiavelli writes *The Prince*
1515	Francis I leads the third French invasion of Italy
1516	Concordat of Bologna between France and the papacy
1527	Sack of Rome by imperial soldiers

Christine de Pisan Instructs Women on How to Handle Their Husbands

Renowned Renaissance noblewoman Christine de Pisan has the modern reputation of being perhaps the first feminist, and her book The Treasure of the City of Ladies *(also known as* The Book of Three Virtues*) has been described as the Renaissance woman's survival manual. Here she gives advice to the wives of artisans.*

How does Christine de Pisan's image of husband and wife compare with other medieval views? Would the church take issue with her advice? As a noblewoman commenting on the married life of artisans, does her high social standing influence her advice? Would she give similar advice to women of her own social class?

All wives of artisans should be very painstaking and diligent if they wish to have the necessities of life. They should encourage their husbands or their workmen to get to work early in the morning and work until late. . . . [And] the wife herself should [also] be involved in the work to the extent that she knows all about it, so that she may know how to oversee his workers if her husband is absent, and to reprove them if they do not do well. . . . And when customers come to her husband and try to drive a hard bargain, she ought to warn him solicitously to take care that

he does not make a bad deal. She should advise him to be chary of giving too much credit if he does not know precisely where and to whom it is going, for in this way many come to poverty. . . . In addition, she ought to keep her husband's love as much as she can, to this end: that he will stay at home more willingly and that he may not have any reason to join the foolish crowds of other young men in taverns and indulge in unnecessary and extravagant expense, as many tradesmen do, especially in Paris. By treating him kindly she should protect him as well as she can from this. It is said that three things drive a man from his home: a quarrelsome wife, a smoking fireplace, and a leaking roof. She too ought to stay at home gladly and not go off every day traipsing hither and yon gossiping with the neighbours and visiting her chums to find out what everyone is doing. That is done by slovenly housewives roaming about the town in groups. Nor should she go off on these pilgrimages got up for no good reason and involving a lot of needless expense.

From *The Treasure of the City of Ladies or The Book of the Three Virtues*, by Christine de Pisan, trans. by Sarah Lawson (Penguin Classics, 1985), pp. 167–168. This translation © Sarah Lawson, 1985.

(d. 1446) directed his students to a disciplined reading of ancient authors, together with physical exercise and intellectual games. Baldassare Castiglione (1478–1529) wrote the *Book of the Courtier*, a how-to book for the cultured nobility. It stressed the importance of integrating the knowledge of language and history with athletic, military, and musical skills, and crowning them all with good manners and moral character.

Cultured noblewomen also had a prominent place at Renaissance courts, among them Christine de Pisan (1363?–1434). An expert in classical, French, and Italian languages and literature, she had married early (at fifteen) and by twenty-seven was the widowed mother of three children. She wrote to support herself, becoming a well-known woman of letters in the courts of Europe. In *The City of Ladies* she describes the great women of history.

The Florentine "Academy" and Revival of Platonism

Of all the important recoveries of the past made during the Italian Renaissance, the revival of Greek studies, especially the works of Plato in fifteenth-century Florence, stands out. A foundation had been laid when many Greek scholars and manuscripts began to enter the west and settle in Florence, especially after the fall of Constantinople to the Turks (1453). This was the background against which the study of Plato developed under the patronage of Cosimo de' Medici and the supervision of Marsilio Ficino (1433–1499) and Pico della Mirandola (1463–1494).

The thinkers of the Renaissance were especially attracted to Platonism and those Church Fathers who had tried to synthesize Plato's philosophy with Christian teaching. In private residences, Florentine humanists met to discuss the works of Plato and the Neoplatonists. This was the so-called "Florentine Academy," not a formal school but productive informal gatherings of scholars.

The appeal of Platonism lay in its flattering view of human nature. Platonism distinguished between an eternal sphere of being and the perishable world in which humans lived. Human reason was believed to belong properly only to the former— having preexisted in the pristine world of being and continuing still to commune with it, as Plato and his followers believed the innate knowledge of mathematical and moral truths attested.

Renaissance Art

In Renaissance Italy, as later in Reformation Europe, the values and interests of the laity were less subordinated to those of the clergy. In education, culture, and religion, the laity assumed a greater role and even established models for the clergy to imitate. This resulted in part from the church's loss of power during the late Middle Ages. But it was also encouraged by the rise of national sentiment, the creation of competent national bureaucracies staffed by laity rather than clerics, and the growth of lay education. Medieval Christian values were adjusting to a more this-worldly spirit. Men and women began again to glorify the secular world, secular learning, and purely human pursuits.

This is especially prominent in the painting and sculpture of the High Renaissance (late fifteenth and early sixteenth centuries), when Renaissance art reached its full maturity. In imitation of Greek and Roman art, painters and sculptors attempted to portray the human form with a glorified realism. Whereas Byzantine and Gothic art had been religious and idealized in the extreme, Renaissance art, especially in the fifteenth century, realistically reproduced nature and human beings as a part of nature.

Renaissance artists took advantage of new skills and materials developed during the fifteenth century: the use of oil paints, using shading to enhance realism (chiaroscuro), and adjusting the size of figures to give the viewer a feeling of continuity with the painting (linear perspective). Re-

Michelangelo's Pietà (made between 1498 and 1500), St. Peter's, Rome. This work of the artist's youth, sculpted between his twenty-third and twenty-fifth years, portrays a Mary who is younger than her son. Unsurpassed in delicacy, realism, and emotional impact, it exemplifies the creativity of the Italian Renaissance. [Scala/Art Resource, N.Y.]

naissance paintings are filled with energy and life and stand out from the canvas in three dimensions. The great masters of the High Renaissance included Leonardo da Vinci (1452–1519), Raphael (1483–1520), and Michelangelo Buonarroti (1475–1564).

Leonardo da Vinci   Leonardo personified the Renaissance ideal of the universal person, one who is not only a jack-of-all-trades but also a master of many. A military engineer and advocate of scientific experimentation, he dissected corpses to learn anatomy and was a self-taught botanist. He constantly moved from one activity to another. As a painter, his great skill lay in conveying inner moods through complex facial features, such as that seen in the most famous of his paintings, the *Mona Lisa*.

Raphael   Raphael is famous for his tender madonnas. Art historians praise his fresco *The School of Athens*, which depicts Plato and Aristotle surrounded by philosophy and science, as a perfect example of Renaissance artistic theory and technique.

Michelangelo   This melancholy genius also excelled in a variety of arts and crafts. His eighteen-foot godlike sculpture

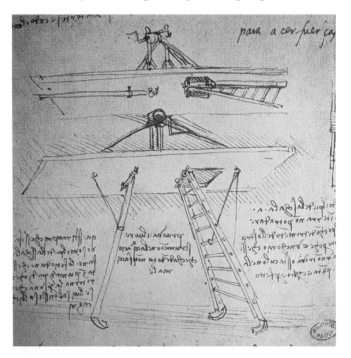

Aviation drawings by Leonardo da Vinci (1452–1519), who imagined a possible flying machine with a retractable ladder for boarding. [David Forbert/SuperStock, Inc.]

David is a perfect example of the Renaissance artist's devotion to harmony, symmetry, and proportion, as well as his glorification of the human form. Four different popes commissioned works by Michelangelo, the best known of which are the frescoes for the Sistine Chapel, painted for Pope Julius II (1503–1513).

His later works mark the passing of High Renaissance painting and the advent of a new, experimental style known as *mannerism*, which reached its peak in the late sixteenth and early seventeenth centuries. A reaction against the simplicity and symmetry of High Renaissance art, which also found expression in music and literature, mannerism made room for the strange and even the abnormal and gave rein to the subjectivity of the artist. It permitted the artist to express his individual perceptions and feelings, to paint, compose, or write in a "mannered" or "affected" way. Tintoretto (d. 1594) and especially El Greco (d. 1614) became its supreme representatives.

Slavery in the Renaissance

Slavery flourished in Renaissance Italy. A Mediterranean slave market had existed since the twelfth century, when the Spanish sold Muslim slaves to Italians and other buyers. After the Black Death (1348–1350) had reduced the supply of laborers in western Europe, the demand for slaves soared. Slaves were taken randomly from conquered people and represented many different races: whites and Asians as well as Africans and Tartars.

In addition to household slavery, plantation slavery following East Asian models had developed in the east Mediterranean. In Sudan and on Venetian estates on Cyprus and Crete, sugar plantations were worked by slaves. Owners had complete dominion over their slaves. A strong, young slave cost the equivalent of the wages paid a free servant over several years. But taking into account a lifetime of free service thereafter, such slaves were good bargains. The Tartars and Africans appear to have been the worst treated. But slaves were generally accepted as family members and integrated into households. Not a few women slaves bore their masters' children. Many children of such unions were raised as legitimate heirs of their fathers. It was also in the interest of their owners to keep slaves healthy and happy; otherwise they would be of little use and could even become a threat. Still, slaves remained a foreign and suspected presence in Italian society.

Italy's Political Decline: The French Invasions (1494–1527)

The Italian city-states had always preserved their safety from foreign invasion by cooperation with each other. Such coop-

This portrait of Katharina, by Albrecht Dürer, provides evidence of African slavery in Europe during the sixteenth century. Katharina was in the service of one João Bradao, a Portuguese economic minister living in Antwerp, then the financial center of Europe. Dürer became friends with Bradao during his stay in the Low Countries in the winter of 1520–1521. [Bildarchiv Foto Marburg/Art Resource, N.Y.]

eration had been maintained during the last half of the fifteenth century. However, in 1494, Naples, supported by Florence and the Borgia pope Alexander VI (1492–1503), prepared to attack Milan. At this point, the Milanese despot Ludovico il Moro (r. 1476–1499) invited the French to revive their dynastic claim to Naples. But France also had dynastic claims to Milan.

Charles VIII's March Through Italy

The French king, Charles VIII (r. 1483–1498) responded to Ludovico's call. He crossed the Alps (August 1495) and raced through Florence and the Papal States into Naples.

Charles's march through Italy alarmed non-Italians. Ferdinand of Aragon (r. 1479–1516), who was also king of Sicily, helped to create a counteralliance: the League of Venice.

Ludovico il Moro meanwhile now saw Milan threatened by the whirlwind he had himself created. He also joined the League of Venice, and this alliance forced Charles to retreat.

Pope Alexander VI and the Borgia Family

The French returned to Italy under Charles's successor, Louis XII (r. 1498–1515), this time assisted by the Borgia pope Alexander VI (1492–1503). Alexander, probably the most corrupt pope who ever sat on the papal throne, promoted the careers of Cesare and Lucrezia, the children he had had before he became pope. Papal policy sought to secure a base in Romagna, part of the Papal States, for Cesare.

In Romagna, several principalities had arisen, and Venice contested the Papal States for their loyalty. Seeing that a French alliance could allow him to reestablish control over the region, Alexander agreed to support a French reconquest of Milan. In exchange, Cesare Borgia got the hand of the sister of the king of Navarre, land grants from Louis XII, and French military aid in Romagna. Such cunning made him the model for Machiavelli's *The Prince*.

This scandalous trade-off enabled both the French king and the pope to realize their ambitions within Italy. Louis took Milan in August 1499. In 1500, he and Ferdinand of Aragon divided Naples between them, while Cesare Borgia conquered Romagna.

Pope Julius II

Cardinal Giuliano della Rovere, a strong opponent of the Borgias, became Pope Julius II (1503–1513). He suppressed the Borgias and the Romagna under papal jurisdiction. Julius was known as the "warrior pope" because he brought the Renaissance papacy to a peak of military prowess and diplomatic intrigue.

Assisted by the French, Pope Julius in 1509 ended Venetian claims in the Romagna. Julius then turned to ridding Italy of the French invaders. Julius, Ferdinand of Aragon, and Venice formed an alliance in October 1511, and soon Emperor Maximilian I (r. 1493–1519) and the Swiss joined them. By 1512, the French were in retreat and were beaten by the Swiss in 1513 at Novara.

The French invaded Italy again under Francis I (r. 1515–1547). French armies massacred Swiss soldiers at Marignano in September 1515, revenging the defeat at Novara. In the Concordat of Bologna (August 1516), the Medici pope Leo X (r. 1513–1521) gave the French king control over the French clergy and the right to collect taxes from them, in exchange for French recognition of the pope's superiority over church councils. This would help to keep France Catholic after the outbreak of the Protestant Reformation. But the new French entry into Italy also led to the first of four major wars with Spain in the first half of the sixteenth century: the Habsburg-Valois wars, none of which France won.

Niccolò Machiavelli

The foreign invasions made a shambles of Italy. One who watched as French, Spanish, and German armies wreaked havoc on his country was Niccolò Machiavelli (1469–1527). He became convinced that Italian political unity and independence justified any means. Machiavelli admired the heroic acts of ancient Roman rulers, what Renaissance people called their *Virtu*, and lamented the absence of heroism among his compatriots.

The juxtaposition of what Machiavelli believed the ancient Romans had been with the failure of contemporary Romans to realize such ideals made him the famous cynic we know in the epithet *Machiavellian*. Only an unscrupulous strongman, he concluded, could impose order on so divided and selfish a people. Machiavelli advised rulers to discover the advantages of fraud and brutality. He apparently hoped to see a strong ruler emerge from the Medici family. However, the second Medici pope, Clement VII (1523–1534), watched helplessly as Rome was sacked by the army of Emperor Charles V (r. 1519–1556) in 1527, the year of Machiavelli's death.[1]

Revival of Monarchy: Nation Building in the Fifteenth Century

With the emergence of sovereign rulers after 1450, unified national monarchies progressively replaced fragmented and divisive feudal governance. The old problem of the one and the many was being decided in favor of monarchy.

In the feudal monarchy of the High Middle Ages, the basic powers of government were divided between the king and his semiautonomous vassals. The nobility and the towns acted through such representative bodies as the English Parliament, the French Estates General, and the Spanish Cortes to thwart the centralization of royal power. However, the landed nobility and the clergy were in decline in the late Middle Ages, and the towns began to ally with the king. Loyal, business-wise townspeople, not the nobility and clergy, became the king's lawyers, bookkeepers, military tacticians, and diplomats. This new alliance between king and town would break the bonds of feudal society and make possible the rise of the modern sovereign state.

In a sovereign state, taxation, war making, and law enforcement are no longer the local right of semiautonomous vassals, but are concentrated in the monarch and exercised

---

[1] To place the western Renaissance in world perspective, see the conclusion of Chapter 17, where the Renaissance and the Reformation are discussed together.

by his agents. Taxes, wars, and laws become national matters. Only as monarchs were able to act independently of the nobility and the representative assemblies could they overcome the decentralization that had blocked nation building.

Monarchies also began to create standing national armies in the fifteenth century. As the infantry and artillery became the backbone of armies, mercenaries were recruited to form the mainstay of the "king's army."

The growing cost of warfare increased the need to develop new national sources of royal income. The expansion of royal revenues was hampered by the belief among the highest classes that they were immune from government taxation. The nobility despised taxation as a humiliation. Royal revenues accordingly grew at the expense of those least able to resist and least able to pay. Monarchs had several options. As feudal lords they could collect rents from their royal domain. They might also levy national taxes on basic food and clothing, such as the *gabelle* or salt tax in France and the *alcabala* or 10 percent sales tax on commercial transactions in Spain. Kings could also levy direct taxes on the peasantry and on commercial transactions in towns under royal protection. This they did through representative assemblies of the privileged classes in which the peasantry did not sit. The French *taille* was such a tax. Sale of public offices and the issuance of high-interest government bonds appeared in the fifteenth century as innovative fund-raising devices. But kings did not tax the powerful nobility. They turned to rich nobles, as they did to the great bankers of Italy and Germany, for loans, bargaining with the privileged classes.

France

There were two cornerstones of French nation building in the fifteenth century. The first was the collapse of the English holdings in France following the Hundred Years' War. The second was the defeat of Charles the Bold (r. 1467–1477) and the duchy of Burgundy. In the mid-fifteenth century, Burgundy aspired to lead a dominant middle kingdom between France and the Holy Roman Empire. But when Charles the Bold was killed at Nancy in 1477, the dream of Burgundian empire died with him.

The dissolution of Burgundy left Louis XI (r. 1461–1483) free to secure the monarchy and double the size of his kingdom. Louis harnessed the nobility, expanded trade and industry, created a national postal system, and established a lucrative silk industry.

A strong nation is a two-edged sword. Such a secure and efficient government enabled Louis's successors to pursue Italian conquests and fight losing wars with the Habsburgs. By the mid-sixteenth century, France was again a defeated nation and almost as divided as it had been during the Hundred Years' War.

Spain

Spain, too, became a strong country in the late fifteenth century. Both Castile and Aragon had been divided kingdoms in the mid-fifteenth century. The marriage of Isabella of Castile (r. 1474–1504) and Ferdinand of Aragon (r. 1479–1516) in 1469 created a formidable European power. Castile had an estimated five million inhabitants to Aragon's less than one million. Castile also had its lucrative sheep-farming industry, which was run by a government-backed organization called the *Mesta*, another example of developing centralized economic planning. Although the two kingdoms were dynastically united by the marriage of Ferdinand and Isabella, each retained its own laws, armies, coinage, taxation, and cultural traditions.

Together, Ferdinand and Isabella could subdue their realms, secure their borders, and venture abroad militarily. Townspeople allied themselves with the crown and replaced the nobility within the royal administration.

Spain had long been remarkable as a place where Islam, Judaism, and Christianity coexisted with some toleration. However, Ferdinand and Isabella made Spain the prime example of state-controlled religion. They exercised almost total control over the Spanish church as they placed religion in the service of national unity. They appointed the higher clergy and the officers of the Inquisition. The Inquisition, run by Tomás de Torquemada (d. 1498), Isabella's confessor, was established in 1479 to monitor the converted Jews (*conversos*) and Muslims (*Moriscos*) in Spain. In 1492, the Jews were exiled and their properties confiscated. In 1502, nonconverting Moors in Granada were driven into exile. Spanish spiritual life remained uniform and regimented, a major reason for Spain's remaining a loyal Catholic country and providing a base for the Counter-Reformation.

Ferdinand and Isabella had wide horizons. They contracted anti-French marriage alliances that determined much of European history in the sixteenth century. In 1496 their eldest daughter, Joanna, later known as "the Mad" (1479–1555), married Archduke Philip (1478–1506), the son of Emperor Maximilian I (1493–1519). Their son, Charles I, the first ruler over a united Spain, came by his inheritance and election as Emperor Charles V in 1519 to rule over a European kingdom almost equal in size to that of Charlemagne. A second daughter, Catherine of Aragon (1485–1536), married King Henry VIII of England. The failure of this latter marriage became the key factor in the English Reformation.

Spanish power was also evident in Ferdinand and Isabella's promotion of overseas exploration. Their patronage of the Genoese adventurer Christopher Columbus (1451–1506) led to the creation of the Spanish empire in Mexico and Peru, whose gold and silver helped to make Spain Europe's dominant power in the sixteenth century.

England

The last half of the fifteenth century was a period of trial for the English. Following the Hundred Years' War, England was subjected to internal warfare between two branches of the royal family, the Houses of York and Lancaster. This conflict, known today as the Wars of the Roses (York's symbol was a white rose, and Lancaster's a red rose), kept England in turmoil from 1455 to 1485.

The Lancastrian monarchy of Henry VI (r. 1422–1461) was challenged by the duke of York and his supporters in the prosperous southern towns. In 1461, Edward IV (r. 1461–1483), son of the duke of York, seized power and bent Parliament to his will. His brother and successor was Richard III (r. 1483–1485), whose reign saw the growth of support for the exiled Lancastrian Henry Tudor. Henry defeated Richard on Bosworth Field in August 1485.

Henry Tudor ruled as Henry VII (r. 1485–1509), the first of the new Tudor dynasty that would endure until 1603. Henry married Edward IV's daughter, Elizabeth of York. He disciplined the English nobility through a feared instrument of the royal will known as the Court of Star Chamber. Henry also used English law to further his own ends. He confiscated so much noble land and fortunes that he governed without dependence on Parliament for funds, always a cornerstone of strong monarchy. Henry thus began to shape a monarchy that became one of early modern Europe's most exemplary governments during the reign of his granddaughter, Elizabeth I (r. 1558–1603).

Review Questions

1. How did the Hundred Years' War, the Black Death, and the great schism in the church affect the course of history? Which had the most lasting effects on the institutions it touched?

2. Was the church an aggressor or a victim in the late Middle Ages and Renaissance? How successful was it in its confrontations with Europe's emerging dynastic states?

3. What was "reborn" in the Renaissance? Were the humanists the forerunners of modern secular education and culture, or eloquent defenders of a still-medieval Christian view of the world against the church's secular and pagan critics?

4. Historians find features of modern states developing in west European lands during the late Middle Ages and Renaissance. What modern features can you identify in the governments of the Italian city-states and the northern monarchies?

Documents CD-ROM

1. *The Chronicle of Jean de Venette*

2. *The Bull Unam Sanctam* of Boniface VIII

3. Propositions of Wycliffe Condemned at London 1382, and at the Council of Constance 1415.

4. Dante: *The Divine Comedy*, Inferno, Canto I

5. Niccolo Machiavelli: *The Prince* and *The Discourses on Titus Livy*

6. Francis Petrarch: Rime

17

THE AGE OF REFORMATION AND RELIGIOUS WARS

CHAPTER TOPICS

- On the Eve of the Reformation
- The Reformation
- The Social Significance of the Reformation in Western Europe
- Family Life in Early Modern Europe

- The Wars of Religion
- England and Spain (1558–1603)
- Superstition and Enlightenment: The Battle Within

In World Perspective The Renaissance and Reformation

In the second decade of the sixteenth century, a powerful religious movement began in Germany and spread throughout northern Europe, affecting society and politics as well as the spiritual lives of men and women. Attacking what they believed to be superstitions that robbed people of their money and peace of mind, Protestant reformers led a revolt against the medieval church. In a short time, hundreds of thousands of people adopted a more simplified religious practice.

Protestantism was not the only reform movement to grow out of the religious grievances and reforms of the late Middle Ages. Within the church itself, reform would win back a great many of its converts. As different groups identified with either Protestantism or Catholicism, 100 years of bloody opposition between Protestants and Catholics darkened the second half of the sixteenth century and the first half of the seventeenth.

For Europe, the late fifteenth and sixteenth centuries were also a period of unprecedented territorial expansion. Permanent colonies were established within the Americas, and American gold and silver spurred scientific invention and a new weapons industry. The new bullion also helped create an international traffic in African slaves.

On the Eve of the Reformation

The Discovery of a New World

The discovery of the Americas set new cultural and economic forces in motion throughout western Europe. Beginning with the voyages of Christopher Columbus (1451–1506) in the late fifteenth century, commercial supremacy started to shift from the Mediterranean and the Baltic to the Atlantic, and western Europe's global expansion began (see Map 17–1).

Gold and Spices   Mercenary motives, reinforced by traditional missionary ideals, had earlier inspired Portuguese exploration of the African coast. By the late fifteenth century, gold from Guinea was entering Europe on Portuguese ships calling at Lisbon and Antwerp, rather than via the traditional Arab overland routes. Antwerp became the financial center of Europe.

The rush for gold expanded into a rush for the spices of India. Spices, especially pepper and cloves, were in great demand as preservatives and to enhance the taste of food.

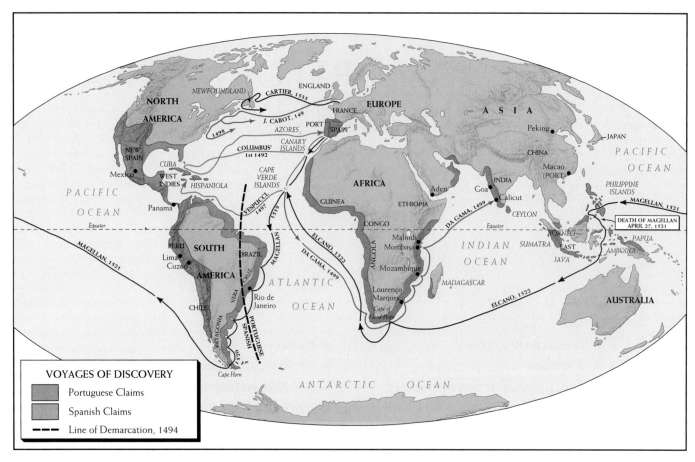

Map 17–1   European voyages of discovery and the colonial claims of Spain and Portugal in the fifteenth and sixteenth centuries.
The map dramatizes Europe's global expansion in the fifteenth and sixteenth centuries.

Bartholomew Dias (d. 1500) opened the Portuguese empire in the East when he rounded the tip of Africa in 1487. In 1498, Vasco da Gama (d. 1524) reached India. Later, the Portuguese established colonies in Goa and Calcutta and challenged the Arabs and the Venetians for control of the European spice trade.

While the Portuguese concentrated on the Indian Ocean, the Spanish set sail across the Atlantic, hoping to establish a shorter route to the East Indies. Instead, Columbus discovered the Americas.

The Voyages of Columbus
On October 12, 1492, Columbus landed in the eastern Bahamas, which he thought was Japan. Columbus called the native people he met Indians, a name that stuck even after it became known that he had discovered a new continent.

On the heels of Columbus, Amerigo Vespucci (1451–1512), after whom America is named, and Ferdinand Magellan (1480–1521) explored the coastline of South America. Their travels documented that the new lands were a new continent that opened on the Pacific Ocean.

Impact on Europe and America
Columbus's voyage of 1492 marked the beginning of more than three centuries of Spanish conquest and administration of an American empire. Voyages of discovery soon became expeditions of conquest that resembled the Christian warfare against the Islamic Moors. Those wars had just ended in 1492, and they imbued Spanish explorers with a zeal for conquering and converting non-Christian peoples.

The voyages to the New World had important consequences for the cultures of both Europe and America. The great wealth from its American possessions financed Spain's commanding role in the age's conflicts while spurring other European countries to undertake their own colonial ventures. It also ignited Europe-wide inflation during the sixteenth century.

For the native peoples of America, the voyages virtually destroyed their civilizations, as warfare, diseases, and exploitation devastated their populations. In both South and North America, Spanish rule set an imprint of Roman Catholicism, economic dependency, and hierarchical social structure still visible today.

Religion and Society

The Protestant Reformation occurred at a time of conflict between the emerging nation-states of Europe, bent on conformity and centralization within their realms, and the self-governing towns and regions, accustomed to running their own affairs. Since the fourteenth century, the king's law and custom had overridden local law and custom almost everywhere. Towns and territories felt the loss of traditional rights and freedoms. Many townspeople and villagers saw the religious revolt as part of their struggle to remain independent. The Reformation came to be identified in the minds of its supporters with what we might call states' rights.

Social and Political Conflict

The Reformation broke out first in the free imperial cities of Germany and Switzerland. There were about sixty-five such cities, each a little kingdom unto itself. Some turned Protestant and remained so. Some were Protestant only for a short time. Others let Catholics and Protestants coexist.

Cities also suffered deep internal social and political divisions. Certain groups favored the Reformation more than others. People who felt pushed around by authority often perceived in the Protestant movement an ally.

Social and political experience thus coalesced with the larger religious issues in both town and countryside. When Martin Luther and his comrades advocated a priesthood of all believers, scorned ecclesiastical landlords, and ridiculed papal laws, they touched political as well as religious nerves in German and Swiss cities. In the villages, the peasants also heard in Protestantism a promise of political liberation and social betterment.

Popular Movements and Criticism of the Church

The Protestant Reformation could not have occurred without the crises of the late medieval church and the Renaissance papacy. The late Middle Ages were marked by lay and clerical efforts to reform local religious practice and by experimentation with religious simplicity in imitation of Jesus.

A variety of factors contributed to the growth of lay criticism of the church. The laity in the cities were becoming increasingly knowledgeable. They traveled widely. New postal systems and the printing press increased the information at their disposal. Laypeople were able to take the initiative in shaping the cultural life of their communities.

Secular Control over Religious Life

On the eve of the Reformation, Rome's international network of church offices began to fall, hurried along by incipient nationalism and secular administrative competence. The late medieval church had permitted important ecclesiastical posts ("benefices") to be sold to the highest bidders and had not enforced residency requirements in parishes.

City governments also sought to restrict the growth of ecclesiastical properties and privileges and to improve religious life by bringing the clergy under the tax code and by endowing new clerical positions for well-trained preachers.

The Northern Renaissance

The works of northern humanists created a climate favorable to reform. Northern humanism was stimulated by Italian learning. The northern humanists tended to come from more diverse backgrounds and to be more devoted to religious reforms than their Italian counterparts. They were also more willing to write for lay audiences.

The growth of schools and lay education combined with the invention of cheap paper to create a mass audience for printed books. In response, Johann Gutenberg (d. 1468) invented printing with movable type in Mainz around 1450. By 1500, printing presses operated in more than 200 cities throughout Europe.

The most famous of the northern humanists was Desiderius Erasmus (1466–1536), who gained fame as an educational and religious reformer. He believed that disciplined study of the classics and the Bible was the best way to reform individuals and society. His ideal was a simple, ethical piety in imitation of Christ. To promote it, Erasmus edited the works of the Church Fathers and made a Greek edition of the New Testament (1516), which became the basis for a more accurate Latin translation (1519). Martin Luther used these works as the basis for his famous German translation.

Both Catholic and Lutheran authorities turned against Erasmus's middle-of-the-road theology. For his part, Erasmus dismissed the teaching of Luther on human sinfulness and bondage to the devil as harshly as he did the corruption of the papacy. Yet despite his alienation from both camps, Erasmus inspired Catholic and Protestant reformers alike.

The best known of early English humanists was Sir Thomas More (1478–1535), a close friend of Erasmus. More's *Utopia* (1516) depicts an imaginary society based on reason and tolerance that requires everyone to work and has rid itself of social and political injustice. Although More would remain staunchly Catholic, humanism in England, as in Germany, paved the way for the English Reformation.

Whereas in Germany, England, and France, humanism helped the Protestants, in Spain it served the Catholic Church. Here the key figure was Francisco Jiménez de Cisneros (1437–1517), the Grand Inquisitor—a position from which he was able to enforce religious orthodoxy. Jiménez founded the University of Alcalá near Madrid in 1509, printed a Greek edition of the New Testament, and translated many religious tracts that aided reform. Such scholarly projects and internal church reforms joined with the repression of Ferdinand and Isabella to keep Spain strictly Catholic.

The printing press made possible the diffusion of Renaissance learning. But no book stimulated thought more at this time than did the Bible. With Gutenberg's publication of a printed Bible in 1454, scholars gained access to a dependable, standardized text, so that Scripture could be discussed and debated as never before. [Huntington Library]

The Reformation

Martin Luther and the German Reformation to 1525

Late medieval Germany lacked the political unity to enforce "national" religious reforms. What happened on a national level in England and France occurred only piecemeal in Germany. As popular resentment of clerical immunities and ecclesiastical abuses, especially the selling of indulgences, spread among German cities, an unorganized "national" opposition to Rome formed, and by 1517 it provided a foundation for Martin Luther's reform.

Luther (1483–1546), the son of a successful Thuringian miner, had entered the Order of the Hermits of Saint Augustine in Erfurt on July 17, 1505. Ordained in 1507, he pursued a traditional course of theological study. In 1510, he journeyed to Rome, where he found justification for the criticisms of the church he had heard in Germany. In 1511, he was transferred to Wittenberg, where he earned his doctorate in theology (1512).

The Attack on Indulgences Reformation theology grew out of the failure of traditional medieval religion to provide personal or intellectual satisfaction. Luther was plagued by the disproportion between his sense of sinfulness and the perfect righteousness that medieval theology taught that God required for salvation. Traditional church teaching and the sacrament of penance were no consolation. Luther wrote that the phrase "righteousness of God" seemed to demand a perfection no human being could achieve. His insight into the meaning of "justification by faith alone" developed between 1513 and 1518. The righteousness God demands, he concluded, came not from religious works and ceremonies but was present in full measure in those who believed and trusted in the work of Jesus Christ, who alone was the perfect righteousness satisfying to God. To believe in Christ was to stand before God clothed in Christ's righteousness.

This new theology made indulgences unacceptable. An indulgence was a remission of the temporal penalty imposed by the priest on penitents as a "work of satisfaction" for their sins. According to medieval theology, after the priest had absolved penitents, God still imposed a temporal penalty, a "work of satisfaction" that the penitent could perform (for example, through prayers, fasting, almsgiving, retreats, and pilgrimages). Penitents who defaulted on such prescribed works of satisfaction would suffer in purgatory.

Indulgences were an aid to a laity made anxious by the belief in suffering in purgatory for neglected penances or unrepented sins. Originally, indulgences had been given only for going on a crusade to the Holy Land. By Luther's time, they were dispensed for small cash payments (modest sums regarded as almsgiving) and were presented to the laity as remitting not only their own future punishments, but also those of their dead relatives.

In 1517, a Jubilee indulgence, proclaimed under Pope Julius II (1503–1513) to raise funds for the rebuilding of Saint Peter's in Rome, was preached near Saxony. John Tetzel (d. 1519) was enlisted to preach the indulgence because he was a seasoned professional who knew how to stir people to action.

When on October 31, 1517, Luther posted his ninety-five theses against indulgences in Wittenberg, he protested especially against the impression created by Tetzel that indulgences released the dead from punishment in purgatory—claims he believed made salvation for sale.

Election of Charles V and the Diet of Worms

Humanists and other proponents of reform made Luther famous overnight and prompted proceedings against him. As sanctions were being prepared against Luther, Emperor Maximilian I died (January 12, 1519), which diverted attention to the contest for a new emperor.

The pope backed the French king, Francis I, but Charles I of Spain, a Habsburg, succeeded his grandfather and became Emperor Charles V (1519–1556).

During the same month in which Charles was elected emperor, Luther entered a debate in Leipzig (June 27, 1519) with John Eck (1486–1543). During this contest Luther challenged the infallibility of the pope and the inerrancy of church councils, appealing to the sovereign authority of Scripture alone. He also defended certain teachings of Jan Hus that had been condemned by the Council of Constance. In 1520, Luther signaled his new direction with the *Address to the Christian Nobility of the German Nation*, which urged the German princes to force reforms on the Roman Church and curtail its power in Germany; the *Babylonian Captivity of the Church*, which attacked the traditional seven sacraments, arguing that only two were proper, and which exalted the authority of Scripture, church councils, and secular princes over that of the pope; and the *Freedom of a Christian*, which summarized the new teaching of salvation by faith alone. Luther was excommunicated on January 3, 1521.

In April 1521, Luther presented his views before a diet of the empire in Worms, over which Charles V presided. Ordered to recant, Luther declared that to do so would be to act against Scripture, reason, and his own conscience. On May 26, 1521, he was placed under the imperial ban and became an "outlaw" to secular as well as to religious authority. Friends hid him in Wartburg Castle, where he translated the New Testament into German.

The Reformation was assisted in these early years by the emperor's war with France and the advance of the Ottoman Turks into eastern Europe. Against both adversaries, Charles V, who also remained a Spanish king with responsibilities outside the empire, needed friendly relations with the German princes. Between 1521 and 1559, Spain (the Habsburg dynasty) and France (the Valois dynasty) fought four major wars. In 1526, the Turks overran Hungary, while in western Europe the French-led League of Cognac formed against Charles for the second Habsburg-Valois war. Thus preoccupied, the emperor agreed at the German Diet of Speyer

A contemporary caricature depicts John Tetzel, the famous indulgence preacher. The last lines of the jingle read: "As soon as gold in the basin rings, right then the soul to heaven springs." It was Tetzel's preaching that spurred Luther to publish his ninety-five theses. [Courtesy Stiftung Luthergedenkstaten in Sachsen-Anhalt/Lutherhalle, Wittenberg]

in 1526 to in effect give the German princes sovereignty in religious matters and the Reformation time to put down deep roots.

The Peasants' Revolt

In its first decade, the Protestant movement suffered more from internal division than from imperial interference. By 1525, Luther had become as much an object of protest within Germany as was the pope. Original allies, sympathizers, and fellow travelers declared their independence from him.

The German peasantry had believed Luther to be an ally. Peasant leaders saw in Luther's teaching about Christian freedom and his criticism of monastic landowners a point of view close to their own, and they solicited Luther's support of their political and economic rights, including their revolutionary request for release from serfdom. But the Lutherans were not social revolutionaries. When the peasants revolted in 1524–1525, Luther urged the princes to crush their revolt without mercy.

For Luther, the freedom of the Christian was an inner release from guilt, not a right to restructure society by revolution. Had Luther supported the Peasants' Revolt, he would have not only contradicted his own belief but also ended any chance that his reform would survive.

Zwingli and the Swiss Reformation

Switzerland and France had independent reform movements, from which developed churches as lasting as the Lutheran. Switzerland was a loose confederacy of autonomous cantons. Some became Protestant, some remained Catholic, and a few compromised. The two preconditions of the Swiss Reformation were the growth of national sentiment and a desire for church reform (see Map 17-2).

The Reformation in Zurich

Ulrich Zwingli (1484–1531), the leader of the Swiss Reformation, had in 1519 become the people's priest in Zurich, from which he engineered the Swiss Reformation. Zwingli's reform guideline was simple and effective: Whatever lacked literal support in Scripture was to be neither believed nor practiced. In 1523, the city government sanctioned Zwingli's Scripture test. Thereafter, Zurich became the center of the Swiss Reformation and one of the first examples of a puritanical Protestant city.

The Marburg Colloquy

Landgrave Philip of Hesse (1504–1567) sought to unite Swiss and German Protestants in a defense pact. His efforts were spoiled, however, by disagreements between Luther and Zwingli over the nature of Christ's presence in the Eucharist. Zwingli maintained that Christ was only spiritually, not bodily, present in the bread and wine of the Eucharist. Luther insisted on Christ's spiritual and bodily presence.

Philip of Hesse brought the two Protestant leaders together in Marburg in 1529, but they could not agree. Luther considered Zwingli a dangerous fanatic. The disagreement splintered the Protestant movement theologically and politically.

Anabaptists and Radical Protestants

Many people desired a more rapid and thorough implementation of primitive Christianity and accused Luther and Zwingli of going only halfway. The most important of these radical groups were the Anabaptists, the sixteenth-century ancestors of the modern Mennonites and Amish. The Anabaptists rejected infant baptism and insisted on only adult baptism (*anabaptism* derives from the Greek word meaning "to rebaptize"), believing that it conformed to Scripture and was respectful of human freedom.

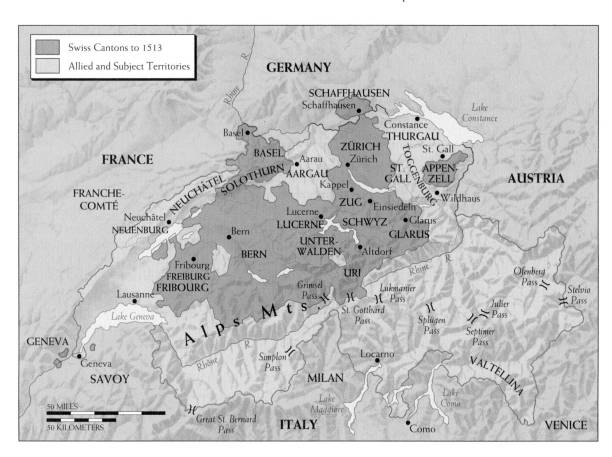

Map 17–2   The Swiss confederation.   While nominally still a part of the Holy Roman Empire, Switzerland grew from a loose defensive union of the central "forest cantons" in the thirteenth century to a fiercely independent association of regions with different languages, histories, and, finally, religions.

Anabaptists separated from society to form a more perfect community in imitation of the first Christians. The political authorities viewed such separatism as a threat to basic social bonds. In 1529, rebaptism became a capital offense throughout the Holy Roman Empire. Between 1525 and 1618, thousands were executed for rebaptizing themselves as adults.

John Calvin and the Genevan Reformation

Calvinism was the religious ideology of political resistance in France, the Netherlands, and Scotland. Believing strongly in both divine predestination and the individual's responsibility to reorder society according to God's plan, Calvinists determined to transform society according to their beliefs. In a famous study, *The Protestant Ethic and the Spirit of Capitalism* (1904), the German sociologist Max Weber argued that this combination of religious confidence and self-disciplined activism produced an ethic that stimulated and reinforced emergent capitalism, bringing Calvinism and later Puritanism into close association with the development of modern capitalist societies.

Political Revolt and Religious Reform in Geneva

Whereas in Saxony religious reform paved the way for a political revolution against the emperor, in Geneva a political revolution laid the foundation for religious change. Genevans revolted against their resident prince-bishop in the 1520s. In 1533, Bern dispatched Protestant reformers to Geneva. On May 21, 1536, the city voted to adopt the Reformation.

John Calvin (1509–1564), a reform-minded humanist and lawyer, arrived in Geneva in July 1536. Before a year had passed, Calvin had drawn up articles for the governance of the church and the people. But these measurees were perceived as going too far too fast, and in February 1538, Calvin was exiled from the city.

Calvin went to Strasbourg, where he wrote a second edition of his *Institutes of the Christian Religion*, which many consider the definitive theological statement of the Protestant faith. He also learned from the Strasbourg reformer Martin Bucer (1491–1551) how to implement the Protestant Reformation successfully.

Calvin's Geneva   In 1540, Geneva invited him to return. Within months of his arrival, new ecclesiastical ordinances provided for cooperation between the magistrates and the clergy.

Calvin and his followers were motivated by a desire to transform society. Faith, Calvin taught, conformed one's every action to God's law. The "elect" should live in a God-pleasing way, if they were truly God's elect. To realize this goal, Calvin spared no effort. The consistory became his instrument of power. It was composed of elders and pastors of the church and was presided over by one of the city's civil magistrates. It enforced the strictest moral discipline, punishing

This seventeenth-century Calvinist church in the Palatinate has no interior decoration to distract the worshipper from the Word of God. The intent was to create an atmosphere of quiet introspection and reflection on one's spiritual life and God's Word. [German National Museum, Nuremberg]

Progress of Protestant Reformation on the Continent

1517	Luther posts ninety-five theses against indulgences
1519	Charles I of Spain elected Holy Roman Emperor (as Charles V)
1519	Luther challenges infallibility of pope and inerrancy of church councils at Leipzig Debate
1521	Papal bull excommunicates Luther for heresy
1521	Diet of Worms condemns Luther
1521-1522	Luther translates the New Testament into German
1524-1525	Peasants Revolt in Germany
1529	Marburg Colloquy between Luther and Zwingli
1530	Diet of Augsburg fails to settle religious differences
1531	Formation of Protestant Schmalkaldic League
1536	Calvin arrives in Geneva
1540	Jesuits, founded by Ignatius of Loyola, recognized as order by pope
1546	Luther dies
1547	Armies of Charles V crush Schmalkaldic League
1555	Peace of Augsburg recognizes rights of Lutherans to worship as they please
1545-1563	Council of Trent institutes reforms and responds to the Reformation

moral and religious transgressions from missing church services to fornication and criticism of Calvin. After 1555, Geneva became home to thousands of exiled Protestants from France, England, and Scotland.

Political Consolidation of the Lutheran Reformation

By 1530, the Reformation was in Europe to stay. It would, however, take decades before all would recognize this. With the triumph of Lutheranism in the empire by the 1550s, Protestant movements elsewhere gained a new lease on life.

Diet of Augsburg   Charles V returned to the empire in 1530 to direct the Diet of Augsburg, a meeting of Protestants and Catholics to resolve religious divisions. The diet ordered Lutherans to revert to Catholicism. But in February 1531, the Lutherans formed the Schmalkaldic League, which achieved a stalemate with the emperor, who was again distracted by war with France and the Turks.

Expansion of the Reformation   In the 1530s, German Lutherans formed regional consistories to replace the old Catholic episcopates. Under the leadership of Philip Melanchthon (1497–1560), educational reforms provided for compulsory primary education, schools for girls, a humanist revision of the curriculum, and instruction in the new religion.

The Reformation also dug in elsewhere. In Denmark, Lutheranism became the state religion under Christian III (r. 1536–1559). In Sweden, Gustavus Vasa (r. 1523–1560), supported by a nobility greedy for church lands, confiscated church property and subjected the clergy to royal authority.

In Poland, Lutherans, Calvinists, and others found room to practice their beliefs. The absence of a central political authority made Poland a model of religious pluralism and toleration in the second half of the sixteenth century.

In 1547, imperial armies crushed the Schmalkaldic League. But the Reformation was too entrenched to be ended by force. Confronted by fierce resistance and weary of war, Charles was forced to relent.

The Peace of Augsburg in 1555 made the division of Christendom permanent. This agreement recognized in law what had already been established in practice: *cuius regio, eius religio*, meaning that the ruler of a land would determine its religion.

Calvinism was not recognized as a legal form of Christian belief by the Peace of Augsburg. Calvinists remained determined not only to secure the right to worship but to shape society according to their convictions. They led national revolutions throughout northern Europe.

The English Reformation to 1553

Late medieval England had a well-earned reputation for maintaining the rights of the crown against the pope. Humanism and anticlerical sentiment prepared the way for Protestant ideas, which sprouted in England in the early sixteenth century. It was, however, King Henry VIII (r. 1509–1547) who ensured the success of those ideas.

The King's Affair   Henry had married Catherine of Aragon (d. 1536), the aunt of Emperor Charles V. By 1527, the union had produced only one child, Mary Tudor. Henry was concerned about having only a female heir. People believed it unnatural for women to rule over men. A woman ruler meant turmoil and revolution. Henry even came to believe that his union with Catherine had been cursed by God, because Catherine had briefly been the wife of his late brother, Arthur.

By 1527, Henry decided to put Catherine aside and marry Anne Boleyn (c. 1504–1536). This he could not do in Catholic England without papal annulment of the marriage to Catherine. And therein lay a problem. In 1527, Pope Clement VII (1523–1534) was a prisoner of Charles V, Catherine's nephew. Even if this had not been the case, it would have been virtually impossible for the pope to grant an annulment. Not only had it survived for eighteen years, but it had been made possible by a papal dispensation required because Catherine had previously been the wife of Henry's brother, Arthur.

After Cardinal Wolsey (1475–1530), Lord Chancellor since 1515, failed to secure the annulment, Thomas Cranmer (1489–1556) and Thomas Cromwell (1485–1540), both of whom harbored Lutheran sympathies, became the king's closest advisers and struck a different course: Why not simply declare the king supreme in English spiritual affairs as he was in English temporal affairs? Then the king could settle his own affair.

Reformation Parliament

In 1531, the clergy recognized Henry as head of the church in England "as far as the law of Christ allows." In 1533 the "Reformation Parliament" passed the Submission of the Clergy, placing the clergy under royal jurisdiction.

In January 1533, Henry wed the pregnant Anne Boleyn. In 1534, Parliament ended payments by the English clergy and laity to Rome and gave Henry jurisdiction over high ecclesiastical appointments. The Act of Succession made Anne Boleyn's children heirs to the throne, and the Act of Supremacy declared Henry "the only supreme head in earth of the church of England."

The Protestant Reformation Under Edward VI

Despite his political break with Rome, Henry remained conservative in his religious beliefs, and Catholic doctrine remained prominent in a country seething with Protestant sentiment. The Six Articles of 1539 reaffirmed transubstantiation, denied the Eucharistic cup to the laity, declared celibate vows inviolable, provided for private masses, and ordered the continuation of auricular confession.

Edward VI (r. 1547–1553) became king when he was only ten years old. Under Edward, England fully enacted the Protestant Reformation. Henry's Six Articles and laws against heresy were repealed, and clerical marriage and communion with cup were sanctioned. An Act of Uniformity imposed Thomas Cranmer's *Book of Common Prayer* on all English churches, which were stripped of their images and altars. A forty-two-article confession of faith was adopted, setting forth a moderate Protestant doctrine.

These changes were short-lived, however. In 1553, Catherine of Aragon's daughter, Mary Tudor (d. 1558), succeeded to the throne and restored Catholic doctrine. It was not until the reign of Anne Boleyn's daughter, Elizabeth I (r. 1558–1603), that a lasting religious settlement was worked out in England.

Catholic Reform and Counter-Reformation

The Protestant Reformation did not take the medieval church completely by surprise. There were many internal criticisms and efforts at reform before there was a Counter-Reformation in reaction to Protestant successes.

Sources of Catholic Reform   Before the Reformation began, ambitious proposals had been made for church reform. But sixteenth-century popes squelched such efforts. Yet, the church was not without reformers. Many new religious orders sprang up in the sixteenth century to revive piety within the church.

Ignatius of Loyola and the Society of Jesus   The most instrumental reform group in the success of the Counter-Reformation was the Society of Jesus, the Jesuits. Organized by Ignatius of Loyola in the 1530s, it was recognized by the church in 1540. Within a century the society had more than 15,000 members, with thriving missions in India, Japan, and the Americas.

Ignatius of Loyola (1491–1556) was a heroic figure. A courtier in his youth, he began his spiritual pilgrimage in 1521 after he had been wounded in battle. During a lengthy convalescence, he read Christian classics and underwent a religious conversion. Henceforth, he would serve the church as a soldier of Christ.

After recuperating, Ignatius developed a program of religious and moral self-discipline that came to be embodied in the *Spiritual Exercises*. This contained mental and emotional exercises to teach one spiritual self-mastery.

The exercises of Ignatius were intended to teach Catholics to submit without question to church authority and spiritual direction through perfect discipline and self-control. To these were added the enthusiasm of traditional spirituality and mysticism and uncompromising loyalty to the church's cause. This potent combination helped win many Protestants back to the Catholic fold, especially in Austria and Germany.

Main Events of the English Reformation

1529	Reformation Parliament convenes
1532	Parliament passes the Submission of the Clergy, an act placing canon law and the English clergy under royal jurisdiction
1533	Henry VIII weds Anne Boleyn
1534	Act of Succession makes Anne Boleyn's children legitimate heirs to the English throne
1534	Act of Supremacy declares Henry VIII the only supreme head of the church of England
1535	Thomas More executed for opposition to Acts of Succession and Supremacy
1535	Publication of Coverdale Bible
1539	Henry VIII imposes the Six Articles, condemning Protestantism and reasserting traditional doctrine
1547	Edward VI succeeds to the throne
1549	First Act of Uniformity imposes *Book of Common Prayer* on English churches
1553–1558	Mary Tudor restores Catholic doctrine
1558–1603	Elizabeth I fashions an Anglican religious settlement

The Council of Trent (1545–1563) The success of the Reformation and the insistence of Charles V forced Pope Paul III (r. 1534–1549) to call a general council of the church, which met in 1545 in Trent in northern Italy. The council's most important reforms concerned church discipline. The selling of church offices and other religious goods was forbidden. Trent strengthened the authority of local bishops so they could discipline popular religious practice. Bishops who resided in Rome were forced to move to their seats. They had to preach regularly and conduct annual visitations. Parish priests were required to be neatly dressed, educated, celibate, and active among their parishioners. To train better priests, Trent also called for a seminary in every diocese.

Not a single doctrinal concession was made to the Protestants, however. Trent reaffirmed the traditional scholastic education of the clergy; the role of good works in salvation; the authority of tradition; the seven sacraments; transubstantiation; the withholding of the Eucharistic cup from the laity; clerical celibacy; the reality of purgatory; the veneration of saints, relics, and sacred images; and the granting of indulgences.

Rulers initially resisted Trent's reform decrees, fearing a revival of papal political power. But in time, parish life revived under the guidance of a better-trained clergy.

The Social Significance of the Reformation in Western Europe

It was a common trait of the Lutheran, Zwinglian, and Calvinist reformers to work within the framework of reigning political power. Scholars characterize them as "magisterial reformers," meaning that they succeeded by the force of the magistrate's sword. They never contemplated reform outside or against the societies of which they were members. Some scholars believe their reforms actually encouraged acceptance of the sociopolitical status quo.

The Reformation and the Changing Role of Women

The Protestant reformers took a positive stand on clerical marriage and opposed monasticism and the celibate life. From this position they opposed the popular antiwoman and antimarriage literature of the Middle Ages. They praised woman in her own right, but especially in her biblical vocation as mother and housewife. Although from a modern perspective, women remained subject to men, new marriage laws gave them greater security and protection.

Relief of sexual frustration and a remedy of fornication were prominent in Protestant arguments for marriage. But the reformers also viewed their wives as indispensable companions in their work. In opposition to the celibate ideal of the Middle Ages, Protestants stressed the sacredness of home and family. This attitude contributed to a more respectful and sharing relationship between husbands and wives and between parents and children.

The ideal of the companionate marriage—that is, of husband and wife as co-workers in a God-ordained family, sharing authority within the household—led to an expansion of the grounds for divorce in Protestant cities. Women now had an equal right with men to divorce and remarry in good conscience—unlike in Catholicism, where only a separation, not divorce and remarriage, was permitted.

Protestant doctrines were as attractive to women as they were to men. Renegade nuns wrote exposés declaring that the nunnery was no special woman's place at all and that supervisory male clergy made their lives as unpleasant as any abusive husband. Some cloistered noblewomen, however, believed the cloister provided them a more independent way of life than they would have known in the secular world.

Because they wanted women to become pious housewives, Protestants encouraged the education of girls to literacy in the vernacular, expecting them to model their lives on the Bible. However, women found biblical passages that suggested they were equal to men in the presence of God. Education also gave some women a role as authors in the Reformation. These may seem like small advances, but they were significant steps toward the emancipation of women.

Family Life in Early Modern Europe

Changes in the timing and duration of marriage, family size, and infant and child care suggest that family life was under social and economic pressure in the sixteenth and seventeenth centuries. The Reformation was only one factor in these changes.

Family life conspires with basic instincts to establish characteristic patterns of behavior, reinforcing natural feelings and building expectations among family members. Time, place, and culture, however, are important. A person raised in a twelfth-century family would be different from one raised in a twentieth-century family, and growing up in Europe is not the same as growing up in China. The differences lie in how different cultures and religions infuse family life with values and influence behavior.

Later Marriages

Between 1500 and 1800, men and women in western Europe married at later ages than they had in previous centuries. Men tended to be in their mid- to late twenties and women in their early to mid-twenties. Late marriage in the West reflected the difficulty couples had supporting themselves. The difficulty arose because of the population growth that occurred during

A German Mother Advises Her Fifteen-Year-Old Son, Who Is Away from Home at School for the First Time (1578)

Although only fourteen miles away from his Nuremberg home, Friedrich Behaim was fifteen and on his own for the first time at the Altdorf Academy, where he would spend the next three years of his life. As there was daily traffic back and forth, mother and son could correspond regularly and Frau Behaim could give her son needed advice and articles of clothing.

What is the mother most concerned about? What do her concerns suggest about life in the sixteenth century? Does she appear to be more strict and demanding of her son than a modern mother would be? Is the son clueless, or adroitly manipulating the mother?

Dear son Friederich . . . You write that you have been unable to get by on the money [I gave you]. I will let it pass this quarter, but see that you manage on it in the future. Enclosed is another gulden.

As for your clothes, I do not have Martin [a servant] here with me now (we are quarreling), but he has begun to work on your clothes. He has made stockings for your leather holiday trousers, which I am sending you with this letter. Since your everyday trousers are so bad, wear these for now until a new pair of woolen ones can be made and sent to you, which I will do as soon as I can. Send me your old trousers in the sack I sent you the pitcher in. As for the smock that you think should be lined [for the winter], I worry that the skirt may be too short and will not keep you warm. You can certainly wear it for another summer if it is not too small for you then and the weather not too warm. Just keep it clean and brushed. I will have a new coat made for you at the earliest.

You also write about [unhappiness with] your food. You must be patient for a while. You may not at the outset lodge a complaint against [your master], and especially while you are sitting at his table. [Only] he may speak out who eats his food and is also an authority in the house. So it would be better if the Inspector, who is there for a reason, reports it to him.

Will you once tell me who your table companions are! Also, let me know by All Saints what you have spent on beer and what you owe the tailor, so I may know how much to send you for the quarter.

As for your [sore] throat, there is nothing you can take for it but warm mead. Gargle often with it and keep your head warm. Put a muffler or scarf around your neck and wear your night coat when you are in your room. Avoid cold drinks and sit perhaps for a while by the fire. And do not forget to be bled on time [people then bled themselves once or twice a year as a health measure] . . . When you need paper, let me know . . .

I am sending some cleaning flakes for your leather pants. After you have worn them three times, put some on the knees . . . I will have your old coat patched and send it to you with the next carter [so that you can wear it] until the new one is made. Send me the two sacks with the next carter. You will find the [aforementioned] gulden in the trouser foot tied with a string.

Nothing more for now. God bless. 14 October, 1578.

Mrs. Paul Behaim

From *Three Behaim Boys: Growing Up in Early Modern Germany: A Chronicle of Their Lives,* ed. and trans. by Steven Ozment, pp. 107–108. Copyright © 1990 Yale University Press. Reprinted by permission of Yale University Press.

---

the late fifteenth and early sixteenth centuries, when western Europe recovered much of the population loss incurred during the Great Plague. Larger families meant a greater division of resources. In Germanic and Scandinavian countries, the custom of a fair sharing of inheritance among all male children worked to delay marriages, for divided inheritances often meant small incomes for the recipients. The average couple took longer to prepare themselves materially for marriage. In the sixteenth century, one in five women never married.

A later marriage meant a shorter marriage, since couples who married in their thirties would spend less time together than couples who married in their twenties. Such marriages also contributed to more frequent remarriage for men because women who bore children for the first time at advanced ages had high mortality rates. Moreover, delayed marriage increased premarital sex and raised the number of illegitimate children.

Arranged Marriages

Marriage tended to be "arranged" in the sense that the parents discussed the terms of the marriage before the bride and bridegroom became party to the discussions. But by the fifteenth century, the two involved people often knew each other in advance and even had had a prior relationship. Also, emotional feeling for one another was increasingly respected by parents, and children had a legal right to resist an unwanted marriage. A forced marriage was invalid, and parents understood that the best marriage was one desired by both parties and their families.

Family Size

The western European family was conjugal, or nuclear; it consisted of a father, a mother, and children who survived into adulthood. This nuclear family lived with a larger household of in-laws, servants, laborers, and boarders. An estimated one-third of children died by age five, and one-half by their teens.

Birth Control

Artificial birth control has existed since antiquity. But early birth control measures were not very effective, and for both historical and moral reasons the church opposed them.

Wet Nursing

The church allied with the physicians of early modern Europe in condemning women who hired nurses to suckle their newborn children, sometimes for as long as a year and a half. Wet nurses were women who had recently had a baby or were suckling a child of their own, and who, for a fee, agreed also to suckle another child. The practice exposed infants to a strange and shared milk supply from women who were usually not as healthy as the infants' own mothers and who often lived under less sanitary conditions. But nursing an infant was a chore some upper-class women found distasteful, and their husbands also preferred that they not do it. Because the church forbade sexual intercourse while a women was lactating, and sexual intercourse was believed to spoil a woman's milk, a nursing wife often became a reluctant lover. In addition, nursing had a contraceptive effect (about 75 percent effective). Some women prolonged nursing their children to delay a new pregnancy, and some husbands cooperated in this form of family planning. For other husbands, however, especially noblemen and royalty who desired more male heirs, nursing seemed to rob them of offspring and jeopardize the patrimony; hence, their support of wet nursing.

Loving Families?

The traditional western European family may seem cold and unloving. When children were between the ages of eight and thirteen, parents routinely sent them out of their homes into apprenticeships, off to school, or into employment. In addition, the emotional ties between spouses seem to have been as tenuous as those between parents and children. Widowers and widows often married again within a few months of their spouses' deaths, and marriages with extreme disparity in age between partners also suggest limited affection.

In response to modern-day criticism, an early modern parent might have asked, "What greater love can parents have for their children than to equip them to make their way in the world?" An apprenticed child was self-supporting, and hence had a future. Considering primitive living conditions, contemporaries could also appreciate the utilitarian and humane side of marriage and understand when widowers and widows quickly married again. Marriages with extreme disparity in age were no more the norm in early modern Europe than wet nursing and received as much criticism and ridicule.

The Wars of Religion

After the Council of Trent adjourned in 1563, Catholics began a Jesuit-led counteroffensive against Protestants. At the time of John Calvin's death in 1564, Geneva had become a refuge for Europe's persecuted Protestants and a school for Protestant resistance.

Genevan Calvinism and the reformed Catholicism of the Council of Trent were dogmatic, aggressive, and irreconcilable church systems. Calvinists may have looked like "new papists" to critics when they dominated cities like Geneva, but when, as minorities, they found their civil and religious rights denied in the empire and elsewhere, they became true firebrands and revolutionaries.

Calvinism adopted a presbyterian organization that magnified regional and local religious authority. By contrast, the Counter-Reformation sponsored a centralized episcopal church system, hierarchically arranged from pope to parish priest and stressing absolute obedience to the person at the top. Calvinism proved attractive to proponents of political decentralization who opposed totalitarian rulers, whereas Catholicism remained congenial to proponents of absolute monarchy.

The wars of religion were both internal national conflicts and international wars. Catholic and Protestant subjects struggled to control France, the Netherlands, and England. The Catholic governments of France and Spain sent armies against Protestant regimes in England and the Netherlands. The Thirty Years' War (1618–1648) drew every major European nation into its net.

French Wars of Religion (1562–1598)

When Henry II (r. 1547–1559) died accidentally during a tournament in 1559, his sickly fifteen-year-old son, Francis II (d. 1560), came to the throne under the regency of the queen mother, Catherine de Médicis (1519–1589). With the monarchy weakened, three powerful families competed to control France: the Bourbons, whose power lay in the south and west; the Montmorency-Châtillons, who controlled the center of France; and the Guises, who were dominant in eastern France. The Guises were the strongest, and were militant, ultra-Catholics. The Bourbon and Montmorency-Châtillon families, in contrast, developed strong Huguenot sympathies, largely for political reasons. (French Protestants were called Huguenots after Besançon Hughes, the leader of Geneva's political revolt in the late 1520s.) The Bourbon Louis I, prince of Condé (d. 1569), and the Montmorency-Châtillon Admiral Gaspard de Coligny (1519–1572) became the political leaders of the French Protestant resistance.

In 1561, Huguenots made up only about one-fifteenth of the population, but held important geographic areas and represented the more powerful segments of French society. Over two-fifths of the French aristocracy became Huguenots. Many apparently hoped to establish within France territorial sovereignty akin to that secured within the Holy Roman Empire by the Peace of Augsburg (1555). Calvinism thus indirectly served the forces of political decentralization.

Catherine de Médicis and the Guises Following Francis II's death in 1560, Catherine de Médicis continued as regent for her second son, Charles IX (r. 1560–1574). Fearing the Guises, Catherine sought allies among the Protestants. Early in 1562, she granted Protestants freedom to worship publicly outside towns—although only privately within them—and to hold church assemblies. In March of the same year, this royal toleration ended when the duke of Guise surprised a Protestant congregation worshipping illegally and massacred several score—an event that marked the beginning of the French wars of religion. Caught between fanatical Huguenot and Guise extremes, Queen Catherine sought to play one side against the other. She wanted a Catholic France but not a Guise-dominated monarchy.

On August 22, 1572, four days after the Huguenot Henry of Navarre had married Charles IX's sister, the Huguenot leader Coligny was wounded by an assassin's bullet. Catherine had apparently been a part of this Guise plot to eliminate Coligny. After its failure, she convinced Charles that a Huguenot coup was afoot, and that only the execution of Protestant leaders could save the crown. On the eve of Saint Bartholomew's Day, August 24, 1572, Coligny and 3,000 Huguenots were butchered in Paris. Within three days, an estimated 20,000 Huguenots were executed throughout France.

This event changed the nature of the struggle between Protestants and Catholics both within and beyond the borders of France. Henceforth, in Protestant eyes, it became an international struggle for survival against an adversary whose cruelty justified any means of resistance.

Rise to Power of Henry of Navarre Henry III (r. 1574–1589), who was Henry II's third son and the last Valois king, found the monarchy wedged between a radical Catholic League, formed in 1576 by Henry of Guise, and

vengeful Huguenots. Henry III sought to steer a middle course and received support from neutral Catholics and Huguenots who put the political survival of France above its religious unity. Such *politiques*, as they were called, were prepared to compromise to save the nation.

In the mid–1580s, the Catholic League, supported by the Spanish, became dominant in Paris. Henry III had to flee. Forced by his weakened position into guerrilla tactics, the king had both the duke and the cardinal of Guise assassinated. The Catholic League reacted with fury, and the king was forced into an alliance with his Protestant cousin and heir, Henry of Navarre, in April 1589.

As the two Henrys prepared to attack Paris, however, a fanatic murdered Henry III. Thereupon the Bourbon Huguenot Henry of Navarre became Henry IV of France (r. 1589–1610). Henry IV came to the throne as a *politique*, prepared to place political peace above absolute religious unity. He believed that a royal policy of tolerant Catholicism would achieve such peace. On July 25, 1593, he publicly embraced the traditional and majority religion of his country. "Paris is worth a Mass," he is reported to have said.

The Edict of Nantes Five years later, on April 13, 1598, Henry IV's famous Edict of Nantes proclaimed a formal religious settlement. The Edict of Nantes recognized minority religious rights within what was to remain an officially Catholic country. This religious truce granted the Huguenots, who numbered over one million, freedom of public worship, the right of assembly, admission to public offices and universities, and permission to maintain fortified towns. Most of the new freedoms, however, were to be exercised within their own localities. The edict transformed a hot war between irreconcilable enemies into a cold war. To its critics, it created a state within a state.

A Catholic fanatic assassinated Henry IV in May 1610. His political and economic policies laid the foundations for the transformation of France into the absolutist state it became in the seventeenth century. Ironically, in pursuit of the political and religious unity that had escaped Henry IV, his grandson Louis XIV (r. 1643–1715) would later revoke the Edict of Nantes in 1685 (see Chapter 21).

Imperial Spain and the Reign of Philip II (1556–1598)

Until the English defeated his mighty Armada in 1588, no one person stood larger in the second half of the sixteenth century than Philip II of Spain. During the first half of his reign, attention focused on Turkish expansion. On October 7, 1571, a Holy League of Spain, Venice, and the pope defeated the Turks at Lepanto in the largest naval battle of the sixteenth century.

Map 17-3 The Netherlands during the Reformation.   The northern provinces of the Netherlands—the United Provinces—were mostly Protestant in the second half of the sixteenth century. The southern provinces—the Spanish Netherlands—made peace with Spain and remained largely Catholic.

Revolt in the Netherlands   The spectacular Spanish military success in southern Europe was not repeated in northern Europe. The resistance of the Netherlands especially proved the undoing of Spanish dreams of world empire.

The Netherlands were the richest area in Europe (see Map 17-3). Its merchant towns were, however, Europe's most independent; many were also Calvinist strongholds. A stubborn opposition to the Spanish overlords formed under William of Nassau, the Prince of Orange (r. 1533–1584), who placed the Netherlands' political autonomy and well-being above religious creeds.

The year 1564 saw the first fusion of political and religious opposition to Spanish rule, the result of Philip II's insistence that the decrees of the Council of Trent be enforced throughout the Netherlands. A national covenant was drawn up to resist the decrees of Trent and the Inquisition.

Philip dispatched the duke of Alba (1508–1582) to suppress the revolt. A special tribunal, known among the Netherlanders as the Council of Blood, reigned over the land. Several thousand suspected heretics were executed. William of Orange now emerged as the leader of a broad movement for the Netherlands' independence from Spain.

After a decade of persecution and warfare, the ten largely Catholic southern provinces (roughly modern Belgium) came together in 1576 with the seven largely Protestant northern provinces (roughly the modern Netherlands) in opposition to Spain. This union declared internal regional sovereignty in matters of religion.

After more fighting, in January 1579 the southern provinces made peace with Spain. The northern provinces formed the Union of Utrecht. Spanish preoccupation with France and England in the 1580s permitted the northern provinces to drive out all Spanish soldiers by 1593. In 1596, France and England recognized the independence of these provinces. In 1609, the Twelve Years' Truce with Spain gave the northern provinces their virtual independence. Full recognition came in the Peace of Westphalia in 1648.

England and Spain (1558–1603)

Elizabeth I   Elizabeth I (r. 1558–1603), the daughter of Henry VIII and Anne Boleyn, was perhaps the most astute politician of the sixteenth century. She guided a religious settlement through Parliament that prevented England from being torn asunder by religious differences in the sixteenth century, as the Continent was.

Catholic extremists hoped to replace Elizabeth with the Catholic Mary Stuart, Queen of Scots. But Elizabeth acted swiftly against Catholic assassination plots and rarely let emotion override her political instincts.

Elizabeth dealt cautiously with the Puritans, Protestants who sought to "purify" the national church of every vestige of "popery" and to make its Protestant doctrine more precise. The Puritans had two special grievances: (1) the retention of Catholic ceremony and vestments within the Church of England, and (2) the continuation of the episcopal system of church governance.

Sixteenth-century Puritans worked through Parliament to create an alternative national church of semiautonomous congregations governed by representative presbyteries (hence, Presbyterians), following the model of Calvin and Geneva. The more extreme Puritans wanted every congregation to be autonomous. They came to be known as Congregationalists. Elizabeth refused to tolerate this group.

Deterioration of Relations with Spain   Events led inexorably to war between England and Spain, despite the desires of both Philip II and Elizabeth to avoid it. Following Spain's victory at Lepanto in 1571, England signed a defense pact with France. Also in the 1570s, Elizabeth's famous seamen, John Hawkins (1532–1595) and Sir Francis Drake (?1545–1596), began to prey on Spanish shipping in the Americas. In 1585, Elizabeth committed English sol-

diers to the Netherlands. These events made a tinderbox of English-Spanish relations. The spark that finally touched it off was Elizabeth's reluctant execution of Mary, Queen of Scots (1542–1587) on February 18, 1587, for complicity in a plot to assassinate Elizabeth. Philip II ordered his Armada to make ready.

On May 30, 1588, a mighty fleet of 130 ships set sail for England. But the swifter English and Netherlands ships, assisted by an "English wind," dispersed the waiting Spanish fleet, over one-third of which never returned to Spain. The Armada's defeat gave heart to Protestant resistance everywhere. Spain never fully recovered from it. The French soon dominated the Continent, while the Dutch and the English whittled away Spain's overseas empire.

Elizabeth died on March 23, 1603, leaving behind her a strong nation poised to expand into a global empire.

The Thirty Years' War (1618–1648)

The Thirty Years' War in the Holy Roman Empire was the last and most destructive of the wars of religion. What made the Thirty Years' War so devastating was the hatred of the various sides and their determination to sacrifice all for their religious beliefs. As the conflicts multiplied, every major European land became involved. When the hostilities ended in 1648, the peace terms shaped much of the map of northern Europe as we know it today.

Fragmented Germany   During the second half of the sixteenth century, Germany was an almost ungovernable land of 360 autonomous political entities. Each levied its own tolls and tariffs and coined its own money, practices that made land travel and trade between the regions difficult. Many of these little "states" also had great power pretensions. Germany was not a unified nation like Spain, England, or even strife-torn France.

Religious Division   Religious conflict accentuated the political divisions (see Map 17–4). The Holy Roman Empire was about equally divided between Catholics and Protestants. There was also religious strife between liberal and conservative Lutherans and between Lutherans and Calvinists (see Map 17-5).

Unrecognized as a legal religion by the Peace of Augsburg (1555), Calvinism established a strong foothold within the empire when Elector Frederick III (r. 1559–1576) made it the official religion within the Palatinate in 1559.

If the Calvinists were active within the Holy Roman Empire, so were the Jesuits. Catholic Bavaria, supported by Spain, became for the Counter-Reformation what the Palatinate was for Protestantism. From Bavaria, the Jesuits launched missions throughout the empire. In 1609, Maximilian, duke of Bavaria

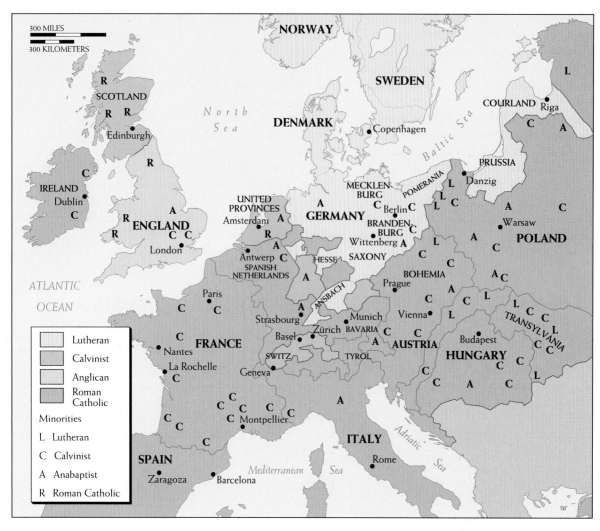

Map 17–4 Religious division about 1600. By 1600 few could expect Christians to return to a uniform religious allegiance. In Spain and southern Italy, Catholicism remained relatively unchallenged, but note the existence elsewhere of large religious minorities, both Catholic and Protestant.

(1573–1651), organized a Catholic League to counter a new Protestant alliance that had been formed by the Calvinist Elector Palatine, Frederick IV (r. 1583–1610). When the league fielded a great army, the stage was set for the Thirty Years' War, the worst European catastrophe since the Black Death of the fourteenth century.

The Treaty of Westphalia   In 1648, all hostilities within the Holy Roman Empire were ended by the Treaty of Westphalia. Rulers were again permitted to determine the religion of their lands. The treaty also gave the Calvinists their long-sought legal recognition. The independence of the Swiss Confederacy and the United Provinces of Holland also became law.

The Treaty of Westphalia perpetuated German division and political weakness into the modern period. Only two German states attained any international significance during the seventeenth century: Austria and Brandenburg-Prussia. The petty regionalism within the empire also reflected the drift of larger European politics. During the seventeenth century, distinctive nation-states, each with its own identity, established the competitive nationalism of the modern world.

Superstition and Enlightenment: The Battle Within

Religious reform and warfare moved intellectuals to rethink human nature and society. One side of that reconsideration was dark and cynical, perhaps because the peak years of religious warfare had also been those of the great European

Map 17–5 The Holy Roman Empire about 1618. On the eve of the Thirty Years' War the Empire was politically and religiously fragmented, as this somewhat simplified map reveals. Lutherans dominated the north and Catholics the south, while Calvinists controlled the United Provinces and the Palatinate and also had an important presence in Switzerland and Brandenburg.

witch hunts. Another side, however, was skeptical and constructive, reflecting the growing scientific movement of the years between 1500 and 1700.

Witch Hunts and Panic

Nowhere is the dark side of the period better seen than in the witch hunts and panics that erupted in almost every western land. Between 1400 and 1700, courts sentenced up to 100,000 people to death for witchcraft.

Eighty percent of the victims were women, most single and between forty-five and sixty years of age. This has suggested to some that misogyny fueled the witch hunts. Occurring at a time when women threatened to break out from under male control, witch hunts, it is argued, were simply woman hunts.

Some also argue that the Reformation was responsible for the witch panics. Having weakened the traditional religious protections against demons and the Devil, while still portraying them as powerful, the Reformation is said to have forced people to protect themselves by executing perceived witches.

End of the Witch Hunts   Many factors helped end the witch hunts. The emergence of a new, more scientific world-view made it difficult to believe in the powers of witches. Witch hunts also tended to get out of hand. Accused witches sometimes implicated important townspeople and even the judges. At this point the trials threatened anarchy.

Although Protestants, like Catholics, hunted witches, the Reformation may also have put the Devil in a more manageable perspective. Ultimately God was the only significant spiritual force, and the Devil became less fearsome.

Writers and Philosophers

By the end of the sixteenth century, many could no longer embrace either old Catholic or new Protestant absolutes. Intellectually as well as politically, the seventeenth century would be a period of transition.

William Shakespeare   William Shakespeare (1564–1616), the greatest playwright in the English language, took the commercialism and the bawdy pleasures of the Elizabethan Age in stride and with amusement. In politics and religion, he was not inclined to offend his queen. By modern standards he was a conservative, accepting the social rankings and the power structure of his day and demonstrating unquestioned patriotism.

Shakespeare was a playwright, actor, and part owner of a theater. His work brought together in an original synthesis the best past and current achievements in the dramatic arts. He mastered the psychology of human motivation and passion and had unique psychological penetration.

Shakespeare wrote histories, comedies, and tragedies. In his lifetime and ever since, he has been immensely popular. As Ben Jonson (1572–1637), a contemporary dramatist put it: "He was not of an age, but for all time."

Thomas Hobbes   Thomas Hobbes (1588–1679) was the most original political philosopher of the seventeenth century. Although he never broke with the Church of England, he came to share basic Calvinist beliefs, especially the low view of human nature and the ideal of a commonwealth based on a covenant, both of which find expression in his political philosophy.

Hobbes was driven to the vocation of political philosophy by the English Civil War (see Chapter 21). In 1651, his *Leviathan* appeared. Its subject was the political consequences of human passions, and its originality lay in (1) its making natural law, rather than common law (i.e., custom or precedent), the basis of all positive law, and (2) its defense of a representative theory of absolute authority against the theory of the divine right of kings. Hobbes maintained that statute law found its justification only as an expression of the law of nature and that rulers derived their authority from the consent of the people.

The key to Hobbes's political philosophy is a brilliant myth of the original state of humankind. According to this myth, human beings in the natural state are generally inclined to a "perpetual and restless desire of power after power that ceases only in death."[1] As all people desire—and in the state of nature have a natural right to—everything, their equality breeds enmity, competition, and diffidence, and the desire for glory begets perpetual quarreling—"a war of every man against every man."[2]

Whereas earlier and later philosophers saw the original human state as a paradise from which humankind had fallen, Hobbes saw it as a corruption from which only society had delivered people. Contrary to the views of Aristotle and of Christian thinkers like Thomas Aquinas, Hobbes saw human beings not as sociable, political animals, but as self-centered beasts, laws unto themselves, utterly without a master unless one is imposed by force.

According to Hobbes, people escape the impossible state of nature only by entering a social contract that creates a commonwealth tightly ruled by law and order. The social contract obliges every person, for the sake of peace and self-defense, to agree to set aside personal rights to all things. We should impose restrictions on the liberty of others only to the degree that we would allow others to restrict our own.

Because words and promises are insufficient to guarantee this state, the social contract also establishes the coercive force necessary to compel compliance with the covenant. Hobbes believed that the dangers of anarchy were far greater than those of tyranny, and he conceived of the ruler's power as absolute and unlimited. There is no room in Hobbes's political philosophy for political protest in the name of individual conscience, nor for resistance to legitimate authority by private individuals.

John Locke   Locke (1632–1704) was the most influential political thinker of the seventeenth century. His political philosophy came to be embodied in the so-called Glorious Revolution of 1688–1689 (Chapter 21). His political writings were a major source of the later Enlightenment criticism of absolutism, and they gave inspiration to both the American and French Revolutions.

Locke's two most famous works are the *Essay Concerning Human Understanding* (1690) (discussed in Chapter 24) and *Two Treatises of Government* (1690). Locke wrote *Two Treatises of Government* against the argument that rulers were absolute in their power. According to Locke, people enter social contracts, empowering legislatures and monarchs to "umpire" their disputes, precisely to preserve their natural rights, and not to give rulers an absolute power over them.

[1]*Leviathan* Parts I and II, ed. by H. W. Schneider (Indianapolis: Bobbs-Merrill, 1958), p. 86.
[2]Ibid., p. 106.

"Whenever that end [namely, the preservation of life, liberty, and property for which power is given to rulers by a commonwealth] is manifestly neglected or opposed, the trust must necessarily be forfeited and the power devolved into the hands of those that gave it, who may place it anew where they think best for their safety and security."[3] From Locke's point of view, absolute monarchy was "inconsistent" with civil society and could be "no form of civil government at all."[4]

Locke's main differences with Hobbes stemmed from the latter's views on the state of nature. Locke believed that the natural human state was one of perfect freedom and equality in which the natural rights of life, liberty, and property were enjoyed, in unregulated fashion, by all. The only thing lacking was a single authority to adjudicate disputes. Contrary to the view of Hobbes, human beings in their natural state were not creatures of monomaniacal passion, but were possessed of extreme goodwill and rationality. They did not surrender their natural rights unconditionally when they entered the social contract; rather, they established a means whereby these rights could be better preserved. The warfare that Hobbes believed characterized the state of nature emerged for Locke only when rulers failed in their responsibility to preserve the freedoms of the state of nature and attempted to enslave people by absolute rule, that is, to remove them from their "natural" condition. Only then were the peace, goodwill, mutual assistance, and preservation, in which human beings naturally live and socially ought to live, undermined, and a state of war was created.

IN WORLD PERSPECTIVE

The Renaissance and Reformation

During the Renaissance, western Europe rediscovered its classical cultural heritage, from which it had been separated for almost eight centuries. No previous world civilization had experienced such alienation from its cultural past. The west owed the recovery of its heritage to the work of Byzantine and Islamic scholars. During the Renaissance, western European lands bound up the wounds of internal warfare and established permanent centralized states and regional governments. Even the great population losses of the fourteenth century were largely recovered by 1500. In the late fifteenth and sixteenth centuries, Europeans sailed far from their own shores, reaching Africa, southern and eastern Asia, and the new world of the Americas. From Japan to Peru, they now directly confronted for the first time the civilizations of the world.

[3]*The Second Treatise of Government*, ed. by T. P. Peardon (Indianapolis: Bobbs-Merrill, 1952), chap. 2, sects. 4–6, pp. 4–6.
[4]Ibid.

Western history between 1500 and 1650 was also powerfully shaped by an unprecedented schism in Christianity, as Protestant groups broke ranks with Rome. The religious divisions contributed to new national and international warfare, which by the seventeenth century had devastated the Holy Roman Empire on a scale unseen since the Black Death.

The other world civilizations moved less dynamically during these centuries, maintaining greater social and political unity and exhibiting a greater tolerance of religious differences. Under Mongol rule (1279–1368), China recognized all indigenous religions as well as Islam and Eastern Christianity. No crises on the scale of those that rocked the west struck China, although plagues between 1586 and 1589 and between 1639 to 1644 killed between a quarter and a third of the inhabitants in populous regions. China moved steadily from Mongol to Ming (1368–1644) to Ching (1644–1911) rule without any major social and political upheavals. Compared to the west, its society was socially stable and its rulers in sure, if despotic, control. While the west also had highly centralized and authoritarian governments between 1350 and 1650, the interests of citizens and subjects were arguably contested more vigorously and accommodated more successfully. That was particularly true in regional and urban governments, where parliaments, estates general, and city councils represented the interests of powerful noblemen, patricians, and well-to-do burghers. But lesser political bodies, too, representing the rights of the middling and lower classes, also had recognized platforms for the expression of their grievances.

Although parallels may be drawn between the court culture of the Forbidden Palace in Peking and that of King Louis XIV in seventeenth-century France, the Chinese government and its official religious philosophy of Confucianism remained more unified and patriarchal than their counterparts in the west. In China, there was never the same degree of political dissent and readiness to fragment society in the name of religion that existed in western societies, even during the west's "Age of Absolutism." On the other hand, the Chinese readily tolerated other religions, as their warm embrace of Jesuit missionaries attests. There is no similar western demonstration of tolerance for Asian religious philosophy.

Voyages of exploration also set forth from Ming China, especially between 1405 and 1433, reaching India, the Arabian Gulf, and East Africa. These voyages did not, however, prove to be commercially profitable as those of the west would be, nor did they spark any notable commercial development in China. It is an open question whether this was because the Chinese were less greedy, curious, or belligerent than the Portuguese and Spanish.

Like the west in the later Middle Ages, Japan experienced its own political and social breakdown after 1467, when the *bakufu* government began to collapse. Japan's old manorial society progressively fell apart, and a new military class of vassalized foot soldiers, armed with spears and muskets, replaced the mounted samurai as the new military force. In 1590, Hideyoshi (r. 1536–1598) disarmed the peasantry and froze the social classes, thereby laying the foundation for a new social and political order in Japan. Building on this achievement, Tokugawa rule (1600–1850) managed to stabilize and centralize the government by 1650. Much as western kings had to "domesticate" their powerful noblemen to succeed, Japanese rulers learned to integrate the many regional daimyo lords into government. Like Louis XIV, Tokugawa shōguns required these lords to live for long periods at court, where their wives and children also remained. As in most western countries, the shōguns of Japan thus avoided both fragmented and absolutist government.

Like the Chinese, the Japanese were also admirers of the Jesuits, who arrived in Japan with the Portuguese in 1543. The admiration was mutual, leading to 300,000 Christian converts by 1600. As in China, the Jesuits treated native religion as a handmaiden and prelude to superior Christian teaching. But the tolerance of Christianity did not last as long in Japan as in China. Christianity was banned in the late sixteenth century as part of Hideyoshi's internal unification program. With the ascent of more-tolerant Confucianism over Buddhism among the Japanese ruling classes, Christianity and western culture would again be welcomed in the nineteenth century.

During the age of Reformation in the west, absolutist Islamic military regimes formed in the Ottoman Empire, among the Safavids in Iran, and among the Mughals in India. In all three cultures religion became tightly integrated into government, so that they never knew the divisiveness and political challenge periodically prompted in the west by Christianity. In opposition to the expansive Ottomans, Shah Abbas I (r. 1588–1629) allied with the Europeans and welcomed Dutch and English traders. Embracing Shi'ite religion and the Persian language (the rest of the Islamic world was mostly Sunni and spoke Arabic or different regional languages), Iran progressively isolated itself. Unlike the west, the Timurid Empire of the Indian Mughals, particularly under Akbar the Great (r. 1556–1605), and extending into the late seventeenth century, encouraged religious toleration even to the point of holding discussions among different faiths at the royal court. Like China and Japan, India too was prepared to live with and learn from the west.

Review Questions

1. What were the main problems of the church that contributed to the Protestant Reformation? Why was the church unable to suppress dissent as it had earlier?

2. How did the theologies of Luther, Zwingli, and Calvin differ? Were their differences only religious, or did they have harmful political consequences for the Reformation as well?

3. Why did the Reformation begin in Germany and not in France, Italy, England, or Spain?

4. What was the Catholic reformation? Did the Council of Trent alter the character of traditional Catholicism?

5. Why did Henry VIII break with the Catholic Church? Was the "new" religion he established really Protestant?

6. Were the wars of religion really over religion?

7. Henry of Navarre (later Henry IV of France), Elizabeth I, and William of Orange have been called *politiques*. What does that term mean, and how might it apply to each?

8. Why was England more successful than other lands in resolving its internal political and religious divisions peacefully during the sixteenth and seventeenth centuries?

9. "The Thirty Years' War is the outstanding example in European history of meaningless conflict." Evaluate this statement and provide specific reasons.

Documents CD-ROM

1. Christopher Columbus: The Letters of Columbus to Ferdinand and Isabel

2. Erasmus: Julius II Excluded

3. Martin Luther: "Ninety-Five Theses or Disputation on the Power and Efficacy of Indulgences"

4. Luther vs. Erasmus: A Reformer's Attack on Free Will

5. John Calvin and the Elect: The Cool Logic of Salvation

18 AFRICA (CA. 1000–1800)

CHAPTER TOPICS

In this chapter we explore, region by region, some salient developments in Africa from 1000 to 1800. While the Atlantic slave trade is treated in Chapter 19, its importance must be kept in mind as we review the period's other developments. We begin with Africa above the equator, where the influence of Islam increased and where substantial empires and kingdoms developed and flourished. Then we discuss west, east, central, and southern Africa and the effects of first Arab-Islamic and then European influence in both regions.

North Africa and Egypt

In politics, this period witnessed the influential dynasties of the Fatimids (909–969 in Tunisia; 969–1171 in Egypt), the Almoravids (1056–1147 in Senegal and the western Sudan; 1062–1118 in Marrakesh and western North Africa; 1086–1147 in Spain), the Almohads (1130–1269 in western North Africa; 1145–1212 in Spain), the Ayyubids (1169–1250 in Egypt), the Mamluks (1250–1517 in Egypt and the eastern Mediterranean); and the Ottomans (from the fourteenth century) across

most of mediterranean Africa. In general, a feisty regionalism characterized states, city-states, and tribal groups north of the Sahara and along the lower Nile, especially vis-à-vis external power centers, such as Baghdad and Spain. No single power controlled them for long. Regionalism persisted even after 1500, when most of North Africa came under the influence—and often direct control—of the Ottoman Empire.

By 1800, the nominally Ottoman domains from Egypt to Algeria were effectively independent principalities. In Egypt, the Ottomans had established direct rule after their defeat of the Mamluks in 1517, but by the seventeenth and eighteenth centuries, power had already passed to Egyptian governors descended from the former ruling Mamluks. The Mediterranean coastlands between Egypt and Morocco were officially Ottoman provinces, or regencies, whether under local governors or Ottoman deputies. By the eighteenth century, however, Algiers, Tripoli (in modern Libya), and Tunisia were virtually independent of the Ottomans.

Morocco was the only North African sultanate to remain fully independent after 1700. Its most important dynasty was that of the Sa'dis (1554–1659).

The Djinguereber mosque in Timbuktu. This mud and wood building is typical of western Sudanese mosques. The distinctive tower of the mosque was a symbol of the presence of Islam, which came to places like Timbuktu in central and West Africa by way of overland trade routes. [Photograph by Eliot Elisofon, National Museum of African Art, Eliot Elisofon Archives, Smithsonian Institution, Washington, D.C.]

The Spread of Islam South of the Sahara

By 1800, Islamic influence in sub-Saharan Africa affected most of the Sudanic belt and the coast of East Africa as far south as modern Zimbabwe. Typically, Islam never penetrated beyond the ruling or commercial classes of a region and tended to co-exist or blend with indigenous ideas. Nevertheless, Islam and its carriers brought commercial and political changes as well as the Qur'an, new religious practices, and literate culture on which innovations, from architecture and technology to intellectual life and administrative practice depended.

In East Africa, Islamic city-states along the coast from Mogadishu to Kilwa became a major factor. By contrast, in the western and central parts of the continent, Islam penetrated south of the Sahara into the Sudan by overland routes, primarily from North Africa and the Nile valley. Its agents were sometimes traders, but primarily emigrants from the east seeking new land.

From the 1030s, zealous militants known as Almoravids began an overt conversion campaign that extended to the western Sahel and Sahara. This movement eventually swept into Ghana, and finally Kumbi in 1076. Farther west, the Fulbe rulers of Takrur along the Senegal became Muslim in the 1030s and propagated their new faith among their subjects.

Sahelian Empires of the Western and Central Sudan

Urbanization and state formation in sub-Saharan Africa did not occur only in response to trans-Saharan trade with the Islamic world, which dates largely from the end of the first millennium. Substantial states had risen in the first millennium C.E. in the Sahel regions just south of the Sahara proper. From about 1000 to 1600, four of these developed into notable and relatively long-lived empires: Ghana, Mali, and Songhai in the western Sudan, and Kanem-Bornu in the central Sudan.

Ghana

Ghana was located north of modern Ghana between and north of the inland Niger delta and the upper Senegal. It emerged as a regional power near the end of the first millennium and flourished for about two centuries. Its capital, Kumbi (or Kumbi Saleh), on the desert's edge, was well sited for the Saharan and Sahelian trade networks. Ghana's major population group were the Soninke. (*Ghana* is the Soninke term for "ruler.")

The Ghanaian rulers were matrilineally descended. The king was supreme judge and held court regularly to hear grievances. The royal ceremonies were embellished with the full trappings of regal wealth and power appropriate to a king held to be divinely blessed if not semidivine himself.

Tribute from the empire's many chieftaincies and taxes on royal lands and crops supplemented the duties levied on all incoming and outgoing trade. This trade involved a variety of goods—notably imported salt, cloth, and metal goods such as copper—probably in exchange for gold and perhaps kola nuts from the south. The regime apparently also controlled the gold (and, presumably, the slave) trade that originated in the savannah to the south and west.

Although the king and court of Ghana did not convert to Islam, they made elaborate arrangements to accommodate Muslim traders and government servants in their own settlement a few miles from the royal preserve in Kumbi Saleh. Muslim traders were prominent in the court, literate Muslims administered the government, and Muslim legists advised the ruler. In Ghana's hierarchical society, slaves were

Ghana and Its People in the Mid-Eleventh Century

The following excerpt is from the geographical work of the Spanish Muslim geographer al-Bakri (d. 1094). In it he describes with great precision some customs of the ruler and the people of the capital of Ghana as he carefully gleaned them from other Arabic sources and travelers (he never visited West Africa himself, it seems).

How did the ruler of Ghana deal with the differing religious groups in his capital?

Ghana is a title given to their kings; the name of the region is Awkar, and their king today, namely in the year 460 [1067–8], is Tanka Manin. . . . This Tanka Manin is powerful, rules an enormous kingdom, and possesses great authority.

The city of Ghana consists of two towns situated on a plain. One of these towns, which is inhabited by Muslims, is large and possesses twelve mosques, in one of which they assemble for the Friday prayer. There are salaried imams and muezzins, as well as jurists and scholars. In the environs are wells with sweet water, from which they drink and with which they grow vegetables. The king's town is six miles distant from this one and bears the name of Al-Ghaba. Between these two towns there are continuous habitations. The houses of the inhabitants are of stone and acacia (*sunt*) wood. The king has a palace and a number of domed dwellings all surrounded with an enclosure like a city wall (*sur*). In the king's town, and not far from his court of justice, is a mosque where the Muslims who arrive at his court . . . pray. Around the king's town are domed buildings and groves and thickets where the sorcerers of these people, men in charge of the religious cult, live. In them too are their idols and the tombs of their kings. . . .

All of them shave their beards, and women shave their heads. The king adorns himself like a woman [wearing necklaces] round his neck and [bracelets] on his forearms, and he puts on a high cap (*tartur*) decorated with gold and wrapped in a turban of fine cotton. He sits in audience or to hear grievances against officials (*mazalim*) in a domed pavilion around which stand ten horses covered with gold-embroidered materials. Behind the king stand ten pages holding shields and swords decorated with gold, and on his right are the sons of the [vassal] kings of his country wearing splendid garments and their hair plaited with gold. The governor of the city sits on the ground before the king and around him are ministers seated likewise. . . . When the people who profess the same religion as the king approach him they fall on their knees and sprinkle dust on their heads, for this is their way of greeting him. As for the Muslims, they greet him only by clapping their hands.

Their religion is paganism and the worship of idols (*dakakir*). When their king dies they construct over the place where his tomb will be an enormous dome of saj wood. Then they bring him on a bed covered with a few carpets and cushions and place him beside the dome. At his side they place his ornaments, his weapons, and the vessels from which he used to eat and drink, filled with various kinds of food and beverages.

From J. F. P. Hopkins, trans.; N. Levtzion and J. F. P. Hopkins, eds., *Corpus of Early Arabic Sources for West African History.* Reprinted with permission of Cambridge University Press, pp. 79–80.

at the bottom; farmers and draftsmen above them; merchants above them; and the king, his court, and the nobility on top.

A huge, well-trained army secured royal control and enabled the kings to extend their sway in the late tenth century to the Atlantic shore and to the south as well (see Map 18–1). Ghanaian troops captured Awdaghast, the important southern terminus of the trans-Saharan trade route to Morocco, from the Berbers in 992. The empire was, however, vulnerable to attack from the desert fringe, as Almoravid Berber forces proved in 1054 when they took Awdaghast in a single raid.

Ghana's rulers may have converted to Islam soon after 1100. Ghana's empire was probably destroyed in the late twelfth century by the actively anti-Muslim Soso people from the mountains southeast of Kumbi Saleh.

Mali

After the Almoravids brought their reform movement to the western Sahel at the end of the eleventh century, their proselytizing zeal led to conversion of many of the region's ruling classes. It was, however, over a half-century after the breakup of Ghana's empire before anyone in the western Sahel, Muslim or non-Muslim, could reestablish an empire of comparable extent. With Ghana's collapse and the Almoravids' failure to build a new empire below the Sahara (largely because of their focus on North Africa), the western Sudan broke up into smaller kingdoms. The former Ghanaian provinces of Mande and Takrur were already independent before 1076, and in the early twelfth century Takrur's control of the Senegal valley and the gold-producing region of Galam made it briefly the strongest state in the western Sudan. Like Ghana, however, it was soon

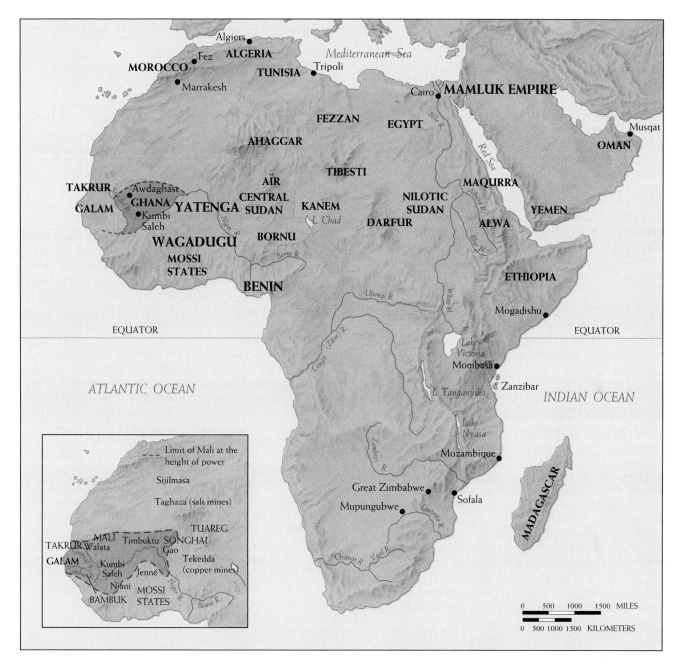

Map 18-1 Africa ca. 900–1500. Shown are major cities and states referred to in the text. The main map shows the region of West Africa occupied by the empire of Ghana from ca. 990 to ca. 1180. The inset shows the region occupied by Mali between 1230 and 1450.

eclipsed by developments to the east, along the upper Niger—first the brief Soso ascendancy and then the rise of Mali.

In the mid-thirteenth century, the Keita ruling clan of a Ghanaian successor kingdom, Mali, forged a new and lasting empire. The Keita kings dominated enough of the Sahel to control the flow of West African gold from the Senegal regions and the forestlands south of the Niger to the trans-Saharan trade routes, and the influx of copper and especially salt in exchange. Because they were farther south, in the fer-

tile land along the Niger, than their Ghanaian predecessors had been, they were better placed to control all trade on the upper Niger and to add to it the Gambia and Senegal trade to the west. They were also able to use war captives for plantation labor in the Niger inland delta to produce surplus food for trade.

Agriculture and cattle farming were the primary occupations of Mali's population and, together with the gold trade, the mainstays of the economy. Rice was grown in the river

Muslim Reform in Songhai

Around 1500 Askia Muhammad al-Turi, the first Muslim among the rulers of Songhai, wrote to the North African Muslim theologian Muhammad al-Maghili (d. 1504) with a series of questions about proper Muslim practices. These excerpts are from the seventh question of al-Turi and the answers given by al-Maghili. Here one sees something of the zeal of the new convert to conform to traditional religious norms, as well as the rather strict and puritanical "official line" of the conservative Maliki ulama *on "pagan" mores. Also evident is the king's desire for bettering social order and his concern for justice in the market and elsewhere. However, also manifest is that many of the more strongly Shari`a-minded* ulama *did not want to compromise at all, let alone allow syncretism to emerge among formerly pagan, newly converted groups.*

What are the problems and corresponding solutions listed in the letter? Which problem did al-Maghili find most serious? Why? Which do you think would have been most serious? Why?

From Al-Turi's Seventh Question

Among the people [of the Songhay Empire said Askia Muhammad], there are some who claim knowledge of the supernatural through sand divining and the like, or through the disposition of the stars . . . [while] some assert that they can write (talismans) to bring good fortune . . . or to ward off bad fortune. . . . Some defraud in weights and measures. . . .

One of their evil practices [continued Askia Muhammad] is the free mixing of men and women in the markets and streets and the failure of women to veil themselves . . . [while] among the people of Djenné [Jenne] it is an established custom for a girl not to cover any part of her body as long as she remains a virgin . . . and all the most beautiful girls walk about naked among people. . . .

So give us legal ruling concerning these people and their ilk, and may God Most High reward you!

From Al-Maghili's Answer

The answer-and God it is who directs to the right course—is that everything you have mentioned concerning people's behavior in some parts of this country is gross error. It is the bounden duty of the commander of the Muslims and all other believers who have the power [replied al-Maghili] to change every one of these evil practices.

As for any who claims knowledge of the supernatural in the ways you have mentioned . . . he is a liar and an unbeliever. . . . Such people must be forced to renounce it by the sword. Then whoever renounces such deeds should be left in peace, but whoever persists should be killed with the sword as an unbeliever; his body should not be washed or shrouded, and he should not be buried in a Muslim graveyard. . . .

As for defrauding in weights and measures [continued al-Maghili] it is forbidden (*haram*) according to the Qur'an, the Sunna and the consensus of opinion of the learned men of the Muslim community. It is the bounden duty of the commander of the Muslims to appoint a trustworthy man in charge of the markets, and to safeguard people's means of subsistence. He should standardize all the scales in each province. . . . Similarly, all measures both large and small must be rectified so that they conform to a uniform standard. . . .

Now, what you mentioned about the free mixing of men and women and leaving the pudenda uncovered is one of the greatest abominations. The commander of the Muslims must exert himself to prevent all these things. . . . He should appoint trustworthy men to watch over this by day and night, in secret and in the open. This is not to be considered as spying on the Muslims; it is only a way of caring for them and curbing evildoers, especially when corruption becomes widespread in the land as it has done in Timbuktu and Djenné [Jenne] and so on.

From *The African Past*, trans. by J. O. Hunwick, reprinted in Basil Davidson (Grosset and Dunlap, The Universal Library), pp. 86–88. Reprinted by permission of Curtis Brown Ltd. Copyright © 1964 by Basil Davidson.

---

valleys and millet in the drier parts of the Sahel. Together with beans, yams, and other agricultural products, this made for a plentiful food supply. Fishing flourished along the Niger and elsewhere. Animal husbandry was strongest among pastoralists of the Sahel, such as the Fulani (or Fulbe), but cattle, sheep, and goats were also plentiful in the Niger valley by the fourteenth century. Many of the Fulani seem to have been attracted by excellent pasturages to the riverine regions.

The chief craft specialties were metalworking (iron and gold) and weaving of cotton grown within the empire.

The Malinke, a southern Mande-speaking people of the upper Niger region, formed the core population of the new state. They apparently lived in walled urban settlements typical of the western savannah region. Each walled town was surrounded by its own agricultural land, and held perhaps 1,000 to 15,000 people.

The Keita dynasty had converted early to Islam (ca. 1100). During Mali's heyday in the thirteenth and fourteenth centuries, its kings often made the pilgrimage to Mecca. From their travel in the central Islamic lands, they brought back new ideas about political and military organization. Through Muslim traders' networks, Islam also connected Mali to other areas of Africa.

Mali's imperial power was built largely by one leader, the Keita King Sundiata (or Sunjaata; r. 1230–1255). Sundiata and his successors, aided by significant population growth in the western savannah, exploited their agricultural resources and Malinke commercial skills to build an empire even more powerful than its Ghanaian predecessor. Sundiata extended his control well beyond the former domains of Ghana, west to the Atlantic coast and east beyond Timbuktu. By controlling the commercial entrepôts of Gao, Walata, and Jenne, he was able to dominate the Saharan as well as the Niger trade. He built his capital, Niani, into a major city. Niani was located on a tributary of the Niger in the savannah at the edge of the forest in a gold- and iron-rich region, well away from the lands of the Sahel nomads and well south of Ghana's capital, Kumbi. It had access to the forest trade products of gold, kola nuts, and palm oil; it was easily defended by virtue of its surrounding small hills; and it was easily reached by river.

The empire that Sundiata and his successors built ultimately encompassed three major regions and language groups of Sudanic West Africa: (1) the Senegal region (including Takrur), occupied by speakers of the West Atlantic Niger-Kongo language group (including Fulbe, Tukulor, Wolof, Serer); (2) the central Mande states between Senegal and Niger, occupied by the Niger-Kongo-speaking Soninke and Mandinke peoples; and (3) the peoples of the Niger in the Gao region who spoke Songhai, the only Nilo-Saharan language west of the Lake Chad basin.

Mali was less a centralized bureaucratic state than the center of a vast sphere of influence that included provinces and tribute-paying kingdoms. Many chieftaincies retained much of their independence but recognized the sovereignty of the supreme, sacred *mansa*, or "emperor," of the Malian realms.

The greatest Keita king proved to be Mansa Musa (r. 1312–1337), whose pilgrimage through Mamluk Cairo to Mecca in 1324 became famous. At home, he consolidated Mali's power, securing peace for most of his reign throughout his vast dominions. Musa's devoutness as a Muslim fostered the further spread of Islam in the empire and beyond. Under his rule, Timbuktu became known far and wide for its *madrasas* and libraries, and for its poets, scientists, and architects, making the city the leading intellectual center of sub-Saharan Islam as well as a major trading city of the Sahel.

Mali's dominance waned in the fifteenth century as the result of rivalries for succession to the throne. As time went on, subject dependencies became independent, and the empire withered. After 1450, a new Songhai power in Gao to the east ended Mali's imperial authority.

Songhai

Gao became an imperial power in the reign of Sonni Ali (1464–1492). Sonni Ali made the Songhai Empire so powerful that it dominated the political history of the western Sudan for more than a century and was arguably the most powerful state in Africa (see Map 18–2).

Askia Muhammad al-Turi (r. 1493–1528) continued Sonni Ali's expansionist policies. Between them, Sonni Ali and Askia Muhammad built an empire that stretched from near the Atlantic into the Sahara and the central Sudan. The ancient caravan trade across the Sahara to the North African coasts provided their major source of wealth.

Muhammad al-Turi was an enthusiastic Muslim. He built up the Songhai state after the model of the Islamic empire of Mali. In his reign, Muslim scholars made Timbuktu a major intellectual and legal training center for the whole Sudan. Nevertheless, his reforms failed to Islamize the empire or to ensure a strong central state under his less able successors.

The last powerful Askia leader was Askia Dawud (r. 1549–1583), under whom Songhai economic prosperity and intellectual life peaked. Still, difficulties mounted. Civil war broke out over succession to the throne in 1586, and the empire was divided. The once-great state became only one among many regional competitors in the western Sudan.

Sahelian Empires of the Western Sudan

ca. 990–ca. 1180?	Empire of Ghana
1076	Ghana loses Awdaghast to Almoravids
1180–1230	Soso clan briefly controls the old Ghanaian territories
ca. 1230–1450	Empire of Mali, founded by Sundiata
1230–1255	Reign of Sundiata
1312–1337	Reign of Mansa Musa
1374	Independent Songhai state emerges in Gao after throwing off Malian rule
ca. 1450–1600	Songhai empire at Gao
1464–1591	Askia dynasty
1464–1492	Reign of Sonni Ali
1493–1528	Reign of Askia Muhammad al-Turi
1549–1583	Reign of Askia Dawud
1590s	Collapse of the Songhai Empire

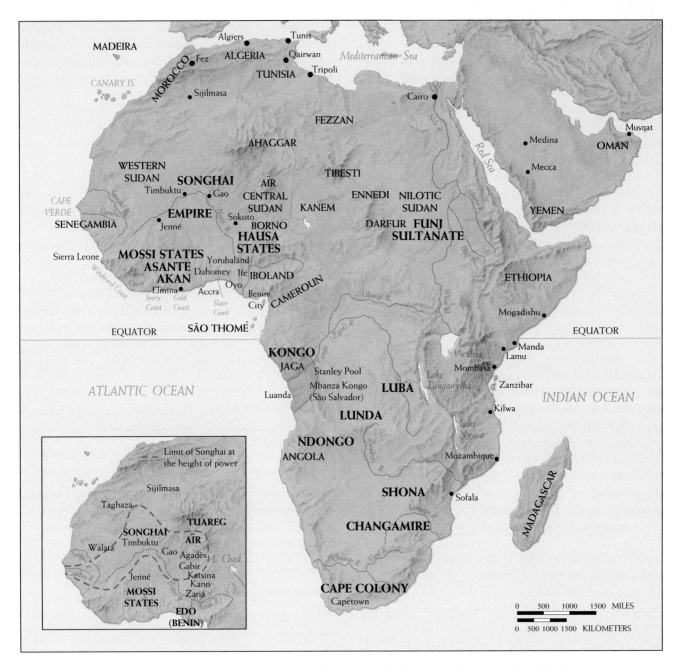

Map 18–2 Africa ca. 1500–1800. Important towns, regions, peoples, and states. The inset shows the empire of Songhai at its greatest extent in the early sixteenth century.

Kanem and Kanem-Bornu

A fourth sizable Sahelian empire, Kanem, in the central Sudan, arose after 1100. Roughly contemporaneous with the Malian Empire to the west, Kanem began as a southern Saharan confederation of the black nomadic tribes known as Zaghawah. Their key leader, Mai Dunama Dibbalemi (r. ca. 1221–1259), was probably the first Kanuri leader to embrace Islam, which appears to have entrenched itself among the Kanuri ruling class during his reign. Dibbalemi used Islam to sanction his rule and provide a rationale for expansion through *jihad*, or holy "struggle" against polytheists.

Dibbalemi and his successors expanded Kanuri power to control important trade routes to Libya and Egypt.

Civil strife, largely over the royal succession, weakened the Kanuri state from the later fourteenth century, and after 1400, the locus of power shifted from Kanem proper westward,

Central Sudanic Empires	
ca. 1100-1500	Kanuri Empire of Kanem
ca. 1220s-1400	Height of Empire of Kanem
1221-1259	Reign of Mai Dunama Dibbalemi
1575-1846	Kanuri Empire of Kanem-Bornu
1575-1610	Reign of Idris Alawma, major architect of the state

to the land of Bornu, southwest of Lake Chad. Near the end of the sixteenth century, firearms and Turkish military instructors enabled the Kanuri leader Idris Alawma (r. ca. 1575–1610) to unify Kanem and Bornu. He set up an avowedly Islamic state and extended his rule even into Hausaland, between Bornu and the Niger River. The center of trading activity as well as political power and security now shifted from the Niger Bend east to the territory under Kanuri control.

Deriving its prosperity from the trans-Saharan trade, Idris Alawma's regional empire survived for nearly a century, but by 1700, its power had been reduced by the Hausa states to the west (see Chapter 31).

The Eastern Sudan

The Christian states of Maqurra and Alwa in the Nilotic Sudan, or Nubia, lasted for more than 600 years from their early seventh-century beginnings. Often thought of as isolated, Christian Nubia in fact maintained political, religious, and commercial contact with Egypt, the Red Sea world, and the east-central and even central Sudan. From late Fatimid times onward, both Maqurra and Alwa were subject to growing Muslim minorities. The result was a long-term intermingling of Arabic and Nubian cultures and the creation of a new Nilotic Sudanese people and culture.

Islam spread slowly with Arab immigration into the upper Nile region. A significant factor in the gradual disappearance of Christianity in Nubia was the apparently elite character of Christianity there and its association with foreign Egyptian Coptic Christianity. Maqurra became officially Muslim at the beginning of the fourteenth century. The Islamization of Alwa came somewhat later, under the Funj sultanate that replaced the Alwa state.

The Funj state flourished from just after 1500 until 1762. The Funj developed an Islamic society whose Arabized character was unique in sub-Saharan Africa. A much-reduced Funj state held out until an Ottoman-Egyptian invasion in 1821.

The Forestlands— Coastal West and Central Africa

West African Forest Kingdoms: The Example of Benin

Many states had developed in West Africa centuries before the first Portuguese reports in 1485. Benin, the best known of these kingdoms, reflects, especially in its art, the sophistication of West African culture before 1500.

Benin State and Society   Some kind of distinct kingdom of Benin likely existed as early as the twelfth century, and the power of the king, or *oba*, at this time was sharply limited by the *uzama*, an order of hereditary indigenous chiefs. Only in the fifteenth century, with King Ewuare, did Benin become a royal autocracy and a large state of major regional importance.

Ewuare apparently established a government in which he had sweeping authority, although he exercised it in light of the deliberations of a royal council formed from the palace *uzama* and the townspeople. He gave each chief specific administrative responsibilities and rank in the government hierarchy. Ewuare and his successors engaged in major wars of expansion and claimed for the office of *oba* an increasing ritual authority.

In the seventeenth century, the *oba* was transformed from a military leader into a religious figure with supernatural powers. Human sacrifice, specifically of slaves, seems to have accompanied the cult of deceased kings. Succession by primogeniture was discontinued, and new *obas* were chosen by the *uzama* from any branch of the royal family.

Benin Art   The lasting significance of Benin lies in its court art, especially its famous brass sculptures. The splendid terra-cotta, ivory, and brass statuary sculpture of Ife-Benin are among the glories of human creativity. These magnificent sculptures, initially realistic or naturalistic and later sometimes highly stylized, seem to be wholly indigenous African products.

The best sculptures are cast bronze plaques depicting legendary and historical scenes. These were mounted on the walls and columns of the royal palace in Benin City. There are

Benin	
ca. 1100-1897	Benin state
ca. 1300	First Ife king of Benin state
1440-1475	Reign of Ewuare

also brass heads, apparently of royalty. Similar sculptures have been found both well to the north and in the Niger delta. Recent excavations east of the Niger at Igbo-Ukwu have unearthed stunning terra cottas and bronzes that belong to the same general artistic culture, which is dated as early as the ninth century. These artifacts testify to the high cultural level attained in traditional African societies that had little or no contact with the extra-African world.

European Arrivals on the Coastlands

Along the coasts of West and central Africa, many changes occurred between 1500 and 1800, including those connected with trade in West African gold and other commodities and the effects associated with the importation and spread in West and central Africa of food crops, such as maize, peanuts, squash, sweet potatoes, cocoa, and cassava (manioc) from the Americas. The gradual involvement of Africa in the emerging global economic system paved the way for eventual colonial domination of the continent, especially its coastal regions, by the Europeans. The European names for segments of the coastline—the Grain (or Pepper) Coast, the Ivory Coast, the Gold Coast, and the Slave Coast—identify the main exports that could be extracted by ship and vividly indicate the nature of the emerging relationship.

Senegambia   In West Africa, Senegambia—which takes its name from the Senegal and Gambia Rivers—was one of the earliest regions affected by European trade. Its maritime trade with European powers, like the older overland trade, was primarily in gold and products such as salt, cotton goods, hides, and copper. Senegambian states also provided perhaps a third of all African slaves exported during the sixteenth century. Thereafter, the focus of the slave trade shifted south and east along the coast. Over time, Portuguese-African mulattos and the British came to control the Gambia River trade, while the French won the Senegal River markets.

This naturalistic brass head (29 cm high), which dates to the thirteenth century, conveys the remarkable power of the art of Benin. [© Frank Willet]

The Gold Coast   The Gold Coast derives its name from its importance after 1500 as the outlet for West Africa's gold fields. Here, beginning with the Portuguese at Elmina in 1481, European states and companies built coastal forts to protect their trade. The trade encouraged the growth of larger states—like the Akan forest states near the coast and the Gonja state just north of the forest—perhaps because they could better control commerce.

The intensive contact of the Gold Coast with Europeans also led to the spread of American crops, notably maize and cassava, into the region, which contributed to substantial population growth. Slaves became big business here in the late seventeenth century, especially in the Accra region. The economy was so disrupted by the slave trade that gold mining declined. Eventually more gold came into the Gold Coast from the sale of slaves than went out from its mines.

Central Africa

The vast center of the subcontinent is bounded by swamps in the north, coastal rain forests to the west, highlands to the east, and deserts in the south. Before 1500, these natural barriers impeded international contact and trade with the interior.

The coming of the Portuguese broke down this isolation, albeit slowly. The Portuguese came looking for gold and silver but found none. Instead, they exported such goods as ivory and palm cloth. Ultimately, their main export was slaves, first to the Portuguese sugar plantations on Sao Thomé island in the Gulf of Guinea, then to Brazil.

The Kongo Kingdom Kongo was the major state with which the Portuguese dealt after coming to central Africa in 1483. Dating from probably the fourteenth century, the Kongo kingdom was located on a fertile, well-watered plateau south of the lower Zaïre River valley, between the coast and the Kwango River in the east. Here, astride the border between forest and grassland, the Kongo kings had built a central government based on a pyramid structure of tax or tribute collection balanced by rewards for those faithful in paying their taxes. Kongo society was dominated by the king, whose authority was tied to acceptance of him as a kind of spiritual spokesman of the gods or ancestors. By 1600, Kongo was half the size of England and alongside farming boasted a high state of specialization in weaving and pottery, salt production, fishing, and metalworking.

The Portuguese brought Mediterranean goods, preeminently luxury textiles from North Africa, to trade for African goods. Such luxuries augmented the prestige and wealth of the ruler and his elites. However, slaves became the primary export that could be used to obtain foreign luxury goods. Imports such as fine clothing, tobacco, and alcohol did nothing to replace the labor pool lost to slavery.

At first the Portuguese put time and effort into education and Christian proselytizing, but the need for more slaves brought a focus on exploiting the human resources of central Africa. Regional rulers sought to procure slaves from neighboring kingdoms, as did Portuguese traders who went inland themselves. As the demand grew, local rulers increasingly attacked neighbors to garner slaves for Portuguese traders (see Chapter 19).

The Kongo ruler Affonso I (r. ca. 1506–1543), a Christian convert, began by welcoming Jesuit missionaries and supporting conversion. But in time he broke with the Jesuits and encouraged traditional practices, even though he himself remained a Christian. Affonso had constant difficulty curbing slaving practices and provincial governors who often dealt directly with the Portuguese, undermining royal authority. Affonso's successor restricted Portuguese activity to Mpinda harbor and the Kongo capital of Mbanza Kongo (São Salvador). A few years later, Portuguese attempts to name the Kongo royal successor caused a bloody uprising against them that led in turn to a Portuguese boycott on trade with the kingdom.

Thereafter, disastrous internal wars shattered the Kongo state. Kongo, however, enjoyed renewed vigor in the seventeenth century. Its kings ruled as divine-right monarchs at the apex of a complex sociopolitical pyramid that rose from district headmen through provincial governors to the court nobility and king. Royal power came to depend on a guard of musket-armed hired soldiers. The financial base of the kingdom rested on tribute from officials holding positions at the king's pleasure and on taxes and tolls on commerce. Christianity, the state religion, was accommodated to traditional beliefs. Kongo sculpture, iron and copper technology, and dance and music flourished.

Angola To the south, in Portuguese Angola, the experience was even worse than in Kongo. By 1600, Angola was exporting thousands of slaves yearly through the port of Luanda. In less than a century, the hinterland had been plundered. The Portuguese arrival had brought economic and social catastrophe.

East Africa

Swahili Culture and Commerce

The participation of East African port towns in the lucrative southern-seas trade was ancient. Arabs, Indonesians, and even Indians had trafficked there for centuries. From the eighth century onward, Islam traveled with Arab and Persian sailors and merchants to these southerly trading centers. In the thirteenth century, Muslim traders from Arabia and Iran began to come in increased numbers and to dominate the coastal cities. Henceforward, Islamic faith and culture were often predominant along the seacoast, from Mogadishu to Kilwa.

By this time, a common language had developed from the interaction of Bantu and Arabic speakers along the coast. This tongue is called *Swahili*, or *Kiswahili*, from the Arabic *sawahil*, "coastlands."

Swahili language and culture probably developed first in the northern towns of Manda, Lamu, and Mombasa, then farther south along the coast to Kilwa. Likewise, the spread of Islam was largely limited to the coastal civilization and did not reach inland. This contrasts with lands farther north, in the Horn of Africa, where Islamic kingdoms developed in the Somali hinterland as well as on the coast.

Swahili civilization reached its apogee in the fourteenth and fifteenth centuries. The harbor trading towns were the administrative centers of the local Swahili states, and most of them were sited on coastal islands or easily defended peninsulas. To these ports came merchants from abroad and from the African hinterlands, some to settle and stay. These towns had impressive mosques, fortress-palaces, harbor fortifications, fancy residences, and commercial buildings.

Central Africa

1300s	Kongo kingdom founded
1483	Portuguese come to central African coast
ca. 1506–1543	Reign of Affonso I as king of Kongo
1571	Angola becomes Portuguese proprietary colony

Today, historians are recognizing that the Swahili states' ruling dynasties were probably African in origin, with an admixture of Arab or Persian immigrant blood. Swahili coastal centers boasted an advanced, cosmopolitan level of culture; by comparison, most of the populace in the small villages lived in mud and sometimes stone houses and earned their living by farming or fishing, the two basic coastal occupations besides trade. Society seems to have consisted of three principal groups: the local nobility, the commoners, and resident foreigners engaged in local commerce. Slaves constituted a fourth class of people, although their local extent (as opposed to their sale) is disputed.

The flourishing trade of the coastal centers was fed mainly by export of inland ivory. Other exports included gold, slaves, turtle shells, ambergris, leopard skins, pearls, fish, sandalwood, ebony, and local cotton cloth. The chief imports were cloth, porcelain, glassware, china, glass beads, and glazed pottery. Certain exports tended to dominate particular ports: cloth, sandalwood, ebony, and ivory at Mogadishu; ivory at Manda; and gold at Kilwa. Cowrie shells were a common currency in inland trade, but coins were used in the major trading centers. The gold trade itself apparently became important only in the fifteenth century.

The Portuguese and the Omanis of Zanzibar

The decline of the original Swahili civilization in the sixteenth century can be attributed primarily to the arrival of the Portuguese and their destruction of the old oceanic trade (in particular, the Islamic commercial monopoly) and the main Islamic city-states along the eastern coast.

In Africa, as everywhere, the Portuguese saw the "Moors" as implacable enemies. Many Portuguese viewed the struggle to wrest the commerce and seaports of Africa and Asia from Islamic control as a Christian crusade.

The initial Portuguese victories along the African coast led to the submission of many small Islamic coastal ports and states. Still, there was no concerted effort to spread Christianity. Thus, the long-term cultural and religious consequences of the Portuguese presence were slight. After 1660, the eastern Arabian state of Oman ejected the Portuguese everywhere north of Mozambique.

The Omanis soon shifted their home base to Zanzibar, which became a major power in East Africa. Their control of the coastal ivory and slave trade seems to have fueled a substantial recovery of prosperity by the later eighteenth century. The domination of the east coast by Omani African sultans, descendants of the earlier invaders, continued until 1856. Thereafter, Zanzibar and its coastal holdings became independent, and then passed to the British. Still, the Islamic impact on the whole coast survives today.

Southern Africa

Southeastern Africa: "Great Zimbabwe"

At about the same time that the east-coast trading centers were beginning to flourish, a purely African civilization was enjoying its heyday inland in modern southern Zimbabwe. It was founded in the tenth or eleventh century by Bantu-speaking Shona people, who still inhabit the same general area today. It seems to have become a large and prosperous state between the late thirteenth and the late fifteenth centuries. We know it only through the archaeological remains of an estimated 150 settlements in the Zambezi-Limpopo region.

The most impressive of these ruins is known today as "Great Zimbabwe"—a huge, sixty-odd-acre site encompassing two major building complexes. One—the so-called acropolis—is a series of stone enclosures on a high hill. It overlooks another, much larger enclosure that contains many ruins and a circular tower, all surrounded by a massive wall some thirty-two feet high and up to seventeen feet thick. The acropolis complex may have contained a shrine, whereas the larger enclosure was apparently the royal palace and fort. The stonework reflects a wealthy and sophisticated society. Artifacts from the site include gold and copper ornaments, soapstone carvings, and imported beads, as well as china, glass, and porcelain of Chinese, Syrian, and Persian origins.

The state itself seems to have had partial control of the increasing gold trade between inland areas and the east coast. We can speculate that this large settlement was the capital city of a prosperous empire and the residence of a ruling elite. Its wider domain was made up mostly of smaller settlements whose inhabitants lived by subsistence agriculture and cattle raising and whose culture was considerably different from that of the capital.

Without written or new archaeological sources, we shall likely never know exactly what allowed this impressive civilization to develop and to dominate its region for nearly 200 years.

The Portuguese in Southeastern Africa

The Portuguese destroyed Swahili control of both the inland gold trade and the overseas trade. Their chief objective was to obtain gold from the interior, though they derived little lasting profit from the enterprise.

All along the Zambezi, however, a lasting and destabilizing consequence of Portuguese intrusion was the creation of quasi-tribal chiefdoms led by mixed-blood Portuguese landholders, who were descended from the first Portuguese estate holders along the Zambezi. By the late eighteenth century, they were too strong for either the Portuguese or the regional African rulers to control. They remind us of how diverse the peoples of modern Africa are.

South Africa: The Cape Colony

In South Africa, the Dutch planted the first European colonials almost inadvertently, yet the consequences of their action were to be ultimately as grave and far-reaching as any European incursion onto African soil. The first Cape settlement was built in 1652 by the Dutch East India Company as a resupply point and way station for Dutch vessels on their way back and forth between the Netherlands and the East Indies. The support station gradually became a settler community, the forebears of the Afrikaners of modern South Africa.

The local Khoikhoi (see Chapter 6) had neither a strong political organization nor an economic base beyond their herds. They bartered livestock freely to Dutch ships. As Company employees established farms to supply the Cape station, they began to displace the Khoikhoi. Conflicts led to the consolidation of European landholdings and a breakdown of Khoikhoi society. Military success led to even greater Dutch control of the Khoikhoi by the 1670s. The Khoikhoi became the chief source of colonial wage labor.

The colony also imported slaves. Slavery set the tone for relations between the emergent, and ostensibly "white," Afrikaner population and the "coloreds" of other races. Free or not, the latter were eventually identified with slave peoples.

Southern Africa

1652	First Cape Colony settlement of Dutch East India Company
1795	British replace Dutch as masters of Cape Colony

This Benin bronze plaque came from the palace of the Obas of Benin and dates to the Edo period of Benin culture, 1575–1625. It depicts two Portuguese males, perhaps a father and son, holding hands. It is likely that they represent the traders or government officials who came to the African coasts in increasing numbers from the end of the fifteenth century on. On the West African coast and in Central Africa they trafficked in a variety of things ranging from ivory to human slaves, the latter gradually displacing everything else. [Art Resource, N.Y.]

After the first settlers spread out around the Company station, nomadic white livestock farmers, or *Trekboers,* moved more widely afield, leaving the richer, but limited, farming lands of the coast for the drier interior tableland. There they contested still wider groups of Khoikhoi cattle herders for the best grazing lands. Again the Khoikhoi lost. By 1700, their way of life was destroyed.

The Cape society in this period was thus a diverse one. The Dutch Company officials (including Dutch Reformed ministers), the emerging Afrikaners (both settled colonists and Trekboers), the Khoikhoi, and the slaves of diverse nationality played differing roles. Intermarriage and cohabitation of masters and slaves added to the complexity. The emergence of

Afrikaans, a new vernacular language of the colonials, shows that the Dutch immigrants themselves were also subject to acculturation processes. By the time of English domination after 1795, the sociopolitical foundations—and the bases of the *Apartheid* doctrine—of modern South Africa were firmly laid.

IN WORLD PERSPECTIVE

Africa, ca. 1000–1800

Developments in African history from 1000 to 1800 varied markedly by region. Along the Mediterranean, the key new factor was the Ottomans' imperial expansion into Egypt and North Africa. The influence of Islam provided a shared arena of expression for some groups in societies from Egypt to Senegambia. At the same time, most Africans from the Sahara south clung to their older traditions. In central and southern Africa, except along the east coast, and in the West African forests, there was little or no evidence of Islam beyond individual Muslims involved in trade. On the east coast, however, Islam influenced the development of the distinctive Swahili culture and language, and Islamic traders linked the region to India, China, and the Indies.

Along the Atlantic and Indian Ocean coasts of Africa, the key development of the fifteenth century was the appearance of ships from the newly potent nations of Christian Europe and the traders and missionaries they carried. First the Portuguese and later other Europeans came by sea in search of commerce and spheres of influence. The European voyages of discovery presaged Africa's involvement in a new, expanding global trading system dominated by Europeans (see Chapter 19). This system generally exploited rather than bolstered African development, as the infamous Atlantic slave trade and the South African experience illustrate.

Review Questions

1. Why did Islam succeed in sub-Saharan and East Africa? How did warfare and trade affect its success?

2. What was the importance of the empires of Ghana, Mali, and Songhai to world history? Why was the control of the trans-Saharan trade so important to these kingdoms? What was the importance of Islamic culture to them? Why did each of these empires break up?

3. How did the Portuguese affect East and central Africa? How did European coastal activities affect the African interior?

4. How did the Portuguese and Dutch differ from or resemble the Arabs, Persians, and other Muslims who came as outsiders to sub-Saharan Africa?

6. Discuss the diversity of Cape society in South Africa before 1800. Who were the Trekboers and what was their conflict with the Khoikhoi? How was the basis for Apartheid formed in this period?

Documents CD-ROM

1. Ibn Battuta in Mali

2. Martín Fernández de Figueroa: Confronting the Moors in Somalia

3. Kilwa, Mombasa, and the Portugese: Realities of Empire

4. *Sundiata*

19 CONQUEST AND EXPLOITATION: THE DEVELOPMENT OF THE TRANSATLANTIC ECONOMY

CHAPTER TOPICS

- Mercantilist Theory of Economic Exploitation
- Establishment of the Spanish Empire in America
- Economies of Exploitation in the Spanish Empire
- Colonial Brazil and Slavery

- French and British North America
- Slavery in the Americas
- Africa and the Transatlantic Slave Trade
- *In World Perspective* The Transatlantic Economy

The late fifteenth-century European encounter with the American continents made the region an area where European languages, legal and political institutions, trade, and religion prevail. These developments in the Americas gave Europe more influence over other world cultures than it would otherwise have achieved.

Within decades of the European voyages of discovery, Native Americans, Europeans, and Africans began to interact in a manner unprecedented in human history. By the close of the sixteenth century, Europe, the Americas, and Africa had become linked in a vast transatlantic economy that extracted wealth from the American continents largely on the basis of the nonfree labor of impressed Native Americans and imported African slaves in a plantation economy that eventually extended from Maryland to Brazil. The slave trade connected the economy of sections of Africa to the transatlantic economy and devastated the African people and cultures involved in it, but it also enriched the Americas with African culture.

Mercantilist Theory of Economic Exploitation

The European empires of the sixteenth through the eighteenth centuries—empires based on commerce—existed primarily to enrich trade. Extensive trade rivalries sprang up around the world. The protection of these empires required naval power, and they depended largely on slave labor. Indeed, the Atlantic slave trade was a major way in which European merchants enriched themselves. That trade in turn forcibly brought the peoples of Africa into the life and culture of the New World.

If any formal economic theory lay behind these empires, it was mercantilism, a system in which governments heavily regulate trade and commerce to increase national wealth. Economic writers of the time believed that a nation had to gain more gold and silver bullion than its rivals.

From beginning to end, the economic well-being of the home country was the primary concern of mercantilist writers.

Colonies existed to provide markets and natural resources for the home country, which furnished military security and political administration for the colonies. For decades, both sides assumed that the colonies were the inferior partner in the relationship. The mercantilist statesmen and traders regarded the world as an arena of scarce resources in which one national economy could grow only at the expense of others. The home country and its colonies were to trade exclusively with each other. National monopoly was the ruling principle.

Mercantilist ideas were always neater on paper than in practice. By the early eighteenth century, mercantilist assumptions were far removed from the realities of the colonies. The colonial and home markets did not mesh. Spain could not produce enough goods for South America. Economic production in the British North American colonies challenged English manufacturing.

Colonists of different countries wished to trade with each other. The governments could not control all their subjects. Clashes among colonists could lead to war between governments. The problems associated with the mercantile empires led to conflicts around the world.

Establishment of the Spanish Empire in America

Conquest of the Aztecs and the Incas

Within twenty years of the arrival of Columbus (1451–1506), Spanish explorers in search of gold had claimed the major islands of the Caribbean and suppressed the native peoples. These actions presaged what was to occur on the continent.

In 1519, Hernan Cortés (1485–1547) landed in Mexico with about 500 men and a few horses. He opened communication with Moctezuma II (1466–1520), the Aztec emperor. Moctezuma hesitated to confront Cortés, attempting at first to appease him with gifts of gold. Cortés forged alliances with subject peoples of the Aztecs. His forces then marched on the Aztec capital of Tenochtitlán (modern Mexico City), where Moctezuma welcomed him. Cortés soon made Moctezuma a prisoner in his own capital. Moctezuma died in unexplained circumstances, and the Spaniards were driven from Tenochtitlán. But they returned, and the Aztecs were defeated in late 1521. Cortés proclaimed the Aztec Empire to be New Spain.

In 1532, Francisco Pizarro (c. 1478–1541) landed on the western coast of South America to take on the Inca Empire. His force included about 200 men armed with guns, swords, and horses, the military power of which the Incas did not understand. Pizarro lured the Inca ruler Atahualpa (c. 1500–1533) into a conference, then seized him and had him garroted in 1533. The Spaniards then captured Cuzco, the Inca capital, ending the Inca Empire.

The conquests of Mexico and Peru are among the most dramatic and brutal events in modern world history. Small military forces armed with advanced weapons subdued, in a brief time, two advanced, powerful peoples. European diseases, especially smallpox, also aided the conquest. The native populations had long lived in isolation, and many succumbed to the new diseases. But beyond the drama and bloodshed, these conquests marked a turning point. Whole civilizations with long histories and enormous social, architectural, and technological achievements were destroyed. Native American cultures endured, but European culture had the upper hand.

The Roman Catholic Church in Spanish America

The Spanish conquest of the West Indies, Mexico, and South America opened that region to the Roman Catholic faith. As it had in the Castilian reconquest of the Iberian peninsula from the Moors, religion played a central role in the conquest of the New World. In both cases, conversion justified military conquest and the extension of political control and dominance. As a consequence of this policy, the Roman Catholic Church in the New World was always a conservative force working to protect the interests of the Spanish authorities.

The relationship between political authority and the propagation of religious doctrine was even closer in the New World than on the Iberian peninsula. The papacy recognized that it could not from its own resources support so extensive a missionary effort and turned over much of the control of the church in the New World to the Spanish monarchy. There was thus always a close relationship between the monarchy and the church. The zeal of both increased in the sixteenth century as the papacy and the Habsburg monarchy determined that Protestantism should have no foothold in America. As a consequence, the Roman Catholicism that spread throughout Spanish America took the form of the zealous faith of the Counter-Reformation.

The Roman Catholic Church, often represented by the Franciscans and Dominicans, and later by the Jesuits, sought to convert the Native Americans and eradicate Indian religious practices. Thus, religious conversion represented, among other things, an attempt to destroy still another part of the Native American culture. Furthermore, conversion did not bring acceptance; even until late in the eighteenth century, there were few Native American Christian priests.

A sixteenth-century Aztec drawing depicts a battle in the Spanish conquest of Mexico. [Corbis-Bettmann]

Tension, however, existed between the early Spanish conquerors and the friars. Without conquest, the church could not convert the Native Americans, but the priests often deplored the harsh conditions imposed on the native peoples. The most outspoken clerical critic of the Spanish conquerors was Bartolomé de Las Casas (1474–1566), a Dominican. He contended that conquest was not necessary for conversion. One result of his campaign was new royal regulations after 1550. Another was the "Black Legend," according to which all Spanish treatment of the Native Americans was inhumane. Those who created this view of Spanish behavior drew heavily on Las Casas's writings. Although substantially true, the "Black Legend" exaggerated the case against Spain. Certainly the rulers of the native empires—as the Aztec demands for sacrificial victims attest—had often themselves been cruel to their subject peoples.

By the end of the sixteenth century, the church in Spanish America had become largely an institution upholding the colonial status quo. Although priests did defend the communal rights of Indian tribes, the colonial church prospered through its exploitation of the resources of the New World. Those who spoke for the church did not challenge Spanish domination, and the church only modestly moderated the forces exploiting human labor and material wealth. By the late eighteenth century, the Roman Catholic Church had become one of the most conservative forces in Latin America.

Economies of Exploitation in the Spanish Empire

Colonial Spanish America had an economy of exploitation in two senses. First, its organization of labor involved dependent servitude or slavery. Second, resources were exploited for the economic advantage of Spain.

Varieties of Economic Activity

The early *conquistadores* ("conquerors") had been interested primarily in gold, but by the middle of the sixteenth century, silver mining provided the chief source of metallic wealth. The great silver mining centers were in Bolivia and northern Mexico. The Spanish crown received one-fifth of all mining revenues. Silver mining for the benefit of Spaniards and the Spanish crown epitomized the extractive economy on which Latin American colonial life was based.

This extractive economy required labor, but there were too few Spanish colonists to provide it, and most of the colonists who came to the Americas were unwilling to provide wage labor. So, the Spaniards looked first to the native population and then to African slaves. Indian labor dominated on the continent and African labor in the Caribbean.

Encomienda   The Spanish devised a series of institutions to exploit Native American labor. The first was the *encomienda*, a formal grant by the crown of the right to the labor of a specific number of Native Americans for a particular time. *Encomienda* as an institution declined by the middle of the sixteenth century. The Spanish crown disliked the *encomienda* system. The monarchy was distressed by reports from clergy that the Native Americans were being mistreated and feared that *encomienda* holders were becoming a powerful nobility in the New World.

Repartimiento   The passing of the *encomienda* led to the *repartimiento*, largely copied from the draft labor practices of the Incas. *Repartimiento* required adult male Native Americans to devote a set number of days of labor annually to Spanish economic enterprises. The time limitation on *repartimiento* led some Spanish managers to use their workers harshly, and Native Americans sometimes did not survive their days of labor rotation.

The Hacienda   The *hacienda*, which dominated rural and agricultural life in Spanish colonies on the continent, developed when the crown made grants of land. These grants led to large landed estates owned by *peninsulares*, whites born in Spain, or creoles, whites born in America. The crown thus continued to use the resources of the New World for patronage without directly impinging on the Native Americans because the grazing that occurred on the *haciendas* required less labor than did the mines. *Haciendas* would become one of the most important features of Latin American life. Laborers on the *hacienda* were usually in formal servitude to the owner and had to buy goods for everyday living on credit from him. They were rarely able to repay the resulting debts and thus could not leave. This system was known as *debt peonage*. The *hacienda* economy produced foodstuffs for mining areas and urban centers.

The Decline of the Native American Population

The conquest, the exploitation, and the forced labor (and European diseases) decimated the Indian population. From the sixteenth century, Native Americans began to die off in huge numbers. In New Spain (Mexico) alone, the population probably declined from approximately 25 million to fewer than 2 million within the first century after the conquest. Thereafter, the Indian population began to expand slowly, but the precipitous drop eliminated the easy supply of exploitable labor.

Commercial Regulation

Because Queen Isabella of Castile (r. 1474–1504) had commissioned Columbus, the legal link between the New World and Spain was the crown of Castile. Government of America was assigned to the Council of the Indies, which nominated the viceroys of New Spain and Peru, the chief executives in the New World. Each of the viceroyalties included subordinate judicial councils known as *audiencias*. A variety of local officers presided over municipal councils. Virtually all political power flowed from the top of this political structure downward; there was little local initiative or self-government (see Map 19–1).

The colonial political structures existed largely to support the commercial goals of Spain. But the system of monopolistic trade regulation was often breached. The Casa de Contratación (House of Trade) in Seville regulated all trade with the New World and was the most influential institution of the Spanish Empire. The entire organization was geared to benefit the Spanish monarchy and privileged merchant groups.

A complicated system of trade and bullion fleets administered from Seville maintained the trade monopoly. Each year a fleet of commercial vessels controlled by Seville merchants, escorted by warships, carried merchandise from Spain to specified ports in America. These included Portobello, Veracruz, and Cartagena. There were no authorized ports on the Pacific Coast. Areas such as Buenos Aires received goods only after the shipments had been unloaded at one of the authorized ports. After selling their wares, the ships were loaded with silver and gold bullion, usually wintered in fortified Caribbean ports, and then sailed back to Spain. Regulations prohibited the Spanish colonists from trading directly with each other and from building their own shipping and commercial industry. Foreign merchants were also forbidden to breach the Spanish monopoly.

Colonial Brazil and Slavery

In 1494, by the Treaty of Tordesillas, the pope divided the seaborne empires of Spain and Portugal by drawing a line west of the Cape Verde Islands. In 1500, a Portuguese explorer landed in present-day Brazil, which extended east of the papal line, and thus Portugal gained a major hold in South America.

Portugal had fewer resources to devote to its New World empire than did Spain. The crown permitted private persons to exploit the region. The native people in the lands that Portugal governed lived in small, nomadic groups. As a result, the Portuguese imported Africans as slaves rather than using the native Indian population, as did the Spanish.

By the mid-sixteenth century, sugar production had gained preeminence in the Brazilian economy. The dominance of sugar meant the dominance of slavery. Slavery became even more important when in the early eighteenth century, gold was discovered in southern Brazil. Nowhere, except perhaps in the West Indies, was slavery so important as it was in Brazil, where it persisted until 1888.

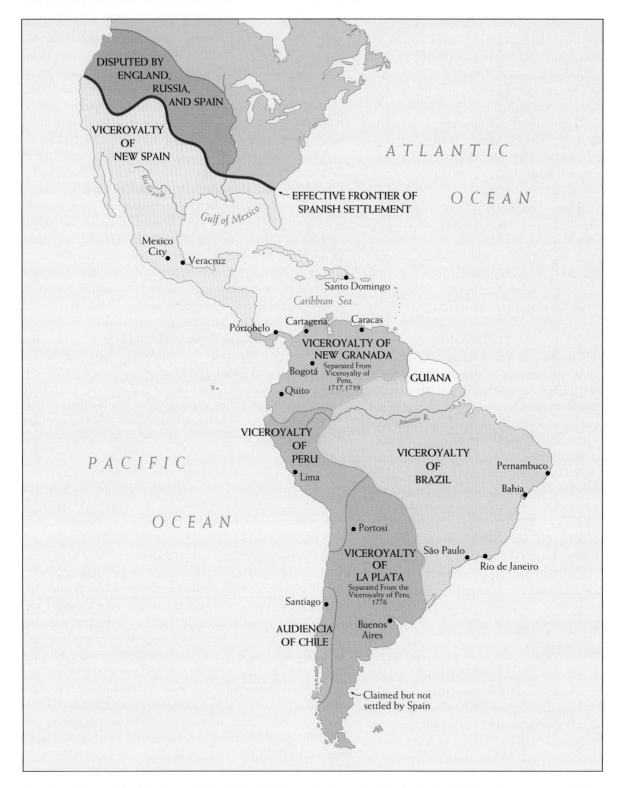

Map 19–1 Viceroyalties in Latin America in 1780.   Spain organized its vast holdings in the New World into viceroyalties, each of which had its own governor and other administrative officials.

The sugar plantations of Brazil and the West Indies were a major source of the demand for slave labor. Slaves are here shown grinding sugar cane and refining sugar, which was then exported to the consumer markets in Europe. [Hulton/Corbis-Bettmann]

The taxation and administration associated with gold mining brought new wealth to the Portuguese monarchy, allowing it to rule without recourse to the Cortés or traditional parliament for taxation. Through transatlantic trade, the new wealth generated from Brazilian gold also filtered into all the major trading nations.

French and British North America

French explorers had pressed down the St. Lawrence River valley in Canada during the seventeenth century. French fur traders and missionaries had followed, with the French government supporting the missionary effort. By the end of the seventeenth century, a sparsely populated French presence existed in Canada. The largest settlement was Quebec, founded in 1608. It was primarily through the fur trade that French Canada functioned as part of the early transatlantic economy.

Beginning with the first successful settlement in Jamestown, Virginia, in 1607, the eastern seaboard of the United States became populated by English colonies. With the exception of Maryland, these colonies were Protestant. The Church of England dominated the southern colonies. In New England, varieties of Protestantism associated with or derived from Calvinism were in the ascendancy. In their religious affiliations, the English-speaking colonies manifested two important traits derived from the English experience. First, much of their religious life was organized around self-governing congregations. Second, their religious outlook derived from those forms of Protestantism that were suspicious of central political authority. In this regard, their cultural and political outlook differed sharply from the cultural and political outlook associated with the Roman Catholicism of the Spanish empire. In a sense, the values of the extreme Reformation and Counter-Reformation confronted each other in the Americas.

The English colonists had complex interactions with the Native American populations. They had only modest interest in missionary enterprise. As in South America, new diseases imported from Europe took a high toll of the native population. Unlike Mexico and Peru, however, North America had no large Native American cities. The Native American populations were dispersed, and intertribal animosity was intense. The

English often used one tribe against another, and the Native Americans also tried to use the English or the French in their own conflicts. From the late seventeenth century through the American Revoution, however, the Native Americans of North America were drawn into the Anglo-French Wars that were fought there as well as Europe. (See Chapter 21.)

The largest economic activity throughout the English-speaking colonies was agriculture. From New England through the Middle Atlantic states, there were mostly small farms tilled by free white labor; from Virginia southward it was the plantation economy, dependent on slavery. The principal ports—Boston, Newport, New York, Philadelphia, Baltimore, and Charleston—were primarily trading centers through which goods moved back and forth between the colonies and England and the West Indies. The commercial economies of these cities were all related to the transatlantic slave trade.

Until the 1760s, the political values of the Americans resembled those of their English counterparts. They were monarchists but suspicious of monarchical power. Their politics involved patronage and individual favors. Their society was hierarchical, with an elite that functioned like a colonial aristocracy and many ordinary people who were dependent on that aristocracy. Throughout the colonies during the eighteenth century, the Anglican church grew in influence and membership. The prosperity of the colonies might eventually have led them to separate from England, but in 1750 few people thought that would occur.

Both England and France had important sugar islands in the Caribbean with plantations worked by African slaves. The trade and commerce of the northern British colonies were closely related to meeting the needs of these islands.

Slavery in the Americas

Black slavery was the final mode of forced or subservient labor in the New World. It extended throughout the Americas.

Establishment of Slavery

As the numbers of Native Americans in South America declined, the Spanish and Portuguese turned to African slaves. By the late 1500s, in the West Indies and the cities of South America, black slaves surpassed the white population.

On much of the South American continent dominated by Spain, slavery declined during the late seventeenth century. It continued to prosper, however, in Brazil and in the Caribbean. Later, starting with the importation of slaves to Jamestown in 1619, slavery became a fundamental institution in British North America.

One of the forces that led to the spread of slavery in Brazil and the West Indies was the cultivation of sugar. Only slave labor could provide enough workers for the sugar plantations. As the production of sugar expanded, so did the demand for slaves.

By 1700, the Caribbean Islands were the world center for sugar production. As the European appetite for sugar grew, the slave population expanded. By 1725, black slaves may have constituted almost 90 percent of the population throughout the West Indies. There and in Brazil and the southern British colonies, prosperity and slavery went hand in hand. The wealthiest colonies were those that raised consumer staples, such as sugar, rice, tobacco, or cotton, by slave labor.

Native Americans in the Saint Lawrence region of North America were drawn into the transatlantic economy through interaction with French fur traders in the early seventeenth century. This illustration shows Samuel de Champlain, the founder of New France, assisting his Huron allies in an attack on the Iroquois in part of an ongoing struggle for control of valuable fur grounds. The palm trees in the background suggest that the artist was unfamiliar with the region. [New York Public Library, Rare Book Division]

The Plantation Economy and Transatlantic Trade

The plantations that stretched from Maryland through the West Indies and into Brazil formed a vast corridor of slave societies. This kind of society, in its total dependence on slave labor and racial differences, had not existed before the European discovery and exploitation of the Americas. The social and economic influence of plantation slavery also touched West Africa, Europe, and New England. It persisted from the sixteenth century through the second half of the nineteenth century. Every society in which it existed still contends with its effects.

The slave trade was part of the larger system of transatlantic trade that linked Europe, Africa, and the European colonies in the Americas. In this system, the Americas supplied labor-intensive raw materials like tobacco, sugar, coffee, precious metals, cotton, and indigo. Europe supplied manufactured goods like textiles, liquor, guns, metal wares, and beads, not to mention cash. And Africa supplied gold, ivory, wood, palm oil, gum, and other products, as well as the slaves who provided the labor to create the American products. By the eighteenth century, slaves were the predominant African export.

Slavery on the Plantations

The plantations in the Americas to which the African slaves arrived produced for an overseas market that was part of a larger integrated transatlantic economy. In turn, plantation owners imported virtually all the finished or manufactured goods they consumed.

The conditions of plantation slaves differed from colony to colony. Vast slave holdings were the exception. Black slaves living in Portuguese areas had the fewest legal protections. In the Spanish colonies, the church provided some protection, but devoted more effort protecting Native Americans. Slave codes in the British and the French colonies provided only the most limited protection. Regulations were intended to prevent slave revolt and favored the master rather than the slave. Masters were permitted to punish slaves by harsh corporal punishment. Slaves were forbidden to gather in large groups lest they plan a revolt. In most slave-owning societies, slave marriages were not recognized by law. The children of slaves were owned by the owner of the parents. Slave families could be separated by sale or inheritance.

The death rate among slaves was high. Their lives were sacrificed to the ongoing expansion of the plantations that made their owners wealthy and that produced goods for consumers in Europe.

The African slaves who were transported to the Americas were converted to Christianity: in the Spanish domains to Roman Catholicism, and in the English colonies to Protestantism. In both cases, they became largely separated from African religious outlooks. Although slaves did manage to mix Christianity with African religion, the conversion of Africans to Christianity represented another example of the crushing of non-European cultural values in the New World.

Europeans were also prejudiced against black Africans. Many Europeans thought Africans were savages or looked down on them because they were slaves. These attitudes had been shared by both Christians and Muslims in the Mediterranean world, where slavery had long existed. Furthermore, many European cultures attached negative connotations to blackness. Although racial thinking in regard to slavery became more important in the nineteenth century, the fact that slaves were differentiated from the rest of the population by race as well as by their status as chattel property was fundamental to the system.

Africa and the Transatlantic Slave Trade

It was the establishment of plantations demanding slave labor that drew Africa into the heart of the transatlantic economy. As Native Americans were decimated by conquest and disease or proved unsatisfactory as plantation laborers, colonial entrepreneurs began to look elsewhere for plantation labor. First the Portuguese, and then the Spanish, Dutch, French, and English turned to Africa for slaves. The Atlantic slave trade was not overtly the result of racist principles, but of the economic needs of the colonial powers and their willingness to exploit weaker peoples to satisfy them. However, this willingness was based on the tacit racist assumption that non-European, nonwhite tribal peoples could be enslaved for European purposes.

The Portuguese were the principal carriers throughout most of the history of the trade. During the eighteenth century, which saw the greatest shipments, the French and English carried almost half the total traffic. Americans were avid slavers who managed to make considerable profits even after Britain and the United States outlawed slaving in 1807.

Slaving was an important part of the massive new overseas trade that financed much European and American economic development that so changed the west during the nineteenth century. This trade, bought at the price of immense human suffering, helped propel Europe and some of its colonial offshoots in the Americas into world dominance.

A Slave Trader Describes the Atlantic Passage

During 1693 and 1694, Captain Thomas Phillips carried slaves from Africa to Barbados on the ship Hannibal. *The financial backer of the voyage was the Royal African Company of London, which held an English crown monopoly on slave trading. Phillips sailed to the west coast of Africa, where he purchased the Africans who were sold into slavery by an African king. Then he set sail westward.*

Who are the various people described in this document who in one way or another were involved in or profited from the slave trade? What dangers did the Africans face on the voyage? What contemporary attitudes could have led this ship captain to treat and think of his human cargo simply as goods to be transported? What are the grounds of his self-pity for the difficulties he met?

Having bought my complement of 700 slaves, 480 men and 220 women, and finish'd all my business at Whidaw [on the Gold Coast of Africa], I took my leave of the old king and his cappasheirs [attendants], and parted, with many affectionate expressions on both sides, being forced to promise him that I would return again the next year, with several things he desired me to bring from England. . . . I set sail the 27th of July in the morning, accompany'd with the East-India Merchant, who had bought 650 slaves, for the Island of St. Thomas . . . from which we took our departure on August 25th and set sail for Barbadoes.

We spent in our passage from St. Thomas to Barbadoes two months eleven days, from the 25th of August to the 4th of November following: in which time there happened such sickness and mortality among my poor men and Negroes. Of the first we buried 14, and of the last 320, which was a great detriment to our voyage, the Royal African Company losing ten pounds by every slave that died, and the owners of the ship ten pounds ten shillings, being the freight agreed on to be paid by the charter-party for every Negro delivered alive ashore to the African Company's agents at Barbadoes. . . . The loss in all amounted to near 6500 pounds sterling.

The distemper which my men as well as the blacks mostly died of was the white flux, which was so violent and inveterate that no medicine would in the least check it, so that when any of our men were seized with it, we esteemed him a dead man, as he generally proved. . . .

The Negroes are so incident to the small-pox that few ships that carry them escape without it, and sometimes it makes vast havock and destruction among them. But tho' we had 100 at a time sick of it, and that it went thro' the ship, yet we lost not above a dozen by it. All the assistance we gave the diseased was only as much water as they desir'd to drink, and some palm-oil to annoint their sores, and they would generally recover without any other helps but what kind nature gave them. . . .

But what the small pox spar'd, the flux swept off, to our great regret, after all our pains and care to give them their messes in due order and season, keeping their lodgings as clean and sweet as possible, and enduring so much misery and stench so long among a parcel of creatures nastier than swine, and after all our expectations to be defeated by their mortality. . . .

No gold-finders can endure so much noisome slavery as they do who carry Negroes; for those have some respite and satisfaction, but we endure twice the misery; and yet by their mortality our voyages are ruin'd, and we pine and fret ourselves to death, and take so much pains to so little purpose.

From Thomas Phillips, *"Journal," A Collection of Voyages and Travels*, Vol. VI, ed. by Awnsham and John Churchill (London, 1746), as quoted in Thomas Howard, ed., *Black Voyage: Eyewitness Accounts of the Atlantic Slave Trade* (Boston: Little, Brown and Company, 1971), pp. 85–87.

The Background of Slavery

Slavery seems to have been a tragic fact of human societies as far back as we can trace it. Although linked to warfare, it cannot be explained by military or economic necessity.

Virtually every premodern state around the globe depended on slavery. The Mediterranean and African worlds were no exception. Slave institutions in sub-Saharan Africa were ancient. The Islamic states of southwestern Asia and North Africa increased this traffic, although they took fewer slaves from Africa than from Eastern Europe and central Asia.

(Hence it is not surprising that the word *slave* is derived ultimately from *Slav*.) Both Mediterranean-Christian and Islamic peoples were using slaves—mostly Greeks, Bulgarians, Turkish prisoners of war, and Black Sea Tartars, but also Africans—before the voyages of discovery opened sub-Saharan sources of slaves for the new European colonies.

Not all forms of slavery were as dehumanizing as the chattel slavery in the Americas. Islamic law, for example, ameliorated slavery. All slavery, however, involved the forceful exploitation and degradation of human beings, the denial of basic freedoms, and the sundering of family ties.

Africa suffered immense social devastation when it was the chief supplier of slaves to the world. The societies that were built on the exploitation of African slavery also suffered enduring consequences, not the least of which is racism.

Slavery and Slaving in Africa

The trade that supplied African slaves to the Islamic lands and Asia has been termed the "oriental" slave trade. The Sudan and the Horn of Africa were the two prime sources of slaves for this trade. The trade managed by Europeans is called the "occidental" slave trade. Voyages beginning in the fifteenth century by first the Portuguese and then other Europeans made the western coasts of Africa as far south as Angola the prime slaving areas.

Before the full development of the transatlantic slave trade by about 1650, slavery and slave trading had been no more significant in Africa than anywhere else.[1] Indigenous African slavery resembled that of other premodern societies. Estimates suggest that about 10,000 slaves per year, most of them female, were taken from sub-Saharan Africa through the oriental trade.

By about 1650, the newer occidental slave trade of the Europeans had become as large as the oriental trade and for the ensuing two centuries far surpassed it. It affected all of Africa, disrupting especially western and central African society. As a result of the demand for young male slaves on the plantations of the Americas, West Africa experienced a sharp drain on its productive male population. Between 1640 and 1690, the number of slaves sold to European carriers doubled, indicating the increasing participation of Africans in the trade. The demand for slaves increased internal warfare in western and central Africa. Moreover, as the external trade destroyed the male-female population balance, an internal market for female slaves arose.

These developments accelerated during the eighteenth century, when African states and slave traders were most heavily involved in the trade. The population declined sharply in the coastal and inland areas hardest hit by the ravages of the trade.

As European and American nations began to outlaw slaving and slavery in the nineteenth century, the oriental and internal trades increased. Slave exports from East Africa and the Sudan and Horn increased after about 1780, and indigenous African slavery also expanded. This traffic was dominated by the same figures—merchants, warlords, and rulers—who had profited from external trade.

Indigenous African slavery began a real decline only at the end of the nineteenth century because of the dominance of European colonial regimes and internal changes. The formal end of African indigenous slavery occurred only in 1928 in Sierra Leone.

[1] The summary follows closely that of P. Manning, *Slavery and African Life: Occidental, Oriental, and African Slave Trades* (Cambridge: Cambridge University Press, 1990), pp. 127–140.

Estimated Slave Imports into the Americas and Old World by Region, 1451–1870	
British North America	523,000
Spanish America	1,687,000
British Caribbean	2,443,000
French Caribbean	1,655,000
Dutch Caribbean	500,000
Danish Caribbean	50,000
Brazil (Portuguese)	4,190,000
Old World	297,000
Total	**11,345,000**

Figures as calculated by James A. Rawley, *The Transatlantic Slave Trade: A History* (New York: W. W. Norton, 1981), p. 428, based on his and other more recent revisions of the careful but older estimates of Philip D. Curtin, *The Atlantic Slave Trade: A Census* (Madison: University of Wisconsin Press, 1969), especially pp. 266, 268.

The African Side of the Transatlantic Trade

Africans were actively involved in the transatlantic slave trade. European slave traders generally obtained their human cargoes from private or government-sponsored African middlemen along the coast. This situation was the result of both the ability of Africans to control inland trade and the vulnerability of Europeans to tropical disease. Thus it was largely African middlemen who undertook the capture or procurement of slaves and the difficult task of marching them to the coast. These middlemen were generally either wealthy merchants or the agents of African chieftaincies or kingdoms.

The media of exchange varied. At first they usually involved barter for goods from gold dust or firearms to alcohol. In time they increasingly involved monetary payments. This exchange drained productive resources (human beings) in return for nonproductive wealth.

The chief West and central African slaving regions provided different numbers of slaves at different times, and the total number of exported slaves varied between periods. When one area could not meet demand, the European traders shifted to other points. Traders went where population density and African merchant or state suppliers promised the best numbers and prices.

The Extent of the Slave Trade

The slave trade varied sharply in extent from period to period. The period of greatest activity, 1701–1810, accounted for over 60 percent of the total, and even the final half-century of slaving until 1870 accounted for over 20 percent of the total. The Portuguese transported more than a million slaves to Brazil between 1811 and 1870. We would do well to remember how long it took the "modern" occidental world to abolish the trade in African slaves.

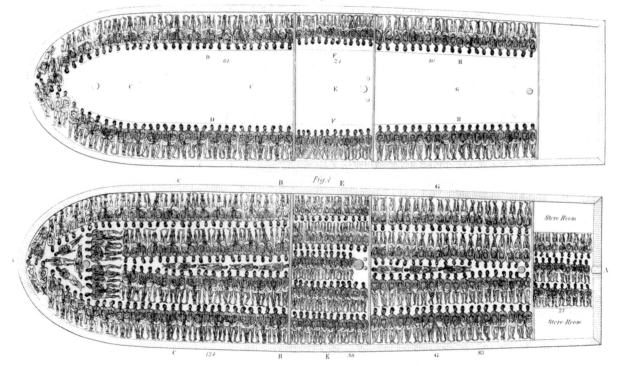

Loading plan for the main decks of the 320-ton slave ship Brookes. The Brookes was only 25 feet wide and 100 feet long, but as many as 609 slaves were crammed on board for the nightmarish passage to the Americas. The average space allowed each person was only about 78 inches by 16 inches. [Photographs and Prints Division, Schomburg Center for Research in Black Culture, The New York Public Library, Astor, Lenox, and Tilder Foundations]

The overall number of African slaves exported during the occidental trade—effectively, between 1451 and 1870—is still debated and must be seen in the larger context of all types of slaving in Africa in the same period. A major unknown is the number of slaves who died under the brutal conditions to which they were subjected when captured and transported overland and by sea. The most reliable estimates pertain only to those slaves who actually landed abroad. As the accompanying table shows, just those who actually reached an American or Old World destination in the occidental trade totaled more than 11 million.

At a minimum, Africa lost some 13 million people to the Atlantic trade alone. Another 5 million or more were lost to the oriental trade. Finally, according to the estimate of one expert, an additional 15 million people were enslaved within African societies themselves.[2]

Consequences of the Slave Trade for Africa

These statistics hint at the massive impact slave trading had on African life. Still, the actual effects remain disputed. We do not know for certain if the Atlantic trade brought net population loss or gain to specific areas of West Africa. The rapid

[2]Manning, pp. 37, 170–171.

spread of maize and cassava cultivation in forest regions after these plants had been imported from the Americas may have fueled African population increases that offset regional human loss through slaving. We know, however, that slaving took away many of the strongest young men and, in the oriental-trade zones, most of the young women.

Similarly, we do not know if more slaves were captured as byproducts of local wars or from pure slave raiding, but we do know they were captured and removed from their societies.

Nor do we know if slaving always inhibited trade or stimulated it because commerce in African products from ivory to wood and hides often accompanied that in slaves. Still, we do know that the exchange of productive human beings for money or goods that were not used to build a productive economy was a loss for African society.

Finally, because we do not yet have accurate estimates of the total population of Africa at different times over the four centuries of the Atlantic slave trade, we cannot determine with certainty its demographic impact. We can, however, make educated guesses. If, for example, tropical Africa had 50 million inhabitants in 1600, it would then have had 30 percent of the combined population of the Americas, the Middle East, Europe, and Africa. If in 1900, after the depredations of the slave trade, it had 70 million inhabitants, its population would have dropped to about 10 percent of the combined population of the same world regions. Current estimates indicate that overall African population growth suffered significantly as a result of the slave trade. Figures like these also give some idea of slavery's probable impact on Africa's ability to keep up with the modern industrializing world.[3]

Even in West and central Africa, which bore the brunt of the Atlantic trade, its impact and the response to it were varied. In a few cases, kingdoms such as Dahomey (the present Republic of Benin) seem to have derived immense economic profit by making slaving a state monopoly. Other kingdoms derived no gain from it. In many instances, including the rise of Asante power or the fall of the Yoruba Oyo Empire, increased slaving was a result as well as a cause of regional change. Increased warfare meant increased prisoners to be sold off; however, whether slaving gave good cause for war is still unclear.

Similarly, if one can establish, as seems evident, a major increase in indigenous slavery as a result of the external trade to occident and orient, we have to assume major social consequences for African society, but the specific consequences would differ according to regional situations. For example, in West Africa more men were taken as slaves than women, whereas in the Sahelian Sudanic regions, more women than men were taken. In the west, the loss of so many men increased the pressures for polygamy and possibly the use of women slaves, whereas in the Sahelian Sudanic regions, the loss of women may have stimulated polyandry and reduced the birthrate.

[3]On all of the preceding points regarding probable impact of the trade, see Manning, pp. 126–148, 168–176.

Conquest of the Americas and the Transatlantic Slave Trade	
1494	The Treaty of Tordesillas divides the seaborne empires of Spain and Portugal
1500	The Portuguese arrive in Brazil
1519–1521	Hernan Cortés conquers the Aztec Empire
1531–1533	Francisco Pizarro conquers the Inca Empire
1607	Jamestown, Virginia, first permanent English settlement in North America founded
1608	The French found Quebec
1619	First African slaves brought to British North America
1650	Transatlantic slave trade becomes bigger than the older oriental slave trade
1700s	Over six million slaves imported from Africa to the Americas
1807	Slavery abolished in British domains
1808	The importation of slaves abolished in the United States
1874–1928	Indigenous African slavery abolished
1888	Slavery abolished in Brazil

Even though slavery existed previously in Africa, the scale of the Atlantic trade was unprecedented and hence had an unprecedented impact. In general, the slave trade changed patterns of life and balances of power in the main affected areas, whether by stimulating trade or warfare, by disrupting market and political structures, by increasing slavery inside Africa, or by disturbing the male-female ratio (and hence the work-force balance and birthrate patterns) and consequently the basic social institution of monogamous marriage.

The overseas slave trade at the least siphoned indigenous energy into counterproductive or destructive directions. This, in turn, inhibited true economic development. The Atlantic slave trade was one of the most tragic aspects of European involvement in Africa.

IN WORLD PERSPECTIVE

The Transatlantic Economy

The contact between the native peoples of the American continents and the European explorers of the fifteenth and sixteenth centuries transformed world history. In the Americas, the native peoples had established a wide variety of civilizations. Some of their most remarkable architectural monuments and cities were constructed during the centuries when European civilizations were reeling from the collapse of Roman power. Until the European explorations, the civilizations of the Americas and Eurasia and Africa had had no significant contact with each other.

Within half a century of the landing of Columbus, millions of America's native peoples had encountered Europeans intent on conquest, exploitation, and religious conversion. Because of their advanced weapons, navies, and the new diseases they brought with them, as well as internal divisions among the Native Americans, the Europeans achieved a rapid conquest.

In both North and South America, economies of exploitation were established. In Latin America, various institutions were developed to extract native labor. From the mid-Atlantic English colonies through the Caribbean and into Brazil, slave-labor plantation systems were established. The slaves were forcibly imported from Africa and sold in America to plantation owners. The economies and peoples of Europe, Africa, and the Americas were thus drawn into a vast worldwide web of production based on slave labor.

The impact of slavery in the Americas was not limited to the life of the black slaves. Whites in the New World numbered about 12 million in 1820, compared to some 6 million blacks. However, only about 2 million whites had migrated there, compared to some 11 million or more Africans forcibly imported as slaves. Such numbers reveal the effects of brutal slave conditions and the high mortality and low birthrates of slave populations.

None of these statistics, however, enables us to assess the role that slavery has played in the Americas or, in particular, the United States. The United States actually received only a bit more than a quarter as many slaves as did Brazil alone or the British and French Caribbean regions together, yet the consequences of the forced migration of just over a half-million Africans remain massive. Consider just the American Civil War and the endurance of racism and inequality or, more positively, the African contribution to American industrial development, language, music, literature, and artistic culture. The Atlantic slave trade's impact continues to be felt at both ends of the original "trade."

Review Questions

1. How were small groups of Spaniards able to conquer the Aztec and Inca Empires?

2. What was the basis of the mercantilist theory of economics? What was the relationship between the colonial economies and those of the homelands?

3. Describe the economies of Spanish America and Brazil. What were the similarities and differences between them and the British and French colonies in the Caribbean and North America? What role did the various colonies play in the transatlantic economy?

4. Why did forced labor and slavery develop in tropical colonies? How was slavery in the Americas different from slavery in earlier societies?

5. What was the effect of the transatlantic slave trade on West African societies? On East Africa? What role did Africans themselves play in the slave trade?

Documents CD-ROM

1. Bernal Díaz del Castillo, *The Conquest of Mexico*

2. Bartholomew de las Casas: Amerindians and the "Garden of Eden"

3. Christopher Columbus, *Journal of First Voyage to America*

4. Bartholoméw de las Casas: Destruction of the Indies and the Only Method of Converting the Indians

5. Olaudah Equiano, *The Life Olaudah Equiano or Gustavus Vassa, The African*

6. Commerce, Slavery and Religion in North Africa

20 EAST ASIA IN THE LATE TRADITIONAL ERA

CHAPTER TOPICS

LATE IMPERIAL CHINA
◆ Ming (1368-1644) and Ch'ing (1644-1911) Dynasties

JAPAN
◆ Warring States Era (1467-1600)
◆ Tokugawa Era (1600-1868)

KOREA AND VIETNAM
◆ Korea
◆ Vietnam

In World Perspective Late Traditional East Asia

This chapter underlines the dynamism of both China and Japan during the centuries between the "medieval" and the "modern" eras. "Late traditional society" does not mean "late static society." In both countries the society became more integrated and the apparatus of government became more sophisticated. These advances shaped Chinese and Japanese responses to the West during the nineteenth century. Even Korea and Vietnam did not lack dynamism. But during these centuries the West was transformed. As we view East Asia from the perspective of Europe, it appears to have been caught in a tar pit of slow motion, but it was actually the West that had accelerated.

LATE IMPERIAL CHINA

Ming (1368–1644) and Ch'ing (1644–1911) Dynasties

The Ming and the Ch'ing were China's last dynasties. The first was Chinese, the second a dynasty of conquest (Manchus). They were nevertheless remarkably similar in their institutions and pattern of rule.

Land and People

China's population reached about 410 million people in the mid-nineteenth century. This population density stimulated commerce and gave new prominence to the scholar-gentry. Population growth was paralleled by an increase in the food supply.

There are many unanswered questions regarding the population growth during these six centuries. Was there a decline in the death rate and, if so, why? Or did the development of new lands and technology enable more mouths to be fed? Certainly the Ming-Ch'ing era was the longest continuous period of good government in Chinese history. But by the early nineteenth century, the Chinese standard of living may have begun to decline. An ever increasing population was no blessing.

China's Third Commercial Revolution

Early Ming emperors, isolationist and agrarian in orientation, operated government monopolies that stifled enterprise and depressed the southeastern coastal region with their restrictions on maritime trade and shipping. In the mid-sixteenth century, commerce started to grow again, buoyed by the surge of population and agriculture and a relaxation of government controls. If the growth during the Han and Sung dynasties may be called China's first and second commercial revolutions, then the expansion between 1500 and 1800 was the third. By the early nineteenth century, China was the most highly commercialized nonindustrial society in the world.

One stimulus to commerce was imported silver. The Chinese balance of trade was favorable. Beginning in the mid-sixteenth century, silver from Japan entered China, and from the 1570s, Spanish galleons brought in Mexican and Peruvian silver. In the eighteenth century, private "Shensi banks" opened branches throughout China to facilitate the transfer of funds and extend credit for trade. Eventually they opened offices in Singapore, Japan, and Russia. As in Europe, so in China, the influx of silver and the overall increase in liquidity led to inflation and commercial growth.

Urban growth between 1500 and 1800 was mainly at the level of market towns. These towns provided the link between the local markets and the larger provincial capitals and cities. The commercial integration of local, intermediate, and large cities spread over all of China. Interregional trade also gained. But China did not develop a national economy. Seven or eight regional economies, each the size of a large European nation, were the focus for most economic activity. But a new level of trade developed among them, especially where water transport made such trade economical.

Women and the Commercial Revolution

The Confucian family ideal changed little during the Ming and Ch'ing dynasties. A woman was expected first to obey her parents, then her husband, and finally her son—when he became the new family head. Physically, women became more restricted as footbinding spread through the upper classes and to some commoners. One exception to the rule was the Manchus. One Manchu (Ch'ing) emperor even issued an edict banning footbinding, but it was ignored by the Chinese.

As population grew and the size of the average landholding shrank, more women worked at home, making products for commercial markets. And as their contribution to the household income grew, their voice in household decisions often became larger than Confucian doctrines would suggest.

Political System

One might expect these massive demographic and economic changes to have produced a profound change in the political superstructure of China. They did not. Government during the Ming and Ch'ing was much like that of the Sung or Yuan, only stronger. The sources of strength of the Ming-Ch'ing system were the spread of education, the use of Confucianism as an ideology, stronger emperors, better government

finances, more competent officials, and a larger gentry class with an expanded role in local society.

Role of Confucianism

Confucian teachings were more widespread in late imperial China than ever before. There were more schools. Academies preparing candidates for the civil service examinations multiplied. Literacy outpaced population growth. The Confucian view of society was patriarchal. The family, headed by the father, was the basic unit. The emperor, the son of Heaven and the ruler-father of the empire, stood at its apex. In between were the district magistrates, the "father-mother officials." The idea of the state as the family writ large carried with it duties and obligations at every level.

In comparison to Europe, where religious philosophies were less involved with the state and where a revolution in science was reshaping religious and political doctrines, the greater unity and integration of the Chinese worldview cannot be denied.

Emperor

Ming-Ch'ing emperors were more powerful than ever and made all important and many unimportant decisions. They wielded despotic powers at their courts. They had secret police and prisons where those who gave even minor offense might be tortured. Even high officials might suffer humiliating and fatal punishment. The dedication and loyalty even of officials who were cruelly mistreated attest to the depth of their Confucian ethical formation.

During the Ch'ing, the life-and-death authority of emperors did not diminish, but officials were generally better treated. As foreign rulers, the Manchu emperors took care not to alienate Chinese officials.

The Forbidden Palace in Peking was an icon of the emperor's majesty. The entire palace complex focused on the ruler. Its massive walls and vast courtyards progress to the audience hall where the emperor sat on an elevated dais above the officials, who knelt before him. Behind the audience hall were the emperor's private chambers and his harem. By the seventeenth century, there were 9,000 palace ladies and perhaps as many as 70,000 eunuchs. The glory of the emperor extended to his family, whose members were awarded vast estates in North China.

Bureaucracy

A second component of the Ming-Ch'ing system was the government itself. At the top were the military, the censorate, and the administrative branch; beneath the administration were the six ministries and the web of provincial, prefectural, and district offices. But government was better financed than during earlier dynasties. As late as the 1580s, huge surpluses were accumulated at both the central and the provincial levels. Only during the last fifty years of the Ming did soaring military expenses bankrupt government finances. Then, in the second half of the seventeenth century, the Manchus reestablished a strong central government and restored the flow of taxes to levels close to those of the Ming.

The good government the Ming-Ch'ing system brought to China was largely a product of the ethical commitment and ability of its officials. No officials in the world today approach in power or prestige those of the Ming and the Ch'ing. When the Portuguese arrived early in the sixteenth century, they called these officials "mandarins." The rewards of an official career were so great that the competition to enter it was intense. As population grew and schools increased, entrance became ever more competitive.

After being screened at the district office, a candidate took the county examination. If he passed, he became a member of the gentry and was exempted from state labor service. Even this examination required years of study. About half a million passed each year. The second hurdle was the provincial examination held every third year. Only one in a hundred was successful. The final hurdle was the metropolitan examination, also held triennially. Fewer than ninety passed each year.

Gentry   A final component in the Ming-Ch'ing system was the gentry class. It was an intermediate layer between the elite bureaucracy above and the village below. The lowest level of bureaucratic government was the district magistrate. Although the population increased sixfold during the Ming and the Ch'ing, the number of district magistrates increased only from 1,171 to 1,470. To prevent conflicts of interest, an outsider was appointed as district magistrate. His office compound had a large staff of secretaries and advisers, but to govern effectively, he had to obtain the cooperation of the local literati or gentry.

By *gentry* we do not mean a rural elite, like English squires. The Chinese gentry was largely urban, living in market towns or district seats. Socially and educationally, its members were of the same class as the magistrate—a world apart from clerks or village headmen. They usually owned land, which enabled them to avoid manual labor and to send their children to private academies. As absentee landlords whose lands were worked by sharecroppers, they were often exploitative. But they also acted as local leaders. They represented community interests vis-à-vis the bureaucracy. They also performed quasi-official functions on behalf of their communities: maintaining schools and Confucian temples; repairing roads, bridges, canals, and dikes. The gentry class was the matrix from which officials arose; it was the local upholder of Confucian values.

Pattern of Manchu Rule   The collapse of the Ming dynasty in 1644 and the establishment of Manchu rule was less of a break than might be imagined. First, the transition was short. Second, the Manchus, unlike the Mongols, were already partially Sinicized. Even before entering China, they had ruled over Chinese who had settled in Manchuria.

The great Manchu emperor Ch'ien Lung (r. 1736–1795). [© Metropolitan Museum of Art, Rogers Fund, 1942 (42.141.8)]

In the late sixteenth century, an able leader unified the Manchurian tribes, proclaimed a new dynasty, and established a Confucian government. When the Ming collapsed, the Manchus presented themselves as the conservative upholders of the Confucian order. The Chinese gentry preferred the Manchus to Chinese rebel leaders, whom they regarded as bandits. After the Manchu conquest, most officials served the new dynasty. The Ch'ing as a Chinese dynasty dates from 1644.

As a tiny fraction of the Chinese population, the Manchus adopted institutions to maintain themselves as an ethnically separate elite group. One was their military organization. Manchu garrison forces were segregated and not put under the jurisdiction of Chinese officials. They were given stipends and lands to cultivate. They were forbidden to marry Chinese, their children had to study Manchu, and they were not permitted to bind the feet of their daughters. In 1668, northern and central Manchuria were closed to Chinese immigrants.

The second institutional feature was the appointment of one Chinese and one Manchu to each key post in the central government. At the provincial level, Chinese governors were overseen by Manchu governor-generals. Most officials and all district magistrates beneath the governors were Chinese.

A particular strength of the Manchu dynasty was the long reigns of two extremely able emperors, K'ang Hsi (1661–1722) and Ch'ien Lung (1736–1795). K'ang Hsi was a man of great vigor. He rose at dawn to read official documents before meeting with officials. He presided over palace examinations. Well versed in the Confucian classics, he won the support of scholars.

K'ang Hsi also displayed an interest in European science, a subject he studied with Jesuit court astronomers. He opened four ports to foreign trade and carried out public works, improving the dikes on the Huai and Yellow Rivers and dredging the Grand Canal. During his reign, he made six tours of China's southern provinces. K'ang Hsi, in short, was a model emperor.

Ch'ien Lung began his reign in 1736. During his reign the Ch'ing dynasty attained its highest level of prosperity and power. Like K'ang Hsi, he was vigorous, wise, conscientious, careful, and hard-working. He visited South China on inspection tours and patronized scholars on a grand scale.

Only in his last years did Ch'ien Lung lose his grip and permit a court favorite to practice corruption on an almost unprecedented scale. In 1796, the White Lotus Rebellion broke out. Ch'ien Lung's successor put down the rebellion, but the ample financial reserves that had existed throughout the eighteenth century were never reestablished. China nevertheless entered the nineteenth century with its government intact and with a peaceful and stable society. There were few signs of what was to come.

Ming–Ch'ing Foreign Relations

Ming The first Ming emperor (r. 1368–1398) oversaw the expansion of China's borders. At his death, China controlled the northern steppe and had regained control of the southern tier of Chinese provinces (see Map 20–1). During the reign of the third Ming emperor (1402–1424), northern Vietnam became a Chinese province for two decades.

The Ming emperors "managed" China's frontiers with the tribute system. In this system, the ambassadors of vassal kings acted out their subordination to the universal ruler of the celestial kingdom. An ambassador approached the emperor, performed the kowtow (kneeling three times and each time bowing his head to the floor three times), and presented his gifts. In return, the vassal kings were sent seals confirming their status, given permission to use the Chinese calendar and year-period names, and appointed to the Ming nobility.

The most far-ranging ventures of the third Ming emperor were the maritime expeditions that sailed to Southeast Asia, India, the Arabian Gulf, and East Africa between 1405 and 1433. They were commanded by the eunuch Cheng Ho, a Muslim from Yunnan (see Map 20–1). The first of these armadas had sixty-two major ships and carried 28,000 sailors, soldiers, and merchants. Trade was not the primary purpose. The expeditions were intended to make China's glory known to distant kingdoms and to enroll them in the tribute system.

The expeditions ended as abruptly as they had begun. They were costly at a time when the dynasty was fighting in Mongolia and building Peking. What was remarkable about these expeditions was not that they came a half-century earlier than the Portuguese voyages of discovery, but that China had the necessary maritime technology and yet decided not to use it. China lacked the combination of restlessness, greed, faith, and curiosity that would motivate the Portuguese.

The chief threat to the Ming dynasty was the Mongols. In the 1430s they captured the emperor, and in 1550 they overran Peking, but were defeated by a Chinese army in the 1560s and signed a peace treaty in 1571.

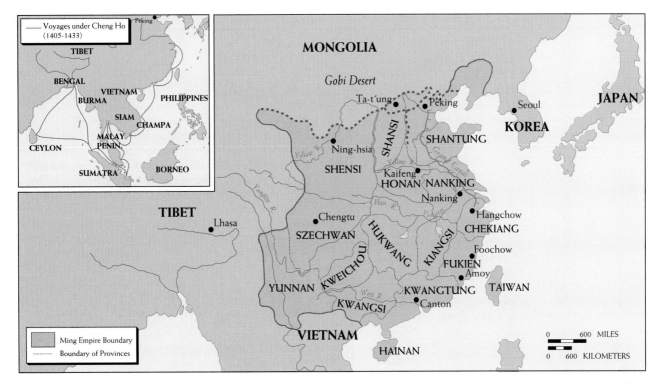

Map 20–1 Ming Empire and the voyages of Cheng Ho. The ships of Cheng Ho, venturing beyond Southeast Asia and India, reached the coast of East Africa.

A second threat came from Japan. Pirates raided the Chinese coast in the fifteenth and sixteenth centuries, and Hideyoshi, after unifying Japan, invaded and occupied Korea in 1592 and 1597–98. Eventually China sent troops. The Japanese withdrew after the death of Hideyoshi. But the strain on Ming finances had weakened the dynasty.

Ch'ing The final and successful foreign threat to the Ming was the Manchus. After coming to power in 1644, the Manchu court spent decades consolidating its rule within China. Chinese generals who had helped the Manchus revolted and were supported by a pirate state on Taiwan. The emperor K'ang Hsi suppressed the revolts; in 1683 he took Taiwan, which became a part of China for the first time.

As always, the principal foreign threats to China came from the north and northwest. By the 1660s, Russian traders, trappers, and adventurers had reached northern Manchuria, where they built forts and traded with the eastern Mongols. During the 1680s, K'ang Hsi drove the Russians from the lower Amur River. This victory led to the 1689 Treaty of Nerchinsk, which excluded Russia from northern Manchuria.

In the west, the situation was more complex, with a three-corner relationship among Russia, the western Mongols, and Tibet. K'ang Hsi, and then Ch'ien Lung, campaigned against the Mongols, invaded Tibet, and in 1727 signed a new treaty with Russia. During the campaigns, the Chinese temporarily came to control millions of square miles of new territories. It is a telling comment on the Chinese concept of empire that ever since that time, even after China's borders contracted during the nineteenth century, the Chinese have insisted that the Manchu conquests of non-Chinese peoples define their legitimate borders. The roots of the present-day contention over borders between China and the countries of the former Soviet Union go back to these events during the eighteenth century, as does the Chinese claim to Tibet.

Contacts with the West Europeans had made their way to China during the T'ang and the Yuan dynasties. But only with Europe's oceanic expansion in the sixteenth century did they arrive in large numbers. Some came as missionaries, of whom the most successful were the Jesuits. They studied Chinese and the Confucian classics and conversed with scholars. They used their knowledge of astronomy, geography, engraving, and firearms to win entry to the court at Peking and appointments in the bureau of astronomy.

When the Manchus came to power in 1644, the Jesuits kept their position. They appealed to the curiosity of the court with instruments such as telescopes, clocks, and clavichords. They tried to propagate Christianity. They attacked Taoism and Buddhism, but argued that Confucianism as a

Ch'ien Lung's Edict to King George III of England

The Chinese emperor rejected the requests of the 1793 Macartney mission for change in the restrictive Canton system. His edict reflects the Chinese sense of their superiority to other peoples and their belief that China was the "central kingdom" of the world.

What philosophical principles underlie the emperor's sense of superiority?

You, O King, are so inclined toward our civilization that you have sent a special envoy across the seas to bring to our Court your memorial of congratulations on the occasion of my birthday and to present your native products as an expression of your thoughtfulness. On perusing your memorial, so simply worded and sincerely conceived, I am impressed by your genuine respectfulness and friendliness and greatly pleased. . . .

The Celestial Court has pacified and possessed the territory within the four seas. Its sole aim is to do its utmost to achieve good government and to manage political affairs, attaching no value to strange jewels and precious objects. The various articles presented by you, O King, this time are accepted by my special order to the office in charge of such functions in consideration of the offerings having come from a long distance with sincere good wishes. As a matter of fact, the virtue and prestige of the Celestial Dynasty having spread far and wide, the kings of the myriad nations come by land and sea with all sorts of precious things. Consequently there is nothing we lack, as your principal envoy and others have themselves observed. We have never set much store on strange or ingenious objects, nor do we need any more of your country's manufactures. . . .

Reprinted by permission of the publisher from *China's Response to the West* by Ssu-yu Teng and John K. Fairbank, Cambridge, MA: Harvard University Press. Copyright © 1954, 1979 by the President and Fellows of Harvard College. Reprinted by permission of Harvard University Press.

---

rational philosophy complemented Christianity, just as Aristotle's teaching complemented Christian theology in Europe. They interpreted the Confucian rites of ancestor worship as secular and nonantagonistic to Christianity. A few high court officials were converted.

Meanwhile, their Franciscan and Dominican rivals had reported to Rome that the Jesuits condoned the Confucian rites. Papal bulls in 1715 and 1742 forbade Chinese Christians to participate in the family rites of ancestor worship. Thereupon the emperor banned Christianity in China.

Other Europeans came to China to trade. The Portuguese came first in the early sixteenth century and were permitted to trade on a tiny peninsula at Macao. They were followed by Dutch from the East Indies (Indonesia), by the British East India Company in 1699, and by Americans in 1784.

By the early eighteenth century, westerners could trade only at Canton, outside its walls along the river. They could not bring their wives to China. They were subject to Chinese law and were under the control of official merchant guilds. Nevertheless, the trade was profitable to both sides.

The British East India Company developed a triangular commerce among China, India, and Britain. For China, this trade produced an influx of specie, and the Chinese officials in charge grew immensely wealthy. Chafing under the restrictions, the British government in 1793 sent the Macartney mission to China to negotiate the opening of other ports, fixed tariffs, representation at Peking, and so on. The emperor Ch'ien Lung permitted Lord Macartney (1736–1806) to present his gifts, which the Chinese described as tribute, but he turned down Macartney's requests. Western trade remained encapsulated at Canton.

Ming-Ch'ing Culture

Chinese culture had begun to turn inward during the Sung in reaction to Buddhism. This tendency continued into the Ming and Ch'ing, when Chinese culture became virtually impervious to outside influences. This reflected a tradition and a social order that had stood the test of time, but it also indicated a closed system of ideas with weaknesses that would become apparent in the nineteenth century.

Ming and Ch'ing Chinese esteemed most highly the traditional categories of high culture: painting, calligraphy, poetry, and philosophy. Porcelains of great beauty were also produced. The pottery industry of Europe was begun during the sixteenth century to imitate these wares, and Chinese and Japanese influences have dominated Western ceramics down to the present. Chinese today, however, see the novel as the characteristic cultural achievement of the Ming and Ch'ing.

The novel in China grew out of plot-books used by earlier storytellers. Like the stories, Chinese novels consisted of episodes strung together. As most novels were written in colloquial Chinese, which was not quite respectable in the society of scholars, their authors wrote under pseudonyms.

JAPAN

The two segments of late traditional Japan could not be more different. The Warring States era (1467–1600), the last phase of Japan's medieval history, saw the unleashing of internal wars and anarchy. Within a century, all vestiges of the old manorial or estate system had been scrapped and almost all of the Ashikaga lords had been overthrown. The Tokugawa era (1600–1868) that followed saw Japan with a stronger government than ever. During the Tokugawa era, Japanese culture was transformed, preparing it for the challenge it would face during the mid-nineteenth century.

Warring States Japan (1467–1600)	
1543	Portuguese arrive in Japan
1575	Battle of Nagashino
1582	Oda Nobunaga is assassinated
1587	Spanish arrive in Japan
1588	Hideyoshi's sword hunt
1590	Hideyoshi unifies Japan
1592, 1597–1598	Hideyoshi sends armies to Korea; battles fought against Chinese troops
1597	Hideyoshi bans Christianity
1598	Hideyoshi dies
1600	Tokugawa victory in Battle of Sekigahara

Warring States Era (1467–1600)

In 1467, a dispute arose over who would be the next Ashikaga shōgun. The dispute led to wars throughout Japan for eleven years. Most of Kyoto was destroyed in the fighting, and the authority of the Ashikaga *bakufu* came to an end. This first war ended in 1477, but the fighting resumed and continued for more than a century.

War of All Against All

Even before 1467, the Ashikaga equilibrium had been precarious. The regional daimyo lords had relied on their relationship to the *bakufu* to hold their stronger vassals in check, while relying on these vassals to preserve their independence against strong neighbors. The collapse of *bakufu* authority after 1467 left the regional lords standing alone, removing the last barrier to internecine wars. The regional lords, however, were too weak to stand alone. They became prey to the stronger among their vassals as well as to powerful neighboring states.

By the end of the sixteenth century, hundreds of little "Warring States daimyo" had emerged, each with his own warrior band. The constant wars among these men were not unlike those of the early feudal era in Europe. The most efficient in revamping their domain for military ends survived. The less ruthless, who clung to old ways, were defeated and absorbed.

As fighting continued, local states gave way to regional states until in the late sixteenth century, all of Japan was brought under the hegemony of a single lord, Toyotomi Hideyoshi (1536–1598). But it was only with the victory of Tokugawa Ieyasu (1542–1616) at the Battle of Sekigahara in 1600 that true unification was finally achieved. Ieyasu's unification was based on a sweeping transformation of Japan's society.

How should one characterize the society that emerged from the Warring States? Does the word *feudal* apply? In some respects, it does: By the late sixteenth century all warriors in Japan were part of a pyramid of vassals and lords headed by a single overlord; warriors of rank held fiefs and vassals of their own.

In other respects, Japan was more like postfeudal Europe. First, most of the military class were soldiers, not aristocrats. Even though they were called samurai and were vassals, they were not given fiefs but were paid with stipends of rice. Second, unlike, say, feudal England, where the military class was about one-quarter of 1 percent of the population, in mid-sixteenth-century Japan it may have reached 7 or 8 percent. It was more of a size with the mercenary armies of Europe during the fifteenth or sixteenth centuries. Third, the recruitment of village warriors gave rise to problems as well. Taxes became harder to collect. Local samurai were often involved in uprisings that sometimes involved whole provinces. Again, the parallels with postfeudal Europe seem closer. Fourth, even in a feudal society, not everything is feudal. Commercial growth continued in the Warring States era.

Foreign Relations and Trade

Japanese pirate-traders plied the seas of East Asia during the fifteenth and sixteenth centuries. To halt their depredations, the Ming emperor invited the third Ashikaga shōgun to trade with China. An agreement was reached in 1404. However, piracy stopped only after Japan was reunified at the close of the sixteenth century.

The content of the trade reflected the progress of Japanese crafts. Early Japanese exports to China were raw materials, but by the sixteenth century, manufactured goods were rising in importance. In exchange, Japan received copper cash, porcelains, paintings, books, and medicines. Then, in 1635, the imposition of seclusion ended Japan's foreign trade: No Japanese could leave Japan, and the construction of large ships was prohibited.

Overlapping Japan's maritime expansion in the seas of East Asia was the arrival of European ships. Portuguese pirate-traders arrived in Japan in 1543. Spanish galleons came in 1587. They were followed by the Dutch and the English after the turn of the century.

The Portuguese became important as shippers. They carried Southeast Asian goods and Japanese silver to China and Chinese silk to Japan, and they used their profits to buy spices for the European market.

Traders brought with them Jesuit missionaries. They directed their efforts toward the samurai. Christian converts numbered about 300,000 in 1600. That is to say, in the late sixteenth century, a higher percentage of Japanese were Christian than today.

It is difficult to explain why Christianity met with greater success in Japan than in other Asian lands. When introduced, it was seen as a new Buddhist sect. There seemed little difference to the Japanese between the cosmic Buddha of Shingon and the Christian God, between the paradise of Amida and the Christian Heaven, or between prayers to Kannon—the female *bodhisattva* of mercy—and to the Virgin Mary. The Japanese also noted the theological similarity between the pietism of the Pure Land sect and that of Christianity. The personal example of the Jesuits was also important.

The fortunes of Christianity began to decline in 1597, when six Spanish Franciscans and twenty Japanese converts were crucified in Nagasaki. It was said that Spanish merchants and priests represented the first step toward the conquest of Japan. Sporadic persecutions continued until 1614, when Tokugawa Ieyasu formally banned the foreign religion. Some Christians recanted. More than 3,000 others were martyred.

The last resistance was an uprising in 1637 and 1638 in which 37,000 Christians died. After that, Christianity survived in Japan only as a hidden religion. A few of these "hidden Christians" reemerged in the later nineteenth century.

Tokugawa Era (1600–1868)

Political Engineering and Economic Growth During the Seventeenth Century

After the unifications of 1590 and 1600, Japan's leaders sought to create a peaceful, stable, orderly society. By the middle or late seventeenth century, Japan's society and political system had been radically reengineered. Vigorous economic and demographic growth had also occurred. This combination of political and economic change made the seventeenth century a period of great dynamism.

Hideyoshi's Rule   In the summer of 1588, Hideyoshi ordered a "sword hunt" to disarm the peasants. Once the hunt was completed, the 5 percent of the population who remained samurai used their monopoly on weapons to control the other 95 percent.

Hideyoshi next moved to freeze the social classes. Samurai were prohibited from quitting the service of their lord. Peasants were barred from abandoning their fields to become townspeople. This policy succeeded. Samurai, farmers, and townspeople tended to marry within their respective classes, and each class developed a unique cultural character.

Having disarmed the peasantry, Hideyoshi ordered surveys to define each parcel of land by location, size, soil quality, product, and cultivator's name. Hideyoshi's survey laid the foundations for a systematic land tax. Domains and fiefs were henceforth ranked in terms of their assessed yield.

Establishment of Tokugawa Rule   Hideyoshi assumed that his vassals would honor their oaths of loyalty to his heir. He was especially trustful of his great ally Tokugawa Ieyasu. His trust was misplaced. After his death in 1598, Hideyoshi's former vassals broke into two opposing camps and fought a great battle in 1600 from which Tokugawa Ieyasu emerged victorious. Ieyasu established his headquarters in Edo (today's Tokyo), in the center of his military holdings in eastern Japan (see Map 20–2). He took the title of shōgun in 1603 and called his government the *bakufu*. Ieyasu then used his military power to reorganize Japan.

Ieyasu's first move was to confiscate the lands of his defeated enemies and to reward his vassals and allies. During the first quarter of the seventeenth century, the *bakufu* confiscated the domains of 150 daimyo and transferred 229 daimyo from one domain to another. The transfers severed long-standing ties between daimyo and their disarmed former village retainers. When a daimyo was transferred to a new fief, he took his samurai retainers with him. The entire arrangement constituted a defensive system, with the staunchest Tokugawa supporters nearest to the center of power.

The Tokugawa also established other controls. Legal codes regulated the imperial court, the temples and shrines, and the daimyo. Military houses were enjoined to use men of ability and to practice frugality. Only with *bakufu* consent could daimyo marry or repair their castles.

A second control was a hostage system that required the wives and children of daimyo to reside permanently in Edo and the daimyo themselves to spend every second year in Edo. This transformed feudal lords into courtiers.

A third key control was the national policy of seclusion. Seclusion was no barrier to cultural imports from China and Korea. But except for small Chinese and Dutch trading contingents at Nagasaki, no foreigners were permitted to enter Japan, and on pain of death, no Japanese were allowed to go abroad. Nor could oceangoing ships be built. This policy was

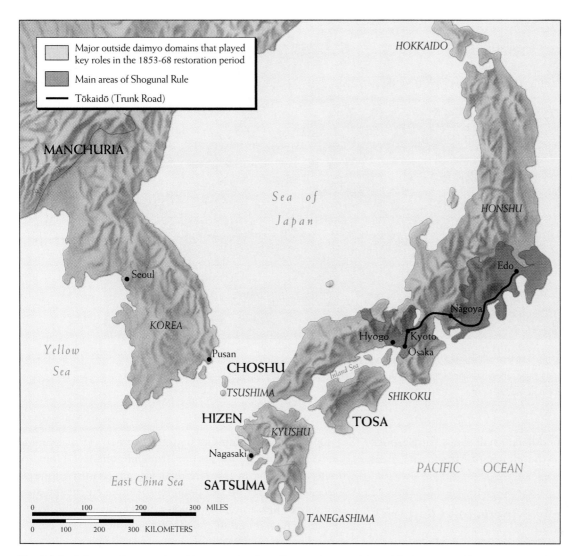

Map 20-2 Tokugawa Japan and the Korean peninsula. The area between Edo and Osaka in central Honshu was both the political base of the Tokugawa *bakufu* and its rice basket. The domains that would overthrow the Tokugawa *bakufu* in the late nineteenth century were mostly in outlying areas of southwestern Japan.

strictly enforced until 1854. Seclusion enclosed the system of Tokugawa rule. Cut off from outside political contacts, for Japanese, Japan became the world.

The Seventeenth-Century Economy   The political dynamism of the period from Hideyoshi through the first century of Tokugawa rule was matched by economic growth. Resources no longer needed for war were allocated to land reclamation and agriculture. The result was a doubling of agricultural production, as well as a doubling of population from about 12 million in 1600 to 24 million in 1700.

Peace also sustained growth in commerce. The medieval guilds were abolished and Japan's central markets freed from monopolistic restrictions. The result was a burgeoning of trade and the formation of a national market network. As this network expanded, economic functions became more differentiated and efficient.

Economic growth and the national integration of the economy led to a richness and diversity in urban life. Townsmen governed their districts. Samurai city managers watched over the city as a whole. Official services were provided by schools, police, and firefighters. But there were also servants, cooks, messengers, restaurant owners, priests, doctors, teachers, sword sharpeners, book lenders, instructors in the martial arts, prostitutes, and bathhouse attendants. In the world of popular arts, there were woodblock printers and artists, book publishers, puppeteers, acrobatic troupes, storytellers, and Kabuki and Nō actors. Merchant establishments included money

The commercial district of Osaka, the "kitchen" of Tokugawa Japan. Warehouses bear the crests of their merchant houses. Ships (upper right) loaded with rice, cotton goods, sake, and other goods are about to depart for Edo (Tokyo). Their captains vied with one another to arrive first and get the best price. [Courtesy A. Craig]

changers, pawnbrokers, peddlers, small shops, single-price retail establishments like the House of Mitsui, and great wholesale merchants.

Eighteenth and Early Nineteenth Centuries

By the late seventeenth century, the political engineering of the Tokugawa state was complete. After that, few important changes were made in governing institutions. In the economy, too, dynamic growth gave way to slower growth within a high-level equilibrium. Yet changes of a different kind were under way.

Cycles of Reform   Most political history of late Tokugawa Japan is written in terms of alternating cycles of laxity and reform. Even during the mid-seventeenth century, the expenses of the *bakufu* and daimyo states were often greater than their income. In part, the reason was structural: Taxes were based on agriculture in an economy that was becoming commercial. In part, it was simple mathematics: After the samurai were paid their stipends, not enough was left for the expenses of domain government and the costs of the Edo establishments. In part, it was the toll of extraordinary costs, such as a *bakufu* levy, the wedding of a daimyo's daughter, or the rebuilding of a castle after a fire. And finally, in part, it was a taste for luxury among daimyo and retainers of rank.

Over the years a familiar pattern emerged. To make ends meet, domains would borrow from merchants. Then, as finances became even more difficult, a reformist clique of officials would return the domain to a more frugal and austere way of life. But since no one likes to practice frugality forever, a new round of spending would begin. The *bakufu* carried out three great reforms:

1716–1733	Tokugawa Yoshimune	17 years
1787–1793	Matsudaira Sadanobu	6 years
1841–1843	Mizuno Tadakuni	2 years

The first two were long and successful; the third was not. Its failure set the stage for the ineffective response of the *bakufu* to the West in the mid-nineteenth century.

Bureaucratization   The balance between centralization and decentralization lasted, until the end of the Tokugawa era. Not a single domain ever tried to overthrow the *bakufu* hegemony. Nor did the *bakufu* ever try to extend its control over the domains. But bureaucracy grew steadily both within the *bakufu* and domains. By 1850, all but the largest samurai fiefs were administered by district officials who collected the standard domain taxes and forwarded to the samurai their income. Along with the growth in bureaucracy was the proliferation of administrative codes and paperwork: records of births, adoptions, name changes, samurai ranks, fief registers, stipend registers, land and tax registers, court proceedings, and so on.

Of course, there were limits to bureaucratization. Only samurai could aspire to official posts. They came to the office wearing their two swords. Decision-making posts were limited to upper-ranking samurai. But periods of financial crises a demand arose for men of ability, and middle- or lower-middle-ranking samurai became staff assistants to bureaucrats of rank.

The Later Tokugawa Economy   By 1700, the economy approached the limit of expansion within the available technology. The population reached 26 million early in the eighteenth century and was at the same figure in the mid-nineteenth century, a period during which the population of China more than doubled.

After 1700, taxes became stabilized and land surveys were few. Evidence suggests little increase in grain production and only slow growth in agricultural byproducts. Some families made conscious efforts to limit their size to raise their standard of living. Contraception and abortion were commonplace, and infanticide was practiced in hard times. But periodic disease, shortages of food, and late marriages among the poor were more important factors.

Some farmers remained independent cultivators, but about a quarter of all cultivated lands were worked by tenants by the mid-nineteenth century. Most landlords were small, and often were village leaders. They were not at all like the Chinese gentry. The misery of the lower stratum of rural society contributed to an increase in peasant uprisings during the late eighteenth and early nineteenth centuries. Authorities had no difficulty quelling them, and no uprising in Japan approached those of late Manchu China.

Commerce grew slowly during the late Tokugawa. In the early eighteenth century, it was reencased within guilds. Merchants paid set fees in return for monopoly privileges in central marketplaces. Guilds were also reestablished in the domains, and some domains established domain-run monopolies on products such as wax, paper, indigo, or sugar. The problem facing domain leaders was how to share in the profits without injuring the competitive standing of domain exports. Most late Tokugawa commercial growth was in countryside industries—*sake*, soy sauce, dyes, silks, or cotton. Some were organized and financed by city merchants. Others competed with city merchants, shipping directly to the end markets to circumvent monopoly controls. The expansion of labor in such rural industries may explain the population shrinkage in late Tokugawa cities.

The largest question about the Tokugawa economy concerns its relation to Japan's rapid industrialization in the late nineteenth century. Some scholars have suggested that Japan had a "running start." Others have stressed Japanese backwardness in comparison with European late developers. The question is still unresolved.

Tokugawa Era (1600–1868)

1600	Tokugawa Ieyasu reunifies Japan
1615	"Laws of Military Houses" issued
1639	Seclusion policy adopted
1642	Edo hostage system in place
1644–1694	Bashō, poet
1653–1724	Chikamatsu Monzaemon, dramatist
1701	The forty-seven rōnin avenge their lord
1853, 1854	Commodore Matthew Perry visits Japan

Tokugawa Culture

Two hundred fifty years of peace and prosperity provided a base for an ever more complex culture and a broader popular participation in cultural life. In the villages, Buddhism became more deeply rooted; new folk religions proliferated; by the early nineteenth century most well-to-do farmers could read and write. The aristocratic culture of the ranking samurai houses also remained vigorous. Nō plays continued to be staged. The medieval tradition of black ink paintings was continued by the Kanō school and other artists.

The Ashikaga tradition of restraint, simplicity, and naturalness in architecture was extended. The imperial villa in Katsura outside of Kyoto has its roots in medieval architecture and to this day inspires Japanese architects. The gilded and colored screen paintings that had surged in popularity during Hideyoshi's rule developed further, culminating in the powerful works of Ogata Kōrin (1658–1716).

Zen Buddhism, having declined during the Warring States period, was revitalized by the monk Hakuin (1686–1769). One of the great cultural figures of the Tokugawa era, Hakuin was also a writer, a painter, a calligrapher, and a sculptor.

Some scholars have argued that Tokugawa urban culture had a double structure. On the one hand were the samurai, serious and high-minded, who produced a vast body of Chinese-style paintings, poetry, and philosophical treatises. On the other hand was the culture of the townspeople: lowbrow, irreverent, secular, satirical, and often scatological. The samurai esteemed Sung-style paintings of mountains and waterfalls, often adorned with quotations from the Confucian classics or T'ang poetry. The townspeople collected prints of local beauties, actors, courtesans, and scenes from everyday life. Samurai moralists saw money as the root of evil. Merchants saw it as their goal in life.

Literature and Drama   Is cultural creativity more likely during periods of economic growth and political change or during periods of stability? The greatest works of literature and philosophy of Tokugawa Japan were produced between

1650 and 1725, just as the initial political transformation was being completed, but the economy still growing and the society not yet set in its ways.

One of the major literary figures and certainly the most entertaining was Ihara Saikaku (1642–1693), who is generally credited with having recreated the Japanese novel. Saikaku was the heir to an Osaka merchant house. He was raised to be its master, but after his wife died he let the head clerk manage the business and devoted himself to poetry, the theater, and the pleasure quarters. At the age of forty he wrote and illustrated *The Life of an Amorous Man*, the story of a modern and bawdy Prince Genji who cuts a swath through bathhouse girls, shrine maidens, courtesans, and boy actors. The success of the work led to a sequel, *The Life of an Amorous Woman*, the tale of a woman undone by passion.

A second major figure of Osaka culture at the turn of the century was the dramatist Chikamatsu Monzaemon (1653–1724). Born a samurai, Chikamatsu wrote for both the Kabuki and the puppet theater. Kabuki had begun early in the seventeenth century as suggestive skits and erotic dances performed by actresses. In 1629, the *bakufu* forbade women to perform on the stage. By the 1660s, Kabuki had evolved into a more serious drama with male actors playing both male and female roles.

The three main types of Kabuki plays were dance pieces, which were influenced by the tradition of the Nō; domestic dramas; and historical pieces. Chikamatsu wrote all three. In contrast to Saikaku's protagonists, the men and women in Chikamatsu's dramas struggle to fulfill the duties and obligations of their stations in life. Only when their passions become uncontrollable do the plays end in tragedy. The emotional intensity of the ending is heightened by the restraint shown by the actors before they reach their breaking point.

It is interesting to compare Kabuki and the Nō drama. Nō is like early Greek drama in that the chorus provides the narrative line. In Nō, the stylization of action is extreme. In Kabuki, as in Elizabethan drama, the actors declaim their lines in the dramatic realism demanded by the commoner theatergoers of seventeenth-century Japan.

In the early eighteenth century, Kabuki was displaced in popularity by the puppet theater (Bunraku). Many of Chikamatsu's plays were written for this genre. In the late eighteenth century, the puppet theater, in turn, declined, and Kabuki again blossomed as Japan's premier form of drama.

Confucian Thought

The most important change in Tokugawa intellectual life was that the ruling elite abandoned the religious worldview of Buddhism in favor of the more secular Confucianism, opening many avenues for further changes.

The great figures of Tokugawa Confucianism lived in the late seventeenth and early eighteenth centuries. They succeeded in adapting Chinese Confucianism to fit Japanese society. One problem, for example, was that in Chinese Confucianism there was no place for a shōgun, whereas in the Japanese tradition of sun-line emperors, there was no room for the Mandate of Heaven. Most Tokugawa thinkers handled this discrepancy by saying that Heaven gave the emperor its mandate and that the emperor then entrusted political authority to the shōgun. One philosopher suggested that the divine emperor acted for Heaven and gave the mandate to the shōgun. Neither solution was very comfortable, for, in fact, the emperor was as much a puppet as those in the Osaka theater.

Another problem was the difference between China's centralized bureaucratic government and Japan's "feudal" system of lord-vassal relationships. Samurai loyalty was clearly not that of a scholar-official to the Chinese emperor. Some Japanese Confucianists solved this problem by saying that it was China that had deviated from the feudal society of the Chou sages, whereas in Japan, Tokugawa Ieyasu had recreated just such a society.

A third problem concerned the "central flowery kingdom" and the barbarians around it. No philosopher could bring himself to say that Japan was the real middle kingdom and China the barbarian, but some argued that centrality was relative, and still others suggested that China under barbarian Manchu rule had lost its claim to universality. These are just a few of a large range of problems related to Japanese political organization, Shinto, and Japanese family practices. By the early eighteenth century, these problems had been addressed, and a revised Confucianism acceptable for use in Japan had come into being.

Another point to note is the continuing intellectual vitality of Japanese thought into the mid-nineteenth century. This vitality is partly explained by the disputes among different schools of Confucianism and partly, perhaps, by Japan's lack of an examination system. The best energies of its samurai youth were not channeled into writing the conventional and sterile "eight-legged essay" that was required for the Chinese examination system. Official preferment—within the constraints of Japan's hereditary system—was more likely to be obtained by writing a proposal for domain reforms.

The intellectual vitality was also a result of the rapid expansion of schools from the early eighteenth century. By the early nineteenth century, every domain had its own official school. Commoner schools (*terakoya*), in which reading, writing, and the rudiments of Confucianism were taught, grew apace. In the first half of the nineteenth century, private academies also appeared throughout the country. By the mid-nineteenth century, about 40 to 50 percent of the male population and 15 to 20 percent of the female population was literate—a far higher rate than in most of the world, and on a par with some European late developers.

Other Developments in Thought For Tokugawa scholars, the emotional problem of how to deal with China was vexing. They praised China as the teacher country and respected its creative tradition. They studied its history, philosophy, and literature. But they also sought to retain a separate Japanese identity. Most scholars dealt with this problem by adapting Confucianism to fit Japan. But two schools, National Studies and Dutch Studies, criticized the Chinese influence on Japanese life and culture.

National Studies began as philological studies of ancient Japanese texts. One source of its inspiration was Shinto. Another was the Neo-Confucian School of Ancient Learning. Just as the School of Ancient Learning had sought to discover the original, true meanings of the Chinese classics before they were contaminated by Sung metaphysics, so the scholars in the National Studies tradition tried to find in the Japanese classics the original true character of Japan before it had been contaminated by Chinese ideas. On studying these works, they found that the early Japanese spirit was free, spontaneous, clean, lofty, and honest, in contrast to the Chinese spirit, which they characterized as rigid, cramped, and artificial. National Studies also reaffirmed Japan's emperor institution.

National Studies became influential during the late Tokugawa era and influenced the Meiji Restoration. Its doctrines continued thereafter as one strain of Japanese ultranationalism.

A second development was Dutch Studies. After Christianity had been proscribed and the policy of seclusion adopted, all Western books were banned in Japan. Some knowledge of Dutch was maintained among the official interpreters who dealt with the Dutch at Nagasaki. The ban on Western books (except for those propagating Christianity) was ended in 1720 by the shōgun Tokugawa Yoshimune (r. 1716–1745).

During the eighteenth century, a school of "Dutch medicine" became established in Japan. Japanese pioneers early recognized that Western anatomy texts were superior to Chinese. The first Japanese dissection of a corpse occurred in 1754. By the mid-nineteenth century, there were schools of Dutch Studies in the main cities of Japan, and instruction was available in some domains as well. Medicine was the primary occupation of those who studied Dutch. But some knowledge of Western astronomy, geography, botany, physics, chemistry, and arts also entered Japan.

From the late eighteenth century, the Japanese began to be aware of the West, and especially of Russia, as a threat to Japan. In 1791, a concerned scholar wrote *A Discussion of the Military Problems of a Maritime Nation*, advocating strong navy and coastal defenses. During the early nineteenth century,

such concerns mounted. A sudden expansion in Dutch Studies occurred after Commodore Matthew Perry's visits to Japan in 1853 and 1854. During the 1860s, Dutch Studies became Western Studies, as English, French, German, and Russian were added to the languages studied at the *bakufu* Institute for the Investigation of Barbarian Books. In sum, Dutch Studies laid a foundation on which the Japanese built quickly when the need arose for knowledge of the West.

KOREA AND VIETNAM

A feature of world history, noted earlier, is the spread of heartland civilizations into their surrounding areas. In East Asia, the heartland civilization was that of China, the surrounding areas that were able to take in Chinese learning were Japan, Korea, and Vietnam. Like the Japanese, Koreans and Vietnamese devised a writing system using Chinese ideographs. They partially modeled their governments on those of China. They accepted Chinese Buddhism and Confucianism, and with them Chinese conceptions of the universe, state, and human relationships. The Confucian definitions of the relations between ruler and minister, father and son, and husband and wife were emphasized in Korea and Vietnam as they were in China. But at the same time, Koreans and Vietnamese, who spoke non-Chinese tongues, saw themselves as separate peoples, and gradually came to take pride in their independence. In Europe, Germany might be a parallel case: it became civilized by borrowing the heartland Greco-Christian culture of the Mediterranean area, but it kept its original tongue and elements from its earlier culture.

Korea

A range of mountains along its northern rim divides the Korean peninsula from Manchuria, making it a distinct geographical unit. Mountains continue south through the eastern third of Korea, while in the west and south are coastal plains and broad river valleys. Two further geographical factors affected Korean history. One was that the northwestern corner of Korea was only 300 miles from the northeastern corner of historical China: close enough for Korea to be vulnerable to invasions by its powerful neighbor but far enough away so that most of the time China found it easier to treat Korea as a tributary than to control it directly. The other factor was that the southern rim of Korea was just 100 miles from Japan.

Early History

During the first millennium B.C.E., agriculture, bronze, and iron were introduced to Korea, transforming its primitive society. But Koreans were still ruled by tribal chiefdoms in 108 B.C.E. when the Han Emperor Wu Ti sent an army into north Korea to menace the flank of the Hunnish (Hsiung Nu) Empire that had spread across the steppe to the north of China. Wu Ti built a Chinese city which survived into the fourth century C.E., and established commanderies and prefectures to administer the land.

Between the fourth and seventh centuries, three archaic states emerged from earlier tribal confederations. Silla, one of the three, together with armies from T'ang China, conquered the other two in the seventh century. Silla was recognized by China in 675 as an autonomous tribute state. The period of Silla rule may be likened to Nara Japan: Korea borrowed Chinese writing, established some government offices on the Chinese model, sent annual embassies to the T'ang court, and took in Chinese Buddhism and Chinese arts and philosophies. Yet within the Silla government, birth mattered more than scholarship and rule by aristocrats continued, while in village Korea, the worship of nature deities was only lightly touched by the Buddhism that spread among the ruling elites.

Silla underwent a normal end-of-dynasty decline, and in 918, a warlord general founded a new dynasty, the Koryo. The English word "Korea" is derived from this dynastic name. This was a creative period. Korean scholars advanced in their mastery of Chinese principles of government. New genres of poetry and literature appeared. Korean potters made celadon vases rivaling those of China. Printing using moveable metallic type was invented during the thirteenth century. But most important was the growth of Buddhism. Temples, monasteries, and nunneries were built throughout the land, and Buddhist arts flourished.

Despite cultural advances, the Koryo state was weak. Its economy was undeveloped: trade was by barter, and Chinese missions commented on the extravagance of officials in the capital and the squalor of commoners and slaves in Korea's villages. The dynasty was aristocratic, and as centuries passed, private estates and armies arose, and civil

officials were replaced by military men. Frequent incursions from across Korea's northern border weakened the state. The cost of wars with the Mongols was particularly high. The Koryo court survived as long as it did by becoming in succession the tributary of the Sung, Liao, Chin, and Mongol dynasties.

The Choson Era: Late Traditional Korea

In 1392, a Koryo general, Yi Songgye, founded a new dynasty. It lasted until 1910; its amazing longevity was directly related to the stability of Ming-Ch'ing China.

After seizing power, Yi carried out an extensive land reform and strengthened his government by absorbing into his officialdom members of the great Koryo families. During the Yi or Choson period, these elite families, known as *yangban*, monopolized education, official posts, and land. Beneath them were the commoners known as "good people," tax-paying free subjects of the king. Beneath the commoners and constituting perhaps one-third of the population were government and private slaves. Korean scholars argue that they were not like slaves in other lands, since there were no slave auctions, and, following Confucian teachings, husbands were not separated from their wives. But Korean slaves were nonetheless property. They were often attached to land, they could be given as gifts, and their children were slaves to be used as their owners willed.

Early Choson culture showed many signs of vigor. Lyrical poetry and then prose reached new heights. The most important intellectual trend was the gradual movement of the *yangban* away from Buddhism and their acceptance of Neo-Confucianism.

But at mid-dynasty, invasions dealt a severe blow to the well-being of Choson society. Hideyoshi, having brought all of Japan under his control, decided to conquer China through Korea. His samurai armies devastated Korea in 1592 and 1596. The invasions ended with his death in 1598. On both occasions the Ming court sent troops to aid its tributary, but the Chinese armies devastated the land almost as much as had the Japanese. A third disaster occurred in 1627 and 1637 when Manchu troops invaded pro-Ming Korea. The result of these multiple incursions was a drop in taxable land to about a quarter of its late-sixteenth-century level. Behind this statistic lay famine, death, and misery.

Had the late-sixteenth-century Choson government been stronger, it might have recovered. But cliques of officials had begun to fight among themselves over official positions. Many in the losing factions were executed or imprisoned. As the struggles became more fierce, the effectiveness of government declined. High officials in Seoul used their power to garner private agricultural estates, and established local academies to prepare their own kinsmen for the official examinations.

From the mid-seventeenth century on, Korea offers a mixed picture. Literacy rose and a new popular fiction of fables, romances, and novels appeared. Women writers became important for the first time. Among some *yangban* there was a philosophic reaction against what was perceived as the emptiness of Neo-Confucianism. Calling for "practical learning" to effect a renewal of Korean society, scholars criticized the Confucian classics and outlined plans for administrative reforms and the encouragement of commerce. Unfortunately, their recommendations were not adopted, and the society continued its decline. More Koreans died in the famine of 1671 than during Hideyoshi's invasions. Overtaxation, drought, floods, pestilence, and famine became commonplace. Robberies occurred in daytime Seoul, and bandits plagued the countryside. Disgruntled officials led peasants in revolts in 1811 and 1862. Because of the concentration of officials, wealth, and military power at Seoul and because of Manchu support for the ruling house, neither revolt toppled the dynasty, but the revolts left Korea unable to meet the challenges it would soon face.

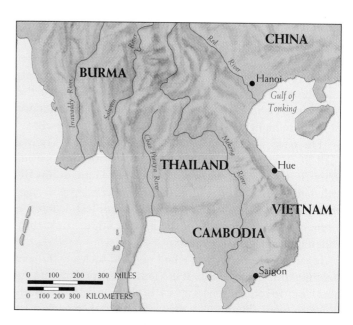

Map 20-3   Vietnam and neighboring Southeast Asia.

Vietnam

Southeast Asia

The historical civilizations of Southeast Asia were shaped by three movements. One was the movement of peoples and languages from north to south. Ranges of mountains rising in Tibet and South China divide Southeast Asia into river valleys. The Mon and Burmese peoples had moved from the southeast slopes of the Tibetan plateau into the Upper Irrawaddy by 500 B.C.E. and continued south, founding the kingdom of Pagan in 847 C.E. Thai tribes moved south from China down the valley of the Chao Phraya River somewhat later, founding the kingdoms of Sukhothai (1238–1419) and Ayutthaya (1350–1767). Even today Thai-speaking tribes are found in south China. The Vietnamese, too, arose in the north and moved into present-day central and south Vietnam only in recent historical times.

A second movement was the Indianization of Southeast Asia. Between the first and fifteenth centuries, Indian traders and missionaries established outposts throughout southeast Asia. As Hinduism and Buddhism spread through the region, Indian-type states with god-kings were established, and Indian scripts, legal codes, literature, drama, art, and music were adopted. Today, Burma, Thailand, and Cambodia retain an Indian-type of Buddhism.

A third movement was of Arab and Indian traders who sailed across the Indian Ocean to dominate trade with the Spice Islands (the Moluccas of present-day Indonesia) between the thirteenth and fifteenth centuries. They married into local ruling families and spread Islam. Local rulers who converted became sultans. Today Malaysia and Indonesia are predominantly Muslim.

Early Vietnamese History

Vietnam, however, was untouched by either Indian or Islamic culture. Most of its higher culture came from China.

To comprehend Vietnamese history, one must distinguish between the people and the land. Until the fifteenth century C.E., the Vietnamese people inhabited only a small portion of what is today Vietnam, the basin of the Red River. Central Vietnam and the southeastern coast were ruled by the state of Champa. Most of the Mekong River delta in the south was ruled by Cambodian empires.

The political history of the Vietnamese began in 208 B.C.E., when a renegade Han dynasty general formed the state of Nan Yueh. It ruled over southeastern China and the Red River basin from its capital, which was near present-day Canton. In Vietnamese, the Chinese ideograph "Yueh" is read "Viet." The name "Vietnam," literally "Viet to the south," is derived from the name of this early state. In 111 B.C.E., Han Wu Ti brought it under Chinese rule.

For more than a millennium after 111 B.C.E., Vietnam was ruled by China. The administrative center was a fort with a Chinese governor and Chinese troops. The governor ruled through Vietnamese who were the heads of powerful local families. Then in 39 C.E., the Truong sisters led a revolt against Chinese rule—the husband of one sister had been executed by the Chinese. Thereafter, more officials were sent from China and direct bureaucratic rule was instituted.

Later Vietnamese historians made the two sisters into national heroes.

During these early centuries, change was slow. Buddhism was introduced into Vietnam from China. Chinese officials and immigrants married Vietnamese women, which led to the formation of a Sino-Vietnamese political elite. The influence of Chinese higher culture was largely confined to this elite.

The pace of change increased during the T'ang dynasty (618–907). Vietnam was still treated as a border region, but Chinese administration became stronger. Vietnam was divided into provinces, which the Chinese referred to as *Annam*, the "pacified south." This name was never lost: when the French came to Vietnam in the nineteenth century, they called its people the *Annamese*.

Japan and Korea also reached out and took in Chinese learning during the T'ang. Was Vietnam's experience a parallel case? In some respects it was. In all three societies, Buddhism entered, flourished in the capitals, and then percolated into local areas, where it absorbed earlier religious traditions. In all three, other aspects of China's higher culture affected mainly the elites. In villages, an older way of life continued. But the differences were also significant. Japanese and Korean rulers reached out for Chinese civilization, and used it for their own ends. In Vietnam, because the rulers were Chinese, no such transformation occurred.

Late Traditional Vietnam

Ten major revolts occurred during Chinese rule—a not unusual number for a Chinese border region with a non-Chinese population. The last revolt, in 939 when China was weak, led to an independent Vietnamese government. Vietnam never again became a part of China.

Several approaches have been used in writing the history of Vietnam's second millennium. One sees it in terms of dynasties:

Ly	1009–1225
Tran	1225–1400
Le	1428–1787
Nguyen	1802–1880s

As in China, dynasties began with strong military figures, who established courts, extended their control over the countryside, and collected taxes. Most founders of dynasties were members of the Sino-Vietnamese elite. Dynasties ended with the decentralization of power, the breakdown of taxation, and the rise of regional armies. But the idea of a "dynastic cycle" of slow administrative decline fits Vietnam less well than China. For one thing, even early in a dynasty, administrations were weaker than in China. Local magnates contested central control for longer periods. For another, each new Chinese dynasty invaded Vietnam, to regain control over an area that had once been ruled by China. These invasions often reshaped dynasties. The Tran dynasty, for example, was extended for twenty extra years by supporting Ming forces. For still another, the dynastic name was sometimes kept even after its ruling house had lost power. During the seventeenth and eighteenth centuries, for example, Vietnam was divided into two states, one ruling from Hanoi and the other from Hue. In short, though the "dynasty" may be a convenient unit for dividing the second millennium into large blocks of time, it is less useful for analysis.

Another approach is to see Vietnam in relation to the Chinese state and Chinese civilization. Although Chinese invasions of Vietnam were unsuccessful, Vietnamese rulers found it easier to "manage" China than to defy it. Every Vietnamese dynasty became a "tributary" of China. Missions were sent to China bearing tribute. The head of the mission professed the Vietnamese ruler's submission to the Chinese emperor and performed the kowtow. In correspondence with the Chinese "emperor," too, the Vietnamese rulers styled themselves as "kings," a title indicating their subordinate status. But this formal submission was little more than a ritual. Within Vietnam, Vietnamese rulers styled themselves as "emperors." They claimed their mandate to rule came directly from Heaven, equal to the mandate received by the Chinese ruler. They denied the universality of the Chinese imperium by referring to China not as the Middle Kingdom but as the Northern Court—their own government being the Southern Court. Yet over the centuries, the imprint of Chinese culture became more pronounced. One highpoint was the era of Le Thanh Tong (1442–1497), one of the strongest figures in Vietnamese history. Le used Chinese culture and institutions as an advanced technology to strengthen his government. He established schools, introduced Neo-Confucianism, institutionalized an examination system, and promulgated a legal code that remained in effect through the rest of the dynasty.

A third approach to Vietnamese history is to see it as a steady "march to the south" between the fifteenth and eighteenth centuries. Vietnam has been likened to two baskets on a carrying pole. One basket is the Red River delta centering on Hanoi in the north, the other the Mekong delta centering on Saigon in the south. The pole is the narrow mountainous strip of central Vietnam. Until the fifteenth century, Vietnamese inhabited only the north. Central and southeastern Vietnam was Champa, the kingdom of the Chams, a Malayan people who engaged in trade and piracy. The Chams converted to Islam. For centuries Vietnamese and Chams waged intermittent wars. In 1357 when Tran Rule was weak, a Cham army pillaged Hanoi. But under Le Thanh Tong, Vietnam destroyed Champa.

Settlers from the crowded Red River delta began to pour into the south. Political authority followed the settlers. During the seventeenth century, the Cambodian empire of Angkor was unable to resist. By 1700, a southern Vietnamese state with a capital at Hue had conquered Saigon, and by 1757 it had occupied present-day southern Vietnam. This chain of events made south Vietnam different from the north. It was less Confucian and, as a frontier society, less educated. It included large minority populations of Muslim Chams and Cambodians, who practiced a Southeast Asian form of Buddhism. Massive emigrations of Chinese into southeast Asia also began during these centuries. Today about 1 million Chinese live in south Vietnam alone and play key roles in its economy. Such ethnic and religious diversity made the south far more difficult to govern than the more homogeneous north.

During the last half of the eighteenth century, Vietnam was wracked by further wars. In 1802, one warlord established Vietnam's last dynasty, the Nguyen. Its capital was at Hue. In coming to power, the new emperor had been aided by French advisors, several of whom were rewarded with high posts. The Nguyen dynasty, nonetheless, became more Chinese than any previous dynasty. It adopted the law codes of Manchu China and established institutions such as the Six Boards, Hanlin Academy, Censorate, and a hierarchy of civil and military officials recruited by examinations. The reasons for these initiatives were to placate Confucian scholars in the north, to strengthen the court, and to weaken the military figures who had helped the dynasty's rise. From the time of the second emperor, it also became anti-French and anti-Christian.

During the first half of the nineteenth century, Vietnam was probably governed better than any other Southeast Asian state. But it had weaknesses. There were tensions between the north, which was overpopulated, well schooled, and furnished most of the official class, and the south, which was ethnically diverse, educationally backward, and poorly represented in government. Trade and artisanal industries were less developed than in China and Japan, only small amounts of specie circulated, and periodic markets were more common than permanent market towns. The government rested on a society composed largely of self-sufficient villages. In sum, Vietnam entered the second half of the nineteenth century even less prepared than China or Japan for the challenges posed by the West.

IN WORLD PERSPECTIVE

Late Traditional East Asia

The history of late traditional East Asia underlines the exceptional nature of the European development from commerce to industry. The arguments and counterarguments as to why this development did not occur in China and Japan are illuminating. One often-cited argument is that East Asia lacked the Protestant ethic that inspired Western capitalism. The counterargument is that all East Asian nations have strong family-centered ethics with an emphasis on frugality, hard work, and saving. Is that not a Protestant ethic of sorts? Moreover, if the problem is as deeply rooted as a religious ethic, why have parts of East Asia been able to achieve such explosive economic growth since the 1960s?

Another argument stresses the absence of a scientific revolution in premodern East Asia. The counterargument is that science made only a minimal contribution to England's early industrialization. Some scholars argue that in China, merchant capital, instead of being put into industry, was invested in land, which was honorable and secure from rapacious officials. But this argument applies to the Ch'ing less well than the Ming and does not apply to Japan, where merchants could not buy land at all.

Still another argument stresses incentives and rewards. In England, the self-educated technicians who invented the water loom and the steam engine reaped enormous rewards and honors. In China, wealth and prestige were reserved largely for officials and gentry, who were literary or political in orientation and despised those who worked with their hands. No patent laws protected inventors. But other scholars ask whether the Ming and Ch'ing were so different from past dynasties during which the Chinese had been brilliantly inventive. Whatever the explanation, all agree that substantial commercial growth in both China and Japan did not lead to an indigenous breakthrough to machine industry.

Another comparison concerns bureaucracy. Bureaucracy does for administration what the assembly line does for manufacturing: It breaks complex tasks into simple ones to achieve huge gains in efficiency. In the West, bureaucracies appeared only in recent centuries. They strengthened first monarchies and then nation-states against landed aristocrats. They are viewed as a sign of modernity, the triumph of ability over hereditary privilege. In some respects, Chinese bureaucracy was similar: It was reasonably efficient, and it strengthened the central state. Would-be officials in nineteenth-century Britain studied the Greek and Roman classics, just as those in China studied the Confucian classics. But in other regards, Western historians of Chinese bureaucracy feel as if they have passed through Alice's looking glass: What was recent in the West had flourished for over a thousand years in China. Chinese officials themselves were a segment of a landed gentry class in a country from which hereditary aristocracies had long since disappeared. Moreover, although Chinese officials were certainly men of talent, they would become a major obstacle to modernity.

A final point to note is the difference between Chinese and Japanese attitudes toward outside civilizations. When the Jesuits tried to introduce science, the Chinese response was occasional curiosity and general indifference. A few Jesuits were appointed as interpreters and court astronomers, or were employed to cast cannon. The Chinese lack of interest in foreign cultures may be explained by the coherence of China's core institutions of government—the emperor, bureaucracy, examination system, gentry, and Confucian schools—which had been in place for centuries. Having proved their worth, they were so deeply rooted and internalized as to approximate a closed system, impervious to outside influences. In contrast, the Tokugawa Japanese, despite a national policy of seclusion, reached out for Dutch science as they earlier had reached out for Chinese Neo-Confucianism. This difference would shape the respective responses of China and Japan to the West during the mid-nineteenth century.

For Korea and Vietnam, the problem is to explain why they were so much less developed in commerce—to say nothing of industry—than China and Japan. Were both the Korean *yangban* and the Vietnamese officials more aristocratic than Chinese gentry? Was the *yangban's* distaste for commerce greater than that of Chinese officials? Vietnam clearly lacked the long periods of peace—a necessary condition for commercial growth—enjoyed by China and Japan. Did the travails and social unrest during the last centuries of Choson rule in Korea also stifle the growth of commerce? These are questions for which scholars have not yet provided answers.

Review Questions

1. Why did the economy grow in late traditional China?

2. Did Manchu rule resemble Mongol rule, or was it different? In what regards were K'ang Hsi and Ch'ien Lung indistinguishable from Chinese emperors?

3. Ming-Ch'ing foreign relations set the stage for China's nineteenth-century encounter with the West. How would you describe the setting?

4. How did military technology in Japan change during the fifteenth and sixteenth centuries? Was unification the consequence or would it have happened anyway?

5. Contrast the dynamism of social engineering in seventeenth-century Japan with the high-level equilibrium of the eighteenth and early nineteenth centuries. How did these influence changes in Japanese thought?

6. In what sense was Chinese culture a "technology" used by Japan, Korea, and Vietnam for state building? Why were the results in each country so different?

Documents CD-ROM

1. Dynastic Change in China Tears a Family Apart
2. Cheng Ho (Zheng He): Ming Maritime Expeditions
3. Wu Chengen: From *Monkey*

4. Murasaki Shikibu: *The Tale of Genji*
5. Nō Theatre, Atsumori

21 EUROPEAN STATE-BUILDING AND WORLDWIDE CONFLICT

CHAPTER TOPICS

Between the early seventeenth and mid-twentieth century no region so dominated other parts of the world as Europe. For three and a half centuries, northwestern Europe became the chief driving force in world historical development. This era of European dominance coincided with a shift in power within Europe itself from the Mediterranean to the states of the northwest and later north-central Europe.

By the mid-eighteenth century, five major states had come to dominate European politics and would continue to do so until at least World War I. They were Great Britain, France, Austria, Prussia, and Russia. Through their military strength, economic development, and in some cases colonial empires, they would affect virtually every other world civilization.

In the mid-eighteenth century, these five successful states entered upon three quarters of a century of warfare among themselves. These wars were fought both in Europe and in the European colonial empires, making them the first extensive world wars arising from conflict in Europe. These conflicts represented the most extensive European impact on the non-European world since the early sixteenth century, when the Spanish had conquered the civilizations of Mexico and Peru.

Two Models of European Political Development

In the second half of the sixteenth century, changes in military organization, weapons, and tactics increased the cost of warfare. Because traditional sources of income could not finance these costs and those of government, monarchs sought new revenues. Only monarchies that built a secure financial base that was not dependent on noble estates, diets, or assemblies achieved absolute rule. The French monarchy succeeded in this effort; the English monarchy failed. That success and failure led to the two models of government—absolutism in France and parliamentary monarchy in England—that shaped subsequent political development in Europe.

In their pursuit of income, English monarchs of the seventeenth century threatened the local interests of the nobility and landed and commercial elite. These groups invoked traditional English liberties to resist the monarchs.

The experience of Louis XIV (r. 1643–1715), the French king, was different. After 1660 he made the French nobility dependent on his goodwill. In turn, he supported their place in a firm social hierarchy. But Louis accepted the authority of the noble-dominated *Parlement* of Paris to register royal decrees before they became law, and he permitted regional *parlements* to exercise authority over local administration and taxation.

Religious factors also affected the political destinies of England and France. In England, Puritanism overturned the Stuart monarchy. Louis XIV, in contrast, crushed the Protestant communities of France.

There were also major institutional differences between the two countries. The English Parliament had long bargained with the monarch. In the early seventeenth century, Parliament was not the strong institution it would become, nor was the transformation it underwent during the century inevitable. The institutional basis for it, however, was in place. Parliament expected to be consulted, and the English had a tradition of liberty to which members of Parliament could appeal against the monarchy.

France lacked similarly strong traditions. The Estates General played no role after 1614. It was not called again until the eve of the French Revolution in 1789. Opposition to the monarchy lacked both an institutional base and a forum in which political skills might have been developed.

Finally, personalities were important. During the first half of the century, France profited from the guidance of two able statesmen, Cardinals Richelieu and Mazarin. Mazarin trained

Louis XIV to be a hard-working monarch. Louis employed capable ministers. The first four Stuart monarchs of England (r. 1603–1689), on the other hand, were distrusted. Their judgment was faulty. They offended significant groups of their subjects. In a strongly Protestant nation, they were suspected of Catholic sympathies.

In both England and France, the nobility and large landowners stood at the top of the social hierarchy and sought to protect their interests. Important segments of the British nobility and landed classes came to believe that the Stuarts sought to undermine their local standing. Parliamentary government was the result of the efforts of these English landed classes to protect their interests and limit the power of the monarchy to interfere with life on the local level. The French nobility under Louis XIV, in contrast, concluded that the best way to secure their interests was to support the throne.

Constitutional Crisis and Settlement in Stuart England

James I

In 1603, James VI of Scotland (r. 1603–1625), the son of Mary Stuart, Queen of Scots, succeeded Elizabeth I as James I of England. He also inherited a royal debt and a divided church. Parliament met only when the monarch summoned it, which James hoped to do rarely. In place of parliamentarily approved revenues, James levied new custom duties known as impositions. Members of Parliament regarded this as an affront to their authority over the royal purse, but they did not seek a serious confrontation.

Puritans within the Church of England had hoped that James would further reform the English church. But he supported the Anglican episcopacy.

James's foreign policy also roused opposition. In 1604, he concluded peace with Spain, England's longtime adversary. His subjects considered this a sign of pro-Catholic sentiment. James's attempt to relax laws against Catholics increased their suspicions, as did his hesitancy in 1618 to rush English troops to the aid of German Protestants at the outbreak of the Thirty Years' War. His efforts to arrange a marriage between his son Charles and a Spanish princess and then Charles's marriage in 1625 to Henrietta Marie of France further increased religious suspicions. In 1624, England again went to war against Spain in response to parliamentary pressures.

Charles I

Parliament had favored the war with Spain but would not adequately finance it because its members distrusted the

England	
1603	James VI of Scotland becomes James I of England
1625	Charles I becomes king of England
1628	Petition of Right
1629	Charles I dissolves Parliament and embarks on eleven years of personal rule
1640	April-May, Short Parliament; November, Long Parliament convenes
1641	Great Remonstrance
1642	Outbreak of the Civil War
1649	Charles I executed
1649-1660	Various attempts at a Puritan Commonwealth
1660	Charles II restored to the English throne
1670	Secret Treaty of Dover between France and England
1672	Parliament passes the Test Act
1685	James II becomes king of England
1688	Glorious Revolution
1689	William III and Mary II come to the throne of England
1701	Act of Settlement provides for Hanoverian Succession
1702-1714	Queen Anne, the last of the Stuarts
1714	George I of Hanover becomes king of England
1721-1742	Ascendancy of Sir Robert Walpole

monarchy. Unable to gain adequate funds from Parliament, Charles I (r. 1625–1649) resorted to extraparliamentary measures. These included levying new tariffs and duties, attempting to collect discontinued taxes, and subjecting English property owners to a so-called forced loan and then imprisoning those who refused to pay. These actions, as well as quartering troops in private homes, challenged local control of nobles and landowners.

When Parliament met in 1628, its members would grant new funds only if Charles recognized the Petition of Right. This required that there should be no forced loans or taxation without the consent of Parliament, that no freeman should be imprisoned without due cause, and that troops should not be billeted in private homes. It thus expressed resentment and resistance to the monarchy on the local level. Charles agreed to the petition.

Years of Personal Rule

In 1629, Parliament declared that religious innovations leading to "popery" and the levying of taxes without parliamentary consent were treason. Charles promptly dissolved Parliament and did not recall it until 1640.

To allow Charles to rule without renegotiating financial arrangements with Parliament, his chief minister, Thomas Wentworth (1593–1641; after 1640, earl of Strafford), instituted a policy known as *thorough*. This policy imposed strict efficiency and administrative centralization in government. Its goal was absolute royal control of England. Its success depended on the king's ability to operate independently of Parliament, which no law required him to summon.

Charles might have ruled indefinitely without Parliament had not his religious policies provoked war with Scotland, where Charles hoped to impose religious conformity. In 1637, Charles and Archbishop William Laud (1573–1645) tried to impose on Scotland the English episcopal system and prayer book. The Scots rebelled, and Charles, with insufficient resources for war, was forced to call Parliament. Parliament refused even to consider funds for war until the king agreed to redress a long list of political and religious grievances. The king, in response, immediately dissolved Parliament. When the Scots defeated an English army at Newburn in the summer of 1640, Charles reconvened Parliament for a long and fateful duration.

The Long Parliament and Civil War

The landowners and the merchant classes represented in Parliament resented the king's financial measures and paternalistic rule. The Puritans in Parliament resented his religious policies. The Long Parliament (1640–1660) thus acted with widespread support when it convened in November 1640.

The House of Commons impeached Strafford and Laud. Both were later executed. Parliament abolished the courts that had enforced royal policy and resolved that no more than three years should elapse between its meetings and that it could not be dissolved without its own consent.

Parliament, however, was divided over religion. Both moderate Puritans (the Presbyterians) and more extreme Puritans (the Independents) wanted to abolish the episcopacy and the *Book of Common Prayer*. The majority Presbyterians sought to reshape England religiously along Calvinist lines, with local congregations subject to higher representative governing bodies (presbyteries). Independents wanted every congregation to be its own final authority. But many conservatives in both houses of Parliament were determined to preserve the English church in its current form. These divisions intensified in October 1641, when Parliament was asked to fund an army to suppress a rebellion in Scotland.

Civil War

On December 1, 1641, Parliament presented the king with the "Grand Remonstrance," a summary of popular and parliamentary grievances against the crown. In January 1642, the king left London and began to raise an army. Shocked, the House of Commons passed the Militia Ordinance, which gave Parliament authority to raise an army of its own. For the next four years (1642–1646), civil war engulfed England. There were nobility, gentry, and townspeople on both sides. The chief factor distinguishing them was religion; the Puritans tended to favor Parliament.

Oliver Cromwell and the Puritan Republic

Two factors led to Parliament's victory. The first was an alliance with Scotland in 1643 that committed Parliament to a Presbyterian church. The second was the reorganization of the parliamentary army under Oliver Cromwell (1599–1658). Cromwell and his "godly men" were willing to tolerate an established majority church, but only if it permitted Protestant dissenters to worship outside it.

Defeated by June 1645, Charles tried to take advantage of divisions within Parliament, but Cromwell and his army foiled him. In 1649, after a trial by a special court, Charles was executed. Parliament then abolished the monarchy, the House of Lords, and the Anglican Church.

From 1649 to 1660, England was dominated by Cromwell. His army conquered Ireland and Scotland. Cromwell, however, was no politician. In 1653, he disbanded Parliament and ruled thereafter as Lord Protector.

Cromwell's military dictatorship, however, was harsh and hated. When he died in 1658, the English were ready to restore both the Anglican Church and the monarchy.

Lady Mary Wortley Montague Advises Her Husband on Election to Parliament

In this letter of 1714, Lady Mary Wortley Montague discussed how her husband might be elected to the House of Commons. Note her emphasis on knowing the right people and on having large amounts of money to spend on voters. Eventually her husband was elected in a borough that was controlled through government patronage.

What are the various ways in which candidates and their supporters used money to campaign? What role did friendships play in the campaigning? How important do the political ideas or positions of the candidates seem to be? Women could not vote in eighteenth-century parliamentary elections, but what kind of influence do they seem to exert?

You seem not to have received my letters, or not to have understood them: you had been chose undoubtedly at York, if you had declared in time; but there is not any gentleman or tradesman disengaged at this time; they are treating every night. Lord Carlisle and the Thompsons have given their interest to Mr. Jenkins. I agree with you of the necessity of your standing this Parliament, which, perhaps, may be more considerable than any that are to follow it; but, as you proceed, 'tis my opinion, you will spend your money and not be chose. I believe there is hardly a borough unengaged. I expect every letter should tell me you are sure of some place; and, as far as I can perceive you are sure of none. As it has been managed, perhaps it will be the best way to deposit a certain sum in some friend's hands, and buy some little Cornish borough: it would, undoubtedly, look better to be chose for a considerable town; but I take it to be now too late. If you have any thoughts of Newark, it will be absolutely necessary for you to enquire after Lord Lexington's interest; and your best way to apply yourself to Lord Holdernesse, who is both a Whig and an honest man. He is now in town, and you may enquire of him if Brigadier Sutton stands there; and if not, try to engage him for you. Lord Lexington is so ill at the Bath, that it is a doubt if he will live 'till the elections; and if he dies, one of his heiresses, and the whole interest of his estate, will probably fall on Lord Holdernesse.

'Tis a surprize to me, that you cannot make sure of some borough, when a number of your friends bring in so many Parliament-men without trouble or expense. 'Tis too late to mention it now, but you might have applied to Lady Winchester, as Sir Joseph Jekyl did last year, and by her interest the Duke of Bolton brought him in for nothing; I am sure she would be more zealous to serve me, than Lady Jekyl.

From Lord Wharncliffe, ed., *Letters and Works of Lady Mary Wortley Montague*, 3rd ed., Vol. 1 (London, 1861), p. 211.

The Restoration of the Monarchy

Charles II (r. 1660–1685) returned to England amid rejoicing. A man of charm and political skill, Charles set a refreshing new tone after eleven years of Puritanism. England returned to the status quo of 1642, with a hereditary monarch, a Parliament that met only when the king summoned it, and the Anglican Church, with its bishops and prayer book, supreme in religion.

The king, however, had secret Catholic sympathies and favored religious toleration. He wanted to allow loyal Catholics and Puritans to worship freely. But in Parliament, even the ultraroyalist Anglicans did not believe patriotism and religion could be separated. Between 1661 and 1665, through a series of laws known as the Clarendon Code, Parliament excluded Roman Catholics, Presbyterians, and Independents from the religious and political life of the nation.

In 1670, England and France allied against the Dutch, their chief commercial competitor. Charles secretly pledged to announce his conversion to Catholicism as soon as conditions in England permitted. In return for this announcement (which was never made), Louis XIV promised to pay Charles a subsidy. As a sign of good faith, Charles issued a Declaration of Indulgence in 1672 suspending all laws against Roman Catholics and non-Anglican Protestants. But Parliament passed the Test Act requiring all officials of the crown, civil and military, to swear an oath against the doctrine of transubstantiation—which no loyal Roman Catholic could honestly do. Parliament had aimed the Test Act at the king's brother, James, duke of York, heir to the throne and a convert to Catholicism.

James II

When James II (r. 1685–1688) became king in 1685, he demanded the repeal of the Test Act. When Parliament balked, he dissolved it and appointed Catholics to high positions. In 1687, he issued another Declaration of

Indulgence suspending all religious tests and permitting free worship. These actions represented a royal attack on the local authority of nobles, landowners, the church, and other corporate bodies whose members believed they possessed legal privileges.

The English had hoped that James would be succeeded by Mary (r. 1689–1694), his Protestant eldest daughter. She was the wife of William III of Orange (1650–1702), *stadtholder* of the Netherlands. But on June 20, 1688, James II's second wife gave birth to a son. There was now a Catholic male heir to the throne. The parliamentary opposition invited William to invade England to preserve the Anglican Church and parliamentary government.

The "Glorious Revolution"

William of Orange arrived with his army in November 1688, and James fled to France. Parliament in 1689 proclaimed William III and Mary II the new monarchs, thus completing the "Glorious Revolution." William and Mary recognized a Bill of Rights that limited the powers of the monarchy and guaranteed the civil liberties of the English privileged classes. Henceforth, England's monarchs would be subject to law and would rule by the consent of Parliament. The Bill of Rights also prohibited Roman Catholics from occupying the English throne. The Toleration Act of 1689 permitted worship by all Protestants and outlawed Roman Catholics.

The Act of Settlement in 1701 provided for the English crown to go to the Protestant House of Hanover in Germany if Anne (r. 1702–1714), the second daughter of James II and the heir to the childless William III, died without issue. At Anne's death, the Elector of Hanover became King George I of England (r. 1714–1727).

The Age of Walpole

George I confronted a challenge to his title. The son of James II landed in Scotland in December 1715 but was soon defeated.

However, the political situation remained in flux until Robert Walpole (1676–1745) took over the government. George I gave Walpole his full confidence. For this reason, Walpole has often been regarded as the first prime minister of Great Britain—although he never bore the title—and the originator of the cabinet system of government.

The source of his power was the combination of the support of the king, Walpole's ability to handle the House of Commons, and his control of government patronage. Through the skillful use of patronage, Walpole bought support from people who wanted jobs, favors, and government contracts. Corruption cemented political loyalty.

The eighteenth-century British House of Commons was neither a democratic nor a representative body. Each county elected two members, but if the more powerful landed families agreed on the candidates, as often happened, there was no contest. Other members were elected from units called *boroughs*, most of which had few electors. Proper management could control the composition of the House of Commons.

The structure of Parliament resulted in the domination of the government of England by the owners of property and especially by wealthy nobles. They were suspicious of an administrative bureaucracy controlled by the crown or its ministers. For this reason, they or their agents served as local government administrators, judges, militia commanders, and tax collectors. In this sense, the British nobility and landowners governed the nation. Moreover, because they regarded Parliament as the political sovereign, there was no absence of central political authority. The supremacy of Parliament provided Britain with the unity that elsewhere in Europe was achieved through absolutism.

British political life was freer than on the Continent. Walpole's power had limits. Parliament could not wholly ignore popular pressure. Many members of Parliament maintained independent views. Newspapers and debate flourished. Free speech could be exercised, as could freedom of association. There was no large standing army. Walpole's enemies could openly oppose his policies.

Walpole's ascendancy, which lasted from 1721 to 1742, brought the nation stability. He maintained peace abroad and promoted the status quo at home. All forms of economic enterprise seemed to prosper. The navy became stronger. As a result, Great Britain became not only a European power of the first order but eventually a world power. Its government and economy were models for progressive Europeans.

Rise of Absolute Monarchy in France: The World of Louis XIV

The groundwork for Louis XIV's absolutism (r. 1643–1715) had been laid first by Cardinal Richelieu (1585–1642), the chief minister for Louis XIII (r. 1610–1643), and then by Cardinal Mazarin (1602–1661). Richelieu and Mazarin had tried to impose direct royal administration on France. These efforts aroused rebellions among French nobles between 1649 and 1652.

These rebellions convinced Louis XIV that heavy-handed policies could endanger the monarchy. Louis would concentrate unprecedented authority in the monarchy, but his genius was to make the monarchy the most powerful institution in France while also assuring the nobles and other wealthy groups of their influence on the local level. Rather than destroying existing institutions, Louis worked through them. Nevertheless, the king was clearly the senior partner in the relationship.

Years of Personal Rule

On the death of Mazarin in 1661, Louis XIV assumed control of the government at the age of twenty-three. He appointed no chief minister and ruled through councils that controlled foreign affairs, the army, domestic administration, and economic regulations. Each day he spent hours with the chief ministers of these councils, whom he chose from families long in royal service or from among people beginning to rise in the social structure. Unlike the more ancient noble families, they depended solely on the king.

Louis made sure, however, that the nobility and other major social groups would benefit from his authority. He never tried to abolish noble institutions or limit their local authority. Local *parlements* enjoyed considerable latitude. Louis did clash with the *Parlement* of Paris, which had the right to register royal laws. In 1673 he curtailed its power.

Versailles

Louis and his advisors became masters of propaganda and political image. Louis never missed an opportunity to impress the grandeur of his crown on the French people. The central element of the image of the monarchy was the palace of Versailles. More than any other monarch, Louis XIV used the physical setting of his court to exert political control. Versailles, on the outskirts of Paris, became Louis's permanent residence after 1682. It was a temple to royalty, designed to proclaim the glory of the Sun King, as Louis was known. With magnificent fountains and gardens, it housed thousands of nobles, officials, and servants. Although it consumed over half Louis's annual revenues, Versailles paid political dividends.

Louis was the chief source of favors and patronage in France. To emphasize his prominence, he organized life at court around his daily routine. Elaborate etiquette governed life at Versailles. The king's rising and dressing were times of rare intimacy, when nobles could whisper in his ear. Fortunate nobles held his candle as they accompanied him to his bed.

Versailles, as painted in 1668 by Pierre Patel the Elder (1605–1676). The central building is the hunting lodge built for Louis XIII earlier in the century. The wings that appear here were some of Louis XIV's first expansions. [Giraudon/Art Resource, N.Y.]

Some nobles avoided Versailles. They managed their estates and cultivated their local influence. Others were too poor to cut a figure at court. The nobility understood, however, that Louis would not threaten their local social standing. Louis supported France's traditional social structure and the social privileges of the nobility.

King by Divine Right

An important source for Louis's concept of royal authority was Bishop Jacques-Bénigne Bossuet (1627–1704). Bossuet defended what he called the "divine right of kings" and cited examples of Old Testament rulers appointed by and answerable only to God. Bossuet argued that only God could judge the king. Although kings might be duty bound to reflect God's will, as God's regents on Earth they were not bound to the dictates of mere nobles and parliaments. Such assumptions lay behind Louis XIV's alleged declaration: *"L'état, c'est moi"* ("I am the state").

Despite these claims, Louis's rule did not exert the oppressive control over the daily lives of his subjects that police states would do in the nineteenth and twentieth centuries. His absolutism functioned primarily in the classic areas of European state action—war and peace, religion, and economic oversight. Even at the height of his power, local institutions retained their administrative authority. The king and his ministers supported the social and financial privileges of these local elites. But Louis prevented them from interfering with his authority on the national level. This system would endure until the end of the eighteenth century.

Louis's Early Wars

By the late 1660s, France was superior to any other European nation in administrative bureaucracy, armed forces, and national unity. Louis could afford to raise and maintain a powerful army and was in a position to dominate Europe. He spent most of his reign looking to extend the borders of his domain and displace the power of the Habsburgs.

The early wars of Louis XIV included conflicts with Spain and the United Netherlands. In 1667, Louis's armies invaded Flanders and the Franche-Comté. By the Treaty of Aix-la-Chapelle (1668) he gained control of certain towns bordering the Spanish Netherlands.[1]

---

[1]The political divisions during the seventeenth and eighteenth centuries in what are today the Netherlands and Belgium were complex. The independence of the United Netherlands, a loosely federated union, was recognized at the Peace of Westphalia in 1648. Most of its population were Protestants. It was often referred to as "Holland." Present-day Belgium was governed by the Habsburgs, first Spanish, then Austrian—after 1714. Its population was Roman Catholic.

France

1649-1652	The Fronde, a revolt of nobility and townspeople against the crown
1661	Louis assumes personal rule
1667-1668	War of Devolution fought over Louis's claims to the Spanish Netherlands
1672	France invades the United Provinces
1678-1679	Peace of Nimwegen
1682	Louis establishes his court at Versailles
1685	Edict of Nantes revoked
1689-1697	Nine Years' War between France and the League of Augsburg
1697	Peace of Ryswick
1702-1714	War of the Spanish Succession
1713	Treaty of Utrecht between England and France
1714	Treaty of Rastadt between the emperor and France
1726-1743	Ascendency of Cardinal Fleury

Louis invaded the Netherlands in 1672. The war ended inconclusively, but France gained more territory.

Revocation of the Edict of Nantes

After the Edict of Nantes in 1598, relations between Catholics (nine tenths of the French population) and Protestants had remained hostile. The Catholic Church supported persecution as pious and patriotic.

Louis was determined to unify France religiously. He hounded the Huguenots out of public life and bribed them to convert to Catholicism. He bullied them by quartering troops in their towns. Finally, Louis revoked the Edict of Nantes in 1685. Protestant churches and schools were closed, ministers exiled, nonconverting laity forced to be galley slaves, and children baptized by Catholic priests.

The revocation was a blunder. Protestants considered Louis a fanatic to be resisted at all costs. The revocation prompted the emigration of more than a quarter million people, who joined the resistance to France in England, Germany, Holland, and the New World.

War of the Spanish Succession

On November 1, 1700, Charles II of Spain (r. 1665–1700) died without direct heirs. He left his inheritance to Louis's grandson, who became Philip V of Spain (r. 1700–1746).

Spain and its American empire appeared to have fallen to France. In September 1701, England, Holland, and the Holy Roman Empire formed the Grand Alliance to preserve the balance of power. Louis increased the political stakes by recognizing the Stuart claim to the English throne.

In 1701, the War of the Spanish Succession (1701–1714) began. France went to war with inadequate finances, a poorly equipped army, and mediocre generals. The English, in contrast, had advanced weaponry and superior tactics. John Churchill, the duke of Marlborough (1650–1722), bested Louis's soldiers in every major engagement, although French arms triumphed in Spain.

France finally made peace with England at Utrecht in 1713 and with Holland and the emperor at Rastadt in 1714. Philip V remained king of Spain but England got Gibraltar, making it a Mediterranean power (see Map 21–1). Louis also recognized the House of Hanover.

After Louis's death, the monarchy weakened. France was exhausted. Louis XV (r. 1715–1774) was only five years old at his accession, and the regency allowed the *Parlement* of Paris greater authority. By 1726, the political direction of the nation had come under Cardinal Fleury (1653–1743). Like Walpole in Britain, he pursued economic prosperity at home and peace abroad.

Russia Enters the European Political Arena

The emergence of Russia as a European power was a new factor in European politics. Russia had been considered part of Europe only by courtesy. Hemmed in by Sweden and the Ottoman Empire, Russia had no warm-water ports. There was little trade. Russia did have vast, largely undeveloped natural and human resources.

Years of Turmoil

Ivan IV (r. 1533–1584), known as Ivan the Terrible, appointed able advisors, undertook sensible revisions of the law and local government, and reorganized the army. Then about 1560, he began to distrust virtually everyone and imprisoned, tortured, and executed *boyars* (nobles) without cause or trial. He even killed his own son.

Ivan's reign was followed by a period of anarchy known as the Time of Troubles. In 1613, an assembly of nobles elected as tsar Michael Romanov (r. 1613–1645), whose dynasty ruled Russia until 1917.

Michael Romanov and his two successors brought stability to Russia. The country, however, remained weak. The *boyars* controlled the bureaucracy. The tsars faced the danger of mutiny from the *streltsy*, or Moscow garrison.

Peter the Great

In 1682, a ten-year-old boy ascended the Russian throne as co-ruler with his half brother. His name was Peter (r. 1682–1725). He and his feeble half brother, Ivan V (d. 1696), had come to power on the shoulders of the *streltsy*. Violence had surrounded the succession. The turmoil of his youth convinced Peter that the power of the tsar must be made secure and that Russian military power had to be increased.

Peter I, who came to be known as Peter the Great, was an imitator of the first order. The products and workers from the West who had filtered into Russia impressed him. In 1697, he made a visit, supposedly in disguise, to western Europe. There he inspected shipyards, docks, and the manufacture of military hardware and returned to Moscow determined to copy what he had seen, for he knew that only warfare would make Russia a great power. The tsar's drive to modernize his nation had four areas of concern: taming the boyars and the *streltsy*, achieving secular control of the church, reorganizing the internal administration, and developing the economy.

Peter pursued each of these goals with ruthlessness. His successes allowed him to expand his military strength. By bringing the boyars, *streltsy*, and church under control, Peter curbed the groups that might have opposed his expansion of the army and navy. Developing Russia's economy enabled him to finance his military ventures.

He made a sustained attack on the *boyars* and demanded they serve his state. In 1722, Peter published a Table of Ranks, which henceforth equated a person's social position and privileges with his rank in the bureaucracy or the army rather than with his position in the nobility. However, the

Rise of Russian Power	
1533–1584	Reign of Ivan the Terrible
1584–1613	Time of Troubles
1613	Michael Romanov becomes tsar
1682	Peter the Great becomes tsar as a boy
1689	Peter assumes personal rule
1697	European tour of Peter the Great
1698	Peter suppresses the *streltsy*
1700	The Great Northern War opens between Russia and Sweden; Russia defeated at Narva by Charles XII
1703	Saint Petersburg founded
1709	Russia defeats Sweden at Poltava
1718	Death of Alexis, son of Peter the Great
1721	Peace of Nystad ends the Great Northern War
1721	Peter establishes control over the Russian church
1722	The Table of Ranks
1725	Peter dies, leaving an uncertain succession

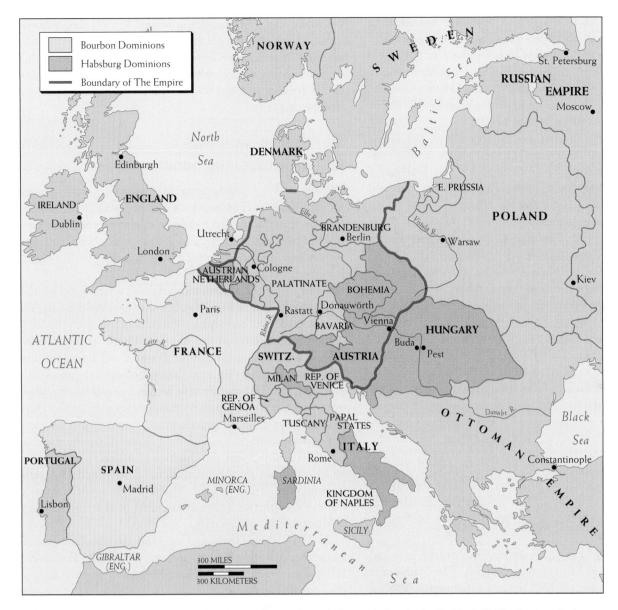

Map 21-1 Europe in 1714. The War of the Spanish Succession ended a year before the death of Louis XIV. The Bourbons had secured the Spanish throne, but Spain had forfeited its possessions in Flanders and Italy.

Russian nobility never became perfectly loyal to the state. It repeatedly sought to reassert its independence.

The *streltsy* fared less well than the boyars. In 1698, they had rebelled while Peter was on his European tour. When he returned, almost 1,200 of the rebels were put to death.

Peter dealt with the Russian Orthodox Church with similar ruthlessness. He wanted to prevent the clergy from opposing westernization and sought to prevent the church hierarchy from making religious reforms that might provoke popular discontent. In 1721, Peter replaced the position of patriarch of the Russian church with a synod headed by a layman.

In his reorganization of domestic administration, Peter looked to Swedish models, creating "colleges," or bureaus, composed of several officials. The colleges were to look after foreign affairs, war, and economic matters. In 1711, Peter created a senate of nine members to direct the central government when the tsar was away with the army. The purpose of these reforms was to establish a bureaucracy that could collect and spend tax revenues to support an efficient army.

Peter's economic policies were closely related to his military needs. He encouraged the establishment of an iron industry in the Ural Mountains. He sent prominent young Russians abroad to acquire technical and organizational skills. He attempted to lure western European craftsmen to Russia. However, these efforts had only marginal success.

Peter was determined to secure warm-water ports that would allow Russia to trade with the West and intervene in European affairs. This led to wars with the Ottoman Empire and Sweden. Peter's armies captured Azov on the Black Sea in 1696, but he had to return it in 1711.

Peter had more success against Sweden in the Great Northern War (1700–1721). In 1721, the Peace of Nystad confirmed the Russian conquest of Estonia, Livonia, and part of Finland. Henceforth, Russia possessed warm-water ports and a permanent influence on European affairs.

At one point, the domestic and foreign policies of Peter the Great intersected. This was at the spot on the Gulf of Finland where Peter founded his new capital of Saint Petersburg. There he built government structures and compelled his *boyars* to construct town houses. Saint Petersburg symbolized a new orientation for Russia toward western Europe.

Despite his success on the Baltic, Peter's reign ended with a great question mark. He had long quarreled with his only son, Alexis, who was imprisoned in 1718 and died mysteriously. When Peter died in 1725, Russia had no firmer policy on succession than it had had when he acceded to the throne. For more than thirty years after his death, soldiers and nobles would determine who ruled Russia. Peter had laid the foundations of a modern Russia, but he had failed to lay the foundations of a stable state.

Central and Eastern Europe

As Russia became a major European power, the political contours of central Europe also changed. The Habsburgs expanded their political base outside of Germany. Within

Austria and Prussia

1640–1688	Reign of Frederick William, the Great Elector
1658–1705	Leopold I rules Austria and resists the Turks and Louis XIV
1683	Turkish siege of Vienna
1701	Frederick I becomes "King in Prussia"
1699	Peace between Turks and Habsburgs
1711–1740	Charles VI rules Austria and secures agreement to the Pragmatic Sanction
1713–1740	Frederick William I builds the military power of Prussia
1740	Maria Theresa succeeds to the Habsburg throne; Frederick II invades Silesia

Germany, the Hohenzollerns forged Prussia into a major state. Thereafter, the Habsburg Empire and Prussia would duel for Germany. By the middle of the century, that conflict would become united with the colonial conflict between Great Britain and France to create the first worldwide European war.

The Habsburg Empire and the Pragmatic Sanction

The close of the Thirty Years' War marked a turning point for the Austrian Habsburgs. In alliance with their Spanish cousins, they had hoped to bring Germany under their control and back to the Catholic fold. In this they had failed, and the decline of Spanish power meant that the Austrian Habsburgs were on their own.

After 1648, the Habsburgs retained a firm hold on the title of Holy Roman Emperor, but the power of the emperor depended on the cooperation he could elicit from the various political bodies in the empire. These included large units (such as Saxony, Hanover, Bavaria, and Brandenburg) and scores of small German cities, bishoprics, and principalities. The Habsburgs also began to consolidate their power within their hereditary possessions outside the Holy Roman Empire, which included the Crown of Saint Wenceslas, encompassing the kingdom of Bohemia (in the modern Czech Republic) and the duchies of Moravia and Silesia; and the Crown of Saint Stephen, which ruled Hungary, Croatia, and Transylvania. Much of Hungary was only liberated from the Turks at the end of the seventeenth century (1699).

In 1714, the Habsburgs received the former Spanish (thereafter Austrian) Netherlands and Lombardy. Thereafter, Habsburgs power would be based primarily on their territories outside Germany.

In each of their many territories, the Habsburgs ruled by virtue of a different title and needed the cooperation of the local nobility. They repeatedly had to bargain with nobles in one part of Europe to maintain their position in another. Their domains and peoples were so diverse that almost no grounds existed on which to unify them politically. Even Roman Catholicism proved ineffective as a common bond, particularly in Hungary, the most recalcitrant province, where many Magyar nobles were Calvinist and seemed ever ready to rebel. Habsburg rulers established central councils to chart common policies for their far-flung domains. Virtually all of these bodies, however, dealt with only a portion of the Habsburg holdings.

Despite these internal difficulties, Leopold I (r. 1658–1705) managed to resist the advances of the Turks into central Europe, which included a siege of Vienna in 1683, and to thwart the aggression of Louis XIV. He also extended his territorial holdings over much of the Balkans. Strength in the east gave the Habsburgs greater political leverage in Germany.

Charles VI (r. 1711–1740) had no male heir and feared that on his death the Habsburg lands might fall prey to the surrounding powers. To prevent that disaster, he devoted most of his reign to seeking the approval of his family, the estates of his realms, and foreign powers for a document called the *Pragmatic Sanction.*

This provided the legal basis for a single line of inheritance within the Habsburg dynasty through Charles VI's daughter Maria Theresa (1740–1780). Other members of the Habsburg family recognized her as the rightful heir. After extracting concessions from Charles, the nobles of the various Habsburg domains and the other European rulers did likewise. Charles VI believed that he had secured legal unity for the Habsburg Empire and a safe succession for his daughter. However, his failure to provide his daughter with a strong army or a full treasury left her inheritance open to foreign aggression. Less than two months after his death, in December 1740, Frederick II of Prussia invaded the Habsburg province of Silesia. Maria Theresa had to fight for her inheritance.

Prussia and the Hohenzollerns

The rise of Prussia occurred within the German power vacuum created by the Peace of Westphalia. It is the story of the extraordinary Hohenzollern family, which had ruled Brandenburg since 1417. Through inheritance, the family had acquired East Prussia and other territories that by the late seventeenth century represented a block of territory within the Holy Roman Empire, second in size only to that of the Habsburgs.

The person who began to forge these areas into a modern state was Frederick William (r. 1640–1688), who became known as the Great Elector. He established himself and his successors as the central uniting power by breaking the medieval parliaments or estates, organizing a royal bureaucracy, and building a strong army.

There was a political and social trade-off between the Elector and his nobles. These *Junkers*, or German noble landlords, in exchange for their obedience to the Hohenzollerns, received the right to demand obedience from their serfs. Frederick William also tended to choose as the local administrators of the tax structure men who would normally have been members of the noble branch of the old parliament. He thus co-opted potential opponents into his service. The taxes fell most heavily on the peasants and the urban classes. As the years passed, *Junkers* dominated the army officer corps. Officials and army officers took an oath of loyalty to the Elector.

The army and the Elector thus came to embody the otherwise absent unity of the state.

Yet even with the considerable accomplishments of the Great Elector, the house of Hohenzollern did not possess a crown. The achievement of a royal title was the accomplishment of Frederick I (r. 1688–1713). In the War of the Spanish Succession, he put his army at the disposal of the Habsburg Holy Roman Emperor Leopold I. In exchange, the emperor permitted Frederick to assume the title of "King in Prussia" in 1701.

His successor, Frederick William I (r. 1713–1740), organized the bureaucracy along military lines. The discipline that he applied to the army was fanatical. The Prussian military grew from about 39,000 in 1713 to over 80,000 in 1740, making it the third- or fourth-largest army in Europe. Prussia's population, in contrast, ranked thirteenth in size. Laws, customs, and royal attention made the officer corps the highest social class of the state. Military service thus attracted the sons of *Junkers*. In this fashion, the army, the *Junker* nobility, and the monarchy became forged into a single political entity. Military priorities and values dominated Prussian government, society, and daily life.

The First Worldwide Wars

The War of the Spanish Succession had been fought mainly in Europe. The wars that Europe fought between 1739 and 1763 were worldwide in scope and impact. By the end of the conflicts, the French had been driven out of North America and the British had established a domination in India that would last until 1947.

The Colonial Arena

The Treaty of Utrecht established the boundaries of empire during the first half of the eighteenth century. Except for Portuguese Brazil, Spain controlled South America, as well as Florida, Mexico, California, Cuba, and half of Hispaniola. The British Empire consisted of the colonies along the North Atlantic seaboard, Nova Scotia, Newfoundland, Jamaica, and Barbados. Britain also possessed trading stations on the Indian subcontinent. The Dutch controlled Surinam, or Dutch Guiana, in South America; trading stations in Ceylon and Bengal; and the trade with Java in what is today Indonesia.

The French had also established an empire in America and southern Asia. It covered the Saint Lawrence River valley; the Ohio and Mississippi River valleys; Saint Domingue (Haiti), Guadeloupe, and Martinique in the West Indies; and stations in India and West Africa. The economy of their West Indian islands resembled those of the Spanish and the British.

Their holdings in Canada were sparsely populated, and the economy was based on agriculture and the fur trade. French and English settlers in North America clashed throughout the eighteenth century.

The Treaty of Utrecht gave the British a thirty-year *asiento*, or contract, to furnish slaves to the Spanish Empire and the right to send one ship each year to the trading fair at Portobello. Little but friction arose from these rights. Much to the chagrin of the British, the Spanish government under the Bourbons maintained coastal patrols that searched English vessels for contraband.

British commercial interests put great pressure on Parliament to do something about Spanish interference in their trade. Robert Walpole could not resist these pressures, and in late 1739, Great Britain went to war with Spain. This might have been a minor clash, but as a result of the Prussian invasion of Silesia, it became the opening encounter in a series of worldwide European wars that lasted off and on until 1815.

The War of the Austrian Succession (1740–1748)

In December 1740, the new king of Prussia, Frederick II, (r. 1740–1786, Frederick the Great) seized the Austrian province of Silesia. The invasion shattered the Pragmatic Sanction and upset the continental balance of power. In response to the Prussian aggression, Maria Theresa of Austria recognized Hungary as the most important of her crowns and promised the Magyars local autonomy. She thus preserved the Habsburg state, but at great cost to the power of the central monarchy.

The war over the Austrian succession and the British-Spanish commercial conflict could have remained separate disputes. What united them was the role of France. A group of aggressive court aristocrats compelled the elderly Cardinal Fleury to support the Prussian aggression against Austria, the traditional enemy of France.

This proved to be one of the most fateful decisions in world history. French aid to Prussia helped to consolidate a powerful German state that later endangered France itself. The French move against Austria also brought Great Britain into the continental war against France and Prussia to assure that Belgium remained in the friendly hands of Austria. The British-French conflict expanded to the New World. The war ended in 1748 with the Treaty of Aix-la-Chapelle. Prussia retained Silesia, but the treaty was a truce rather than a permanent peace.

The Seven Years' War (1756–1763)

Before the rivalries again erupted into war, a shift of alliances took place. In 1756, Prussia and Great Britain signed a defensive alliance aimed at preventing the entry of foreign troops into the Germanies. Great Britain, the ally of Austria since the wars of Louis XIV, had now joined forces with Austria's major enemy. Later in 1756, Austria achieved a defensive alliance with France.

Conflict between France and Great Britain had continued unofficially in the Ohio River valley and in upper New England. These skirmishes were the prelude to what is known in American history as the French and Indian War. Once again, however, the king of Prussia opened a general European war that extended into a colonial theater.

In August 1756, what would become the Seven Years' War opened when Frederick II invaded Saxony in a preemptive strike against a conspiracy by Saxony, Austria, and France to destroy Prussian power. In 1757, France and Austria were joined by Sweden, Russia, and the smaller German states. Two factors, in addition to Frederick's strong leadership, saved Prussia—British financial aid and the death in 1762 of Empress Elizabeth of Russia (r. 1741–1762). Her successor Tsar Peter III (d. 1762), a fervent admirer of Frederick, immediately made peace with Prussia, thus allowing Frederick to hold off Austria and France. The Treaty of Hubertusburg of 1763 closed the continental conflict with no significant changes in prewar borders.

More impressive than the survival of Prussia were the victories of Great Britain. The architect of victory was William Pitt the Elder (1708–1778). Pitt pumped huge subsidies to Frederick the Great. But North America was Pitt's real concern. He wanted all of North America east of the Mississippi for Great Britain, and he directed unprecedented resources into the overseas colonial conflict. The French government was unwilling and unable to direct similar resources against the English in America. In September 1759, the British took

Quebec City. Montreal fell the next year. The French Empire in Canada was over.

Pitt's colonial vision, however, was global. The French West Indies fell to British fleets. On the Indian subcontinent, British forces under Robert Clive (1725–1774) defeated the French in 1757 at the Battle of Plassey. This victory opened the way for the eventual conquest of all India by the British East India Company. Never had any other European power experienced such a complete worldwide military victory. Never had a European military victory affected so many non-Europeans.

By the Treaty of Paris of 1763, Pitt was no longer in office. George III (r. 1760–1820) had replaced Pitt with the Earl of Bute (1713–1792) in 1762. The new minister was responsible for the peace settlement, in which Britain received Canada, the Ohio River valley, and the eastern half of the Mississippi River valley. France retained footholds in India and regained West Indies sugar islands.

The mid-century wars among European powers resulted in a new balance of power on the European continent and the high seas. Great Britain gained a world empire, and Prussia was recognized as a great continental power. With the surrender of Canada, France retreated from North America and thus opened the way for a continent dominated by the English language and Protestantism. By contrast, Latin America would be dominated by the Spanish and Portuguese languages and Roman Catholicism. For many years, West Africa would continue to furnish slaves to both Americas. On the subcontinent of Asia, the foundations were laid for almost two centuries of British dominance. By 1760, therefore, a true world economy had been established in which political and economic developments in one region could affect others.

IN WORLD PERSPECTIVE

Eighteenth-Century European States and Warfare

By the second quarter of the eighteenth century, the major European powers were not yet nation-states in which the citizens felt themselves united by community, culture, language, and history. They were still monarchies in which the personality of the ruler and the personal relationships of the great noble families shaped public affairs.

These European states displayed problems that also characterized China and Japan during the same epochs. In particular, as in Japan, the problem of a balance between centralization and decentralization arose in virtually all the European states. In France, Russia, and Prussia, the forces of centralization proved strong. In Austria, the forces of decentralization were powerful. England achieved a delicate balance. Furthermore, as in Tokugawa Japan, European states of the eighteenth century saw an increase in legal codification and bureaucracy. Only in Prussia did the military influence on society resemble that in Japan.

The role of the personality of the monarch in Europe bore some resemblance to that of Manchu emperors in China, such as K'ang Hsi (1662–1722) and Ch'ien Lung (r. 1736–1795). Louis XIV and Peter the Great had no less influence on their nations than did these great Manchu emperors. All of them built up military strength and fostered innovation. However, European bureaucracies were less brilliant than those who administered China.

The global commercial empires of France, Spain, and England gave rise to fierce commercial rivalries. The drive for empire and commercial supremacy propelled these states into contact with Africa, Latin America, India, China, and Japan. Spain and Portugal had long exploited Latin America as their own monopoly. France and England fought for commercial supremacy in India, and by the 1760s England had, in effect, conquered the subcontinent. The slave trade between Africa and the New World flourished throughout the eighteenth century. European merchants and navies also sought to penetrate East Asia. As a result of these developments, European commerce would dominate the world for the next two centuries. Europe and its colonists extracted labor and other natural resources from other continents. The European military, especially naval dominance, made all this possible.

By the mid-eighteenth century, the European states that just two centuries earlier had only started to settle the Americas and to engage in limited long-range trade had made their power and influence felt throughout the world. Beginning in the early eighteenth century, the political power of the European states became linked to a qualitatively different economic base than any seen elsewhere in the world. That political and economic combination allowed Europe to dominate the world from the 1750s to the Second World War.

Review Questions

1. By the end of the seventeenth century, England and France had different systems of government with different religious policies. What were the main differences? Similarities? Why did each nation develop as it did?

2. Why did the English king and Parliament come into conflict in the 1640s? What were the most important issues behind the war between them? What was the Glorious Revolution? What role did religion play in each event?

3. How did Louis XIV consolidate his monarchy? What limits were there on his authority? What was Louis's religious policy? What were the goals of his foreign policy?

4. How did the Hohenzollern family forge diverse land holdings into the state of Prussia? Why was the military so important in Prussia? Compare how the Hohenzollerns and Habsburgs each handled their problems. Which family was more successful and why?

5. How and why did Russia emerge as a great power? Discuss the character of Peter the Great. How were his domestic reforms related to his military ambitions? To what extent did he succeed?

6. What were the main points of conflict between Britain and France in North America, the West Indies, and India? Which countries emerged stronger from the Seven Years' War and why?

Documents CD-ROM

1. James I: From *Anglicanism*

2. Thomas Macauley: From *History of England*, Volume I

3. G. M. Trevelyan: Chapter I from *History of England*, Volume I

4. Louis XIV: *Mémoires for the Instruction of the Dauphin*

5. Peter the Great: Correspondence with His Son

6. Parliament Takes Control: England's Bill of Rights of 1689

22 EUROPEAN SOCIETY UNDER THE OLD REGIME

At the opening of the eighteenth century, European merchants and traders dominated the transatlantic economy and European states governed much of the American continents. During the century, the peoples living primarily in northwestern Europe undertook a series of economic advances that laid the foundation for the social and economic transformation of the world. These developments, known collectively as the Industrial Revolution, gave Europe a productive capacity previously unknown in human history. That economic advance enabled Europeans to dominate much of the world both economically and militarily. At the same time, the industrial achievement of Europe became an example that less economically advanced areas of the world would seek to imitate. This potential for change emerged in a society whose institutions had been designed to inhibit social and economic change.

During the French Revolution and its aftermath, the patterns of social, political, and economic relationships that had existed in France before 1789 were referred to as the *ancien régime*, or the "Old Regime." The term has come to be applied generally to the life and institutions of prerevolutionary continental Europe. Tradition, hierarchy, corporateness, and privilege were the chief social characteristics of the Old Regime. Yet change and innovation were fermenting in its midst

Major Features of Life in the Old Regime

Socially, prerevolutionary Europe was based on (1) aristocratic elites with many inherited legal privileges; (2) established churches intimately related to the state and the aristocracy; (3) an urban labor force usually organized into guilds; and (4) a rural peasantry subject to high taxes and feudal dues.

Few outside the political, commercial, and intellectual elite wanted change. This was especially true of social relationships. Both nobles and peasants called for the restoration of traditional or customary rights. The nobles asserted what they considered their ancient rights against the expanding monarchical bureaucracies. The peasants, through petitions and revolts, called for their customary manorial rights.

Except for the early industrial development in Britain, the economy was also traditional. The grain harvest remained crucial for both the population and governments.

Hierarchy and Privilege

The medieval sense of hierarchy became more rigid during the century. It was enforced by the corporate nature of social relationships. Each state or society was considered a community composed of smaller communities. Eighteenth-century Europeans did not enjoy what Americans regard as individual rights. Instead, persons enjoyed such rights and privileges as were guaranteed to whatever communities or groups of which they were a part. The "community" might include the village, the municipality, the nobility, the church, the guild, a university, or the parish. In turn, each of these bodies enjoyed certain privileges, such as exemption from taxation or degrading punishment, the right to practice a trade or pursue a particular occupation, or, for the church, the right to collect the tithe.

Aristocracy

The eighteenth century was the great age of the aristocracy. The nobility constituted 1 to 5 percent of the population of any given country. It was the single wealthiest sector of the population; possessed the most power; and dominated society. Land provided the aristocracy with its largest source of income, but the influence of aristocrats was felt in every area of life. To be an aristocrat was a matter of birth and legal privilege, but aristocracies differed from country to country.

Great Britain

The smallest, wealthiest, and most socially responsible aristocracy resided in Great Britain. It consisted of about 400 families, whose eldest male members sat in the House of Lords. These families also controlled most seats in the House of Commons and owned one-fourth of the arable land in Britain. Increasingly, they invested in commerce, canals, urban real estate, mines, and industrial ventures. Because only the eldest son inherited the title and the land, younger sons moved into commerce, the army, the professions, and the church. Most members of the House of Commons were also landowners. They paid taxes and had few legal privileges, but their control of local government gave them immense power. Socially and politically, the aristocracy dominated the English counties.

France

In France, the nobility was theoretically divided between nobles of the sword and those of the robe. The former families' nobility derived from military service; the latter had gained their titles either by serving in the bureaucracy or by purchasing them.

The nobility who held favor with the royal court at Versailles reaped the wealth that came from holding high office. By the late 1780s, appointments to the church, the army, and the bureaucracy tended to go to the court aristocracy. Other

Painted by the English artist Francis Wheatley (1747–1801) near the close of the eighteenth century, this scene is part of a series illustrating a day in the life of an idealized farm family. Note the artist's assumptions about the division of labor by gender. Men work in the fields, women work in the home or look after the needs of men and children. As other illustrations in this chapter show, many eighteenth-century women in fact worked outside the home, but considerable social pressure was developing at this time to restrict them to domestic roles. This painting and the others in the series are thus more prescriptive than descriptive, intended in part to persuade their viewers that women belonged in their separate family sphere. Many, perhaps most, families living in the countryside could not maintain the closeness that these paintings extol. To survive, many had to send members to work on other farms or even to other regions. [Francis Wheatley (RA)(1747–1801), "Evening," signed and dated 1799, oil on canvas, 17 x 21 in. (44.5 x 54.5 cm), Yale Center for British Art, Paul Mellon Collection, B1977.14.118]

nobles, known as *hobereaux*, lived in the provinces and were sometimes no better off than well-to-do peasants.

All French aristocrats enjoyed hereditary privileges. They were exempt from many taxes and were not subject to the royal *corvées*, or labor donations. Moreover, they could collect feudal dues from their tenants and enjoyed exclusive hunting and fishing rights.

Eastern Europe

In Poland, thousands of nobles were entirely exempt from taxes. Until 1768 they could legally execute their serfs. A few rich nobles dominated the Polish state.

In Austria and Hungary, the nobility had broad judicial powers over the peasantry and enjoyed exemptions from taxation. In Prussia, after the accession of Frederick the Great in 1740, the position of the *Junkers* became stronger. Frederick's wars required their support. He drew his officers and bureaucrats almost wholly from the *Junker* class. Prussian nobles also enjoyed extensive authority over their serfs.

In Russia, a new, service nobility arose in the eighteenth century. Peter the Great linked noble status to state service through the Table of Ranks (1722). Resistance to state service created among Russian nobles a self-conscious class identity. In 1785, in the Charter of the Nobility, Catherine the Great granted a legal definition of noble rights and privileges in exchange for assurances of voluntary state service from the nobility. The noble privileges included the right of transmitting noble status to one's wife and children, the judicial protection of noble rights and property, power over the serfs, and exemption from personal taxes.

Throughout the century, in a European-wide *aristocratic resurgence*, the various nobilities sought to protect their social position and privileges. First, all nobilities attempted to restrict entry into their ranks. Second, they attempted to monopolize appointments to the officer corps, the government, and the church. The nobles thus hoped to control the power of the monarchies. Third, they attempted to use institutions they already controlled—the British Parliament, the French *parlements*, local aristocratic estates, and provincial diets—against the monarchies. Fourth, the aristocracies pressed the peasantry for higher rents or forgotten feudal dues.

The Land and Its Tillers

Land was the economic basis of eighteenth-century life. Over three-fourths of Europeans lived on the land, and most never traveled more than a few miles from their birthplaces. Except for the nobility and the wealthier landowners, the dwellers on the land were poor and led hard lives.

Peasants and Serfs

The major forms of rural social dependency related to the land. Those who worked the land were subject to immense influence or direct control by the landowners who also controlled local government and the courts.

Landlord power increased as one moved from west to east. Most French peasants owned some land, but a few were serfs. However, nearly all peasants were subject to feudal dues and forced labor on the lord's estate for a number of days each year.

In Prussia and Austria, despite attempts by the monarchies to improve the lot of the serfs, the landlords continued to exercise almost complete control over them. Moreover, throughout continental Europe the burden of state taxation fell on the tillers of the soil. Many agricultural laborers were forced to undertake supplemental work to pay the tax collector. Through legal privileges and the ability to demand concessions from the monarchs, the landlords escaped numerous taxes. They also presided over the manorial courts.

The condition of the serfs was the worst in Russia. They were regarded merely as economic commodities. Their services were attached to an individual lord rather than to a particular plot of land. Russian landlords could demand as many as six days a week of labor, and like Prussian and Austrian landlords, they could punish their serfs. However, custom, tradition, and law did provide a few protections. For example, the marriages of serfs, unlike those of most slaves throughout the world, were legally recognized. The landlord could not disband the family of a serf.

The Russian monarchy contributed to the degradation of the serfs. Peter the Great (r. 1682–1725) gave whole villages to favored nobles. Catherine the Great (r. 1762–1796) confirmed the authority of the nobles over their serfs in exchange for the nobility's political cooperation. This situation led to unrest. There were over fifty peasant revolts between 1762 and 1769.

Western Europe was more tranquil, but England experienced numerous enclosure riots. Rural rebellions were violent, but the peasants and serfs normally directed their wrath against property rather than persons. The rebels usually sought to reassert traditional or customary rights against practices they perceived as innovations. In this respect, the peasant revolts were conservative in nature.

Family Structures and the Family Economy

In preindustrial Europe, the household was the basic unit of production and consumption. Other than in cities, few productive establishments employed more than a handful of people not belonging to the owner's family. This mode of economic organization is known as the *family economy*.

Priscilla Wakefield Demands More Occupations Be Opened to Women

At the end of the eighteenth century, several English women writers began to demand a wider life for women. Priscilla Wakefield was among such authors. She was concerned that women found themselves able to pursue only occupations that paid poorly. Often they were excluded from work on the grounds of their alleged physical weakness. She also believed that women should receive equal wages for equal work. Many of the issues she raised have yet to be adequately addressed on behalf of women.

From reading this passage, what do you understand to have been the arguments at the end of the eighteenth century to limit the kinds of employment that women might enter? Why did women receive lower wages for work similar to or the same as that done by men? What occupations traditionally filled by men does Wakefield believe women might also pursue?

Another heavy discouragement to the industry of women, is the inequality of the reward of their labor, compared with that of men; an injustice which pervades every species of employment performed by both sexes.

In employments which depend on bodily strength, the distinction is just; for it cannot be pretended that the generality of women can earn as much as men, when the produce of their labor is the result of corporeal exertion; but it is a subject of great regret, that this inequality should prevail even where an equal share of skill and application is exerted. Male stay-makers, mantua-makers, and hairdressers, are better paid than female artists of the same professions; but surely it will never be urged as an apology for this disproportion, that women are not as capable of making stays, gowns, dressing hair, and similar arts, as men; if they are not superior to them, it can only be accounted for upon this principle, that the prices they receive for their labor are not sufficient to repay them for the expense of qualifying themselves for their business; and that they sink under the mortification of being regarded as artisans of inferior estimation. . . .

Besides these employments which are commonly performed by women, and those already shown to be suitable for such persons as are above the condition of hard labor, there are some professions and trades customarily in the hands of men, which might be conveniently exercised by either sex.—Watchmaking requiring more ingenuity than strength, seems peculiarly adapted to women; as do many parts of the business of stationer, particularly, ruling account books or making pens. The compounding of medicines in an apothecary's shop, requires no other talents than care and exactness; and if opening a vein occasionally be a indispensable requisite, a woman may acquire the capacity of doing it, for those of her own sex at least, without any reasonable objection. . . . Pastry and confectionery appear particularly consonant to the habits of women, though generally performed by men; perhaps the heat of the ovens, and the strength requisite to fill and empty them, may render male assistants necessary; but certain women are most eligible to mix up the ingredients, and prepare the various kinds of cakes for baking.—Light turnery and toy-making depend more upon dexterity and invention than force, and are therefore suitable work for women and children. . . . .

Farming, as far as respects the theory, is commensurate with the powers of the female mind: nor is the practice of inspecting agricultural processes incompatible with the delicacy of their frames if their constitution be good.

From Priscilla Wakefield, *Reflections on the Present Condition of the Female Sex* (1798), (London, 1817), pp. 125–127, as quoted in Bridget Hill, ed., *Eighteenth-Century Women: An Anthology.* Copyright © 1984 George Allen & Unwin, pp. 227–228.

Households

What was a household under the Old Regime? There were two basic models, one characterizing northwestern Europe and the other eastern Europe.

Northwestern Europe   Here, the household usually consisted of a married couple, their children through their early teenage years, and servants. Except for the wealthy, households were small. High mortality and late marriage meant that grandparents rarely lived in the same household as their grandchildren. The family structure of northwestern Europe was thus nuclear rather than extended; that is to say, these families consisted of parents and children rather than of several generations under the same roof.

Children lived with their parents only until their early teens. Then they normally left home to enter the work force of young servants. A child of a skilled artisan might remain with his or her parents to acquire the skill, but only rarely would more than one child do so because their labor was more valuable elsewhere.

These young men and women who had left home would eventually marry and form independent households of their own. This practice of moving away from home is known as *neolocalism.* The effort to acquire the economic resources to establish a household meant the age of marriage would be relatively late: for men, over twenty-six, and for women, over twenty-three. The marriage often occurred at the end of a long courtship when the woman was pregnant. The new couple would soon employ a servant, and everyone, including the children, would help the household support itself.

In preindustrial Europe, a servant—either male or female—was hired, often under a contract, to work for the head of the household in exchange for room, board, and wages. The servant was usually young and not socially inferior to his or her employer. Normally, the servant was an integral part of the household and ate with the family. Young men and women became servants when their labor was no longer needed in their parents' household or when they could earn more money for their family outside it. Being a servant for several years allowed young people to acquire skills and save enough to begin their own households. This period of working as a servant between leaving home and beginning a new household largely explains the late age of marriage in northwestern Europe.

Eastern Europe   As one moved east, the structure of the household and the pattern of marriage changed. In Russia and elsewhere in eastern Europe, marrying involved not starting a new household but continuing in and expanding one already established. Consequently, marriage occurred early, before the age of twenty for both men and women. Children were born to parents of a much younger age than in western Europe. Eastern European households tended to be larger than those in the west. The rural Russian household could have more than twenty members, with three or even four generations living together.

The landholding pattern in eastern Europe accounted, at least in part, for these patterns of marriage and the family. The lords of the manor who owned land wanted to ensure that it would be cultivated so that they could receive their rents. They discouraged single-generation family households because the death or serious illness of a person in such a household might mean that the land assigned to it would go out of cultivation.

The Family Economy

Throughout Europe, the household was the fundamental unit of production and consumption. People thought and worked in terms of sustaining the economic life of the family, and family members saw themselves as working together in an interdependent rather than an independent or individualistic manner. The goal of the family household was to produce or secure through wages enough food to support its members. In the countryside, that effort virtually always involved farming. In cities and towns, artisan production or working for another person was the usual pattern. Almost everyone lived within a household because ordinary people could rarely support themselves independently. Indeed, except for members of religious orders, people living outside a household were viewed with suspicion.

Everyone in the household had to work. On a farm, much of the effort went into raising food or producing agricultural goods that could be exchanged for food. In western Europe, however, few people had enough land to support their households from farming alone, so one or more family members might work elsewhere and send wages home. Within this family economy, all of the goods and income produced went to the benefit of the household rather than to the individual family member. The need to survive poor harvests or economic slumps meant that no one could be idle.

The family economy also dominated the life of skilled urban artisans. The father was usually the chief craftsman with one or more servants in his employ. He would also expect his children to work in the enterprise. His eldest child was usually trained in the trade. His wife often sold the wares, or had a small shop. The wife of a merchant also often ran the husband's business, especially when he traveled to purchase new goods. In any case, everyone in the family was involved. If business was poor, family members would look for employment elsewhere, not to support themselves but to help the family unit survive.

In western Europe, the death of a father could destroy the economy of the household. The family's economic life usually depended on his land or skills. The widow might take on the farm or the business, or her children might do so. She usually sought to remarry quickly to have the labor and skills of a male in the household and to prevent herself from falling into dependence. The high mortality rate meant that many households were second family groups with stepchildren. But some households simply dissolved. In desperate situations, survivors resorted to crime or begging. The personal, emotional, and economic vulnerability of the family economy cannot be overemphasized.

In eastern Europe, the family economy existed in the context of serfdom and landlord domination. Peasants thought in terms of their families and of expanding the land available for cultivation. The village structure may have mitigated the pressures of the family economy, as did the multigenerational family. Dependence on the land was the chief fact of life, and there were fewer artisan and merchant households and far less mobility than in western Europe.

Women and the Family Economy

The family economy established the chief constraints on the lives and personal experiences of women in preindustrial society. In western Europe, a woman's life experience was largely the function of her capacity to establish and maintain a household. For women, marriage was an economic necessity. A woman outside a household was vulnerable. Unless she was an aristocrat or a member of a religious order, she probably could not support herself by her own efforts. Much of a woman's life was devoted first to aiding her parents' household and then to getting her own household as an adult. Bearing and rearing children were subordinate to these goals.

By the age of seven, a girl was expected to contribute to the household work. On a farm, she might look after chickens or water animals or carry food to adult workers. In an urban artisan's household, she would do light work. The girl would remain at home as long as she made a real contribution to the family enterprise or her labor elsewhere was not more valuable to the family. An artisan's daughter might not leave home until marriage because she could learn valuable skills from her parents.

On farms, most girls would leave home between the ages of twelve and fourteen. They might go to another farm, but were more likely to migrate to a town or city. They would rarely travel more than thirty miles from their parents' household and would then normally become servants.

The young woman's chief goal was to accumulate a dowry. Marriage within the family economy was a joint economic undertaking, and the wife was expected to make an immediate contribution of capital to establish the household. A young woman might work for ten years or more to accumulate a dowry.

Within the marriage, earning enough money or producing enough farm goods to ensure an adequate food supply was the dominant concern. Domestic duties, childbearing, and child rearing were subordinate to economic survival. Consequently, couples would often practice birth control, usually through *coitus interruptus,* or withdrawal of the male before ejaculation. Young children were often placed with wet nurses so the mother could continue to contribute to the household economy. The wet nurse, in turn, was contributing to her own household. The child would be reintegrated into its family when it was weaned.

A married woman's work was a function of her husband's occupation. If the peasant household possessed enough land to support itself, the wife literally carried things for her husband—water, food, seed, grain, and the like. But few peasants had such landholdings. If the husband had to do work other than farming, such as fishing or migrant labor, the wife might plow, plant, and harvest. In the city, the wife of an artisan or merchant often acted like a business manager. When her husband died, she might take over the business, perhaps hiring an artisan.

Finally, if economic disaster struck, often it was the wife who organized what Olwen Hufton has called the "economy of expedients,"[1] within which family members might be sent off to find work elsewhere or even to beg.

In all phases of life within the family economy, women led active, often decisive roles. Finding a functional place in the household was essential to their well-being, but their function was also essential to its ongoing well-being.

Children and the World of the Family Economy

Childbirth was a time of danger to both mother and infant. Puerperal fever and other infections from unsterilized medical instruments were common. Not all midwives were skillful. The poverty and wretched housing of most Europeans endangered the newborn child and the mother.

However, the birth of a child was not always welcome. The child might be illegitimate or an economic burden. Through at least the end of the seventeenth century, infanticide was practiced, especially among the poor. Unwanted infants might be smothered or exposed to the elements. These practices were one result of the ignorance and prejudice surrounding contraception. Although many married couples seem to have succeeded in limiting their families, unmarried young people whose sexual relationships may have been the result of a fleeting acquaintance were less fortunate. Numerous young women, especially among servants, found themselves pregnant and without husbands. This situation and the consequent birth of illegitimate children seem to have become more frequent during the eighteenth century. It probably arose from the more frequent migration of young people from their homes and the disturbance of traditional village life through enclosures (to be discussed later), the commercialization of agriculture, wars, and the late-century revolutions.

In the late seventeenth and early eighteenth centuries, reflecting a new interest in preserving the lives of abandoned children, large foundling hospitals were established in the major nations. Sadness and tragedy were the lot of abandoned children. Most were illegitimate infants, but many seem to have been left with the foundling hospitals because their parents could not support them. Parents would sometimes leave personal tokens on the abandoned baby in the vain hope that they might reclaim the child. Few children were so reclaimed. Leaving a child at a foundling hospital did not guarantee its survival. In Paris, only about 10 percent of all abandoned children lived to the age of ten years.

Despite these perils, children did grow up across Europe. The world of the child may not have received the kind of

---

[1] "Women and the Family Economy in Eighteenth-Century France," *French Historical Studies* 9 (1975): 19.

attention it does today, but during the eighteenth century the seeds of that modern sensibility were sown. Particularly among the upper classes, new interest arose in the education of children. However, most education remained in the hands of the churches. Most Europeans remained illiterate. Not until the late nineteenth century did childhood and education become inextricably linked. Then children would be reared to become members of a national citizenry. In the Old Regime, they were reared to contribute to the economy of their parents' family and then to set up their own households.

Growth of Agriculture and Population

Thus far, this chapter has examined those groups who sought stability and resisted change. Other groups, however, pursued new directions in social and economic life that would during the next century transform first Europe and then much of the rest of the world. These developments first appeared in agriculture.

The Revolution in Agriculture

The main goal of traditional European peasant society was to ensure the local food supply. That supply was never certain and became more uncertain the farther east one traveled. A failed harvest meant starvation. Food was often harder to find in the country than in cities because city governments usually stored reserves of grain.

Poor harvests also raised grain prices. Even small increases in the cost of food could squeeze peasant or artisan families. If prices increased sharply, many of those families fell back on poor relief from their local government or the church. Peasants felt helpless before the whims of nature and the marketplace, and resisted changes that they felt might endanger the sure supply of food, which they believed traditional cultivation practices ensured.

During the century, bread prices slowly but steadily rose, spurred largely by population growth. This put pressure on the poor. Prices rose faster than urban wages and brought no appreciable advantage to the small peasant producer. Instead, the rise in grain prices benefited landowners and those wealthier peasants who had surplus grain to sell.

The increasing price of grain allowed landlords to improve their income and lifestyle. They began a series of innovations in farm production that are known as the *agricultural revolution*.

New Crops and New Methods   This movement began during the sixteenth and seventeenth centuries in the Low Countries, where Dutch landlords and farmers devised better ways to drain land so that they could farm more areas.

They also experimented with new crops, such as clover and turnips, that would increase the supply of animal fodder and replenish the soil.

In England during the early eighteenth century, new methods of farming, crops, and modes of landholding led to greater productivity. This advance in food production was necessary for an industrial society to develop. It ensured adequate food for the cities and freed surplus agricultural labor for industrial production. The changing modes of agriculture sponsored by the landlords undermined the assumptions of traditional peasant production. Farming now took place not only to provide the local food supply but to earn the landlord a profit.

Enclosure Replaces Open-Field Method   Many of the agricultural innovations, which were adopted only slowly, were incompatible with the existing organization of land in Britain. Small cultivators in village communities farmed most of the soil. Each farmer tilled an assortment of unconnected strips. The two- or three-field systems of rotation left much land unproductive each year. Animals grazed on the common land in the summer and on the stubble of the harvest in the winter. Until at least the middle of the eighteenth century, the decisions about what crops would be planted were made communally. The system discouraged improvement and favored the poorer farmers, who needed the common land and stubble fields for their animals. Traditional methods aimed to produce a steady but not a growing supply of food.

In the second half of the eighteenth century, the rising price of wheat encouraged landlords to consolidate or enclose their lands to increase production. The enclosures were intended to use land more rationally and raise profits. The process involved the fencing of common lands, the reclamation of untilled waste, and the transformation of strips into block fields. These procedures disrupted economic and social life. Riots often ensued. Because many British farmers either owned their strips or rented them in a manner that amounted to ownership, the landlords had to resort to parliamentary acts to legalize the enclosure of the land, which they owned but rented to the farmers. Because the large landowners controlled Parliament, such measures passed easily. In 1801, a general enclosure act streamlined the process.

The enclosures have remained controversial. They increased food production on larger agricultural units but also disrupted small traditional communities and forced many off the land. However, the enclosures did not depopulate the countryside. In some counties where the enclosures took place, the population increased. New soil had come into production, and services subsidiary to farming expanded.

Limited Improvements in Eastern Europe   In Prussia, Austria, Poland, and Russia, agricultural improvement was minimal. There, the chief method of increasing production was to farm previously untilled lands. By extending tillage, the great landlords sought to squeeze more labor from their serfs rather than greater productivity from the soil. As in the west, the goal was increased profits for the landlords. The only significant nutritional gain landlords achieved was the introduction of maize and the potato.

Population Expansion

Agricultural improvement was both a cause and a result of an immense expansion in the population of Europe. Our current population explosion seems to have had its origins in the eighteenth century. In 1700, Europe's population, excluding the Ottoman Empire, was between 100 million and 120 million people. By 1800, the figure had risen to almost 190 million, and by 1850 to 260 million. Such extraordinary growth put new demands on resources and pressure on social organizations.

The population expansion occurred in both the country and the cities. Only a limited consensus exists about the causes of this growth. There was a decline in the death rate. There were fewer wars and epidemics in the eighteenth century. Hygiene and sanitation improved. But changes in the food supply may have been the chief reason for sustained population growth. One contributing factor was expanding grain production. Even more important was the widespread cultivation of the potato. An acre of potatoes could feed one peasant's family for an entire year. With this more certain food supply, more children could survive.

The Eighteenth-Century Industrial Revolution

An Event in World History

In the late eighteenth century, the European economy began to industrialize. This development distinguished Europe and eventually North America from the rest of the world for the next two centuries. The consumer products of the industrializing businesses gave Europeans new goods to sell throughout the world and thus encouraged more international trade in which Western nations supplied the finished goods in exchange for raw materials. The prosperity of other areas of the globe became economically dependent on European and American demand. The wealth achieved through this uneven commerce allowed Europeans to dominate world markets for two centuries.

Furthermore, iron and steel production and the new technologies allowed European states and the United States to build more powerful military forces, especially navies, than those of Africa, Latin America, or Asia. The economic

and military dominance of the West arose from the industrial achievement.

Much of the history of the non-Western world from the middle of the eighteenth century to the present can be understood in terms of how it reacted to its penetration by Europeans and Americans made wealthy and powerful through industrialized economies. Africa and Latin America became dependent economies. Japan successfully imitated the European pattern. China did not and became indirectly ruled by Europeans. The Chinese revolutions of the twentieth century are efforts to achieve self-direction. Southeast Asia and the Middle East became drawn into the network of resource supply to the West; they could move toward economic independence only through imitation or, like Arab nations in the early 1970s, by refusing to supply oil to the West. The industrialization that commenced in small factories in eighteenth-century Europe has changed the world more than any other single development in the last two centuries.

The European Industrial Revolution of the eighteenth century achieved sustained economic growth. Previously, production had been limited. The economy of a province or a country might grow, but soon reached a plateau. However, since the late eighteenth century, the economy of Europe has expanded relatively uninterruptedly. Even during economic downturns the Western economy has continued to grow.

At considerable social cost and dislocation, industrialism produced more goods and services than ever before. Industrialism in Europe overcame the economy of scarcity. The new means of production demanded new skills and discipline in work and a large labor force. The produced goods met consumer demand and created new demands. In the long run, industrialism raised the standard of living; the poverty in which most Europeans had always lived was overcome. Industrialization provided human beings greater control over nature than they had ever known.

The wealth produced by industrialism upset the political and social structures of the Old Regime and led to reforms. The economic elite of the emerging industrial society would challenge the dominance of the aristocracy. Industrialization undermined communities and displaced many people. These processes repeated themselves wherever industrialization occurred during the next two centuries.

Industrial Leadership of Great Britain

Great Britain was the home of the Industrial Revolution and, until the late nineteenth century, remained the industrial leader of the world. Several factors contributed to early industrialization in Britain. Britain was the largest free-trade area in Europe, with good roads and waterways without internal trade barriers. There were rich deposits of coal and iron ore. The political structure was stable, and property was secure. Sound banking and public credit created a good investment climate. Taxation was heavy, but it received legal approval from Parliament. Taxes were efficiently and fairly collected, largely from indirect taxes with all regions and persons from all classes paying the same taxes. Besides satisfying domestic consumer demand, the British economy also benefited from the demand for goods from the North American colonies.

Finally, British society was relatively mobile. Persons who had money could rise socially. The British aristocracy would accept people who had amassed large fortunes. The combination of these factors plus the progressive state of British agriculture provided the nation with a marginal advantage in the creation of a new mode of economic production. No less important, the wars and revolutions of the late eighteenth and early nineteenth centuries disrupted those parts of the Continent where an industrialized economy might also have begun to develop.

New Methods of Textile Production   Although eighteenth-century society was devoted primarily to agriculture, manufacturing permeated the countryside. Peasants often spun thread or wove textiles in winter. Under the *domestic* or *putting-out* system, urban textile merchants took wool or other unfinished fiber to peasants, who spun it into thread. The agent then transported the thread to other peasants, who wove it into the finished product. The merchant sold the wares. Sometimes the spinners or weavers owned their own equipment, but more often the merchant capitalist owned the machinery as well as the raw material.

Eighteenth-century industrial development took place within a rural setting. The peasant family living in a cottage, not the factory, was the basic unit of production. The family economy, not the industrial factory economy, characterized the century.

However, by mid-century, demand for cotton textiles was growing more rapidly than production, particularly in Great Britain, whose growing population wanted cotton textiles, as did its colonies in North America. The most famous inventions of the Industrial Revolution were devised in response to consumer demand for cotton textiles.

Cotton textile weavers had the technical capacity to produce enough fabric to satisfy demand, but the spinners could not produce as much thread as the weavers needed. This imbalance had been created during the 1730s by James Kay's flying shuttle, which increased the productivity of the weavers. To eliminate this bottleneck, in about 1765 James Hargreaves (d. 1778) invented the spinning jenny, which by the close of the century allowed as many as 120 spindles of thread to be spun.

The spinning jenny was still used in the cottage. The invention that took cotton textile manufacture from the home to the factory was Richard Arkwright's (1732–1792)

water frame, patented in 1769. It was a water-powered device to produce a purely cotton fabric rather than one containing linen for durability. Numerous factories sprang up in the countryside near the necessary water power. From the 1780s onward, the cotton industry could meet an ever-expanding demand. By 1815, cotton composed 40 percent of the value of British domestic exports.

The Steam Engine   The new technology in textile manufacture revolutionized a major consumer industry. But the invention that more than any other enabled industrialization to grow on itself and expand into one area of production after another was the steam engine. This machine provided for the first time in human history an unlimited source of inanimate power. Unlike engines powered by water or wind, the steam engine, driven by burning coal, was a portable source of industrial power that did not fail or falter as the seasons changed. Unlike human or animal power, the steam engine depended on mineral energy that never tired. Finally, the steam engine could be applied to many industrial and, eventually, transportation uses.

The first practical engine using steam power was invented by Thomas Newcomen (1663–1729) in the early eighteenth century. It was large, inefficient, and practically untransportable. Nonetheless, English mine operators used it to pump water out of coal and tin mines.

During the 1760s, James Watt (1736–1819) understood that if the condenser were separated from the piston and the cylinder, much greater efficiency would result. In 1769, he patented his new invention, and in 1776, the Watt steam engine found its first commercial application pumping water from mines. By the early nineteenth century, the steam engine had become the prime mover for industry. With its application to ships and then to wagons on iron rails, it also revolutionized transportation.

Iron Production   High-quality iron has been basic to industrial development. It constitutes the chief element of heavy industry and land or sea transport and is the material out of which most productive machinery has been manufactured. During the early eighteenth century, British ironmakers

---

Major Inventions in the Textile-Manufacturing Revolution

1733	James Kay's flying shuttle
1765	James Hargreaves's spinning jenny (patent 1770)
1769	James Watt's steam engine patent
1769	Richard Arkwright's water frame patent
1787	Edmund Cartwright's power loom

produced less than 25,000 tons annually. Three factors held back production. First, charcoal rather than coke was used to smelt the ore. Charcoal, which is derived from wood, was becoming scarce, and it did not burn at as high a temperature as coke, which is derived from coal. Second, until the perfection of the steam engine, insufficient blasts could be achieved in the furnaces. Finally, the demand for iron was limited. The elimination of the first two problems eliminated the third.

In the course of the century, British ironmakers began to use coke, and the steam engine provided new power for the blast furnaces. Coke was abundant because of Britain's large coal deposits. The steam engine improved iron production and increased the demand for iron.

In 1784, Henry Cort (1740–1800) introduced a new method for melting and stirring the molten ore. Cort's process produced a purer iron. He also developed a rolling mill that shaped the still-molten metal into bars, rails, or other forms. Previously, the metal had been pounded into these forms.

These innovations achieved a better, more versatile, and cheaper product. The demand for iron grew as its price fell. By the early nineteenth century, annual British iron production amounted to over a million tons. The lower cost of iron in turn lowered the cost of steam engines and allowed them to be used more widely.

Cities

Patterns of Preindustrial Urbanization

Remarkable changes occurred in city growth between 1500 and 1800. In 1500, 156 cities within Europe (excluding Hungary and Russia) had a population greater than 10,000. Only Paris, Milan, Venice, and Naples had more than 100,000 inhabitants. By 1800, 363 cities had 10,000 or more inhabitants, and 17 of those had populations larger than 100,000. The percentage of the European population living in urban areas had risen from over 5 percent to over 9 percent. The urban concentration had also shifted from Mediterranean Europe to the north.

These raw figures conceal changes that took place in how cities grew and the population distributed itself. Urban development in the sixteenth century was followed in the seventeenth by leveling and decline. New growth began in the early eighteenth century and accelerated thereafter.

Growth of Capitals and Ports   Capitals and ports were the urban areas that displayed the most growth and vigor between 1600 and 1750. This reflects the success of monarchical state building and the burgeoning of groups related to the process of government who lived in the capitals. The growth of port cities reflects the expansion of European overseas trade and especially that of the Atlantic routes. With the

exception of Lyons, France, significant growth did not take place in industrial cities. Furthermore, between 1600 and 1750, cities with populations of fewer than 40,000 inhabitants declined. These cities included older landlocked trading centers, medieval industrial cities, and ecclesiastical centers. They contributed less to the new political regimes, and since rural labor was cheaper than urban labor, cities with concentrations of labor declined as production sites were moved from urban workshops into the countryside.

New Cities and Growth of Small Towns   After 1750, large cities grew more slowly. New cities arose, and older smaller cities began to grow. Several factors were at work. First was the overall population increase. Second, the early stages of the Industrial Revolution, particularly in Britain, occurred in the countryside and aided the growth of smaller towns and cities near the factories. Factory organization itself fostered new concentrations of population. But cities also grew because of the new prosperity of European agriculture. Greater agricultural production aided the growth of nearby market towns and other urban centers. This new pattern of urban growth—new cities and the expansion of smaller existing cities—would continue into the nineteenth century.

Urban Classes

Social divisions were as marked in the cities of the eighteenth century as they were in the industrial centers of the nineteenth.

The Upper Classes   At the top of the urban social structure stood a small group of nobles, large merchants, bankers, financiers, clergy, and government officials. These men (and they were always men) controlled the affairs of the town through its corporation or city council. These rights of self-government had generally been granted by a royal charter that gave the city corporation the power to select its own members.

The Middle Class   The prosperous merchants, tradesmen, bankers, and professional people were the most dynamic element of the urban population and constituted the middle class, or *bourgeoisie*. Middle-class people lived in the cities and towns, and their sources of income had little to do with the land. The middle class normally supported reform, change, and economic growth. Middle-class businessmen and professionals often found their pursuit of profit and prestige blocked by aristocratic privilege and social exclusiveness. The bourgeoisie (and some progressive aristocrats) also wanted more rational regulations for trade and commerce.

During the eighteenth century, the middle class and the aristocracy frequently collided. The former often imitated the lifestyle of the latter, and nobles increasingly embraced the commercial spirit of the middle class. Both were seeking to enhance their existing power and prestige. However, tradition and political connection gave the advantage to the nobility. Consequently, the middle class increasingly resented the aristocracy, especially as the bourgeoisie grew wealthier and more numerous and the aristocratic control of power tightened.

On the other hand, the middle class also tended to fear the lower urban classes. The lower orders constituted a potentially violent threat to property and, in their poverty, a drain on national resources. The lower orders, however, were much more varied than either the city aristocracy or the middle class cared to admit.

Artisans Shopkeepers, artisans, and wage earners constituted the single largest group in any city. They had their own culture, values, and institutions. Like the peasants, they were conservative. Their economic position was vulnerable. If a poor harvest raised the price of food, their businesses suffered.

The life of these artisans and shopkeepers centered on their work. They usually lived near or at their place of employment. Most of them worked in shops with fewer than a half-dozen other craftsmen. Their primary institution had been the guild, but most guilds had lost influence.

Nevertheless, the guilds played a conservative role. They did not seek economic growth or innovation. They attempted to preserve the jobs and the skills of their members and to prevent too many people from learning a particular skill. The guilds also provided a framework for social and economic advancement. A young boy might become an apprentice to learn a craft or trade. After several years he would be made a journeyman. Still later, he might become a master. The artisan could also receive social benefits from the guilds, including aid for his family during sickness or the promise of admission into the guild for his son. The guilds constituted the chief protection for artisans against the commercial market.

The Age of the Ghetto

Most European Jews lived in Eastern Europe. In the eighteenth century, 3 million Jews dwelled in Poland, Lithuania, and Ukraine. There were perhaps 150,000 in the Habsburg lands around 1760. Fewer than 100,000 lived in Germany and approximately 40,000 in France. England and Holland had Jewish populations of fewer than 10,000. Even fewer Jews lived in Italy.

Jews dwelled in most nations without enjoying the rights and privileges of other subjects, unless such rights were specifically granted to them. They were aliens whose status might be changed at the whim of rulers.

The Jews of Europe under the Old Regime lived apart from non-Jews. In cities they usually lived in distinct districts known as *ghettos;* in the countryside, in Jewish villages. Thus, this period in Jewish history is known as the age of the ghetto, or separate community. Jews were also treated as a distinct people religiously and legally. In Poland for much of the century they were virtually self-governing. Elsewhere they lived under the burden of discriminatory legislation. Except in England, Jews could not mix in the mainstream of the societies in which they dwelled.

During the seventeenth century, a few Jews helped finance the wars of rulers. These financiers came to be known as "court Jews." They tended to marry among themselves. Their position at court and their financial abilities may have brought them privilege and fame, but court Jews often failed to have their loans repaid.

However, most European Jews lived in poverty. They occupied the most undesirable sections of cities or poor rural villages. A few were money lenders, but most worked at the lowest occupations. Their religious beliefs, rituals, and community set them apart. A wall of laws and social institutions—as well as the physical walls of the ghetto—kept them in positions of social inferiority.

Under the Old Regime, this discrimination was based on religious separateness. Jews who converted to Christianity were welcomed into the major political and social institutions of European society. But until the late eighteenth century, those Jews who remained loyal to their faith were not free to pursue the professions or often change residence and stood outside the political structures of the nations in which they lived. Jews could be expelled from the cities where they dwelled and their property confiscated. They were regarded as socially and religiously inferior. Their children could be taken away from them and given Christian instruction. And their non-Jewish neighbors might turn violently against them.

IN WORLD PERSPECTIVE

The European Old Regime

Eighteenth-century European society was traditional, hierarchical, corporate, and privileged. These features had characterized Europe and the world for centuries. All societies also confronted the scarce food supplies.

The eighteenth century witnessed important changes in all these societies. The population explosion was not limited to Europe. Whether in Europe or China, an improved food supply helped support the larger population. In China, marginal lands were settled. Agricultural techniques improved in Europe, but emigration to the New World also opened vast expanses of land. In contrast to Europe, the farmland of China continued to be cultivated by clans or communities. But in all cases, the vast, expanding population created pressures on social structures.

In both China and Europe, commerce grew during the eighteenth century. In both cultures banking and the money supply improved. Agriculture became more commercialized, with more money payments. As in Europe, Chinese cities expanded, and Chinese trade grew.

Eighteenth-century Japan stood, of course, in marked contrast to both Europe and China. Tokugawa rule had achieved stability, but Japan did not enter the world-trading network, except as a depot for Dutch and Chinese goods. The population and economy seem to have grown slowly. As in many European cities, guilds controlled manufacture. Japan in the eighteenth century sought to spurn innovation and preserve stable tradition.

Throughout the eighteenth century, the slave trade drew Africa deeply into the transatlantic economy.

Latin America remained, at least in theory, the preserve of Spain and Portugal. But their monopoly could not survive the determination of Britain to enter the Latin American market. At the same time, British forces established a hegemony in mid-eighteenth-century India that would last almost two centuries.

Seen in this world context, European society stood on the brink of a new era in which the social, economic, and political relationships of centuries would be destroyed. The commercial spirit and the values of the marketplace clashed with the traditions of peasants and guilds. That commercial spirit brought social change; by the early nineteenth century it led to a conception of human beings as individuals rather than as members of communities.

The expansion of the European population further stimulated change and challenge to tradition, hierarchy, and corporateness. The traditional economic and social organization had presupposed a stable or declining population. A larger population meant that new ways had to be devised to solve old problems. The social hierarchy had to accommodate itself to more people. Corporate groups, such as the guilds, had to confront an expanded labor force. New wealth meant that birth would cease to determine social relationships.

Finally, the conflicting political ambitions of the monarchies, the nobilities, and the middle class generated innovation. The monarchies wanted to make their nations rich enough to wage war. The nobilities wished to reassert their privileges. The middle class wanted social prestige and influence.

As these social and economic changes became connected to the world economy, the transformation of Europe led to the transformation of much of the non-European world. For the first time in history, major changes in one region left virtually no corner of the globe untouched. By the close of the eighteenth century, a movement toward world interconnectedness and interdependence that had no real precedent in terms of depth and extent had begun, and it has not ended.

Review Questions

1. Describe the privileges of the various European nobilities. What was the economic basis of the life of the nobility? What authority did they have over other groups in their various societies?

2. How would you define the term *family economy*? What were some of the particular characteristics of the northwestern European household as opposed to that in eastern Europe? How were the lives of women constrained by the family economy?

3. What caused the Agricultural Revolution? How did technological innovations help change European agriculture? To what extent did the English aristocracy contribute to the Agricultural Revolution?

4. What factors explain the increase in Europe's population in the eighteenth century? What were the effects of the population explosion?

5. What caused the Industrial Revolution of the eighteenth century? What were some of the technological innovations and why were they important? Why did Great Britain take the lead in the Industrial Revolution?

6. During the eighteenth century, were all European cities of the same character? What changes took place in the distribution of population in cities and towns?

Documents CD-ROM

1. G. M. Trevelyan: Chapter XIII from *English Social History*
2. Jonathan Swift: A Description of a City Shower

3. Mary Astell: From "Some Reflections upon Marriage"

23 THE LAST GREAT ISLAMIC EMPIRES (1500–1800)

Between 1450 and 1650, Islamic culture and statecraft blossomed. The creation of the Ottoman, Safavid, and Mughal Empires marked the global apogee of Islamic culture and power. (see Map 23–1).

In 1600, Islamic civilization seemed as strong and vital as that of western Europe, China, or Japan. Yet by the late seventeenth century, Islamic power was in retreat before the rising tide of western European military and economic imperialism, even though Islamic cultural life and Muslim religion flourished.

ISLAMIC EMPIRES

The Ottoman Empire

Origins and Development of the Ottoman State before 1600

The Ottomans were a Turkish dynasty that reached Anatolia (Asia Minor) in the time of the Seljuks of Rum (1098–1308)[1]. In the fourteenth century, the Ottomans expanded into central Anatolia and west across the Dardanelles (in 1356) onto European soil. The Ottomans built a formidable fighting force.

By 1402, Ottoman control extended as far as the Danube. Constantinople fell in 1453 to Sultan Mehmed II, "the Conqueror" (r. 1451–1481). It became the Ottoman capital and was renamed "Istanbul." After hundreds of years, Byzantium, the center of eastern Christendom, was no more.

By 1512, Ottoman rule was secure in southeastern Europe. Under Selim I (r. 1512–1520) and Süleyman, "the Lawgiver" ("Süleyman the Magnificent"; r. 1520–1566), this sovereignty was greatly expanded. Selim subjugated Egypt (1517), Syria-Palestine, and most of North Africa. The Yemen and western Arabia, including Mecca and Medina, also were brought under Ottoman rule. Süleyman extended Ottoman control in the Caucasus and Mesopotamia. He also brought most of Hungary under Ottoman rule.

The Ottoman ruler could now claim to be the caliph for all Muslims. This claim was symbolized by the title "Protector of the Sacred Places [Mecca and Medina]" and emperor (*padishah*).

[1]The Ottomans are named after Osman (1259–1326), said to have founded the dynasty about 1288 in northwestern Anatolia.

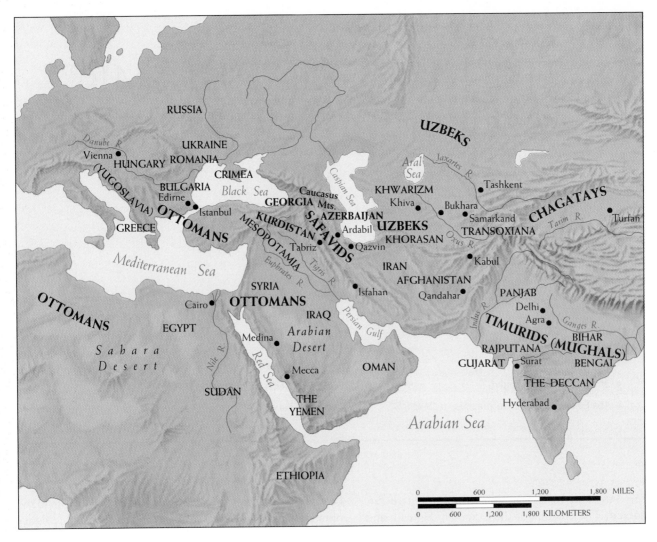

Map 23–1 Sixteenth-century Islamic empires. Major Islamic dynasties in the central Islamic lands, ca. 1600.

The "Classical" Ottoman Order

The entire Ottoman state was organized as one vast military institution. It was supported by the productivity of its Muslim and non-Muslim subjects. The ruling class were Muslims and had to give utter allegiance to the sultan. The state organization included the palace and the administrative, military, and religious or learned institutions.

Several measures helped ensure the strength of the sultan. Young Ottoman princes were given leadership training in the provinces, which gave them experience of life outside the capital. Stability of succession was guaranteed by fratricide in the ruling family, which continued until the late sixteenth century. The succession was theoretically left to God, the strongest aspirant to the sultanate having to seize power, after which he was expected to execute his brothers to eliminate claims to the throne.

By institutionalizing the religious institution, the Ottomans made the religious scholars, or *ulama*, an arm of the government under a single religious authority, the Grand Mufti or "Shaykh of Islam." This branch of the state was open only to Muslim men and included the entire system of courts and judges.

Although the religious establishment upheld the *Shari'a* and the sultan recognized its authority, the functional law of the land was the state administrative law, or *Qanun*, established by the ruler. This had been a de facto characteristic of most Islamic states, but under the Ottomans, administrative law was highly organized.

As for the military institution, the Ottoman rulers kept its loyalty by checks on the power of the old landed aristocracy and by the use of slave soldiers with allegiance only to the sultan. To sustain the quality of these slave troops, the Ottomans developed the provincial slave levy, or *devshirme*. This selected Christian boys from the peasantry to be raised as

Muslims. They were trained to serve in both army and bureaucracy. The most famous slave corps was the Janissaries, the elite infantry of the empire.

After Süleyman: Challenges and Change

The reign of Süleyman marked the peak of Ottoman prestige and power. Beginning with his weak son, Selim II (1566–1574), the empire was plagued by corruption, decentralization, and maritime setbacks. Agricultural failures, commercial imbalances, and inflation were hard to check. Yet culturally, the seventeenth and eighteenth centuries were impressive. Overall, the two centuries seesawed between decline and vitality.

Political and Military Developments The post–Süleyman era began with the loss of territory in the east to the Persian Safavids (1603). By this time the Ottoman military apparatus was weakened, partly from fighting two-front wars with the Safavids and the Habsburgs and partly because of European advances in technology. The Janissaries, once the backbone of Ottoman power, became disruptive and tried to influence decision making and even dynastic succession. Finally, the increasing employment of mercenaries resulted in peacetime in the release of masses of unemployed armed men into the countryside, which led to the sacking of provincial towns, banditry, and revolts.

Economic Developments Financing the Ottoman state grew ever more difficult. The increase in the Janissary corps from 12,000 to 36,000 men by 1600 drained state coffers. Fluctuations in silver caused inflation. The Ottomans encouraged imports, since too many exports would have raised domestic prices. This damaged the Ottoman economy in the long run. The population doubled in the sixteenth century, which led to increased unemployment. Decentralization paved the way for the rise of provincial notables (*ayan*), who became virtually independent in the eighteenth century.

Culture and Society The seventeenth and eighteenth centuries were an era of vitality in culture, but the *ulama* became an aristocratic social elite. Major religious posts were controlled by a handful of families and became hereditary sinecures that were often sold or leased.

In literature, Katib Chelebi (d. 1657) was only the most illustrious of many polymaths who wrote histories, social commentary, geographies, and encyclopedic works. Ottoman art in the latter sixteenth century produced distinctively Ottoman artistic and architectural forms. The greatest name here is that of the imperial master architect Sinan (d. 1578). The first half of the eighteenth century was the golden age of Ottoman poetry and art; it also saw the first Ottoman printing press.

The Ottoman Empire	
ca. 1280	Foundation of early Ottoman principality in Anatolia
1356	Ottomans Cross Dardanelles into Europe
1451–1481	Rule of Sultan Mehmed II, "the Conqueror"
1453	Fall of Constantinople to Mehmed the Conqueror
1512–1520	Rule of Selim I
1517	Ottoman conquest of Egypt, assumption of claim to Abbasid caliphal succession from Mamluks
1520–1566	Rule of Süleyman, "the Lawgiver"
1578	Death of Ottoman master architect, Sinan
1683	Ottoman siege of Vienna
1699	Treaty of Karlowitz, loss of Hungarian and other European territory
1774	Loss of Crimea to Russia; tsar becomes formal protector of Ottoman Orthodox Christians
1918	End of empire

Socially, the period saw the consolidation of Ottoman society as a multi-ethnic and multi-religious state. Considerable Jewish immigration into Ottoman societies following their expulsion from Spain (1492) had brought new craftsmen, physicians, bankers, scholars, and entertainers. The large Christian population of the empire was well treated, but in the seventeenth century they began to suffer increasing discrimination. As a result, the Christians looked to Europe and Russia for liberation.

Overall, in the eighteenth century strained relations between Muslims and non-Muslims increased, in part because of the rise in the economic and social status of non-Muslims—in particular the rich mercantile middle class. Non-Muslims monopolized foreign trade, and in the eighteenth century, European countries gave many of them citizenship, which allowed them the trade privileges granted to foreign governments by the sultan.

One of the major social institutions of later Ottoman society, the coffeehouse, flourished from the mid-sixteenth century on. The Ottoman coffeehouse rapidly became a major common space for socializing. Here people gathered to drink coffee, play games, read, and discuss public affairs. The coffeehouse stimulated the development of a common Ottoman urban culture among lower and middle classes.

The Decline of Ottoman Military and Political Power

After the failure in 1683 of a second siege of Vienna, the Ottomans were driven out of Hungary and Belgrade and never again threatened Europe. The treaty of Karlowitz sealed the loss of Hungary to Austria (1699). Defeat by Russia cost the Ottomans the Crimea, which made the tsar the protector of the Orthodox Christians of the Islamic empire (1774). Henceforth, the Ottomans were prey to the West, never regaining their earlier power and influence before their final demise in 1918.

Outflanked by Russia to their north and by European sea power to the south and west, the Ottomans found themselves blocked in the east by their Shi'ite foes in Iran. They could not support their expensive wars. Ultimately, their dependence on an agrarian economy proved insufficient to face the commercial and industrial powers of Europe.

The Safavid Shi'ite Empire

Origins

As noted in Chapter 14, Iranian history changed under the Safavid dynasty after 1500. The Safavids had begun in the fourteenth century as hereditary Turkish spiritual leaders of a Sunni Sufi order in the northwestern Iranian province of Azerbaijan. In the fifteenth century, the Safavid order evolved a new and militant Shi'ite ideology. The Safavid spiritual masters (*shaykhs*, or *pirs*) of the order claimed descent from the seventh imam of the Twelver Shia (see Chapter 14), which made them (the *pirs*) the focus of Shi'ite religious allegiance.

The growing strength of the Safavids brought about conflict with the dominant Sunni groups around Tabriz. The Safavids emerged victorious in 1501 under the leadership of the young Safavid master-designate Isma'il, who extended his sovereignty over the southern Caucasus, Azerbaijan, the Tigris-Euphrates valley, and western Iran by 1506. In the east, by 1512 the Safavids had taken eastern Iran from the Uzbek Turks. The Uzbeks, however, became implacable foes of the Safavids and throughout the ensuing century often forced them to fight a debilitating two-front war, with Uzbeks in the east, and Ottomans in the west.

Strong central rule now united Iran for the first time since the Abbasid caliphate. It was a regime based on the existing Persian bureaucratic institutions. Shah Isma'il enforced Shi'ite

The Safavid Empire

ca. 1500	Rise of Safavids under Shah Isma'il
1501-1512	Safavid conquest of greater Iran; Shi'ite state founded
1588-1629	Rule of Shah Abbas I
1722	Forced abdication of last Safavid ruler
1736-1747	Rule of the Sunni Afghan leader, Nadir Shah; revival of Sunni monarchy in Iran
1739	Nadir Shah sacks Delhi

conformity on the Sunni majority, and Shi'ite conformity slowly took root across the realm—perhaps bolstered by Persian self-consciousness in the face of the Sunni Ottomans, Arabs, Uzbeks, and Mughals who surrounded Iran.

In the west, however, the better-armed army of Selim I defeated the Safavids in 1514, marking the beginning of a series of Ottoman-Safavid conflicts over the next two centuries. This defeat gave the Ottomans control of the Fertile Crescent and forced the Safavids to move their capital and their focus eastward to Isfahan.

Shah Abbas I

Tahmasp I (r. 1524–1576) managed to survive attacks by both Ottomans and Uzbeks. In part, the strength of Shi'ite religious feeling and the allegiance of the bureaucracy enabled the regime to survive. A few years later, the greatest Safavid ruler, Shah Abbas I (r. 1588–1629), brought able leadership to the Safavid domains. He pushed the Ottomans out of Azerbaijan and Iraq and turned back Uzbek invasions in Khorasan. He also sought alliances with the Ottomans' European enemies. This latter tactic, used by several Safavid rulers, reflects the division the new militant Persian Shi'ism had brought to the Islamic world. Abbas also opened trade with the English and Dutch. His reign brought prosperity to Iran, symbolized by the magnificent capital he built at Isfahan.

Safavid Decline

After Shah Abbas, with the exception of Abbas II (1642–1666) and Husayn I (1694–1722), the empire never again enjoyed able leadership. This led finally to its decline and collapse, the chief causes of which were (1) continued pressure from Ottoman and Uzbek armies; (2) the concentration of wealth at the center of, and the corresponding economic decline in, the empire; and (3) the power and bigotry of the Shi'ite *ulama*. The conservative *ulama* introduced a Shi'ite legalism and emphasized their own authority over that of the Safavid monarch. They also persecuted religious minorities and encouraged hatred of Sunni Muslims.

One result of Shi'ite exclusivism was tribal revolts among the Sunni Afghans. An Afghan leader took Qandahar (in modern Afghanistan) and then captured Isfahan and forced the abdication of Husayn I in 1722. Safavid princes managed to retake western Iran, but the empire's greatness was past. A revived, but officially Sunni, monarchy under Nadir Shah (r. 1736–1747) restored much of Iran's lost territories. However, his military ventures, which included the conquest of Delhi, sapped the empire's finances. After his despotic reign, Iran could not regain stability for another half-century.

Culture and Learning

The most impressive aspect of Safavid times, besides the conversion of Iran to Shi'ism, was the cultural renaissance of the sixteenth and seventeenth centuries. The traditions of painting, with their origins in the powerful miniatures of the preceding century, were cultivated and modified in Safavid times. Portraiture and scenes from everyday life became popular. Among the most developed crafts were ceramic tiles, porcelain, and carpets. In architecture, the magnificent public squares, parks, palaces, hospitals, caravanserais, mosques, and other buildings of Isfahan constructed in Shah Abbas's time give evidence of Safavid taste.

The Safavid age also saw a distinctively Shi'ite piety develop. It focused on commemorating the suffering of the imams and loyalty to the Shi'ite *ulama*, who (through their knowledge of the Qur'an and the traditions from Muhammad and the Imams) alone provided guidance in the absence of the hidden imam (see Chapter 11).

The Empire of the Indian Timurids, or "Mughals"

Invaders from the northwest in the early sixteenth century ended the political fragmentation that had reduced the Delhi sultanate to only one among many Indian states. These invaders were descended from Timur (Tamerlane) and known, not entirely correctly, as the *Mughals* (a Persianate form of *Mongol*). In 1525–1527, the founder of the Mughal dynasty, Babur, marched on India. Before his death in 1530, he ruled an empire stretching from the Himalaya to the Deccan. Akbar "the Great" (r. 1556–1605), however, was the real founder of the Mughal Empire, and the greatest Indian ruler since Ashoka (ca. 264–223 B.C.E.).

Akbar's Reign

Akbar added North India and the northern Deccan to the Mughal dominions. Even more significant, however, were his governmental reforms, cultural patronage, and religious toleration. He reorganized government and rationalized the tax system. His marriages with Rajput princesses and his appointment of Hindus to power eased Muslim-Hindu tensions. So did his cancellation of the poll tax on non-Muslims (1564). Under his leadership, the Mughal Empire became a truly Indian empire.

Akbar showed unusual interest in different religious traditions. He frequently brought together representatives of all faiths to discuss religion. Akbar tried to promulgate among his intimates a new monotheistic creed that subsumed Muslim, Hindu, and other viewpoints. However, his ideas died with him.

The Last Great Mughals

Akbar's three immediate successors were Jahangir (r. 1605–1627), Shah Jahan (r. 1628–1658), and Awrangzeb (r. 1658–1707). Although each left behind significant achievements, none matched Akbar. The problems of sustaining an Indian empire took their toll on Mughal power. The reigns of Jahangir and Shah Jahan were the golden age of Mughal culture. But the burdens imposed by military campaigns and the erosion of Akbar's administrative and tax reforms led to economic decline. Jahangir set a fateful precedent in permitting English merchants to establish a trading post at Surat on the western coast in Gujarat. No less a burden on the treasury were Shah Jahan's elaborate building projects, the most magnificent of which was the Taj Mahal (built 1632–1653), the unparalleled tomb that he built for his beloved consort, Mumtaz.

With Shah Jahan, religious toleration retreated; under Awrangzeb, religious fanaticism reversed Akbar's earlier policies. The resulting disorder hastened the decline of Mughal power. Awrangzeb persecuted non-Muslims, destroying Hindu temples, reimposing the poll tax (1679), and alienating the Rajput leaders, whose forebears Akbar had cultivated. His intransigent policies coincided with the spread of the militant Sikh movement and the rise of Hindu Maratha nationalism.

Sikhs and Marathas

In the late sixteenth and early seventeenth centuries, the Sikhs, who trace their origins to the irenic teachings of Guru Nanak (d. 1538), developed into a distinctive religious movement. Neither Muslim nor Hindu, they had their own scripture, ritual, and ideals. Angered by their rejection of Islam, Awrangzeb earned their lasting enmity by persecution. Thereafter, the Sikhs developed into a formidable military force. Awrangzeb and his successors had to contend with repeated Sikh uprisings.

The Hindu Marathas, led by Shivaji (d. 1680), rose in religious and nationalistic fervor to found their own empire about 1646. On Shivaji's death, the Maratha army was the most disciplined force in India. After Awrangzeb's death, the Marathas brought about a confederation of the Deccan States under their leadership. While acknowledging Mughal sovereignty, the Marathas controlled far more of India after 1740 than did the Mughals.

Political Decline

In addition to these wars, other factors sealed the fate of the Mughal Empire after Awrangzeb's death in 1707: the rise in the Deccan of the powerful Islamic state of Hyderabad in 1724; the Persian invasion of North India by Nadir Shah in

Some Reforms of Akbar

Akbar (r. 1556–1605) was certainly one of history's great rulers, but some of his fame is surely due to the laudatory quality of the voluminous Persian chronicle of his reign written by Abu'l-Fazl (d. 1602). The often exaggerated praise was, however, a convention of such Persian works. It would not have hidden from its readers Abu'l-Fazl's message about the statecraft and significant achievements of his ruler.

What does this excerpt suggest might have been some practical reasons for Akbar's reforms? How does this document compare to others concerned with law, leadership, and government? See for example: "Hammurabi's Code on Women, Marriage, and Divorce in Babylonia" (Chapter 1), "Athenian Democracy: An Unfriendly View" (Chapter 3), and "The Edicts of Ashoka" (Chapter 4).

One of the glorious boons by His Majesty the Shahinshah which shone forth in this auspicious year was the abolition of enslavement. The victorious troops which came into the wide territories of India used in their tyranny to make prisoners of the wives and children and other relatives of the people of India, and used to enjoy them or sell them. His Majesty the Shahinshah, out of his thorough recognition of and worship of God, and from his abundant foresight and right thinking gave orders that no soldier of the victorious armies should in any part of his dominions act in this manner. Although a number of savage natures who were ignorant of the world should make their fastnesses a subject of pride and come forth to do battle, and then be defeated by virtue of the emperor's daily increasing empire, still their families must be protected from the onset of the world-conquering armies. No soldier, high or low, was to enslave them, but was to permit them to go freely to their homes and relations. It was for excellent reasons that His Majesty gave his attention to this subject, for although the binding, killing or striking the haughty and the chastising the stiff-necked are part of the struggle for empire—and this is a point about which both sound jurists and innovators are agreed—yet it is outside of the canons of justice to regard the chastisement of women and innocent children as the chastisement of the contumacious. If the husbands have taken the path of insolence, how is it the fault of the wives, and if the fathers have chosen the road of opposition what fault have the children committed? Moreover the wives and innocent children of such factions are not munitions of war! In addition to these sound reasons there was the fact that many covetous and blindhearted persons from vain imaginings or unjust thoughts, or merely out of cupidity attacked villages and estates and plundered them, and when questioned about it said a thousand things and behaved with neglect and indifference. But when final orders were passed for the abolition of this practice, no tribe was afterwards oppressed by wicked persons on suspicion of sedition. As the purposes of the Shahinshah were entirely right and just, the blissful result ensued that the wild and rebellious inhabitants of portions of India placed the ring of devotion in the ear of obedience, and became the materials of world-empire. Both was religion set in order, for its essence is the distribution of justice, and things temporal were regulated, for their perfection lies in the obedience of mankind.

From Abu'l-Fazl ibn Mubarak, *The Akbarnama*, trans. by H. Beveridge (Calcutta: The Asiatic Society, 1905–1939); reprinted in W. H. McNeill and M. R. Waldman, *The Islamic World*. Copyright © 1973 Oxford University Press, pp. 360–361.

1739; the invasions (1748–1761) by the Afghan tribal leader Ahmad Shah Durrani (r. 1747–1773); and the British victories over Bengali forces at Plassey in Bengal (1757) and over the French on the southeastern coast (1740–1763). By 1819, the dominance of the British East India Company had eclipsed Indian power, even though the Mughal line came to an official end only in 1858.

Religious Developments

The period from about 1500 to 1650 was of major importance for Indian religious life. In the sixteenth century, a number of religious figures preached a piety that transcended the legalism of both the *ulama* and the Brahmans and rejected caste distinctions. In these ideas, we can see both Muslim Sufi and Hindu *bhakti* influences at work. Guru Nanak, the spiritual father of the Sikh movement, preached faith and devotion to one loving and merciful God. He opposed narrow allegiance to particular creeds or rites and excessive pride in external religious observance. Dadu (d. 1603) preached a similar message. He was born a Muslim but strove to get people to go beyond Muslim or Hindu allegiance.

There was also a Hindu revival epitomized by Chaitanya (d. ca. 1533), who stressed total devotion to Lord Krishna. The forebears of present-day Hare Krishna devotees, his followers spread his ecstatic public praise of God and his message of the equality of all in God's sight. Tulasidas's (d. 1623) retelling of the *Ramayana* remains among the most popular works of

Indian literature. Tulasidas used the story of Rama's adventures to present *bhakti* ideas that remain alive in Hindu life.

Muslim eclectic tendencies came primarily from the Sufis. By 1500, the Chishtiya Sufi order especially had won many converts to Islam. Such Sufis were, however, often opposed by the *ulama*, many of whom were royal advisers and judges responsible for upholding the religious law. The more intolerant side of the spirit of Awrangzeb's time eventually won the day. The possibilities for Hindu-Muslim rapprochement waned, presaging the communal strife that has so marred southern Asian history in our own century.

ISLAMIC ASIA

Central Asia: Islamization and Isolation

The solid footing of Islam in Central Asia can be traced to the fifteenth century. Even in the preceding century, as the peoples of western Central Asia had begun to shift to a settled existence, the familiar pattern of Islamic diffusion from trading and urban centers had set in. Islamization was slowed only in the late sixteenth century by the conversion of Mongolia proper to Buddhism. In the region between the Aral and Caspian Seas, the most important states were founded by Uzbek and Chaghatay Turks.

Uzbeks and Chaghatays

During the fifteenth century, a new steppe khanate had been formed by the unification in 1428 of assorted clans of Turks and Mongols known as the Uzbeks. In time, an Uzbek leader who was descended from Genghis Khan, Muhammad Shaybani (d. 1510), invaded Transoxiana (1495– 1500) and founded an Uzbek Islamic empire. Muhammad's line continued Uzbek rule in Transoxiana at Bukhara into the eighteenth century, while another Uzbek line ruled the khanate of Khiva in western Turkestan from 1512 to 1872.

Of the other Central Asian Islamic states after 1500, the most significant was that of the Chaghatay Turks. From about 1514, a revived Chaghatay state in eastern Turkestan lasted until 1678.

Consequences of the Shi'ite Rift

On the face of it, the Ottoman, Mughal, Safavid, and Central Asian were Islamic states that had much in common. Yet the deep religious division between the Shi'ite Safavids and their Sunni neighbors proved stronger than their common bonds. The result was a geographic division that isolated Central Asian Muslims.

Shi'ite-Sunni political competition was sharpened by Safavid militancy, to which the Sunni states responded in kind. Attempts to form alliances with non-Muslim states became a commonplace of Shi'ite and Sunni tactics. Although trade went on, the international flow of Islamic commerce was hurt by a militant Shi'ite state astride the overland trade routes of the larger Islamic world. The Safavid Shi'ite schism also ruptured the cultural traditions of the "abode of Islam." The militant Shi'ism of Iran isolated Central Asia from the rest of the Muslim world after 1500. However healthy Islam remained in this region, its contact with the Islamic heartlands shrank. Contact came primarily through pilgrims, Sufis, *ulama*, and students. Central Asian Islam mostly developed in isolation, peripheral to the Islamic mainstream.

Power Shifts in the Southern Seas

Along the southern rim of Asia, from the Red Sea and East Africa to the South China Sea, the first half of the second millennium witnessed the spread of Islamic religion and culture. In port cities, Islamic traders established thriving communities that often became the dominant presence. Typically this first stage of conversion was followed by Islam's transmission to surrounding areas and inland centers of Hindu, Buddhist, or pagan culture. In this transmission, Sufi orders played the main role. However, conquest by Muslim coastal states quickened the process in Indonesia and East Africa.

Hindus were the chief religious group the Muslims displaced. Islam never ousted the Indian Buddhist cultures of Burma, Thailand, and Indochina. Islam did, however, win most of Malaysia, Sumatra, Java, and the "Spice Islands" of the Moluccas. By the end of the fifteenth century, Islam had also spread along the East African coast.

India: The Mughals and Contemporary Indian Powers

1525-1527	Rule of Babur, founder of Indian Timurid state
1538	Death of Guru Nanak, founder of Siteh religious tradition
1556-1605	Rule of Akbar "the Great"
1605-1627	Rule of Jahangir
1628-1658	Rule of Shah Jahan, builder of the Taj Mahal
1646	Founding of Maratha Empire
1658-1707	Rule of Awrangzeb
1680	Death of Maratha leader, Shivaji
1708	Death of tenth and last Sikh guru, Gobind Singh
1724	Rise of Hyderabad state
1739	Iranian invasion of North India under Nadir Shah
1757	British East India Company victory over Bengali forces at Plassey

The Taj Mahal. Probably the most beautiful tomb in the world, the Taj was built from 1631 to 1653 by Shah Jahan for his beloved wife, Mumtaz Mahal. Located on the south bank of the Yamuna River at Agra, the Mughal capital, the Taj Mahal remains the jewel of Mughal architecture.

[Michael Gotin]

Control of the Southern Seas

The Portuguese reached the East African coast in 1498. In the following three centuries, the history of the lands along the trade routes of the southern Asian seas was bound not only with Islamic networks but with the rising power of Christian western Europe. The key attractions of these diverse lands were their commercial and strategic possibilities.

In the sixteenth century, the Europeans began to displace by force the Muslims who dominated the maritime southern rim of Asia. European success was based on national support systems and superior warships. The effectiveness of this combination was evident along the west coast of India, where the Portuguese carved out a power base in the early sixteenth century at the expense of Muslim traders. They did so through superior naval power, exploitation of indigenous rivalries, and terror.

However, Islamization continued apace, even in the face of Christian proselytizing and European power. The Muslims rarely abandoned their faith, which proved generally attractive to new peoples they encountered. The result was usually an Islamicized and racially mixed population.

The upshot of these developments was that while European imperialism had considerable military and economic success, European culture and Christian missionary work made little headway against Islam. Only in the Philippines did a substantial population become Christian.

The Indies: Acheh

In Indonesian archipelago, substantial Islamic sultanates arose in the sixteenth and seventeenth centuries, of which the most powerful was Acheh, in northwestern Sumatra (ca. 1524–1910).

Acheh provided the only counterweight to the Portuguese presence across the straits in Malacca (Malaysia). The Portuguese subdued it, and Acheh thrived until the end of the sixteenth century. In the first half of the seventeenth century, the sultanate controlled both coasts of Sumatra and parts of the Malay peninsula. Meanwhile, also in the seventeenth century, the Dutch replaced the Portuguese. In the early twentieth century, the Dutch finally won full control after nearly forty years of war with Acheh (1873–1910).

IN WORLD PERSPECTIVE
The Last Islamic Empires

In the period from 1500 to 1800, we have focused on the cultural and political blossoming of Islamic societies and their sharp decline. We have also seen the beginning of new kinds of European intrusion upon the Islamic heartlands and Africa, India, and Southeast Asia. By contrast, in the sixteenth and seventeenth centuries, Japan and China were not subject to much influence from either the Islamic empires or European imperialism.

The Islamic vitality in the first half of this period was exemplified in the Ottoman, Safavid, and Mughal Empires. All three built vast bureaucracies and arguably the greatest cities in the world of their time. They patronized the arts. Yet they were conservative societies. Economically they remained tied to agricultural production and taxation based on land. Much like contemporaneous China and Japan, they did not undergo the social or religio-political revolutions that rocked the West after 1500 or the sort of generative changes in material and intellectual life that the Western world experienced during the same period. There was no compelling challenge to traditional Islamic ideals, even though numerous Islamic movements of the eighteenth century did call for reform.

By the latter half of this period, all these empires were in economic, political, and military decline, even if intellectual and artistic vigor held on.

Thus, it is not surprising that European expansionism impinged in these centuries upon Africa, India, Indonesia, and the Islamic heartland, rather than the reverse. Neither the Islamic states, the Hindu kingdoms, nor the varied African states (let alone the societies of Africa, the Americas, and the

The Southern Seas: Arrival of the Portuguese	
1498	The Portuguese come to the East African coast and to the west coast of India
1500–1512	The Portuguese establish bases on west Indian coast, replace Muslims as Indian Ocean power
early 1500s	Muslim sultanates replace Hindu states in Java, Sumatra
1524–1910	State of Acheh in northwestern Sumatra
1600s	Major increase in Islamization and connected spread of Malay language in the archipelago
1641	Dutch conquest of Malacca
ca. 1800	Dutch replace Muslim states as main archipelago power
1873–1910	War between Holland and Acheh

South Pacific) fared well in their encounters with Europeans during this age. Their growing domination of the world's seas allowed Europeans to contain or to bypass the major Islamic lands in their quest for commercial empires.

Industrial development joined economic wealth and political stability by the late 1700s to give the West global military supremacy for the first time. Before 1800, the Europeans were able to bring only minor Islamic states under colonial administrations. However, the footholds they gained in Africa, India, and Southeast Asia laid the groundwork for rapid colonial expansion after 1800. The age of the last great Muslim empires was the beginning of the first great modern European empires. The colonialism of the nineteenth century accompanied the relentless advance of Western industrial, commercial, and military power that would hold sway globally until the mid-twentieth century.

Review Questions

1. Why did the Ottoman Empire expand into Europe? What brought about this rapid expansion? Why did the empire fail to hold certain areas in Europe?

2. What were the most important reasons for the success of the Safavid Empire in Iran? Who were its major foes?

3. What were the most important elements that united all Islamic states? Why was there a lack of unity between these states from 1500 to 1800?

4. What were Akbar's main policies toward the Hindu population? Why did his followers fail in this area? How and why did the Sikhs develop into a formidable military power?

5. Why were outside powers attracted to the South Seas lands? Why were the European powers able to win out in the long struggle for control of this area?

Documents CD-ROM

1. The Ottomans: Empire-Builders at the Crossroads of Three Continents

2. Konstantin Mihailovic, *Memoirs of a Janissary*

3. Kritovoulos, *History of Mehmed the Conquerer*

4. Shah Abbas the Great: The Resurgence of the Persian Empire

5. Albert Hourani: Changing Relations with Europe

ENLIGHTENMENT AND REVOLUTION IN THE WEST

Between approximately 1750 and 1850, most of the intellectual, political, economic, and social characteristics associated with the *modern* world came into being in Europe. Europe became the great exporter of ideas and technologies that in time transformed the world.

The *Enlightenment* drew confidence from the scientific worldview. Its exponents applied the spirit of critical rationalism to social and political life. As a result of their labors, the idea of change, so important in modern life, for the first time became a positive notion.

Commencing in 1789, the French Revolution brought *the people* to the forefront of world political history. The revolution gave rise to both *liberalism* and *nationalism*, the most powerful ideology of the modern world. Nationalism became a secular religion that aroused a degree of loyalty and self-sacrifice previously called forth only by the great religions.

Finally, between 1750 and 1850, Europe became an exporter not only of reform and revolution but also of manufactured commodities. Europeans achieved a productive capacity that, in cooperation with their naval power, permitted them to dominate the markets of the world. Thereafter, to be strong, independent, and modern would mean to become industrialized and to imitate the manufacturing techniques of Europe and later of the United States.

But industrialism fostered immense social problems, among which the major intellectual and political response was *socialism*.

Enlightenment, revolution, and industrialism permitted Europe to dominate the world. Yet those same movements fostered critiques and skills that twentieth-century non-European peoples would turn against their European masters.

1750–1800

July 14, 1789, Bastille prison, Paris. (Giraudon/Art Resource, N.Y.)

1762–1796 Catherine II, "the Great" reigns
    in Russia
1763 Peace of Paris; Seven Years' War
1772 First partition of Poland
1789 French Revolution begins
1793 and 1795 Last partitions of Poland

1757 British victory at Plassey, in Bengal
1761 English oust French from India
1772–1784 Warren Hastings' administration
    in India
1772–1833 Ram Mohan Roy, Hindu reformer
    in India
1794–1925 Qajar shahs in Iran
1805–1849 Muhammad Ali in Egypt

1800–1850

1804–1814 Napoleon's empire
1814–1815 Congress of Vienna
1830–1848 Louis Philippe reigns in France
1832 First British Reform Act
1837–1901 Queen Victoria of England
1848 Revolutions across Europe

1835 Introduction of English education in India

British colonial rule in India (1880). (E.T. Archive, Victoria and Albert Museum)

ca. 1839-1897 Tanzimat reforms, Ottoman Empire
1839–1897 Muslim intelluctual, Jamal al-Din
    Al-Afghani
1845–1905 Muhammad Abduh

1753–1806 Kitagawa Utamaro, Tokugawa era artist
1787–1793 Matsudaira Sadanobu's reforms in Japan
1789 White Lotus Rebellion in China
1823–1901 Li Hung-chang, powerful Chinese governor-general

Utamaro woodblock print. (The Nelson-Atkins Museum of Art, Kansas City, MO, © The Nelson Gallery Foundation. All rights reserved.)

1754–1817 Usman Dan Fodio, founder of Sultanate in northern and central Nigeria
1762 End of Funj sultanate in eastern Sudanic region

1759–1788 Spain reorganizes government of its America Empire
1776 American Declaration of Independence
1791 First ten amendments to U.S. Constitution (Bill of Rights) ratified
1791 Negro slave revolt in French Santo Domingo
1791 Canada Constitutional Act divides the country into Upper and Lower Canada

1835–1908 Empress Dowager Tz'u-hsi
1839–1842 Opium War; 1842, Treaty of Nanking grants Hong Kong to the British and allows them to trade in China
1844 Similar treaties made between China and France and the United States

1804 Fulani Jihad into Hausa lands
1806 British take Cape Colony from Dutch
1817–1828 Zulu chief Shaka reigns
1830–1847 French invasion of Algeria
1830s Dutch settlers, the Boers, expand northward from Cape Colony
1848–1885 Sudanese Madhi, Muhammad Ahmad

1804 Haitian independence
1808–1824 Wars of independence in Latin America
1822 Brazilian independence
1847 Mexican War

Simón Bolivar. (Hulton/Corbis)

24 THE AGE OF EUROPEAN ENLIGHTENMENT

CHAPTER TOPICS

- The Scientific Revolution
- The Enlightenment
- The Enlightenment and Religion

- The Enlightenment and Society
- Enlightened Absolutism

In World Perspective The Enlightenment Heritage

No intellectual force during the past three centuries has so transformed the world as western science and technology. Today, the impact of science on human life remains dominant and scientific knowledge, for military advantage as well as medical and economic advance, is a goal of modern states. The emergence of science as this culturally transforming force began in Europe during the sixteenth century in a process known as the *Scientific Revolution*, which gained momentum during the next two centuries.

The impact of science could make itself felt only when the conviction spread that change and reform were possible and desirable. This attitude came into its own in Europe only after 1700. The movement that fostered such thinking is called the *Enlightenment*. It combined confidence in the human mind inspired by the Scientific Revolution and faith in the power of rational criticism to challenge tradition and revealed religion. The rationality of the physical universe became a standard against which the traditions of society could be measured and criticized. As a result, the spirit of innovation and improvement came to characterize modern Western society. This outlook would become perhaps the most important European cultural export to the rest of the world.

The Scientific Revolution

The sixteenth and seventeenth centuries witnessed a sweeping change in the scientific view of the universe. From being the center of the universe, the Earth was seen as only a planet orbiting the sun, which itself became one of millions of stars. This transformation led to a rethinking of moral and religious matters as well as of scientific theory. Science and the scientific method set a new standard for evaluating knowledge in the West.

The process by which this new view of scientific knowledge came to be established is termed the Scientific Revolution. It was a long, complex movement that never involved more than a few hundred people. However, it ultimately revolutionized how Europeans thought about nature and themselves. This new outlook would be exported to the world.

Nicolaus Copernicus

Copernicus (1473–1543), a Polish astronomer, published *On the Revolutions of the Heavenly Spheres*. Before Copernicus, the standard explanation of the Earth and the heavens was that associated with Ptolemy's (ca. 90–168) *Almagest* (150 C.E.). The Ptolemaic system assumed that the Earth was the center of the universe. Above the Earth lay a series of crystalline spheres, containing the moon, the sun, the planets, and the stars. Aristotelian physics underpinned the Ptolemaic systems. The Earth had to be the center because of its heaviness. The other heavenly bodies had to be enclosed in the crystalline spheres to move. Nothing could move unless something was moving it. The state of rest was natural; motion required explanation.

However, the planets could be seen moving in noncircular patterns around the Earth. At times they appeared to be going backward. The Ptolemaic systems explained that these strange motions occurred primarily through *epicycles*: The planets made a second revolution in an orbit tangent to their primary orbit around the Earth. The Ptolemaic explanations were effective as long as one assumed Aristotelian physics and the Christian belief that the Earth rested at the center of the created universe.

Copernicus challenged this picture in the most conservative manner possible. He suggested that if the Earth were assumed to move about the sun in a circle, the difficulties with the Ptolemaic systems would become simpler. His motive was to construct a more mathematically elegant basis for astronomy: With the sun at the center of the universe, mathematical astronomy would make more sense. It meant that the planets were actually moving in circular orbits and only seemed to be doing otherwise as a result of the position of observers on Earth.

Except for the modification in the position of the Earth, most of Copernicus's book was Ptolemaic, but it allowed others who were discontented with the Ptolemaic systems to think in new directions.

Copernicus's fusion of mathematical astronomy with empirical data and observation became the model for the new scientific thought.

Tycho Brahe and Johannes Kepler

The Danish astronomer Tycho Brahe (1546–1601) advocated a different kind of Earth-centered system in which the moon and the sun revolved around the Earth, and the other planets revolved around the sun. His major weapon against Copernican astronomy was accurate tables of astronomical observations, made with the naked eye.

When Brahe died, these tables came into the possession of Johannes Kepler (1571–1630), a German astronomer. Kepler was a convinced Copernican, but after much work, he discovered that to keep the sun at the center of things, he must

abandon Copernicus's circular orbits. The mathematical relationships that emerged from Brahe's observations suggested that the orbits of the planets were elliptical. Kepler published his findings in 1609. He had solved the problems of planetary orbits by using Copernicus's sun-centered universe and Brahe's empirical data, but the available theories could not explain why the planetary orbits were elliptical. That solution awaited the work of Sir Isaac Newton.

Galileo Galilei

In 1609, the Italian scientist Galileo Galilei (1564–1642) first turned a telescope on the heavens. He saw stars where none had been known to exist, mountains on the moon, spots moving across the sun, and moons orbiting Jupiter. The heavens were far more complex than anyone had suspected, and the Ptolemaic system could not accommodate these new phenomena.

Galileo publicized his findings and arguments for the Copernican system in his *Dialogues on the Two Chief Systems of the World* (1632). He was condemned by the Roman Catholic Church and compelled to recant his opinions. However, he is reputed to have muttered, "It [the Earth] still moves."

Galileo articulated the concept of a universe totally subject to mathematical laws. He believed that the smallest atom behaved with the same mathematical precision as the largest heavenly sphere.

Galileo championed the application of mathematics to scientific investigation and the goal of reducing phenomena to mathematical formulas. However, the English philosopher Francis Bacon advocated a method based solely on empiricism. Both empirical induction and mathematical analysis proved fundamental to scientific investigation.

Francis Bacon

Bacon (1561–1626) attacked the scholastic belief that most truth had already been discovered and the scholastic reverence for tradition and the work of the ancients. He urged contemporaries to strike out on their own in search of a new understanding of nature.

Bacon was one of the first major European writers to champion innovation and change. Most people in Bacon's day thought that the best era of human history lay in antiquity. Bacon dissented from that view. He looked to a future of material improvement achieved through the empirical examination of nature. His great achievement was persuading thinkers that scientific thought must conform to empirical experience.

Isaac Newton

Isaac Newton (1642–1727) solved the major remaining problem of planetary motion and established a basis for physics that endured for more than two centuries. In 1687, he published *The Mathematical Principles of Natural Philosophy*, better known by its Latin title, *Principia Mathematica*. Newton was indebted to Galileo's view that inertia could exist in either a state of motion or a state of rest, and Galileo's mathematical bias permeated Newton's thought. Newton reasoned that all physical objects moved through mutual attraction. Every object in the universe affected every other object through gravity, which explained why the planets moved in an orderly manner. Newton demonstrated the effect of gravity mathematically, but did not explain gravity itself.

Newton was a mathematical genius, but he also upheld the importance of empirical data and observation. The final test of any theory for him was whether it described what could actually be observed.

With the work of Newton, the natural universe became a realm of law and regularity. Spirits and divinities were no longer necessary to explain it, a point of view that contributed to skepticism about witchcraft. Thus, the Scientific Revolution liberated human beings from the fear of a chaotic universe. Most of the scientists were devout. For them, God, the Creator of a rational, lawful nature, must also be rational. To study nature was to better understand that Creator. Science and faith were mutually supporting.

This reconciliation of faith and science allowed the new physics and astronomy to spread rapidly. Faith in a rational God encouraged faith in the rationality of human beings and in their capacity to improve their lot. The Scientific Revolu-

tion provided the model for the desirability of change and for criticizing inherited views.

John Locke

John Locke (1632–1704) attempted to achieve a lawful picture of the human mind similar to that which Newton had presented of nature. In the *Essay Concerning Human Understanding* (1690), Locke envisioned the human mind as being blank at the time of birth. People were born with no innate ideas; all knowledge is derived from sense experience. Each individual mind grows through experience as it confronts sensation. What people know is not the external world in itself but the results of the interaction of their minds with the outside world. Human nature can be molded by modifying the environment. Locke also rejected the Christian view that human beings were flawed by original sin. Human beings do not need to wait for divine aid. They can take charge of their own destiny.

The Enlightenment

The movement known as the Enlightenment included writers living at different times in various countries. Its early exponents, known as the *philosophes*, popularized the rationalism and scientific ideas of the seventeenth century. They exposed contemporary social and political abuses and argued that reform was necessary and possible. They confronted oppression and religious condemnation. Yet by the mid-century they had convinced Europeans that change was a good idea.

Voltaire

The most influential of the *philosophes* was François Marie Arouet, known as Voltaire (1694–1778). During the 1720s, Voltaire had offended the French authorities and been briefly imprisoned. In 1733, after visiting England, he published *Letters on the English*, which praised English intellectual and political freedom and indirectly criticized French society. In 1738, he published *Elements of the Philosophy of Newton*, which popularized the thought of the great scientist. Both works enhanced his reputation.

Thereafter, Voltaire lived either in France or near Geneva, just across the French border, where the royal authorities could not bother him. His essays, history, plays, stories, and letters made him the literary dictator of Europe. He turned the venom of his satire against one evil after another in French and European life. In *Candide* (1759), he attacked war, religious persecution, and unwarranted optimism about the human condition. Like most *philosophes*, Voltaire believed

---

Major Publication Dates of the Enlightenment

1687	Newton's *Principia Mathematica*
1690	Locke's *Essay Concerning Human Understanding*
1733	Voltaire's *Letters on the English*
1738	Voltaire's *Elements of the Philosophy of Newton*
1748	Montesquieu's *Spirit of the Laws*
1750	Rousseau's *Discourse on the Moral Effects of the Arts and Sciences*
1751	First volume of the *Encyclopedia* edited by Diderot and d'Alembert
1755	Rousseau's *Discourse on the Origin of Inequality*
1762	Rousseau's *Social Contract*
1763	Voltaire's *Treatise on Toleration*
1776	Smith's *Wealth of Nations*
1779	Lessing's *Nathan the Wise*
1792	Wollstonecraft's *A Vindication of the Rights of Woman*

that human society could and should be improved. But he was never certain that reform, if achieved, would be permanent. Enlightenment optimism constituted a tempered hopefulness rather than a glib certainty. Pessimism was an undercurrent in most Enlightenment works.

The Encyclopedia

The mid-century witnessed the publication of the *Encyclopedia*, one of the greatest monuments of the Enlightenment. Under the leadership of Denis Diderot (1713–1784) and Jean le Rond d'Alembert (1717–1783), the first volume appeared in 1751. When completed in 1772, it numbered seventeen volumes of text and eleven of plates. The *Encyclopedia* was the product of more than 100 authors, and its editors had solicited articles from the major French *philosophes*. The project reached fruition only after attempts to censor it and halt its publication. The *Encyclopedia* set forth the most advanced critical ideas in religion, government, and philosophy. The articles represented a plea for freedom of expression but also provided information on manufacturing, canal building, and agriculture.

The *Encyclopedia* had been designed to secularize learning, and the articles concentrated on humanity and its well-being. The encyclopedists looked to antiquity rather than to the Christian centuries for their intellectual and ethical models. The welfare of humankind lay in the application of reason to human relationships. The *Encyclopedia* diffused enlightened thought over the Continent, drawing in German and Russian thinkers.

Charles de Secondat, Baron de Montesquieu (1689–1755) was the author of *The Spirit of the Laws*, possibly the most influential work of political thought of the eighteenth century. [Hulton/UPI/Corbis]

The Enlightenment and Religion

In the eyes of the *philosophes*, the chief enemy of the improvement and happiness of humankind was the church. Roman Catholicism especially invited their criticism. But all the churches perpetuated a religious view of humankind and nature and taught that human beings were sinful and required divine grace. Religion turned human interest away from this world to the world to come. For the *philosophes*, the churches fostered intolerance and bigotry.

Deism

The *philosophes* believed that religion should be reasonable and lead to moral behavior. The Newtonian worldview had convinced many that nature was rational. Therefore, the God who had created nature must also be rational, and the religion through which that God was worshiped should be rational. Lockean philosophy, which limited human knowledge to empirical experience, cast doubt on divine revelation. These considerations gave rise to a movement for enlightened religion known as *deism*.

There were two major points in the deists' creed. The first was a belief in a rational God, which they thought could be empirically deduced from nature. Because a rational God must also favor rational morality, the second point was a belief in life after death, when rewards and punishments would be meted out according to the virtue of the life a person had led.

Deism was empirical, tolerant, reasonable, and capable of encouraging virtuous living. It was the major positive religious component of the Enlightenment.

Toleration

Such a life required religious toleration. Voltaire championed this cause. In 1762, the French authorities ordered the execution of a Huguenot named Jean Calas (1698–1762) for having allegedly murdered his son to prevent him from

Maria Theresa and Joseph II of Austria Debate Toleration

In 1765, Joseph, the eldest son of the Empress Maria Theresa, had become co-regent with his mother. He began to believe that some measures of religious toleration should be introduced into the Habsburg realms. Maria Theresa, whose opinions on many political issues were quite advanced, adamantly refused to consider adopting a policy of toleration. This exchange of letters sets forth their sharply differing positions. The toleration of Protestants in dispute related only to Lutherans and Calvinists. Maria Theresa died in 1780; the next year Joseph issued an edict of toleration.

How does Joseph define toleration, and why does Maria Theresa believe it is the same as religious indifference? Why does Maria Theresa fear that toleration will bring about political as well as religious turmoil? Why does Maria Theresa think the belief in toleration has come from Joseph's acquaintance with wicked books? Compare the positions for and against religious toleration expressed in this correspondence to the actions of previous European rulers.

Joseph to Maria Theresa, July 20, 1777

. . . [I]t is only the word "toleration" which has caused the misunderstanding. You have taken it in quite a different meaning [from mine expressed in an earlier letter]. God preserve me from thinking it a matter of indifference whether the citizens turn Protestant or remain Catholic, still less, whether they cleave to, or at least observe, the cult which they have inherited from their fathers! I would give all I possess if all the Protestants of your states would go over to Catholicism.

The word "toleration," as I understand it, means only that I would employ any persons, without distinction of religion, in purely temporal matters, allow them to own property, practice trades, be citizens, if they were qualified and if this would be of advantage to the State and its industry. Those who, unfortunately, adhere to a false faith, are far further from being converted if they remain in their own country than if they migrate into another, in which they can hear and see the convincing truths of the Catholic faith. Similarly, the undisturbed practice of their

religion makes them far better subjects and causes them to avoid irreligion, which is a far greater danger to our Catholics than if one lets them see others practice their religion unimpeded. . . .

Maria Theresa to Joseph, Late July, 1777

Without a dominant religion? Toleration, indifference are precisely the true means of undermining everything, taking away every foundation; we others will then be the greatest losers. . . . He is no friend of humanity, as the popular phrase is, who allows everyone his own thoughts. I am speaking only in the political sense, not as a Christian; nothing is so necessary and salutary as religion. Will you allow everyone to fashion his own religion as he pleases? No fixed cult, no subordination to the Church—what will then become of us? The result will not be quiet and contentment; its outcome will be the rule of the stronger and more unhappy times like those which we have already seen. A manifesto by you to this effect can produce the utmost distress and make you responsible for many thousands of souls. And what are my own sufferings, when I see you entangled in opinions so erroneous? What is at stake is not only the welfare of the State but your own salvation. . . . Turning your eyes and ears everywhere, mingling your spirit of contradiction with the simultaneous desire to create something, you are ruining yourself and dragging the Monarchy down with you into the abyss. . . . I only wish to live so long as I can hope to descend to my ancestors with the consolation that my son will be as great, as religious as his forebears, that he will return from his erroneous views, from those wicked books whose authors parade their cleverness at the expense of all that is most holy and most worthy of respect in the world, who want to introduce an imaginary freedom which can never exist and which degenerates into license and into complete revolution.

From *The Habsburg and Hohenzollern Dynasties in the Seventeenth and Eighteenth Centuries*, C. A. Macartney, ed., Copyright © 1980, Walker and Company, pp. 151–153. Reprinted by permission.

converting to Roman Catholicism. Calas had been tortured and publicly strangled without confessing his guilt.

Voltaire made the dead man's cause his own. In 1763 he published a *Treatise on Toleration* and hounded the authorities until in 1765 the decision against Calas was reversed. For

Voltaire, the case illustrated religious fanaticism and the need for rational judicial reform. In 1779, the German writer Gotthold Lessing (1729–1781) wrote *Nathan the Wise* as a plea for toleration of all religious faiths. All of these calls for toleration argued that secular values were more important than religious ones.

The Enlightenment and Society

The *philosophes* believed that the application of human reason to society would reveal laws in human relationships similar to those found in physical nature. The discovery of social laws would remove the inhumanity that existed through ignorance of them.

Adam Smith

The most important Enlightenment exposition of economics was Adam Smith's (1723–1790) *An Inquiry into the Nature and Causes of the Wealth of Nations* (1776). Smith urged that the mercantile system of England be abolished. These modes of economic regulation by the state were intended to preserve the wealth of the nation and capture wealth from other nations. But Smith believed that they constricted wealth and production. He wanted to unleash individuals to pursue their own economic interest. The free pursuit of economic self-interest would ensure economic expansion as each person sought enrichment by meeting the demands of the marketplace.

Smith saw nature as a boundless expanse of physical resources to be exploited for the benefit of humankind. This idea, which dominated western life until recent years, stemmed from the Enlightenment. When Smith wrote, the population of the world was smaller, its people were poorer, and the quantity of undeveloped resources per capita was much greater. For people of the eighteenth century, the improvement of the human condition seemed to lie in the uninhibited exploitation of natural resources.

Smith is usually regarded as the founder of *laissez-faire* economics, which has argued for a limited role for government in economic life. However, Smith was not opposed to all government activity in the economy. The state should provide schools, armies, navies, and roads and undertake commercial ventures that were desirable but too risky for private enterprise. Indeed, most of the *philosophes* were less doctrinaire than any brief summary of their thought may suggest. They recognized human passions as well as reason. They adopted reason and nature as tools to create a climate of opinion that would allow humanity to flourish.

Montesquieu and *The Spirit of the Laws*

Charles Louis de Secondat, Baron de Montesquieu (1689–1755), was a French noble magistrate. His work *The Spirit of the Laws* (1748) was perhaps the most influential book of the century. Montesquieu pursued an empirical method, taking examples from both ancient and modern nations. He concluded that no single set of political laws could apply to all peoples at all times and in all places. Only a careful examination and evaluation of many variables could reveal what

mode of government would prove most beneficial to a particular people. A century later, such speculations would have been classified as sociology.

For France, Montesquieu believed in a monarchy whose power was tempered and limited by intermediary institutions, including the aristocracy, the towns, the *parlements*, and other corporate bodies that enjoyed liberties that the monarch must respect. Their role was to limit the power of the monarchy and thus to preserve the liberty of the subjects. Montesquieu was a political conservative, but he hoped to achieve reform, for he considered the oppressive and inefficient absolutism of the monarchy responsible for degrading French life.

One of Montesquieu's most influential ideas was the division of power. He took Great Britain for his model: executive power resided in the king, legislative power in the Parliament, and judicial power in the courts. Any two branches could check and balance the power of the other. His perception of the eighteenth-century British constitution was incorrect, but the analysis illustrated his sense of the need to limit power through a constitution, and for legislatures, not monarchs, to make laws. Montesquieu's ideas had an enduring effect on the liberal democracies of the next two centuries.

Rousseau

Jean-Jacques Rousseau (1712–1778) had a deep antipathy toward the society in which he lived. In 1750, in his *Discourse on the Moral Effects of the Arts and Sciences,* he contended that civilization and enlightenment had corrupted human nature. In 1755, in a *Discourse on the Origin of Inequality,* Rousseau blamed much of the evil in the world on maldistribution of property. Rousseau felt that the real purpose of society should be to nurture better people. His vision of reform was much more radical than that of other philosophers.

The Social Contract (1762) outlines the kind of political structure that Rousseau believed would overcome the evils of contemporary society. Most eighteenth-century political thinkers regarded society as a collection of independent individuals pursuing selfish goals. They wished to liberate these individuals from the undue bonds of government. Rousseau suggested that society is more important than its individual members, because they are what they are only as a result of their relationship to the larger community. Independent human beings living alone can achieve little. Through their relationship to the larger community, they become moral creatures capable of significant action. Rousseau drew on Plato and Calvin to define freedom as obedience to law. In his case, the law to be obeyed was that created by the general will. This concept normally indicated the will of the majority of voting citizens who acted with adequate information and under the influence of virtuous customs and morals. Rousseau believed that the general will must always be right and that to obey it was to be free. This argument led him to conclude that some people must be forced to be free. He thus justified radical direct democracy and collective action against individual citizens.

Women in the Thought and Practice of the Enlightenment

Women, especially in France, helped to promote the careers of the *philosophes*. In Paris, the salons of women such as Marie-Thérèse Geoffrin (1699–1777), Julie de Lespinasse (1733–1776), and Claudine de Tencin (1689–1749) gave the *philosophes* a receptive environment for their ideas. These women were well connected to political figures who could help protect the *philosophes*. The Marquise de Pompadour (1721–1764), the mistress of Louis XV, for example, helped overcome efforts to censor the *Encyclopedia*.

Nonetheless, the *philosophes* advocated no radical changes in the social condition of women. Montesquieu, for example, believed women were not naturally inferior to men and should have a wider role in society. Yet he expected men to dominate marriage and family. Furthermore, although he supported the right of women to divorce and opposed laws that oppressed them, he upheld the ideal of female chastity.

In the *Encyclopedia*, the articles that dealt with women emphasized their physical inferiority, usually attributed to menstruation or childbearing, and conveyed the sense that women were reared to be frivolous. The encyclopedists discussed women primarily as daughters, wives, and mothers, and considered motherhood their most important occupation. The encyclopedists also upheld a double standard of sexual behavior. However, illustrations in the *Encyclopedia* showed women, many of them lower- and working-class, deeply involved in economic activity.

Rousseau urged a traditional role for women. In his novel *Émile* (1762) he declared that women should be educated to be subordinate to men, emphasizing their function in bearing and rearing children. He portrayed them as weaker and inferior to men, except perhaps for their capacity for feeling and giving love, and excluded them from political life. Women were assigned the domestic sphere alone.

Despite these views and his own ill treatment of the women who bore his many children, Rousseau achieved a vast following among women in the eighteenth century, perhaps because his writings stressed women's emotions and subjective feelings. He portrayed the domestic life and the role of wife and mother as a noble vocation, giving middle- and upper-class women a sense that their lives had purpose.

In 1792, in *A Vindication of the Rights of Woman*, Mary Wollstonecraft (1759–1797) brought Rousseau before the judgment of the rational Enlightenment ideal of progressive knowledge. Wollstonecraft accused Rousseau and others who upheld traditional roles for women of attempting to narrow women's vision and limit their experience. She argued that to confine women to the separate domestic sphere because of their supposed physiological limitations was to make them the sensual slaves of men and prevent them from achieving their own moral or intellectual identity. Denying good education to women would impede human progress. Wollstonecraft was demanding for women the kind of intellectual liberty that male writers of the Enlightenment were championing for men.

Enlightened Absolutism

During the last third of the century, several European rulers embraced many of the *philosophes'* reforms. *Enlightened absolutism* is the term used to describe this phenomenon. The phrase indicates monarchical government dedicated to the rational strengthening of the central absolutist administration at the cost of lesser centers of power. The monarchs most closely associated with it—Frederick II of Prussia, Joseph II of Austria, and Catherine II of Russia—often found that the political and social realities of their realms caused them to moderate both their enlightenment and their absolutism. They corresponded with *philosophes*, invited them to court, and imposed reforms that contemporaries believed derived from suggestions of the *philosophes*.

However, the relationship between these rulers and the writers of the Enlightenment was more complicated. The rulers sought the rational economic and social integration of their realms to achieve military strength. They and their

Russia from Peter the Great through Catherine the Great	
1725	Death of Peter the Great
1741–1762	Elizabeth
1762	Peter III
1762	Catherine II (the Great) becomes empress
1767	Legislative Commission summoned
1768	War with Turkey
1771–1774	Pugachev's Rebellion
1772	First Partition of Poland
1774	Treaty of Kuchuk-Kainardji ends war with Turkey
1775	Reorganization of local government
1783	Russia annexes the Crimea
1785	Catherine issues the Charter of the Nobility
1793	Second Partition of Poland
1795	Third Partition of Poland
1796	Death of Catherine the Great

advisers used "enlightened" reforms to pursue many goals admired by the *philosophes* but also to further what the *philosophes* considered irrational militarism.

Joseph II of Austria

No eighteenth-century ruler so embodied rational, impersonal force as the emperor Joseph II of Austria, the son of Maria Theresa (r. 1740–1780). He prided himself on a narrow, passionless rationality, which he sought to impose on the Habsburg domains. Joseph II genuinely wished to improve the lot of his peoples. His well-intentioned efforts led to aristocratic and peasant rebellions from Hungary to the Austrian Netherlands.

Austria was the most diverse state of the eighteenth century. The Habsburgs never succeeded in creating a unified administrative structure or strong aristocratic loyalty. The price of preserving the monarchy during the War of the Austrian Succession (1740–1748) had been guarantees of aristocratic independence, especially in Hungary.

During and after the conflict, however, Maria Theresa had strengthened her powers in Austria and Bohemia. She imposed a more efficient system of tax collection that extracted funds even from the clergy and the nobles, and she established central councils to deal with governmental problems. She tried to bring all educational institutions into the service of the crown so that she could have enough educated officials, and she expanded primary education.

Maria Theresa was also concerned about the peasants and serfs and limited the services that landowners could demand from them. This concern arose from her desire to assure a good military recruitment pool. In her desire to stimulate prosperity and military strength by royal initiative, Maria Theresa anticipated the policies of her son.

However, his reforms were more wide ranging than his mother's. His greatest ambition was to overcome the pluralism of the Habsburg holdings by increasing the power of the central monarchy that Maria Theresa had wisely not disturbed. In particular, Joseph sought to lessen Hungarian autonomy. He refused to have himself crowned king of Hungary and thus avoided having to guarantee Hungarian privileges in a coronation oath. He reorganized local government in Hungary to increase the authority of his own officials, and he required the use of German in government. But the Magyar nobility resisted, and in 1790 Joseph had to rescind most of his centralizing measures.

In religion, Joseph extended freedom of worship to Lutherans, Calvinists, and the Greek Orthodox, and relieved the Jews of signs of personal degradation and gave them the right of private worship. Joseph also sought to control the Roman Catholic Church. He forbade direct communication between bishops and the pope. He dissolved over 600 monasteries and confiscated their lands, and replaced the traditional Roman Catholic seminaries with eight general seminaries that emphasized parish duties. Joseph's policies made Roman Catholic priests the employees of the state and ended the independent influence of the church. These ecclesiastical policies, known as *Josephinism*, prefigured those of the French Revolution.

Joseph believed that reducing traditional burdens would make the peasants more productive and industrious. He abolished the servile status of serfdom and gave peasants more personal freedom. They could marry, engage in skilled work, or have their children trained in skills without permission of the landlord. The manorial courts were reformed, and peasants could appeal to royal officials. Joseph also encouraged landlords to change land leases, so that it would be easier for peasants to inherit them or to transfer them to another peasant.

In 1789, Joseph proposed a new system of land taxation. All proprietors were to be taxed, regardless of social status. But in 1790 Joseph died, and the system never went into effect. However, his measures had stirred up turmoil. Peasants revolted over disagreements about their newly granted rights. The nobles protested the taxation scheme. His brother Leopold II (r. 1790–1792), although sympathetic to Joseph's goals, had to repeal many of the most controversial decrees.

Catherine the Great of Russia

Joseph II never grasped the necessity of cultivating support for his policies. Catherine II (r. 1762–1796) understood the fragility of the Romanov dynasty's power.

After the death of Peter the Great in 1725, the court nobles and the army had determined the Russian succession. Peter's daughter Elizabeth (r. 1741–1762) was succeeded by Peter III, one of her nephews. He was a weak and possibly insane ruler who had been married in 1745 to a young German princess, the future Catherine the Great. After a few months, Peter III was deposed and murdered with Catherine's approval, and she was proclaimed empress.

Catherine's familiarity with the Enlightenment and western Europe convinced her that Russia must make reforms to remain a great power. Since she had come to the throne through a palace coup, she understood that any major reform must enjoy wide support.

Consequently, in 1767 Catherine summoned a Legislative Commission to advise her on revising the government of Russia. There were over 500 delegates from all sectors of Russian life. Catherine wrote a set of *Instructions*, containing ideas drawn from the *philosophes*. Catherine dismissed the commission before several of its key committees reported, but it had gathered a vast amount of information about conditions in Russia, and its debates suggested that most

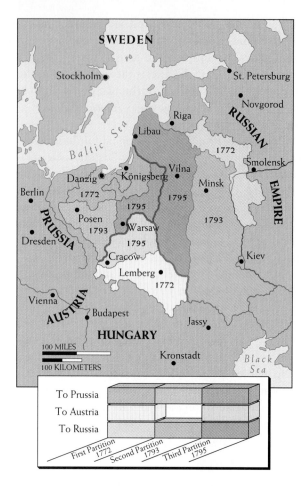

Map 24–1 Partitions of Poland, 1772, 1793, and 1795. The callous eradication of Poland from the map displayed eighteenth-century power politics at its most extreme. Poland, without a strong central government, fell victim to the strong absolute monarchies of central and eastern Europe.

to the crown. So Catherine strengthened her crown by a convenient alliance with her nobles and urban leaders.

Catherine continued the Russian drive for warm-water ports. This led to warfare with the Turks between 1768 and 1774, when the Treaty of Kuchuk-Kainardji gave Russia a direct outlet on the Black Sea. Catherine annexed the Crimea in 1783.

The Partition of Poland

These Russian military successes made the other states of eastern Europe uneasy. Their anxieties were allayed by the First Partition of Poland (see Map 24–1). Frederick the Great made a proposal to Russia and Austria that would give each something it wanted, prevent conflict among them, and save appearances. After complicated, secret negotiations among the three powers, the Polish state lost approximately one-third of its territory. Two additional partitions of Poland in 1793 and 1795 removed it from the map of Europe until 1919. Poland's political weakness made the country and its resources ripe for plunderous aggression.

IN WORLD PERSPECTIVE

The Enlightenment Heritage

No other movements of European thought have remained as influential as the Scientific Revolution and the Enlightenment. Wherever modern science and technology are pursued and their effects felt, the spirit of the Enlightenment persists.

The Enlightenment *philosophes* used reason as a weapon for reform and the basis for a more productive economic life. In the two centuries since the Enlightenment, such a use of critical reason has become a mark of reforming and progressive social and intellectual movements. One strand of Enlightenment political thought contributed to constitutionalism and modes of government that limited the power and authority of the central government. Montesquieu, for example, influenced the Constitution of the United States. Another strand of Enlightenment political thought, found in Voltaire, contributed to the growth of strong central governments to formulate and impose rational solutions to political or social problems. Still another, arising from Rousseau, led to the socialist concern with inequality of wealth. Modern liberal, socialist, and authoritarian governments all partake of the Enlightenment heritage.

Russians saw no alternative to an autocratic monarchy. Catherine herself had no intention of departing from absolutism.

Catherine carried out limited reforms on her own authority. In 1775, she reorganized local government to solve problems brought to light by the Legislative Commission. She put most local offices into the hands of nobles rather than creating a royal bureaucracy. In 1785, Catherine issued the Charter of the Nobility, which guaranteed noble rights and privileges. She issued a similar charter to the towns of her realms. The empress had to favor the nobles. She had too few educated subjects to establish an independent bureaucracy, and the treasury could not afford an army strictly loyal

Review Questions

1. Discuss the contributions of Copernicus, Brahe, Kepler, Galileo, and Newton to the Scientific Revolution. Which do you think made the most important contributions? Define the term *Scientific Revolution*. In what ways was it truly revolutionary?

2. How did the Enlightenment change Western attitudes toward reform, faith, and reason? How important were Voltaire and the *Encyclopedia* in the success of the Enlightenment?

3. Why did the *philosophes* consider organized religion to be their greatest enemy? Discuss the basic tenets of deism.

4. What were the separate spheres Rousseau imagined men and women occupying? What were Mary Wollstonecraft's criticisms of his view?

5. Discuss the political views of Montesquieu and Rousseau. Did Rousseau value the individual or society more?

6. Were the enlightened monarchs true believers in the ideal of the *philosophes*? What motivated their reforms?

Documents CD-ROM

1. John Locke, *The Second Treatise of Civil Government*
2. Jean-Jacques Rousseau, *The Social Contract*
3. Adam Smith: From *The Theory of Moral Sentiments*

4. Charles Montesquieu, Book 4 from *The Spirit of the Laws*
5. Catherine the Great, *The Instruction to the Commissioners for Composing a New Code of Laws*

25 REVOLUTIONS IN THE TRANSATLANTIC WORLD

Between 1776 and 1824, a world-transforming series of revolutions occurred in France and the Americas. In a half century, the peoples of the two American continents established their independence of European political control. In Europe, the French monarchy collapsed. All the revolutionary leaders sought to establish new governments based largely on Enlightenment principles. The era also witnessed the commencement of an international crusade to abolish first the slave trade and then slavery in the transatlantic world.

Revolution in the British Colonies in North America

Resistance to the Imperial Search for Revenue

After the Treaty of Paris in 1763 ended the Seven Years' War, the British government faced two imperial problems. The first was the cost of empire, which the British felt they could no longer carry alone. The second was the need to organize a vast new territory: all of North America east of the Mississippi.

The British drive for revenue began in 1764 with the Sugar Act, which attempted to produce more revenue from imports into the colonies by the rigorous collection of what was actually a reduced tax on sugar. Smugglers were to be tried in admiralty courts without juries. The next year, Parliament passed the Stamp Act, which put a tax on legal documents and other items. The British considered these taxes just because they had been approved by Parliament and because the revenue was to be spent in the colonies. The Americans responded that they alone had the right to tax themselves and that they were not represented in Parliament.

In the face of protest and disorder in America, Parliament repealed the Stamp Act in 1766 but claimed the power to legislate for the colonies.

American Political Ideas

The American colonists believed that the English Revolution of 1688 had established their own fundamental liberties. They claimed that George III (r. 1760–1820) and the British Parliament were attacking those liberties and dissolving the bonds of allegiance that had united the two peoples. The colonists thus employed a theory that had been developed to justify an aristocratic rebellion in England to support their own popular revolution.

In addition to these Whig political ideas, largely derived from John Locke (1632–1704), the Americans had also become familiar with British political writers called the *Commonwealthmen*, who held republican political ideas that had their roots in the radical thought of the Puritan revolution. They regarded much parliamentary taxation as a means of financing political corruption and attacked standing armies as instruments of tyranny. The policy of Great Britain toward America after the Treaty of Paris made many colonists believe that the worst fears of the Commonwealthmen were coming true.

Crisis and Independence

In May 1773, Parliament allowed the East India Company to import tea directly into the American colonies. Although the law lowered the price of tea, it retained a tax on it without the colonists' consent. In Boston, a shipload of tea was thrown into the harbor, known since as the Boston Tea Party.

The British ministry of Lord North (1732–1792) was determined to assert the authority of Parliament over the colonies. In 1774, Parliament closed the port of Boston, reorganized the government of Massachusetts, allowed troops to be quartered in private homes, and removed the trials of royal customs officials to England. Parliament also extended the boundaries of Quebec to include the Ohio River valley which the Americans regarded as an attempt to prevent the extension of their mode of self-government westward beyond the Appalachian Mountains.

During these years, committees of correspondence, composed of citizens critical of Britain, had been established throughout the colonies. In September 1774, these committees organized the First Continental Congress in Philadelphia. This body failed to persuade Parliament to abandon its attempt at direct supervision of colonial affairs. In 1775, the battles of Lexington, Concord, and Bunker Hill were fought, and the Second Continental Congress undertook the government of the colonies. In August 1775, George III declared the colonies in rebellion. During the winter, Thomas Paine's (1737–1809) pamphlet *Common Sense* galvanized public opinion in favor of separation from Great Britain. A colonial army and navy were organized. Finally, on July 4, 1776, the Continental Congress adopted the Declaration of Independence. The War of the American Revolution continued until 1781, when the forces of George Washington (1732–1799) defeated those of Lord Cornwallis

The American Revolution

1760	George III becomes king
1763	Treaty of Paris concludes the Seven Years' War
1764	Sugar Act
1765	Stamp Act
1766	Stamp Act repealed and Declaratory Act passed
1770	Lord North becomes George III's chief minister
1773	Boston Tea Party
1774	First Continental Congress
1775	Second Continental Congress
1776	Declaration of Independence
1778	France enters the war on the side of America
1781	British forces surrender at Yorktown
1783	Treaty of Paris concludes War of the American Revolution

(1738–1805) at Yorktown. In 1778, however, the war had widened into a European conflict when the French government supported the rebellion. In 1779, Spain also came to the aid of the colonies. The 1783 Treaty of Paris concluded the conflict, and the thirteen American colonies had established their independence.

As the crisis with Britain unfolded, the American colonists came to see themselves as first preserving traditional English liberties and then as developing a new sense of liberty. By the mid-1770s, the colonists had embraced republican political ideals. After the Constitution was adopted in 1788, Americans insisted on a bill of rights to protect civil liberties. The Americans would reject the aristocratic social hierarchy that had existed in the colonies. They would embrace democratic ideals, even if the franchise remained limited. They would assert the equality of white male citizens before the law and in social relations. They would reject social status based on birth and inheritance and assert the necessity of liberty for all citizens to improve their social standing and economic lot by engaging in free commercial activity. They did not free their slaves, nor did they address the rights of women or Native Americans, but the American Revolution produced a society freer than any the world had seen, one that would expand political and social liberty. The American Revolution was a radical movement, the influence of which would increase as Americans moved across the continent and as other peoples began to question traditional European government. The American Revolution would inspire the Wars of Independence in Latin America and liberal and radical political movements in Europe.

Revolution in France

The French monarchy emerged from the Seven Years' War defeated and deeply in debt. Support for the American Revolution exacerbated its financial difficulties. Given the economic vitality of France, the government debt was not overly large, but the government could not collect sufficient taxes to service and repay the debt.

Between 1786 and 1788, Louis XVI's (r. 1774–1792) ministers failed to persuade the aristocracy and the church to pay more taxes. As these negotiations dragged on, the *parlement* of Paris declared that only the Estates General could institute new taxes. The Estates General had not met since 1614. In July 1788, Louis agreed to convene the Estates General.

Revolutions of 1789

The Estates General Becomes the National Assembly

The Estates General had three divisions: the First Estate of the clergy, the Second Estate of the nobility, and the Third Estate, representing everyone else. The Estates General met at Versailles in May 1789. On June 1, the Third Estate, composed largely of local officials, professional men, and lawyers, invited the clergy and nobles to join it in organizing a new legislative body. A few of the lower clergy did so. On June 17, that body declared itself the National Assembly.

Three days later, finding themselves accidentally locked out of their usual meeting place, the National Assembly moved to a nearby tennis court, where its members took the famous Tennis Court Oath to sit until they had given France a constitution. Louis XVI ordered the National Assembly to desist, but most of the clergy and many nobles joined the assembly. On June 27, the king capitulated and the National Assembly became the National Constituent Assembly.

Fall of the Bastille

Two new factors soon intruded. First, Louis XVI attempted to regain the initiative by mustering troops near Versailles and Paris. This was the beginning of a poorly executed, royal attempt to halt the revolution. Most of the National Constituent Assembly wished to create a constitutional monarchy, but Louis's refusal to cooperate thwarted that effort.

The second new factor was the populace of Paris. The mustering of royal troops created anxiety in the city, where there had been several bread riots. By June, the Parisians were organizing a citizen militia and collecting arms.

On July 14, a crowd marched to the Bastille in search of weapons for the militia. This great fortress had once held political prisoners. The troops in the Bastille fired into the crowd which then stormed the fortress, released its seven prisoners, none of whom was there for political reasons, and killed the governor. They found no weapons.

This was the first of many *journées*, or days when the populace of Paris would redirect the course of the revolution. Similar disturbances took place in the provincial cities. Louis XVI came to Paris and recognized the new elected government of the city and its National Guard.

The Great Fear and Surrender of Feudal Privileges

As disturbances erupted in various cities, the *Great Fear* swept across the French countryside. Peasants were reclaiming rights and property that they had lost through the aristocratic resurgence of the last quarter century, as well as venting their anger against the injustices of rural life. The Great Fear witnessed the burning of châteaux, the destruction of documents, and the refusal by peasants to pay feudal dues.

On the night of August 4, 1789, aristocrats in the assembly attempted to halt the disorder. By prearrangement, liberal nobles and churchmen surrendered hunting and fishing rights, judicial authority, tithes, and special exemptions. These nobles gave up what they had already lost and what they could not have regained without civil war. Later, many would also be compensated for their losses. Nonetheless, after August 4 all French citizens were subject to the same laws.

Declaration of the Rights of Man and Citizen

On August 27, 1789, the assembly issued the *Declaration of the Rights of Man and Citizen*. It proclaimed that all men were born free and equal with natural rights to liberty, property, and personal safety. Governments existed to protect those rights. All political sovereignty resided in the nation and its representatives. All citizens were to be equal before the law and to be equally admissible to public offices according to their natural abilities and character. There were to be due process of law and presumption of innocence until proof of guilt. Freedom of religion was affirmed. Taxation was to be apportioned equally according to capacity to pay. Property was a sacred right.

Louis XVI stalled before ratifying the declaration and the aristocratic renunciation of feudalism. His hesitations fanned suspicions that he might try to resort to force. Moreover, bread shortages continued. On October 5, several thousand Parisian women marched to Versailles, demanding more bread. This was one of several occasions when women played a major role in the Parisian crowd. The king agreed to sanction the decrees of the assembly, but the Parisians demanded that Louis and his family return to Paris. The monarch had no choice. On October 6, 1789, he and his family followed the crowd and settled in the palace of the Tuileries. The assembly went too. Thereafter, both Paris and France remained relatively stable until the summer of 1792.

French Women Petition to Bear Arms

The issue of women serving in the revolutionary French military appeared early in the revolution. In March 1791, Pauline Léon presented a petition to the National Assembly on behalf of more than 300 Parisian women asking the right to bear arms and train for military service for the revolution. Similar requests were made during the next two years. Some women did serve in the military, but in 1793, legislation specifically forbade it on the grounds that women belonged in the domestic sphere and that military service would lead them to abandon family duties.

Citoyenne is the feminine form of the French word for citizen. How does this petition seek to challenge the concept of citizenship in the *French Declaration of the Rights of Man and Citizen*? How do these petitioners relate their demand to bear arms to their role as women in French society? How do the petitioners relate their demands to the use of all national resources against the enemies of the revolution?

Patriotic women come before you to claim the right which any individual has to defend his life and liberty.

. . . We are *citoyennes* [female citizens], and we cannot be indifferent to the fate of the fatherland.

. . . Yes, Gentlemen, we need arms, and we come to ask your permission to procure them. May our weakness be no obstacle; courage and intrepidity will supplant it, and the love of the fatherland and hatred of tyrants will allow us to brave all dangers with ease. . . .

No, Gentlemen, We will [use arms] only to defend ourselves the same as you; you cannot refuse us, and society cannot deny the right nature gives us, unless you pretend the *Declaration of Rights* does not apply to women and that they should let their throats be cut like lambs, without the right to defend themselves. For can you believe the tyrants would spare us? . . . Why then not terrorize aristocracy and tyranny with all the resources of civic effort and the pure zeal, zeal which cold men can well call fanaticism and exaggeration, but which is only the natural result of a heart burning with love for the public weal? . . .

. . . If, for reasons we cannot guess, you refuse our just demands, these women you have raised to the ranks of *citoyennes* by granting that title to their husbands, these women who have sampled the promises of liberty, who have conceived the hope of placing free men in the world, and who have sworn to live free or die—such women, I say, will never consent to concede the day to slaves; they will die first. They will uphold their oath, and a dagger aimed at their breasts will deliver them from the misfortunes of slavery! They will die, regretting not life, but the uselessness of their death; regretting moreover, not having been able to drench their hands in the impure blood of the enemies of the fatherland and to avenge some of their own!

But, Gentlemen, let us cast our eyes away from these cruel extremes. Whatever the rages and plots of aristocrats, they will not succeed in vanquishing a whole people of united brothers armed to defend their rights. We also demand only the honor of sharing their exhaustion and glorious labors and of making tyrants see that women also have blood to shed for the service of the fatherland in danger.

Gentlemen, here is what we hope to obtain from your justice and equity:

1. Permission to procure pikes, pistols, and sabres (even muskets for those who are strong enough to use them), within police regulations.

2. Permission to assemble on festival days and Sundays on the Champ de la Fédération, or in other suitable places, to practice maneuvers with these arms.

3. Permission to name the former French Guards to command us, always in conformity with the rules which the mayor's wisdom prescribes for good order and public calm.

From "French Women Petition to Bear Arms" in *Women in Revolutionary Paris 1789–1795*, trans. by Darline Gay Levy, Harriet Branson Applewhite, and Mary Durham Johnson. © 1979 by the Board of Trustees of the University of Illinois. Used with permission of the authors and the University of Illinois Press.

Reconstruction of France

The National Constituent Assembly set about reorganizing France. The assembly was determined to protect property and limit the impact on national life of small-property owners as well as of the unpropertied elements of the nation. While championing equality before the law, the assembly spurned social equality and extensive democracy. It thus charted a course that nineteenth-century liberals across Europe and in other areas of the world would follow.

Political Reorganization The Constitution of 1791 established a constitutional monarchy. There was a unicameral Legislative Assembly. The monarch could delay but not halt legislation. Voting was restricted to about 50,000 citizens of the French nation of 26 million.

The exclusion of women from both voting and holding office did not pass unnoticed. In 1791, Olympe de Gouges (d. 1793), a butcher's daughter who became a radical in Paris, composed a *Declaration of the Rights of Woman*, which she ironically addressed to Queen Marie Antoinette (1755–1793). Much of the document added the word *woman* to the *Declaration of the Rights of Man and Citizen*. That strategy demanded that women be regarded as citizens and not merely as daughters, sisters, wives, and mothers of citizens. Olympe de Gouges further outlined rights that would permit women to own property and require men to recognize the paternity of their children. She called for equality of the sexes in marriage and improved education for women. Her demands illustrated how the public listing of rights in the *Declaration of the Rights of Man and Citizen* created expectations even among those it did not cover.

The National Constituent Assembly replaced the ancient French Provinces with eighty-three departments *(départements)*. The ancient judicial courts, including the *parlements*, were replaced by uniform courts with elected judges and prosecutors. Legal procedures were simplified, and the most degrading punishments abolished.

Economic Policy The National Constituent Assembly suppressed the guilds, liberated the grain trade, and established the metric system of uniform weights and measures. In 1790, the assembly placed the burden of proof on the peasants to rid themselves of the residual feudal dues for which compensation was to be paid. In 1791, it enacted the Chapelier Law forbidding worker associations, thereby crushing the attempts of urban workers to protect their wages. Peasants and workers were to be left to the mercy of the free marketplace.

The assembly decided to pay the troublesome royal debt by confiscating and selling the lands of the Roman Catholic Church. The assembly authorized the issuance of *assignats*, or government bonds, the value of which was guaranteed by the revenue generated from the sale of church property. When the *assignats* began to circulate as currency, the assembly issued even larger quantities of them to liquidate the national debt. However, the value of *assignats* soon began to fall. Inflation increased and put new stress on the urban poor.

Civil Constitution of the Clergy In July 1790, the assembly issued the Civil Constitution of the Clergy, which transformed the Roman Catholic Church into a branch of the state. This measure reduced the number of bishoprics, made borders of dioceses conform to those of the new departments, and provided for the election of priests and bishops, who became salaried employees of the state. The assembly consulted neither the pope nor the French clergy about these changes. The king approved the measure reluctantly.

The Civil Constitution of the Clergy roused immense opposition within the French church. The assembly ruled that all clergy must take an oath to support the Civil Constitution. Only about half the clergy did so. In reprisal, the assembly designated the clergy who had not taken the oath as "refractory" and removed them from their clerical functions. Refractory priests immediately attempted to celebrate mass.

In February 1791, the pope condemned not only the Civil Constitution of the Clergy but also the *Declaration of the Rights of Man and Citizen*. That condemnation marked the opening of a Roman Catholic offensive against liberalism and revolution that continued for over a century. Within France itself, the pope's action meant that religious devotion and revolutionary loyalty became incompatible for many people. French citizens divided between supporters of the constitutional priests and of the refractory clergy. Louis XVI favored the latter.

Counterrevolutionary Activity In the summer of 1791, the queen and some nobles persuaded Louis XVI to flee. The escape failed. Thereafter, the leaders of the National Constituent Assembly knew that the chief counterrevolutionary sat on the French throne.

On August 27, 1791, Leopold II of Austria (r. 1790–1792), who was the brother of Marie Antoinette, and Frederick William II (r. 1786–1797) of Prussia issued the Declaration of Pillnitz. They promised to intervene in France to protect the royal family if the other major European powers agreed. The latter provision rendered the statement meaningless because Great Britain would not consent. However, the revolutionaries felt surrounded by aristocratic and monarchical foes.

In September 1791, the National Constituent Assembly forbade its members to sit in the Legislative Assembly then being elected. This new body met on October 1.

A Second Revolution

Since the earliest days of the revolution, clubs of politically like-minded persons had organized themselves in Paris. The best organized were the *Jacobins,* who were linked to clubs in the provinces. In the Legislative Assembly, a group of Jacobins known as the *Girondists* (because many came from the department of the Gironde) led it on April 20, 1792, to declare war on Austria.

End of the Monarchy The war radicalized the revolution and led to the *second revolution,* which established a republic. The war went poorly, and the revolution seemed in danger. Late in July, under radical working-class pressure, the government of Paris passed to a committee, or commune, of representatives from the municipal wards. On August 10, 1792, a large crowd invaded the Tuileries and forced Louis

XVI and Marie Antoinette to take refuge in the Legislative Assembly. During the disturbance, royal guards and many Parisians died. Thereafter, the royal family was imprisoned, and the king suspended from his political functions.

The Convention and the Role of Sans-Culottes

In early September, the Paris Commune killed about 1,200 people in the city jails. Most were common criminals whom the crowd had assumed were counterrevolutionaries. The Commune then compelled the Legislative Assembly to call for the election, by universal manhood suffrage, of a new assembly to write a democratic constitution. That body, called the Convention, met on September 21, 1792.

The Convention declared France a republic. The second revolution had been the work of radical Jacobins and of the people of Paris known as the *sans-culottes*, meaning "without breeches," from the long trousers that, as working people, they wore instead of aristocratic knee breeches. The *sans-culottes* were shopkeepers, artisans, wage earners, and a few factory workers. The politics of the Old Regime had ignored them, and the National Constituent Assembly had left them victims of unregulated economic liberty.

The *sans-culottes*, sought price controls for food. They resented most forms of social inequality and were hostile to the aristocracy and the original leaders of the revolution. They advocated a community of small property owners. They were antimonarchical, republican, and suspicious of government.

In contrast, the Jacobins were republicans who favored representative government and an unregulated economy. However, once the Convention began its deliberations, the more extreme Jacobins, known as the Mountain, worked with the *sans-culottes* to carry the revolution forward and win the war.

In December 1792, Louis XVI was put on trial and convicted of conspiring against the state. He was beheaded on January 21, 1793.

France was now at war with virtually all Europe. Civil war soon followed. In March 1793, aristocratic officers and priests commenced a royalist revolt in western France with local popular support.

The Reign of Terror and Its Aftermath

The Reign of Terror is the name given to the months of quasi-judicial executions and murders from autumn 1793 to midsummer 1794. The Terror can be understood only in the context of the internal and external wars on the one hand, and the revolutionary expectations of the Convention and the *sans-culottes* on the other.

Committee of Public Safety   In April 1793, the Convention established a Committee of Public Safety that eventually enjoyed almost dictatorial power to save the revolution

On the way to her execution in 1793, Marie Antoinette was sketched from life by Jacques-Louis David as she passed his window. [Bibliotheque Nationale, Paris, France/Giraudon/Art Resource, N.Y.]

from enemies at home and abroad. It generally enjoyed a working political relationship with the *sans-culottes* of Paris.

In June 1793, the Parisian *sans-culottes* invaded the Convention and secured the expulsion of the Girondists. That gave the Mountain complete control. August 23 saw a *levée en masse*, or general military requisition of population, which conscripted males into the army and directed economic production for military purposes. On September 29, a maximum on prices was established in accord with *sans-culottes'* demands. During these same months, the armies of the revolution crushed many of the counterrevolutionary disturbances in the provinces.

The Society of Revolutionary Republican Women

In May 1793, Pauline Léon and Claire Lacombe founded the Society of Revolutionary Republican Women, which became increasingly radical. Its members sought stricter price controls, worked to ferret out food hoarders, and brawled with market women thought to be insufficiently revolutionary.

The women of the Society also demanded the right to wear the revolutionary cap worn only by male citizens. By October 1793, the Jacobins in the Convention had begun to fear the turmoil the Society was causing and banned all women's clubs and societies.

There were other examples of repression of women in 1793. Olympe de Gouges opposed the Terror. She was tried and guillotined in November 1793. Women were excluded from the French army and from attending the galleries of the Convention.

Dechristianization
In October 1793, the Convention proclaimed a new calendar dating from the first day of the French Republic. There were twelve months of thirty days with names associated with the seasons and climate. In November 1793, the Convention decreed the Cathedral of Notre Dame to be a Temple of Reason. The legislature then sent trusted members, known as deputies-on-mission, into the provinces to enforce dechristianization by closing churches and persecuting clergy and believers. This religious policy roused much opposition and separated the provinces from the revolutionary government in Paris.

Progress of the Terror
During late 1793 and early 1794, Maximilien Robespierre (1758–1794) emerged as the chief figure on the Committee of Public Safety. The Jacobin Club provided his base of power. A shrewd politician, he depended on the support of the sans-culottes of Paris and opposed dechristianization as a political blunder.

The Reign of Terror manifested itself through a series of revolutionary tribunals established by the Convention during the summer of 1793. The tribunals were to try the enemies of the republic, but the definition of enemy shifted as the months passed. Marie Antoinette, other members of the royal family, and aristocrats were executed in October 1793. They were followed by Girondist politicians.

By early 1794, the Terror had moved to the provinces, where the deputies-on-mission presided over the execution of thousands of people. In Paris during the winter of 1794, Robespierre turned the Terror against republican political figures of the left and right and exterminated the leaders who might have threatened his own position. On June 10, he secured a law that permitted the revolutionary tribunal to convict suspects without evidence.

In May 1794, at the height of his power, Robespierre, considering the worship of reason too abstract for most citizens, abolished it and established the Cult of the Supreme Being. He did not long preside over this new religion. On July 27 (the Ninth of Thermidor), members of the Convention, by prearrangement, shouted him down when he rose to speak. Robespierre was executed the next day.

The Reign of Terror had claimed 40,000 victims. Most were peasants and sans-culottes who had rebelled against the revolutionary government. By the late summer of 1794, provincial uprisings had been crushed and the war against foreign enemies was going well. Those factors and the feeling that the revolution had consumed enough of its own children brought the Terror to an end.

The Thermidorian Reaction: End of the Terror and Establishment of the Directory
The tempering of the revolution, called the Thermidorian Reaction, began in July 1794. It set up a new constitutional regime. The influence of wealthy middle-class and professional people replaced that of the sans-culottes. Many of the people responsible for the Terror were removed from public life. The Jacobin Club was closed.

The Thermidorian Constitution of the Year III was a conservative document that provided for a bicameral legislative government favoring property owners. The executive body, consisting of a five-person Directory, was elected by the upper legislative house.

True to their belief in an unregulated economy, the Thermidorians repealed the ceiling on prices. When food riots resulted during the winter of 1794–1795, the Convention put them down to prove that the era of the sans-culottes journées had ended. On October 5, 1795, Paris rebelled. A general named Napoleon Bonaparte (1769–1821) dispersed the crowd with artillery. Other enemies of the Directory would be more difficult to disperse.

The Napoleonic Era

Napoleon Bonaparte was born in 1769 to a poor noble family in Corsica. France had annexed Corsica in 1768, and he obtained a commission as a French artillery officer. He was a fiery Jacobin. In 1793, he played a leading role in recovering the port of Toulon from the British. As a reward, the government appointed him a brigadier general. His defense of the new regime in 1794 won him a command in Italy. By October 1797, he had crushed the Austrians and concluded the Treaty of Campo Formio, which took Austria out of the war. Italy and Switzerland lay under French domination.

In November 1797, the triumphant Bonaparte returned to Paris to confront France's only remaining enemy, Britain. Judging it impossible to invade England at that time, he chose to capture Egypt from the Ottoman Empire and cut off British communication with India. But the invasion of Egypt was a failure. Admiral Horatio Nelson (1758–1805) destroyed the French fleet, and the French army was stranded. The Russians, Austrians, and Ottomans joined Britain to form the Second Coalition. In 1799, the Russian and Austrian armies defeated the French in Italy and Switzerland and threatened to invade France.

Napoleon returned to France in October 1799. On November 10, 1799 (19 Brumaire) he overthrew the Directory. Bonaparte issued the Constitution of the Year VII in December 1799, establishing himself as the First Consul. The constitution received approval from the electorate in a rigged plebiscite. The Consulate closed the revolution in France.

The Consulate in France (1799–1804)

Bonaparte quickly achieved peace. Russia had already left the Second Coalition. A victory over Austria at Marengo in Italy in 1800 took Austria out of the war. In 1802, Britain concluded the Treaty of Amiens, which temporarily brought peace to Europe.

Bonaparte also restored peace and order at home. Although he used generosity, flattery, and bribery to win over some of his enemies, issued a general amnesty, and employed persons from all political factions, Bonaparte suppressed political opposition. He established centralized administration in which all departments were managed by prefects appointed by the central government in Paris. He employed secret police. He stamped out royalist rebellions and plots.

Napoleon also alleviated the hostility of French Catholics. In 1801, he concluded a concordat with Pope Pius VII (r. 1800–1823). Both refractory and constitutional clergy were forced to resign. Their replacements received their spiritual investiture from the pope, but the state named the bishops and paid their salaries and the salary of one priest in each parish. In return, the church gave up its claims to its confiscated property. The clergy had to swear an oath of loyalty to the state, and the Organic Articles of 1802 established the supremacy of state over church. Similar laws applied to the Protestant and Jewish communities.

In 1802, another plebiscite appointed Napoleon consul for life. He transformed the basic laws and institutions of France on the basis of both liberal principles derived from the Enlightenment and the revolution and conservative principles going back to the Old Regime, on the one hand, and the spirit that had triumphed at Thermidor, on the other. This was especially true of the Civil Code of 1804, usually called the Napoleonic Code. However, these laws stopped far short of the full equality advocated by liberal rationalists. Fathers were granted extensive control over their children and men over their wives. Labor unions were forbidden, and the rights of workers were inferior to those of employers.

In 1804, Bonaparte seized on a bomb attack on his life to make himself emperor. Another new constitution, ratified by a plebiscite, designated Napoleon Emperor of the French. Napoleon summoned the pope to Notre Dame to take part in the coronation, but Napoleon crowned himself.

The French Revolution

1789

May 5	Estates General opens at Versailles
June 17	Third Estate declares itself the National Assembly
June 20	National Assembly takes the Tennis Court Oath
July 14	Fall of the Bastille
July	Great Fear spreads in the countryside
August 4	Nobles surrender their feudal rights in a meeting of the National Constituent Assembly
August 27	*Declaration of the Rights of Man and Citizen*
October 5–6	Parisian women march to Versailles and force Louis XVI and his family to return to Paris

1790

July 12	Civil Constitution of the Clergy adopted
July 14	New constitution accepted by the king

1791

June 20–24	Louis XVI and his family attempt to flee France
August 27	Declaration of Pillnitz
October 1	Legislative Assembly meets

1792

April 20	France declares war on Austria
August 10	Tuileries palace stormed, and Louis XVI takes refuge with the Legislative Assembly
September 2–7	September Massacres
September 21	Convention meets, and monarchy abolished

1793

January 21	Louis XVI executed
February 1	France declares war on Great Britain
March	Counterrevolution breaks out
April 6	Committee of Public Safety formed
July	Robespierre enters Committee of Public Safety
August 23	*Levée en masse* proclaimed
September 29	Maximum prices set on food and other commodities
October 16	Queen Marie Antoinette executed
November 10	Cult of Reason proclaimed; revolutionary calendar

1794

May 7	Cult of the Supreme Being proclaimed
July 27	Ninth of Thermidor and fall of Robespierre
July 28	Robespierre executed

1795

August 22	Constitution of the Year III adopted, establishing the Directory

Napoleon's Empire (1804–1814)   Between his coronation as emperor and his final defeat at Waterloo (1815), Napoleon conquered most of Europe. France's victories ended the Old Regime and its feudal trappings in western Europe, and forced the eastern European states to reorganize themselves. Everywhere, Napoleon's advance unleashed nationalism.

The Treaty of Amiens with Britain (1802) could not last, and Britain declared war again in May 1803. William Pitt the Younger (1759–1806) returned to office as prime minister in 1804 and persuaded Russia and Austria to move again against French aggression. On October 21, 1805, Lord Nelson destroyed the French and Spanish fleets at the Battle of Trafalgar just off the Spanish coast. Nelson was killed, but Trafalgar guaranteed British control of the sea.

On land, however, between October 1805 and July 1807, Napoleon defeated the armies of Austria, Prussia, and Russia. He forced Austria to withdraw from northern Italy, where Napoleon became king. He replaced the Holy Roman Empire with the Confederation of the Rhine. Prussia and Russia became his allies.

Napoleon could not be secure until he had defeated Britain. Unable to compete with the British navy, he adopted economic warfare to cut off British trade with Europe. He hoped to cripple British commercial and financial power and drive the British from the war. Nonetheless, the British economy survived because of its access to the Americas and the eastern Mediterranean. Known as the Continental System, Napoleon's policies harmed the European economies and roused resentment.

The Wars of Liberation   In 1807, a French army invaded the Iberian Peninsula to force Portugal to abandon its alliance with Britain. When a revolt broke out in Madrid in 1808, Napoleon deposed the Spanish Bourbons and placed his brother Joseph (1768–1844) on the Spanish throne. Attacks on the church increased public outrage.

In Spain, Napoleon faced guerrilla warfare, and the British landed an army under Sir Arthur Wellesley (1769–1852), later the duke of Wellington, to support the Spanish. Thus began the long peninsular campaign that would play a critical role in Napoleon's defeat.

The Austrians renewed the war in 1809, but the French won the battle of Wagram. The resulting peace deprived Austria of 3.5 million subjects. Another spoil of victory was the Archduchess Marie Louise (1791–1847), Francis I's (r. 1792–1835) eighteen-year-old daughter, whom Napoleon married for dynastic purposes after divorcing Josephine de Beauharnais (1763–1814), who had borne him no children.

The Franco-Russian alliance was faltering. The Continental System had harmed the Russian economy, and Napoleon's organization of a Polish state, the Grand Duchy of Warsaw, on the Russian doorstep angered Tsar Alexander I (r. 1800–1825). In 1810, Russia withdrew from the Continental System and began to prepare for war.

To stifle the Russian military threat, Napoleon amassed an army of over 600,000 men, but the Russians retreated before his advance and destroyed all food and supplies as well. The so-called Grand Army of Napoleon could not live off the country, and Russia was too vast for supply lines.

In September 1812, Russian public opinion forced the army to fight. At Borodino, the French lost 30,000 casualties and the Russians almost twice as many. Yet the Russian army was not destroyed. By October, after occupying Moscow, the Grand Army was forced to retreat. Perhaps only 100,000 lived to tell the tale.

In 1813, patriotic pressure and national ambition brought together the last and most powerful coalition against Napoleon. Financed by the British, the Russians drove westward to be joined by Prussia and Austria. From the west, Wellington marched his peninsular army into France. Napoleon waged a skillful campaign but met decisive defeat in October at Leipzig. At the end of March 1814, the allied army marched into Paris. Napoleon abdicated and went into exile on the island of Elba off the coast of Italy.

The Congress of Vienna and the European Settlement

Once Napoleon was removed, the allies began to pursue their own separate ambitions. The key person among the allies was Viscount Castlereagh (1769–1822), the British foreign secretary. Even before the victorious armies had

---

Napoleonic Europe

1797	Napoleon concludes Treaty of Campo Formio
1799	Consulate established
1801	Concordat between France and papacy
1802	Treaty of Amiens
1803	War renewed between France and Britain
1804	Napoleonic Civil Code issued; Napoleon crowned emperor
1805	Nelson defeats French fleet at Trafalgar
1806	Continental System
1808	Beginning of Spanish resistance to Napoleonic domination
1809	Wagram; Napoleon marries Archduchess Marie Louise of Austria
1812	Invasion of Russia
1813	Leipzig
1814	Congress of Vienna convenes (September)
1815	Waterloo (June 18); Holy Alliance formed (September 26)
1821	Napoleon dies on Saint Helena

Map 25-1 Europe 1815, after the Congress of Vienna. The Congress of Vienna achieved the post-Napoleonic territorial adjustments shown on the map. The most notable arrangements dealt with areas along France's borders (the Netherlands, Prussia, Switzerland, and Piedmont) and in Poland and northern Italy.

entered Paris, he achieved the Treaty of Chaumont on March 9, 1814, providing for the restoration of the Bourbons to the French throne and the contraction of France to its 1792 frontiers. Remaining problems were left for a conference at Vienna.

The Congress of Vienna met from September 1814 until November 1815. The victors agreed that no single state should be allowed to dominate Europe. They constructed a series of states to prevent French expansion (see Map 25–1). Thus, they established the kingdom of the Netherlands in the north and added Genoa to Piedmont in the south. Prussia was given new territories in the west to deter French aggression along the Rhine River. Austria was given full con-

trol of northern Italy to prevent a repetition of Napoleon's conquests there. Most of Napoleon's arrangements in the rest of Germany were left untouched. The Holy Roman Empire was not revived. The Congress established the rule of legitimate monarchs and rejected any hint of the republican and democratic politics that had flowed from the French Revolution.

However, eastern Europe divided the victors. Alexander I wanted Russia to govern all of Poland. Prussia wanted all of Saxony. Austria, however, refused to see Prussian power grow and Russia penetrate deeper into Europe. The Polish-Saxon question enabled France to rejoin the great powers. The French Foreign Minister Talleyrand (1754–

1838) negotiated a secret treaty with Britain and Austria. When the news leaked out, the tsar agreed to become ruler of a smaller Poland, and Prussia settled for part of Saxony. Thereafter, France was included as a fifth great power in all deliberations.

Napoleon's escape from Elba on March 1, 1815, further restored unity among the victors. The allies sent their armies to crush him. Wellington and the Prussians defeated Napoleon at Waterloo in Belgium on June 18, 1815. Napoleon was exiled to Saint Helena, a tiny island off the coast of Africa, where he died in 1821.

The main outlines of the Vienna Settlement remained in place. The alliance between England, Austria, Prussia, and Russia was renewed on November 20, 1815. Henceforth, it was a coalition for the maintenance of peace. Its existence and later operation represented an important departure in European affairs. The statesmen at Vienna, unlike their eighteenth-century counterparts, had seen the armies of the French Revolution change borders and overturn the political and social order of the continent. They were determined to prevent a recurrence of those upheavals. Their purpose was to establish a framework for stability, not to punish defeated France. The great powers through the Vienna Settlement framed international relations so that the major powers would respect that settlement and not, as in the eighteenth century, use military force to change it.

The Congress of Vienna arranged an acceptable settlement for Europe that produced a long-lasting peace. Its work has been criticized for failing to recognize and provide for the great forces that would stir the nineteenth century—nationalism and democracy—but such criticism is inappropriate. The settlement, like all such agreements, was aimed at solving past ills, and in that it succeeded. The Vienna settlement spared Europe a general war until 1914.

Wars of Independence in Latin America

The wars of the French Revolution and Napoleon sparked movements for independence throughout Latin America. Between 1804 and 1824, France was driven from Haiti, Portugal lost control of Brazil, and Spain was forced to withdraw from all of its American empire except for Cuba and Puerto Rico. Three centuries of Iberian colonial government over the South American continent ended.

Eighteenth-Century Developments

Spain was one of the defeated powers in 1763. Charles III (r. 1759–1788) was convinced that the American colonial system had to be changed. After 1765, the monarch abolished the monopolies of Seville and Cádiz, and opened more South American and Caribbean ports to trade, and authorized commerce between American ports. In 1776 he organized a fourth viceroyalty that included much of present-day Argentina, Uruguay, Paraguay, and Bolivia. Charles III also attempted to make tax collection more efficient and to eliminate bureaucratic corruption. To achieve those ends, he introduced into the empire *intendents*, who were royal bureaucrats loyal only to the crown.

These reforms returned the empire to direct Spanish control. Many *peninsulares*, whites born in Spain, went to the New World to fill new posts at the expense of Creoles, whites born in America. Expanding trade brought more Spanish merchants to Latin America. Economic life continued to be organized for the benefit of Spain.

First Movements Toward Independence

Haiti achieved independence from France in 1804, following a slave revolt that commenced in 1794 led by Toussaint L'Ouverture (1746–1803). Haiti's revolution involved the popular uprising of a repressed social group, which proved the great exception in the Latin American drive for liberty from European masters. On the South American continent it was the Creole elite who led the movements against Spain and Portugal. Few Indians, blacks, mestizos, mulattos, or slaves became involved or benefited from the end of Iberian rule. The Creoles were determined that political independence from Spain and Portugal should not cause social disruption or the loss of their privileges. In this respect they were not unlike American revolutionaries in the southern colonies who wanted to reject British rule but keep their slaves, or French revolutionaries who did not want to extend liberty to the French working class.

Creole complaints resembled those of the American colonists against Great Britain. Merchants wanted to trade more freely within the region and with North America and Europe. They wanted commercial regulations that would benefit them rather than Spain. Creoles also feared that Spanish imperial regulations would harm their interests, and they resented Spanish policies favoring *peninsulares* for political patronage.

From the 1790s onward, Spain suffered reverses in the wars associated with the French Revolution and Napoleon, and the commercial situation turned against the inhabitants of the Spanish Empire. The military pressures led the Spanish monarchy into a desperate search for new revenues, including increased taxation and the confiscation of property in the American Empire. The policies harmed the economic life of the Creole elite.

Creole leaders had read the Enlightenment *philosophes* and regarded their reforms as potentially beneficial to the region.

They were also well aware of the political philosophy of the American Revolution. The event that transformed Creole discontent into revolt against the Spanish government occurred when Napoleon toppled the Portuguese monarchy in 1807 and the Spanish government in 1808, and then placed his own brother on the throne of Spain. The Portuguese royal family fled to Brazil, but the Bourbon monarchy of Spain seemed vanquished.

The Creole elite feared that a liberal Napoleonic monarchy in Spain would harm their economic and social interests and would drain the region of resources for Napoleon's wars. To protect their interests, Creole juntas, or political committees, between 1808 and 1810 claimed the right to govern regions of Latin America. The Spanish would not again directly govern the continent and after ten years of warfare had to recognize Latin American independence.

San Martín in Río de la Plata

The first region to assert its independence was the Río de la Plata, or modern Argentina. In 1810, the junta in Buenos Aires thrust off Spanish authority and sent liberation forces against Paraguay and Uruguay. The armies were defeated, but Paraguay asserted its own independence, and Uruguay was absorbed by Brazil.

The Buenos Aires government then determined to liberate Peru, the greatest stronghold of royalist power and loyalty on the continent. By 1814, José de San Martín (1778–1850) had led an army over the Andes Mountains. By early 1817, he had occupied Santiago in Chile, and established, Bernardo O'Higgins (1778–1842) as supreme dictator. In 1821, he drove royalist forces from Lima and assumed the title of Protector of Peru.

Simón Bolívar's Liberation of Venezuela

In 1810, as a firm advocate of both independence and republicanism, Simón Bolívar (1783–1830) had helped organize a liberating junta in Caracas, Venezuela. Between 1811 and 1814, civil war broke out as royalists, slaves, and cowboys challenged the authority of the republican government. Bolívar had to go into exile. In 1819, with help from Haiti, he captured Bogotá, capital of New Granada (including modern Colombia, Bolivia, and Ecuador), as a base for attacking Venezuela. In 1821, his forces captured Caracas, and he was named president.

In July 1822, the armies of Bolívar and San Martín liberated Quito. The two leaders disagreed about the future political structure of Latin America. San Martín believed that monarchies were required; Bolívar maintained his republicanism. Not long thereafter San Martín went into exile in Europe. In 1823, Bolívar sent troops to Peru. On December

Toussaint L'Ouverture (1743–1803) began the revolt that led to Haitian independence in 1804. [Historical Pictures Collection/Stock Montage, Inc.]

9, 1824, at the battle of Ayacucho, the Spanish royalist forces were defeated. The battle marked the end of Spain's effort to retain its American empire.

Independence in New Spain

The drive for independence in New Spain, which included present-day Mexico as well as Texas, California, and the rest of the southwestern United States, illustrates the socially conservative outcome of the Latin American colonial revolutions. As elsewhere, a local governing junta was organized. But before it had undertaken any significant measures, a Creole priest, Miguel Hidalgo y Costilla (1753–1811), issued a call for rebellion to the Indians in his parish. They and other repressed groups responded. Father Hidalgo set forth a program of social change. Soon he had 80,000 followers, but in July 1811 he was captured and executed. Leadership of his movement then fell to José María Morelos y Pavón (1765–1815), a more radical mestizo priest. He was executed in 1815.

In 1820, however, a revolution in Spain forced Ferdinand VII (r. 1813–1833) to accept a liberal constitution. Conservative Mexicans feared that the new liberal monarchy would attempt to impose liberal reforms on Mexico. Therefore, for the most conservative of reasons, they created an independent Mexico governed by persons determined to resist social reform.

Great Britain was sympathetic to the independence movements in Latin America. Independence opened the markets of the continent to British trade. In 1823, Britain supported the American Monroe Doctrine that prohibited further intervention by European powers in America. Britain soon recognized the Spanish colonies as independent states. Through the rest of the century, British commercial interests dominated Latin America.

Brazilian Independence

Brazilian independence came relatively peacefully. As already noted, the Portuguese royal family and several thousand officials took refuge in Brazil in 1807. Their arrival transformed Rio de Janeiro into a court city. The prince regent Joao (r. 1816–1826) in 1815 made Brazil a kingdom; it was no longer

merely a colony of Portugal. Then in 1820 a revolution occurred in Portugal, and its leaders demanded Joao's return to Lisbon and the return of Brazil to colonial status. Joao, who had become Joao VI in 1816, returned to Portugal but left his son Pedro (r. 1822–1831) as regent in Brazil. In 1822, Pedro embraced Brazilian independence and became emperor of Brazil, which remained a monarchy until 1889.

Toward the Abolition of Slavery in the Transatlantic Economy

In 1750, few questioned the institution of slavery; by 1888, slavery no longer existed in the transatlantic economy. This transformation of economic and social life occurred as the result of an international effort, first to abolish the slave trade and then to abolish slavery itself. No previous society had attempted to abolish slavery. Its abolition in the transatlantic world is one of the most permanent achievements of the eighteenth-century Enlightenment and revolutions.

The eighteenth-century crusade against slavery originated among writers of the Enlightenment and religious critics. The general Enlightenment rhetoric of equality stood in sharp contrast to the radical inequality of slavery. Adam Smith's emphasis in *The Wealth of Nations* on free labor and free markets undermined economic defenses of slavery. Some Europeans also looked on African slaves as having been robbed of an original innocence. In such a climate, slavery grew to be regarded as unacceptable.

Just as the slave system was a transatlantic affair, so was the crusade against it. The initial religious protest against slavery originated among eighteenth-century English Quakers. But Quaker communities in America soon also wrote and organized against the institution. By the earliest stages of the American Revolution, small groups of reformers, usually spearheaded by Quakers, had established an antislavery network. Emancipation gradually spread among the northern states. In 1787, the Continental Congress forbade slavery in the Northwest Territory north of the Ohio River.

However, Great Britain became the center for the antislavery movement. During the early 1780s, the antislavery reformers in Britain decided to work toward ending the slave trade rather than slavery itself. To many, the slave trade appeared a more obvious crime than the holding of slaves. Furthermore, attacking slavery itself involved serious issues of property rights. The antislavery groups also believed that if the trade were ended, planters would have to treat their remaining slaves more humanely.

While the British reformers worked for the abolition of the slave trade, some slaves took matters into their own hands. The slave revolt in Haiti was a warning to slave owners throughout the West Indies. Other slave revolts occurred in

The Wars of Latin American Independence	
1759–1788	Charles III of Spain carries out imperial reforms
1794	Toussaint L'Ouverture leads slave revolt in Haiti
1804	Independence of Haiti
1807	Portuguese royal family flees to Brazil
1808	Spanish monarchy falls to Napoleon
1808–1810	Creole Committees organized to govern much of Latin America
1810	Buenos Aires junta sends forces to liberate Paraguay and Uruguay
1811	Miguel Hidalgo y Costilla leads rebellion in New Spain and is executed
1811–1815	José María Morelos y Pavón leads rebellion in New Spain and is executed
1814	San Martín organizes army
1815	Brazil declared a kingdom
1817	San Martín occupies Santiago, Chile
1820	Revolution in Spain
1821	
February 24	New Spain declares independence
June 29	Bolívar captures Caracas, Venezuela
July 28	San Martín liberates Peru
1822	
July 26–27	San Martín goes into exile
September 7	Dom Pedro declares Brazilian independence
1824	Battle of Ayacucho—final Spanish defeat

Virginia, South Carolina, and British-controlled Demarra. Each of these was suppressed.

For economic reasons, some British West Indies planters began to consider abolition of the slave trade useful to their interests. The planters were experiencing soil exhaustion and increased competition. There was a glut of sugar on the market, and the price was falling. Without new slaves, competing French planters would lack the labor they needed to exploit their islands.

By 1807, abolition sentiment was strong enough for Parliament to prohibit slave trading from any British port. Thereafter, the suppression of this trade became a pillar of nineteenth-century British foreign policy. The British navy maintained a squadron off West Africa to halt slave traders.

Sentiment to abolish slavery itself increased. In 1833, following the passage of the Reform Bill in Great Britain, Parliament abolished the right of British subjects to hold slaves. In the British West Indies, 750,000 slaves were freed within a few years.

Leaders of the Latin American wars of independence, disposed by Enlightenment ideas to disapprove of slavery, had sought the support of slaves by promises of emancipation. The newly independent nations slowly freed their slaves to maintain good relations with Britain, from whom they needed economic support. Slavery disappeared from Latin America by the middle of the century, with the important exception of Brazil.

The other old colonial powers in the New World were slower to abolish slavery. Portugal did nothing about slavery in Brazil, and its independent government continued slavery. Portugal ended slavery elsewhere in its American possessions in 1836; the Swedes, in 1847; the Danes, in 1848, but the Dutch not until 1863. France had a significant antislavery movement, but did not abolish slavery in its West Indian possessions until 1848.

Despite all of these achievements, during the first thirty years of the nineteenth century slavery achieved new footholds in the transatlantic world. These areas included the lower south of the United States for the cultivation of cotton, Brazil for the cultivation of coffee, and Cuba for the cultivation of sugar. World demand for those products made the slave system economically viable in those regions. Slavery would end in the United States only after the Civil War. In Cuba it would persist until 1886, and full emancipation would occur in Brazil only in 1888. (See Chapters 26, 27, and 30.)

The emancipation crusade, like slave trading itself, drew Europeans into African affairs. In 1787, the British established a colony for free blacks from Britain in Sierra Leone. The French established a smaller experiment at Libreville in Gabon. The most famous and lasting attempt to settle former black slaves in Africa was the establishment of Liberia through the efforts of the American Colonization Society after 1817.

Liberia became an independent republic in 1847. These efforts to move former slaves back to Africa had only modest success, but they did affect the future of West Africa itself.

Other antislavery reformers were less interested in establishing outposts for settlement of former slaves than in transforming the African economy itself. These reformers attempted to spread both Christianity and free trade to Africa, hoping to exchange British manufactured goods for tropical goods produced by Africans. These commercial efforts of the antislavery movement marked the first serious intrusions of European powers into the heart of Africa.

After the American Civil War finally halted any large-scale demand for slaves from Africa, the antislavery reformers began to focus on ending the slave trade in East Africa and the Indian Ocean. This new drive against slavery and the slave trade in Africa itself became one of the rationales for the establishment of the late-nineteenth century colonial empires.

IN WORLD PERSPECTIVE

The Transatlantic Revolutions

The revolutions and the crusade against slavery that occurred throughout the transatlantic world between 1776 and the 1830s transformed three continents. In North America, in France and other parts of Europe, and in South America, political experiments challenged government by both monarchy and aristocracy. The foundations of modern liberal democracy were laid. The largest republic since ancient times had been established in North America. In France, written constitutions and elected legislatures remained essential parts of the government. In Latin America, republicanism triumphed everywhere except Brazil. Never again could government be undertaken in these regions without some form of participation by the governed.

The expanding forms of political liberty found their counterparts in an economic life freed from the constraints of the old colonial empires and the slavery that marked their plantations. The new American republic constituted a vast free trade zone. Its commerce was open to the world. And for the first time since the encounter with Europe, Latin America could trade freely among its own peoples and those of the rest of the world. In France and Europe, where the Napoleonic armies had carried the doctrines of the rights of man, economic life had been rationalized and freed from the domination of local authorities and local weights and measures. National law formed the framework for economic activity. The movement to abolish slavery fostered a wage economy of free laborers. That kind of economy would generate its own set of problems and social dislocation, but it was nonetheless an economy of free human beings.

Finally, the age of transatlantic revolutions saw the emergence of nationalism as a political force. All of the revolutions, because of their popular political base, had given power to the idea of nations defined by their own character and historical past rather than by dynastic rulers. The Americans saw themselves as forming a new kind of nation. The French had demonstrated the power of a nation mobilized for military purposes. In turn, the aggression of France had aroused national sentiment, especially in Great Britain, Spain, and Germany. The new nations of Latin America also sought to define themselves by their heritage and historical experience rather than by their past in the Spanish and Portuguese Empires.

These various revolutions, their political doctrines, and their social and economic departures provided examples to peoples elsewhere in the world. But even more important, the transatlantic revolutions and eventual abolition of slavery meant that new political classes and independent nations would become actors on the world scene. Europeans would have to deal with a score of new nations in the Americas. The rest of the world confronted new nations freed from the direction and authority of European powers. The political changes in Europe meant that those nations and their relationships with the rest of the world would be directed by a broader range of groups than in the past.

Review Questions

1. To what extent were the American colonists influenced by their position in the transatlantic economy? To what extent were they influenced by European ideas and political developments? How did their demands for liberty compare with the ideas of liberty championed during the French Revolution?

2. How was the Estates General transformed into the National Assembly? How does the *Declaration of the Rights of Man and Citizen* reflect the social and political values of the eighteenth-century Enlightenment? How were France and its government reorganized in the early years of the revolution? Why was the Civil Constitution of the Clergy a blunder?

3. Why did the revolution of 1792 occur? What were the causes of the Reign of Terror and what made it possible?

4. How did Napoleon rise to power? What were his major domestic achievements? Why did he decide to invade Russia? What were the major outlines of the peace settlement achieved by the Congress of Vienna?

5. What political changes took place in Latin America between 1804 and 1824? What were the main reasons for Creole discontent with Spanish rule? How were the movements to Latin American independence influenced by the American and French Revolutions? What factors made the Latin American Wars of Independence different from those two revolutions?

6. What intellectual and religious factors contributed to the rise of the antislavery movement? Why did slavery receive a new lease on life during the same years that the antislavery movement emerged?

Documents CD-ROM

1. Edmund Burke: From "Speech on Conciliation with America"

2. Thomas Paine: From *Common Sense*

3. John Adams: "Thoughts on Government"

4. "The Declaration of the Rights of Man and Citizen," 1789

5. Robespierre's Theory of Revolutionary Government, 1793

6. Edmund Burke: The Moral Imagination

26 EUROPE AND NORTH AMERICA 1815–1850: POLITICAL REFORM, ECONOMIC ADVANCE, AND SOCIAL UNREST

CHAPTER TOPICS

- ◆ Nationalism and Liberalism
- ◆ Efforts to Liberalize Early-Nineteenth-Century European Political Structures
- ◆ Testing the New American Republic

- ◆ Europe Moves Toward an Industrial Society
- ◆ 1848: Year of Revolutions

In World Perspective Early-Nineteenth-Century Europe and the United States

---

The decades immediately after the Congress of Vienna ushered in political and social departures throughout the transatlantic world. In Europe, the defeat of Napoleon and the Congress of Vienna had restored a conservative political and social order. But the conservatives regarded themselves as standing on the defensive against the forces of liberalism, nationalism, and popular sovereignty. New social forces were creating new sources of political discontent as industrialization began to expand and people from the countryside crowded into cities, seeking work in factories. The result was considerable social tension. By 1848, those tensions, enhanced by nationalistic stirrings, erupted as revolutions spread across much of the continent.

In Latin America, the newly independent states sought, often unsuccessfully, to organize stable political and economic structures. In the United States, Americans began to move in large numbers across the Appalachians, and an industrialized economy began to grow from New England to Delaware. At the same time, the plantation economy moved west across the lower South, where cotton became king and black slaves provided the labor. The dispute over slavery in the United States coincided with the first conflicts over industrial labor in Europe. Thus by the 1850s, the politics of both Europe and the United States stood sharply divided over the issues of labor and what it meant for laborers to be free.

Nationalism and Liberalism

The Emergence of Nationalism

Nationalism is based on the relatively modern concept that a nation is composed of people who are joined together by the bonds of common language, customs, culture, and history, and who, because of those bonds, should share the same government. That is to say, political and ethnic boundaries should coincide. This idea came into its own during the late eighteenth and early nineteenth centuries.

Opposition to the Vienna Settlement Nationalists opposed the principle upheld at the Congress of Vienna that legitimate monarchies or dynasties should provide the basis for political unity. Nationalists protested multinational states such as the Austrian or Russian Empires. They also objected to peoples of the same ethnic group, such as Germans and Italians, dwelling in political units smaller than that of the ethnic nation.

Creating Nations Nationalists actually created nations in the nineteenth century. During the first half of the century, nationalistically minded writers spread a nationalistic concept of the nation. Many were historians who chronicled a people's past or literary scholars who established a national literature by collecting and publishing earlier writings in the people's language. In effect, they gave a people a sense of their past and a literature of their own, which schoolteachers spread.

The language to be used in schools and government was a point of contention for nationalists. In France and Italy, official versions of the national language were imposed in the schools. In eastern Europe, nationalists attempted to resurrect the national language. Often these resurrected languages were virtually invented by scholars. This process led to far more linguistic uniformity within European nations than had existed before the nineteenth century. Proficiency in the official language became a path to advancement. A uniform language helped to persuade people who had not thought of themselves as constituting a nation that they were a nation.

Meaning of Nationhood Nationalists used a variety of arguments to express what they meant by nationhood. Some argued that gathering, for example, Italians into a unified Italy would promote economic and administrative efficiency. Others claimed that nations, like biological species, were distinct creations of God.

A significant difficulty for nationalism was, and is, determining which ethnic groups could be considered nations, with claims to territory and political autonomy. In theory, any of them could, but nationhood came to be associated with groups that were large enough to support an economy, that had a history of significant cultural association, that possessed a cultural elite that could nourish the national language, and that could conquer other peoples to protect their own independence. Many smaller ethnic groups claimed to fulfill these criteria but could not achieve either independence or recognition. They could and did, however, create unrest within the political units they inhabited. Such was the situation in Europe.

Regions of Nationalistic Pressure in Europe During the nineteenth century, nationalists challenged the political status quo in six major areas of Europe. Irish nationalists wanted independence or at least self-government from Britain. German nationalists sought political unity for all German-speaking peoples, challenging the multinational Austrian Empire and pitting Prussia and Austria against each other. Italian nationalists sought to unify the peninsula and drive out the Austrians. Polish nationalists struggled, primarily against Russia, to restore Poland as an independent nation. In eastern Europe, Hungarians, Czechs, Slovenes, and others sought either autonomy or formal recognition within the Austrian Empire. Finally, in the Balkans, national groups sought independence from Ottoman and Russian control. In each area, nationalist activity ebbed and flowed. The dominant governments often thought they needed only to repress the activity or ride it out. During the century, however, nationalists changed the map and political culture of Europe.

Early-Nineteenth-Century Liberalism

Politics European liberals derived their political ideas from the Enlightenment, the example of English liberties, and the French *Declaration of the Rights of Man and Citizen*. Liberals sought to establish a framework of legal equality, religious toleration, and freedom of the press, and to limit the arbitrary power of the government. They believed that the legitimacy of government emanated from the freely given consent of the governed expressed through elected parliaments. Most important, free government required that state or crown ministers be responsible to the representatives of the nation rather than to the monarch.

These goals were limited. The people who espoused them tended to be those who were excluded from the existing political processes but whose wealth and education made them believe such exclusion was unjustified. Liberals were often academics, members of the learned professions, and people involved in commerce and manufacturing. They were products of the career open to talent. The existing monarchical and aristocratic regimes often failed to recognize their status and interests.

European liberals were not democrats. They despised the lower classes. Liberals transformed the eighteenth-century concept of aristocratic liberty into a new concept of privilege based on wealth and property. By the mid-century, this meant that throughout Europe, liberals had separated themselves from the working class. In the first half of the nineteenth century, political liberals generally did not support political rights for women, but liberal political principles provided women with strong arguments to do so.

Economics The economic goals of the liberals also furthered their separation from the working class. Here, the Enlightenment and the economic thought deriving from Adam Smith set the pattern. The landed and commercial middle class wanted to be able to manufacture and sell goods freely. They thus favored the removal of barriers to trade and, from the 1830s onward, the construction of railways as well.

European economic liberals opposed the old paternalistic legislation that established wages and labor practices by governments or guilds. Labor was simply a commodity to be bought and sold freely. Liberals sought an economic structure in which people were free to use their talents and property to enrich themselves. The liberals contended that this would lead to more goods and services for everyone at lower prices.

The economic goals of European liberals found many followers outside Europe among groups who favored the expansion of free trade, new transport systems, and a free market in labor. In the United States, people of this outlook often attacked slavery as inefficient and paternalistic. In Latin America, political liberals sought to remove paternalistic legislation that had protected Native Americans under Spanish rule.

The idea of the career open to talent could be applied to suppressed national groups who were not permitted to realize their cultural or political potential. The efficient government and administration required by commerce and industry would mean replacing the small German and Italian states with larger political units. Moreover, nationalist groups could gain the sympathy of liberals by espousing representative government and political liberty.

Efforts to Liberalize Early-Nineteenth-Century European Political Structures

Russia: The Decembrist Revolt and Nicholas I

In the process of driving Napoleon's army across Europe, officers in the Russian army were introduced to the ideas of the French Revolution and the Enlightenment. They realized how backward Russia was. Groups within the officer corps then formed small, secret societies to affect a change in the government of Russia through a coup d'état.

In late November 1825, Tsar Alexander I suddenly died without a direct heir. His brother Constantine stood next in line to the throne. However, Constantine, who was the commander of Russian forces in Poland, had renounced any claim to be tsar, and Alexander had secretly named his younger brother, Nicholas (r. 1825–1855), as the new tsar. Once Alexander was dead, the legality of the succession became uncertain. Constantine acknowledged Nicholas as tsar, and Nicholas acknowledged Constantine. For about three weeks, Russia had no ruler. Then, in early December, the army command reported to Nicholas that a conspiracy existed among certain officers. Able to wait no longer, Nicholas had himself declared tsar.

On December 26, 1825, the army was to take the oath of allegiance to Nicholas, who was regarded as more conservative than Constantine. Nearly all of the regiments did so. But one regiment, whose chief officers, surprisingly, were not secret society members, marched into the Senate Square in Saint Petersburg and refused to swear allegiance. They called for Constantine and a constitution. Attempts to settle the situation peacefully failed, and Nicholas ordered the cavalry and artillery to attack the insurgents. Five plotters were executed and over 100 other officers exiled to Siberia.

Liberalism in Russia was crushed. Nicholas I also became the policeman of Europe, ever ready to provide troops to suppress liberal and nationalist movements.

Revolution in France (1830)

In 1824, Louis XVIII (r. 1814–1824), the Bourbon restored to the throne by the Congress of Vienna, was succeeded by his brother, Charles X (r. 1824–1830), who considered himself king by divine right. Charles favored the aristocracy and the Roman Catholic Church. In 1830, his ultraroyalist ministry lost the elections to the liberals. Instead of attempting to accommodate the new Chamber of Deputies, the king and his ministers decided on a royalist seizure of power. On July 25, 1830, Charles issued the Four Ordinances, which restricted freedom of the press, dissolved the new Chamber of Deputies, and called for new elections under a franchise restricted to the wealthiest people in the country.

Liberal newspapers immediately called on the nation to resist. The laboring populace of Paris, burdened since 1827 by an economic downturn, took to the streets, and over 1,800 people died during the ensuing battles. On August 2, Charles X abdicated and left France for exile in England. The liberals in the Chamber of Deputies proclaimed Louis Philippe (r. 1830–1848) the head of the liberal branch of the royal family, the new monarch. Under what became known as the July Monarchy, Louis Philippe was called the king of the French rather than of France and became a constitutional monarch. The revolutionary tricolor replaced the white flag of the Bourbons. Catholicism was recognized only as the religion of the majority. Censorship was abolished. The franchise, though still restricted, was extended.

Socially, however, the Revolution of 1830 proved conservative. The landed oligarchy retained its influence. Money became the path to power. There was much corruption. The liberal monarchy displayed scant sympathy for the lower classes.

The Great Reform Bill in Britain (1832)

The passage of the Great Reform Bill in Britain, which became law in 1832, was the result of compromise between the forces of conservatism and reform. English determination to maintain the union with Ireland caused the first step in the reform process. After the Act of Union in 1800 between England and Ireland, only Protestant Irishmen could be elected to represent overwhelmingly Catholic Ireland.

During the 1820s, under the leadership of Daniel O'Connell (1775–1847), Irish nationalists agitated for legal rights for Roman Catholics. In 1828, O'Connell was elected to Parliament but could not legally take his seat. The British ministry of the duke of Wellington (1769–1852) realized that civil war might erupt. In 1829, Wellington and Robert Peel (1788–1850) steered the Catholic Emancipation Act through Parliament. Roman Catholics could now become members of Parliament. In 1830, the Wellington ministry fell and King William IV (r. 1830–1837) turned to the Whigs under Earl Grey (1764–1845) to form a government.

The Whig ministry soon presented the House of Commons with a major reform bill that had two broad goals: to replace "rotten" boroughs, which had few voters, with representatives for the unrepresented manufacturing districts and cities, and to increase the number of voters in England and Wales. After considerable agitation, the measure became law in 1832.

The Great Reform Bill was not a democratic measure. The electorate increased by almost 50 percent, but the basis of voting remained a property qualification. New urban boroughs gave the growing cities a voice in the House of Commons. Yet for every new urban electoral district, a new rural district was also drawn, which the aristocracy were expected to dominate.

Testing the New American Republic

Toward Sectional Conflict

While Western Europe moved slowly toward political liberalism, the United States was continuing its republican political experiment. However, sectional tensions had arisen, especially over black slavery in the southern states. By 1820, the number of slave and free states was evenly divided. That year, Missouri was admitted as a slave state and Maine as a free one. It was also decided that no slave states would be carved out of land north of the southern border of Missouri. For the time being, this compromise ended congressional debate over slavery. Nonetheless, the economies of the North and South were rapidly diverging.

Northern Economic Development   Family farms, free labor, commerce, and industrialization in textiles characterized the economy of the northern states. The political spokesmen for the North tended to favor tariffs to protect their young industries from cheaper foreign competition. In favoring of tariffs, many Americans whose political views otherwise often resembled European liberals differed from their European counterparts.

The North was the site of the earliest textile factories in the United States. Much of the early industrialization of the United States depended on technological transfers from Britain and Europe. By the second decade of the nineteenth century, there were hundreds of cotton factories in the North.

Throughout the North, a labor force developed that was divided along class lines. There were some early attempts at labor unions in crafts such as printing, hat making, and tailoring, and strikes occurred as owners introduced more efficient machinery or lowered wages during economic downturns. Nonetheless, virtually all of these early labor organizations collapsed during major recessions when workers sought scarce jobs despite low wages. American businessmen, like their European counterparts, opposed unionization.

During the second quarter of the century, innovations in transportation led to the fuller integration of different parts of the northern economy. By the late 1840s, railways linked the Northeast and the West. Midwest agricultural products were sold in the Northeast and exported from northern ports. Few major lines ran north and south, so former ties between the sections based on the rivers weakened. The railways also aided the development of the northern coal and iron industries. The expansion of railways at mid-century caused new sectional tensions, as it became clear the railways could open for settlement vast territories and thus could also open debate about the future of slavery. That prospect sharpened the sectional debate and led to civil war.

The North also possessed vast farming resources. Thousands of small farms raised corn, wheat, and livestock that could be shipped on the expanding transportation system. In this sense, much of the northern economy was as rural and agricultural as the southern. What most distinguished the two regions was their differing labor systems. Free wage labor characterized the northern economy and its expansion. Slavery characterized the southern economy, which could expand only if slavery were allowed to expand.

The Southern Economy   The economy of the South was dependent on cotton and slavery. In those respects, the southern economy resembled those of Latin American countries that were based on exporting a single crop or natural resource and on slave labor. The South had to export goods, primarily raw cotton, either to the North or to Europe—primarily to Great Britain—to maintain its standard of living.

Cotton was king. The invention of the cotton gin by Eli Whitney (1765–1825) in 1793 made cotton cultivation much more profitable. The industrial revolution in textiles kept cotton prices high. The South profited from growing the cotton, New England from shipping it, and other parts of the North from supplying the manufacturing needs of the South. The South had little incentive to diversify its agriculture.

Slavery   Slavery was abolished in the North by the early nineteenth century largely in response to the egalitarian values of the American Revolution. But in the South, the

Daniel A. Payne Denounces American Slavery

Daniel A. Payne was an African American who became an ordained Lutheran minister. He delivered this speech in June 1839, on the occasion of his ordination. Though born in Charleston, South Carolina, he was the son of free African Americans. As a young man he had opened a school in that state to educate African-American children. He had to abandon this effort after the legislature passed a law imposing fines for the teaching of either free or enslaved African Americans to read and write. Later he became president of Wilberforce University in Xenia, Ohio, dedicated to the education of African Americans.

On what grounds does Payne condemn slavery? What are the examples of moral brutalization that Payne associates with slavery? How does Payne bring religious arguments against the evils of slavery?

. . . I am opposed to slavery, not because it enslaves the black man, but because it enslaves *man*. And were all the slaveholders in this land men of color, and the slaves white men, I would be as thorough and uncompromising an abolitionist as I now am; for whatever and whenever I may see a being in the form of a man, enslaved by his fellow man, without respect to his complexion, I shall lift up my voice to please his cause, against all the claims of his proud oppressor; and I shall do it not merely from the sympathy which man feels towards suffering man, but because *God, the living God*, whom I dare not disobey, has commanded me to open my mouth for the dumb, and to plead the cause of the oppressed.

Slavery brutalizes man. . . . This being God created but a little lower than the angels, and crowned him with glory and honor; but slavery hurls him down from his elevated position, to the level of brutes, strikes this crown of glory from his head and fastens upon his neck the galling yoke, and compels him to labor like an ox, through summer's sun and winter's snow, without remuneration. Does a man take the calf from the cow and sell it to the butcher? So slavery tears the child from the arms of the reluctant mother, and barters it to the soul trader for a young colt, or

some other commodity! Does the bird catcher tear away the dove from his mate? So slavery separates the groaning husband from the embraces of his distracted and weeping wife! . . . The very moment that a man conceives the diabolic design of enslaving his brother's body, that very moment does he also conceive the still more heinous design of fettering his will, for well does he know that in order to make his dominion supreme over the body, he must fetter the living spring of all its motions. Hence, the first lesson the slave is taught is to yield his will unreservedly and exclusively to the dictates of his master. And if a slave desire to educate himself or his children, in obedience to the dictates of reason or the laws of God, he does not, he cannot do it without the consent of his master. . . .

In view of the moral agency of man, God hath most wisely and graciously given him a code of laws, and certain positive percepts, to control and regulate moral actions. This code of laws, and these positive percepts, with the divine influence which they are naturally calculated to exert on the mind of man, constitutes his moral government. . . .

Now, slavery nullifies these laws and percepts—weakens and destroys their influence over the human mind, and hinders men from yielding universal and entire obedience to them; therefore slavery subverts the moral government of God. This is the climax of the sin of slavery. . . .

. . . Slavery never legislates for the religious instruction of slaves, but, on the contrary, legislates to perpetuate their ignorance; and there are laws this very moment in the statute books of South Carolina and other states, prohibiting the religious instruction of slaves. . . .

In a word, slavery tramples the laws of the living God under its unhallowed feet—weakens and destroys the influence which those laws are calculated to exert over the mind of man, and constrains the oppressed to blaspheme the name of the Almighty.

Speech originally printed in the *Lutheran Herald and Journal of the Fort Plain, N. Y., Franckean Synod*, Vol. 1, No 15 (August 1, 1839) as reprinted in Philip S. Foner, ed., *The Voice of Black America: Major Speeches by Negroes in the United States, 1797–1971.* Copyright © 1972, New York: Simon & Schuster, pp. 67–71.

expansion of the cotton empire gave slavery a new lease on life. Although most southern families never owned slaves and most slave owners possessed a few slaves, slavery survived for many reasons: It was economically viable, and no one could devise a way acceptable to white southerners to abolish it. The strong commitment to the protection of private property throughout American society included slaves. But perhaps the most basic reason for the

endurance of slavery was racist thinking that saw blacks as inferior to whites.

All American slaves were nonwhite, the descendants of Africans who had been captured and shipped to the United States (see Chapter 19). Despite much miscegenation among Africans and their white slaveowners and Native Americans, slave codes defined as black virtually anyone who had African antecedents. Slaves were regarded as chattel property: They could be disposed of like any other piece of property. They had no recourse to law or constitutional protections. Whipping and beating were permitted. Slaves lived with no serious protection from the law or legal authorities.

Their standard of living was poor. Slaves suffered from diseases associated with poor nutrition, sanitation, and housing. Slaves worked primarily in the fields, where they cultivated cotton, rice, tobacco, or corn. They were usually organized into work gangs supervised by white overseers. During planting or harvest seasons, labor would persist from sunrise to sunset. Children would work in the fields as helpers. Older or more privileged slaves might work in the house, cleaning, cooking, or taking care of children.

The slave communities helped to preserve the family life and inner personalities of the slaves. Some African culture persisted in the slave communities. African legends were passed on orally. Religion was also important, and slaves often combined elements of African religion with evangelical Protestantism.

Yet despite these efforts to preserve a sense of community and family, marriages and family lives of slaves had no legal recognition. White masters often sexually exploited black slave women. Families could be, and were, separated by sale or after an owner's death.

The Abolitionist Movement

During the 1830s, a militant antislavery movement emerged in the North. Abolitionists such as William Lloyd Garrison condemned the Union and the Constitution as structures that perpetuated slavery. Former slaves, such as Frederick Douglas and Sojourner Truth, and freeborn black Americans also joined the cause. Abolitionism profited from the general climate of reform at the time. From the 1820s onward, movements for temperance reform, women's rights, education improvement, and the like attracted many supporters. These movements had persuaded many people that the life of the nation needed to be changed.

The antislavery movement gained new adherents during the 1840s. Victory in the Mexican War opened debate on the extension of slavery into the huge new territory it created. Southerners feared that the changing climate of national debate and the opening of territories where slavery might be prohibited would give the South a minority status and thus eventually overturn its political and social culture. The Compromise of 1850 restored political stability and reassured the South. But many northerners came to believe that the compromise only demonstrated the strength of a slave power conspiracy in Washington.

Europe Moves Toward an Industrial Society

As the United States expanded across North America and debated slavery, Europe headed toward a more fully industrial society. However, what characterized the second quarter of the century was less the triumph of industrialism than the final gasps of those economic groups that opposed it and were displaced by it. Intellectually, the period saw the formulation of the major creeds supporting and criticizing the new society.

Proletarianization of Factory Workers and Urban Artisans

In much of northern Europe, both artisans and factory workers underwent *proletarianization*. This term indicates the entry of workers into a wage economy and their loss of ownership of the means of production, such as tools and equipment, and of control over their trades. The process occurred wherever the factory system arose. The factory owner provided the financial capital to construct the factory, purchase machinery, and secure raw materials. The factory workers contributed their labor for a wage and submitted to factory discipline, which meant that work conditions became determined by the operation of the machines. Factory workers had no direct say over the quality of the product or its price.

Urban artisans in the nineteenth century experienced proletarianization more slowly than factory workers, and machinery had little to do with the process. It became difficult for artisans to exercise corporate or guild direction and control over their trades. The French Revolution had outlawed such organizations in France. Liberals disapproved of labor and guild organizations and attempted to ban them.

Other destructive forces were also at work. The masters often found themselves under increased competitive pressure from larger, more heavily capitalized establishments or from the introduction of machine production into a craft-dominated industry. In many workshops, masters began to follow a practice whereby goods such as shoes, clothing, and furniture were produced in standard sizes and styles rather than for individual customers. This practice increased the division of labor in the workshop. Masters also attempted to increase production and reduce their costs for piecework. Migrants from the countryside or small towns into the cities were often willing to work for lower wages or under less favorable and protected conditions than traditional artisans. The dilution of skills and lower wages, caused not by machinery but by changes in the organization of artisan production, made it much more difficult for urban journeymen to become masters with their own workshops. Increasingly, these artisans became lifetime wage laborers whose skills were simply bought and sold in the marketplace.

Family Structures and the Industrial Revolution

It is more difficult to generalize about European family structure in the age of early industrialism than under the Old Regime. Yet the process of factory expansion, proletarianization, and growth of commercial and service sectors related to industrialism did change the structures of much family life and gender roles within families.

The adoption of new machinery and factory production did not destroy the working-class family. In the domestic system of the family economy, parents and children had worked in textile production as a family unit. Their home and economic lives were largely the same. In the early factories, the father was permitted to employ his wife and children as his assistants. Education and discipline were not removed from the workplace or from the family.

A major shift in this family and factory structure began in the mid-1820s in England and was more or less completed by the mid-1830s. The newer machines required fewer skilled operators but more unskilled attendants. Machine tending became the work of unmarried women and children. Factory wages for skilled adult males, however, became sufficiently high to allow some fathers to remove their children from the factory and to send them to school. The children who were now working in the factories as assistants were often the children of the economically depressed handloom weavers. Wives of the skilled operatives tended not to work in the factories. The links of the family in the British textile factory that had existed for over a quarter century disappeared.

The English Factory Act of 1833, passed to protect children by limiting their workday to eight hours and requiring two hours of education paid for by the factory owner, further divided work and home life. The workday for adult males remained twelve hours, but children often worked in relays of four or six hours, so the parental link was thoroughly broken. The education requirement began the process of removing nurturing and training from the home and family and setting them into a school, where a teacher rather than the parents was in charge of education.

After this act was passed, many of the working-class demands for shorter workdays for adults related to the desire of adults to spend more hours with their children. In 1847, Parliament mandated a ten-hour day. This allowed parents and children more time together as a domestic unit because their relationship as a work or production unit had ceased wherever the factory system prevailed. By the middle of the 1840s, for industrial workers the roles of men as breadwinners, fathers, and husbands had become distinct in the British textile industry. With the spread of the factory system, the European family became the chief unit of consumption rather than the chief unit of both production and consumption.

Women in the Early Industrial Revolution

The industrial economy ultimately produced an immense impact on the home and the family life of women. First, it took virtually all productive work out of the home and allowed many families to live on the wages of the male spouse alone. That transformation prepared the way for a new concept of gender-determined roles in domestic life. Women came to be associated with domestic duties such as housekeeping and child rearing. Men came to be associated with breadwinning. Children were reared to match these patterns. Previously, this domestic division of labor had prevailed only among the middle and gentry classes. During the nineteenth century, it came to characterize the working class as well. Second, industrialization allowed many young women to earn enough money to marry or support themselves. Third, industrialism, although fostering more employment for women, lowered the skills required of them.

As textile production became increasingly automated in the nineteenth century, textile factories required fewer skilled workers and more unskilled attendants. To fill these unskilled positions, factory owners turned increasingly to unmarried women and widows, who worked for lower wages than men and were less likely to form labor organizations.

[Bildarchiv Preussischer Kulturbesitz]

Because the early Industrial Revolution had begun in textile production, women and their labor were deeply involved from the start. When production moved into factories and involved large machines, however, women tended to be displaced by men. The higher wages for male factory workers allowed many married women to stop working or to work only to supplement their husbands' wages. Factory owners also disliked employing married women because of the likelihood of pregnancy, the influence of husbands, and the duties of child rearing.

In Britain and elsewhere by mid-century, industrial factory work accounted for less than half of all employment for women. The largest group of employed women in France continued to work on the land. In England they were domestic servants. Domestic industries, such as lace, glove, and garment making and other kinds of needlework, employed many women. Their conditions of labor were harsh. Generally work done by women commanded low wages and involved low skills. They had virtually no way to protect themselves from exploitation.

One of the most serious problems facing working women was the uncertainty of employment. Because they virtually always did the least skilled jobs, their employment was never secure. This was one reason working-class women feared they might have to turn to prostitution. On the other hand, movement to cities and entrance into the wage economy also gave women wider opportunities for marriage. Marriage also generally meant that a woman could live on her husband's earnings. That arrangement might improve her situation, but if the husband became ill, died, or deserted her, she would have to reenter the market for unskilled labor at an advanced age.

Nonetheless, many of the traditional practices associated with the family economy survived into the industrial era. As a young woman came of age, both family needs and her desire to marry still directed what she would do with her life. The most likely early occupation for a young woman was domestic service. As in the past, she would attempt to earn enough to give herself a dowry so that she might marry and establish her own household. If she became a factory worker, she would probably live in a supervised dormitory. The life of young women in the cities seems to have been more precarious than it had been earlier. There seem to have been fewer family and community ties. There were also perhaps more available young men. In any case, illegitimate births increased. Fewer women who became pregnant before marriage found the father willing to marry them.

Marriage in the wage industrial economy was less an economic partnership: The husband might be able to support the entire family. The wage economy and the industrialization separating workplace and home made it difficult for women to combine domestic duties with work. When married women worked, it was usually not in industry. More often

than not, children rather than the wife went to work, which may help explain the increase of fertility within marriages, since children in the wage economy tended to be an economic asset. Married women worked outside the home only when family needs required them to.

Within the home, the domestic duties of working-class women were essential for the family wage economy. Homemaking came to the fore when a life at home had to be organized that was separate from the place of work. Wives were concerned with food and cooking, but they often also managed the family's finances. The role of the mother expanded when the children still living at home became wage earners. She then provided home support for her entire wage-earning family. The longer period of home life of working children may also have strengthened the affection between them and their mothers.

Marxist Critique of the Industrial Order

The 1840s, according to Karl Marx, produced the most influential critique of the new industrial order. His analysis was adopted by the leading socialist political party in Germany, which in turn influenced other European socialist parties, including a small group of exiled Russian socialists led by V. I. Lenin. Marx (1818–1883) was born in the Rhineland of Jewish middle-class parents. He became deeply involved in radical politics until the German authorities drove him, after 1849, into exile in London.

In 1844, Marx met Friedrich Engels (1820–1895), whose father owned a textile factory in Manchester, England. The two men became fast friends. Late in 1847, they were asked to write a pamphlet for a secret communist league. *The Communist Manifesto*, published in German, appeared in 1848. The name *communist* was adopted because it was much more radical than *socialist*. *Communism* implied the outright abolition of private property rather than a less extensive rearrangement of society. The *Manifesto* would in time become the most influential political document of modern European history.

In *The Communist Manifesto*, Marx and Engels contended that human history must be understood rationally and as a whole. According to their analysis, history is the record of humankind's coming to grips with physical nature to produce the goods necessary for survival. That basic productive process determines the structures, values, and ideas of a society. Historically, the organization of the means of production has always involved conflict between the classes who owned and controlled the means of production and those classes who worked for them. That necessary conflict has provided the engine for historical development; it is not an accidental byproduct of mismanagement or bad intentions. Only a radical transformation, not piecemeal reforms, can eliminate the social and economic evils inherent in the structures of production. Such a revolution will occur as the inevitable outcome of capitalism.

In Marx's and Engels's eyes, during the nineteenth century the class conflict had become a struggle between the bourgeoisie and the proletariat. Capitalism ensured the sharpening of the struggle. Capitalist production and competition would increase the size of the unpropertied proletariat. Large-scale mechanical production crushed both traditional and smaller industrial producers into the ranks of the proletariat. As the business structures grew larger, smaller middle-class units would be squeezed out. Competition among the few remaining gigantic concerns would lead to intense suffering by the proletariat, who would foment revolution and overthrow the remaining owners of the means of production. The workers would organize the means of production through a dictatorship of the proletariat, which would eventually give way to a propertyless and classless communist society.

This proletarian revolution was inevitable, according to Marx and Engels. Capitalism required competition and consolidation. Unlike earlier class conflicts, the struggle between the capitalistic bourgeoisie and the industrial proletariat would culminate in a new society that would be free of class conflict. The victorious proletariat, by its very nature, they contended, could not be a new oppressor class. The victory of the proletariat over the bourgeoisie represented the culmination of human history. For the first time, one group of people would not be oppressing another.

Capitalism did not collapse as Marx predicted, nor did the middle class ever become proletarianized. Rather, more and more people came to benefit from the industrial system. Nonetheless, within a generation Marxism had captured the imagination of many socialists and much of the working class. Its doctrines were allegedly based on hard economic fact. This much-proclaimed scientific aspect of Marxism helped the ideology, as science became more influential. Marx had made the ultimate victory of socialism seem certain. His works also suggested that the path to socialism lay with revolution rather than reform. As Marxist thought permeated the international socialist movement, it would provide the ideological basis for some of the most momentous and repressive political movements in the history of the modern world.

1848: Year of Revolutions

In 1848, a series of liberal and nationalistic upheavals spread across the Continent. No single factor caused this revolutionary ground swell, but similar conditions existed in several countries: food shortages due to poor harvests, economic recession, and widespread unemployment. However, the dynamic for change in 1848 originated with the political liberals, who were generally middle class. Throughout the Con-

The Revolutionary Crisis of 1848–1851	
1848	
February 22–24	Revolution in Paris forces the abdication of Louis Philippe
February 26	National workshops established in Paris
March 3	Kossuth attacks Habsburg domination of Hungary
March 13	Revolution in Vienna
	Revolution in Berlin
March 18	Frederick William IV of Prussia promises a constitution
	Revolution in Milan
March 22	Piedmont declares war on Austria
April 23	Election of French National Assembly
May 18	Frankfurt Assembly gathers to prepare a German constitution
June 17	Czech revolution in Prague is suppressed
June 23–26	Workers' insurrection in Paris is suppressed
July 24	Austria defeats Piedmont
November 25	Pius IX flees Rome
December 2	Franz Joseph becomes emperor of Austria
December 10	Louis Napoleon elected president of the second French Republic
1849	
January 5	Austrian troops occupy Budapest
February 2	Roman Republic is proclaimed
March 12	War resumes between Piedmont and Austria
March 23	Piedmont is defeated; Charles Albert abdicates in favor of Victor Emmanuel II
April 21	Frederick William IV of Prussia rejects crown offered by Frankfurt Parliament
June 18	Frankfurt Parliament dispersed by troops
July 3	French troops overthrow Roman Republic
1851	
December 2	Coup d'état of Louis Napoleon

tinent, liberals were pushing for representative governments, civil liberty, and unregulated economic life.

To put additional pressure on their governments, the liberals began to appeal for the support of the urban working classes, even though the two groups had different goals. The working classes sought improved employment and better working conditions rather than political reform for its own sake. The liberals refused to follow political revolution with social reform and thus isolated themselves from their working-class allies. Once separated from potential mass support, the liberal revolutions became easy prey to the armies of reactionary governments. As a result, the revolutions of 1848 failed to establish genuinely liberal or national states.

France: The Second Republic and Louis Napoleon

Early in 1848, liberal political opponents of Louis Philippe organized political banquets to criticize the regime. On February 21, 1848, the government forbade further banquets. Fighting soon occurred between the citizenry and the municipal guards in Paris. On February 24, Louis Philippe abdicated and fled to England.

The liberal opposition organized a provisional government. Under pressure by working-class groups seeking social as well as political revolution, the provisional government organized national workshops to provide work and relief for unemployed workers. The election held on April 23 produced a National Assembly dominated by moderates and conservatives who considered the expensive national workshops socialistic. By late June, barricades appeared in Paris and more than 3,000 people died in street fighting.

The so-called June Days confirmed the political predominance of conservative property owners in French life. Their search for social order led, in 1848, to the election to the presidency of Louis Napoleon Bonaparte (1808–1873), a nephew of the great emperor. His election doomed the Second Republic. For three years he quarreled with the National Assembly; then, on December 2, 1851, he seized power in a military coup. In a plebiscite, over 7.5 million voters supported his actions, with only 640,000 disapproving. In December 1852, another plebiscite, made France an empire. Louis Napoleon became Emperor Napoleon III (r. 1852–1870) in deference to the first Napoleon's deceased young son.

The Habsburg Empire: Nationalism Resisted

The events of February 1848 in Paris reverberated throughout the Habsburg domains. In 1848, the regime confronted rebellions in Vienna, Prague, Hungary, and northern Italy.

The Habsburg troubles commenced on March 3, 1848, when Louis Kossuth (1802–1894), a Magyar nationalist, attacked Austrian domination of Hungary. Shortly thereafter, student riots broke out in Vienna. After the army failed to restore order, Metternich fled the country. In December, Emperor Ferdinand (r. 1835–1848) abdicated in favor of his nephew Franz Joseph (1848–1916).

The Habsburg government most feared an uprising of the serfs. After the Vienna riots, the government emancipated the serfs in most of Austria. The Hungarian Diet also abolished serfdom. This smothered the most serious threat to order.

In Hungary and Prague, the Habsburg government confronted revolution by making concessions that it later repudiated after Habsburg forces suppressed the revolution. In Italy, nationalists drove the Austrians from Milan in March 1848. King Charles Albert of Piedmont (r. 1831–1849) supported them, but by July the Habsburg army had defeated Piedmont and suppressed the revolution. The Habsburg government had survived its gravest internal challenge as a result of the divisions among its enemies and its willingness to use force.

Italy: Unification Defeated

The defeat of Piedmont disappointed Italian nationalists who had hoped to unify the peninsula. In November 1848, political disturbances erupted in Rome, and Pope Pius IX (1846–1878) fled to Naples. In February 1849, radicals proclaimed the Roman Republic. In March, Charles Albert renewed the patriotic war against Austria. Piedmont was quickly defeated and Charles Albert abdicated in favor of his son Victor Emmanuel II (r. 1849–1878). In early June, French troops overthrew the Roman Republic and restored the pope; French troops remained in Rome until 1870 to protect the pope.

Germany: Liberalism Frustrated

In Germany, revolution occurred in Prussia in March 1848. Frederick William IV (r. 1840–1861) had to call a constituent assembly to write a constitution and to appoint a liberal cabinet. In April 1849, he dissolved the assembly and proclaimed his own conservative constitution.

On May 18, 1848, representatives from all the German states gathered in Frankfurt to write a moderately liberal constitution. However, it lost the support of German workers and artisans by refusing to restore the economic protection once afforded by the guilds.

The Frankfurt Parliament also floundered over whether to include Austria in a united Germany. Austria, however, rejected the whole notion of German unification, which raised too many nationality problems within the Habsburg domains. So the Frankfurt Parliament looked to Prussian leadership. However, Frederick William IV refused to accept the crown of a united Germany from the liberal parliament. On his refusal in the spring of 1849, the Frankfurt Parliament began to dissolve. Not long afterward, troops dispersed the members. German liberalism never recovered from the failures of the Frankfurt Parliament.

The turmoil of 1848 through 1850 ended the era of liberal revolution that had begun in 1789. Liberals and nationalists had discovered that rational argument and small insurrections would not help them achieve their goals. The working class also adopted new tactics and organization. In the future, workers would turn to trade unions and political parties to achieve their goals. Finally, after 1848, the political initiative in Europe passed for a time to conservative political groups.

IN WORLD PERSPECTIVE

Early-Nineteenth-Century Europe and the United States

The first half of the nineteenth century witnessed three major developments in Europe that would affect the entire world. First, the modern industrial economy permanently established itself. This gave Europeans a disproportionate economic and military influence throughout the world. Europe also experienced social dislocation that foreshadowed the pressures on family and community that would arise elsewhere in the world when agricultural economies made the transition to industrialized ones.

Second, Europeans developed political ideologies that eventually spread over most of the globe. The ideas associated with liberalism would come to be used against traditional forms of government elsewhere in the world. In the non-European world, nationalism would display itself in the twentieth century against European colonial rule. Marxism would spread around the world during the twentieth century as poor and underdeveloped nations sought to reject the dominance of wealthy, industrialized ones.

Third, the defeat of liberal political forces in 1848 and the triumph of conservative powers influenced the modernization of Japan. When Japan emerged from its long self-imposed isolation after the Meiji Restoration, its new leaders looked to European examples of successful modern nations and most clearly copied the conservative, militaristic Germany that emerged after the defeat of the liberals of 1848.

During this same era, the United States continued to pursue the most politically advanced democratic experiment of any nation in the world. It saw itself as an arena where reform and progress could fully manifest themselves. Part of that drive to reform led to its debate over slavery, which would ultimately result in civil war. Its economy prospered in a manner that differed from its neighbors in Latin America. That prosperity, along with its democratic politics, attracted immigrants from Europe, an attraction that would grow stronger in the second half of the century.

Review Questions ———

1. Define nationalism. What were the goals of nationalists? What were the difficulties they confronted in realizing those goals? Why was nationalism a special threat to the Austrian Empire?

2. What were the tenets of liberalism? Who were the liberals and how did liberalism affect the political developments of the early nineteenth century? What relationship does liberalism have to nationalism?

3. Why did France experience political change by revolution in 1830 and England achieve political change through parliamentary reform in 1832?

4. What economic differences between the American North and South gave rise to sectional conflict? Why was slavery the core issue in that conflict?

5. What changes did industrialism make in society? Why were the years covered in this chapter so difficult for artisans? What does "the proletarianization of workers" mean?

6. How did the industrial economy change the working-class family? What roles and duties did various family members assume? How did the role of women change in the new industrial era?

7. What factors, old and new, led to the outbreak of revolutions in 1848? Why did these revolutions fail throughout Europe?

Documents CD-ROM

1. Thomas MacAulay: "A Radical War Song"

2. Alexis de Tocqueville: The New Social Morality

3. Women Miners in the English Coal Pits

4. Thomas Carlyle: From "Signs of the Times"

5. Karl Marx and Friedrich Engels, *The Communist Manifesto*

INTO THE
MODERN WORLD

Between about 1850 and 1945, Europe achieved an unprecedented measure of political, economic, and military power. The century may thus be regarded as the European era of world history. But by 1945 much of Europe lay in ruins. Soon the United States and the Soviet Union emerged as superpowers with whom no European state could compete. Furthermore, Asia, Africa, and Latin America thrust off colonial status. The rise and decline of European dominance fostered violence and exploitation all over the world.

Late-nineteenth-century European civilization dominated the globe because of its economic and technological base. Europeans and Americans possessed unrivaled productive capacity. Their banks controlled vast amounts of capital. Their military technology, especially their navies, allowed them to back up economic power with armed force. Other centers of world civilization were left vulnerable by political decay and their less advanced technology.

The one exception was Japan, which succeeded in imitating the technological and political structures of Europe.

Two major developments emerged during the century of European dominance. First, the entire globe became economically and politically interdependent. Second, peoples who were subjected to the dominance of Europe and North America began to resist that dominance.

In 1900, many Europeans and Americans regarded their position of dominance as permanent. They did not grasp the special circumstances that had allowed them to achieve their power and the resentment that it fostered. Nor did they realize that modern technology and ideas would transform other parts of the world no less than they had Europe and America.

1850–1899

German Empire proclaimed (Bildarchiv Preussischer.
Original: Friedrichsruh, Bismark Museum)

1852–1870 The Second French Empire, under
Napoleon III
1854–1856 The Crimean War
1861 Italy unified
1861 Emancipation of Russian serfs
1866 Austro-Prussian War; creation of Dual
Monarchy of Austria-Hungary in 1867
1870–1871 Franco-Prussian War; German Empire
proclaimed in 1871
1873 Three Emperors League
1882 Triple Alliance
1890 Bismarck dismissed by Kaiser Wilhelm II

1857–1858 Sepoy Rebellion: India placed directly
under the authority of the British government
in 1858
1869 Suez Canal completed; 1875, British
purchase controlling interest
1869–1948 Mohandas (Mahatma) Gandhi
1876–1949 Muhammad Ali Jinnah, "founder
of Pakistan"
1882 English occupation of Egypt
1886 India National Congress formed
1889–1964 Jawaharlal Nehru
1899 Ottoman sultan Abdulhamid II grants
concession to Kaiser Wilhelm II to extend
railway to Baghdad ("Berlin-to-Baghdad"
Railway)

1900–1914

1902 Entente Cordiale
1905 January 22, "Bloody Sunday"
1905 Revolution in Russia
1914 War begins in Europe

1908 "Young Turk" Revolt

EAST ASIA	AFRICA	THE AMERICAS
1850–1873 Taiping and other rebellions	**1856–1884** King Mutasa of Buganda reigns	**1854** Kansas-Nebraska Act
1853–1854 Commodore Perry "opens" Japan to the West, ending seclusion policy	**1870** British protectorate in Zanzibar	**1856** Dred Scott Decision
1859 French seize Saigon	**1879–1880** Henry M. Stanley gains the Congo for Belgium	**1859** Raid on Harper's Ferry
1860s Establishment of treaty ports in China	**1880s** Mahdist revival and uprising in Sudan	**1860** Abraham Lincoln elected U.S. president
1864 French protectorate over Cambodia	**1880** French protectorate in Tunisia and the Ivory Coast	**1861–1865** U.S. Civil War
1868 Meiji Restoration in Japan	**1884–1885** International Conference in Berlin to prepare rules for further acquisition of African territory; the Congo free State declared	**1862–1867** French invasion of Mexico
1870s Civilization and Enlightenment movement in Japan	**1884** German Southwest Africa	**1863** Emancipation Proclamation in United States
1870s–1890s Self-Strengthening movement in China	**1885** British control Nigeria and British East Africa	**1865–1877** Reconstruction
1889 Meiji Constitution in Japan	**1894** French annex Dahomey	**1865–1870** Paraguayan War
1894–1895 Sino-Japanese War; Japan gets Taiwan as colony	**1899** German East Africa; British in Sudan	**1879–1880** Argentinian conquest of the desert
1898–1900 Boxer Rebellion in China	**1899–1902** Boer War	**1880s** Slavery eliminated in Cuba and Brazil
		1898 Spanish-American War

Abraham Lincoln (Library of Congress)

The empress dowager Tz'u-hsi, Manchu court
(Hutton Picture Library/Corbis)

EAST ASIA	AFRICA	THE AMERICAS
1904–1905 Russo-Japanese War	**1900** Nigeria a British crown colony	**1901** Theodore Roosevelt elected U.S. president
1910 Japan annexes Korea	**1907** Orange Free State and the Transvaal join with Natal and Cape Colony to form the Union of South Africa	**1910–1917** Mexican Revolution
1911 Republican Revolution begins in China; Ch'ing dynasty overthrown	**1911** Liberia becomes a virtual U.S. protectorate	**1912** Woodrow Wilson elected U.S. president
	1914 Ethiopia the only independent state in Africa	

27 POLITICAL CONSOLIDATION IN EUROPE AND NORTH AMERICA

CHAPTER TOPICS

- ◆ The Crimean War (1854–1856)
- ◆ Italian Unification
- ◆ German Unification
- ◆ France: The Third Republic
- ◆ The Habsburg Empire
- ◆ Russia: Emancipation and Revolutionary Stirrings

- ◆ Great Britain: Toward Democracy
- ◆ The United States: Civil War, Reconstruction, and Progressive Politics
- ◆ The Canadian Experience

In World Perspective European and North American Political Consolidation

---

Between 1850 and 1875, Europe and North America underwent political consolidation that strengthened the authority of central governments. In Europe, the defeat of the revolutions of 1848 entrenched conservative, authoritarian regimes except in Britain. Yet only twenty-five years later, conservative governments carried out many of the goals of early-nineteenth-century liberals and nationalists. At the end of this process, Britain, France, Italy, and Germany—but not the Habsburg Empire or Russia—had achieved considerable political stability.

The same quarter century witnessed similar political consolidation and centralization in North America. By 1861, the sectional conflict in the United States had erupted into civil war. That conflict led to new authority for the federal government and the abolition of slavery. During the same decade, Canada achieved self-government, and in both North American nations, the westward movement continued.

The various nations of the North Atlantic region became the most powerful political units in the world and would soon dominate much of the rest of the world.

The Crimean War (1854–1856)

As is so often true in history, war made change possible. In this case, a conflict disrupted the international balance that had prevailed in Europe since 1815 and unleashed forces that upset the political status quo.

The Crimean War (1854–1856), named after the Black Sea peninsula on which it was largely fought, originated from a long-standing rivalry between Russia and the Ottoman Empire. In 1853, Russia went to war against the Ottomans. The next year, France and Great Britain supported the Ottoman Empire to protect their interests in the eastern Mediterranean. In March 1856, a peace conference in Paris concluded a treaty unfavorable to Russia.

The Crimean War shattered the image of an invincible Russia that had prevailed since the Napoleonic wars. It also shattered the power of the Concert of Europe to deal with international relations on the Continent. The major European powers were no longer willing to cooperate. For the next twenty-five years, instability prevailed in European affairs.

Italian Unification

Italian nationalists had long wanted to unite the small principalities of the peninsula into one state, but could not agree on how to do it. Romantic republicans such as Giuseppe Mazzini (1805–1872) and Giuseppe Garibaldi (1807–1882) sought to drive out the Austrians and establish a republic. They failed, but frightened more moderate Italians. It was Count Camillo Cavour (1810–1861), the prime minister of Piedmont, who achieved unification.

Piedmont (officially the "Kingdom of Sardinia"), was the most independent state on the peninsula (see Map 27–1). It had fought Austria in 1848 and 1849. Following the second defeat, Charles Albert (r. 1831–1849) abdicated in favor of his son, Victor Emmanuel II (r. 1849–1878). In 1852, the new monarch chose Cavour—a moderate liberal in economics and a strong monarchist—as his prime minister. Cavour believed that Italy could be unified only with the aid of France.

Cavour joined the French and British side in the Crimean War to be able to raise the question of Italian unification at the peace conference. There he gained the sympathy of Napoleon III (r. 1852–1870) of France. In 1858, Cavour and the French Emperor plotted to start a war with Austria.

In 1859, Piedmont mobilized its army. In late April 1859, war erupted. In June, the Austrians were defeated at Magenta and Solferino. Fearing too extensive a Piedmontese victory, Napoleon III concluded a separate peace on July 11. Piedmont received Lombardy, but the Veneto remained under Austrian control. Cavour felt betrayed by France, but Parma, Modena, Tuscany, and Romagna voted to unite with Piedmont.

At this point, the forces of romantic republican nationalism compelled Cavour to pursue the complete unification of Italy. In May 1860, Garibaldi landed in Sicily and captured Palermo. By September, the kingdom of Naples lay under his control. To forestall a republican victory, Cavour rushed troops south. On the way, they conquered the Papal States except for the area around Rome, which remained under the control of the pope.

Garibaldi accepted the Piedmontese domination. In late 1860, the southern Italian state voted to join the northern union forged by Piedmont. In March 1861, Victor Emmanuel II was proclaimed king of Italy. Three months later Cavour died. Italy gained the Veneto in 1866 as a result of the war between Austria and Prussia, and Rome in 1870 during the Franco-Prussian War.

The Italian state confronted difficulties that would continue to affect it throughout the twentieth century. Unification did not produce economic power or political strength to match the great nation-states. The north was economically advanced, but the south remained rural and poor. The parliamentary system was unstable. The new state also had an ongoing conflict with the Roman Catholic Church, whose leader regarded himself as a prisoner in the Vatican.

German and Italian Unification

1859	War of Piedmont and France against Austria
1860	Garibaldi conquers southern Italy
1861	March 17, Proclamation of the Kingdom of Italy
	June 6, death of Cavour
1862	Bismarck becomes prime minister of Prussia
1864	Danish War
1866	Austro-Prussian War; Veneto ceded to Italy
1867	North German Confederation formed
1870	June 19–July 12, crisis over Hohenzollern candidacy for the Spanish throne
	July 19, France declares war on Prussia
	September 1, France defeated at Sedan and Napoleon III captured
	September 4, French Republic proclaimed
	October 2, Italian state annexes Rome
1871	January 18, Proclamation of the German Empire at Versailles
	March 18–May 28, Paris Commune
	May 10, Treaty of Frankfurt between France and Germany

German Unification

A united German nation was the single most important political development in Europe between 1848 and 1914. Germany was united by conservative Prussia and its prime minister, who sought to outflank the Prussian liberals. William I (r. 1861–1888) regarded the Prussian army as his first concern. In 1860, the Prussian Parliament refused to approve taxes to strengthen the army. A deadlock continued for two years between the monarch and the Parliament dominated by liberals.

Bismarck

In September 1862, William I turned for help to Otto von Bismarck (1815–1898). Bismarck came from *Junker* stock and shared the most traditional Prussian values, including admiration for the monarchy, the nobility, and the army.

After being appointed minister president and foreign minister, Bismarck immediately moved against the liberal

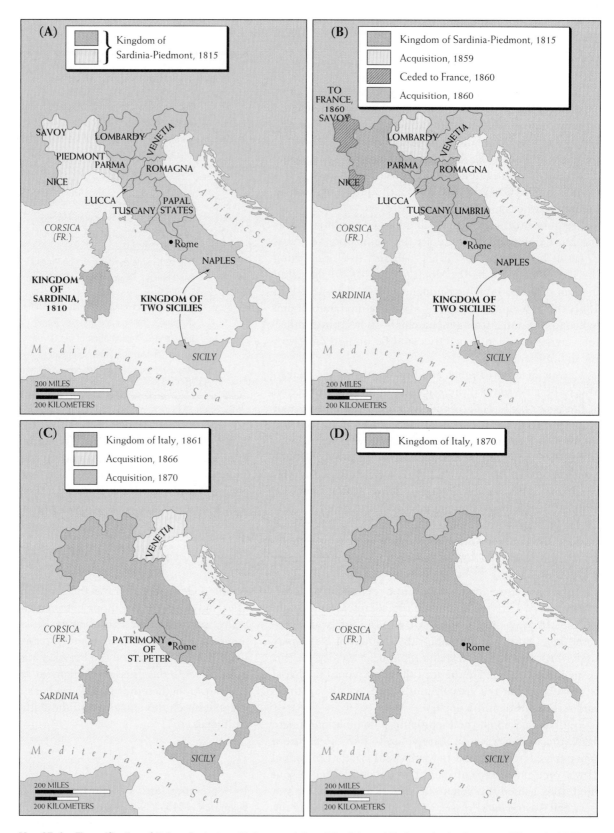

Map 27–1   The unification of Italy.   Beginning with the association of Sardinia and Piedmont by the Congress of Vienna in 1815, unification was achieved through the expansion of Piedmont between 1859 and 1870. Both Cavour's statesmanship and the campaigns of ardent nationalists played large roles.

Parliament. He contended that the Prussian constitution permitted the government to function on the basis of previously granted taxes. Therefore, taxes could be collected and spent, despite the parliamentary refusal to vote them. However, in 1863 elections sustained the liberal majority in the Parliament. To attract popular support away from the liberals, Bismarck set about uniting Germany through the conservative institutions of Prussia, thus diverting public attention from domestic matters to foreign affairs. Prussia now assumed a position of leadership in the effort to unify Germany.

Bismarck pursued a *kleindeutsch*, or small German, solution to unification. Austria was to be excluded from German affairs. To achieve that end, Bismarck undertook two brief wars.

In 1864, he went to war with Denmark over the question of Schleswig and Holstein, German-speaking areas that had long been administered by the Danish monarchy (see Map 27–2). The Austrians helped defeat Denmark. Bismarck then gained the support of France and Italy against Austria. War

between Prussia and Austria broke out in the summer of 1866. This Seven Weeks' War led to the decisive defeat of Austria at Koniggratz. The Prussian victory excluded the Habsburgs from German affairs. Prussia became the only major power among the German states.

In 1867, Hanover, Hesse, Nassau, and Frankfurt, all of which had supported Austria during the war, were annexed by Prussia and their rulers deposed. Prussia and the German states north of the Main River constituted the North German Confederation. Prussia was its undisputed leader. The constitution of the confederation, which after 1871 became the governing document of the German Empire, possessed only the appearance of liberalism. Bismarck provided for a lower legislative house, or Reichstag, to be chosen by universal manhood suffrage because he sensed that the peasants would vote conservatively. The Reichstag had little power, and its members knew that the army would always support the king. Germany was, in effect, a military monarchy dominated by Prussia.

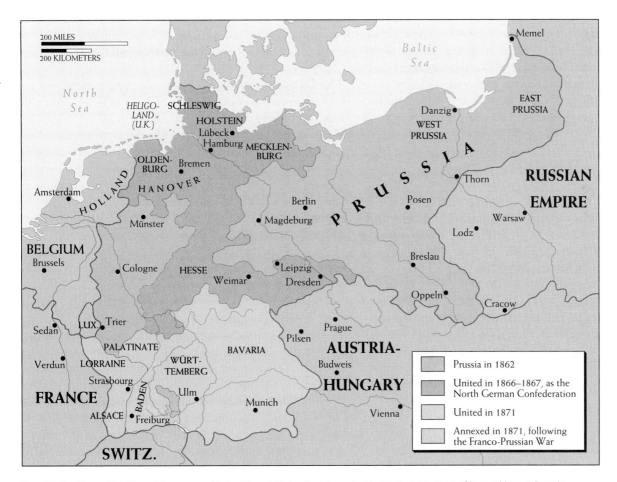

Map 27–2 The unification of Germany.   Under Bismarck's leadership, and with the strong support of its royal house, Prussia used diplomatic and military means, on both the German and international stages, to forcibly unify the German states into a strong national entity.

The Franco-Prussian War and the German Empire (1870–1871)

Bismarck now awaited an opportunity to complete unification by bringing the states of southern Germany into the confederation. The occasion arose as a result of complex diplomacy surrounding the possibility of a cousin of William I of Prussia becoming king of Spain. France opposed the idea of a second state on its borders ruled by a Hohenzollern. Bismarck edited a press dispatch to make it appear that William I had insulted the French ambassador, even though such had not been the case. Bismarck intended to goad France into war.

The French government declared war on July 19. Napoleon III hoped that victory would give his regime a stronger popular base. The states of southern Germany supported Prussia. On September 1, at Sedan, the Germans defeated the French army and captured Napoleon III. By late September, Paris was besieged. It capitulated on January 28, 1871. Ten days earlier, at the Palace of Versailles, the German Empire had been proclaimed. The rulers of the states of South Germany had requested William I to accept the imperial title. They, in turn, retained their thrones.

The unification of Germany established a strong state in the middle of Europe. It had been forged by the Prussian army and its center of power rested on the Prussian monarchy and the military. It possessed enormous economic resources and nationalistic ambitions. For the next eighty years, Europe would have to come to grips with this new political reality.

France: The Third Republic

After his coup in December 1851, Napoleon III kept a close rein on the legislature, controlled the press, and harassed dissidents. His support came from property owners, the Catholic Church, and businessmen. From the late 1850s onward, Napoleon III became less authoritarian, but his liberal concessions, such as the relaxation of the press laws, were attempts to compensate for an unsuccessful foreign policy. First he lost control of Italian unification. Then, between 1861 and 1867, he supported an expedition against Mexico led by Archduke Maximilian of Austria (1832–1867) (see Chapter 30) that ended in Maximilian's execution. The war of 1870 against Germany was Napoleon III's most disastrous attempt to shore up French foreign policy and secure domestic popularity.

Paris Commune

Shortly after the news of Sedan reached Paris, a republic was proclaimed. Paris surrendered to the Germans in January 1871, but France itself had been ready to sue for peace much earlier.

The division between the provinces and Paris deepened after the fighting stopped. Monarchists dominated the new National Assembly, which met at Versailles. Under the leadership of Adolphe Thiers (1797–1877), the assembly negotiated a peace settlement that required France to pay a large indemnity and surrender Alsace-Lorraine to Germany.

Paris resented this settlement. On March 26, 1871, the Parisians elected a new municipal government, called the Paris Commune. It intended to administer Paris separately from the rest of France. Political radicals of all stripes participated in the Paris Commune. The National Assembly reacted rapidly. Its army broke through the city's defenses on May 21 and killed about 20,000 Parisians. Others were slain by the communards.

The Third Republic

The National Assembly created a republic against its will. Its monarchist majority was divided between adherents of the House of Bourbon and the House of Orléans. In 1875, unable to agree on a candidate for the throne, the assembly adopted a law that provided for a chamber of deputies elected by universal manhood suffrage, a senate chosen indirectly, and a president elected by the two legislative houses.

The Dreyfus Affair   The greatest trauma of the new republic occurred over the Dreyfus affair. In 1894, a French military court found Captain Alfred Dreyfus (1859–1935) guilty of spying for the German army. The flimsy evidence for his guilt was forged. Someone in the officer corps had been passing documents to the Germans, and it suited the army to accuse Dreyfus, who was Jewish. In 1896, French counterintelligence found evidence of forgery. A different officer was implicated, but a military court acquitted him. The officer who had discovered the forgeries was transferred.

By then the matter had provoked near-hysterical public debate. The army, the Catholic Church, political conservatives, and anti-Semitic newspapers contended that Dreyfus was guilty. In 1898, however, the novelist Emile Zola (1840–1902) published a newspaper article entitled *"J'accuse"* ("I Accuse"), in which he contended that the army had denied due process to Dreyfus and had plotted to suppress and forge evidence. Zola was convicted of libel but fled to England.

Liberals, radicals, and socialists demanded a new trial for Dreyfus. They realized that his cause could aid theirs. They portrayed the conservative institutions of the nation as having denied Dreyfus the rights belonging to any citizen of the republic and claimed that Dreyfus had been singled out to protect the guilty persons, who were still in the army. In August 1898, further evidence of forged material came to light. The officer responsible for those forgeries committed suicide. In a new military trial, Dreyfus was again found guilty by officers who refused to admit the original mistake. The president of France immediately pardoned him, and in 1906 a civilian court set aside the results of both military trials.

The Dreyfus case profoundly divided France. By its conclusion, the conservatives stood on the defensive. They had persecuted an innocent person and manufactured evidence against him to protect themselves from disclosure. They had also embraced anti-Semitism. On the political left, radicals, republicans, and socialists developed an informal alliance that outlived the fight over the Dreyfus case itself. Most French citizens understood that their rights and liberties were safer under a republic. The divisions growing out of the Dreyfus affair would mark the Third Republic until its defeat by Germany in 1940. The anti-Semitism associated with the attack on Dreyfus would manifest itself in the Vichy regime during World War II.

The Habsburg Empire

During the 1850s, Emperor Francis Joseph (r. 1848–1916) attempted to impose a centralized administration on the multinational empire (see Map 27-3). The system amounted to a military and bureaucratic government dominated by German-speaking Austrians. The defeats in 1859 and 1866 compelled Francis Joseph to come to terms with the Hungarian nobility. The *Ausgleich*, or Compromise, of 1867 transformed the Habsburg Empire into a dual monarchy. Except for the common monarch, foreign policy, and army, Austria and Hungary became almost separate states.

Many of the other national groups within the empire opposed the Compromise because it permitted the German-speaking Austrians and the Magyars to dominate all other nationalities in their respective states. The Czechs of Bohemia were the most vocal group. By the turn of the century, they

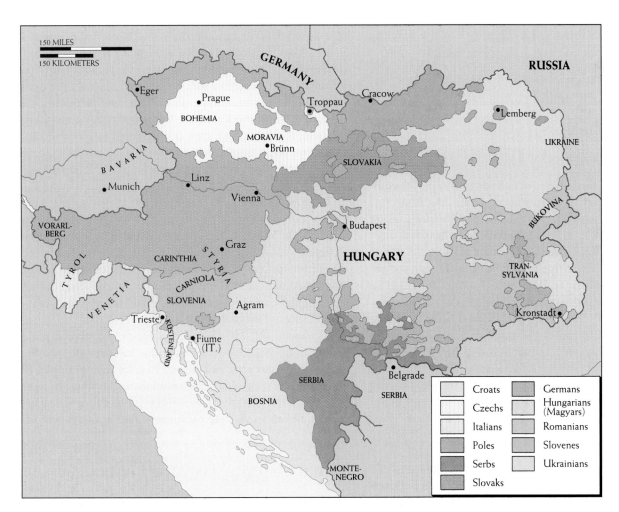

Map 27-3 Nationalities within the Habsburg Empire.   The patchwork appearance reflects the unusual problem of the numerous ethnic groups that the Habsburgs could not, of course, meld into a modern national state. Only the Magyars were recognized in 1867, leaving nationalist Czechs, Slovaks, and the others chronically dissatisfied.

and German-speaking groups disrupted parliament rather than permit a compromise on language issues. The emperor ruled thereafter by imperial decree. Constitutionalism was dead in Austria. It flourished in Hungary only because the Magyars used it to dominate competing national groups.

Unrest of Nationalities

Nationalist unrest touched each of the three great central and eastern European empires—the German, the Russian, and the Austrian. All had Polish populations and other major national groups. Each nationality regarded its own aspirations and discontents as more important than the larger good or even survival of the empire they inhabited. Nationalism affected the fate of all three empires from the 1860s through the outbreak of World War I. The government of each would be overturned during the war, and the Austrian Empire would disappear. These same unresolved problems of central and eastern European nationalism would then lead to World War II. During more recent years, they have led to civil war in the former Yugoslavia and to the breakup of Czechoslovakia.

Russia: Emancipation and Revolutionary Stirrings

Reforms of Alexander II

Defeat in the Crimean War compelled the Russian government to reconsider its domestic situation. Alexander II (r. 1855–1881) was familiar with the chief difficulties facing Russia. The debacle of the war had made reform both necessary and possible. Alexander II took advantage of this to institute the most extensive restructuring of Russian society and administration since Peter the Great (r. 1682–1725). Like Peter, Alexander imposed his reforms from the top.

In March 1856, Alexander II announced his intention to abolish serfdom. He had decided that only abolition would permit Russia to organize its human and natural resources so as to remain a great power. Serfdom was economically inefficient; there was always the threat of revolt; serfs in the army had performed poorly in the Crimean conflict; and moral opinion increasingly condemned serfdom. In February 1861, against opposition from the landlords, Alexander II ended serfdom in Russia.

The procedures of emancipation were so complicated and the immediate benefits so limited that many serfs believed real emancipation was still to come. They received the personal rights to marry without their landlord's permission as well as to purchase and sell property freely, to engage in court actions, and to pursue trades. But they did not receive free

title to their land. Instead, they had to pay for the land over a period of forty-nine years. The redemption payments led to endless resentment. Facing widespread unrest following the defeat of Russia by Japan in 1905, the tsarist government grudgingly cancelled the remaining debts.

The abolition of serfdom required the reorganization of local government and the judicial system. Village elders now settled family quarrels, imposed fines, and collected taxes. In 1864, nobles were authorized to form *zemstvos*, or councils, to oversee local matters, such as road repairs and education. Inadequate funding meant that the local governments never became vigorous. Also in 1864, Alexander II introduced principles of western European legal systems into Russia. They included equality before the law, impartial hearings, uniform procedures, judicial independence, and trial by jury.

Revolutionaries

The initial reforms of Alexander II raised great hopes among Russian students and intellectuals, but they soon became discontented with the limited character of the restructuring. These students formed a revolutionary movement known as Populism. They sought a social revolution based on the communal life of the Russian peasants. The chief radical society was called Land and Freedom. In the early 1870s, hundreds of young Russians, both men and women, took their revolutionary message into the countryside. They intended to teach the peasants about the coming revolution. The bewildered peasants turned most of the youths over to the police.

In 1879, Land and Freedom split into two groups. One group, known as People's Will, decided to assassinate the tsar himself. On March 1, 1881, a bomb hurled by a member of People's Will killed Alexander II. The emergence of such revolutionary opposition constituted as much a part of the reign of Alexander II as did his reforms, for the limited character of those reforms convinced many that the autocracy would never redirect Russian society.

Alexander III (1881–1894) was autocratic and repressive. He sought to roll back his father's reforms and strengthened the secret police and press censorship. In effect, he confirmed all the evils that the revolutionaries saw inherent in autocratic government. Under his son, Nicholas II (r. 1894–1917), the autocracy would not survive the pressures of the twentieth century.

Great Britain: Toward Democracy

Great Britain continued to symbolize the confident liberal state. A large body of ideas emphasizing competition and individualism was accepted by all classes. Even the leaders of trade unions during these years asked only to receive the fruits of prosperity and to prove their own social respectability. Parliament itself continued to absorb new groups and interests.

The Second Reform Act passed by a Conservative government in 1867 increased the number of voters from approximately 1,430,000 to 2,470,000. Britain had taken a major step toward democracy. Benjamin Disraeli (1804–1881), who led the Conservatives, thought much of the working class would support Conservative candidates who were responsive to social issues. He also thought the growing suburban middle class would become more conservative.

Gladstone and Disraeli

In 1868, however, William Gladstone (1809–1898) became prime minister. His ministry of 1868–1874 witnessed the culmination of classical British liberalism. Gladstone introduced competitive examinations into the civil service, abolished the purchase of army officers' commissions, and introduced the secret ballot. He opened Oxford and Cambridge Universities to students of all religious denominations and, by the Education Act of 1870, made the British government responsible for elementary schools.

The liberal policy of creating popular support for the nation by extending political liberty and reforming abuses had its conservative counterpart in concern about social reform. Disraeli succeeded Gladstone as prime minister in 1874. Whereas Gladstone looked to individualism, free trade, and competition to solve social problems, Disraeli believed the state should protect weaker citizens. In his view, paternalistic legislation would alleviate class antagonism. He extended sanitary legislation and provided housing for the working class.

The Irish Question

The major issue of the 1880s was Ireland. From the late 1860s onward, Irish nationalists had sought to achieve home rule for Ireland, by which they meant more Irish control of local government. The leader of the movement for home rule was Charles Stewart Parnell (1846–1891). By 1885, Parnell had organized eighty-five Irish members of the House of Commons into a tightly disciplined party that held the balance of power between the English Liberals and Conservatives. When Gladstone announced support for home rule for Ireland, Parnell gave his votes to the formation of a Liberal ministry. However, the issue split the Liberal Party and in 1886, Gladstone's Home Rule Bill was defeated.

In 1892, Gladstone sponsored a second Home Rule Bill that was defeated in the House of Lords. With the failure of this bill, further action on the Irish question was suspended until a Liberal ministry passed the third Home Rule Bill in the summer of 1914. However, its implementation was suspended for the duration of World War I.

The Irish question affected British politics in a manner not unlike that of the Austrian nationalities problem. Normal British domestic issues could not be adequately addressed because of the political divisions created by Ireland. The split of the Liberal Party hurt the cause of social and political reform. The people who could agree about reforms could not agree on Ireland, and Ireland seemed more important. As the two traditional parties failed to deal with the social questions, by the turn of the century the new Labour Party began to fill the vacuum.

The United States: Civil War, Reconstruction, and Progressive Politics

While European nations consolidated and unified themselves, the United States reforged the character of its union and democracy through a civil war that ended with the abolition of slavery. The abolition of slavery in the United States occurred in the same decade as the abolition of serfdom in Russia. Both processes left the groups who were freed—Russian serfs and black American slaves—in precarious positions. The war also ended with the triumph of the federal government. The southern states' attempt to forge their own nation had failed and a wider nationalism succeeded. That victory, however, left a North-South economic and political problem similar to that in Italy after its unification.

During the 1850s, The American debate over slavery became more extreme. Northern abolitionists resented the federal Fugitive Slave Law, which required the return of escaped slaves to their owners. Southerners feared that the North was determined to dominate the South economically and politically.

In 1854, the Kansas-Nebraska Bill galvanized the antislavery forces. The principle of the bill, introduced by Stephen A. Douglas (1813–1861), was that of popular sovereignty. The people of each new territory would decide whether to permit slavery within its borders. Douglas was thus willing to repeal the Missouri Compromise, which had prohibited slavery in most of the Louisiana Territory.

In 1857, in the Dred Scott decision, the Supreme Court declared that Congress could not prohibit slavery in the territories and that slaves did not become free by living in free states or have rights that others were bound to respect. For radical antislavery northerners, the decision raised the most serious questions about the morality of the Union itself, and it demonstrated again a Southern conspiracy to protect slavery. Thereafter, slavery dominated national political debate.

In 1859, John Brown seized the federal arsenal at Harpers Ferry, Virginia to foment a slave rebellion. He was captured

Lincoln States the Ideals of American Liberty at Gettysburg

The battle of Gettysburg in 1863 was the largest battle of the American Civil War and marked the farthest intrusion of Confederate forces into the North. The Union won the battle after great losses to both sides. A few months later, President Lincoln journeyed to Gettysburg to participate in the dedication of a military cemetery. There he delivered one of his very few public speeches during the war. In it he set forth what he considered to be the ideals of democratic government that he had come to believe constituted the goals for which the Union stood and fought. Note that he traced American liberty to the Declaration of Independence rather than to the Constitution, which had actually embraced slavery.

How did this speech transform the Union position in the American Civil War from an effort to suppress a rebellion into a war for human liberty? What would Lincoln have included in the unfinished work that the living must continue? What did he mean by "a new birth of freedom"?

Four score and seven years ago our fathers brought forth on this continent, a new nation, conceived in Liberty, and dedicated to the proposition that all men are created equal.

Now we are engaged in a great civil war, testing whether that nation or any nation so conceived and so dedicated, can long endure. We are met on a great battlefield of that war. We have come to dedicate a portion of that field, as a final resting place for those who here gave their lives that that nation might live. It is altogether fitting and proper that we should do this.

But, in a larger sense, we cannot dedicate—we cannot consecrate—we cannot hallow—this ground. The brave men, living and dead, who struggled here, have consecrated it, far above our poor power to add or detract. The world will little note, nor long remember what we say here, but it can never forget what they did here. It is for us the living, rather, to be dedicated here to the unfinished work which they who fought here have thus far so nobly advanced. It is rather for us to be here dedicated to the great task remaining before us—that from these honored dead we take increased devotion to that cause for which they gave the last full measure of devotion—that we here highly resolve that these dead shall not have died in vain—that this nation, under God, shall have a new birth of freedom—and that government of the people, by the people, for the people, shall not perish from the earth.

From Abraham Lincoln, *The Gettysburg Address, November 19, 1863*, as quoted in Henry Steele Commager, *Documents of American History*, 8th ed., Vol. 1. Copyright © 1968 Appleton-Century-Crofts, pp. 428–429.

---

and hanged, further increasing sectional polarization. Radical southerners feared more than ever a northern conspiracy to attack slavery, while northern radicals feared that the South controlled the federal government and would use it to protect slavery. Thus the politics of both sections became radicalized.

The Republican Party had become the party that opposed slavery. In 1860, Abraham Lincoln (1809–1865), the Republican candidate, was elected president. Neither he nor the Republican Party had campaigned for the abolition of slavery, but southerners perceived his election as the victory of a party and a president dedicated to its eradication. In 1860-1861, southern states seceded and formed the Confederate States of America. Attempts at compromise failed, and when confederate forces fired on Fort Sumter in Charleston Harbor in April 1861, the Civil War began.

A different nation emerged from the violence. In 1863, two years after Alexander II ended Russian serfdom, Lincoln emancipated the slaves in the rebelling states. By the time the Confederacy was defeated in 1865, the South was occupied by northern armies and was economically devastated. The Thirteenth, Fourteenth, and Fifteenth Amendments recast the character of the Union. The Thirteenth abolished slavery; the Fourteenth granted citizenship to the former slaves; and the Fifteenth allowed them to vote. These amendments resolved the issues of slavery and the relative roles of the state and federal governments.

Within the context of world history, the American Civil War is important for several reasons. It was the greatest war that occurred between the defeat of Napoleon in 1815 and the onset of World War I in 1914. It represented the triumph of the same kind of central or centralizing political authority that also triumphed in Italy, Germany, and France in the 1860s. It resulted in the establishment of a continent-wide free labor market, even though freed blacks lived in poverty and an economic dependence not unlike that of the rural classes of Latin America. The free labor market, purged of slavery, helped to open all of North America to economic development. The war also allowed America to develop without the distraction of the debates over states rights and slavery. Free labor became the American norm, and the debates over the role of industrial labor in the United States resembled those in Europe.

Dashed Hopes of Equality

The most visible result of the Civil War was the end of slavery in the South. However, in the quarter century following the war, the fruits of liberty for blacks proved ephemeral and the liberty of Native Americans was even more curtailed.

Emergence of Segregation of Black Americans

Throughout the era of Reconstruction (1865–1877), freedmen, as former slaves were called, voted, held office, and owned property. These years proved to be a false spring of political liberty for blacks.

In 1876, the last federal troops were removed from the South. Simultaneously, in the North, concern for the freedmen diminished. Northerners who had wanted to end slavery retreated from the promise of extending full civil rights to free blacks.

Racism backed by legislation grew to dominate the political and social life of the South. Within the states of the old Confederacy, the border states, and, to a lesser extent, elsewhere, a system of legalized discrimination against blacks arose in the form of segregation. Laws passed by city councils and state legislatures divided social life into black and white spheres. Race defined nearly every institution and limited access to every public facility. In 1896, the Supreme Court declared these arrangements to be constitutional in *Plessy v. Ferguson*. That decision remained in force until 1954.

American blacks were subject to discrimination simply on the basis of the color of their skin. Furthermore, southern states legalized poll taxes and literacy tests, depriving blacks of their right to vote. American blacks were also subject to physical intimidation and terrorism. Waves of lynchings spread across the South. Most victims were blacks.

In the late nineteenth century, many black leaders argued that their fellow blacks should wait for better times, submit to the discrimination, and practice economic virtues such as hard work and thrift that might lead them out of poverty. Drawing on the ideas of European economic liberalism that admonished against government action, they contended that by behaving in a careful, deferential manner, blacks might convince whites of their worthiness for inclusion in political activity.

After the turn of the century, W. E. B. DuBois (1868–1963), who had been educated at Harvard and in Berlin, urged more direct claims to political rights and the establishment of a well-educated black leadership. He understood that racism was spreading and had penetrated the North. Deference had achieved nothing. In 1909, DuBois and others organized the National Association for the Advancement of Colored People. In time, that organization would spearhead the effort of black Americans toward equality, but almost half a century would pass before segregation was declared illegal.

The Native American Experience

During the second half of the nineteenth century, European powers gained military and administrative control over peoples in Africa and Asia. The United States pursued similar policies toward Native Americans during the westward migration across North America. In the early nineteenth century, the Native Americans who lived east of the Mississippi were pushed west. These forced removals by the federal government became known as the Trail of Tears. By the close of the Civil War, there were more than 300,000 Native Americans, most of whom lived west of the Mississippi.

The virtual end of the Native American way of life took place between 1865 and the 1890s. While the transcontinental railways opened the West to white settlement, the buffalo and other food supplies of the Native Americans were destroyed. The technologically better-armed troops of the U.S. Army suppressed opposition and even massacred women and children.

The federal policy against Native Americans had much in common with that of the southern states against blacks. Both policies were antidemocratic and calculated to make social and economic life safe and profitable for white Americans. Racist thinking played a major role. Blacks were segregated and excluded from political life and their labor extracted at low wages. Native Americans were, in effect, segregated from the rest of the nation and excluded from political life, and their lands were appropriated. In 1867, the federal government began to place Native Americans on reservations. The land assigned to them was almost invariably of poor quality and far removed from areas that white Americans wished to develop.

The Canadian Experience

Under the Treaty of Paris of 1763, all of Canada came under the control of Great Britain. Canada then, as now, included both English- and French-speaking populations. The latter was concentrated primarily in Quebec. The Quebec Act of 1774 made the Roman Catholic Church the established church in Quebec. During the American Revolution, 30,000 English loyalists fled the colonies and settled in Canada. They thus established a larger English presence and were strongly loyal to the British crown.

The Constitutional Act of 1791 divided the colony into Upper Canada (primarily English in ethnic composition) and Lower Canada (primarily French). Each section had its own legislature, and a governor-general presided over the two provinces. Newfoundland, Nova Scotia, New Brunswick, Cape Breton Island, and Prince Edward Island remained separate colonies.

In the early nineteenth century, relations with the United States were often tense. Fear that the United States would dominate Canada, along with the Anglo-French ethnic divisions, were two of the major themes of Canadian history.

By the late 1830s, the political situation in Canada was generating internal pressure. There were economic tensions between long-established families and new settlers, and quarrels over the influence of the British crown. In 1837, abortive rebellions occurred in both Upper and Lower Canada.

Road to Self-Government

The British government was determined to avoid another North American revolution. It sent the Earl of Durham (1792–1840) to Canada with extensive powers to make reforms. In 1839, he advocated responsible government for Canada and uniting both Canadian provinces into one political unit. He thought that such political unification would lead to a thoroughly English culture throughout Canada that would overwhelm the French influence in Quebec. He also believed that most Canadian affairs should be in the hands of a Canadian legislature and that only foreign policy and defense should remain under British control. His policy was carried out in the Canada Act of 1840, which gave the nation a single legislature composed of two houses.

The Durham Report established the political pattern that the British government would follow with its other English-speaking colonies during the nineteenth century in Australia, New Zealand, and South Africa. The Canadian experience thus had a considerable impact throughout the world. But, until well into the twentieth century, the British government, like other Western imperial powers, also generally believed that nonwhite peoples, such as those of India, required direct British colonial administration.

Keeping a Distinctive Culture

Canadians did exercise self-government, but distinct English and French cultures persisted. Within the legislature there were almost always trade-offs between the eastern and western sections of the nation. During the American Civil War, fears that the American republic might seek to invade or dominate Canada led to considerations of the desirability for a stronger federation among all the parts of Canada.

The result was the British North America Act of 1867, which created a Canadian federation. Canadians hoped to avoid what they regarded as flaws in the constitution of the United States. The Canadian system of government was federal, but with less emphasis on states' rights than in the United States. Canadians established a parliamentary government, but also retained the British monarchy in the person of the

governor-general as head of state. The person who was most responsible for establishing this new government and who led it for most of the period between 1867 and 1891 was John A. MacDonald (1815–1891).

Like settlers in the United States, Canadians during the nineteenth century pressed westward. The path for the settlement of the western prairies and the Canadian Northwest was provided by the construction of the Canadian Pacific Railway, completed in 1885. The railroad crossed the continent as a kind of spine along which settlements grew. In turn, the Canadian economy became highly integrated with that of the United States. This situation, which persists today, created fears of being dominated economically by Canada's southern neighbor.

As Canadians established a nation that stretched across a continent, British domination diminished. The link with the British Crown remained, but Canada established its own foreign policy. Political power resided in the Canadian political parties and parliament. Canada supported Great Britain in the Boer War, World War I, and World War II—but as an ally, not a colony.

The Canadian transition from colony to self-governing nation was thus different from that of the United States. The British government and its representatives were actively involved. Furthermore, the presence of a strong French culture in which the Roman Catholic Church played a major role led to real cultural differences between French- and English-speaking Canada. English-speaking Canadians dominated both political and economic life. French-speaking Canadians virtually always felt like second-class citizens.

IN WORLD PERSPECTIVE

European and North American Political Consolidation

The movement toward strong, centralized national states in Europe and North America during the nineteenth century had its counterparts elsewhere in the world. In Asia, Japan sought to imitate the power of the European states. Latin America enjoyed one of its most successful periods. Its governments established centralized regimes on the basis of relatively prosperous economies.

In the United States, the Civil War established the power of the federal government over the states. The role of the war in forging a single American nation was similar to the role that military force played in the unifications of Italy and Germany and the suppression of the Paris Commune.

Many people regarded the triumph of nationalism as a positive achievement. However, the last half of the century also saw national and ethnic groups and national governments use the power of a national state to repress or dominate other groups. Throughout the world, nationalism involved the extension of liberty to some peoples and its denial to others. In almost all cases, this repression generated problems that would haunt the twentieth century.

Finally, the emergence of strong European nation-states set the stage for the transfer of their rivalry from Europe to other areas of the globe. The militarily and economically strong states of Europe soon turned to foreign adventures that would subjugate vast areas of Africa and Asia. This imperialism led many of the colonialized peoples to believe that only strong nationalistic movements of their own could end subjugation by the militarily stronger Europeans. During the first quarter of the twentieth century, the nationalistic principle that less than fifty years earlier had stirred European politics began to influence the politics of the peoples on whom Europeans had imposed their sway. The United States would be drawn into those conflicts.

Review Questions

1. Why was it so difficult to unify Italy? What did Cavour and Garibaldi contribute to Italian unification?

2. What was Bismarck's method of unification of Germany and why did he succeed? What effect did the unification of Germany have on the rest of Europe?

3. How did the Third Republic become established in France?

4. What unique problems did Austria confront? Why was nationalism a pressing problem for Austria?

5. What reforms were instituted by Tsar Alexander II? Were they effective in solving Russia's domestic problems? Was Alexander II a "visionary" reformer?

6. How would you contrast the British Liberal and Conservative parties between 1860 and 1890? How did British politicians handle the Irish Question?

7. Compare the results of the American Civil War with Italian and German unification. Compare the situation of freed American slaves and freed Russian serfs.

Documents CD-ROM

1. Guiseppe Mazzini: Global Rebirth Through Risorgimento

2. "Napoleon the Little": A Revised Agenda for Bonapartism

3. Isaiah Berlin: Alexander Herzen

4. John Henry Newman: Who's to Blame?

5. Benjamin Disraeli: Utilitarian Follies

6. Irish National Identity and Destiny: Three Views

28

THE BUILDING OF NORTHERN TRANSATLANTIC SUPREMACY:
SOCIETY AND POLITICS TO WORLD WAR I

CHAPTER TOPICS

EUROPE

◆ The Middle Classes in Ascendancy

◆ Jewish Emancipation

◆ Late-Nineteenth-Century Urban Life

◆ Late-Nineteenth-Century Women's Experience

◆ Labor, Socialism, and Politics to World War I

NORTH AMERICA

◆ The New Industrial Economy

◆ The Progressives

In World Perspective The Building of Northern Transatlantic Supremacy

---

Between 1860 and 1914, European and American life assumed many characteristics of our present-day world. On both sides of the north Atlantic, business adopted large-scale corporate structures, and the labor force organized itself into trade unions. The numbers of white-collar laborers grew as urban life became predominant. During this period, too, women began to assert new political awareness and to become politically active. Socialism became a major ingredient in the political life of all European nations, but made few inroads in the United States.

During this half century, the extensive spread of industrialism created an unparalleled productive capacity in Europe and the United States. European goods flowed into markets across the globe.

The Europe of this era became the model for much of the rest of the world, but the United States retained its own political direction, spurning socialism and other radical political alternatives.

EUROPE

The Middle Classes in Ascendancy

The sixty years before World War I were the age of the middle classes. They became the arbiter of consumer taste and ceased to be revolutionary. Property owners across the Continent moved to protect what they possessed against demands from working-class groups.

The middle classes grew increasingly diverse. Their most prosperous members lived in splendor that rivaled that of the aristocracy. Beneath them were the comfortable small entrepreneurs and professional people, whose incomes permitted private homes, large quantities of consumer goods, journals, education for their children, and vacations. Also in this group were the shopkeepers, schoolteachers, librarians, and others who had a bit of property or a skill that provided respectable, nonmanual employment.

Finally, there was a new element, white-collar workers, who formed the lower middle class or petite bourgeoisie. They included secretaries, retail clerks, and lower-level bureaucrats. They often had working-class origins, but they had middle-class aspirations and sought to distance themselves from a lower-class lifestyle. They pursued educational opportunities and career advancement for themselves and their children. Many of them spent their disposable income on consumer goods that were middle class in appearance.

Tensions and social anxieties marked relations among the various middle-class groups. Small shopkeepers resented the power of the great capitalists. The professions may have become overcrowded. People who had attained a middle-class lifestyle feared losing it in bad economic times. Nonetheless, the middle classes set the values and goals for society.

Jewish Emancipation

One of the important social changes to occur throughout Europe during the nineteenth century was the emancipation of European Jews from the ghetto into a world of equal or nearly equal citizenship and social status. This transformation represented a major impact of political liberalism.

Early Steps to Equal Citizenship

Emancipation moved at different paces in different countries. But by the first half of the nineteenth century, Jews in western Europe and to a lesser extent in eastern Europe had begun to acquire equal citizenship.

In Russia, however, prejudice and discrimination continued until World War I. Jews were treated as aliens. The government restricted areas where Jews might live, required internal passports from Jews, and banned them from many forms of state service and institutions of higher education. The police and others were allowed to conduct pogroms—organized riots—against Jews.

Broadened Opportunities

In western Europe, from approximately 1850 to 1880 there was relatively little organized or overt prejudice toward Jews. They entered the professions and other occupations once closed to them. They participated in the literary and cultural life of their nations. They were active in the arts. They became leaders in science and education. Jews intermarried freely with non-Jews.

Outside of Russia, Jewish political figures served in the highest offices of the state. Politically they tended to align with liberal parties because such groups championed equal rights. Later in the century, many Jews became associated with the socialist parties.

The prejudice that had been associated with religious attitudes toward Jews seemed to have dissipated, although it still appeared in rural Russia and eastern Europe. From these regions, hundreds of thousands of European Jews immigrated to the United States. Almost anywhere in Europe Jews might encounter personal prejudice. But in western Europe, the Jews seem to have felt secure from the old dangers of persecution and discrimination.

That began to change during the last two decades of the nineteenth century. In the 1870s, anti-Semitic sentiments attributing the economic stagnation of that decade to Jewish financial interests began to be voiced. In the 1880s, organized anti-Semitism erupted in Germany as it did in France at the time of the Dreyfus Affair (see Chapter 27). As will be seen in the next chapter, those developments gave birth to Zionism, the movement to establish a Jewish state in Palestine. However, most Jewish leaders believed the attacks on Jewish life to be temporary recurrences; they felt that their communities would remain safe under the legal protections that had been extended during the century.

Late-Nineteenth-Century Urban Life

After 1850, Europe became more urbanized than it ever had been. Migration within the Continent and Great Britain continued to move toward the cities. The rural migrants to the cities were largely uprooted from traditional social ties. They often confronted poor housing, social anonymity, and unemployment. The difficulties that peoples from different ethnic backgrounds had in mixing socially and the competition for too few jobs generated political and social discontent.

Redesign of Cities

The inward urban migration placed new social and economic demands on city resources and transformed the patterns of urban living. The central portions of many major European cities were redesigned during the second half of the century. These areas had been places where many people from all social classes lived and worked. From the middle of the century onward, they became districts where relatively few people resided and where businesses, government offices, stores, and theaters were located.

Development of Suburbs The commercial development of the central portions of cities, the clearing of slums, and the extension of railways into cities raised the price of centrally located urban land and of the rents charged on buildings there. Both the middle classes and the working class began to seek housing elsewhere. The middle classes sought to avoid urban congestion, the working class to find affordable housing. As a result, outside the urban centers proper, suburbs arose to house the families whose breadwinner worked in the city.

The expansion of railways with cheap workday fares and the introduction of tramways allowed thousands of workers to move daily between the city and the outlying suburbs. For hundreds of thousands of Europeans, home and work became physically separated as never before.

The New Paris This remarkable social change and the values it reflected became embodied in the new designs of many European cities. The most famous and extensive transformation occurred in Paris. Paris had expanded from the Middle Ages with little or no planning. Great public buildings and squalid hovels stood near each other. The Seine River was an open sewer. The streets were narrow, crooked, and crowded. It was impossible to cross easily from one part of Paris to another. Moreover, those streets had for sixty years provided the battleground for urban insurrections that had often, most recently in 1848, toppled French governments.

Napoleon III (r. 1852–1870) determined that Paris must be redesigned. He wished the city to be beautiful and to reflect the achievements of his regime and modern technology. He put Georges Haussmann (1809–1891) in charge of the rebuilding program. As prefect of the Seine from 1853 to 1870, Haussmann oversaw a vast urban reconstruction program. Whole districts were destroyed to create broad boulevards and streets. The wide vistas not only were beautiful but also allowed troops to put down riots and remove areas where barricades had been erected. Parks and major public buildings were also constructed. All of these projects created thousands of jobs.

Further rebuilding and redesign took place under the Third Republic. There was much private construction of department stores, offices, and middle-class apartment buildings. By the late 1870s, mechanical trams were operating in Paris. A subway system (the Métro) was begun in 1895, long after that of London (1863). New railway stations were erected near the close of the century. This transport linked the refurbished central city to the suburbs. In 1889, the Eiffel Tower was built, originally as a temporary structure for an international exposition.

Urban Sanitation

The efforts of governments and of the middle classes to maintain order after 1848 led to a growing concern with public health and housing for the poor. A feeling arose that

Growth of Major European Cities (in thousands)

	1850	1880	1910
Berlin	419	1,122	2,071
Birmingham	233	437	840
Frankfurt	65	137	415
London	2,685	4,470	7,256
Madrid	281	398	600
Paris	1,053	2,269	2,888
Vienna	444	1,104	2,031

the health of the middle classes and political stability depended on improving the health and housing of the working class.

Impact of Cholera These concerns first manifested themselves as a result of the great cholera epidemics of the 1830s and 1840s, during which thousands of Europeans, especially those in cities, had died from this disease of Asian origin, previously unknown in Europe. Cholera struck persons from all classes and thus generated middle-class demand for a solution. Before the development of the bacterial theory of disease late in the century, cholera and other diseases were thought to spread through infection from miasmas in the air. The miasmas, identified by their foul odors, were believed to arise from filth.

New Water and Sewer Systems The proposed solution to the urban health hazard was cleanliness, to be achieved through new water and sewer systems. The building of these systems constituted one of the major health and engineering achievements of the second half of the nineteenth century. Wherever these sanitary reforms were undertaken, the mortality rate decreased.

Expanded Government Involvement in Public Health This concern with public health led to an expansion of governmental power. In Britain, France, and the German states, legislation introduced new restraints on private life and enterprise. This legislation allowed medical officers and building inspectors to enter homes and businesses in the name of public health. Private property could be condemned for health hazards. Private land could be excavated to construct the sewers and water mains required to protect the public. New building regulations restrained contractors.

When the bacterial theory of disease was accepted at the close of the century, the necessity of cleanliness became greater. The discoveries of Louis Pasteur (1822–1895), Robert Koch (1843–1910), and Joseph Lister (1827–1912) paved the way for the acceptance of the use of antiseptics in medicine and public health policy. Throughout Europe, the maintenance of public health and the physical well-being of national populations opened the way for government intervention in the lives of citizens and vastly expanded the role of scientific experts and governmental bureaucracies.

Housing Reform and Middle-Class Values

The wretched dwellings of the poor were a cause of poor sanitation and thus one of the newly perceived health hazards. Middle-class reformers were shocked by the domestic arrangements of the poor, whose large families often lived in a single room. One toilet might serve a whole block of tenements. After the revolutions of 1848, the social discontent that overcrowding generated also appeared to be politically dangerous.

Middle-class reformers thus turned to housing reform to solve the medical, moral, and political dangers posed by slums. Decent housing would foster a good home life, which would in turn lead to a healthy, moral, and politically stable population. It was also believed that the personal saving required for owning a home would lead the working class to adopt the thrifty habits of the middle classes.

The first attacks on the housing problem came from private philanthropy. Industrial firms also constructed model housing projects and industrial communities in all the major European nations to ensure a contented, healthy, and stable work force. These early efforts reflected the usual liberal tendency to favor private rather than governmental enterprise.

By the mid-1880s, as a result of mass migration, governmental action seemed inescapable. Policies differed in each country, but all were hesitant. No government undertook large-scale housing experiments before World War I. Most legislation facilitated the construction of cheap housing by the private sector.

By 1914, the necessity for planning and action was fully recognized if not adequately addressed. The middle-class housing reformers had defined the debate. The values and character of the middle-class family house and home had become the ideal. The goal of housing reform across western Europe came to be that of a dwelling that would allow the working class to enjoy a family life along the lines of the middle classes.

Late-Nineteenth-Century Women's Experience

In this period, European women, like men, led lives that reflected their social rank. Yet within each rank, the experience of women was distinct from that of men. Women remained economically dependent and legally inferior, whatever their social class. Their position thus resembled that of women around the world in that all women found their lives circumscribed by traditional roles.

Social Disabilities Confronted by All Women

At mid-century, European women faced social and legal disabilities in property rights, family law, and education. By the close of the century, each area had shown improvement.

Women and Property   Until the last quarter of the century, in most European countries no married women could own property in their own names. In effect, upon marriage women lost to their husbands' control any property they owned, might inherit, or earn. Their legal identities were subsumed into their husbands', and they had no independent standing before the law. Because European society was based on private property and wage earning, these disabilities limited married women's freedom to work, save, and relocate.

Reform of women's property rights came slowly. By 1882, Britain allowed married women to own property in their own right. In France, however, not until 1907 were married women granted possession of their own wages. In 1900, a German husband still retained control of most of his wife's property except for her wages. Similar laws prevailed elsewhere.

Family Law   Family law also worked to the disadvantage of women. Legal codes required wives to obey their husbands. The Napoleonic Code and the remnants of Roman law made women legal minors throughout Europe. Divorce was difficult or forbidden. Across Europe extramarital sexual relations of husbands were more tolerated than those of wives. Everywhere, divorce required legal hearings and proof, making it expensive and difficult for women who did not control their own property.

The authority of husbands also extended to children. A husband could take children away from their mother. Only the husband, in most countries, could permit his daughter to marry. In cases of divorce and separation, the husband normally assumed authority over children.

The sexual and reproductive rights of women could hardly be discussed in the nineteenth century. Contraception and abortion were illegal. The law on rape normally worked against women. Wherever they turned, women confronted a world controlled by men.

Educational Barriers   Throughout the nineteenth century, most women were educated only enough for the domestic careers expected of them. University and professional education remained reserved for men until at least the third quarter of the century.

The absence of a system of secondary education for women prevented most of them from gaining the qualifications they needed to enter a university whether or not the university prohibited them. Evidence suggests that educated men feared the challenge educated women posed to traditional gender roles in the home and workplace. Restricting their access to secondary and university education helped bar women from advancement. Women would benefit only marginally from the expansion of professional employment that occurred during the late nineteenth and early twentieth centuries.

Schoolteaching at the elementary level, which was seen as a female job because of its association with the nurturing of children, became a professional haven for women. Trained at institutions that were equivalent to normal schools, women schoolteachers were regarded as educated, but not as university educated. Secondary education remained largely the province of men.

The few women who pioneered in the professions and on government commissions or who dispersed birth control information faced humiliation and bigotry. These women and their male supporters were challenging the separation of life into male and female spheres that had emerged in middle-class European society during the nineteenth century. Many women themselves had been so acculturated into the recently stereotyped roles that they saw a conflict between family responsibilities and feminism.

New Employment Patterns for Women

During the late nineteenth century, two major developments affected the economic lives of women. The first was an expansion in the variety of jobs available outside the learned professions. The second was a withdrawal of married women from the work force.

Availability of New Jobs The expansion of governmental bureaucracies and the emergence of large-scale businesses and retail stores opened new employment opportunities for women. The need for women elementary school teachers grew with compulsory education. Technological innovations, such as the typewriter and the telephone exchange, also fostered female employment. Women by the thousands became secretaries, clerks, and shop assistants. These jobs required low-level skills and training. Few women had prominent positions.

Employers paid women low wages because they assumed, often knowing better, that a woman could expect financial support from her father or husband. A woman who did need to support herself could rarely find a job paying an adequate income or that paid as well as one held by a man. Women were nearly always treated as casual workers in Europe.

Withdrawal from the Labor Force Most of the women filling these new service positions were young and unmarried. After marriage or the birth of her first child, a woman normally either did not work or worked at home. This pattern was not new, but it had become more common by the end of the nineteenth century. The industrial occupations that women had filled in the mid-nineteenth century were shrinking. Employers in offices and retail stores preferred young, unmarried women whose family responsibilities would not interfere with work.

Male workers' earnings increased during this period, thus reducing families' need for a second income. Also, thanks to improving health conditions, men lived longer, so wives were less often thrust into the work force by an emergency. Smaller families also lowered the need for supplementary wages. Working children stayed at home longer and contributed to the family's income.

Finally, the cultural dominance of the middle class, with its generally idle wives, established a pattern of social expectations. The more prosperous a working-class family became, the less involved in employment its women were supposed to be.

Yet behind these generalities, social class largely determined womens' individual experiences.

Poverty and Prostitution

Nineteenth-century cities had a surplus of working women who did not fit the stereotype of wife or daughter supplementing a family's income. More women were almost always seeking employment than there were jobs. The economic vulnerability of women and the poverty many of them faced were among the chief causes of prostitution. Any large European city had thousands of prostitutes.

Prostitution, of course, had always been one way for poor women to earn money. In the late nineteenth century, however, it was closely related to the difficulty encountered by poor women who were trying to enter an overcrowded female labor force. On the Continent, prostitution was generally subject to governmental regulations passed and enforced by male legislatures, police, and physicians. In Great Britain, prostitution received minimal regulation.

In England, most prostitutes were active on the streets only from their late teens to about age twenty-five. Certain cities—those with garrisons, naval ports, or those, like London, with large transient populations—attracted prostitutes. There were fewer prostitutes in manufacturing towns, where there were more opportunities for steady employment and community life was more stable.

Prostitutes usually came from families of unskilled workers and had minimal skills and education. Many had been servants. They also often were from broken homes or were orphaned. Child prostitutes were rare. Furthermore, women were seldom seduced into prostitution by middle-class men. Most customers of poor working-class prostitutes were working-class men.

Women of the Middle Class

A vast social gap separated poor working-class from middle-class women. As their fathers' and husbands' incomes permitted, middle-class women participated in the vast expansion of consumerism and domestic comfort that marked the late nineteenth and early twentieth centuries.

The Cult of Domesticity For the middle classes, the distinction between work and family, defined by gender, had become complete and constituted the model for all other social groups. Middle-class women, if at all possible, did not work. They became limited to the roles of wife and mother. They might enjoy domestic luxury and comfort, but their lives were circumscribed.

Middle-class women became the product of a particular understanding of social life. The home was to be a private place of refuge from business and the marketplace, a view set forth in women's journals across Europe.

As studies of middle-class women in northern France suggest, this image of the middle-class home and of the role of women in it is different from the one that had existed earlier in the nineteenth century. During the first half of the century, the spouse of a middle-class husband might contribute directly to the business. These women also frequently left child rearing to nurses and governesses. The reasons for the change during the century are not certain, but it appears that men began to insist on doing business with other men. Magazines and books began to praise motherhood, domesticity, religion, and charity as women's proper separate spheres.

For middle-class women, the home came to be seen as the center of virtue, children, and the proper life. Marriages were usually arranged for the family's economic benefit. Romantic marriage was viewed as a danger to social stability. Most middle-class women in northern France married by the age of twenty-one. The first child was often born within the first year after marriage. Rearing and nurturing her children were a woman's chief task. She would receive no experience or training for any role other than that of dutiful daughter, wife, and mother.

Within the home, a middle-class woman largely ran the household. She oversaw domestic management and child care. She was in charge of the home as a unit of consumption, which is why so much advertising was directed toward women. This domestic activity, however, occurred within the limits of the approved middle-class lifestyle. In her conspicu-

ous idleness, a woman symbolized first her father's and then her husband's success.

Religious and Charitable Activities The cult of domesticity assigned religious duties to women, which the Roman Catholic Church supported. Women were expected to attend mass, assure the religious instruction of their children, and participate in religious observances. Prayer was a major part of their lives. They internalized those portions of the Christian religion that stressed meekness and passivity. Because religious activities became part of the expected work of women, political liberals regarded women as susceptible to the influence of priests. This association between religion and a strict domestic life for women led later to tension between feminism and religious authorities.

Another important role for middle-class women was the administration of charity, because of their presumed innate spirituality and capacity to instill domestic and personal discipline. Women were supposed to be particularly interested in the problems of poor women, their families, and their children. Charity from middle-class women often required the recipient to demonstrate good character. By the end of the century, middle-class women seeking to expand their activity became social workers for the church, private charities, or the government. These vocations were an extension of the roles socially assigned to them.

Sexuality and Family Size Diaries, letters, and early medical and sociological surveys indicate that sexual enjoyment was fundamental to middle-class marriages. Much of the inhibition about sexuality stemmed from the dangers of childbirth, not from dislike or disapproval of sex.

One of the major changes during the second half of the century was the acceptance of small family size among the middle classes. The fertility rate in France dropped throughout the nineteenth century. It began to fall in England from the 1870s onward. During the last decades of the century, new contraceptive devices became available. One reason to limit family size was to maintain a high level of material consumption. Children had become much more expensive to rear, while more material comforts had become available. Fewer children probably meant more attention for each of them, possibly bringing mothers and their children emotionally closer.

The Rise of Political Feminism

Liberal society and its values did not inevitably improve the lot of women. In particular, it did not give them the vote or access to political activity. Male liberals feared that granting the vote to women would benefit conservatives, because women were thought to be unduly controlled by the clergy. Anticlerical liberals often had difficulty working with feminists.

Obstacles to Achieving Equality But women also were often reluctant to support feminist causes. Political issues relating to gender were only one of several priorities for many women. Some were sensitive to their class and economic interests. Others subordinated feminist political issues to national unity and patriotism. Still others would not support feminist organizations because of differences over tactics. The social and tactical differences among women often led to divisions among the feminists. Except in England, it was often difficult for working-class and middle-class women to cooperate. Roman Catholic feminists were uncomfortable with radical secularist feminists.

Although liberal society and law presented women with obstacles, they also provided feminists with intellectual and political tools. The arguments for utility and efficiency so dear to middle-class liberals could be used to expose the human and social waste implicit in the inferior role assigned to women.

Furthermore, the socialist criticism of capitalist society often included a harsh indictment of the position to which women had been relegated. The earliest statements of feminism were often associated with people who had unorthodox opinions about sexuality, family life, and property. This hardened resistance to the feminist message.

These difficulties prevented continental feminists from mounting the large demonstrations that feminists in Britain and the United States did. Everywhere in Europe, however, the feminist cause was divided over goals and tactics.

Votes for Women in Britain Europe's most advanced women's movement was in Britain, where Millicent Fawcett (1847–1929) led the moderate National Union of Women's Suffrage Societies. She believed Parliament would grant women the vote only when convinced that they would be responsible in their political activity. In 1908, this organization rallied almost half a million women in London. Her tactics were those of English liberals.

Emmeline Pankhurst (1858–1928) led a more radical branch of British feminists. In 1903, Pankhurst and her daughters founded the Women's Social and Political Union, known derisively as *suffragettes*. By 1910, they turned to the violent tactics of arson, window breaking, and sabotage of postal boxes. They marched en masse on Parliament. The Liberal government of Herbert Asquith (1852–1928) imprisoned many of the demonstrators and force-fed those who went on hunger strikes in jail. The government refused to extend the franchise. Only in 1918, and then as a result of their contribution to the war effort, did some British women receive the vote.

Political Feminism on the Continent The contrast of France and Germany shows how advanced the British women's movement was. In France, when Hubertine Auclert (1848–1914) began campaigning for the vote in the 1880s, she stood virtually alone. In 1901, the National Council of French Women (CNFF) was organized among upper-middle-class women, but it did not support the vote for women for several years. French Roman Catholic feminists supported the franchise. French feminists, however, rejected violence. They never organized mass rallies. Their leaders believed that the vote could be achieved through careful legalism. French women did not receive the right to vote until after World War II.

In Germany, feminist awareness and action were even more underdeveloped. Because no group in the German empire enjoyed extensive political rights, women were not certain that they would benefit from demanding them. Any such demand would be regarded as subversive of the state and society.

In 1894, the Union of German Women's Organizations (BDFK) was founded. By 1902 it was calling for the right to vote. But it was largely concerned with improving women's social conditions, their access to education, and their right to other protections. The German Social Democratic Party supported women's suffrage, but that socialist party was so disdained by the authorities and German Roman Catholics that this support only made suffrage more suspect in their eyes. Women received the vote in Germany only in 1918 under the constitution of the Weimar Republic. Before World War I, only in Norway (1907) could women vote on national issues.

Labor, Socialism, and Politics to World War I

The Working Classes

The late-century industrial expansion wrought further changes in the labor force. Proportionally, there were fewer artisans and skilled workers. Factory wage earners predominated. Work became more impersonal. Factories were located in cities, and most links between employment and home life dissolved. Large corporate enterprise meant less personal contact between employers and their workers.

Trade Unionism Workers still had to look to themselves to improve their situation. However, after mid-century, the labor force accepted the fact of modern industrial production and attempted to receive more benefits from that system. Workers turned to new institutions and ideologies: trade unions, democratic political parties, and socialism.

Trade unionism came of age as legal protections were extended to unions throughout the second half of the century. Most trade unions were slow to enter the political process directly. As long as the traditional governing classes looked after labor interests, members of the working class rarely sought office.

The mid-century organizational efforts of the unions aimed to improve the wages and working conditions of skilled workers. By the close of the century, large industrial unions for unskilled workers were also being organized. They confronted extensive opposition from employers, and were often recognized only after long strikes. In the decade before 1914, strikes were common throughout Europe as the unions attempted to raise wages to keep up with inflation. However, despite the advances of unions and the growth of their membership, they never included a majority of the industrial labor force. The unions represented a new collective fashion in which workers could associate to confront the economic difficulties of their lives and attain better security.

Democracy and Political Parties   The democratic franchise gave workers direct political influence, which meant they could no longer be ignored. Except for Russia, the major European states adopted broad-based electoral systems. Democracy brought popular pressure to bear on governments. Discontented groups could now voice their grievances and advocate programs within government rather than from outside it.

The advent of democracy witnessed the formation for the first time in Europe of organized mass political parties. The expansion of the electorate brought into the political processes many people whose level of political consciousness and interest was low. The organized political party mobilized the new voters. The largest single group in these mass electorates was the working class. The democratization of politics presented the socialists with opportunities and required the traditional ruling class to vie with them for the support of the new voters.

Marx and the First International

Karl Marx (1818–1883) himself accommodated the new practical realities that developed during the third quarter of the century. He did not abandon the revolutionary doctrines of *The Communist Manifesto*, and in *Capital* (Vol. 1, 1867), he continued to predict the disintegration of capitalism. But his practical, public political activity reflected a different approach.

In 1864, a group of British and French trade unionists founded the International Working Men's Association, known as the First International. Marx wrote its inaugural address. In it, he approved efforts by workers and trade unions to reform the conditions of labor within the existing political and economic processes. He urged revolution but tempered the means.

During the late 1860s, the First International gathered statistics, kept labor groups informed of mutual problems, provided a forum for the debate of socialist doctrine, and proclaimed its own size and influence. From these debates and activities, Marxism emerged as the most important strand of socialism. In 1872, Marx and his supporters drove the anarchists out of the First International. Marx was determined to preserve the role of the state against the anarchist attack on authority. German socialists became impressed by Marx's thought. Because they became the most important socialist party in Europe, they were the chief channel for Marxism.

The First International was destroyed by the events surrounding the Paris Commune. Only one real Marxist was involved in the Commune, but Marx glorified it as a proletarian uprising. British trade unionists, who in 1871 were finally receiving new legal protection, wanted no connection with the crimes of the Parisians. Throughout Europe the events in Paris cast a pall over socialism. The First International was dissolved in 1876. Thereafter, the fate of Marxism, socialism, and the labor movement depended largely on the economic and political conditions of the individual European countries.

Germany: Social Democrats and Revisionism

The German Social Democratic Party (SPD) kept Marxist socialism alive. Founded in 1875, the SPD suffered twelve years of persecution by Otto von Bismarck (1815–1898), who believed socialism would undermine German politics and society. Nonetheless, the SPD polled more votes in elections to the *Reichstag*.

Repression having failed, Bismarck enacted social welfare legislation to wean German workers from socialist loyalties. These measures provided health and accident insurance, and old age and disability pensions. The German state thus organized a system of social security that did not change the system of property holding or politics.

In 1891, the SPD was allowed to operate as a legalized party. Its new direction was announced in the Erfurt Program. In Marxist fashion, the program declared the imminent doom of capitalism and the necessity of socialist ownership of the means of production. However, these goals were to be achieved by legal political participation. The revolution was inevitable, but the immediate task of socialists was to improve workers' lives. In theory, the SPD was hostile to the German Empire, but the party functioned within its institutions.

This situation of the SPD, however, generated the most important internal socialist challenge to the orthodox Marxist analysis of capitalism and the socialist revolution. Eduard Bernstein (1850–1932) wrote what was regarded as this socialist heresy. Bernstein questioned whether Marx and his orthodox followers had been correct in their pessimistic appraisal of capitalism and the necessity of revolution. Bernstein pointed to the rising standard of living in Europe, the ongoing power of the middle class, and the opening of the franchise to the working class. He argued that a humane socialist society required not revolution but more democracy and social reform. Bernstein's doctrines, known as *revisionism*, were condemned as theory by German socialists, although the party actually pursued a peaceful, reformist program. In theory, the SPD continued to advocate revolution.

The SPD was the most successful prewar socialist party. Its rejection of reform socialism in favor of revolutionary socialism influenced all socialists who looked to the German example. Most significant, Lenin and the leaders of the Russian revolution adopted this position. Thereafter, wherever Soviet Marxism was influential, the goal would be revolution rather than reform.

France: "Opportunism" Rejected

French socialism gradually revived after the suppression of the Paris Commune. The major problem for French socialists was their own internal division. There were no fewer than five separate parties. They managed to elect approximately forty members to the Chamber of Deputies by the early 1890s.

At the turn of the century, the two major factions of French socialism were led by Jean Jaurès (1859–1914) and Jules Guesde (1845–1922). Jaurès believed, like the revisionists in Germany, that socialists should cooperate with radical middle-class ministries to enact social legislation. Guesde argued that socialists could not support a bourgeois Cabinet that they were dedicated to overthrowing. The quarrel came to a head as a byproduct of the Dreyfus Affair (see Chapter 27) in 1899, when the socialist Alexander Millerand (1859–1943) was appointed to the Cabinet.

By 1904, "opportunism," the term applied to such Cabinet participation by socialists, was debated at the Congress of the Second International. This organization had been founded in 1889 to unify the national socialist parties and trade unions. The Congress condemned "opportunism" and ordered the French socialists to form a single party. Jaurès accepted the decision. By 1914, the united Socialist Party was the second largest in the Chamber of Deputies. But Socialist Party members would not again serve in a French Cabinet until 1936.

Great Britain: The Labour Party and Fabianism

No form of socialism made significant progress in Britain, the most advanced industrial society of the day. The growing trade unions normally supported Liberal Party candidates. The "new unionism" of the 1880s and 1890s organized the dock workers, the gas workers, and similar unskilled groups. Employer resistance heightened class antagonism. In 1892, Keir Hardie (1856–1915) became the first independent worker elected to Parliament.

In 1901, however, a decision by the House of Lords (Britain's supreme court) removed the legal protection accorded union funds. The Trades Union Congress responded by launching the Labour Party, which elected twenty-nine members to Parliament in 1906. Their goals did not yet encompass socialism. The British labor movement also became more militant. In scores of strikes, workers fought for wages to meet the rising cost of living. The government intervened to mediate these strikes.

British socialism itself remained primarily the preserve of intellectuals. The most influential socialists were from the Fabian Society, founded in 1884. The society took its name from Q. Fabius Maximus (d. 203 B.C.E.), the Roman general who defeated Hannibal by waiting before attacking. It favored a gradualist, peaceful, democratic approach to social reform. Its leading members were Sydney (1859–1947) and Beatrice (1858–1943) Webb, H. G. Wells (1866–1946), and George Bernard Shaw (1856–1950). The Fabians were particularly interested in collective ownership on the municipal level, or so-called gas-and-water socialism.

Russia: Industrial Development and the Birth of Bolshevism

In the late nineteenth century, the tsarist government was determined to make Russia an industrial power. It favored heavy industries such as railways, iron, and steel. By 1900, Russia had approximately 3 million factory workers, whose working and living conditions were bad.

New political departures accompanied this economic development. In 1901, the Social Revolutionary Party was founded. It opposed industrialism and looked to the communal life of rural Russia as an economic model. In 1903, the Constitutional Democratic Party, or Cadets, was formed. It was drawn from people who participated in the *zemstvos* (local governments). They wanted a parliamentary regime with responsible ministries, civil liberties, and economic progress. The Cadets hoped to model themselves on the liberal parties of western Europe.

Lenin's Early Thought and Career The situation for Russian socialists differed radically from that in other major European countries. Russia had no representative political institutions and only a small working class. The compromises and accommodations achieved elsewhere were meaningless in Russia, where socialism in both theory and practice had to be revolutionary. The Russian Social Democratic Party, established in 1898, was Marxist, and its members

A Russian Social Investigator Describes the Condition of Children in the Moscow Tailoring Trade

E. A. Oliunina was a young Russian woman who had been active among union organizers during the Revolution of 1905. Later, as a student at the Higher Women's Courses in Moscow, a school for women's postsecondary education, she began to investigate and to write about child garment workers. The clothes produced by these children might have ended up in Russian department stores.

Why might the parents of these children have allowed them to work in these sweatshops? Why was alcoholism so prevalent? Why does Oliunina regard schools as the solution to this problem?

Children begin their apprenticeship between the ages of twelve and thirteen, although one can find some ten- and eleven-year-olds working in the shops. . . .

Apprenticeship is generally very hard on children. At the beginning, they suffer enormously, particularly from the physical strain of having to do work well beyond the capacity of their years. They have to live in an environment where the level of morality is very low. Scenes of drunkenness and debauchery induce the boys to smoke and drink at an early age.

For example, in one subcontracting shop that made men's clothes, a fourteen-year-old boy worked together with twelve adults. When I visited there at four o'clock one Tuesday afternoon, the workers were half-drunk. Some were lying under the benches, others in the hallway. The boy was as drunk as the rest of them and lay there with a daredevil look on his face, dressed only in a pair of longjohns and a dirty, tattered shirt. He had been taught to drink at the age of twelve and could now keep up with the adults.

"Blue Monday" is a custom in most subcontracting shops that manufacture men's clothes. The whole workshop gets drunk, and work comes to a standstill. The apprentices do nothing but hang around. Many of the workers live in the workshop, so the boys are constantly exposed to all sorts of conversations and scenes. In one shop employing five workers and three boys, "Blue Monday" was a regular ritual. Even the owner himself is prone to alcoholic binges. In these kinds of situations, young girls are in danger of being abused by the owner or his sons. . . .

In Russia, there have been no measures taken to improve the working conditions of apprentices. As I have tried to show, the situation in workshops in no way provides apprentices with adequate training in their trade. The young workers are there only to be exploited. Merely limiting the number of apprentices would not better their position, nor would it eradicate the influx of cheap labor. An incomparably more effective solution would be to replace apprenticeship with a professional educational system and well-established safeguards for child workers. However, the only real solution to the exploitation of unpaid child labor is to introduce a minimum wage for minors.

From Victoria E. Bonnell, *The Russian Worker: Life and Labor Under the Tsarist Regime.* Copyright © 1983 The Regents of California. Published and reprinted by permission of the University of California Press. Excerpts from pp. 177, 180–181, 182–183.

---

greatly admired the SPD, but tsarist repression meant that it had to function in exile.

The leading late-nineteenth-century Russian Marxist was Georgii Plekhanov (1857–1918), based in Switzerland. His chief disciple was Vladimir Illich Ulyanov (1870–1924), who took the name of Lenin. In 1895, he was exiled to Siberia for revolutionary activity. After his release in 1900, Lenin spent most of the next seventeen years in Switzerland.

There Lenin became involved with the exiled Russian Social Democrats. They all considered themselves Marxists, but quarrelled about the nature of a Marxist revolution in primarily rural Russia and the structure of their own party. The Social Democrats favored further industrial development. Most believed that Russia must develop a large proletariat before the revolution could come. They hoped to mold a mass political party like the SPD.

Lenin dissented from both positions. In *What Is to Be Done?* (1902), he condemned any accommodations. He also criticized a trade unionism that settled for short-term gains rather than revolution. Lenin rejected the concept of a mass party composed of workers. Revolutionary consciousness must be carried to the working class by a small, elite party of professional revolutionaries.

Establishment of the Bolsheviks   In 1903, at the London Congress of the Russian Social Democratic Party, Lenin split the party ranks. Although it lost most of the votes during the congress, near the close Lenin's group mustered a slim majority. Thereafter, it assumed the name *Bolsheviks,* meaning "majority," and the more moderate, democratic revolutionary faction became known as the *Mensheviks,* or "minority." In 1905, Lenin urged that the socialist revolution unite the proletariat and the peasants. He understood the profound discontent in the Russian countryside and knew that an alliance of workers and peasants in rebellion probably could not be suppressed. Lenin's two principles of an elite party and a dual social revolution allowed the Bolsheviks, in late 1917, to capture the leadership of the Russian Revolution and transform the political face of the modern world.

The Revolution of 1905 and Its Aftermath   The quarrels among the Russian socialists had no immediate influence within Russia itself. In 1904, Russia went to war with Japan, but the result was defeat and political crisis. On January 22, 1905, a priest named Father Gapon (1870–1906) led thousands of workers to petition the tsar for improvements in industrial conditions. As they approached the Winter Palace in Saint Petersburg, troops killed about 100 people.

Revolutionary disturbances spread throughout Russia: Sailors mutinied, peasants revolted, and property was attacked. Liberal Constitutional Democrat leaders from the *zemstvos* demanded political reform. In October 1905, strikes broke out in Saint Petersburg, and worker groups, called *soviets*, virtually controlled the city. Nicholas II (r. 1894–1917) promised Russia constitutional government.

Early in 1906, the tsar announced the election of a parliament, the Duma. However, he reserved for himself ministerial appointments, financial policy, and military and foreign affairs. Nicholas named as his chief minister P. A. Stolypin (1862–1911). Neither was sympathetic to the Duma. In 1906, the government canceled any redemptive payments the peasants still owed from the emancipation of the serfs in 1861. Thereafter, Stolypin repressed rural discontent.

After Stolypin's assassination in 1911, the tsarist government muddled along. But the imperial family became surrounded by scandal over the influence of Grigori Rasputin (1871?–1916), who seemed able to heal the tsar's hemophilic son, the heir to the throne. The undue influence of this uncouth man, the continued social discontent, and the conservative resistance to liberal reforms rendered the position and policy of the tsar uncertain after 1911.

NORTH AMERICA

The New Industrial Economy

The full industrialization of the United States followed a pattern not unlike that of nineteenth-century Europe, but with significant differences. The United States industrialized later than Britain. Its major expansion in iron and steel took place after the Civil War and was approximately contemporary to the economic rise of the newly united Germany. In the United States, entre-preneurial enterprise had always been respected. American manufacturers and commercial developers encountered little of the prejudice against trade and commerce that existed among the European aristocracy. Wealthy American businessmen had political influence. The United States possessed an immense internal market that functioned without trade restraints for the shipment of unprocessed goods to factories or of finished products to their markets. Much of the capital for American industrial expansion came from British bankers who saw the United States as an area of secure investment. Finally, the United States had a relative shortage of labor and consequently relatively high wages, the factors that attracted so many immigrants to the industrial sector during the second half of the century.

In America as in Europe, however, the railways spurred the most intense industrial growth. Railway miles increased from approximately 50,000 in the mid-1860s to almost 200,000 by 1900. Much of the construction was made possible by European investments. The railways created demand for iron, steel, coal, and lumber. They also stimulated settlement, expanded markets, and helped knit the country together.

European Immigration to the United States

The same conditions that made American life so difficult for blacks and Native Americans (see Chapter 27) turned the United States into a land of opportunity for white immigrants. These immigrants faced religious and ethnic discrimination and poverty, but for many of them and their children, the social and economic structures of the United States allowed for assimilation and upward social mobility. This was especially true of those immigrants, mostly from northern and western Europe, who arrived between approximately 1840 and 1890—the great period of German, British, and Irish immigration. Among this group, the Irish encountered the most difficulties and resistance.

Toward the end of the century and well into the next, millions of people arrived from the Mediterranean and eastern Europe. Most of them left economically depressed areas and financed their immigration themselves.

These new immigrants, who generally worked in the growing industrial cities, were seen and treated as of a lower class and inherently more difficult to assimilate than the earlier immigrants. Predominately Roman Catholic, Orthodox, and Jewish, they encountered intolerance. The same kind of racial theory that spread through Europe during these years was present in the United States. The new immigrants were often regarded as being from less desirable racial stocks. They often endured enormous poverty and settled into communities of people from their own ethnic background. What ultimately held them together were private organizations, such as churches and synagogues, clubs, newspapers in their own languages, and social agencies they organized for themselves.

Although none of these immigrants faced the same legal discrimination as did American blacks, the Jews encountered restricted covenants on real estate, obstacles to joining private clubs, and quotas for admission to many schools and universities. Asian immigrants to the West Coast faced harsher prejudice.

Unions: Organization of Labor

The expansion of industrialism led to labor unions. In America as in Europe, workers faced resistance from employers and those who feared that labor unions might lead to socialism. Another difficulty arose from the social situation of the labor force itself. White laborers would not organize alongside blacks. Different ethnic minorities would not cooperate. The flood of immigration ensured a supply of workers willing to work for low wages. The owners of businesses could often divide and conquer the ethnically mixed labor force.

In 1881, the American Federation of Labor (AFL) was founded. Unlike the advanced European socialist movement, it did not seek to transform the life of workers in a radical fashion but rather focused on higher wages and better working conditions. The AFL concentrated on organizing skilled workers; it did not seek to organize whole industries. Among its most effective leaders was Samuel Gompers (1850–1924). Other unions, such as the United Mine Workers and the Railway Brotherhoods, organized workers by industry.

The industrialization of the United States—again, like that of Europe—saw business crises or downturns. Depressions occurred in the 1870s and 1890s. What little relief there was came from local authorities and private charities. This pattern would continue until the Great Depression of the 1930s. The economic turmoil of the 1880s and 1890s spawned violent strikes. The major goal of labor thereafter was to win the full legal right to organize. This was achieved only during Franklin Roosevelt's (1882–1945) New Deal in the 1930s.

Socialism was a path not taken by American labor and one not allowed to be taken. The leaders of the conservative unions worked against socialists, and spokesmen for business sought to block their influence. The federal and state governments tried to repress socialist activities. After the Bolshevik Revolution of 1918, American socialists were persecuted as Bolshevists. The United States thus became the land where many social issues tended to be addressed by trade unions rather than by socialist parties. Furthermore, unions were not legally attacked in America as they were in Britain, which led to the founding of the British Labour Party.

In many European countries, socialist parties, or ministers like Bismarck who attempted to outflank the socialists, had pressed their governments to provide social services. No significant legislation of this kind was passed in the United States until the New Deal.

The Progressives

Political bosses controlled much of the power in American politics after the Civil War, especially in cities. This system depended on patronage. In return for jobs and favors, the boss received political support. Government was a vehicle for distributing spoils. Boss politics was a way, however crude and unattractive, of organizing the disorderly social and economic forces of the great cities.

Toward the close of the century, reformers from the white upper-middle classes feared that people such as themselves might lose political and social influence. Disturbed by the corruption of political life, they found the urban environment with its slums unacceptable. They wanted more efficient and less corrupt government. They also wanted the government to become a direct agent of change and reform. Pursuing these goals, they ushered in the progressive era, which lasted from approximately 1890 through 1914. The progressives were not always liberal by later standards. For example, progressives in the South often disenfranchised blacks and poor whites by imposing literacy tests.

The progressives began their reform work on the local level before they launched into national politics. The disorder and poverty in the cities disturbed them. Urban reformers believed that bosses robbed cities of the money needed to make them livable. In place of patronage, they demanded social and municipal services to clean up the cities. They attacked special interests who blocked reform. Progressive mayors called for lower utility rates and streetcar fares and attacked police corruption.

Social Reform

Churches also began to advocate social reform. It was in this era that the "Social Gospel" was first preached, with its message that Christianity involved civic action. Young people began to work in settlement houses in the slums. Other young persons from the middle class became active in housing and health reform, education, and charities. They conducted surveys of the urban slums. Their vision of social order was that of the white middle class.

In the mid-nineties, progressivism began to affect state governments. There the impulse toward reform involved attempts to protect whole classes of persons who were perceived as unable to protect themselves against exploitation, especially children and women working under unwholesome conditions for low wages. Other aspects of progressivism at the state level involved the civil service and the regulation of railways. These reformers partook of the late nineteenth century cult of science. They believed that the problems of society were susceptible to scientific, rational management. The general public interest should replace special interests.

This picture, taken in 1910, shows women working in a New England shoe factory. Women were also working in similar factory workshops in Europe. [The Granger Collection, N.Y.]

The Progressive Presidency

Roosevelt   Theodore Roosevelt became president in 1901 after the assassination of William McKinley (1843–1901). He had been a reforming governor of New York State. Roosevelt created the modern American presidency. By force of personality and intelligence, he began to make the presidency the most powerful branch of government. As president, he began to set the agenda for national affairs and to define the problems that the federal government was to address. He surrounded himself with strong advisers.

Roosevelt was determined to control the powerful business trusts. No centers of economic power should be stronger than the federal government. He moved against some of the most powerful financiers in the country, such as J. P. Morgan and John D. Rockefeller. Through legislation associated with the term "Square Deal," Roosevelt attempted to assert the public interest over that of powerful special interests. He wanted big business to operate according to rules established by the government for the public good.

In 1902, Roosevelt brought the moral power of the presidency to the aid of mine workers who were on strike. He appointed a commission to arbitrate the dispute. This was a major intrusion of the federal government into the economic system. A decade earlier, the government had used troops to break strikes. Roosevelt sought to make the presidency and the federal government the guarantor of fairness in economic relations. Thus he fostered the passage of the Pure Food

and Drug Act and the Meat Packing Act in 1906, which protected the public against adulterated foodstuffs. Here again, the regulatory principle came to the fore. His conservation policies ensured that millions of acres of national forests came under the care of the federal government.

Roosevelt was associated with a vigorous, imperialistic foreign policy that had roots in the 1890s. In 1898, McKinley had led the nation into the Spanish-American War, and the United States had acquired control of Cuba, Puerto Rico, Guam, and the Philippines. Roosevelt believed that the United States should be a world power. In Latin America, naval intervention assured the success of the Panamanian revolt of 1903 against Colombia. A treaty with the new Panamanian government allowed the United States to construct and control a canal across Panama. The United States was thus following the model of the European great powers, which had been intervening in Africa and Asia. Like the other great powers, the imperialist policies of the United States were built on a conviction of racial superiority.

Wilson   In 1913, Woodrow Wilson, a Democrat, brought a different concept of progressivism to the White House. Wilson (1856–1924) was a former reforming governor of New Jersey, where he had battled the bosses. Like Roosevelt, he accepted a modern industrialized nation. However, unlike Roosevelt, Wilson disliked big business almost in and of itself. He believed in economic competition in which the weak would receive protection from the government. Wilson termed his policy the New Freedom. In office, however, he followed a policy of moderate regulation of business.

Wilson saw the presidency as responsible for leading Congress to legislative decisions, and he admired the British parliamentary system. He presented Congress with a vast agenda of legislation and then worked to see that it was passed. Although Wilson appeared to be an advanced reformer, he reinstated racial segregation in the federal civil service and opposed female suffrage.

War broke out in Europe in August 1914. Although Wilson was reelected in 1916 on the slogan "He Kept Us Out of War!," in April 1917 he led the nation into the European conflict. The expertise that progressives had brought to the task of efficient domestic government was then turned to making the nation an effective military force. These two impulses—the first toward domestic reform, the second toward a strong international role—marked the progressive movement and would shape American history after the war.

The American progressives resembled political leaders of their generation in Great Britain. The Conservative Benjamin Disraeli (1804–1881) and liberals William Gladstone (1809–1898) and David Lloyd-George (1863–1945) had supported various social reforms. Political leaders in France and Germany had undertaken reforms to forestall the advance of socialism and address the problems of industrialization and urbanization. These leaders had favored unprecedented use of central government authority.

IN WORLD PERSPECTIVE

The Building of Northern Transatlantic Supremacy

Between 1850 and 1914, Europe had more influence throughout the world than it had ever before or since. Europe and North America were the most industrially advanced regions of the world. But Europe's industrial base was more advanced than that of the still-developing United States. European banks exercised vast influence across the globe. Europeans financed the building of railways in Africa, Asia, and the Americas. Financial power brought political influence. The armaments industry gave European armies and navies power over the peoples of Africa and Asia. The United States had begun to exercise such power as a result of the Spanish-American War. These economic developments established a pattern that still persists. First European and later American banks, companies, and corporations penetrated the economies and societies of Asia, Africa, and Latin America. They often expected their governments to protect their interests.

Thus, what started as commercial contact often evolved into direct political influence.

During these years, European culture was also probably enjoying its greatest influence. Capital cities in Latin America adopted European-style architecture. Paris became synonymous with high fashion. Paris, London, and Vienna were world intellectual centers. The advanced industrial and urban civilization of Europe was regarded as a model.

The emerging role of women in western Europe and the United States would also affect the rest of the world. In particular, the demand for the entrance of women into the political process and the professions would become a hallmark of the next century. On both sides of the Atlantic, women became leaders in social reform movements.

The nation that most understood the nature of European power and sought to imitate it was Japan. Its administrators and intellectuals after the Meiji restoration (1868) came to Europe to study the new technology, political structures, and military organizations. The Japanese defeated Russia in 1905, the first non-European nation using Western weapons, organizations, and economic power to defeat a European nation. In the twentieth century, other non-European nations would find ways to import or manufacture technology that would allow them to challenge European and later American hegemony. Today the proliferation of weaponry usually developed in the United States or Europe has allowed regional powers to challenge Western dominance. This destabilizing trade began in the latter nineteenth century.

Unlike Japan, China, India, the countries of the Middle East, and Africa were overwhelmed by the economic and military power of Europe. In time, however, the peoples of those lands who were dominated by the European powers embraced the ideologies of revolutionary protest, particularly those of nationalism and socialism. As people from the colonial world came to work or study in Europe, they encountered ideas and criticisms of Western culture that they adapted and then turned against their colonial governors.

World War I destroyed the late-nineteenth-century European self-confidence. The Bolsheviks brought revolution to Russia. After the war, anticolonial movements began to grow, especially in India, in a manner that most Europeans in 1900 could not have imagined. Those movements found supporters in Europe as a result of the spread of socialist ideas regarding social justice and public policy. Furthermore, because the political and economic systems of the world had become so interconnected during the second half of the nineteenth century, the influence and impact of the European conflict could not be limited to Europe. The United States would be drawn into World War I and would never again be able to avoid worldwide responsibilities.

Review Questions

1. What were the chief features of the late-nineteenth-century European middle-class society?

2. Why were European cities redesigned during the late nineteenth century? Why were housing and health key issues for urban reform?

3. What were the major characteristics of Jewish emancipation in the nineteenth century? Why did women grow discontented with their lot? How had they improved their position by 1914? Was the emancipation of women inevitable? How did women approach their situation differently from country to country?

4. What caused the emergence of trade unions and organized mass political parties in Europe? How did the American progressives, as reformers, differ from the various European socialists? Why were the debates of "opportunism" and "revisionism" important to the socialist parties?

5. How did Lenin's view of socialism differ from that of socialists in western Europe? Why did socialism not emerge as a major political force in the United States?

Documents CD-ROM

1. Sarah Stickney Ellis 1799–1872: From *The Women of England: Their Social Duties and Domestic Habits* (The Influence of Women)

2. John Stuart Mill: From *The Subjection of Women*

3. Bernard Shaw: Act III From *Mrs. Warren's Profession*

4. Gertrude Himmelfarb: From *Poverty and Compassion*

5. Oscar Wilde: From "The Soul of Man Under Socialism"

29 THE BIRTH OF CONTEMPORARY WESTERN THOUGHT

The second half of the nineteenth century, when the modern nation-state developed and the industrial growth that laid the foundations for the modern material lifestyle occurred, was also the age in which the ideas and concepts that marked Western thought for much of the twentieth century took shape.

The impact of these advanced ideas did not remain limited to Europe. They found a wide audience in the United States, as well as among the numerous students from regions in Africa and Asia that were governed by Europe, and students from Latin America who studied in European universities. They took home the ideas they encountered there, which they associated with modern society and politics, and often attempted to apply them in their homelands. Consequently, for much of the twentieth century, people around the world who regarded themselves as educated, who wished their nations to become modern, and who wished to be politically active drew upon the new world of European ideas discussed in this chapter as well as the ideas of European socialism discussed earlier. They often saw the application of such ideas, most particularly science and technology, as a path to power and wealth and as weapons that could be turned against their European colonial administrators. In both the Western and the non-Western worlds, the ideas that em-

anated from Europe in the second half of the nineteenth century thus became powerful vehicles for challenging traditional thought and society.

The Prestige of Science

In about 1850, the basic Newtonian picture of nature as a vast machine that operated according to mechanical principles still prevailed. Its laws could be ascertained objectively through experiment and observation. Scientific theory purportedly described physical nature as it really existed. Most scientists also believed, like Newton and the deists of the eighteenth century, that their knowledge of nature demonstrated the existence of a supreme being.

Darwin and Natural Selection

In 1859, Charles Darwin (1809–1882) published *The Origin of Species*, which carried the mechanical interpretation of physical nature into the world of living things. The book was one of the seminal works of Western thought. Darwin did not originate the concept of evolution, which had been discussed widely before he wrote. What he and Alfred Russel Wallace (1823–1913) did, working independently, was to formulate the principle of natural selection, which explained how species had changed or evolved over time. Earlier writers had believed that evolution might occur; Darwin and Wallace explained how it *could* occur.

The two scientists contended that organisms come into existence in numbers greater than those able to survive in their environment. Those organisms possessing a marginal advantage in the struggle for existence live long enough to propagate. This principle of survival of the fittest Darwin called *natural selection*. The principle was naturalistic and mechanistic. Its operation required no guiding mind. What neither Darwin nor anyone else in his day could explain was the origin of those chance variations that provided some members of a species with a better chance for survival than others. Only when the work on heredity by the Austrian monk Gregor Mendel (1822–1884) received public attention after 1900 did the mystery of those variations begin to be unraveled.

Darwin's and Wallace's theory represented the triumph of naturalistic explanation, which removed the idea of purpose from organic nature. Thus, it not only contradicted the biblical Creation, but also undermined the deistic argument that the design of the universe indicated the existence of God. Darwin's work also undermined the whole concept of fixity in nature or the universe. The world was a realm of flux and change. The fact that physical and organic nature might be constantly changing allowed people to believe that society, values, customs, and beliefs should also change.

In 1871, in *The Descent of Man*, Darwin applied the principle of evolution by natural selection to human beings. Darwin was hardly the first person to treat human beings as animals, but his arguments brought greater plausibility to that point of view. He contended that humankind's moral nature and religious sentiments, as well as its physical frame, had developed naturalistically in response to the requirements of survival. Within Darwin's thought, neither the origin nor the character of humankind required the existence of a God for its explanation.

Darwin's theory of evolution by natural selection encountered criticism from the religious and scientific communities. By 1900, evolution was widely accepted by scientists, but the acceptance of Darwin's mechanism of natural selection within the scientific community really dates from the 1920s and 1930s, when it became combined with modern genetics. The role of natural selection is still controversial within the scientific community.

Auguste Comte and Intellectual Development

The French philosopher Auguste Comte (1798–1857), a late child of the Enlightenment, developed a philosophy of human intellectual development that regarded science as its final or positive stage. Comte thought that positive laws of social behavior could be discovered in the same fashion as laws of physical nature. He is therefore generally regarded as the father of sociology. Comte helped to convince learned Europeans that knowledge in any field must resemble scientific knowledge.

Comte's thinking achieved considerable impact in Latin America. Many people associated with business, technology, railway building, and the military there saw themselves guided by Comtean ideas as did those who opposed the influence of the church. Comteanism was attractive because it advocated achieving scientific, technological advance in a generally nondemocratic manner. Those who wanted their countries to become modern but feared disorder turned to Comte's thought.

Social Darwinism

Theories of ethics were modeled on science during the last half of the century. The concept of the struggle for survival was applied to human social relationships. The phrase "survival of the fittest" predated Darwin and reflected the competitive outlook of classical economies. Darwin's use of the phrase gave it the prestige of advanced science.

The most famous advocate of evolutionary ethics was Herbert Spencer (1820–1903), who believed that human society progressed through competition. If the weak received too much protection, humankind was the loser. In Spencer's work, struggle against one's fellow human beings became a kind of ethical imperative. The concept could be applied to justify not aiding the poor and the working class or dominating colonial peoples, or to urge aggressively competitive relationships among nations. Evolutionary ethics and similar concepts, all of which are usually termed *social Darwinism*, came close to saying "Might makes right." Spencer's ideas attracted business groups in the United States, Latin America, and Asia who considered themselves well suited to guide their nations in the struggle for economic existence.

One of the chief opponents of such thinking was Thomas Henry Huxley (1825–1895), the great defender of Darwin. In 1893, Huxley declared that the physical cosmic process of evolution was at odds with the process of human ethical development. The struggle in nature only demonstrated how human beings should not behave.

During the last half of the century, scientists believed that they had discovered all the principles that might be discovered. However, in the twentieth century, that confident, self-satisfied world vanished. But the pursuit of science and technology became associated with the military and economic dominance of Europe. By the late nineteenth century, political leaders around the world who wished their nations to resist European inroads or to see their peoples become more prosperous embraced what often amounted to a cult of science. Often their model was Germany. The most important example of such new departures were the events in late-nineteenth-century Japan that led to a vast reorganization of its society and government.

Christianity Under Siege

The nineteenth century was a difficult period for the organized Christian churches. Many European intellectuals left the faith. The secular, liberal nation-states attacked the influence of the church. The expansion of population and the growth of cities challenged its organizational capacity. Yet the churches remained popular, and thousands of missionaries labored in the non-Western world.

The Intellectual Attack

The intellectual attack on Christianity challenged its historical credibility, scientific accuracy, and morality. The *philosophes* of the Enlightenment had delighted in pointing out contradictions in the Bible. The historical scholarship of the nineteenth century cast doubts on the historical validity of the Bible and caused many literate people to lose faith in Christianity.

Science also undermined Christianity. Many eighteenth-century writers had led Christians to believe that the scientific examination of nature buttressed their faith. But Charles Lyell (1797–1875) suggested that the Earth was much older than the biblical records contended, and Darwin's theory and the ideas of other writers suggested that the moral nature of humankind could be explained without God. Anthropologists, psychologists, and sociologists suggested that religion and religious sentiments were just natural phenomena.

Other intellectuals questioned the morality of Christianity. The moral character of the Old Testament God came under fire. His cruelty and unpredictability clashed with the progressive, tolerant, rational values of liberals. They also wondered about the morality of the New Testament God, who would sacrifice for His own satisfaction the only perfect being ever to walk the Earth. Many of the clergy began to ask themselves if they could preach doctrines they felt to be immoral.

These skeptical intellectual currents seem to have directly influenced only the upper levels of educated society. Yet they created a climate in which Christianity lost its intellectual respectability. Fewer educated people joined the clergy. More people found that they could lead their lives without reference to Christianity. The secularism of everyday life proved as harmful to the faith as direct attacks. This situation prevailed especially in the cities, which were growing faster than the churches' ability to meet the challenge. Whole generations of the urban poor grew up with little experience of the church as an institution or of Christianity itself.

Conflict of Church and State

The secular state of the nineteenth century clashed with both the Protestant and the Roman Catholic Churches. Liberals disliked the dogma and the political privileges of the established churches. National states were often suspicious of the supranational character of the Roman Catholic Church. However, the primary area of conflict was education. The churches feared that future generations would emerge without religious teaching. The advocates of secular education feared that future generations would be more loyal to religion or the churches than to the nation. From 1870 through the turn of the century, religious education was debated in every major European country.

France   In France, a dual system of Catholic and public schools existed. Under the Falloux Law of 1850, the local priest provided religious education in the public schools. The conservative French Catholic Church and the Third Republic detested each other. Between 1878 and 1886, the government passed educational laws sponsored by Jules Ferry (1832–1893) that replaced religious instruction in the public schools with civic training. Members of religious orders were no longer permitted to teach in the public schools, the number of which was to be expanded. After the Dreyfus Affair (1894–1899), the government of René Waldeck-Rousseau (1846–1904), drawn from pro-Dreyfus groups, suppressed the religious orders. In 1905, the Napoleonic Concordat was terminated, and church and state were separated.

Germany and the *Kulturkampf*   The most extreme church-state conflict occurred in Germany during the 1870s. Bismarck felt threatened by the Roman Catholic Church and the Catholic Center Party. He removed Catholic and Protestant clergy from overseeing local education in Prussia and set education under state direction. This was merely the beginning of a concerted attack on the Catholic Church in Germany.

The "May Laws" of 1873, which applied only to Prussia, required priests to be educated in German schools and universities and to pass state-administered examinations. The state could veto the appointments of priests. The disciplinary power of the pope and the church over the clergy was transferred to the state. When the bishops and many of the clergy refused to obey these laws, Bismarck used force, but in the end his *Kulturkampf* ("cultural struggle") against the Catholic Church failed. By 1880, the chancellor had abandoned his attack. He had gained state control of education only at the price of Catholic resentment against the German state. The *Kulturkampf* was probably Bismarck's greatest blunder.

Church-State Conflict Outside of Europe   Conflict between church and state also constituted one of the chief elements in nineteenth-century Latin American politics. By the time of the Wars of Independence, the Roman Catholic Church had become a major landholder in much of Latin America and a force for social conservatism. After the Wars of Independence, liberal political movements tended to oppose the church as they worked to expand education and reform landholding. Violent anti-clericalism often marked Latin American social and political life in the middle and late nineteenth century.

Areas of Religious Revival

German Catholic resistance to the secular state illustrates the continuing vitality of Christianity. In Great Britain, both the Anglican church and the Nonconformist denominations grew. In France, pilgrimages and the cult of the miracle of Lourdes became popular. Churches of all denominations tried to give more attention to the urban poor.

The Missionary Effort

The churches also attempted to spread the Christian faith around the world. During the nineteenth century, Protestant denominations in Great Britain and the United States initiated the modern missionary movement. This effort occurred during the very decades when many intellectuals had begun to doubt the Christian faith. Nonetheless, throughout the century thousands of missionaries preached Christianity in Africa, Asia, and the Pacific. Most of these missionaries were Protestant, but by 1900 the Roman Catholic Church was also active.

The missionary societies at home that sponsored this activity acted as political pressure groups. As a result, the home governments took considerable interest in their missionaries, helping to give them more influence and impact.

Roman Catholic missionary work was directed primarily by the hierarchy. Pope Gregory XVI (1831–1846) sent out priests to new areas and established bishoprics in Africa and Asia. Christian missionaries were often among the first Westerners to interact with Africans and Asians. Europeans and Americans frequently learned about non-Western peoples through their reports. Some missionaries were sympathetic to the peoples whom they hoped to convert. For others, spreading the Christian faith primarily meant spreading their own culture. There were long debates among missionaries about how much of local religious belief and prac-

tice to tolerate. There were also difficulties about allowing indigenous leadership to grow. By 1900, many people associated the missionary effort with the general determination of Europeans and Americans to dominate the rest of the world.

The Roman Catholic Church and the Modern World

Perhaps the most striking example of religious revival amidst intellectual skepticism and political hostility was the resilience of the papacy. In 1864, Pius IX (1846–1878), embittered by the effects of Italian unification, issued the *Syllabus of Errors*, which condemned the major tenets of political liberalism and modern thought. He set the Roman Catholic Church squarely against contemporary science, philosophy, and politics. In 1870, the First Vatican Council promulgated the dogma of the infallibility of the pope when speaking officially on matters of faith and morals. No earlier pope had gone so far.

Pius IX was succeeded by Leo XIII (1878–1903), who sought to make accommodation with the modern age and to address the great social questions. He looked to the philosophical tradition of Thomas Aquinas (1225–1274) to reconcile faith and reason. He permitted Catholics to participate in the politics of liberal states. In the encyclical *Rerum Novarum* (1891) he defended private property, religious education, and religious control of the marriage laws, and condemned socialism and Marxism. But he also declared that employers should treat their employees justly, pay them proper wages, and permit them to organize labor unions. The pope urged that modern society be organized in corporate groups, including people from various classes, who might cooperate according to Christian principles. The corporate society, derivative of medieval social organization, was to be an alternative to both socialism and competitive capitalism. On the basis of Leo XIII's pronouncements, democratic Catholic parties and trade unions were founded throughout Europe.

The post–World War II era has seen momentous changes in the church. These began in 1959 when Pope John XXIII (r. 1958–1963) summoned the twenty-first Ecumenical Council, which came to be called Vatican II. The Council ended the practice of celebrating the mass in Latin, requiring it instead to be said in the vernacular. It also permitted freer relations with other Christian denominations and gave more power to bishops. In recognition of the growing importance to the church of the world outside Europe and North America, the church has also transformed itself into a truly world body. However, the popes have upheld the celibacy of priests, maintained the church's prohibition on contraception, and opposed the ordination of women.

John Paul II (r. 1978–m) has pursued a three-pronged policy. First, he has maintained traditional doctrine, stressing the authority of the papacy and attempting to limit religious experimentation. Second, he took a firm stand against communism and contributed to the spirit of freedom in Eastern Europe that destroyed the communist regimes. Finally, he has encouraged the expansion of the church in the non-Western world, stressing the need for social justice while limiting the political activity of priests, especially in Latin America.

Toward a Twentieth-Century Frame of Mind

The late nineteenth century and the early twentieth century constituted the crucible of contemporary Western and European thought. Philosophers, scientists, psychologists, and artists began to portray physical reality and human nature and society in new ways. Their concepts challenged the presuppositions of mid-nineteenth-century science, rationalism, liberalism, and bourgeois morality.

Science: The Revolution in Physics

Modifications in the scientific worldview originated within the scientific community itself. By the late 1870s, critics suggested that the belief of many scientists—that their mechanistic models, solid atoms, and theories about absolute time and space actually described the real universe—was not well-founded. By World War I, few scientists believed any longer that they could portray the "truth" about physical reality. Rather, they saw themselves as recording the observations of instruments and as setting forth useful hypothetical or symbolic models of nature.

New discoveries in the laboratory paralleled the philosophical challenge to nineteenth-century science. With those discoveries the comfortable world of supposedly "complete" nineteenth-century physics vanished forever. In December 1895, Wilhelm Roentgen (1845–1923) published a paper on his discovery of X rays, a form of energy that penetrated various opaque materials. His paper was soon followed by major steps in the exploration of radioactivity.

The discovery of radioactivity and discontent with the existing mechanical models led to revolutionary theories in physics. In 1905, Albert Einstein (1879–1955) published his first papers on relativity. He contended that time and space exist not separately but rather as a combined continuum. Moreover, the measurement of space and time depends on the observer as well as on the entities being measured. In 1927, Werner Heisenberg (1901–1976) set forth the uncertainty principle, according to which the behavior of subatomic particles is a matter of statistical probability rather than of exactly determinable cause and effect. Much that only fifty years earlier had seemed certain and unquestionable about the physical universe now became problematical.

Nineteenth-century popularizers of science had urged its importance as a path to rational living and decision making. By the early twentieth century, the developments in the scientific world itself had dashed such hopes. The mathematical complexity of twentieth-century physics meant that science would rarely again be successfully popularized. However, through applied technology and further research in physics and medicine, science also affected daily living more than ever before. Consequently, nonscientists in legal, business, and public life have been called on to make decisions involving technological matters that they rarely can or do understand in depth or detail and have thus become increasingly dependent upon persons with scientific expertise.

Philosophy: Revolt Against Reason

Philosophical circles were questioning whether rational thinking could adequately address the human situation.

Friedrich Nietzsche No late-nineteenth-century writer better exemplified this new attitude than the German philosopher Friedrich Nietzsche (1844–1900). He was at odds with the predominant values of the age. He attacked Christianity, democracy, nationalism, rationality, science, and progress. He sought less to change values than to probe their sources in the human mind and character. He wanted not only to tear away the masks of respectable life but also to explore how human beings made such masks.

Major Scientific Publication Dates: The Nineteenth and Early Twentieth Centuries

1830	Lyell's *Principles of Geology*
1830–1842	Comte's *The Positive Philosophy*
1853–1854	Gobineau's *Essay on the Inequality of the Human Races*
1859	Darwin's *The Origin of Species*
1871	Darwin's *The Descent of Man*
1872	Neitzsche's *The Birth of Tragedy*
1883	Nietzsche's *Thus Spake Zarathustra*
1896	Herzl's *The Jewish State*
1899	Chamberlain's *The Foundations of the Nineteenth Century*
1900	Freud's *The Interpretation of Dreams*
1905	Weber's *The Protestant Ethic and the Spirit of Capitalism*

In *The Birth of Tragedy* (1872), he insisted on the positive function of instinct and ecstasy in human life. To limit life to strictly rational behavior was to impoverish it. The strength for the heroic life and the highest artistic achievement arose from sources beyond rationality.

In later works, such as *Thus Spake Zarathustra* (1883), Nietzsche criticized democracy and Christianity as leading only to the mediocrity of sheepish masses. He announced the death of God and proclaimed the coming of the Overman *(Ubermensch)*, who would embody heroism and greatness. Nietzsche did not intend this term to refer to superman or superrace. He was critical of contemporary racism and anti-Semitism. He sought a return to the heroism that he associated with Greek life in the Homeric age. He thought that the values of Christianity and bourgeois morality prevented humankind from achieving life on a heroic level. Those moralities forbade too much of human nature from fulfilling itself. Christianity demanded a useless and debilitating sacrifice of the flesh and spirit rather than full-blooded heroic living and daring. He believed that war had accomplished more than philanthropy.

Sigmund Freud forced a reconsideration of the role of rationality in human motivation. After Freud it was no longer possible to see reason as the sole determinant of behavior. [Bildarchiv Preussischer Kulturbesitz]

Nietzsche sought to discover not what is good and what is evil but the social and psychological sources of the judgment of good and evil. In his view, morality was a human convention that had no independent existence. For Nietzsche, this discovery liberated human beings to create life-affirming values that would glorify pride, assertiveness, and strength rather than meekness, humility, and weakness.

Birth of Psychoanalysis

The major figures of late-nineteenth-century science, art, and philosophy sought to discern the undercurrents, tensions, and complexities that lay below the smooth surfaces of hard atoms, respectable families, rationality, and social relationships. As a result of their theories and discoveries, educated Europeans could never again view the surface of life with smugness, complacency, or even much confidence. The emergence of psychoanalysis through the work of Sigmund Freud (1856–1939) exemplified this trend.

Freud was born into an Austrian Jewish family. In 1886, he opened his medical practice in Vienna, where he continued to live until driven out by the Nazis in 1938. All of Freud's research and writing were done from the base of his medical practice. His earliest medical interests had been psychic disorders, to which he sought to apply the critical method of science. In 1885, he had studied in Paris with Jean-Martin Charcot (1825–1893), who used hypnosis to treat hysteria. In 1895, Freud and another physician published *Studies in Hysteria*.

In the mid-1890s, Freud abandoned hypnosis and allowed his patients to talk spontaneously about themselves. He found that they associated their neurotic symptoms with experiences going back to childhood. He also noticed that sexual matters were significant in his patients' problems. By 1897, he formulated a theory of infantile sexuality, according to which sexual drives and energy exist in infants and do not simply emerge at puberty. In Freud's view, human beings are creatures of sexuality from birth through adulthood. He thus radically questioned the concept of childhood innocence. He also portrayed sex as one of the bases of mental order and disorder.

Freud also examined the psychic phenomena of dreams. As a good rationalist, he believed that the irrational content of dreams must have a reasonable, scientific explanation. His examination led him to reconsider the general nature of the human mind. He concluded that during dreams, unconscious wishes, desires, and drives that were excluded from everyday conscious life and experience enjoyed relatively free play in the mind. He argued that during the waking hours, the mind repressed those wishes, which were as important to one's psychological makeup as conscious thought. In fact, those unconscious drives and desires contributed to conscious behavior. Freud related these concepts to his idea of infantile sexuality in *The Interpretation of Dreams* (1900), his most important book.

In later writings, Freud developed a new model of the internal organization of the mind in which the mind is an arena for struggle and conflict among the id, the ego, and the superego. The id consists of amoral, irrational, driving instincts for aggression and physical and sensual pleasures. The superego embodies the external moral imperatives and expectations imposed on the personality by society and culture. The ego is the mediator between the impulses of the id and the asceticism of the superego. The ego allows the personality to cope with the inner and outer demands of its existence. One's personality reflects the result on the ego of the partial and unconscious repression of the impulses of the id to satisfy the demands of the external world embodied in the superego. Freud believed that excessive repression could lead to mental disorder, but that some repression of sexuality and aggression was necessary for civilized living.

Freud was a son of the Enlightenment. Like the *philosophes*, he was a realist who wanted human beings to live free of fear and illusions by rationally understanding themselves and their world. He saw the personalities of human beings as determined by finite physical and mental forces in a finite world. He spoke of religion as an illusion. Freud, like the writers of the eighteenth century, wished to see civilization and humane behavior prevail. However, he also understood the immense sacrifice of instinctual drives required for civilized behavior and how many obstacles lay in the way of rationality. Freud believed that the sacrifice and struggle were worthwhile, but he was pessimistic about the future of civilization in the West.

Freud's work marked the beginning of the psychoanalytic movement. By 1910 he had attracted a small but able group of disciples, some of whom developed theories of which Freud disapproved. The most important dissenter was Carl Jung (1875–1961).

Psychoanalysis touched not only twentieth-century psychology but also sociology, anthropology, religious studies, and literary theory. However, despite its impact on Western thought, psychoanalysis exerted only modest influence elsewhere in the world. Recently, psychoanalysis has come under much criticism, and its future influence remains uncertain.

Political and Social Thought

Retreat from Rationalism in Politics

Both nineteenth-century liberals and socialists agreed that rational analysis could solve the problems of society. They felt that once given the franchise, individuals would vote in their own rational self-interest. Education could improve the human condition. By 1900, these views were under attack. Political scientists and sociologists painted politics as frequently irrational. Racial theorists questioned whether rationality and education could affect society at all.

However, one social theorist remained impressed by the role of reason in human society. The German sociologist Max Weber (1864–1920) regarded the emergence of rationalization as the major development of human history. According to this view, rationalization displayed itself in both scientific knowledge and the rise of bureaucratic organization. Weber saw bureaucratization, not capitalism, as the most fundamental feature of modern society. Bureaucratization involved the extreme division of labor, requiring individuals to fit themselves into a small role in a large organization. Weber believed that in modern society people derived their own sense of personal worth from their positions in these organizations. Weber also contended, in contrast to Marx, that noneconomic factors might account for major developments in human history. In his most famous essay, *The Protestant Ethic and the Spirit of Capitalism* (1905), Weber traced much of the rational character of capitalist enterprise to the ascetic religious doctrines of Puritanism. The Puritans, in his opinion, had accumulated wealth less for its own sake than to assure themselves that they stood among the elect of God.

In emphasizing the individual and rationality, Weber differed from many contemporary social scientists who argued that instinct, habit, and affections, not reason, directed human behavior. These theorists also emphasized the role of collective groups in politics rather than the individual championed by the liberals.

Racial Theory

The same tendencies to question or deny the role of reason in human affairs and to sacrifice the individual to the group manifested themselves in theories of race. Racial thinking had long existed in Europe. Since at least the eighteenth century, biologists and anthropologists had classified human beings according to the color of their skin, their language, and their stage of civilization. Linguistic scholars had observed similarities between European languages and Sanskrit. They then postulated the existence of an ancient race called the *Aryans*, who had spoken the original language from which the rest derived. During the Romantic period, writers had called the different cultures of Europe *races*. The debates over slavery in the European colonies and the United States had also involved racial theory. However, in the late nineteenth century, race emerged as a dominant explanation of the history and character of large groups of people.

Arthur de Gobineau (1816–1882), a reactionary French diplomat, enunciated the first important theory of race as the major determinant of history. In his *Essay on the Inequality of the Human Races* (1853–1854), Gobineau portrayed the troubles of Western civilization as resulting from of the long degeneration of the original white Aryan race. It had unwisely intermarried with the inferior yellow and black races, thus diluting the greatness and ability that originally existed in its blood. Gobineau saw no way to reverse this degeneration.

A growing literature by anthropologists and explorers helped to spread racial thinking. In the wake of Darwin's theory, the concept of survival of the fittest was applied to races and nations. The recognition of the animal nature of humankind made the racial idea more persuasive. Houston Stewart Chamberlain (1855–1927), an Englishman who settled in Germany, drew together these strands of racial thought into his *Foundations of the Nineteenth Century* (1899). He championed the concept of biological determinism through race, but he was more optimistic than Gobineau. Chamberlain believed that through genetics, a superior race could be developed. Chamberlain also pointed to the Jews as the major enemy of European racial regeneration. Chamberlain's book thus aided the spread of anti-Semitism. Other writings in Germany emphasized the supposed racial and cultural dangers that the Jews posed to German national life.

Anti-Semitism and the Birth of Zionism

Political and racial anti-Semitism emerged in part from this racial thought and the retreat from rationality in politics. Religious anti-Semitism dated from at least the Middle Ages. Popular anti-Semitism, which identified the Jewish community with economic exploitation, persisted. During the last third of the century, as finance capitalism changed the economic structure of Europe, people pressured by the changes became hostile toward the Jewish community. This was especially true of the insecure middle class. In Vienna, Mayor Karl Lueger (1844–1910) used this kind of anti-Semitism for his Christian Socialist Party. In Germany, the ultraconservative Lutheran chaplain Adolf Stoecker (1835–1909) revived anti-Semitism. The Dreyfus Affair in France fanned hatred toward the Jews.

To this already ugly atmosphere, racial thought contributed the belief that no matter to what extent Jews assimilated themselves into the culture of their country, their Jewishness—and thus their alleged danger to the society—would remain. The problem of race was not in the character but in the blood of the Jew. An important Jewish response to this new, rabid outbreak of anti-Semitism was the launching in 1896 of the Zionist movement to found a separate Jewish state. Its founder was the Austro-Hungarian Theodor Herzl (1860–1904). The conviction in 1894 of Captain Dreyfus in France and Karl Lueger's election in 1895 as mayor of Vienna, as well as Herzl's personal experiences of discrimination, convinced him that the liberal state could not protect the Jews in Europe.

In 1896, Herzl published *The Jewish State*, in which he called for a separate state in which the Jews of the world might be assured of those rights and liberties that they should be enjoying in the liberal states of Europe. Herzl followed the tactics of late-century mass democratic politics by appealing to poor Jews who lived in the ghettos of eastern Europe and the slums of western Europe. The original call to Zionism thus combined a rejection of the anti-Semitism of Europe with a desire to establish some of the ideals of liberalism and socialism in a state outside Europe.

Late-Century Nationalism

Racial thinking and anti-Semitism were part of a wider late-century aggressive nationalism. Nationalism had been a literary and liberal movement. Writers had sought to develop what they regarded as the historically distinct qualities of national or ethnic literatures. Liberal nationalists had hoped to redraw the map of Europe to reflect ethnic boundaries.

From the 1870s onward, however, nationalism became a mass movement with well-financed political parties. Nationalists tended to redefine nationality in terms of race and blood. The new nationalism opposed the internationalism of liberalism and socialism and the pluralism of class, religion, and geography. The nation and its duties sometimes became a secular religion. This aggressive, racist nationalism was the most powerful ideology of the early twentieth century.

Women and Modern Thought

Despite the often radical new ideas that shook European thought after 1850, views of women and their roles in society remained unchanged.

Antifeminism in Late-Century Thought

Much of the biological thought that challenged religious ideas and the received wisdom in science reinforced the traditional view of women as weaker than men. Darwin himself expressed such views. Medical thought concurred.

This conservative and hostile understanding of women manifested itself within the scientific community. Male scientists believed women should not discuss sexual matters. T. H. Huxley, the great defender of Darwin, claimed to have scientific evidence for the inferiority of women to men. Late Victorian anthropologists tended to assign women, as well as nonwhite races, an inferior place in the human family.

The position of women in Freud's thought is controversial. Critics have claimed that Freud portrayed women as incomplete human beings who might be inevitably destined to unhappy mental lives. He saw the natural destiny of women

Virginia Woolf Urges Women to Write

In 1928, Virginia Woolf, the English novelist, delivered two papers at women's colleges at Cambridge University. Those papers provided the basis for A Room of One's Own, *published a year later. In this essay, Woolf discussed the difficulty a woman writer confronted in finding previous women authors as models. She also outlined many of the obstacles that women faced in achieving the education, the time, and the income that would allow them to write. At the close of her essay, she urged women to begin to write so that future women authors would have models. She then set forth an image of Shakespeare's sister who, lacking such models, had not written anything, but who through the collective efforts of women might in the future emerge as a great writer because she would have the literary models of the women Woolf addressed to follow and to imitate.*

How does Woolf's fiction of Shakespeare's sister establish a benchmark for women writers? What does Woolf mean by the common life through which women will need to work to become independent writers? Why does she emphasize the need for women to have both income and space if they are to become independent writers?

A thousand pens are ready to suggest what you should do and what effect you will have. My own suggestion is a little fantastic, I admit; I prefer, therefore, to put it in the form of fiction.

I told you in the course of this paper that Shakespeare had a sister; but do not look for her in Sir Sidney Lee's life of the poet. She died young—alas, she never wrote a word. She lies buried where the omnibuses now stop, opposite the Elephant and Castle [a London intersection]. Now my belief is that this poet who never wrote a word and was buried at the crossroads still lives. She lives in you and in me, and in many other women who are not here tonight, for they are washing up the dishes and putting the children to bed. But she lives; for great poets do not die; they are continuing presences; they need only the opportunity to walk among us in the flesh. This opportunity, as I think, it is now coming within your power to give her. For my belief is that if we live another century or so—I am talking of the common life which is the real life and not of the little separate lives which we live as individuals—and have five hundred [pounds income] a year each of us and rooms of our own; if we have the habit of freedom and the courage to write exactly what we think; if we escape a little from the common sitting-room and see human beings not always in their relation to each other but in relation to reality; and the sky, too, and the trees or whatever it may be in themselves; . . . if we face the fact, for it is a fact, that there is no arm to cling to, but that we go alone and that our relation is to the world of reality and not only to the world of men and women, then the opportunity will come and the dead poet who was Shakespeare's sister will put on the body which she has so often laid down. Drawing her life from the lives of the unknown who were her forerunners, as her brother did before her, she will be born. As for her coming without that preparation, without that effort on our part, without that determination that when she is born again she shall find it possible to live and write her poetry, that we cannot expect, for that would be impossible. But I maintain that she would come if we worked for her, and that so to work, even in poverty and obscurity, is worth while.

From Virginia Woolf, *A Room of One's Own.* Copyright © 1974 The Hogarth Press, pp. 170–172.

---

as motherhood, and their greatest fulfillment the rearing of sons. The first psychoanalysts were trained as medical doctors, and their views of women reflected contemporary medical education, which tended to portray women as inferior. Women psychoanalysts, such as Karen Horney (1885–1952) and Melanie Klein (1882–1960), would later challenge Freud's views on women, and other writers would try to establish a psychoanalytic basis for feminism. Nonetheless, the psychoanalytic profession and academic psychology would remain dominated by men. Since psychology would increasingly influence child-rearing and domestic relations law in the twentieth century, it would, ironically, give men a large impact in the one area of social activity that women had dominated.

The social sciences of the era similarly reinforced traditional gender roles. Most major theorists believed that women's role in reproduction and child rearing demanded a social position inferior to men and took a conservative view of marriage, the family, child rearing, and divorce.

New Directions in Feminism

The feminists of the turn of the century set forth much of the feminist agenda for the twentieth century. They urged equal treatment of women under the law and the right to vote, but they also contended that the relationship of men and women within marriage and the family required rethinking.

Sexual Morality and the Family   Middle-class women began to challenge the double standard of sexual morality and the traditional male-dominated family. Often this challenge took the form of action relating to prostitution.

Between 1864 and 1886, English prostitutes were subject to the Contagious Diseases Acts. The police in certain cities with naval or military bases could require any woman suspected of being a prostitute to undergo immediate internal medical examination for venereal disease. Those found to have a disease could without legal recourse be confined for months to women's hospitals for treatment. The law took no action against their male customers. Indeed, the purpose of the laws was to protect men, not the women themselves, from infection.

These laws angered English middle-class women who believed that the working conditions and the poverty imposed on so many working-class women were the true causes of prostitution. They framed the issue in the context of their own efforts to prove that women were as human and rational as men and thus deserved equal treatment. They saw poor women as victims of the same kind of discrimination that prevented themselves from entering the universities and professions. The Contagious Diseases Acts assumed that women were inferior to men and put women's bodies under the control of male customers, medical men, and the police. They denied to poor women the freedoms that men enjoyed in English society.

By 1869, the Ladies' National Association for the Repeal of the Contagious Diseases Acts, a middle-class organization, began to oppose these laws. The acts were suspended in 1883 and repealed in 1886. Government and police regulation of prostitution roused similar movements in other nations.

The feminist groups that demanded the abolition of laws that punished prostitutes without questioning the behavior of their customers were challenging the double standard and, by extension, the traditional relationship of men and women in marriage. In their view, marriage should be a free union of equals with men and women sharing responsibility for their children.

Virtually all turn-of-the-century feminists supported wider sexual freedom for women, often claiming that it would benefit society as well as improve women's lives. Many of the early advocates of contraception had also been influenced by social Darwinism. They hoped that limiting the number of children would allow more healthy and intelligent children to survive. Such was the outlook of Marie Stopes (1880–1958), who pioneered contraceptive clinics in the poor districts of London.

Women Defining Their Own Lives   For many British and Continental feminists, achieving legal and social equality for women would help transform Europe from a male-dominated society to one in which both men and women could control their own destinies. Increasingly, feminists would concentrate on freeing and developing women's personalities through better education and government financial support for women engaged in traditional social roles, whether or not they had gained the vote.

Some women also became active within socialist circles. There they argued that the socialist transformation of society should include major reforms for women. Socialist parties usually had all-male leadership. Most male socialist leaders, including Lenin and later Stalin, were intolerant of demands for changes in the family or greater sexual freedom for either men or women. Nonetheless, socialist writings began to include calls for improving the economic situation of women that were compatible with more advanced feminist ideals.

It was within literary circles, however, that feminist writers often most clearly articulated the problems that they now understood themselves to face. Women authors, such as Virginia Woolf (1882–1941), were actually doing, on an equal footing, something that men had always done: leading some to wonder whether simple equality was the main issue. Woolf's *A Room of One's Own* (1929) became a fundamental text of twentieth-century feminist literature. In it she discussed the difficulties that women of brilliance and social standing encountered in being taken seriously as writers and intellectuals. She concluded that a woman who wished to write required both a room of her own, meaning a space not dominated by male institutions, and an independent income. But she also asked whether women writers should bring to their endeavors separate intellectual and psychological qualities that they possessed as women. She challenged some of the received notions of feminist thought by concluding that male and female writers must be able to think as both men and women and share the sensibilities of each. She thus sought to open the whole question of gender definition.

By World War I, feminism in Europe had become associated with challenges to traditional gender roles and sexual morality and with either socialism or political radicalism. So when extremely conservative political movements arose between the world wars, their leaders often emphasized traditional roles for women and traditional sexual morality.

Ideas associated with feminism encountered a mixed reception in the non-Western world. Feminist voices have appeared on every continent, but they have often encountered resistance. In some areas, such as India and Pakistan, women have achieved the highest political office and entered the professions. The fundamentalist Islamic revival, by contrast, has asserted a traditional role for women. Worldwide, women still stand far behind men in education, economic advance, and healthcare.

IN WORLD PERSPECTIVE

Intellectual Change

The scientific achievements of Europe during the second half of the nineteenth century were exported with mixed results. Social Darwinism and racism came to undergird the ideology of imperialism. The concept of survival of the fittest provided for many Europeans a pattern for their relations with the rest of the world. In both Europe and the United States, nonwhites were regarded as inferior. State governments in the southern United States enacted segregation laws based in part on racial thinking. Some scientific writers contended that non-European peoples stood on a lower level of the evolutionary ladder. When European states conquered and administered much of Africa and Asia, they justified their actions partly on the grounds that the native peoples were less fit than Europeans to govern themselves. Racial thinking of this kind affected most colonial administrators.

The technology and scientific theories that had made the Second Industrial Revolution possible also provided the technological superiority that allowed Europe and the United States to dominate the world between 1850 and 1945. That technological domination made the conclusions of racial

thinking plausible. However, science and technology could be copied and turned against its originators. Japan after the Meiji restoration (1858) copied the science and political administration associated with modern Western thought. It thus succeeded in defending itself against the intrusions of the West.

China failed to embrace modern science and technology and fell victim to both the Western powers and Japan. However, at the turn of the century China began to abandon its dedication to Confucian education. Reformers embraced Western ideas, including social Darwinism and socialism. By the end of World War I, a strong sense of nationalism also permeated China. The need to embrace science and a concern for social reform combined in China to contribute to the appeal of Marxism, which was viewed as a form of scientific socialism.

The emergence of a strong industrialized Japan and of a China stirred by nationalism and Marxist revolution illustrates the double influence of late-nineteenth-century Western ideas. Those scientific and political ideas first led to the degradation of those Asian peoples. In turn, other Western ideas, along with long-standing Asian ideas and values, provided the technological and ideological basis for national revivals leading those nations to challenge Western imperialism.

Review Questions

1. How would you account for the dominance of science in the thought of the second half of the nineteenth century? What were some of the major changes in scientific outlook between 1850 and 1914? How would you define positivism? Describe Darwin and Wallace's theory of natural selection. How did it affect ethics, Christianity, and European views of human nature?

2. How and why did Christianity come under attack in the late nineteenth century? Why was Leo XIII regarded as a liberal pope? How do you account for the resilience of the papacy during this period of attack on the church?

3. How did Nietzsche and Freud challenge traditional middle class and religious morality? Would you describe Freud more as a product of the Enlightenment or of Romanticism?

4. Why did many late-nineteenth-century intellectuals display fear and hostility toward women? How did Freud view the position of women? What were some of the social and political issues affecting women in the late nineteenth and early twentieth centuries and how did reformers confront them? What new directions did feminism take?

5. What was the character of late-nineteenth-century racial theory? How did it become associated with anti-Semitism? What led Herzl to develop the idea of Zionism?

Documents CD-ROM

1. Charles Darwin: From *The Descent of Man*

2. Auguste Comte: From "The Age of Ideology"

3. Pope Leo XIII: Rerum Novarum

4. Friedrich Nietzsche: From *Beyond Good and Evil*

5. David Friedrich Strauss: From *The Life of Jesus Critically Examined*

6. Wollestonecraft's Torch: Emmeline Pankhurst and Militant Suffragism

30 LATIN AMERICA: FROM INDEPENDENCE TO THE 1940S

By the mid-1820s, Latin Americans had driven out their colonial rulers and broken the colonial trade monopolies (see Map 30–1). Although rich in natural resources, the region did not achieve widespread prosperity and political stability for more than a century after independence.

The explanations for why Latin America has been less stable and prosperous than Europe and North America appear to lie in the role it played in the integrated global economic system that began to develop when it achieved political independence. This system prevented Latin Americans from achieving economic independence. The region's leaders thought their nations could prosper by providing raw materials to the world economy. Most Latin American nations developed export economies devoted to raw materials or semi-finished goods. This decision made their export products vulnerable to worldwide fluctuations in demand. They were also susceptible to influence from foreign business interests and interference by the governments of the United States and Europe.

Latin America had much in common with Africa and Asia during the nineteenth and early twentieth centuries. In all three regions, nations or areas would specialize by filling a niche by supplying a particular raw product to the increasingly integrated world economy. This might bring initial prosperity but provided too narrow a base for sustained economic well-being. In contrast, the economic advance of the United States and Europe was largely due to their ability to dominate and exploit niche economies around the globe.

Independence Without Revolution

The Wars of Independence liberated Latin America from direct European control but left it economically exhausted and politically unstable. Only Brazil tended to prosper immediately after independence. In contrast, the new republics of the former Spanish Empire felt themselves vulnerable. Because the Wars of Independence had been civil wars, the new governments knew that many of their populations might welcome their collapse. Economic life contracted: In 1830 overall production was lower than in 1800. Difficult terrain over vast distances made interregional trade difficult. The old patterns of overseas trade had been disrupted. There was an absence of funds for investment. Many wealthy *peninsulares* departed. Consequently, Latin American governments and businesses looked to Britain for protection, markets, and investment.

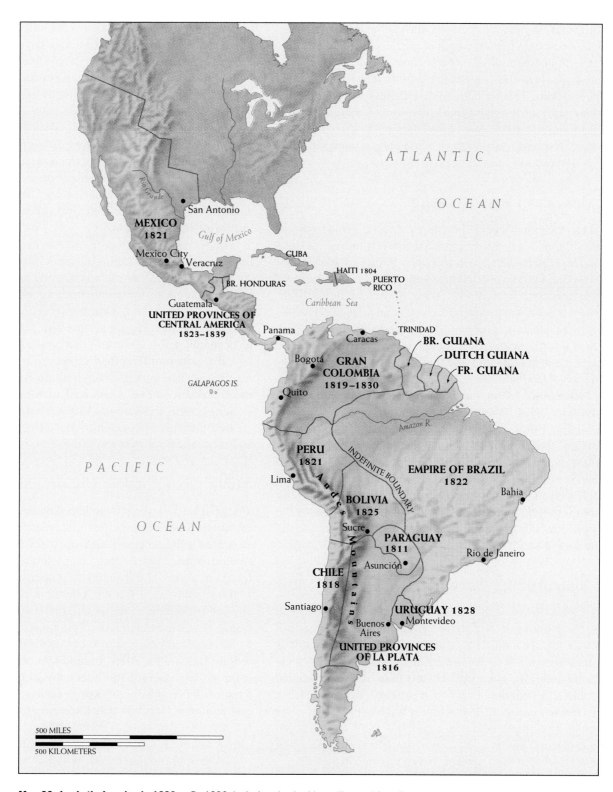

Map 30-1 Latin America in 1830. By 1830, Latin America had been liberated from European government. This map shows the initial borders of the states of the region with the dates of their independence. The United Provinces of La Plata formed the nucleus of what later became Argentina.

Independence also created new sources of discontent. There was much disagreement about the character of the future government. Institutions, such as the Roman Catholic Church, sought to maintain their privileges. Indian communities found themselves subject to new exploitation. Quarrels arose between the Creole elites of different regions of the new nations. The agricultural hinterlands resented the predominance of the port cities. Investors or merchants from one Latin American nation found themselves in conflict with those of others over tariffs or mining regulations. Civilians became rivals of the military.

Absence of Social Change

Yet all the elites opposed social reform. The Creole victors in the Wars of Independence granted equal rights to all persons and, except for Brazil, had abolished slavery by 1855. However, the right to vote depended on a property qualification, and peasants remained subservient to their landlords. Colonial racial codes disappeared, but not racial prejudice. Persons of white or nearly white complexion tended to constitute the elite of Latin America. Most important, there were no major changes in landholding; the ruling classes protected the interests of landholders.

Except for Mexico in 1910, no Latin American nation until the 1950s experienced a revolution that overthrew the social and economic structures dating from the colonial period. The absence of such social revolution is perhaps the most important factor in Latin American history during the first century of independence. The rise and fall of political regimes represented quarrels among the elite. Everyday life for most of the population did not change. Throughout the social structure, there was no mutual trust or allegiance to the political system.

Control of the Land

Most Latin Americans during the nineteenth century lived in the countryside. Agriculture was dominated by large *haciendas*, or plantations. The landowners ruled these estates as small domains. The *latifundia* (the large rural estates) grew larger during the nineteenth century from confiscated church lands and conquered Indian territories. Work was labor intensive because little machinery was available. For some products—salted meats, for example—there was a limited manufacturing stage in Latin America. Most crops, including grains, tobacco, sugar, coffee, and cacao, were exported.

Landowners constituted a society of their own. They sometimes formed family alliances with the wealthy urban classes who were involved in export commerce or the law. Younger sons might enter the army or the church. The landowners served in the national parliaments. Their wealth, literacy, and social connections made them the rulers of the countryside, and the army would protect them from any social uprising.

The rural work force was socially and economically dependent on the landowners. In Brazil, slavery persisted until 1888. In other rural areas, many people lived as virtual slaves. Debt peonage was widespread and often tied a peasant to the land like a serf. Later in the nineteenth century, the new lands that were opened were generally organized as large holdings with tenants rather than as small land holdings with independent farmers. This was different from both the United States and Canada. Poor transportation made internal travel difficult and kept many people on the land. Little effort was made to provide education, leaving Latin American peasants ignorant, lacking technological skills, and incapable of improving their condition.

The second half of the nineteenth century witnessed a remarkable growth in Latin American urban life. There was some movement from the countryside to the city and an influx of European and even Asian immigrants. Throughout this period there arose a political and social trade-off between the urban and rural elites. Each permitted the other to pursue its economic self-interest and repress discontent. Nonetheless, the growth of the urban centers shifted political influence to the cities and gave rise to an urban working class and the social discontents associated with many poor people working in difficult situations. Urban growth in Latin America created difficulties not unlike those that arose in Europe and the United States at about the same time.

Submissive Political Philosophies

The political philosophies embraced by the Creole elites also discouraged challenges to the social order. The political ideas associated with European liberalism, which flourished in Latin America after independence, supported republican government but limited the franchise to property holders. Thus in Latin America, as in Europe, liberalism protected property and tended to ignore the social problems of the poor. The Creole elite also exhibited racial prejudice toward nonwhites.

Economic liberalism and the need for British investment led to free trade. After independence, Latin America exported less than it had under colonial rule and achieved a trade balance only by exporting precious metals. The general economic view was that Latin America would produce raw materials for export in exchange for manufactured goods imported from Europe, especially from Britain.

For most of the nineteenth century, the landed sector of the economy dominated because cheap imports and a shortage of local capital discouraged indigenous industrialism. Latin American liberals championed the great landed estates and the social dependence associated with them. The produce of the new land could contribute export goods to pay for the import of finished goods. Liberals thus favored confiscating land owned by the church and the Indians, because they did not exploit their lands in a progressive manner, according to the liberals.

During the second half of the century, the political ideas of the French positivist philosopher Auguste Comte (1798–1857) swept across Latin America. Comte and his followers (see Chapter 29) had advocated the cult of technological progress. This undemocratic outlook suggested that either technocrats or authoritarians could best achieve modernization. It was popular among military officers and influenced the ongoing Latin American struggle between civilian and military elites. The great slogan of Latin American positivism, emblazoned on the flag of the Brazilian republic, was "Order and Progress." Groups that challenged the existing social order were unprogressive.

Toward the close of the century, the officer corps was often the most important educated elite in a country. Their education and attachment to the army gave them influence, generally conservative.

Finally, European theories of "scientific" racism were used to preserve the Latin American social status quo. Racial theory could attribute the economic backwardness of the region to its vast nonwhite or mixed blood population. This explanation shifted responsibility for the economic difficulties of Latin America away from the mostly white governing elites toward Indians, blacks, mestizos, and mulattos, who had long been exploited or repressed.

This conservative intellectual heritage affected twentieth-century political thought. First, it can be seen in the tendency of military groups in Latin America to view themselves as the guarantors of order. They were ready to seize control from civilians to thwart social change. Second, it can be seen in the way the political elites of Latin America opposed communism after the Russian Revolution. Governments used the fear of communism to resist political movements—communist or not—that advocated social reform or questioned property arrangements. Communism would become an even more powerful issue after the Cuban Revolution of 1957 installed a communist state in Latin America.

Economy of Dependence

The Wars of Independence destroyed the colonial trade monopolies. But Latin America remained dependent on non-Latin American economies. Trade was free and the nations were independent, but other nations continued to shape Latin American economic life.

One of the chief reasons for this dependence was the absence of large internal markets. Trade after independence flowed in the same direction that it had flowed before independence because Europe remained the source of imports of finished goods. Furthermore, then as now, geographical barriers hindered internal trade, and European and American investments in railways facilitated exports.

New Exploitation of Resources

The Wars of Independence disrupted the Latin American economy. Mines were flooded; machinery was in disrepair; labor was dispersed. Agricultural production was also disrupted. To restore old industries such as mining, and gain access to steamships and railroads, Latin Americans had to turn to Europe and North America. For decades, Britain economically dominated Latin America. The desire to pour manufactured goods into Latin America led Britain and other nations to discourage the development of manufacturing industries there.

To pay for foreign imports, Latin American nations produced agricultural commodities. Production for the export market led governments to expand into unsettled territory and to confiscate the lands of the church.

After 1850, the Latin American republics became relatively more prosperous. Chile exported copper and nitrates as well as wheat. Peru exported guano for fertilizer. Coffee was becoming king in Venezuela, Brazil, Colombia, and Central America. Sugar continued to be produced in the West Indies and Cuba, which remained under Spanish control. Argentina supplied hides and tallow. But this limited prosperity was based on the export of agricultural commodities or raw materials and the importation of finished goods. Yet the export economy seemed to foster genuine economic growth.

Both the trading patterns for these goods and internal improvements in Latin American production linked the economy of the region to Europe and, after 1900, to the United States. Europeans and North Americans provided capital and the technological skills to build bridges, roads, railroads, steam lines, and mines. But whenever the economy of Europe or the United States floundered, Latin America was hurt. The region could not control its own economic destiny.

Increased Foreign Influence

During the late nineteenth century, the relative prosperity of the export sector increased the degree of dependence. The growing European demand gave Latin Americans a false sense of security. The vast profits to be made through mining and agricultural exports discouraged investment in local industry. Foreigners saw no reason to capitalize local industry that might replace imported goods. By late in the century, the wealthy in Latin America had, in effect, lost control of valuable sectors of their economy. For example, in 1901 British and other foreign investors owned approximately 80 percent of the Chilean nitrate industry.

Foreign powers also used their political and military influence to protect their economic interests. Britain, as the dominant power until the turn of the century, was frequently involved in the political affairs of the Latin American nations. From the Spanish American War of 1898 onward, the United States began to exercise more direct influence in the region. In 1903, to facilitate its plans to build a canal across Panama, the United States participated in the rebellion that allowed Panama to separate from Colombia. The U.S. military intervened in the Caribbean and Central America. By the 1920s, the United States had replaced Britain as the dominant trading partner of Latin America.

United States interventions were one cost to Latin America of being a dependent economy. More significant costs, however, arose from fundamental shifts in world trade that were brought on by World War I and continued through the 1920s. First, the amount of trade carried on by European countries decreased. Second, during the 1920s world prices of agricultural commodities dropped. Latin American nations had to produce more goods to pay for their imports. Third, synthetic products manufactured in Europe or North America replaced the natural products supplied by Latin America. Finally, petroleum began to replace other natural products as an absolute percentage of world trade. This shift meant that petroleum-exporting countries, such as Mexico, gained a greater share of export income.

Economic Crises and New Directions

The Great Depression produced a crisis in this *neocolonial economy*. Commodity prices collapsed. The republics of Latin America could not repay their debts to foreign banks. The Depression led to the beginning of a new economic era in Latin America after the conclusion of World War II. It was marked by economic nationalism and a determination to create national economies that were not wholly dependent on foreign events and wealth.

With the Depression, it became necessary to substitute domestic manufactured goods for those imported from abroad. Various nations pursued policies called *import substitution*, and by the mid-1940s there were three varieties of manufacturing in Latin America. First, there were industries that, as in the past, transformed raw materials for export, such as food processing, mining, and petroleum refining. Second, there were industries addressing local demands, such as power plants and machine shops. Third, there were industries, basically assembly plants, that transformed imported materials to take advantage of cheap labor. None of this manufacturing involved heavy industry.

Search for Political Stability

The new states of independent Latin America had no experience in self-government. The Spanish Empire had been ruled directly by the monarchy and by Spanish-born bureaucrats. This monarchical or paternalistic heritage survived in the proclivity of the Latin American political elites to tolerate or support strong executives. The early republic constitutions were frequently suspended or rewritten, so that a strong leader could consolidate his power. Such figures were called *caudillos*. They usually came from the officer corps or enjoyed strong ties to the army. The real basis of their rule was force. *Caudillos* might support conservative causes, such as protection of the church or strong central government, or they might pursue liberal policies, such as the confiscation of church land, the extension of landed estates, and the development of education.

Even when *caudillos* were forced from office and parliamentary government was restored, the regimes that replaced them were neither genuinely liberal nor democratic. Parliamentary governments usually ruled by courtesy of the military and in the interest of the elites. No matter who ruled, the lives of most of the population changed little. Except for the Mexican Revolution of 1910, Latin American politics was run by and for the elite.

Three National Histories

Argentina, Mexico, and Brazil possess over 50 percent of the land, people, and wealth of the region. Their histories illustrate the general themes of Latin American history.

Argentina

Argentine history from independence to World War II can be divided into three eras. From the rebellion against Spain in 1810 until mid-century, the question of which region of the nation would be dominant was foremost. From 1853 until 1916, Argentina experienced economic expansion and large-scale immigration from Europe, which transformed its society and its world position. From 1916 to 1943, Argentines failed to establish a democratic state and struggled with an economy they did not control.

Buenos Aires versus the Provinces   In 1810, the junta in Buenos Aires overturned Spanish government. However, the other regions of the viceroyalty of Río de la Plata refused to accept its leadership. Paraguay, Uruguay, and Bolivia went their separate ways. Conflicts between Buenos Aires and the remaining provinces dominated the first seventy years of Argentine history. Eventually Buenos Aires established its primacy because it dominated trade on the Río de la Plata.

A commercial treaty in 1823 established Great Britain as a dominant trading partner. Thus began a deep intermeshing of trade and finance between the two nations that would continue for over a century. In 1831, the *caudillo* of the province of Buenos Aires, Juan Manuel de Rosas (1793–1877), negotiated the Pact of the Littoral, whereby Buenos Aires was put in charge of foreign relations and trade while the other provinces ran their own internal affairs. Within Buenos Aires, Rosas set up dictatorial rule. His major policies were expansion of trade and agriculture, suppression of the Indians, and nationalism.

Expansion and Growth of the Republic
Rosas' success in strengthening Buenos Aires bred resentment in other provinces. In 1852, Rosas was overthrown. The next year a federal constitution was promulgated for the Argentine Republic, but Buenos Aires remained economically and politically dominant.

The Argentine economy was agricultural, the chief exports at mid-century being animal products. Internal transportation was poor and the country was sparsely populated. Technological advances changed this situation during the last quarter of the century. In 1876, the first refrigerator ship steamed into Buenos Aires. Henceforth, it would be possible to transport Argentine beef to Europe. Furthermore, it became clear that wheat could be farmed throughout the pampas. In 1879 and 1880, the army carried out a major campaign against the Indian population known as the *Conquest of the Desert*. The British soon began to construct and manage railways to carry wheat to the coast, where it would be loaded on British and other foreign steamships. Government policy made the purchase of land by wealthy Argentines simple and cheap. The owners, in turn, rented the land to tenants. The predominance both of large landowners and of foreign business interests thus continued throughout the most significant economic transformation in Argentine history.

The vastly increased production of beef and wheat made Argentina one of the wealthiest nations of Latin America and an agricultural rival of the United States. The opening of land, even if only for tenant farming and not ownership, encouraged many Europeans, particularly from Spain and Italy, to emigrate to Argentina. The immigrants also provided workers for the food-processing, service, and transportation industries in Buenos Aires. By 1900, Argentina had become much more urbanized and industrialized. More people had reason to be politically discontent. Moreover, the children of the immigrants often became the strongest Argentine nationalists during the twentieth century.

Prosperity quieted political opposition for a time. The conservative landed oligarchy governed under presidents who perpetuated a strong export economy. Like similar groups elsewhere, they ignored the social questions raised by urbanization and industrialization.

However, the urban middle and professional classes wanted a greater share in political life and an end to corruption. In 1890, these groups founded the Radical Party. Its leader, Hipólito Irigoyen (1850–1933), was elected president in 1916. Without significant support in the legislature, his presidency brought few changes. In World War I, Argentina traded with both sides. Nonetheless, the war put pressure on the economy, and labor agitation resulted. Irigoyen used troops against strikers. Thereafter, the Radical Party pursued policies that benefited landowners and urban business interests. This was possible because of the close relationship between agricultural producers and processors and because both the landed and the middle classes resisted concessions to the working classes.

The Military in Ascendence
By the end of the 1920s, the Radical Party had become corrupt and directionless. The worldwide commodity depression hurt exports. In 1930, the military staged a coup. The officers returned power to conservative civilians, and Argentina remained dependent on the British export market.

In the 1930s, a right-wing nationalistic movement, *nacionalismo*, arose among writers, journalists, and a few politicians. It resembled the fascist political movements then active in Europe. Its supporters equated British and American domination of the economy with imperialism. They rejected liberalism, detested communism, were anti-Semitic, and supported the Roman Catholic Church. *Nacionalismo* was associated with a relatively progressive social policy rooted in the social values of Pope Leo XIII (see Chapter 29). It advocated social reforms that recognized the needs of workers and the poor, but that also sought to promote social harmony rather than communist revolution or socialist reconstruction of the economy. In effect, these groups were anti-imperialistic, socially concerned, authoritarian, and sympathetic to the rule of a modern *caudillo*. World War II gave these attitudes and their supporters new influence.

The war closed most of Europe to Argentine exports, creating an economic crisis. In 1943, the military again seized control. Many of the officers were fiercely nationalistic children of immigrants. Some had become impressed by the fascist and Nazi movements and were hostile to Britain. They contended that the government must address social questions, industrialize the country, and liberate it from foreign economic control. In these respects, they echoed the *nacionalistas*.

Between 1943 and 1946, Juan Perón (1895–1974), one of the colonels involved in the 1943 coup, forged this social discontent

Eva Perón Explains the Sources of Her Popularity

The Perónist movement in Argentina drew broad support from workers and the poor. The movement involved a cult of personality around both Perón and his wife Eva. In 1951, Eva Perón published a book entitled My Mission in Life (La razón de mi vida). *Here she explains how she sought to relate to her husband's political supporters.*

Why was Eva Perón's accepting the name "Evita" a political act? How did her use of this name separate her from the ruling elites of Argentina? What is the role she projects for herself in her relationship to various social groups in Argentina? Do you believe her discussion of herself to be sincere or politically opportunistic?

When I chose to be "Evita," I chose the path of my people. . . .

Only the people call me "Evita." Only the *descamisados* [the "unshirted," as Perón's working-class followers were termed] learned to call me so. . . .

I appeared to them thus the day I went to meet the humble of my land, telling them that I preferred being "Evita" to being the wife of the president, if that "Evita" could help to mitigate some grief, or dry a tear.

If a man of the government, a leader, a politician, an ambassador, who normally calls me "Señora," should call me "Evita," it would sound as strange and out of place to me as if a street-urchin, a workingman, or a humble person of the people should call me "Señora." . . .

Now, if you ask me which I prefer, my reply would be immediately that I prefer the name by which I am known to the people.

When a street-urchin calls me "Evita," I feel as though I were the mother of all urchins, and of all the weak and the humble of my land.

When a working man calls me "Evita," I feel glad to be the companion of all the workingmen of my country and even of the whole world.

When a woman of my country calls me "Evita," I imagine myself her sister, and that of all the women of humanity,

And so, almost without noticing it, I have classified in these three examples the principal activities of "Evita" relating to the humble, the workers, and women.

The truth is that, without any artificial effort, at no personal cost, as though I had been born for all this, I feel myself responsible for the humble as though I were the mother of all of them; I fight shoulder to shoulder with the workers as though I were another of their companions from the workshop or factory; in front of the women who trust in me, I consider myself something like an elder sister, responsible to a certain degree for the destiny of all of them who have placed their hopes in me.

And certainly I do not deem this an honor but a responsibility. . . .

Yes. I confess that I have an ambition, one single, great personal ambition: I would like the name of "Evita" to figure somewhere in the history of my country.

From Lourdes Arizpe, "Peasant Women and Silence," translated by Laura Beard Milroy in *Women's Writing in Latin America: An Anthology* by Sara Castro-Klarén, Sylvia Malloy, and Beatriz Sarlo. Copyright © 1992 by Westview Press. Reprinted by permission of the author.

Chronology of Argentina

1810	Junta in Buenos Aires overthrows Spanish government
1827–1852	Era of Rosas's dictatorial government
1876	Ship refrigeration makes possible export of beef around the world
1879–1880	Conquest of the Desert against the Indian population
1914–1918	Argentina remains neutral in World War I
1930s	Period of strong influence of nationalist military
1943–1956	Era of Juan and Eva Perón

and authoritarianism into a political movement known as Perónism. It was authoritarian, anti-communist, and socially progressive. Perón understood that political power could be exerted by appeals to the Argentine working class. He gained the support of the trade unions that were opposed to communism. In 1946, he made himself the voice of working-class democracy, even though he created an authoritarian regime that only marginally addressed industrial problems. He was aided by his wife, the former actress Eva Duarte (1919–1952), who enjoyed charismatic support among the working class.

Perón was the supreme twentieth-century embodiment of the *caudillo*. His power and appeal were rooted in the antiliberal attitudes that had been fostered by the corruption and aimlessness of Argentine politics during the Depression. He was ousted in 1956, but stability would continue to elude Argentine politics.

Mexico

For the first century of Mexican independence, conservative forces held sway, but in 1910, the Mexican people launched the most far-reaching revolution in Latin American history.

Turmoil Follows Independence The years from 1820 to 1876 were a time of turmoil, economic floundering, and humiliation. Independent Mexico attempted no liberal political experiments. Its first ruler was Agustín de Iturbide (1783–1824), who ruled until 1823 as an emperor. Thereafter, Mexico was governed by a succession of *caudillo* presidents, who depended on the army for support. The strongest of these figures was Antonio López de Santa Anna (1795–1863), a general and political opportunist who was finally exiled in 1855.

The mid-century movement against Santa Anna's autocracy was called *La Reforma*. In theory, its supporters were liberal, but Mexican liberalism was associated with anticlericalism, confiscation of church lands, and opposition to military influence on national life and politics. *La Reforma* aimed to produce political stability and civilian rule and attract foreign capital and immigrants. Its attack on the church led to further civil war. In January 1861, Benito Juárez (1806–1872) entered Mexico City as the temporary victor.

Political instability was matched by economic stagnation. The mines that had produced Mexico's colonial wealth were in poor condition, and the country could not repair them. The *hacienda* system left farming in a backward condition. Cheap imports of manufactured goods stifled domestic industries. Transportation was primitive. The government's remedy was massive foreign borrowing; as a result, interest payments ate up the national budget.

Foreign Intervention Political weakness and economic disarray invited foreign intervention. The territorial ambitions of the United States led to war with Mexico in 1846 and the US army occupied Mexico City. Mexico lost a vast portion of its territory, including what is now New Mexico, Arizona, and California.

Further foreign intervention occurred as a result of Juárez's liberal victory in 1861. Mexican conservatives and clerics invited the Austrian Archduke Maximilian (1832–1867) to become the emperor of Mexico. Napoleon III (r. 1852–1870) of France, who portrayed himself as a defender of the Roman Catholic Church, provided support for this venture. In May 1862, French troops invaded Mexico. Maximilian became emperor, but was unable to gain support from much of the population. In 1867, Juárez captured the unhappy emperor and executed him.

This twentieth-century portrait of Benito Juárez (oil on canvas, 1948, from Presidential Collection of Portraits of Mexican Presidents) emphasizes his major accomplishments. The foreground shows him drafting the Constitution of 1857. In the background to the left is the execution of Maximilian; to the right are scenes of road construction and farmers (who, thanks to Juárez's reforms, were given clear title to their lands) working their fields. [Corbis-Bettmann]

Díaz and Dictatorship The liberal leaders continued their measures against the church but also failed to rally popular support. In 1876, Porfirio Díaz (1830–1915), a liberal general, seized power and retained it until 1911. He maintained one of the most successful dictatorships in Latin American history by giving almost every political sector something it wanted. He allowed landowners to purchase public land cheaply; he cultivated the army; and he made peace with the church. He used repression against opponents and bribery to cement the loyalty of his supporters. Wealthy Mexicans grew even richer, and Mexico became a respectable member of the international financial community. Foreign capital, especially from the United States, flooded the nation.

Chronology of Mexico

1820–1823	Agustín de Iturbide rules as emperor
1833–1855	Santa Anna dominates Mexican political scene
1846–1848	Mexico defeated by United States and loses considerable territory
1861	Victory of liberal forces under Juárez
1862–1867	French troops led by Archduke Maximilian of Austria invade Mexico
1876–1911	Era of Porfirio Díaz
1911	Beginning of Mexican Revolution
	Zapata proclaims Plan of Ayala
1917	Forces of Carranza proclaim constitution
1929	Institutional Revolutionary Party organized

Yet problems remained. The peasants wanted land. Many Mexicans were malnourished. Labor unrest afflicted the textile and mining industries. Real wages for the working class declined. The Panic of 1907 in the United States disrupted the Mexican economy. By 1910, the *Pax Porfiriana* was unravelling.

Revolution

Revolution In 1911, Francisco Madero (d. 1913), a wealthy landowner and moderate liberal, led an insurrection that drove Díaz into exile. Shortly thereafter, Madero was elected president. He recognized the right of unions to strike, but was unwilling to undertake agrarian reform that might have changed the pattern of landholding. More radical leaders called for social change. Pancho Villa (1874–1923) in the north and Emiliano Zapata (1879–1919) in the south rallied mass followings of peasants who demanded fundamental changes in rural landholding. In late 1911, Zapata proclaimed his Plan of Ayala, which set forth a program of large-scale peasant confiscation of land. Much of the struggle during the next ten years would be between supporters and opponents of such agrarian reform.

Madero was squeezed between conservatives and the radical peasant revolutionaries. No one trusted him. In early 1913, he was overthrown by General Victoriano Huerta (1854–1916), who had help from the United States. In the meantime, Venustiano Carranza (1859–1920), a wealthy landowner, put himself at the head of a large army that initially received the support of both Zapata and Villa. On August 15, 1914, Carranza's forces entered Mexico City. Thereafter, disputes between Carranza, Villa, and Zapata arose both from political rivalry and from Carranza's refusal to embrace radical agrarian reform. Carranza eventually won out.

Carranza's political skills helped him build a broad base and edge out Villa and Zapata as the chief leader of the revolution. He separated the concerns of urban industrial workers from the land hunger of rural peasants, and thus doomed the effort to implement an agrarian revolution.

In early 1915, Carranza's army attacked Villa and Zapata. The peasant leaders still commanded regional support but could not win control of the nation. During 1916, Carranza confronted US military intervention along the border that continued until early 1917, when the United States became involved in World War I in Europe. Throughout the turmoil in Mexico, the government of the United States attempted to protect American interests through diplomacy and military intervention.

By 1917, after years of civil war, Carranza's forces wrote a constitution. The Constitution of 1917 set forth a program for ongoing social revolution—never pursued with vigor—and political reform. Years would pass before all the provisions of the constitution could be enforced, but it provided the goals and ideals toward which Mexican governments were expected to strive.

Carranza and his subordinates recognized the agrarian problem but were cautious about addressing it. They admired the economic development they had seen in California and were determined to modernize Mexican political life and attract capital investment; Mexican leaders would share these goals from that time onward. Thus, despite the radical rhetoric and the upheaval among peasants that the revolution involved, the Mexican revolution saw the victory of a middle-class elite who would attempt to govern through enlightened paternalism.

The decade after 1917 witnessed both confusion and consolidation. In 1919, Zapata was killed. Carranza was assassinated in 1920, Villa in 1923. In this turmoil, Carranza's generals provided stability. During the 1920s, they served as presidents. They moved cautiously and hesitated to press land redistribution but were opposed by the Roman Catholic Church. In 1929, Plutarco Elías Calles (1877–1945) organized the PRI, the Institutional Revolutionary Party, which remains the most important political force in the nation today. Despite criticism and tensions, the PRI has overseen the longest period of political stability experienced by any Latin American nation in this century.

In 1934, Lázaro Cárdenas (1895–1970) was elected president and moved to fulfill the promises of 1917. He turned tens of millions of acres of land over to peasant villages and nationalized the oil industry.

With the election of Manuel Ávila Camacho (1897–1955) in 1940, the era of revolutionary politics ended. Thereafter, the major issues in Mexico were those associated with postwar economic development. But unlike other Latin American nations, Mexico, because of its revolution, could confront those issues with a democratic perspective and a sense of social responsibility.

Brazil

Postcolonial Brazil differed from other newly independent nations in the region. Its language and heritage were Portuguese, not Spanish. For the first sixty-seven years of its independence, it had a stable monarchical government. And it retained slavery until 1888.

Brazil became an independent empire in 1822. The first emperor, Pedro I (r. 1822–1831), while serving as regent for his father, the king of Portugal, had put himself at the head of the independence movement. Although he granted Brazil a constitution in 1823, Pedro's high-handed rule led to his abdication in 1831. Brazilians then took hold of their own destinies.

His fifteen-year-old son, Pedro II (r. 1831–1889), assumed power in 1840 and governed Brazil until 1889. Pedro II established a reputation as a constitutional monarch by asking leaders of both the conservative and the liberal political parties to form ministries. Consequently, Brazil enjoyed political stability.

The Slavery Issue The great divisive issue in Brazil was slavery. Sugar production remained the mainstay of the economy until the 1850s, when coffee cultivation began to dominate Brazilian agriculture. Like sugar planters, coffee producers also used slave labor, but their profits were much larger than those of the sugar producers, so a transition to free labor would have been easier for them. Coffee planters also tended to see themselves as economic progressives. Hence, people investing in coffee were more open to emancipation than those who had invested in sugar, which depended on slave labor to be profitable.

By 1850, Brazil had virtually ceased importing slaves. The end of slave imports doomed the institution of slavery because the slave population could not reproduce itself. It was nonetheless one thing to face this inevitability and another to abolish slavery.

The Paraguayan War of 1865–1870 postponed consideration of the slave question. This conflict pitted Brazil, Argentina, and Uruguay against Paraguay. The dictator of Paraguay, Francisco Solano López (1827–1870), fought a war of attrition. His death in battle ended the war, but only after more than half of the adult male population of Paraguay had been killed.

The end of the war returned slavery to the forefront of Brazilian politics. Brazil and the Spanish colonies of Puerto Rico and Cuba were now the only slaveholding countries in the hemisphere. The emperor favored gradual emancipation. A law of 1871 freed slaves owned by the crown and decreed legal freedom for future children of slaves, but it required them to work on plantations until the age of twenty-one. However, throughout the 1870s and 1880s, the abolition

movement grew in Brazil. In 1888, Pedro II was in Europe and his daughter was regent. She favored abolition and signed a law abolishing slavery without compensation to the slave owners. Thus ended slavery in Brazil.

A Republic Replaces Monarchy It also brought to a head other issues that in 1889 ended the monarchy. Planters who received no financial compensation for their slaves were resentful. Roman Catholic clerics were disaffected by disputes with the emperor over education. Pedro II was unwell; his daughter, the heir to the throne, was unpopular. The officer corps of the army wanted more political influence. In November 1889, the army sent Pedro II into exile.

The Brazilian republic lasted from 1891 to 1930. Like the monarchy, it was dominated by a small group of wealthy persons. The political arrangement that allowed the republic to function smoothly was an agreement among the state governors. The president was to be chosen alternately from the states of São Paulo and Minas Gerais. In turn, the other eighteen governors had local political control. Fixed elections and patronage kept the system going. Literacy tests left few people qualified to vote. There was little organized opposition.

From the 1890s onward, the coffee industry dominated the nation. Around 1900, Brazil was producing over three-fourths of the world's coffee. The crop's success led to overproduction. To meet this problem, the government subsidized prices with loans from foreign banks and taxes on the rest of the economy, which felt exploited by the coffee interests. Throughout the life of the republic, Brazil produced essentially a single product for export and few goods for internal consumption.

Economic Problems and Military Coups The end of slavery, the expansion of coffee production, and the beginning of urban industry attracted foreign immigrants. They tended to settle in the cities and constituted the core of the early industrial labor force. In Brazil, as elsewhere, World War I caused major economic disruption. Urban labor discontent appeared. The failure to address urban and industrial social problems and the political corruption led to attempted military coups. The revolts demonstrated that segments of the military wanted a modern nation that was not dependent on a single exportable product and a political system that recognized interests besides those of the coffee planters.

Coffee had ruled as the economic "king" of the Brazilian republic, and its collapse brought the republic down with it. In 1929, coffee prices hit record lows, and the economic structure of the republic lay in shambles. In October 1930, a military coup installed Getulio Vargas (1883–1954) in the presidency. Vargas governed Brazil until 1945.

The Vargas years represent a major turning point in Brazilian history. Vargas was initially supported by the reform elements in the military, middle-class groups, and urban workers. In office, he was a pragmatist who wanted to hold on to power and modernize Brazil. Vargas recognized the new social and economic groups shaping Brazilian political life. First with constitutionalism and then with dictatorship, he attempted to allow the government to act on behalf of those groups without allowing them to influence or direct the government in a democratic manner. However, he did not form his own political party or movement as Perón would later do in Argentina. Vargas rather attempted to function like a ringmaster directing the various forces in Brazilian life. His failure to establish a genuinely stable institutional political framework for a Brazil that included many interest groups besides the coffee planters still influences Brazil.

Vargas and his supporters sought to lessen dependence on coffee by fostering industries that would produce domestically goods that had previously been imported from abroad. The policy succeeded, and by the mid-1930s, domestic manufacturing was increasing. Vargas also established a legal framework for labor relations that included an eight-hour day and a minimum wage.

In the Brazilian context, these measures appeared reformist, if not necessarily liberal. However, in the late 1930s, Vargas confronted major political opposition and assumed dictatorial power in 1937. His regime thereafter was repressive. He claimed to have established an *Estado Novo* ("new state"). He presented himself as the protector of national stability against factions that would foster instability and of the national interest against international opponents.

Like the European dictators of the same era, Vargas used censorship, secret police, and torture. He also diversified and modernized the economy. In 1940, a five-year plan provided more state direction for the economy. His government favored the production of goods from heavy industry that would be used in Brazil itself. To maintain the support of trade unions, the state issued a progressive labor code. Siding with the Allies in World War II, Brazil built up large reserves of foreign currency through the export of foodstuffs. This economic activity and imposed political stability allowed the government to secure foreign loans for further economic development. By the end of the war, Brazil was becoming the major Latin American industrial power.

Participation in World War II on the side of the Allies had led many in Brazil to believe that they should not remain under a dictatorship. This attitude was widespread in the military, which had fought in Europe and established close contact with the United States. In 1945, the military carried out a coup, and Vargas retired temporarily from political life.

The new regime, which was democratic, continued the policy of economic development through foreign-financed industrialization. When in 1950 Vargas was elected president, his return to office was anticlimactic. He was elderly and past his prime. When a member of his staff became involved in the assassination of a journalist, the military demanded that Vargas resign. Instead, he took his own life in 1954.

In the decade after Vargas's death, Brazil remained a democracy, although an unstable one. The government began to undertake vast projects such as the costly construction of the new capital of Brasília, begun in 1957. The rapid growth of cities and the expansion of a working class radicalized political life. The political system could not readily accommodate itself to the concerns of workers and the urban poor. Poverty and illiteracy plagued both the cities and the countryside.

By the early 1960s, when President João Goulert (1918–1977) took office, Brazilian political life was in turmoil. Goulert's predecessors, including Vargas, had attempted to balance interests and political forces. However, Goulert committed himself to the left. In 1964, he announced his support for land reform, which was anathema to conservatives. Goulert also questioned the authority of the military hierarchy. In March 1964, the military, claiming to protect Brazil from communism, seized control of the government, ending its post–World War II experiment with democracy.

IN WORLD PERSPECTIVE

Latin American History

Since the early nineteenth century, Spanish- and Portuguese-speaking America stretching from the Rio Grande to Cape Horn has posed a paradox. Languages, religion, economic ties, and political institutions render the area part of the Western world. Yet its economics, politics, and social life have developed differently from other parts of the West. A region exceedingly rich in natural resources has been plagued with poverty. As other Western nations have moved toward liberal democracy and social equality, the states of Latin America have had millions of citizens living in poverty and social dependence. For over a century and a half, the political life of Latin America has been authoritarian and unstable. Three major explanations try to account for these difficulties, which have led to so much human suffering.

The most widely accepted view contends that after the Wars of Independence, the new states of Latin America remained economically and culturally dependent. In effect, the colonial framework was never abolished. Under colonial rule, Latin America's wealth was extracted and exported for the benefit of Spain and Portugal. After independence, the Creole elite turned toward foreign investors, first British and then American, to finance economic development and to provide technology. As a result, Latin America became dependent on foreign powers for investment and markets.

A second explanation emphasizes the Iberian heritage. Its advocates contend that Latin America should be viewed as a region on the periphery of the Western world in the same manner that Spain, Portugal, and Italy lie on the Mediterranean periphery of Europe. All of these Latin nations, dominated by Roman Catholicism, have had similar unstable governments. They have often tended toward dictatorship, uneven development, anticlericalism, and social cleavage between urban and rural areas and between wealthy elites and poor peasants. In this Iberian-Mediterranean context, Latin America is less puzzling than when it is viewed in the context of northern Europe.

A third explanation emphasizes decisions taken by the Latin American elite after independence. It contends that the elite sought to enrich themselves and maintain their positions at the cost of the population. These leaders aligned their national economies with the industrializing regions of Europe and North America. They also adopted the liberal political and economic ideologies of Europe to justify exploitation of economic resources on the basis of individualistic enterprise. They embraced European concepts of progress to dismiss the legitimacy of the culture and the communal values of the Indians or peasants.

None of these interpretations excludes the others. To understand the region and its past, all three viewpoints seem necessary. It also helps to view Latin America within a global perspective. Beginning in the nineteenth century, much of the region, like much of Asia and Africa, was drawn into an integrated worldwide economic system dominated by Europe and North America. Many nations in Latin America and elsewhere developed narrow economies based on the export of raw materials or semi-finished products. They were vulnerable to fluctuations in worldwide demand for these products and to interference from Europe and North America. The result was often economic turbulence and political instability.

Review Questions

1. What was the condition of the Latin American economies after independence? What was their relation to Britain? Why were most Latin American states slow to develop an industrial base? What role did their economies play in the worldwide economy that developed in the nineteenth century?

2. Did the structure of Latin American societies change after independence? What role did the traditional elites play in the economic and political life of their nations? What was the condition of the mass of the population?

3. How did European and US investment in Latin America affect the region economically? Politically?

4. Why did Latin American nations find it difficult to develop stable regimes? What role did the military play?

5. How did European immigration affect Argentina? How did the Argentine elite cope with urbanization and industrialization? Why was Juan Perón able to hold power?

6. Did Mexico experience a real revolution in the early twentieth century? How does this experience distinguish Mexico from other Latin American countries?

7. Why was the Brazilian experience of independence and early nationhood different from that of Spanish-speaking Latin America? What was the role of coffee in Brazil's economy? How did the Vargas regime change the Brazilian economy? Why did Brazilian democracy end in a military coup in 1964?

Documents CD-ROM

1. Domingo Faustino Sarmiento: From *Life in the Argentine Republic in the Days of the Tyrants*

2. José Hernández: From *The Gaucho Martin Fierro*

3. An Exiled Idealist Ignites the Mexican Revolution

4. Ariel: The Dualistic Nature of the Americas

31

INDIA, THE ISLAMIC HEARTLANDS, AND AFRICA: THE ENCOUNTER WITH THE MODERN WEST (1800–1945)

CHAPTER TOPICS

The encroachment of the European nations on the rest of the world from the late fifteenth century onward brought radical changes. In the West itself, spiritual and material disruption accompanied the Renaissance, the Reformation, the Enlightenment, and the Industrial and Scientific Revolutions. The effects of these watershed European developments on the Indian, Asian, and African worlds came more rapidly, in greater concentration, and with less preparation than they had in the West.

To call these complex processes of "modernization" does not reflect the acute differences between the relatively lengthy and gradual processes of change in western Europe and the more rapid and disruptive changes that European imperialism and colonialism brought to other parts of the world. The very concept of "modernity" has been appropriated by the West. Western dominance has led it to a specific and novel notion of modernity: namely, as a special set of ideas and institutions that evolved in Europe between the Renaissance and the early twentieth century and was then gradually exported to, or imposed upon, other societies. The expression "the impact of modernity" refers to how the introduction of "modern" Western civilization affected traditional cultures.

The consequences of the spread of Western culture have been so massive that today non-Western peoples are often merely its passive recipients. The American or European view of the world often portrays the West as the active, creative, dominant force in recent history, as though the rest of the world were some monolithic, archaic entity.

As parochial as such chauvinistic generalizations are, the impingement of the West has been a major element in the recent history of African, Asian, and Indian civilizations. Yet in all of these "Third World" areas, Western modernity entered cultures that had ancient and highly developed traditions of their own. These traditions did not simply melt away on the arrival of the westerners. Islamic, Hindu, and other regions of the Third World maintained continuity with the past. Much of the history of the twentieth-century Asian and African societies hit hardest by the new "modernity" has been shaped by their peoples' realization of the importance of their own traditions.

THE INDIAN EXPERIENCE

British Rule

In the eighteenth century, Britain became the dominant naval and commercial power in the Southern Seas. In India by the early nineteenth century, the British had built the largest European colonial empire in the Afro-Asian world. India was the "jewel in the crown" of that empire.

Building the Empire: The First Half of the Nineteenth Century

As we saw in Chapter 23, before the British crown asserted direct rule over India in 1858, the British wielded effective imperial control through the East India Company. Those areas not annexed were recognized as independent princely states. They retained their status only so long as they remained faithful to Britain. The India that resulted was a polyglot mixture of tributary states and provinces that the British administered directly.

The economic impact of Company rule was extensive. The need for ever higher revenues squeezed peasants. In addition, demand for Indian indigo, cotton, and opium in the China and British trade also slacked off in the 1830s, and famines brought widespread suffering.

Company rule also affected the physical face of India. Company policies encouraged settled agriculture and small commodity production at the expense of the nomadic and pastoralist cultures of North and central India. British "pacification" involved the clearing of land to deny natural cover to military enemies and the often forced settlement of peasants in new regions. Early in the nineteenth century, European loggers caused extensive deforestation as, after 1840, did the tracts leveled for tea and coffee plantations in Assam and the Bengal hills. This ecological destruction was part of the transformation of India into a more homogeneous peasant farming society that provided a better base for colonial administration.

The Indians were by no means passive in the face of this exploitation. The first half of the nineteenth century saw almost constant revolt in one place or another. The revolts included peasant movements of noncooperation, Muslim farm workers' attacks on British and Hindu estate owners, grain riots, tribal revolts, and other actions. They culminated in the Indian Revolt of 1857.

The immediate trigger of the Revolt was the concern among Bengal troops that animal grease on newly issued rifles exposed them to ritual pollution. Behind this issue, however, lay other grievances, including the addition of Sikhs, Gurkhas, and lower-caste soldiers to the army; deteriorating economic conditions; outrage at excessive tax rates; and anger at the 1856 British annexation of the princely state of Awadh. One can also see in the revolt the desire to rebuild a pre-British political order in North India. The revolt was not an all-India affair. It centered on Delhi, where the last Mughal emperor joined in the rebel cause.

The British eventually won the day. With their forces augmented by Sikhs from the Panjab and Gurkhas from Bengal, they overcame the divided Indian opposition. By the end of 1857, the revolt was broken, often with great brutality. In 1858, the East India Company was dissolved, and India came under direct rule of the British Crown.

The "Mutiny" of 1857 was not a nationalist revolution. Still, it highlighted resentment of the burdens of foreign domination that were to grow increasingly oppressive for Indians of all regions and religions over the ensuing ninety years of Crown rule.

British-Indian Relations

The overall impact of British presence on the Indian masses was brutal but impersonal and largely economic. India was effectively integrated into Britain's economy, becoming a market for British goods, providing Britain with raw materials and other products, and helping Britain maintain a healthy balance of trade.

British cultural imperialism was never a major nor even an official policy of the East India Company. Nonetheless, the British-Indian relationship had a paternalistic and patronizing dimension, both before and after the events of 1857. The ethos of the British rulers included the understanding that they had the task of governing an inferior "race" that could not handle the job by itself. Even Indians whose university degrees or army training were impeccable by British standards were never accepted as equals. From army to civil-service ranks, the upper echelon of command was British.

Despite this unequal relationship, British ideas influenced a small but powerful Indian elite in both their business and political life and their manners and customs. Conversion to Christianity was rare, but Christian and secular values associated with the European Enlightenment influenced Hindu and Muslim educated classes.

In the nineteenth century, probably the most influential member of the Indian elite to engage the British on their own ground was Ram Mohan Roy (1772–1833). Roy, a Bengali Hindu, rose to the top of the native ranks of East India Company service and became a strong voice for reform, both of Hindu life and of British colonial policy. Roy was a modernist who wanted to meld the best of European-Christian morality and thought with the best of Hindu piety and thought. He opposed autocratic and unfair British legal and commercial practices and campaigned in India and England to reform the Company's India policies. He studied the Christian scriptures and the great thinkers of European civilization and drew upon these sources in his Hindu reform efforts. His public campaigns for education, political involvement, and social progress and against the "backward" practices and ideas of many of his Hindu compatriots alienated most of the leading Hindu thinkers of his age, but twentieth-century Indians have often seen him as a visionary.

If many Indians sought to acquire British ways and join the British in business and administration, many more resented their subordinate status. The anti-imperial sentiment that blossomed into the nationalist movement at the end of the nineteenth century extended to the grass-roots level—among tribal groups, peasant farmers, and workers. Whatever their status, the distrust and animosity most Indians felt continued to grow.

Gandhi on Passive Resistance and Swarāj

Gandhi's powerful thinking and prose were already evident in his Hind Swarāj, *or* Indian Home Rule *of 1909. This work was to remain his basic manifesto. The following excerpts reflect important points in his philosophy.* Swadeshī *refers to reliance only on what one produces at home (rather than on foreign goods).*

How does Gandhi relate the ideas of passive resistance and *swarāj* to his theory of Indian self-rule? What are the advantages and disadvantages of his strategy for effecting political and social change? How does this document compare with others concerned with movements of independence and nationalism?

Passive resistance is a method of securing rights by personal suffering; it is the reverse of resistance by arms. When I refuse to do a thing that is repugnant to my conscience, I use soul-force. For instance, the government of the day has passed a law which is applicable to me. I do not like it. If by using violence I force the government to repeal the law, I am employing what may be termed body-force. If I do not obey the law and accept the penalty for its breach, I use soul-force. It involves sacrifice of self.

Everybody admits that sacrifice of self is infinitely superior to sacrifice of others. Moreover, if this kind of force is used in a cause that is unjust, only the person using it suffers. He does not make others suffer for his mistakes. . . .

. . . The real meaning of the statement that we are a law-abiding nation is that we are passive resisters. When we do not like certain laws, we do not break the heads of law-givers but we suffer and do not submit to the laws. . . .

If man will only realize that it is unmanly to obey laws that are unjust, no man's tyranny will enslave him. This is the key to self-rule or home-rule. . . .

Let each do his duty. If I do my duty, that is, serve myself, I shall be able to serve others. Before I leave you, I will take the liberty of repeating:

1. Real home-rule is self-rule or self-control.

2. The way to it is passive resistance: that is soul-force or love-force.

3. In order to exert this force, *Swadeshī* in every sense is necessary.

4. What we want to do should be done, not because we object to the English or because we want to retaliate, but because it is our duty to do so. Thus, supposing that the English remove the salt-tax, restore our money, give the highest posts to Indians, withdraw the English troops, we shall certainly not use their machine-made goods, nor use the English language, nor many of their industries. It is worth noting that these things are, in their nature, harmful; hence we do not want them. I bear no enmity towards the English but do towards their civilization.

In my opinion, we have used the term *Swarāj* without understanding its real significance. I have endeavored to explain it as I understand it, and my conscience testifies that my life henceforth is dedicated to its attainment.

From *Sources of Indian Tradition* edited by William Theodore de Bary. Copyright © 1958 by Columbia University Press. Reprinted with permission of the publisher.

From British Raj to Independence

The Burden of Crown Rule

The Revolt of 1857 had numerous consequences beyond the transfer of the administration of India to the British Crown. The bloody conflict exacerbated mutual fear and hatred. Before the revolt, the British had maintained a largely native army under British officers. After the revolt, they tried to maintain a ratio of at least one British to three Indian soldiers. The army was financed by Indian, not British, revenues. This imposed a huge economic burden on India, diverting one-third of its annual revenues to pay for its own occupation.

British economic policies and accelerating population growth put great strains on India's poor. Cheap British goods were exchanged for Indian raw materials and the products of its home industries, harming Indian craft industries and forcing multitudes into poverty or onto the land. Industrialization, which might have provided work for India's unemployed masses, was avoided. Finally, many peasants lost their hereditary lands because of other British policies, forcing thousands to emigrate to Britain's dominions in South Africa, where they worked as indentured servants.

The Revolt of 1857 also created a poisonous distrust of Indians within the British colonial administration. "Cantonments" segregating white masters from natives became the rule in Indian cities. Despite the intentions expressed in royal statements and the opening of the civil service, at least nominally, to Indian candidates, the raj discouraged equality between Indian and Britisher.

Indian Resistance

Indians soon took up political activism. Late in the nineteenth century, they founded the institutions that would help overcome regionalism, build national feeling, and end colonial rule. In 1885, Indian modernists formed The Indian National Congress. The Muslim League developed as a counterbalance to the Hindu-dominated Congress. The League ultimately worked for, and gained, a separate independent Muslim state, Pakistan. Erratic British policies strengthened the desire for independence.

Besides the British themselves, Indian internal divisions were the major obstacle to independence. These divisions included the many language groups and subject princely states of the subcontinent. These, however, were not even the most critical divisions. For much of British rule, every Indian politician was first a representative of his own region or state and second an Indian nationalist. Furthermore, the Indian elite had little in common with the masses beyond antagonism to foreign rule, making unified resistance difficult. Conflict among Hindus, Muslims, Sikhs, and Jains also impeded concerted political action.

Yet a nationalist movement took root. Three principal elements within the independence movement led to the creation of India and Pakistan in 1947.

The first consisted of those in the National Congress who sought gradual reform and progress toward Indian self-governance, or *swarāj*. This position did not preclude opposition to the British, but it did mean trying to change the system from within. Among the proponents of this approach were the spiritual and political genius Mohandas K. Gandhi (1869–1948) and his follower Jawaharlal Nehru (1889–1964), who became the first prime minister of India. Gandhi was the principal Indian leader after World War I and directed the all-India drive that finally forced the British out. Himself an English-trained lawyer, Gandhi drew on not only his own Hindu (and Jain and Buddhist) heritage, but also on the ideas of Western liberal and Christian thinkers. In the end, Gandhi became a world figure.

The second element consisted of the militant Hindu nationalists, whose leader, the extremist B. G. Tilak (1856–1920), stressed the use of Indian languages and a revival of Hindu culture and learning. Tilak also subscribed to an anti-Muslim, Hindu communalist vision of Indian "self-governance." The Hindu extremists looked to a return to traditional Indian values and self-sufficiency. Their ideas still influence Indian political life, as the resurgence of Hindu extremist groups in recent years and communal strife, especially with Muslims, are unhappy testimony.

Muslims made up the third element. The subcontinent held many divergent regional and sectarian Muslim constituencies. Their leaders could be brought to make common cause only by the fear that, as a minority, Muslims stood to lose what power they had in a Hindu-majority, all-India state. Muslims had been slower than the Hindus to take up British ideas and education and thus lagged behind the Hindu intelligentsia in numbers and influence with the British or other Indians.

India	
1772–1833	Ram Mohan Roy, Hindu reformer
1857–1858	Revolt, or "Mutiny," followed by direct Crown rule as a British colony
1885	Indian National Congress formed
1869–1948	Mohandas K. Gandhi
1873–1938	Muhammad Iqbal
1876–1949	Muhammad Ali Jinnah
1889–1964	Jawaharlal Nehru
1947	Independence and partition

Hindu-Muslim Friction

In the twentieth century, the rift between Muslims and Hindus in the subcontinent grew wider. In the end, the great Indo-Muslim poet and thinker, Muhammad Iqbal (1873–1938), and the "founder of Pakistan," Muhammad Ali Jinnah (1876–1949), helped move Muslims to separatism.

The independence of India and Pakistan from Western domination was only achieved with violence. Blood was spilled in the long battle with the British, in communal violence between Hindus and Muslims that accompanied partition in 1947, and in the still festering dispute over Kashmir between India and Pakistan. Still, the victory of 1947 gave the peoples of the subcontinent, Indians and Pakistanis, at last a sense of participation in the world of nations on their own terms instead of on those dictated by a foreign power. The British left a legacy of unity and egalitarian and democratic ideals that Indian nationalists turned to their own uses.

THE ISLAMIC EXPERIENCE

Islamic Responses to Declining Power and Independence

The eighteenth century saw the weakening of the great Muslim empires and the increasing ascendancy of the West. The diverse Islamic peoples and states were thrust into a struggle for survival. The decline of Islamic preeminence was also the result of internal problems.

By the eighteenth century, the largest Muslim empires had declined from their heydays in the sixteenth and seventeenth centuries. They had grown decentralized, were less stable economically and politically, and were increasingly dominated by entrenched hereditary elites, including those among the gentry, palace guards, military castes, local princes, urban guilds, and even religious leaders (the *ulama*) and the Sufi orders.

During the eighteenth century, reform movements sought to revive Islam as a comprehensive guide for living and to purify it from the more stultifying developments in Islamic societies during the preceding centuries. Most of these movements emphasized inner piety and a puritanical stress on external practice.

The most famous of these movements was that of the Wahhabis, the followers of Ibn Abd al-Wahhab (1703–1792) in Arabia. It sought to combat excesses of popular and Sufi piety to break the stranglehold of the *ulama*'s conformist interpretations of legal and religious issues. The only authorities were to be the Qur'an and the traditions of the Prophet. Allied with a local Arab prince, Sa'ud, the Wahhabi movement swept much of the Arabian peninsula. It was crushed in the early

nineteenth century by the Ottomans. It finally saw victory under a descendant of Sa'ud at the onset of this century and has become the guiding ideology of Saudi Arabia.

Other Muslim reform movements reflected similar revivalist and even militantly pietist responses to Islamic decadence and decline. This call continues to rally movements from Africa to Indonesia. In Islamic societies everywhere in recent times, it has provided a response to the challenge of Western-style "modernity" and a model for cultural and religious life.

Western Political and Economic Encroachment

From the late 1700s until World War II, the political fortunes of Islamic states were increasingly dictated from outside by Western powers. Western governments extracted capitulations favorable to their own interests from indigenous governments in exchange for promises of military protection or other considerations. These capitulations took the form of treaty clauses granting commercial concessions, special protection, and "extraterritorial" legal status to European merchant enclaves. Such concessions had originally been reciprocal and had served the commercial purposes of Muslim rulers and some merchants as well as Western traders. However, they eventually provided Western powers with pretexts for direct intervention in Ottoman, Iranian, Indian, and African affairs. The Ottoman Empire suffered from internal disunity; its provincial rulers, or *pashas*, were virtually independent. This, combined with the economic problems facing all the agrarian societies of Asia and Africa, made it easy for the Western powers—with their industrializing economies and militaries—to take control. Repeated Ottoman diplomatic and military defeats made that once, great imperial power "the sick man of Europe" after 1800; similar weakness allowed westerners to control Indian and Iranian states.

Napoleon Bonaparte's (1769–1821) unsuccessful invasion of Egypt in 1798 heralded a new era of European imperialism and colonialism in the region. By this date, the British had already wrested control over India and the Persian Gulf from the French; they now became the preeminent European power in the eastern Mediterranean as well. The Russians presented the most serious nineteenth-century challenge to Britain's colonial empire. Russia sought to gain as much territory and influence in the Iranian and Central Asian regions as possible. Afghanistan, an independent kingdom established by Ahmad Shah Durrani (r. 1737–1773), acted as a buffer that prevented Russia from penetrating southwestward into British India. In the Iranian and Ottoman regions, however, Russia and Britain—with French involvement—struggled with each other for supremacy. The Crimean War of 1854–1856 (see Chapter 27) was one result of this conflict.

The Western Impact

Beyond the overt political and commercial impact of the West, Western political ideology, culture, and technology proved critical factors for change in Islamic societies. Outside of India, this effect was most strongly felt in Egypt, Lebanon, North Africa, and Turkey. The Islamic states least and last affected by Western "modernity" were Iran, Afghanistan, and the Central Asian khanates.

The rulers of Iran from 1794 to 1925 were the Qajar shahs, whose absolutist reign was not unlike that of the Safavids. However, the Qajars did not claim, as had the Safavids, to descent from the Shi'ite *imams*. Under Qajar rule, the *ulama* of the Shi'ite community became less strongly connected with the state apparatus. This period also saw the emergence of a Shi'i traditionalist doctrine that encouraged all Shi'ites to choose a *mujtahid*—a qualified scholarly guide—from among the *ulama* and follow his religious-legal interpretations. As a result, the *ulama* were often the chief critics of the government (not least for its attempts to admit Western influences) and exponents of the people's grievances.

A demonstration of *ulama* power occurred when in 1890 the Qajar Shah granted a fifty-year monopoly on tobacco sales to the British. In 1891, the *ulama* decreed a tobacco boycott to protest the concession. This popular action was supported by modernist-nationalist opponents of the Qajar regime who had strong connections to Iran's commercial, or *bazaari*, middle classes. It forced the Shah to rescind the concession.

Subject as it was to the machinations of outsiders, such as Russia, Britain, and France, Iran felt the impact of Western ideas, especially in the latter half of the century, when younger Iranian intellectuals began to warm to Western liberalism. As in other Islamic countries, the seeds of secular nationalism were being sown where religious sentiments had held sway. It worked with a desire among larger sectors of the populace for a voice in government. An uneasy alliance of Iranian modernists with conservative *ulama* proved, on occasion, an effective counterforce to Qajar absolutism, as in the tobacco boycott and in the early stages of the effort to force the Qajars to accept a constitution in 1906–1911. Yet such alliances did not bridge the inherent ideological divisions of the two groups.

Islamic Responses to Foreign Encroachment

As the Iranian case shows, Western impingement on the Islamic world in the nineteenth and twentieth centuries elicited varied responses. Every people or state had a different experience. Yet we can point to at least three typical styles of reaction: (1) a tendency to emulate and adopt Western ideas and institutions; (2) the attempt to join Western innovations with traditional Islamic institutions; and (3) a traditionalist rejection of things Western in favor of either the status quo or return to a purified Islamic community.

Emulation of the West

A strategy of emulation is exemplified in the career of the virtually independent Ottoman viceroy Muhammad Ali (ca. 1769–1849), pasha of Egypt from 1805 to 1849. He set out to rejuvenate Egypt's agriculture, to introduce modern industry, to modernize the army with European help, and to introduce European education and culture in government schools. Although he did not bring Egypt to a position of power equal to the European states, and his successors' financial and political catastrophes led the British to occupy Egypt (1882–1922), Muhammad Ali did set his country on the path to becoming a modern national state. Hence he is rightly called "the father of modern Egypt."

Efforts to appropriate Western experience and success were made by several Ottoman sultans and viziers after the defeat of the Turks by Russia in 1774. Most notable were the reforms of Selim III (r. 1762–1808), Mahmud II (r. 1808–1839), and the so-called Tanzimat, or beneficial "legislation" era from about 1839 to 1880. Selim made serious efforts at economic as well as administrative and military reform. Mahmud's reforms were much like those of Muhammad Ali. Most important were his destruction of the Janissary corps, his tax and bureaucratic reforms, and his encouragement of Western military and educational methods. Like Muhammad Ali, he was less interested in promoting European enlightenment ideas about citizen rights and equity than in building a stronger, more modern government.

Islamic Lands	
1703-1792	Ibn Abd al-Wahhab
1737-1773	Rule of Ahmad Shah Durrani, founder of modern Afghanistan
1794-1925	Qajar shahs of Iran
1798	Invasion of Egypt by Napoleon Bonaparte
1805-1849	Rule of Muhammad Ali in Egypt
ca. 1839-1880	Era of the Tanzimat reforms of the Ottoman Empire
1839-1897	Jamal al-Din al-Afghani
1845-1905	Muhammad Abduh
1882-1922	British occupation of Egypt
1908	"Young Turk" revolution
1922-1938	Mustafa Kemal, "Atatürk" in power

Kemal Atatürk (right) giving instruction in the Latin alphabet. This 1928 photograph reflects the personal engagement of Mustafa Kemal in the many reform efforts he instituted. [Historical Pictures Collection/Stock Montage Inc.]

The Tanzimat reforms, introduced by several liberal Ottoman ministers of state, continued the efforts of Selim and Mahmud. They were intended to bring the Ottoman state into line with ideals espoused by the European states, to give European powers less cause to intervene in Ottoman affairs, and to regenerate confidence in the state.

The nineteenth-century Ottoman reforms failed to save the empire. Nevertheless, they paved the way for the rise of Turkish nationalism, the "Young Turk" revolution of 1908, and the nationalist revolution of the 1920s that produced modern Turkey.

The creation of the Turkish republic out of the ashes of the Ottoman state after World War I is probably the most extreme example of an effort to modernize and nationalize an Islamic state on a Western model. This state was largely the child of Mustafa Kemal (1881–1938), known as "Atatürk" ("father of the Turks"), its first president (1922–1938). Atatürk's major reforms ranged from the introduction of a European-style code of civil law to the abolition of the caliphate, Sufi orders, Arabic script, and the Arabic call to prayer. These changes constituted a radical attempt to secularize an Islamic state and to separate religious from political

and social institutions. Nothing quite like it has ever been repeated. Despite some adjustments and even reversals of Atatürk's measures, Turkey has maintained its independence, reaffirmed its commitment to democratic government, and emerged with a unique but still distinctly Islamic identity.

Integration of Western and Islamic Ideas

The attempt to join modernization with traditional Islamic institutions and ideas is exemplified in the thought of famous Muslim intellectuals, such as Jamal al-Din al-Afghani (1839–1897), and Muhammad Abduh (1845–1905). These thinkers argued for a progressive Islam rather than a materialist Western secularism as the best answer to life in the modern world.

Afghani is best known for his emphasis on the unity of the Islamic world, or "pan-Islamism," and on a populist, constitutionalist approach to political order.

Purification and Revival of Islam

A third kind of Muslim reaction to Western domination has focused on recourse to Islamic values and ideals to the exclusion of "outside" forces. This approach includes reformist revivalism like Wahhabism and the kind of conservatism often associated with Sunni or Shi'ite "establishment" *ulama*, as in Iran since 1979. The conservative spirit has often been the target of revivalist reformers who see in it the worst legacy of medieval Islam. Still, both conservative and revivalist Muslim thinkers look answers to the questions facing Muslims in the modern world within, not outside, the Islamic tradition.

Nationalism

Nationalism is a product of modern history. Nationalist movements in the Islamic world have been either stimulated by Western models or produced in reaction to Western exploitation and colonial occupation. Indeed, the often arbitrary or artificial division of the colonial world by European administrators has frequently produced national units where none had existed—notably in Africa, but also in Syria, Jordan, Iraq, and Central Asia. In Turkey in the 1920s, nationalism took a secularist form; in Libya, Iran, and elsewhere since the 1970s and 1980s, it has taken an Islamic-revivalist form. As an Afro-Asian phenomenon, it will reappear in the next section and in Chapter 38.

THE AFRICAN EXPERIENCE

Between 1800 and 1945, virtually every part of Africa changed, but nowhere more than sub-Saharan Africa. With the exception of South Africa below the Transvaal, tropical and southern Africa came under major influence and finally colonial control from outside only after 1880. Before then, internal developments—demographic and power shifts and then the rise of Islamic reform movements—overshadowed the European presence in the continent.

New States and Power Centers

Southern Africa

In the south, below the Limpopo River, the first quarter of the nineteenth century saw devastating internal warfare, depopulation, and forced migrations of many Bantu peoples in what is known as the *mfecane*, or "crushing" era. Likely brought on by a population explosion and economic competition, the *mfecane* was marked by the rise of military states among the northern Nguni-speaking Bantu. Its result was a period of warfare and chaos; depopulation; and the creation of multitribal, multilingual Bantu states in modern Zimbabwe, Mozambique, Malawi, Zambia, and Tanzania.

The Nguni warrior-king Dingiswayo formed the first of the new military states between ca. 1800 and 1818. The most important state was formed by his successor, Shaka, leader of the Nguni-speaking Zulu nation and kingdom (ca. 1818–1828). Shaka's brutal military tactics led to the Zulu conquest of a vast dominion in southeastern Africa and the depopulation of some 15,000 square miles. Refugees fled north into Sotho-speaking Bantu territory or south to put increasing pressure on the southern Nguni peoples. Chaos ensued north and south of Zululand and even in the high veld above the Orange River.

The net result was the creation of diverse states. Some people tried to imitate the military state of Shaka; others fled to the mountains; others even went west into the Kalahari. The most famous of these was Lesotho, the Sotho kingdom of King Mosheshwe, which survived as long as he lived (from the 1820s until 1870). Mosheshwe defended his people from the Zulu and held off the Afrikaners, missionaries, and British. After his death, the latter groups became Lesotho's chief predators.

The new state-building spawned by the *mfecane* was nullified by Boer expansion and British annexation of the Natal province (1843). These developments stemmed from the Great Trek of Boer *voortrekers*, which took place between 1835 and 1843. This migration brought about 6,000 Afrikaners from the eastern Cape Colony northeastward into the more fertile regions of southern Africa, Natal, and the high veld above the Orange River. It resulted in the creation after 1850 of two Afrikaner republics: the Orange Free State between the Orange and Vaal Rivers and the South African Republic north of the Vaal.

Southern Africa

ca. 1800-1818	Dingiswayo, Nguni Zulu king, forms new military state
1800-1825	The *mfecane* among the Bantu of southeastern Africa
1795	British take Cape Colony from the Dutch
ca. 1818-1828	Shaka's reign as head of the Nguni state; major warfare, destruction, and expansion
ca. 1825-1870	Sotho kingdom of King Mosheshwe in Lesotho region
1835-1843	Great Trek of Boers into Natal and north onto the high veld beyond the Orange
1843	British annexation of Natal province
1852-1860	Creation of the Orange Free State and South African Republic

East and Central Africa

In East and East Central Africa, external trade resulted in the formation of strong states. In the Lakes region, peoples such as the Nyamwezi to the east of Lake Tanganyika and the Baganda west of Lake Victoria gained regional power from as early as the late eighteenth century through trade with the Arab-Swahili eastern coast and the eastern Congo to the west. This east–west commerce involved slaves; ivory; copper; and, from the outside, Indian cloth, firearms, and manufactured goods.

West Africa

In West Africa, the slave trade was replaced by European demand for palm oil and gum arabic by the 1820s. In the first half of the century, *jihad* (holy struggle) movements of the Fulbe (or Fulani) and others shattered the stability of the western savannah and forest regions from modern Senegal and Ghana through southern Nigeria. Wars and dislocation resulted in the rise of regional kingdoms, such as those of Asante and Dahomey (modern Benin). These eventually succumbed to internal dissension and the colonial activities of Britain and France later in the century.

Islamic Reform Movements

The vitality of Islam was a significant agent of change in sub-Saharan Africa before the European rush for colonies in the 1880s. It is still a factor. In 1800, Islam was already well established from West Africa across the Sudan to the Red Sea and along the East African coast. Islam was the law of the land in states such as the sultanate of Zanzibar on the eastern coast and the waning Funj sultanate on the Blue Nile in the eastern

Sudan. But in many "Islamic" states in Africa, the rural populace were still semi- if not wholly pagan; and even the urban elites were only nominally Muslim.

The nineteenth century is notable for the militant Islamic revivalist and reform movements of *jihad*, which fixed and spread Islam as a lasting part of the African scene. The most important *jihad* movement was led by a Fulbe Muslim scholar from Hausa territory in the central Sahel. Usman Dan Fodio (1754–1817) was influenced by the reformist ideas that spread throughout the Muslim world in the eighteenth century. Shortly after 1804, he gathered an army and conquered most of the Hausa lands of northern and central Nigeria, bringing an explicitly Islamic order to the area. Dan Fodio left behind a sultanate centered on the new capital of Sokoto and governed by one of his sons, Muhammad Bello, until 1837. The Fulbe became the ruling class in the Hausa regions, and Islam spread into the countryside, where it still predominates.

Other nineteenth-century reform movements had similar success in spreading a revivalist, reformist Islamic message among the masses. Most notable were the Sanusi of Libya and the eastern Sahara (after about 1840) and the Mahdist uprising of the eastern Sudan (1880s and 1890s). The Libyan movement provided the focus for resistance to the Italian invasion of 1911. The Sudanese Muhammad Ahmad (1848–1885) condemned the corruption of basic Muslim ideals and declared himself the awaited deliverer, or Mahdi, in 1881. He led the northern Sudan in rebellion against Ottoman-Egyptian control. His successor governed the Sudan until the British destroyed the young Islamic state in 1899.

Increasing European Involvement

Muslim reform movements were not the only important developments in Africa during the nineteenth century. Another was the growing involvement of Europe, which led to European domination of the continent. Before the mid-1800s, the penetration of white outsiders had been limited largely to coastal areas, although their slave trade had had significant effects inland (see Chapter 19). This changed as trading companies, explorers, missionaries, and then colo-

nial troops and governments moved into Africa. Ironically, the elimination of the slave trade (primarily through Britain's efforts) was accompanied by increased European exploration and Christian missionizing, which ushered in imperial and colonial ventures that were to have even more disastrous consequences than slaving for Africa's future.

Exploration

The nineteenth-century European explorers—mostly English, French, and German—uncovered for westerners the "secrets" of Africa: the sources and courses of the Niger, Nile, Zambezi, and Congo Rivers; natural wonders such as Mount Kilimanjaro and Lake Tanganyika; and fabled places like Timbuktu, the once, great Berber trading gateway and center of Islamic learning. The history of European exploration is one of fortune hunting, self-promotion, violence, and mistakes, but also of patience and perseverance, bravery and dedication.

The explorers stimulated European interest and opened the way for traders, missionaries, and finally soldiers and governors from the Christian West. One of the greatest explorers was Dr. David Livingstone (1813–1873), who was a missionary dedicated to Africa and its peoples as few other westerners have been.

Christian Missions

The late nineteenth century saw an influx of Christian missionaries, both Protestant and Catholic (by 1900, perhaps as many as 10,000). The missionaries came to know the African peoples far better than did the explorers. Their accounts of Africa contained chauvinistic and misleading descriptions of the "degraded" state of African culture and religion, but they brought real knowledge of and interest in Africa to Europe. Their schools also brought some alphabetic culture and literacy to the African tribal world. Although their settlements, often in remote areas, provided European governments with convenient pretexts for intervention, the missionaries themselves were more often idealists than opportunists. Half of those who went into the tropical regions succumbed to diseases, such as malaria, yellow fever, and sleeping sickness. If they were often paternalistic and instruments of the imperialism of their home countries, they also sought to provide Africans with medicine and education. Through the ideals of their faith, they provided Africans—sometimes inadvertently—with a weapon of principle to use against their European exploiters. African Christian churches, for example, played a leading role in resisting apartheid in South Africa, despite white Christian oppression and collusion with racism in that country and elsewhere in Africa (see Chapter 38). As this discussion suggests, the role of Africans in the European domination of Africa was neither simple nor wholly positive.

Central Sudan	
1754–1817	Usman Dan Fodio, Fulbe leader of major Islamic *jihad*
1810	Dan Fodio founds Islamic sultanate in lands of former Hausa states of northern and central Nigeria
1817–1837	Reign at Sokoto of Muhammad Bello, son of Dan Fodio

The Colonial "Scramble for Africa"

Before 1850, the only significant European attempts to take African territory were in South Africa and Algeria. In South Africa, as we have noted, the Boers came into conflict with Bantu tribes on their Great Trek. The French invaded Algeria in 1830, settled Europeans on choice farmlands, and waged war on native resistance fighters (1830-1847). Over most of the continent, however, the European presence was felt with real force only from the 1880s. Yet by World War I, all of Africa except Ethiopia and Liberia was divided arbitrarily into a patchwork of European colonial administrations (see Map 31–1).

This takeover was supported by mounting European popular and commercial interest fueled by the publicity given African exploration and missionary work. The European desire for the markets and resources of Africa, together with intra-European competition for power and prestige, pushed one European state after another to lay claim to whatever segments of Africa they could.

What made this wholesale takeover possible was the superior power the West commanded. In particular, European technical expertise opened up the interior of the continent. Except for the Nile and the Niger, the great African rivers have impassible waterfalls near the sea. Steamboats above the falls and railroads around them provided access to the African interior and opened its riches to exploitation.

Britain and France were the colonial vanguard. The British had the largest involvement. On one axis, it ranged from their South African holdings (begun when they took the Cape Colony from the Dutch in 1795) to their protectorate in Egypt (from 1882). On another axis, it extended from trading interests in West Africa to colonies such as Sierra Leone and Gambia, to protectorate rule, as in the Niger districts after 1885, and to a Zanzibar-based sphere of influence in East Africa.

The British preferred "indirect" to "direct" colonial administration. Their rule was only slightly more enlightened than that of the French, who carved out a colonial empire under their direct control. The French had long had government-supported trading outposts in West Africa. Tunisia and the Ivory Coast became French protectorates in the 1880s; Dahomey was bloodily annexed in 1894; and the colony of French Equatorial Africa was proclaimed in 1910.

Beginning in the mid-1880s, the European powers began to seek mutual agreement to their claims on segments of Africa. Leopold II of Belgium (r. 1865–1909) and Otto von Bismarck (1815–1898) in Germany established their claims to parts of South, Central, and East Africa. France and England set about consolidating their African interests. Italy took African colonial territory in Eritrea, Somaliland, and Libya. But the Italian design on Ethiopia was thwarted when Ethiopia defeated an Italian invasion in 1896. The Italians eventually conquered Ethiopia in 1935. The "scramble for Africa" was over by the outbreak of World War I. In the

Colonial Africa	
1830	French invasion of Algeria
1890	British protectorate in Zanzibar
ca. 1880	French protectorate in Tunisia and Ivory Coast
1880s–1890s	Mahdist uprising in eastern Sudan
1882	British protectorate in Egypt
1894	French annexation of Dahomey
1910	French colony of Equatorial Africa

aftermath of the war, Germany lost its African possessions to other colonial powers. Europe's colonies in Africa did not gain independence (see Chapters 36 and 38) until after World War II beginning in the 1950s.

European colonial rule in Africa is one of the uglier chapters of modern history. The paternalistic attitudes of late-nineteenth-century Europe and America amounted to racism when applied in Africa. The regions with large-scale white settlement produced the worst exploitation at the expense of vastly greater native populations. The worst legacy of the European presence was the white racist state of modern South Africa, which only ended in 1994. No Western nation can have a clear conscience about its involvement in Africa.

African Resistance to Colonialism: The Rise of Nationalism

African states were not, however, passive objects of European manipulation. Astute native rulers sought to use the European presence to their own advantage. Some, like the Bagandan king Mutesa in the 1870s (in what is today Uganda), succeeded for some time. Direct armed resistance was doomed (even Ethiopia's) because of European technological superiority. Nevertheless, such resistance was widespread. In the end, however, other factors brought an end to most foreign rule on African soil.

The most prominent factor was the rise of nationalism across Africa, especially after World War I. However little the colonial partition of Africa reflected native divisions, it still influenced nationalist movements and the eventual shape of African states. The "national" consciousness of the diverse peoples of a given colonial unit was fueled by common opposition to foreign rule, use of a common European tongue, and the assimilation of European thought and culture by an educated native elite. These elites were educated in mission schools and foreign universities. Their ranks increased in the early twentieth century. From them came the leaders of Africa's nationalist movements between the two world wars and of Africa's independent nations after World War II.

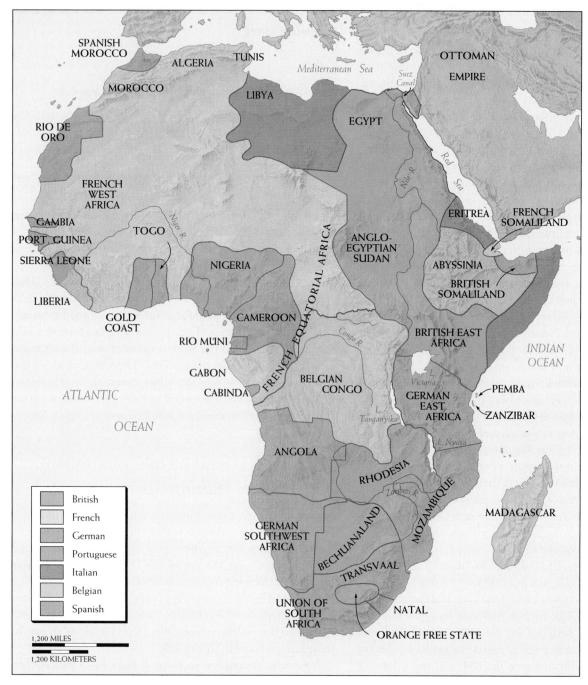

Map 31–1 Partition of Africa, 1880–1914. By 1914, the only countries in Africa that remained independent were Liberia and Abyssinia (Ethiopia). The occupying powers included most large European states.

The severest indigenous critiques of the Western treatment of Africa often drew on Western religious and political ideals. The process culminated in the creation of over forty self-governing African nations after 1945 (see Chapter 38). African independence movements were based on modern nationalist models from Europe and America rather than ancient ones derived from native tradition. The nationalist and independence movements sought to eject the colonial intruders, not to return to an earlier status quo. Their aim was to take over and run for themselves the Western institutions that colonialism had introduced. This legacy from the West is still visible today.

India, the Islamic Heartlands, and Africa, 1800–1945

The century and a half following the French Revolution was a bleak one for the Indian subcontinent, Africa, and the Islamic societies. For centuries there had been a rough balance in material and intellectual culture, commerce, and political stability among the major cultural regions of the world. Suddenly, over 150 years, the European sector of the global community came to dominate the rest of the world.

The Middle East, Africa, Iran, Central Asia, India, and Indonesia-Malaysia, along with Central and South America—what is today referred to as "the Third World" of "developing nations"—were most drastically affected by European imperialism and colonialism. Regardless of indigenous developments in these regions, the decisive development of this era was unprecedented domination by a single segment of the global community. Western dominance, sometimes positive, often sordid and ugly, was by no means synonymous with "progress," as westerners have often liked to think. Nevertheless, it has been a hallmark of the "modern" age in most of Asia, Africa, and South America.

The vitality of so many of the cultures and traditions that bore the brunt of the Western onslaught has been striking. Arab, Iranian, Indian, African, and other encounters with Western material and intellectual domination produced different responses and initiatives. These have borne full fruit in political, economic, and intellectual independence only since 1945; however, most began much earlier, some even well before 1800. For example, modern Islamic reform and resurgence began in the eighteenth century, although it has become a major global factor only in recent years. Indian national consciousness also developed from the eighteenth century onward in response to British domination, even though it led to national union and independence only after World War II.

One result of the imperial-colonial experience almost everywhere has been the sharpening of cultural self-consciousness and self-confidence among those peoples most negatively affected by Western dominance. The imperial-colonial experiences of the Third World nations may well prove to have been not only ones of misery and reversal, but also of transition to positive development and resurgence, despite the looming economic, educational, and demographic problems that plague many of them.

Review Questions

1. What does the "impact of modernity" mean to traditional cultures of the Afro-Asian-Indian world? What patterns of reaction can you discern? Why was the West able to impose itself on these other cultures?

2. Why was India called the "jewel in the crown" of the British Empire? What kind of policies did the British follow in government and economics?

3. What kinds of political activism against British rule were there in India after 1800? What success did they have?

4. How was the Islamic world internally divided after 1800? How did those divisions influence the coming of European powers?

5. How did nationalism affect European control in south Asia, Africa, and the Middle East? How and when did it arise? Were there any successful "national states" from these regions before 1945?

6. Why was there a failure to develop a modern state in sub-Saharan Africa before 1870? What role did Islam and trade play in the development of new entities?

7. What were the three main interests of Europeans in the "Dark Continent"? Why were native Africans unable to stop the "scramble for Africa"?

8. What was the role of African nationalism in resisting foreign control?

Documents CD-ROM

1. Lord William Bentinck: Comments on Ritual Murder and the Limits of Religious Toleration

2. Gandhi: Facing the British in India

3. Rudyard Kipling, "The White Man's Burden"

4. Gandhi: The Gentle Violence of "Soul Force"

5. Jawaharlal Nehru: The Second "Founding-Father"

6. Zulu War: The Fury of Resistance to Imperialism

32 MODERN EAST ASIA

CHAPTER TOPICS

MODERN CHINA (1839–1949)

◆ Close of Manchu Rule

◆ From Dynasty to Warlordism (1895–1926)

◆ Cultural and Ideological Ferment: The May Fourth Movement

◆ Nationalist China

MODERN JAPAN (1853–1945)

◆ Overthrow of the Tokugawa *Bakufu* (1853–1868)

◆ Building the Meiji State (1868–1890)

◆ Growth of a Modern Economy

◆ The Politics of Imperial Japan (1890–1945)

◆ Japanese Militarism and German Nazism

In World Perspective Modern East Asia

From the mid-nineteenth century, the West was the expanding, aggressive, imperialistic force in world history; it was the trigger for change throughout the world. But the response to the Western impact depended on internal forces in each country. Japan and China were both relatively successful in their responses, for neither became a colony.

The two countries' governing elites were educated in Confucianism, which was just secular enough to crumble in the face of the more powerful secularism of nineteenth-century science and the doctrines associated with it. In both countries, one of the "breakdown products" of the Confucian sociopolitical identity was a strong new nationalism.

But in most other respects, modern Japan and China could hardly be more different. The coming of Commodore Matthew Perry (1794–1858) in 1853–1854 precipitated rapid change in Japan. The old Tokugawa regime collapsed, and the Japanese built a modern state. Economic growth followed. By 1900, Japan had defeated China and was about to defeat Russia. After the Great Depression, Japan, like Italy and Germany, became an aggressive and militarized state and was

defeated in World War II. But after the war, Japan reemerged more stable and productive, and with a stronger parliamentary government than ever before.

In contrast, the hold of tradition in China was remarkable. But in one sense, its strength was China's weakness, for only after the overthrow of Manchu rule in 1911 was China willing to begin the modernization that Japan had started in 1868. Even then it was unsuccessful. Along with warlordism, new ills arose from the rending of the very fabric of the dynastic pattern. That China "failed" during this modern century is the view held by the Chinese themselves.

MODERN CHINA (1839–1949)

China's modern century was not the century in which it became modern, but the one in which it encountered the modern West. Its first phase, from the Opium War to the fall of the Ch'ing or Manchu dynasty (1911), was little affected by Western impact. Only during the decade before 1911 did the

Confucian tradition begin to be discarded in favor of new ideas from the West. The second phase, from 1911 to the establishment of a communist state in 1949, was a time of turmoil: decades of warlord rule; war with Japan; and then four years of civil war.

Close of Manchu Rule

The Opium War

The eighteenth-century three-country trade—British goods to India, Indian cotton to China, and Chinese tea to Britain—was in China's favor. Then the British replaced cotton with Indian opium, and by the 1820s, the balance of trade was reversed.

To check the evil of opium and the outflow of silver, the Chinese government banned opium in 1836. In 1839, the government sent Lin Tse-hsu (1785–1850) to Canton to superintend the ban. He destroyed a six-month supply of opium belonging to foreign merchants, leading to a confrontation with the British.

War broke out in November 1839. For the next two years, the British fought battles and attempted negotiations. The Chinese troops were ineffective. The war was finally ended in August 1842 by the Treaty of Nanking, the first of the "unequal treaties."

The treaty ended the "tribute system," and gave Britain the island of Hong Kong and a huge indemnity. It also opened five ports: Canton, Shanghai, Amoy, Ningpo, and Foochow. British merchants and their families could reside in the ports and engage in trade; Britain could appoint a consul for each city; and British residents were subject to British, not Chinese, law. The treaty also contained a "most-favored-nation" clause: any further rights gained by any other nation would automatically accrue to Britain as well. In 1844, similar treaties followed with the United States and France.

After the signing of the British treaty, Chinese imports of opium increased, but other kinds of trade did not grow as much as had been hoped. Western merchants blamed the lack of growth on Chinese officials. They also complained that Canton remained closed to trade. The Chinese authorities were incensed by the export of coolies to work in Cuba and Peru. A second war broke out in 1856, and the British captured Peking in 1860. New treaties provided for indemnities, the opening of eleven new ports, the stationing of foreign diplomats in Peking, the propagation of Christianity anywhere in China, and the legalization of the opium trade.

Meanwhile, the Russians were encroaching on China's northern frontier. In 1858, China ceded the north bank of the Amur to Russia, and in 1860, China gave Russia the Maritime Province between the Ussuri River and the Pacific. China still claims these lands.

Rebellions Against the Manchu

More serious threats to Manchu rule were the Taiping, Nien, and Muslim rebellions that convulsed China between 1850 and 1873. The torment and suffering they caused were unparalleled in world history. China's population dropped by 60 million.

The Taipings were begun by Hung Hsiu-ch'uan (1814–1864), a schoolteacher from the southern province of Kwangtung. Influenced by Protestant tracts, Hung announced that he was the younger brother of Jesus and that God had told him to rid China of Manchus, Confucians, Taoists, and Buddhists. Like earlier rebels, the Taipings combined moral reform, religious fervor, and a vision of egalitarian society. The Taipings were soon joined by peasants, miners, and workers. The fighting spread until the Taipings controlled most of the Yangtze basin and had entered sixteen of the eighteen Chinese provinces. Their army numbered close to a million.

The other rebellions were of lesser note. The Nien were located north of the Taipings along the Huai River. They were organized in secret societies and raided the countryside. Eventually they built an army, collected taxes, and ruled 100,000 square miles. A longer revolt was of Muslims against Chinese in the southwest and the northwest. These rebellions took advantage of the weakened state of the dynasty. They occurred in areas that had few officials and no Ch'ing military units.

Against the rebellions, the imperial forces proved helpless: In 1852, the court sent Tseng Kuo-fan (1811–1872) to south-central China to organize a local army. Tseng, a product of the Confucian examination system, saw the Manchu government, of which he was an elite member, as the upholder of morality and the social order, and Chinese rebels as would-be destroyers of that order. He recruited members of the gentry as officers. They were Confucian, and as landlords had the most to lose from rebel rule. They recruited soldiers from their local areas and stopped the Taipings' advance.

In 1860, when the British and French occupied Peking, a reform government began internal changes, adopted a policy of cooperation with the Western powers, and put Tseng in charge of suppressing all the rebellions. Tseng appointed able officials to raise regional armies. Foreigners and Shanghai merchants gave their support. The Taipings collapsed when Nanking was captured in 1864. The Nien were suppressed by 1868 and the Muslim rebellion was put down five years later. Scholar-officials, relying on local gentry, had saved the dynasty.

Self-Strengthening and Decline (1874–1895)

In view of the dynasty's advanced stage of administrative decentralization, the Chinese resiliency and capacity to rebuild in the two decades after the suppression of the rebellions were impressive. But if we ask how effective China's response was to the West, or if we compare China's progress with that of Japan, then China during the same decades looks almost moribund. Historians often call these years the period of "self-strengthening," yet China was relatively weaker at the end of the period than at the start.

The Court at Peking   China's inability to act effectively is explained partly by the situation at the court. Prince Kung (1833–1898) and the empress dowager (1835–1908) were coregents for the young emperor. Prince Kung was a man of ideas. In 1861, he established a new office to handle the court's relations with foreign diplomats in Peking. The following year, he established a school to train Chinese in foreign languages. However, outmaneuvered by the empress dowager, he was ousted in 1884.

The empress dowager had produced the only male child of the former emperor. She had no conception of how to reform China, her single goal was power. She acquired it by forging a political machine of conservative bureaucrats, military commanders, and eunuchs, and by maintaining a balance between the court and the regional governor-generals. The result was a court just able to survive but too weak to govern effectively.

Regional Governments   The most vital figures during these decades were a handful of able governors-general. Each had an army and was in charge of two or three provinces. They were loyal to the dynasty that they had restored in the face of almost certain collapse and were allowed great autonomy.

Their first task was reconstruction. Millions were hungry or homeless. The leaders' response was massive and effective. Just as they had mobilized the gentry to suppress the rebellions, now they obtained their cooperation in rebuilding. They set up refugee centers, reduced taxes in the devastated Yangtze valley, reclaimed lands gone to waste, began water-control projects, and built granaries. By the early 1890s, well-being had been restored to Chinese society.

Their second task was self-strengthening—the adoption of Western arms and technology. They built arsenals and ship-yards, a telegraph company, railways, and cotton mills. The formula applied in running these enterprises was "official supervision and merchant operation." The major decisions were made by scholar-officials, but day-to-day operations were left to the merchants.

Treaty Ports   The treaty ports, of which there were fourteen by the 1860s, were little islands of privilege and security, under the rule of foreign consuls, where capital was safe from confiscation, trade was free, and "squeeze" (extortion by officials) was the exception. Foreign companies naturally located in the ports, as did Chinese merchants who were also attracted by these conditions. Well into the twentieth century, the foreign concessions (treaty-port lands leased in perpetuity by foreigners) remained the vital sector of China's modern economy.

The effects of the treaty ports and of Western imperialism on China were largely negative. Under the low tariffs mandated by the treaties, Chinese industries had little protection from imports. Native cotton spinning was almost destroyed by imports of yarn. Chinese tea lost ground to Indian tea and Chinese silk to Japanese silk. China found few products to export. The level of foreign trade stayed low, and China's interior markets were affected only slightly.

By the 1870s, the foreign powers had reached an accommodation with China. They counted on the court to uphold the treaties; in return, they became a prop for the dynasty. By 1900, for example, the court's revenues from customs fees were larger than those from any other source. The fees were collected by the Maritime Customs Service, an efficient and honest treaty-port institution headed by an Irishman. In 1895, the Maritime Customs Service had 700 Western and 3,500 Chinese employees.

The Borderlands: The Northwest, Vietnam, and Korea

China's other foreign relations were with fringe lands that China claimed by right of past conquest or as tributaries. The tributaries were the mirrors in which China saw reflected its own self-image as a universal empire. During the late nineteenth century, this image was strengthened in the northwest but dealt a fatal blow in Vietnam and Korea.

The Northwest   In the northwest, China confronted imperial Russia. Caught between them, the independent nomadic tribes were rendered impotent. By 1878, China had reconquered Chinese Turkestan, which was renamed Sinkiang, or the "New Territories." A treaty signed with Russia in 1881 restored most of the Ili region in western Mongolia to Chinese control. The victories strengthened court conservatives who wished to take a stronger stance toward the West.

Vietnam   Vietnam had retained its independence from China since 935. It saw itself as an independent state but used the Chinese writing system, modeled its laws and government on those of China, and traded with China. China simply saw Vietnam as a tributary.

During the 1840s, the second emperor of the Nguyen dynasty, which had begun in 1802, moved to reduce French influences and suppress Christianity. Thousands were killed, including French and Vietnamese priests. The French responded by seizing Saigon and Cochin China in 1859, establishing a protectorate over Cambodia in 1864, and taking Hanoi in 1882. China in 1883 sent troops to aid its tributary, but after a two year war with France China was forced, in 1885, to abandon its claims to Vietnam. By 1893, France had brought together Vietnam, Cambodia, and Laos to form the Federation of Indochina, which remained a French colony until 1940.

Korea Unlike Vietnam, Korea saw itself as a tributary of China on Chinese terms. The Korean ruler styled himself as a king and not an emperor.

During the last decades of the long (1392–1910) Choson dynasty, the Korean state was weak. It hung on to power in part by enforcing a policy of seclusion almost as total as that of Tokugawa Japan, winning it the name of the Hermit Kingdom. Its only foreign ties were with China and Japan. In 1876, Japan "opened" Korea to international relations, using much the same tactics that Perry had used against Japan. Japan then contended with China for influence in Korea.

In 1893, a popular religious sect unleashed a rebellion against the Seoul government. When the government requested Chinese help to suppress the rebellion, China sent troops, but Japan sent more, and in 1894, war broke out between China and Japan. Taiwan became Japan's first colony. The defeat convinced many in China that basic changes were inevitable.

From Dynasty to Warlordism (1895–1926)

China was ruled by officials who had mastered the Confucian classics. This intellectual formation was resistant to change. For most officials living in China's interior, the foreign crises of the nineteenth century were "coastal phenomena," soon forgotten. Few officials realized the magnitude of the foreign threat.

China's defeat by Japan in 1895 came as a shock. The response within China was a new wave of reform proposals. The most influential thinker was K'ang Yu-wei (1858–1927), who described China as "enfeebled" and blamed the "conservatives." They did not understand, K'ang argued, that Confucius himself had been a reformer who had invented the idea of a golden age to persuade the rulers of his own age to adopt his ideas. History was evolutionary—a march forward from absolute monarchy to constitutional monarchy to democracy. K'ang's reinterpretation of Confucianism removed a major barrier to the entry of Western ideas into China.

In 1898, the emperor himself became sympathetic to K'ang's ideas and launched "one hundred days of reform."

He took as his models Peter the Great (r. 1682–1725) and the Japanese Meiji Emperor (r. 1867–1912). Edicts were issued to reform China's schools, railroads, police, laws, military, bureaucracy, post offices, and examination system. But conservative resistance was nationwide. At court, the empress dowager regained control and ended the reforms. K'ang fled to Japan. One reformer was executed.

The response of the Western powers to China's 1895 defeat was to define spheres of interest, which usually consisted of a leasehold along with railway rights and commercial privileges. Russia gained a leasehold at Port Arthur; Germany acquired one in Shantung. Britain got the New Territories adjoining Kowloon at Hong Kong. New ports and cities were opened to foreign trade. The United States was in a weaker position, so it enunciated an "open-door" policy: equal commercial opportunities for all powers and the preservation of the territorial integrity of China.

There was in China at this time a religious society known as the Boxers. They rebelled first in Shantung in 1898, and, gaining court support, entered Peking in 1900. There followed a two-month siege of the foreign legation quarter. The rebellion was fueled by pent-up resentments against decades of foreign encroachments. Eventually an international force captured Peking, and the Russians occupied Manchuria.

The defeat of the Boxers convinced even conservative Chinese leaders of the futility of clinging to old ways. A more powerful reform movement began, with the empress dowager in its vanguard. But the dynasty could not control the movement and eventually was bypassed.

Sun Yat-sen (1866–1925), father of China's 1911 republican revolution. [Brown Brothers]

Educational reforms began in 1901. Women were admitted to newly formed schools. In place of Confucianism, the instructors taught science, mathematics, geography, and an anti-imperialist version of Chinese history. Western doctrines, such as classical economics, liberalism, socialism, anarchism, and social Darwinism, were introduced into China. By 1906, there were 8,000 Chinese students in Japan, which became a hotbed of Chinese reformist and revolutionary societies.

Military reforms were begun by Yuan Shih-k'ai (1859–1916), whose New Army drew on Japanese and Western models. Young men from gentry families, spurred by patriotism, joined the New Army as officers. Their loyalty was to their commanders and their country, not to the dynasty.

In 1905, the examination system was abolished; officials were to be directly recruited from the schools and those who had studied abroad. Provincial assemblies were formed in 1909, and a consultative assembly was established in Peking in 1910.

These changes sparked the 1911 revolution. It began with an uprising in Szechwan province against a government plan to nationalize the main railways. The key figures were:

1. Gentry who stood to lose their investments in the railways.

2. Ch'ing military commanders, who declared their provinces independent.

3. Sun Yat-sen (1866–1925), a republican revolutionary. He organized the Revolutionary Alliance in Tokyo in 1905 and was associated with the Nationalist Party (Kuomintang) formed in 1912.

4. Yuan Shih-k'ai, who arranged for the last child emperor to abdicate, for Sun to step aside, and for himself to become president of the new Republic of China.

In 1916, Yuan proclaimed a new dynasty with himself as emperor. The idea of another dynasty, however, met opposition from all quarters. Yuan died in June 1916. China then fell into the hands of warlord armies. The years until the late twenties were a time of agony for the Chinese people. Yet they were also in a time of intense intellectual ferment.

Cultural and Ideological Ferment: The May Fourth Movement

A period of freedom and vigorous experimentation with new doctrines began in 1914 and extended into the 1920s. It is called the May Fourth Movement after an incident in Peking in 1919 in which thousands of students protested the settlement at Versailles that awarded former German possessions in Shantung to Japan. The nationalist fervor that led the students to demonstrate in the streets changed the complexion of Chinese thought. Leading thinkers began to judge ideas in terms of their value in solving China's problems.

During the May Fourth era, the center of advanced thought was Peking. Ideas propounded there quickly spread to the rest of China, especially to its urban centers. Protest demonstrations against imperialist privilege broke out in Shanghai, Wuhan, and Canton, as they had in the capital. Nationalism and anti-imperialist sentiment were stronger than liberalism, although most thinkers spoke of democracy. Only members of an older generation of reformers, appalled by the slaughter of World War I and what they saw as Western materialism, advocated a return to traditional philosophies.

After the Russian Revolution of 1917, Marxism-Leninism entered China. The Leninist definition of imperialism as the last crisis stage of capitalism put the blame for China's ills on the West and offered "feudal" China the possibility of leapfrogging over capitalism to socialism. Marxist study groups formed in Peking and other cities. In 1919, a student from Hunan, Mao Tse-tung, who had worked in the Peking University library, returned to Changsha to form a study group. The Chinese Communist Party was formed in Shanghai in 1921; Chou En-lai (1898–1976) formed a similar group in Paris the same year.

Nationalist China

Kuomintang Unification of China and the Nanking Decade (1927–1937)

Sun Yat-sen had fled to Japan during the 1913–1916 rule by Yuan Shih-k'ai. He returned to Canton in 1916, but he was a poor organizer, and his Kuomintang (KMT)—or Nationalist Party—made little headway. From 1923, Sun began to receive Soviet support. He reorganized his party on the Leninist model, with an executive committee on top of a national party congress, provincial and county organizations, and local party cells.

Since 1905, Sun had enunciated his "three principles of the people": nationality, livelihood, and rights. Sun's nationalism was now directed against Western imperialism. The principle of people's livelihood was defined in terms of equalizing land holdings and nationalizing major industries. By "people's rights" Sun meant democracy, although he argued that it must be preceded by a preparatory period of single-party dictatorship. Sun sent his loyal lieutenant Chiang Kai-shek (1887–1975) to the Soviet Union for study. Chiang returned after four months with a cadre of Russian advisers and established a military academy at Whampoa south of Canton in 1924. Sun died in 1925. By 1926, the Whampoa

Ch'en Tu-hsiu's "Call to Youth" in 1915

Struggle, natural selection, and organic process are the images used by Ch'en Tu-hsiu. How different from those of Confucianism!

How does Ch'en's "Call to Youth" relate to the political conditions in China in 1915?

The Chinese compliment others by saying, "He acts like an old man although still young." Englishmen and Americans encourage one another by saying, "Keep young while growing old." Such is one respect in which the different ways of thought of the East and West are manifested. Youth is like early spring, like the rising sun, like trees and grass in bud, like a newly sharpened blade. It is the most valuable period of life. The function of youth in society is the same as that of a fresh and vital cell in a human body. In the processes of metabolism, the old and the rotten are incessantly eliminated to be replaced by the fresh and living. . . . According to this standard, then, is the society of our nation flourishing, or is it about to perish? I cannot bear to answer. As for those old and rotten elements, I shall leave them to the process of natural selection. . . . I only, with tears, place my plea before the young and vital youth, in the hope that they will achieve self-awareness, and begin to struggle.

What is the struggle? It is to exert one's intellect, discard resolutely the old and the rotten, regard them as enemies and as the flood or savage beasts, keep away from their neighborhood and refuse to be contaminated by their poisonous germs. Alas! Do these words really fit the youth of our country? I have seen that, out of every ten youths who are young in age, five are old in physique; and out of every ten who are young in both age and physique, nine are old in mentality. Those with shining hair, smooth countenance, a straight back and a wide chest are indeed magnificent youths! Yet if you ask what thoughts and aims are entertained in their heads, then they all turn out to be the same as the old and rotten, like moles from the same hill. . . . It is the old and rotten air that fills society everywhere. One cannot even find a bit of fresh and vital air to comfort those of us who are suffocating in despair.

Reprinted by permission of the publisher from *China's Response to the West* by Ssu-Yu Teng and John K. Fairbank, Cambridge, MA: Harvard University Press. Copyright © 1954, 1979 by the President and Fellows of Harvard College.

Academy had graduated several thousand officers, and the KMT army numbered almost 100,000. The KMT had become the major political force in China.

The growth of the party was spurred by changes within Chinese society. Industries arose in the cities. Labor unions were organized. New ventures were begun outside the treaty ports. A politically conscious middle class developed.

The quicksilver element in cities was the several million students. In May 1925, students demonstrated in Shanghai. Police in the international settlement fired on the demonstrators. The incident inflamed national and anti-imperialist feelings. Strikes and boycotts of foreign goods were called throughout China.

Under these conditions the Chinese Communist Party (CCP) also grew and was influential in student organizations, labor unions, and even within the KMT. Sun had permitted CCP members to join the KMT as individuals, but had enjoined them from organizing CCP cells within it. Moscow approved of this policy. It felt that the CCP was too small to accomplish anything on its own.

By 1926, Chiang Kai-shek felt ready to march against the warlords. He worried about the growing communist strength, however, and before setting off he ousted the Soviet advisers and CCP members from the KMT offices in Canton. The march north began in July. By the spring of 1927, Chiang's army had reached the Yangtze, defeating warlord armies as it advanced.

After entering Shanghai in April 1927, Chiang carried out a sweeping purge of the CCP. Many were killed. The surviving CCP members fled to the mountainous border region of Hunan and Kiangsi to the southwest and established the "Kiangsi Soviet." Chiang's army took Peking and gained the nominal submission of most northern Chinese warlords during 1928. Most foreign powers recognized the KMT regime as the government of China.

Chiang Kai-shek was the key figure in the government. He believed in military force. He was unimaginative, strict, and incorruptible. Chiang venerated Sun Yat-sen and his three "people's principles." But where Sun was a revolutionary, Chiang was conservative and, though a Methodist, often appealed to Confucian values. The New Life Movement begun by Chiang in 1934 was an attempt to revitalize these values.

Chiang's power rested on the army, the party, and the bureaucracy. The army was dominated by the Whampoa clique, which was loyal to Chiang, and by officers trained in

Japan. After 1927, German advisers reorganized Chiang's army along German lines with a general staff system. The larger part of KMT revenues went to the military, which was expanded into a modernized force of 300,000. Whampoa graduates also controlled the secret military police and used it against communists and any others who opposed the government. The KMT was a dictatorship under a central committee. Chiang became president of the party in 1938.

The densely populated central and lower Yangtze provinces were the area of KMT strength. The party, however, was unable to control the outlying areas occupied by warlords, communists, and Japanese. Warlords ruled some areas until 1949. In 1931, Chiang attacked the Kiangsi Soviet. In 1934, the communists were forced to flee to the southwest and then to Shensi province in northwestern China in the epic "Long March." During this march Mao Tse-tung wrested control of the CCP from the Moscow-trained, urban-oriented leaders and established his unorthodox view that a Leninist party could base itself on the peasantry.

The Japanese had held special rights in Manchuria since the Russo-Japanese War of 1905. When Chiang's march north and Chinese nationalism threatened the Japanese position, Japan's Kwantung Army engineered a military coup in 1931 and in 1932 proclaimed the independence of Manchukuo, their puppet state. In the years that followed, Japanese forces moved south as far as the Great Wall. Chinese nationalism demanded that Chiang resist. Chiang, well aware of the disparity between his armies and those of Japan, said that the internal unification of China must take precedence. In 1937, however, a full-scale war with Japan broke out, and China's situation changed.

Modern China

1839–1842	Opium War
1850–1873	Taiping and other rebellions
1870s–1880s	Self-strengthening movement
1894–1895	Sino-Japanese War
1898	One hundred days of reform
1898–1900	Boxer Rebellion
1911	Republican revolution overthrows Ch'ing dynasty
1912–1916	Yuan Shih-k'ai president of Republic of China
1916–1928	Warlord era
1919	May Fourth incident
1924	Founding of Whampoa Military Academy
1926–1928	March north and Kuomintang reunification of China
1934–1935	Chinese Communists' Long March to Yenan
1937–1945	War with Japan
1945–1949	Civil war and the establishment of the People's Republic of China

War and Revolution (1937–1949)

The war with Japan began in July 1937 as an unplanned clash at Peking and then quickly spread. Peking and Tientsin fell to Japan within a month, Shanghai was attacked in August, and Nanking fell in December. During the following year, the Japanese took Canton and set up puppet regimes in Peking and Nanking. In 1940, the leader of the left wing of the KMT and many of his associates joined the Japanese puppet government. Japan proclaimed its "New Order in East Asia." It expected Chiang to submit. Instead, in 1938 he relocated his capital to Chungking, far to the west, and was joined by thousands of Chinese.

Chiang's stubborn resistance won admiration from all sides. But the withdrawal to Chungking cut the KMT off from most of the Chinese population; programs for modernization ended; and the KMT's former tax revenues were lost. Inflation increased geometrically and exacerbated the already widespread corruption.

The United States sent advisers and military equipment to strengthen Chiang's forces after the start of the Pacific War. However, Chiang wanted not to fight the Japanese but to husband his forces for a postwar confrontation with the Communists. Within his own army a gap appeared between officers and men. Conditions in the camps were primitive, food poor, and medical supplies inadequate. The young saw conscription almost as a death sentence. Chiang's unwillingness to commit his troops against the Japanese also meant that the surge of anti-Japanese patriotism was not converted to popular support for the KMT.

For the communists, the Japanese occupation was an opportunity. Headquartered at Yenan, they began campaigns to promote literacy and self-sufficiency. Soldiers farmed so as not to burden the peasants. The CCP abandoned its earlier policy of expropriating lands in favor of reductions in rents and interest. They took only those offices needed to ensure their control and shared the rest with the KMT and other parties. They expanded village councils to include tenants. But they also strengthened their party internally.

Party membership expanded from 40,000 in 1937 to 1.2 million in 1945. Schools were established in Yenan to train party cadres. Orthodoxy was maintained by a rectification campaign. Those tainted by impure tendencies were made to repent at public meetings. Mao's thought was supreme. To the Chinese at large, Mao represented himself as the successor to Sun Yat-sen, but within the Communist Party he presented himself as a theoretician in the line of Marx (1818–1883), Engels (1820–1895), Lenin (1870–1924), and Stalin (1879–1953).

The communists learned to operate at the grass-roots level. They infiltrated Japanese-controlled areas and KMT organizations and military units. CCP armies were built up from

90,000 in 1937 to 900,000 in 1945. These armies were supplemented by a rural people's militia and by guerrilla forces. The Yenan leadership and its party, army, and mass organizations possessed a cohesion, determination, and morale that were lacking in Chungking.

But the strength of the Chinese communists as of 1945 should not be overstated. When the war in the Pacific ended in 1945, China's future was unclear. Even the Soviet Union recognized the KMT as the government of China and expected it to win the postwar struggle. The Allies directed Japanese armies to surrender to the KMT forces in 1945. The United States flew Chiang's troops to key eastern cities. His armies were by then three times the size of the communists' and far better equipped.

A civil war broke out immediately. Efforts by US General George Marshall (1880–1959) to mediate were futile. Until the summer of 1947, KMT armies were victorious—even capturing Yenan. But the tide turned in July as CCP armies went on the offensive in north China. In January 1949, Peking and Tientsin fell. A few months later all of China was in communist hands. Many Chinese fled with Chiang to Taiwan or escaped to Hong Kong. In China, apprehension was mixed with anticipation. The feeling was widespread that the future of China was once again in the hands of the Chinese.

MODERN JAPAN (1853–1945)

Overthrow of the Tokugawa *Bakufu* (1853–1868)

From the seventeenth century into the nineteenth, the natural isolation of the islands of Japan was augmented by its policy of seclusion, making Japan into a little world of its own. The 260-odd domains were the states of this world, the *bakufu* in Edo was its hegemon, and the imperial court in Kyoto provided a religious sanction for the *bakufu*-domain system. Then at mid-century, the American ships of Commodore Perry came and forced Japan to sign a treaty opening it to foreign intercourse. Fourteen years later, the entire *bakufu*-domain system collapsed, and a group of talented leaders seized power. Seclusion, like the case of a watch, had been necessary to preserve the Tokugawa political mechanism. With the case removed, the inner workings flew apart.

Little changed during the first four years after Perry. The break came in 1858 when the *bakufu*, ignoring the imperial court's disapproval, was persuaded to sign a commercial treaty with the United States. Some daimyo, who wanted a voice in national policy, criticized the treaty as contravening the hallowed policy of seclusion. Younger samurai, frustrated by their exclusion from office, started a movement to "honor the emperor." The *bakufu*, in turn, responded with a purge. But in 1860, the head of the *bakufu* council was assassinated by extremist samurai. His successors lacked the nerve to continue his tough policies.

In 1861, two domains, Chōshū and Satsuma, emerged to heal the breach between the *bakufu* and the court. First, Chōshū officials proposed a policy that favored the *bakufu* but made concessions to the court. Next, Satsuma advocated a policy that made further concessions and ousted Chōshū as "the friend of the court." In response, the moderate reformist government of Chōshū adopted the pro-emperor policy of its extremist faction and, in turn, ousted Satsuma. Satsuma then seized the court in 1863 in a military coup.

Several points may be noted about the 1861–1863 diplomatic phase of domain action: (1) Even after 250 years of *bakufu* rule, several domains could still act when the opportunity occurred. (2) The two domains that acted first and most of the others that followed had many samurai and substantial financial resources. (3) Both Satsuma and Chōshū had fought against the Tokugawa in 1600 and remembered an earlier independence. (4) By 1861–1863, the new politics had opened decision making to middle-ranking samurai officials in a way that would have been impossible before 1853.

The 1863 Satsuma coup at the Kyoto court initiated a military phase of politics in which battles would determine every turning point. As long as Satsuma and Chōshū remained enemies, politics stalemated and the *bakufu* continued as hegemon. But when the two domains became allies in 1866, the *bakufu* was overthrown in less than two years.

One factor contributing to this process was the movement for a "union of court and camp"; daimyo campaigned for a new counciliar rule in which they would participate together with the emperor and withdrew support from the *bakufu*. A second feature of the years between 1863 and 1868 was antiforeignism. Extremists assassinated foreigners as well as *bakufu* officials; one of their slogans was "expel the barbarians." A third was the formation of new rifle units, commanded mostly by lower samurai. These units transformed political power in Japan. A fourth development during 1867 and 1868 was a cultural shift in the way Japanese saw themselves. During the Tokugawa era, the Japanese saw themselves as civilized Confucians and much of the rest of the world as barbarians. But in the face of Western gunboats, this view seemed hollow. The West, with its technology, science, and humane laws, was seen as "civilized and enlightened"; China, Japan, and countries like Turkey were seen as half civilized; and other areas were barbarian.

Building the Meiji State (1868–1890)

The idea of a "developing nation" did not exist in the mid-nineteenth century. Yet Japan after the 1868 Meiji restoration was just such a nation. (The years from 1868 to 1912 are referred to as the Meiji period, after the name of the emperor.) It was committed to progress, by which it meant achieving wealth and power of the kind possessed by Western industrial nations. There was no blueprint for progress. The government advanced by trial and error. It also demanded that the Japanese people make sacrifices for the sake of the future.

The announcement of the restoration of rule by an emperor was made on January 3, 1868. In the battles that followed, Chōshū and Satsuma troops defeated those of the *bakufu*. Edo surrendered and was renamed Tokyo, the "eastern capital." Edo castle became the imperial palace. A year later, the last *bakufu* holdouts surrendered. At the start the Meiji government was only a small group of samurai leaders from Chōshū, Satsuma, and a few other domains. They have been described, only half humorously, as twelve bureaucrats in search of a bureaucracy. But their vision defined the goals of the new government.

Centralization of Power

Their immediate goal was to centralize political power. By 1871, the young leaders had replaced the domains with prefectures controlled from Tokyo. To ensure a break with the past, each new prefectural governor was chosen from samurai of other regions.

Having centralized political authority, about half of the most important Meiji leaders went abroad for a year and a half to study the West. On their return to Japan in 1872, they discovered that officials were planning war with Korea. They quashed the plan, insisting that priority be given to domestic development.

The second goal or task of the Meiji leaders was to stabilize government revenues that, because the land tax was collected mostly in grain, fluctuated with the price of rice. The government converted the grain tax to a money tax. But a third of the revenues still went to pay for samurai stipends, so in 1873 the government raised a conscript army and abolished the samurai class. The samurai were paid off in government bonds; but as the bonds fell during the inflation of the 1870s, most former samurai became impoverished. What had begun as a reform of government finance ended as a social revolution.

Some samurai rebelled. The last and greatest uprising was in 1877. When it was suppressed in 1878, the Meiji government became militarily secure.

Political Parties

Other samurai opposed the government by forming political parties and campaigning for popular rights, elections, and a constitution. They drew heavily on liberal Western models.

National assemblies, they argued, were the means used by advanced societies to tap the energies of their peoples. Parties in a national assembly would unite the emperor and the people, thereby curbing the Satsuma-Chōshū clique. Samurai were the mainstay of the early party movement, despite its doctrines proclaiming all classes to be equal. In 1881, the government promised a constitution and a national assembly within ten years. As the date for national elections approached, the parties gained strength, and the ties between party notables and local men of influence grew closer.

The Constitution

The government viewed the party movement with distaste but was not sure how to counter it. Itō Hirobumi (1841–1909), originally from Chōshū, went abroad to shop for a constitution that would serve the needs of the Meiji government. He brought home a German jurist to help adapt the conservative Prussian constitution of 1850 to Japanese uses. As promulgated in 1889, the Meiji Constitution granted extensive powers to the emperor and severely limited the powers of the lower house in the Diet (the English term for Japan's bicameral national assembly).

The emperor was sovereign. According to the constitution, he was "sacred and inviolable," and in Itō's commentaries this was defined in Shinto terms. The emperor was given direct command of the armed forces. Yamagata Aritomo (1838–1922) had set up a German-type general staff system in 1878. The emperor had the right to name the prime minister and to appoint the Cabinet. He could dissolve the lower house of the Diet and issue imperial ordinances when the Diet was not in session. The Imperial Household Ministry, which was outside the Cabinet, administered the great wealth given to the imperial family during the 1880s—so that the emperor would never have to ask the Diet for funds. It was understood that the Meiji leaders would act for the emperor in all of these matters. Finally, the constitution itself was presented as a gift from the emperor to his subjects.

The lower house of the Diet was given the authority only to approve budgets and pass laws, and both of these powers were hedged. The previous year's budget would remain in effect if a new budget was not approved. The appointive House of Peers, the upper house of the Diet, had to approve any bill to become law. Furthermore, the vote was given only to adult males paying fifteen yen or more in taxes. In 1890 this was about 5 percent of the adult male population. In sum, Itō's intention was to create not a parliamentary system, but a constitutional system that included a parliament as one of its parts.

During the 1880s, the government also created institutions to limit the future influence of the political parties. In

1884, it created a new nobility with which to stock the future House of Peers. The nobility was composed of ex-nobles and the Meiji leaders themselves. Itō, born a lowly foot soldier, ended as a prince. In 1885, he established a cabinet system and became the first prime minister. In 1887, Itō established a Privy Council, with himself as its head, to approve the constitution he had written. In 1888, laws were passed and civil-service examinations instituted to insulate the imperial bureaucracy from the tawdry concerns of politicians.

Growth of a Modern Economy

The late Tokugawa economy was not markedly different from the economies of other East Asian countries. Almost 80 percent of the population lived in the countryside at close to a subsistence level. Taxes were high, and two-thirds of the land tax was paid in kind. Money had only partially penetrated the rural economy. Japan had not developed factory production with machinery, steam power, or large accumulations of capital.

Early Meiji reforms unshackled the late Tokugawa economy. Occupations were freed, which meant that farmers could trade and samurai could farm. Barriers on roads were abolished, as were the monopolistic guilds. The abolition of domains threw open regional economies. There followed a groundswell of new commercial ventures and traditional agriculturally based industries.

Silk was the wonder crop. The government introduced mechanical reeling, enabling Japan to win markets previously held by the hand-reeled silk of China. Silk production rose from 2.3 million pounds in the post-Restoration era to 93 million in 1929.

A parallel unshackling occurred on the land. The land tax reform of the 1870s created an incentive for growth by giving farmers a clear title to their land and by fixing the tax in money. The freedom to buy and sell land led to a rise in tenancy from perhaps 25 percent in 1868 to about 44 percent at the turn of the century. Progressive landlords bought fertilizer and farm equipment. Rice production rose from 149 million bushels a year during 1880–1884 to 316 million during 1935–1937. More food, combined with a drop in the death rate—the result of better hygiene—led to population growth: from about 30 million in 1868 to 45 million in 1900 to 73 million in 1940. Because the farm population remained constant, the extra hands were available for factory and other urban jobs.

First Phase: Model Industries

The modern sector of the economy was the government's greatest concern. It developed in four phases. The first was the era of model industries, which lasted until 1881. With military strength as a major goal, the Meiji government expanded arsenals and shipyards, built telegraph lines, made a start on railroads, developed mines, and established factories. The quantitative output of these early industries was insignificant, however. They were pilot-plant operations that doubled as "schools" for technologists and labor.

Just as important to economic development were banks, post offices, ports, roads, commercial laws, a system of primary and secondary schools, a government university, and so on. They were patterned after European and American examples.

Second Phase: 1880s–1890s

More substantial growth in the modern sector took place during the 1880s and 1890s. It was marked by the appearance of what would later become the great industrial combines known as *zaibatsu*. One of the first industries to benefit was cotton textiles. By 1896, the production of yarn had reached 17 million pounds, and by 1913 it was over ten times that amount. Production of cotton cloth rose from 22 million square yards in 1900 to 2.7 billion in 1936.

Another area of growth was railroads. Railroads gave Japan an internal circulatory system, opening up hitherto isolated regions. In 1872, Japan had 18 miles of track; in 1894, 2,100 miles; and by 1934, 14,500 miles.

Cotton textiles and railroads were followed during the 1890s by cement, bricks, matches, glass, beer, chemicals, and other private industries. The government created a favorable climate for growth: The society and the polity were stable, the yen was sound, capital was safe, and taxes on industry were low. In every respect, the conditions enjoyed by Japan's budding entrepreneurs differed from those of China.

Third Phase: 1905–1929

Economic growth spurted ahead during World War I. But an economic slump followed the war, and the economy grew slowly during the twenties. One factor was renewed competition from a Europe at peace; another was the earthquake that destroyed Tokyo in 1923. Agricultural productivity also leveled off during the twenties: It became cheaper to import food from the colonies than to invest in new agricultural technology at home.

By the twenties, Japanese society, especially in the cities, was becoming modern. The Japanese were healthier and lived longer. Personal savings rose with the standard of living. Even factory workers drank beer, went to movies, and read newspapers. By 1925, primary school education was universal. Japan had done what no other non-Western nation had even attempted: It had achieved universal literacy. Nevertheless, an immense cultural and social gap remained between the majority who had only a primary school education and the 3 percent who attended university. This gap was a basic weakness in the political democracy of the twenties.

It should also be noted that the costs of growth were sometimes high. Because textiles played a large role in the early phase of Japan's modern economic growth, well into the twentieth century more than half of the industrial labor force was women. They went to the mills after leaving primary school and returned to their villages before marrying. Their working hours were long, their dormitories crowded, and their movements restricted. Some contracted tuberculosis, the plague of late-nineteenth and early-twentieth-century Japan, and were sent back to their villages to die.

Fourth Phase: Depression and Recovery

A Japanese bank crisis in 1927, followed by the worldwide Great Depression in 1929, plunged Japan into unemployment and suffering. The political consequences were enormous. Yet most of Japan recovered by 1933, more rapidly than any other industrial nation.

The recovery was fueled by an export boom and military procurements. During the 1930s, the production of pig iron, raw steel, and chemicals doubled. By 1937, Japan had a merchant fleet of 4.5 million tons, the third largest and the newest in the world. The quality of Japan's manufacturers also rose. The outcry in the West against Japanese exports at this time was not so much because of volume—a modest 3.6 percent of world exports in 1936—but because Japanese products had become competitive in terms of quality.

The Politics of Imperial Japan (1890–1945)

Parliaments began in the West and have worked better there than in the rest of the world. Even so cautious a constitution as that of Meiji had no precedent outside the West at the time. How are we then to view the Japanese political experience after 1890?

One view is that because Japanese society was not ready for constitutional government, the militarism of the thirties was inevitable. From the perspective of an ideal democracy, Japanese society had many weaknesses: a small middle class, weak trade unions, an independent military under the emperor, a strong emperor-centered nationalism, and so on. But these weaknesses did not prevent the Diet from growing in importance, nor did they block the transfer of power from the bureaucratic Meiji leaders to the political party leaders. The transfer fell short of full parliamentary government. However, had it not been derailed by the Great Depression and other events, the advance toward parliamentary government might well have continued.

From Confrontation to the Founding of the Seiyūkai (1890–1900)

In 1890, the Meiji leaders—sometimes called *oligarchs*, the few who rule—were concerned with nation building, not politics. They saw the cabinet as serving the emperor and nation above the ruck of partisan interests. They viewed the political parties as ineffective and irresponsible. They saw the lower house of the Diet as a place to let off steam without interfering in the government's work of building a new Japan. But the oligarchs had miscalculated: The authority of the lower house to approve or turn down the budget made it more powerful than they had intended. This involved the oligarchs, willy-nilly, in the political struggles.

The first act of the parties in the new 1890 Diet was to slash the government's budget. Prime Minister Yamagata had to make concessions to get part of the cut restored. This pattern continued for ten years. Rising costs meant that the previous year's budget was never enough. The government tried to intimidate and bribe the parties, but failed. The opposing political parties maintained their control of the lower house. They also had the support of the voters, mostly well-to-do landowners, who opposed the government's heavy land tax.

In 1900, Itō Hirobumi formed a new party, called the Rikken Seiyūkai, or "Friends of Constitutional Government." It was composed of ex-bureaucrats associated with Itō and of politicians from the Liberal Party that Itagaki Taisuke (1837–1919) had formed in 1881. For most of the next twenty years it was the most important party in Japan, providing parliamentary support for successive governments through its control of the lower house. This arrangement was satisfactory to both sides: Prime ministers got the Diet support necessary for the government to function smoothly. The party politicians got cabinet posts and pork barrel legislation with which to reward their supporters.

The Golden Years of Meiji

The years before and after the turn of the century represented the culmination of what the government had striven for since 1868. Economic development was under way. Japan got rid of extraterritoriality in 1899 and regained control of its own tariffs in 1911. However, it was international events that won Japan recognition as a world power.

The first event was a war with China in 1894–1895 over Korea. From its victory, Japan secured Taiwan, the Pescadores Islands, the Kwantung Peninsula in southern Manchuria, an indemnity, and a treaty giving it the same privileges in China as those enjoyed by the Western powers (see Map 32–1). Russia, however, with French and German support, forced Japan to give up the Kwantung Peninsula, which included Port Arthur. Three years later, Russia took Kwantung for itself.

Map 32–1 Formation of the Japanese Empire. The Japanese Empire grew in three stages: the Sino-Japanese War of 1894–1895, the Russo-Japanese War of 1904–1905, and Japanese conquests in Manchuria and northern China after 1931.

The second event was Japan's participation in 1900 in the international force that relieved the Boxers' siege of the foreign legations in Peking. A third development was the Anglo-Japanese Alliance of 1902. For Britain, this alliance ensured Japanese support for its East Asian interests and warded off the likelihood of a Russian-Japanese agreement over spheres of influence in Northeast Asia. For Japan, the alliance meant it could fight Russia without fear of intervention by a third party.

The fourth event was the war with Russia that began in 1904. Japanese armies drove the Russians from their railway zones in Manchuria and seized Mukden in March 1905. The Russians sent their Baltic fleet to join the battle, but it was annihilated by Admiral Tōgō (1847–1934)

at the Straits of Tsushima. After months of war, both countries were worn out, and Russia was plagued by revolution. President Theodore Roosevelt (1858–1919) proposed a peace conference at Portsmouth, New Hampshire. The resulting treaty gave Japan the Russian lease in the Liaotung Peninsula, the Russian railway in south Manchuria, the southern half of Sakhalin, and a recognition of Japan's "paramount interest" in Korea, which was annexed in 1910.

Japan joined the imperialist scramble for colonies because it wanted equality with the great Western powers, and military power and colonies were the best credentials. Enthusiasm for empire was shared by political party leaders, most liberal thinkers, and conservative leaders alike.

Rise of the Parties to Power

The founding of the Seiyūkai by Itō in 1900 ended a decade of confrontation between the Diet and the government. The aging oligarch Itō found it intolerable to deal with party politicians, who, unlike the bureaucrats, neither obeyed him nor paid him the respect that he thought his due. In 1903, he relinquished the presidency of the party to Saionji Kinmochi (1849–1940), who passed the post to Hara Takashi (1856–1921) in 1914. With Hara, the office found the man.

Hara was an outsider. Born a generation after the founding fathers of the Meiji state, he helped Itō to found the Seiyūkai and was the most able politician in Japan. His goals for Japan centered on the expansion of national wealth and power and were no different from those of Itō or Yamagata. But he felt that they should be achieved by party government, not oligarchic rule, and worked to expand the power of his party. The years between 1905 and 1921 were marked by the struggle between these two alternative conceptions of government.

The struggle can be represented as a rising curve of party strength and a descending curve of oligarchic influence. The rising curve had two vectors: a buildup of the Seiyūkai party machine that enabled it to win elections and maintain itself as the majority (or plurality) party in the Diet, and the strengthening of the Diet vis-à-vis other elites within the government in Tokyo. For the former, Hara obtained campaign funds from moneyed interests. He also promoted pork barrel legislation. Constituencies that supported Seiyūkai candidates got new schools, bridges, dams, roads, or even railroad lines. Hara was even willing to call on the police and local officials to aid Seiyūkai election campaigns.

In co-opting other governmental elites, the Seiyūkai had mixed success. The party increased its representation in the Cabinet and gained some patronage appointments in the bureaucracy, although most bureaucrats remained professionals and resisted the intrusion of political appointees. The House of Peers and the Privy Council, which ratified treaties, remained independent bodies. The Seiyūkai had no success in penetrating the military services.

The descending curve of weakening oligarchic control reflected the aging of the "men of Meiji." In 1900, Itō was the last oligarch to become prime minister. From 1901 to 1912, Katsura Tarō (1847–1913), a Chōshū general and Yamagata's protégé, and Saionji, Itō's protégé, took turns in the post. Both had Seiyūkai support. The oligarchs were also weakened by changes within the elites. A younger generation of officers in the military services chafed at the continuing domination by the old cliques. In the civil bureaucracy, younger officials who had graduated from the Law Faculty of Tokyo Imperial University were achieving positions of responsibility. They saw the bureaucracy as an independent service and resisted oligarchic control almost as much as they resisted that of the parties.

The oligarchs maintained their power to act for the emperor in appointing prime ministers. With the deaths of Itō in 1909 and Yamagata in 1922, this vital function was taken over by Saionji and, later, by ex-prime ministers.

As the rising and descending curves approached each other, the political parties advanced. Several turning points were critical. One came in 1912. When the army's demands for a larger budget were refused, it withdrew its minister, causing Saionji's cabinet to collapse. Katsura tried to govern using imperial decrees in place of Diet support. This infuriated the parties, and even the Seiyūkai withdrew its support. Massive popular demonstrations broke out. Katsura was forced to resign in 1913. The lower house had defeated an oligarchic prime minister.

The curves finally crossed in 1918 when Hara became prime minister. It was the first time a politician who was not a Meiji founding father or a protégé of one had obtained the post. He enacted reforms but did nothing to remedy the parliamentary shortcomings of the Meiji Constitution.

A third development was the wave of liberalism that began during World War I and culminated in the period of party governments from 1924 to 1932. Joining the Allies in World War I, Japan had been influenced by democratic thought from England and America. Scholars discussed revising the Meiji Constitution. Labor unions were organized, at first liberal and often Christian, and later Marxist. A social movement was launched to improve conditions in Japan's industrial slums and to pass social and labor legislation. Japan's second political party, the Kenseikai, which had been out of power since 1916, grew steadily more liberal and adopted several of the new social causes as its own, such as universal manhood suffrage. When Hara cut the tax qualification for voting from ten to three yen—a considerable extension of the franchise—the Kenseikai criticized the change as insufficient.

In 1924, the Kenseikai and the Seiyūkai formed a coalition government. For the next eight years, the presidents of one or the other of the two major parties were appointed as prime ministers.

The cabinets (1924–1926) of Katō Kōmei are considered the peak of parliamentarianism in prewar Japan. Blunt, cold, and haughty, Katō was respected, if not liked. He was an Anglophile who advocated a British model of government. His ministry passed universal manhood suffrage, increased academic appointments to the House of Peers, and cut the military budget. He also enacted social and labor legislation. In effect, he legalized the moderate socialist movement and outlawed revolutionary socialism. Katō's cabinet brought Japan close to a true parliamentary government.

Militarism and War (1927–1945)

The future of Japan's parliamentary coalition seemed assured during the mid-1920s. The economy was growing; society was stable; the party leaders were experienced. Japan's international position was secure. By a decade later, however, the party leaders had lost the gains of thirty-five years. By 1945, Japan had been defeated in a devastating war and was occupied by foreign troops for the first time in its history. How did this come about?

Simply put, a small shift in the balance of power among the governmental elites established by the Meiji Constitution had produced a major change in Japan's foreign policy. The parties had been the obstreperous elite between 1890 and 1926 and had advanced by forcing the other elites to compromise. From the late 1920s, the military became the obstreperous elite and did the same. Beginning in 1932, military men replaced party presidents as prime ministers. In 1937, Japan went to war with China; and by the end of 1941, Japan was allied with Germany and Italy and had gone to war with the United States.

From their inception, the military services in Japan had been constructed on different principles from Japan's civilian society. Soldiers were not samurai. Universal conscription had put the new military on a changed footing. But the armed services had their own schools, which inculcated the values of discipline, bravery, loyalty, and obedience. The military saw themselves as the heirs of those who had founded the modern Japanese state and the guardians of Japanese tradition. They contrasted their loyalty to the emperor and their concern for all Japanese with the pandering to special interests by the political parties.

They resented their diminished national stature during the 1920s, when military budgets were cut and the prestige of a military career declined. But even during the liberal 1920s there had been no change in the constitutional position of the services. The general staffs remained directly responsible to the emperor. With the passing of the Meiji oligarchs, this meant they were responsible to no one but themselves.

A Crisis in Manchuria   The new multilateral treaties (the 1924 Washington Conference and the 1930 London Conference) that replaced the earlier system of bilateral treaties (such as the Anglo-Japanese Alliance) recognized the existing colonies of the victors in World War I but opposed new colonial ventures. Japan's position in Manchuria was ambiguous. Because Japan maintained its rule through a tame Chinese warlord, Manchuria was not, strictly speaking, a colony. But because Japan had gained its special position in Manchuria at the cost of 100,000 lives in the 1905 Russo-Japanese War, it saw its claim to Manchuria as similar to that of Western nations to their colonies.

From the late 1920s, the Kuomintang unification of China and the blossoming of Chinese nationalism threatened Japan's special position. Japanese army units tried to block the march north and murdered the Manchurian warlord when he showed signs of independence. In this crisis, the party government in Tokyo equivocated, hoping to preserve a status quo that was crumbling before its eyes. The army saw Manchuria as a buffer between the Soviet Union and the Japanese colony of Korea. In 1931, the army provoked a crisis, took over Manchuria, and proclaimed it an independent state in 1932. When the League of Nations condemned Japan, Japan withdrew from the League in 1933.

The Great Depression   Japan's government acted effectively to counter the Depression, as noted earlier, but the recovery came too late to help the political parties. By 1936, political trends that had begun during the worst years of the Depression had become irreversible.

Modern Japan

Overthrow of Tokugawa *Bakufu*

1853–1854	Perry obtains Treaty of Friendship
1858	*Bakufu* signs commercial treaty
1861–1863	Chōshū and Satsuma mediate
1866	Chōshū defeats *bakufu* army
1868	Meiji Restoration

Nation Building

1868–1871	Shaping a new state
1873–1878	Social revolution from above
1877–1878	Satsuma rebellion
1889	Meiji Constitution promulgated
1890	First Diet session

Imperial Japan

1894–1895	Sino-Japanese War
1900	Seiyūkai formed
1904–1905	Russo-Japanese War
1910	Korea annexed

Era of Party Government

1918	Hara becomes prime minister
1924	Katō becomes prime minister
	Universal manhood suffrage passed

Militarism

1931	Japan takes Manchuria
1937	War with China
1941	Japan attacks Pearl Harbor
1945	Japan surrenders

The Depression galvanized the political left and right. The political left was composed mainly of socialist moderates, who won eight Diet seats in 1928 and thirty-seven in 1937. Supported by unionists and white-collar workers, they would reemerge as an even stronger force after World War II. The radical left consisted of many little Marxist parties led by intellectuals and of the Japanese Communist Party. Although small and subject to governmental repression, the radical parties were influential in intellectual and literary circles during the twenties and thirties.

The Radical Right and the Military

The political right in pre-World War II Japan is difficult to define. Most Japanese, even socialists, were imbued with an emperor-centered nationalism. During the 1930s, however, a new array of right-wing organizations went beyond the usual nationalism to challenge the status quo. Civilian ultranationalists used Shinto myths and Confucian values to attack Western liberalism in Japan's urban society. Some bureaucrats looked to the example of Nazi Germany and argued for the exclusion of party politicians from government. Military officers envisioned a "defense state" guided by themselves. They argued for military expansion and an autarchic colonial empire insulated from the uncertainties of the world economy. Young officers of the revolutionary right advocated "direct action" against the elites of the parliamentary coalition. They called for a second restoration of imperial power.

The last group precipitated political change. On May 15, 1932, junior army and navy officers attacked the Seiyūkai offices, the Bank of Japan, and the Tokyo police headquarters, and murdered Prime Minister Inukai. The attack occurred at the peak of right-wing agitation and the pit of the Depression. Saionji decided that it would be unwise to appoint another party president as the new prime minister; and chose instead a moderate admiral. For the next four years, cabinets were led by moderate military men, but with party participation. These cabinets satisfied neither the parties nor the radical young officers.

During 1936 and 1937, Japanese politics continued to drift to the right. In the election of February 1936, the opposition overturned the Seiyūkai-dominated Diet with the slogan, "What shall it be, parliamentary government or Fascism?" A week later, young officers attempted a coup in Tokyo. They killed cabinet ministers and occupied the Diet and other government buildings. They wanted their army superiors to form a new government. Saionji and other men about the emperor stood firm; the navy opposed the rebellion; and within three days it was suppressed. It was the last "direct action" by the radical right in prewar Japan. The ringleaders were tried and executed, and generals sympathetic to them were retired. The officers in charge of the purge within the army were tough-minded elitist technocrats. They included General Tōjō Hideki (1884–1948), who would lead Japan into World War II.

But the services interfered more than ever in the formation of cabinets. From 1936 on, moderate prime ministers gave way to more outspokenly militaristic figures.

Opposition to militarism remained substantial nonetheless. In the 1937 election, the two major centrist parties, which had joined in opposition to the government, won 354 Diet seats. The Japanese people were more level-headed than their leaders. But the centrists' victory proved hollow. The Diet could not oppose a government in wartime, and by summer, Japan was at war in China.

The Road to Pearl Harbor

Between the outbreak of the war with China and World War II, in the Pacific, there were three critical junctures. The first was the decision in January 1938 to strike a knockout blow at the Nationalist Party (KMT) government. The war had begun as an unplanned skirmish between Chinese and Japanese troops in the Peking area but had quickly spread. The Japanese army's leaders disagreed on whether to continue. Many held that the only threat to Japanese interests in Korea and Manchuria was the Soviet Union, and that a long war in China was foolish. But as the Japanese armies advanced, the general staff argued that the only way to end the war was to convince the Nationalists that fighting was hopeless. The army occupied most of the cities and railroads of eastern China, but Chiang Kai-shek refused to give in. A stalemate ensued that lasted until 1945. China was never a major theater of the war in the Pacific.

The second critical decision was the signing of the Tripartite Pact with Germany and Italy in September 1940. Japan had long admired Germany. In 1936, it had joined Germany in the Anti-Comintern Pact directed against international communism. It also wanted an alliance with Germany against the Soviet Union. Germany insisted, however, that any alliance would also have to be directed against the United States and Britain. The Japanese disagreed. The Japanese navy saw the American Pacific fleet as its only potential enemy and was not willing to risk being dragged into a German war. When Japanese troops battled Russian troops in an undeclared mini-war from May to September 1939 on the Mongolian border, sentiment rose in favor of an alliance with Germany, but then Germany "betrayed" Japan by signing a nonaggression pact with the Soviet Union. For a time Japan decided to improve its relations with the United States, but America insisted that Japan get out of China. By the late spring of 1940 German victories in Europe—the fall of Britain appeared imminent—again led military leaders in Japan to favor an alliance with Germany.

When Japan signed the Tripartite Pact, it had three objectives: to isolate the United States, to inherit the Southeast Asian colonies of the countries defeated by Germany in Europe, and to improve its relations with the Soviet Union through the good offices of Germany. The last objective was reached when Japan signed a neutrality pact with the Soviet Union in April 1941. Two months later, Germany attacked the Soviet Union without consulting its ally, Japan. It compounded this second "betrayal" by asking Japan to attack the Soviet Union in the east. Japan waited and watched. When the German advance was stopped short of Moscow, Japan decided to honor the neutrality pact and turn south. This decision marked, in effect, the end of Japan's participation in the Axis. Thereafter, it fought its own war in Asia. Yet instead of deflecting American criticism as intended, the pact, by linking Japan to Germany, led to a hardening of America's position on China.

The third and fatal decision was to go to war with the United States. In June 1940, following Germany's defeat of France, Japanese troops had moved into northern French Indochina . The United States retaliated by limiting strategic exports to Japan. When Japanese troops took southern Indochina in July 1941, the United States embargoed all exports to Japan; this cut Japanese oil imports by 90 percent. The navy's general staff argued that oil reserves would last only two years; after that the navy would lose its capability to fight. Its general staff pressed for the capture of the oil-rich Dutch East Indies. But it was too dangerous to move against Dutch and British colonies in Southeast Asia with the United States on its flank in the Philippines. The navy, therefore, planned a preemptive strike against the United States, and on December 7, 1941, it bombed Pearl Harbor. The Japanese decision for war wagered Japan's land-based air power, shorter supply lines, and what it saw as greater will power against American productivity. The navy's chief of staff compared the war with the United States to a dangerous operation that might save the life of a critically ill patient. In the end, the war left Japan defeated and in ruins.

Japanese Militarism and German Nazism

Some of the salient features of Japanese militarism may be revealed by a comparison with Nazi Germany. Both countries were late developers with elitist, academic bureaucracies and strong military traditions. Both had authoritarian family systems. The parliamentary systems of both were shallowly rooted. Both were stricken by the Great Depression and sought a solution in territorial expansion, justifying it in terms of being have-not nations. Both persecuted socialists and then liberals. Both were modern enough in their military services, schools, governments, and communications to implement authoritarian regimes, but their values were not modern enough or democratic enough to resist their antiparliamentary forces.

The differences between Japan and Germany were also striking. Japan was more homogeneous than Germany. It had no

Catholic-Protestant split or powerful *Junker* class; nor was its socialist movement a serious contender for political power. The political process during the 1930s was also different. In Germany, parliament ruled, so that to come to power the Nazis had to win an election. In this, they were helped by the combination of the Great Depression and a runaway inflation that destroyed the German middle class and the centrist parties along with it. In Japan's constitutional system, the Diet was weaker. Control of the government was taken away from the parties even while they continued to win elections. The parties remained strong at the polls partly because Japan did not suffer from inflation and its middle class was not hurt by the Depression.

The process by which the two countries went to war was also different. In Germany, the Nazis rose as a mass party, created a totalitarian state, and then made war. The authority of the Nazi Party lasted until Hitler died. In Japan, there was neither a mass party nor a single group of leaders in continuous control of the government. Moreover, in Japan it was not the totalitarian state that made war as much as it was war that made the state totalitarian.

The Allies depicted General Tōjō, who was prime minister and his own army minister, as the Japanese Hitler. Yet when American planes began to bomb Japan in 1944, the elder statesmen close to the emperor removed Tōjō from office and appointed moderate prime ministers. The military continued to prosecute the war. Even after the two atomic bombs, the Imperial Conference on August 14, 1945, was split three to three over the Allied ultimatum demanding unconditional surrender. The emperor broke the deadlock, saying that the unendurable must be endured. It was the only important decision that he had ever been allowed to make.

IN WORLD PERSPECTIVE

Modern East Asia

From the late nineteenth century, most countries wanted to become modern. They coveted the wealth and power that science and industry had produced in the West. They did not wish to become Western, for that would have denied them their own cultural identity. However, it was difficult to separate what was modern from what was merely recent Western.

We note three stages in Japan's development as the world's first non-Western modernizer. First, even before its contact with the modern West, it had some of the *preconditions* needed to adopt modern technology: a fairly high literacy, an ethic of duty and hard work, a market economy, a shift from religious to secular thought, an adequate bureaucracy, and political orientations resembling nationalism. These preconditions provided a base for an "external modernization."

Second, after 1868 Japan *Westernized*. The Meiji leaders introduced a wide range of new institutions. Japanese thinkers brought in modern ideas and values. Third, Japan began to *assimilate* the ideas and institutions it had borrowed from the West.

Japan may serve as a useful model in that its modernization has gone further than that in any other non-Western country. We note the absence of comparable preconditions in India or the Islamic world. Even after the end of colonialism, countries in these areas had to create the necessary preconditions while borrowing the new technologies. That difficulty explains their limited success. In Africa the dearth of preconditions was even more pronounced.

In comparison to most of the non-Western world, the Chinese tradition was advanced. Like Japan, it had already achieved many of the preconditions for modernization: a high level of literacy, a belief in education as the means for advancement, the ingredients for shaping a modern nationalism, a family system that adapted well to small enterprises, and a market economy. But when it came to borrowing Western ideas and institutions, the government by Confucian literati that had long been China's outstanding asset became its greatest liability. It took decades to topple the dynasty and to advance beyond Confucian ideas.

Then, in the maelstrom of the May Fourth Movement, intellectual changes occurred at a furious pace. But in the chaos following the breakdown of the ancient regime, doctrines alone could not provide a stable polity. Nationalism was the common denominator of most Chinese thought. Sun Yat-sen appealed to it. The Kuomintang drew on it at the Whampoa Academy, during the march north, and in founding their government. Yet other groups could also appeal to nationalism, and eventually the Chinese Communist Party (CCP) won out.

It is beguiling to view the CCP cadres as a new class of literati operating the machinery of a monolithic, centralized state, with the teachings of Marx and Lenin replacing those of Confucius, and local party organization replacing the Confucian gentry. But this interpretation is too simple. Communism stressed science, materialism, and class conflict. It broke with the Chinese past.

Communism itself was also modified in China. Marx had predicted that socialist revolutions would break out in advanced economies where the contradictions of capitalism were sharpest. Lenin had shifted the emphasis from spontaneous revolutions by workers to the small but disciplined revolutionary party, the vanguard of the proletariat. He thereby changed communism into what it has been ever since: a movement capable of seizing power only in backward nations. Mao Tse-tung slightly modified Lenin's ideas by theorizing that "progressive" peasants were a part of the proletariat. But in practice, he virtually ignored city workers and relied on China's villages for recruits for his armies, who were then indoctrinated using Leninist techniques. Despite its low level of technology, the People's Liberation Army—the communist equivalent of a "citizen's army," was formidable. It was also modern in the sense that it did not loot and despoil the areas it occupied.

Yet, the organizational techniques that were so effective in creating a party and army would prove less so for economic development. It soon became clear that mass mobilization was no substitute for individual incentives.

Review Questions

1. Which had the greater impact on China, the Opium War or the Taiping Rebellion?

2. How did the Ch'ing (or Manchu) dynasty recover from the Taiping Rebellion? Why did the recovery not prevent the overthrow of the dynasty in 1911?

3. Did the May Fourth Movement prepare the way for the nationalist revolution? The communist revolution? Or was it incidental to both?

4. After the Meiji restoration, what steps did Japan's leaders take to achieve their goal of "wealth and power"?

5. What were the strengths and weaknesses of Japan's prewar parliamentary institutions? What led to the sudden rise of militarism during the thirties?

Documents CD-ROM

1. The Taiping Rebellion

2. The Chinese Boxer Uprising: Atrocities of Frustration

3. Manifesto of the Chinese United League

4. Quotations from Chairman Mao Tse-tung: Chapter 1, *Little Red Book*

5. Itō Hirobumi: Reminiscences on the Drafting of the New Constitution

6. Tōjō Makes Plea of Self-Defense

GLOBAL CONFLICT AND CHANGE

The twentieth century saw unprecedented global conflict and interaction. Growing trade forged economic links among nations tighter than any in the past. The imperialistic ambitions of Europe and the United States during the late nineteenth century linked the world politically. As a result, conflict in Europe drew in the rest of the world.

World War I unleashed political, social, and economic turmoil around the world. After World War II, Europe ceased to dominate the world. The peoples of Asia, Africa, and Latin America adopted the European ideologies of nationalism and revolutionary socialism to solve their own problems, turning them against their source. Independent nations replaced the European and Japanese Empires.

After the war, the hopes of many for peace and stability rested with the United Nations (UN). But a period of competition and sometimes open hostility called the Cold War began between the West and the Soviet Union and spread around the world.

The Cold War ended in the late 1980s when Soviet power, and the Soviet Union itself, dissolved.

What now lies before the nations of the world is the challenge to establish a new order in the face of ethnic and national tensions and the efforts of powerful governments to dominate others. The closing years of the century were witness to both types of conflict, and an increasing reliance on the UN to solve them.

1914–1940

Nazi brutality poster by Ben Shahn.
(The Granger Collection)

1914–1918 World War I
1917 Bolsheviks seize power, Russia
1919 Versailles Settlement
1922 Mussolini seizes power, Italy
1925 Locarno Pact
1933 Hitler comes to power
1936 Spanish Civil War begins
1938 Munich Conference
1939 World War II begins

1922 British leave Egypt
1922–1938 Mustafa Kemal first president of Turkey
1928 The Muslim Brotherhood founded by Hasan Al-Banna

1941–1959

1944 D-Day
1945 World War II ends
1948 Berlin blockade and airlift
1949 NATO treaty; Russia detonates atomic bomb
1953 Death of Stalin
1955 Warsaw Pact
1956 Soviets crush Hungarian revolt
1957 EEC founded
1958 Charles de Gaulle comes to power in France

1947 Indian Independence; creation of Pakistan
1948 Assassination of Mahatma Gandhi
1949 State of Israel founded
1953 Mosaddeq overthrown in Iran
1954–1970 Abdel Nasser leads Egypt
1956 Suez crisis

1960–1979

1960 Paris Summit Conference collapses after U-2 incident
1961 Berlin Wall erected
1964 Khrushchev replaced as Soviet prime minister by Kosygin; as Party Secretary by Brezhnev
1968 Soviets invade Czechoslovakia
1972 British impose direct rule on Northern Ireland
1972 Israeli Olympic athletes killed by Arab terrorists
1974 End of military rule in Greece
1974 Portuguese dictatorship deposed; democratic reforms begin
1977 Brezhnev president of USSR
1979 Margaret Thatcher becomes British prime minister

1966 Indira Ghandi becomes prime minister of India
1967 Israeli-Arab June War
1969 Golda Meir becomes prime minister of Israel
1969 Arafat elected P.L.O. chairman
1971 India-USSR friendship treaty
1973 Arab-Israeli October War
1972 Independence for Bangladesh
1973 OPEC oil embargo
1977 Menachem Begin becomes prime minister of Israel
1978 Iranian revolution under Khomeini's leadership
1979 Egyptian-Israeli Peace Treaty
1979 Iran takes US hostages
1979 Soviets invade Afghanistan

1980–1999

Opening of the Berlin Wall, 1989.
(R. Bossu/Corbis/Sygma)

1980 Solidarity Movement in Poland
1981 Crackdown against Solidarity
1984–1985 Bitter strikes by miners in England
1984 Mikhail Gorbachev introduces *glasnost* in USSR
1989 Berlin Wall demolished
1990 Germany unified
1991 Failed coup in Soviet Union; Yeltsin emerges as leader of Russia
1991 Major replaces Thatcher as England's prime minister
1993 Czechoslovakia divides into two republics
1995 Dayton Peace Accords end war in Bosnia
1999 NATO military campaign against Serbia

1980–1988 Iran-Iraq War
1981 Hostages released in Iran
1981 Egypt's Sadat assassinated; succeeded by Hosni Mubarak
1982 Israel invades Lebanon
1984 Indira Gandhi assassinated
1989 Soviets leave Afghanistan
1989 Death of Khomeini
1990 Central Asian States become independent on fall of USSR
1990–1991 Gulf War
1991 Indian prime minister Rajiv Ghandi assassinated

EAST ASIA

1916–1928 Warlord era in China
1919 May 4th Movement in China
1925 Universal male suffrage in Japan
1928–1937 Nationalist government in China at Nanking
1931 Japan occupies Manchuria
1937–1945 Japan at War with China

1941 Japan attacks Pearl Harbor
1945 Japan surrenders after US atomic bombs
1945–1949 Civil War in China; People's Republic founded
1950 N. Korea invades S. Korea
1952 US ends occupation of Japan
1953–1972 Double-digit growth in Japan
1955 Liberal-Democratic Party formed in Japan
1959–1960 Sino-Soviet split

1959–1975 Vietnam War
1965–1976 Cultural Revolution devastates China
1968 Death of Ho Chi Minh, president of North Vietnam
1971 Lin Piao killed in China
1972 President Nixon visits China
1973 Economic growth slows in Japan
1976 Death of Mao Tse-tung
1978–1989 New Economic policies of Teng Hsiao-p'ing in China
1978–1989 Vietnam occupies Cambodia

1980s Double-digit economic growth in South Korea and Taiwan
1988 Japan's GNP second in world
1989 Vietnam pledges to withdraw from Cambodia
1989 China crushes pro-democracy demonstrations in Peking
1991–1992 Political scandals and plummeting stock market in Japan
1992 Kim Young Sam, civilian party leader, elected S. Korean president

A student confronts tanks in Tienanmen Square, China, May 1989. (Reuters/Archive Photos)

AFRICA

1935 Mussolini invades Ethiopia

1942–1945 World War II engulfs North Africa
1955–1962 Wars of independence in French Algeria
1956 Sudan gains independence from Britain and Egypt
1956 Morocco and Tunisia gain independence from France
1957 Ghana an independent state under Kwame Nkrumah

1960 Belgian Congo granted independence as Zaire
1963 Kenya becomes an independent republic
1964 Zanzibar, the Congo, and Northern Rhodesia (Zambia) become independent republics
1965 Revolution in Kenya
1967–1970 Nigerian Civil War
1974 Drought and famine in Africa
1974 Emperor Haile Selassie of Ethiopia is deposed
1974–1975 Portugal grants independence to Guinea, Angola, Mozambique, Cape Verde

1980 Southern Rhodesia (Zimbabwe) gains independence from Britain
1984 Bishop Desmond Tutu awarded Nobel Peace Prize
1985 US economic sanctions against South Africa result in more repression
1989 Conservative Botha government resigns in South Africa; DeKlerk becomes president
1992 Nelson Mandela freed from prison in South Africa
1994 Nelson Mandela elected President of South Africa

THE AMERICAS

1917 US enters World War I
1929 Wall Street Crash; the Great Depression begins
1930–1945 Vargas dictatorship in Brazil
1932 F. D. Roosevelt elected US president
1938 Mexico nationalizes oil

1941 US enters World War II
1945 Death of F. D. Roosevelt
1946 Peron elected president in Argentina
1954 US Supreme Court outlaws segregation
1955 Peron overthrown
1956 Montgomery bus boycott
1959 Fidel Castro comes to power in Cuba

1960 Kennedy elected president
1962 Cuban Missile Crisis
1963 Kennedy assassinated
1964 Passage of Civil Rights Act
1965 US expands Vietnam commitment
1968 Martin Luther King and Robert Kennedy assassinated; campus unrest
1968 Nixon elected
1970 Allende elected in Chile
1972 Nixon visits China and USSR; is re-elected president
1973 Watergate Scandal breaks
1973 Peron re-elected, Argentina
1973 Chile's Allende overthrown
1974 Nixon resigns presidency
1979 Revolution in Nicaragua and El Savador

1980 Iran hostage crisis
1980 Reagan elected president
1982 War between Argentina and Great Britain over Islas Malvinas (Falkland Islands)
1983 Argentine military government overthrown; elected government restored
1983 End of Mexican oil boom
1988 Major arms agreement between US and USSR
1991 Gulf War
1992 Clinton elected president
1994 Revolt in Chiapas, Mexico
1998 Pope visits Cuba

33 IMPERIALISM AND WORLD WAR I

During the second half of the nineteenth century, Europe exercised unprecedented control over the rest of the world. The Americas, Australia, and New Zealand almost became part of the European world as streams of European immigrants populated them. Africa was divided among European nations (see Chapter 31), and Europe imposed its power across Asia (see Map 33–1 and Chapter 32). By 1900, European dominance had brought every part of the globe into a single world economy.

But these developments helped to foster competition and hostility among the great powers of Europe and to bring on a terrible war. The frenzy for imperial expansion that seized Europeans in the late nineteenth century did much to destroy its peace, prosperity, and dominant place in the world.

The "New Imperialism"

The explosive developments in nineteenth-century science, technology, industry, agriculture, transportation, communication, and weapons enabled a few Europeans (and Americans) to impose their will on other peoples many times their number. The growth of national states permitted the European nations to deploy their response in the most effective way. The Europeans also believed that their civilization and way of life were superior to all others. This gave them a confidence and often a cultural arrogance that fostered the expansionist mood.

After 1870, the European states swiftly spread their control over about a fifth of the world's land area and a tenth of its population. The movement has been called the New Imperialism.

The New Imperialism

Imperialism can be defined as extending a nation's power by some form of power over foreign peoples. The usual pattern of the New Imperialism was for the European nation to invest capital in the "backward" country and thereby to transform its economy and culture. To guarantee their investments, the European states would establish different degrees of political control ranging from full annexation as a colony, to protectorate status (whereby the local ruler was controlled by the dominant European state), to "spheres-of-influence" status (whereby the European state received special privileges without direct political involvement).

Motives for the New Imperialism

There is still no agreement about the motives for the New Imperialism. Economic motives certainly played a part, but the new colonies were never major markets for European goods and investments. It is not even clear that control of them was profitable. Some advocates of imperialism argued that the European nations had a responsibility to bring the benefits of their superior civilization and Christianity to the people of "backward" lands, but few people were influenced by such arrogant arguments, although many shared the assumptions behind them. Nor did the new colonies attract many European emigrants. Most of them went to the Americas and Australia.

Strategic and prestige considerations seem to have been more important in bringing on the New Imperialism. Thus, the completion of the Suez Canal in 1869 made Egypt vital to the British because it sat astride the shortest route to India. When Egypt's stability was threatened in the 1880s, the British established a protectorate. Then, to protect Egypt, they advanced into the Sudan.

Other European nations equated status (Britain was the model) with the possession of colonies. They sought colonies as evidence of their own importance. This explains much of the scramble for Africa (see Chapter 31). In Asia, the emergence of Japan as a great power with claims on China and Korea frightened the other powers, and they pressed feverishly for concessions in China.

By 1900, most of the world had thus come under the control of the industrialized West. The greatest remaining vulnerable area was the Ottoman Empire, but its fate was tied up with European developments (see Map 33-1).

Emergence of the German Empire

Formation of the Triple Alliance (1873–1890)

Prussia's victories over Austria and France and its creation of the German Empire in 1871 revolutionized European diplomacy. The sudden appearance of a powerful new state posed problems.

The balance of power created at the Congress of Vienna was altered radically. Britain and Russia retained their position. Austria, however, had lost ground and was threatened by nationalism within the Austro-Hungarian Empire. French power and prestige were badly damaged by the Franco-Prussian War and the German annexation of Alsace-Lorraine. The French were both afraid of Germany and resentful of their loss of territory and of France's traditional dominance in western Europe.

Bismarck's Leadership (1873–1890)

Until 1890 Otto von Bismarck (1815–1898) continued to guide German policy. He insisted after 1871 that Germany wanted no further territorial gains, and he meant it. He wanted to avoid a war that might undo his achievement. He tried to assuage France by cultivating friendly relations and supporting its colonial aspirations. He also prepared for the worst. If France could not be conciliated, it must be isolated. Bismarck sought to prevent an alliance between France and any European power—especially Austria or Russia—that would threaten Germany with a war on two fronts.

War in the Balkans Bismarck's first move was to establish the Three Emperors' League in 1873. It brought together the three great conservative empires of Germany, Austria, and Russia. The league collapsed when Russia went to war with Turkey in 1877. The tottering Ottoman Empire was preserved chiefly by the competing aims of those powers who awaited its demise. Ottoman weakness encouraged its Slavic subjects in the Balkans to rebel.

When Russia entered the fray, it created an international crisis. The Russians hoped to gain control of Constantinople. Russian intervention also reflected the influence of the Pan-Slavic movement, which sought to bring all the Slavs, even those under Austrian or Ottoman rule, under the protection of Holy Mother Russia.

The Ottoman Empire was forced to sue for peace. The Treaty of San Stefano of March 1878 was a Russian triumph. The Slavic states in the Balkans were freed of Ottoman rule, and Russia obtained territory and an indemnity. But the terms of the Russian victory alarmed the other great powers. Austria feared that the new Slav states and the increase in Russian influence would threaten its own Balkan provinces. The British were alarmed by the possible Russian control of Constantinople. Disraeli (1804–1881) was determined to resist, and British public opinion supported him.

Congress of Berlin Disraeli sent a fleet to Constantinople, and Britain and Austria forced Russia to agree to an international conference at which the provisions of San Stefano would be reviewed by the other great powers. The resulting Congress of Berlin met in June and July of 1878 under the presidency of Bismarck.

The decisions of the Congress were a blow to Russian ambitions. Bulgaria lost two-thirds of its territory. Austria-Hungary was given Bosnia and Herzegovina to "occupy and administer" under formal Ottoman rule. Britain received Cyprus, and France gained permission to occupy Tunisia. These were compensations for the gains that Russia was

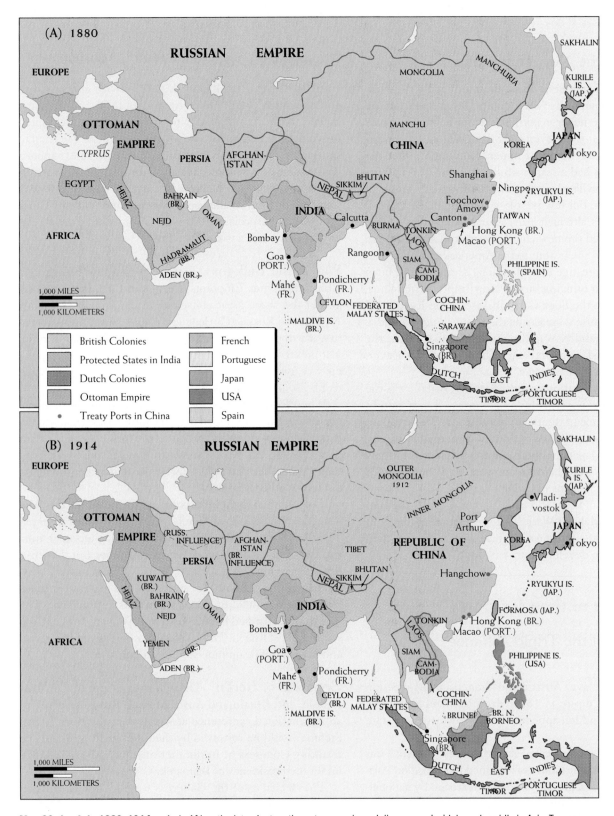

Map 33-1 Asia 1880-1914. As in Africa, the late nineteenth century saw imperialism spread widely and rapidly in Asia. Two new powers, Japan and the United States, joined the British, French, and Dutch in extending control both to islands and to the mainland and in exploiting an enfeebled China.

permitted to keep. Germany asked for nothing, but the Russians were angry. The Three Emperors' League was dead.

The south Slavic states of Serbia and Montenegro resented the Austrian occupation of Bosnia and Herzegovina. The south Slavic question, no less than the estrangement between Russia and Germany, was a threat to the peace of Europe.

German Alliances with Russia and Austria
Bismarck could ignore the Balkans, but not Russia. He concluded a secret treaty with Austria in 1879. This Dual Alliance provided that if either Germany or Austria were attacked by Russia, the ally would help the attacked party. If either was attacked by someone else, each promised at least to maintain neutrality. The treaty was renewed every five years until 1918.

Bismarck never allowed the alliance to drag Germany into Austria's Balkan quarrels. He made it clear to the Austrians that Germany would never attack Russia.

Bismarck expected the Austro-German negotiations to frighten Russia into seeking closer relations with Germany, and he was right. By 1881, he had renewed the Three Emperors' League on a firmer basis.

The Triple Alliance
In 1882, Italy, annoyed by the French preemption of Tunisia, asked to join the Dual Alliance. Bismarck was now allied with three of the great powers and friendly with Great Britain, which held aloof from all alliances. France was isolated. Although the Three Emperors' League was allowed to lapse, the Triple Alliance (Germany, Austria, and Italy) was renewed for another five years in 1887. To restore German relations with Russia, Bismarck negotiated the Reinsurance Treaty that same year, in which both powers promised to remain neutral if either was attacked. However, a change in the German monarchy overturned Bismarck's system.

In 1888, William II (r. 1888–1918) came to the German throne. Like many Germans of his generation, he was filled with a sense of Germany's destiny as the leading power of Europe. To achieve a "place in the sun," he wanted a navy and colonies like Britain's. These aims, of course, ran counter to Bismarck's policy. In 1890, William dismissed Bismarck.

During Bismarck's time, Germany was a force for European peace. This position would not have been possible without its great military power. But it also required a statesman who could exercise restraint and understand what his country needed and what was possible.

Forging the Triple Entente (1890–1907)

Franco-Russian Alliance
After Bismarck's retirement, his system of alliances collapsed. His successor refused the Russian request to renew the Reinsurance Treaty, which he considered incompatible with the Austrian alliance. Political isolation and the need for foreign capital then drove the Russians toward France. The French, who were even more isolated, were glad to pour capital into Russia if it would help produce security against Germany. In 1894, the Franco-Russian alliance was signed.

Britain and Germany
Britain now became the key to the international situation. Colonial rivalries pitted the British against the Russians in Central Asia and against the French in Africa. Traditionally, Britain had also opposed Russian control of Constantinople and French control of the Low Countries. There was no reason to think that Britain would soon become friendly to its traditional rivals or abandon its friendliness toward the Germans. Yet within a decade of William II's accession, Germany had become the enemy in the minds of the British. The problem lay in Germany's foreign and naval policies.

At first Germany tried to win the British over to the Triple Alliance, but when Britain clung to "splendid isolation," Germany sought to demonstrate its worth as an ally by making trouble for Britain. The Germans began to exert pressure against Britain in Africa by barring British attempts to build a railroad from Capetown to Cairo. They also openly sympathized with the Boers of South Africa in their resistance to British expansion.

In 1898, William's dream of a German navy began to achieve reality with the passage of a naval law providing for nineteen battleships. In 1900, a second law doubled that figure. The architect of the new navy, Admiral Alfred von Tirpitz (1849–1930), proclaimed that Germany's naval policy was aimed at Britain. As the German navy grew and German policies seemed to become more threatening, the British abandoned their traditional policies.

Entente Cordiale
In 1902, Britain concluded an alliance with Japan to help defend British interests in the Far East against Russia. Next, Britain in 1904 made a series of agreements with the French, collectively called the Entente Cordiale. It was not a formal treaty and had no military provisions, but it settled all outstanding colonial differences between the two nations. The Entente Cordiale went far toward aligning the British with Germany's great potential enemy.

First Moroccan Crisis
In March 1905, William II landed at Tangier and challenged the French predominance there in a speech in favor of Moroccan independence. Germany's chancellor, Prince Bernhard von Bülow (1849–1929), intended to show France how weak it was and how little it could expect from Britain; he also hoped to gain colonial concessions.

The Germans might have achieved their aims, but they demanded an international conference to exhibit their power. The conference met in 1906 at Algeciras in Spain. Austria sided with its German ally, but Spain, Italy, and the United States voted with Britain and France. The French were confirmed in their position in Morocco, and German bullying had driven Britain and France closer together. Sir Edward Grey (1862–1933), the British foreign secretary, without making a firm commitment, authorized conversations between the British and French general staffs. By 1914, French and British military and naval plans were so mutually dependent that the two countries were effectively, if not formally, allies.

British Agreement with Russia   Hardly anyone believed that Britain and Russia could ever be allies. The Russo-Japanese war of 1904–1905 made such a development seem even less likely because Britain was allied with Russia's enemy. But defeat and the Russian Revolution of 1905 left Russia weak and reduced British apprehensions. The British were also concerned that Russia might drift into the German orbit.

With French support, in 1907 an agreement settled Russo-British quarrels in Central Asia and Persia and opened the door for wider cooperation. The Triple Entente, an informal but powerful association of Britain, France, and Russia, was now ranged against the Triple Alliance. Because Italy was unreliable, Germany and Austria-Hungary stood surrounded by two great land powers and Great Britain.

William II and his ministers had turned Bismarck's nightmare of the prospect of a two-front war with France and Russia into a reality and had added Britain to the hostile coalition. Bismarck's alliance system had been intended to maintain peace, but the new one increased the risk of war and made the Balkans, where Austrian and Russian ambitions clashed, a likely spot for it.

World War I

The Road to War (1908–1914)

Except for the Greeks and the Romanians, most of the inhabitants of the Balkans were Slavs and felt a kinship with one another and with Russia. For centuries they had been ruled by Austrians, Hungarians, or Turks, and the nationalism that characterized late-nineteenth-century Europe made many of them eager for liberty or at least autonomy. The more radical among them longed for a union of the south Slavic, or Yugoslav, peoples in a single nation led by independent Serbia. They hoped to detach all the Slavic provinces (especially Bosnia, which bordered on Serbia) from Austria. Serbia

was to unite the Slavs at the expense of Austria, as Piedmont had united the Italians and Prussia the Germans.

In 1908, modernizing reformers called the Young Turks overthrew the Ottoman government. This threatened to revive the empire and precipitated a series of Balkan crises that would lead to world war.

The Bosnian Crisis   In 1908, Austria and Russia decided to act before Turkey became stronger. They agreed to call an international conference in which each of them would support the other's demands. Russia would agree to the Austrian annexation of Bosnia and Herzegovina, and Austria would support Russia's request to open the Dardanelles to Russian warships.

Austria, however, declared the annexation unilaterally before any conference was called. The British, concerned about their own position in the Mediterranean, rejected the Russian demand. The Russians were furious. The Serbs were enraged by the annexation of Bosnia. The Russians were too weak to do anything but accept the new situation. The Germans were unhappy because Austria's action threatened their relations with Russia. But Germany felt so dependent on the Dual Alliance that it assured Austria of its support. To an extent, German policy was being made in Vienna. It was a dangerous precedent. At the same time, the failure of Britain and France to support Russia strained the Triple Entente and made it harder for them to oppose Russian interests again if they wanted to retain Russian friendship.

Second Moroccan Crisis   The second Moroccan crisis, in 1911, emphasized the French and British need for mutual support. When France sent an army to Morocco to put down a rebellion, Germany took the opportunity to extort colonial concessions in the French Congo by sending the gunboat *Panther* to the port of Agadir in Morocco, allegedly to protect German citizens there. As in 1905, the Germans went too far.

Anglo-German relations had already been deteriorating, chiefly because of the naval race. The British now mistakenly believed that the Germans meant to turn Agadir into a naval base on the Atlantic. The crisis passed when France yielded bits of the Congo and Germany withdrew from Morocco. The main result was to draw Britain closer to France. Plans were formulated for a British expeditionary force to help defend France against German attack, and the British and French navies agreed to cooperate.

The Balkan Wars   After the second Moroccan crisis, Italy feared that France would move into Ottoman Libya. Consequently, in 1911 Italy attacked the Ottoman Empire to forestall the French, and obtained Libya and the Dodecanese Islands in the Aegean. The Italian victory encouraged the Balkan states to try their luck. In 1912, Bulgaria, Greece,

Montenegro, and Serbia attacked the Ottoman Empire and won easily. The Serbs and the Bulgarians then quarreled about the division of Macedonia, and in 1913, Turkey and Romania joined Greece and Serbia against Bulgaria, which lost much of what it had gained since 1878.

The Austrians were determined to limit Serbian gains and prevent the Serbs from obtaining a port in Albania on the Adriatic. An international conference sponsored by Britain in early 1913 resolved the matter in Austria's favor and called for an independent kingdom of Albania. But Austria felt humiliated by the public airing of Serbian demands and in October unilaterally forced Serbia to withdraw from Albania. Russia again let Austria have its way.

The lessons learned from this affair influenced behavior in the final crisis of 1914. The Russians had, as in 1908, been embarrassed by their passivity, and their allies were now more reluctant to restrain them. The Austrians were determined not to accept an international conference again. They and their German allies had seen that better results might be obtained from a threat of force.

Sarajevo and the Outbreak of War (June–August 1914)

The Assassination   On June 28, 1914, a Bosnian nationalist killed the Austrian Archduke Francis Ferdinand (1863–1914), heir to the throne, and his wife in the Bosnian capital of Sarajevo. The assassin was a member of a conspiracy hatched by a political terrorist society. The chief of intelligence of the Serbian army had helped plan the crime. Even though his role was unknown at the time, it was generally believed that Serbian officials were involved.

Germany and Austria's Response   The assassination was condemned throughout Europe. To those Austrians who had long favored an attack on Serbia as a solution to the empire's Slavic problem, the opportunity seemed irresistible. But Count Stefan Tisza (1861–1918), speaking for Hungary, resisted. Count Leopold Berchtold (1863–1942), the Austro-Hungarian foreign minister, knew that German support would be required if Russia should decide to protect Serbia and to persuade the Hungarians to accept a war. The question of peace or war, therefore, had to be answered in Berlin.

William II and Chancellor Theobald von Bethmann-Hollweg (1856–1921) promised German support for an attack on Serbia. They urged the Austrians to move swiftly, while the other powers were still angry at Serbia. They also indicated that a failure to act would be evidence of Austria-Hungary's uselessness as an ally. Therefore, the Austrians determined to attack Serbia. They hoped, with the protection of Germany, to avoid a general European conflict, but were

prepared to risk one. The Germans also knew that they risked a general war, but hoped to "localize" the fight between Austria and Serbia.

These calculations proved to be incorrect. Bethmann-Hollweg hoped that the Austrians would present the powers with a *fait accompli* while the outrage of the assassination was still fresh. He also hoped that German support would deter Russian involvement. Failing that, he was prepared for a continental war that would bring rapid victory over France and allow a full-scale attack on the Russians, who were always slow to bring their strength into action. The German chancellor convinced himself that the British would stand aloof.

However, the Austrians were slow to act. They did not even deliver their deliberately unacceptable ultimatum to Serbia until July 24, when the general hostility toward Serbia had begun to subside. Serbia returned a conciliatory answer, but the Austrians were determined not to turn back. On July 28 they declared war on Serbia, even though they could not field an army until mid-August.

The Triple Entente's Response   The Russians, responded angrily to the Austrian demands on Serbia. The government ordered partial mobilization to pressure Austria to hold back its attack on Serbia.

Coming of World War I	
1871	End of the Franco-Prussian War; creation of the German Empire; German annexation of Alsace-Lorraine
1873	Three Emperors' League (Germany, Russia, and Austria-Hungary)
1875	Russo-Turkish War
1878	Congress of Berlin
1879	Dual Alliance between Germany and Austria
1881	Three Emperors' League is renewed
1882	Italy joins Germany and Austria in Triple Alliance
1888	William II becomes German emperor
1890	Bismarck dismissed
1894	Franco-Russian alliance
1898	Germany begins to build battleship navy
1902	British alliance with Japan
1904	Entente Cordiale between Britain and France
1904–1905	Russo-Japanese War
1905	First Moroccan crisis
1907	British agreement with Russia
1908–1909	Bosnian crisis
1911	Second Moroccan crisis; Italy attacks Turkey
1912–1913	First and Second Balkan wars
1914	Outbreak of World War I

Mobilization of any kind, however, was generally understood to be equivalent to an act of war. It was especially alarming to General Helmuth von Moltke (1848–1916), head of the German general staff. Russian mobilization could upset the delicate timing of Germany's battle plan—the Schlieffen Plan, which required an attack on France first—and would endanger Germany. From this point on, Moltke pressed for war. The pressure of military necessity became irresistible.

The western European powers were not eager for war. But the French gave the Russians the same assurances that Germany had given its ally. The British worked hard for another conference of the powers, but Austria would not hear of it. The Germans privately supported the Austrians but were publicly conciliatory in the hope of keeping the British neutral.

When Bethmann-Hollweg realized that if Germany attacked France, Britain would fight, he tried to persuade the Austrians to negotiate, but the Austrians could not retreat without losing their own self-respect and that of the Germans.

On July 30, Austria ordered mobilization against Russia. Russia and Germany then ordered general mobilization. The Schlieffen Plan went into effect. The Germans invaded Belgium on August 3, which violated the treaty of 1839, in which the British had guaranteed Belgian neutrality. This undermined sentiment in Britain for neutrality and united the nation against Germany. Germany then invaded France. On August 4, Britain declared war on Germany.

The Great War had begun. Europe would never be the same.

Women munitions workers in England. The First World War demanded more from the civilian populations than had previous wars, resulting in important social changes. The demands of the munitions industries and a shortage of men (so many of whom were in uniform) brought many women out of traditional roles at home and into factories and other war work. [Hulton Getty Picture Collection/Tony Stone Images]

Strategies and Stalemate (1914–1917)

Throughout Europe jubilation greeted the outbreak of war. No general war had been fought since Napoleon, and the horrors of modern warfare were not yet understood. The dominant memory was of Bismarck's swift and decisive campaigns, in which costs and casualties were light and the rewards great.

Both sides expected to take the offensive and win a quick victory. The Triple Entente powers—or the Allies, as they came to be called—had superior numbers and financial resources as well as command of the sea. Germany and Austria, the Central Powers, had the advantages of internal lines of communication and of having launched their attack first.

The War in the West   After 1905, Germany's war plan was the one developed by Count Alfred von Schlieffen (1833–1913), chief of the German general staff from 1891 to 1906. It aimed to sweep through Belgium to the Channel, then wheel to the south and east to envelop the French and crush them against the German fortresses in Lorraine. In the east, the Germans planned to stand on the defensive against Russia until France had been beaten, a task they thought would take only six weeks.

The execution of his plan, however, was left to Helmuth von Moltke, a gloomy and nervous man, who made enough tactical mistakes to cause it to fail by a narrow margin. As a result, the French and British were able to stop the Germans at the Battle of the Marne in September 1914.

Thereafter, the war in the west became one of position. Both sides dug in behind a wall of trenches protected by barbed wire that stretched from the North Sea to Switzerland. Machine-gun nests made assaults dangerous. Both sides, nonetheless, attempted massive attacks initiated by artillery bombardments of unprecedented force and duration. Still, the defense always prevented a breakthrough.

The War in the East   In the east, the Russians advanced into Austrian territory and inflicted heavy casualties, but Russian incompetence and German energy soon reversed the situation. General Erich Ludendorff (1865–1937), under the command of the elderly Paul von Hindenburg (1847–1934), destroyed or captured an entire Russian army at the Battle of Tannenberg. In 1915, the Central Powers drove into the Baltic states and western Russia, inflicting over 2 million casualties. Russian confidence was shaken.

Both sides sought new allies. Turkey and Bulgaria joined the Central Powers. Italy joined the Allies in 1915 after they agreed to give it *Italia Irredenta* (i.e., the Trentino, the South Tyrol, Trieste, and some of the Dalmatian Islands) from Austria after victory. Romania joined the Allies in 1916 but was quickly driven from the war. In the Far East, Japan honored its alliance with Britain and overran the German colonies in China and the Pacific.

In 1915, the Allies undertook to break the deadlock in the fighting by going around it. The idea came chiefly from Winston Churchill (1874–1965), First Lord of the British Admiralty. He proposed to attack the Dardanelles and capture Constantinople. This policy would knock Turkey from the war and ease communication with Russia. Success depended on daring leadership, but the attack was inept. Before the campaign was abandoned, the Allies lost almost 150,000 men.

Return to the West   Both sides turned back to the west in 1916. Erich von Falkenhayn (1861–1922), who had succeeded Moltke in September 1914, sought success by an attack on the French stronghold of Verdun. It failed. The Allies in turn launched a major offensive along the River Somme in July. The only result was enormous casualties on both sides.

The War at Sea   As the war continued, control of the sea became more important. The British imposed a strict blockade to starve out the enemy, regardless of international law. The Germans responded with submarine warfare to destroy British shipping and starve the British. They declared the waters around the British Isles a war zone, where even neutral ships would not be safe. Both policies were unwelcome to neutrals, and especially to the United States. But the sinking of neutral ships by German submarines was both more dramatic and offensive than Britain's blockade.

In 1915, the British liner *Lusitania* was torpedoed by a German submarine. Among the 1,200 drowned were 118 Americans. President Woodrow Wilson (1856–1924) protested, and the Germans desisted rather than further anger the United States. This development gave the Allies a considerable advantage. The German fleet that had cost so much money and had caused so much trouble played no significant part in the war.

America Enters the War   In December 1916, President Wilson attempted to bring about a negotiated peace. But neither side would give up its hopes for total victory. The war seemed likely to continue until one or both sides reached exhaustion. Two events early in 1917 changed the situation. On February 1, the Germans announced the resumption of unrestricted submarine warfare, which led the United States to declare war on Germany on April 6.

One of the deterrents to an earlier American intervention had been the presence of autocratic czarist Russia among the Allies. Wilson could conceive of the war only as an idealistic crusade "to make the world safe for democracy." That problem was resolved in March 1917 by a revolution in Russia that overthrew the czarist government.

The Russian Revolution

The March Revolution in Russia was neither planned nor led by political faction. It was the result of the collapse of the monarchy's ability to govern. Military and domestic failures produced massive casualties, hunger, strikes, and disorganization. All political factions were discontented.

In early March 1917, strikes and demonstrations erupted in Petrograd, as Saint Petersburg had been renamed. The ill-disciplined troops in the city refused to fire on the demonstrators, and the tsar abdicated on March 15. The Duma formed a provisional government composed chiefly of Constitutional Democrats with Western sympathies. The various socialists also began to organize the workers into councils called *soviets*. They became estranged as the Constitutional Democratics failed to control the army or purge "reactionaries" from the government.

The provisional government decided to continue the war against Germany, but a new offensive in the summer of 1917 collapsed. Disillusionment with the war, shortages of food and other necessities, and the demand for land reform undermined the government, even after its leadership had been taken over by the moderate socialist Alexander Kerensky (1881–1970).

Ever since April the Bolsheviks had been working against the provisional government. The Germans had rushed V. I. Lenin (1870–1924) in a sealed train from his exile in Switzerland to Petrograd in the hope that he would cause trouble for the revolutionary government. The Bolsheviks demanded that all political power go to the soviets, which they controlled. They attempted a coup, but it failed. Lenin fled to Finland, and his chief collaborator, Leon Trotsky (1877–1940), was imprisoned.

An abortive right-wing countercoup gave the Bolsheviks another chance. Trotsky, released from prison, led the powerful Petrograd Soviet. Lenin returned in October and insisted that the time was ripe to take power. On November 6, the Bolsheviks seized power.

The victors moved to fulfill their promises and to assure their own security. The provisional government had decreed an election for late November to select a Constituent Assembly. The Social Revolutionaries won a large majority over the Bolsheviks. When the assembly gathered in January, the Red Army, controlled by the Bolsheviks, dispersed it. All other political parties ceased to function in any meaningful fashion. The Bolshevik government nationalized the land and turned it over to its peasant proprietors. Factory workers were put in charge of their plants. Banks were seized for the state, and the debt of the tsarist government was repudiated. The property of the church was also seized.

The Bolsheviks signed an armistice with Germany in December 1917. On March 3, 1918, they accepted the Treaty of Brest-Litovsk, by which Russia yielded Finland, Poland, the Baltic states, and the Ukraine. Some territory in the

Lenin Establishes His Dictatorship

After the Bolshevik coup in October, elections for the Constituent Assembly were held in November. The results gave a majority to the Social Revolutionary Party and embarrassed the Bolsheviks. Using his control of the Red Army, Lenin closed the Constituent Assembly in January 1918, after it had met for only one day, and established the rule of a revolutionary elite and his own dictatorship. Here is the crucial Bolshevik decree.

What reasons does Lenin give for closing the legitimately elected Constituent Assembly? What other reasons might he have had? What were the soviets? Did they have a legitimate claim to the monopoly of political power? Was the dissolution of the assembly a temporary or permanent measure? What defense can be made for the Bolsheviks' action? Is it enough to justify that action?

. . . The Constituent Assembly, elected on the basis of lists drawn up prior to the October Revolution, was an expression of the old relation of political forces which existed when power was held by the compromisers and the Cadets. When the people at that time voted for the candidates for the Socialist-Revolutionary Party, they were not in a position to choose between the Right Socialist-Revolutionaries, the supporters of the bourgeoisie, and the Left Socialist-Revolutionaries, the supporters of Socialism. Thus, the Constituent Assembly, which was to have been the crown of the bourgeois parliamentary republic, could not become an obstacle in the path of the October Revolution and the Soviet power.

The October Revolution, by giving the power to the Soviets, and through the Soviets to the toiling and exploited classes, aroused the desperate resistance of the exploiters, and in the crushing of this resistance it fully revealed itself as the beginning of the socialist revolution . . . the majority in the Constituent Assembly which met on January 5 was secured by the party of the Right Socialist-Revolutionaries, the party of Kerensky, Avksentyev and Chernov. Naturally, this party refused to discuss the absolutely clear, precise and unambiguous proposal of the supreme organ of Soviet power, the Central Executive Committee of the Soviets, to recognize the program of the Soviet power, to recognize the "Declaration of Rights of the Toiling and Exploited People," to recognize the October Revolution and the Soviet power . . .

The Right Socialist-Revolutionary and Menshevik parties are in fact waging outside the walls of the Constituent Assembly a most desperate struggle against the Soviet power. . . .

Accordingly, the Central Executive Committee resolves: The Constituent Assembly is hereby dissolved.

Text excerpt from "Lenin, Draft Decree on the Dissolution of the Constituent Assembly" in *A Documentary History of Communism*, Vol. 1, R. V. Daniels, ed. Copyright © University Press of New England, pp. 71–72. Reprinted by permission of the editor.

Transcaucasus region went to Turkey. The Bolsheviks also agreed to pay an indemnity. These terms were a high price to pay for peace, but the Bolsheviks needed time to impose their rule on Russia.

Until 1921, the Bolsheviks confronted massive domestic resistance. A civil war erupted between the "Red" Russians supporting the revolution and the "White" Russians, who opposed the Bolsheviks and received aid from the Allies. In the summer of 1918, the tsar and his family were murdered. However, led by Trotsky, the Red Army overcame the opposition. By 1921, Lenin and his supporters were in firm control.

End of World War I

Military Resolution

The Treaty of Brest-Litovsk brought Germany to the peak of its success. In 1918, they decided to gamble everything on a last offensive. But the German army could not get beyond the Marne. Germany was exhausted. The Allies, on the other hand, were bolstered by the arrival of American troops in ever increasing numbers. They launched a counteroffensive that was irresistible. As the Austrian fronts in the Balkans and Italy collapsed, the German high command knew that the end was imminent but wanted peace to be made before the army could be thoroughly defeated in the field, so that the responsibility should fall on civilians. The army therefore allowed a new government to be established on democratic principles to seek peace. The new government, under Prince Max of Baden (1867–1928), asked for peace on the basis of the Fourteen Points that President Wilson had declared as the American war aims. These were idealistic principles, but Wilson insisted that he would deal only with a democratic German government that spoke for the German people.

The disintegration of the German army forced William II to abdicate on November 9, 1918. The Social Democratic Party proclaimed a republic to prevent the establishment of a soviet government under the control of their Leninist wing. Two days later this republican, socialist-led government signed an armistice and accepted German defeat. The German people were, in general, unaware that their army had been defeated. No foreign soldier stood on German soil. Many Germans expected a mild settlement. The real peace embittered the German people, many of whom came to believe that Germany had been stabbed in the back by republicans and socialists at home.

The casualties on all sides came to about 10 million dead and twice as many wounded. The financial resources of the European states were badly strained. The victorious Allies, formerly creditors to the world, became debtors to the new American colossus.

The old international order, moreover, was dead. Russia was ruled by a Bolshevik dictatorship that preached world revolution. Germany was in chaos. Austria-Hungary had disintegrated. These kinds of change stirred the colonial empires ruled by the European powers; they would never again be as secure as they had seemed before the war. Europe was no longer the center of the world, free to interfere when it wished or to ignore the outer regions if it chose. Its easy confidence in progress was shattered by four years of horrible war. The memory of that war shook the nerve of the victorious Western powers in the postwar world.

Settlement at Paris

The Peacemakers The representatives of the victorious states gathered at Versailles and other Parisian suburbs in the first half of 1919. Wilson speaking for the United States, David Lloyd George (1863–1945) for Britain, Georges Clemenceau (1841–1929) for France, and Vittorio Emanuele Orlando (1860–1952) for Italy made up the Big Four. Japan also had an important part in the discussions.

Wilson's idealism came into conflict with the war aims of the victorious powers and with the secret treaties that had been made before and during the war. The British and French people had been told that Germany would be made to pay for the war. Romania had been promised Transylvania at the expense of Hungary. Italy and Serbia had competing claims in the Adriatic. During the war, the British had encouraged Arab hopes of an independent Arab state carved out of the Ottoman Empire; those plans conflicted with the Balfour Declaration (1917), in which the British also seemed to accept Zionism and to promise the Jews a national home in Palestine. Both of these plans conflicted with an Anglo-French agreement to divide the Near East between themselves.

The national goals of the victors presented further obstacles to an idealistic "peace without victors." France was eager to achieve a settlement that would permanently weaken Germany and preserve French political and military superiority. Italy sought to acquire *Italia Irredenta*; Britain looked to its imperial interests; Japan pursued its own advantage in Asia; and the United States insisted on freedom of the seas, which favored American commerce, and on its right to maintain the Monroe Doctrine.

Finally, the peacemakers of 1919 faced a world in turmoil. The greatest immediate threat appeared to be Bolshevism. While Lenin and his colleagues were distracted by civil war, the Allies landed small armies in Russia to help overthrow the Bolshevik regime. Communist governments were established in Bavaria and Hungary. Berlin also experienced an abortive communist uprising. The Allies were so worried that they supported the suppression of these communist movements by right-wing forces. They even permitted an army of German volunteers to fight the Bolsheviks in the Baltic states. But fear of Germany remained the chief concern for France, and traditional interests governed the policies of the other Allies.

The Peace The Paris settlement consisted of five separate treaties between the victors and the defeated powers. The Soviet Union (as Russia was now called) and Germany were excluded from the peace conference. The Germans were simply presented with a treaty and compelled to accept it. The principle of national self-determination was violated often, as was unavoidable. The undeserved adulation accorded Wilson on his arrival turned into equally undeserved scorn. He had not abandoned his ideals but had given way to the irresistible force of reality.

The League of Nations Wilson put great faith in the new League of Nations. Its covenant was an essential part of the peace treaty. The league was not intended as an international government but as a body of sovereign states that agreed to pursue common policies. If war threatened, the members promised to submit the matter to an international court or the League Council. Refusal to abide by this agreement would justify league intervention in the form of economic or military sanctions.

But the league had no armed forces. Action required the unanimous consent of its council, consisting of Britain, France, Italy, the United States, Japan, and four other states that had temporary seats. The league was generally seen as a device to ensure the security of the victorious powers. The exclusion of Germany and the Soviet Union further undermined the league's claim to evenhandedness.

Provisions of the covenant that dealt with colonial areas and disarmament were ineffective. Members of the league remained fully sovereign and pursued their national interests.

Germany In the west, the main territorial issue was the fate of Germany (see Map 33–2). The French would have

Austria-Hungary, 1914

Germany, 1914

Areas lost by Germany in 1919

Areas lost by Bulgaria

Areas lost by Russia

Areas lost by The Ottoman Empire

Map 33-2 World War I peace settlement in Europe and the Middle East.   The map of central and eastern Europe, as well as that of the Middle East, underwent drastic revision after World War I. The enormous territorial losses suffered by Germany, Austria-Hungary, the Ottoman Empire, Bulgaria, and Russia were the other side of the coin represented by gains for France, Italy, Greece, and Romania and by the appearance, or reappearance, of at least eight new independent states from Finland in the north to Yugoslavia in the south. The mandate system for former Ottoman territories outside Turkey proper laid foundations for several new, mostly Arab, states in the Middle East.

liked to set up the Rhineland as a buffer state, but Lloyd George and Wilson would not permit that. But France did received Alsace-Lorraine and the right to work the coal mines of the Saar for fifteen years. Germany west of the Rhine, and fifty kilometers east of it, was to be a demilitarized zone; Allied troops could stay on the west bank for fifteen years. The treaty also provided that Britain and the United States would guarantee to aid France if it were attacked by Germany. Such an attack was made more unlikely by the permanent disarmament of Germany. Its army was limited to 100,000 men; its fleet was all but eliminated; and it was forbidden to have war planes, submarines, tanks, heavy artillery, or poison gas. As long as these provisions were observed, France would be safe.

The East   The settlement in the east ratified the collapse of the empires that had ruled it for centuries. Germany lost part of Silesia, and East Prussia was cut off from the rest of Germany by a corridor carved out to give the revived state of Poland access to the sea. The Austro-Hungarian Empire disappeared. Most of its German-speaking people in the small Republic of Austria were forbidden to unite with Germany. The Magyars occupied the much-reduced kingdom of Hungary.

The Czechs of Bohemia and Moravia joined with the Slovaks and Ruthenians to form Czechoslovakia, which also included several million unhappy Germans. The southern Slavs were united in the kingdom of Serbs, Croats, and Slovenes, or Yugoslavia. Italy gained the Trentino and Trieste. Romania gained Transylvania from Hungary and Bessarabia from Russia. Bulgaria lost territory to Greece and Yugoslavia. Finland, Estonia, Latvia, and Lithuania became independent states, and much of Poland was carved out of formerly Russian soil.

The old Ottoman Empire also disappeared. The new republic of Turkey was limited to little more than Constantinople and Asia Minor. Palestine and Iraq came under British control and Syria and Lebanon under French control as mandates under the purely theoretical authority of the League of Nations. Germany's former colonies in Africa and the Pacific were divided among the victors.

Reparations   Before the armistice, the Germans promised to pay compensation "for all damages done to the civilian population of the Allies and their property." However, France and Britain were eager to have Germany pay the full cost of the war. No sum was fixed at the conference. Germany was to pay $5 billion annually until 1921, when a final figure would be set, which Germany would have to pay within thirty years. The French calculated that either Germany would be bled into impotence or refuse to pay and justify French intervention.

To justify these huge reparation payments, the Allies inserted the notorious war guilt clause into the treaty, which placed the responsibility for the war solely on Germany. The

Germans bitterly resented the charges but had to accept the treaty as it was written by the victors without negotiation. The German government led by the Social Democrats and the Catholic Center Party signed the treaty. These parties formed the backbone of the German Republic, but they never overcame the stigma of accepting the treaty.

Evaluation of the Peace

Few peace settlements have been more attacked than the Treaty of Versailles, but many of the attacks on it are unjustified. Germany was neither dismembered nor ruined. Reparations were scaled down, and until the Great Depression of the 1930s, the German economy recovered. The attempt at achieving self-determination for nationalities was less than perfect, but it was the best Europe had ever accomplished.

The peace, nevertheless, was unsatisfactory. The elimination of the Austro-Hungarian Empire, however inevitable, created serious problems. Economically it was disastrous, for it separated raw materials from manufacturing areas and producers from their markets. Poland and especially Czechoslovakia contained unhappy German minorities. Disputes over territories in eastern Europe promoted further tension. The peace also rested on a defeat that Germany did not admit. The Germans believed they had been cheated, not defeated.

Finally, the peace failed to accept reality. Germany and Russia must inevitably play an important part in European affairs, yet they were excluded from the settlement and from the League of Nations. Given the many discontented parties, the peace was not self-enforcing; yet no satisfactory machinery for enforcing it was established. The league was never a serious force for this purpose. It was left to France, with no guarantee of support from Britain and no hope of help from the United States, to defend the new arrangements. France was simply not strong enough for the task if Germany were to rearm. The Treaty of Versailles was neither conciliatory enough to remove the desire for change, nor harsh enough to make another war impossible.

IN WORLD PERSPECTIVE

Imperialism and World War I

European imperialism in the last part of the nineteenth century brought the Western countries into contact with most of the world. By 1914, European nations had divided Africa among themselves and controlled large parts of Asia and the islands of the Pacific. Much of the Middle East was under the nominal control of the Ottoman Empire, which was in its death throes and under European influence. The Monroe Doctrine made Latin America a protectorate of the United

States. Japan had become an imperial power at the expense of China and Korea.

The emergence of a new, powerful German state at the center of Europe upset the old balance of power. Bismarck, however, preserved the peace for as long as he remained in power. The new German emperor, William II, abandoned the policy of restraint and sought more power and influence for his country. The result was a system of alliances that divided Europe into two armed camps. What began as yet another Balkan War involving the European powers became a world war that influenced the rest of the world. As the terrible war of 1914–1918 dragged on, the real motives that had driven the European powers to fight gave way to public affirmations of the principles of nationalism and self-determination. The peoples under colonial rule took these statements seriously and sought to win their own independence and nationhood. For the most part they were disappointed by the peace settlement. The British and French Empires were larger than ever. The Americans added to the islands they controlled in the Pacific. Japanese imperial ambitions were rewarded at the expense of China.

However, the old imperial nations, especially Britain and France, had paid an enormous price in lives, money, and will for their victory in the war. Colonial peoples pressed for the rights that were proclaimed as universal by the West but denied to their colonies; influential minorities in the countries that ruled them sympathized with colonial aspirations for independence. Tension between colonies and their ruling nations was a cause of instability in the world created by the Paris treaties of 1919.

Review Questions

1. What role did Bismarck envisage for the new Germany after 1871? Was he wise to tie Germany to Austria-Hungary?

2. Why and in what stages did Britain abandon "splendid isolation?" Were the policies it pursued wise ones?

3. How did developments in the Balkans lead to the outbreak of World War I? Did Germany want a general war?

4. Why did Germany lose World War I? Assess the settlement of Versailles. What were its benefits to Europe, and what were its drawbacks? Was it too harsh or too conciliatory? How might it have been improved?

5. Why was Lenin successful in establishing Bolshevik rule in Russia? What role did Trotsky play?

Documents CD-ROM

1. Selected Poetry

2. The Perversion of Technology: War in "No Man's Land"

3. World War I: A Frenchman's Recollections

4. Sir Henry McMahon: Letter to Ali Ibn Husain

5. The Balfour Declaration

6. Woodrow Wilson, Speech on the Fourteen Points

34 DEPRESSION, EUROPEAN DICTATORS, AND THE AMERICAN NEW DEAL

CHAPTER TOPICS

- ◆ After Versailles: Demands for Revision and Enforcement
- ◆ Toward the Great Depression in Europe
- ◆ The Soviet Experiment
- ◆ The Fascist Experiment in Italy

- ◆ German Democracy and Dictatorship
- ◆ The Great Depression and the New Deal in the United States

In World Perspective The Economic and Political Crisis

In the two decades that followed the Paris Settlement, the western world saw a number of experiments in politics and economic life. Two broad factors accounted for these experiments. First, the war, the Russian Revolution, and the peace treaty had transformed the political face of Europe. The new regimes that emerged in the wake of the collapse of the monarchies of Germany, Austria-Hungary, and Russia faced economic dislocation and nationalistic resentments.

Second, the Great Depression caused political instability and economic crisis. In Europe this often produced authoritarian regimes. In the United States it led to an increased role for the federal government.

After Versailles: Demands for Revision and Enforcement

The Paris settlement fostered resentments that counted among the chief political factors in Europe for the next two decades. The arrangements for reparations led to endless haggling. National groups in eastern Europe felt that injustice had been done to them and demanded border adjustments. The victorious powers, especially France, often believed that the treaty was being inadequately enforced. Too many political figures were willing to fish in these troubled international waters for domestic votes.

Toward the Great Depression in Europe

Three factors combined to bring about the severity and the extended length of the Great Depression. First, a financial crisis stemmed directly from the war and the peace settlement. To this was added a crisis in the production and distribution of goods in the world market. Finally, these difficulties were exacerbated because no major western European country or the United States provided responsible economic leadership.

Financial Tailspin

France was determined to collect reparations from Germany. The United States was no less determined that its allies repay the wartime loans it had extended to them. German reparations were to provide the means of repaying these debts.

The quest for payment of German reparations caused one of the major diplomatic crises of the 1920s; the crisis itself resulted in further economic upheaval. In early 1923, the Allies—and France in particular—declared Germany to be in default of its reparation payments. On January 11, French troops occupied the Ruhr mining and manufacturing district. The Weimar Republic ordered passive resistance. Confronted with this tactic, the French ran the German mines and railroads. The Germans paid, but Britain became more sympathetic to Germany. The cost of the Ruhr occupation, moreover, damaged the French economy.

The political and economic turmoil of the Ruhr invasion led to international attempts to ease the German payment of reparations. The most famous of these were the Dawes Plan of 1924 and the Young Plan of 1929, both devised by Americans. At the same time, American investment capital was pouring into Europe. However, the crash of Wall Street in October 1929—the result of unregulated speculation—saw the loss of large amounts of money. Thereafter, little American capital was available for investment in Europe.

In May 1931, the Kreditanstalt collapsed. It was a primary lending institution for much of central and eastern Europe. The German banking system then came under severe pressure. As the German difficulties increased, US president Herbert Hoover (1874–1964) announced in June 1931 a one-year moratorium on all payments of international debts. The Hoover moratorium was a prelude to the end of reparations. In the summer of 1932, the Lausanne Conference, in effect, ended the era of reparations.

Problems in Agricultural Commodities

The 1920s witnessed a contraction in the market demand for European goods. The difficulty arose from agriculture. Better methods of farming and more extensive transport facilities all over the globe vastly increased the quantity of grain. Wheat prices fell to record lows. This decreased the income of European farmers, while the cost of the industrial goods they used rose. Consequently, they had great difficulty paying off their debts. These problems were especially acute in central and eastern Europe and abetted farmers' disillusionment with liberal politics.

Outside Europe similar problems affected producers of wheat, sugar, coffee, rubber, wool, and lard. The people who produced these goods in underdeveloped nations could no longer make enough money to buy finished goods from industrial Europe. Commodity production had outstripped world demand.

The result was stagnation and depression for European industry. Coal, iron, and textiles had depended largely on international markets. Unemployment spread from these industries to those producing consumer goods. Unemployment in Britain and Germany during the 1920s had created "soft" domestic markets. The policies of reduced spending with which the governments confronted the Depression further weakened domestic demand. By the early 1930s the Depression was feeding on itself.

Depression and Government Policy

The Depression did not mean absolute economic decline or total unemployment. However, the economic downturn made people insecure. Even the employed often seemed to make no progress, and their anxieties created discontent.

The governments of the late 1920s and the early 1930s were not well suited to confront these problems. The electorates demanded action. The government response depended largely on the severity of the Depression in a particular country and on the self-confidence of its political system.

Great Britain and France undertook moderate political experiments. In 1924, the Labour Party in Great Britain established itself as a viable governing party. Under the pressure of the Depression, the Labour prime minister Ramsay MacDonald (1866–1937) organized a National Government, which was a coalition of the Labour, Conservative, and Liberal Parties. It remained in power until 1935, when a Conservative ministry led by Stanley Baldwin (1867–1947) replaced it.

The most important French political experiment was the Popular Front Ministry, which came to office in 1936. It was composed of socialists, radicals, and communists—the first time that socialists and communists had cooperated in a ministry. It addressed major labor problems in the French economy, but by 1938 the Popular Front was at an end.

The political experiments of the 1920s and 1930s that reshaped world history involved a Soviet government in Russia, a Fascist regime in Italy, and a Nazi dictatorship in Germany.

The Soviet Experiment

The Bolshevik Revolution in Russia led to the most durable of all twentieth-century authoritarian governments. The Communist Party of the Soviet Union retained power from 1917 until the end of 1991, and it influenced the history of much of the world like no other single factor. Unlike the Italian fascists or the German national socialists, the bolsheviks seized power violently through revolution. Their leaders long felt insecure about their hold on the country. The

A Communist Woman Demands a New Family Life

While Lenin sought to consolidate the Bolshevik Revolution against internal and external enemies, there existed within the young Soviet Union a vast utopian impulse to change and reform virtually every social institution that had existed before the revolution or that communists associated with capitalist society. Alexandra Kollontai (1872–1952) was a spokesperson of the extreme political left within the early Soviet Union. There had been much speculation on how the end of bourgeois society might change the structure of the family and the position of women. In this passage written in 1920, Kollontai states one of the most idealistic visions of this change. During the years immediately after the revolution, extreme rumors circulated in both Europe and America about sexual and family experimentation in the Soviet Union. Statements such as this fostered such rumors. Kollontai herself later became a supporter of Stalin and a Soviet diplomat.

Why did Kollontai see the restructuring of the family as essential to the establishment of a new kind of Communist society? Would these changes make people loyal to that society? What changes in society does the kind of economic independence she seeks for women presuppose? What might childhood be like in this society?

There is no escaping the fact: the old type of family has seen its day. It is not the fault of the Communist State, it is the result of the changed conditions of life. The family is ceasing to be a necessity of the State, as it was in the past; on the contrary, it is worse than useless, since it needlessly holds back the female workers from more productive and far more serious work. . . . But on the ruins of the former family we shall soon see a new form rising which will involve altogether different relations between men and women, and which will be a union of affection and comradeship, a union of two equal members of the Communist society, both of them free, both of them independent, both of them workers. No more domestic "servitude" of women. No more inequality within the family. No more

fear on the part of the woman lest she remain without support or aid with little ones in her arms if her husband should desert her. The woman in the Communist city no longer depends on her husband but on her work. It is not her husband but her robust arms which will support her. There will be no more anxiety as to the fate of her children. The State of the Workers will assume responsibility for these. Marriage will be purified of all its material elements, of all money calculations, which constitute a hideous blemish on family life in our days. . . .

The woman who is called upon to struggle in the great cause of the liberation of the workers—such a woman should know that in the new State there will be no more room for such petty divisions as were formerly understood: "These are my own children, to them I owe all my maternal solicitude, all my affection; those are your children, my neighbour's children; I am not concerned with them. I have enough to do with my own." Henceforth the worker-mother, who is conscious of her social function, will rise to a point where she no longer differentiates between yours and mine; she must remember that there are henceforth only our children, those of the Communist State, the common possession of all the workers.

The Worker's State has need of a new form of relation between the sexes. The narrow and exclusive affection of the mother for her own children must expand until it embraces all the children of the great proletarian family. In place of the indissoluble marriage based on the servitude of woman, we shall see rise the free union, fortified by the love and mutual respect of the two members of the Workers' State, equal in their rights and in their obligations. In place of the individual and egotistic family there will arise a great universal family of workers, in which all the workers, men and women, will be, above all, workers, comrades.

From *Communism and the Family* by Alexandra Kollontai, as reprinted in Rudolf Schlesinger, ed. and trans., *The Family in the USSR*, London: Routledge and Kegan Paul, 1949, pp. 67–69. Reprinted by permission.

Communist Party was not a mass party nor a nationalistic one. The bolsheviks confronted a much less industrialized economy than that in Italy or Germany. They believed in and practiced the collectivization of economic life attacked by the right-wing dictatorships. The Marxist-Leninist ideology was broader than the nationalism of the fascists and the racism of the Nazis. Communism was an exportable commodity. The communists regarded their government and their revolution as epoch-making events in the development of humanity. Fear of communism and determination to stop its spread were

leading political forces in western Europe and the United States for most of the rest of the century and would influence their relationships to much of the rest of the world.

War Communism

Within months of the revolution, a new secret police, known as *Cheka*, appeared. Throughout the Russian civil war Lenin had declared that the Bolshevik Party, as the vanguard of the revolution, was imposing the dictatorship of the proletariat.

Under the economic policy of "War Communism," the revolutionary government confiscated the banks, the transport facilities, and heavy industry. The state also requisitioned grain and shipped it from the countryside to feed the army and the cities.

"War Communism" helped the Red Army defeat its opponents. The revolution had survived and triumphed. The policy, however, generated domestic opposition. Many Russians were no longer willing to make the sacrifices demanded by the central party bureaucrats. In 1920 and 1921, strikes occurred. Peasants resisted the requisition of grain. In March 1921, the navy mutinied. Each of these incidents suggested that the proletariat itself was opposing the dictatorship of the proletariat. Also, by late 1920 it had become clear that revolution would not sweep across the rest of Europe. The Soviet Union was a vast island of revolutionary socialism in a sea of worldwide capitalism.

The New Economic Policy

Lenin made a strategic retreat. In March 1921, he outlined the New Economic Policy, or NEP. Apart from "the commanding heights" of banking, heavy industry, transportation, and international commerce, private economic enterprise was allowed and peasants could farm for a profit. The countryside became more stable, and a secure food supply seemed assured for the cities. Similar free enterprise flourished within light industry and retail trade. The revolution seemed to have transformed Russia into a land of small farms and private shops and businesses.

Stalin Versus Trotsky

The NEP had caused sharp disputes within the Politburo, the highest governing committee of the Communist Party. These frictions increased when Lenin suffered a stroke in 1922 and died in 1924. An intense struggle for leadership of the party commenced. Two factions emerged. One was led by Trotsky; the other by Joseph Stalin (1879–1953), who had become general secretary of the party in 1922.

The struggle was fought over the question of Russia's path toward industrialization and the future of the communist revolutionary movement. Trotsky, speaking for what became known as the left wing, urged rapid industrialization and looked to voluntary collectivization of farming by poor peasants as a means of increasing agricultural production. Trotsky further argued that the revolution in Russia could succeed only if new revolutions took place elsewhere.

A right-wing faction opposed Trotsky. Stalin was its manipulator. This group pressed for the continuation of Lenin's NEP.

Stalin was the ultimate victor. His power lay in his command of bureaucratic and administrative methods. He mastered the crucial details of party structure, including admission and promotion. He had the support of the lower levels of the party when he clashed with other leaders.

In 1924, Stalin enunciated, in opposition to Trotsky, the doctrine of "socialism in one country." Russian success did not depend on the fate of the revolution elsewhere. Stalin thus nationalized the previously international scope of the Marxist revolution. By 1927, Trotsky had been ousted from the party. In 1929, he was expelled from Russia and was eventually murdered in 1940 by one of Stalin's agents. With the removal of Trotsky, Stalin was firmly in control of the Soviet state.

Decision for Rapid Industrialization

During the Depression, the Soviet Union registered tremendous industrial advance. As usual in Russia, the direction and impetus came from the top. Stalin far exceeded the tsars in the coercion and terror he brought to the task. Russia achieved its economic growth during the 1930s only at the cost of millions of human lives.

Through 1928, Lenin's NEP had steered Soviet economic development. A few farmers, the *kulaks*, had become prosperous. During 1928 and 1929, they and other farmers withheld grain from the market because prices were too low. Food shortages in the cities caused unrest. Stalin came to a momentous decision. Russia must industrialize rapidly to match the power of the West. Agriculture must be collectivized to produce sufficient grain for food and export and to free peasant labor for the factories. This program, which basically embraced Trotsky's earlier economic position, unleashed a second Russian revolution.

Agricultural Policy   In 1929, Stalin ordered party agents to confiscate hoarded wheat. As part of the general plan to collectivize farming, the government undertook to eliminate the *kulaks* as a class. A *kulak*, however, soon came to mean any peasant who opposed Stalin's policy. In the countryside, peasants at all levels of wealth resisted stubbornly. They wreaked their vengeance on the policy of collectivization by slaughtering more than 100 million horses and cattle between 1929 and 1933. The situation in the countryside amounted to open warfare.

As many as 10 million peasants were killed, and millions of others were sent to labor camps. Because of the turmoil, there was famine in 1932 and 1933. Yet Stalin persevered. Peasants had their lands incorporated into large collective farms. The state controlled the machinery for these units.

The government now had primary direction over the food supply. The peasants could no longer determine whether there would be stability or unrest in the cities. Stalin and the Communist Party had won the battle of the wheat fields, but the problem of producing enough grain still plagues the former Soviet Union.

Five-Year Plans The revolution in agriculture had been undertaken for the sake of industrialization. The increased grain supply was to feed the labor force and provide exports to finance the imports required for industrial development. The industrial achievement of the Soviet Union between 1928 and World War II was one of the most striking accomplishments of the twentieth century. Russia made a more rapid advance toward economic growth than any other nation in the western world has ever achieved during a similar period of time. Soviet industrial production rose approximately 400 percent between 1928 and 1940. Few consumer goods were produced. The labor for this development was supplied internally. Capital was raised from the export of grain, even at the cost of internal shortage. The technology was borrowed from industrialized nations.

The organizational vehicle for industrialization was a series of five-year plans first begun in 1928. The State Planning Commission, or Gosplan, set goals of production and organized the economy to meet them. Coordinating all facets of production was difficult and complicated. A vast program of propaganda was undertaken to sell the five-year plans to the Russian people. The industrial labor force became subject to regimentation similar to that being imposed on the peasants. The accomplishment of the three five-year plans probably allowed the Soviet Union to survive the German invasion.

Many non-Russian contemporaries looked at the Soviet economic experiment uncritically. While the capitalist world lay in the throes of the Depression, the Soviet economy had grown at an unprecedented pace. These observers seem to have had little idea of the social cost of the Soviet achievement. Millions had been killed or uprooted. The suffering and human loss during those years will probably never be known; it far exceeded anything described by Marx and Engels in relation to nineteenth-century industrialization in western Europe.

The Purges

Stalin's decisions to industrialize rapidly and to move against the peasants aroused internal political opposition because they were departures from the policies of Lenin. In 1933, Stalin began to fear that he would lose control over the party apparatus. These fears were probably paranoid. Nevertheless, they resulted in the Great Purges, among the most mysterious and horrendous political events of this century.

On December 1, 1934, Sergei Kirov (1888–1934), the popular party chief of Leningrad (formerly Saint Petersburg) was assassinated. In the wake of the shooting, thousands of people were arrested, and still more were expelled from the party and sent to labor camps. It now seems certain that Stalin himself authorized Kirov's assassination to forestall any threat from him.

The purges after Kirov's death were just the beginning. Between 1936 and 1938, spectacular show trials were held in Moscow. Previous high Soviet leaders publicly confessed political crimes and were executed. Their confessions were palpably false. Other leaders and party members were tried in private and shot. Thousands of people received no trial at all. It is inexplicable why some were executed, others sent to labor camps, and still others left unmolested. After the civilian party members had been purged, important officers, including heroes of the civil war, were killed. The exact numbers of executions and imprisonments are unknown but ran into the millions.

The scale of the political turmoil was unprecedented. The Russians themselves did not comprehend what was occurring. The only rational explanation is found in Stalin's concern for his own power. The purges created a new party structure absolutely loyal to him.

Despite the violence and repression, the Soviet experiment found many sympathizers. The Soviet Union after the Bolshevik seizure of power had fostered Communist Parties subservient to Moscow throughout the world. Others who were not members of these parties sympathized with what they believed were the goals of the Soviet Union. During at least the first fifty years of its existence, the Soviet Union managed to capture the imagination of some intellectuals around the globe who hoped for a utopian egalitarian transformation of society. During much of the 1930s, the Soviet Union also appeared as an enemy to the fascist experiments in Italy and Germany. The Marxist ideology championed by the Soviet Union appeared to many people living in the European colonial empires as a vehicle for freeing themselves. The Soviet Union welcomed and trained many such anti-colonial leaders. With what is now known about Soviet repression, it is difficult to understand the power its presence exercised over many people's political imaginations, but that attraction was a factor in world politics from the 1920s through at least the early 1970s.

The Fascist Experiment in Italy

The first authoritarian political experiment in western Europe that arose in part from fears of the spread of bolshevism occurred in Italy. The general term *fascist*, which has been used to describe the various right-wing dictatorships that arose between the wars, was derived from the Italian fascist movement of Benito Mussolini (1883–1945).

The governments regarded as fascist were antidemocratic, anti-Marxist, antiparliamentary, and frequently anti-Semitic. They hoped to hold back the spread of bolshevism, which seemed a real threat at the time. They sought a world that would be safe for the middle class and small farmers. The fascist regimes rejected the political ideas of the French

Revolution and of liberalism. Their adherents believed that parliamentary politics and parties sacrificed national greatness to petty party disputes. They wanted to overcome the class conflict of Marxism and the party conflict of liberalism by consolidating all classes within the nation for great national purposes. Fascist governments were usually single-party dictatorships rooted in mass political parties and characterized by terrorism and police surveillance.

Rise of Mussolini

The Italian *Fasci di Combattimento* ("Band of Combat") was founded in 1919 in Milan. Most of its members were veterans who felt that the sacrifices of World War I had been in vain. They resented Italy's failure to gain the city of Fiume at the Paris conference. They feared socialism, inflation, and labor unrest.

Their leader, Benito Mussolini, had been active in Italian socialist politics but broke with the socialists in 1914 and supported Italian entry into the war. He then established his own paper, *Il Popolo d'Italia*, and was wounded in the army. As a politician, Mussolini was an opportunist. He could change his ideas and principles to suit any occasion. Action for him was always more important than thought. His goal was political survival.

Many Italians were dissatisfied with the parliamentary system. They felt that Italy had not been treated as a great power at the peace conference or received the territories it deserved. The main spokesman for this discontent was the extreme nationalist writer Gabriele D'Annunzio (1863–1938). In 1919, he captured Fiume with a force of patriotic Italians. The Italian army drove him out, but this made the parliamentary ministry seem unpatriotic.

Between 1919 and 1921, Italy was also wracked by social turmoil. Numerous strikes occurred, and workers occupied factories. Peasants seized land. Parliamentary government seemed incapable of dealing with this unrest. Many Italians believed that a communist revolution might break out.

Mussolini first supported the factory occupations and land seizures, but soon reversed himself. He had discovered that many upper-class and middle-class Italians who were pressured by inflation and feared property loss had no sympathy for the workers or peasants. They wanted order. Consequently, Mussolini and his fascists took direct action in the face of the government inaction. They terrorized socialist supporters, attacked strikers and farm workers, and protected strikebreakers. Conservative land and factory owners were grateful. The government ignored these crimes. By early 1922, the fascists controlled the local government in much of northern Italy.

In 1921, Mussolini and thirty-four of his followers had been elected to the Chamber of Deputies. The fascist movement now had hundreds of thousands of supporters. In October 1922, the fascists, dressed in their characteristic black shirts, began a march on Rome. King Victor Emmanuel III (r. 1900–1946) refused to authorize using the army against them, which ensured a fascist seizure of power. The Cabinet resigned. On October 29, the king telegraphed Mussolini in Milan and asked him to become prime minister. The next day Mussolini arrived in Rome by train and, as head of the government, greeted his followers when they entered the city.

Technically, Mussolini had come into office by legal means. The monarch had the power to appoint the prime minister. Mussolini, however, had no majority in the Chamber of Deputies. Behind the legal facade lay the months of terrorist intimidation and the threat of the fascists' October march.

The Fascists in Power

Mussolini, who had not expected to be appointed prime minister, succeeded because of the impotence of his rivals, his use of his office, his power over the masses, and his ruthlessness. On November 23, 1922, the king and Parliament granted Mussolini dictatorial authority for one year to restore order. Wherever possible, Mussolini appointed fascists to office. In 1924, Parliament changed the election law so that the party that gained the largest popular vote (with at least 25 percent) received two-thirds of the seats in the chamber. Coalition government, with all its compromises and hesitations, would no longer be necessary. In the election of 1924, the fascists won complete control of the Chamber of Deputies. They used that majority to end legitimate parliamentary life. Laws permitted Mussolini to rule by decree. In 1926, Italy was transformed into a single-party, dictatorial state.

One domestic initiative brought Mussolini significant political dividends and respectability. Through the Lateran Accord of February 1929, the Roman Catholic Church and the Italian state made peace with each other. The agreement recognized the pope as the temporal ruler of Vatican City. The Italian government agreed to pay an indemnity to the papacy for confiscated land. The state also recognized Catholicism as the religion of the nation, exempted church property from taxes, and allowed church law to govern marriage.

German Democracy and Dictatorship

The Weimar Republic

The Weimar Republic was born from the defeat of the imperial army, the revolution of 1918, and the hopes of German Liberals and Social Democrats. Its name derived from the city of Weimar where its constitution was written in August 1919. While the constitution was being debated, the republic, headed by the Social Democrats, accepted the hated Versailles Treaty. Although its officials had signed only under duress, the republic was permanently associated with the national disgrace. Throughout the 1920s, the government was required to fulfill the economic and military provisions imposed by the Paris settlement. Nationalists and military figures whose policies had brought on the tragedy and defeat of the war blamed the young republic and the socialists for its results. In Germany, the desire to revise the treaty was related to a desire to change the form of government.

The Weimar Constitution was an enlightened document. It guaranteed civil liberties and provided for direct election, by universal suffrage, of the Reichstag and the president. It also, however, contained structural flaws that eventually allowed it to be overthrown. A complicated system of proportional representation made it relatively easy for small political parties to gain seats in the Reichstag, which resulted in instability. The president appointed and removed the chancellor, the head of the cabinet. Article 48 allowed the president, in an emergency, to rule by decree. This permitted a possible presidential dictatorship.

In March 1920, a right-wing putsch, or armed insurrection, erupted in Berlin. It failed, but only after government officials had fled the city. In the same month, strikes took place in the Ruhr, and the government sent in troops. Such extremism from both the left and the right would haunt the republic. In May 1921, the Allies presented a reparations bill for 132 billion gold marks. The German government accepted this preposterous demand only after new Allied threats. Throughout the early 1920s, there were assassinations or attempted assassinations of republican leaders. Violence was the hallmark of the first five years of the republic.

Invasion of the Ruhr and Inflation   Inflation brought on the major crisis of this period. The war and postwar deficit spending generated an immense rise in prices. The value of German currency fell. By early 1921, the German mark traded against the American dollar at a ratio of 64 to 1, compared with a ratio of 4.2 to 1 in 1914. The German financial community contended that the mark could not be stabilized until the reparations issue had been solved. Meanwhile, the government kept issuing paper money, which it used to redeem government bonds.

The French invasion of the Ruhr in January 1923, to secure the payment of reparations, and the German response of passive economic resistance produced cataclysmic inflation. Unemployment spread, creating a drain on the treasury and reducing tax revenues. The printing presses had difficulty providing enough paper currency to keep up with the daily rise in prices. Money was literally not worth the paper it was printed on. Stores were unwilling to exchange goods for the worthless currency, and farmers hoarded produce.

Major Political Events of the 1920s and 1930s

1919	August, Constitution of the Weimar Republic promulgated
1920	Putsch in Berlin
1921	March, Lenin initiates his New Economic Policy
1922	October, fascist march on Rome leads to Mussolini's assumption of power
1923	January, France invades the Ruhr
	November, Hitler's Beer Hall Putsch
1924	Death of Lenin
1925	Locarno Agreements
1928	Kellogg-Briand Pact; first five-year plan launched in USSR
1929	January, Trotsky expelled from USSR
	February, Lateran Accord between the Vatican and the Italian state
	October, New York stock market crash
	November, Stalin's power affirmed
1930	March, Bruning government begins in Germany
	September, Nazis capture 107 seats in German Reichstag
1931	August, National Government formed in Britain
1932	March 13, Hindenberg defeats Hitler for German presidency
	May 31, Franz von Papen forms German Cabinet
	July 31, German Reichstag election
	November 6, German Reichstag election
	December 2, Kurt von Schleicher forms German Cabinet
1933	January 30, Hitler made German chancellor
	February 27, Reichstag Fire
	March 5, Reichstag election
	March 23, Enabling Act consolidates Nazi power
1934	June 30, Blood purge of the Nazi Party
	August 2, Death of Hindenburg
	December 1, Assassination of Kirov leads to the beginning of Stalin's purges
1936	May, Popular Front government in France
	July–August, Most famous of public purge trials in Russia

The values of thrift and prudence were undermined. Middle-class savings, pensions, insurance policies, and investments in government bonds were wiped out. Debts and mortgages could not be paid off. Speculators made fortunes, but to the middle class and the lower middle class, the inflation was another trauma coming hard on the heels of military defeat and the peace treaty. This social and economic upheaval was behind the later German desire for order and security at almost any cost.

Hitler's Early Career   In 1923, Adolf Hitler (1889–1945) made his first significant appearance on the German political scene. The son of a minor Austrian customs official, his hopes of becoming an artist had been dashed in Vienna. Hitler absorbed the rabid German nationalism and extreme anti-Semitism that flourished there. He came to hate Marxism, which he associated with Jews. During World War I, Hitler fought in the German army, was wounded, rose to the rank of corporal, and won the Iron Cross for bravery. The war gave him his first sense of purpose.

After the conflict, Hitler settled in Munich and became associated with a small nationalistic, anti-Semitic party that in 1920 adopted the name of National Socialist German Workers Party, better known as the Nazis. The group paraded under a red banner with a black swastika. Its program called for the repudiation of the Versailles Treaty, the unification of Austria and Germany, the exclusion of Jews from German citizenship, agrarian reform, the prohibition of land speculation, the confiscation of war profits, state administration of the giant cartels, and the replacement of department stores with small retail shops.

The "socialism" that Hitler and the Nazis had in mind had nothing to do with traditional German socialism. It meant not state ownership of the means of production but the subordination of all economic enterprise to the welfare of the nation. It often implied protection for small economic enterprises. The Nazis discovered that their social appeal was to the lower middle class, which found itself squeezed between big business and socialist labor unions. The Nazis tailored their message to this troubled economic group.

The Nazi Stormtroopers, or SA *(Sturm Abteilung)*, were organized under the leadership of Captain Ernst Roehm (1887–1934). The Stormtroopers were the chief Nazi instrument for terror and intimidation before the party controlled the government. The existence of such a private party army was a sign of the potential for violence in the Weimar Republic and of contempt for the republic.

The social and economic turmoil following the French occupation of the Ruhr and the German inflation gave the Nazis an opportunity for direct action against the Weimar Republic. By this time, Hitler dominated the Nazi Party. On November 9, 1923, Hitler and a band of followers, accompanied by General Erich Ludendorff (1865–1937), attempted an unsuccessful putsch at a beer hall in Munich. The local authorities crushed the rising, and sixteen Nazis were killed. Hitler and Ludendorff were tried for treason. The general was acquitted. Hitler made himself into a national figure. In his defense, he condemned the republic, the Versailles Treaty, and the Jews. He was sentenced to five years in prison but spent only a few months in jail before being paroled. During this time, he dictated *Mein Kampf* ("My Struggle"). Another result of the brief imprisonment was his decision to seize political power by legal methods.

The Stresemann Years   Gustav Stresemann (1878–1929) was primarily responsible for the reconstruction of the republic and its achievement of a sense of self-confidence. Stresemann

abandoned the policy of passive resistance in the Ruhr. With the aid of banker Hjalmar Schacht (1877–1970), he introduced a new German currency. The rate of exchange was one trillion of the old German marks for one new Rentenmark. Stresemann also moved against challenges from both the left and the right. He supported the crushing of both Hitler's abortive putsch and smaller communist disturbances. In late November 1923, after four months as chancellor, he became foreign minister, a post he held until his death in 1929.

In 1924, the Weimar Republic and the Allies renegotiated the reparation payments. French troops left the Ruhr in 1925. The same year, Field Marshal Paul von Hindenburg (1847–1934), a military hero and a conservative monarchist, was elected president and governed in strict accordance with the constitution. The prosperity of the latter 1920s seemed to reconcile conservative Germans to the republic. Foreign capital flowed into Germany, and employment improved smartly. Giant industrial combines spread.

In foreign affairs, Stresemann pursued a conciliatory course. He fulfilled the provisions of the Versailles Treaty but attempted to revise it by diplomacy. He accepted the settlement in the west but aimed to recover German-speaking territories lost to Poland and Czechoslovakia and possibly to unite with Austria, chiefly by diplomatic means.

Locarno   These developments gave rise to the Locarno Agreements of October 1925. Foreign ministers Austen Chamberlain (1863–1937) for Britain and Aristide Briand (1862–1932) for France accepted Stresemann's proposal for a fresh start. France and Germany accepted the western frontier established at Versailles. Britain and Italy agreed to intervene against the aggressor if either side violated the frontier or if Germany sent troops into the demilitarized Rhineland. No such agreement was made about Germany's eastern frontier, but the Germans made arbitration treaties with Poland and Czechoslovakia, and France strengthened its alliances with those countries. France supported German membership in the League of Nations and agreed to withdraw its occupation troops from the Rhineland in 1930, five years earlier than specified at Versailles.

The Locarno Agreements brought new hope to Europe. Chamberlain, Briand, and Stresemann received the Nobel Peace Prize. The spirit of Locarno was carried even further when the leading European states, Japan, and the United States signed the Kellogg-Briand Pact in 1928, renouncing "war as an instrument of national policy." The joy and optimism were not justified. France had merely recognized its inability to coerce Germany without help. Britain had shown its unwillingness to uphold the settlement in the east. Germany was not reconciled to the eastern settlement.

In both France and Germany, moreover, the conciliatory politicians represented only a part of the nation. In Germany especially, most people continued to reject Versailles and regarded Locarno as only an extension of it. Despite these problems, war was by no means inevitable. Europe, aided by American loans, was returning to prosperity. German leaders like Stresemann would certainly have continued to press for change, but not through force, much less a general war. Continued prosperity and diplomatic success might have won the loyalty of the German people for the Weimar Republic and moderate revisionism, but the Great Depression of the 1930s brought new forces to power.

Depression and Political Deadlock

The outflow of foreign, and especially American, capital from Germany that began in 1928 undermined the prosperity of the Weimar Republic. The resulting economic crisis brought parliamentary government to a halt. In 1928, a coalition of center parties and the Social Democrats governed. When the Depression struck, the coalition partners differed sharply on economic policy, and the coalition dissolved in March 1930. President von Hindenburg appointed Heinrich Brüning (1885–1970) as chancellor. Lacking a majority in the Reichstag, the new chancellor governed through emergency presidential decrees. The Weimar Republic had become a presidential dictatorship.

German unemployment rose from 2,258,000 in March 1930 to over 6,000,000 in March 1932. The economic downturn and the parliamentary deadlock worked to the advantage of extremists. In the election of 1928, the Nazis had won only 12 seats in the Reichstag and the communists 54. In the election of 1930, Nazis won 107 seats and the communists, 77.

The power of the Nazis in the streets also rose. The unemployment fed thousands of men into the Stormtroopers, which had almost 1 million members in 1933. The SA attacked communists and Social Democrats. For the Nazis, politics meant the capture of power through terror and intimidation as well as through elections. Decency and civility in political life vanished. Nazi rallies resembled religious revivals. They paraded through the streets and the countryside. They gained powerful supporters in the business, military, and newspaper communities. Some intellectuals were also sympathetic. The Nazis transformed this discipline and enthusiasm born of economic despair and nationalistic frustration into electoral results.

Hitler Comes to Power

For two years, Brüning governed with the confidence of Hindenburg. The economy did not improve, and the political situation deteriorated. In 1932, the eighty-three-year-old president stood for reelection. Hitler ran against him and Hindenburg won. But Hitler got 36.8 percent of the final vote. The vote convinced Hindenburg that Brüning had lost

the confidence of conservative Germans. In May 1932, he appointed Franz von Papen (1878–1969) chancellor. Papen was one of a small group of extremely conservative advisers on whom Hindenburg had become dependent. With the continued paralysis in the Reichstag, their influence over the president amounted to control of the government.

Papen and the circle around the president wanted to draw the Nazis into cooperation with them without giving Hitler effective power. The government needed the popular support on the right that only the Nazis seemed able to generate. The Hindenburg circle decided to convince Hitler that the Nazis could not come to power on their own. Papen removed the ban on Nazi meetings that Brüning had imposed and called a Reichstag election for July 1932. The Nazis won 230 seats and polled 37.2 percent of the vote. Hitler would only enter the Cabinet if he were made chancellor. Hindenburg refused. Another election was called in November. The Nazis gained only 196 seats, and their percentage of the popular vote dipped to 33.1 percent.

In early December 1932, Papen resigned, and General Kurt von Schleicher (1882–1934) became chancellor. People were now afraid of civil war between the extreme left and the far right. Schleicher tried to fashion a coalition of conservatives and trade unionists. The Hindenburg circle did not trust Schleicher's motives, which have never been clear. They persuaded Hindenburg to appoint Hitler chancellor. To control him, Papen was named vice-chancellor, and other traditional conservatives were appointed to the Cabinet. On January 30, 1933, Adolf Hitler became the chancellor of Germany.

Hitler had come into office by legal means. The proper procedures had been observed. This permitted the civil service, courts, and other government agencies to support him in good conscience. He had forged a rigidly disciplined party structure and had mastered the techniques of mass politics and propaganda. His support appears to have come from across the social spectrum. Pockets of resistance appeared among Roman Catholic voters in the country and small towns. Otherwise, support for Hitler was strong among farmers, veterans, and the young, who had suffered from the insecurity of the 1920s and the Depression. Hitler promised them security, effective government in place of petty politics, and a strong, restored Germany.

There is little evidence that business contributions made any crucial difference to the Nazis' success. Hitler's supporters were frequently suspicious of business and giant capitalism. They wanted a simpler world in which small property would be safe from both socialism and large-scale capitalist consolidation. These people looked to Hitler and the Nazis rather than to the Social Democrats because the latter never appeared sufficiently nationalistic. The Nazis won out over other conservative nationalistic parties because, unlike those conservatives, the Nazis addressed the problem of social insecurities.

Hitler's Consolidation of Power

Once in office, Hitler moved swiftly to consolidate his control. This process had three facets: the capture of full legal authority, the crushing of alternative political groups, and the purging of rivals within the Nazi Party itself. On February 27, 1933, a mentally ill Dutch Communist set fire to the Reichstag building in Berlin. The Nazis turned the incident to their own advantage by claiming that the fire proved the existence of a communist threat to the government. To the public, this seemed plausible. Under Article 48, Hitler suspended civil liberties and arrested communists or alleged communists. This decree was not revoked for as long as Hitler ruled Germany.

In early March, another Reichstag election took place. The Nazis still received only 43.9 percent of the vote. However, the arrest of communist deputies and the fear aroused by the fire meant that Hitler could control the Reichstag. On March 23, 1933, the Reichstag passed an Enabling Act, which permitted Hitler to rule by decree. Thereafter, there were no legal limits on his power. The Weimar Constitution was never formally repealed.

Hitler understood that he and his party had come to power because his potential opponents had stood divided between 1929 and 1933. To prevent them from regrouping, Hitler outlawed or undermined any German institutions that might have served as rallying points for opposition. By the close of 1933, all major institutions of potential opposition—trade unions, other political parties, the federal state governments—had been eliminated.

The final element in Hitler's personal consolidation of power involved the Nazi Party itself. Ernst Roehm, the commander of the SA, was a possible rival to Hitler. The German officer corps, whom Hitler needed to rebuild the army, were jealous of the SA. To protect his own position and to shore up support with the army, Hitler ordered the murder of key SA officers, including Roehm. Between June 30 and July 2, 1934, more than 800 people were killed, including the former chancellor Kurt von Schleicher and his wife. The German army, which might have prevented the murders, did nothing. On August 2, 1934, President Hindenburg died, and the offices of chancellor and president were combined. Hitler was now the sole ruler of Germany and of the Nazi Party.

The Police State

Terror and intimidation had helped propel the Nazis to office. As Hitler consolidated his power, he oversaw the organization of a police state. The chief vehicle of police surveillance was the SS *(Schutzstaffel)*, or security units, commanded by Heinrich Himmler (1900–1945). This group was a more elite paramilitary organization than the larger SA. In 1933, the SS had approximately 52,000 members. It was the instrument that carried out the blood purges of the party in 1934. By 1936, Himmler had become head of all police matters in Germany.

The police character of the Nazi regime was all-pervasive, but the people who most consistently experienced its terror were the Jews. Anti-Semitism had been a key plank of the Nazi program—anti-Semitism based on biological racial theories stemming from late-nineteenth-century thought rather than from religious discrimination. Before World War II, the Nazi attack on the Jews went through three stages. In 1933, the Nazis excluded Jews from the civil service and attempted to enforce boycotts of Jewish businesses. The boycotts won little public support. In 1935, the Nuremberg Laws robbed German Jews of their citizenship. All persons with at least one Jewish grandparent were defined as Jews. The professions and major occupations were closed to Jews. Marriage and sexual intercourse between Jews and non-Jews were prohibited. Legal exclusion and humiliation of the Jews became the norm.

The persecution of the Jews increased again in 1938. In November, under orders from the Nazi Party, thousands of Jewish stores and synagogues were destroyed. The Jewish community itself had to pay for the damage that occurred on this Kristallnacht because the government confiscated the insurance money. In both large and petty ways, the German Jews were harassed. This persecution allowed the Nazis to inculcate the rest of the population with the concept of a master race of pure German "Aryans" and also to display their own contempt for civil liberties.

After the war broke out, Hitler decided in 1942 to destroy the Jews in Europe. It is thought that over 6 million Jews, mostly from eastern Europe, died as a result of that decision, unprecedented in its scope and implementation.

Women in Nazi Germany

The Nazis believed in separate social spheres for men and women. Men belonged in the world of action, women in the home. The two spheres should not mix. Respect for women should arise from their function as wives and mothers.

These attitudes conflicted with the social changes that German women, like women elsewhere in Europe, had experienced during the first three decades of the twentieth century. German women had become much more active and assertive. They worked in factories or were independently employed, and had begun to enter the professions. Under the Weimar constitution, they voted. Throughout the Weimar period, there was also a lively discussion of women's emancipation. For the Nazis, these developments were signs of cultural weakness.

The Nazis' point of view was supported by women of a conservative outlook and women who followed traditional roles as housewives. In a period of high unemployment, the Nazi attitude also appealed to many men because it discouraged women from competing with them in the workplace. Such competition had begun during World War I, and many Nazis considered it symptomatic of the social confusion that had followed the German defeat.

The Nazi discussion of the role of women was also rooted in Nazi racism. It was the special task of German mothers to preserve racial purity. Hitler championed this view of women. They were to breed strong sons and daughters for the German nation. Nazi journalists often compared the role of women in childbirth to that of men in battle. Each served the state in particular gender roles. In both cases, the good of the nation was superior to that of the individual.

The Nazis also attacked feminist outlooks. Women were encouraged to bear many children, because the Nazis believed the declining German birth rate was the result of emancipated women who had spurned their natural roles as mothers. The Nazis sponsored schools that taught women how to rear children.

The Nazis also saw women as educators of the young and thus the protectors of German cultural values. Through cooking, dress, music, and stories, mothers were to instill a love for the nation. As consumers for the home, women were to buy German goods and avoid Jewish merchants.

The Nazis realized that in the midst of the Depression many women would need to work, but the party urged them to pursue employment that the Nazis considered natural to their character. These tasks included agriculture, teaching, nursing, social work, and domestic service. Nonetheless, the percentage of women employed in Germany changed little from the Weimar to the Hitler years: It was 37 percent in 1928 and in 1939. Thereafter, because of the war, many more women were recruited into the German work force.

The Great Depression and the New Deal in the United States

The United States emerged from the First World War as a world power. However, it retreated from that role when the Senate refused to ratify the Versailles Treaty and failed to join the League of Nations. In 1920, Warren Harding (1865–1923) became president and urged a return to what he termed "normalcy," which meant minimal involvement abroad and conservative economic policies at home. Business interests remained in the ascendent, and the federal government took a relatively inactive role in national life, especially under Harding's successor, Calvin Coolidge (1872–1933).

The first seven or eight years of the decade witnessed remarkable American prosperity. New electrical appliances such as the radio, phonograph, washing machine, and vacuum cleaner appeared on the market. Real wages rose for many workers. Industry grew at a robust rate. Automobile manufacturers assumed a major role in national economic life. Fac-

tories became mechanized. Engineers and efficiency experts were the heroes of the business world. The stock market boomed. This activity stood in marked contrast to the economic dislocations of Europe.

The material prosperity appeared, however, in a divided society. Segregation remained a basic fact of life for black Americans. The Ku Klux Klan, which sought to terrorize blacks, Roman Catholics, and Jews, enjoyed a resurgence. The Prohibition Amendment of 1919 (repealed in 1933) forbade the manufacture and transport of alcoholic beverages. In the wake of this divisive national policy, major criminal operations arose to supply liquor and disrupt civic life. Many immigrants came from Mexico and Puerto Rico. They settled in cities where their labor was desired but where they were often not welcomed or assimilated. Finally, the wealth of the nation was concentrated in too few hands.

Economic Collapse

In March 1929, Herbert Hoover became president, the third Republican in as many elections. On October 29, 1929, the New York stock market crashed. The other financial markets also went into a tailspin. During the next year the stock market continued to fall. The banks that had loaned people money with which to speculate in the market suffered great losses.

The financial collapse of 1929 triggered the Great Depression in America, although there were other underlying domestic causes. Manufacturing firms had not made sufficient capital investment. The disproportionate amount of profits going to about 5 percent of the US population undermined the purchasing power of other consumers. Agriculture was in trouble. Finally, the economic difficulties in Europe and Latin America, which predated those in the United States, meant foreigners were less able to purchase American products.

The most pervasive problem of the Great Depression was unemployment. Joblessness hit unskilled workers first but then worked its way up the job ladder to touch factory and white-collar workers. As unemployment spread, small retail businesses suffered. In the major American manufacturing cities, hundreds of thousands of workers could not find jobs. The price of corn fell so low in some areas that it was not profitable to harvest it. By the early 1930s, banks began to fail, and people lost their savings.

The federal government was not equipped to address the emergency. There was no tradition of federal action to alleviate economic distress. President Hoover organized economic conferences and encouraged the Federal Reserve to make borrowing easier. He supported the ill-advised Hawley-Smoot Tariff Act of 1930, which hoped to protect American industry by a high tariff barrier. Hoover believed relief was a matter for local government and voluntary organizations; however, many local relief agencies had run out of money by 1931.

New Role for Government

The election of 1932 was one of the most crucial in American history. The Democrat Franklin Delano Roosevelt (1882–1945) promised a "new deal for the American people." He overwhelmingly defeated Hoover, and quickly redirected federal policy toward the Depression.

Roosevelt had been born into a moderately wealthy New York family and was a distant cousin of Theodore Roosevelt (1858–1919). After serving in World War I as Assistant Secretary of the Navy, in 1920 he ran as the Democratic vice-presidential candidate. The next year, however, he was struck with polio and his legs became paralyzed, but he went on to be elected governor of New York in 1928. As president he attempted to convey to the nation the same kind of optimistic spirit that had informed his own struggle of the 1920s.

Roosevelt's first goal was to give the nation a sense that the federal government was meeting the economic challenge. The first hundred days of his administration became legendary. He immediately closed all the banks and permitted only sound institutions to reopen. Congress rapidly passed a new banking act and then enacted the Agricultural Adjustment Act and the Farm Credit Act to aid the farmers. To provide jobs, Roosevelt sponsored the Civilian Conservation Corps. The Federal Emergency Relief Act funded state and local relief agencies. To restore confidence, Roosevelt began making speeches, known as "fireside chats," to the American people.

Roosevelt's most ambitious program was the National Industrial Recovery Act (NIRA), which established the National Recovery Administration (NRA). This agency attempted to foster codes written by various industries to regulate wages and prices to monitor competition and thus protect jobs and assure production.

The NIRA and other New Deal legislation, such as the Wagner Act of 1935, which established the National Labor Relations Board and the Fair Labor Standards Act of 1938, provided a larger role in the American economy for organized labor. It became easier for unions to organize. Union membership grew, and American unionism took on a new character. Most unions had been organized by craft and were affiliated with the American Federation of Labor (AFL). In the 1930s, however, whole industries composed of workers in various crafts were organized in a single union. The most important of these organizations were the United Mine Workers and United Automobile Workers. These new unions organized themselves into the Congress of Industrial Organizations (CIO). The CIO and the AFL merged in the 1950s. These strong industrial labor organizations introduced a new force into the American economic scene.

In 1935, the US Supreme Court declared the NRA unconstitutional. Thereafter, Roosevelt deemphasized centralized economic planning. The number of federal agencies increased, but they operated in general independence from each other.

Through New Deal legislation, the federal government was far more active in the economy than it had ever been. The government itself attempted to provide relief for the unemployed in the industrial sector. The major institution of the relief effort was the Works Progress Administration. Created in 1935, the WPA began a massive program of public works.

The programs of the New Deal years also involved the federal government directly in economic development rather than turning such development over to private enterprise. Through the Tennessee Valley Authority (TVA), the government became directly involved in the economy of the four states of the Tennessee River valley. The TVA built dams and then produced and sold hydroelectricity. Never had the government undertaken so extensive an economic role. Another major new function for the government was providing security for the elderly, through the establishment of the Social Security Administration in 1935.

In one area of American life after another, it was decided that the government must provide personal economic security. These actions established a mixed economy in the United States—that is, one in which the federal government would play an active role alongside the private sector.

Yet the New Deal did not solve the unemployment problem. In the late 1930s, the economy began to falter again. Only the entry of the nation into World War II brought the US economy to full employment.

The experience of the United States under the New Deal stood in marked contrast to the economic and political experiments in Europe. Many business people found Roosevelt too liberal and his policies too activist. Nonetheless, the New Deal preserved capitalism in a democratic setting, where, again in contrast to Europe, there was free political debate—much of it critical of the administration. The United States had demonstrated that a nation with a vast industrial economy could confront its gravest economic crisis and still preserve democracy.

IN WORLD PERSPECTIVE

The Economic and Political Crisis

The two decades between the great wars were a period of transition around the globe. Many regions endured political turmoil and economic instability, followed by the establishment of authoritarian regimes. In Italy it was the fascists; in Germany, the Nazis; in the Soviet Union, Stalin's regime. In East Asia, Japan had a right-wing militaristic government. China saw over twenty years of civil war and revolution. Most of Latin America came under the sway of dictators or governments influenced by the military. In the late 1930s, the day of liberal parliamentary democracy appeared to be ending. The disruptions arising from World War I and the Depression seemed to pose problems that liberal governments could not address.

The interwar period also departed from the nineteenth-century ideal of economies in which central governments assumed little responsibility. The German inflation of the early 1920s, the worldwide financial collapse of the late 1920s, the vast unemployment of the early 1930s, and the agricultural crisis of both decades roused demands for government action. One reason for these demands was that more governments throughout the world were responsible to mass electorates. Governments that did not seek to address the problems were put out of office. This happened to the Republicans in the United States, the socialist and liberal parties in Germany, the left-wing parties in Japan, and various political parties in Latin America that failed to deal with the Depression. Paradoxically, many democratic electorates turned themselves over to authoritarian regimes as they searched for social and economic stability. That would be an important lesson in the years after World War II. Then, in response to the experience of the 1920s and 1930s, democratic governments around the globe would seek to provide economic and social security to protect democracy.

The authoritarian governments of Germany, Italy, and Japan all had agendas of nationalistic aggression. They were prepared to move wherever they saw fellow nationals living outside their borders or where they could become imperial powers. Japan moved against Manchuria and other areas of Asia. Italy invaded Ethiopia. Germany sought union with Germans in Austria and Czechoslovakia and then sought to expand throughout eastern Europe. Those actions challenged the imperial dominance of Great Britain and the security of the United States. By the end of the 1930s, the authoritarian regimes and the liberal democracies stood on the brink of a major confrontation.

During these years, the United States and the Soviet Union remained relatively withdrawn from the world scene. The former pursued the democratic experiment of the New Deal, while the latter underwent the equally bold experiment of central-government planning and repression. The aggression of other powers would draw the United States and the Soviet Union directly into the world conflict. Because of their vast economic resources, they would emerge as the two strongest postwar powers. The United States attained that economic role through democracy, the Soviet Union through repression. The relative virtues of those two modes of political and social life would form the issues on which much of the postwar great power rivalry would center.

Review Questions

1. Explain the causes of the Great Depression. Why was it more severe and why did it last longer than previous economic downturns? Could it have been avoided?

2. How did Stalin achieve supreme power in the Soviet Union? Why did he decide that Russia had to industrialize rapidly? Why did this require the collectivization of agriculture? Was the policy a success? How did it affect the Russian people? What were the causes of the great purges?

3. Why was Italy unstable after World War I? How did Mussolini achieve power? What were the characteristics of the fascist state?

4. Why did the Weimar Republic collapse in Germany? Which groups in Germany supported Hitler and why were they pro-Nazi? How did he consolidate his power?

5. What characteristics did the authoritarian regimes in the Soviet Union, Italy, and Germany have in common?

6. Why did the US economy collapse in 1929? How did Roosevelt combat the Depression? How did his policies affect the role of the federal government?

Documents CD-ROM

1. V. I. Lenin: "Tasks of the Youth Leagues": Bourgeois and Communist Morality

2. Nodezhda K. Krupskaya: "What a Communist Ought to Be Like"

3. Anna Akhmatova: *Requiem*

4. Benito Mussolini: From "The Political and Social Doctrine of Fascism"

5. Franklin Delano Roosevelt: Praising the First Hundred Days and Boosting the NRA

35 WORLD WAR II

The more idealistic survivors of the First World War, especially in the United States and Britain, thought of it as "the war to end all wars" and "a war to make the world safe for democracy." Only thus could they justify the slaughter, expense, and upheaval. Yet only twenty years after the peace treaties, a second great war broke out that was more truly global than the first. In this war, the democracies would be fighting for their lives against militaristic, nationalistic, authoritarian, and totalitarian states in Europe and Asia. Britain and the United States would be allied with the Communist Soviet Union. The defeat of the militarists and dictators would lead to a Cold War in which the European states became second-class powers, subordinate to the Soviet Union and the United States.

The Road to War (1933–1939)

Hitler's Goals

The Nazi destruction of political opposition meant that German foreign policy lay in Hitler's hands. From first to last, Hitler's racial theories and goals were central in his thought. He intended to bring the entire German people (*Volk*), understood as a racial group, together into a single nation. The new Germany would include all the Germanic parts of the old Habsburg Empire, including Austria. This virile nation would need more space to live (*Lebensraum*), which would be taken from the Slavs, a lesser race. The new Germany would be purified by the removal of the Jews, the most inferior race in Nazi theory. The plan required the conquest of Poland and the Ukraine to settle Germans and provide badly needed food. However, neither *Mein Kampf* nor later statements of policy were blueprints for action. Hitler exploited opportunities as they arose. But he never lost sight of his goal, which would almost certainly require a major war.

Destruction of Versailles

When Hitler came to power, Germany was weak. The first problem was to shake off the fetters of Versailles and make Germany a formidable military power. In October 1933, Germany withdrew from an international disarmament conference and from the League of Nations. These acts were merely symbolic, but in March 1935, Hitler renounced the disarmament provisions of the Versailles Treaty with the formation of a German air force. Soon he reinstated conscription, which aimed at an army of half a million men.

His path was made easier because the League of Nations was ineffective. In September 1931, Japan occupied Manchuria. China appealed to the league, which condemned the Japanese for resorting to force. But the powers would not impose sanctions. Japan withdrew from the league and kept Manchuria.

The league condemned Hitler's decision to rearm Germany, but took no steps to prevent it. France and Britain met with Mussolini in June 1935 to form the so-called Stresa Front and agreed to maintain the status quo in Europe by force if necessary. But Britain was desperate to maintain superiority at sea. Contrary to the Stresa accords, Britain soon made a separate naval agreement with Hitler, allowing him to rebuild the German fleet to 35 percent of the British navy.

Italy Attacks Ethiopia

The Italian attack on Ethiopia in October 1935 made the impotence of the League of Nations and the timidity of the Allies even clearer. Using a border incident as an excuse, Mussolini's intent was to avenge a humiliating defeat that the Italians had suffered in 1896 and perhaps to divert Italians from fascist corruption and Italy's economic troubles.

The League of Nations voted economic sanctions and imposed an arms embargo. But Britain and France were afraid of alienating Mussolini, so they refused to place an embargo on oil, the one economic sanction that could have prevented Italian victory. Nor did the British prevent the movement of Italian troops and munitions through the Suez Canal. This wavering policy was disastrous. The League of Nations and collective security were discredited, and Mussolini turned to Germany.

Remilitarization of the Rhineland

On March 7, 1936, Hitler took his greatest risk yet, sending a small armed force into the demilitarized Rhineland. This was a breach of the Versailles Treaty and of the Locarno Agreements. It also removed an important element of French security. Yet Britain and France made only a feeble protest.

A Germany that was rapidly rearming and had a defensible western frontier presented a new problem to the western powers. Their response was "appeasement." It was based on the assumption that Germany had real grievances, that Hitler's goals were limited, and that the correct policy was to make concessions before a crisis could lead to war. Behind this approach was the horror of another war. As Germany armed, the French huddled behind their defensive wall, the Maginot Line, and the British hoped for the best.

The Spanish Civil War

The new European alignment that found the western democracies on one side and the fascist states on the other was made clearer by the Spanish Civil War, which broke out in July 1936. In 1931, the Spaniards had established a republic. Elections in February 1936 brought to power a government of the left. The defeated groups, especially the falangists, the Spanish version of fascists, would not accept defeat at the polls. In July, General Francisco Franco (1892–1975) led an army against the republic.

Thus began a civil war that lasted almost three years. Germany and Italy aided Franco with troops and supplies. The Soviet Union sent equipment and advisers to the republicans. Leftists from Europe and America volunteered to fight against fascism.

The civil war, fought on ideological lines, brought Germany and Italy closer together, leading to the Rome-Berlin Axis Pact in 1936. They were joined in the same year by Japan in the Anti-Comintern Pact, ostensibly against communism. In western Europe, the appeasement mentality reigned. By early 1939, the fascists had won control of Spain.

Austria and Czechoslovakia

In 1934, Mussolini, not yet allied with Hitler, had frustrated a Nazi coup in Austria by threatening military intervention. In March 1938, the new diplomatic situation encouraged Hitler to try again. Mussolini made no objection, and Hitler marched into Vienna to the cheers of his Austrian sympathizers.

The *Anschluss*, or union of Germany and Austria, had great strategic significance. Czechoslovakia was now surrounded by Germany on three sides. It was allied both to France and the Soviet Union but contained about 3.5 million ethnic Germans who lived in the Sudetenland near the German border. Supported by Hitler, they agitated for privileges and autonomy within the Czech state. The Czechs made concessions; but Hitler's motivation was to destroy Czechoslovakia.

The French, as usual, deferred to British leadership. The British prime minister Neville Chamberlain (1869–1940) was determined not to allow Britain to go to war again. In September 1938, German intervention seemed imminent. Chamberlain sought to appease Hitler at Czech expense and avoid war. But Hitler wanted the immediate occupation of the Sudetenland by the German army.

Munich

France and Britain prepared for war. At the last moment, Mussolini proposed a conference of Germany, Italy, France, and Britain. It met on September 29 at Munich. Hitler received almost everything he had demanded. The Sudetenland became part of Germany, thus depriving the Czechs of any chance of self-defense. In return, the rest of Czechoslovakia was spared. Hitler promised, "I have no more territorial demands to make in Europe." Chamberlain told a cheering crowd that "I believe it is peace for our time."

Soon, however, Poland and Hungary tore bits of territory from Czechoslovakia, and the Slovaks demanded autonomy. Finally, on March 15, 1939, Hitler broke his promise and occupied Prague, putting an end to Czech independence. Munich remains an example of short-sighted policy that helped bring on a war in disadvantageous circumstances as a result of the very fear of war and the failure to prepare for it.

Hitler's occupation of Prague discredited appeasement in Britain. Poland was the next target of German expansion. In the spring of 1939, the Germans put pressure on Poland to restore the formerly German city of Danzig and allow a railroad and a highway through the Polish Corridor to connect East Prussia with the rest of Germany. When the Poles would not yield, the pressure mounted. On March 31, Chamberlain announced a Franco-British guarantee of Polish independence. Hitler did not take the guarantee seriously. He knew that both countries were unprepared for war and that much of their populations opposed war for Poland.

Moreover, France and Britain could not get effective help to the Poles. The only way to defend Poland was to bring Russia into the alliance against Hitler, but a Russian alliance posed problems. Each side was suspicious of the other. The French and British were hostile to communism, and since Stalin's purge of the officer corps of the Red Army, they questioned Russia's military abilities. Besides, both Poland and Romania were suspicious of Russian intentions—with good reason. As a result, western negotiations with Russia were slow and cautious.

The Nazi-Soviet Pact

The Russians resented being left out of the Munich agreement and were annoyed by the low priority that the west seemed to give to negotiations with Russia. They feared, rightly, that the western powers meant them to bear the burden of the war against Germany. As a result, they opened negotiations with Hitler, and on August 23, 1939, the world was shocked to learn of a Nazi-Soviet nonaggression pact. Its secret provisions divided Poland between them and allowed Russia to annex the Baltic states and take Bessarabia from Romania. Communist parties in the west changed their line overnight from advocating resistance to Hitler to a policy of peace and quiet.

The Nazi-Soviet Pact sealed the fate of Poland. On September 1, 1939, the Germans invaded Poland. Two days later, Britain and France declared war on Germany. World War II had begun.

World War II (1939–1945)

German Conquest of Europe

The speed of the German victory over Poland astonished everyone, and the Russians hastened to collect their share of the booty before Hitler could deprive them of it. On September 17 they invaded Poland from the east, dividing the country with the Germans. They then absorbed Estonia, Latvia, and Lithuania. In November 1940, the Russians invaded Finland, but the Finns fought back and retained their independence.

Meanwhile, the western front was quiet. The French remained behind the Maginot Line. Britain imposed the traditional naval blockade. Cynics in the west called it the phony war, but in April 1940, the Germans invaded Denmark and Norway. A month later, a combined land and air attack struck the Low Countries. The Dutch surrendered in a few days, and the Belgians less than two weeks later. The British and French armies in Belgium were forced to flee to the English Channel to seek escape from the beaches of Dunkirk. Over 200,000 British and 100,000 French soldiers were saved, but valuable equipment was abandoned.

The Maginot Line ran from Switzerland to the Belgian frontier. Hitler's swift advance through Belgium therefore circumvented France's main line of defense. The French army, poorly led, collapsed. Mussolini attacked France on June 10, though without success. Less than a week later, the French government, under the ancient hero of Verdun, Henri Philippe Pétain (1856–1951), asked for an armistice.

The terms of the armistice, signed June 22, 1940, allowed the Germans to occupy more than half of France, including the Atlantic and English Channel coasts. To prevent the French from fleeing to North Africa to continue the fight, Hitler left southern France unoccupied. Pétain set up a dictatorial regime at the resort city of Vichy and collaborated with the Germans to preserve as much autonomy as possible. The French were too stunned to resist. Many thought that Hitler's victory was certain and saw no alternative to collaboration. A few, notably General Charles de Gaulle (1890–1969), fled to Britain and organized the French National Committee of Liberation, or "Free French." As expectations of a quick German victory faded, French resistance arose.

Battle of Britain

Hitler expected the British to come to terms. Any chance that the British would consider terms disappeared when Winston Churchill (1874–1965) replaced Chamberlain as prime minister in May 1940.

Churchill established a close relationship with the American president Franklin D. Roosevelt. In 1940 and 1941, before the United States was at war, America sent military supplies and even convoyed ships across the Atlantic to help the British survive.

As Britain remained defiant, Hitler was forced to contemplate an invasion, which required control of the air. The German air force (*Luftwaffe*) destroyed much of London, and about 15,000 people were killed. But the Royal Air Force (RAF), aided by the newly developed radar, inflicted heavy losses on the *Luftwaffe*. Hitler was forced to abandon his plans for invasion.

German Attack on Russia

Operation Barbarossa, the code name for the invasion of Russia, was aimed at knocking Russia out of the war before winter could set in. Success depended in part on an early start, but here Hitler's Italian alliance proved costly. Mussolini had launched an attack against the British in Egypt and also invaded Greece. But in North Africa the British counterattacked and drove into Libya, and the Greeks repulsed the Italians. In March 1941, the British sent help to the Greeks, and Hitler was forced to divert his attention to the Balkans and to Africa. General Erwin Rommel (1891–1944) soon drove the British back into Egypt. In the Balkans, the German army occupied Yugoslavia and crushed Greek resistance, but the price was a delay of six weeks for Barbarossa. This proved to be costly the following winter.

Operation Barbarossa was launched against Russia on June 22, 1941, and it almost succeeded. Stalin panicked. By November, the German army stood at the gates of Leningrad, on the outskirts of Moscow, and on the Don River. A German victory seemed imminent.

But the Germans could not deliver the final blow before winter struck the German army, which was not equipped to face it. In November and December, the Russians counterattacked. The *Blitzkrieg* had turned into a war of attrition.

Hitler's Europe: The Holocaust

The demands of war and Hitler's defeat prevented him from fully carrying out his plans. But the measures he took before his death give evidence of a regime unmatched in history for planned terror and inhumanity. Hitler regarded the conquered lands merely as a source of plunder and slave labor. But the most horrible aspect of the Nazi rule in Europe arose from the inhumanity inherent in Hitler's racial doctrines. He considered the Slavs *Untermenschen*, subhuman creatures like beasts. In Poland, the upper and professional classes were jailed, deported, or killed, and harsh living conditions were imposed. In Russia, things were even worse. Hitler spoke of his Russian campaign as a war of extermination. The SS formed extermination squads to eliminate 30 million Slavs

Coming of World War II		
1919	June, Versailles Treaty	
1923	January, France occupies the Ruhr	
1925	October, Locarno Agreements	
1931	Spring, Onset of Great Depression in Europe	
1933	January, Hitler comes to power	
	October, Germany withdraws from League of Nations	
1935	March, Hitler renounces disarmament, starts an air force, and begins conscription	
	October, Mussolini attacks Ethiopia	
1936	March, Germany reoccupies and remilitarizes the Rhineland	
	July, Outbreak of Spanish Civil War	
	October, Formation of the Rome-Berlin Axis	
1938	March, *Anschluss* with Austria	
	September, Munich Conference and partition of Czechoslovakia	
1939	March, Hitler occupies Prague; France and Great Britain guarantee Polish independence	
	August, Nazi-Soviet pact	
	September 1, Germany invades Poland	
	September 3, Britain and France declare war on Germany	

to make room for the Germans. Some 6 million Russian prisoners of war and civilians may have died under Nazi rule.

Hitler meant to make Europe *Judenrein* ("free of Jews"). Eventually he decided on the "final solution of the Jewish problem": extermination. The Nazis built extermination camps in Germany and Poland and killed millions of men, women, and children just because they were Jews. Before the war was over, 6 million Jews had died in what is called the Holocaust.

America's Entry into the War

The war took on global proportions in 1941. On Sunday morning, December 7, 1941, even while Japanese representatives were negotiating in Washington, Japan launched an air attack on Pearl Harbor, Hawaii, the chief American naval base in the Pacific. (see Chapter 32.) The next day, the United States and Britain declared war on Japan. Three days later, Germany and Italy declared war on the United States.

The Tide Turns

Its potential power was enormous, but America was ill prepared for war. The army was tiny, inexperienced, and poorly supplied. American industry was not ready for war. By the summer of 1942, the Japanese Empire stretched from the Aleutian Islands south almost to Australia, and from Burma east to the Gilbert Islands in the mid-Pacific (see Map 35–1).

An Observer Describes the Mass Murder of Jews in Ukraine

After World War II some German officers and officials were put on trial at Nuremberg by the victorious powers for crimes they were charged with having committed in the course of the war. The following selections from the testimony of a German construction engineer who witnessed the mass murder of Jews at Dubno in the Ukraine on October 5, 1942, reveal the brutality with which Hitler's attempt at a "final solution of the Jewish problem" was carried out.

Why did the German government commit these atrocities? Why were they directed chiefly at Jews? Was there a cost to Germany in pursuing such a policy? Why did ordinary Germans participate?

On October 5, 1942, when I visited the building office at Dubno, my foreman told me that in the vicinity of the site, Jews from Dubno had been shot in three large pits, each about 30 metres long and 3 metres deep. About 1,500 persons had been killed daily. All the 5,000 Jews who had still been living in Dubno before the pogrom were to be liquidated. As the shooting had taken place in his presence, he was still much upset.

Thereupon, I drove to the site accompanied by my foreman and saw near it great mounds of earth, about 30 metres long and 2 metres high. Several trucks stood in front of the mounds. Armed Ukrainian militia drove the people off the trucks under the supervision of an S.S. man. The militiamen acted as guards on the trucks and drove them to and from the pit. All these people had the regulation yellow patches on the front and back of their clothes, and thus could be recognized as Jews.

My foreman and I went directly to the pits. Nobody bothered us. Now I heard rifle shots in quick succession from behind one of the earth mounds. The people who had got off the trucks—men, women and children of all ages—had to undress upon the orders of an S.S. man, who carried a riding or dog whip. They had to put down their clothes in fixed places, sorted according to shoes, top clothing and underclothing. I saw a heap of shoes of about 800 to 1,000 pairs, great piles of underlinen and clothing.

Without screaming or weeping, these people undressed, stood around in family groups, kissed each other, said farewells, and waited for a sign from another S.S. man, who stood near the pit, also with a whip in his hand. During the fifteen minutes that I stood near I heard no complaint or plea for mercy. I watched a family of about eight persons, a man and a woman both about fifty with their children of about one, eight and ten, and two grown-up daughters of about twenty to twenty-nine. An old woman with snow-white hair was holding the one-year-old child in her arms and singing to it and tickling it. The child was cooing with delight. The couple were looking on with tears in their eyes. The father was holding the hand of a boy about ten years old and speaking to him softly; the boy was fighting his tears. The father pointed to the sky, stroked his head, and seemed to explain something to him.

At that moment the S.S. man at the pit shouted something to his comrade. The latter counted off about twenty persons and instructed them to go behind the earth mound. Among them was the family which I have mentioned. I well remember a girl, slim and with black hair, who, as she passed close to me pointed to herself and said "23." I walked around the mound and found myself confronted by a tremendous grave. People were closely wedged together and lying on top of each other so that only their heads were visible. Nearly all had blood running over their shoulders from their heads. Some of the people shot were still moving. Some were lifting their arms and turning their heads to show that they were still alive. The pit was already two-third full. I estimated that it already contained about 1,000 people.

From the *Nuremberg Proceedings*, as quoted in Louis L. Snyder, *Documents of German History.* © 1958 by Rutgers, The State University, pp. 462–464. Reprinted by permission of Rutgers University Press.

In the same year, the Germans almost reached the Caspian Sea. In Africa, Rommel drove the British back toward the Suez Canal. Relations between the democracies and their Soviet ally were not close; German submarines were threatening British supplies.

The tide turned at the Battle of Midway in June 1942. American planes destroyed four Japanese aircraft carriers. Soon American Marines landed on Guadalcanal in the Solomon Islands and began to reverse the momentum of the war. Japan was checked sufficiently to allow the Allies to concentrate their efforts first in the West.

Allied Landings in Africa, Sicily, and Italy In November 1942, an Allied force landed in French North Africa. Even before that landing, the British Field Marshal Bernard Montgomery (1887–1976), after stopping Rommel at El Alamein, had begun a drive to the west. The American general Dwight D. Eisenhower (1890–1969) pushed eastward through Morocco and Algeria. The German army was trapped in Tunisia and crushed. In July and August 1943, the Allies took Sicily. Mussolini was driven from power, the Allies landed in Italy, and Marshal Pietro Badoglio (1871–1956), the leader of the new Italian government, declared war on Germany. German resis-

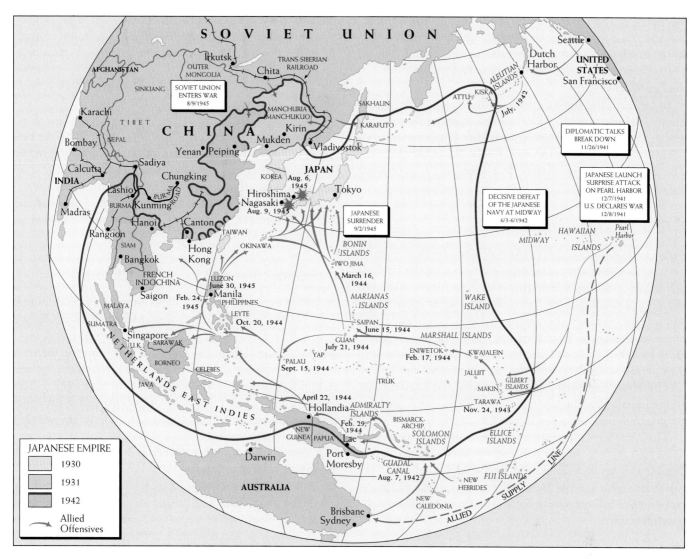

Map 35–1 The war in the Pacific.   As in Europe, the Allies initially had trouble recapturing areas that the Japanese had quickly seized early in the war. The map shows the initial expansion of the Japanese and the long struggle of the Allies to push them back to their homeland and defeat them.

tance in Italy was tough and determined, but the need to defend it further strained the Germans' energy and resources.

Stalingrad

The Russian campaign became especially demanding. In the summer of 1942, the Germans resumed the offensive. Their goal was the oil fields near the Caspian Sea, and they got as far as Stalingrad on the Volga. Hitler was determined to take the city and Stalin to hold it. The Battle of Stalingrad raged for months. The Russians lost more men than the Americans lost in combat during the entire war, but their defenses prevailed. Hitler overruled his generals and would not allow a retreat. An entire German army was lost.

Stalingrad marked the turning point of the Russian campaign. Thereafter, as German resources dwindled, the Russians advanced westward inexorably.

Strategic Bombing

In 1943, the Allies also gained ground in production and logistics. The industrial might of the United States came into play. New technology and tactics began eliminating the submarine menace. In the same year, the American and British air forces began massive bombardments of Germany by night and day. In 1944, the Americans introduced long-range fighters that could protect the bombers and allow accurate missions by day. By 1945, the Allies could bomb at will.

Defeat of Nazi Germany

On June 6, 1944 (D-Day), Allied troops landed in Normandy (see Map 35–2). By September, France had been liberated. In December, the Germans launched a counterattack called the Battle of the Bulge through the Forest of Ardennes. It was their last gasp. The Allies recovered and crossed the Rhine in March 1945. German resistance crumbled. There could be no doubt that the Germans had lost the war on the battlefield.

In the east, the Russians were within reach of Berlin by March 1945. Because the Allies insisted on unconditional surrender, the Germans fought on until May. Hitler committed suicide in an underground hideaway in Berlin on May 1, 1945. The Russians occupied Berlin. The Third Reich had lasted only a dozen years.

Fall of the Japanese Empire

The war in Europe ended on May 8, 1945. By then victory over Japan was in sight. The Japanese attack on the United States had been a calculated risk. The longer the war lasted, the greater the impact of American superiority in industry and human resources. Beginning in 1943, American forces began a campaign of "island hopping," selecting places strategically located along the enemy supply line. Relentlessly, they moved northeast toward the Japanese homeland. American bombers destroyed Japanese industry and disabled the Japanese navy. But the Japanese government, dominated by a military clique, refused to surrender.

The Americans made plans for an assault on the Japanese homeland, which, they calculated, would cost huge casualties. At this point, science and technology presented the Americans with another choice. Since early in the war a secret program had been working to use atomic energy for military purposes.

On August 6, 1945, an American plane dropped an atomic bomb on the city of Hiroshima. More than 70,000 of its 200,000 residents were killed. Two days later, the Soviet Union declared war on Japan and invaded Manchuria. The next day, a second atomic bomb fell on Nagasaki. The Japanese were still prepared to face an invasion, but Emperor Hirohito (r. 1926–1989) forced the government to surrender on August 14. Even then, the Cabinet made the condition that Japan could keep its emperor. President Harry S. Truman (1884–1972), who had come to office on April 12, 1945, on the death of Franklin D. Roosevelt, accepted the condition. Peace was formally signed on September 2, 1945.

The Cost of War

World War II was the most terrible war in history. Military deaths are estimated at 15 million, and at least as many civilians were killed. If deaths linked indirectly to the war are included, 40 million may have died. Most of Europe and parts of Asia were devastated. Yet the end of the war brought little opportunity for relaxation. The dawn of the Atomic Age

made people conscious that another major war might destroy humanity. Everything depended on the conclusion of a stable peace, but the victors soon quarreled.

The Domestic Fronts

World War II represented an effort of total war by all the belligerents. One result was the carnage that occurred in the fighting. Another was an unprecedented organization of civilians on the various home fronts. Each domestic effort and experience was different, but few escaped the impact of the conflict. Shortages, propaganda, and new political developments were ubiquitous.

Germany: From Victory to Defeat

Hitler had expected to defeat all his enemies by rapid strokes, or *blitzkrieg*. Such campaigns would scarcely have affected Germany's society and economy. During the first two years of the war, Hitler demanded few sacrifices from the German people. Spending on domestic projects continued; food was plentiful; the economy was not on a full wartime footing. The failure to knock out the Soviet Union changed everything. Germany had to mobilize for total war, and the government demanded major sacrifices.

A great expansion of the army and military production began in 1942. Albert Speer (1905–1981) guided the economy, and Germany met its military needs instead of making consumer goods. German businesses aided the growth of wartime production. Between 1942 and late 1944, the output of military products tripled; but as the war went on, the army absorbed more men from industry, hurting the production of even military goods.

Beginning in 1942, everyday products became scarce. The standard of living fell. Food rationing began in April 1942, and shortages were severe until the Nazi government seized food from occupied Europe. To preserve their own home front, the Nazis passed on the suffering to their defeated neighbors.

By 1943, there were serious labor shortages. The Nazis required German teenagers and the elderly to work in the factories, and many women joined them. To achieve total mobilization, the Germans closed retail businesses, made more women do compulsory service, shifted non-German domestic workers to wartime industry, moved artists and entertainers into military service, closed theaters, and reduced basic public services. Finally, the Nazis forced thousands of people from conquered lands to labor in Germany.

Hitler assigned women a special place in the war effort. The celebration of motherhood continued, with an emphasis on the mothers of military figures. Films portrayed ordinary women who became brave and patriotic during the war

The Axis
Allied with the Axis
Occupied by the Axis
1 AXIS TROOPS OCCUPY VICHY FRANCE, NOV. 10 and 11, 1942.
2 AXIS TROOPS EVACUATED, MAY, 1943
3 ALLIES INVADE SICILY & ITALY, JULY–SEPT., 1943
4 ITALIAN SURRENDER SEPT. 8, 1943
5 NORMANDY INVASION JUNE 5, 1944
6 RUSSIAN FRONT JUNE 23, 1944
7 ALLIES LAND IN PROVENCE AUG. 15, 1944
8 BATTLE OF THE BULGE DEC., 1944
9 RHINE CROSSING, MARCH 7, 1945
10 GERMAN SURRENDER IN REIMS, MAY 7, 1945 AND BERLIN MAY 8, 1945
FARTHEST AXIS ADVANCE, DEC., 1941
FARTHEST AXIS ADVANCE, NOV., 1942
ATLANTIC OCEAN
North Sea
Baltic Sea
Black Sea
Mediterranean Sea
Adriatic Sea
Caspian Sea
EIRE
UNITED KINGDOM
NORWAY
SWEDEN
FINLAND
DENMARK
NETH.
BELG.
FRANCE
SPAIN
SWITZ.
ITALY
GREATER GERMANY
AUSTRIA
HUNGARY
SLOVAKIA
ROMANIA
BULGARIA
YUGOSLAVIA
ALBANIA
GREECE
SOVIET UNION
UKRAINE
BYELORUSSIA
ESTONIA
LATVIA
LITHUANIA
EAST PRUSSIA
POSEN
BOHEMIA
MORAVIA
CROATIA
SERBIA
MONTE-NEGRO
BESSARABIA
CRIMEA
TRANSCAUCASUS
IRAN
IRAQ
SYRIA
LEBANON
ALGERIA (VICHY)
TUNISIA (VICHY)
CORSICA (VICHY)
SARDINIA
SICILY
CALABRIA
CRETE
RHODES
CYPRUS (U.K.)
MALTA (U.K.)
TYROL
Kuibyshev (Wartime Capital)
300 MILES
300 KILOMETERS

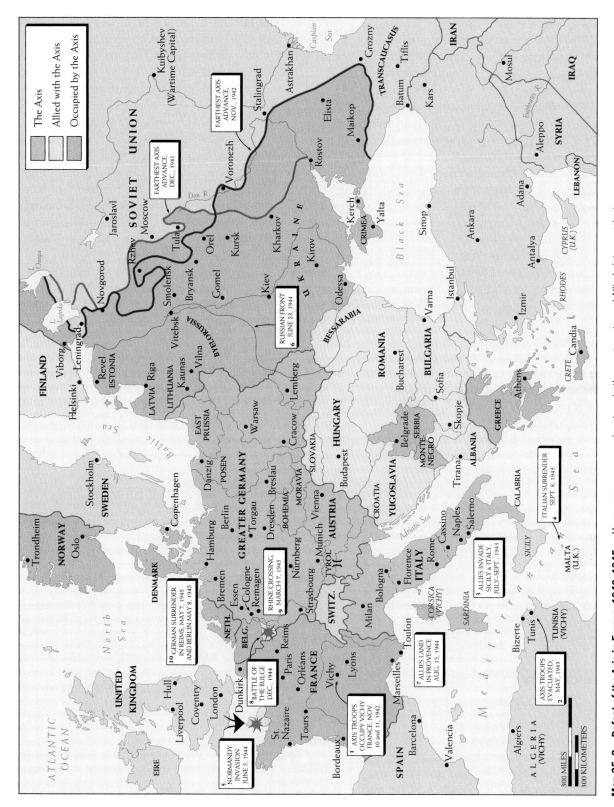

Map 35–2 Defeat of the Axis in Europe, 1942–1945. Here we see some major steps in the progress toward Allied victory against Axis Europe. From the south through Italy, the west through France, and the east through Russia, the Allies gradually conquered the continent to bring the war in Europe to a close.

and remained faithful to their soldier husbands. The government portrayed other wartime activities of women as the natural fulfillment of their maternal roles. As air raid wardens they protected their families; as workers in munitions plants they aided their sons on the front lines. Women working on farms were feeding their soldier sons and husbands; as housewives they were helping to win the war by managing their households frugally. Finally, by their faithful chastity, German women were protecting racial purity.

The war years also saw an intensification of political propaganda. The Nazis believed that weak domestic support had led to Germany's defeat in World War I, and they were determined that this would not happen again. Propaganda Minister Josef Goebbels (1897–1945) used radio and films to boost the Nazi cause. Movies demonstrated German military might. As the German armies were checked on the battlefield, especially in Russia, propaganda became a substitute for victory. The propaganda also aimed to frighten the German population about the consequences of defeat.

After May 1943, when the Allies began their major bombing offensive over Germany, one German city after another endured bombing, fires, and destruction. But the bombing did not undermine German morale—on the contrary, it may have confirmed the fear of defeat by such savage opponents and increased German resistance.

World War II brought increased power to the Nazi party. Every area of the economy and society came under its influence or control. The Nazis were determined that they, rather than the German officer corps, would profit from the new authority flowing to the central government because of the war effort. Throughout the war years there was little serious opposition to Hitler or his ministers. In 1944, a small group of army officers attempted to assassinate Hitler; they failed, and had no significant popular support.

The war brought great changes to Germany, but what transformed the country afterward was the experience of defeat accompanied by destruction, invasion, and occupation. A new state with new political structures emerged.

France: Collaboration and Resistance

In France, the Vichy government cooperated with the Germans for a variety of reasons. Some collaborators believed that the Germans were sure to win. A few sympathized with the ideas and plans of the Nazis. Many conservatives regarded the French defeat as a judgment on what they saw as the corrupt Third Republic. But most of the French were not active collaborators and remained demoralized by defeat.

Many conservatives and extreme rightists saw the Vichy government as a device to reshape the French national character and halt the decadence they associated with liberalism. The Roman Catholic clergy gained status under Vichy. The church supported Pétain; his government supported religious education. Vichy adopted the church's views of the importance of family and spiritual values. Divorce was made difficult; large families were rewarded.

The Vichy regime embraced a chauvinistic nationalism. It persecuted foreigners who were not regarded as genuinely French. The chief victims were French Jews. Anti-Semitism was not new in France. Even before Germany undertook Hitler's "final solution" in 1942, the French had begun to remove Jews from government, education, and publishing. In 1941, the Germans began to intern Jews living in occupied France. In 1942, they began deporting Jews, ultimately over 60,000, to the extermination camps. The Vichy government made no protest, and its own anti-Semitic policies facilitated the process.

Serious internal resistance to the German occupiers and the Vichy government developed only late in 1942. The Germans attempted to force young French people to work in German factories; some fled and joined the Resistance, but the total number of resisters was small. Many were deterred by fear. Some disliked the violence that resistance entailed. So long as it appeared that the Germans would win the war, moreover, resistance seemed imprudent and futile. In all, less than 5 percent of the adult French population appear to have been involved.

By early 1944, an Allied victory appeared inevitable, and the Vichy government was clearly doomed. Only then did an active resistance assert itself. From Algiers on August 9, 1944, the Committee of National Liberation declared the authority of Vichy illegitimate. French soldiers joined in the liberation of Paris and established a government for Free France. On October 21, 1945, France voted to adopt a new constitution as the basis of the Fourth Republic.

Great Britain: Organization for Victory

On May 22, 1940, Parliament gave the government emergency powers. The government could institute compulsory military service, food rationing, and economic controls.

Churchill and the British war cabinet mobilized the nation. By the end of 1941, British production had already surpassed Germany's. Factory hours were extended, and women were brought into the work force in great numbers. Unemployment disappeared, and the working classes had more money to spend than they had enjoyed for many years.

The bombing "blitz" conducted by the *Luftwaffe* against British cities from 1940 to 1941 was the most immediate and dramatic experience of the war for the British people. Many homes were destroyed; families removed their children to the countryside; more than 30,000 people were killed. This toll was much smaller than the number of Germans killed by Allied bombing. In England as in Germany, however, the bombing seems to have made the people more determined.

Winston Churchill cheered and encouraged the British people. They had to make many sacrifices: Transportation facilities were strained; food, clothing, and gasoline for civilians were in short supply.

The British established their own propaganda machine. The British Broadcasting Company (BBC) sent programs to every country in Europe to encourage resistance. At home the government used the radio to unify the nation. Soldiers heard the same programs as their families.

For most of the population the standard of living actually improved during the war, as did the general health of the nation. These gains should not be exaggerated, but many connected them with the active involvement of the government in the economy and the lives of the citizens. This wartime experience may have contributed to the Labour Party's victory in 1945; many feared that Conservative rule would revive the economic misery of the 1930s.

The Soviet Union: "The Great Patriotic War"

No nation suffered more deaths or destruction during World War II than the Soviet Union. Perhaps 16 million people were killed. Hundreds of cities and towns and well over half of the industrial and transportation facilities of the country were devastated.

In the decade before the war, Stalin had already made the Soviet Union a highly centralized nation (see Chapter 34). The country was thus on what amounted to a wartime footing long before the conflict erupted.

Soviet propaganda differed from that of other nations. Because the Soviet government distrusted the loyalty of its citizens, it confiscated radios. Instead, loudspeakers broadcast to the people. Soviet propaganda emphasized Russian patriotism: The struggle was called "The Great Patriotic War."

Stalin even made peace with the Russian Orthodox Church. He hoped that this would give him more support at home and make the Soviet Union more popular in eastern Europe where the Orthodox church predominated.

Within occupied portions of the Soviet Union, resistance arose against the Germans. The swiftness of the German invasion had stranded thousands of Soviet troops, some of whom escaped and carried on irregular warfare behind enemy lines. Stalin supported partisan forces for two reasons: He wanted to cause difficulty for the Germans; and the Soviet-sponsored resistance reminded the peasants in the conquered regions that the Soviet government had not disappeared. Stalin feared that the peasants' hatred of the communist government might lead them to collaborate with the invaders.

As the Soviet armies reclaimed the occupied areas and then moved across eastern and central Europe, the Soviet Union established itself as a world power second only to the United States. Stalin had been a reluctant belligerent, but he emerged a major victor. The war and the extraordinary patriotic effort and sacrifice it generated consolidated the power of Stalin and the party more effectively than had the political and social policies of the 1930s.

Preparations for Peace

The split between the Soviet Union and its wartime allies that followed the war should cause no surprise. As the self-proclaimed center of world communism, the Soviet Union was dedicated to the overthrow of the capitalist nations. The western allies were no less open about their hostility to communism and its chief purveyor, the Soviet Union.

Although cooperation against a common enemy and strenuous propaganda helped improve western feeling toward the Soviet ally, Stalin remained suspicious and critical of the western war effort. Likewise, Churchill never ceased planning to contain the Soviet advance into Europe. Roosevelt seems to have hoped that the Allies could continue to work together after the war. But even he was losing faith by 1945. Differences in historical development and ideology, as well as traditional conflicts over power and influence, dashed hopes of a satisfactory peace settlement and continued cooperation.

The Atlantic Charter

In August 1941, even before America entered the war, Roosevelt and Churchill had agreed to the Atlantic Charter. A broad set of principles in the spirit of Wilson's Fourteen Points, it provided a theoretical basis for the peace they sought. When Russia and the United States joined Britain in the war, the three powers entered a military alliance, leaving political questions aside. In Moscow in October 1943, their foreign ministers reaffirmed earlier agreements to fight on until the enemy surrendered unconditionally and to continue cooperating after the war in a united-nations organization.

Tehran

The first meeting of the three leaders took place at Tehran, the capital of Iran, in 1943. Western promises to open a second front in France the next summer (1944) and Stalin's agreement to join in the war against Japan (when Germany was defeated) created an atmosphere of goodwill in which to discuss a postwar settlement. Stalin wanted to retain what he had gained in his pact with Hitler and to dismember Germany. Roosevelt and Churchill made no firm commitments. The most important decision was for the western allies to attack Germany from Europe's west coast. This decision meant, in retrospect, that Soviet forces would occupy eastern Europe and control its destiny. At Tehran in 1943, the western allies did not foresee this clearly, for the Russians were still fighting deep within their own frontiers.

But by August 1944, Soviet armies were in sight of Warsaw, which had risen in expectation of liberation. But the Russians allowed the Polish rebels to be annihilated. The Russians also gained control of Romania and Hungary. Alarmed by these developments, Churchill went to Moscow and met with Stalin in October. They agreed to share power in the Balkans on the basis of Soviet predominance in Romania and Bulgaria, western predominance in Greece, and equality of influence in Yugoslavia and Hungary. But the Americans were hostile to such un-Wilsonian devices as "spheres of influence."

The three powers agreed on Germany's disarmament and denazification and on its division into four zones of occupation by France and the Big Three (the USSR, Britain, and the United States). Churchill, however, began to balk at Stalin's plan to dismember Germany and to his demands for $20 billion in reparations and forced labor. These matters caused dissension in the future.

Eastern Europe remained a problem. Everyone agreed that the Soviet Union deserved neighboring governments that were friendly, but the West insisted that they also be independent and democratic. However, Stalin knew that freely elected governments in Poland and Romania would not be safely friendly to Russia. He had already established a subservient government in Poland. Under pressure, Stalin agreed to include some Poles friendly to the West. He also promised self-determination and free democratic elections. He probably thought it worth endorsing some meaningless principles as the price of continued harmony. In any case, he soon violated these agreements.

Yalta

The next meeting of the Big Three was at Yalta in the Crimea in February 1945. The western armies had not yet crossed the Rhine. The war with Japan continued, and no atomic explosion had yet taken place. Roosevelt, faced with an invasion of Japan and heavy losses, was eager to bring the Russians into the Pacific war.

As a true Wilsonian, Roosevelt also suspected Churchill's determination to maintain the British Empire. The Americans thought that Churchill's plan to set up British spheres of influence in Europe would encourage the Russians to do the same and lead to war. To encourage Russian participation in the war against Japan, Roosevelt and Churchill made extensive concessions to Russia in Asia. Again in the tradition of Wilson, Roosevelt wanted a United Nations. Soviet agreement on these points seemed well worth concessions elsewhere.

Potsdam

The Big Three met for the last time in the Berlin suburb of Potsdam in July 1945. Much had changed. Germany was defeated, and news of a successful atomic weapon reached the American president during the meetings. President Truman had replaced Roosevelt; and Clement Attlee (1883–1967), leader of the Labour Party, replaced Churchill during the conference. Progress on undecided questions was slow.

Russia's western frontier was moved far into what had been Poland and German East Prussia. In compensation, Poland was moved about a hundred miles west, at the expense of Germany. The Allies agreed that Germany would be divided into occupation zones until the final peace treaty was signed, and the country remained divided until the end of the Cold War more than forty years later.

A Council of Foreign Ministers was established to draft peace treaties for Germany's allies. Disagreements made the job difficult, and it was not until February 1947 that Italy, Romania, Hungary, Bulgaria, and Finland signed treaties. The Russians signed their own agreements with the Japanese in 1956.

IN WORLD PERSPECTIVE
World War II

The second great war of the twentieth century (1939–1945) grew out of the unsatisfactory resolution of the first. In retrospect, the two wars appear to some people to be one continuous conflict, with the two main periods of fighting separated by an uneasy truce. To others, that point of view distorts the situation by implying that the second war was the inevitable result of the first and its inadequate peace treaties.

The latter opinion seems more sound. Whatever the flaws of the treaties of Paris, the world suffered an even more terrible war than the first as a result of failures of judgment and will on the part of the victorious democratic powers. The United States, which had become the wealthiest and potentially the strongest nation in the world, disarmed almost entirely and withdrew into foolish isolation; it could play no important part in restraining the ambitious dictators who would bring on the war. Britain and France refused to face the threat posed by the Axis powers until the most deadly war in history was required to put it down. If the victorious democracies had remained strong, responsible, and realistic, they could have remedied whatever injustices or mistakes arose from the treaties without endangering the peace.

The second war itself was plainly a world war. The Japanese occupation of Manchuria in 1931 was a precursor. Italy attacked Ethiopia in 1935. Italy, Germany, and the Soviet

Union intervened in the Spanish Civil War (1936–1939). Japan attacked China in 1937. These developments revealed that aggressive forces were on the march around the globe and that the defenders of the world order lacked the will to stop them. The formation of the Axis among Germany, Italy, and Japan guaranteed that the war would be fought around the world. There was fighting and suffering in Asia, Africa, the islands of the Pacific, and Europe. The use of atomic weapons brought the struggle to a close, but what are called conventional weapons did almost all the damage. The survival of civilization was threatened even without the use of nuclear devices.

This was ended not with unsatisfactory peace treaties but with no treaty at all in the European area where it had begun. The world quickly split into two unfriendly camps: the western led by the United States, and the eastern led by the Soviet Union. This division hastened the liberation of former colonial territories. The bargaining power of these new nations was increased, as the two rival great powers tried to gain their friendship or allegiance. It became customary to refer to these nations as "the Third World," with the Soviet Union and the United States and their allies being the first two. In time, differences among these newer nations became so great as to make the name almost meaningless.

One of the most surprising aspects of the second war, the treatment received by the defeated powers, was also largely the result of the emergence of the Cold War. Instead of holding them back, the western powers installed democratic governments in Italy, West Germany, and Japan, took them into the western alliances designed to contain communism, and helped them recover economically. Japan and reunified Germany are among the richest nations in the world, and Italy is more prosperous than it has ever been. Meanwhile, state control of the economy in communist countries ultimately produced disastrous results around the world. As a result, the threat posed by communism, so feared soon after the war, has waned. The former Soviet Union, the original motherland of communism, has dissolved along with its satellite empire in Eastern Europe, and the states that made up the Union and the empire have rejected the discredited system. Even communist China has turned increasingly to free enterprise to achieve economic prosperity. China, however, remains formally committed to communism, and former communists remain influential in some of the states of the former Soviet empire. It may be too early to be sure that communism in some form is a thing of the past.

Review Questions

1. What were Hitler's foreign policy aims? Was he bent on conquest in the east and dominance in the west, or did he simply want to return Germany to its 1914 boundaries?

2. Why did Britain and France adopt a policy of appeasement in the 1930s? What were its main features? Did the appeasers buy the west valuable time to prepare for war by their actions at Munich in 1938?

3. How was Hitler able to defeat France so easily in 1940? Why did Hitler invade Russia? Why did the invasion fail?

4. What was the significance of American intervention in the war? Why did the United States drop atomic bombs on Japan?

5. What impact did World War II have on the civilian population of Europe? How did experiences on the domestic front of Great Britain differ from those of Germany and France? What impact did "The Great Patriotic War" have on the people of the Soviet Union? Did participation in World War II solidify Stalin's hold on power?

6. What was Hitler's "final solution" to the Jewish problem? Why did Hitler want to eliminate Slavs as well? Some historians have looked at the twentieth century and have seen a period of great destruction as well as of great progress. Is this truly a "century of Holocaust"? Discuss the ramifications of these questions.

Documents CD-ROM

1. Adolph Hitler: "The Obersalzberg Speech"

2. Winston Churchill: "Their Finest Hour–House of Commons, 18 June 1940"

3. Franklin Delano Roosevelt: "A Call for Sacrifice–28 April 1942"

4. Eleanor Roosevelt: From "My Day"

5. Hidecki Tōjō's Imperial War Conference: Casting the Die

6. "The Atlantic Charter"

36 THE WEST SINCE WORLD WAR II

CHAPTER TOPICS

- The Cold War Era
- European Society in the Second Half of the Twentieth Century
- Postwar America
- The Soviet Union to 1989
- 1989: Year of Revolutions in Eastern Europe
- The Collapse of the Soviet Union
- The Collapse of Yugoslavia and Civil War
- Problems in the Wake of the Collapse of Communism

In World Perspective The West Since 1945

Since the conclusion of World War II, Europe's influence on the world scene has been transformed. The destruction of the war itself left Europe incapable of exercising the kind of power it had formerly exerted. The Cold War between the United States and the Soviet Union made Europe a divided and contested territory. Furthermore, Europeans soon began to lose control of their overseas empires.

The decision by the United States to take an activist role in world affairs touched every aspect of the postwar world. American domestic politics and foreign policy became intertwined as in no previous period of American history.

Like virtually every other part of the world, Europe experienced the impact of American culture through military alliances, trade, tourism, and popular entertainment. Europeans also began to build structures for greater economic cooperation.

While Western Europe enjoyed increased democratization and unprecedented prosperity, Eastern Europe experienced economic stagnation and Soviet domination. Yet from the late 1970s onward, there were political stirrings in the east. These culminated in 1989 with revolutions throughout Eastern Europe

and in 1991 with the collapse of communist government in the Soviet Union itself. For over a decade since those events, Europeans have been seeking to forge a new political direction.

The Cold War Era

Initial Causes

The tense relationship between the United States and the Soviet Union that dominated world history during the second half of the twentieth century originated in the closing months of World War II.

The split arose from basic differences of ideology and interest. The Soviet Union's attempt to extend its control westward into Europe and southward into the Middle East was a continuation of the policy of tsarist Russia. It had been Britain's traditional role to restrain Russian expansion into these areas; the United States inherited that task as Britain's power waned. The alternative was to permit a major increase in power by a huge, traditionally hostile state. That state, dedicated in its official ideology to the overthrow of nations like the United States, was governed by Stalin (1879–1953), an absolute dictator, with a proven record for horrible cruelties. Few nations would take such risks.

However, the Americans made no attempt to roll back Soviet power where it already existed, even though American military forces were the greatest in their history, American industrial power was unmatched, and America had a monopoly on atomic weapons. In less than a year from the war's end, the Americans reduced their forces in Europe from 3.5 million to half a million. The speedy withdrawal was fully in accord with America's peacetime goals. These goals included support for self-determination, autonomy, and democracy in the political sphere; and free trade, freedom of the seas, no barriers to investment, and the Open Door in the economic sphere. As the strongest, richest nation in the world, the United States would benefit from an international order based on such goals.

However, the Soviets saw American resistance to their expansion as a threat to their security and their legitimate aims. American objections over Poland and other states were seen as attempts to undermine regimes friendly to Russia and encircle the Soviet Union with hostile neighbors.

The growth in France and Italy of communist parties taking orders from Moscow led the Americans to believe that Stalin was engaged in a worldwide plot to subvert capitalism and democracy. We do not know for certain if these suspicions were justified, but most people in the West considered them plausible.

Early Cold War Conflict

The new mood of hostility among the former allies appeared quickly. In February 1946, both Stalin and his foreign minister, Vyacheslav Molotov (1890–1986), publicly spoke of the Western democracies as enemies. A month later, Churchill (1874–1965) delivered a speech in Fulton, Missouri, in which he spoke of an Iron Curtain dividing a free and democratic West from an East under totalitarian rule. In this atmosphere, difficulties grew.

The attempt to deal cooperatively with the problem of atomic energy was an early victim of the Cold War. The United States continued to develop its own atomic weapons in secrecy, and the Russians did the same. By 1949, the Soviet Union had exploded its own atomic bomb, and the race for nuclear weapons was on.

The resistance of westerners to what they perceived as Soviet intransigence and communist subversion took clearer form in 1947. Since 1944, civil war had been raging in Greece between the royalist government restored by Britain and insurgents supported by the communist countries. In 1947,

Britain informed the United States that it was financially no longer able to support the Greeks. On March 12, President Truman (1884–1972) asked Congress to provide funds to support Greece and Turkey, which was also under Soviet pressure. Congress complied. In what became known as the Truman Doctrine, the American president advocated a policy of supporting "free people who are resisting attempted subjugation by armed minorities or by outside pressures," by implication anywhere in the world.

For Western Europe, where the menacing growth of communist parties was fueled by postwar poverty and hunger, the Americans devised the European Recovery Program. Named the Marshall Plan after George C. Marshall (1880–1959), the secretary of state who introduced it, this program provided broad economic aid to European states on condition only that they work together. The Soviet Union forbade its satellites to take part.

The Marshall Plan helped restore prosperity to Western Europe and set the stage for its unprecedented economic growth. It also led to the establishment there of solid democratic regimes.

Stalin's answer was to replace all multiparty governments behind the Iron Curtain with thoroughly communist regimes under his control. He also organized in 1947 the Communist Information Bureau (Cominform) dedicated to spreading revolutionary communism throughout the world.

Major Dates in the Era of the Cold War

1948	Berlin Blockade
1949	Formation of the North Atlantic Treaty Organization (NATO)
1950	Outbreak of the Korean War
1953	Death of Stalin
1956	July, Egypt seizes the Suez Canal
	October, Anglo-French attack on the Suez Canal; Hungarian Revolution
1957	Treaty of Rome establishes the European Economic Community (EEC)
1960	Paris Summit Conference collapses
1961	Berlin Wall erected
1962	Cuban missile crisis
1963	Russian-American Test Ban Treaty
1968	Russian invasion of Czechoslovakia
1975	Helsinki Accords
1979	Russian invasion of Afghanistan
1981	Military crackdown on Solidarity Movement in Poland
1985	Reagan-Gorbachev summit
1987	Major American-Soviet Arms Limitation Treaty
1989	Berlin Wall comes down

In February 1948, a brutal display of Stalin's policy took place in Prague. The communists expelled the democratic members of what had been a coalition government and murdered the foreign minister. Czechoslovakia was brought fully under Soviet rule.

These Soviet actions increased America's determination to make its own arrangements in Germany. The Russians dismantled German industry in the eastern zone, but the Americans tried to make Germany self-sufficient, which meant restoring its industrial capacity. To the Soviets the restoration of a powerful industrial Germany was unacceptable.

When the Western powers agreed to go forward with a separate constitution for the western sectors of Germany in February 1948, the Soviets walked out of the joint Allied Control Commission. Berlin, although well within the Soviet zone, was governed by all four powers. The Soviets sealed the city off by closing all railroads and highways to West Germany. Their purpose was to drive the Western powers out of Berlin.

The Western allies responded to the Berlin Blockade with an airlift of supplies that lasted almost a year. In May 1949, the Russians were forced to reopen access to Berlin. The incident hastened the separation of Germany into two states, which prevailed for forty years. West Germany became the German Federal Republic in September 1949, and the eastern region became the German Democratic Republic a month later.

NATO and the Warsaw Pact

Meanwhile, Western Europe was coming closer together. The Marshall Plan encouraged international cooperation. In April 1949, Belgium, the Netherlands, Luxembourg, France, Britain, Italy, Denmark, Norway, Portugal, and Iceland signed a treaty with Canada and the United States that formed the North Atlantic Treaty Organization (NATO) for mutual assistance in case of attack. NATO formed the West into a bloc. A few years later West Germany, Greece, and Turkey joined the alliance (see Map 36–1).

Unlike the NATO states, the states of Eastern Europe were under direct Soviet domination through local communist parties controlled from Moscow and overawed by the Red Army. The Warsaw Pact of May 1955, which included Albania, Bulgaria, Czechoslovakia, East Germany, Hungary, Poland, Romania, and the Soviet Union, merely gave formal recognition to a system that already existed. Europe stood divided into two unfriendly blocs.

Crises of 1956

The events of 1956 had considerable significance both for the Cold War and for what they implied about the realities of European power in the postwar era.

Suez   In July 1956, President Gamal Abdel Nasser (1918–1970) of Egypt nationalized the Suez Canal. Britain and France feared that this action would imperil their supplies of oil in the Persian Gulf. In October 1956, war broke out between Egypt and Israel. The British and French intervened; however, the United States refused to support them. The Soviet Union protested vehemently. The Anglo-French forces had to be withdrawn, and control of the canal remained with Egypt. The Suez intervention proved that without the support of the United States, the nations of Western Europe could no longer impose their will on the rest of the world.

Poland   Developments in Eastern Europe demonstrated similar limitations on independent action among the Soviet bloc nations. When the prime minister of Poland died, the Polish Communist Party refused to choose a successor selected by Moscow. Considerable tension developed. In the end, Wladyslaw Gomulka (1905–1982) emerged as the new communist leader of Poland. He proved acceptable to the Soviets because he promised to keep Poland in the Warsaw Pact. However, he halted the collectivization of Polish agriculture and improved relations with the Polish Roman Catholic Church.

Uprising in Hungary   Hungary provided the second trouble spot for the Soviet Union. In late October, fighting erupted in Budapest. A new ministry headed by Imre Nagy (1896–1958) was installed. Nagy was a communist who sought an independent position for Hungary. Unlike Gomulka, he called for Hungarian withdrawal from the Warsaw Pact. Soviet troops deposed Nagy, who was later executed, and imposed Janos Kadar (1912–1989) as premier.

The Cold War Intensified

The events of 1956 ended the era of fully autonomous action by the European nation-states. The two superpowers had demonstrated the new political realities. After 1956, the Soviet Union began to talk about "peaceful coexistence" with the United States. In 1959, tensions relaxed sufficiently for Soviet Premier Nikita Khrushchev (1894–1971) to tour the United States. A summit meeting was scheduled for May 1960 in Paris, and American President Dwight D. Eisenhower (1890–1969) was to go to Moscow.

Just before the gathering, the Soviet Union shot down an American U–2 aircraft that was flying reconnaissance over Soviet territory. Khrushchev refused to take part in the summit conference, and Eisenhower's trip to the Soviet Union was canceled.

In fact, the Soviets had long been aware of the American flights. They chose to protest at this time for two reasons. Khrushchev had hoped that the leaders of Britain, France, and the United States would be so divided over the future of

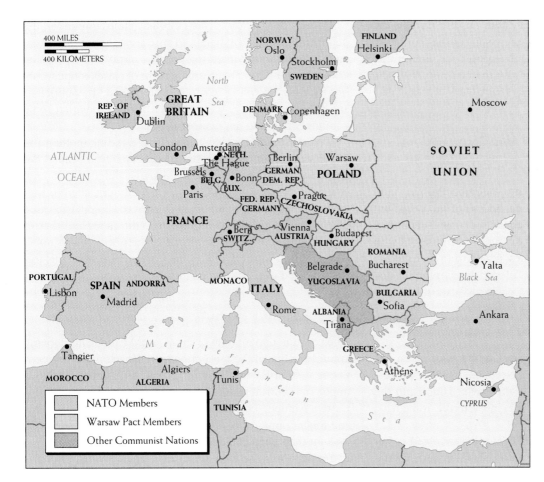

Map 36–1 Major Cold War European alliance systems. The North Atlantic Treaty Organization, which includes both Canada and the United States, stretches as far east as Turkey. By contrast, the Warsaw Pact nations were the contiguous communist states of Eastern Europe, with the Soviet Union, of course, as the dominant member.

Germany that a united Allied front would be impossible. The divisions did not arise, so the conference would have been of little use to him. Second, by 1960 the communist world had become split between the Soviets and the Chinese, who accused the Russians of lacking revolutionary zeal. Khrushchev's action was an attempt to show the hard-line attitude of the Soviet Union toward the capitalist world.

The abortive Paris conference opened the most difficult period of the Cold War. Throughout 1961, thousands of refugees from East Germany had fled to West Berlin. To stop this outflow, in August 1961 the East Germans erected a concrete wall along the border between East and West Berlin that remained until November 1989.

A year later, the Cuban missile crisis brought the most dangerous days of the Cold War. The Soviet Union placed missiles in Cuba, a nation friendly to Soviet aims lying less than a hundred miles from the United States. The United States blockaded Cuba, halted the shipment of new missiles, and demanded the removal of existing installations. After a tense week, the Soviets backed down and the crisis ended.

Detente and Afterward

In 1963, the two powers concluded a Nuclear Test Ban Treaty. This agreement marked the start of a detente, or lessening in tensions, between the United States and the Soviet Union that intensified during the presidency of Richard Nixon (1913–1994). This policy involved trade agreements and mutual reduction of strategic armaments. But the Soviet invasion of Afghanistan in 1979 hardened relations between Washington and Moscow, and the US Senate refused to ratify the Strategic Arms Limitation Treaty of 1979.

However, President Ronald Reagan (b. 1911) and Soviet leader Mikhail S. Gorbachev (b. 1931) held a friendly summit meeting in 1985, the first East-West summit in six years. Other meetings followed. In December 1987, the United States and the Soviet Union agreed to dismantle over 2,000 medium- and shorter-range missiles. The treaty provided for mutual inspection. This action represented the most significant agreement since World War II between the two superpowers.

Thereafter, the political upheavals in Eastern Europe and the Soviet Union overwhelmed the issues of the Cold War. The Soviet Union abandoned its support for communist governments in Eastern Europe. By the close of 1991, the Soviet Union itself had collapsed. The Cold War was over.

European Society in the Second Half of the Twentieth Century

The sharp division of Europe into a democratic west and communist east for most of the second half of the twentieth century makes generalizations about social and economic developments difficult. Prosperity in the west contrasted with shortages in the eastern economies, which were managed to benefit the Soviet Union. Most of the developments discussed in this chapter have taken place in Western Europe.

Toward Western European Unification

Since 1945, the nations of Western Europe have taken unprecedented steps toward economic cooperation. The process is not completed. The collapse of the Soviet Union and the emergence of new free governments in Eastern Europe have further complicated it.

The Marshall Plan and NATO gave the involved countries new experience in working with each other and demonstrated the gains from cooperative action. In 1950, France, West Germany, Italy, Belgium, the Netherlands, and Luxembourg organized the European Coal and Steel Community. Its success reduced suspicions about the concept of coordination and economic integration.

In 1957, through the Treaty of Rome, the six members of the Coal and Steel Community agreed to form a new organization: the European Economic Community, or Common Market. The members sought to achieve the eventual elimination of tariffs, a free flow of capital and labor, and similar wage and social benefits in all the participating countries. The chief institution of the EEC was a High Commission composed of technocrats.

The Common Market was a stunning success. By 1968, all tariffs among the six members had been abolished. Trade and labor migration among the members grew steadily. Moreover, nonmember states began to seek membership. In 1973, Great Britain, Ireland, and Denmark became members, and Spain, Portugal, Greece, Sweden, Finland, and Austria were eventually admitted.

In 1988, the leaders of the Community decided to create a virtual free-trade zone throughout the Community. In 1991, the Treaty of Maastricht called for a unified currency and a strong central bank. The European Community was renamed the European Union.

However, as the prospect of unity becomes imminent, the people of Europe have begun to raise issues about the democratic nature of the emerging political entity they are being asked to join. They are clearly in favor of closer cooperation, but they are unwilling to see it set forth only by politicians and bureaucrats. They want a wider European market to be genuinely free and not overregulated.

The most striking element of the expanding momentum of economic cooperation is the common currency, called the Euro. In 1999, the currencies of Austria, Belgium, Finland, France, Germany, Ireland, Italy, Luxembourg, the Netherlands, Portugal, and Spain were fixed according to the value of the Euro. By 2002, their national currencies and that of Greece will have been replaced by new coins and notes denominated in the Euro. Such a common currency is unprecedented in European history.

A Consumer Society

The consumer orientation of the Western European economy emerged as one of the most important characteristics differentiating it from Eastern Europe. Those differences produced important political results. Throughout the Soviet Union and Eastern Europe, economic planning favored capital investment and military production. Those nations produced inadequate food for their people and few and shoddy consumer goods.

Yet people in the East grew increasingly aware of the discrepancy between their lifestyle and that of the West. They saw Western consumerism clearly linked to democratic governments, free societies, and economic policies that favored the free market. Thus the expansion of consumerism in the West, deplored by many, helped generate the discontent that brought down the communist governments of Eastern Europe and the Soviet Union.

The Movement of Peoples

Many people have migrated from, to, and within Europe during the past half century.

External Migration   In the decade and a half after 1945, approximately a half million Europeans each year settled elsewhere in the world. Many of these migrants were educated city dwellers.

Decolonization in the postwar period contributed to an inward flow of European colonials and non-European inhabitants of the former colonies to Europe. This influx has caused social tension and conflict. In Great Britain, for example, during the 1980s there were clashes between the police and non-European immigrants. France has had similar difficulties. Moreover, large Islamic populations now exist in several European nations and have become political factors in France and Germany.

Internal Migration The major motivation for internal migration from the late 1950s onward was economic opportunity. The prosperous nations of northern and Western Europe had jobs that paid good wages and provided excellent benefits. Thus, there was a flow of workers from the poorer countries of Turkey, Greece, Yugoslavia, Italy, Spain, and Portugal into the wealthier countries of France, West Germany, Switzerland, and the Benelux nations. The establishment of the EEC in 1957 facilitated this movement.

The migration of workers into northern Europe snowballed after 1960. Several hundred thousand workers would enter France and Germany each year. They were usually welcomed during years of prosperity, and resented when economies began to slow in the mid-1980s. In Germany during the early 1990s, they were attacked.

In the late 1980s, politics again became a major factor in European migration. With the collapse of the communist governments of Eastern Europe in 1988 and 1989, people from all over Eastern Europe have migrated to the West. The civil war in the former Yugoslavia has also created many refugees. However, the new migrants are generating resentment. Several nations have taken steps to restrict migration.

New Patterns for Women

Since World War II, the work patterns and social expectations of women have changed markedly. In all social ranks, women have begun to assume larger economic and political roles. They have entered the professions and are filling major managerial positions.

New Work Patterns In the late twentieth century, the work pattern of European women has displayed much more continuity than it did in the nineteenth century. Single women enter the work force after their schooling and continue to work after marriage. The number of married women in the work force has risen sharply. Both middle-class and working-class married women have sought jobs outside the home. They might withdraw from the work force to care for young children but return when the children begin school.

Several factors created this new pattern, but women's increasing life expectancy is one of the most important. The lengthening life span has meant that child rearing occupies much less of women's lives. Women throughout the Western world have new concerns about how they will spend those years when they are not rearing children. The age at which women have decided to bear children has risen. In urban areas, childbearing occurs later and the birthrate is lower than elsewhere.

Many women have begun to limit the number of children they bear or to forgo childbearing altogether. Both men and women continue to expect to marry. But the new careers open to women and the desire of couples for a higher standard of living have contributed to a declining birthrate.

Women in the New Eastern Europe Many paradoxes surround the situation of women in Eastern Europe now that it is no longer governed by communists. Under communism women generally enjoyed social equality as well as a broad spectrum of government benefits. Well over 50 percent of women worked in these societies both because they could and because it was expected of them. There were, however, no significant women's movements since they, like all independent associations, were frowned on.

The new governments of the region are free, but have shown little concern toward women's issues. Economic difficulties may endanger the funding of various health and welfare programs that benefit women and children, like the extensive maternity benefits they used to enjoy. Moreover, the high proportion of women in the work force could leave them more vulnerable than men to the region's economic troubles.

Postwar America

Three major themes have characterized the postwar American experience—opposition to the spread of communism, expansion of civil rights to blacks and other minorities at home, and a determination to achieve economic growth.

Truman and Eisenhower Administrations

The foreign policy of President Harry Truman was directed against communist expansion in Europe and East Asia (see Chapter 37). Domestically, the Truman administration tried to continue the New Deal. However, Truman encountered opposition from conservative Republicans, who in 1947 passed the Taft-Hartley Act, which limited labor-union activity. Truman won the 1948 election against great odds. Through policies he termed the Fair Deal, he sought to extend economic security.

Those efforts, however, were frustrated by fears of a domestic communist menace fanned by Senator Joseph McCarthy (1909–1957) of Wisconsin. That development, a frustration with the war in Korea, and perhaps the natural weariness of the electorate after twenty years of Democratic Party government, led to the election of war hero Dwight Eisenhower in 1952.

The Eisenhower years now seem a period of calm. Eisenhower ended the Korean War. The country was generally prosperous. The president was less activist than either Roosevelt or Truman had been.

Beneath the apparent quiet, however, stirred forces that would lead to the disruptions of the 1960s.

Civil Rights

In 1954, the US Supreme Court, in *Brown v. Board of Education of Topeka*, declared racial segregation unconstitutional. Shortly thereafter, the Court ordered the desegregation of schools. For the next ten years, the struggle over school integration and civil rights for black Americans stirred the nation. Southern states attempted to resist desegregation. American blacks began to protest it. In 1955, Reverend Martin Luther King, Jr. (1929–1968) organized a boycott in Montgomery, Alabama, against segregated buses that marked the beginning of the use of civil disobedience to fight racial discrimination in the United States. The civil rights struggle continued well into the 1960s. The greatest achievements of the movement were the Civil Rights Act of 1964, which desegregated public accommodations, and the Voting Rights Act of 1965, which cleared the way for blacks to vote. Black citizens were brought nearer to the mainstream of American life than they had ever been.

However, much remained undone. In 1967, race riots occurred in American cities. Those riots, followed by the assassination of Martin Luther King, Jr., in 1968, weakened the civil rights movement. Furthermore, as other groups, particularly Latino Americans, began to raise issues on behalf of their own communities, racial relations became more complicated. Black Americans and other minorities continue to lag behind white Americans economically.

New Social Programs

The advance of the civil rights movement in the late 1950s and early 1960s represented the cutting edge of a new advance of political liberalism. In 1960, John F. Kennedy (1917–1963) narrowly won the presidential election. He attempted unsuccessfully to expand medical care under the social security program, but the reaction to his assassination in 1963 allowed his successor, Lyndon Johnson (1908–1973), to press for activist legislation. Johnson's domestic program, known as the War on Poverty, established major federal programs to create jobs and provide job training. It also added new entitlements to the social security program, including Medicare, which provides medical services for the elderly and disabled. Johnson's drive for what he termed the Great Society ended the era of major federal initiatives that had begun under Franklin Roosevelt. By the late 1960s, the electorate had become more conservative.

The Vietnam War and Domestic Turmoil

Johnson's activist domestic vision was overshadowed by the US involvement in Vietnam (see Chapter 37). By 1965, Johnson had decided to send American troops to Vietnam.

This policy led to the longest of American wars. At home, the war and the draft provoked large-scale protests on the streets and on college campuses. The Vietnam War divided the nation as had no conflict since the Civil War.

Lyndon Johnson decided not to seek reelection in 1968. Richard Nixon led the Republicans to victory. His election marked the beginning of an era of American politics dominated by conservative policies. Perhaps the most important act of his administration was to establish diplomatic relations with the People's Republic of China. Although half of the casualties in the Vietnam War occurred under Nixon's administration, he concluded the war in 1972. That same year he was reelected, but the Watergate scandal began to erode his administration.

The Watergate Scandal

On the surface, the Watergate scandal involved only the burglary of the Democratic party national headquarters by White House operatives in 1972. The deeper issues related to presidential authority and the right of the government to intrude into the lives of citizens. In 1973, Congress established a committee to investigate the scandal. Testimony revealed that President Nixon had recorded conversations in the White House. In the summer of 1974, the newly released tapes showed that Nixon had ordered federal agencies to try to cover up White House participation in the burglary. After this revelation, Nixon resigned.

The Watergate scandal further shook public confidence in the government. It was also a distraction from the major problems facing the country, especially inflation, which had resulted from fighting the war in Vietnam while expanding federal domestic expenditures. The administrations of Gerald Ford (1974–1977; b. 1913) and Jimmy Carter (1977–1981; b. 1924) battled inflation and high interest rates without success.

The Triumph of Political Conservatism

In 1980, Ronald Reagan was elected president by a large majority and reelected four years later. Reagan was the first fully ideological conservative to be elected in the postwar era. He sought to reduce the role of the federal government in American life through major tax cuts. This plus vastly increased defense spending produced the largest fiscal deficit in American history, but inflation was controlled, and the economy expanded.

In 1988, George Bush (b. 1924) was elected to succeed Reagan. In the summer of 1990, in response to the invasion of Kuwait by Iraq, he initiated the largest mobilization of American troops since the Vietnam War and forged a worldwide coalition, which forced Iraq out of Kuwait in 1991.

But Bush stumbled in the face of serious economic problems. In 1992, the Democratic nominee, Governor William Clinton (b. 1946) of Arkansas, won the election.

In 1994, the Republic Party won majorities in both houses of Congress in an election that marked a major conservative departure in American political life. This Congress continued the conservative redirection of federal policy that had begun under Ronald Reagan.

President Clinton and a Republican dominated Congress were reelected in 1996, but scandals plagued both parties. Because of a personal sexual scandal and allegations of perjury, President Clinton was impeached in 1998 but acquitted in early 1999 by the Senate. In terms of policy, Clinton was seen as moving the Democractic party into a more conservative stance.

The Soviet Union to 1989

The major themes of Soviet history after 1945 were the rivalry with the United States for world leadership, the rivalry with China for the leadership of communist nations, the effort to sustain Soviet domination of Eastern Europe, and a series of unsuccessful attempts to reform the Stalinist state, which ended in 1991 with the collapse of the Soviet Union.

The Soviet Union emerged from World War II as a major world power, but Stalin did not modify the repressive regime he had fostered. The central bureaucracy grew. Heavy industry was still favored at the expense of consumer goods. Agriculture remained troubled. Stalin's authority was unchallenged. He solidified Soviet control over Eastern Europe.

The Khrushchev Years

Stalin died on March 6, 1953. No single leader immediately replaced him, but by 1956, Nikita Khrushchev (1894–1971) became premier, but without the extraordinary powers of Stalin.

In 1956, at the Twentieth Congress of the Communist Party, Khrushchev denounced Stalin and his crimes. The speech shocked party circles and opened the way for limited internal criticism of the Soviet government.

Under Khrushchev, intellectuals were somewhat freer to express their opinions. In economic policy, Khrushchev made moderate efforts to decentralize economic planning, but the consumer sector improved only marginally. The ever growing defense budget and the space program made major demands on the nation's productive resources.

Khrushchev redirected Stalin's agricultural policy. The Soviet Union could not feed its own people. Khrushchev removed the most restrictive regulations on private cultivation, but the agricultural problem continued to grow.

By 1964, Communist Party leaders had concluded that Khrushchev had tried to do too much too soon and had done it poorly. His foreign policy, culminating in the backdown over the Cuban missile crisis, appeared a failure. On October 16, 1964, Khrushchev was forced to resign. Leonid Brezhnev (1906–1982) emerged as his successor.

Brezhnev

The Soviet government became more repressive after 1964. Intellectuals enjoyed less freedom. Jewish citizens of the Soviet Union were harassed.

The internal repression gave rise to a dissident movement. A few Soviet citizens dared to criticize the regime for violating the human rights provisions of the 1975 Helsinki Accords. The dissidents included the Nobel Prize–winning physicist Andrei Sakharov (1921–1989). The Soviet government responded with more repression.

In foreign policy, the Brezhnev years witnessed attempts both to reach accommodation with the United States and to continue to expand Soviet influence and maintain Soviet leadership of the communist movement. Growing spending on defense sqeezed the consumer side of the economy.

In December 1979, the Soviet Union invaded Afghanistan for reasons that still remain unclear. The Afghanistan invasion exacerbated tensions with the United States and tied the hands of the Soviet government in Eastern Europe. Soviet hesitation to react to events in Poland during the 1980s stemmed in part from the military committment in Afghanistan and from the condemnation the invasion provoked from Western European communists and from many governments. The Soviet government also lost support at home as its army became bogged down and suffered steady losses.

Solidarity in Poland

In July 1980, the Polish government raised meat prices. The result was strikes across the country. In August, a strike at the Lenin shipyard at Gdansk spread to other shipyards, transport facilities, and factories. The strikers, led by Lech Walesa (b. 1944), refused to negotiate through the government-controlled unions. The Gdansk strike ended on August 31 after the government promised the workers the right to organize an independent union, Solidarity. Less than a week later the Polish communist head of state was replaced.

In the summer of 1981, for the first time in any European communist state, secret elections for the Polish party congress permitted real choices among the candidates. Poland remained a communist state, but real debate was temporarily permitted within the party congress. This experiment ended in December 1981. General Wojciech Jaruzelski (b. 1923) became head of the party, and martial law was declared.

Khrushchev Denounces the Crimes of Stalin: The Secret Speech

In 1956, Khrushchev denounced Stalin in a secret speech to the Party Congress. The New York Times *published a text of that speech smuggled from Russia.*

What are the specific actions on the part of Stalin that Khrushchev denounced? Why does Khrushchev pay so much attention to Stalin's creation of the concept of an "enemy of the people"? Why does Khrushchev draw a distinction between the actions of Stalin and those of Lenin?

Stalin acted not through persuasion, explanation, and patient cooperation with people, but by imposing his concepts and demanding absolute submission to his opinion. Whoever opposed this concept or tried to prove his viewpoint and the correctness of his position was doomed to removal from the leading collective [group] and to subsequent moral and physical annihilation. . . .

Stalin originated the concept of "enemy of the people." This term automatically rendered it unnecessary that the ideological errors of a man or men engaged in a controversy be proved; this term made possible the usage of the most cruel repression violating all norms of revolutionary legality, against anyone who in any way disagreed with Stalin, against those who were only suspected of hostile intent, against those who had bad reputations.

This concept "enemy of the people" actually eliminated the possibility of any kind of ideological fight or the making of one's views known on this or that issue, even those of a practical character. In the main, and in actuality, the only proof of guilt used, against all norms of current legal science, was the "confession" of the accused himself; and, as a subsequent probing proved, "confessions" were acquired through physical pressures against the accused. . . .

Lenin used severe methods only in the most necessary cases, when the exploiting classes were still in existence and were vigorously opposing the revolution, when the struggle for survival was decidedly assuming the sharpest forms, even including civil war.

Stalin, on the other hand, used extreme methods and mass repressions at a time when the revolution was already victorious, when the Soviet State was strengthened, when the exploiting classes were already liquidated and Socialist relations were rooted solidly in all phases of national economy, when our party was politically consolidated and had strengthened itself both numerically and ideologically. It is clear that here Stalin showed in a whole series of cases his intolerance, his brutality and his abuse of power. Instead of proving his political correctness and mobilizing the masses, he often chose the path of repression and physical annihilation, not only against actual enemies, but also against individuals who had not committed any crimes against the party and the Soviet Government. . . .

The New York Times, June 5, 1956, pp. 13–16.

Gorbachev Attempts to Redirect the Soviet Union

By the time of Brezhnev's death in 1982, the Soviet system seemed incapable of meeting the needs of its people or pursuing a successful foreign policy. But no observers expected rapid change in the Soviet Union or its satellites.

However, in 1985, Mikhail S. Gorbachev (b. 1931) came to power and immediately set about making the most remarkable changes that the Soviet Union had witnessed since the 1920s. His reforms unleashed forces that within seven years would force him to retire and end both communist rule and the Soviet Union itself.

Initially, Gorbachev and his supporters challenged the way the party and bureaucracy managed the Soviet government and economy. Under the policy of *perestroika*, or restructuring, they proposed major economic and political reforms. The centralized economic ministries were streamlined. By early 1990, Gorbachev had even begun to advocate private ownership of property. He and his advisers considered policies to move the economy rapidly toward a free market. However, the Soviet economy, instead of growing, stagnated and even declined. Shortages of food, consumer goods, and housing became chronic. Old-fashioned communists blamed these results on the abandonment of centralized planning, while democratic critics blamed them on overly slow reform.

Gorbachev also allowed public criticism of Soviet history and Soviet Communist Party policy. This development was termed *glasnost*, or openness. In factories, workers were permitted to criticize party officials and the economic plans of the party and the government. Censorship was relaxed and free expression encouraged. Dissidents were released from prison. In 1988, a new constitution permitted contested elections. After real political campaigning, the Congress of People's Deputies was elected in 1989 and then formally elected Gorbachev as president.

The Soviet Union was a vast empire of diverse nationalities. Some had been conquered under the tsars; others had been seized by Stalin. Glasnost quickly brought to the fore the discontents of all such peoples. Gorbachev proved inept in addressing these ethnic complaints.

1989: Year of Revolutions in Eastern Europe

In 1989, Soviet domination and communist rule in Eastern Europe ended. None of these revolutions could have taken place without the refusal of the Soviet Union to intervene militarily as it had done in 1956 and 1968. For the first time since the end of World War II, the peoples of Eastern Europe could shape their own political destiny. Once they realized the Soviets would stand back, thousands of citizens denounced Communist Party domination and asserted their desire for democracy.

The generally peaceful character of most of these revolutions was not inevitable. It may have resulted from the shock with which the world responded to the violent repression of prodemocracy protesters in Beijing's Tienanmen Square in May 1989. The Communist Party officials of Eastern Europe and the Soviet Union clearly decided that they could not offend world opinion with a similar attack.

Solidarity Reemerges in Poland

During the mid-1980s, Poland's government relaxed martial law. By 1984, leaders of Solidarity began again to work for free trade unions and democratic government. New dissenting organizations emerged. Poland's economy continued to deteriorate. In 1988, new strikes occurred. This time the communist government failed to reimpose control. Solidarity was legalized.

Jaruzelski, with the tacit consent of the Soviet Union, promised free elections to parliament. When elections were held in 1989, the communists lost overwhelmingly to Solidarity candidates. On August 24, 1989, after negotiating with Lech Walesa, Jaruzelski named Tadeusz Mazowiecki (b. 1927) the first non-communist prime minister of Poland since 1945. The appointment was made with the express approval of Gorbachev.

Hungary Moves Toward Independence

Hungary had for some time shown the greatest national economic independence of the Soviet Union in Eastern Europe. The Hungarian government had emphasized the production of food and consumer goods. In early 1989, as events unfolded in Poland, the Hungarian communist government permitted independent political parties and free travel between Hungary and Austria, opening the first breach in the Iron Curtain. Thousands of East Germans then moved through Hungary and Austria to West Germany.

In May 1989, Premier Janos Kadar (1912–1989) was voted from office by the parliament. In October, Hungary promised free elections. By 1990, a coalition of democratic parties governed the country.

German Reunification

In the autumn of 1989, demonstrations erupted in East German cities. The streets filled with people demanding an end to Communist Party rule.

Gorbachev told the leaders of the East German Communist Party that the Soviet Union would no longer support them. They resigned, making way for a younger generation of Communist Party leaders who promised reforms. They convinced few East Germans, however. In November 1989,

The collapse of Communist Party governments in Eastern Europe and the Soviet Union is the most important political event of the closing years of the twentieth century. It was accompanied by the destruction of the public symbols of those governments. Throughout the region gigantic statues of Communist Party leaders were torn down. Here, Hungarians explore a toppled statue of Lenin. [Corbis-Sygma]

the government of East Germany ordered the opening of the Berlin Wall, and thousands of East Berliners crossed into West Berlin. By early 1990, the communist government of East Germany had been swept away.

The citizens of the two Germanies were determined to reunify. By February 1990, reunification had become a foregone conclusion, accepted by the United States, the Soviet Union, Great Britain, and France.

The Velvet Revolution in Czechoslovakia

Late in 1989, in "the velvet revolution," communist rule in Czechoslovakia unraveled. In November, under popular pressure from street demonstrations and well-organized political opposition, the Communist Party began to retreat from office. The patterns were similar to those occurring elsewhere. The old leadership resigned, and younger communists replaced them. The changes they offered were inadequate.

The popular new Czech leader was Vaclav Havel (b. 1936), a playwright of international standing whom the government had imprisoned. Havel and his group, which called itself Civic Forum, negotiated changes with the government that included an end to the political dominance of the Communist Party and the inclusion of non-communists in the government. In late December 1989, Havel was elected president.

Violent Revolution in Romania

The most violent upheaval of 1989 occurred in Romania, where President Nicolae Ceausescu (1918–1989) had governed without opposition for almost a quarter century. Romania was a corrupt, one-party state with total centralized economic planning. Ceausescu, who had long been at odds with the Soviet government, maintained his Stalinist regime in the face of Gorbachev's reforms. He was supported by a loyal security force.

On December 15, troubles erupted in the city of Timisoara in western Romania. The security forces fired on demonstrators, and casualties ran into the hundreds. By December 22, Bucharest was in full revolt. Fighting broke out between the army, which supported the revolution, and the security forces. Ceausescu and his wife attempted to flee the country but were captured and executed on December 25. His death ended the fighting. The provisional government in Bucharest announced the first free elections since the end of World War II.

The Collapse of the Soviet Union

Gorbachev believed that the Soviet Union could no longer afford to support communist governments in Eastern Europe. He was beginning to realize that the Communist Party within the Soviet Union was also going to lose power.

Renunciation of Communist Political Monopoly

In early 1990, Gorbachev formally proposed that the Soviet Communist Party abandon its monopoly of power. After intense debate, the Central Committee abandoned the Leninist position that only a single elite party could act as the vanguard of the revolution and forge a new Soviet society.

Gorbachev confronted challenges from three major political forces by 1990. One group—considered conservative in the Soviet context—wanted to maintain the influence of the Communist Party and the Soviet army. They were disturbed by the country's economic stagnation and disorder. They appeared to have significant support. During late 1990 and early 1991, Gorbachev, who himself seems to have been disturbed by the nation's turmoil, began to appoint members of this group to government posts. In other words, Gorbachev seemed to be making a strategic retreat. He apparently believed that these more conservative forces could give him the support he needed against opposition from a second group, led by Boris Yeltsin (b. 1931), who wanted to move quickly to a market economy and a more democratic government. In 1990, Yeltsin was elected president of the Russian Republic, the most important of the Soviet Union's constituent republics. That position gave him a firm political base from which to challenge Gorbachev's authority and increase his own.

The third force was regional unrest, especially from the three Baltic republics of Estonia, Latvia, and Lithuania. During 1989 and 1990, the parliaments of the Baltic republics tried to increase their independence, and Lithuania actually declared itself independent. Discontent also arose in the Soviet Islamic republics in central Asia. Gorbachev sought to negotiate new constitutional arrangements between the republics and the central government but failed. That may have been the most important reason for the rapid collapse of the Soviet Union.

The August 1991 Coup

The turning point came in August 1991 when the conservative forces that Gorbachev had brought into the government attempted a coup. Armed forces occupied Moscow, and Gorbachev himself was placed under house arrest in the Crimea. Yeltsin denounced the coup and asked the world for help.

Within two days the coup collapsed. Gorbachev returned to Moscow, but in humiliation, having been victimized by the groups he had turned to for support. From that point on, Yeltsin steadily became the dominant political figure in the nation. The Communist Party, compromised by its participation in the coup, collapsed. On December 25, 1991, the Soviet Union ceased to exist, Gorbachev left office, and the Commonwealth of Independent States came into being.

The Yeltsin Years

As president of Russia, Boris Yeltsin was head of the largest and most powerful of the new states, but by 1993 he faced serious problems. Opposition to Yeltsin personally and to his economic and political reforms grew in the Russian Parliament. Its members were mostly former communists who wanted to slow or halt the movement toward reform. In September 1993, Yeltsin suspended Parliament, which responded by deposing him. The military, however, backed Yeltsin and surrounded the Parliament building. On October 4, 1993, after pro-Parliament rioters rampaged through Moscow, Yeltsin ordered tanks to attack the Parliament building, crushing the revolt.

These actions consolidated Yeltsin's position and authority. The major Western powers supported him. The crushing of Parliament left Yeltsin far more dependent on the military. And the country's continuing economic problems bred unrest. In the December 1993 parlimentary elections, radical nationalists made an uncomfortably strong showing. In 1994 and again in 1999–2000, the central government found itself at war in the province of Chechnya. In December 1999, Yeltsin, who suffered from poor health, resigned and was succeeded as president by Vladimir Putin. Putin was elected to a full term in April 2000, promising strong leadership

However, the future course of Russia remains highly confused. Its economic life has remained stagnant at best. In 1998, Russia defaulted on its debt payments. Political assassinations have occurred. The economic downturn has contributed to further political unrest and social misery.

The Collapse of Yugoslavia and Civil War

Yugoslavia was created after World War I. Its borders included six major national groups—Serbs, Croats, Slovenes, Montenegrins, Macedonians, and Bosnians (Muslims)—among whom there have been ethnic disputes for centuries. The Croats and Slovenes are Roman Catholic and use the Latin alphabet. The Serbs, Montenegrins, and Macedonians are Eastern Orthodox and use the Cyrillic alphabet. The Bosnians are Islamic. Most members of each group reside in a region with which they are associated historically—Serbia, Croatia, Slovenia, Montenegro, Macedonia, and Bosnia-Herzegovina—and these regions constituted individual republics within Yugoslavia. Many Serbs, however, lived outside Serbia proper.

Yugoslavia's first communist leader, Marshal Tito (1892–1980), had acted independently of Stalin in the late 1940s and pursued his own foreign policy. He muted ethnic differences by encouraging a cult of personality around himself and by complex power sharing. After his death, economic difficulties undermined the central government, and Yugoslavia dissolved into civil war.

In the late 1980s, the old ethnic differences came to the fore again in Yugoslav politics. Nationalist leaders—most notably Slobodan Milošević (b. 1941) in Serbia and Franjo Tudjman (1922–1999) in Croatia—gained authority. The Serbs contended that Serbia did not exercise sufficient influence in Yugoslavia and that Serbs living in Yugoslavia but outside Serbia encountered discrimination, especially from Croats. Ethnic tension and violence soon resulted. During the summer of 1991, in the wake of the changes in the former Soviet bloc nations, Slovenia and Croatia declared independence from the central Yugoslav government and were recognized by the European community.

From this point on, violence escalated. By June 1991, full-fledged war had erupted between Serbia and Croatia. At its core, however, the conflict was ethnic; as such, it highlights the potential for violent ethnic conflict within the former Soviet Union.

The conflict took a new turn in 1992 as Croatian and Serbian forces determined to divide Bosnia-Herzegovina. The Muslims in Bosnia—who had lived alongside Serbs and Croats for generations—soon became crushed between the opposing forces. The Serbs in particular, pursuing a policy called "ethnic cleansing," a euphemism redolent of some of the worst horrors of World War II, killed or forcibly moved many Bosnian Muslims.

The United Nations attempted unsuccessfully to mediate the conflict and imposed sanctions, which had little influence. But in 1995, NATO forces carried out strategic air strikes. Later that year, under the leadership of the United States, the leaders of the warring forces completed a peace agreement in Dayton, Ohio, which recognized an independent Bosnia. The terms of the agreement were enforced by the presence of NATO troops.

The Breakup of Yugoslavia

June 1991	Slovenia declares independence
June 1991	Croatia declares independence
April 1992	War erupts in Bosnia and Herzegovina after Muslims and Croats vote for independence
November 1995	Peace agreement reached in Dayton, Ohio
January 1992	Macedonia declares independence
April 1992	Serbia and Montenegro proclaim a new Federal Republic of Yugoslavia
March 1998	War breaks out in Kosovo, a province of Serbia
March 1999	NATO bombing of Serbia begins

An elderly parishioner walks through the ruins of Saint Mary's Roman Catholic Church in Sarajevo. The church was destroyed by Serb shelling in May 1992. [Reuters/Corbis-Bettmann]

The situation in the former Yugoslavia remained dangerous and deadly. During 1997 and 1998, Serbia moved against ethnic Albanians living in its province of Kosovo. In 1999, NATO again undertook air strikes against Serbian forces, and forced Serbia to withdraw from Kosovo. In 2000, a popular revolution swept the non-democratic government of Yugoslavia.

Problems in the Wake of the Collapse of Communism

The collapse of communism has presented Europe with new problems and opportunities. The opportunities include the possibility of establishing democratic governments and market economies throughout the region. They also include the restoration of civil liberties in countries where they have not been known for over a half century. If the countries of the former Soviet bloc reorganize their economies successfully, their citizens may come to enjoy the kinds of consumer goods—and the standard of living they make possible—that have long been available in Western Europe. Realizing these opportunities, however, will require enormous patience. Such patience may be in short supply. Already in Poland, Lech Walesa in 1995 lost the presidential election to a former communist. In other parts of Eastern Europe, former communists have become a major political force.

The problems in the new political and economic situation are enormous. Unemployment is widespread throughout the former Soviet Union and Eastern Europe. The plants and factories that the communist governments had built are obsolete and have caused some of the worst environmental problems in the world. These nations also now recognize that by the standards of Western Europe, they are poor. Thousands of people are migrating from Eastern to Western Europe to look for work. In western countries, however, the migrants have encountered resentment, opposition, and violence.

The nations of Western Europe, facing considerable public resentment over the costs already incurred from the collapse of communism, are hesitant to send economic aid to the east. This is especially true in Germany, where the costs of unification have been high. Western Europeans are also grappling with another issue: How should the former communist economies relate to the European Union?

The political challenges of the collapse of communism are no less great than the economic. Civil war has ravaged Yugoslavia. The potential for ethnic violence threatens the former Soviet Union, where nuclear weapons are still available. The Czechs and the Slovaks, unable to establish a unified state, divided Czechoslovakia into two separate nations in 1993. The liberty made possible by the end of the communist governments has thus far tended to be used in pursuit of ethnic goals, leading to domestic political turmoil. The key question is whether democratic governments can survive or whether they will succumb to illiberal alternatives.

Under these rapidly changing conditions, NATO has expanded its membership to include Poland, the Czech Republic, and Hungary. Yet the exact purpose of NATO remains ill defined. Although initially reluctant to settle the civil war in the former Yugoslavia, NATO eventually assumed the role of internal peacekeeper in the new Europe.

IN WORLD PERSPECTIVE

The West Since 1945

The history of the West since the end of World War II has been full of paradoxes. Europe, which gave birth to Western civilization and remained its center until the war, has declined in world influence. During the four decades immediately after the war, the United States and the Soviet Union replaced Western Europe as the major powers on the world scene. But they did so in conflict with each other.

The Cold War dominated political struggles throughout the world for more than half a century. It divided Europe between the NATO and Warsaw Pact alliances and forced nations outside Europe to side with one or the other of the superpowers.

In the later 1980s, however, the Cold War unexpectedly ended as the Soviet Union and the nations of Eastern Europe experienced enormous internal political changes. These changes have opened a new epoch of Western history. The United States has emerged from the Cold War as the single remaining superpower. Western Europe stands on the brink of new unity, but its peoples and governments are hesitant to press the process too far too rapidly. Eastern Europe and the former Soviet Union are experiencing economic turmoil and political uncertainty.

A new world order is emerging in which regional conflict will pose many of the gravest dangers. It remains to be seen whether the United States will be able to maintain its position of leadership in the West or whether Western Europe will take a more independent course. It also remains to be seen whether Europe, in response to economic pressures and the turmoil in the east, withdraws somewhat from world involvement during the next decade.

Review Questions

1. What were the causes of the Cold War? How did the United States and the Soviet Union each react to what it perceived to be the other's hostility? What was the effect of the Cold War on Europe?

2. How did the outcome of World War II affect Europe's position in the world? What were the factors behind the movement toward European unification? How successful has this movement been?

3. What were the chief characteristics of Western European society in the decades since 1945? What was the experience of Eastern Europe during the same period and why was it different?

4. Describe the Soviet economy between 1945 and 1990. Did it meet the needs of the Soviet people? What were the causes for the collapse of the Soviet Union? What role did Gorbachev play in that process?

5. Describe the collapse of communist rule in Eastern Europe. Why was it a relatively bloodless revolution? What problems has the collapse of communist rule led to?

6. Was the old Yugoslavia a national state? Why did it break apart and slide into civil war? How did the West respond to this crisis?

Documents CD-ROM

1. Whitaker Chambers: Foreward in the Form of a Letter to My Children

2. George Kennan: From Memoirs: 1925–1950

3. Address by President Kennedy on the Cuban Missile Crisis

4. Murray Kempton: From *Rebellions, Perversities, and Main Events*

5. Francis Fukuyama: From *The End of History*

6. Pope John Paul II: "Centesimus Annus"

37 EAST ASIA IN THE LATE TWENTIETH CENTURY

CHAPTER TOPICS

- Japan
- China
- Taiwan

- Korea
- Vietnam

In World Perspective East Asia

The history of East Asia since the end of World War II (see Map 37–1) may be divided into two phases. In the first, from 1945 to 1980, several East Asian nations became communist but achieved only a small improvement in the conditions of their peoples. In stark contrast, the nations that used a mixture of state guidance and market-oriented economies made the region as a whole the most dynamic in the postwar world.

The second phase of postwar East Asian history was the eighties and nineties. During the eighties, those nations that had prospered earlier continued to grow. But during the nineties, a recession rippled through East Asia and growth halted or slowed.

The most marked change occurred in China, which, even while maintaining a communist dictatorship, introduced many features of a market economy. The result was explosive growth and social change.

Japan

By early 1945, Japan was poor, hungry, and ill-clothed. Cities were burnt out, factories scarred by bombings; shipping had been sunk, railways were dilapidated, and trucks and cars were scarce. On August 15, 1945, the emperor broadcast Japan's surrender to the Japanese people. They expected a harsh and vindictive occupation, but when they found it constructive, their receptivity to new democratic ideas and their repudiation of militarism led one Japanese writer to label the era "the second opening of Japan."

The Occupation

General Douglas MacArthur was the Supreme Commander for the Allied Powers in Japan, and the occupation forces were mostly American. The chief concern of the first phase of the occupation was demilitarization and democratization. Civilians and soldiers abroad were returned to Japan and the military was demobilized. Wartime leaders were brought to trial for "crimes against humanity." Shinto was disestablished as the state religion, labor unions were encouraged, and the holding companies of *zaibatsu* combines were dissolved. Land reform expropriated landlord holdings and sold them to landless tenants at a fractional cost.

The new constitution, written by MacArthur's headquarters and passed into law by the Japanese Diet, fundamentally changed Japan's polity in five respects:

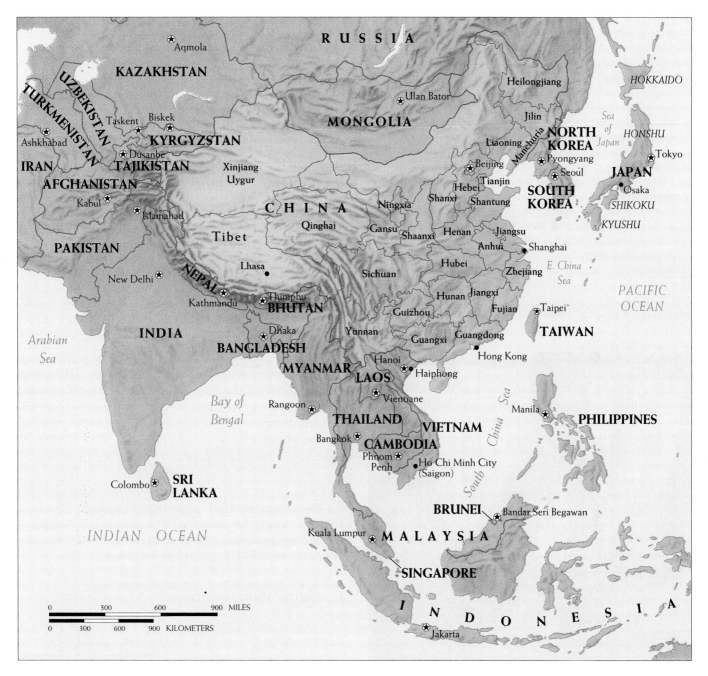

Map 37-1　Contemporary Asia.

1. A British-style parliamentary state was established along with an American-style independent judiciary and a federal system of prefectures with elected governors.

2. Women were given the vote.

3. The rights to life, liberty, the pursuit of happiness, a free press, and free assembly were guaranteed.

4. Article 9, the no-war clause, stipulated, "The Japanese people forever renounce war as a sovereign right of the nation."

5. The constitution defined a new role for the emperor as "the symbol of the state deriving his position from the will of the people with whom resides sovereign power."

The Occupation of Japan

There are occupations, and then there are occupations. Former Prime Minister Yoshida Shigeru presents his view.

Is this an objective appraisal, or an attempt by Yoshida to justify his own role in the Allied Occupation?

There are some now in Japan who point to similarities between the Allied, and predominantly American, Occupation of Japan, and our Occupation of Manchuria, China and other countries of Asia—the idea apparently being that, once an Occupation régime has been established, the relationship between victors and vanquished is usually found to be the same. I regret that I cannot subscribe to this opinion. Japan's Occupation of various Asian countries, carried out by Army officers of no higher rank than colonel and more often by raw subalterns, became an object of hatred and loathing among the peoples of the occupied countries, and there is none to dispute that fact. The Americans came into our country as our enemies, but after an Occupation lasting little less than seven years, an understanding grew up between the two peoples which is remarkable in the history of the modern world.

Criticism of Americans is a right accorded even to Americans. But in the enumeration of their faults we cannot include their Occupation of Japan.

From *The Yoshida Memoirs*, Yoshida Shigeru. Copyright © 1961 Heineman Books, p. 60.

Women, newly enfranchised, voting in postwar Japan. [UPI/Corbis-Bettmann]

The Japanese people accepted the new constitution and embraced democracy with uncritical enthusiasm. To create a climate in which the new democracy could flourish, the occupation in its second phase turned to Japan's economic recovery. It dropped plans to deconcentrate big business further, encouraged the Japanese government to curb inflation, and cracked down on communist unions. The United States also gave Japan $2 billion in economic aid.

When Japan regained its sovereignty in April 1952, the changeover was hardly noticeable in the daily life of the Japanese people. On the same day as the peace treaty, Japan signed a security treaty with the United States which became the cornerstone of Japan's minimalist defense policy.

Parliamentary Politics

Japan's postwar politics can be divided into three periods. The first, from 1945 to 1955, was the continuation of prewar party politics as modified to fit the new political environment. Two conservative parties, the Liberals and the Democrats, and the Japanese Socialist Party emerged. For most of this first decade, the Liberals held power.

In the long second period from 1955 to 1993, the Liberal Democratic Party (LDP), which was formed by a merger of the two conservative parties, held power and the Japanese Socialist Party was the permanent opposition.

The LDP became identified as the party that was rebuilding Japan and maintaining Japan's security through close ties with the United States. Despite the cozy relationships that developed between the LDP and business, periodic scandals, and a widespread distrust of politicians, the Japanese people voted to keep it in power. Rule by a single party for such a long period provided for an unusual continuity in government policies.

A third era of politics began with the 1993 election, in which established parties lost ground. The LDP lost its majority in the lower house of the Diet. But since other smaller conservative parties gained, the change inaugurated an era of conservative multiparty politics. The biggest loser in the election was the Japanese Socialist Party, which ended the socialists' role as the major opposition party.

Economic Growth

The extraordinary story of the economic rise of East Asia after World War II began with Japan. Several factors explain this growth. An infrastructure of banking, marketing, and manufacturing skills had carried over from prewar Japan. The international situation was also favorable: oil was cheap, access to raw materials and export markets was easy, and American sponsorship gained Japan early entry into international organizations. A rate of savings close to 20 percent helped reinvestment.

A revolution in education contributed as well. By the early 1980s, almost all middle school graduates went on to high school, and almost 40 percent of high school graduates went on to higher education. This upgrading of human capital and channeling of its best minds into productive careers let Japan tap the huge backlog of technology that had developed in the United States during and after the war years. After "improvement engineering," Japan sold its products to the world.

Another factor was an abundance of high-quality, cheap labor. The government also aided manufacturers with tariff protection, foreign exchange, and special depreciation allowances. Industries engaged in advanced technologies benefited from cheap loans, subsidies, and research products of government laboratories. Critics who spoke of "Japan Inc." as though Japan were a single gigantic corporation overstated the case, but government was more supportive of business than it was regulative.

By 1973, the Japanese economy had become "mature." Double-digit growth gave way to 4 percent growth. Smokestack industries declined while service industries, pharmaceuticals, specialty chemicals, scientific equipment, computers, and robots grew. Japan's trade began to generate huge surpluses. The surpluses were generated mainly by the appetite of world markets for Japanese products, but they were also a result of protectionist policies that led to demands from the United States and Europe that they be abolished.

Even slower growth, or no growth at all, characterized the nineties. Banks and individuals retrenched. Unemployment rose from the usual 1.5 to 4.4 percent, and hidden unemployment was higher. But exports continued to boom, and Japan's favorable balance of trade remained large. Like other countries in Asia, Japan hoped to export its way out of recession.

Whatever the future may hold, the economic weight of Japan in Asia is huge. The second largest economy in the world after the United States, the Japanese economy is half again as large as the combined economies of most of the rest of Asia—as can be seen in the following table.

Alternatively, Japan may be viewed as a "Western" economy and compared to France and Germany. Japan's economy is larger than that of France and Germany combined, and its per capita product is greater. Of course, land, food, and clothing are so expensive in Japan that the per capita product does not simply equate with standard of living. Still, the important fact is that Japan achieved its present affluence through the peaceful development of human resources in a free society.

Society and Culture

The triple engines of change in postwar Japan were occupation reforms, economic growth, and a rapid expansion of higher education. Taken together, one might have expected them to produce deep cultural strains and social dislocations. Yet the ability of the society—the family, the school, the office, and the workshop—to absorb the strains and to lend support to the individual was impressive. Lifetime employment gave workers and salaried employees a feeling of security. The divorce rate was less than one-third of that in the United States. Infant mortality was the lowest in the world and longevity the highest. Japan also had far less crime. By most objective measures the society was stable and healthy.

A Comparison of the Projected 1999 Gross Domestic Products of Japan and Other Asian Countries (in billions of dollars)			
China	$1,088	Japan	$4,528
South Korea	491		
Taiwan	318		
Hong Kong*	201		
Singapore	103		
Thailand	138		
Malaysia	82		
Indonesia	132		
India	384		
Pakistan	69		
TOTAL	$3,006		$4,528

*Hong Kong considered as a separate economic entity.

Comparison of Japan with France and Germany, Projected 1999 Figures

	GDP (in billions)	Population (in millions)	Per Capita GDP
France	$1,530	59	$25,932
Germany	2,284	82	27,854
Japan	4,528	126	35,937

China

Civil war in China ended in 1949 as the last troops of Chiang Kai-shek fled to Taiwan. The People's Republic of China was proclaimed in October. In the decade that followed, the Soviet model was adopted for the government, the army, the economy, and higher education.

Areas inhabited by Tibetans, Uighur Turks, Mongols, and other minorities were occupied by the Chinese army and settled by Chinese immigrants. The Communist Party held the key levers of power in the government, army, and security forces. Mao was chairman of the party and head of state. The Soviet Union sent financial aid as well as engineers and planners.

Rural society underwent two fundamental changes: land redistribution and then collectivization. In the early fifties, hundreds of thousands of landlords were killed and their holdings redistributed to the landless. Subsequently, all lands were seized by the state and collectivized.

During the early fifties, intellectuals and universities also became a target for thought reform. The Chinese slang term was "brainwashing." This involved study and indoctrination in Marxism, group pressures to produce an atmosphere of insecurity and fear, followed by confession, repentance, and reacceptance by society. The indoctrination was intended to strengthen party control and mobilize human energies on behalf of the state.

In 1958, Mao abandoned the Soviet model in favor of a mass mobilization to unleash the productive energies of the people, called the Great Leap Forward. The results were disastrous. Between 1958 and 1962, 20 to 30 million Chinese reportedly starved to death.

Sino-Soviet relations also deteriorated. Disputes arose over borders. China was dissatisfied with Soviet aid. The Soviet Union condemned the Great Leap Forward as "leftist fanaticism" and resented Mao's view of himself, after Stalin's death, as the foremost exponent of world communism. In 1960, the Soviet Union halted economic aid and withdrew its engineers from China. Each country deployed about a million troops along their mutual border.

The years between 1960 and 1965 saw conflicting trends. The failure of the Great Leap Forward led some Chinese leaders to turn away from Mao's reckless radicalism toward more moderate policies. Mao remained head of the party but had to give up his post as head of state. Yet even as the government moved toward realistic goals and stable bureaucratic management, a new mass movement was also begun to transform education.

The Great Proletarian Cultural Revolution (1965–1976)

In 1965, Mao again emerged to dominate Chinese politics. He feared that the Chinese revolution—his revolution—would end up as a Soviet-style bureaucratic communism run for the benefit of officials. So he called for a new revolution to create a truly egalitarian culture.

Obtaining army support, Mao urged students and teenagers to form bands of Red Guards. Universities were shut down as student factions fought. Teachers were beaten, imprisoned, and humiliated. Books were burned and art destroyed. Homes were ransacked for foreign books and Chinese who had studied abroad were persecuted. Red Guards beat to death persons viewed as reactionaries. High officials were purged.

Eventually Mao tired of the violence and near anarchy. In 1968 and 1969 he called in the army. Violence came to an end. Worsening relations with the Soviet Union also made China's leaders desire greater stability at home. When President Nixon proposed a renewal of ties, China responded. Nixon visited Peking in 1972, opening a new era of diplomatic relations.

The second phase of the Cultural Revolution between 1969 and 1976 was moderate only in comparison with what had gone before. On farms and in factories, ideology was still a substitute for economic incentives. Universities reopened, but students were admitted by class background. The so-called Gang of Four, which included Mao's wife and was abetted by the aging Mao, revived class struggle.

China After Mao

Political Developments   Mao's death in 1976 brought immediate changes. The Gang of Four and their radical supporters were arrested. In their place, Teng Hsiao-p'ing (Deng Xiaoping, 1904–1997) emerged as the dominant figure in Chinese politics. Teng ousted his enemies, rehabilitated those purged during the Cultural Revolution, and put his supporters in power. After the lunacy of the Cultural Revolution, a "normal" Communist Party dictatorship was a relief. The people could now enjoy a measure of security and material improvement. There continued, however, a tension between the determination of the ruling party to maintain its grip on power and its desire to obtain the benefits of liberalization.

Universities returned to normal in 1977. Entrance examinations were reinstituted, purged teachers returned to their classrooms, and scholars were sent to study in Japan and the West. Students began to demand still greater freedoms with the hope that they would lead to political democracy.

The new spirit came to a head in April and May of 1989, when hundreds of thousands of students, workers, and people from all walks of life demonstrated for democracy in Tienanmen Square in Peking and in dozens of other cities. The government sent in tanks and troops. Hundreds of students were killed, and leaders who did not escape abroad were jailed. The event defined the political climate in China for the decade that followed: freedom was allowed in most areas of life, but no challenge to Communist Party rule was tolerated.

Economic Growth   Developments in the economy were more promising. Teng's great achievement in the years after 1978 was to demonstrate in China the superiority of market incentives to central planning.

In China's villages, as the farm household became the basic unit of production, grain production rose but agriculture still had problems. Because the government bought up 30 percent of farmers' grain output at an artificially low price, farmers living near cities abandoned grain production in favor of specialty crops such as fruit or the feedgrain required by China's rising consumption of meat. China already imported some of its food, and there were gloomy estimates of more serious food shortages after the turn of the century.

State-operated enterprises, which often ran at a loss and employed twice the labor needed to run them efficiently, were a constant drain on China's state-owned banks. As the free market sector grew faster, their share of production declined. Finally, the government announced that "state ownership" would give way to "public ownership." The costs of such privatization would be high—defaulted loans, bankruptcies, unemployed workers, and a sudden rise in pensioners, but the drain on the state budget would end.

The main driver of the new economy was the free market sector. After 1980, the Chinese economy grew faster than any other Asian economy. Exports skyrocketed.

The factors that fueled this growth were clear: China used tariffs to shield its markets, while making use of cheap labor to flood foreign markets with goods and build up its currency reserves.

Social Change   During the Mao years, farmers had been tied to their collective or village. Cities were closed to those without residence permits. City dwellers were members of

The Chinese Cultural Revolution of the 1960s. Marchers hold a banner of Mao Tse-tung. [Archive Photos]

"units" that provided their members with jobs, housing, food, child care, medical services, and pensions. Party cadres exercised near total control over the unit's members. Block organizations reported any infractions of "socialist morality" to the authorities.

Under Teng, controls were loosened. The "unit" diminished in importance as food became widely available in free markets and apartments were sold to their inhabitants on easy terms. As workers with higher salaries began to provide for their own needs, life became freer and more enjoyable. The market economy placed a premium on individual decisions and initiatives.

The new prosperity and changing mores became increasingly evident. By the nineties, Chinese designers were holding fashion shows in Shanghai and Peking. Young people associated freely. The "household treasures" of the sixties, radios and bicycles, gave way to stoves and refrigerators, washing machines and color televisions. Motorbikes and privately owned cars competed in crowded streets with the flow of bicycles. Private restaurants opened, and travel for pleasure became commonplace.

But the new wealth was unevenly distributed. The more successful entrepreneurs bought houses, cars, microwaves, computers, and cell phones. They traveled abroad and sent their children to private schools. But many barely scraped by, and in the hinterlands, poverty and hardship remained the rule.

China's Relations with the World

From the fifties to the seventies, China isolated itself from the rest of the world. During the eighties, trade ties with the non-communist world led China to look outward and adopt more moderate policies. In the nineties, China emerged as the military and political heavyweight of East Asia, though Japan remained, even in recession, the predominant economic power.

China's relations with the United States were difficult. US military alliances with Japan, South Korea, Taiwan, and the non-communist nations of Southeast Asia were the main countervailing force to Chinese hegemony in the region. From the 1980s, trade with the United States was vital to China's economic growth, and it became more so during the mid-nineties as the rest of East Asia slipped into recession. Despite areas of contention, the United States worked to better relations, hoping that a deeper Chinese engagement with the United States and the rest of the world would lead to a freer Chinese society.

Taiwan

Taiwan is a mountainous island less than a hundred miles off the coast of central China. A little larger than Massachusetts, it has a population of 22 million. Originally a remote and backward part of the Ch'ing Empire, it became a Japanese colony in 1895. The Japanese colonial government suppressed opium and bandits, eradicated epidemic diseases, built roads and railroads, reformed the land system, and improved agriculture. It also introduced mass education and light industries.

Anticolonial feelings rose slowly, but the Taiwanese were happy to see the Japanese leave in 1945. Kuomintang (Guomindang) officials however, looted the economy and ruled harshly. By the time Chiang Kai-shek and 2 million more military and civilian mainlanders fled to the island in 1949, its economy and society were in disarray. Taiwanese hated their new rulers and even compared them unfavorably to the Japanese.

In the mid-1950s, order was restored, and rapid economic growth followed. By the late nineties, Taiwan had the healthiest economy in recession-ridden Asia.

Taiwan's politics was authoritarian until Chiang Kai-shek died in 1976. Taiwan then moved toward representative government. In 1987, martial law ended and opposition parties were permitted.

In 1996, Lee Teng-hui, a native Taiwanese, was elected president in what was, as he put it, "the first free election in 5000 years of Chinese history."

Ever since 1949, the communist government in Peking had claimed that Taiwan was a province of China controlled by a "bandit" government. It did not rule out taking Taiwan by force and refused diplomatic ties with any nation maintaining such ties with Taiwan. From the outbreak of the Korean War in 1950 until 1979, Taiwan was a protégé of the United States. In 1979, however, the United States broke off relations with Taipei and recognized Peking as the sole government of a China that included Taiwan. But the United States continued to trade with Taiwan and to sell it arms. In the late nineties, both China and the United States were apprehensive about Taiwan. China worried that a democratically elected government would give Taiwan a claim to legitimacy, and spoke of taking back the island. The United States felt it could not see this prosperous and democratic state it had helped to create be forcibly taken over by China.

Korea

Korea became a Japanese colony in 1910. Annexation was followed by changes designed to make Korea into a model colony. A land survey and land tax reform clarified land ownership. Infectious diseases dropped, and the population grew from 14 million in 1910 to 24 million in 1940. Attendance at schools became widespread. New money was issued and banks established. A huge investment was made in roads, railways, telegraph lines, hydroelectric power, nitrogenous fertilizer plants, and mining. Koreans who studied at Japanese universities brought new knowledge back to Korea. By the 1930s a modern culture was forming in Korea's cities.

Nonetheless, the colonial government was authoritarian. Its goal was to make Korea a subordinate part of Imperial Japan. Any benefits to the Koreans were incidental. Education was given in Japanese. In government, banking, or industry, Koreans were relegated to the lower echelons. The colonial regime suppressed all nationalist movements and political opposition. The police were brutal. Koreans were pressured to adopt Japanese names, drafted to fight in Japan's wars, and sent to labor in Japan. The legacy of colonial rule in Korea was an animosity that has persisted to this day.

North and South

With Japan's defeat in 1945, US forces occupied Korea south of the thirty-eighth parallel and Soviet troops occupied the north. Two separate states developed. In the south, the United States settled for the anti-communist government of

Syngman Rhee (1875–1965), a long-term nationalist leader whose party won the May 1948 election. Many of Rhee's officials and officers had served the Japanese. His government was strongly supported by conservative Koreans and those who had fled the north.

In the north, the Russians established a communist government under Kim Il-sung (1912–1994) in 1948 and withdrew its troops from North Korea. The United States also withdrew its troops from the south.

Civil War and US Involvement

On June 25, 1950, North Korea invaded the south. The North Korean leader had received Stalin's permission for the invasion and a promise from Mao to send Chinese troops if the United States entered the war. His plan was for a quick victory, but the United States saw the invasion as an act of aggression by world communism. It rushed troops from Japan to South Korea and obtained United Nations backing.

During the first months of the war, the unprepared American and South Korean forces were driven southward into a small area around Pusan (see Map 37–2). But then, amphibious units landed at Inchon and drove deep into North Korea. China then sent in "volunteers" to rescue the beleaguered North Koreans and pushed the overextended UN forces back to a line close to the thirty-eighth parallel. The war ended with an armistice on July 27, 1953.

Recent Developments

North Korea remained a closed, authoritarian state with a planned economy. It stressed heavy industry, organized its farmers in collectives, and controlled education and the media. Shortages of food, clothing, and other necessities were chronic. The cult of personality surrounding "the great leader" Kim Il-sung developed beyond that of even Stalin or Mao. His son, "the beloved leader" Kim Jong-il (b. 1942), succeeded his father in 1994—the only hereditary succession in a communist state.

In South Korea, Rhee was forced to retire in 1960. There followed twenty-seven years of rule by two generals, Park Chung-hee and Chun Doo-hwan. Their rule was semi-authoritarian: Opposition parties were legal and active but their leaders were often jailed. Park and Chun promoted economic growth. They supported business and expanded higher education, emphasizing science and technology. Labor was disciplined, hard-working, and cheap. The United States gave large amounts of aid and provided an open market for Korean exports. These factors produced double-digit growth. By the 1990s, South Korea had moved into the ranks of developed nations.

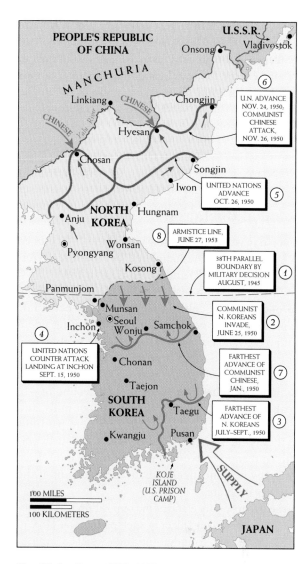

Map 37–2 Korea, 1950–1953. This map indicates the major developments in the bitter three-year struggle that followed the North Korean invasion of South Korea in 1950.

Industrialization and urbanization produced an affluent and educated middle class that resented authoritarian rule. In 1987, Chun agreed to step down, and a free and direct election was held. Although Chun's hand-picked successor, Roh Tae-woo, became president, most Koreans saw the election as an opening to democracy. This was confirmed four years later when Kim Young-sam, a moderate politician, was elected as president. He was pro-labor and a populist, but his liberal programs were constrained by the severe recession that gripped Korea from 1996.

Korean international relations have changed only slowly. South Korea's primary ties were with the United States, its long-time ally, which guaranteed its defense. The country's economic weight in the world grew with its trade. By 1999, it was the world's eleventh largest economy. North Korea's principal ties were with the Soviet Union and China. But with the collapse of the Soviet Union, Russia lost interest in its former ally. China, too, established diplomatic relations with South Korea in 1992. Since then, trade between the two nations has flourished. North Korea was increasingly an orphan. Its future is unclear.

Vietnam

The Colonial Backdrop

The Nguyen dynasty that reunited Vietnam in 1802 proved no match for France. France completed its conquest of Vietnam and Cambodia by 1883 and added Laos in 1893.

In many ways, Indochina was a classic case of colonialism: people of one race and culture, for the sake of economic benefits and national glory, controlling and exploiting a people of another race and culture in a far-off land. To obtain access to the country's natural resources, the French built harbors, roads, and a railway. They established rubber and tea plantations, introduced modern mining technology to extract coal, and built breweries, rice and paper mills, and glass and cement factories. Native workers were paid low wages. In the south, 3 percent of landowners owned 45 percent of the land and received 60 percent of the crop. Rice consumption by peasants declined. Over 80 percent of the population was illiterate.

Under the French, only clandestine opposition parties survived. The most skilled organizer of such parties was Ho Chi Minh (1892–1969), who founded the Indochinese Communist Party in 1930. Shortly before the outbreak of the Pacific War, the Japanese occupied Vietnam. Ho, who in 1941 had formed the Viet Minh (League for the Independence of Vietnam) as a popular front organization to resist the Japanese, proclaimed the Democratic Republic of Vietnam in 1945. Since then, the history of Vietnam can be seen in terms of three cycles of war followed by two decades of peace.

The Anticolonial War

The first war lasted from 1946 to 1954. On one side was the Viet Minh, led by Ho. It was controlled by communists but also included representatives of nationalist parties. On the other side were the French and their conservative Vietnamese allies. The French lost a major battle at Dien Bien Phu in 1954 and departed in defeat.

A conference at Geneva divided the country into a communist north and a non-communist south. In the south, Ngo Dinh Diem, a non-communist nationalist, established the Republic of Vietnam.

The Vietnam War

The second cycle of war was from 1959 to 1975 and involved the United States. Fighting began with guerrilla warfare in the south and eventually became a full-scale war between the north and the south. The north received material aid from the Soviet Union and China. The south was aided by the United States, whose forces increased to over half a million in 1969. Despite such massive support, South Vietnam—and the United States—lost the war.

In January 1973, a ceasefire was arranged in Paris, and two months later the last US troops left. Fighting broke out anew between north and south, the South Vietnamese forces collapsed in 1975, and the country was reunited under the Hanoi government in the north.

War with Cambodia

Vietnam's third cycle of war was with its neighbor, Cambodia. Pol Pot (1926–1998) and the communist Khmer Rouge ("Red Cambodia") had come to power in 1975. His government evacuated cities and towns, abolished money and trade, banned Buddhism, and killed an estimated 1 million persons, roughly 15 percent of the total population.

Clashes occurred between Khmer Rouge troops and Vietnamese troops along their common border. Historically, Vietnam was Cambodia's traditional enemy, as China was Vietnam's. In 1978, Vietnam occupied much of Cambodia, and the next year, set up a puppet government.

In its international relations, the unified Vietnam of 1975 became an ally of the Soviet Union. Relations with China, never good, worsened. In 1979, China invaded four northern provinces. Vietnamese troops repelled the invaders, but losses were heavy on both sides.

Recent Developments

The collapse of the Soviet Union destroyed Vietnam's primary international relationship. Vietnam's leaders also became aware that victories in wars were hollow so long as their people remained destitute.

In 1989, Vietnam withdrew from its costly occupation of Cambodia, and by the mid-nineties, Vietnam's relations with China improved. In 1995, Vietnam joined ASEAN (Association of Southeast Asian Nations) and reestablished diplomatic relations with the United States.

At home, the Communist Party-dominated government monopolized political power, controlled the army, police, and media, and supported a large sector of state-run industries. But it also encouraged the growth of a market economy, and the production of consumer goods grew. Between 1991 and 1996, the economy achieved an average growth of over

8 percent and received more offers of foreign investment than it could absorb.

But all was not rosy. Foreign investors were drawn to Vietnam by cheap labor but often encountered shortages, delays, red tape, and financial bottlenecks. Inflation was high. About 70 percent of labor was still employed in agriculture, and in the countryside barter was common. The gap in standard of living between urban and rural Vietnamese grew. In 1995, the per capita income of Vietnam was $240, less than one hundredth of Singapore's. It was still unclear where the balance would be struck between communist conservatives and reformers in the government.

IN WORLD PERSPECTIVE

East Asia

The industrialization of East Asia raises five issues that will powerfully affect future relations between nations.

One question is whether nations with high wages can compete with those low-wage nations that have found the formula for growth. Until recently, the advanced nations assumed that their technological advantage was permanent, that they could always stay sufficiently ahead of the less-developed nations to maintain their high wages. This assumption has now been challenged. Since the sixties, Taiwan, South Korea, Hong Kong, and Singapore have not only achieved modern economic growth but have moved rapidly into high technology—well before their wages reached Western levels. This made them formidable competitors in just those areas in which the West felt it was preeminent. China, the most recent East Asian industrializer, is now moving toward higher levels of technology and will possess the economic advantages of cheap labor for decades. If it succeeds in its developmental goals, the impact on high-wage nations will be massive.

A second issue concerns natural resources, and particularly, oil. As the nations of East Asia and elsewhere industrialize, the demand for oil rises inexorably. When eventually, it outstrips supply, how will resource-poor Japan, Taiwan, and South Korea be affected?

A third issue is population. Japan's population quadrupled during its industrialization and then began to level off. Its pattern was similar to that of advanced nations in the West. China, in contrast, already had a huge population when it began its recent industrialization and adopted tough policies to limit births. Whether other less-developed nations in the world follow the Japanese or Chinese model will depend on their circumstances, but for many, the tougher Chinese model seems unavoidable.

A fourth issue concerns the political consequences of economic growth. The recent history of Taiwan and South Korea suggests that East Asian dictatorships can evolve toward democracy as standards of living rise. Will the same thing happen in China?

A final issue is pollution. Automobile fumes, industrial effluents, chimney gases, pesticides, garbage, and sewage cause lakes to die, forests to wither, and levels of toxins to rise. In some areas, the damage is already near irreversible.

Review Questions

1. Is postwar Japan better understood in terms of a return to the liberalism of the 1920s, or as a fresh start based on occupation reforms?
2. Is China after 1949 better understood as an outgrowth of its earlier history, or in the context of a comparison with the Soviet Union and other communist states?
3. Examine the precolonial and colonial eras of Korea and Vietnam. What background factors shaped each in the period after World War II?
4. How did the Cold War affect the postwar histories of Korea and Vietnam?
5. If you were the American secretary of state, what long-term China policy would you propose?

Documents CD-ROM

1. Postwar Japan
2. Mao Zedong: Poems
3. Beijing 1989: The Square of Shattered Hopes
4. Mang Ke: *Ape Herd*
5. Marguerite Higgins: An Interview with Ngo Dinh Diem
6. Views of a Viet Cong Official

38 THE EMERGING NATIONS OF AFRICA, ASIA, AND LATIN AMERICA SINCE 1945

The post–World War II decades have witnessed the end of the age of Western colonialism and sharp challenges to European and superpower imperialism. This waning of colonial and imperial dominance must, however, be set within a larger historical perspective. Since the sixteenth century the various non-European portions of the globe had been drawn steadily into the European sphere of economic and political influence. Those areas to be treated here—Africa, the Middle East, Southwest and Southeast Asia, and Latin America—were the regions not only influenced but often subjected, exploited, and colonized by European powers. The period of colonialism that began in earnest in the seventeenth century was a relatively brief episode in world history. The last significant colonial holdings were given their independence within two decades after the Second World War.

The Postcolonial Era

It could be argued that with the passing of apartheid South Africa, the postcolonial era has also ended. What we shall witness in the future are waves of economic growth, such as that of the early 1990s in much of East Asia; the forging of dramatic new political alignments, both regional and transregional; and internal struggles in country after country to build political systems that allow the development of civil society and limit the destructive domination of oligarchic or dictatorial regimes.

Since 1945, two distinct developments have occurred in the postcolonial world. The first—in a process that is generally termed *decolonization*—is the emergence of the various parts of Africa and Asia from the direct administration of foreign powers, and the organization of those previous colonial dependencies into independent states (see Map 38–1).

The second development has been the forging of new relationships between the emerging nations and the Western nations and superpowers. These relationships have been of three kinds. First, until the recent breakup of the Soviet Union, its rivalry with the United States manifested itself on every continent and added to the tensions and turmoil of the era. New, emerging nations tended to be under the patronage of one or the other superpower (or, less often, that of China).

Second, the character of the world economy, including issues of both trade and resource allocation, has led to new modes of economic interdependence. Third, the ideas of civil society and participatory government have gained ground.

AFRICA, THE MIDDLE EAST, AND ASIA

Throughout the Afro-Asian world, except for much of East Asia, the dominant notes of postwar history have been independence and self-determination. Today the Afro-Asian world encompasses nearly a hundred sovereign states, whereas before 1939 there were only twelve. The rise of new nationalisms in these areas goes back to the nineteenth century, but it was only after World War II that nationalist movements emerged forcefully and found themselves strong enough—and their colonial masters weak (or receptive) enough—to win independence. Ironically, what came to define a "country" or a "nation" was less a communal affinity than the arbitrary boundaries of colonial administrations. As the colonial administrations themselves had been the principal targets of liberation and nationalist agitation, pre-independence boundaries naturally provided the geographical frameworks for most new nation-states.

The difficulties and instability these new states have faced are clear evidence of how little the older colonial powers really did for human development and self-governance in the countries they profited from and ruled. Few of the new nations have had the educational, technological, commercial, and political bases for self-sufficiency. Driving almost all other problems has been that of spiraling overpopulation, which has typically outpaced indigenous food production and even natural resources. Latin American and the Afro-Asian "Third World" peoples (including China, but not Japan) now make up about three-quarters of the world's population, which is approaching 5 billion.

In the waning decades of colonial rule and in the subsequent postcolonial era, the small elites of the former colonies have commonly been educated abroad, usually in Europe, America, and the former Soviet Union. Politically, socially, and economically, they have been too cut off from the masses of their own people to be able to lead their new independent states well. The absence of a well-educated middle class has

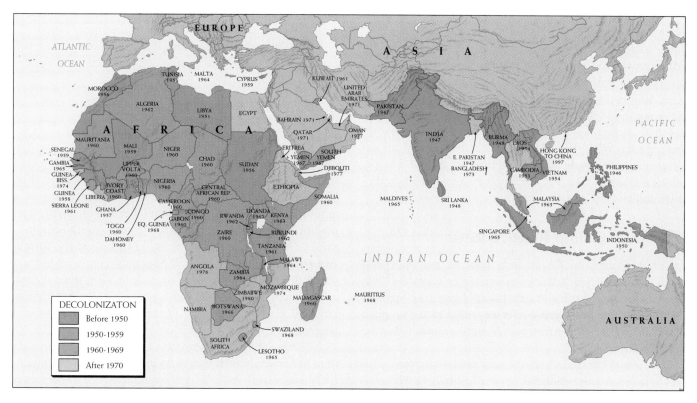

Map 38-1 Decolonization since World War II. The Western Powers' rapid retreat from imperialism after World War II is graphically shown on this outline map covering half the globe—from West Africa to the Southwest Pacific.

exacted a high price. Populist movements have foundered on internal rivalries and lack of modern political experience. Class differences have pitted one group against another. Tribal or other groups have found it hard to pull together with rival groups. For many of the new nations, the price of independence has been high—in bloodshed; political, ethnic, and religious strife; economic and social chaos; and continuing inequities in the distribution of wealth.

Yet there have also been hopeful signs. Some of these states have made progress in combatting illiteracy, poverty, disease, and authoritarianism. Some have been able to develop a sense of cultural, political, or religious continuity with their precolonial pasts without retreating from the realities of modern challenges. Most African and Asian peoples can now pursue their own course into the twenty-first century. Even if that course is difficult, at least it is not one forced on them by foreign armies and bureaucracies.

Postcolonial Africa

Nowhere is the dramatic continuity between often arbitrary colonial territories and emergent independent states clearer than in Africa. Most of its modern nations are direct inheritors of their colonial predecessors' boundaries, and the former colonial capitals have become the new national capitals, even though the colonial frontiers had little to do with the boundaries of traditional tribal territories or indigenous states. If nationalism was a European export to the rest of the world, Africa provides striking examples of how attractive it can be as a motive for supra-tribal and transregional state formation.

African nationalism can be dated generally to the period between the two world wars, when regional opposition to colonial occupation began to be replaced by larger-scale movements. World War II proved a catalyst for African nationalism, both among Africans themselves and for Europe, which was largely disposed to renounce white supremacy theories and give up its colonial empires after the war.

The Transition to Independence

In 1950, apart from Egypt, only Liberia, Ethiopia, and white-controlled South Africa were sovereign states. By 1980, no African state (with the exception of two tiny Spanish holdings on the Moroccan coast) was ruled by a European state, although South Africa and Namibia continued to be white dominated.

The actual transition from colonial administrative territories to independent national states was less fraught with conflict and bloodshed than one might have expected. The most protracted and bloody wars of independence from European overlords were the guerrilla struggles fought in French Algeria from 1955 to 1962; in Portuguese Angola and Mozambique from 1961 to 1975; and in Zaire (formerly the Belgian Congo), Zambia (formerly Northern Rhodesia), and Zimbabwe (formerly Southern Rhodesia) from 1960 to 1980. Usually, however, the transfer of power was relatively peaceable.

The same cannot be said of the internal conflicts that often arose after colonial withdrawal. Much of the instability in emergent African states has been a legacy of both the colonial powers' minimal efforts to prepare their subjects for self-government and the haphazard nineteenth-century division of the continent into often arbitrary colonial units. The establishment of new African governments often succeeded only after substantial civil strife.

Few African states had the numbers of educated and experienced native citizens that were needed to staff the apparatuses of a sovereign country, and this alone made for difficult times after independence. Corruption and military coups were rife; the attempt to implement planned economies on a socialist model often brought economic catastrophe; and tribal and regional revolts at times led to civil war.

Most dangerous and costly were the separatist struggles, civil wars, and border clashes between new states that grew out of the independence struggles. The Nigerian civil war of 1967–1970, in which more than 1 million people died, was a bloody example (see next section). However, these conflicts tended to ratify the postcolonial state divisions that had almost always kept to the old colonial boundaries (instead of regional or tribal/linguistic divisions within these units).

Every African state has had a different history in the half century since World War II; here we shall look at two cases: Nigeria and South Africa.

The Nigerian Case

Nigeria is the most populous state in Africa, with about 100 million inhabitants. It was formed when the British joined their protectorates of Northern and Southern Nigeria in 1914. Nigeria achieved independence in 1960 and ratified a republican constitution in 1964 that federated the three major provincial regions—the Eastern, Western, and Northern—under a national government based in Lagos, the former British administrative capital. Nigeria's largest ethnic and linguistic groups are the major ones of the same three regions or provinces: Igbo (Ibo) in the Eastern, Yoruba in the Western, and Hausa and Fulani in the Northern. The official language is English.

Nowhere was the aftermath of independence bloodier than in Nigeria, which was, at its inception, the most potentially successful state in independent Africa. The three-province federation soon proved to be unworkable, and a 1966 coup brought a military government into power. Its leader, an Ibo, was assassinated within seven months, and

Lt. Colonel Yakubo Gawon (b. 1934) took over amid ethnic unrest that ended in massacres in the fall of 1966. Gawon's government subdivided the three provinces into states, but in May 1967, the Eastern Province's assembly empowered its leader, Lt. Colonel Odumegwu Ojukwu (b. 1933), to form the independent state of Biafra out of the three states of the Eastern Province. Ojukwu was an Ibo nationalist but aspired to control lands beyond those of the Ibos—especially the offshore oil reserves of the Eastern Province. The new Biafran state gained recognition from several African states; and arms and support from France, South Africa, and Portugal. Worldwide propaganda depicted Biafra as a small, brave, mostly Christian country fighting for its survival.

The ensuing two and one-half years saw a bloody civil war. The larger federal forces slowly chipped away at first the non-Ibo regions, then the Ibo heartland of the Biafran state. Famine was a major cause of casualties, and the estimated death toll soared above a million by the time the Biafrans surrendered in January 1970. Out of this brutal conflict, however, came a sense of Nigerian unity, along with a major role for the military in Nigerian politics. The struggle also contributed to the development of African diplomacy and of international aid efforts in Africa.

Gawon was overthrown by another commander in 1975. In the ensuing twenty-five years, Nigeria has been plagued by political instability, with its leadership passing usually from one military ruler to another. The regime of General Sani Abacha (1993–1998) was especially brutal.

Abacha died in June 1998. Civilian rule was restored in 1999 but ethnic and religious violence soon broke out between Northerns and Southerns, Muslims and Christians.

All of this offers little promise. A great opportunity for successful transition to economic and political independence and leadership of less well-endowed African countries has been squandered.

The South African Case

One of the most tragic chapters in the history of modern Africa has finally been closed: that of white minority rule in South Africa, with its radical separation of white from nonwhite peoples in all areas of life as official government policy for nearly fifty years. In the rest of East and southern Africa, minority white-settler governments tried in vain in the postwar period to put down African independence movements. Only in South Africa did they manage, until the 1990s, to sustain a white supremacist state.

From the time the Afrikaner-led National Party (NP) came to power in 1948, the Union of South Africa was governed according to the racist policy of *apartheid* ("apartness"). Until the dismantling of this policy after 1991, the country's white minority (in 1991, 5.4 million persons) ran the country. Its

31 million blacks, 3.7 million "coloreds" (of mixed blood), and 1 million Indians were kept strictly segregated—treated, at best, as second-class citizens or, in the case of blacks, as noncitizens or even nonhumans. This system was maintained by repression, to quell dissent and enforce apartheid laws.

The history of apartheid and its passing is a bloody but triumphant one. In part as a result of worldwide opposition, South Africa saw itself become isolated from the 1960s onward. Meanwhile, the rest of Africa—including other white-run states like Rhodesia (now Zimbabwe)—progressed to majority, African rule. In 1961, South Africa withdrew from the British Commonwealth of Nations. In the sixties and seventies, the government created three tiny "independent homelands" for blacks inside the country, allowing the white minority to treat blacks as immigrant "foreigners" in the parts of South Africa where most had to work. The international community refused to recognize the homelands, or "Bantustans." South Africa's isolation was further dramatized when two anti-apartheid black leaders, the Zulu chief Albert Luthuli in 1960 and the Anglican archbishop Desmond Tutu in 1984, were awarded the Nobel Prize for their work against apartheid.

By 1978, when Pieter Botha (b. 1916) came to power, apartheid was failing: The homelands were economic and political catastrophes; the country was in a recession; skilled whites were emigrating; and South Africa was becoming an international pariah. In the 1980s, internal opposition to apartheid grew.

Beginning in 1986, many nations imposed economic sanctions against the government. Anti-apartheid movements in the United States and elsewhere had convinced companies and individuals to divest themselves of investments in South Africa. Strikes by black workers in 1987 led the government to give virtually unlimited power to its security forces, but the violence created support in the West for a trade embargo of South Africa.

In June 1988, more than 2 million black workers went on strike to protest new repressive labor laws and a ban on political activity by trade unions and anti-apartheid groups. President Botha resigned in August 1989. His replacement, F. W. de Klerk (b. 1936) (also of the NP, but younger and more ready for accommodation), began to dismantle white-only rule and the official structures of apartheid. In February 1990, de Klerk announced radical changes, and a series of landmark government actions followed: the lifting of the ban on the African National Congress (ANC), the main anti-apartheid organization; the release of ANC leader Nelson Mandela after twenty-seven years of imprisonment; and the repeal of the Separate Amenities Act, the legal basis for segregation in public places. In 1991, the race registration law was repealed. In March 1992, a whites-only referendum voted to grant constitutional equality to all races. The NP government under de Klerk's leadership also negotiated with the ANC leader Mandela, and despite terrorist attempts from both black and white extremists to derail the talks, the two leaders brought their own and eighteen other parties of both sides to endorse an interim constitution, which was to be implemented once national elections could be held in which all citizens of South Africa would be enfranchised. (Mandela and de Klerk shared the Nobel Peace Prize for 1993.)

The elections were held in April 1994. The ANC won 63 percent of the vote, and the NP 20 percent, thus relegating apartheid to the slag heap of history. The nonracial constitution of December 1996 offers a new basis for the future, but the new state faces huge problems: one of the world's most extreme income inequalities; insufficient education and economic infrastructure; rampant black poverty; high unemployment; militant extremist groups; inadequate public services in much of the country; potentially severe water supply and water quality problems; and difficulties in attracting foreign investment. The obstacles will, however, no longer include a state system that holds the majority of the population in bondage.

While the new independent states of Africa have been anything but models, nevertheless Africa did not revert to tiny tribal and regional political units. However, some struggles—such as those in the Sudan, Somalia, Rwanda, Sierra Leone, Congo, and Liberia—are still ongoing, their human consequences catastrophic, and their ultimate outcomes not clear.

The African Future

Most African states have not achieved peace and prosperity. On the other hand, the last fifty years have seen radical change and development. The prospects for government stability are not entirely bleak. Economic problems loom large, but even here progress is being made. In any case, every African state is different; each faces unique problems and must draw on its unique resources. Probably the most serious problems are those with which almost all of Africa's new nations have to contend: overpopulation, poverty, disease, famine, lack of professional and technical expertise, and general economic underdevelopment. In particular, the explosive growth of new urban centers at the expense of rural areas has brought disruptive changes in the continent's traditionally agrarian-based societies, age-old family and tribal allegiances, religious values, and sociopolitical systems. The challenge for African nations in the twenty-first century is to build a truly civil society and achieve economic health and political stability in the face of internal divisions, exploding population growth, and world-market competition.

The Postcolonial Middle East and Central Asia

The lands still dominated or marked by Islamic culture and containing either Muslim majority populations or large Muslim minorities stretch from North and West Africa to the Philippines.

Since 1945, six major developments have affected these widespread regions: (1) the emergence of new national states and international alignments, (2) the creation of the state of Israel, (3) the increase in importance of oil, (4) a resurgence of religious, political, and social Islamic reform movements, (5) the Iranian Revolution, and (6) the collapse of Soviet control in Central Asia.

New Nations in the Middle East

Saudi Arabia, Iraq, and Egypt obtained sovereign status after World War I, and Lebanon and Syria during World War II. Yet these states only became truly independent of European control after World War II. Others soon followed: Jordan in 1946; Libya in 1951; Morocco and Tunisia in 1956; Algeria in 1962; and, by 1971, the two Yemens and the Arabian Gulf states. Political instability and autocratic rule have been constants in most of these states. All share the Arabic language and the Muslim faith (although Lebanon has many Druze and Christians), but attempts to create pan-Arab alliances or federations have been abortive. Historical, regional, and national factors give each country a distinctive character. The oil wealth and strategic importance of the region have attracted foreign interest and interference, further complicating relations among the Arab states and between them and the rest of the world.

Turkey dates its existence from the 1920s rather than the 1950s. It represents a modernist republican experiment that has managed to allow a civil society and a democratically elected government to be the norm. It has, however, been plagued with ongoing intervention from the military, which has repeatedly deposed existing elected governments. Turkey, along with Israel, is still the most economically advanced Middle Eastern country. With the creation of new Turkic-language-speaking states in Central Asia after the breakup of the Soviet Union, Turkey is making a bid to strengthen its ties there.

The Arab-Israeli Conflict

Nowhere has the presence of the superpowers and Europe been more sharply felt than in the 1948 creation of the state of Israel in the former British mandate territory of Palestine, intended as a national homeland for the Jewish people. This event was the achievement of the world Zionist movement founded in 1897 by Theodor Herzl (1860–1904) in Europe (see Chapter 29). The British Balfour Declaration of 1917 had already favored a national homeland for the Jews in Palestine. But the potential for difficulties was great.

The interwar years saw growing communal conflict. Immigration of Jews, largely from eastern Europe, increased until Britain tried in 1936 to restrict it, which prevented many European Jews from escaping the Holocaust. Because of the Nazi attempt to exterminate European Jewry, after the war the Zionist movement received a tremendous boost from the Allied nations.

The concept of return to the Holy Land had a long history in the Jewish religion. However, for centuries, the land had been the home of Arabic-speaking Palestinians, who were without voice in the matter. The Palestinians have not been able to see why they should be persecuted, whether because of another people's historic religious attachment to the land or to pay for Europe's sins against the Jews. On the other hand, Jews themselves rightly felt the desperate need for a homeland where they might be safe and to which Jews everywhere might flee from future persecutions.

In 1945, Britain found itself beset in Palestine by Jews seeking to settle there and by Jewish terrorist organizations. In 1947, the British washed their hands of the problem, and the United Nations called for partition into a Jewish and an Arab state. The existing Arab states refused to accept the UN resolution, but in May 1948, the independent state of Israel was proclaimed. This declaration led to the Israeli-Arab war of 1948–49, in which Syria, Lebanon, Jordan, Egypt, and Saudi Arabia attacked Israel but lost to the better-armed and more resolute Israelis, ceding much territory designated by the UN for a Palestinian state.

Since then there has been, at best, an armed truce between Israel and its neighbors. The Arab nations and the Palestinian people displaced by the new state have generally not wanted to accept Israel's right to exist, and Israel (with the support of the United States) has taken aggressive measures to ensure its survival. The most serious military confrontations were the Suez crisis of 1956; the 1967 June War, when Israel attacked and occupied the Sinai, the Golan Heights, and the West Bank (of the Jordan River); the October War of 1973 in which the Egyptians staged a surprise attack on Israel in the Sinai that ended in a standoff; and the Israeli invasions of Lebanon in 1978 and 1982.

Even in periods without overt war, bloodshed has become commonplace. Arab terrorism grew out of Palestinian frustration. The Palestine Liberation Organization (PLO) and more radical groups carried on determined guerrilla battles within and along Israel's borders for decades.

Simultaneously, the frustrations of an embattled Israel have made it ready to meet terrorist atrocities with pre-emptive military actions and reprisals. Israel has responded to terrorist attacks and civilian resistance such as the Intifada, or Arab uprising, in the occupied territories with air and commando raids and punitive measures against the Arab populations in the occupied territories.

Arab states have supported guerrilla groups attacking Israel and long refused to deal directly with Israel to reach a Middle East solution. Egypt was the first notable exception to this policy. In the late 1970s, under President Anwar Sadat (1918–1981), and through the mediation of US President Jimmy Carter (b. 1924), Egypt entered into direct negotiations with Israel's prime minister Menachem Begin (1913–1994). The two countries reached an agreement—the Camp David Accords—in 1978, and in 1979 signed a formal peace treaty. Sadat was assassinated in 1981 by Egyptian Muslim extremists, but the treaty has held up under his successor, Husni Mubarak (b. 1928). Nonetheless, the cycle of violence has continued even as peace initiatives have increased.

Added to this bleak history is the ugly legacy of hate instilled in many on both sides over the past fifty years. Many Muslims have come to label all Jews as oppressors and enemies, making virtually no distinction among them. Many Israelis and some Jews around the world have similarly vilified all Arabs and Muslims. In many ways, Arab-Israeli and Muslim-Jewish relations are at an all-time low. The human crisis is far from over, even if peace were to arrive tomorrow.

In the offices of the first Iranian women's daily newspaper, *Rooznameh Zan*. Despite the reactionary adoption of a conservative dress code for women after the 1978 Iranian revolution, women in Iran today are pursuing a variety of careers and taking an active part in public discourse. This is not to argue that women's equality is being implemented, but only that women will not likely be long suppressed in Iranian society and economy. [Eslami Rad/Liaison Agency, Inc.]

Some events of recent years have given at least faint hope for an eventual resolution to the conflict. In 1991, in the wake of the Gulf War that followed Iraq's invasion of Kuwait, the parties to the Arab-Israeli conflict began peace negotiations, which led to the September 1993 Middle East Peace Agreement. This raised hopes for a negotiated settlement and the creation of a secular Palestinian state alongside the Jewish state of Israel.

Although parts of the West Bank and Gaza have been turned over to the PLO, there have been fits and starts in the process and ongoing danger that it might break down altogether. Jordan and Egypt agreed in 1994 to a peace treaty with Israel, but other Arab states—notably Syria—have still not been willing to come to an accord with Israel. Extremists on both sides have tried to derail the peace initiative.

Middle Eastern Oil

The oil wealth of the Arab and Iranian world has been another significant factor in its recent history. Since Saudi Arabia's first oil production in 1939, the world demand for oil has soared. Oil has become a major bargaining chip in international diplomacy for Arab and other oil-rich Third World states—such as Venezuela, Nigeria, Iran, and Indonesia. In the Arab countries of North Africa and especially of Arabia and the Gulf, oil production and wealth have changed every aspect of life. Oil has propelled formerly peripheral countries of the Sahara or the Arabian deserts into major roles in international banking and finance. Oil also has boosted the damaged self-confidence of the Arab world after a century and a half of Western domination. A testimony to the global importance of Middle Eastern oil was the willingness of the United States and European nations to form a coalition with Arab countries and commit massive forces to expel Iraq from Kuwait in 1991.

Islamism and Politics

The increase in the global importance of the oil-producing states of the Middle East has coincided with efforts to revive pristine Muslim values and standards and to reform Muslim societies. In the spirit, and often in the footsteps, of earlier Muslim resurgents, many Muslims have sought to return to the "fundamentals" of Islamic life, faith, and society. They see this as a means of rejuvenation, of social and economic as well as political justice, and of defense against Western secularist values. A great part of the appeal of Islamist groups is their willingness and ability to address the needs of the underclasses. Islamic groups have provided social services such as housing, medical care, education, and jobs, under the banner of a just, moral Muslim societal ideal. The political actions of "Islamist reformism" range from revolutionary action (Iran) to democratic participation (Turkey) to complete political quietism (the

Tablighi international revivalist movement begun in Pakistan). Whether these movements will bring lasting change to Islamic societies is an open question.

The background to modern Islamist reform lies in the European expansion over much of the globe since the late 1400s. This expansion brought far more social and political change than religious or even cultural change to the Islamic world. It saw the emergence globally of European-style nationalism and the idea of the nation-state; of post-Enlightenment ideals of individual liberties and rights and representative government; and of the concept of religious faith and affiliation as a private, "religious" matter and citizenship as a public, "secular" matter. Such ideas proved revolutionary in the Islamic world.

The twentieth century in Islamic parts of the world presented a checkered history of autocratic governments. Experiments with European-style parliamentary government have only rarely taken hold, nor have either liberal democratic or Marxist-Socialist political and social ideals. Even so, until recently, little of the political discourse in Islamic lands has given serious attention to specifically *Islamic* alternatives.

With the rise and postcolonial independence of numerous national states and the flourishing of diverse nationalisms, politics became often theoretically as well as actually divorced from Islamic religious tradition and its norms in overt ways that it had not been before. Where leaders had previously claimed Muslim faith and allegiance, some came to espouse secular ideologies and virtually ignored religion except as a political weapon. And used as a weapon it was: Islamic religious allegiance has commonly been invoked to bolster a ruler's claim to legitimacy and often to cloak in pious garb more mundane objectives.

In short, the twentieth century saw no realization of an "ideal" Islamic state in which religious and political authority are conjoined. If anything, the gap widened between Islamic norms and ideals on the one hand and political and social realities on the other. Even the postrevolutionary Islamic Republic of Iran saw a clear division between political necessity and reality and religious values and standards.

When we look at the Islamist movements of recent decades, we find that the calls for a congruence of religion and politics in the Islamic world trace less to some kind of ideal model of a religious state or so-called "theocracy" than to a need for social and political justice, such as that which Islam has always demanded. The cries for a new "jihad" of Muslims are aimed much less often outward than inward at domestic tyrants, corruption, and injustice. Indeed, perhaps the most international and influential of contemporary Islamic revivalist or reform movements, that of the Tabligh-i Jama'at, is explicitly apolitical in its tenets; it looks to convert the individual person of faith to true submission (*islam*) rather than lip service: Reform of the world begins with oneself.

Iran

Iran was ruled from 1925 to 1941 as a monarchy by a former army commander, Reza Khan, who had come to power by military takeover and governed under the old Persian title Shah Reza Pahlavi. He attempted to introduce modernist reforms, not unlike those of Atatürk (1881–1938). By the time Russian and British forces deposed Reza in 1941 and installed his son, Muhammad Reza, as shah, the power of the Shi'ite religious leaders, or *ulama*, had been muted and a strong, centralized state established. The son, like his father, sought to ground the legitimacy of Pahlavi rule on the ancient, pre-Islamic dynasties of greater Iran, especially the Achaemenids (see Chapter 4). He continued his father's secularist state building from the end of World War II until 1978.

In the 1960s, Muhammad Reza Shah was finally forced by popular opposition to institute land reform and other socialist or populist reforms. However, his repressive measures against the leftist and especially the religious opposition alienated the Iranian masses. His reign failed to narrow the gap between them and the wealthy elites.

Finally, in 1978, religious leaders and secularist revolutionaries joined forces to end the Shah's regime with a revolution fueled by Shi'ite feeling and symbolism. In 1979, the constitution of a new Islamic republic was adapted under the guidance of the major Shi'ite religious leader, or *ayatollah*, Ruhollah Khomeini (Khumayni; 1902–1989). Subsequent years have seen a protracted war with Iraq (1980 to 1988) and the institution of repressive and violent measures against enemies of the regime not unlike those used under the Shah. Still, the new state—with religious leaders exercising a degree of influence over politics not seen since early Safavid times in the sixteenth century—has survived. Khomeini and his successor, Hashemi Rafsanjani (b. 1934) had to struggle to find a new formula for combining Muslim values and norms with twentieth-century *Realpolitik*, and this will continue to challenge their successors.

The successor to Rafsanjani, Mohammad Khatami, was elected in 1997 by a resounding majority. Khatami, a moderate cleric with a reputation as a relative liberal, has tried to steer Iran on a moderate and more liberal course. Many think his election and administration represent a key step in Iran's movement toward a more stable government.

Central Asia

North of Iran, 40 million Central Asian Muslims predominate in the south-central reaches of the former USSR, and 30 million or more Muslims live in Chinese Central Asia. They have had to sustain their traditions in the face of Russian and Chinese imperialism. In the 1980s, both Soviet and Chinese Muslims appeared to be asserting themselves. The 1979 Soviet occupation of Afghanistan reflected the potential importance of this movement. The withdrawal of Soviet forces from Afghanistan in 1988 looked surprisingly like the US withdrawal from South Vietnam. It was soon followed by the collapse of the Soviet Union in 1990 into the loosely connected Commonwealth of Independent States (CIS). Suddenly the Central Asian Islamic republics of the former USSR found themselves effectively independent states, yet with little of the infrastructure to manage such a transition successfully. The great challenge is whether they can attain political viability without being destroyed by economic collapse or ethnic or regional conflict. Islamist reformism will surely play a role in these states, but so can civil-society ideals of democratic governance and free-market economies.

South and Southeast Asia

Five major southern and Southeast Asian nations—India, Pakistan, Bangladesh, Indonesia, and Malaysia—that together contain well over half of all Muslims in the world, came into being after World War II. India, a largely Hindu state, and Pakistan, a largely Muslim state, gained independence in 1947. Much of their subsequent history has involved mutual antagonism. The two states have still not resolved their differences, including their conflicting claims to Kashmir. Their rivalry has been exacerbated recently by a new round of sabre-rattling, this time a nuclear one, when both India and Pakistan carried out underground nuclear tests in 1998.

Indonesia and Malaysia, the two largest states of Southeast Asia, have long histories that link them to the wider Islamic world, to Indian culture and religion, and to China.

Pakistan and Bangladesh

The architect and first president of Pakistan, Muhammad Ali Jinnah (1876–1948), oversaw the creation of a Muslim state in the two predominantly Muslim areas of northwest India and East Bengal. In 1971, East Pakistan seceded and became the new Islamic nation of Bangladesh. However, the main political division in the subcontinent remains that between India and Pakistan.

Pakistan's groping efforts to create a fully Islamic society and to solve its massive economic problems have been hampered by periodic lapses into military dictatorship, the latest in 1999. Pakistan, like most Asian societies, faces enormous economic and demographic challenges. The Pakistanis must try to create a modern economic and political system that will meet their physical needs while allowing them to maintain their commitment to remain an Islamic society. Overpopulation, poverty, and a massive military are all major obstacles to Pakistan's progress.

India

India has been directed for most of its existence by the Congress Party, first under Jawaharlal Nehru (1889–1964), who developed India's famous theory of political neutrality vis-à-vis world alignments. He was able to make some headway in reducing the communal hatreds, religious zealotry, and regional tensions of the postpartition era and in the huge task of economic development. Hindi and English were set as the national languages, with fourteen major regional languages, recognized for regional official use. Nehru's resolute opposition to caste privilege also helped to improve equality of citizenship.

Nehru's daughter, Indira Gandhi (1917–1984; prime minister, 1966–1977, 1980–1984; no familial relation to Mohandas Gandhi), carried on most of her father's policies and managed to steer a tricky course of neutralism during the Cold War. India's 1971 victory over Pakistan and the subsequent creation of Bangladesh to replace East Pakistan cemented her political control; this war and the development, with Russian help, of an atomic bomb confirmed India as the major power in South Asia. After her efforts to assume virtual dictatorial power, in 1977 she and the Congress Party were ousted by the voters for three years. She was reelected prime minister and served until her efforts to quell Sikh separatism brought about her assassination in 1984.

Indira Gandhi's son, Rajiv Gandhi (1944–1991), was elected prime minister after her, but charges of corruption led to his party's temporary fall, and in May 1991 he was also assassinated. In the 1990s, Congress Party rule alternated with governments dominated by a coalition of Hindu nationalists.

India's problems remain large. Poverty and disease remain widespread. Separatist movements based on regional linguistic affinity, such as that of the Tamil peoples of the south, or religious affinity, such as that of the Sikhs of the Punjab, have pulled at the unity of the Indian state. Industrialization and agricultural modernization have made great strides, yet the neutralizing force of runaway population growth has not been countered. India's population is now about 1 billion and growing at nearly 2 percent per year. The growing strength of militant Hindu nationalists and fundamentalists and new outbreaks of communal violence between Hindus and the large Muslim minority pose serious threats to stability. As the world's largest functioning democracy, India will be an important model of representative government and pluralistic society if it succeeds in staying together and reducing its overpopulation and mass poverty.

LATIN AMERICA SINCE 1945

During the last half century, the nations of Latin America have experienced divergent paths of political and economic change. Their leaders have tried to alleviate their people's dependence on the more developed nations. At best, these efforts have had mixed results; at worst, they have led to repression and tragedy.

Before World War II, the states of Latin America had been economically dependent on the United States and western Europe. Beginning in the 1950s, Latin America became an arena for confrontations between the United States and the Soviet Union.

During this era attempts were made to expand the industrial base and agricultural production of the various national economies. The financing came from US and Western European banks or from Soviet subsidies. Enormous debts were contracted that made Latin American economies virtual prisoners to the fluctuations of world interest rates and international banks or to Soviet subsidies. These new relationships, however, did not alter the underlying character of most Latin American economies, which remain exporters of agricultural commodities and mineral resources.

A culture of poverty continues to be the most dominant social characteristic of the area. Migration into the cities from the countryside has caused urban overcrowding and slums inhabited by the desperately poor. The standards of health and nutrition have often fallen. The growth of service industries in the cities has also fostered the emergence of a professional, educated middle class that often wants to imitate the lifestyle of their social counterparts in the United States and Western Europe. This new professional middle class has displayed little taste for radical politics, social reform, or revolution. They and the more traditional elites were willing, especially during the 1960s and 1970s, to support military governments pledged to maintain the status quo.

Political events in Latin America led to the establishment of authoritarian governments of both the left and the right and to a retreat from the model of parliamentary democracy. Only Mexico, Colombia, Venezuela, and Costa Rica remained parliamentary states throughout this period. Elsewhere, two paths of political development were followed. In Cuba and Nicaragua, and briefly in Chile, revolutionary socialist governments with close ties to the Soviet Union were established. Elsewhere, often in response to the fear of revolution or communism, military governments held power, sometimes punctuated with brief interludes of civilian rule. Such were the situations in Chile, Brazil, Argentina, Bolivia, Peru, and Uruguay. Governments of both the left and the right engaged in political repression.

These political changes fostered new roles for the military and the Roman Catholic Church. Latin American armies have played key political roles since the Wars of Independence. But since World War II, they have frequently assumed the direct government of nations rather than using indirect influence. Many Roman Catholic priests and bishops have protested inequalities and attacked political repression. Certain Roman

Catholic theologians have combined traditional Christian concern for the poor with Marxist ideology to formulate what is called a liberation theology. This Latin American theological initiative has been attacked by the Vatican.

Since the 1980s, Latin America has changed significantly. Several nations have moved toward democratization and free-market economies. This marks a sharp departure from the 1930s and 1940s, when the state itself was seen as largely responsible for economic development. Yet in most nations, the military keeps a watchful eye on democratic developments and possible disorder. The end of the Cold War brought to a close one source of external political challenge, but the internal social problems of these nations continue to raise difficulties for their governments. In several nations, drug-producing cartels have challenged the authority of governments themselves.

Revolutionary Challenges

There were three major attempts among the nations of Latin America to establish revolutionary governments pursuing major social and economic change. They occurred in Cuba in 1959, in Chile in 1970, and in Nicaragua in 1979. Each involved a Marxist political organization and a close relationship with the Soviet Union. The establishment of these governments provoked active resistance by the United States and opposition from traditional elites.

The Cuban Revolution

Cuba had remained a colony until the Spanish-American War of 1898. Thereafter, it achieved independence within a sphere of US influence that took the form of economic domination and military intervention. The governments of the island were ineffective and corrupt. During the 1950s, Fulgencio Batista (1901–1973), a dictator supported by the United States, ruled Cuba.

Historically, Cuba had been politically restive. On July 26, 1953, Fidel Castro Ruz (b. 1926), the son of a wealthy landowner, and others attacked a government army barracks. The revolutionary movement that he thereafter came to lead in exile took its name from that date: the Twenty-Sixth of July Movement. In 1956, Castro and a handful of followers landed in Cuba. They took refuge in the Sierra Maestra mountains and attacked Batista's forces. Batista fled Cuba on New Year's Day in 1959. In January, Castro arrived in Havana as the revolutionary victor.

Castro undertook the most extensive political, economic, and social reconstruction seen in recent Latin American history. He rejected parliamentary democracy and governed Cuba in an authoritarian manner. The revolutionary government carried out major land redistribution. Both small landowners and large state farms were established.

The Cuban Revolution spurned an industrial economic model and concentrated on the agricultural sector. Sugar preserved its leading role, and the Cuban economy remained monocultural. The sugar industry depended on large Soviet subsidies and on the Soviet-bloc nations for its market. In that respect, the Cuban economy did not escape the cycle of external dependence.

In foreign affairs, the Cuban Revolution was characterized by a sharp break with the United States and a close relationship with the Soviet Union. Castro aligned himself with the Cuban Communist Party and with the Soviet bloc. The United States was hostile toward Castro and toward the presence of a communist state less than a hundred miles from Florida. In 1961, the United States and Cuban exiles launched the unsuccessful Bay of Pigs invasion. The close Cuban relationship to the Soviet Union led to the missile crisis of 1962, the most dangerous incident of the Cold War. In the late 1970s and the 1980s, a dialogue of sorts was undertaken between Cuba and the United States, but mutual distrust continues.

With the collapse of the Soviet Union and the end of the Cold War, the future of Castro's Cuba has become uncertain. Cuba remains the only state closely associated with the former Soviet bloc that has not experienced political or economic reform. The subsidies that flowed from the Soviet Union to support the Cuban economy, however, have ended, creating a shortage of consumer goods. The Marxist political and economic ideology stands discredited throughout the world, but the aging Castro's leadership remains intact. Cuba must confront the need for a successor to Castro. It also must confront the need for economic reform and find a new role in a Latin American order in which the issues of the Cold War are no longer relevant. One hint of new direction came in 1998 when the Castro government permitted a highly publicized visit from Pope John Paul II.

Throughout the Cold War, Cuba assumed an importance far greater than its size might suggest. After 1959, it served as a center for the export of communist revolution and it sent troops to Angola in the late 1970s. The US government sought to prevent the establishment of a second Cuba in Latin America. That goal led to intervention in other revolutionary situations and to support for authoritarian governments in Latin America.

Chile

Until the 1970s, Chile was the most enduring model of parliamentary democracy in Latin America. During the 1960s, however, Chilean politics became polarized. Unemployment rose alarmingly. There was labor unrest and popular resentment of the economic domination of Chile by large US corporations.

The situation came to a head in 1970 when Salvador Allende (1908–1973), the candidate of the left-wing political coalition and a Marxist, was elected president. His coalition did not control the Chilean congress, nor did it have the support of the military. The center and right-wing political groups took a watch-and-wait attitude. Allende nationalized some businesses. Other policies were blocked in the congress, and Allende had to govern by decree. By this device he began to expropriate foreign property, much of which belonged to US corporations. This policy frightened the Chilean owners of small and medium-sized businesses, but did not satisfy workers. Inflation ballooned. Harvests were poor.

In the autumn of 1973, Allende found himself governing a nation in turmoil without significant domestic political support and with many foreign enemies. He proved unwilling to make political compromises or to change his policies. The army became hostile. The government of the United States was disturbed by the prospect of a Marxist nation on the western coast of South America. The Nixon administration supported the discontent within the Chilean army. In mid-September 1973, an army coup overthrew Allende, who was killed in the presidential palace.

Thereafter, for fifteen years Chile was governed by a military junta under General Augusto Pinochet (b. 1915). The military government pursued a close relationship with the United States and resisted Marxism in the hemisphere. It established a state-directed free-market economy and reversed the expropriations of the Allende years. There was also harsh political repression.

In a referendum held in late 1988, Chileans rejected Pinochet's bid for another term as president. Democratization was relatively smooth. Civilian rule has included efforts to investigate the political repression of the Pinochet years. Thousands of cases of torture and murder have been revealed. The Chilean government itself moved slowly, not wishing to revisit the most controversial era of the nation's history.

The Sandinista Revolution in Nicaragua

In the summer of 1979, a Marxist guerrilla force, the Sandinistas, overthrew the corrupt dictatorship of the Somoza family in Nicaragua. The Somozas had governed Nicaragua as their personal preserve since the 1930s with support from the United States. The Sandinistas established a collective government that pursued social and economic reform and reconstruction. The movement—with Roman Catholic priests on its leadership council—epitomized the new political and social forces in Latin America. However, the revolutionary government confronted significant domestic political opposition and military challenge from the contra guerrilla movement.

The government of the United States, particularly under the Reagan administration (1981–1989), was hostile toward the Sandinistas. It provided both direct and indirect aid to the opposition guerrillas. The US government feared the spread of Marxist revolutionary activity in Central America, a fear reinforced by the close ties between the revolutionary government and the Soviet Union. For the United States, the Sandinista government represented in Central America a problem analogous to that of Cuba a generation earlier.

Sandinista rule came to a relatively quick end. In early 1990, after a negotiated peace settlement with the contras, they lost the presidential election to an opposition coalition and relinquished power peacefully.

Pursuit of Stability

Argentina

In 1955, the Argentine army revolted against the Perón dictatorship, and Juan Perón (1895–1974) went into exile. Two decades of economic stagnation and social unrest followed. In 1973, Perón was recalled from exile in a desperate attempt to restore stability, but died about a year later.

By 1976, the army had undertaken direct rule. There was widespread repression; thousands of citizens disappeared, never to be heard of again. In April 1982, General Leopoldo Galtieri (b. 1926) launched a disastrous invasion of the Islas Malvinas (Falkland Islands). Argentina was defeated by Britain, and the military junta discredited.

In 1983 civilian rule was restored, and Argentina set out on the road to democratization. Under President Raul Alfonsín (b. 1927), many of the former military figures responsible for the years of repression received prison sentences. Alfonsín also sought to turn more real political authority over to the Argentine congress. Argentina has provided the most extensive example in Latin America of the restoration of democratic practices after military rule. Peaceful elections and transitions of governments have occurred for two decades.

Brazil

In 1964, the military assumed the direct government of Brazil and did not fully relinquish it until the mid-1980s. The military government stressed order and used repression to maintain it. The army itself, however, was divided. Many officers were concerned that the corruption of everyday politics would undermine the army's reputation and esprit de corps. Consequently, within the army itself, certain forces sought to restore a more democratic government. In 1985, civilian government returned under the military's watchful eye.

Lourdes Arizpe Discusses the Silence of Peasant Women

Lourdes Arizpe, a Mexican anthropologist, wrote extensively on the plight of peasant women in the 1970s. In this passage she discusses how the lives and history of Mexican peasant women are shrouded in silence. Though her remarks are directed toward the situation in Mexico, they may well apply to peasant women in other cultures as well.

What are the factors that Arizpe cites as leading to the historical silence of peasant women? Why does she believe it is important for such women to learn to speak with their own voices? How do the stereotypes of Mexican peasant women both contribute to the silence and arise from the silence? Why does she believe peasant women to be the most marginalized of all women?

History has imposed a greater silence on peasant women than on any other social group. Perhaps it is the solitude of the plains or the obligatory circumspection of their gender or merely political repression, but circumstances combine to force them to live in a secret world. Doubtless there are those who would assert that their tie to nature leads them to express themselves with actions rather than words. But the male peasant lives in the natural world without being silenced.

Silence, when not deliberate (although, how can we be sure it isn't?) could be anger or wisdom or, simply, a gesture of dignity. When there is no one worth talking to, I stay silent. If someone doesn't want to recognize my existence, I stay silent. In the spectrum of invisibility that his-tory has imposed on women, perhaps the most invisible of the invisibles have been the peasants.

When direct expression is not permitted, the possibility of knowledge is lost and we fill that disturbing vacuum with phantoms. It is therefore not surprising that the Mexican mentality is filled with myths and stereotypes about peasant women. There is the submissive Indian woman who is a product of condescending maternalism; the wild woman both fantasized about and feared by men; the brazen hussy of melodramatic soap operas; the faint-hearted but treacherous small-town woman invented by the urban mind. Silence is also created by everyone's desire to hear what they want to hear rather than listen to what women are trying to say.

Today it seems that everyone mouths concerns about peasant women without any sincere interest.

. . . What is important today is to create opportunities for peasant women to speak.

It is not that they have never spoken, only that their words have never been recognized. Because their words are discomforting when they denounce exploitation; disturbing when they display a deep understanding of the natural world not shared by their city sisters; strange when they describe an integrating vision of the universe; and because, being women's words, they are not important to androcentric [male-centered] history. Of all the marginalized peoples, peasant women are the most marginalized.

From Lourdes Arizpe, "Peasant Women and Silence," translated by Laura Beard Milroy in *Women's Writing in Latin America: An Anthology* by Sara Castro-Klarén, Sylvia Malloy, and Beatriz Sarlo. Copyright © 1992 by Westview Press. Reprinted by permission of the author.

The military government fostered denationalized industrial development. Non-Brazilian corporations were invited to spearhead the drive toward industrialization. Brazil opted for an industrialism guided and dominated from the outside. One result was a massive foreign debt, the servicing and repayment of which have become perhaps Brazil's most important national problem. Brazil also became the major industrialized nation in Latin America. The question now is how the social changes wrought by industrialism, such as growing urbanization, will receive political accommodation. In Brazil, as in Argentina, economic and social pressures have spawned conditions ripe for political agitation. It was just that possibility that led both the traditional and the new professional elites to support authoritarian government in the past.

Mexico

Institutionally, Mexico has undergone few political changes since World War II. In theory, the government continued to pursue the goals of the revolution. Power remained in the control of the Partido Revolucionario Institucional (PRI).

Yet shifts had occurred under this apparently stable surface. The government retreated from some of the aims of the revolution and appeared conservative when compared to Marxist states. In the early 1950s, certain large landowners were exempted from the expropriation and redistribution of land. The Mexican government maintained relations with Cuba and the other revolutionary regimes of Latin America but also resisted Marxist doctrines in Mexico. When necessary, it arrested malcontents.

Mexico experienced an oil boom from 1977 to 1983, but the world oil glut burst that bubble. The aftermath revealed the absence of stable growth. Like so many other states in the region, Mexico amassed large foreign debts and thus surrendered real economic independence.

In 1988, the PRI encountered a challenge at the polls. Opposition candidates received much of the vote in a hotly contested election. The PRI remained in power but with the knowledge that it would not be able to dominate the political scene as it had done. Thereafter, the leadership began to decentralize the party. President Carlos Salinas moved to privatize economic enterprise. He also favored free-trade agreements. The most important of these was the North American Free Trade Agreement (NAFTA), which created a vast free-trade area including Mexico, Canada, and the United States. In 1991, Salinas made new accommodations with the Roman Catholic Church, thus moving away from the traditional anticlericalism of Mexican politics. By 1991, the PRI appeared to have regained its former political ascendancy.

However, in 1994 Mexico underwent political shocks. Troops had to quell armed rebellion in Chiapas. During the election of that year the leading candidate was assassinated and party members were charged with complicity in the deed. Party corruption received increased publicity. Early in 1995, Mexico suffered a major economic downturn, and only loans from the United States saved the economy. Ernesto Zedillo, elected president in 1994, blamed Salinas and his family for the situation, and the corruption of the Salinas government became public. The government faced further unrest in Chiapas, growing power among drug lords, and turmoil within the governing party itself. In 2000, the PRI lost the election for the presidency. A new era may have begun.

Continuity and Change in Recent Latin American History

What is most striking about the history of the past four decades in Latin America is its tragic continuity with the region's previous history. Revolution has brought moderate social change, but at the price of authoritarian government, economic stagnation, and dependence on foreign powers. Real independence has not been achieved. Throughout the region for much of the period, parliamentary democracy has been fragile; it was the first element of national life to be sacrificed to the conflicting goals of socialism, economic growth, or resistance to revolution.

The recent trends toward democratization and market economics may, however, mark a break in that pattern. The region could enjoy healthy economic growth if inflation can be contained and investment fostered. The challenge will be to see that the fruits of any new prosperity are shared in a way

that prevents resentment and turmoil. Furthermore, as in the past, economic turmoil far from Latin America may harm it. Each time such turmoil has occurred, the governments of Latin America, like the current government of Mexico, have found themselves economically dependent upon either the United States or Europe.

IN WORLD PERSPECTIVE

The Emerging Nations: Opportunities and Frustrations of Global Democratization

During the past quarter century, on one continent after another, democratic political rights have expanded. Authoritarian political regimes of both the left and the right have undergone reform or collapsed. Dictatorships, military governments, and one-party communist states have been replaced by more nearly democratic governments. Progress has not been uniform, but more people everywhere have a voice in their governments.

This process of political change, usually termed *democratization*, involves the expansion of the numbers of people who participate in the selection of executive and legislative leaders, orderly elections, and reduced governmental control over the daily lives of citizens. The movement has also tended to involve a shift from regulated to free-market economies. Despite many continuing autocracies, at no time in history have so many nations seen such an extension of democratic government.

Initially, many believed that democratization would almost necessarily lead to liberal governments. However, in many nations, especially those of Eastern Europe, the frustrations and economic hardships of the move from centrally planned to market economies have seen the return to political office of former communists who long opposed democracy. Resurgent nationalism has also come to the fore.

The developments of the past two decades must be seen against the backdrop of democratic achievements that followed World War II. The Atlantic Charter drawn up by the United States and Great Britain in 1942 asserted a democratic vision that was first realized among the defeated nations: Germany, Italy, and Japan. All three soon became among the most stable democracies in the world.

Elsewhere, the years immediately following World War II were less hopeful. Eastern Europe fell under the domination of the Soviet Union. In Yugoslavia, Marshall Tito's more or less independent communist government resisted Stalin but was still authoritarian. On the Iberian peninsula, the older dictatorships of Antonio Salazar (1889–1970) and General

Francisco Franco (1892–1975) held sway. In 1967, Greece fell under military rule. In the Middle East, authoritarian rule has been the norm.

From the late 1940s through the 1970s, Latin America was studded with repressive regimes, usually dominated by the military. In Cuba, a communist dictatorship governed after 1957. One of the ongoing justifications of these Latin American authoritarian regimes was the necessity to oppose communist insurrections sponsored from Cuba. Similar appeals had long been used by Salazar in Portugal and Franco in Spain.

In South Africa, the policy of apartheid, which was imposed formally in the 1940s, established a racially divided society in which a white minority held all political and social power. Black South Africans enjoyed no political rights.

Decolonization, which saw the withdrawal of European powers from their colonial empires, also failed to fulfill early democratic expectations. India, after the withdrawal of the British in 1947, became the largest democracy on Earth. But in sub-Saharan Africa, former European colonies generally declined into dictatorships. Across northern postcolonial Africa, authoritarian governments arose whose power often resided in the military or in the use of referenda to confirm authoritarian power. In the former French colonies of Southeast Asia, stable democratic governments failed to establish themselves, and in North Vietnam, a communist government prevailed. But the early democratic vision of the postcolonial world remained as an ideal toward which groups opposing the authoritarian governments could point.

As a result of these developments, some observers believed that the rest of the century might see only a few functioning democracies survive. Democracy appeared secure in North America above the Mexican border, in Western Europe, Japan, Israel, and a few other isolated nations. The rest of the world seemed condemned to authoritarianism.

The political pessimists were proved wrong around the globe. The movement toward an expansion of political participation that culminated in two decades of steady democratization commenced during the mid-1960s. The civil rights movement in the United States fostered a new role for African Americans. The Civil Rights Act of 1964 allowed them entry into areas of social life that had been closed to them since before the turn of the century. Even more important, the Voting Rights Act of 1965 permitted new participation of African-American voters in many southern states where their activity had been barred. Thereafter, the number of African-American elected officials grew in the South and the entire nation.

The next area that witnessed major movement toward democratization was the Mediterranean. Four years after Salazar's death in 1970, an army revolt led to the beginning of a democratic movement that soon brought free elections. General Franco's fascist regime was followed, as he had decreed, by a monarchy. The new king, Juan Carlos (b. 1938), understood that Spain could achieve a new political and economic status in Europe and domestic and political stability only if it moved toward democratic government. His determination to bring democratic government to Spain made his succession stable and lasting. A functioning multiparty system quickly developed.

In some cases, unsuccessful military ventures opened the way to democratic government. Portugal under Salazar, in an attempt to retain colonial rule, had long been involved in an unwinnable war in Angola, undermining enthusiasm for his government. In 1974, the Greek military government collapsed after an unsuccessful confrontation with Turkey over Cyprus. Another important factor turning these nations toward democracy was that the European Economic Community restricted membership to democracies. Any European nation hoping for prosperity had to participate in it.

In Latin America, the Brazilian military allowed elections for the presidency in 1985. Argentina elected a civilian president in 1983; Chile followed in 1990.

Elsewhere in Latin America, the tide of democracy has also continued to rise. Dictatorships and one-party governments, including the Sandinista government in Nicaragua, have generally given way to democratic governments, although the long-term stability of some of them is uncertain.

Worldwide communications technology has often contributed to democratization. Today it is more difficult for repressive governments to hide their repression or to prevent opponents from communicating with the outside world through radio, television, and fax machines. In Asia, the eighties saw an expansion of democracy in South Korea and the Philippines. In South Africa, the repressive apartheid regime was dismantled in the early 1990s.

Despite democratization elsewhere, it was generally assumed that the authoritarian governments of Eastern Europe and the Soviet Union would survive indefinitely. For that reason, the events of the 1980s and early 1990s in that region were astounding. During 1989, all of the Communist Party regimes in Eastern Europe collapsed with amazing rapidity. The Soviet Union itself dissolved in 1991. Democratic governments embracing free-market policies emerged in place of single-party governments and planned economies in all these states.

Yet the new governments of Eastern Europe and the former Soviet Union face constant antidemocratic pressures. There are the former communists who constitute the largest group with political experience. There are ethnic nationalists who feel Russia has been displaced as a great power. The role of the military is uncertain. Throughout Eastern Europe and the former Soviet Union anti-Semitism has reappeared. These nondemocratic forces may display new strength. To fend them off, the democratic governments may resort to repressive measures.

The civil war in the former Yugoslavia displays the violence and disorder that may arise when an authoritarian regime collapses. There the forces of ethnic nationalism have led to civil war, civilian atrocities, deprivation, and nondemocratic government. That conflict could lead to similar disorder elsewhere in Europe.

Not only in Eastern Europe and the former Soviet Union does the drive toward greater democracy throughout the world remain incomplete and uncertain. Communist dictatorships remain in power in Cuba, North Korea, and Vietnam. The People's Republic of China, still dominated by the Chinese Communist Party, repressed a drive toward democracy in 1989 with a massacre of protesters in Tienanmen Square. In Iraq, Iran, Saudi Arabia, and other parts of the Middle East, repressive governments prevail. In much of Africa, the early attempts at democracy have given way to dictatorship.

In the new democracies, the extent of democracy differs from nation to nation. Impatient voters or military leaders may turn to older authoritarian structures. Yet more opportunities now exist for the emergence of democratic governments around the globe than at any time in history.

Review Questions

1. What factors contributed to the spread of decolonization in sub-Saharan Africa? Why were the newly independent states so fragile? Has postcolonial Nigeria lived up to its potential? Why is Nigeria's record significant for Africa as a whole?

2. Describe the apartheid regime in South Africa. Why was it dismantled in the 1990s? What problems does the new South Africa face?

3. Describe the creation of the State of Israel. What has been the response of the Arab nations of the Middle East? What is the current state of Arab-Israeli relations?

4. How has Muslim fundamentalism affected the various Muslim nations? Is Muslim fundamentalism a monolithic movement?

5. Are the nations of Latin America still economically dependent on the United States and Western Europe? Why is this so? How did the superpower rivalry of the Cold War affect Latin America?

6. How successful has the worldwide trend toward democratization been in Latin America? Describe the transition from military rule to civilian democracy in Brazil, Argentina, and Chile. Has Mexico made a similar transition?

Documents CD-ROM

1. Kwame Nkrumah, *I Speak of Freedom: A Statement of African Ideology*

2. Amilcar Cabral: The Force of the Intellect

3. Julius Nyerere's Path of Ujamaa

4. Nelson Mandela: The Ultimate Conquest

5. African Women: An Overlooked Factor?

6. Moncada: The Beginnings of Fidelismo

SUGGESTED READINGS

Chapter 1

General Prehistory

V. GORDON CHILDE, *What Happened in History* (1946). A pioneering study of human prehistory and history before the Greeks from an anthropological point of view.

M. EHRENBERG, *Women in Prehistory* (1989). An account of the role of women in early times.

D. C. JOHNSON AND M. R. EDEY, *Lucy: The Beginning of Mankind* (1981). An account of the African origins of humans.

CHARLES L. REDMAN, *The Rise of Civilization* (1978). An attempt to use the evidence provided by anthropology, archaeology, and the physical sciences to illuminate the development of early urban society.

Near East

M. E. AUBER, *The Phoenicians and the West* (1996). A new study of an important sea-going people who served as a conduit between east and west.

BEN-TOR, ED., *The Archaeology of Ancient Israel* (1992). A useful and up-to-date survey.

H. CRAWFORD, *Sumer and the Sumerians* (1991). A discussion of the oldest Mesopotamian civilization.

HENRI FRANKFORT, *Ancient Egyptian Religion: An Interpretation* (1948). A brief but masterful attempt to explore the religious conceptual world of ancient Egyptians in intelligible and interesting terms.

HENRI FRANKFORT ET AL., *Before Philosophy* (1949). A brilliant examination of the mind of the ancients from the Stone Age to the Greeks.

ALAN GARDINER, *Egypt of the Pharaohs* (1961). A sound narrative history.

W. W. HALLO AND W. K. SIMPSON, *The Ancient Near East: A History* (1971). A fine survey of Egyptian and Mesopotamian history.

THORKILD JACOBSEN, *The Treasures of Darkness: A History of Mesopotamian Religion* (1976). A superb and sensitive recreation of the spiritual life of Mesopotamian peoples from the fourth to the first millennium B.C.E.

J. N. POSTGATE, *Early Mesopotamia* (1992). An excellent study of Mesopotamian economy and society from the earliest times to about 1500 B.C.E., helpfully illustrated with drawings, photos, and translated documents.

JAMES B. PRITCHARD, ED., *Ancient Near Eastern Texts Relating to the Old Testament* (1969). A good collection of documents in translation with useful introductory material.

D. B. REDFORD, *Akhenaten* (1987). A study of the controversial religious reformer.

W. F. SAGGS, *Everyday Life in Babylonia and Assyria*, rev. ed. (1987). A new edition of a classic work.

W. F. SAGGS, *The Might That Was Assyria* (1984). A history of the northern Mesopotamian Empire and a worthy companion to the author's account of the Babylonian Empire in the south.

B. G. TRIGGER ET AL., *Ancient Egypt: A Social History* (1982).

JOHN A. WILSON, *Culture of Ancient Egypt* (1956). A fascinating interpretation of the civilization of ancient Egypt.

India

D. P. AGRAWAL, *The Archaeology of India* (1982). A fine survey of the problems and data. Detailed, but with excellent summaries and brief discussions of major issues.

B. AND R. ALLCHIN, *The Birth of Indian Civilization: India and Pakistan Before 500 B.C.* (1968). A one-volume summary of prehistoric India from an archaeological perspective.

W. T. DE BARY ET AL., COMP., *Sources of Indian Tradition* (1958; 2nd rev. ed., 2 vols., New York, 1988). A fine anthology of original texts in translation from all periods of Indian civilization.

A. L. BASHAM, *The Wonder That Was India*, 2nd rev. ed. (1963). Chapters 1 and 2 provide a readable and carefully done introduction to ancient India through the Aryan culture. Still the classic survey.

E. C. L. DURING CASPERS, "Sumer, Coastal Arabia and the Indus Valley in Protoliterate and Early Dynastic Eras," *JESHO* 22, 2 (1979): 121–135.

C. CHAKRABORTY, *Common Life in the Rigveda and Atharvaveda—An Account of the Folklore in the Vedic Period* (1977). An interesting attempt to reconstruct everyday life in the Vedic period from the principal Vedic texts.

D. D. KOSAMBI, *Ancient India: A History of Its Culture and Civilization* (1965). The most readable survey history of India to the fourth century C.E. See Chapters 2–4 on prehistoric, Indus, and Aryan culture.

W. D. O'FLAHERTY, *The Rig Veda: An Anthology* (1981). An excellent selection of Vedic texts in prosaic but very careful translation, with helpful notes on the texts.

J. E. SCHWARTZBERG, ED., *A Historical Atlas of South Asia* (1978). The definitive reference work for historical geography. Includes chronological tables and substantive essays.

R. L. SINGH, ED., *India: A Regional Geography* (1971). An excellent reference source for each of the major regions of the subcontinent.

China

K. C. CHANG, *The Archeology of Ancient China*, 4th ed. (1986). The standard work on the subject.

K. C. CHANG, *Art, Myth, and Ritual, The Path to Political Authority in Ancient China* (1984). A study of the relation between shamans, gods, agricultural production, and political authority during the Shang and Chou dynasties.

K. C. CHANG, *Shang Civilization* (1980).

D. HAWKES, *Ch'u Tz'u, The Songs of the South* (1985). Chou poems from the southern state of Ch'u, superbly translated.

C. Y. HSU, *Ancient China in Transition: An Analysis of Social Mobility 722–222 B.C.* (1965). A study of the Eastern Chou dynasty.

C. Y. HSU, *Western Chou Civilization* (1988).

X. Q. LI, *Eastern Zhou and Qin Civilizations* (1986). This work includes fresh interpretations based on archaeological finds.

Americas

R. L. BURGER, *Chavín and the Origins of Andean Civilization* (1992). A lucid and detailed account of the rise of civilization in the Andes.

M. D. COE, *America's First Civilization* (1968). Examines the earliest civilizations of Mesoamerica.

L. S. CRESSMAN, *Prehistory of the Far West: Homes of Vanished Peoples* (1977). Examines the earliest history of native Americans in the Pacific Northwest.

V. W. FITZHUGH AND A. CROWELL, *Crossroads of Continents: Cultures of Siberia and Alaska* (1988). Covers the area where the immigration from Eurasia to the Americas began.

R. FORD, ED., *Prehistoric Food Production in North America* (1985). Examines the origins of agriculture in the Americas.

D. HEYDEN AND P. GENDREP, *Precolumbian Architecture of Mesoamerica* (1975). A discussion of the architecture of Mesoamerica.

P. D. HUNT, *Indian Agriculture in America: Prehistory to the Present* (1987). Includes a discussion of preconquest agriculture.

J. D. JENNINGS, ED., *Ancient South Americans* (1983). Articles on Andean prehistory.

S. MASUDA, I. SHIMADA, AND C. MORRIS, *Andean Ecology and Civilization* (1985). Includes coverage of the earliest civilizations in the Andes.

C. MORRIS AND A. VON HAGEN, *The Inka Empire and Its Andean Origins* (1993). An overview of Andean civilization with excellent illustrations.

M. MOSELEY, *The Incas and Their Ancestors: The Archaeology of Ancient Peru* (1992). An overview of Peruvian archaeology.

J. A. SABLOFF, *The New Archaeology and the Ancient Maya* (1990). A lively account of recent research in Mayan archaeology.

Chapter 2

China

H. G. CREEL, *What Is Taoism? And Other Studies in Chinese Cultural History* (1970).

W. T. DE BARY ET AL., *Sources of Chinese Tradition* (1960). A reader in China's philosophical and historical literature. It should be consulted for the later periods as well as for the Chou.

Y. L. FUNG, *A Short History of Chinese Philosophy*, ED. D. Bodde (1948). A survey of Chinese philosophy from its origins to recent times.

D. C. LAU, trans., *Lao-Tzu, Tao Te Ching* (1963).

D. C. LAU, trans., *Confucius, The Analects* (1979).

F. W. MOTE, *Intellectual Foundations of China* (1971).

B. I. SCHWARTZ, *The World of Thought in Ancient China* (1985).

A. WALEY, *Three Ways of Thought in Ancient China* (1956). An easy yet sound introduction to Confucianism, Taoism, and Legalism.

A. WALEY, *The Book of Songs* (1960).

B. WATSON, trans., *Basic Writings of Mo Tzu, Hsun Tzu, and Han Fei Tzu* (1963).

B. WATSON, trans., *The Complete Works of Chuang Tzu* (1968).

H. WELCH, *Taoism, The Parting of the Way* (1967).

India

A. L. BASHAM, *The Wonder That Was India*, rev. ed. (1963). Still unsurpassed by more recent works. Chap. VII, "Religion," is a superb introduction to the Vedic-Aryan, Brahmanic, Hindu, Jain, and Buddhist traditions of thought.

W. N. BROWN, *Man in the Universe: Some Continuities in Indian Thought* (1970). A penetrating yet brief reflective summary of major patterns in Indian thinking.

W. T. DE BARY ET AL., *Sources of Indian Tradition* (1958). 2 vols. Vol. I, *From the Beginning to 1800*, ed. and rev. Ainslie T. Embree (1988). Excellent selections from a variety of Indian texts, with good introductions to chapters and individual selections.

PETER HARVEY, *An Introduction to Buddhism* (1990). Chapters 1–3 provide an excellent historical introduction.

T. J. HOPKINS, *The Hindu Religious Tradition* (1971). A first-rate, thoughtful introduction to Hindu religious ideas and practice.

JOHN M. KOLLER, *The Indian Way* (1982). A useful, wide-ranging handbook of Indian thought and religion.

W. RAHULA, *What the Buddha Taught*, 2nd ed. (1974). A readable introduction to Buddhist thought from a Theravadin viewpoint, with primary-source selections.

R. H. ROBINSON AND W. L. JOHNSON, *The Buddhist Religion*, 3rd ed. (1982). An excellent first text on the Buddhist tradition, its thought and development.

R. C. ZAEHNER, *Hinduism* (1966). One of the best general introductions to central Indian religious and philosophical ideas.

Israel

J. BRIGHT, *A History of Israel* (1968), 2nd ed. (1972). One of the standard scholarly introductions to biblical history and literature.

W. D. DAVIES AND L. FINKELSTEIN, EDS., *The Cambridge History of Judaism.* Vol. I, *Introduction: The Persian Period* (1984). Excellent essays on diverse aspects of the exilic period and later.

J. NEUSNER, *The Way of Torah: An Introduction to Judaism* (1979). A sensitive introduction to the Judaic tradition and faith.

L. W. SCHWARZ, ED., *Great Ages and Ideas of the Jewish People* (1956). Especially the first section, "The Biblical Age," by Yehezkel Kaufmann.

Greece

J. BURNET, *Early Greek Philosophy* (1963). Stresses the rational aspect of Greek thought and its sharp break with mythology.

F. M. CORNFORD, *From Religion to Philosophy* (1912). Emphasizes the elements of continuity between myth and religion on the one hand and Greek philosophy on the other.

B. FARRINGTON, *Greek Science* (1953). A lively interpretation of the origins and character of Greek scientific thought.

G. B. KERFERD, *The Sophistic Movement* (1981). An excellent description and analysis.

J. LEAR, *Aristotle: The Desire to Understand* (1988). A brilliant yet comprehensible introduction to the work of the philosopher.

J. M. ROBINSON, *An Introduction to Early Greek Philosophy* (1968). A valuable collection of the main fragments and ancient testimony to the works of the early philosophers, with excellent commentary.

G. VLASTOS, *The Philosophy of Socrates* (1971). A splendid collection of essays illuminating the problems presented by this remarkable man.

G. VLASTOS, *Platonic Studies*, 2nd ed. (1981). A similar collection on the philosophy of Plato.

G. VLASTOS, *Socrates, Ironist and Moral Philosopher* (1991). The results of a lifetime of study by the leading interpreter of Socrates in our time.

Chapter 3

The Rise of Greek Civilization

A. R. BURN, *Persia and the Greeks*, 2nd ed. (1984). A thorough narrative and analysis of the conflict between the Persians and the Greeks down to 479 B.C.E.

J. B. BURY AND R. MEIGSS, *A History of Greece*, 4th ed., (1975). A thorough and detailed one-volume narrative history.

P. CARTLEDGE, *Sparta and Lakonia* (1979).

J. CHADWICK, *The Mycenaean World* (1976). A readable account by a man who helped decipher Mycenaean writing.

R. DREWS, *The Coming of the Greeks* (1988). A fine discussion of the Greeks' arrival as part of the movements of the Indo-European peoples.

V. EHRENBERG, *The Greek State* (1964). A good handbook of constitutional history.

J. V. FINE, *The Ancient Greeks* (1983). An excellent survey that discusses historical problems and the evidence that gives rise to them.

M. I. FINLEY, *World of Odysseus*, REV. ED. (1965). A fascinating attempt to reconstruct Homeric society.

P. GREEN, *Xerxes at Salamis* (1970). A lively and stimulating history of the Persian War.

V. D. HANSON, *The Western Way of War* (1989). A brilliant and lively discussion of the rise and character of the hoplite phalanx and its influence on Greek society.

V. D. HANSON, *The Other Greeks* (1995). A revolutionary account of the Greek invention of the family farm and its centrality for the shaping of the *polis*.

S. HOOD, *The Minoans* (1971). A sketch of Bronze Age civilization on Crete.

D. KAGAN, *The Great Dialogue: A History of Greek Political Thought from Homer to Polybius* (1965). A discussion of the relationship between the Greek historical experience and political theory.

W. K. LACEY, *The Family in Ancient Greece* (1984).

J. F. LAZENBY, *The Defense of Greece, 490–479 B.C.* (1993). A new and valuable study of the Persian wars.

J. F. McGLEW, *Tyranny and Political Culture in Ancient Greece* (1993). A recent account of political developments in the Archaic Age.

O. MURRAY, *Early Greece* (1980). A lively and imaginative account of the early history of Greece to the end of the Persian War.

C. ROEBUCK, *Economy and Society in the Early Greek World* (1984). A valuable study.

B. SNELL, *Discovery of the Mind* (1960). An important study of Greek intellectual development.

A. M. SNODGRASS, *The Dark Age of Greece* (1972). A good examination of the archaeological evidence.

C. G. STARR, *The Economic and Social Growth of Early Greece, 800–500 B.C.* (1977).

EMILY VERMEULE, *Greece in the Bronze Age* (1972). A study of the Mycenaean period.

A. G. WOODHEAD, *Greeks in the West* (1962). An account of the Greek settlements in Italy and Sicily.

W. J. WOODHOUSE, *Solon the Liberator* (1965). A discussion of the great Athenian reformer.

D. C. YOUNG, *The Olympic Myth of Greek Athletics* (1984). A lively challenge to the orthodox view that Greek athletes were amateurs.

Classical and Hellenistic Greece

M. AUSTIN AND P. VIDAL-NAQUET, *The Economic and Social History of Classical Greece* (1977). A combination of documents and explanation.

W. BURKERT, *Greek Religion* (1987). An excellent study by an outstanding student of the subject.

G. Cawkwell, *Philip of Macedon* (1978). A brief but learned account of Philip's career.

J. K. Davies, *Democracy and Classical Greece* (1978). Emphasizes archeological evidence and social history.

J. R. Lane Fox, *Alexander the Great* (1973). An imaginative account that does more than the usual justice to the Persian side of the problem.

Y. Garlan, *Slavery in Ancient Greece* (1988). An up-to-date survey.

Peter Green, *Alexander to Actium: The Historical Evolution of the Hellenistic Age* (1990). A remarkable synthesis of political and cultural history.

C. D. Hamilton, *Agesilaus and the Failure of Spartan Hegemony* (1991). An excellent biography of the king who was the central figure in Sparta during its domination in the fourth century B.C.E.

N. G. L. Hammond, *Philip of Macedon* (1994). A new biography of the founder of the Macedonian Empire.

N. G. L. Hammond and G. T. Griffith, *A History of Macedonia*, Vol. 2, *550–336 B.C.* (1979). A thorough account of Macedonian history that focuses on the careers of Philip and Alexander.

R. Just, *Women in Athenian Law and Life* (1988). An account of women's place in Athenian society.

D. Kagan, *The Outbreak of the Peloponnesian War* (1969). A study of the period from the foundation of the Delian League to the coming of the Peloponnesian War that argues that war could have been avoided.

B. M. W. Knox, *The Heroic Temper: Studies in Sophoclean Tragedy* (1964). A brilliant analysis of tragic heroism.

D. M. Lewis, *Sparta and Persia* (1977). A valuable discussion of relations between Sparta and Persia in the fifth and fourth centuries B.C.E.

G. E. R. Lloyd, *Greek Science After Aristotle* (1974).

A. A. Long, *Hellenistic Philosophy: Stoics, Epicureans, Sceptics* (1974). An account of Greek science in the Hellenistic and Roman periods.

R. Meiggs, *The Athenian Empire* (1972). A fine study of the rise and fall of the empire, making excellent use of inscriptions.

H. W. Parke, *Festivals of the Athenians* (1977). A fine discussion of the religious practices of the Athenians.

J. J. Pollitt, *Art and Experience in Classical Greece* (1972). A scholarly and entertaining study of the relationship between art and history in classical Greece, with excellent illustrations.

J. J. Pollitt, *Art in the Hellenistic Age* (1986). An extraordinary analysis that places the art in its historical and intellectual context.

M. I. Rostovtzeff, *Social and Economic History of the Hellenistic World*, 3 vols. (1941). A masterpiece of synthesis by a great historian.

D. M. Schaps, *Economic Rights of Women in Ancient Greece* (1981).

B. S. Strauss, *Athens After the Peloponnesian War* (1987). An excellent discussion of Athens' recovery and of the nature of Athenian society and politics in the fourth century B.C.E.

B. S. Strauss, *Fathers and Sons in Athens* (1993). An unusual synthesis of social, political and intellectual history.

W. W. Tarn, *Alexander the Great*, 2 vols. (1948). The first volume is a narrative account, the second a series of detailed studies.

W. W. Tarn and G. T. Griffith, *Hellenistic Civilization* (1961). A survey of Hellenistic history and culture.

V. Tcherikover, *Hellenistic Civilization and the Jews* (1970). A fine study of the impact of Hellenism on the Jews.

G. Vlastos, *Socrates, Ironist and Moral Philosopher* (1991). The results of a lifetime of study by the leading interpreter of Socrates in our time.

F. W. Walbank, *The Hellenistic World* (1981).

Chapter 4

Iran

M. Boyce, *Zoroastrians: Their Religious Beliefs and Practices* (1979). The most recent survey, organized historically and based on extensive research.

M. Boyce, ed. and trans., *Textual Sources for the Study of Zoroastrianism* (1984). Well-translated selections from a broad range of ancient Iranian materials.

J. M. Cook, *The Persian Empire* (1983). Survey of the Achaemenid period.

John Curtis, *Ancient Persia* (1989). Excellent portfolio of photographs of artifacts and sites, with a clear historical survey of the arts and culture of ancient Iran.

W. D. Davies and L. Finkelstein, ed., *The Cambridge History of Judaism*, Vol. 1 (Introduction; The Persian Period). Good articles on Iran and Iranian religion as well as Judaism.

J. Duchesne-Guillemin, trans., *The Hymns of Zarathushtra*, trans. M. Henning (1952, 1963). The best short introduction to the original texts of the Zoroastrian hymns.

R. N. Frye, *The Heritage of Persia* (1963, 1966). A first-rate survey of Iranian history to Islamic times: readable but scholarly.

R. Ghirshman, *Iran* (1954). Good material on culture, society, and economy as well as politics and history.

W. W. Malandra, trans. and ed., *An Introduction to Ancient Iranian Religion: Readings from the Avesta and Achaemenid Inscriptions* (1983). Helpful especially for texts of inscriptions relevant to religion.

India

A. L. Basham, *The Wonder That Was India*, rev. ed. (1963). Excellent material on Mauryan religion, society, culture, and history.

A. L. Basham, ed., *A Cultural History of India* (1975). A fine collection of historical-survey essays by a variety of scholars. See Part I, "The Ancient Heritage" (Chapters 2–16).

N. N. Bhattacharyya, *Ancient Indian History and Civilization: Trends and Perspectives* (1988). Covers Mauryan and Gupta times as well as earlier periods, with chapters on political systems, cities and villages, ideology and religion, and art.

W. T. de Bary et al., comp., *Sources of Indian Tradition*, 2nd ed. (1958). Vol. I: *From the Beginning to 1800*, ed. and rev. Ainslie T. Embree (1988). Excellent selections from a wide variety of Indian texts, with good introductions to chapters and selections.

B. Rowland, *The Art and Architecture of India: Buddhist/Hindu/Jain*, 3rd rev. ed. (1970). The standard work, lucid and easy to read. Note Part Three, "Romano-Indian Art in North-West India and Central Asia."

V. A. Smith, ed., *The Oxford History of India*, 4th rev. ed. by Percival Spear et al. (1981), pp. 71–163. A dry, occasionally dated historical survey. Includes useful reference chronologies.

R. Thapar, *Ashoka and the Decline of the Mauryans* (1973). The standard treatment of Ashoka's reign.

R. Thapar, *A History of India, Part I* (1966), pp. 50–108. Three chapters that provide a basic survey of the period.

Stanley Wolpert, *A New History of India*, 2nd ed. (1982). A basic survey history. Chapters 5 and 6 cover the Mauryans, Guptas, and Kushans.

Greek and Asian Dynasties

A. K. Narain, *The Indo-Greeks* (1957. Reprinted with corrections, 1962). The most comprehensive account of the complex history of the various kings and kingdoms.

F. E. Peters, *The Harvest of Hellenism* (1970), pp. 222–308. Helpful chapters on Greek rulers of the Eastern world from Seleucus to the last Indo-Greeks.

J. W. Sedlar, *India and the Greek World: A Study in the Transmission of Culture* (1980). A basic work that provides a good overview.

D. Sinor, ed., *The Cambridge History of Early Inner Asia* (1990). See especially Chapters 6 and 7.

Chapter 5

From Republic to Empire

F. E. Adcock, *The Roman Art of War Under the Republic* (1940). An analysis of Roman military procedures.

E. Badian, *Foreign Clientelae* (1958). A brilliant study of the Roman idea of a client-patron relationship extended to foreign affairs.

E. Badian, *Roman Imperialism in the Late Republic*, 2nd ed. (1968).

A. H. Bernstein, *Tiberius Sempronius Gracchus: Tradition and Apostacy* (1978). A new interpretation of Tiberius's place in Roman politics.

J. Boardman, J. Griffin, and O. Murray, *The Oxford History of the Roman World* (1990). An encyclopedic approach to the varieties of the Roman experience.

P. A. Brunt, *Social Conflicts in the Roman Republic* (1971).

T. J. Cornell, *The Beginnings of Rome. Italy and Rome from the Bronze Age to the Punic Wars, c. 1000–264 B.C.* (1995). A consideration of the royal and early republican periods of Roman history.

T. Cornell and J. Matthews, *Atlas of the Roman World* (1982). Much more than the title indicates, this book presents a comprehensive view of the Roman world in its physical and cultural setting.

S. Dixon, *The Roman Mother* (1988). Describes the place of women within the Roman family.

D. C. Earl, *The Moral and Political Tradition of Rome* (1967).

R. M. Errington, *The Dawn of Empire: Rome's Rise to Power* (1972). An account of Rome's conquest of the Mediterranean.

M. Gelzer, *Caesar: Politician and Statesman*, trans. by P. Needham (1968). The best biography of Caesar.

E. S. Gruen, *The Last Generation of the Roman Republic* (1973). An interesting but controversial interpretation of the fall of the republic.

E. S. Gruen, *The Hellenistic World and the Coming of Rome* (1984). A new interpretation of Rome's conquest of the eastern Mediterranean.

W. V. Harris, *War and Imperialism in Republican Rome, 327–70 B.C.* (1975). An analysis of Roman attitudes and intentions concerning imperial expansion and war.

A. Keaveney, *Rome and the Unification of Italy* (1988). The story of how Rome organized her defeated opponents.

A. Keaveney, *Lucullus: A Life* (1992). A biography of the famous Roman epicure.

J. F. Lazenby, *Hannibal's War: A Military History of the Second Punic War* (1978). A careful and thorough account.

F. B. Marsh, *A History of the Roman World from 146 to 30 B.C.*, 3rd ed., rev. by H. H. Scullard (1963). An excellent narrative account.

C. Nicolet, *The World of the Citizen in Republican Rome* (1980).

M. Pallottino, *The Etruscans*, 6th ed. (1974). Makes especially good use of archaeological evidence.

R. T. Ridley, *The History of Rome* (1989). A solid general history.

E. T. Salmon, *Roman Colonization Under the Republic* (1970).

E. T. Salmon, *The Making of Roman Italy* (1982). The story of Roman expansion on the Italian peninsula.

H. H. Scullard, *A History of the Roman World 753–146 B.C.*, 4th ed. (1980). An unusually fine narrative history with useful critical notes.

H. H. Scullard, *From the Gracchi to Nero*, 5th ed. (1982). A work of the same character and quality.

A. N. SHERWIN-WHITE, *Roman Citizenship* (1939). A useful study of the Roman franchise and its extension to other peoples.

D. STOCKTON, *Cicero: A Political Biography* (1971). A readable and interesting study.

D. STOCKTON, *The Gracchi* (1979). An interesting analytic narrative.

L. R. TAYLOR, *Party Politics in the Age of Caesar* (1949). A fascinating analysis of Roman political practices.

B. H. WARMINGTON, *Carthage* (1960). A good survey.

G. WILLIAMS, *The Nature of Roman Poetry* (1970). An unusually graceful and perceptive literary study.

Imperial Rome

J. P. V. D. BALSDON, *Roman Women* (1962).

T. BARNES, *The New Empire of Diocletian and Constantine* (1982).

K. R. BRADLEY, *Slavery and Society at Rome* (1994). A study of the role of slaves in Roman life.

P. BROWN, *Augustine of Hippo* (1967). A splendid biography.

P. BROWN, *The World of Late Antiquity, A.D. 150–750* (1971). A brilliant and readable essay.

J. BURCKHARDT, *The Age of Constantine the Great* (1956). A classic work by the Swiss cultural historian.

E. R. DODDS, *Pagan and Christian in an Age of Anxiety* (1965). An original and perceptive study.

A. FERRILL, *The Fall of the Roman Empire, The Military Explanation* (1986). An interpretation that emphasizes the decline in the quality of the Roman army.

A. FERRILL, *Caligula: Emperor of Rome* (1991). A biography of the monstrous young emperor.

E. GIBBON, *The History of the Decline and Fall of the Roman Empire*, 2nd ed., 7 vols., ed. by J. B. Bury (1909–1914). One of the masterworks of the English language.

M. GRANT, *The Fall of the Roman Empire* (1990). A lively, well-written account.

N. HANNESTAD, *Roman Art and Imperial Policy* (1988). An analysis of how the emperors used the arts to further their own and imperial interests.

A. H. M. JONES, *The Later Roman Empire*, 3 vols. (1964). A comprehensive study of the period.

D. KAGAN, ED., *The End of the Roman Empire: Decline or Transformation?* 3rd ed. (1992). A collection of essays discussing the problem of the decline and fall of the Roman Empire.

J. LEBRETON AND J. ZEILLER, *History of the Primitive Church*, 3 vols. (1962). From the Catholic viewpoint.

J. E. LENDON, *Empire of Honor, The Art of Government in the Roman World* (1997). An original and path-breaking interpretation.

H. LIETZMANN, *History of the Early Church*, 2 vols. (1961). From the Protestant viewpoint.

F. LOT, *The End of the Ancient World and the Beginnings of the Middle Ages* (1961). A study that emphasizes gradual transition rather than abrupt change.

E. N. LUTTWAK, *The Grand Strategy of the Roman Empire* (1976). An original and fascinating analysis by a keen student of modern strategy.

R. MACMULLEN, *Paganism in the Roman Empire* (1981).

R. MACMULLEN, *Roman Social Relations, 50 B.C. to A.D. 284* (1981).

R. MACMULLEN, *Corruption and the Decline of Rome* (1988). A study that examines the importance of changes in ethical ideas and behavior.

R. W. MATHISON, *Roman Aristocrats in Barbarian Gaul: Strategies for Survival* (1993). An unusual slant on the late empire.

W. A. MEEKS, *The Origins of Christian Morality. The First Two Centuries*. An account of the shaping of Christianity in the Roman Empire.

F. G. B. MILLAR, *The Emperor in the Roman World, 31 B.C.–A.D. 337* (1977). A study of Roman imperial government.

F. MILLAR, *The Roman Empire and Its Neighbors*, 2nd ed. (1981).

A. MOMIGLIANO, ED., *The Conflict Between Paganism and Christianity* (1963). A valuable collection of essays.

H. M. D. PARKER, *A History of the Roman World from A.D. 138 to 337* (1969). A good survey.

M. I. ROSTOVTZEFF, *Social and Economic History of the Roman Empire*, 2nd ed. (1957). A masterpiece whose main thesis has been much disputed.

V. RUDICH, *Political Dissidence Under Nero, The Price of Dissimulation* (1993). A brilliant exposition of the lives and thoughts of political dissidents in the early empire.

E. T. SALMON, *A History of the Roman World, 30 B.C. to A.D. 138* (1968). A good survey.

R. SYME, *The Roman Revolution* (1960). A brilliant study of Augustus, his supporters, and their rise to power.

R. SYME, *The Augustan Aristocracy* (1985). An examination of the new ruling class shaped by Augustus.

L. A. THOMPSON, *Romans and Blacks* (1989).

Chapter 6

P. BOHANNAN AND P. CURTIN, *Africa and Africans*, rev. ed. (1971). An enjoyable and enlightening discussion of African history and prehistory and of major African institutions (e.g., arts, family life, religion).

P. CURTIN, S. FEIERMANN, L. THOMPSON, AND J. VANSINA, *African History* (1978). Probably the best survey history. The relevant portions are chaps. 1, 2, 4, 8, and 9.

T. R. H. DAVENPORT, *South Africa: A Modern History*, 3rd rev. ed. (1987). Chapter 1 gives excellent summary coverage of prehistoric southern Africa, the Khoisan peoples, and the Bantu migrations.

B. DAVIDSON, *The African Past* (1967). A combination of primary-source selections and brief secondary discussions trace sympathetically the history of the diverse parts of Africa.

J. D. Fage, *A History of Africa* (1978). A fine general history. The relevant segment here is Part I, "The Internal Development of African Society" (chaps. 1–5).

P. Garlake, *The Kingdoms of Africa* (1978). A lavishly illustrated set of photographic essays that provide a helpful introduction to the various historically important areas of precolonial Africa.

R. W. July, *Precolonial Africa: An Economic and Social History* (1975). A very readable, topically arranged study. See especially "The Savannah Farmer," "The Bantu," "Cattlemen," and "The Traders" chapters.

R. W. July, *A History of the African People*, 3rd ed. (1980). Part I, "Ancient Africa," covers the precolonial centuries and offers a very readable historical introduction to African civilization.

J. Ki-Zerbo, *Methodology and African Prehistory*. Vol. I of *UNESCO General History of Africa* (1981). Useful summary and interpretive articles (but of very uneven quality) treat diverse topics, including sources, languages, geography, and prehistory.

H. Loth, *Woman in Ancient Africa*. Trans. S. Marnie (1987). An interesting survey of legal, familial, cultural, and other aspects of women's roles.

G. Mokhtar, *Ancient Civilizations of Africa*. Vol. II of *UNESCO General History of Africa* (1981). As in other volumes, the quality of articles varies greatly. Relevant chaps. are 8–16 on Nubia, Meroe, and Aksum; 17–20 on the Saharan region in ancient times; and 22–29 on the early history of sub-Saharan Africa.

R. Oliver, *The African Experience* (1991). A masterly, balanced, and engaging sweep through African history. The chapters on prehistory and early history are outstanding summaries of the results and implications of recent research.

I. Van Sertima, *Black Women in Antiquity* (1984, 1988). Studies of queens, goddesses, matriarchy, and other aspects of the role and status of women in Egyptian, Ethiopian, and other African societies of the past.

Chapter 7

D. Bodde, *China's First Unifier* (1938). A study of the Ch'in unification of China, viewed through the Legalist philosopher and statesman Li Ssu.

T. T. Ch'u, *Law and Society in Traditional China* (1961). Treats the sweep of Chinese history from 202 b.c.e. to 1911 c.e.

T. T. Ch'u, *Han Social Structure* (1972).

A. Cotterell, *The First Emperor of China* (1981).

R. Coulborn, *Feudalism in History* (1965). One chapter interestingly compares the quasi-feudalism of the Chou with that of the Six Dynasties period.

J. K. Fairbank, E. O. Reischauer, and A. M. Craig, *East Asia: Tradition and Transformation* (1989). A widely read single-volume history covering China, Japan, and other countries in East Asia from antiquity to recent times.

J. Gernet, *A History of Chinese Civilization* (1982). An excellent survey of Chinese history.

C. Y. Hsu, *Ancient China in Transition* (1965). On social mobility during the Eastern Chou era.

C. Y. Hsu, *Han Agriculture* (1980). A study of the agrarian economy of China during the Han dynasty.

J. Levi, *The Chinese Emperor* (1987). A novel about the First Ch'in Emperor based on scholarly sources.

M. Loewe, *Everyday Life in Early Imperial China* (1968). A social history of the Han dynasty.

J. Needham, *The Shorter Science and Civilization in China* (1978). An abridgment of the multivolume work on the same subject with the same title—minus Shorter—by the same author.

C. Schirokauer, *A Brief History of Chinese and Japanese Civilizations* (1978). A standard text, especially good on literature and art.

M. Sullivan, *The Arts of China* (1967). An excellent survey history of Chinese art.

D. Twitchett and M. Loewe eds., *The Ch'in and Han Empires, 221 b.c.–a.d. 220* (1986). (Vol. 1 of *The Cambridge History of China*.)

Z. S. Wang, *Han Civilization* (1982).

B. Watson, *Ssu-ma Ch'ien, Grand Historian of China* (1958). A study of China's premier historian.

B. Watson, *Records of the Grand Historian of China*, Vols. 1 and 2 (1961). Selections from the Shih-chi by Ssu-ma Ch'ien.

B. Watson, *The Columbia Book of Chinese Poetry* (1986).

A. Wright, *Buddhism in Chinese History* (1959).

Y. S. Yu, *Trade and Expansion in Han China* (1967). A study of economic relations between the Chinese and their neighbors.

Chapter 8

General

J. Cahill, *Chinese Painting* (1960). An excellent survey.

J. K. Fairbank, *China: A New History* (1992). The summation of a lifetime engagement with Chinese history.

F. A. Kierman, Jr., and J. K. Fairbank, eds., *Chinese Ways in Warfare* (1974). Chapters by different authors on the Chinese military experience from the Chou to the Ming.

Sui and T'ang

P. B. Ebrey, *The Aristocratic Families of Early Imperial China* (1978).

S. Owen, *The Great Age of Chinese Poetry: The High T'ang* (1980).

E. G. Pulleyblank, *The Background of the Rebellion of An Lushan* (1955). A study of the 755 rebellion that weakened the central authority of the T'ang dynasty.

E. O. Reischauer, *Ennin's Travels in T'ang China* (1955). China as seen through the eyes of a ninth-century Japanese Marco Polo.

E. H. SCHAFER, *The Golden Peaches of Samarkand* (1963). A study of T'ang imagery.

D. TWITCHETT, ED., *Sui and T'ang China, 589–906, Part 1* (1984). (Part 2, also in *The Cambridge History of China*, is forthcoming.)

G. W. WANG, *The Structure of Power in North China During the Five Dynasties* (1963). A study of the interim period between the T'ang and the Sung dynasties.

A. F. WRIGHT, *The Sui Dynasty* (1978).

Sung

C. S. CHANG AND J. SMYTHE, *South China in the Twelfth Century* (1981). China as seen through the eyes of a twelfth-century Chinese poet, historian, and statesman.

J. GERNET, *Daily Life in China on the Eve of the Mongol Invasion* (1962).

J. W. HAEGER, ED., *Crisis and Prosperity in Sung China* (1975).

R. HYMES, *Statesmen and Gentlemen* (1987). On the transformation of officials into a local gentry elite during the twelfth and thirteenth centuries.

J. T. C. LIU AND P. J. GOLAS, EDS., *Change in Sung China: Innovation or Renovation?* (1969).

M. ROSSABI, *China Among Equals* (1983). A study of the Liao, Ch'in, and Sung empires and their relations.

W. M. TU, *Confucian Thought, Selfhood as Creative Transformation* (1985).

K. YOSHIKAWA, *An Introduction to Sung Poetry*, trans. by B. Watson (1967).

Yuan

T. T. ALLSEN, *Mongol Imperialism* (1987).

J. W. DARDESS, *Conquerors and Confucians: Aspects of Political Change in Late Yuan China* (1973).

H. FRANKE AND D. TWITCHETT, EDS., *Alien Regimes and Border States, 710–1368* (to appear soon as Vol. 6 of *The Cambridge History of China*).

J. D. LANGLOIS, *China Under Mongol Rule* (1981).

R. LATHAM, TRANS., *Travels of Marco Polo* (1958).

H. D. MARTIN, *The Rise of Chingis Khan and His Conquest of North China* (1981).

D. MORGAN, *The Mongols* (1986).

Chapter 9

C. BLACKER, *The Catalpa Bow* (1975). A fascinating study of folk Shinto.

R. BORGEN, *Sugawara no Michizane and the Early Heian Court* (1986). A study of a famous courtier and poet.

D. BROWN AND E. ISHIDA, EDS., *The Future and the Past* (1979). A translation of a history of Japan written in 1219.

M. COLLCUTT, *Five Mountains* (1980). A study of the monastic organization of medieval Zen.

P. DUUS, *Feudalism in Japan* (1969). An easy survey of the subject.

W. W. FARRIS, *Population, Disease, and Land in Early Japan, 645–900* (1985). An innovative reinterpretation of early history.

W. W. FARRIS, *Heavenly Warriors: The Evolution of Japan's Military, 500–1300* (1992).

K. F. FRIDAY, *Hired Swords: The Rise of Private Warrior Power in Early Japan* (1991). The interpretation in this book may be compared to that in Farris's *Heavenly Warriors*.

J. W. HALL, *Government and Local Power in Japan, 500–1700: A Study Based on Bizen Province* (1966). The best book on Japanese history to 1700.

J. W. HALL AND J. P. MASS, EDS., *Medieval Japan* (1974). A collection of topical essays on medieval history.

J. W. HALL AND T. TOYODA, *Japan in the Muromachi Age* (1977). Another collection of essays.

D. KEENE, ED., *Anthology of Japanese Literature from the Earliest Era to the Mid-Nineteenth Century* (1955).

D. KEENE, ED., *Twenty Plays of the Nō Theatre* (1970).

J. M. KITAGAWA, *Religion in Japanese History* (1966). A survey of religion in premodern Japan.

I. H. LEVY, *The Ten Thousand Leaves* (1981). A fine translation of Japan's earliest collection of poetry.

J. P. MASS, *The Development of Kamakura Rule, 1180–1250* (1979).

J. P. MASS AND W. HAUSER, EDS., *The Bakufu in Japanese History* (1985). Topics in *bakufu* history from the twelfth to the nineteenth centuries.

I. MORRIS, *The World of the Shining Prince: Court Life in Ancient Japan* (1964). A study of the court during the age in which *The Tale of Genji* was written.

I. MORRIS, TRANS., *The Pillow Book of Sei Shōnagonō* (1967). Observations about the Heian court life by the Jane Austen of ancient Japan.

S. MURASAKI, *The Tale of Genji*, trans. by A. Waley (1952). A comparison of this translation with that of Seidensticker is instructive.

S. MURASAKI, *The Tale of Genji*, trans. by E. G. Seidensticker (1976). The world's first novel and the greatest work of Japanese fiction.

R. J. PEARSON ET AL., EDS., *Windows on the Japanese Past: Studies in Archaeology and Prehistory* (1986).

D. L. PHILIPPI, TRANS., *Kojiki* (1968). Japan's ancient myths.

E. O. REISCHAUER AND A. M. CRAIG, *Japan: Tradition and Transformation* (1989). A widely used text covering the total sweep of Japanese history from the early beginnings to the present day.

D. T. SUZUKI, *Zen and Japanese Culture* (1959).

R. TSUNODA, W. T. DEBARY, AND D. KEENE, COMPS., *Sources of the Japanese Tradition* (1958). A collection of original religious, political, and philosophical writings from each period of Japanese history. The best reader.

H. P. VARLEY, *Imperial Restoration in Medieval Japan* (1971). A study of the 1331 attempt by an emperor to restore imperial power.

A. WALEY, TRANS., *The Nō Plays of Japan* (1957). Medieval dramas.

K. YAMAMURA, ED., *Medieval Japan* (1990), Vol. 5 of the *Cambridge History of Japan*.

Chapter 10

Iran

M. BOYCE, *Zoroastrians: Their Religious Beliefs and Practices* (1979). A detailed survey by the current authority on Zoroastrian religious history. See Chapters 7–9.

M. BOYCE, ED. AND TRANS., *Textual Sources for the Study of Zoroastrianism* (1984). A valuable anthology with an important introduction that includes Boyce's arguments for a revision of the dates of Zoroaster's life (to between 1400 and 1200 B.C.E.).

R. N. FRYE, *The Heritage of Persia* (1963). Still one of the best surveys. Chapter 6 deals with the Sasanid era.

R. GHIRSHMAN, *Iran* (1954 [orig. ed. 1951]). An introductory survey of similar extent to Frye, but with differing material also.

R. GHIRSHMAN, *Persian Art: The Parthian and Sasanid Dynasties* (1962). Superb photographs, and a very helpful glossary of places and names. The text is minimal.

GEO WIDENGRAN, *Mani and Manichaeism* (1965). Still the standard introduction to Mani's life and the later spread and development of Manichaeism.

India

A. L. BASHAM, *The Wonder That Was India* (1963). The best survey of classical Indian religion, society, literature, art, and politics.

W. T. DE BARY ET AL., COMP. *Sources of Indian Tradition*, 2nd ed. (1958). Vol. I, *From the Beginning to 1800*, ed. and rev. by Ainslie T. Embree (1988). Excellent selections from a wide variety of Indian texts, with good introductions to the text selections.

S. DUTT, *Buddhist Monks and Monasteries of India* (1962). The standard work. See especially Chapters 3 ("Bhakti") and 4 ("Monasteries Under the Gupta Kings").

D. G. MANDELBAUM, *Society in India* (1972). 2 vols. The first two chapters in Volume I of this study of caste, family, and village relations are a good introduction to the caste system.

B. ROWLAND, *The Art and Architecture of India: Buddhist/Hindu/Jain*, 3rd rev. ed. (1970). See the excellent chapters on Sungan, Andhran, and other early Buddhist art (6–8, 14), the Gupta period (15), and the Hindu Renaissance (17–19).

V. A. SMITH, *The Oxford History of India*, 4th rev. ed. (1981). See especially pages 164–229 (the Gupta period and following era to the Muslim invasions).

R. THAPAR, *A History of India, Part I* (1966), pp. 109–193. Three chapters covering the rise of mercantilism, the Gupta "classical pattern," and the southern dynasties to ca. C.E. 900.

P. YOUNGER, *Introduction to Indian Religious Thought* (1972). A sensitive attempt to delineate classical concerns of Indian religious thought and culture.

Chapter 11

J. ASHTIANI, T. M. JOHNSTONE, J. D. LATHAM, R. B. SERGEANT, AND G. R. SMITH, EDS., *Abbasid Belles Lettres* (1990). A wide-ranging survey of Arabic letters between 750 and 1258 C.E., arranged by genres and major writers.

A. F. L. BEESTON, T. M. JOHNSTONE, R. B. SERGEANT, AND G. R. SMITH, EDS., *Arabic Literature to the End of the Umayyad Period* (1983). The most comprehensive survey of the early Arabic historical, religious, poetic, and other literary sources.

K. CRAGG AND R. MARSTON SPEIGHT, EDS., *Islam from Within: Anthology of a Religion* (1980). One of the best and most sensitive collections of selections from Islamic primary sources.

F. M. DONNER, *The Early Islamic Conquests* (1981). The introduction and first chapter are especially good for an introduction to many important issues in the origin and spread of Islam.

H. A. R. GIBB, *Studies on the Civilization of Islam*, ed. by S. J. Shaw and W. R. Polk (1962). This volume of selected essays by Gibb has some very helpful general studies on Islamic political order and religion.

H. A. R. GIBB, *Mohammedanism: An Historical Survey* (1970). Despite the offensive title, still the best brief introduction to Islam as a religious tradition.

O. GRABAR, *The Formation of Islamic Art* (1973). A critical and creative interpretation of major themes in the development of distinctively Islamic forms of art and architecture.

G. E. VON GRUNEBAUM, *Classical Islam: A History 600–1258*, trans. by K. Watson (1970), pp. 1–140. A competent, culturally oriented introductory survey of formative developments.

M. G. S. HODGSON, *The Classical Age of Islam* (1974). 3 vols. Vol. I, *The Venture of Islam*. The most thoughtful and comprehensive attempt to deal with classical Islamic civilization as a whole and in relation to contemporaneous non-Islamic cultures.

A. HOURANI, *A History of the Arab Peoples* (1991). A masterly survey of the Arabs down through the centuries and a clear picture of many aspects of Islamic history and culture that extend beyond the Arab world.

B. LEWIS, ED., *Islam and the Arab World* (1976). A large-format, heavily illustrated volume with many excellent articles on diverse aspects of Islamic (not simply Arab, as the misleading title suggests) civilization through the pre-modern period.

F. RAHMAN, *Major Themes of the Qur'an* (1980). The best introduction to the basic ideas of the Qur'an and Islam, seen through the eyes of a perceptive Muslim modernist scholar.

M. A. SHABAN, *Islamic History: A New Interpretation (1971–76)*. 2 vols. An influential reassessment of the course of Islamic history to 1055 C.E.

D. SOURDEL, *Medieval Islam* (1979). Eng. trans. by W. M. Watt (1983). A brief but excellent survey of the world of medieval Islam with emphasis on social, religious, and political institutions.

Chapter 12

R. BARTLETT, *Trial by Fire and Water: The Medieval Judicial Ordeal* (1986). Makes sense of these seemingly bizarre ways of letting God decide guilt or innocence.

R. BARTLETT, *The Making of Europe, 950–1350* (1992). A study of the way immigration and colonial conquest shaped the Europe we know.

M. BLOCH, *Feudal Society*, Vols. 1 and 2, trans. by L. A. Manyon (1971). A classic on the topic and as an example of historical study.

P. BROWN, *Augustine of Hippo: A Biography* (1967). Late antiquity seen through the biography of its greatest Christian thinker.

P. BROWN, *The Body and Society* (1988). Understanding late antiquity through people's attitudes toward the physical body.

J. H. BURNS, *The Cambridge History of Medieval Political Thought c. 350–c. 1450* (1991).

H. CHADWICK, *The Early Church* (1967). Among the best treatments of early Christianity.

B. CUNLIFFE, *Greeks, Romans and Barbarians* (1988). A quantitative account.

R. H. C. DAVIS, *A History of Medieval Europe: From Constantine to St. Louis* (1972). Unsurpassed in clarity.

K. F. DREW, ED., *The Barbarian Invasions: Catalyst of a New Order* (1970). Collection of essays that focus on the issues.

G. DUBY, *The Early Growth of the European Economy: Warriors and Peasants from the Seventh to the Twelfth Century* (1974). Readable, authoritative account of rural society.

F. DVORNIK, *Byzantium and the Roman Primacy* (1966).

H. FICHTENAU, *The Carolingian Empire: The Age of Charlemagne*, trans. by Peter Munz (1964). Strongest on the political history of the era.

JOHN V. A. FINE, *The Early Medieval Balkans: Sixth–Twelfth Centuries* (1983). The formation of multiculturalism in the region.

F. L. GANSHOF, *Feudalism*, trans. by Philip Grierson (1964). A profound brief analysis of the subject.

P. GEARY, *Before France and Germany* (1988). The medieval evolution of these territories.

A. F. HAVIGHURST, ED., *The Pirenne Thesis: Analysis, Criticism, and Revision* (1958). Excerpts from the scholarly debate over the extent of western trade in the East during the early Middle Ages.

RICHARD HODGES ET AL., *Mohammed, Charlemagne, and the Origins of Europe* (1982). Good on the society and economy of early medieval Europe.

GEORGE HOLMES, ED., *The Oxford History of Medieval Europe* (1992). Overviews of Roman and northern Europe during the "Dark Ages."

A. HOURANI, *A History of the Arab Peoples* (1991). A comprehensive text that includes an excellent overview of the origins and early history of Islam.

D. KNOWLES, *Christian Monasticism* (1969). Sweeping survey with helpful photographs.

R. KRAUTHEIMER, *Early Christian and Byzantine Architecture* (1965). Makes the developments clear and interesting.

M. L. W. LAISTNER, *Thought and Letters in Western Europe, 500 to 900* (1957). Among the best surveys of early medieval intellectual history.

C. H. LAWRENCE, *Medieval Monasticism* (1989). Comprehensive survey.

J. LECLERCQ, *The Love of Learning and the Desire for God: A Study of Monastic Culture*, trans. by Catherine Misrahi (1962). Lucid, delightful, absorbing account of the ideals of monks.

J. LECLERCQ, F. VANDENBROUCKE, AND L. BOUYER, *The Spirituality of the Middle Ages* (1968). Perhaps the best survey of medieval Christianity, East and West, to the eve of the Protestant Reformation.

C. MANGO, *Byzantium: The Empire of New Rome* (1980).

JANET MARTIN, *Medieval Russia 980–1584* (1995). A concise narrative history.

M. McCORMICK, "Byzantium and the West, A.D. 700–900," in *The New Cambridge Medieval History*, Vol. 2: *The Early Medieval West 700–900* (1993). Up-to-date framing of events and political developments.

R. McKITTERNICK, *The Frankish Kingdoms Under the Carolingians, 751–987* (1983).

P. MUNZ, *The Age of Charlemagne* (1971). Penetrating social history of the period.

T. NOBLE, *The Republic of St. Peter* (1988). How the church became an empire.

H. PIRENNE, *A History of Europe, I: From the End of the Roman World in the West to the Beginnings of the Western States*, trans. by Bernhard Maill (1958). Comprehensive survey, with now-controversial views on the demise of western trade and cities in the early Middle Ages.

S. RUNCIMAN, *Byzantine Civilization* (1970). Succinct, comprehensive account by a master.

P. SAWYER, *The Age of the Vikings* (1962). The best account.

R. W. SOUTHERN, *The Making of the Middle Ages* (1973). Originally published in 1953, but still a fresh account by an imaginative historian.

C. STEPHENSON, *Medieval Feudalism* (1969). Excellent short summary and introduction.

A. A. VASILIEV, *History of the Byzantine Empire 324–1453* (1952). The most comprehensive treatment in English.

S. F. WEMPLE, *Women in Frankish Society: Marriage and the Cloister 500–900* (1981). The impact of Christian marriage customs on the Franks.

L. WHITE, JR., *Medieval Technology and Social Change* (1962). Often fascinating account of how primitive technology changed life.

Chapter 13

EMILIE AMT, ED., *Women's Lives in Medieval Europe: A Sourcebook* (1992). Outstanding collection of sources.

P. ARIES, *Centuries of Childhood: A Social History of Family Life*, trans. by Robert Baldick (1962). Profound and controversial pioneer effort on the subject.

J. W. BALDWIN, *The Scholastic Culture of the Middle Ages: 1000–1300* (1971). Best brief synthesis available.

J. W. BALDWIN, *The Government of Philip Augustus* (1986). A scholarly feat.

M. W. BALDWIN, ED., *History of the Crusades, I: The First Hundred Years* (1955). Basic historical narrative.

G. BARRACLOUGH, *The Origins of Modern Germany* (1963). Penetrating political narrative.

G. BARRACLOUGH, *The Medieval Papacy* (1968). Brief, comprehensive survey, with pictures.

R. BARTLETT, *Trial by Fire and Water: The Medieval Judicial Ordeal* (1986).

R. BARTLETT, *The Making of Medieval Europe* (1992). Sees the interaction of different cultures as the decisive factor in the creation of West European civilization.

M. BLOCH, *French Rural Society*, trans. by J. Sondheimer (1966). A classic by a great modern historian.

J. BONY, *French Gothic Architecture of the Twelfth and Thirteenth Centuries* (1983).

J. BRUNDAGE, *Law, Sex, and Christian Society in Medieval Europe* (1987). Everything about the topic of sex in all its scholastic subtlety.

C. BYNAM, *Holy Feast, Holy Fast: The Religious Significance of Food to Medieval Women* (1987). An analysis of the mind-set of cloistered women through their attitudes toward food.

A. CAPELLANUS, *The Art of Courtly Love*, trans. by J. J. Parry (1941). Translation of this classic along with other documents from the court of Marie de Champagne.

M. CLAGETT, G. POST, AND R. REYNOLDS, EDS., *Twelfth-Century Europe and the Foundations of Modern Society* (1966). Demanding but stimulating collection of essays.

F. COPLESTON, *A History of Philosophy, III/1: Ockham to the Speculative Mystics* (1963). The best introduction to Ockham and his movement.

F. C. COPLESTON, *Aquinas* (1965). Best introduction to Aquinas's philosophy.

R. H. C. DAVIS, *A History of Medieval Europe: From Constantine to St. Louis, Part 2* (1972).

G. DUBY, *Rural Economy and Country Life in the Medieval West* (1968). Slice-of-life analysis.

G. DUBY, *The Three Orders: Feudal Society Imagined*, trans. by Arthur Goldhammer (1981). Large, comprehensive, and authoritative.

R. AND J. GIES, *Marriage and Family in the Middle Ages* (1983).

E. GILSON, *Heloise and Abelard* (1968). An analysis and defense of medieval scholarly values.

J. GOODY, *The Development of the Family and Marriage in Europe* (1983). Bold interpretation of the church's marital legislation, ascribing unflattering, materialistic motives to the church.

ELIZABETH M. HALAM, *Capetian France 987–1328* (1980). Especially good on politics and heretics.

B. HANAWALT, *The Ties That Bound: Peasant Families in Medieval England* (1986). Analysis of family structure and relationships.

C. H. HASKINS, *The Renaissance of the Twelfth Century* (1927). Still the standard account.

C. H. HASKINS, *The Rise of Universities* (1972). A short, minor classic.

D. HERLIHY, *Medieval Households* (1985). Sweeping survey of Middle Ages that defends the medieval family against modern caricatures.

D. HERLIHY, *Opera Muliebria* (1990). Brief, pioneer effort to describe the many vocational and employment opportunities of medieval women.

J. C. HOLT, *Magna Carta*, 2nd ed. (1992). The famous document and its interpretation by succeeding generations.

E. H. KANTOROWICZ, *The King's Two Bodies* (1957). Controversial analysis of political concepts in the High Middle Ages.

G. LEFF, *Paris and Oxford Universities in the Thirteenth and Fourteenth Centuries: An Institutional and Intellectual History* (1968). Very good on debates on Scholasticism.

J. LE GOFF, *The Birth of Purgatory* (1981).

K. LEYSER, *Rule and Conflict in Early Medieval Society: Ottonian Saxony* (1979). Basic and authoritative.

K. LEYSER, *Medieval Germany and Its Neighbors, 900–1250* (1982). Basic and authoritative.

R. S. LOOMIS, ED., *The Development of Arthurian Romance* (1963). A basic study.

R. S. LOPEZ AND I. W. RAYMOND, EDS., *Medieval Trade in the Mediterranean World* (1955). An illuminating collection of sources, concentrated on southern Europe.

E. MÂLE, *The Gothic Image: Religious Art in France in the Thirteenth Century* (1913). A classic.

P. MANDONNET, *St. Dominic and His Work* (1944). The origins of the Dominican Order.

H. E. MAYER, *The Crusades*, trans. by John Gilligham (1972). Extremely detailed, and the best one-volume account.

R. I. MOORE, *The Formation of a Persecuting Society: Power and Deviance in Western Europe, 950–1250* (1987). A sympathetic look at heresy and dissent.

J. MOORMAN, *A History of the Franciscan Order* (1968). The best survey.

J. B. MORRALL, *Political Thought in Medieval Times* (1962). A readable and illuminating account.

J. T. NOONAN, *Contraception: A History of Its Treatment by the Catholic Theologians and Canonists* (1967). A fascinating account of medieval theological attitudes toward sexuality and sex-related problems.

E. PANOFSKY, *Gothic Architecture and Scholasticism* (1951). A controversial classic.

C. PETIT-DUTAILLIS, *The Feudal Monarchy in France and England from the Tenth to the Thirteenth Century*, trans. by E. D. Hunt (1964). A political narrative.

H. PIRENNE, *Medieval Cities: Their Origins and the Revival of Trade*, trans. by Frank D. Halsey (1970). A minor classic.

J. M. POWELL, *Innocent III: Vicar of Christ or Lord of the World* (1963). Excerpts from the scholarly debate over Innocent's reign.

F. W. POWICKE, *The Thirteenth Century* (1962). An outstanding treatment of English political history.

H. RASHDALL, *The Universities of Europe in the Middle Ages*, Vols. 1–3 (1936). Dated but still a standard comprehensive work.

J. RILEY-SMITH, *The Crusades: A Short History* (1987). Up-to-date, lucid, and readable.

F. RORIG, *The Medieval Town*, trans. by D. J. A. Matthew (1971). Excellent on northern Europe.

S. SHAHAR, *The Fourth Estate: A History of Women in the Middle Ages* (1983). Readable survey.

O. VON SIMSON, *The Gothic Cathedral* (1956).

R. W. SOUTHERN, *Medieval Humanism and Other Studies* (1970). Provocative and far-ranging essays on topics in the intellectual history of the High Middle Ages.

B. TIERNEY, *The Crisis of Church and State 1050–1300* (1964). A very useful collection of primary sources on key Church-State conflicts.

W. L. WAKEFIELD AND A. P. EVANS, EDS., *Heresies of the High Middle Ages* (1969). A major document collection.

J. WEISHEIPL, *Friar Thomas* (1980). Biography of Thomas Aquinas that attempts to do justice to the human side of the story as well as to the theological.

S. WILLIAMS, ED., *The Gregorian Epoch: Reformation, Revolution, Reaction* (1964). Variety of scholarly opinion on the significance of Pope Gregory's reign presented in debate form.

R. L. WOLFF AND H. W. HAZARD, EDS., *History of the Crusades 1189–1311* (1962).

Chapter 14

The Islamic Heartlands

C. E. BOSWORTH, *The Islamic Dynasties: A Chronological and Genealogical Handbook* (1967). A handy reference work for dynasties and families important to Islamic history in all periods and places.

J. A. BOYLE, ED., *The Cambridge History of Iran*, Vol. 5, *The Saljuq and Mongol Periods* (1968). Useful and reasonably detailed articles on political, social, religious, and cultural developments.

P. K. HITTI, *History of the Arabs*, 8th ed. (1964). Still a useful English resource, largely for factual detail. See especially Part IV, "The Arabs in Europe: Spain and Sicily."

M. G. S. HODGSON, *The Expansion of Islam in the Middle Periods*, Vol. 2 of *The Venture of Islam*. 3 vols. (1964). The strongest of Hodgson's monumental three-volume survey of Islamic civilization and the only English work of its kind to give the period 945–1500 such broad and unified coverage.

A. HOURANI, *A History of the Arab Peoples* (1991). The newest survey history and the best, at least for the Arab Islamic world.

S. K. JAYYUSI, ED., *The Legacy of Muslim Spain*, 2 vols. (1994). A comprehensive survey of the arts, politics, literature, and society by experts in various fields.

B. LEWIS, ED., *Islam and the Arab World* (1976). A large-format, heavily illustrated volume with many excellent articles on diverse aspects of Islamic (not simply Arab, as the misleading title indicates) civilization through the pre-modern period.

D. MORGAN, *The Mongols* (1986). A recent and readable survey history.

J. J. SAUNDERS, *A History of Medieval Islam* (1965). A brief and simple, if sketchy, introductory survey of Islamic history to the Mongol invasions.

D. SOURDEL, *Medieval Islam*, trans. by W. M. Watt (1983). The synthetic, interpretive chapters on Islam and the political and social orders (4, 5) and on towns and art (6) are especially helpful.

B. SPULER, *The Muslim World: A Historical Survey*, trans. by F. R. C. Bagley (1960). 3 vols. Volumes I and II are handy references offering a highly condensed chronicle of Islamic history from Muhammad through the fifteenth century.

B. SPULER, *The Mongols in History*, trans. by Geoffrey Wheeler (1971). A short introductory survey of Mongol history, of which Chapters 2–5 are most relevant.

India

W. T. DE BARY ET AL., COMP., *Sources of Indian Tradition*, 2nd ed. (1958). Vol. I, *From the Beginning to 1800*, ed. and rev. by Ainslie T. Embree (1988). Excellent selections from a wide variety of Indian texts, with good introductions to chapters and individual selections.

S. M. IKRAM, *Muslim Civilization in India* (1964). The best short survey history, covering the period 711 to 1857.

R. C. MAJUMDAR, GEN. ED., *The History and Culture of the Indian People*, Vol. VI, *The Delhi Sultanate*, 3rd ed. (1980). A comprehensive political and cultural account of the period in India.

M. MUJEEB, *The Indian Muslims* (1967). The best cultural study of Islamic civilization in India as a whole, from its origins onward.

F. ROBINSON, ED., *The Cambridge History of India, Pakistan, Bangladesh, Sri Lanka, Nepal, Bhutan, and the Maldives* (1989). A recent and very helpful quick reference source with brief but well-done survey essays on a wide range of topics relevant to South Asian history down to the present.

A. WINK, *Al-Hind: The Making of the Indo-Islamic World*, Vol. 1 (1991). The first of five promising volumes to be devoted to the Indo-Islamic world's history. This volume treats the seventh to eleventh centuries.

Chapter 15

B. S. BAUER, *The Development of the Inca State* (1992). An important new work that emphasizes archaeological evidence over the Spanish chronicles in accounting for the emergence of the Inca Empire.

F. F. BERDAN, *The Aztecs of Central Mexico: An Imperial Society* (1982). An excellent introduction to the Aztecs.

R. E. BLANTON, S. A. KOWALEWSKI, G. FEINMAN, AND J. APPEL, *Ancient Mesoamerica: A Comparison of Change in Three Regions* (1981). Concentrates on ancient Mexico.

K. O. BRUHNS, *Ancient South America* (1994). A clear discussion of the archaeology and civilization of the region with emphasis on the Andes.

R. L. BURGER, *Chavín and the Origins of Andean Civilization.* (1992). A detailed study of early Andean prehistory by one of the leading authorities on Chavín.

R. M. CARMACK, J. GASCO, AND G. H. GOSSEN, *The Legacy of Mesoamerica: History and Culture of a Native American Civilization* (1996). A survey of Mesoamerica from its origins to the present.

I. CLENDINNEN, *Aztecs: An Interpretation* (1995). A fascinating attempt to reconstruct the Aztec world.

M. D. COE, *Breaking the Maya Code* (1992). The story of the remarkable achievement of deciphering the ancient Maya language.

M. D. COE, *The Maya* (1993). The best introduction.

M. D. COE, *Mexico from the Olmecs to the Aztecs* (1994). A wide-ranging introductory discussion.

G. CONRAD AND A. A. DEMAREST, *Religion and Empire: The Dynamics of Aztec and Inca Expansionism* (1984). An interesting comparative study.

S. D. GILLESPIE, *The Aztec Kings* (1989).

R. HASSIG, *Aztec Warfare*.

J. HYSLOP, *Inka Settlement Planning* (1990). A detailed study.

M. LEÓN-PORTILLA, *Fifteen Poets of the Aztec World* (1992). An anthology of translations of Aztec poetry.

M. E. MILLER, *The Art of Mesoamerica from Olmec to Aztec* (1986). A well-illustrated introduction.

C. MORRIS AND A. VON HAGEN, *The Inka Empire and Its Andean Origins* (1993). A clear overview of Andean prehistory by a leading authority. Beautifully illustrated.

M. E. MOSELY, *The Incas and Their Ancestors: The Archaeology of Peru* (1992). Readable and thorough.

J. A. SABLOFF, *The Cities of Ancient Mexico* (1989). Capsule summaries of ancient Mesoamerican cultures.

J. A. SABLOFF, *Archaeology and the Maya* (1990). A look at changing views of the ancient Maya.

L. SCHELE and M. E. MILLER, *The Blood of Kings* (1986). A rich and beautifully illustrated study of ancient Maya art and society.

R. S. SHARER, *The Ancient Maya*, 5th ed. (1994). A classic. Readable, authoritative, and thorough.

M. P. WEAVER, *The Aztecs, Maya, and Their Predecessor.* A classic textbook.

Chapter 16

L. B. ALBERTI, *The Family in Renaissance Florence*, trans. by R. N. Watkins (1962). A contemporary humanist, who never married, explains how a family should behave.

M. ASTON, *The Fifteenth Century: The Prospect of Europe* (1968). Crisp social history, with pictures.

H. BARON, *The Crisis of the Early Italian Renaissance*, Vols. 1 and 2 (1966). A major work, setting forth the civic dimension of Italian humanism.

B. BERENSON, *Italian Painters of the Renaissance* (1901). Still incisive.

G. BRUCKER, *Renaissance Florence* (1983). Considered the best introduction to the subject.

G. BRUCKER, *Giovanna and Lusanna: Love and Marriage in Renaissance Florence* (1986). A tale of unhappy marriage and extramarital love, more in the spirit of Bergman than of Fellini, and apparently typical of much of Renaissance Italy.

J. BURCKHARDT, *The Civilization of the Renaissance in Italy* (1867). The old classic that still has as many defenders as detractors.

C. CIPOLLA, *Before the Industrial Revolution: European Society and Economy, 1000–1700* (1976). Readable, sweeping account.

W. K. FERGUSON, *The Renaissance* (1940). A brief, stimulating summary of the Renaissance in both Italy and northern Europe.

W. K. FERGUSON, *Europe in Transition 1300–1520* (1962). A major survey that deals with the transition from medieval to Renaissance society.

F. GILBERT, *Machiavelli and Guicciardini* (1984). The two great Renaissance historians compared.

M. GILMORE, *The World of Humanism 1453–1517* (1952). A comprehensive survey, especially strong in intellectual and cultural history.

J. R. HALE, *Europe in the Renaissance* (1994). New, learned survey focusing on social and cultural history.

D. HAY, *The Italian Renaissance* (1977). For those who want the subject in a nutshell.

D. HERLIHY, *The Family in Renaissance Italy* (1974). Excellent on family structure and general features.

D. HERLIHY AND C. KLAPISCH-ZUBER, *Tuscans and Their Families* (1985). Important work based on unique demographic data that gives the reader an appreciation of quantitative history.

A. HUDSON, *The Premature Reformation: Wycliffite Texts and Lollard History* (1988). The teaching of John Wycliffe and the movement it stimulated.

J. HUIZINGA, *The Waning of the Middle Ages: A Study of the Forms of Life, Thought, and Art in France and The Netherlands in the Dawn of the Renaissance* (1924). A classic study of "mentality" at the end of the Middle Ages.

G. HUPPERT, *After the Black Death* (1986). A social historian's perspective on the transition from the Renaissance to modern times.

D. JENSEN, *Renaissance Europe: Age of Recovery and Reconciliation* (1981). Up-to-date textbook.

R. KELSO, *Doctrine of the Lady of the Renaissance* (1978). Noblewomen in the Renaissance.

R. KIECKHEFER, *Unquiet Souls* (1984). Penetrating and sympathetic study of fourteenth-century religious life.

C. KLAPISCH-ZUBER, *Women, Family, and Ritual in Renaissance Italy* (1985). Sober essays, stressing the negative status of women and unfairness of male treatment of them.

R. J. KNECHT, *Francis I* (1982). Up-to-date biography of the French king.

P. O. KRISTELLER, *Renaissance Thought: The Classic, Scholastic, and Humanist Strains* (1961). A master shows the many sides of Renaissance thought.

I. MACLEAN, *The Renaissance Notion of Women* (1980). A study of largely unflattering theories about women found in learned tracts on theology, philosophy, law, and medicine.

W. H. MCNEILL, *Plagues and Peoples* (1976). The Black Death in a broader context.

L. MARTINES, *Power and Imagination: City States in Renaissance Italy* (1980). Stimulating account of cultural and political history.

H. A. MISKIMIN, *The Economy of Early Renaissance Europe 1300–1460* (1969). Shows the interaction of social, political, and economic change.

E. MUIR, *Civic Ritual in Renaissance Venice* (1981). A study of the use of pageantry for political purposes.

F. OAKLEY, *The Western Church in the Later Middle Ages* (1979). Vigorous defense of the integrity of late medieval religion.

E. PERROY, *The Hundred Years' War*, trans. by W. B. Wells (1965). The most comprehensive one-volume account.

Q. SKINNER, *The Foundations of Modern Political Thought I: The Renaissance* (1978). A broad survey, very comprehensive.

M. SPINKA, *John Hus's Concept of the Church* (1966). Intellectual history with documents.

J. W. THOMPSON, *Economic and Social History of Europe in the Later Middle Ages 1300–1530* (1958). A bread-and-butter account.

B. TIERNEY, *The Crisis of Church and State 1050–1300* (1964). Part 4 provides the major documents in the clash between Boniface VIII and Philip the Fair.

W. ULLMANN, *Origins of the Great Schism* (1948). A basic study by a controversial interpreter of medieval political thought.

P. ZIEGLER, *The Black Death* (1969). A highly readable journalistic account.

Chapter 17

R. ASHCRAFT, *Revolutionary Politics and Locke's Two Treatises of Government* (1986). The most important study of Locke to appear in recent years.

R. H. BAINTON, *Here I Stand: A Life of Martin Luther* (1957). The most readable and positive biography of the reformer.

R. H. BAINTON, *Erasmus of Christendom* (1960). Charming, readable presentation.

W. BOUWSMA, *John Calvin. A Sixteenth Century Portrait* (1988). Interpretation of Calvin against the background of Renaissance intellectual history.

C. BOXER, *Four Centuries of Portuguese Expansion 1415–1825* (1961). A comprehensive survey by a leading authority.

F. BRAUDEL, *The Mediterranean and the Mediterranean World in the Age of Philip the Second*, Vols. 1 and 2 (1976). A widely acclaimed work by a French master.

K. C. BROWN, *Hobbes Studies* (1965). A collection of important essays.

E. CAMERON, *The European Reformation* (1990). Large synthesis of recent studies, with most attention given to the German Reformation.

O. CHADWICK, *The Reformation* (1964). Among the best short histories; especially strong on theological and ecclesiastical issues.

J. DELUMEAU, *Catholicism Between Luther and Voltaire: A New View of the Counter Reformation* (1977). Programmatic essay for a new social history of the Counter Reformation.

A. G. DICKENS, *The Counter Reformation* (1969). A brief narrative with pictures.

A. G. DICKENS, *The English Reformation* (1974). The best one-volume account.

B. DIEFENDORF, *Beneath the Cross: Catholics and Huguenots in Sixteenth Century Paris* (1991). Stresses the primary forces of popular religion in the French wars of religion.

G. DONALDSON, *The Scottish Reformation* (1960). A dependable, comprehensive narrative.

R. DUNN, *The Age of Religious Wars 1559–1689* (1979). An excellent brief survey of every major conflict.

M. DURAN, *Cervantes* (1974). Detailed biography.

J. H. ELLIOTT, *Europe Divided 1559–1598* (1968). A direct, lucid narrative account.

G. R. ELTON, *England Under the Tudors* (1955). A masterly account.

G. R. ELTON, *Reformation Europe 1517–1559* (1966). Among the best short treatments, especially strong on political issues.

H. O. EVENNETT, *The Spirit of the Counter Reformation* (1968). An essay on the continuity of Catholic reform and its independence from the Protestant Reformation.

J. H. FRANKLIN, ED. AND TRANS., *Constitutionalism and Resistance in the Sixteenth Century: Three Treatises by Hotman, Beza, and Mornay* (1969). Three defenders of the right of people to resist tyranny.

HANS-JÜRGEN GOERTZ, *The Anabaptists* (1996). Best treatment of minority Protestants.

P. GEYL, *The Revolt of The Netherlands, 1555–1609* (1958). The authoritative survey.

M. GREENGRASS, *The French Reformation* (1987). Summary account, pulling everything together succinctly.

C. HAIGH, *The English Reformation Revised* (1988). Argues that the English Reformation was less revolutionary than historians have traditionally argued.

R. HSIA, *The German People and the Reformation* (1989). Collection illustrative of the new social history of the German Reformation.

H. JEDIN, *A History of the Council of Trent*, Vols. 1 and 2 (1957–1961). Comprehensive, detailed, and authoritative.

D. JENSEN, *Reformation Europe, Age of Reform and Revolution* (1981). An excellent, up-to-date survey.

T. F. JESSOP, *Thomas Hobbes* (1960). A brief biographical sketch.

W. K. JORDAN, *Edward VI: The Young King* (1968). The basic biography.

R. KIECKHEFER, *European Witch Trials: Their Foundations in Popular and Learned Culture 1300–1500* (1976). One of the best treatments of the subject.

R. J. KNECHT, *The French Wars of Religion, 1559–1598* (1989).

A. KORS AND E. PETERS, EDS., *European Witchcraft, 1100–1700* (1972).

P. LASLETT, *Locke's Two Treatises of Government*, 2nd ed. (1970). Definitive texts with very important introductions.

CARTER LINDBERG, *The European Reformations* (1996). New survey with traditional strengths and clarity.

A. MACFARLANE, *The Family Life of Ralph Josselin: A Seventeenth Century Clergyman* (1970). Exemplary family history.

J. MCNEILL, *The History and Character of Calvinism* (1954). The most comprehensive account, very readable.

G. MATTINGLY, *The Armada* (1959). A masterpiece, novellike in style.

H.C. ERIK MIDELFORT, *The Mad Princes of Renaissance Germany* (1996).

K. MOXLEY, *Peasants, Warriors, and Wives* (1989). The English Reformation through popular art.

CHARLES G. NAUERT, JR., *Humanism and the Culture of Renaissance Europe* (1995). Lucid up-to-date overview.

J. NEALE, *Queen Elizabeth I* (1934). A superb biography.

J. E. NEALE, *The Age of Catherine de Medici* (1962). A short, concise summary.

D. NUGENT, *Ecumenism in the Age of Reformation: The Colloquy of Poissy* (1974). A study of the last ecumenical council of the sixteenth century.

J. W. O'MALLEY, *The First Jesuits* (1993). Extremely detailed account of the creation of the Society of Jesus and its original purposes.

S. OZMENT, *The Age of Reform 1250–1550: An Intellectual and Religious History of Late Medieval and Reformation Europe* (1980). Broad, lucid survey.

S. OZMENT, *When Fathers Ruled: Family Life in Reformation Europe* (1983). Effort to portray the constructive side of Protestant thinking about family relationships.

S. OZMENT, *Protestants: The Birth of a Revolution* (1992). Original synthesis of the German Reformation with critical analysis of reigning scholarly views.

S. OZMENT, *Three Behaim Boys: Growing Up in Early Modern Germany* (1990). Teenagers and young adults in their own words.

S. OZMENT, *The Bürgermeister's Daughter: Scandal in a Sixteenth Century German Town* (1996). A woman's struggle for justice.

GEOFFREY PARKER, *The Thirty Years' War* (1984). Large, lucid survey.

J. H. PARRY, *The Age of Reconnaissance* (1964). A comprehensive account of explorations from 1450 to 1650.

E. F. RICE, JR., *The Foundations of Early Modern Europe 1460–1559* (1970). A broad, succinct narrative.

J. H. M. SALMON, ED., *The French Wars of Religion: How Important Were the Religious Factors?* (1967). Scholarly debate over the relation between politics and religion.

J. J. SCARISBRICK, *Henry VIII* (1968). The best account of Henry's reign.

A. SOMAN, ED., *The Massacre of St. Bartholomew's Day: Reappraisals and Documents* (1974). The results of an international symposium on the anniversary of the massacre.

L. SPITZ, *The Religious Renaissance of the German Humanists* (1963). Comprehensive and entertaining.

G. STRAUSS, *Luther's House of Learning: The Indoctrination of the Young in the German Reformation* (1978). Account of Protestant efforts to rear children in the new faith, stressing the authoritarian elements.

G. STRAUSS, ED. AND TRANS., *Manifestations of Discontent in Germany on the Eve of the Reformation* (1971). A rich collection of sources for both rural and urban scenes.

R. H. TAWNEY, *Religion and the Rise of Capitalism* (1947). Advances beyond Weber's arguments relating Protestantism and capitalist economic behavior.

K. THOMAS, *Religion and the Decline of Magic* (1971). Something of a classic on the subject.

E. TROELTSCH, *The Social Teaching of the Christian Churches*, Vols. 1 and 2, trans. by Olive Wyon (1960).

M. WEBER, *The Protestant Ethic and the Spirit of Capitalism*, trans. by Talcott Parsons (1958). First appeared in 1904–1905; it has continued to stimulate debate over the relationship between religion and society.

C. V. WEDGWOOD, *The Thirty Years' War* (1939). The authoritative account.

C. V. WEDGWOOD, *William the Silent* (1944). An excellent political biography.

F. WENDEL, *Calvin: The Origins and Development of His Religious Thought*, trans. by Philip Mairet (1963). The best treatment of Calvin's theology.

MERRY WIESNER, *Working Women in Renaissance Germany* (1986). Sketch of women's opportunities in six German cities.

G. H. WILLIAMS, *The Radical Reformation* (1962). A broad survey of the varieties of dissent within Protestantism.

HEIDE WUNDER, *He Is the Sun, She Is the Moon: Women in Early Modern Germany* (1998). The best book in any language on the subject to date.

Chapter 18

J. ABUN-NASR, *A History of the Maghrib in the Islamic Period* (1987). The most recent North African survey. Pages 59–247 are relevant to this chapter.

D. BIRMINHAM, *Central Africa to 1870* (1981). Chapters from the *Cambridge History of Africa* that give a brief, lucid overview of developments in this region.

P. BOHANNAN AND P. CURTIN, *Africa and Africans*, rev. ed. (1971). Accessible, topical approach to African history, culture, society, politics, and economics.

P. D. CURTIN, S. FEIERMANN, L. THOMPSON, AND J. VANSINA, *African History* (1978). An older but masterly survey. The relevant portions are chapters 6–9.

R. ELPHICK, *Kraal and Castle: Khoikhoi and the Founding of White South Africa* (1977). An incisive, informative interpretation of the history of the Khoikhoi and their fateful interaction with European colonization.

R. ELPHICK AND H. GILIOMEE, *The Shaping of South African Society, 1652–1820* (1979). A superb, synthetic history of this crucial period.

J. D. FAGE, *A History of Africa* (1978). Still a readable survey history.

M. HISKETT, *The Development of Islam in West Africa* (1984). The standard survey study of the subject. Of the relevant sections (chapters 1–10, 12, 15), that on Hausaland, which is treated only in passing in this text, is noteworthy.

R. W. JULY, *Precolonial Africa: An Economic and Social History* (1975). Chapter 10 gives an interesting overall picture of slaving in African history.

R. W. JULY, *A History of the African People*, 3rd ed. (1980). Chapters 3–6 treat Africa before about 1800 area by area; chapter 7 deals with "The Coming of Europe."

I. M. LEWIS, ED., *Islam in Tropical Africa* (1966), pp. 4–96. Lewis's introduction is one of the best brief summaries of the role of Islam in West Africa and the Sudan.

D. T. NIANI, ED. *Africa from the Twelfth to the Sixteenth Century, UNESCO General History of Africa*, Vol. IV (1984). Many survey articles cover the various regions and major states of Africa in the centuries noted in the title.

R. OLIVER, *The African Experience* (1991). A masterly, balanced, and engaging survey, with outstanding syntheses and summaries of recent research.

J. A. RAWLEY, *The Transatlantic Slave Trade: A History* (1981). Impressively documented, detailed, and well-presented survey history of the Atlantic trade; little focus on African dimensions.

A. F. C. RYDER, *Benin and the Europeans: 1485–1897* (1969). A basic study.

JOHN K. THORNTON, *The Kingdom of Kongo: Civil War and Transition, 1641–1718* (1983). A detailed and perceptive analysis for those who wish to delve into Kongo state and society in the seventeenth century.

M. WILSON AND L. THOMPSON, EDS., *The Oxford History of South Africa*, Vol. I., *South Africa to 1870* (1969). Relatively detailed, if occasionally dated, treatment.

Chapter 19

P. BAKEWELL, *A History of Latin America* (1997). A recent accessible survey.

L. BETHWELL, *The Cambridge History of Latin America*, Vols. 1 and 2 (1984). Excellent essays by leading scholars.

B. COBO, *History of the Inca Empire* (1979). A major discussion.

G. A. COLLIER, R. I. ROSALDO, AND J. D. WIRTH, *The Inca and Aztec States 1400–1800* (1982). An important collection of advanced essays.

M. CRATON, ED., *Roots and Branches: Current Directions in Slave Studies* (1979). Diverse articles by scholars such as Curtin and Lovejoy; note especially those on the European plantation system by S. M. Greenfield.

P. D. CURTIN, *The Atlantic Slave Trade: A Census* (1969). Still a basic work, and useful for an overview of the trade, even though figures in many areas have since been refined or amended by other work.

P. D. CURTIN, *Economic Change in Precolonial Africa: Senegambia on the Eve of the Slave Trade* (1975). The chapter on slave trading is an illuminating treatment of the topic with respect to one area of Africa.

D. B. DAVIS, *The Problem of Slavery in Western Culture* (1966). A brilliant and far-ranging discussion.

H. A. GEMERY AND J. S. HOGENDORN, EDS., *The Uncommon Market: Essays in the Economic History of the Atlantic Slave Trade* (1979). Useful statistics on trans-Saharan and particular African regions of the Atlantic slave trade.

C. GIBSON, *The Aztecs Under Spanish Rule: A History of the Native Americans of the Valley of Mexico* (1964). An exceedingly interesting book.

C. GIBSON, *Spain in America* (1966). A splendidly clear and balanced discussion.

S. GRUZINSKI, *The Conquest of Mexico: The Incorporation of Indian Societies into the Western World, 16th–18th Centuries* (1993). Interprets the experience of native Americans, from their own point of view, during the time of the Spanish conquest.

L. HANKE, *Bartolomé de Las Casas: An Interpretation of His Life and Writings* (1951). A classic work.

J. HEMMING, *The Conquest of the Incas,* (1970). A lucid account of the conquest of the Inca Empire and its aftermath.

J. HEMMING, *Red Gold: The Conquest of the Brazilian Native Americans, 1500–1760* (1978). A careful account with excellent bibliography.

M. LEON-PORTILLA, ED., *The Broken Spears: The Aztec Account of the Conquest of Mexico* (1961). A collection of documents recounting the experience of the Aztecs from their own point of view.

J. LOCKHARDT AND S. B. SCHWARTZ, *Early Latin America: A History of Colonial Spanish America and Brazil* (1983). The new standard work.

J. R. MCNEIL, *Atlantic Empires of France and Spain: Louisbourg and Havana, 1700–1763* (1985). An examination of imperial policies in terms of two key overseas outposts.

P. MANNING, *Slavery and African Life: Occidental, Oriental, and African Slave Trades* (1990). An admirably concise yet probing and careful economic-historical synthesis of the evidence, with multiple tables and statistics to supplement the magisterial analysis. An indispensible attempt at presenting the "big picture" of African slavery.

S. W. MINTZ, *Sweetness and Power: The Place of Sugar in Modern History* (1985). Traces the role of sugar in the world economy and sugar's impact on world culture.

A. PAGDEN, *Lords of All the World: Ideologies of Empire in Spain, Britain, and France c. 1500–c. 1800* (1955). An effort to explain the imperial thinking of the major European powers.

R. PARES, *War and Trade in the West Indies* (1936). Relates the West Indies to Britain's larger commercial and naval concerns.

J. H. PARRY, *Trade and Dominion: The European Overseas Empires in the Eighteenth Century* (1971). A comprehensive account with attention to the European impact on the rest of the world.

J. A. RAWLEY, *The Transatlantic Slave Trade: A History* (1981). Impressively documented, detailed, and well-presented survey history of the Atlantic trade; little focus on African dimensions.

C. D. RICE, *The Rise and Fall of Black Slavery* (1975). An excellent survey of the subject with careful attention to the numerous historiographical controversies.

S. B. SCHWARTZ, *Sugar Plantations in the Formation of Brazilian Society: Bahia, 1550–1835* (1985). A broad-ranging study of the emergence of the plantation economy.

I. K. STEELE, *The English Atlantic, 1675–1740s: An Exploration of Communication and Community* (1986). An exploration of culture and commerce in the transatlantic world.

R. L. STEIN, *The French Sugar Business in the Eighteenth Century* (1988). A study that covers all aspects of the French sugar trade.

S. J. STEIN, *Peru's Indian Peoples and the Challenge of Spanish Conquest: Huamanga to 1640* (1933). A work that examines the impact of the conquest of the Inca empire over the scope of a century.

H. THOMAS, *Conquest: Montezuma, Cortés, and the Fall of Old Mexico* (1993). A splendid modern narrative of the event with careful attention to the character of the participants.

J. THORNTON, *Africa and Africans in the Making of the Atlantic World, 1400–1680* (1992). A discussion of the role of Africans in the emergence of the transatlantic economy.

N. WACHTEL, *The Vision of the Vanquished: The Spanish Conquest of Peru Through Indian Eyes, 1530–1570* (1977). A presentation of Incan experience of conquest.

Chapter 20

China

D. BODDE AND C. MORRIS, *Law in Imperial China* (1967). Focuses on the Ch'ing dynasty (1644–1911).

C. S. AND S. L. H. CHANG, *Crisis and Transformation in Seventeenth Century China: Society, Culture, and Modernity* (1992).

W. T. DE BARY, *Learning for One's Self: Essays on the Individual in Neo-Confucian Thought* (1991). A useful corrective to the view that Confucianism is simply a social ideology.

M. ELVIN, *The Pattern of the Chinese Past: A Social and Economic Interpretation* (1973). A controversial but stimulating interpretation of Chinese economic history in terms of technology. It brings in earlier periods as well as the Ming, Ch'ing, and modern China.

J. K. FAIRBANK, ED., *The Chinese World Order: Traditional China's Foreign Relations* (1968). An examination of the Chinese tribute system and its varying applications.

H. L. KAHN, *Monarchy in the Emperor's Eyes: Image and Reality in the Ch'ien-lung Reign* (1971). A study of the Chinese court during the mid-Ch'ing period.

LI YU, *The Carnal Prayer Mat*, trans. by P. Hanan (1990).

F. MOTE AND D. TWITCHETT, EDS., *The Ming Dynasty 1368–1644*, Part 1 of *The Cambridge History of China*, Vol. 7 (1987).

S. NAQUIN AND E. S. RAWSKI, *Chinese Society in the Eighteenth Century* (1987).

J. B. PARSONS, *The Peasant Rebellions of the Late Ming Dynasty* (1970).

P. C. PERDUE, *Exhausting the Earth, State and Peasant in Hunan, 1500–1850* (1987).

D. H. PERKINS, *Agricultural Development in China, 1368–1968* (1969).

M. RICCI, *China in the Sixteenth Century: The Journals of Matthew Ricci, 1583–1610* (1953).

W. ROWE, *Hankow* (1984). A study of a city in late imperial China.

G. W. SKINNER, *The City in Late Imperial China* (1977).

J. D. SPENCE, *Ts'ao Yin and the K'ang-hsi Emperor: Bondservant and Master* (1966). An excellent study of the early Ch'ing court.

J. D. SPENCE, *Emperor of China: A Self-Portrait of K'ang-hsi* (1974). The title of this readable book does not adequately convey the extent of the author's contribution to the study of the early Ch'ing emperor.

F. WAKEMAN, *The Great Enterprise* (1985). On the founding of the Manchu dynasty.

Japan

M. E. BERRY, *Hideyoshi* (1982). A study of the sixteenth-century unifier of Japan.

H. BOLITHO, *Treasures Among Men: The Fudai Daimyo in Tokugawa Japan* (1974). A study in depth.

C. R. BOXER, *The Christian Century in Japan, 1549–1650* (1951).

M. CHIKAMATSU, *Major Plays of Chikamatsu*, trans. by D. Keene (1961).

R. P. DORE, *Education in Tokugawa Japan* (1965).

C. J. DUNN, *Everyday Life in Traditional Japan* (1969). A descriptive study of Tokugawa society.

G. S. ELISON, *Deus Destroyed: The Image of Christianity in Early Modern Japan* (1973). A brilliant study of the persecutions of Christianity during the early Tokugawa period.

J. W. HALL, ED., *Early Modern Japan*, Vol. 4 of *The Cambridge History of Japan* (1991).

J. W. HALL AND M. JANSEN, EDS., *Studies in the Institutional History of Early Modern Japan* (1968). A collection of articles on Tokugawa institutions.

J. W. HALL, K. NAGAHARA, AND K. YAMAMURA, EDS., *Japan Before Tokugawa* (1981).

H. S. HIBBETT, *The Floating World in Japanese Fiction* (1959). An eminently readable study of early Tokugawa literature.

M. JANSEN, ED., *The Nineteenth Century*, Vol. 5 in *The Cambridge History of Japan* (1989).

D. KEENE, TRANS., *Chushingura, The Treasury of Loyal Retainers* (1971). The puppet play about the forty-seven rōnin who took revenge on the enemy of their former lord.

M. MARUYAMA, *Studies in the Intellectual History of Tokugawa Japan*, trans. by M. Hane (1974). A seminal work in this field by one of modern Japan's greatest scholars.

K. W. NAKAI, *Shogunal Politics* (1988). A brilliant study of Arai Hakuseki's conceptualization of Tokugawa overnment.

P. NOSCO, ED., *Confucianism and Tokugawa Culture* (1984). A lively collection of essays.

H. OOMS, *Tokugawa Ideology* (1985). A study of seventeenth-century Confucianism.

I. SAIKAKU, *The Japanese Family Storehouse*, trans. by G. W. Sargent (1959). A lively novel about merchant life in seventeenth-century Japan.

G. B. SANSOM, *The Western World and Japan* (1950).

C. D. SHELDON, *The Rise of the Merchant Class in Tokugawa Japan* (1958).

T. C. SMITH, *The Agrarian Origins of Modern Japan* (1959). On the evolution of farming and rural social organization in Tokugawa Japan.

R. P. TOBY, *State and Diplomacy in Early Modern Japan: Asia in the Development of the Tokugawa Bakufu* (1984).

C. TOTMAN, *Tokugawa Ieyasu: Shōgun* (1983).

C. TOTMAN, *Green Archipelago, Forestry in Preindustrial Japan* (1989).

H. P. VARLEY, *The Ōnin War: History of Its Origins and Background with a Selective Translation of the Chronicle of Ōnin* (1967).

K. YAMAMURA AND S. B. HANLEY, *Economic and Demographic Change in Preindustrial Japan, 1600–1868* (1977).

Korea

T. HATADA, *A History of Korea* (1969).

W. E. HENTHORN, *A History of Korea* (1971).

KI-BAIK LEE, *A New History of Korea* (1984).

PETER LEE, *Sourcebook of Korean Civilization*, Vol. I (1993).

Vietnam

J. BUTTINGER, *A Dragon Defiant, a Short History of Vietnam* (1972).

NGUYEN DU, *The Tale of Kieu* (1983).

N. TARLING, ED., *The Cambridge History of Southeast Asia* (1992).

K. TAYLOR, *The Birth of Vietnam* (1983).

A. B. WOODSIDE, *Vietnam and the Chinese Model* (1988).

Chapter 21

M. S. ANDERSON, *Europe in the Eighteenth Century*, 1713–1783 (1988). A good one-volume introduction to the individual states.

T. M. BARKER, *Army, Aristocracy, Monarchy: Essays in War, Society and Government in Austria, 1618–1780* (1982). Examines the intricate power relationships among these major institutions.

W. BEIK, *Absolutism and Society in Seventeenth-Century France* (1985). An important study that questions the extent of royal power.

J. BLACK, *Eighteenth-Century Europe 1700–1789* (1990). An excellent survey.

R. BONNEY, *Political Change in France Under Richelieu and Mazarin 1624–1661* (1978). An important examination of the emergence of French absolutism.

J. BREWER, *The Sinews of Power: War, Money, and the English State, 1688–1783* (1989). A study that emphasizes the financial power behind British military success.

G. BURGESS, *Absolute Monarchy and the Stuart Constitution* (1996). A new study that challenges many of the traditional interpretative categories.

P. BURKE, *The Fabrication of Louis XIV* (1992). Examines the manner in which the public image of Louis XIV was forged in art.

F. L. CARSTEN, *The Origins of Prussia* (1954). Discusses the groundwork laid by the Great Elector in the seventeenth century.

J. C. D. CLARKE, *English Society: 1688–1832: Social Structure and Political Practice During the Ancien Régime* (1985). An important, controversial work that emphasizes the role of religion in English political life.

L. COLLEY, *Britons: Forging the Nation, 1707–1837* (1992) A major study of the making of British nationhood.

WALTER DORN, *Competition for Empire, 1740–1763* (1940). Still one of the best accounts of the mid-eighteenth-century struggle.

W. DOYLE, *The Old European Order, 1660–1800* (1992). The most thoughtful treatment of the subject.

P. DUKES, *The Making of Russian Absolutism: 1613–1801* (1982). An overview based on recent scholarship.

R. J. W. EVANS, *The Making of the Habsburg Monarchy, 1550–1700: An Interpretation* (1979). Places much emphasis on intellectual factors and the role of religion.

F. FORD, *Robe and Sword: The Regrouping of the French Aristocracy after Louis XIV* (1953). Remains an important book for political, social, and intellectual history.

P. GOUBERT, *Louis XIV and Twenty Million Frenchmen* (1966). A fine overview of seventeenth-century French social structure.

R. HATTEN, ED., *Louis XIV and Europe* (1976). Covers foreign policy.

D. HIRST, *Authority and Conflict: England 1603–1658* (1986). Scholarly survey integrating history and historiography.

J. M. HITTLE, *The Service City: State and Townsmen in Russia, 1600–1800* (1979). Examines the relationship of cities in Russia to the growing power of the central government.

L. HUGHES, *Russia in the Age of Peter the Great* (1998). A major new account.

H. C. JOHNSON, *Frederick the Great and His Officials* (1975). An excellent recent examination of the Prussian administration.

P. LANGFORD, *A Polite and Commercial People: England 1717–1783* (1989). An excellent survey of mid-eighteenth-century Britain based on the most recent scholarship covering social history as well as politics, the overseas wars, and the American revolution.

A. LOSSKY, *Louis XIV and the French Monarchy* (1994). The most recent major analysis.

R. K. MASSIE, *Peter the Great: His Life and His World* (1980). A good popular biography.

R. MIDDLETON, *The Bells of Victory: The Pitt-Newcastle Ministry and the Conduct of the Seven Years' War, 1757–1762* (1985). A careful study of the intricacies of eighteenth-century cabinet goverment that questions the centrality of Pitt's role in the British victory.

J. H. PLUMB, *Sir Robert Walpole*, 2 vols. (1956, 1961). A masterful biography ranging across the sweep of European politics.

J. H. PLUMB, *The Growth of Political Stability in England, 1675–1725* (1969). An important interpretive work.

J. G. A. POCOCK, ED., *Three British Revolutions: 1641, 1688, 1776* (1980). An important collection of essays.

N. V. RIASANOVSKY, *The Image of Peter the Great in Russian History and Thought* (1985). Examines the ongoing legacy of Peter in Russian history.

J. C. RILEY, *The Seven Years' War and the Old Regime in France: The Economic and Financial Toll* (1986). An analysis of pressures that would undermine the French monarchy.

H. ROSENBERG, *Bureaucracy, Aristocracy, and Autocracy: The Prussian Experience, 1660–1815* (1960). Emphasizes the organization of Prussian administration.

C. RUSSELL, *The Fall of the English Monarchies, 1637–1642* (1991). A major revisionist account, which should be read with Stone's book.

D. L. RUBIN, *The Sun King: The Ascendancy of French Culture During the Reign of Louis XIV* (1992). A collection of useful essays.

K. Sharpe, *The Personal Rule of Charles I* (1992). A major narrative work.

L. Stone, *The Causes of the English Revolution 1529–1642* (1972). Survey stressing social history and ruminating over historians and historical method.

G. Treasure, *Mazarin: The Crisis of Absolutism in France* (1996). An examination not only of Mazarin, but also of the larger national and international background.

D. Underdown, *Fire from Heaven: Life in an English Town in the Seventeenth Century* (1992). A lively account of how a single English town experienced the religious and political turmoil of the century.

J. West, *Gunpower, Government, and War in the Mid-Eighteenth Century* (1991). A study of how warfare touched much government of the day.

J. B. Wolf, *Louis XIV* (1968). Authoritative and readable.

Chapter 22

I. T. Berend and G. Ranki, *The European Periphery and Industrialization, 1780–1914* (1982). Examines the experience of eastern and Mediterranean Europe.

J. Blum, *Lord and Peasant in Russia from the Ninth to the Nineteenth Century* (1961). A thorough and wide-ranging discussion.

J. Blum, *The End of the Old Order in Rural Europe* (1978). The most comprehensive treatment of life in rural Europe, especially central and eastern, from the early eighteenth through the mid-nineteenth centuries.

F. Braudel, *The Structures of Everyday Life: The Limits of the Possible*, trans. by M. Kochan (1982). A magisterial survey by the most important social historian of our time.

J. Cannon, *Aristocratic Century: The Peerage of Eighteenth-Century England* (1985). A useful treatment based on the most recent research.

G. Chaussinand-Nogaret, *The French Nobility in the Eighteenth Century* (1985). Suggests that culture, not class, was the decisive element in late eighteenth-century French society.

P. Deane, *The First Industrial Revolution*, 2nd ed. (1979). A well-balanced and systematic treatment.

J. De Vries, *The Economy of Europe in an Age of Crisis, 1600–1750* (1976). An excellent overview that sets forth the main issues.

J. De Vries, *European Urbanization 1500–1800* (1984). The most important and far-ranging of recent treatments of the subject.

W. Doyle, *Venality: The Sale of Offices in Eighteenth-Century France* (1997). Examines the manner in which the phenomena characterized much of the society.

P. Earle, *The Making of the English Middle Class: Business, Community, and Family Life in London, 1660–1730* (1989). The most careful study of the subject.

M. W. Flinn, *The European Demographic System, 1500–1820* (1981). A major summary.

F. Ford, *Robe and Sword: The Regrouping of the French Aristocracy after Louis XIV* (1953). An important treatment of the growing social tensions within the French nobility during the eighteenth century.

R. Forster and O. Ranum, *Deviants and the Abandoned in French Society* (1978). This and the following volume contain important essays from the French journal *Annales*.

R. Forster and O. Ranum, *Medicine and Society in France* (1980).

D. V. Glass and D. E. C. Eversley, eds., *Population in History: Essays in Historical Demography* (1965). Fundamental for an understanding of the eighteenth-century increase in population.

P. Goubert, *The Ancien Regime: French Society, 1600–1750*, trans. by Steve Cox (1974). A superb account of the peasant social order.

D. Hay et al., *Albion's Fatal Tree: Crime and Society in Eighteenth-Century England* (1976). Separate essays on a previously little-explored subject.

D. Hay and N. Rogers, *Eighteenth-Century English Society: Shuttles and Swords* (1997). Explores the social experience of the lower orders.

O. H. Hufton, *The Poor of Eighteenth-Century France, 1750–1789* (1975). A brilliant study of poverty and the family economy.

C. Jones, *Charity and Bienfaisance: The Treatment of the Poor in the Montpellier Region, 1740–1815* (1982). An important local French study.

E. L. Jones, *Agriculture and Economic Growth in England, 1650–1815* (1968). A good introduction to an important subject.

A. Kahan, *The Plow, the Hammer, and the Knout: An Economic History of Eighteenth-Century Russia* (1985). An extensive and detailed treatment.

H. Kamen, *European Society, 1500–1700* (1985). A useful one-volume treatment.

P. Laslett, *The World We Have Lost* (1984). Examination of English life and society before the coming of industrialism.

R. K. McClure, *Coram's Children: The London Foundling Hospital in the Eighteenth Century* (1981). A moving work that deals with the plight of all concerned with the problem.

N. McKenderick, ed., *The Birth of a Consumer Society: The Commercialization of Eighteenth-Century England* (1982). Deals with several aspects of the impact of commercialization.

F. E. Manuel, *The Broken Staff: Judaism Through Christian Eyes* (1992). An important discussion of Christian interpretations of Judaism.

M. A. Meyer, *The Origins of the Modern Jew: Jewish Identity and European Culture in Germany, 1749–1824* (1967). A general introduction organized around individual case studies.

S. POLLARD, *The Genesis of Modern Management: A Study of the Industrial Revolution in Great Britain* (1965). Treats industrialization from the standpoint of factory owners.

S. POLLARD, *Peaceful Conquest: The Industrialization of Europe, 1760–1970* (1981). A useful survey.

A. RIBEIRO, *Dress in Eighteenth-Century Europe, 1715–1789* (1985). An interesting examination of the social implication of style in clothing.

G. RUDE, *The Crowd in History 1730–1848* (1964). A pioneering study.

G. RUDE, *Paris and London in the Eighteenth Century* (1973).

H. SCHMAL, ED., *Patterns of European Urbanization Since 1500* (1981). Major essays.

L. STONE, *An Open Elite?* (1985). Raises important questions about the traditional view of open access to social mobility in England.

T. TACKETT, *Priest and Parish in Eighteenth-Century France: A Social and Political Study of the Cures in a Diocese of Dauphine, 1750–1791* (1977). An important local study that displays the role of the church in the fabric of social life in the old regime.

L. A. TILLY AND J. W. SCOTT, *Women, Work, and Family* (1978). An excellent survey of the issues in western Europe.

D. VALENZE, *The First Industrial Woman* (1995). An elegant work exploring the manner in which industrialization transformed the work of women.

A. VICKERY, *The Gentleman's Daughter: Women's Lives in Georgian England* (1998). Argues that women experienced expanding social horizons in the eighteenth century.

R. WALL, ED., *Family Forms in Historic Europe* (1983). Essays that cover the entire continent.

C. WILSON, *England's Apprenticeship, 1603–1763* (1984). A broad survey of English economic life on the eve of industrialism.

E. A. WRIGLEY, *Continuity, Chance and Change: The Character of the Industrial Revolution in England* (1988). A major conceptual reassessment.

E. A. WRIGLEY AND R. S. SCHOFIELD, *The Population History of England, 1541–1871: A Reconstruction* (1982). One of the most ambitious demographic studies ever undertaken.

Chapter 23

A. L. BASHAM, ED., *A Cultural History of India* (1975). Part II, "Age of Muslim Dominance," is of greatest relevance here.

S. S. BLAIR AND J. BLOOM, *The Art and Architecture of Islam, 1250–1800* (1994). A fine survey of the period for all parts of the Islamic world.

K. CHELEBI, *The Balance of Truth* (1957). A marvelous volume of essays and reflections by probably the major intellectual of Ottoman times.

M. A. COOK, ED., *A History of the Ottoman Empire to 1730* (1976). Articles from *The Cambridge History of Islam* and *The New Cambridge Modern History*, with a brief introduction by Cook.

W. T. DE BARY ET AL., COMP., *Sources of Indian Tradition*, 2nd ed. (1958). Vol. I, *From the Beginning to 1800*, ed. and rev. by Ainslie T. Embree (1988). Excellent selections from a wide variety of Indian texts, with good introductions to chapters and individual selections.

C. H. FLEISCHER, *Bureaucrat and Intellectual in the Ottoman Empire: the Historian Mustafa Ali (1541–1600)* (1986). A major study of Ottoman intellectual history.

G. HAMBLY, *Central Asia* (1966). Excellent survey chapters (9–13) on the Chagatay and Uzbek (Shaybanid) Turks.

R. S. HATTOX, *Coffee and Coffee-houses: The Origins of a Social Beverage in the Medieval Near East* (1985). A fascinating piece of social history.

M. G. S. HODGSON, *The Gunpowder Empires and Modern Times*, Vol. 3 of *The Venture of Islam*, 3 vols. (1974). Less ample than Vols. 1 and 2 of Hodgson's monumental history, but a thoughtful survey of the great post–1500 empires.

P. M. HOLT, ANN K. S. LAMBTON, AND BERNARD LEWIS, *The Cambridge History of Islam*, 2 vols. (1970). A traditional, somewhat compartmentalized history useful for reference. Vol. I has important surveys on the Ottoman empire and Safavid Iran. Vol. II includes chapters on post–1500 India, Southeast Asia, and Africa.

S. M. IKRAM, *Muslim Civilization in India* (1964). Still the best short survey history, covering the period from 711 to 1857.

H. INALCIK, *The Ottoman Empire: The Classical Age 1300–1600* (1973). An excellent, if dated, survey with solid treatment of Ottoman social, religious, and political institutions.

H. INALCIK, *An Economic and Social History of the Ottoman Empire, 1300–1914* (1994). A masterly survey by the dean of Ottoman studies today.

C. KAFADAR, *Between Two Worlds: The Construction of the Ottoman State* (1995). A readable analysis of theories of Ottoman origins and early development.

N. R. KEDDIE, ED., *Scholars, Saints, and Sufis: Muslim Religious Institutions in the Middle East Since 1500* (1972). A collection of interesting articles well worth reading.

R. C. MAJUMDAR, GEN. ED., *The History and Culture of the Indian People*, Vol. VII, *The Mughal Empire* (1974). A thorough and readable political and cultural history of the period in India.

M. MUJEEB, *The Indian Muslims* (1967). The best cultural study of Islamic civilization in India as a whole, from its origins onward.

G. NECIPOGLU, *Architecture, Ceremonial, and Power: the Topkapi Palace in the Fifteenth and Sixteenth Centuries* (1991). A superb analysis of the symbolism of Ottoman power and authority.

S. A. A. RIZVI, *The Wonder That Was India*, Vol. II (1987). A sequel to Basham's original *The Wonder That Was India*; treats Mughal life, culture, and history from 1200 to 1700.

F. ROBINSON, *Atlas of the Islamic World Since 1500* (1982). Brief, excellent historical essays, color illustrations with detailed accompanying text, and chronological tables, as well as precise maps, make this a refreshing general reference work.

R. SAVORY, *Iran Under the Safavids* (1980). A solid and readable survey.

S. J. SHAW, *Empire of the Gazis: The Rise and Decline of the Ottoman Empire, 1280–1808*, Vol. I of *History of the Ottoman Empire and Modern Turkey* (1976). A solid historical survey with excellent bibliographic essays for each chapter and a good index.

J. O. VOLL, *Islam: Continuity and Change in the Modern World* (1982). Chapter 3 provides an excellent overview of eighteenth-century revival and reform movements in diverse Islamic lands.

Chapter 24

R. ASHCRAFT, *Revolutionary Politics and Locke's Two Treatises of Government* (1986). The most important study of Locke to appear in recent years.

R. P. BARTLETT, *Human Capital: The Settlement of Foreigners in Russia 1762–1804* (1979). Examines Catherine's policy of attracting farmers and skilled workers to Russia.

D. BEALES, *Joseph II: In the Shadow of Maria Theresa, 1741–1780* (1987). The best treatment in English of the early political life of Joseph II.

C. BECKER, *The Heavenly City of the Eighteenth Century Philosophers* (1932). An influential but very controversial discussion.

T. BESTERMANN, *Voltaire* (1969). A biography by the editor of Voltaire's letters.

M. BIAGIOLI, *Galileo Courtier: The Practice of Science in the Culture of Absolutism* (1993). A major revisionist work that emphasizes the role of the political setting on Galileo's career and thought.

D. D. BIEN, *The Calas Affair: Persecution, Toleration, and Heresy in Eighteenth-Century Toulouse* (1960). The standard treatment of the famous case.

R. CHARTIER, *The Cultural Origins of the French Revolution* (1991). A wide-ranging discussion of the emergence of the public sphere and the role of books and the book trade during the Enlightenment.

H. CHISICK, *The Limits of Reform in the Enlightenment: Attitudes Toward the Education of the Lower Classes in Eighteenth-Century France* (1981). An attempt to examine the impact of the Enlightenment on nonelite classes.

I. B. COHEN, *Revolution in Science* (1985). A general consideration of the concept and of historical examples of change in scientific thought.

R. DARNTON, *The Literary Underground of the Old Regime* (1982). Essays on the world of printers, publishers, and booksellers.

I. DE MADARIAGA, *Catherine the Great: A Short History* (1990). A good brief biography.

J. DUNN, *The Political Thought of John Locke: An Historical Account of the "Two Treatises of Government"* (1969). An excellent introduction.

M. A. FINOCCHIARO, *The Galileo Affair: A Documentary History* (1989). A collection of all the relevant documents with an introductory commentary.

J. GAGLIARDO, *Enlightened Despotism* (1967). Remains a useful discussion.

P. GAY, *The Enlightenment: An Interpretation*, 2 vols. (1966, 1969). The most important and far-reaching treatment.

A. GOLDGAR, *Impolite Learning: Conduct and Community in the Republic of Letters, 1680–1750* (1995). A lively survey of the structure of the European intellectual community.

D. GOODMAN, *The Republic of Letters: A Cultural History of the French Enlightenment* (1994). Concentrates on the role of salons.

I. HARRIS, *The Mind of John Locke: A Study of Political Theory in Its Intellectual Setting* (1994) The most comprehensive recent treatment.

M. C. JACOB, *Living the Enlightenment: Freemasonry and Politics in Eighteenth-Century Europe* (1991). The best treatment in English of Freemasonry.

R. KREISER, *Miracles, Convulsions, and Ecclesiastical Politics in Early Eighteenth-Century Paris* (1978). An important study of the kind of religious life that the *philosophes* opposed.

T. S. KUHN, *The Copernican Revolution* (1957). Remains the most influential treatment.

D. LINDBERG AND R. L. NUMBERS, EDS., *Good and Nature: Historical Essays on the Encounter Between Christianity and Science* (1986). The best collection of essays on the subject.

C. A. MACARTNEY, *The Habsburg Empire, 1790–1918* (1971). Provides useful coverage of major mid-eighteenth-century developments.

F. MANUEL, *The Eighteenth Century Confronts the Gods* (1959). A broad examination of the *philosophes'* treatment of Christian and pagan religion.

R. R. PALMER, *Catholics and Unbelievers in Eighteenth-Century France* (1939). A discussion of the opponents of the *philosophes*.

G. RITTER, *Frederick the Great* (trans. 1968). A useful biography.

R. O. ROCKWOOD, ED., *Carl Becker's Heavenly City Revisited* (1958). Important essays qualifying Becker's thesis.

H. M. SCOTT, ED., *Enlightened Absolutism: Reform and Reformers in Later Eighteenth-Century Europe* (1990). A useful collection that incorporates recent scholarship.

S. SHAPIN, *The Scientific Revolution* (1996). An important revisionist survey emphasizing social factors.

J. N. SHKLAR, *Men and Citizens, a Study of Rousseau's Social Theory* (1969). A thoughtful and provocative overview of Rousseau's political thought.

D. SPADAFORA, *The Idea of Progress in Eighteenth Century Britain* (1990). A recent major study that covers many aspects of the Enlightenment in Britain.

L. STEINBRÜGGE, *The Moral Sex: Woman's Nature in the French Enlightenment* (1995). Emphasizes the conservative nature of Enlightenment thought on women.

L. STEWART, *The Rise of Public Science: Rhetoric, Technology, and Natural Philosophy in Newtonian Britain, 1660–1750* (1992). Examines how science became related to public life and economic development.

R. S. WESTFALL, *Never at Rest: A Biography of Isaac Newton* (1981). A very important major study.

A. M. WILSON, *Diderot* (1972). A splendid biography of the person behind the project for the *Encyclopedia* and other major Enlightenment publications.

L. WOLFF, *Inventing Eastern Europe: The Map of Civilization on the Mind of the Enlightenment* (1994). A remarkable study of the manner in which Enlightenment writers recast the understanding of this part of the Continent.

Chapter 25

R. ANSTEY, *The Atlantic Slave Trade and British Abolition, 1760–1810* (1975). A standard overview that emphasizes the role of religious factors.

B. BAILYN, *The Ideological Origins of the American Revolution* (1967). An important work illustrating the role of English radical thought in the perceptions of the American colonists.

K. M. BAKER, *Inventing the French Revolution: Essays on French Political Culture in the Eighteenth Century* (1990). Important essays on political thought before and during the revolution.

K. M. BAKER AND C. LUCAS, EDS., *The French Revolution and the Creation of Modern Political Culture*, 3 vols. (1987). A splendid collection of important original articles on all aspects of politics during the revolution.

R. J. BARMAN, *Brazil: The Forging of a Nation, 1798–1852* (1988). The best coverage of this period.

C. BECKER, *The Declaration of Independence: A Study in the History of Political Ideas* (1922). Remains an important examination of the political and imperial theory of the Declaration.

J. F. BERNARD, *Talleyrand: A Biography* (1973). A useful account.

L. BETHELL, *The Cambridge History of Latin America*, Vol. 3 (1985). Contains an extensive treatment of independence.

R. BLACKBURN, *The Overthrow of Colonial Slavery, 1776–1848* (1988). A major discussion quite skeptical of the humanitarian interpretation.

T. C. W. BLANNING, ED., *The Rise and Fall of the French Revolution* (1996). A wide-ranging collection of essays illustrating the debates over the French Revolution.

J. BROOKE, *King George III* (1972). The best biography.

R. COBB, *The People's Armies* (1987). The major treatment in English of the revolutionary army.

O. CONNELLY, *Napoleon's Satellite Kingdoms* (1965). The rule of Napoleon and his family in Europe.

E. V. DA COSTA, *The Brazilian Empire* (1985). Excellent coverage of the entire nineteenth-century experience of Brazil.

D. B. DAVIS, *The Problem of Slavery in the Age of Revolution, 1770–1823* (1975). A transatlantic perspective on the issue.

F. FEHÉR, *The French Revolution and the Birth of Modernity* (1990). A wide-ranging collection of essays on political and cultural facets of the revolution.

A. FORREST, *The French Revolution and the Poor* (1981). A study that expands consideration of the revolution beyond the standard social boundaries.

M. GLOVER, *The Peninsular War, 1807–1814: A Concise Military History* (1974). An interesting account of the military campaign that so drained Napoleon's resources in western Europe.

J. GODECHOT, *The Counter-Revolution: Doctrine and Action, 1789–1804* (1971). An examination of opposition to the revolution.

A. GOODWIN, *The Friends of Liberty: The English Democratic Movement in the Age of the French Revolution* (1979). A major work that explores the impact of the French Revolution on English radicalism.

L. HUNT, *Politics, Culture, and Class in the French Revolution* (1986). A series of essays that focus on the modes of expression of the revolutionary values and political ideas.

W. W. KAUFMANN, *British Policy and the Independence of Latin America, 1802–1828* (1951). A standard discussion of an important relationship.

E. KENNEDY, *A Cultural History of the French Revolution* (1989). An important examination of the role of the arts, schools, clubs, and intellectual institutions.

M. KENNEDY, *The Jacobin Clubs in the French Revolution: The First Years* (1982). A careful scrutiny of the organizations chiefly responsible for the radicalizing of the revolution.

M. KENNEDY, *The Jacobin Clubs in the French Revolution: The Middle Years* (1988). A continuation of the previously listed study.

H. KISSINGER, *A World Restored: Metternich, Castlereagh and the Problems of Peace, 1812–1822* (1957). A provocative study by an author who became an American secretary of state.

G. LEFEBVRE, *The Coming of the French Revolution* (trans. 1947). A classic examination of the crisis of the French monarchy and the events of 1789.

G. LEFEBVRE, *Napoleon*, 2 vols., trans. by H. Stockhold (1969). The fullest and finest biography.

J. LYNCH, *The Spanish American Revolutions, 1808–1826* (1986). An excellent one-volume treatment.

G. MASUR, *Simón Bolívar* (1969). The standard biography in English.

P. MAIER, *American Scripture: Making the Declaration of Independence* (1997) Stands as a major revision of our understanding of the Declaration.

S. E. MELZER AND L. W. RABINE, EDS., *Rebel Daughters: Women and the French Revolution* (1992). A collection of essays exploring various aspects of the role and image of women in the French Revolution.

M. MORRIS, *The British Monarchy and the French Revolution* (1998). Explores the manner in which the British monarchy saved itself from possible revolution.

R. MUIR, *Tactics and the Experience of Battle in the Age of Napoleon* (1998). Examines the wars from the standpoint of the soldiers in combat.

H. NICOLSON, *The Congress of Vienna* (1946). A good, readable account.

T. O. OTT, *The Haitian Revolution, 1789–1804* (1973). An account that clearly relates the events in Haiti to those in France.

R. R. PALMER, *Twelve Who Ruled: The Committee of Public Safety During the Terror* (1941). A clear narrative and analysis of the policies and problems of the committee.

R. R. PALMER, *The Age of the Democratic Revolution: A Political History of Europe and America, 1760–1800*, 2 vols. (1959, 1964). An impressive survey of the political turmoil in the transatlantic world.

C. PROCTOR, *Women, Equality, and the French Revolution* (1990). An examination of how the ideas of the Enlightenment and the attitudes of revolutionaries affected the legal status of women.

A. J. RUSSELL-WOOD, ED., *From Colony to Nation: Essays on the Independence of Brazil* (1975). A series of important essays.

P. SCHROEDER, *The Transformation of European Politics, 1763–1848* (1994). A fundamental treatment of the diplomacy of the era.

T. E. SKIDMORE AND P. H. SMITH, *Modern Latin America*, 4th ed. (1997). A very useful survey.

A. SOBOUL, *The Parisian Sans-Culottes and the French Revolution, 1793–94* (1964). The best work on the subject.

A. SOBOUL, *The French Revolution* (trans. 1975). An important work by a Marxist scholar.

D. G. SUTHERLAND, *France, 1789–1825: Revolution and Counterrevolution* (1986). A major synthesis based on recent scholarship in social history.

T. TACKETT, *Religion, Revolution, and Regional Culture in Eighteenth-Century France: The Ecclesiastical Oath of 1791* (1986). The most important study of this topic.

T. TACKETT, *Becoming a Revolutionary: The Deputies of the French National Assembly and the Emergence of a Revolutionary Culture (1789–1790)* (1996). The best study of the early months of the revolution.

J. M. THOMPSON, *Robespierre*, 2 vols. (1935). The best biography.

D. K. VAN KEY, *The Religious Origins of the French Revolution: From Calvin to the Civil Constitution, 1560–1791* (1996). Examines the manner in which debates within French Catholicism influenced the coming of the revolution.

M. WALZER, ED., *Regicide and Revolution: Speeches at the Trial of Louis XVI* (1974). An important and exceedingly interesting collection of documents with a useful introduction.

I. WOLOCH, *The New Regime: Transformations of the French Civic Order, 1789–1820s* (1994). An important overview of just what had and had not changed in France after the quarter-century of revolution and war.

G. WOOD, *The Radicalism of the American Revolution* (1991). A major interpretation.

Chapter 26

B. ANDERSON, *Imagined Communities*, rev. ed. (1991). A discussion of the forces that have fostered national identity.

R. M. BERDAHL, *The Politics of the Prussian Nobility: The Development of a Conservative Ideology, 1770–1848* (1988). A major examination of German conservative outlooks.

I. BERLIN, *Karl Marx: His Life and Environment*, 4th ed. (1996). A volume that remains an excellent introduction.

J. BLASSINGAME, *The Slave Community* (1975). Emphasizes the manner in which slaves shaped their own community.

S. G. CHECKLAND, *The Rise of Industrial Society in England, 1815–1885* (1964). Strong on economic institutions.

A. CLARKE, *The Struggle for the Breeches: Gender and the Making of the British Working Class* (1995). An examination of the manner in which industrialization made problematical the relationships between men and women.

W. COLEMAN, *Death Is a Social Disease: Public Health and Political Economy in Early Industrial France* (1982). One of the first works in English to study this problem.

I. DEAK, *The Lawful Revolution: Louis Kossuth and the Hungarians, 1848–1849* (1979). The most significant study of the topic in English.

M. DUBERMAN, ED., *The Anti-Slavery Vanguard* (1965) Important essays.

T. DUBLIN, *Women at Work: The Transformation of Work and Community in Lowell, Massachusetts, 1826–1860* (1979). The best work on this important setting of early American industrialization.

J. ELSTER, *An Introduction to Karl Marx* (1985). The best volume to provide a discussion of Marx's fundamental concepts.

E. GENOVESE, *Roll Jordan Roll* (1974). The best overview of American slavery.

L. GREENFIELD, *Nationalism: Five Roads to Modernity* (1992). A major comparative study.

T. HAMEROW, *Restoration, Revolution, and Reaction: Economics and Politics in Germany, 1815–1871* (1958). Traces the forces that worked toward the failure of revolution in Germany.

R. F. HAMILTON, *The Bourgeois Epoch: Marx and Engels on Britain, France, and Germany* (1991). Examines Marx's and Engels's observations against what is known to have been the situation in each nation.

G. HIMMELFARB, *The Idea of Poverty: England in the Early Industrial Age* (1984). A major work covering the subject from the time of Adam Smith through 1850.

E. J. HOBSBAWM, *The Age of Revolution, 1789–1848* (1962). A very comprehensive survey emphasizing the social ramifications of the liberal democratic and industrial revolutions.

E. J. HOBSBAWM, *Nations and Nationalism Since 1780: Programme, Myth, Reality*, rev. ed. (1992). The best recent introduction to the subject.

A. JARDIN AND A. J. TUDESQ, *Restoration and Reaction, 1815–1848* (1984). Surveys this period in France.

K. KOLAKOWSKI, *Main Currents of Marxism: Its Rise, Growth, and Dissolution*, 3 vols. (1978). A very important and comprehensive survey.

D. LANDES, *The Unbound Prometheus: Technological Change and Industrial Development in Western Europe from 1750 to the Present* (1969). The best one-volume treatment of technological development in a broad social and economic context.

W. L. LANGER, *Political and Social Upheaval, 1832–1852* (1969). A remarkably thorough survey strong in both social and intellectual history as well as political narrative.

R. MAGRAW, *A History of the French Working Class*, 2 vols. (1992). A major overview based on the most recent literature.

H. PERKIN, *The Origins of Modern English Society, 1780–1880* (1969). A provocative attempt to look at the society as a whole.

M. D. PETERSON, *The Great Triumvirate: Webster, Clay, and Calhoun* (1988). A splendid narrative of American politics from the 1820s through the 1850s.

D. H. PINKNEY, *Decisive Years in France, 1840–1847* (1986). A detailed and careful examination of the years leading up to the Revolution of 1848.

P. ROBERTSON, *An Experience of Women: Pattern and Change in Nineteenth-Century Europe* (1982). A useful survey.

W. H. SEWELL, JR., *Work and Revolution in France: The Language of Labor from the Old Regime to 1848* (1980). A very fine analysis of French artisans.

J. SHEEHAN, *German History, 1770–1866* (1989). A very long work that is now the best available survey of the subject.

N. SMELZER, *Social Change in the Industrial Revolution: An Application of Theory to the British Cotton Industry* (1959). Important sections on the working-class family.

P. STEARNS, *Eighteen Forty-Eight: The Tide of Revolution in Europe* (1974). A good discussion of the social background.

E. P. THOMPSON, *The Making of the English Working Class* (1964). An important, influential, and controversial work.

L. A. TILLY AND J. W. SCOTT, *Women, Work, and Family* (1978). A useful and sensitive survey.

A. B. ULAM, *Russia's Failed Revolutionaries* (1981). Contains a useful discussion of the Decembrists as a background for other nineteenth-century Russian revolutionary activity.

S. WILLENTZ, *Chants Democratic: New York City and the Rise of the American Working Class, 1788–1850* (1984). An important examination of labor and politics.

A. S. WOHL, *Endangered Lives: Public Health in Victorian Britain* (1983). An important and wide-ranging examination of the health problems created by urbanization and industrialization.

Chapter 27

M. BENTLEY, *Politics Without Democracy, 1815–1914* (1984). A well-informed survey of British development.

R. BLAKE, *Disraeli* (1967). The best biography.

J. BLUM, *Lord and Peasant in Russia from the Ninth to the Nineteenth Century* (1961). A clear discussion of emancipation in the later chapters.

M. BURNS, *Rural Society and French Politics: Boulangism and the Dreyfus Affair, 1886–1900* (1984). An examination of the subject from the rural perspective.

G. CHAPMAN, *The Dreyfus Affair: A Reassessment* (1955). A detached treatment of a subject that still provokes strong feelings.

D. G. CREIGHTON, *John A. MacDonald* (1952, 1955). Major biography of the first Canadian prime minister.

G. CRAIG, *Germany, 1866–1945* (1978). An excellent survey.

D. DONALD, *Lincoln* (1995). Now the standard biography.

S. EDWARDS, *The Paris Commune of 1871* (1971). A useful examination of a complex subject.

D. FEHRENBACHER, *The Dred Scott Case* (1978). A brilliant study that goes far beyond the subject of the title.

D. K. FIELDHOUSE, *The Colonial Experience: A Comparative Study from the Eighteenth Century* (1966). An excellent study.

E. HOBSBAWM, *The Age of Empire, 1875–1914* (1987). A stimulating survey that covers cultural as well as political developments.

I. V. HULL, *The Entourage of Kaiser Wilhelm II, 1888–1918* (1982). An important discussion of the scandals of the German court.

R. A. KANN, *The Multinational Empire*, 2 vols. (1950). The basic treatment of the nationality problem of Austria-Hungary.

G. KITSON CLARK, *The Making of Victorian England* (1962). The best introduction.

W. L. LANGER, *The Diplomacy of Imperialism* (1935). A major study of the diplomatic intricacies of late-century imperialism.

R. R. LOCKE, *French Legitimists and the Politics of Moral Order in the Early Third Republic* (1974). An excellent study of the social and intellectual roots of monarchist support.

P. MAGNUS, *Gladstone: A Biography* (1955). A readable biography.

A. J. MAY, *The Habsburg Monarchy, 1867–1914* (1951). Narrates in considerable detail and with much sympathy the fate of the dual monarchy.

M E. MCGERR, *The Decline of Popular Politics: The American North, 1865–1928* (1986). A study of the decline in popular political participation.

F. MCMILLAN, *Napoleon III* (1991). The best recent study.

J. M. MCPHERSON, *The Battle Cry of Freedom: The Civil War Era* (1988). An excellent one-volume treatment.

W. N. MEDLICOTT, *Bismarck and Modern Germany* (1965). An excellent brief biography.

W. J. MOMMSEN, *Theories of Imperialism* (1980). A study of the debate on the meaning of imperialism.

W. E. MOSSE, *Alexander II and the Modernization of Russia* (1958). A brief biography.

N. M. NAIMARK, *Terrorists and Social Democrats: The Russian Revolutionary Movement Under Alexander III* (1983). Based on the most recent research.

M. E. NEELY, JR., *The Fate of Liberty: Abraham Lincoln and Civil Liberties* (1991). A major discussion of the issue.

C. C. O'BRIEN, *Parnell and His Party* (1957). An excellent treatment of the Irish question.

J. P. PARRY, *The Rise and Fall of Liberal Government in Victorian Britain* (1994). An outstanding study.

O. PFLANZE, *Bismarck and the Development of Germany*, 3 vols. (1990). Carries the story from the achievement of unification to the end of Bismarck's career.

A. PLESSIS, *The Rise and Fall of the Second Empire, 1852–1871* (1985). A useful survey of France under Napoleon III.

D. M. POTTER, *The Impending Crisis, 1848–1861* (1976).

R. SHANNON, *Gladstone: 1809–1865* (1982). Best coverage of his early career.

D. M. SMITH, *Cavour* (1984). An excellent biography.

C. P. STACEY, *Canada and the Age of Conflict* (1977, 1981). A study of Canadian foreign relations.

A. J. P. TAYLOR, *The Habsburg Monarchy, 1809–1918* (1941). An opinionated but highly readable work.

R. TOMBS, *The War Against Paris, 1871* (1981). Examines the role of the army in suppressing the Paris Commune.

A. B. ULAM, *Russia's Failed Revolutionaries* (1981). A recent study of revolutionary societies and activities before the Revolution of 1917.

R. M. UTLEY, *The Indian Frontier and the American West, 1846–1890* (1984). A broad survey of the pressures of white civilization agaibt Native Americans.

F. VENTURI, *The Roots of Revolution* (trans. 1960). A major treatment of late-nineteenth-century revolutionary movements.

H. S. WATSON, *The Russian Empire, 1801–1917* (1967). A far-ranging narrative.

H. U. WEHLER, *The German Empire, 1871–1918* (1985). An important, controversial work.

C. B. WOODHAM-SMITH, *The Reason Why* (1953). A lively account of the Crimean War and the charge of the Light Brigade.

C. V. WOODWARD, *The Strange History of Jim Crow* (1966). A clear discussion of the imposition of racial segregation in the United States.

T. ZELDIN, *France: 1848–1945*, 2 vols. (1973, 1977). Emphasizes the social developments.

R. E. ZELNICK, *Labor and Society in Tsarist Russia: The Factory Workers of St. Petersburg, 1855–1870* (1971). An important volume that considers the early stages of the Russian industrial labor force in the era of serf emancipation.

Chapter 28

J. ALBISETTI, *Secondary School Reform in Imperial Germany* (1983). Examines the relationship between politics and education.

I. M. ARONSON, *Troubled Waters: The Origins of the 1881 Anti-Jewish Pogroms in Russia* (1990). The best discussion of this subject.

J. H. BATES, *St. Petersburg: Industrialization and Change* (1976). Impact of industrialization on the capital of imperial Russia.

G. BEHLMER, *Child Abuse and Moral Reform in England, 1870–1908* (1982). An important study of changes in the treatment of children.

L. R. BERLANSTEIN, *The Working People of Paris, 1871–1914* (1985). Interesting and comprehensive.

P. BRANCA, *Silent Sisterhood: Middle Class Women in the Victorian Home* (1975). A well-researched work.

N. BULLOCK AND J. READ, *The Movement for Housing Reform in Germany and France, 1840–1914* (1985). An important and wide-ranging study of the housing problem.

A. D. CHANDLER, JR., *The Visible Hand: Managerial Revolution in American Business* (1977). The best discussion of the innovative role of American business.

J. M. COOPER, JR., *The Warrior and the Priest: Woodrow Wilson and Theodore Roosevelt* (1983). An interesting dual biography.

W. CRONIN, *Nature's Metropolis: Chicago and the Great West, 1848–1893* (1991). The best examination of any major American nineteenth-century city.

P. GAY, *The Dilemma of Democratic Socialism: Eduard Bernstein's Challenge to Marx* (1952). A clear presentation of the problems raised by Bernstein's revisionism.

D. F. GOOD, *The Economic Rise of the Habsburg Empire, 1750–1914* (1985). The best available study.

S. C. HAUSE, *Women's Suffrage and Social Politics in the French Third Republic* (1984). A wide-ranging examination of the question.

G. HIMMELFARB, *Poverty and Compassion: The Moral Imagination of the Late Victorians* (1991). The best examination of late Victorian social thought.

E. J. Hobsbawm, *The Age of Capital* (1975). Explores the consolidation of middle-class life after 1850.

L. Holcombe, *Wives and Property: Reform of the Married Women's Property Law in Nineteenth-Century England* (1983). The standard work on the subject.

S. Kern, *The Culture of Time and Space, 1880–1918* (1983). A lively discussion of the impact of the new technology.

S. Kern, *The Culture of Love: Victorians to Moderns* (1992). A major discussion of how Europeans have thought and behaved in regard to love, family, and sexuality.

L. Kolakowski, *Main Currents of Marxism: Its Rise, Growth, and Dissolution*, 3 vols. (1978). Especially good on the last years of the nineteenth century and the early years of the twentieth.

P. Krause, *The Battle for Homestead, 1880–1892* (1992). Examines labor relations in the steel industry.

D. Landes, *The Wealth and Poverty of Nations: Why Some Are So Rich and Some So Poor* (1998). A major international discussion of the subject.

A. H. McBriar, *Fabian Socialism and English Politics, 1884–1918* (1962). The standard discussion.

A. MacLaren, *Sexuality and Social Order: The Debate over the Fertility of Women and Workers in France, 1770–1920* (1983). Examines the debate over birth control in France.

G. L. Mosse, *German Jews Beyond Judaism* (1985). Sensitive essays exploring the relationship of Jews to German culture in the nineteenth and early twentieth centuries.

R. A. Nye, *Crime, Madness, and Politics in Modern France: The Medical Concept of National Decline* (1984). Relevant to issues of family and women.

H. Pelling, *The Origins of the Labour Party, 1880–1900* (1965). Examines the sources of the party in the activities of British socialists and trade unionists.

D. H. Pinkney, *Napoleon III and the Rebuilding of Paris* (1958). A classic study.

F. K. Prochaska, *Women and Philanthropy in Nineteenth-Century England* (1980). Studies the role of women in charity.

J. Rendall, *The Origins of Modern Feminism: Women in Britain, France and the United States, 1780–1860* (1985). A well-informed introduction.

T. Richards, *The Commodity Culture of Victorian England: Advertising and Spectacle, 1851–1914* (1990). A study of how consumers were persuaded of their need for new commodities.

H. Rogger, *Russia in the Age of Modernization and Revolution, 1881–1917* (1983). The best synthesis of the period.

H. Rogger, *Jewish Policies and Right-Wing Politics in Imperial Russia* (1986). A very learned examination of Russian anti-Semitism.

M. L. Rozenblit, *The Jews of Vienna, 1867–1914: Assimilation and Identity* (1983). Covers the cultural, economic, and political life of Viennese Jews.

C. E. Schorske, *German Social Democracy, 1905–1917* (1955). Remains a brilliant study of the difficulties of the Social Democrats under the empire.

A. L. Shapiro, *Housing the Poor of Paris, 1850–1902* (1985). Examines what happened to working-class housing during the remodeling of Paris.

B. G. Smith, *Ladies of the Leisure Class: The Bourgeoises of Northern France in the Nineteenth Century* (1981). Emphasizes the importance of the reproductive role of women.

R. A. Soloway, *Birth Control and the Population Question in England, 1877–1930* (1982). An important book that should be read with MacLaren *(listed above)*.

N. Stone, *Europe Transformed* (1984). A sweeping survey that emphasizes the difficulties of late-nineteenth-century liberalism.

S. Trachtenberg, *The Incorporation of America: Culture and Society in the Gilded Age* (1982). Studies the manner in which corporate organization affected various aspects of American life outside the realm of business.

A. B. Ulam, *The Bolsheviks: The Intellectual and Political History of the Triumph of Communism in Russia* (1965). Early chapters discuss prewar developments and the formation of Lenin's doctrines.

A. M. Verner, *The Crisis of Russian Autocracy: Nicholas II and the 1905 Revolution* (1990). A major study of this crucial event.

J. R. Walkowitz, *Prostitution and Victorian Society: Women, Class, and the State* (1980). A work of great insight and sensitivity.

E. Weber, *Peasants into Frenchmen: The Modernization of Rural France, 1870–1914* (1976). An important and fascinating work on the transformation of French peasants into self-conscious citizens of the nation-state.

M. J. Wiener, *English Culture and the Decline of the Industrial Spirit, 1850–1980* (1981). The best study of the problem.

Chapter 29

R. Aron, *Main Currents in Sociological Thought*, 2 vols. (1965, 1967). An introduction to the founders of the science.

S. Aschheim, *The Nietzsche Legacy in Germany* (1992). Important study of the influence of Nietzsche's thought.

S. Avineri, *The Making of Modern Zionism: The Intellectual Origins of the Jewish State* (1981). An excellent introduction to the development of Zionist thought.

S. Barrows, *Distorting Mirrors: Visions of the Crowd in Late Nineteenth-Century France* (1981). An important and imaginative examination of crowd psychology as it related to social tension in France.

M. D. Biddis, *Father of Racist Ideology: The Social and Political Thought of Count Gobineau* (1970). Sets the subject in the more general context of nineteenth-century thought.

D. BLACKBOURNE, *Marpingen: Apparitions of the Virgin Mary in Nineteenth-Century Germany* (1993). A major study of popular religious movements and the religious revival of the late century.

P. BOWLER, *The Eclipse of Darwinism: Anti-Darwinian Evolution Theories in the Decades Around 1900* (1983). A major study of the fate of Darwinian theory in the nineteenth-century scientific community.

P. BOWLER, *Evolution: The History of an Idea* (1989). An outstanding survey of the subject.

O. CHADWICK, *The Secularization of the European Mind in the Nineteenth Century* (1975). The best available treatment.

A. DANTO, *Nietzsche as Philosopher* (1965). A very helpful and well-organized introduction.

A. DESMOND AND J. MOORE, *Darwin* (1992). A brilliant biography.

J. EFRON, *Defenders of the Race: Jewish Doctors and Race Science in Fin-de-Siecle Europe* (1994). A study of the manner in which Jewish physicians responded to late-century antisemitic racial thought.

P. GAY, *Freud: A Life for Our Time* (1988). A major new biography.

C. C. GILLISPIE, *Genesis and Geology* (1951). A classic discussion of the impact of modern geological theory during the early nineteenth century.

R. HELMSTADTER, *Freedom and Religion in the Nineteenth Century* (1997). A series of important essays primarily on church-state relations.

H. S. HUGHES, *Consciousness and Society: The Reorientation of European Social Thought, 1890–1930* (1958). A wide-ranging discussion of the revolt against positivism.

W. IRVINE, *Apes, Angels, and Victorians* (1955). A lively and sound account of Darwin and Huxley.

C. JUNGNICKEL AND R. MCCORMMACH, *Intellectual Mastery of Nature: Theoretical Physics from Ohm to Einstein*, 2 vols. (1986). A demanding but powerful exploration of the creation of modern physics.

W. A. KAUFMANN, *Nietzsche: Philosopher, Psychologist, Antichrist*, rev. ed. (1968). An exposition of Neitzsche's thought and its sources.

J. T. KLOPPENBERG, *Uncertain Victory: Social Democracy and Progressivism in European and American Thought* (1986). An extremely important comparative study.

W. LACQUER, *A History of Zionism.* (1989). The most extensive one-volume treatment.

K. S. LATOURETTE, *A History of the Expansion of Christianity (1837–1945)* (1975). Remains the most extensive coverage of the missionary movement.

B. LIGHTMAN, *The Origins of Agnosticism: Victorian Unbelief and the Limits of Knowledge* (1987). The best study of the subject.

J. MORRELL AND A. THACKRAY, *Gentlemen of Science: Early Years of the British Association for the Advancement of Science* (1981). An important study that examines the role of science in early and mid-nineteenth-century Britain.

G. L. MOSSE, *Toward the Final Solution: A History of European Racism* (1978). A sound introduction.

S. NEIL, *A History of Christian Missions* (1986). A good introduction with excellent guides to further reading.

L. POLIAKOV, *The Aryan Myth: A History of Racist and Nationalist Ideas in Europe* (1971). The best introduction to the problem.

P. G. J. PULZER, *The Rise of Political Anti-Semitism in Germany and Austria* (revised, 1989). A sound discussion of antisemitism in the world of central European politics.

A. RABINBACH, *The Human Motor: Energy, Fatigue, and the Origins of Modernity* (1990). A broad study of the impact of metaphors of energy as related to the study of human nature.

C. E. SCHORSKE, *Fin de Siecle Vienna: Politics and Culture* (1980). Major essays on the explosively creative intellectual climate of Vienna.

W. SMITH, *Politics and the Sciences of Culture in Germany, 1840–1920* (1991). A major survey of the interaction between sciences and the various social sciences.

F. STERN, *The Politics of Cultural Despair: A Study in the Rise of the German Ideology* (1965). An important examination of antimodern and antisemitic thought in imperial Germany.

F. M. TURNER, *Contesting Cultural Authority: Essays in Victorian Intellectual Life* (1993). Essay dealing with the relationship of science and religion and the problem of faith for intellectuals.

J. P. VON ARX, *Progress and Pessimism: Religion, Politics, and History in Late Nineteenth Century Britain* (1985). A major study that casts much new light on the nineteenth-century view of progress.

C. WELCH, *Protestant Thought in the Nineteenth Century*, 2 vols. (1972, 1985). The most extensive recent study.

R. WOHL, *A Passion for Wings: Aviation and the Western Imagination, 1908–1918* (1994). An examination of the relationship of technology, art, and culture.

Chapter 30

S. ARROM, *The Women of Mexico City, 1790–1857* (1985). A pioneering study.

E. BERMAN, ED., *Women, Culture, and Politics in Latin America* (1990). Useful essays.

L. BETHELL, ED., *The Cambridge History of Latin America*, 8 vols. (1992). The single most authoritative coverage, with extensive bibliographical essays.

V. BULMER-THOMAS, *The Economic History of Latin America Since Independence* (1994). A major study in every respect.

E. B. Burns, *The Poverty of Progress: Latin America in the Nineteenth Century* (1980). Argues that the elites suppressed alternative modes of cultural and economic development.

E. B. Burns, *A History of Brazil* (1993). The most useful one-volume treatment.

D. Bushnell and N. Macaulay, *The Emergence of Latin America in the Nineteenth Century* (1994). A survey that examines the internal development of Latin America during the period.

R. Conrad, *The Destruction of Brazilian Slavery, 1850–1889* (1971). A good survey of the most important problem in Brazil in the second half of the nineteenth century.

R. Conrad, *World of Sorrow: The African Slave Trade to Brazil* (1986). An excellent survey of the subject.

E. V. Da Costa, *The Brazilian Empire: Myths and Histories* (1985). Essays that provide a thorough introduction to Brazil during the period of the empire.

H. S. Ferns, *Britain and Argentina in the Nineteenth Century* (1968). Explains clearly the intermeshing of the two economies.

M. Font, *Coffee, Contention, and Change in the Making of Modern Brazil* (1990). Extensive discussion of the problems of a single-commodity economy.

R. Graham, *Britain and the Onset of Modernization in Brazil* (1968). Another study of British economic dominance.

S. H. Haber, *Industry and Underdevelopment: The Industrialization of Mexico, 1890–1940* (1989). Examines the problem of industrialization before and after the revolution.

G. Hahner, *Emancipating the Female Sex: The Struggle for Women's Rights in Brazil, 1850–1940* (1990). An extensive examination of a relatively understudied issue in Latin America.

C. H. Haring, *Empire in Brazil: A New World Experiment with Monarchy* (1958). Remains a useful overview.

J. Hemming, *Amazon Frontier: The Defeat of the Brazilian Indians* (1987). A brilliant survey of the experience of Native Americans in modern Brazil.

R. A. Humphreys, *Latin America and the Second World War*, 2 vols. (1981–1982). The standard work on the topic.

F. Katz, ed., *Riot, Rebellion, and Revolution in Mexico: Social Base of Agrarian Violence, 1750–1940* (1988). Essays that put the violence of the revolution in a longer context.

A. Knight, *The Mexican Revolution*, 2 vols. (1986). The best treatment of the subject.

S. Mainwaring, *The Catholic Church and Politics in Brazil, 1916–1985* (1986). An examination of a key institution in Brazilian life.

M. C. Meyer and W. L. Sherman, *The Course of Mexican History* (1995). An excellent survey.

M. Morner, *Adventurers and Proletarians: The Story of Migrants in Latin America* (1985). Examines immigration to Latin America and migration within it.

J. Page, *Perón: A Biography* (1983). The standard English treatment.

D. Rock, *Politics in Argentina, 1890–1930: The Rise and Fall of Radicalism* (1975). The major discussion of the Argentine Radical Party.

D. Rock, *Argentina, 1516–1987: From Spanish Colonization to Alfonsin* (1987). Now the standard survey.

D. Rock, ed., *Latin America in the 1940s: War and Postwar Transitions* (1994). Essays examining a very difficult decade for the continent.

R. M. Schneider, *"Order and Progress": A Political History of Brazil* (1991). A straightforward narrative with helpful notes for further reading.

T. E. Skidmore, *Black into White: Race and Nationality in Brazilian Thought* (1993). Examines the role of racial theory in Brazil.

P. H. Smith, *Argentina and the Failure of Democracy: Conflict among Political Elites, 1904–1955* (1974). An examination of one of the major political puzzles of Latin American history.

S. J. and B. H. Stein, *The Colonial Heritage of Latin America: Essays on Economic Dependence in Perspective* (1970). A major statement of the dependence interpretation.

D. Tamarin, *The Argentine Labor Movement, 1930–1945: A Study in the Origins of Perónism* (1985). A useful introduction to a complex subject.

H. J. Wiarda, *Politics and Social Change in Latin America: The Distinct Tradition* (1974). Excellent essays that stress the ongoing role of Iberian traditions.

J. D. Wirth, ed., *Latin American Oil Companies and the Politics of Energy* (1985). A series of case studies.

J. Wolfe, *Working Women, Working Men: São Paulo and the Rise of Brazil's Industrial Working Class, 1900–1955* (1993). Pays particular attention to the role of women.

J. Womack, *Zapata and the Mexican Revolution* (1968). A classic study.

Chapter 31

India

A. Ahmad, *Islamic Modernism in India and Pakistan, 1857–1964* (1967). The standard survey of Muslim thinkers and movements in India during the period.

C. A. Bayly, *Indian Society and the Making of the British Empire, The New Cambridge History of India*, II.1 (Cambridge, UK: Cambridge University Press, 1988). One of several major contributions of this author to the ongoing revision of our picture of modern Indian history since the eighteenth century.

R. Guha, ed., *Subaltern Studies: Writings on South Asian History and Society* (1982). Essays on the colonial period that focus on the social, political, and economic history of "subaltern" groups and classes (hill tribes, peasants, etc.) rather than the elites of India only.

S. N. Hay, ED., "Modern India and Pakistan," Part VI of Wm. Theodore de Bary et al., eds., *Sources of Indian Tradition*, 2nd ed. (1988). A superb selection of primary-source documents with brief introductions and helpful notes.

D. Kopf, *British Orientalism and the Bengal Renaissance: The Dynamics of Indian Modernization, 1773–1835* (1969). An intriguing study of British-Indian interchange and mutual influence in the heyday of the East India Company.

F. Robinson, ED., *The Cambridge Encyclopedia of India, Pakistan, Bangladesh, Sri Lanka, Nepal, Bhutan, and the Maldives* (1989). A fine collection of survey articles by various scholars, organized into topical chapters ranging from "Economies" to "Cultures."

W. C. Smith, *Modern Islam in India: A Social Analysis* (1943). A Marxist critique. Still the best survey and analysis of Indian Muslim thought from Sayyid Ahmad Khan to the early 1940s.

P. Spear, *The Oxford History of Modern India, 1740–1947* (1965). Still a helpful quick reference tool.

M. N. Srinivas, *Social Change in Modern India* (1966). An older but highly influential treatment of topics such as "sanskritization," "westernization," and "secularization."

E. Stokes, *The Peasant Armed: The Indian Revolt of 1857* (1986). The basic starting point for study of the revolt. A posthumously edited work on the battles and the involvement of rural districts of North India in what Stokes saw as a "peasant revolt."

S. Wolpert, *A New History of India*, 2nd ed. (1982). Chapters 14–25. A solid survey and useful quick reference source.

Central Islamic Lands

K. Cragg, *Counsels in Contemporary Islam* (1965). A brief survey of intellectual trends in the modern Islamic world in the nineteenth and twentieth centuries.

J. J. Donahue and J. L. Esposito, EDS., *Islam in Transition: Muslim Perspectives* (1982). An interesting selection of primary-source materials on Islamic thinking in this century.

D. F. Eickelman, *Knowledge and Power in Morocco: The Education of a Twentieth-Century Notable* (1985). A fascinating study of traditional Islamic education and society in the twentieth century through a social biography of a Moroccan religious scholar and judge.

M. G. S. Hodgson, *The Venture of Islam* (1974). Vol. 3, The Gunpowder Empires and Modern Times. Although less ample than his first two volumes, this volume still provides a solid interpretative introduction.

A. Hourani, *Arabic Thought in the Liberal Age, 1798–1939* (1967). The standard work, by which all subsequent scholarship on the topic is to be judged.

N. R. Keddi, *An Islamic Response to Imperialism* (1968). A brief study of al-Afghani, the great Muslim reformer, with translations of a number of his writings.

N. R. Keddi, ED., *Religion and Politics in Iran* (1983). A collection of essays with a helpful historical introduction by the editor and varied articles on modern Iran.

M. H. Kerr, *Islamic Reform: The Political and Legal Theories of Muhammad 'Abduh and Rashid Rida* (1966). A fine study of two major Muslim reformers in the colonial period in Egypt.

B. Lewis, *The Emergence of Modern Turkey*, 2nd ed. (1968). A concise but thorough history of the creation of the Turkish state, including nineteenth-century background.

E. Mortimer, *Faith and Power: The Politics of Islam* (1982). A fine survey of contemporary Islamic countries by a knowledgeable and thoughtful journalist.

F. Rahman, *Islam* (1966). Chapters 12 and 13. These two chapters from a fine introductory survey of Islam by a major modern Muslim historian and thinker deal with reform movements and other modern developments in the Islamic world.

J. C. B. Richmond, *Egypt, 1798–1952: Her Advance Towards a Modern Identity* (1977). A basic history, with focus on political change.

S. J. Shaw and E. K. Shaw, *History of the Ottoman Empire and Modern Turkey* (1977). Vol. II, *Reform, Revolution, and Republic: The Rise of Modern Turkey, 1808–1975.* Detailed and careful analytic and survey history of the modern period.

W. C. Smith, *Islam in Modern History* (1957). Dated, but still the most penetrating analysis of the dilemmas facing Muslim individuals and states in the twentieth century.

J. O. Voll, *Islam: Continuity and Change in the Modern World* (1982). Chapters 1–6. An interpretive survey of the Islamic world since the eighteenth century. Its emphasis on eighteenth-century reform movements is especially noteworthy.

Africa

A. A. Boahen, *Africa Under Colonial Domination, 1880–1935* (1985). Vol. VII of the UNESCO *General History of Africa.* Excellent chapters on various regions of Africa in the period. Chapters 3–10 detail African resistance to European colonial intrusion in diverse regions.

W. Cartey and M. Kilson, EDS., *The Africa Reader: Colonial Africa* (1970). Original source materials give a vivid picture of African resistance to colonial powers, adaptation to foreign rule, and the emergence of the African masses as a political force.

P. Curtin, S. Feiermann, L. Thompson, and J. Vansina, *African History* (1978). The relevant portions are chapters 10–20.

B. Davidson, *The African Genius: An Introduction to African Social and Cultural History* (1969). A sensitive analysis of Africa from the standpoint of African rather than European thought and action. Especially interesting are African responses to imperial and colonial penetration.

J. D. Fage, *A History of Africa* (1978). The relevant chapters, which give a particularly clear overview of the colonial period, are 12–16.

D. Fode and P. M. Kaberry, eds., *West African Kingdoms in the Nineteenth Century* (1967). Very useful treatments of the different West African states such as Benin, Asante, and Gonja.

B. Freund, *The Making of Contemporary Africa: The Development of African Society Since 1800* (1984). A refreshingly direct synthetic discussion and survey that take an avowedly, but not reductive, materialist approach to interpretation.

R. Hallett, *Africa Since 1875: A Modern History* (1974). Detailed survey of modern African history from the outset of the colonial period.

R. W. July, *A History of the African People*, 3rd ed. (1980). The strongest portions of the book are those on the nineteenth and twentieth centuries.

M. A. Klein, *Islam and Imperialism in Senegal: Sine-Saloum, 1847–1914* (1968). A first-rate study of the shift in the Serer states of Senegal from traditional authority to that of the colonial French.

B. A. Ogot and J. A. Kieran, eds., *Zamani: A Survey of East African History*, 2nd rev. ed. (1974). Good material on the nineteenth century and colonial period in the various regions.

A. D. Roberts, ed., *The Colonial Moment in Africa: Essays on the Movement of Minds and Materials, 1900–1940* (1986). Chapters from *The Cambridge History of Africa* treating various aspects of the colonial period in Africa, including economics, politics, and religion.

Chapter 32

China

P. M. Coble, *The Shanghai Capitalists and the Nationalist Government, 1927–1937* (1980).

L. E. Eastman, *The Abortive Revolution: China Under Nationalist Rule, 1927–1937* (1974).

L. E. Eastman, *Seeds of Destruction: Nationalist China in War and Revolution, 1937–1949* (1984).

M. Elvin and G. W. Skinner, *The Chinese City Between Two Worlds* (1974). A study of the late Ch'ing and the Republican eras.

J. W. Esherick, *The Origins of the Boxer Rebellion* (1987).

S. Etō, *China's Republican Revolution* (1994).

J. K. Fairbank, *China, a New History* (1992). A survey of the entire sweep of Chinese history; especially strong on the modern period.

J. K. Fairbank and D. Twitchett, eds., *The Cambridge History of China*. Like the premodern volumes in the same series, the volumes on modern China represent a survey of what is known. Volumes 10–15, which cover the history from the late Ch'ing to the People's Republic, have been published, and the others will be available soon. The series is substantial. Each volume contains a comprehensive bibliography.

C. Hao, *Chinese Intellectuals in Crisis: Search for Order and Meaning, 1890–1911* (1987).

Lu Hsun, *Selected Works* (1960). Novels, stories, and other writings by modern China's greatest writer.

P. A. Kuhn, *Rebellion and Its Enemies in Late Imperial China; Militarization and Social Structure, 1796–1864* (1980). A study of how the Confucian gentry saved the Manchu dynasty after the Taiping Rebellion.

J. Levenson, *Liang Ch'i-ch'ao and the Mind of Modern China* (1953). A classic study of a major Chinese reformer and thinker.

E. O. Reischauer, J. K. Fairbank, and A. M. Craig, *East Asia: Tradition and Transformation* (1989). The most widely read text on East Asian history. Contains ample chapters on Japan and shorter chapters on Korea and Vietnam, as well as coverage of China.

H. Z. Schiffrin, *Sun Yat-sen, Reluctant Revolutionary* (1980). A biography.

B. I. Schwartz, *Chinese Communism and the Rise of Mao* (1951). A classic study of Mao, his thought, and the Chinese Communist Party before 1949.

B. I. Schwartz, *In Search of Wealth and Power: Yen Fu and the West* (1964). Study of a late-nineteenth-century thinker who introduced Western ideas into China.

J. D. Spence, *The Gate of Heavenly Peace: The Chinese and Their Revolution, 1895–1980* (1981). Historical reflections on twentieth-century China.

J. D. Spence, *The Search for Modern China* (1990). A thick text that reads remarkably well.

S. Y. Teng and J. K. Fairbank, *China's Response to the West* (1954). Translations from Chinese thinkers and political figures, with commentaries.

T. H. White and A. Jacoby, *Thunder Out of China* (1946). A view of China during World War II by two who were there.

Japan

G. C. Allen, *A Short Economic History of Modern Japan* (1958).

W. G. Beasley, *Japanese Imperialism, 1894–1945* (1987).

G. M. Berger, *Parties Out of Power in Japan, 1931–1941* (1977). An analysis of the condition of political parties during the militarist era.

A. M. Craig, *Chōshū in the Meiji Restoration* (1961). A study of the Chōshū domain, a Prussia of Japan, during the period from 1840 to 1868.

P. Duus, *Party Rivalry and Political Change in Taisho Japan* (1968). A study of political change in Japan during the 1910s and 1920s.

P. Duus, ed., *The Cambridge History of Japan* (1988). Vol. 6, *The Twentieth Century*.

Y. FUKUZAWA, *Autobiography* (1966). Japan's leading nineteenth-century thinker tells of his life and of the birth of modern Japan.

C. N. GLUCK, *Japan's Modern Myths: Ideology in the Late Meiji Period* (1988).

A. GORDON, *The Evolution of Labor Relations in Japan: Heavy Industry, 1853–1955* (1985).

T. R. H. HAVENS, *The Valley of Darkness: The Japanese People and World War II* (1978).

A. IRIYE, *After Imperialism: The Search for a New Order in the Far East, 1921–1931* (1965). (See also other works by the same author.)

D. KEENE, ED., *Modern Japanese Literature, An Anthology* (1960). A collection of modern Japanese short stories and excerpts from novels.

J. W. MORLEY, ED., *The China Quagmire* (1983). A study of Japan's expansion on the continent between 1933 and 1941. (See also other works on diplomatic history by the same author.)

R. H. MYERS AND M. R. PEATTIE, EDS., *The Japanese Colonial Empire, 1895–1945* (1984).

T. NAJITA, *Hara Kei in the Politics of Compromise, 1905–1915* (1967). A study of one of Japan's greatest party leaders.

K. OHKAWA AND H. ROSOVSKY, *Japanese Economic Growth: Trend Acceleration in the Twentieth Century* (1973).

R. H. SPECTOR, *Eagle Against the Sun: The American War with Japan* (1985).

Chapter 33

L. ALBERTINI, *The Origins of the War of 1914*, 3 vols. (1952, 1957). Discursive but invaluable.

V. R. BERGHAHN, *Germany and the Approach of War in 1914* (1973). A work similar in spirit to both of Fischer's (see below) but stressing the importance of Germany's naval program.

R. BOSWORTH, *Italy and the Approach of the First World War* (1983). A fine analysis of Italian policy.

L. CECIL, *Wilhelm II: Prince and Emperor 1859–1900* (1989). The first part of a projected two-volume history of the Kaiser.

V. DEDIJER, *The Road to Sarajevo* (1966). The fullest account of the assassination that provoked World War I and its Balkan background.

S. B. FAY, *The Origins of the World War*, 2 vols. (1928). The best and most influential of the revisionist accounts.

F. FISCHER, *Germany's Aims in the First World War* (1967). An influential interpretation that stirred a great controversy in Germany and around the world by emphasizing Germany's role in bringing on the war.

F. FISCHER, *War of Illusions* (1975). A long and diffuse book that tries to connect German responsibility for the war with internal social, economic, and political developments.

I. GEISS, *July 1914* (1967). A valuable collection of documents by a student of Fritz Fischer. The emphasis is on German documents and responsibility.

M. GILBERT, *The First World War* (1994). A lively narrative that combines discussion of the battlefields with accounts of the home front.

O. J. HALE, *The Great Illusion 1900–1914* (1971). A fine survey of the period, especially good on public opinion.

M. B. HAYNE, *The French Foreign Office and the Origins of the First World War* (1993). An examination of the work of the influence on French policy of the professionals in the foreign service.

J. N. HORNE, *Labour at War: France and Britain, 1914–1918* (1991). An examination of a major issue on the home fronts.

J. JOLL, *The Origins of the First World War* (1984). A brief but thoughtful analysis.

P. KENNEDY, *The Rise of the Anglo-German Antagonism 1860–1914* (1980). An unusual and thorough analysis of the political, economic, and cultural roots of important diplomatic developments.

J. M. KEYNES, *The Economic Consequences of the Peace* (1920). The famous and influential attack on the Versailles Treaty.

L. LAFORE, *The Long Fuse* (1965). A readable account of the origins of World War I that focuses on the problem of Austria-Hungary.

W. L. LANGER, *The Diplomacy of Imperialism* (1935). A continuation of the previous study for the years 1890–1902.

W. L. LANGER, *European Alliances and Alignments*, 2nd ed. (1966). A splendid diplomatic history of the years 1871–1890.

B. H. LIDDELL HART, *The Real War 1914–1918* (1964). A fine short account by an outstanding military historian.

D. C. B. LIEVEN, *Russia and the Origins of the First World War* (1983). A good account of the forces that shaped Russian policy.

E. MANTOUX, *The Carthaginian Peace* (1952). A vigorous attack on Keynes's view (see Keynes, above).

J. STEINBERG, *Yesterday's Deterrent* (1965). An excellent study of Germany's naval policy and its consequences.

Z. STEINER, *Britain and the Origins of the First World War* (1977). A perceptive and informed account of the way British foreign policy was made in the years before the war.

A. J. P. TAYLOR, *The Struggle for Mastery in Europe, 1848–1918* (1954). Clever but controversial.

L. C. F. TURNER, *Origins of the First World War* (1970). Especially good on the significance of Russia and its military plans.

S. R. WILLIAMSON, JR., *Austria-Hungary and the Origins of the First World War* (1991). A valuable new study of a complex subject.

Chapter 34

W. S. ALLEN, *The Nazi Seizure of Power: The Experience of a Single German Town, 1930–1935*, rev. ed. (1984). A classic treatment of Nazism in a microcosmic setting.

J. BARNARD, *Walter Reuther and the Rise of the Auto Workers* (1983). A major introduction to the new American unions of the 1930s.

K. D. BRACHER, *The German Dictatorship* (1970). A comprehensive treatment of both the origins and the functioning of the Nazi movement and government.

A. BULLOCK, *Hitler: A Study in Tyranny*, rev. ed. (1964). The best biography.

M. BURLEIGH AND W. WIPPERMAN, *The Racial State: Germany 1933–1945* (1991). Emphasizes the manner in which racial theory influenced numerous areas of policy.

R. CONQUEST, *The Great Terror: Stalin's Purges of the Thirties* (1968). The best treatment of the subject to this date.

G. CRAIG, Germany, *1866–1945* (1978). A major survey.

I. DEUTSCHER, *The Prophet Armed* (1954), *The Prophet Unarmed* (1959), and *The Prophet Outcast* (1963). Remains the major biography of Trotsky.

I. DEUTSCHER, *Stalin: A Political Biography*, 2nd ed. (1967). The best biography in English.

B. EICHENGREEN, *Golden Fetters: The Gold Standard and the Great Depression, 1919–1939* (1992). A remarkable study of the role of the gold standard in the economic policies of the interwar years.

E. EYCK, *A History of the Weimar Republic*, 2 vols. (trans. 1963). The story as narrated by a liberal.

M. S. FAUSOLD, *The Presidency of Herbert Hoover* (1985). An important treatment.

G. FELDMAN, *The Great Disorder: Politics, Economics, and Society in the German Inflation, 1914–1924* (1993). The best work on the subject.

S. FITZPATRICK, *Stalin's Peasants: Resitance and Survival in the Russian Village after Collectivization* (1994). A pioneering study.

P. FUSSELL, *The Great War and Modern Memory* (1975). A brilliant account of the literature arising from World War I during the 1920s.

K. GALBRAITH, *The Great Crash* (1979). A well-known account by a leading economist.

R. GELLATELY, *The Gestapo and German Society: Enforcing Racial Policy, 1933–1945* (1990). A discussion of how the police state supported Nazi racial policies.

H. J. GORDON, *Hitler and the Beer Hall Putsch* (1972). An excellent account of the event and the political situation in the early Weimar Republic.

R. HAMILTON, *Who Voted for Hitler?* (1982). An examination of voting patterns and sources of Nazi support.

J. HELD, ED., *The Columbia History of Eastern Europe in the Twentieth Century* (1992). Individual essays on each country.

P. KENEZ, *The Birth of the Propaganda State: Soviet Methods of Mass Mobilization, 1917–1929* (1985). An examination of the manner in which the communist government inculcated popular support.

B. KENT, *The Spoils of War: The Politics, Economics, and Diplomacy of Reparations, 1918–1932* (1993). A comprehensive account of the intricacies of the reparations problem of the 1920s.

D. LANDES, *The Unbound Prometheus: Technological Change and Industrial Development in Western Europe from 1750 to the Present* (1969). Includes an excellent analysis of both the Great Depression and the few areas of economic growth.

B. LINCOLN, *Red Victory: A History of the Russian Civil War* (1989). An excellent narrative account.

M. MCAULEY, *Bread and Justice: State and Society in Petrograd, 1917–1922* (1991). A study that examines the impact of the Russian Revolution and Leninist policies on a major Russian city.

D. J. K. PEUKERT, *Inside Nazi Germany: Conformity, Opposition, and Racism in Everyday Life* (1987). An excellent discussion of life under Nazi rule.

R. PIPES, *The Unknown Lenin: From the Secret Archives* (1996). A collection of previously unpublished documents that indicated the repressive character of Lenin's government.

P. PULZER, *Jews and the German State: The Political History of a Minority, 1848–1933* (1992). A detailed history by a major historian of European minorities.

L. J. RUPP, *Mobilizing Women for War: German and American Propaganda, 1839–1945* (1978). Although concentrating on a later period, it includes an excellent discussion of general Nazi attitudes toward women.

A. M. SCHLESINGER, JR., *The Age of Roosevelt*, 3 vols. (1957–1960). The most important overview.

D. M. SMITH, *Mussolini's Roman Empire* (1976). A general description of the Fascist regime in Italy.

D. M. SMITH, *Italy and Its Monarchy* (1989). A major treatment of an important neglected subject.

A. SOLZHENITSYN, *The Gulag Archipelago*, 3 vols. (1974–1979). A major examination of the labor camps under Stalin by one of the most important of contemporary Russian writers.

R. J. SONTAG, *A Broken World, 1919–1939* (1971). An exceptionally thoughtful and well-organized survey.

A. J. P. TAYLOR, *English History, 1914–1945* (1965). Lively and opinionated.

H. A. TURNER, JR., *German Big Business and the Rise of Hitler* (1985). An important major study of the subject.

H. A. TURNER, *Hitler's Thirty Days to Power* (1996). A narrative of the events leading directly to the Nazi seizure of power.

L. YAHIL, *The Holocaust: The Fate of European Jewry, 1932–1945* (1990). A major study of this fundamental subject in twentieth-century history.

Chapter 35

A. ADAMTHWAITE, *France and the Coming of the Second World War, 1936–1939* (1977). A careful account making good use of the newly opened French archives.

E. R. BECK, *Under the Bombs: The German Home Front, 1942–1945* (1986). An interesting examination of a generally unstudied subject.

A. BULLOCK, *Hitler: A Study in Tyranny,* rev. ed. (1964). A brilliant biography.

R. CARR, *The Civil War in Spain* (1986). A thorough and careful study.

W. S. CHURCHILL, *The Second World War,* 6 vols. (1948–1954). The memoirs of the great British leader.

L. DAWIDOWICZ, *The War Against the Jews, 1933–1945* (1975). An excellent account of the Holocaust.

H. FEIS, *From Trust to Terror: The Onset of the Cold War, 1945–1950* (1970). The best general account.

H. W. GATZKE, *Stresemann and the Rearmament of Germany* (1954). An important monograph.

M. GILBERT AND R. GOTT, *The Appeasers,* rev. ed. (1963). A revealing study of British policy in the 1930s.

M. HARRISON, *Soviet Planning in Peace and War, 1938–1945* (1985). An examination of the Soviet wartime economy.

K. HILDEBRAND, *The Foreign Policy of the Third Reich* (1970).

J. KEEGAN, *The Second World War* (1990). A lively account of the war written by a brilliant military historian.

M. KNOX, *Mussolini Unleashed* (1982). An outstanding study of Fascist Italy's policy and strategy in World War II.

G. KOLKO, *The Politics of War* (1968). An interesting example of the new revisionist school that finds the causes of the Cold War in economic considerations and emphasizes American responsibility.

W. L. LANGER AND S. E. GLEASON, *The Challenge of Isolation* (1952). American foreign policy in the 1930s.

D. C. LARGE, ED., *Contending with Hitler: Varieties of German Resistance in the Third Reich* (1992). Essays that examine the efforts of resistance to Hitler and their limits.

B. H. LIDDELL HART, *History of the Second World War,* 2 vols. (1971). A good military history.

S. MARKS, *The Illusion of Peace* (1976). A good discussion of European international relations in the 1920s and early 1930s.

V. MASTNY, *Russia's Road to the Cold War* (1979). Written by an expert on the Soviet Union and Eastern Europe.

W. MURRAY, *The Change in the European Balance of Power 1938–1939* (1984). A brilliant study of the relationship between strategy, foreign policy, economics, and domestic politics in the years before the war.

R. PIPES, *The Russian Revolution* (1991). A full and thoroughly up-to-date narrative and analysis.

N. RICH, *Hitler's War Aims,* 2 vols. (1973–1974).

M. SHERWIN, *A World Destroyed: The Atomic Bomb and the Grand Alliance* (1975). An analysis of the role of the atomic bomb in the years surrounding the end of World War II.

R. J. SONTAG, *A Broken World 1919–1939* (1971). An excellent survey.

A. J. P. TAYLOR, *The Origins of the Second World War* (1966). A lively, controversial, even perverse study.

C. THORNE, *The Approach of War 1938–1939* (1967). A careful analysis of diplomacy.

H. A. TURNER, JR., *Hitler's Thirty Days to Power* (1996). A compelling account of the lack of inevitability of Hitler's gaining control of Germany.

A. ULAM, *The Bolsheviks* (1968). An outstanding account of Lenin's faction and its rise to power.

P. WANDYCZ, *The Twilight of French Eastern Alliances, 1926–1936* (1988). A well-documented account of the diplomacy of central and eastern Europe in a crucial period.

D. C. WATT, *How War Came* (1989). A thorough study of the diplomatic history of the origins of World War II.

G. WRIGHT, *The Ordeal of Total War 1939–1945* (1968). An excellent survey.

Chapter 36

B. S. ANDERSON AND J. P. PINSSER, *A History of Their Own: Women in Europe from Prehistory to the Present,* Vol. 2 (1988). A broad-ranging survey.

T. S. ASH, *The Uses of Adversity* (1989). Important essays on central European culture and politics prior to the events of 1989.

P. BALDWIN, *The Politics of Social Solidarity: Class Bases of the European Welfare State 1875–1975* (1990). An excellent analysis of the political forces that allowed the welfare state to come into being.

I. BANAC, ED., *Eastern Europe in Revolution* (1992). Excellent articles on the events of 1989 and afterward.

J. H. BILLINGTON, *Russia Transformed: Breakthrough to Hope, Moscow, August, 1991* (1992). A thoughtful essay on the attempted coup.

E. BOTTOME, *The Balance of Terror: Nuclear Weapons and the Illusion of Security, 1945–1985* (1986). A review of the issues that dominated the Cold War era.

A. BROWN, *The Gorbachev Factor* (1996). An important commentary by an English observer.

A. N. DRAGNICH, *Serbs and Croats: The Struggle in Yugoslavia* (1992). An introduction to the historical roots of the current struggle.

M. ELLMAN AND V. KONTOROVICH, *The Disintegration of the Soviet Economic System* (1992). An overview of the economic strains that the Soviet Union experienced during the 1980s.

H. FEIS, *From Trust to Terror: The Onset of the Cold War, 1945–1950* (1970). The best general account.

J. L. GADDIS, *What We Know Now* (1997). Examines the Cold War in light of newly released documents.

D. J. GARROW, *Bearing the Cross: Martin Luther King, Jr. and the Southern Leadership Conference 1955–1968* (1986). The best work on the subject.

M. GLENNY, *The Fall of Yugoslavia: The Third Balkan War* (1992). An overview by a British journalist.

B. GWERTZMAN AND M. T. KAUFMAN, *The Collapse of Communism* (1991). A collection of contemporary news accounts.

B. GWERTZMAN AND M. T. KAUFMAN, *The Decline and Fall of the Soviet Empire* (1992). A collection of contemporary news accounts.

D. HOLLOWAY, *The Soviet Union and the Arms Race* (1985). Excellent treatment of internal Soviet decision making.

L. JOHNSON, *Central Europe: Enemies & Neighbors & Friends* (1996). Explores the complexities of relationships in the region.

R. G. KAISER, *Why Gorbachev Happened* (1992). A useful overview.

D. KEARNS, *Lyndon Johnson and the American Dream* (1976). A useful biography.

J. KEEP, *The Last of the Empires: A History of the Soviet Union, 1956–1991* (1995). A clear narrative.

R. F. LESLIE, *The History of Poland Since 1863* (1981). An excellent collection of essays that provide the background for later events in Poland.

F. LEWIS, *Europe: Road to Unity* (1992). A discussion of contemporary Europe by a thoughtful journalist.

R. MALTBY, ED., *Passing Parade: A History of Popular Culture in the Twentieth Century* (1989). A collection of essays on a topic just beginning to receive scholarly attention.

P. H. MERKL, *German Unification in the European Context* (1992). The first major essay on the impact of German unity.

C. MURRAY, *Losing Ground: American Social Policy 1950–1980* (1983). A pessimistic assessment.

P. PULZER, *German Politics, 1945–1995* (1996). An important overview.

L. SCHAPIRO, *The Communist Party of the Soviet Union* (1960). A classic analysis of the most important institution of Soviet Russia.

A. M. SCHLESINGER, JR., *A Thousand Days: John F. Kennedy in the White House* (1965). A biography by an adviser and major historian.

H. SIMONIAN, *The Privileged Partnership: Franco-German Relations in the European Community (1969–1984)* (1985). An important examination of the dominant role of France and Germany in the EEC.

J. STEELE, *Soviet Power: The Kremlin's Foreign Policy–Brezhnev to Andropov* (1983). A broad Survey.

D. STOCKMAN, *The Triumph of Politics: The Inside Story of the Reagan Revolution* (1987). A critical memoir by one of Reagan's aides.

G. Stokes, ed., *From Stalinism to Pluralism: A Documentary History of Eastern Europe since 1945* (1996). An important collection of documents which are not easily accessible elsewhere.

H. A. Turner, Jr., *Germany from Partition to Reunification* (1992). The best and most recent introduction.

M. WALKER, *The Cold War and the Making of the Modern World* (1994). A major survey.

B. WOODWARD AND C. BERNSTEIN, *The Final Days* (1976). A discussion of the Watergate scandal by the reporters who uncovered it.

Chapter 37

China

F. BUTTERFIELD, *China, Alive in the Bitter Sea* (1982). Observations about China by a Chinese-speaking *New York Times* reporter.

A. CHAN, R. MADSEN, AND J. UNGER, *Chen Village: A Recent History of a Peasant Community in Mao's China* (1984). An account of the postwar history of a Chinese village.

J. CHANG, *Wild Swans: Three Daughter's of China* (1991). An inside look at recent Chinese society.

B. M. FROLIC, *Mao's People: Sixteen Portraits of Life in Revolutionary China* (1987).

T. GOLD, *State and Society in the Taiwan Miracle* (1986). The story of economic growth in postwar Taiwan.

H. LIANG, *Son of the Revolution* (1983). An autobiographical account of a young man growing up in Mao's China.

B. LIU, *People or Monsters? and Other Stories and Reportage from China After Mao* (1983). Literary reflections on China.

F. W. MOTE AND D. TWITCHETT, EDS., *The Cambridge History of China* (1987). Vol. 14, *The People's Republic Part I*. A summary of the best recent research.

M. WOLF, *Revolution Postponed: Women in Contemporary China* (1985).

ZHANG X. AND SANG Y., *Chinese Lives: An Oral History of Contemporary China* (1987).

Japan

G. BERNSTEIN, *Haruko's World: A Japanese Farm Woman and Her Community* (1983). A study of the changing life of a village woman in postwar Japan.

T. BESTOR, *Neighborhood Tokyo* (1989). A portrait of contemporary urban life in Japan.

H. HIBBETT, ED., *Contemporary Japanese Literature: An Anthology of Fiction, Film, and Other Writing Since 1945* (1977). Translations of postwar short stories.

D. OKIMOTO, *Between MITI and the Market* (1989). A discussion of the respective roles of government and private enterprise in Japan's postwar growth.

E. O. REISCHAUER, *The Japanese* (1977). The best overall account of contemporary Japanese society and politics.

E. F. VOGEL, *Japan as Number One: Lessons for America* (1979). A sociological analysis of the sources of Japan's early postwar economic growth.

Korea and Vietnam

B. CUMINGS, *Korea, The Unknown War* (1988).

B. CUMINGS, *The Two Koreas: On the Road to Reunification?* (1990).

B. CUMINGS, *The Origins of the Korean War* (Vol. 1, 1981; Vol. 2, 1991).

C. J. ECKERT, *Korea Old and New, A History* (1990). The best short history of Korea, with extensive coverage of the postwar era.

C. J. ECKERT, *Offspring of Empire: The Koch'ang Kims and the Colonial Origins of Korean Capitalism, 1876–1945* (1991).

G. M. T. KAHIN, *Intervention: How America Became Involved in Vietnam* (1986).

S. KARNOW, *Vietnam: A History,* (rev. ed.) (1996).

L. KENDALL, *Shamans, Housewives, and Other Restless Spirits: Women in Korean Ritual and Life* (1985).

K. B. LEE, *A New History of Korea* (1984). A translation by E. Wagner and others of an outstanding Korean work, covering the full sweep of Korean history.

T. LI, *Nguyen Cochinchina: South Vietnam in the Seventeenth and Eighteenth Centuries* (1998).

D. MARR, *Vietnam 1945: The Quest for Power* (1995).

C. W. SORENSEN, *Over the Mountains Are Mountains* (1988). How peasant households in Korea adapted to rapid industrialization.

A. WOODSIDE, *Vietnam and the Chinese Model* (1988). Provides the background for Vietnam's relationship to China.

Chapter 38

Africa

A. BOYD, *An Atlas of World Affairs,* 9th ed. (1991). A simple and brief, but useful, quick reference book on the current shape of world nations, alliances, and major political issues. Especially useful for keeping up with the changing political units of contemporary Africa.

B. DAVIDSON, *Let Freedom Come* (1978). A broad-ranging study of modern Africa, using incisive specific examples to support thoughtful analyses of trends and events across the continent since the nineteenth century.

B. FREUND, *The Making of Contemporary Africa: The Development of African Society Since 1800* (1984). The final three chapters give excellent treatment of decolonization after 1940, tropical Africa since independence, and southern Africa into the 1980s.

R. W. JULY, *A History of the African People,* 3rd ed. (1980). Chapters 14–22. The last part of the book provides a careful and clear survey of post-World War I history, including chapters on the various regions of the continent and on topics like nationalism.

A. J. H. LATHAM, *Africa, Asia, and South America since 1800: A Bibliographic Guide* (1995). A valuable tool for finding materials on the topics in this chapter.

R. OLIVER, *The African Experience* (1991). The closing chapters give a thoughtful and probing overview of postcolonial Africa.

C. M. TURNBULL, *The Lonely African* (1962). A haunting and vivid series of case studies of post-World War II Africans caught in the upheavals of modernization and rapid change.

India and Pakistan

W. T. DE BARY ET AL., EDS., *Sources of Indian Tradition,* 2nd ed. (1988). The final chapters offer selections from major modern Indian political and literary figures, accompanied by solid introductions.

N. MAXWELL, *India's China War* (1970). A fascinating, detailed study of the Sino-Indian border war of the early 1960s. It is illuminating especially about the intricacies of Indian politics of the time.

D. E. SMITH, *India as a Secular State* (1963). Still pertinent today for the vexed question in South Asia of how to deal with secularism and religion in the political arena.

F. ROBINSON, ED., *The Cambridge Encyclopedia of India, Pakistan, Bangladesh, Sri Lanka, Nepal, Bhutan, and the Maldives* (1989). A sweeping and detailed reference source for the South Asian world to 1988.

S. WOLPERT, *A New History of India,* 3rd ed. (1988). The closing chapters of this fine survey history are particularly helpful in orienting the reader in postwar Indian history until the mid-1980s.

Islam and the Middle East

J. J. DONOHUE AND J. L. ESPOSITO, EDS., *Islam in Transition: Muslim Perspectives* (1982). Selections from Muslim writers, including many since World War II, on issues of social, political, and religious change in the Islamic world.

J. ESPOSITO, *The Islamic Threat: Myth or Reality,* 2nd ed. (1992). A useful corrective to some of the polemics against Islam and Muslims today.

N. R. KEDDIE, *Roots of Revolution: An Interpretive History of Modern Iran* (1981). Chapters 6–9 focus on Iran from 1941 through the first years of the 1978 revolution and provide a solid overview of history in this era.

T. MOSTYN AND A. HOURANI, EDS., *The Cambridge History of the Middle East and North Africa* (1988). A detailed reference source on the entire region to the mid-1980s.

H. MUNSON, JR., *Islam and Revolution in the Middle East* (1988). Based on numerous specific studies of recent years, this little book offers a good general picture, especially for students, of the historical and ideological background of contemporary Islamic religion-political movements and on the Iranian revolution in particular.

P. Sluglett and M. Faroule-Sluglett, eds. *Tuttle Guide to the Middle East* (1992). A superb handbook arranged by country, with useful appendices.

W. C. Smith, *Islam in Modern History* (1957). Old, but still the most thoughtful and comprehensive treatment of issues facing Muslim peoples from the Arab world to India.

J. O. Voll, *Islam: Continuity and Change in the Modern World* (1982). Chapters 5–8. A brief yet detailed survey of trends and major events in recent Islamic history from Indonesia to Africa.

Latin America

S. De Vylder, *Allende's Chile* (1976). A sound introduction to a difficult and controversial subject.

J. Dominguez, *Cuba: Order and Revolution* (1978). A useful overview. Essential for understanding the background of the present tensions in the area.

C. Fuentes, *A New Time for Mexico* (1996). A commentary by an influential contemporary writer.

R. Kagan, *A Twilight Struggle: American Power and Nicaragua, 1977–1990* (1996). A major discussion.

W. Lafeber, *The Panama Canal: The Crisis in Historical Perspective* (1981). An important and far-ranging consideration of US policy in Latin America.

P. Lowden, *Moral Opposition to Authoritarian Rule in Chile* (1996). A discussion of Chilean politics from the standpoint of human rights.

S. D. Morris, *Political Reformers in Mexico: An Overview of Contemporary Mexican Politics* (1995). An examination of a rapidly changing scene.

L. H. Oppenheim, *Politics in Chile: Democracy, Authoritarianism, and the Search for Development* (1993). Examines the controversial course of Chilean politics during the last quarter century.

A. Stepan, *The Breakdown of Democratic Regimes* (1978). An overview of the collapse of Latin American democracies in the third quarter of the twentieth century.

D. KL. Van Cott, ed., *Indigenous People and Democracy in Latin America* (1994). Examination of an often neglected subject.

H. Wirarda, *Democracy and Its Discontents: Development, Interdependence, and U.S. Policy in Latin America* (1995). A useful overview.

G. W. Wynia, *Argentina: Illusion and Realities* (1992). Essays on recent developments.

INDEX

religion, 201, 203
society, 203
Spanish conquest of, 261
Tenochtitlán, 200, 203

Babur, 321
Babylon:
Cyrus and, 52
Old dynasty, 4, 5
religion, 4
Babylonian captivity, 22, 216
Babylonian Captivity of the Church (Luther), 229
Babylonian Exile of the Jews, 52
Bacchus, 66
Bacon, Francis, 331
Bactria, Indo-Greeks of, 59
Baden, Max, 460
Badoglio, Pietro, 482
Baghdad, 186
Bahmanids in the Deccan, 190
Bakufu, 120
Ashikaga, 122–123
Tokugawa, 279, 280, 282, 439
Baldwin, Stanley, 466
Balfour Declaration (1917), 461, 519
Balkans, war in, 453, 456–457
Bangladesh, 521
Bantu, 86–87, 427
Basel, Council of (1431–1449), 217
Basil the Great, 150
Basra, 139
Bastille, fall of, 342
Batista, Fulgencio, 523
Batu Khan, 178
Bavaria, 239–240
Baybars, 186
Becket, Thomas, 174
Begin, Menachem, 519
Beguine houses, 169
Beligum, Congress of Vienna and, 350
Bello, Muhammad, 428
Benedictines, 150
Benedict of Nursia, 150, 161
Benefice, 152, 157
Benin, 253–254
Berbers, 138, 185
Berchtold, Leopold, 457
Berke, 189
Berlin Blockade, 492
Berlin Wall, 493, 500
Bernard of Clairvaux, Saint, 164
Bernstein, Eduard, 389–390
Bessus, 46
Bethmann-Hollweg, Theobald von, 457, 458
Bhagavad Gita, 58, 133
Bhakti, 132, 190–191
Biafra, 517
Bible:
Erasmus' translation of, 227
Hebrew, 22, 24
Jiménez de Cisneros' translation, 227
Luther's translation of, 227, 228, 229
Vulgate, 77

Bindusara, 55
Birth control:
eighteenth-century, 310
impact of Reformation on, 236
infanticide, 172–173
in Japan (Tokugawa), 283
nineteenth-century, 385, 387
Birth of Tragedy, The (Nietzsche), 402
Biruni, al-, 187, 192
Bismarck, Otto von, 371, 373, 389, 399–400, 429, 453, 455
Black Death:
in Arab Middle East, 186
causes of, 215
remedies, 215
social and economic consequences, 215–216
spread of, 215
Black Legend, 262
Boccaccio, Giovanni, 218
Bodhisattva, 132
Bohemia, 300
Boleyn, Anne, 232, 233
Bolívar, Simón, 351
Bologna:
Concordat of (1516), 222
universities in, 166–167
Bolshevism, 390–392, 459–460
Bonaventure, Saint, 175
Boniface VIII, pope, 216
Book of Common Prayer (Cranmer) 233, 293
Book of the Courtier (Castiglione), 219
Book of the Han, The (Pan Ku), 96
Borgia family, 222
Bosnia, 453, 455
crisis of 1908, 456
war in 1992, 501
Bosnia-Herzegovina, 501
Bossuet, Jacques-Bénigne, 297
Boston Tea Party, 341
Botha, Pieter, 517
Bourbons, 236
Bouvines, 175
Boxer Rebellion, 435
Brahe, Tycho, 331
Brahman, 18, 19
Brahmanas, 9, 10, 18
Brahmanic age, 9, 10
Brandenburg-Prussia, 301
Brazil:
civilian government in, 524–525
conditions in, following independence, 408, 410
economic problems and military coups, 417–418
events/dates, major, 418
exploitation of resources, 411
independence for, 352
monarchy replaced with a republic, 417
Paraguayan War (1865–1870), 417
slavery in, 263–265, 417
Brest-Litovsk, treaty of (1918), 459–460
Brezhnev, Leonid, 497
Briand, Aristide, 472

Britain:
See also England
Africa, colonial rule in, 429, 453
Battle of Britain, 480–481
Disraeli and Gladstone, 377
Egypt, colonial rule of, 425
Entente Cordiale, 455
Great Reform Bill (1832), 357–358
India, colonial rule of, 421–424
Irish question, 377
Labour Party and Fabianism, 390
Latin America, relations with, 411, 412
World War I, 456–459
World War II, 480–481, 482–484, 486–487
British North America Act (1867), 380
Bronze Age, 3, 10–12
on Crete, 32–33
Brown, John, 377–378
Brown v. Board of Education, 496
Bruni, Leonardo, 218
Brüning, Heinrich, 473
Bucer, Martin, 231
Buddha (Siddhartha Gautama), 20, 132
Buddhism:
dharma, 19–22
dukkha, 20–22
Han dynasty and, 96–97
in India, 18, 20–22, 132–133
in medieval Japan, 123–124
Nara and Heian, 120
Nichiren, 124
post-Mauryan, 58
Pure Land, 124
Shingon sect, 120
T'ang dynasty, 105–106
Tendai sect, 120
T'ien-t'ai sect, 97, 105
Zen, 105–106, 124, 125
Buenos Aires, 351, 412–413
Bunker Hill, battle of, 341
Bülow, Bernhard von, 455
Burgundians, 213
Bush, George, 496–497
Bute, Earl of, 303
Buyids, 143, 186–187
Byzantine/Byzantine Empire, 76
Islamic conquest of, 138, 149
Middle Ages and, 147–149

Caesar, Julius, 68
Caesar, meaning of term, 70
Cahuachi, 204
Cairo, 186
Calas, Jean, 333–334
Calendar:
Mayan, 198, 199
Mesoamerican, 196, 198
Muslim, 137
Shang dynasty, 11
Caligula, 70
Caliphate, 139–140
high, 142–143
Calixtus II, pope, 162
Calles, Plutarco Elías, 416
Calvin, John, 231–232, 236

Louis XIV, king of France, 237, 291–292, 294, 295–297
Louis XV, king of France, 298
Louis XVI, king of France, 343–345
Louis XVIII, king of France, 357
Louis Philippe, king of the French, 357, 364
Louis the German, 155, 157
Louis the Pious, 155, 158
L'Ouverture, Toussaint, 350, 351
Loyang, 12, 94, 102
Lucretius, 70
Ludendorff, Eich, 458, 472
Ludovico il Moro, 221, 222
Lueger, Karl, 404
Lusitania, 459
Luther, Martin, 227, 228–229
Lutheranism, political consolidation of the reformation, 232
Luthuli, Albert, 517
Lwo, 88
Lyceum (Aristotle), 26
Lyell, Charles, 399
Lysander, 43

Maasai, 88
Maastricht, treaty of (1991), 494
MacArthur, Douglas, 504
Macartney, Lord, 278
MacDonald, John A., 380
MacDonald, Ramsay, 466
Macedon/Macedonia, 46, 65
Macedonians, 1021
Machiavelli, Niccolò, 222
Madero, Francisco, 416
Madrasa, 182, 186
Magellan, Ferdinand, 226
Magi, 52, 59
Maginot Line, 480
Magna Carta (1215), 164, 174–175
Magna Graecia, 35
Magnesia, 65
Magyars, 157, 375, 376
Mahabharata, 9, 58
Mahavira Vardhamana, 20
Mahayana Buddhism, 132–133
Mahdi, 141
Mahmud II, 425–426
Mahmud of Ghazna, 187
Maimonides (ibn Maymun), 184, 185
Maitreya, 105
Mali, 80, 248–251
Malinke, 250–251
Mamakuna, 206–207
Mamluks, 142, 186
Ma'mun, al-, 142, 143
Manchu dynasty:
    rule, end of, 433
    rule, pattern of, 275–276
    women, 274
Manchuria, 445
Mande, 248
Mandela, Nelson, 517–518
Mani, 129
Manichaeism, 129
Mannerism, 221

Manors and serfdom, 154, 155, 170–171
Mansa Musa, 251
Mao Tse-tung (Mao Zedong), 438, 508, 509
Maqurra, 84, 253
Marathas, 321
Marathon, 40
Marburg Colloquy, 230
Marco Polo, 112
Marcus Antonius, 68
Marcus Aurelius, 70, 72–73
Mardonius, 40
Maria Theresa of Austria, 301, 302, 334, 337
Marie, countess of Champagne, 174
Marie Antoinette, Queen of France, 344, 345, 346
Marie Louise, Archduchess, 348
Maritime Customs Service, 434
Marius, Gaius, 67
Mark Anthony, 68
Marriage(s):
    arranged, 235
    Athenian, 42
    eighteenth-century, 308
    feminism and views on, 406
    impact of Industrial Revolution on, 362
    impact of Reformation on, 234–235
    medieval, 172
    Mesopotamian, 4–5
    nineteenth-century, 387
    timing of, 234–235
    Vedic Aryan, 9–10
Marshall, George C., 491
Marshall Plan, 491, 492
Martin V, pope, 217
Marx, Karl, 362–363, 389
Mary II, 295
Mary Stuart, 239, 292
Mary Tudor, 232, 233
Master K'ung, 16
Matara, 84
Mathematical Principles of Natural Philosophy (Newton), 332
Mathematics:
    Gupta, 131
    Hellenistic, 49
    Mayan, 199
Mauryans, 51, 55–58
Maximilian, archduke of Austria, 374, 415
Maximilian, duke of Bavaria, 239
Maximilian I, emperor, 222, 223, 229
Mayapan, 200
Mayas, 195, 198–200
May Fourth movement, 436
May Laws (1873), 399
Mazarin, Cardinal, 295, 296
Mazdak, 129
Mazdakite movement, 129
Mazowiecki, Tadeusz, 499
Mazzini, Giuseppe, 371
McCarthy, Joseph, 495
McKinley, William, 394
Meat Packing Act (1906), 394
Mecca, 135, 136, 137–138
Medes, 52, 53
Medici, Cosimo de', 218, 219

Médicis, Catherine de, 236, 237
Medina, 137–138
Mehmed II, 317
Meiji period (1868–1890), 435, 439–444
Mein Kamf (Hitler), 472, 478
Melanchthon, Philip, 232
Menander, 59
Mencius, 17
Mendel, Gregor, 398
Mercantilism, 260–261
Merchants, rise of, 164
Meroitic empire, 82–83
Merovingians, 151–152
Mesoamerica:
    Aztecs, 200–203
    classic, 196–200
    events/dates, major, 13, 196
    formative (pre-classic), 196
    human sacrifice, 196, 198, 199, 200, 201, 203
    Mayas, 195, 198–200
    meaning of name, 195
    Monte Alban, 196
    Neolithic societies, 3
    Olmec, 14, 196
    periods of, 14, 195–196
    post-classic, 200–203
    range of, 13–14
    Teotihuacán, 197–198
    Toltecs, 200
    Valley of Oaxaca, 196
    writing and use of a calendar in, 196
Mesopotamia, 3
    Alexander the Great conquest of, 46
    cities, 4
    civilization, 4–5
    government, 4
    key events and people in, 4
    marriage, 4–5
    religion, 4
    slavery, 5
    society, 4–5
    women, 4–5
Messenia, 37
Mesta, 223
Metamorphoses (Ovid), 70
Metternich, Klemens, 364
Mexico (New Spain):
    Chiapas, rebellion in, 526
    Díaz and dictatorship, 415–416
    events/dates, major, 416
    foreign intervention, 415
    independence for, 351–352
    Partido Revolucionario Institucional (PRI), 416, 525–526
    revolution (1911), 416
    turmoil following independence, 415
Michelangelo, 220–221
Middle Ages, early:
    See also Japan, medieval
    Byzantine Empire, 147–149
    decline of Roman authority, 146–147
    development of Roman Catholic church, 150–151
    Franks, 151–157

SINGLE PC LICENSE AGREEMENT AND LIMITED WARRANTY

READ THIS LICENSE CAREFULLY BEFORE OPENING THIS PACKAGE. BY OPENING THIS PACKAGE, YOU ARE AGREEING TO THE TERMS AND CONDITIONS OF THIS LICENSE. IF YOU DO NOT AGREE, DO NOT OPEN THE PACKAGE. PROMPTLY RETURN THE UNOPENED PACKAGE AND ALL ACCOMPANYING ITEMS TO THE PLACE YOU OBTAINED THEM.

1.   GRANT OF LICENSE and OWNERSHIP: The enclosed computer programs ("Software") are licensed, not sold, to you by Prentice-Hall, Inc. ("We" or the "Company") and in consideration of your purchase or adoption of the accompanying Company textbooks and/or other materials, and your agreement to these terms. We reserve any rights not granted to you. You own only the disk(s) but we and/or our licensors own the Software itself. This license allows you to use and display your copy of the Software on a single computer (i.e., with a single CPU) at a single location for *academic* use only, so long as you comply with the terms of this Agreement. You may make one copy for back up, or transfer your copy to another CPU, provided that the Software is usable on only one computer.

2.   RESTRICTIONS: You may *not* transfer or distribute the Software or documentation to anyone else. Except for backup, you may *not* copy the documentation or the Software. You may *not* network the Software or otherwise use it on more than one computer or computer terminal at the same time. You may *not* reverse engineer, disassemble, decompile, modify, adapt, translate, or create derivative works based on the Software or the Documentation. You may be held legally responsible for any copying or copyright infringement which is caused by your failure to abide by the terms of these restrictions.

3.   TERMINATION: This license is effective until terminated. This license will terminate automatically without notice from the Company if you fail to comply with any provisions or limitations of this license. Upon termination, you shall destroy the Documentation and all copies of the Software. All provisions of this Agreement as to limitation and disclaimer of warranties, limitation of liability, remedies or damages, and our ownership rights shall survive termination.

4.   LIMITED WARRANTY AND DISCLAIMER OF WARRANTY: Company warrants that for a period of 60 days from the date you purchase this SOFTWARE (or purchase or adopt the accompanying textbook), the Software, when properly installed and used in accordance with the Documentation, will operate in substantial conformity with the description of the Software set forth in the Documentation, and that for a period of 30 days the disk(s) on which the Software is delivered shall be free from defects in materials and workmanship under normal use. The Company does *not* warrant that the Software will meet your requirements or that the operation of the Software will be uninterrupted or error-free. Your only remedy and the Company's only obligation under these limited warranties is, at the Company's option, return of the disk for a refund of any amounts paid for it by you or replacement of the disk. THIS LIMITED WARRANTY IS THE ONLY WARRANTY PROVIDED BY THE COMPANY AND ITS LICENSORS, AND THE COMPANY AND ITS LICENSORS DISCLAIM ALL OTHER WARRANTIES, EXPRESS OR IMPLIED, IN-CLUDING WITHOUT LIMITATION, THE IMPLIED WARRANTIES OF MERCHANTABILITY AND FITNESS FOR A PARTICULAR PURPOSE. THE COMPANY DOES NOT WARRANT, GUARANTEE OR MAKE ANY REPRESENTATION REGARDING THE ACCURACY, RELIABILITY, CURRENTNESS, USE, OR RESULTS OF USE, OF THE SOFTWARE.

5.   LIMITATION OF REMEDIES AND DAMAGES: IN NO EVENT, SHALL THE COMPANY OR ITS EMPLOYEES, AGENTS, LICENSORS, OR CONTRACTORS BE LIABLE FOR ANY INCIDENTAL, INDIRECT, SPECIAL, OR CONSEQUENTIAL DAMAGES ARISING OUT OF OR IN CONNECTION WITH THIS LICENSE OR THE SOFTWARE, INCLUDING FOR LOSS OF USE, LOSS OF DATA, LOSS OF INCOME OR PROFIT, OR OTHER LOSSES, SUSTAINED AS A RESULT OF INJURY TO ANY PERSON, OR LOSS OF OR DAMAGE TO PROPERTY, OR CLAIMS OF THIRD PARTIES, EVEN IF THE COMPANY OR AN AUTHORIZED REPRESENTATIVE OF THE COMPANY HAS BEEN ADVISED OF THE POSSIBILITY OF SUCH DAMAGES. IN NO EVENT SHALL THE LIABILITY OF THE COMPANY FOR DAMAGES WITH RESPECT TO THE SOFTWARE EXCEED THE AMOUNTS ACTUALLY PAID BY YOU, IF ANY, FOR THE SOFTWARE OR THE ACCOMPANYING TEXTBOOK. BECAUSE SOME JURISDICTIONS DO NOT ALLOW THE LIMITATION OF LIABILITY IN CERTAIN CIRCUMSTANCES, THE ABOVE LIMITATIONS MAY NOT ALWAYS APPLY TO YOU.

6.   GENERAL: THIS AGREEMENT SHALL BE CONSTRUED IN ACCORDANCE WITH THE LAWS OF THE UNITED STATES OF AMERICA AND THE STATE OF NEW YORK, APPLICABLE TO CONTRACTS MADE IN NEW YORK, AND SHALL BENEFIT THE COMPANY, ITS AFFILIATES AND ASSIGNEES. THIS AGREEMENT IS THE COMPLETE AND EXCLUSIVE STATEMENT OF THE AGREEMENT BETWEEN YOU AND THE COMPANY AND SUPERSEDES ALL PROPOSALS OR PRIOR AGREEMENTS, ORAL, OR WRITTEN, AND ANY OTHER COMMUNICATIONS BETWEEN YOU AND THE COMPANY OR ANY REPRESENTATIVE OF THE COMPANY RELATING TO THE SUBJECT MATTER OF THIS AGREEMENT. If you are a U.S. Government user, this Software is licensed with "restricted rights" as set forth in subparagraphs (a)-(d) of the Commercial Computer-Restricted Rights clause at FAR 52.227-19 or in subparagraphs (c)(1)(ii) of the Rights in Technical Data and Computer Software clause at DFARS 252.227-7013, and similar clauses, as applicable.

Should you have any questions concerning this agreement or if you wish to contact the Company for any reason, please contact in writing: History Media Editor, Prentice Hall, One Lake Street, Upper Saddle River, NJ 07458.